CHILDREN AND ADULTS WITH ATTENTION DEFICIT DISORDERS

ADD & Adults: Strategies for Success from CH.A.D.D.

CH.A.D.D.®

Graphic Design by: Kall Graphics, Inc.
Editorial and Publication Management by: Rosenberg Communications, Inc.

Queries regarding rights and permissions should be addressed to:
CH.A.D.D.
499 N.W. 70th Avenue, Suite 101
Plantation, Florida 33317
phone   954.587.3700
e-mail   http://www.chadd.org/

Printed in the United States of America

Library of Congress Catalog Number: 97-69554

ISBN 0-9634875-2-3

Table of Contents

INTRODUCTION I

FOREWORD II

CHAPTER 1: ASSESSMENT & DIAGNOSIS 1
   Introduction
   Common Sense about Adult ADD 3
   Getting Professional Help for Problems of Inattention 7
   Diagnosing ADD in Adults 8
   Assessment of AD/HD in Adults 12

CHAPTER 2: MANAGEMENT OF ADD 15
   Introduction
   Coping Strategies for Adults with AD/HD 17
   50 Tips on the Management of Adult ADD 20
   Coaching – An Interview with Nancy Ratey, EDM 24
   Get Ready, Get Set, Get Organized 26
   Anger Management Training 28
   A New Generation of Time Management? 30

CHAPTER 3: MEDICAL MANAGEMENT OF ADD 33
   Introduction
   Pharmacoptherapy of Adult AD/HD 35
   Psychopharmacologic Treatment of AD/HD
      in Young Adults 41

CHAPTER 4: ON THE JOB 45
   Introduction
   Top Ten Traps for Adults with ADD in the Workplace:
      How to Avoid Getting Caught By Them! 47
   Succeeding in the Workplace with ADD 50
   Equal Employment Opportunity Commission Issues
      New Guidance on Psychiatric
      Disabilities and the ADA 54
   Adults with ADD and the Military: An Overview 57

CHAPTER 5: EDUCATING AND TRAINING 59
   Introduction
   Career and Life Planning with ADD:
      After Diagnosis and Treatment... What's Next? 61

Table of Contents, continued

Planning for the Future: Alternatives to College 63
The Key Steps to Selecting a College:
    For Students with ADD 66
Legal Rights and Accommodations for
    College Students with ADD 72
Documenting ADD for College Accommodations 75
Using Strategies and Services for Success in College 79
Where There's A Will, There's A Way 81

CHAPTER 6: RELATIONSHIPS 83
Introduction
The Impact of ADD Upon Couples 85
Living and Loving with ADD 88
Interpersonal and Social Problems
    in Adults with ADD 92
Acclimated to AD/HD 95
The Search 96

CHAPTER 7: TOPICS OF SPECIAL INTEREST 99
Introduction
ADD and Substance Abuse:
    An Intoxicating Combination 100
ADD in Females: From Childhood to Adulthood 103
ADD Research: An Interview
    with Russell A. Barkley, Ph.D. 107
Adults with AD/HD and the Driving Performance of
    Adolescents with AD/HD:
    An Interview with Kevin Murphy, Ph.D. 109
Parenting a Child with AD/HD:
    Hope and Help for the Harried and Hassled 111
A Touch of Real Life 115

Introduction
ADD – Not Just A Children's Problem Anymore

There has been a growing realization that Attention Deficit Disorders (ADD, AD/HD) persist into adulthood for many individuals. The core symptoms of ADD, inattention, impulsivity, and overactivity are most evident during childhood, but it is now known that they continue into adulthood for a significant percentage of children with ADD. Unfortunately, relatively few adults have been identified or treated for ADD.

ADD in adults is a "hidden disorder" in which symptoms are often obscured by problems with relationships, staying organized, and holding a steady job. A number of adults who are diagnosed with ADD are first recognized as having problems with substance abuse or impulse control. Another factor relating to the under-diagnosis of ADD in adults is that many mental health practitioners have received little training in childhood disorders or were trained during a time when it was assumed that children with ADD "grew out" of their symptoms.

The growth of CH.A.D.D. as a national organization, recognition of ADD as a significant disorder by parents and professionals, and increased media attention to ADD have contributed to the growing interest in adult ADD. In adulthood, the symptoms of ADD affect not only individuals, but their family, friends, and others with whom they come into daily contact. Adults who are diagnosed with ADD can learn how the disorder has influenced their development and how they can cope with their symptoms in order to live more successfully.

Characteristics of Adults with ADD

Most adults grew up at a time when clinicians, educators, parents, and the general public knew little or nothing about ADD, and even less about its diagnosis or treatment. As a result, adults who are living with the condition, and especially those who are undiagnosed and untreated, may be experiencing a number of problems, some of which stem directly from the disorder, and others which are the result of associated adjustment patterns. Their presenting concerns may include:

- Distractibility
- Disorganization
- Forgetfulness
- Procrastination
- Chronic lateness
- Chronic boredom
- Anxiety
- Depression
- Low self-esteem
- Mood swings

- Employment problems
- Restlessness
- Substance abuse or addiction
- Relationship problems

The central or associated features of ADD range from mild to severe – ADD can affect only a few areas of functioning, or it can impair nearly all. The symptoms of ADD can be variable and situational, or constant and unremitting.

There is no one "ADD personality profile." Some persons with ADD can concentrate if they are interested or excited, while others have difficulty concentrating under any circumstances. Some avidly seek stimulation, while others avoid it. Some become oppositional, ill-behaved and, later, antisocial; others may become ardent people-pleasers. Some are gregarious, and others, withdrawn.

Prevalence

We are in the beginning stages of learning about this disorder in adults. Studies of children indicate that 3 to 5 percent have ADD. Although it is diagnosed more often in school-age boys than in girls, this may be related to the identification of hyperactive and/or aggressive behavior, which is more frequently demonstrated by boys. The prevalence of ADD in adults is unknown; very few have been studied. In the few treatment studies of adults, there does not appear to be a significant sex difference.

About two-thirds of the children who are diagnosed in or before elementary school with ADD continue to have behavioral symptoms in adolescence. During this time period, associated behavioral, learning, and emotional problems also manifest themselves. Approximately one-third to one-half of these adolescents continue to have symptoms of ADD during their adult years.

What Causes ADD?

The exact cause or causes of ADD are not conclusively known. Scientific evidence suggests that in many cases, the disorder is genetically transmitted and is caused by an imbalance or deficiency in certain chemicals that regulate the efficiency with which the brain controls behavior. A 1990 study at the National Institute of Mental Health correlated ADD with a series of metabolic abnormalities in the brain, providing further evidence that ADD is a neurobiological disorder.

While heredity is often indicated, problems in prenatal development, birth complications, or later neurological damage can contribute to ADD. There is little scientific evidence to suggest that environmental factors, dietary factors such as food dyes or sugar, middle ear problems, or "visual motor" difficulties are the underlying cause of ADD.

Diagnosis of ADD in Adults

A multi-factored evaluation of an individual is important in the diagnosis of ADD. Diagnostic assessment of adults should be made by a clinician or team of clinicians with experience and expertise in the area of attentional dysfunction and related conditions.

ADD with hyperactivity is characterized by symptoms of inattention, impulsivity, and hyperactivity which have an onset before age seven, which persist for at least six months, and which are not due primarily to other psychiatric disorders or environmental circumstances, such as reaction to family stresses.

The primary characteristic of ADD without hyperactivity is significant inattentiveness. Studies of children with this diagnosis indicate that they show more signs of anxiety and learning problems and qualitatively different inattention. Although there have been no adult follow-up studies, it is projected that children who have ADD without hyperactivity may have different outcomes than the hyperactive group, who show more externalizing behavior problems associated with oppositional and conduct disorders.

Various symptoms of ADD may reflect developmental variations in some individuals, while in others, they may indicate that other conditions co-exist with ADD, including specific learning disabilities, anxiety disorders, affective disorders, Tourette's Syndrome, borderline personality disorders, and obsessive compulsive disorder.

The assessment is designed to look for the presence of life-long patterns of behavior that indicate underlying attention and impulse problems. An evaluation of an adult should make use of information from a variety of sources. These may include:

- a thorough medical and family history;
- a physical examination;
- interviews or rating scales completed by others who can comment on the person's behavior, such as a parent, friend, or spouse;
- observation of the individual; and
- psychological tests that measure cognitive abilities, social and emotional adjustment, as well as screen for learning disabilities.

Why Identify ADD in Adults?

Identification of adults who have ADD and appropriate management of their educational, personal, and social development improves their chances for a successful outcome. Effective intervention can improve self-esteem, work performance and skills, and educational achievement.

A proper diagnosis of ADD can help an adult put his or her difficulties into perspective. These individuals have often developed low self-esteem and negative perceptions of themselves as a result of cumulative academic, social, and vocational failures. Many have been labeled as "having a bad attitude," "a slow learner," "lacking motivation," "immature," "lazy," "spacey," or "self-centered." Rather than viewing their difficulties as the result of an inherited or acquired neurobiological disorder, many have come to accept the unsubstantiated belief that they themselves are to blame for their problems.

After Diagnosis: What Then?

Many adults with ADD have been assisted to lead more satisfying and productive lives through appropriate diagnostic and treatment services. In addition to ADD, they may have a variety of behavioral, social, academic, vocational, and family concerns to be addressed. The methods of treatment supported by professionals may include a combination of education for the adult and his or her family and close friends, educational/employment accommodations, medication, and counseling. Appropriate treatment is determined according to the severity of an individual's disorder and the type and number of associated problems.

Many people have benefited from a treatment plan that includes medication. Used in conjunction with education and counseling, it can provide a base from which adults can build new successes. The purpose of medication is to help the adult to help him or herself. It provides the biological support needed for self-control. As such, the individual is not "controlled" by medication; the efforts to succeed are his or her own. Many adults feel a sense of relief following diagnosis. The uncertainty over what was "wrong" is replaced with information and hope for the future. Some tips that adults with ADD have found useful include:

- **Using external structure.** Once in place, structure helps the adult stay on track. This includes using datebooks, lists, notes to oneself, color-coding, routines, reminders, and files.
- **Choosing "good" addictions.** Select exercise or other healthy, favorite activities for a regular structured "blow-out" time.
- **Setting up a rewarding environment.** Design projects, tasks, etc., to minimize or eliminate frustration. Break large tasks into smaller ones; prioritize.
- **Using Time-outs.** Take time to calm down and regain perspective when upset, overwhelmed or angry. Walk away from a situation, if needed.
- **Using Humor.** It's useful if partners and colleagues are constantly providing an aggressive push to help one stay on track – as long as it's done with humor and sensitivity. Learn to view symptoms of ADD with humor and to joke with close friends and relatives about symptoms, such as getting lost, forgetfulness, etc.
- **Getting a Coach.** A friend, spouse, counselor, etc. can help you with organization, point out what needs to be done, and provide encouragement.
- **Becoming educated and an educator.** Read books. Talk to professionals. Talk to other adults who have ADD. Let people who matter know about personal strengths and weaknesses related to ADD. Be an advocate.

New Directions

CH.A.D.D. is working to increase the understanding of ADD in adults. In 1993, it changed its name to Children and Adults with Attention Deficit Disorders. In addition to increasing public and professional awareness of this previously "hidden" disorder, additional research and training is needed to develop diagnostic and treatment procedures. In this collection of articles – some of which have appeared in CH.A.D.D. publications or have been presented at CH.A.D.D. conferences, and some of which are being published for the first time – adults with ADD, their family members, and friends, will find valuable information and strategies for successfully managing ADD.

Adult Issues Committee
CH.A.D.D. National Board of Directors

Editor's Note: You will note that this book uses the terms Attention Deficit Disorder (ADD) and Attention Deficit/Hyperactivity Disorder (AD/HD). Most of the time, we use the term ADD to refer to all sub-types of this disorder. However, some authors prefer to use AD/HD – in those cases, we have respected the author's wishes.

Foreword

Kevin Murphy, Ph.D.
University of Massachusetts Medical Center
Worcester, Massachusetts

Until relatively recently, Attention Deficit Disorder (ADD) was thought to exist only in children. The belief was that ADD was a childhood disorder, which, by definition, remitted during adolescence and certainly by adulthood. We now know that this is not the case for most. Numerous prospective and retrospective studies of children diagnosed with ADD followed into adulthood have demonstrated that from 50 to 80 percent continue to have significant ADD symptoms and associated impairment into their adult lives. Although there are still some who question the validity or even the existence of the diagnosis of ADD in adults, those of us who live, work, and do research with this population have no question that it is indeed a bona fide disorder that can cause significant disruption in all aspects of adult functioning including work, school, social, family, and daily adaptive functioning.

Why has this disorder in adults suddenly become so visible and popular? One reason is the frequent and sometimes controversial media exposure on the subject. ADD in adults has been featured on numerous prime time television and radio shows, news broadcasts, in local and major newspapers and magazines, and in documentaries. Further, an explosion of popular books on adult ADD has contributed to making this term practically a household name. In short, what was once a rather obscure and relatively unknown diagnosis has now become far more visible in our society – almost a part of our culture.

This explosion of publicity about ADD in adults has, in my view, both a positive and a negative side. On the one hand, the greater exposure and awareness has resulted in many adults being accurately identified and treated for the first time in their lives. The quality of life for many of these adults has been vastly improved, and they are leading more productive and satisfying lives. The knowledge that there is a name for their lifelong struggles, and that it is neurobiological in origin and is treatable has offered hope to millions. The downside is that the widespread publicity of the disorder in adults has given rise to much confusion and controversy. Skepticism abounds in large part due to the difficulty in accurately assessing and diagnosing the condition and the fact that almost everyone can identify with at least some of the symptoms.

So who has the real disorder and who doesn't? Where do we draw the line? The boundaries can get blurred if we are not careful. Rendering the adult ADD diagnosis too liberally can have significant social, academic, vocational, and/or legal implications and can potentially undermine the efforts of those who actually do have the disorder in their bid for social acceptance of their condition. Indeed, accurate diagnosis of this disorder has huge implications. For example, whether or not somebody meets diagnostic criteria can impact areas such as special education budgets, school and workplace accommodations, eligibility for test accommodations, and eligibility for legal protection under the Americans with Disabilities Act. It is therefore critically important to be tight in our methodology, rigorous in our assessments, consistent in our application of diagnostic criteria, and conservative in our diagnostic judgments so that this legitimate disorder does not become tarnished or trivialized.

At this point in time, there is little scientific data available to guide us in the assessment and treatment of ADD in adults. To date, we have largely relied on clinical anecdotes and impressions, case illustrations, trial and error, and common sense in working with this population. Consequently, there are presently many more questions than answers.

The questions that we are wrestling with include:

- Are the current *DSM-IV* criteria adequate for diagnosing the condition in adults?

- What are the best methods for assessment?

- How much testing is necessary and which tests are most useful in identifying ADD symptomatology?

- How do we differentiate "true" ADD from simply being a product of today's busy world?

- What kinds of impairment are evident in adults with ADD at work, in school, in family/marital life, or in social and daily adaptive functioning?
- Are there differences between adults who are self-referring for evaluation versus those who were diagnosed as children and followed to adulthood?
- How do we determine the threshold of impairment/deviance required for a clinical diagnosis?
- What are the most common comorbidities associated with adult ADD?
- What kinds of psychosocial treatments are most effective?
- How many adults have ADD?
- What are the variables associated with positive outcomes in this population?
- What are the differences between ADD with and without hyperactivity? Are they the same disorder?
- Are there gender differences and if so, what are they?
- How do we best serve college students with ADD?
- Which treatments work best for whom and under what conditions?

These and many other questions are difficult to answer at this time. Continued scientific inquiry is essential to shed more definitive light on these issues. We are in great need of sound empirical research to help drive our assessment and treatment interventions with this population. As the field grows and matures and as we await the results of future scientific inquiry, we will continue to wrestle with these and other questions.

Although we still have many challenges left to conquer, the future has never been brighter and more hopeful for both children and adults with ADD. With the efforts of advocacy organizations such as CH.A.D.D. and increasing numbers of professionals devoting their efforts to studying this disorder, we are sure to make continued and steady progress in better understanding this often misunderstood disorder.

The following collection of articles is an excellent starting point for understanding many of the issues before us. CH.A.D.D. has compiled a wealth of information that summarizes what we know about adult ADD up to this point in time. The articles herein are an invaluable resource for clinicians, families, patients, and educators and are written by a variety of national experts on ADD in adults. The reader will find useful and practical information on a wide range of topics including assessment, medication and psychosocial treatments, coaching, college and workplace/career issues, ADD and the law, social/interpersonal issues, and even ADD in the military!

Congratulations to CH.A.D.D. for this extraordinary contribution and for once again demonstrating its commitment to improving the lives of individuals with ADD and those who care for them.

CHAPTER 1

ASSESSMENT AND DIAGNOSIS

An Introduction by Russell A. Barkley, Ph.D.

University of Massachusetts Medical Center,

Director of Psychology and Professor of Psychiatry & Neurology

The increasing number of adults seeking clinical evaluations for attention deficit hyperactivity disorder (AD/HD) has placed an unusual burden on mental health providers specializing in adult treatment, who are quickly trying to get up to speed on the nature, evaluation, and management of the disorder, which were unlikely to have been a part of their formal training. Yet even now, the number of referrals for such evaluations probably have barely scratched the surface of the considerably larger population that likely has the disorder, estimated in some studies to be at least 3 percent or more of the adult population (Murphy & Barkley, 1996). We can anticipate, then, that as the general population becomes more aware of the existence of AD/HD in its midst, even more referrals for evaluation and treatment will occur, further taxing mental health providers working with adults. The chapter that follows provides some excellent advice and admonitions on the appropriate procedures to follow in the assessment and diagnosis of AD/HD in adults that should help to fulfill this need for state-of-the-art information.

As these articles make clear, the assessment and diagnosis of AD/HD in adults is fraught with more difficulties than are involved in diagnosing children with AD/HD. For one reason, attempting to find a clinician who may be reasonably knowledgeable about AD/HD as it expresses in adults is no simple matter – clinicians specializing in children do not like to evaluate and treat adult cases because of their relatively lesser degree of training and experience in adult mental disorders, while clinicians focusing on adult mental disorders are far less likely to recognize or respect the legitimacy of AD/HD as an adult disorder in its own right.

Secondly, evaluating adults is a more taxing endeavor given that adults who present themselves to clinics for evaluation of AD/HD are self-referred and often come to clinics alone. Children with AD/HD are typically not self-referred but are accompanied by at least one adult who knows them well (most often a parent) and the ready availability of others with information about them, such as teachers. Therefore, while children with AD/HD may be interviewed about their symptoms, history, domains of potential impairments, etc., there is the handy availability of other sources of information to corroborate or supersede these self-reports. On the other hand, this is less likely to be the case for an adult unless the clinician takes active steps to speak with others who know him or her well. As this chapter duly notes, this is a critical aspect of diagnosis that, while cumbersome, is absolutely essential.

A further reason that the assessment and diagnosis

of AD/HD in adults may be a more complex enterprise is the fact that the very criteria developed for rendering the diagnosis seems to become increasingly less sensitive to the disorder with advancing age of the patient (Barkley, 1996; Murphy & Barkley, 1996). This should not be surprising given that the formal diagnostic criteria in the *DSM-IV* were developed using only children (ages 4-16 years), yet many clinicians first learning of this caveat about the *DSM-IV* do seem surprised by this developmental limitation.

As the articles that follow make apparent, the assessment and diagnosis of adults with AD/HD is a most-thoughtful and sobering endeavor, demanding more of the clinician than is often the case with most other readily accepted adult mental disorders. And as the authors here admonish us, there can be no shortcuts taken in this process, and no great liberties taken with the diagnostic criteria themselves without gutting the very integrity of the disorder and its legitimacy as a true condition of adulthood. The authors here are to be commended for helping to blaze a better trail in the venture of assessment and diagnosis of adult AD/HD, giving us guideposts along the way so that a more sure route to our goal may be obtained more swiftly and reliably than has previously been the case. The reader would do well to heed their sage advice.

REFERENCES

Barkley, R. A. (1996). Attention deficit hyperactivity disorder. In E. J. Mash & R. A. Barkley (Eds.), *Child psychopathology* (pp. 63-112). New York: Guilford.

Fischer, M. (1997). The persistence of childhood AD/HD into adulthood: It depends on who you ask. *The AD/HD Report*, 5 (4), 1 0- 11.

Murphy, K., & Barkley, R. A. (1996). Prevalence of DSM-IV AD/HD symptoms in adult licensed drivers. *Journal of Attention Disorders*, 1, 147-161.

Common Sense about Adult AD/HD

by Stephen P. McDermott, M.D., Thomas Spencer, M.D., and Timothy E. Wilens, M.D.

Much has been written recently about attention-deficit/hyperactivity disorder (AD/HD) in adults, in both the medical and general press. The literature has ranged from descriptions so broadly-based that one might question whether anyone could escape a diagnosis of AD/HD, to articles mocking those who even suggest its existence. Yet, between these extreme views of AD/HD, there exists a reasonable common ground based on research and common sense.

Given the vast amount of conflicting information (and opinion framed as fact) circulating in the general press today, patients may be uncertain about their AD/HD diagnosis. This can perplex family members trying to deal with their symptoms. It also can create a quandary for employers, who are confused about whether they are dealing with a legitimate psychiatric disorder, or just problematic personality styles. Confusion is apparent on occasion even in the medical literature; as a result, doctors and other clinicians may be reluctant to diagnose AD/HD in their patients, even though they meet the diagnostic criteria for the disorder.

As psychiatrists who specialize in the treatment of patients with AD/HD, we see the need to address the common misconceptions about AD/HD in adults. We have encountered all of these misconceptions among patients, their families, and referring clinicians. These misunderstandings often create problems for patients who receive this diagnosis, and can raise questions among clinicians regarding their own diagnostic abilities and the best treatment course for their patients.

AD/HD: WHAT IT IS AND WHAT IT IS NOT

AD/HD is a disorder generally characterized by three core symptoms: hyperactivity, inattention/distractibility, and impulsivity. These frequently lead to complaints of disorganization and interpersonal conflict in personal and work lives.

Studies show that adults with AD/HD often complain of stubbornness, low frustration tolerance, and chronic conflicts in social relations with peers, spouses, and authorities. Studies also show higher rates of separation and divorce, and poor academic and occupational achievement despite adequate intellectual abilities, compared to people without this disorder. Adults with AD/HD commonly describe their work difficulties and frequent job changes as stemming from dissatisfaction, easy frustration, boredom, and impulsiveness. Employers of these adults, when asked to compare them with other employees, report they have poor levels of work performance, impairment in task completion, lack of independent skills, and poor relationships with supervisors.

In addition to the problems that result directly from the effects of AD/HD, adults with AD/HD also show increased incidence of psychoactive substance use, anxiety, and mood and conduct disorders.

Psychiatrists have developed a set of criteria for each major psychiatric disorder, which allows them to distinguish one disorder from another and make certain that what one clinician describes as a disorder in a patient is readily understood by another. These criteria are presented in the *Diagnostic and Statistical Manual of Mental Disorders, Version IV, (DSM-IV)* of the American Psychiatric Association.

The diagnosis of AD/HD is made definitively in adults if the patient has had six or more of the nine symptoms listed in *DSM-IV* for either the inattention or hyperactive/impulsive subtypes. These symptoms must have been present before age seven, and be continuous through adolescence and adulthood. They must be, "to a degree that is maladaptive and inconsistent with their developmental level," and there must be "clear evidence of clinically significant impairment in social, academic, or occupational functioning." Also, these symptoms must not occur exclusively during the course of other disorders, nor be better accounted for by another mental disorder.

It is important to understand the diagnostic criteria describe symptoms that may not always be present (just as some individuals with anxiety disorders are not constantly nervous). Individuals with AD/HD may find themselves as engrossed in their favorite movie or sport as individuals without AD/HD. Where these two groups vary is in their ability to concentrate on tasks which are not inherently attention-grabbing.

Some authors have written about other signs and symptoms that they believe may be associated with AD/HD, such as personality styles, emotional components, or temperament, but these more broadly-based descriptions are not part of the criteria for AD/HD as defined by the *DSM-IV*, the "gold-standard" of psychiatric diagnosis.

THE MYTHS OF ADULT AD/HD

The misinformation one commonly encounters about adult AD/HD has led to a confusing and pervasive mythology about it. Some of these myths, and the more accurate responses to them, are presented here.

"The criteria are so loose and broad that anyone can have it."

Much has been made of the rather broad and pervasive quality of the core symptoms. Obviously, most individuals have, at some time, acted impulsively or been distractible or disorganized. Some authors have used these broad definitions to dispute the validity of AD/HD as a diagnosis.

The *DSM-IV* attempts to more narrowly and precisely define a disorder by requiring a specific number of concrete, observable behaviors in order to make the diagnosis (for example, six out of nine behaviors).

Also, while much attention has been focused on the diagnostic criteria related to "attention-deficit" and "hyperactivity," some individuals fail to understand that the mere presence of symptoms does not mean that one has a disorder. *DSM-IV* requires that the symptoms be present "to a degree that is maladaptive and inconsistent with (the individual's) developmental level." This means that these characteristics must be of greater severity, duration and/or frequency than for the average individual (who does not have the disorder), and that they cause "clinically significant impairment in social, academic, or occupational functioning" in order to be classified as AD/HD.

While any individual may have periods of hyperactivity, impulsivity, or distractibility, the individual with AD/HD shows this as a pervasive pattern. That is, these core symptoms are accurate descriptions of their baseline functioning, and not merely occasional variances from a better level of functioning.

Research shows that adults can make these distinctions. Joseph Biederman, M.D. and his colleagues reported that a sample of adults who were not at increased risk for AD/HD were no more likely to "see" themselves as exhibiting AD/HD symptoms than would be expected given the prevalence of AD/HD in the general population. Their study suggests that adults can accurately determine whether they have symptoms related to AD/HD, and if so, whether these symptoms are beyond what is reasonably expected for adults (Biederman, 1993).

Not all hyperactivity, impulsivity, or distractibility is AD/HD. Each and all of these symptoms can be caused by other physical or psychological processes, such as mood and anxiety disorders, neurological disorders, substance abuse, and medication effects. The diagnosis of AD/HD will not meet *DSM-IV* criteria if the symptoms are "better accounted for" by these other disorders.

On the other hand, AD/HD can co-exist with other disorders. Biederman and his coworkers reported higher rates of anxiety, mood, and antisocial disorders in adults with AD/HD. Because the symptoms of these disorders can overlap, consultation with a mental health professional who is experienced in the evaluation of AD/HD may be helpful.

Even if AD/HD is present, it may not be the most significant problem for the individual. For example, individuals with AD/HD may also have problems with anxiety, depression, or substance abuse, which have far greater impact on their functioning than their AD/HD. These disorders can interfere with the treatment of the AD/HD, which can also complicate the treatment of the other disorders. The full impact of the AD/HD on an individual – whether minimal, severe, or somewhere in between – may not become apparent until these disorders are treated first. This further reinforces the need for the comprehensive evaluation of an individual presenting with co-existing conditions.

"AD/HD is just the 'fad' diagnosis of this decade."

Some writers have questioned the validity of the diagnosis of AD/HD in adults merely because it is diagnosed (and discussed) so much more frequently today. Their logic seems to be, "How can this disorder be so common now, yet be previously unknown?"

In fact, AD/HD is a disorder which has been described in different forms for almost one hundred years. It has been known by various names, including hyperactivity, hyperkinesis, minimal brain dysfunction, and attention deficit disorder (ADD). Each name change reflected increased knowledge about the disorder.

Much of the initial clinical work and research has involved child populations. According to Martha B. Denckla, M.D. (as quoted by Paul Wender, M.D., in his book, *The Hyperactive Child, Adolescent, and Adult:*

Attention Deficit Disorder Through the Lifespan), "As for adults, since they were either lost to follow-up (or never seen) by pediatricians, child psychiatrists, or child-oriented clinics, their 'hyperactivity' was not appreciated." Due in part to the work of Dr. Wender and his associates, who started to describe children diagnosed with AD/HD after reaching adulthood, the concept of "attention-deficit/hyperactivity disorder – residual type" became better understood.

As research on adult AD/HD advances further, we will be better able to distinguish subtypes and develop ways of differentiating it from similar and comorbid conditions. In order for this to happen, though, we must first accept AD/HD as a valid diagnosis in adults. To quote Spencer and his colleagues in the *Harvard Review of Psychiatry*:

"The validity of the diagnosis of AD/HD in adults is of more than academic interest. This disorder is not benign....(G)iven the longer duration of psychopathology and the increased demands for independent functioning, the level of dysfunction may be even more severe in adults than in children. A lifetime of interpersonal, academic, and occupational failure may be qualitatively and quantitatively different than a limited experience in childhood in a more protected family setting."

"AD/HD is just an excuse for not dealing with one's problems."

Some authors in the popular press and the psychiatric literature have expressed concern that a diagnosis of AD/HD is an excuse that allows individuals to blame their daily dilemmas and problematic life events on something over which they have no control, instead of accepting the responsibility for dealing with them.

Most adults with AD/HD lead active and productive lives. They don't use their disorder to excuse themselves from dealing with their problems. Instead, they seek treatment because they seem to have to work so much harder than other people to accomplish the same tasks.

As with any other disorder, some adults have AD/HD that severely affects their daily functioning to the point where it is almost disabling. But AD/HD is no more an excuse for being unable to do something than is any other disorder. Although certain things may be more difficult to do, they still can be done once the individual has the proper "tools" and motivation for using them. These "tools" may be new skills learned through psychotherapy, self-help materials, support groups, and/or medications.

However, as with many other disorders, the motivation of individuals with AD/HD to develop new ways to tackle their problems can be "disabled" by the beliefs they hold about themselves. These beliefs are often the result of a lifetime of mislabeling by those around them. Sometimes the most damaging aspects of AD/HD are the labels which these individuals have received, such as "lazy," "stupid," and "unmotivated." These mistaken categorizations are usually attached by well-meaning family members, teachers, friends, and employers. Patients treated in the mental health system often are told erroneously that their symptoms are due to "resistance," "masochism," and "secondary gain." Even in some segments of the AD/HD treatment and self-help communities, patients' difficulties are ascribed to such poorly-defined concepts as "the need for chaos."

These labels not only inaccurately reflect the cause of these individuals' problems, they also imply an inability or unwillingness to change. "Laziness" or "stupidity" are usually seen as deeply-ingrained personality traits (with the implication that these are virtually impossible to modify), while being "unmotivated" suggests one merely needs to decide to "just do it" and all will be well. Yet the descriptions themselves have the effect of diminishing the likelihood that the individual *will* change. The pervasive, unchanging quality of these labels increases patients' hopelessness about their condition, decreasing their motivation for treatment.

These representations are harmful to individuals with AD/HD and to those with whom they interact, for in reality, the situation is both more hopeful and more complicated than these labels suggest. New medication regimens and psychotherapy protocols specifically developed for AD/HD, such as cognitive therapy, provide promise even for individuals with previously treatment-resistant disorders.

But what of the excuse, "I can't do it – I have AD/HD"? This explanation for not attempting something is based on the fear of failure many of these individuals experience due to decades of past failure experiences. Through thoughtful, competent treatment, such individuals can learn to turn their "inability" into a "difficulty" that may diminish with further practice.

AD/HD is a common psychiatric disorder of children and adults. It can take a severe toll on individuals, their families and friends, and their employers. The encouraging news is that this sometimes difficult disorder can be treated successfully. In order to do so, we need not only recognize its presence in an individual, but acknowledge its existence as a valid psychiatric disorder.

This article first appeared in the Fall 1995 issue of ATTENTION!

Stephen P. McDermott, M.D. is Director of the Cognitive Therapy and Research Program at Massachusetts

General Hospital and Instructor in Psychiatry at Harvard Medical School.

Thomas Spencer, M.D. is the Assistant Director, Pediatric Psychopharmacology; the Assistant Chief, Pediatric Psychopharmacology Clinic; and the Assistant Chief, Pediatric Psychopharmacology Research Program at Massachusetts General Hospital.

Timothy E. Wilens, M.D. is Staff at the Pediatric Psychopharmacology unit at Massachusetts General Hospital, and Associate Professor of Psychiatry at Harvard Medical School.

REFERENCES

American Psychiatric Association (1994), *Diagnostic and Statistical Manual of Mental Disorders*, 4th ed. Washington, DC, American Psychiatric Association.

Biederman J, Faraone SV, Spencer T, Wilens TE, Norman D, Lapey KA, Mick E, Lehman B, Doyle A (1993), Patterns of psychiatric comorbidity, cognition, and psychosocial functioning in adults with attention deficit hyperactivity disorder. *Am J Psychiatry* 150: 1792-1798.

Mannuzza S, Klein RG, Bessler A, Malloy P, LaPadula M. (1993), Adult outcome of hyperactive boys: Educational achievement, occupational rank, and psychiatric status. *Arch Gen Psychiatry* 50: 565-576.

Spencer T, Biederman J, Wilens T, Faraone S. (1994), Is attention deficit hyperactivity disorder in adults a valid diagnosis? *Harvard Review of Psychiatry* 1: 326-35.

Wender P, Reimherr F, Wood D. (1981), Attention deficit disorder ('minimal brain dysfunction') in adults. *Arch Gen Psychiatry* 38: 449-456.

Wood D, Reimherr F, Wender P, Johnson G. (1976), Diagnosis and treatment of minimal brain dysfunction in adults. *Arch Gen Psychiatry* 33: 1453-1460.

Weiss G, Hechtman, L. (1986), *Hyperactive children grown up*. New York, The Guilford Press.

McDermott S, Wilens T. (In Press), Cognitive and emotional impediments to treating the adult with AD/HD: a cognitive therapy perspective. In Brown T (ed), *Attention deficit disorders and comorbidity in children, adolescents, and adults*. Washington, DC, American Psychiatric Press.

Biederman J, Faraone S, Knee D, Munir K. (1990), Retrospective assessment of DSM-III attention deficit disorder in non-referred individuals. *J Clin Psychiatry* 51: 102-7.

Wender P. (1987), *The Hyperactive Child, Adolescent, and Adult: Attention Deficit Disorder Through the Lifespan*. New York, Oxford University Press.

Wilens TE, Spencer TJ, Biederman, J. (In press), J: *Pharmacotherapy of adult AD/HD*. In Nadeau KG (ed), A Comprehensive Guide to Attention Deficit Disorders in Adults.

Vatz RE. (1994), Attention deficit delirium, *The Wall Street Journal*. New York, , A16.

Shaffer D (1994), Attention deficit hyperactivity disorder in adults (editorial). *Am J Psychiatry* 151: 633-638.

Getting Professional Help for Problems of Inattention

by The Program Committee, CH.A.D.D. National Board of Directors

ADD is a disorder in which the primary symptoms are impairment of an individual's ability to sustain attention, focus, and concentrate. A number of conditions other than ADD can interfere with attention. Therefore, if an individual is experiencing problems related to inattention, it is important that he or she seek professional help to determine the cause and discuss options for treatment.

The treatment of ADD includes hope, education, and good professional assessment. The following questions are suggested for use in interviewing professionals regarding their qualifications and practices with regard to the assessment and treatment of patients with ADD and co-existing conditions.

QUESTIONS TO ASK POTENTIAL PROVIDERS OF CLINICAL SERVICES FOR ADD

Name of professional: _____

Phone: _____

Address:_____

_____

1. Type of Professional:
   ☐ Pediatrician   ☐ Neurologist   ☐ Psychiatrist
   ☐ Family Practice Doctor   ☐ Other M.D. or D.O.
   (Physician)   ☐ Psychologist
   ☐ Other:_____

2. Do you assess and treat adults with ADD? Yes No

3. Would you say that patients with ADD are a large part of your practice? Yes No

4. Have you had training related to the assessment and treatment of ADD? Yes No

5. For non-physicians: Do you ever refer patients for assessment for medication as a part of the treatment of ADD? Yes No

6. For physicians: Do you recommend medication in the treatment of ADD? Yes No

7. Do you work with other professionals in treating patients with ADD? Yes No
   If yes, with what types of professionals do you routinely work?   ☐ physicians
   ☐ educational specialists   ☐ counselors
   ☐ social workers   ☐ psychologists

8. What types of therapies do you recommend for the treatment of ADD?_____
   _____

9. Do you provide assessment and treatment for related problems?
   ☐ learning disabilities   ☐ anxiety   ☐ head injury
   ☐ behavior disorders   ☐ Tourette's Syndrome
   ☐ mood disorders

10. Do you offer counseling or psychotherapy for patients with ADD or their families? Yes No

11. Do you provide couples therapy for adults with ADD and their partners? Yes No

12. Do you teach parenting skills to parents of children with ADD? Yes No

13. Do you work with patients/schools to address related educational issues? Yes No

14. Do you provide group therapy or support groups related to ADD? Yes No

15. Do you refer patients with ADD or their families to support groups? Yes No

16. What is your fee or hourly rate? _____

17. Additional comments:_____
    _____
    _____
    _____
    _____

Diagnosing ADD in Adults

by Timothy E. Wilens, M.D., Thomas J. Spencer, M.D., and Jefferson Prince, M.D.

INTRODUCTION

There is an increasing recognition of adults with ADD in both mental health, general medical, and addiction domains (Spencer, 1994; Wilens, 1994). Despite this awareness, many practitioners remain reluctant to assess individuals for ADD. This article will review salient characteristics of ADD and provide diagnostic information.

Approximately 4 percent of adults are estimated to have ADD (Murphy, 1996). The disorder commonly impacts all aspects of life including work, relationships, and psychological status. Although historically ADD has been considered only a disorder of children, more recent reports have documented the persistence of ADD in up to 50 percent of young adults diagnosed as having ADD in childhood (Gittelman, 1985; Weiss, 1993; Mannuzza, 1993). The persistent inability to concentrate, multiple failures, disapproval, and demoralization may contribute to low self-esteem. Recent studies confirm that ADD is commonly associated not only with antisocial disorders, but also with anxiety and depressive disorders (Biederman, 1993). While its etiology remains unknown, family, adoption, and twin studies have indicated that there is a genetic link to the disorder (Farone, 1992).

Adults may be identified as having ADD through several means: they may recognize their own behaviors when their children are diagnosed with ADD (between one-quarter and one-half of parents of children with ADD have the disorder themselves); they may be receiving treatment for psychological disorders when it is discovered they also have ADD; or they may seek diagnostic and treatment consultation on their own, having access to the abundance of information on the disorder now available to the general public.

Although there are a number of general guides used to assist in the identification of ADD symptoms in adults, potential confusion with other psychological and neurological problems makes it necessary to carefully tease out the specific symptoms and developmental course of ADD and identify any other co-occur-

ring disorders an adult may have. Simply stated, it is important for individuals suspicious of having ADD to receive a comprehensive assessment for the disorder by a medical or mental health professional knowledgeable about ADD. At our center, we often see adults referred for ADD who have other problems, including bipolar disorder, seizures, and pre-senile dementia. Only through a systematic and careful evaluation are we able to determine that other problems exist, which results in a very different treatment strategy for these individuals. In conducting these assessments, we are particularly attentive to many of the symptoms of ADD in adults noted in the following sections.

CORE ADD SYMPTOMS

The "core" ADD symptoms in adults appear to be related to those in children and adolescents. The classic triad of ADD symptoms – namely inattention/distractibility, impulsivity, and hyperactivity – is also experienced by adults (Table 1). Among the most common symptoms of ADD in adults are marked inattention, easy distractibility, and a frequent shifting of activities. In fact, many adults with ADD who do not have reading disabilities report difficulties in reading text, having to repeat paragraphs because of poor concentration, and the inability to complete a book. They also commonly report frequent daydreaming, "spacing out," and excessive boredom, and forgetfulness. These adults appear to have less ability to attend to and encode information in their short-term memory. Although less defined within ADD, organizational difficulties and procrastination are common, as well.

Adults with ADD also report significant degrees of impulsivity and impatience. For instance, many report the inability to tolerate being in traffic or standing in lines, and often have a low frustration tolerance and exhibit severe temper tantrums. Socially, many adults report excessive talking and inappropriate intrusiveness into other people's conversations. Although less common in adults with

ADD, hyperactivity (such as the inability to stay seated for reasonable lengths of time) and fidgeting may be present.

DIAGNOSTIC CONSIDERATIONS

Although the symptoms of ADD may be seen as non-specific, it is important to ascertain the pervasiveness, context, and impairment of each of the symptoms described in Table 1. As with any psychological disorder, ADD symptoms are outside of "normal difficulties" and are both persistent (since childhood) and impairing. Since many adults have integrated adaptive mechanisms in order to live with their ADD symptoms, it is important to evaluate underlying "urges" for which they may be compensating (i.e. impulsivity).

Diagnostic information should be gathered from the patient and, whenever possible, from significant others such as partners, parents, siblings, and close friends. If ancillary data are not available, information from an adult is acceptable for diagnostic and treatment purposes as adults with ADD are appropriate reporters of their own condition. Careful attention should be paid to the childhood onset of symptoms, longitudinal history of the disorder, and differential diagnosis including medical/neurological and psychosocial factors contributing to the clinical presentation. There are no specific laboratory or neuropsychiatric tests available to diagnose ADD, although certain findings on testing (i.e. coding difficulties) may be suggestive of ADD.

Numerous rating scales are available to assist in the diagnosis of adult ADD such as the Wender Utah Rating Scales, which is an extensive patient-rated questionnaire focusing on childhood symptoms and dysfunction (Ward, 1993). More recently published were the Brown ADD Scales (Brown, 1995), which assess for the core symptoms of ADD in addition to suggesting other comorbid (co-occurring) conditions that are often problematic in adults. Both scales have been scientifically validated.

It is important to note, however, that the *DSM-IV* – the American Psychiatric Association's diagnostic manual – continues to be the "gold standard" and serves as an adequate and helpful guide for directing the assessment of ADD (1994). Many practitioners have reproduced the ADD section of the *DSM-IV* and run down the list of symptoms indicated, asking their adult patients if they have experienced the symptoms as a child, as an adult, or both. When assessing the presence or absence of symptoms using developmentally appropriate *DSM-IV* criteria, particular attention should be paid to the onset of symptoms during early childhood. For instance, many adults with ADD will remember a clear history of academic or behavioral difficulties. Although ADD symptoms may not be present during direct interviews with the patient, if present, they are suggestive of more severe ADD. Adults with mixed symptoms of attentional difficulties and impulsivity and/or hyperactivity may have a combined subtype of ADD, whereas those with promi-

---

TABLE ONE
Clinical Symptoms of ADD in Adults

Core Symptoms	Complaints
Inattention/Distractibility	Poor concentration Inability to complete reading, other cognitive tasks Shifting activities frequently Daydreaming Easily distracted by external stimuli or events Distracted by internal thoughts Forgetful (apparent short-term memory problem) Organizational problems Poor attention to detail
Impulsivity	Acts without thinking Talks out of turn Impulsive urges Temper tantrums Impatience
Hyperactivity	Restless feeling Motoric hyperactivity Difficulty remaining seated during meetings, dinner Difficulty working quietly Fidgety

nent inattention and distractibility may be given a diagnosis of a predominantly inattentive type of ADD.

In addition to the "core" ADD symptoms, adults with ADD may also have a number of associated traits. These include stubbornness and chronic conflicts in social relationships with peers, spouses, and authorities. This may be related to their high rates of separation and divorce, and poor academic and occupational achievement despite adequate intellectual abilities. Adults with ADD commonly describe their work difficulties and frequent job changes as stemming from dissatisfaction, easy frustration, boredom, and impulsiveness. Employers of these adults report they have poor levels of work performance, impairment in task completion, lack of independent skills, and poor relationships with supervisors.

COMORBIDITY WITH ADD

Complicating the diagnostic process, ADD commonly co-occurs (comorbid) with other psychopathologic conditions. Surprisingly, when carefully and systematically assessed, there are few symptoms that overlap between ADD and other disorders. The co-occurrence of ADD and mood disorders occurs in approximately one-third of adults and most often includes major depression and minor, long-standing depression (dysthymia). Although less frequent, up to 10 percent of adults with ADD have bipolar disorder. Despite the similarities between the presentations of the disorders, ADD can be distinguished from bipolar disorder by carefully ascertaining lifelong ADD symptoms beginning in childhood. The presence of pervasive mood lability/irritability, cycling of mood, and psychotic symptoms may be more indicative of bipolarity.

Anxiety disorders are also commonly seen in adults with ADD and are easily distinguished by carefully selecting for specific ADD symptoms. The only shared symptoms include "restlessness" or "feeling on edge." In addition, adults with ADD may have an anxiety toward performing cognitive tasks that are affected adversely by their ADD. The careful ascertainment of childhood symptoms will assist in reducing potential diagnostic inaccuracy because of symptom redundancy.

Many adults with ADD also experience learning disorders, further exacerbating academic performance difficulties. In cases where learning disorders are suspected, additional specialized cognitive testing is recommended. Since learning disorders are not responsive to the pharmacological treatments for ADD, this evaluation may assist in the design and implementation of a remedial educational plan for the adult who may be returning to school, or serve as an aid for structuring the current work environment.

Since alcohol and drug use disorders are frequently encountered by adults with ADD, a careful history of substance use should be completed. However, it is important to note that ADD appears to be over-represented in alcohol and drug abusing groups (Wilens, 1995). Therefore, a careful history of childhood dysfunction and ADD symptoms should be taken. Particular attention should be paid to evaluating for drug disorders such as cocaine use, which may mimic or cause ADD symptoms (impulsivity, hyperactivity, distractibility) (Levin, 1996). Individuals with suspected ADD who are actively abusing substances should be entered into a course of treatment to stabilize their addiction. After an appropriate stabilization period of at least one month, during which the patient has an intact sensory system and memory, ADD symptoms should be reassessed. Since ADD developmentally occurs before the use of abusive substances, prominent ADD symptoms should have become evident prior to any substance use disorder.

MANAGEMENT

Having thoroughly evaluated the presence of ADD and other comorbid psychological disorders in adults, clinicians should strategize the intervention plan hierarchically – treating the most severe disorder first. Drug and alcohol misuse should be addressed prior to introducing any medications used to treat ADD, since there are no data that these medications reduce substance use. In fact, the premature use of medications commonly used to treat ADD by the active substance abuser may cause adverse effects (Wilens, 1997). In adults with depression and ADD, the initial intervention should be directed to the treatment of the mood disorder. Likewise, in adults with prominent mood swings and ADD, the stabilization of mood symptoms should precede treatment of the ADD.

While there is data that supports the efficacy of medications such as stimulants and antidepressants (Wilens, 1995), the non-pharmacological treatment of ADD in adults remains more speculative (McDermott, 1997). Adults with the disorder who have an addiction, or those who report psychological distress related to their ADD (i.e., self esteem issues, self-sabotaging patterns, interpersonal disturbances) should be directed to appropriate psychotherapeutic intervention with clinicians who are knowledgeable about the disorder. Cognitive-behavioral based psychotherapeutic interventions, which are gaining popularity in treating adult ADD, appear particularly useful in those adults who have a history of addiction.

CONCLUSION

Adult ADD is an important disorder that adversely impacts various aspects of a patient's life. The disorder commonly co-occurs with substance abuse, mood, anxiety, and/or antisocial disorders. In diagnosing an adult with ADD, careful attention should be paid to the childhood onset of symptoms and continuation of the syndrome from childhood to the present. In cases of potential overlap between disorders, careful attention needs to be paid to overlapping symptoms and the onset of ADD-like symptoms. Treatment for adults with ADD needs to take into consideration the specific needs of the individual and may include both psychotherapeutic and psychopharmacologic intervention.

This article originally appeared in the Spring 1997 issue of ATTENTION!

Timothy E. Wilens, M.D. is Staff at the Pediatric Psychopharmacology unit at Massachusetts General Hospital, and Associate Professor of Psychiatry at Harvard Medical School.

Thomas J. Spencer, M.D. is assistant Director of the Pediatric Psychopharmacology unit at Massachusetts General Hospital, and Assistant Professor of Psychiatry at Harvard Medical School.

Jefferson Prince, M.D. is Staff at the Pediatric Psychopharmacology unit and at Massachusetts General Hospital and Harvard Medical School.

REFERENCES

Biederman J, Faraone SV, Spencer T, Wilens TE, Norman D, Lapey KA, Mick E, Lehman B, Doyle A. Patterns of psychiatric comorbidity, cognition, and psychosocial functioning in adults with attention deficit hyperactivity disorder. *American Journal of Psychiatry.* 1993; 150: 1792-1798.

Brown T. Brown Attention Deficit Disorder Scales. San Antonio, TX: The Psychological Corporation; 1995.

Diagnostic and Statistical Manual of Mental Disorders IV. Washington, D.C.: American Psychiatric Association Press; 1994.

Faraone SV, Biederman J, Chen WJ, Kritcher B, Keenan K, Moore C, Sprich S, Tsuang MT. Segregation analysis of attention deficit hyperactivity disorder. Psychiatric Genetics. 1992;2:257-275.

Gittelman R, Mannuzza S, Shenker R, Bonagura N. Hyperactive boys almost grown up, I: Psychiatric status. Archives of General Psychiatry. 1985,42:937-947.

Levin F, Evans SM, Lugo L, Seham J, Baird D, Kleber H: ADD in cocaine abusers: Psychiatric comorbidity and pattern of drug use. College on Problems of Drug Dependence. San Juan, 1996.

Mannuzza S, Klein RG, Bessler A, Malloy P, LaPadula M. Adult outcome of hyperactive boys: Educational achievement, occupational rank, and psychiatric status. *Archives of General Psychiatry.* 1993;50:565-576.

Murphy K, Barkley R. Prevalence of DSM-IV symptoms of ADD in adult licensed drivers: Implications for clinical diagnosis. *Journal of Attention Disorders.* 1996;1:147-161.

McDermott SP, Wilens TE: Cognitive and emotional impediments to treating the adult with ADD: A cognitive therapy perspective. In Brown T, eds. *Subtypes of Attention Deficit Disorders in Children, Adolescents, and Adults.* Washington, DC: American Psychiatric Press, Inc; 1997: In Press.

Spencer T, Biederman J, Wilens TE, Faraone SV, Li T. Is attention deficit hyperactivity disorder in adults a valid diagnosis? *Harvard Review of Psychiatry.* 1994; 1:326-335.

Ward MF, Wender PH, Reimherr FW. The Wender Utah rating scale: an aid in the retrospective diagnosis of childhood attention deficit hyperactivity disorder. *American Journal of Psychiatry.* 1993;150:885-890.

Weiss G, Hechtman LT. *Hyperactive children grown up.* New York: The Guilford Press; 1986.

Wilens T, Spencer T, Biederman J. Are attention-deficit hyperactivity disorder and the psychoactive substance use disorders really related? *Harvard Review of Psychiatry.* 1995;3:260-262.

Wilens TE, Biederman J, Spencer TJ. Case study: Adverse effects of smoking marijuana while receiving tricyclic antidepressants. *Journal of the American Academy of Child and Adolescent Psychiatry.* 1997;36:45-48.

Wilens TE, Biederman J, Spencer TJ, Frances RJ. Comorbidity of attention deficit hyperactivity disorder and the psychoactive substance use disorders. *Hospital and Community Psychiatry.* 1994;45:421-435.

Wilens TE, Prince JB, Biederman J, Spencer TJ. Pharmacotherapy of adult Attention-Deficit/ Hyperactivity Disorder: A review. *Journal of Clinical Psychopharmacology.* 1995;15:270-279.

Assessment of AD/HD in Adults

by Kevin Murphy, Ph.D.

A number of questions frequently arise for both clinicians and consumers in this era of managed care and cost containment: What constitutes a sound and thorough assessment to determine an accurate Adult AD/HD diagnosis? How much and what kind of testing is necessary? How long should it take? How does one differentiate between true AD/HD and "normal" variations of symptoms that are part and parcel of what might be considered "life in the 90s?" Is there a better explanation for the symptoms than AD/HD? What kind of historical data is helpful to have? How do we really know who has it and who doesn't?

Oftentimes, these are not easy questions to answer. Adults seeking an AD/HD evaluation frequently present a complex diagnostic puzzle. For example, it is not uncommon for adults to qualify for multiple co-existing diagnoses in addition to their AD/HD. Differentiating AD/HD from a mood, anxiety, or substance abuse disorder or determining such things as where depression or anxiety or substance abuse ends and AD/HD begins are not easy tasks. The purpose of this article is to discuss what I believe are some reasonable guidelines for what is involved in a credible Adult AD/HD evaluation. This information comes largely from what I have learned over several years of clinical and research experience in working with this population.

A few general principles to bear in mind are the following:

1. A childhood onset needs to be established. To qualify for the AD/HD diagnosis as an adult, one must have had it as a child. AD/HD is not, by definition, an adult onset disorder.

2. Obtaining information from multiple sources is critical. Including parents, spouses, or significant others in the evaluation whenever possible either in person, through written questionnaires/rating scales, or by telephone contributes additional and important perspectives.

3. Obtaining historical records documenting past behavior is also critical. This can add valuable data and increase the degree of confidence the clinician has in rendering a diagnosis.

4. Other psychiatric diagnoses or circumstances that may be better explanations for the symptoms must be ruled out.

It should be stated up front that diagnosing AD/HD in adults is not an exact science. Only a very limited number of well designed and well controlled scientific studies have been conducted on adults with AD/HD to date. Our methods of assessment and treatment have not been well studied and need further inquiry. However, we do know that there is no single neurological or psychological test or test battery that can conclusively determine an AD/HD diagnosis. Furthermore, the absence of objective records attesting to past school, social, or psychological functioning is a frequent problem. In some cases, the clinician may be faced with relying almost exclusively on the person's retrospective recall of past childhood behavior to establish the chronic nature and pervasiveness of the core symptoms of the disorder. This data can be subjective, influenced by many variables, and, from a scientific standpoint, is, therefore, not the most reliable or valid method of arriving at a diagnosis.

The fact that the symptoms of AD/HD exist on a continuum and virtually everyone experiences them at times can also contribute to diagnostic uncertainty. How then, does the clinician differentiate the threshold of impairment necessary to warrant a clinical diagnosis versus symptoms or behavior falling within the "normal" range? This decision is often quite arbitrary and unscientific with respect to adults.

IMPORTANCE OF PAST RECORDS

To make this decision less subjective, it is critically important to obtain any and all objective information from the past including report cards, past testing reports, performance reviews from work, college transcripts, or even baby books and the like. These kinds of documents often describe and highlight a pattern of behavior consistent with AD/HD symptomatology and add crucial corroborating data that can go a long way towards substantiating the diagnosis. I am often amazed at the written comments teachers have made in describing the classroom behavior and work habits of many of my patients – even on report cards from many years ago when awareness of AD/HD was extremely limited. The semantics are often similar emphasizing themes of chronic underachievement, inattention, incomplete or missing homework, easy distractibility, inconsistent effort, and problems with disruptive behavior and excessive talking. This kind of objective documentation is enormously helpful in validating the diagnosis.

COMPREHENSIVE INTERVIEW

A comprehensive clinical interview should be conducted, surveying past and present AD/HD symptomatology, developmental and medical history, school history, work history, psychiatric history including any medications prescribed, social adjustment, and general day-to-day adaptive functioning (i.e., how they are doing in meeting the demands of daily life). This should not simply be a brief surface level exam; it should take a minimum of one to two hours. Beware of the clinician who gives a positive diagnosis after only a cursory set of questions lasting only a few minutes. This is simply not sufficient. Ideally, the interview should rely on several informants (a parent if possible) and survey behavior from multiple settings (e.g., work, school, home). It is also important that the clinician attempt to rule in or rule out other psychiatric diagnoses that may be a better explanation for the presenting symptoms. This may involve the use of a published structured psychiatric interview such as the SCID (Structured Clinical Interview for *DSM*). Doing so not only helps in the differential diagnosis of AD/HD but also may establish the existence of one or more additional diagnoses (such as depression or substance abuse) that may co-occur with the AD/HD.

RATING SCALES

The use of behavior rating scales for patients and significant others is also useful in assessment. For example, using the *DSM-IV* AD/HD items in the form of a four point rating scale (rarely, sometimes, often, very often) to assess the number of symptoms endorsed for both present functioning and during childhood is essential to determine if the accepted *DSM-IV* thresholds for diagnosis are met. Other symptom rating scales that have been used for assessing adults for AD/HD include the Wender Utah Rating Scale, the Brown Attention-Activation Disorder Scale (BAADS), the Copeland Symptom Checklist for

Adult Attention Deficit Disorder, and Triolo's Attention-Deficit Scales for Adults (ADSA). However, the *DSM-IV* items remain the most commonly recognized, accepted, and scientifically verified set of criteria. Despite the relative lack of normative data on most of these scales for adults, they do help to establish the type and degree of symptomatology present. A number of other rating scales that are not specific to AD/HD may also be useful, such as depression and anxiety scales or marital satisfaction scales.

TESTING

Neuropsychological tests (including Continuous Performance Tests) have not been shown to be especially useful in either supporting or refuting an AD/HD diagnosis. Although they can provide additional data regarding patterns of strengths and weaknesses that can be helpful, they cannot be relied upon to actually make the diagnosis. Abnormal scores do not necessarily mean one has the diagnosis, just as "normal" scores do not mean one does not have it. Again, in my experience, the diagnosis of AD/HD is best made through a careful and comprehensive interview and history taking; not by relying exclusively on a battery of tests.

A standardized intelligence test, or at least a screen for general intelligence, is a particularly useful component of an adult assessment. Correlating one's native intelligence with one's overall school achievement over the years can provide important clues in understanding school problems. For example, a pattern seen frequently in adults and children with AD/HD is academic underachievement relative to native potential. When someone scores in the average range of intelligence or better, yet has a chronic history of C's, D's, and F's on their report cards, AD/HD related problems may be a plausible explanation. An intellectual assessment also helps to rule out whether one's symptoms of AD/HD may be due to mental retardation, helps to identify the existence of possible learning disabilities, and may help guide treatment strategies and decisions.

No specific medical or neurological tests are routinely necessary in the assessment of AD/HD in adults. However, if the history suggests symptoms of a more severe nature that may be associated with, for example, dementia, Alzheimer's, or another neurological condition, then an appropriate referral should be made. A thorough medical history, however, is essential to fully understand possible medical conditions that may be contributing to or may better explain the symptoms. Certain medical conditions may have important implications regarding treatment decisions, especially with respect to the proper use of medication.

How much impairment is necessary to warrant a clinical diagnosis of AD/HD? The level of impairment required is somewhat subjective, but it must interfere in one's occupational, academic, social, and/or daily adaptive functioning to a "significant" degree. If one truly has AD/HD, there should, in most cases, be a "paper trail" or other observable, measurable, objective evidence of impairment in one or more of these domains. Simply having a subjective sense that one is not satisfied with his/her achievement or having a few of the symptoms to a mild degree that does not interfere appreciably in one's functioning is not sufficient for a diagnosis. It is important to remember that only the extreme end of the continuum truly qualifies for a clinical diagnosis. As my friend and colleague Michael Gordon, Ph.D. states in his book, *The Down and Dirty Guide to Adult ADD*, "the ADD diagnosis makes sense for only a very few people – not for everyone in a zip code." AD/HD is a neurobiological disorder characterized by developmentally inappropriate levels of sustained attention, impulsivity, and in some cases, hyperactivity. There should be evidence that a sufficient number of the symptoms have been present since childhood, that they continue to exist to a significant degree presently, that they are producing significant impairment in the areas mentioned above, and that the symptoms are not better explained by some other psychiatric or organic condition.

It is preferable to have the assessment conducted by a licensed professional (psychiatrist, psychologist, social worker, neurologist) or team of professionals who are experienced and well-trained not only in adult AD/HD, but also in the differential diagnosis of adult psychopathology in general.

In summary, the very limited extent of controlled research, the relative lack of well-normed rating scales, the fact that everyone experiences symptoms of AD/HD to a degree, and the high degree of comorbidity all make the assessment and diagnosis of AD/HD in adults a formidable task. Clinicians should attempt to gather as much historical data and input from others as possible. Based on the data from rating scales, testing, interviews with the patient and significant others, and inspection of prior records, clinicians must make their best judgments as to whether criteria are met. Clinicians are cautioned to be comprehensive, careful, and conservative in their approach to diagnosing AD/HD in adults. Rendering the diagnosis too liberally will not only subject the diagnosis to further skepticism, but will potentially undermine the needs of those who legitimately have the disorder.

This article first appeared in the Winter 1996 issue of ATTENTION!

Kevin Murphy, Ph.D. is Chief of the Adult AD/HD Clinic at the University of Massachusetts Medical Center and is an assistant professor in the department of psychiatry. He provides diagnostic and treatment services to adolescents and adults with AD/HD and conducts didactic training and clinical supervision for psychiatry residents.

CHAPTER 2

MANAGEMENT OF ADD

An Introduction by Sam Goldstein, Ph.D.

Clinical Instructor, Department of Psychiatry, University of Utah School of Medicine

Staff Member, Primary Children's Hospital and the University Neuropsychiatric Institute

For many adult practitioners, the concept of AD/HD as an adult disorder is new and the challenges facing support and treatment for these individuals often appears overwhelming. The concepts of AD/HD in adults was originally studied by Paul Wender and his colleagues at the University of Utah. For a very long time it was an ignored phenomenon. More recently, the adult AD/HD field and the concept of the disorder as one of adulthood have been embraced by the public. There has been an almost evangelical movement to popularize the idea of adult AD/HD, at times leaving limited room for scientific study or debate.

In a number of texts and articles, I, along with my colleagues, have made a conscientious effort to distinguish science from non-science and to distinguish nonsense from either of these. Well-controlled research, though difficult, is necessary if physicians, allied health professionals, mental health practitioners, and educators are to make diagnostic decisions and ethically offer treatment for adults with AD/HD. However, such research, especially in the field of adult AD/HD, will require long and arduous effort. In the meantime, those of us in the helping profession must be capable of offering practical, though untested, suggestions without unethically recommending nonsense under the rubric "if it can't hurt, let's try it."

Along this line of reasoning, this section contains seven practical articles authored by well-respected experts in the field of AD/HD. Many of the suggestions offered reflect a blend of clinical judgment, common sense, and experience. They offer a means of organizing one's life, managing daily events, coping with stress and anger, staying organized, and managing relationships. A number of the articles emphasize the role of the professional helper as that of a "coach." Although the precise definition of coaching as it relates to adult AD/HD has yet to be defined, the concept holds intuitive appeal. In my work with children and adults, I have long offered myself as a "coach." I explain that while a therapist or counselor's job may be to locate problems and help the client fix them, a coach's job is to identify assets and strengthen them. If a team member plays a particular position well, say second base, a coach is not going to make that individual an outfielder but rather teach the individual to be an even better second baseman.

The responsibility of balancing what is known and what is not known with what can be realistically done falls on the practitioner's shoulders. To be effective with adults with AD/HD, practitioners must be aware and believe that the phenomenon exists, that many individuals with AD/HD utilize other strengths to compensate for their disabilities and develop a variety of coping strategies, and that for some, AD/HD represents a significant lifetime disability.

Despite increasing knowledge and greater availability of programs, demand outpaces supply in the adult ADD field. Knowledgeable practitioners can provide their clients with a powerful sense of hope by being available and providing accurate information, understanding, and support. Much of the science remains in the future, but common sense and clinical judgment are undeniable. Advocacy and education are making and will continue to make a positive difference in the lives of adults with AD/HD.

Coping Strategies for Adults with AD/HD

by Kevin Murphy, Ph.D.

Historically, AD/HD has been considered a childhood disorder that children would outgrow by adolescence. However, more recent findings have established that symptoms of the disorder are often present through adolescence and into adulthood. Moreover, these symptoms in adults can cause significant interference and disruption in their day to day lives.

Many adults with AD/HD were not diagnosed as children and never knew they had it. The same degree of awareness about AD/HD by parents and teachers, and the more sophisticated assessment methods that exist today did not exist when they were children. This fact, combined with the large percentage of children who were diagnosed in childhood and continue to have symptoms as adults suggests that there are substantial numbers of adults who are affected by the disorder. Most are undiagnosed, untreated, and unaware that help is available.

The symptoms that occur in adults vary in type and severity and can cause significant impairments in interpersonal relations, marriage, emotional well-being, employment, as well as in daily adaptive functioning. Despite their symptoms, some adults have learned to successfully compensate for their difficulties and function very well. However, most adults with AD/HD are restless, easily distracted, have trouble focusing, concentrating and sustaining attention, are impulsive and impatient, have inconsistent work performance, are often unorganized and fail to plan ahead, often fail to finish tasks they have started, have frequent mood swings and a short temper, and often have a chronic pattern of underachievement. It is not surprising that many adults, after years of frustration with their academic, work, and social lives, have developed low self-esteem. They often have a nagging sense of knowing something is wrong but never knowing exactly what it is. In many cases, they have sought help with various mental health professionals who have overlooked AD/HD and have never gotten to the bottom of what has been troubling them.

Once they have been accurately diagnosed by a professional who understands AD/HD, there is often a sense of tremendous relief at finally having an explanation for their longstanding difficulties. However, as with children, there is no "cure" for adult AD/HD. Therefore, learning how to cope with the manifestations of the disorder is critical to its effective management. The following strategies may be helpful in learning to live with adult AD/HD and cope more successfully.

EDUCATION

Perhaps the most important strategy for adults with AD/HD is to seek education about the disorder. Many adults have little knowledge of AD/HD and do not fully understand the implications it may have on their lives. Education can help adults make sense of what has been troubling them, can help them set realistic and attainable goals, and ease their frustration somewhat. Reading literature, talking with other adults with AD/HD, and talking with experienced professionals can help. Developing an informed awareness of how AD/HD manifests itself in their lives may assist them in structuring their lives in ways that will minimize the negative effects of their deficits. Having a framework from which to understand what has been happening to them over the years can assist them in making sense of the past and empower them to cope more effectively in the future. The realization that many of the problems they have experienced stem from neurological causes rather than from laziness or deficits in character or ability, can begin to enhance self-esteem. Educating spouses, family members, and friends is also important so they can understand and be better able to help.

COMPENSATORY BEHAVIORAL STRATEGIES

Adults with AD/HD are frequently unorganized, forgetful, and underproductive. Implementing selected behavioral strategies can be an effective way to combat these deficits and help the person feel more organized, in control, and efficient. Each person has to determine which ones work best for him and practice them until they become part of a normal routine. Here are some suggestions:

- Make a daily list of what you want to accomplish that day and keep it with you at all times.

- Keep an appointment book/planning calendar.

- Keep notepads in strategic places (car, bathroom, by your bed) so when an idea hits you or you want to remember something, you can capture it.

- Use a portable Dictaphone to help you remember, if making written lists doesn't work for you.

- Post schedules, appointments, errand lists, etc. on strategically placed bulletin boards in your home or office.

- Learn and practice time management skills.

- Break down large tasks or projects into a series of smaller, more manageable ones. This will reduce discouragement and lessen the feeling of being over-whelmed.

- Use desk, drawer, or closet organizers; storage boxes; or file cabinets – anything that helps you to organize and add structure to your life.

- Set up a self reward system. For example, set goals and establish corresponding rewards for yourself such as buying something you have wanted. When you attain the goal you had set, reward yourself.

PSYCHOLOGICAL THERAPIES

Not surprisingly, adults with AD/HD often have coexisting problems with depression, anxiety, marriage, family issues, job problems, interpersonal relations, and/or low self-esteem. To address some of these problems, individual, marital, group, or vocational counseling may be helpful. Target goals might be improving interpersonal and social skills, learning stress management and relaxation skills, learning anger control strategies and self organization skills, and improving selfesteem.

It is important to work towards building a success identity with adults who have AD/HD. Encouragement and positive reinforcement are crucial. Many have had a long history of frustration and failure in school, work, and interpersonal arenas. It is important to identify strengths and work with them. For instance, in the vocational domain, these adults sometimes have jobs that are very inconsistent with their strengths and almost guarantee failure. Vocational counseling aimed at matching them to jobs that maximize their strengths and are consistent with their skills can help them experience a greater sense of mastery and accomplishment. In short, rebuilding self-confidence and self-esteem are the major goals.

Group therapy can also be useful. Hearing how others cope and manage their symptoms, realizing there are others with similar problems, having a "laboratory" for learning and trying out new social and interpersonal skills, as well as the group support can be helpful.

Marriage counseling can also be useful. Spouses are clearly affected and are often confused, angry, and frustrated. A spouse of an adult with AD/HD may complain that his/her partner does not listen, is not dependable, always seems distant or preoccupied, or behaves irresponsibly. Understanding the disorder and realizing that many of the problems do not stem from "willful misconduct" may enable the couple to reframe their difficulties, stop blaming, and begin to work together as a team to improve their relationship.

MEDICATION

Many adults with AD/HD benefit from pharma-cotherapy. The same medications used for children are often effective for adults. Although this is not common knowledge among many physicians, it is true. Stimulants and antidepressants can assist adults with their inattention, distractibility, restlessness, and concentration. It also may help with the inner sense of chaos, disorganization, and mood and temper problems that some adults experience. A positive response to medication can enable adults to be more successful in implementing the compensatory behavioral strategies listed above.

OTHER COPING STRATEGIES

- Schedule regular physical exercise into your routine. The benefits are indisputable. It helps to burn off excess energy and aggression in a positive way, reduces stress, clears the mind, and calms the body.

- Maintain or develop a sense of humor. Learn to joke, poke fun at yourself, and not take yourself or your symptoms too seriously. If you can accept yourself and have a sense of humor, others will likely accept and understand you much more readily.

- Work at eliminating negative self statements. Adults with AD/HD are usually very talented at putting themselves down, which only serves to validate and confirm their low self-esteem. Train yourself to recognize and acknowledge your strengths and begin substituting positive self statements (i.e., I accomplished something. Just because I didn't get it all done doesn't mean I wasn't productive) for the negative ones (i.e., I messed up again. I can never get anything done). Try to become your own best friend. This may require some professional counseling.

- Reduce or eliminate alcohol or other drug use. Excessive use does not help moods, temper, work performance, or interpersonal relations. Reducing use will increase chances for improvement and prevent additional problems.

• Many adults with AD/HD have an on-going need for highly stimulating activities. They crave the excitement and enjoy the challenge. Accept this and proactively schedule these kinds of activities for yourself in a positive and healthy way. This will reduce the "need" to create negative excitement if things get too boring.

• Since many adults with AD/HD become bored easily and often lack the proper motivation to complete uninteresting tasks, it is often helpful to obtain on-going feedback about your behavior, both positive and constructive. Enlist a friend, spouse, family member, or therapist to help motivate and encourage you to stay on task, get things done, remind you of commitments, and give you feedback. Ideally, that person should provide lots of support and encouragement, praise you when appropriate, and have a sense of humor. This kind of influence can be invaluable. Learn and practice effective communication skills. For instance, the common complaints that spouses of adults with ADD have (forgetfulness, being unreliable, not following through on tasks) can be helped when partners with ADD learn to listen more effectively. Remind your spouse to maintain eye contact when communicating or making requests and have you reflect back what you heard. This can help to ensure that the message was actually received. Also, ask your spouse to make requests or give directions during times when outside distractions are not competing for your attention.

• Be aware of community resources available, such as academic support services for college students, vocational assessment and training services, self-help groups, and professional organizations like CH.A.D.D.

SUMMARY

The consequences of undiagnosed and untreated AD/HD in adults can cause a great deal of pain, frustration, and conflict in social, career, and family domains. However, many adults with AD/HD function quite well in spite of their continuing symptoms. They have learned to compensate for their deficits by developing effective coping strategies and finding suitable jobs that "fit" for them. Medication may also provide assistance. With the help and support of those around them, a commitment to working hard at making changes, and armed with knowledge and awareness of their disorder, many adults with AD/HD can learn to work around their difficulties and enjoy more productive and satisfying lives.

This article first appeared in the Fall/Winter 1992 issue of CH.A.D.D.er.

Kevin Murphy, Ph.D. is Chief of the Adult AD/HD Clinic at the University of Massachusetts Medical Center and is an assistant professor in the department of psychiatry. He provides diagnostic and treatment services to adolescents and adults with AD/HD and conducts didactic training and clinical supervision for psychiatry residents.

50 Tips on the Management of Adult ADD

by Edward Hallowell, M.D. and John Ratey, M.D.

The treatment of ADD begins with hope. Most people who discover they have ADD, whether they be children or adults, have suffered a great deal of pain. The emotional experience of ADD is filled with embarrassment, humiliation, and self-castigation. By the time the diagnosis is made, many people with ADD have lost confidence in themselves Many have consulted with numerous specialists, only to find no real help. As a result, many have lost hope.

The most important step at the beginning of treatment is to instill hope once again. Individuals with ADD may have forgotten what is good about themselves. They may have lost, long ago, any sense of the possibility of things working out. They are often locked in a kind of tenacious holding pattern, bringing all theory, considerable resiliency, and ingenuity to just keeping their heads above water. It is a tragic loss, the giving up on life too soon. But many people with ADD have seen no other way than repeated failures. For them, to hope is only to risk getting knocked down once more.

And yet, their capacity to hope and to dream is immense. More than most people, individuals with ADD have visionary imaginations. They think big thoughts and dream big dreams. They can take the smallest opportunity and imagine turning it into a major break. They can take a chance encounter and turn it into a grand evening out. They thrive on dreams, and they need organizing methods to make sense of things and keep them on track.

But like most dreamers, they go limp when the dream collapses. Usually, by the time the diagnosis of ADD has been made, this collapse has happened often enough to leave them wary of hoping again. The little child would rather stay silent than risk being taunted once again. The adult would rather keep his mouth shut than risk flubbing things up once more.

We break down the treatment of ADD into five basic areas:

    (1) diagnosis
    (2) education
    (3) structure, support, and coaching
    (4) various forms of psychotherapy
    (5) medication.

In this article, we will outline some general principles that apply both to children and adults concerning the non-medication aspects of the treatment of ADD. One way to organize the non-medication treatment of ADD is through practical suggestions or "tips" on management. Fifty such tips are presented below:

I. INSIGHT AND EDUCATION

(1) **Be sure of the diagnosis**. Make sure you're working with a professional who really understands ADD and has excluded related or similar conditions such as anxiety states, agitated depression, hyperthyroidism, manic-depressive illness, or obsessive-compulsive disorder.

(2) **Educate yourself.** Perhaps the single most powerful treatment for ADD is understanding ADD in the first place. Read books. Talk with professionals. Talk with other adults who have ADD. You'll be able to design your own treatment to fit your own version of ADD.

(3) **Coaching**. It is useful for you to have a coach, for some person near to you to keep after you in a supportive way. Your coach can help you get organized, stay on task, give you encouragement, or remind you to get back to work. Friend, colleague, or therapist (it is possible, but risky, for your coach to be your spouse), a coach is someone to stay on you to get things done, exhort you as coaches do, keep tabs on you, and in general, be in your corner. A coach can be tremendously helpful in treating ADD.

(4) **Encouragement.** Adults with ADD need lots of encouragement. This is in part due to their having many self-doubts that have accumulated over the years. But it goes beyond that. More than the average person, the adult with ADD withers without encouragement and positively thrives when given it. The adult with ADD will often work for another person in a way he won't work for himself. This is not "bad," it

just is. It should be recognized and taken advantage of.

(5) **Realize what ADD is NOT**, i.e., conflict with mother, etc.

(6) **Educate and involve others.** Just as it is key for you to understand ADD, it is equally, if not important, for those around you to understand it – family, friends, people at work or at school. Once they get the concept, they will be able to understand you much better and to help you out as well. It is particularly helpful if your boss can be aware of the kinds of structures that help people with ADD.

(7) **Give up guilt over high-stimulus-seeking behavior.** Understand that you are drawn to high stimuli. Try to choose them wisely, rather than brooding over the "bad" ones.

(8) **Listen to feedback from trusted others.** Adults (and children, too) with ADD are notoriously poor self-observers. They use a lot of what can appear to be denial.

(9) **Consider joining or starting a support group.** Much of the most useful information about ADD has not yet found its way into books but remains stored in the minds of the people who have ADD. In groups, this information can come out. Plus, groups are very helpful in giving the kind of support that is so badly needed.

(10) **Try to get rid of the negativity** that may have infested your system if you have lived for years without knowing what you had was ADD. A good psychotherapist may help in this regard. Learn to break the tapes of negativity that can play relentlessly in the ADD mind.

(11) **Don't feel chained to conventional careers or conventional ways of coping.** Give yourself permission to be yourself. Give up trying to be the person you always thought you should be – the model student or the organized executive, for example – and let yourself be who you are.

(12) **Remember that what you have is a neuro-biological condition.** It is genetically-transmitted. It is caused by biology, by how your brain is wired. It is NOT a disease of the will, nor a moral failing. It is NOT caused by a weakness in character, nor by a failure to mature. It's cure is not to be found in the power of the will, nor in punishment, nor in sacrifice, nor in pain. ALWAYS REMEMBER THIS. Try as they might, many people with ADD have great trouble accepting the syndrome as being rooted in biology rather than weakness of character.

(13) **Try to help others with ADD.** You'll learn a lot about the condition in the process, as well as feel good to boot.

II. PERFORMANCE MANAGEMENT

(14) **External structure.** Structure is the hallmark of the non-pharmacological treatment of the child with ADD. It can be equally useful with adults. Tedious to set up, once in place, structure works like the walls of the bob-sled slide, keeping the sled from careening off the track. Make frequent use of:
    lists
    notes to self
    color-coding
    rituals
    reminders
    files.

(15) **Color-coding.** Mentioned above, color-coding deserves emphasis. Many people with ADD are visually-oriented. Take advantage of this by making things memorable with color: files, memoranda, texts, schedules, etc. Virtually anything in the black and white of type can be made more memorable, arresting, and therefore attention-getting, with color.

(16) **Use pizzazz.** In keeping with #15, try to make your environment as peppy as you want it to be without letting it boil over.

(17) **Set up your environment to reward rather than to deflate**. To understand what a deflating environment is, all most adults with ADD need to do is think back to school. Now that you have the freedom of adulthood, try to set things up so you will not constantly be reminded of your limitations.

(18) **Acknowledge and anticipate** the inevitable collapse of a certain percentage of projects undertaken, relationships entered into, obligations incurred.

(19) **Embrace challenges.** People with ADD thrive with many challenges. As long as you know they won't all pan out, as long as you don't get too perfectionistic and fussy, you'll get a lot done and stay out of trouble.

(20) **Make deadlines.** Think of deadlines as motivational devices rather than echoes of doom. If it helps, call them lifelines instead of deadlines. In any case, make them and stick to them.

(21) **Break down large tasks into small ones.** Attach deadlines to the small parts. Then, like magic, the large task will get done. This is one of the simplest and most powerful of all structuring devices. Often, a large task will feel overwhelming to the person with ADD. The mere thought of trying to perform the task makes one turn away. On the other hand, if the large task is broken down into small parts, each component may feel quite manageable.

(22) **Prioritize.** Avoid procrastination. When things get busy, the adult with ADD loses perspective – paying an unpaid parking ticket can feel as pressing as putting out the fire that just got started in the wastebasket.

Prioritize. Take a deep breath. Put first things first. Procrastination is one of the hallmarks of adult ADD. You have to really discipline yourself to watch out for it and avoid it.

(23) **Accept fear of things going too well.** Accept edginess when things are too easy, when there's no conflict. Don't gum things up just to make them more stimulating.

(24) **Notice how and where you work best:** in a noisy room, on the train, wrapped in three blankets, listening to music, whatever. Children and adults with ADD can do their best under rather odd conditions. Let yourself work under whatever conditions are best for you.

(25) **Know that it is okay to do two things at once:** carry on a conversation and knit, or take a shower and do your best thinking, or jog and plan a business meeting. Often, people with ADD need to be doing several things at once in order to get anything done at all.

(26) **Do what you're good at.** Again, if it seems easy, that's okay. There is no rule that says you can only do what you're bad at.

(27) **Leave time between engagements to gather your thoughts.** Transitions are difficult for adults with ADD, and mini-breaks can help ease the transition.

(28) **Keep a notepad in your car, by your bed, and in your pocketbook or jacket.** You never know when a good idea will hit you, or you'll want to remember something else.

(29) **Read with a pen in hand**, not only for marginal notes and underlining, but also for the inevitable cascade of "other" thoughts that will occur to you.

III. MOOD MANAGEMENT

(30) **Have structured "blow-out" time.** Set aside some time in every week for just letting go. Whatever you like to do – listening to music, taking a trip to the race track, having a feast – pick some kind of activity from time to time where you can let loose in a safe way.

(31) **Recharge your batteries.** Related to #30, most adults with ADD need, on a daily basis, some time to waste without feeling guilty about it. One guilt-free way to conceptualize it is to call it time to recharge your batteries. Take a nap, watch TV, meditate. Something calm, restful, at ease.

(32) **Choose "good," helpful addictions** such as exercise. Many adults with ADD have an addictive or compulsive personality such that they are always hooked on something. Try to make this something positive.

(33) **Understand mood changes** and ways to manage these. Know that your moods will change willy-nilly, independent of what's going on in the external world.

Don't waste your time ferreting out the reason why or looking for someone to blame. Focus rather on learning to tolerate a bad mood, knowing that it will pass, and learning strategies to make it pass sooner. Changing sets, i.e., getting involved with some new activity (preferably interactive) such as a conversation with a friend or a tennis match or reading a book will often help.

(34) **Related to #33, recognize the following cycle, which is very common among adults with ADD:**

a. Something "startles" your psychological system, a change or transition, a disappointment, or even a success. The precipitant may be quite trivial.

b. This "startle" is followed by a mini-panic with a sudden loss of perspective, the world being set topsy-turvy.

c. You try to deal with this panic by falling into a mode of obsessing and ruminating over one or another aspect of the situation. This can last for hours, days, even months.

(35) **Plan scenarios to deal with the inevitable "blahs."** Have a list of friends to call. Have a few videos that always engross you and get your mind off things. Have ready access to exercise. Have a punching bag or pillow handy if there's extra angry energy. Rehearse a few pep talks you can give yourself, like, "You've been here before. These are the ADD blues. They will soon pass. You are okay."

(36) **Expect depression after success.** People with ADD commonly complain of feeling depressed, paradoxically, after a big success. This is because the high stimulus of the chase or the challenge or the preparation is over. The deed is done. Win or lose, the adult with ADD misses the conflict, the high stimulus, and feels depressed.

(37) **Learn symbols, slogans, sayings** – shorthand ways of labeling and quickly putting into perspective slip-ups, mistakes, or mood swings. When you turn left instead of right and take your family on a twenty-minute detour, it is better to be able to say, "There goes my ADD again," than to have a six-hour fight over your unconscious desire to sabotage the whole trip. These are not excuses. You still have to take responsibility for your actions. It is just good to know where your actions are coming from and where they're not.

(38) **Use "time-outs" as with children.** When you are upset or over-stimulated, take a time-out. Go away. Calm down.

(39) **Learn how to advocate for yourself.** Adults with ADD are so used to being criticized, they are often unnecessarily defensive in putting their own case forward. Learn to get off the defensive.

(40) **Avoid premature closure of a project**, a conflict, a

deal, or a conversation. Don't "cut to the chase" too soon, even though you're itching to.

(41) **Try to let the successful moment last** and be remembered, become sustaining over time. You'll have to consciously and deliberately train yourself to do this because you'll just as soon forget.

(42) **Remember that ADD usually includes a tendency to overfocus or hyperfocus at times.** This hyperfocus can be used constructively or destructively. Be aware of its destructive use: a tendency to obsess or ruminate over some imagined problem without being able to let it go.

(43) **Exercise vigorously and regularly.** You should schedule this into your life and stick with it. Exercise is positively one of the best treatments for ADD. It helps work off excess energy and aggression in a positive way, it allows for noise-reduction within the mind, it stimulates the hormonal and neurochemical system in a most therapeutic way, and it soothes and calms the body. When you add all that to the well-known health benefits of exercise, you can see how important it is. Make it something fun so you can stick with it over the long haul.

IV. INTERPERSONAL LIFE

(44) **Make a good choice in a significant other.** Obviously, this is good advice for anyone. But it is striking how the adult with ADD can thrive or flounder depending on the choice of mate.

(45) **Learn to joke with yourself and others** about your various symptoms – from forgetfulness, to getting lost all the time, to being tactless or impulsive. If you can be relaxed about it and to have a sense of humor, others will forgive you much more easily.

(46) **Schedule activities with friends.** Adhere to these schedules faithfully. It is crucial for you to keep connected to other people.

(47) **Find and join groups** where you are liked, appreciated, understood, enjoyed. People with ADD take great strength from group support.

(48) **Reverse #47: Don't stay too long where you aren't understood or appreciated.** Just as people with ADD gain a great deal from supportive groups, they are particularly drained and demoralized by negative groups.

(49) **Pay compliments.** Notice other people. In general, get social training, as from your coach.

(50) **Set social deadlines.** Without deadlines and dates, your social life can atrophy. Just as you will be helped by structuring your business week, so too will you benefit from keeping your social calendar organized. This will help you stay in touch with friends and get the kind of social support you need.

This article first appeared in the January 1993 issue of CH.A.D.D.er Box.

Edward Hallowell, M.D. is on the faculty of Harvard Medical School and is in private practice as a child and adult psychiatrist. He is the founder and director of The Hallowell Center for Cognitive and Emotional Health, an outpatient diagnosis and treatment center for children and adults located in Concord, Massachusetts, and is the author of several books.

John J. Ratey, M.D. is an assistant professor of psychiatry at Harvard Medical School, Director of Research at Medfield State Hospital, and has a private practice in Cambridge, Massachusetts. He has lectured and published many articles on the topic of treating ADD in adults using psychoeducation and pharmacotherapy.

Coaching
An Interview with Nancy Ratey, EDM

Nancy Ratey, a professional coach in private practice in the Boston area, is one of the leaders, indeed one of the pioneers, in the coaching profession. She has worked with dozens of adults with ADD over the years. In the following interview, Ms. Ratey was asked to discuss the practice of coaching and how it applies to adults with ADD.

One area that seems to be getting a lot of interest these days is the concept of coaching. Could you explain exactly what the term coaching means?

Ms. Ratey: According to the Personal and Professional Coaches Association based in California – an organization I was involved in creating a few years ago – the definition of coaching is an ongoing relationship that focuses on the client taking action toward the realization of his or her vision, goals, and desires. Coaching uses the process of inquiry and personal discovery to build the client's level of awareness and responsibility and provides the client with structure, support, and feedback. When I coach people, I first conduct an extensive, two-hour intake with them, which creates a base from which we can work and develop a long-term relationship. During the initial two-hour intake, I help define and clarify goals and then develop, with my clients, action steps and steps for accountability. I try to understand their strengths and weaknesses and their preferred learning modality. From that basis, we develop strategies – based on what has and hasn't worked for them in the past – that will help move them forward.

How do you and your clients determine the goals of your work?

It really depends on what their goals are. I work with a wide array of clients – high school and college students, professionals, mothers who are simply trying to organize their time – so it greatly depends on the individual's situation. In all cases, however, setting goals involves clarifying and identifying "places" that they want to be but have not had the tools, support, or reminders to get there. And that's the most important thing that a coach offers: serving as that constant reminder, helping to keep the client's focus on what his or her goals are. Most people with ADD know that can be one of the primary areas of difficulty. My clients with ADD typically get side-tracked and forget what their goals are. My job is to help them maintain better organizational skills and keep track of their progress toward their goals.

To do this, I use a process called "co-engineering." My clients sign an agreement saying that they are willing to move forward; I don't facilitate backwards movement, and I don't facilitate inaction. Together, we identify what it is that they need in terms of structure and to help them move forward.

What kind, and how much, interaction do you have with your clients on a regular basis?

Typically, I have an hour's worth of contact with a client each week, usually through four fifteen-minute "check-ins" or two half-hour appointments. In addition to that, I'll sometimes see a client for another one-hour appointment during the week. Each coach-client relationship is, obviously, different, depending on the client's situation. If I'm working with a student, for instance, throughout the week we will have regular "check-ins." During the check-ins, I ask questions such as, "What are your study targets today?"; "How are you going to accomplish them?"; "What strategies are you going to use?" One day during the week, we will have a face-to-face meeting at which we construct a more detailed plan.

What is the average length of time you tend to work with a client?

It really varies. I've worked with some for as long as three years. During that span of time, the degree of contact I have with them usually shifts; if they have a project they need to complete, we increase the contact. When things are going well, we decrease the contact. However, coaching is an ongoing relationship, similar to that of a personal trainer. It's not a "quick-fix."

You have worked with dozens of adults with ADD – are there challenges that these adults tend to have in common that can effectively be addressed through coaching?

Organization, time management, better self-understanding – these are issues that many adults with ADD struggle with. Coaching can be a very successful strategy for these adults.

How can a person determine whether coaching is something that would work for him or her?

If a person wants to take action in his life and the attempts that he's made haven't worked, coaching is for him. Those who seek a coach, however, must be willing to move forward and they have to want to be coached. People usually come to me when they've realized they need constant reminders, and they don't want to draw any more on their current relationships for help. This can be especially true for adults with ADD, who often have experienced extreme stress in their personal relationships.

If I came to you and said my goal is to be more successful in the workplace, where would we start?

I would start out by having you define success.

Let's say my definition of success is to get my tasks accomplished so I'm able to go out to lunch, not have a mountain of paperwork on my desk, and impress my supervisors with my work.

Since it seems that organization is a major hurdle, I would first find out what organizational system you were using and what has worked for you in the past. Then, I would probably want to go to your work site and actually see how you keep your desk organized. My guess is that a person who has the problems you described probably doesn't have a system or gets distracted because of his office environment. It's also possible that he's expecting too much from himself or is in the wrong job.

Based on the individual particulars of a person's situation, we would develop strategies for accomplishing the desired goals. If a person is distracted by her work environment, for example, she may need to ask her employer if she can come in earlier, when there are less people and, thus, less distractions. If a person gets distracted reading, she might want to stand up to read or lift the book up higher so she could have it at eye-level as opposed to having to look down.

Earlier you mentioned accountability. How do you use accountability in coaching?

Basically, I have my clients make themselves accountable for completing their projects and letting me know about it during regular "check-ins." In addition, I ask them to call and leave messages about their projects or send me a note about their project via fax or e-mail.

If you are interested in working with a coach, Ms. Ratey recommends calling the American Coaching Association at 610-825-4505.

This article first appeared in the Spring 1997 issue of ATTENTION!

Get Ready, Get Set, Get Organized

by Jan Sagal

Just about everyone's list of things to do includes the entry, "get organized." Being well organized allows you to spend more time doing the things you enjoy and less time with the drudgery. Becoming organized simply enables you to keep your priorities in order so you can accomplish the most important tasks; it does not mean being compulsive or having things absolutely perfect.

Unfortunately, for a person with ADD, getting and staying organized can be as arduous a task as climbing the face of El Capitan without a rope. But there is hope and help for those who want to make getting organized a reality. This article provides several simple but effective tips.

Many adults with ADD have a tendency to begin tackling a project before thinking it through. Instead of organizing thoughts and ideas first, they may be more prone to think about the project on more creative terms, and use their energy and enthusiasm to jump right into it. Oftentimes, they may even leap into several projects at a time. However, their distractibility and short attention span often impair their ability to bring tasks they started to completion – resulting in a pile of projects that contain creative ideas but incomplete thoughts.

How should a person with ADD combat this obstacle? Using lists, reminders, simple filing systems, appointment books, and daily planning can greatly reduce the disorganization many individuals with ADD experience. However, getting organized doesn't happen overnight, and it's not a one-time event. Changing personal habits is no easy task. The secret to becoming organized lies in learning and applying specific skills, systems, and shortcuts. Good organization is a learning skill that can be developed with commitment and self-discipline.

Here are some quick tips to help individuals with ADD start getting organized:

MAKE LISTS OF EVERYTHING.

Keep a small memo book to write everything down that comes to mind. Make a list of people to call, things to do, promises to keep, and places to be.

USE COLORED FOLDERS.

For example, use red for papers needing immediate attention, yellow for papers needing attention within the next week, and green for those that can wait.

DO ONE THING EACH DAY THAT YOU'VE BEEN PUTTING OFF.

The satisfaction of removing that annoying entry from your "to do" list provides encouragement to tackle the next task.

PLAN YOUR DAY ACCORDING TO YOUR ENERGY LEVEL.

Schedule top priorities when your energy level is at its peak. If sluggishness happens at certain times of the day, schedule projects that require less concentration during those times.

CHOOSE A COACH.

Recruit a professional organizer, friend, colleague, or therapist to provide reminders, periodic check-ups, and motivation to complete tasks.

SET REALISTIC GOALS.

Remember, goals are not dreams with deadlines. Rather, they should be challenging, specific, and achievable. Put goals in writing and review them often.

BREAK DOWN LARGE TASKS INTO SMALL ONES.

ALLOW TIME FOR INTERRUPTIONS.

When estimating the amount of time a task will take, allow 50 percent for interruptions.

Because carving out the time to get organized can be burdensome to many individuals with or without

ADD, hiring a professional organizer may be the best way to conquer the simplest to the most complex organization problems. Professional organizers can assist in designing and implementing an effective paperwork system, creating a functional working environment through efficient use of space, and developing and setting up a customized filing system suited to the needs of even the most disorganized individuals.

Most importantly, individuals trying to get organized should keep one thing in mind: do what works for you. There's no one system that is geared toward everyone. Once you become better organized, you'll be more productive and more efficient – and with the work you have accomplished, you'll feel like you've

reached the top of El Capitan. With the right organizational equipment, you too can scale the heights of success.

This article first appeared in the Winter 1997 issue of ATTENTION!

Jan Sagal is a professional organizer and coach specializing in paper management systems, productivity improvement, and office organization. She is also owner of The Paper Wizard, a Sacramento, California-based company providing a variety of organizing services to individuals and professionals.

Anger Management Training

by Arthur L. Robin, Ph.D.

A. The Nature of Anger - A Stress Reaction with Three Components: Cognitive, Physiological, Behavioral.

B. Why do Adults with ADD Have Trouble Managing Anger?
1. Biology of ADD
2. Lifetime of criticism and low self-esteem
3. Cognitive distortions
4. Behavioral skill deficits

C. Anger Management: A Family of Techniques. Use what works best for you. Designed to enhance control of emotional and impulse responding; encourage appropriate expression of anger.
1. Relaxation training
2. Self-assessment of anger: ABC Model
3. Refuting aggressive beliefs
4. Assertion techniques
5. Self-instructional statements
6. Problem-solving

D. Relaxation Training – Initial Coping Response
1. Take a few deep breaths. Learn to tense and release various muscles in your body.
2. This technique reduces physiological arousal; refocuses attention away from provoking stimuli; delays your response so you can think more clearly.

E. Self-Assessment of Anger: ABC Model. Analyze your anger.
1. Antecedents. What provokes/triggers your anger?
   a. Direct triggers. Being told what to do (verbal) or being pushed, hit, or given the finger (non-verbal).
   b. Indirect triggers. Interpretations or attributions about events. Perceived unfairness, malicious intent.
2. Behavior/ Reactions. What do you do when angry?
   a. Negative statements to self: "I want to kill him."

3. Aggressive behavior
4. Physiological cues - muscles, posture, etc.
5. Consequences. What happens as a result of your anger? Negative and positive consequences.

F. Refute Aggressive Beliefs.
1. We hold beliefs as to why other people treat us the way they do. Hostility bias, unfairness, restrictiveness.
2. We often interpret their actions with distortions.
3. We may be incorrect. Our distorted interpretations spur an angry response. Aggressive interpretations.
4. Examine the accuracy of your interpretations. Learn to interpret things in a non-aggressive way.
5. Brainstorm all the reasons why the person acted that way and evaluate how likely each reason is.

G. Assertion Techniques. Respond assertively to a provoking stimulus. Stand up for yourself, but don't be aggressive. Examples:
1. Broken record – monotone repetition of what you want.
2. Empathic assertion – sensitive listening but sticking to your position; Boss says, "This report is overdue. Get to work on it right now." You may say, "I know you're upset with the report being late, but I've been doing the best I can with a limited staff and budget."
3. Escalating assertion – sequence of responses increasing in assertiveness to obtain a desired outcome. When your child won't clean up her room, you might say: (1) Please clean your room; (2) I asked you to clean your room; (3) I want you to clean your room now; (4) Go to time-out for ten minutes.

H. Self-Instructional Training.
1. Reminders – things we say to ourselves to guide our behavior or remember to do certain things.
2. Reminders can be useful in high-pressure situations.

3. Recognize you are getting angry, press the "pause" button, remind yourself to stay calm, and continue.
4. Examples: "Chill out," "Stay calm," "I'm starting to lose it; let's get with it," "I'm not going to let him get to me." Keep up an internal dialogue of calming, rational thoughts.

I. **Problem-solving Techniques.** Find alternative actions after you stop and think when provoked to anger.
   1. Define the problem.
   2. Brainstorm alternative solutions.
   3. Evaluate the consequences of the solutions.
   4. Decide upon the best solution.
   5. Plan the details.
   6. See how it worked.

Arthur L. Robin, Ph.D. is a professor of psychiatry and pediatrics at Wayne State University School of Medicine and the Chief of Psychology at Children's Hospital in Detroit, Michigan.

Best Reference: E. Feindler & J. Guttman, Cognitive-Behavioral Anger Control Training. In C.W. LeCroy (1994) *Handbook of Child and Adolescent Treatment Manuals*. New York: Lexington Books.

A New Generation of Time Management?

by Jeffrey Rosenberg

Lists of things to get done, notes strategically taped and tacked about the home and office, and elaborate planners and organizers – these are some of the tools and products of traditional time management. They can be both helpful and, sometimes, a source of frustration as lists seem to pile on top of lists in a constant reminder of what hasn't gotten done. Stephen Covey, renowned author of *The 7 Habits of Highly Effective People*, and his colleagues Roger and Rebecca Merrill say that traditional time management strategies may be good for beating the clock but bad for achieving anything important. In another of their books, *First Things First*, these authors introduce the "fourth generation of time management." We interviewed Roger Merrill and asked him about this new generation of time management.

"The first three generations of time management basically grew out of an efficiency paradigm... the 'more, faster, smarter, better' approach with the idea that, if you do that, then your life is going to be better. We really challenge that whole assumption," says Merrill. A long time trainer of time management, Merrill is vice president and founding member of the Covey Leadership Center based in Provo, Utah, and a contributing author to the business best-seller *Principle-Centered Leadership*.

"An underlying assumption of the first three generations of time management is the idea of control – 'If I can control things and people and myself; if I can get everything lined up and know what's going on... the better my life will be.' We're suggesting that that's just not a realistic or valid approach to begin with."

It's basically the difference between a compass and a clock. Do you want the pace and direction of your life to be set by a "compass" of important values and inner principles or by a clock that ticks twenty-four hours, 1,440 minutes, and 86,400 seconds day after day after day? Covey and the Merrills ask. In *First Things First*, they put the choice this way:

Option 1 is the traditional time management approach. "Consider this question. If someone were to wave a magic wand and suddenly grant you the 15 or 20 percent increase in efficiency promised by traditional time management, would it solve your time management concerns?"

Option 2 is their fourth generation of time management. "Rather than offering you another clock, this approach provides you with a compass – because more important than how fast you're going, is where you're headed."

So figure out what's important and manage towards that, they suggest. It comes down to understanding what's really important and what's not. Covey and the Merrills believe that too many people attend to what's urgent but forget what's important. They've identified four quadrants of living. Quadrant I is Important & Urgent, Quadrant II is Important & Not Urgent, Quadrant III is Urgent & Not Important, and Quadrant IV is Not Important & Not Urgent. (see Figure 1)

The key is to spend as much time in Quadrant II (the Important & Not Urgent) as possible. Getting there is basically a two-step process. "The first step in putting first things first," says Merrill, "is to develop the passion of vision. [We're talking about] the passion of giving or contributing. The process for helping to identify your uniqueness and what you really want to do in life, the thing that may evoke some kind of a passion is writing a personal mission statement. That's a classic practice... [The simplest way to think about it] would be, 'What if you had no limits in terms of time, help, resources; what would you do with your life?'"

The second step is to *not* rely *only* on daily planning. Daily planning gives just a limited view, Covey and the Merrills believe. It's too "close up", so what's important gets replaced with what's urgent. Do weekly planning, as well.

"The purpose of a weekly schedule is to set up a framework to make quality decisions in the moment of choice," says Merrill. "That's the emphasis we try to make – you have to make moment by moment, day by day, hour by hour decisions. And the key is integrity in the moment of choice. Integrity to your purposes. Integrity to your conscience. " In this fourth generation of time management, that's the connection between the mission statement and planning.

Like many others, Covey and the Merrills suggest that you identify your primary roles – like employee, spouse, parent – as part of writing a mission statement. What's different is that they urge you to put activities that support your personal mission on your schedule before anything else, to put first things first. "You would come with some 'to dos' and some activities," says Merrill, "usually no more than one or two per role to start with, and then you look at the week ahead and say, 'When am I likely to do those?' Put them [on the schedule] to provide a framework. Now, as you move through the week you may have to move them around, but by putting those in first, you put them center stage."

As a result, your weekly schedule is going to include things like, "Have lunch with my wife" or "Have a good conversation with my teenage daughter" or "Talk to Beth, my co-worker, about our working relationship." And reminders like these would be written down and posted in conspicuous places in the home and office. Because, as Covey and the Merrills ask, what's going to make for a better life one year from today – getting through 365 daily lists of tasks, or having fifty-two quiet lunches with a spouse?

This brings us to one of the last points that Merrill made during his interview: "In *The 7 Habits of Highly Effective People* we introduced something called the 'emotional bank account.' It says that, basically, in a relationship with someone, we kind of have a joint bank account. There are some things you do that tend to make withdrawals from the account. There are some things you do that tend to make deposits. The strength of the relationship at any point in time is equal to that balance. Some of the deposits are, for example, authentic listening and making and keeping commitments. "

Don't overdraw YOUR emotional bank account.

This article first appeared in the Fall 1994 issue of ATTENTION!

Jeff Rosenberg is President of Rosenberg Communications, Inc., a firm located in the Washington, D.C. area that specializes in media relations and publications. He is the Executive Editor of ATTENTION! magazine and Managing Editor of CH.A.D.D.er Box newsletter.

FIGURE 1

Reprinted with permission of the Covey Leadership Center, 3507 N. University Avenue Suite 100 Provo, UT 84604 1-800-331-7716

MEDICAL MANAGEMENT OF ADD

An Introduction by Walid O. Shekim, M.D.

Director, AD/HD and Psychopharmacology Institute

Professor Emeritus, UCLA Neuropsychiatric Institute and Hospital

In 1985, some twelve years ago, when the word got out that I started working with adults with attention deficit/hyperactivity disorder (AD/HD), a student of mine made a memorable comment. A child and adolescent psychiatry fellow enrolled in the psychopharmacology cource I was giving at UCLA Neuropsychiatric Institute and Hospital (UCLA NPI & H), he said to me, "I hope you know what you are getting into; you are going to be called the pill pusher of Los Angeles." We have come a long way since then.

Today, the diagnosis of AD/HD in adults is firm. Assessment instruments are widely used, the disorder is becoming more widely recognized, and, conversely and unfortunately, is sometimes even over-diagnosed in individuals who want to have the label of AD/HD for whatever reason. However, there is much work to be done; the phenomenology and boundaries for AD/HD in adults are far from being resolved and delineated. New criteria for AD/HD in adults are constantly being discussed, and the impact of AD/HD on those with the disorder – in their interpersonal relationships at home, in the family, with their social network, and in the workplace – is being explored. Additionally, gender differences in the clinical presentation, comorbidities, prognosis, and treatments are being scrutinized. In effect, AD/HD in adults is becoming a sub-specialty that clinicians and professionals get interested in, research, teach, and upon which they focus their career.

Comorbidities of AD/HD in adults have been delineated, and we are gaining more understanding of these co-occurring conditions. This is important because these comorbidities determine, to a large extent, the choice, success, and failure of modalities used to treat the symptoms of AD/HD. For instance, the presence of depression, anxiety, alcohol, or drug problems in addition to AD/HD will determine the choice of medication used to treat symptoms, and often require that more than one medication be prescribed. On the other hand, difficulties with school may require that educational accommodations be put in place, such as tutoring or help with time management and study skills.

One major concern that exists in the field of adult AD/HD is the presence of anecdotal work and statements that are affecting the progress of our understanding of the disorder. To emphasize the danger of anecdotal material and how it can delay progress, I cite one example: In the 1950s, some prominent pediatricians in the field of AD/HD in children (hyperactivity, as it was called then) made the anecdotal statement based on their clinical experience that they had never seen AD/HD continue in the few patients they followed to adult years. Hence forth, the view that hyperactivity is outgrown in adolescence and adulthood prevailed for over thirty years. Fortunately, more current research has revealed that AD/HD can continue into adulthood, and there is some good scientific work being conducted in the area

of treatment modalities, though more work is still needed. The writers in this chapter are among those who have done excellent work in their field and their articles provide a valuable description of the medical management of AD/HD.

Pharmacotherapy of Adult AD/HD

by Timothy E. Wilens, M.D., Joseph Biederman, M.D., and Thomas J. Spencer, M.D.

Attention deficit hyperactivity disorder (AD/HD) in adults is an increasingly recognized disorder associated with substantial impairment. While adults with AD/HD may display similar symptoms to those in juveniles with AD/HD, such as inattention, distractibility, hyperactivity, and impulsivity, adults with AD/HD often have co-existing conditions such as mood, anxiety, substance use, and antisocial disorders. As it is with many juveniles, pharmacotherapy can be a main part of a treatment regimen for adult AD/HD.

Unlike the vast amount of data available on AD/HD in children, a limited number of medication studies are available for adult AD/HD. In fact, there are only a total of nine studies of psychostimulants and sixteen studies of non-stimulant medications on AD/HD in adults. A review of the literature indicates that the majority of controlled studies were with psychostimulants. These studies show that there tends to be a dose-related improvement in AD/HD symptoms when stimulant medications were used and that stimulants are the most effective available agents for adults with AD/HD and remain the treatment of choice.

In cases of psychiatric comorbidity, continued symptoms after medication treatment, or adverse effects, some literature suggests combining medications. However, future controlled studies are necessary to further define the range of pharmacotherapeutic options for adults with AD/HD.

TREATMENT

Despite the increasing recognition of adult AD/HD, the effectiveness, types, and order of treatment of AD/HD in adults remains unclear. Although the effectiveness of various psychotherapeutic interventions remains to be established, a retrospective assessment of adults with AD/HD indicated that traditional methods for exploring childhood issues that may be causing current conflicts were not helpful for adults with AD/HD (Ratey JJ,

Greenberg MS, et al., 1992). A structured, proactive, interactive form of therapy addressing an individual's beliefs and perceptions adapted for adults with AD/HD has been developed, which preliminary data suggests is effective when used with pharmacotherapy (McDermott SP, Wilens TE, 1997). In this review we evaluate the existing literature of medication treatment for adults with AD/HD. To this end we conducted a systematic computerized search of all studies available in English relevant to the treatment of AD/HD in adults.

STIMULANTS

In comparison to the more than over 200 controlled studies of stimulant effectiveness in pediatric AD/HD (Spencer T, Biederman J, et al., 1996), only ten total stimulant trials have been conducted on adults with AD/HD. (See Table 1.) In contrast to the consistent positive responses to stimulants of approximately 70 percent experienced by children and adolescents (Wilens TE, Biederman J, 1992), controlled studies in adults have shown more uncertain responses to stimulants – ranging from 25 percent (Mattes JA, Boswell L, et al., 1994) to 78 percent (Spencer T., Wilens, T, et al., 1995) of adults responding to treatment.

This fluctuation in the response rate appears to be related to several factors including the diagnostic criteria used to determine AD/HD, varying stimulant doses, high rates of comorbidity, and differing methods of assessing overall response. The dosages of stimulants given to study participants, for example, appears important to the outcome for several reasons: (1) controlled investigations using higher stimulant dosing resulted in more favorable outcomes (Spencer T, Wilens TE, et al., 1995; Iaboni F, Bouffard R, et al., 1996) than those using lower stimulant dosing (Weeder PH, Reimher FW, et al., 1981; Mattes JA, Boswell L, et al., 1984), and (2) the response to stimulants was dependent on the dosage in two of the studies on adults with AD/HD (Spencer T, Wilens TE, et al., 1995; Wilens T, Frazier J, et al., 1996). It appears that the shorter acting stimulants and methylphenidate may be more effective than pemoline for AD/HD in adults.

Studies have shown that adults with AD/HD using stimulants experience mild side effects such as insomnia, edginess, diminished appetite, weight loss, obsessiveness, tics, and headaches (Wilens TE, Biederman J, 1992). Despite the theoretical potential for abuse of stimulants, no studies of adults with AD/HD have reported such abuse (Larger DW, Sweeny KP, et al, 1986). However, mild side effects, such as minimal elevations of heart rate and blood pressure, have been correlated with stimulant dosage (Spencer T, Wilens TE, et al., 1995). Adults receiving pemoline should have periodic blood tests to check their liver function. Additionally, despite the increasing use of stimulants for adults with AD/HD, up to 50 percent do not respond, experience unfavorable side effects, or have a comorbid condition that stimulants may exacerbate or be ineffective in treating (Biederman J, Farone SV, et al., 1993; Shekim WO, Asarnow RF, et al., 1990; Taylor E, Schachar R, et al., 1987).

NON-STIMULANTS

Reports of non-stimulant treatments for adult AD/HD have included the use of antidepressants, antihypertensives, and amino acids. (See Table 2). The results of studies conducted on the use of these types of medications in the treatment of AD/HD in adults are discussed below.

ANTIDEPRESSANTS

Within the past two decades, tricyclic anti-depressants (desipramine, imipramine, and nortripty-line) have been used as alternatives to stimulants for the treatment of AD/HD in children (Spencer T, Biederman J, et al., 1996). Despite the array of studies that have been conducted on the effectiveness of tricyclic antidepressants in treating children and adolescents (Spencer T, Wilens TE, et al., 1995), only two studies of these agents have been conducted on adults with AD/HD. Compared to stimulants, tricyclic antidepressants have insignificant abuse potential, single daily dosing, and effectiveness in treating comorbid anxiety and depression.

An initial review of the medical charts of thirty-seven adults with AD/HD treated routinely in our clinics indicated that desipramine and nortriptyline, often in combination with other psychotropics including stimulants, resulted in moderate improvement (Wilens TE, Biederman J, et al., 1995). In one scientific trial in which desipramine was dispensed at a dose of 200 mg daily, significant reductions in AD/HD symptoms were reported after a two week period (Wilens T, Biederman J, et al., 1996) and sustained through the end of the study (six weeks).

The stimulant-like antidepressant bupropion has also been reported to be helpful in reducing AD/HD symptoms in adults (Weeder PH, Reimher FW, 1990). In a study of nineteen adults treated with an average of 360 mg of bupropion for six to eight weeks, the majority of participants experienced a positive response (Weeder PH, Reimher FW, 1990).

Monoamine oxidase inhibitor antidepressants have also been studied for the treatment of AD/HD. Studies of pargyline and deprenyl in adult AD/HD showed moderate improvements (Weeder PH, Wood DR, et al., 1983; Wender PH, Wood DR, et al., 1985). However, a more recent study of selegeline (deprenyl) yielded less enthusiastic findings (Ernst M, Liebenauer L, et al., 1996). Although a pilot child-based study demonstrated effectiveness of the reversible monoamine oxidase inhibitor antidepressant, moclobemide, which is not yet available in the U.S., data of its effectiveness for AD/HD in adults is not available.

An investigational antidepressant called tomoxe-tine has been shown in one controlled trial to have mild to moderate effectiveness for AD/HD in adults, although the authors of the study noted that the short duration of the study may have limited its full therapeutic benefit (Spencer T, Biederman J, et al., 1997). The investigational antidepressants S-adenosyl-methionine and nomifensen have also been shown to be effective for AD/HD in adults, but again, they remain unstudied under controlled conditions (Shekim WO, Masterson A, et al., 1989) and thus, are not currently available.

ANTIHYPERTENSIVES

The antihypenensives clonidine and guanfacine have been used to treat AD/HD in children, especially in cases where children with AD/HD displayed marked hyperactivity or aggressiveness (Spencer T, Biederman J, et al, 1997). However, because of a lack of efficacy data and concerns about their effect on blood pressure, their use in adults remains questionable. Beta-blockers may be helpful in adult AD/HD but remain unstudied under controlled conditions (Mattes JA, 1986); Reimherr FW, Wender PH, et al., 1987). One small open study of propanolol used to treat adults with AD/HD and temper outbursts indicated improvement in both the AD/HD symptoms and outbursts when daily doses of up to 640 mg were taken (Mattes JA, 1986). Propanolol has also been shown to be helpful in counteracting side effects of stimulants, such as edginess.

AMINO ACIDS

Trials with the amino acids were in part undertaken with the assumptions that AD/HD may be related to a deficiency in certain neurotransmitters and that administration of the amino acids would make more neurotransmitters available. Unfortunately, the results of open studies with LDOPA and tyrosine and controlled studies of phenylalanine in adults with AD/HD have generally been disappointing despite powerful dosing and adequate trial duration (See Table 2) (Reimherr FW, Wender PH, et al., 1987; Wood D, Reimherr J, et al., 1982; Wood DR, Reimherr FW, et al., 1985). In these studies, any improvement of AD/HD symptoms was lost after two weeks of treatment.

More recently, the relationship of nicotine and AD/HD has attracted attention, including findings of higher than expected overlap of cigarette smoking in individuals with AD/HD. One very brief study found that the nicotine patch significantly reduced AD/HD symptoms (Corners C, Levine ED, et al., 1996). Further research on the relationship between AD/HD and nicotine must be conducted to establish meaningful correlations, as well as the use of nicotine-like compounds to treat AD/HD.

COMBINED PHARMACOTHERAPY

Although carefully collected scientific information assessing the effectiveness and safety of combining agents for AD/HD in adults is lacking, combination treatment may be necessary for those individuals who continue to have AD/HD symptoms when using single agents or have psychiatric comorbidity. For example, in a recent report on desipramine or nortriptyline used to treat adults with AD/HD, 84 percent of adults were receiving additional psychoactive medications with 59 percent receiving additional stimulants (Wilens TE, Biederman J, et al., 1995). These findings are similar to studies of children with AD/HD in which the combination of methylphenidate and desipramine improved AD/HD symptoms more than either agent did when taken individually (Rapport MD, Carlson GA, et al., 1993). The use of methylphenidate in combination with fluoxetine has been reported to be well tolerated and useful in improving depression in adolescents with AD/HD (Gammon GD, Brown TE, 1993) and appears to have similar results in adults with these comorbid conditions.

SUGGESTED MANAGEMENT STRATEGIES

Once an adult has been diagnosed with AD/HD, he or she should become familiar with the risks and benefits of pharmacotherapy, the availability of alternative treatments, and the likely adverse effects. The individual's expectations need to be explored and realistic goals of treatment need to be clearly delineated. Likewise, physicians should review with their patients the various pharmacological options available and that each will require systematic trials of the available

medications for reasonable durations of time and at appropriate doses. Treatment-seeking adults with AD/HD who have psychiatric comorbidity, have continued symptoms with treatment, or report psychological issues related to their AD/HD (i.e., self-esteem issues, self-sabotaging patterns, interpersonal disturbances) should be directed to appropriate psychotherapy with clinicians knowledgeable in AD/HD treatment.

Adults with AD/HD often require more comprehensive treatment for their AD/HD given the longterm problems such as demoralization and underachievement, its effect on psychological development, and continued symptoms even after treatment with medication. To this end, the use of structured psychotherapy appears helpful, especially when used in conjunction with pharmacotherapy (Wilens T, McDermott S, et al., 1997). Groups focused on coping skills, support, and interpersonal psychotherapy also may be very useful for these adults.

SUMMARY

The literature on AD/HD supports the proposition that pharmacotherapy provides an effective treatment for adults with AD/HD. To date, effective pharmacological treatments for adults with AD/HD have included the use of the psychostimulants, antidepressants, and antihypertensives. Psychotherapy may be effective when used in conjunction with medications. Further controlled investigations assessing the efficacy of single and combination agents for adults with AD/HD are necessary with careful attention to specific symptom reduction (ie. inattention vs overactivity) and development of tolerance.

Timothy E Wilens, M.D. is Staff at the Pediatric Psychopharmacology unit at Massachusetts General Hospital, and Associate Professor of Psychiatry at Harvard Medical School.

Joseph Biederman, M.D. is Associate Professor of Psychiatry at Harvard Medical School and an Associate Editor of the Journal of the American Academy of Child and Adolescent Psychiatry.

Thomas Spencer, M.D. is the Assistant Director, Pediatric Psychopharmacology; the Assistant Chief, Pediatric Psychopharmacology Clinic; and the Assistant Chief, Pediatric Psychopharmacology Research Program at Massachusetts General Hospital.

Acknowledgment: This work was supported by USPHS MH01175-03 (T.W.)

REFERENCES

Biederman J, Faraone SV, Spencer T, Wilens TE, Norman D, Lapey KA, Mick E, Lehman B, Doyle A. Patterns of psychiatric comorbidity, cognition, and psychosocial functioning in adults with attention deficit hyperactivity disorder. *American Journal of Psychiatry*. 1993; 150: 17921798.

Conners C, Levin ED, Sparrow E, Hinton S, Erhardt D, Meck W, Rose J, March J. Nicotine and attention in adult attention deficit hyperactivity disorder. *Psychopharmacology Bulletin*. 1996;32:67-73.

Ernst M, Liebenauer L, Jons P, Tebeka D, Cohen R, Zametkin A. Selegiline in adults with attention deficit hyperactivity disorder: Clinical efficacy and safety. *Psychopharmacology Bulletin*. 1996;32:327-334.

Iaboni F, Bouffard R, Minde K, Hechtman L: The efficacy of methylphenidate in treating adults with attention-deficit/hyperactivity disorder. American Academy of Child and Adolescent Psychiatry. Philadelphia, PA, 1996.

Gammon GD, Brown TE. Fluoxetine and methylphenidate in combination for treatment of attention deficit disorder and comorbid depressive disorder. *Journal of Child and Adolescent Psychopharmacology*. 1993;3: 1 -10.

Langer DH, Sweeney KP, Bartenbach DE, Davis PM, Menander KB. Evidence of lack of abuse or dependence following pemoline treatment: results of a retrospective survey. *Drug and Alcohol Dependency*. 1986;17:213-227.

Mattes JA, Boswell L, Oliver H. Methylphenidate effects on symptoms of attention deficit disorder in adults. *Archives of General Psychiatry*. 1984;41: 1059-1063.

Mattes JA. Propanolol for adults with temper outbursts and residual attention deficit disorder. *Journal of Clinical Psychopharmacology*. 1986;6:299-302.

McDermott SP, Wilens TE: Cognitive and emotional impediments to treating the adult with AD/HD: A cognitive therapy perspective. In Brown T, eds. *Subtypes of Attention Deficit Disorders in Children, Adolescents, and Adults*. Washington, DC: American Psychiatric Press, Inc; 1997: In Press.

Rapport MD, Carlson GA, Kelly KL, Pataki C. Methylphenidate and desipramine in hospitalized children: I. Separate and combined effects on cognitive function. *Journal of the American Academy of Child and Adolescent Psychiatry*. 1993;32:333-342.

Ratey JJ, Greenberg MS, Bemporad JR, Lindem KJ. Unrecognized attention-deficit hyperactivity disorder in adults presenting for outpatient psychotherapy. *Journal of Child and Adolescent Psychopharmacology*. 1992;2:267-275.

Reimherr FW, Wender PH, Wood DR, Ward M. An open trial of L-tyrosine in the treatment of attention deficit hyperactivity disorder, residual type. *American Journal of Psychiatry*. 1987;144: 1071-1073.

Shekim WO, Asarnow RF, Hess E, Zaucha K, Wheeler N. A clinical and demographic profile of a sample of adults with attention deficit hyperactivity disorder, residual state. *Comprehensive Psychiatry*. 1990;31 :416-425.

Shekim WO, Masterson A, Cantwell DP, Hanna GL, McCracken JT. Nomifensine maleate in adult attention deficit disorder. *The Journal of Nervous and Mental Disease*. 1989;177:296-299.

Spencer T, Biederman J, Wilens T, Faraone S, Prince J, Hatch M, Harding M. Tolerability and efficacy of tomoxetine for adults with attention deficit hyperactivity disorder. *American Journal of Psychiatry*. 1997; Manuscript submitted:

Spencer T, Biederman J, Wilens T, Harding M, O'Donnell D, Griffin S. Pharmacotherapy of attention deficit disorder across the life cycle. *The Journal of the American Academy of Child and Adolescent Psychiatry*. 1996;35:409-432.

Spencer T, Wilens TE, Biederman J, Faraone SV, Ablon S, Lapey K. A double blind, crossover comparison of methylphenidate and placebo in adults with childhood onset attention deficit hyperactivity disorder. *Archives of General Psychiatry*. 1995;52:434-443.

Taylor E, Schachar R, Thorley G, Wieselberg HM, Everitt B, Rutter M. Which boys respond to stimulant medication? A controlled trial of methylphenidate in boys with disruptive behaviour. *Psychological Medicine*. 1987;17: 121-143.

Wender PH, Reimherr FW, Wood DR. Attention deficit disorder ('minimal brain dysfunction') in adults: A replication study of diagnosis and drug treatment. *Archives of General Psychiatry*. 1981;38:449-456.

Wender PH, Reimherr FW. Bupropion treatment of attention deficit hyperactivity disorder in adults. *American Journal of Psychiatry*. 1990;147:1018-1020.

Wender PH, Wood DR, Reimherr FW. Pharmacological treatment of attention deficit disorder residual type (ADD, RT, "minimal brain dysfunction", "hyperactivity") in adults. *Psychopharmacology Bulletin*. 1985;21 :222-230.

Wender PH, Wood DR, Reimherr FW, Ward M. An open trial of pargyline in the treatment of attention deficit disorder, residual type. *Psychiatry Research*. 1983;9:329-336.

Wilens TE, Biederman J: The stimulants. In Shafer D,

eds. *The Psychiatric Clinics of North America.* Philadelphia: W.B. Saunders; 1992: 191 -222.

Wilens TE, Biederman J, Mick E, Spencer T. A systematic assessment of tricyclic antidepressants in the treatment of adult attention-deficit hyperactivity disorder. *Journal of Nervous and Mental Disease.* 1995;184:48-50.

Wilens T, Biederman J, Prince J, Spencer T, Schleifer D, Harding M, Linehan C, Hatch M. A double blind, placebo controlled trial of desipramine for adults with AD/HD. *American Journal of Psychiatry.* 1996;153: 1147-1153.

Wilens T, Frazier J, J. P, Spencer T, Bostic J, Hatch M, Abrantes A, Sienna M, Soriano J, Millstein R, Biederman J: A double blind comparison of pemoline in adults with AD/HD: Preliminary results. Scientific proceedings of the American Academy of Child and Adolescent Psychiatry. Philadelphia, 1996.

Wilens T, McDermott S, Biederman J, Abrantes A, Spencer T. Combined cognitive therapy and pharmacotherapy for adults with attention deficit hyperactivity disorder: A systematic chart review of 26 cases. *Manuscript submitted.* 1997.

Wood D, Reimherr J, P.H. W. Effects of levodopa on attention deficit disorder, residual type. *Psychiatry Research.* 1982;6: 13-20.

Wood DR, Reimherr FW, Wender PH. The treatment of attention deficit disorder with d,lphenylalanine. *Psychiatry Research.* 1985;16:21-26.

TABLE 1. STUDIES OF STIMULANT PHARMACOTHERAPY IN ADULT AD/HD

Study (year)	N	Design	Medication	Total Dose (Wt-corrected)	Response	Comments
Wood et al. (1976)	15	Controlled	MPH	27 mg 0.4 mg/kg*	73%	Dx criteria not well defined
		Open	Pemoline	37.5-70 mg (0.5-1.0 mg/kg)*	33%	Low doses of Pemoline Mild side effects
Wender et al. (1981)	51	Controlled	Pemoline	65 mg 0.9 mg/kg*	50% in those with childhood onset	Dx criteria not well defined, high rates of dysthymia; moderate side effects
Mattes et al. (1984)	26	Controlled	MPH	48 mg 0.7 mg/kg*	25%	Moderate rate of comorbidity Mild side effects
Wender et al. (1985)	37	Controlled	MPH	43 mg 0.6 mg/kg*	57%	68% dysthymia 22% cyclothymia Mild side effects
Gualtieri et al. (1985)	8	Contolled	MPH	42 mg* 0.6 mg/kg	Mild-moderate response	No plasma level-response associations
Shekim et al. (1990)	33	Open	MPH	40 mg 0.6 mg/kg*	70% responded "favorably"	Problematic outcome measures
Spencer et al. (1995)	23	Controlled	MPH	30-100 mg 0.5, 0.75, & 1.0 mg/kg	78% response rate, dose relationship	No plasma level associations, no effects gender or comorbidity
Iaboni et al. (1996)	30	Controlled	MPH	30-45 mg =0.6 mg/kg*	Moderate response	Improvement in neuropsych & anxiety
Wilens et al. (1996)	42	Controlled	Pemoline	150 mg 2 mg/kg	61% response rate	35% reduction in ADHD symptoms; moderate side effects mg/kg
TOTAL	265	Controlled N=8; Open: N=2	MPH & Pemoline	40 mg (MPH) 0.6 mg/kg* 105 mg (Pem) 1.5 mg/kg*	Variable responses	Dx not well defined High rate of comorbidity Side effects in 30%

Duration of medication trial includes placebo phase. Abbreviations used: MPH=methylphenidate, Dx=diagnosis
*Weight-normalized dose using 50th percentile weight for age

TABLE 2. STUDIES OF NONSTIMULANT PHARMACOTHERAPY IN ADULT AD/HD

Study (year)	N	Design	Medication	Total Dose (Wt-corrected)	Response	Comments
Wood et al. (1982)	8	Open	L-DOPA (+carbidopa)	625 mg (63 mg)	no benefit at end of trial	Side effects: nausea, sedation, low doses
Wender et al. (1983)	22	Open	Pargyline	30 mg	13/22 moderate improvement	Delayed onset, short lasting
Wender et al. (1985)	11	Open	Doprenyl	30 mg	6/9 responded, 2 dropouts	Amphetamine metabolite
Wood et al. (1985)	19	Controlled	Phenylalanine	587 mg	6/14 responded, initially (mood)	Transient mood improvement only
Mattes et al. (1986)	13	Open	Propanolol	528 mg	11/13 improved	Part of "temper" study
Reimherr et al. (1987)	12	Open	Tyrosine	150 mg	8 initial response, 4 dropouts	Delayed onset Tolerance developed
Shekim et al. (1989)	18	Open	Nomifensine maleate	<300 mg	All had AD/HD reduction	Immediate response Not available in US
Shekim et al. (1990)	19	Open	S-adenosyl-L-methionine	<2400 mg	75% of patients responded	Mild adverse effects
Wender et al. (1990)	19	Open	Buproprion	360 mg	Moderate response	Sustained response 5 dropouts
Wilins et al. (1995)	37	Open	Desipramine Nortriptyline	183 92	68% response rate	60% on stimulants Sustained response
Reimherr et al. (1995)	20	Open	Venlafaxine	109	8/12 responded	Side effects led to 40% drop out rate
Spencer et al. (1995)	22	Controlled	Tomoxetine	76	52% response rate	Adrenergic agent Well tolerated
Findling et al. (1996)	9	Open	Venlafaxine	150	7/9 reduction in AD/HD	Improved anxiety scores
Ernst et al. (1996)	24	Controlled	Selegeline	20 & 60	Mild improvement	High placebo response
Wilens et al. (1996)	43	Controlled	Desipramine	147	68% response rate	Comorbidity levels unrelated to response
TOTAL	297	4 Controlled 12 Open	Mixed	Moderate doses	Variable responses	Side effects common Often loss of effect

Psychopharmacologic Treatment of AD/HD in Young Adults

by Patricia O. Quinn, M.D.

Considerable focus has recently been directed to the problems associated with AD/HD in young adults. This phenomenon has occurred as a direct result of an increase in the general overall awareness that the symptoms of this disorder do not disappear in adolescence.

SYMPTOMS OF AD/HD IN YOUNG ADULTS

The disappearance of the overt symptom of hyperactivity and its replacement with motor restlessness led some previously to mistakenly think that the disorder was outgrown. We now know this is not the case and that as many as 40 to 60 percent of individuals with ADD continue to demonstrate symptoms into adulthood. In some adolescents and young adults, these symptoms may not be bothersome but they are still present, affecting overall performance and achievement. Adolescents with ADD may be seen as underachieving in school and to have mood swings, irritability, and even depression. Sleep disorder and problems with arousal mechanisms in the brain are commonly seen in both adults and adolescents. Individuals with AD/HD may need little sleep or always feel sleepy.

Adolescents and young adults frequently report procrastination, lack of focus, and difficulty with time management. These symptoms are becoming hallmarks for the disorder in these age groups. ADD without hyperactivity can be more difficult to diagnose but is probably more common than previously thought. During the controlled, structured environment of elementary school, the bright child with ADD without hyperactivity can cope fairly well. However, as more demands are made during adolescence, problems arise and performance usually declines. It may not be until college that the individual's performance deteriorates to the point of seeking professional help. This situation, however, can be avoided by recognizing any attention problems early on and seeking a proper diagnosis and treatment.

PSYCHOPHRAMACOLOGIC TREATMENT OF AD/HD

Stimulant medication can be a useful tool in dealing with AD/HD as part of a total treatment program. While the use of medications does not cure the disorder, it certainly can reduce many of the symptoms. Stimulants can be very effective in both teenagers and adults with AD/HD. Higher doses may be necessary in this population with best results occurring at a level of 1.0 mg/kg/day dose. This higher dose correlates somewhat to the need for moderate (20 mg/day) and higher dose (30 mg/day) methylphenidate treatment in 71 percent of the subjects with AD/HD reported by Barkley and his colleagues in 1991. In this sample, 95 percent were found to be positive responders to the stimulant medication. In fact, methylphenidate is the most commonly used medication for AD/HD. Dextroamphetamine is also commonly prescribed, particularly to adults (Ella and Rapoport 1991).

USING A NEUROBIOCHEMICAL BASIS TO DETERMINE TREATMENT REGIME

While we don't know the exact mechanism of action of the stimulants, they appear to improve symptoms of AD/HD by allowing better use of the catecholamines. Those individuals with AD/HD who appear to have mainly frontal lobe deactivation have been found to respond best to stimulants. These medications may regulate and stabilize the catecholamine neurobiochemical system and thus improve brain functioning. The frontal lobes become "stimulated" and are able to perform their inhibitory role. Motor restlessness is also decreased. In 1978, Rapoport and colleagues reported that a single dose of dextroamphetamine given to a group of boys without AD/HD resulted in a marked decrease in motor activity and reaction time and improved performance on cognitive tests, ending the theory that children with AD/HD had a "paradoxical" response to stimulants that changed at puberty.

Other individuals who manifest symptoms of

overarousal and hypervigilance as part of their ADD may be more responsive to alpha-2-noradrenergic agonist drugs such as clonidine and guanfacine. Since the work of Hunt in 1985, clonidine has been proposed as an alternative treatment in patients with AD/HD. Clonidine also can be highly effective in controlling tics and therefore has been proposed as an alternative medication in patients with AD/HD and a comorbid tic disorder. In studies conducted by Steingard, Biederman, Spencer, Wilens, and Gonzalez (1993), Clonidine resulted in improvement in both AD/HD (72%) and tic symptoms (75%).

Clonidine may be used alone or in conjunction with stimulants. It appears to be particularly effective in treating the overaroused, hypervigilant, and/or aggressive patient. Its main side effect of sedation necessitates initial therapy at bedtime with general introduction during the day in very small doses. Individual doses should be increased very gradually over several weeks to months until effective levels are reached. Clonidine has proven particularly useful for the patient with AD/HD and tics.

The role of serotonin in AD/HD has not been clearly established biochemically, yet newer serotonin agents such as fenfluaraime and fluoxetine have been useful in treating comorbid symptomatology such as depression and anxiety when they occur in individual's diagnosed with AD/HD. These medications, however, do not appear to address the core symptoms of inattention and disorganization.

Additionally, tricyclic antidepressants have been used for many years as an alternative psychopharmacologic treatment for the symptoms of AD/HD in children (Biederman, et al, 1989). Dosages in adults for treatment of AD/HD have not yet been well established with two opposing camps advocating effectiveness at either 3mg/kg/day or higher, or low dose therapy of between 10 to 30 mg/day as advocated by Dr. John Ratey (1992).

SPECIFIC ISSUES RELATED TO THE TREATMENT OF YOUNG ADULTS

In treating young adults with AD/HD, it is critical to achieve a working relationship that allows for careful follow-up, optimal adjustment of medication dosages, and management of side effects. This relationship will also allow the clinician the opportunity to address problems particular to these age groups such as diet, exercise, motor vehicle accidents, and

---

TABLE 1

Medications Currently Used in the Treatment of AD/HD in Young Adults

Name	Dose available (range)	Onset/Duration
Stimulants		
Methylphenidate	5, 10, 20 mg tablets (5-80 mg/day)	20 minutes lasts 3-5 hours
Ritalin SR	20 mg sustained release (20-80 mg/day)	45-60 minutes lasts 6-8 hours
Dextroamphetamine	5 mg tablets (2.5-40 mg/day)	20-30 minutes lasts 3-5 hours
Dexedrine Spansules	5, 10, 15 mg capsules (5-40 mg/day)	60 minutes lasts 6-10 hours
Adderall	10, 20 mg (5-40 mg/day)	30-60 mins lasts 8-12 hours
Pemoline	18.75, 37.5, 75 mg (18.75-112.5 mg/day)	lasts 12-24 hours*
Non-Stimulants		
Clonidine	0.1, 0.2, 0.3 mg tablets (0.1-0.3 mg/day)	8-12 hours*
Catapres TTS	1,2,3 patches (0.1-0.3 mg/day)	lasts 5-7 days*
Guanfacine	1,2 mg tablets (0.5-2 mg/day)	8-12 hours*

*takes several days to weeks to reach effective levels

Name	Dose available (range)	Onset/Duration
Antidepressants		
Imipramine	10, 25, 50 mg tablets (25-200 mg/day)	12-24 hours*
Desipramine	10, 25, 50, 75 mg tablets (25-200 mg/day)	12-24 hours*
Fluoxetine	10, 20 mg pulvules Liquid 20 mg/5ml (10-60 mg/day)	onset 2-4 weeks half-life of several days
Sertraline	50, 100 mg tablets (50-200 mg/day)	onset 2-3 weeks half-life 24 hours
Paroxetine	20,30 mg tablets (10-40 mg/day)	onset 2-3 weeks half-life 14 hours
Burproprion	75, 100 mg (100-450 mg/day)	onset 3-4 weeks doses 6 hours apart

Table 1 adapted with permission from Adolescents and ADD: Gaining the Advantage *by Patricia Quinn, 1995, New York: Magination Press, p 10 & 11. Copyright 1995, Patricia Quinn. May not be reproduced without the written permission of the author.*

alcohol/substance abuse (Klein and Manuzza, 1991; Weiss and Hecthman, 1993).

Exercise plays an important role in the lives of many patients with AD/HD who report that they need to burn off extra energy by running, jogging, or swimming. A regular exercise regime also keeps them fit, helps them to feel better, and improves self-esteem. Young adults report that they are less hyperactive and can sit for longer periods after exercising vigorously.

One of the rites of passage for all teens is obtaining a driver's license, as it assures a sense of accomplishment and conveys independence. However, symptoms of AD/HD, particularly distractibility and impulse control issues, significantly affect the adolescent's driving skills and judgment. Medication is therefore essential to address symptoms while driving. Additional supervision and practice may also be necessary to assure skill level and competence.

Alcohol and drug abuse arise as particular problems that need to be addressed in adolescents and young adults with ADD. Unfortunately, abuse of medications used to treat ADD is not uncommon. Therefore, those taking one of the prescribed medications for the treatment of ADD should be cautioned about the dangers that are involved.

Side effects are commonly seen during medication treatment but need not be a reason for discontinuing treatment if properly addressed. Table 2 provides suggested strategies for the management of these common side effects.

Patricia O. Quinn, MD. is a developmental pediatrician and a clinical assistant professor at Georgetown University Medical Center in Washington, D.C.

TABLE 2

Common Side Effects of Medications Used to Treat AD/HD with Suggested Strategies for Management

Stimulants

Side Effect	Action to be Taken
Appetite decrease/nausea	Take medication after meals with a full glass of juice or water; increase regular exercise
Stomach aches/headaches	Usually relieved by eating
Weight loss	Increase calories or add supplements
Insomnia	Decrease later doses; clonidine at bed; increase regular exercise
Irritability	Decrease caffeine intake; try dexexrine; overlap doses if rebound phenomenom
Tics	Decrease dose; add clonidine; change medication
Depress mood/social withdrawal	Reevaltuation of medication and possible additional diagnosis

Antidepressants*

Sedation/fatigue	Will gradually decrease over time; begin by taking medications at bedtime
Dry mouth/dizziness	Drink plenty of liquids
Gastrointestinal distress	Take after meals/increase fiber
Nervousness/tremor/anxiety	Decrease dose; change medications
Induction of mania	Discontinue
Insomnia	Decrease dose; change medications

*Monitor cardiac status for tricyclics and liver functions for pemoline.

Always contact your prescribing physician before making changes in your medication or to report serious side effects.

Table 2 reprinted with permission from Adolescents and ADD: Gaining the Advantage *by Patricia Quinn, 1995, New York: Magination Press, p 10 & 11. Copyright 1995, Patricia Quinn. May not be reproduced without the written permission of the author.*

FURTHER READINGS

Quinn, PO *Adolescents and ADD: Gaining the Advantage.* Washington, D.C.: Magination Press; 1995.

Quinn, PO (Ed), *ADD and the College Student.* Washington, D.C.: Magination Press; 1994.

Rosenberg, DR, Holttum, J., & Gershon, S. *Textbook of Pharmacotherapy for Child and Adolescent Psychiatric Disorders.* New York: Brunner/Mazel., Inc.; 1994.

Copeland, E. *Medication for Attention Disorders (AD/HD/ADD) and Related Medical Problems: For Parents, Educators, and Health Professionals.* ADD Warehouse.

Greenhill, LL & Osman, BB (Eds). *Ritalin: Theory and Patient Management.* ADD Warehouse.

Shenker, A. The mechanism of action of drugs used to treat attention deficit hyperactivity disorder: focus on catecholamine receptor pharmacology. *Advances in Pediatrics;* 39; 337382.

Wilens, TE & Biederman, J. The stimulant. *Pediatric Clinics of North America.* 1992; 15(1); 191-222.

Greenhill, L. Pharmacologic treatment of attention deficit hyperactivity disorder. *Pediatric Clinics of North America.* 1992; 15(1); 1-27.

REFERENCES

Barkley, RA, DuPaul, GJ, McMurray, MD. Attention deficit disorder with and without hyperactivity: clinical response to three dose levels of methylphenidate. *Pediatrics.* 1991; 87(4); 519-531.

Biederman, J, Baldessarini, RJ, Wright, V, et al. A double-blind placebo controlled study of desipramine in the treatment of ADD: I. Efficacy. *Journal of the American Academy of Child and Adolescent Psychiatry.* 1989; 28; 777-784.

Elia, J & Rapoport, J. Methylphenidate versus dextroamphetamine: why both should be tried. In B. Osman & LL Greenhill (Eds)., *Ritalin: Theory and Patient Management* (pp. 243-265). New York: Mary Ann Liebert.

Hunt, RD. The therapeutic effect of clonidine in attention deficit disorder with hyperactivity: a comparison with placebo and methylphenidate. *Psychopharmacology Bulletin.* 1986; 22(1); 229-236.

Klein, RG & Mannuzza, S. Long term outcome of hyperactive children: a review. *Journal of the American Academy of Child and Adolescent Psychiatry.* 1991; 30; 383387.

Rapoport, JL, Buchsbaum, MD, Weingartner, H, Zahn, TP, Ludlow, C, Mikkelsen, EJ. Dextroamphetamine: Its cognitive and behavioral effects in normal and hyperactive boys end normal men. *Archives of General Psychiatry.* 1980; 37;933.

Ratey, JJ, Greenburg, MS, & Lindem, KJ. Combination of treatments for attention deficit hyperactivity disorder in adults. *Journal of Nervous and Mental Diseases.* 1991; 179; 699701.

Steingard, Biederman, Spencer, Wilens, & Gonzales. 1993.

Weiss, G & Hecthman LT. *Hyperactive Children Grown up,* 2nd ed. New York: Guilford Press; 1993.

CHAPTER 4

ON THE JOB

An Introduction by Kathleen G. Nadeau, Ph.D.

Director, Chesapeake Psychological Services of Maryland

Member, CH.A.D.D. Professional Advisory Board

As children with ADD enter adulthood, many of them continue to struggle with the same types of issues that posed difficulties for them during their elementary school and high school years. However, the arena of challenge shifts from the classroom to the workplace. While we now have a large body of literature available to us to help children with ADD in the classroom, we are only beginning to develop knowledge about the best ways to help older individuals with ADD meet workplace challenges.

Many of the things we do at work require the same types of skills that were taught to us during school years. On the job, most of us must read, write, calculate, plan, organize, listen, remember, and recall. In fact, jobs that do not call upon these higher level cognitive skills are rapidly reducing in number, and the importance of these higher level skills is rapidly increasing as our culture becomes more and more technologically oriented. Additionally, statistics show that work patterns are changing rapidly so that most young adults entering the marketplace today will have to update skills and retrain repeatedly throughout the course of their work life.

Fortunately for young adults, the range of choices available to them is very broad, allowing them, as they were not allowed during school years, to make choices that are best suited to their strengths, areas of difficul-

ty, interests, and optimal level of stimulation.

Peter and Patricia Latham, who are recognized experts in disability law as it pertains to ADD and Learning Disabilities, emphasize in their article "Succeeding in the Workplace with ADD," the importance of this greater range of choices. They discuss the protection that American workers now enjoy from discrimination due to invisible disabilities such as ADD, but also emphasize the critical importance of learning how to manage and compensate for the workplace problems often posed by ADD.

The educational laws contained in IDEA, which were written to support and to protect the needs of children with disabilities within the public school system, are familiar to many of us. There are parallel laws, specifically the Rehabilitation Act of 1973 and the Americans with Disabilities Act, which have been passed to extend protection against discrimination into the workplace. Under these laws, reasonable accommodations are mandated in most work environments to assist qualified but disabled individuals to perform their job. The Lathams, elucidate in their article "Equal Employment Opportunity Commission Issues new Guidance on Psychiatric Disabilities and the ADA," more specifically how these guidelines pertain to individuals with attentional and learning problems (which are subsumed under the general heading of psychiatric disabilities by the EEOC). These protective laws, and the accommodations for which these laws provide, are very appropriate and supportive of individuals with ADD in the workplace. The Lathams counsel, however, that it is essential that individuals with ADD do not view as their employer's responsibility the task of defining and supplying needed accommodations. As other articles in this chapter emphasize, the adult with ADD in the workforce must take a very informed and pro-active position toward seeking accommodations and appropriate supports and developing compensatory techniques.

My article, "Top Ten Traps for Adults with ADD in the Workplace," emphasizes very concrete, practical steps that an adult with ADD can take to avoid falling into typical ADD workplace "traps." "Taking charge" of ADD patterns and problems is critical for adults with ADD. Along with the extensive choices open to young adults as they enter the workforce, they are also faced with significant challenges. The management of their ADD patterns is no longer shouldered by parents, teachers, or tutors, but becomes their own responsibility to manage.

Sheila Lachs writes about the critical issue of ADD in the military. Ironically, in the past, before ADD was widely recognized and treated, the military often served as an ideal environment for many young adults with ADD. The clear guidelines, predictability and structure of military life often allowed them to function at an optimal level that they were ill-equipped to reach in the less structured civilian workforce. Now the military has, at least for the moment, taken the stance that anyone with a neurological disorder, such as ADD, requiring treatment, including medication, is unfit for military duty. CH.A.D.D. is playing an important and effective role in educating the military about ADD, and in working with them to recognize the very positive and important contributions that members of the military with ADD have made in the past and can make in the future. Encouragingly, the military is studying the experiences of young adults with ADD who have been admitted to the armed forces through a waiver, with an eye toward considering a modification of their exclusionary policy regarding ADD.

As a group, the articles in this chapter present a very positive and practical message: adults with ADD are able to achieve very high levels of success in their work life if they learn to make "ADD-savvy" decisions and choices. They enjoy a broad range of protection under the Rehabilitation Act of 1973 and the Americans with Disabilities Act, but must never abdicate responsibility for identifying and employing workplace accommodations, assistive technologies, and compensatory techniques. The adult who educates himself, who makes "ADD-friendly" workplace choices, and assumes the responsibility to take charge of his ADD has excellent chances for success in his chosen career path.

Top Ten Traps for Adults with ADD in the Workplace: How to Avoid Getting Caught By Them!

by Kathleen G. Nadeau, Ph.D.

Many people with ADD ask, "What are the best jobs for someone like me?" If you talk to several different ADD experts you will receive a jumble of responses. Some, like Thom Hartmann, feel that entrepreneurial activities, which allow maximum freedom, are best for those with ADD. Others will recommend stimulating, action-oriented jobs – pilot, fireman, rescue worker. If you poll a large group of adults with ADD who are successful in their work, you will discover that adults with ADD are achieving positive results in a wide array of careers including teaching, computer science, law, photo-journalism, and almost any other type of career you can name. A better question to ask in seeking career advice is "What are the characteristics that make a particular job right for me?" Almost every career path contains jobs that are very good for someone with ADD, as well as those that could be disastrous for someone with ADD. The key is to find or create ADD friendly jobs within your career track.

Step one is to find a career track that is a good match for you. To do this you need to consider your:

interests

personality type

areas of strength

areas of weakness

level of training.

Once you have honed in on a career track and have received the type of training you need to pursue this career, it is time to think about "ADD Traps" at work and how to minimize or avoid them in your job search. What are some of those typical traps? Not surprisingly, many of those "traps" read like a list of ADD symptoms. Dealing with potential traps not only requires careful consideration before you accept a job, but also that you become "ADD-savvy" once you are on the job. And remember, if at first you don't succeed..... Don't lose heart. You may need to go through a series of jobs, either within an organization or among several organizations, before you have learned enough about your own patterns and needs to make the very best choice.

THE "TOP TEN TRAPS" AT WORK AND WHAT TO DO ABOUT THEM

1. Distractibility

Distractions can be "external" (in the environment) or "internal" (a meandering train of thought). External distractions are rampant in the current open office environment, which is very ADD-unfriendly. Here are a few ideas for coping with external distractions:

- Ask for flex-time in order to have some less-distracting time at work;
- Ask for permission to work at home part of the time;
- Use head phones or a white noise machine to muffle sounds;
- Face your desk away from the line of traffic;
- Ask to use private offices or conference rooms for periods of time.

Internal distractions can be even tougher to avoid, but here are some tips.

- Write down your intrusive ideas so you can get back to task;
- Use a beeper to sound at regular intervals to remind you to come back "to task;"
- Work at a particular task for briefer intervals, and shift to a new task when you find your attention wandering. This technique may work best at tasks which you find boring and repetitive.

2. Impulsivity

Impulsivity can take a number of forms at work, but the common denominator is lack of thought before action! Following are some suggestions for tackling impulsivity:

- If you impulsively commit to projects and then can't follow through, develop the habit of saying, "I'd like to, but let me check my schedule;"

- If you are an impulsive job-hopper, catch yourself before you "take this job and shove it." It may help to talk your dissatisfactions over with a friend or spouse, and look for less drastic solutions;

- If you impulsively blurt out comments in meetings that you later regret, learn to take notes and write down what you're thinking of saying. This will give you time to consider, "Is this a good thing to say?" and consider the best way to say it;

- If you impulsively jump into complex projects without a plan, which can lead to enormous inefficiency and increased cost, team up with someone who is better at planning and organizing. That way your energy and enthusiasm can be put to positive use!

3. Hyperactivity

Many jobs today are sedentary and are poorly suited to adults with ADD on the hyperactive end of the continuum. If you tend to tap, pace, or wander throughout the building aimlessly, your hyperactivity may be misconstrued negatively as boredom or poor motivation. Here are some coping techniques:

- Engage in "intentional fidgeting" by taking notes during meetings. You'll look interested, not bored (but don't doodle!);

- Plan your day to include productive movement – picking up the mail, talking to a colleague, walking to a meeting the long way;

- Bring your lunch and exercise during your lunch break;

- Look for work that requires movement, such as multiple contract jobs or work that is outdoors or on your feet.

4. Memory problems

"Forgetfulness" is often a daily problem for adults with ADD. The more complex or high stress your day is, the more likely you are to forget. Here are some hints:

- Live by the rule, "Do it now or write it down;"

- Don't just write it on a scrap of paper, keep your agenda with you at all times;

- Learn to check your agenda often during the day;

- Set beepers or timers to remind you of times to make a phone call or leave for a meeting.

5. Boredom

Many adults with ADD comment that they "can't stand to be bored" but that they are very prone to boredom. The first and most important step to avoid boredom is to select a career path that is of high interest to you. Unfortunately, you may still occasionally become bored in a job that interests you. Here are some tips for overcoming boredom:

- Do the boring stuff at high energy times of the day.

Don't wait until you are tired;

- Delegate boring tasks whenever possible. What is intolerable to you may seem like an easy task to someone else;

- Break boring tasks up into small pieces;

- Recognize your need for change and stimulation and actively work to introduce more change or challenge into your work life.

6. Time management problems

There are several types of time management problems that are classic to adults with ADD. You may recognize yourself in some of these dilemmas:

Hyperfocusing – "Oh, no! It's what time? I should have left twenty minutes ago!" If you get caught up in what you're doing and lose track of time, develop the habit of setting a beeper to go off when you should leave.

Running late – Also often known as "just-one-more-thing-itis." Plan to be early, and take something to do when you get there (a book, paperwork) to counteract your "I-hate-to-wait-itis". Catch yourself answering the phone or doing one last little task. Stop. And remind yourself that "It's time to leave. I'll do that later."

Over-commitment – Many adults with ADD tend to cram far too many things into each day. This leads them to be highly stressed and usually late to each of the day's commitments. Try to consciously under-commit your time. There are always things you can do if you find free time on your hands, and you'll find you're doing things more effectively because you're not always rushed.

7. Procrastination

Procrastination can be a tremendous stumbling block for adults with ADD. Although everyone procrastinates to some extent, it is often a huge problem for those with ADD. Deadlines serve as starting points rather than finishing points leading to huge time crunches, all-nighters, and projects and proposals turned in late, time after time – not a good way to promote yourself as an effective, responsible professional. Here's what to do:

- Look for work that requires more immediate responses by its very nature. This eliminates the possibility of procrastination;

- Build in rewards for completing undesirable tasks;

- Request closer supervision. Procrastination flourishes in secrecy!

8. Difficulty with long-term projects

Problems completing long-term projects are often related to a cluster of difficulties including poor time management, procrastination tendencies, and difficulty with planning and organization. For adults with ADD, participation in long-term projects usually works best if you can:

- Team up with others to work in close cooperation. Daily or weekly team-meetings can help you stay on-track;

- Break the project down into stages and estimate the time required by each stage;

- In planning, start at the due-date and then work backwards in your calendar, setting dates for the completion of each part of the project;

- Review your progress regularly with your supervisor;

- Identify parts of the project that you are having trouble with and actively identify a solution. Ask yourself, "Do I have the knowledge or resources for this portion, or do I need the help of another team member?"

9. Paperwork

Paperwork is typically the "black hole" in the workplace for adults with ADD. Paperwork requires organization, self-discipline, and attention to detail – all of which are typically difficult for those with ADD. To get a handle on paperwork:

- Look for work that minimizes paperwork;

- Look for ways to streamline your paperwork. Can you dictate and have someone else type your notes for you?;

- Do your paperwork FIRST – before you are tired and frustrated from other events of the day;

- Ask for help before you have created an insurmountable mountain of paperwork;

- Develop a filing system that is SIMPLE; then USE IT!

10. Interpersonal difficulties

Many adults with ADD engage in behaviors on the job that bother co-workers and about which they are completely unaware! Feedback from a trusted friend or spouse can help build awareness. Here are some typical ADD interpersonal patterns that you may need to monitor in order to minimize:

Monologuing – Some individuals with ADD become so engrossed when they are talking about a topic that interests them that they forget to monitor the reactions of their audience; "Are they interested in what I'm saying, or are they giving signs that they would like to shift the topic or leave the interaction?".

Interrupting – This is a widespread pattern, rarely meant to be rude, but which often results in irritation and resentment over time. In meetings, write your comment down if you're afraid you'll forget. In conversation, monitor yourself, and apologize and stop talking if you catch yourself interrupting.

Being blunt – This gets back to that old truism, "It's not what you say, but how you say it." Some adults with ADD blurt out a reaction without taking the time to phrase it in a sensitive fashion. If you are one of those adults who congratulates yourself on your "refreshing honesty," you may want to ask for a little feedback about how your comments are taken.

Now that we've covered the top ten traps at work, I hope that you come away with the message that these traps are manageable, both through careful job selection, and through honest self-assessment and self-management. If you are in a job where you are experiencing serious difficulties, don't immediately assume that you are in the "wrong job." Try some of the coping tips mentioned in this article before deciding that you need to move on. Don't get caught in the biggest trap of all – that dream that somewhere the "perfect" job exists that won't require any efforts or adjustments on your part. Yes, you need to make an "ADD-savvy" job choice, but you also need to take charge of your ADD by understanding your needs, knowing your limits, knowing when to ask for help, and learning how to emphasize your strengths and talents!

This article was excerpted from Kathleen Nadeau's book, ADD in the Workplace, *which was published in April 1977 by Brunner/Mazel. It appeared in the Spring 1997 issue of* ATTENTION!

Kathleen G. Nadeau, Ph.D. is Director of Chesapeake Psychological Services of Maryland, a private clinic that specializes in diagnosing and treating adolescents and adults with ADD. She is editor of A Comprehensive Guide to Attention Deficit Disorder in Adults: Research, Diagnosis, and Treatment, *the first guide for professionals on adults with ADD, and is the author of several books on ADD. Dr. Nadeau serves on CH.A.D.D. s Professional Advisory Board.*

Succeeding in the Workplace with ADD

by Patricia H. Latham, J.D. and Peter S. Latham, J.D.

An article that appeared in the Wall Street Journal explored the world of contract workers. The article, entitled "High-Tech Nomads Write a New Program for the Future of Work," points out that, increasingly, work in America is project-oriented and that projects promote a blend of traditional employees and contract workers. This trend away from traditional jobs has many implications – decreased emphasis on job security and increased focus on one's own mastery of the field. The article quotes a software engineer who recently left the corporate world for life as an independent contractor as saying that now "I'm really independent... I'm attached only to what I know" (*Wall Street Journal*, August 19, 1995, page 1).

This evolving workplace may offer young adults with ADD greater opportunities for success. Trends giving more options as to work arrangements and greater control to the worker may have appeal to many persons with ADD. Similarly, greater flexibility in where and at what times work will be performed may prove beneficial to those persons with ADD who have difficulty with time management, relationships with supervisors, and social interactions in the workplace.

The workplace, as it is now and as it may become, offers greater opportunities to many adults with ADD than they have known before. A key advantage to the workplace, and difference from school, is choice. In the world of education, there are few choices and many demands in the early years. As we advance into secondary and post-secondary education, we have more choices but by no means the range of choice available in the workplace.

What choices do adults with ADD have in the workplace? They may choose a career (type of work), a particular job or work arrangement, a change in position, a career change, or perhaps, even starting a business. The type of work should play to the strengths of the individual and not impact heavily on the weak areas. With a good job match, traits that have caused problems in the past may prove to be assets.

Individuals with ADD may also have legal rights to accommodations in the workplace that may prove helpful in the quest for success. Statistics released by the U. S. Equal Opportunity Employment Commission (EEOC) indicate that disability related discrimination charges are increasing. The most often alleged act of employment discrimination is discharge. The EEOC enforces the ADA as well as various other Acts that prohibit discrimination.

Let's review in greater depth legal rights, accommodations, and strategies to promote success.

LEGAL RIGHTS

Adults with ADD that substantially limits a major life activity such as learning or working are considered individuals with disabilities (for purposes of legal protection) and enjoy the right to be free from discrimination in the workplace. The bar against discrimination applies to recruitment, advertising and job application procedures, hiring, upgrading, promotion, award of tenure, discharge, demotion, transfer, layoff, rehiring, compensation, leave, and various benefits. The right to be free from discrimination in the workplace is provided under two important federal laws: The Americans with Disabilities Act (ADA) and the Rehabilitation Act of 1973 (RA).

To invoke the protection of these federal statutes, the individual must establish that the statute applies and that he or she (1) is an individual with a disability, (2) is otherwise qualified with or without reasonable accommodation for the job, promotion, employment benefit, or privilege being sought, and (3) was denied it by reason of the disability.

Note that to obtain these protections, one must disclose that he or she has a disability. The individual may decide if and when to disclose. Where accommodations in the applications and entry testing process are not needed, many individuals will disclose at some time after they have commenced employment and have determined that they do need work accommodations.

When an individual discloses and requests accommodations, he or she must be prepared to submit professional documentation of the disability. Ordinarily, this documentation should set forth a diagnosis, evaluation of impact of ADD on the individual's functioning, and recommended accommodations.

When do the ADA and RA apply? Both prohibit discrimination against individuals with disabilities in employment, but the ADA has broader application. The RA basically follows federal dollars. It applies to the federal government, federal government contractors, and federal grant recipients. The ADA applies to virtually all employers except those with fewer than fifteen employees.

Who is an individual with a disability? Any individual who has a physical or mental impairment that substantially limits one or more major life activities qualifies as an individual with a disability. Learning disabilities are expressly recognized under regulations as impairments. ADD has been recognized in cases, letters of findings, and U. S. Department of Education memoranda. Note that, in order to qualify as a disability, the impairment must substantially limit a major life activity.

In addition to learning and working, in 1995, the EEOC recognized concentrating, thinking, and interacting with others as major life activities. Recognition of these specific processes may be helpful to individuals with ADD.

When is an individual "otherwise qualified"? One is "otherwise qualified" for a job when he or she can perform the essential functions of the job with or without reasonable accommodations. A reasonable accommodation is one that does not create an "undue hardship" for the employer. An accommodation that alters the essential nature of the job or results in significant difficulty or expense to the employer would create an undue hardship.

A few examples may be helpful in understanding reasonableness. A waiter with a vision impairment that makes it difficult for him to see in dim lighting may not compel a nightclub to accommodate him by providing bright lighting throughout its dining and lounge areas, as this would change the nature of the club and harm its trade. In another case, a school district that required that its teachers take turns driving school buses did have to restructure its job requirements to allow the hiring of a qualified teacher who had a disability that

prevented him from driving. Bus driving is not an essential part of a teaching job.

When is the discharge (or other act giving rise to a complaint) by reason of the disability? The disability must be the reason for the employer's act. In one case, a surgeon with narcolepsy (controlled by medication) had her hospital privileges terminated by a hospital. The termination was held lawful because the surgeon had verbally abused staff members for years, and there was no evidence that this behavior was related to the disability.

ACCOMMODATIONS

Individuals with ADD who meet the tests described above are entitled to reasonable accommodations in the workplace.

What accommodations may be helpful to persons with ADD? The answer depends on the individual case. ADD does not present in exactly the same way in each individual. For example, hyperactivity may be an issue for some and not for others. Also, many persons with ADD have co-existing learning disabilities and/or other disabilities. Recognizing that an accommodation plan is an individual matter, we have listed below accommodations that may be helpful to many persons with ADD.

- Reduce distractions in the work area.
- Give instructions orally and in writing.
- Break tasks down into manageable parts.
- Give frequent and specific feedback.
- Provide training course accommodations.
- Provide test accommodations (e.g., extra time, quiet room).
- Provide job restructuring.
- Allow job reassignment.

STRATEGIES TO PROMOTE SUCCESS

The process of achieving success in the workplace involves the efforts of the employer in providing needed reasonable accommodations and of the individual with ADD in using strategies that will promote success. Like accommodations, strategies should be tailored to the needs of the individual, taking into account how ADD presents in the particular case and any co-existing learning disabilities or other disabilities. We will explore below some strategies that may be helpful to many persons with ADD.

KNOW YOURSELF AND ADD

The individual with ADD must seek to know his or her strengths and weaknesses and to understand ADD and any co-existing conditions. Reading books concerning ADD and obtaining information from disability organizations such as CH.A.D.D. is most helpful. Evaluations and recommendations from medical, educational, psychological, and/or career counseling professionals may further promote understanding, facilitate coping with the disability, and assist self-advocacy efforts.

SELECT A GOOD JOB MATCH.

In general, the type of work an individual with ADD selects should play to his or her strengths and not impact heavily on the weak areas. It's usually best to avoid work with high paperwork and record keeping requirements, considerable supervisory or monitoring responsibilities, high stress, demands for rapid performance, and expectation for rapid learning, especially in large group situations.

Certain career areas seem to work well for some individuals with ADD: the media, the arts, trades, sales, law enforcement, and fire safety. Many individuals will be most comfortable with an expertise in a particular area so that expectations are clear, and there are few surprises. A career that allows a high degree of autonomy may be better than one that will involve close and constant personal supervision. A high degree of structure is a must for some individuals with ADD.

Some young adults with ADD wish to consider the military. Possible advantages include structure, clarity of expectations, and training opportunities. (See "Adults with ADD and the Military" in this chapter.)

The positive side to ADD may open up possibilities. For example, the intensity about interests that may have led earlier to a seeming obsession about toy cars or music tapes may be channeled in adult life to yield great success. One adult turned an interest in antique cars into several successful businesses he owns and operates.

Remember, there are many paths to success – some traditional and others not so traditional. The adult with ADD must consider a range of options and discover what works best. For some individuals with ADD, one job may prove boring, so they may change jobs frequently or hold several part-time jobs simultaneously. Some may return to school in connection with a new career interest. Remember, some adults with ADD do better than ever before in the educational arena with added maturity, courses that are in their area of interest, and increased accommodations in post-secondary education. A number of individuals with ADD have observed that they enjoyed more success as adults in courses with specific career related objectives and clear expectations.

USE AIDS.

Today, more than ever, there are aids that promote success in the workplace. A few of these are:

- tape recorder to record meetings, conferences, training courses, etc.
- day planner (plan book, electronic scheduler, or voice organizer) to keep track of work deadlines, meetings, appointments, and other obligations
- computer and software (e.g., spell check and grammar check)
- calculator or talking calculator.

Sometimes such aids may be provided by employers as workplace accommodations. Consider a case in which a special computer and software were provided by an employer to a research scientist with ADD to accommodate his disability and increase his writing productivity. This arrangement allowed the scientist to dictate to the computer and see the dictated material in print on the computer screen. The research scientist, a Ph.D. in Chemistry, had struggled for years with the research report writing part of his job. After initially getting little response to his request for accommodations and finding himself on the verge of being fired, he filed a complaint with his agency's Equal Employment Opportunity office and, as a result of a mediation process, obtained the requested accommodations.

USE COMPENSATORY TECHNIQUES.

There are various compensatory techniques for specific deficits. A few are explored below.

- If chronic lateness is a problem, leave fifteen minutes early for work, appointments, and interviews. Do not become diverted unless there is an emergency.
- If hyperactivity is a problem, use breaks and your lunch period to get physical movement and exercise to refresh yourself.
- If impulsive statements and loss of temper are problems, listen to others and take time before responding, especially if angry or negative feelings are present. If necessary, take time out to cool down and focus on what is important.

An example of a compensatory technique improving work performance involves a police officer. He had struggled with ADD through his school years and then found law enforcement to be the career for him. Soon, a problem emerged. He was often late to work – usually by just a few minutes. Why was he late? In part because he would become easily diverted, but also because early arrival would mean waiting to go on duty and feeling bored. The solution that worked for him: leaving fifteen minutes early and bringing along one of his many electronic gadgets so that he could enjoy using it while waiting.

In conclusion, young adults with ADD should seek

to know themselves and their disabilities, become informed about their legal rights in the workplace, find an appropriate job match, use helpful strategies, and request reasonable accommodations, if needed. With all of this in place, they will be well positioned to move forward with enthusiasm to make contributions and reap rewards in the workplace. If, despite the best efforts, there is a setback, remember that succeeding in the workplace does not mean succeeding in every job but rather succeeding overall. What is learned from a disappointing experience may help focus in on what will work better in the future.

This article first appeared in the Spring 1995 issue of ATTENTION!

Patricia H. Latham, J.D. and Peter S. Latham, J.D. are partners in the Washington, D.C. law firm Latham & Latham, directors of JKL Communications, and founders and directors of the National Center for Law and Learning Disabilities (NCLLD). They have authored six books, contributed chapters to six additional books, and written numerous articles on ADD and learning disabilities.

Equal Employment Opportunity Commission Issues New Guidance on Psychiatric Disabilities and the ADA

by Peter S. Latham, J.D. and Patricia H. Latham, J.D.

INTRODUCTION

The Americans with Disabilities Act of 1990 (ADA) protects qualified individuals with disabilities from discrimination in employment, eligibility for government programs, and access to places of public accommodation. Since its enactment in 1990, the ADA has been the subject of much debate, which has resulted in the issuance of a number or regulations and interpretations. However, the guidance has been largely concerned with physical disabilities, e.g. back injuries, vision impairments, and hearing impairments.

Now the Equal Employment Opportunity Commission (EEOC) has issued a pamphlet entitled *EEOC Guidance on the Americans With Disabilities Act and Psychiatric Disabilities.* The purpose of this document is to set forth the Commission's position on this topic, and to provide guidance to its personnel in enforcing Title I of the ADA. Title I deals with employment only, but the Commission's position on the proper interpretation of the ADA is respected (and often followed) by the Courts in interpreting other portions of the ADA.

The EEOC's major points are discussed below. It should be noted that the EEOC does not discuss ADD as such, but the principles considered are nonetheless applicable to ADD.

PSYCHIATRIC DISABILITY UNDER THE ADA

The Americans with Disabilities Act of 1990 (ADA) protects individuals with physical or mental impairments that substantially limit one or more of a person's major life activities. The EEOC confirms that, in its view, a "mental impairment" includes any "mental or psychological disorder," together with "emotional or mental illness." These include major depression, bipolar disorder, anxiety disorders, panic disorders, obsessive compulsive disorder, and post-traumatic stress disorder, schizophrenia, and personality disorders. Also covered (but not considered psychiatric disabilities by the EEOC) are "mental retardation,"

"organic brain syndrome" and "specific learning disabilities," as well as other neurological disorders such as Alzheimer's Disease.

The EEOC believes that the ADA should be interpreted in light of current mental health knowledge as reflected in the American Psychiatric Association's *Diagnostic and Statistical Manual of Mental Disorders* (now in its fourth edition, *DSM-IV*).

DSM-IV is relevant for identifying these disorders; it has been recognized as an important reference by courts and is widely used by American mental health professionals for diagnostic and insurance reimbursement purposes.

However, the EEOC cautions that not every condition listed in the *DSM-IV* is a disability under the ADA. Some are nothing more than personality traits, for example. Others are behaviors, not disorders.

SUBSTANTIAL LIMITATION OF A MAJOR LIFE ACTIVITY

Each physical or mental impairment must substantially limit a major life activity in order to constitute a disability. While the EEOC agrees that the "major life activities limited by mental impairments differ from person to person," it also makes clear that it considers "learning, thinking, concentrating, interacting with others, caring for oneself, speaking, performing manual tasks," working, and sleeping as the most likely ones to be affected by mental impairments.

How badly must a disorder affect these activities? It must prevent an individual from performing a major life activity or significantly restrict the manner or duration of performing the activity as compared to the average person in the general population. Here are the EEOC's views on major life activities of particular interest to many individuals with ADD:

Ability to interact with others. An individual would be considered to have a substantial limitation in the ability to interact with others "if his/her relations with others were characterized on a regular basis by severe problems; for example, consistently high levels of hostility, social withdrawal, or failure to communicate when necessary."

Concentration. An individual would be considered to have a substantial limitation in the ability to concentrate "if s/he was easily and frequently distracted, meaning that his/her attention was frequently drawn to irrelevant sights or sounds or to intrusive thoughts; or if s/he experienced his/her 'mind going blank' on a frequent basis."

Ability to care for oneself. An individual would be considered to have a substantial limitation in the ability to care for "him/herself if s/he is significantly restricted as compared to the average person in the general population in performing basic activities such as getting up in the morning, bathing, dressing, and preparing or obtaining food."

Ability to work. The EEOC advises that an individual need not show that he/she is substantially limited in the major life activity of working in order to obtain the protection of the ADA if a substantial limitation in another major life activity can be shown.

REASONABLE ACCOMMODATIONS

The EEOC reminds employers that:

> Reasonable accommodations for individuals with disabilities must be determined on a case-by-case basis because workplaces and jobs vary, as do people with disabilities. Accommodations for individuals with psychiatric disabilities may involve changes to workplace policies, procedures, or practices. Physical changes to the workplace or extra equipment also may be effective reasonable accommodations for some people.

The EEOC suggests that some or all of the following may be reasonable accommodations for individuals with psychiatric disabilities. They are of particular interest to many individuals with ADD.

- Time off. Use of accrued paid leave or additional unpaid leave for treatment or recovery related to a disability. Occasional leave (e.g. a few hours at a time) or a leave of absence may prove appropriate.

- Modified work schedules.

- Physical changes to workplace or equipment. Accommodations recommended for "individuals who have disability-related limitations in concentration" might include room dividers, partitions, soundproofing, or visual barriers. Moving the individual to a quieter location, lowering the pitch of telephones, or permitting use of headphones to block distractions are also possibilities.

- Modification of a workplace policy. The EEOC suggests that "...it would be a reasonable accommodation to allow an individual with a disability, who has difficulty concentrating due to the disability, to take detailed notes during client presentations even though company policy discourages employees from taking extensive notes during such sessions."

- Adjusting supervisory methods to ensure that assignments, instructions, and training are delivered "by the medium that is most effective for a particular individual (e.g., in writing, in conversation, or by electronic mail)." Increased feedback and structure are also reasonable accommodations. However, employer monitoring to ensure that required medications are taken is not a reasonable accommodation.

- Job coaches. The EEOC recommends the use of "a temporary job coach to assist in the training of a qualified individual with a disability" as a reasonable accommodation.

- Reassignment to a vacant position must be considered as a reasonable accommodation when accommodation in the individual's present job would constitute an undue hardship.

HOW TO PROVE IT

The EEOC has provided excellent guidance on the key question. "How do I prove that I am eligible for accommodations?"

The determination that a particular individual has a substantially limiting impairment should be based on information about how the impairment affects that individual and not on generalizations about the condition. Relevant evidence from EEOC investigators includes descriptions of an individual's typical level of functioning at home, at work, and in other settings, as well as evidence showing that the individual's functional limitations are linked to his or her impairment. Expert testimony about substantial limitation is not necessarily required. Credible testimony from the individual with a disability and his or her family members, friends, or co-workers may suffice.

CONCLUSION

The ADA requires that an individual who seeks its protection prove that he or she has a physical or mental impairment that substantially limits one or more major life activities, compared to the average member of the general population AND at the same time is qualified to perform the essential functions of the job in question with or without a reasonable accommodation. In short, the individual's impairment must be serious enough to constitute a disability but mild enough not to interfere with his/her ability to meet the essential job requirements with no more than a reasonable accommodation. The EEOC's new guidance offers individuals with ADD much needed help in navigating between these two obstacles.

This article first appeared in the Fall 1997 issue of ATTENTION!

Peter S. Latham, J.D. and Patricia H. Latham, J.D. are partners in the Washington, D.C. law firm Latham & Latham, directors of JKL Communications, and founders and directors of the National Center for Law and Learning Disabilities (NCLLD). They have authored six books, contributed chapters to six additional books, and written numerous articles on ADD and learning disabilities.

Adults with ADD and the Military:
An Overview

by Sheila Lachs, Esq.

One of the most common issues about which CH.A.D.D. is asked is whether or not individuals with ADD are eligible for military service. This is an extremely important issue because many young adults with ADD seek to join the military, and for these young adults, the environment could not be better suited to them. Many individuals with ADD thrive in structured environments, and it would be difficult to find a more structured environment than that supplied by basic training and eventual service in one of the branches of the military.

CH.A.D.D. also receives calls from adults who are already serving in the military. Many will have just received a diagnosis of ADD and want to know how that will affect their careers if they disclose that they have the disorder.

The military is not subject to such civil rights laws as the Americans with Disabilities Act (ADA), which protects qualified individuals with disabilities from discrimination by most private employers and state and local governments. Instead, federal agencies, such as the Department of Defense, are covered by the Rehabilitation Act of 1973, which prohibits discrimination on the basis of disability by federal agencies, federal contractors, or recipients of federal financial assistance. However, the Department of Defense is not subject to the provisions of the Rehabilitation Act with respect to active duty military personnel because of the unique function such individuals serve. The Department of Defense can require that recruits and active duty personnel meet certain physical fitness standards, including standards that may exclude individuals with ADD.

YOUNG ADULTS WITH ADD

Unfortunately, officially, the military is not receptive to applicants with ADD. The Department of Defense (DOD) Accession Standards, which set forth physical and mental conditions that are not accepted by the military, clearly state that anyone with a "chronic history of academic skills or perceptual defects secondary to organic or functional mental disorders that interferes with work or school after age twelve," will not be admitted to the service. In addition, the standards add that "current use of medication to improve or maintain academic skills (e.g., methylphenidate hydrochloride) is disqualifying." It would seem, then, that anyone with ADD after age twelve or anyone currently taking medication for their ADD would not be admitted to the service.

However, in practice, selected individuals who would otherwise be disqualified by their ADD may still enter the military through the waiver process. In order to receive a waiver, they would have had to score in the top two-thirds of individuals taking the ASVAB, which is the standardized test the military gives to high school students. The award of a waiver is based on expert opinion, but that expert must be affiliated with the military. For example, a waiver might be granted to an individual with ADD by a military doctor if that individual scored well on the ASVAB, had good grades in high school, participated in high school athletics, and is otherwise qualified for service. It would not be advisable for individuals to enter the military in the hopes of obtaining a waiver, however, as they are the exception more than the rule.

In a November 1996 meeting with Lieutenant Colonel Ed Baldwin, Deputy Director of Prevention and Standards for the Department of Defense, CH.A.D.D. learned that the Department was just beginning the process of revising their accession standards. One of the main reasons for the revision was the large number of applicants who had ADD and the need for recruits. Over the following year, the DOD planned to track the success of individuals with ADD who had entered the service under waivers and compare their experiences to those of recruits without ADD. After the data is gathered, the DOD will have sufficient information on the performance of individuals with ADD to revise their accession standards accordingly. Potential revisions included specifying how long an individual would have had to have been off medication before he or she could be admitted to military service.

ADULTS WITH ADD

Since ADD has come under much greater scrutiny in recent years, many adults with ADD who are currently serving in the military may have been able to gain admission during a time when there was less awareness of the disorder. Further, many adults with ADD who were never diagnosed as children may be being diagnosed as adults.

What does an adult with ADD do when he or she is diagnosed with ADD? Should the individual disclose his condition to superiors? Indeed, many adults with ADD have had lengthy and distinguished careers in the military. Although these individuals' careers exemplify the success that individuals with ADD can and do have in the service, many are reluctant to share that they have ADD for fear that they will be asked to step down. The decision is a personal choice, but no one should make that decision without considering the potential risks of disclosure.

Lt. Col. Ed Baldwin stated that an adult who is diagnosed with ADD while serving in the military and reveals his or her condition would be "separated" and sent before a medical board for a thorough assessment of his or her condition. The board would consider whether to classify the individual as "non-deployable" and allow him or her to continue to serve. However, that individual would not be able to be sent to war. If the officer is not considered "non-deployable," he or she would be sent to the Personnel Evaluation Board (PEB) to determine compensation and separation.

Thus, it is clear that disclosure carries with it potentially significant consequences. Individuals must consider the risks and weigh carefully the best action to take.

WHAT CH.A.D.D. IS DOING TO WORK WITH THE DEPARTMENT OF DEFENSE

CH.A.D.D. is continuing to work with the Department of Defense on the issue of individuals with ADD who want to enter the military. We have made clear that individuals with ADD can make successful contributions to the military and currently are doing so. We have advocated for revisions to the accession standards that would make it easier for individuals with ADD to enter and remain in the military. In addition, we have worked with several U. S. Senators on increasing understanding of ADD by the military. We are currently awaiting the revisions to the accession standards and will continue to work with the DOD on their accession process. With every effort we engage in, however, we must carefully determine whether action would serve to help our members and not hurt their chances of entering or remaining in the service.

Sheila Lachs is CH.A.D.D.'s Government Relations Liaison who works in Washington, D.C. to monitor events important to individuals with ADD.

CHAPTER 5

EDUCATING AND TRAINING

An Introduction by Mary McDonald Richard

Member, CH.A.D.D. National Board

Coordinator of Services for Students with Learning Disabilities at the

Office of Student Disability Services at the University of Iowa

This chapter focuses on a number of education and training issues that are of growing interest to many adults who have ADD. Unlike the relatively homogeneous motivations of eighteen-year-olds just out of high school, adults enter education and career programs on the basis of a much wider range of interests and purposes. Some wish to earn new or advanced degrees, while others are seeking personal development opportunities. Work-related motivations may include plans for a dramatic career shift or efforts to ensure continuing employment with a current employer. For some, the decision to take classes has been made with the assistance of vocational counseling. Others may have decided to take a course in order to test the waters, for fun, or as a part of a larger exploratory process. Adults with ADD might fit into any of these scenarios.

Every adult student approaches the classroom with a combination of interests, skills, anxiety, and hope. Each one is aware that new learning experiences have the potential to bring out and increase their strengths, as well as test their weaker skills. Adults may be worried about encountering problems that occurred in former programs prior to diagnosis and treatment. Some will be pleased to find that the insights and skills they have developed to manage ADD symptoms in daily life will similarly empower them in the classroom.

As adult learners, they will find that they have lots of company – over half of the students enrolled in post-secondary programs are of "nontraditional" age. There is a strong likelihood that men and women will encounter other "middle-aged" students upon returning to the classroom. This may be encouraging to those who are thinking about giving school a try. Adults diagnosed with ADD may also be encouraged to learn about the programs and services for students with disabilities available at many schools. For individuals who have not attended a college or training program in more than ten years, they may be pleased with new developments in this area. Students with "non-visible" disorders, such as ADD and learning disabilities, are in the most rapidly growing disability category in post-secondary education. Thus, adult learners often find they are not alone in facing the challenges of returning to the classroom either as an adult or as a person with a disability.

An adult student who qualifies for disability services must have a documented disability that significantly impairs his or her ability to benefit from the program's education or training without reasonable accommodations. Students who meet these criteria are generally protected by federal laws. Section 504 of the

Rehabilitation Act of 1973 and, more recently, the Americans with Disabilities Act (ADA) require education and training programs to provide appropriate assistance to students, provided they carry out certain responsibilities. Students are required to: disclose the disability and provide an appropriate professional report documenting the diagnosis and containing information to demonstrate that the student's functioning is impaired to the degree that reasonable accommodations are needed to "level the playing field." Reasonable modifications are those that are supported by the student's documentation and do not fundamentally alter the program or impose an undue administrative or financial burden on the institution. Both the student's request for accommodations and their provision should be timely.

While programs and services are often helpful and important, students ultimately own the responsibility for their performance. The outcome of students with ADD, and of all students substantially depends upon their abilities and efforts to meet the standards of the program they are attending. Among today's adult students are those who enjoy the fruits of equal educational opportunity by making appropriate use of the accommodations available at their schools. They are not looking for a quick fix for their situations, but are committed to completing the work required to build a bridge to their futures.

The presence of successful adult students with ADD in education and training programs should be encouraging for persons who are considering a similar move. As others cross this bridge, they will add to the number of adults who are proving that, by combining their abilities with strategies, resources and effort, they are able to achieve their personal best.

Career and Life Planning with ADD: After Diagnosis and Treatment... What's Next?

by Wilma R. Fellman, M.Ed., LPC

I'm standing on my soap box frequently lately. While there has been tremendous progress made in the diagnosis and treatment of ADD, careful follow-through must not be neglected. Since ADD affects one's career, relationships, and life, we cannot expect that awareness of limitations and/or medication will be enough to assist individuals in reaching their fullest potential. Further support is available.

Career and life planning are not only important for individuals with ADD, but also for the general population. We live in a rapidly changing world today in which most people who work can expect to change careers at least once in their lifetimes and change jobs as many as eight times. Compare that with our grandparents' lifetimes of choosing a career when they reached adulthood (around age seventeen) and working at it day after day for fifty years. They didn't consider words like "fulfillment" or "reaching their potential." Instead, they tended to accept that whatever they chose to do – which was often what their parents did for a living – was going to be done until retirement. In addition, they did not have to deal with such life-altering events as layoffs, downsizing, rightsizing, or organizational reorganization.

Approximately 22,000 jobs are defined in the *Dictionary of Occupational Titles*. With so many choices open to young adults today, the selection process often feels overwhelming. Therefore, career development assistance can be of tremendous help to adolescents and adults in sorting through the variables that affect decision-making. Career counseling consists of more than a simplistic process of matching an individual's interests to a job; it looks at the whole person when solving this puzzle. Some pieces of the puzzle are: interests, aptitudes, personality traits, values, accomplishments, energy patterns, and challenges.

Only when we look at each of these areas can we actually see the whole person. Despite the human tendency to grab for solutions in order to end tormenting confusion, individuals need to research options they are considering before jumping into them.

In other words, they should "try a career on for size" before "buying it."

We can accomplish this through a three-step process of: (1) reading about a career; (2) talking about it with a handful of people in that field; and (3) if possible, observing the work environment.

While there are few guarantees in life, this process gets us about as close to a realistic picture as possible. The method is not an instant one; it does take time. But jumping into life's work without research can be disastrous.

For the adult with ADD, the process described above is exactly the same. However, it will be additionally important to assess energy patterns (what times of the day, days of the week, etc. are most effective time-slots) and challenges. How these factors affect comfort in the workplace will be different for each individual with ADD. We need to focus on the strengths that will carry and enhance these challenges because many adults with ADD can easily recite their many limitations but have often lost sight of their strengths. It becomes extremely important for adults with ADD to become involved in career counseling to identify their special gifts and accomplishments. While many adults with ADD share common struggles, each also possesses uncommon talents, passions, and skills. Career counselors should support, guide, and encourage these individuals, and then stand back and watch them blossom.

Another important factor for adults with ADD to consider is laws protecting them against discrimination in the workplace. An individual with ADD has the right to be provided "reasonable accommodations" if he or she is the best candidate for the job. However, it should be kept in mind that individuals with ADD should not expect to win out in a competitive job market simply because the law says they must be hired. Individuals with ADD should identify the potential pitfalls and plan accommodations or modifications for the best possible job performance. The law cannot do this for them. A good career counselor can provide assistance in this area, empowering adults with ADD and presenting them with a realistic picture of what will work most comfortably over time. Additional stumbling blocks down the road can also be offset by the counseling process.

Once the facts necessary for good career decision-making have been gathered, the picture that once looked chaotic and lacked direction becomes beautifully clear, and adults with ADD can believe in their potential. The career counseling process can be a great longterm help. It is an insurance policy for the future. After diagnosis and treatment, it is what's next.

Wilma Fellman is a licensed professional counselor with over fifteen years of experience in career and life planning counseling. She specializes in helping young adults with ADD make initial career decisions and mature adults with work-related transitions. Ms. Fellman is the author of The Other Me, *a collection of poems about how ADD affects one's life as an adult, a parent, and a child. A former high school teacher, she combines her personal struggles and triumphs with her aim to touch the heart through humor and the strength of systematic planning.*

Planning for the Future: Alternatives to College

by Robin Hawks

"I probably should be going to college – all of my friends are and that's what my parents want me to do. But I never liked school, and I don't know how I'll be able to deal with it for another four years!" Statements like these are common of high school seniors with ADD. For many, school has been difficult and unenjoyable and the thought of going through more schooling after graduating from high school is often unbearable. The prevalence rates of ADD in childhood is estimated to be approximately 3 to 5 percent (APA). A substantial number of children who have ADD will continue to experience symptoms in adulthood. One of these symptoms, according to research, manifests itself in a substantial comorbidity between ADD and learning disorders (Hooper & Olley, 1996). In fact, one study found that 63 percent of a learning disabled sample population also had ADD (Cantwell, 1991). While individuals with ADD can certainly achieve success in college, it is not always the best – nor the only – option. There are a number of alternatives to the college environment that may be more suitable for those with ADD. Several of these alternatives are highlighted below.

TRADE AND TECHNICAL SCHOOLS

One alternative for individuals with ADD who do not choose to attend college is to attend a trade or technical school. In keeping with comorbidity rates between ADD and learning disorders, nearly 30 percent of adults with a learning disability receive a degree from a trade or technical school, according to *LDA Newsbriefs*. The National Association of Trade and Technical Schools reports that there are over 10,000 such schools in the United States. These schools offer training in 100 different careers, such as cosmetology, automotive repair, and computer training. There are a number of benefits for individuals who choose to attend a trade or technical school. Not only do they receive hands-on experience and guided practice in and learn the special skills that are required for the occupations of their choice, but they are also receiving training that is the most up-to-date; most trade and technical schools have connections with the labor force so their curriculums are updated based on the requirements of local employers.

MILITARY SERVICE

Individuals with ADD who receive passing scores of the Armed Services Vocational Aptitude Battery (ASVAB) may want to consider the military as an alternative to college. Military service is an option for individuals with ADD who perform well in structured and routine environments. Those individuals who have significant difficulty following rules and are oppositional to authority figures will not want to pursue this option, as a willingness to adhere to strict regulations and disciplinary standards is an essential ingredient for military success. It is important to note that adults with ADD who require medication to manage their disorder may not be eligible for military service. Failure to disclose any pre-existing condition may result in discharge from the military. (See "Adults with ADD and the Military: An Overview" in Chapter 5.)

APPRENTICESHIPS

Another alternative for individuals with ADD who do not wish to attend college is to enroll in an apprenticeship program. Apprenticeship programs provide an opportunity for participants to learn a trade while in the work environment. Administered by the Department of Labor, apprenticeship programs are available in over 425 occupational areas, such as heating and air conditioning (Levinson, 1993). The specifics of the arrangement are worked out between the apprentice and the employer; however, general guidelines regarding the hours of training, wage, evaluation methods, and related academic instruction are provided. For more information, contact your local labor department.

EMPLOYMENT

For some individuals with ADD, seeking employment opportunities may be the best option to pursue following graduation from high school. Employment can be obtained through a number of channels, including state employment commissions, newspaper advertisements, job lines, and the individual's network of family and friends. Many states have automated labor exchange systems that assist in the job search process. Those choosing this alternative should recognize, however, that employment brings its own unique set of demands. Common weaknesses for the individual with ADD in the employment arena include:

failure to report to work on time;

failure to listen and follow instructions properly;

taking on responsibilities not assigned as job tasks;

being sensitive to criticism;

taking too long to complete job tasks.

The Americans with Disabilities Act "guarantees all citizens with disabilities equal access to employment, public accommodations, state and local governmental services, transportation, and communication" (Krieg, Brown & Ballard, 1995). This act requires that employers make reasonable accommodations for the disabled employee. To learn more about accommodations and strategies for success in the workplace, consult *Succeeding in the Workplace*, by Patricia Horan Latham, J.D. and Peter S. Latham, J.D. (See Chapter 5 of this book.) In addition, the Job Accommodations Network, which can be accessed by calling 1-800-AOA-WORK, is also a valuable source of information regarding employment issues.

VOCATIONAL REHABILITATION SERVICES

Rehabilitation services are available for individuals with ADD provided that the condition constitutes a substantial barrier to employment. Section 504 of the Rehabilitation Act of 1973 affords individuals with disabilities, including ADD, consideration for services. Individuals qualifying for these services, which include vocational counseling, evaluation, training, and job placement assistance, often benefit greatly. There is no upper age limit for application to vocational rehabilitation. There are three important points that individuals seeking vocational rehabilitation services should be aware of, however: (1) there is no legal obligation on the part of the rehabilitation agency to pay all of an individual's training costs; (2) vocational rehabilitation is an eligibility program – not an entitlement program; and (3) the application process can be intimidating, as there is a set of involved procedures to follow. For additional information regarding vocational rehabilitation services, readers are encouraged to contact their local or state vocational rehabilitation program. HEATH Resources Center also publishes *Vocational Rehabilitation Services – A Student Consumer's Guide*.

SELF AND OCCUPATIONAL AWARENESS

Before choosing a post-secondary pursuit, it is critical for young adults with ADD to take into account their personal characteristics as well as the characteristics of the environment in which they are considering. ADD is as much a part of an individual as his likes and dislikes, and must be considered when choosing alternatives after high school. It is the author's experience that individuals who "own," "embrace," and "attend to" their ADD are the most successful in any environment when compared to their peers who deny the impact of the disorder in settings other than academic one.

Sources such as the *Dictionary of Occupational Titles* (U.S. Employment Service, 1981) and the *Occupational Outlook Handbook* (U.S. Department of Labor, 1982) can be used to promote occupational awareness (Levinson, 1993). Career interest inventories can also provide individuals who have ADD with a time efficient method of matching interests to various job titles. For example, *Holland Self Directed Search* (Holland, 1985) takes approximately fifteen minutes to complete and results in an occupational code that pinpoints the individual's most dominant career interests (i.e., realistic, social, investigative, enterprising, artistic, and conventional). The individual then matches the code to the appropriate job titles that correspond with the code. While this system does not address aptitude, it does provide a direction for self and job exploration. Other sources, such as computerized career information systems, (e.g., SIGI) may be beneficial for individuals to explore. These systems generally guide the individual through a series of career-based interest questions resulting in a code that is matched to various career types. Information pertaining to the job duties, qualifications, occupational outlooks, and salaries of a particular career are also often provided.

Additional information about careers that cannot be accessed through written means can be obtained via informational interviews or job shadowing. Individuals with ADD are encouraged to contact persons who have careers they may be interested in pursuing and ask if they can arrange for an informational interview or a job shadowing experience. Job shadowing allows the individual with ADD the opportunity to follow a professional of his or her choice for a day to gain first-hand experience about a particular job. For persons with ADD, this arrangement can be an extremely valuable experience as their often limited attention span makes gaining career information through books or other written resources troublesome. Informational interviews or job shadowing experiences are informal, arranged easily, and expose the individual to the subtle nuances of a job.

For individuals with ADD, planning for the future beyond high school can be a stressful time, as many graduates dread the thought of enduring more schooling. It is important for these individuals to realize that success is not only achieved through a college degree – there are a number of options that high school graduates with ADD can pursue other than attending college. The items highlighted in this article serve as an example of the many alternatives to college individuals with ADD have available to them.

This article first appeared in the Fall 1996 issue of ATTENTION!

Robin Hawks is in private practice as Director of the Center for Learning Potential and a part-time instructor of special education at James Madison University.

RESOURCES

HEATH Resource Center
One Dupont Circle, Suite 800
Washington, DC 20036
800 544-3284

Job Accommodations Network
West Virginia University
809 Allen Hall
Morgantown, WV 26506
800 ADA-WORK

REFERENCES

Adelman, P. B. & Vogel, S. A. (1993). Issues in the employment of adults with learning disabilities. *Journal of Learning Disabilities.* 16, 219-232.

Americans with Disabilities Act of 1990, 42 U.S.C.A. 12101 et seq. (West 1993). American Psychiatric Association. (1994). *Diagnostic and Statistical Manual of Mental Disorders - 4th Edition.* Washington D. C.: Author

Cantwell, D. P. & Baker, L. (1991). Association between attention deficit-hyperactivity disorder and learning disorders. *Journal of Learning Disabilities.* 24(2), 88-95.

Holland, J. L. (1985). *The Self Directed Search.* Odessa, FL: Psychological Assessment Resources, Inc.

Hooper, S. R. & Olley, J. G. (1996). Psychological comorbidity in adults with learning disabilities. In N. Gregg, C. Hoy & A. Gay. *Adults with learning disabilities: Theoretical and practical perspectives.* New York: Guilford Press.

Levinson, E. M. (1993). *Transdisciplinary vocational assessment: Issues in school based programs.* Brandon, Vermont: Clinical Psychology Publishing Co., Inc.

Krieg, F.J., Brown, P. & Ballard, J. (1995). *Transition: School to work.* Bethesda MD: National Association of School Psychologists.

Rehabilitation Act of 1973. Public Law 93-112, 87 Stat. 355 91973).

Robin, A. L. Attention Deficit Hyperactivity Disorder in adults: Assessment and management. Professional Advancement Seminars. Unpublished Manuscript.

Smith, J.O. (1992). Falling through the cracks: Rehabilitation services for adults with learning disabilities. *Exceptional Children.* March 451-460.

United States Department of Defense. (1984). *Test manual for the Armed Services Vocational Aptitude Battery.* North Chicago, IL: United States Military Entrance Processing Command.

United States Department of Labor. (1982). *Occupational Outlook Handbook.* Washington, DC: U.S. Department of Labor.

United States Employment Service. (1981). *Dictionary of Occupational Titles.* Washington, DC: U.S. Employment Service.

Weiss, L. (1992). *Attention deficit disorder in adults.* Dallas, Texas: Taylor Publishing Co.

The Key Steps to Selecting a College: For Students with ADD

by Marybeth Kravets

The college search process for students with ADD requires many of the same strategies, techniques, and assessments that it does for students who do not have ADD. However, students who have special needs have special reasons why they need to be selective with their college choices. Any college receiving federal funds must comply with the law and provide reasonable accommodations. However, finding the right fit goes beyond reasonable accommodations. There is no crystal ball that can look into the future, but there are several key steps that should help students with ADD search and select colleges that are well suited for their individual needs. These key steps are:

> accepting
> assessing
> prioritizing
> disclosing
> testing
> identifying criteria
> exploring
> touring
> interviewing
> applying
> selecting
> accommodating
> succeeding.

ACCEPTING

The most important ingredient in selecting a college is accepting the diagnosis of ADD. This process could be affected significantly by the length of time that has elapsed since the diagnosis was made. A recently-made diagnosis may have a greater emotional effect than a diagnosis made at an earlier age. Students diagnosed in elementary school have had time to learn about their disorder and make adjustments to enhance their behavior and learning. Students diagnosed later, however, have not had time to understand the disorder and master all of the compensatory skills and techniques.

However difficult it may be, acceptance is essential for success in life. Acceptance means that the student with ADD and his or her family understand the diagnosis and the accommodations that will be necessary in college. Acceptance and understanding are fundamental to the student's ability to self advocate. It is important that college-bound students with ADD be comfortable with their disability. The student should be able to:

- **Articulate** the disability and the impact on his or her learning;

- **Identify** his or her strengths and weaknesses;

- **Accept** accommodations;

- **Describe** accommodations used in high school; and

- **Identify** services needed in college.

ASSESSING

Students may be socially, chronologically, and emotionally ready, but not academically ready for college-level work. It is important to do an assessment on all levels to determine overall readiness.

To assess emotional/social readiness, students should evaluate their:

___ Ability to make and keep friends

___ Ability to deal with setbacks

___ Appropriateness in conversations

___ Ability to read body language

___ Level of interaction with peers and teachers

___ Ability to describe feelings

___ Level of independence

___ Ability to follow rules

___ Coping skills

___ Self-esteem & self-image

To assess academic readiness, students should:

___ Review the high school curriculum

___ Evaluate the degree of difficulty of courses

___ Look for signs of upward grade trend

___ Look for mainstream courses

___ Look for willingness to take risks

___ Look for willingness to accept accommodations

Not every student will begin high school taking college preparatory courses, and many colleges admit students who were enrolled in modified, remedial, or special education courses. However, most four-year colleges will ultimately look for evidence of upward challenge and mainstream college preparatory courses by the student's junior year. Students and parents must remember that:

• college professors are not trained to teach to different levels of academic ability; students are responsible for what they needed to learn in high school;

• students need to be prepared to tackle difficult college level courses;

• reviewing college entrance *and* exit course requirements is imperative; very few colleges offer remedial or individualized courses; and

• students need to experience mainstream, college prep courses during high school.

PRIORITIZING

College brochures and promotional materials typically show pictures of students smiling and having fun on campus and feature the institution's outstanding facilities; videos highlight academic offerings, activities, residential life, and comments from happy students and faculty. All of this information is important in establishing selection criteria. However, students with ADD must begin their search by identifying and prioritizing the *most* important criteria in their ultimate selection. To do this, students should rank their priorities. What is most important?

___ Extended testing time

___ Distraction free environment for testing

___ Small classes

___ Priority registration

___ Advising system

___ Counseling available

___ Course substitution

___ Advocacy available

___ Tutoring

___ Readers

___ Scribes

___ Note-takers

___ Audio tapes of lectures and texts

___ Use of calculator on exams

___ Use of word processor with spell check/ thesaurus on exams

___ Time extension for assignments

___ Skills Courses

___ Support groups

___ Distance from home

___ Psychologist available

___ Particular major

___ Fraternities/sororities

___ Warm /cold climate

___ Sports

___ Other

DISCLOSING

Colleges cannot ask any questions on a college application regarding disabilities. They can, however, suggest that students provide additional information that may be useful in the admission process, or they can provide information about the resource people on campus who can discuss disability services with the student. Thus, the decision to disclose or not remains with the student. Although a student's willingness to disclose his or her ADD on a college application indicates acceptance of the disorder, many students and parents fear that this information could be detrimental in the admission process. The truth of the matter is that colleges cannot deny admission solely based on information about a disability, and in fact, at many colleges, self-disclosure is used in a positive way to be more flexible in an admission decision. Following are a few common questions students with ADD and their parents typically ask:

Will colleges look negatively at this disclosure?

NO. Colleges are far more interested in academic success and ability to compensate.

Will the admission staff understand the disability?

YES /NO. If they don't, they should be provided with information.

Do colleges deny admission because a student has ADD?

NO. Not only is this illegal, it is impractical. Students with ADD can be as successful in college as students without ADD.

Should students disclose the disability?

YES. Disclose the disability and provide supportive documentation describing when it was diagnosed, as well as strategies used to compensate.

Should students submit a personal statement about the ADD?

YES. Students should show their acceptance of ADD and a perspective of their learning history, strengths, weaknesses, and goals.

TESTING

Many students – whether or not they have ADD – are concerned about the importance of standardized testing (ACT or SAT). Following is a list of tips that may serve as an aid in taking standardized tests:

• Familiarity could result in better performance, so student should be prepared

• Untimed tests don't benefit all students; students are encouraged to seek guidance

• ACT/SAT grant permission to take tests non-standardized

• Official documentation of the disability must be submitted to ACT/SAT

• All colleges accept non-standardized administration of the ACT/SAT

• Most colleges require ACT/SAT

• Not all colleges use the results in the same way

• Rarely will an admission decision be based solely on an ACT/SAT

Students who were diagnosed with ADD late in their high school years and very close to the time for taking ACT/SAT, and students who do not take other high school tests/exams in an untimed setting, should be aware that these circumstances often raise a "red flag" from the college's perspective. Colleges might question why ADD suddenly "appeared" in the student's junior year or why the student didn't take other high school tests untimed. This caution is just a reminder that it is very important for all students to provide documentation and explanation to colleges that identify their reasons for the submission of non-standardized test scores.

RECOMMENDING

Students should ask for recommendations from teachers and counselors who know them well and can describe them in positive terms. The purpose of a recommendation is not necessarily to "recommend" admission for a candidate, but rather to provide a 3-D picture of the student. The recommendation can come from a teacher in a course that was difficult, but one in which the student showed perseverance, motivation, and a willingness to keep working in spite of problems. The important aspect of recommendations is to identify where the student was and is now – not to predict where the student will be tomorrow, next week, or next year.

Recommendations should:

• Provide a "user friendly" explanation of ADD.

• Highlight the student's strengths and weaknesses.

• Describe strategies used to cope and compensate.

• Demonstrate motivation and determination.

• Show evidence of creativity.

• Assess maturity.

• Use specific examples.

• Discuss challenges of curriculum and academic success.

INTERVIEWING

College interviews can be an important part of admission decisions. If interviews are optional and a student interviews well, then he or she should, by all means, request one. If, on the other hand, face to face interviews cause the student great anxiety and are not required, then he or she should opt for a group orientation or a tour of the campus. By law, colleges cannot require an interview with students with ADD unless they require interviews with all candidates. However, if the college has a special admission process for students with ADD or the interview may be used to help the student who does not meet admission criteria, then an interview can be requested. Interviews provide students an opportunity to research a particular college and determine if it would be a good match, and they allow the interviewer to learn about the student, answer the student's questions, and gather information to help in the admission decision.

The interviewer may ask:

(1) When was the ADD diagnosed?

(2) Can the student describe the disability?

(3) How does ADD affect the student's learning?

(4) What services or accommodations will be needed in college?

The interviewer will be documenting whether:

(1) Questions are answered by the student or parent.

(2) The student exhibits motivation.

(3) The student has realistic goals.

(4) The student shows signs of being independent and a self-advocate.

Students and parents may ask:

(1) What is the philosophy of the college regarding students with ADD?

(2) What are the admission requirements?

(3) Can entrance course requirements be waived or substituted?

(4) Is there an alternative admission plan?

(5) What documentation is required?

(6) Who is responsible for admission decisions?

(7) Are there fees for services?

(8) Is there a limit on tutoring?

(9) How are professors notified of the student's disability?

(10) What services and accommodations are available?

(11) How many students on campus are identified as having ADD?

(12) What is the success rate of students with ADD?

(13) How is the faculty provided in-service training on working with students with ADD?

TOURING

Most people would not buy a house sight unseen. This is also true in selecting a college. Students need to identify what they want and need in a college environment before making a decision to attend. Videos and view books are useful, but pictures might convince a student that it never snows in Minnesota or that all college classes are taught in small groups outside on a beautiful spring day. Therefore, students are encouraged to visit colleges they are interested in to get a true perspective about its environment. While touring campuses, students should:

- meet with service providers;
- verify that necessary services will be available;
- walk the campus;
- observe the surrounding area;
- talk with students;
- taste the food;
- visit residence halls;
- read about "hot topics" in the school newspaper;
- take a formal tour;
- attend classes;

- talk with professors in their major of interest;
- take notes;
- take pictures;
- attend a social activity (while parents do something else); and
- keep a chart to rank colleges.

Sample Criteria Chart

Criteria	College A	College B	College C
General Information			
1. # of students	_____	_____	_____
2. Location	_____	_____	_____
3. Competitiveness	_____	_____	_____
4. Cost	_____	_____	_____
5. Fee for services	_____	_____	_____
6. Majors offered	_____	_____	_____
7. Admission criteria	_____	_____	_____
8. Documentation required & how recent	_____	_____	_____

Accommodations

1. _____

2. _____

3. _____

4. _____

5. _____

6. _____

Student's Thoughts

1. Pros _____

2. Cons _____

3. Parents' Thoughts _____

SELECTING

If students with ADD follow the key steps outlined in this college search process, they should ultimately be prepared to select a reasonable number of colleges that would be the right match. In making a selection, students should make sure they have:

- talked with their counselor, teachers, and family;
- verified their comfort level in articulating their disability;
- understood their needs;
- prioritized the criteria for success in college; assessed academic and emotional readiness;
- read college materials;
- taken ACT/SAT standardized or non-standardized tests;
- written a personal statement disclosing their ADD;
- identified appropriate colleges;
- requested recommendations from teachers/counselors;
- visited campuses for interview/tour;
- submitted applications;
- submitted official ACT/SAT scores;
- and given permission to release ADD documentation to colleges.

Once the student's role in the application process is complete, colleges begin their selection process to determine the student's admissibility.

ADMITTING

Colleges make admission decisions based on different factors and in different ways:

- computer-generated test scores, class rank, grades, and courses
- committee evaluations assessing each applicant individually
- flexible admissions for students who self-disclose a disability
- special admission for students deficient in admission requirements
- student interview with the director of support services
- decision by director of admission
- decision by admissions and support services
- faculty admission committee
- "Open door admissions"

Even a denial does not necessarily mean the student cannot attend that college. If a student with ADD is denied admission to a college, he or she should inquire about an "appeal process" that allows admission in different ways, such as through summer admit, conditional/probationary admit, limited course load admit, or concurrent enrollment in a community college and four-year college with a limited number of credits at each institution.

YES, STUDENTS WITH ADD SHOULD CONSIDER COLLEGE

Colleges pledge that they are dedicated to assuring each student an opportunity to experience equity in education. The law guarantees access to "reasonable accommodations" as long as these accommodations do not compromise the academic integrity of the program.

Examples of "Reasonable Accommodations" include:

- additional time to complete tests, coursework, or graduation;
- substitution/modification of specific courses for degree requirements not essential to program of study;
- adaptation of course instruction;
- note-takers;
- calculators; and
- auxiliary aids, taped texts, readers, computers, scribes, and recorders.

SUCCEEDING

Students should keep in mind that the first college they are admitted into does not have to be the only one they attend. They do not have to give a four year commitment to the first college they attend. On the contrary, the "college road" can be taken in several steps. For instance, a student may begin at a college that provides the appropriate environment and support and complete a successful first year or two, and then transfer to another college. There are many colleges that offer "open door admission," admitting any student with a high school diploma. Sometimes these colleges provide the most appropriate services and/or accommodations for students with ADD. It is important that students stay focused on attaining a college diploma – not on what college they'll be receiving their degree from or which college decal will be displayed on their car bumper.

In summary, to be successful in college, students should:

- be self-advocates;
- be independent;
- be able to articulate their disability;
- have an understanding of themselves;

- develop compensatory strategies;
- learn better organization skills;
- learn how to manage their time;
- make a schedule for study time and stick to it;
- plan ahead for lengthy or difficult assignments;
- know their strengths and weaknesses;
- be realistic;
- be able to take notes or know how to get notes;
- develop writing skills;
- develop reading skills;
- be computer literate;
- tape lectures and clearly mark each tape;
- review class notes as soon as possible and review often;
- be comfortable with their disability;
- have good judgment;
- attend all classes;
- sit in the front of the classroom;
- be willing to work longer and harder;
- plan three hours of study time for each hour in class;
- be willing to ask for assistance;
- check their understanding of assignments;
- seek advice from their advisor;
- develop a four year plan for their college courses; and
- visit a career counseling center early in their college careers.

Parents need to:

- stay involved;
- know their child's rights;
- promote self-esteem;
- be proud of their child's accomplishments; and
- encourage motivation, taking some academic risks, and independent learning.

There are thousands of students diagnosed with ADD. The good news is that the future for these individuals is bright. College-bound individuals with ADD are typically talented, intelligent, capable students who have developed strategies for compensating for their disorder. However, to ensure success, students need to be open-minded to educational interventions, including classroom accommodations, compensatory instruction, or in some cases, placement in special classes or resource programs. If students with ADD can establish realistic goals and learn to channel their energy appropriately, they can pursue their dreams and achieve success in college.

This article first appeared in the Fall 1996 issue of ATTENTION!

Marybeth Kravets is the College Consultant at Deerfield High School in Deerfield, Illinois. She is the President of the Illinois Association For College Admission Counseling, has appeared as a guest on several television and radio shows including the "Today Show" on NBC, has published many articles in journals and magazines, and has presented at major national conferences on learning disabilities. She is also the coauthor of The K&W Guide To Colleges For The Learning Disabled.

Legal Rights and Accommodations for College Students with ADD

by Lei Ann Marshall-Cohen, Esq.

College students today have more clearly defined legal rights and access to more reasonable modifications of the policies and practices of the school they attend than they did in the past. The Americans with Disabilities Act of 1990 (ADA), a landmark federal law prohibiting discrimination on the basis of disability nationwide, includes specific protections for college students. The ADA applies to both public and private colleges and universities. If a college or university is a recipient of federal funds, it is also prohibited from discrimination on the basis of disability under the Rehabilitation Act of 1973. Additionally, state law or city or county ordinances may be available that prohibit discrimination on the basis of disability. Each of these avenues of protection will be discussed below.

The ADA is divided into substantive sections called titles that establish the rights of people with disabilities and the responsibilities of public and private entities to provide services in a nondiscriminatory manner. It is these provisions of the ADA that are of great significance for students with ADD. The threshold question in determining whether the law is applicable is whether the student meets the definition of a person with a disability. The ADA defines a person with a disability as an individual who:

(1) has a physical or mental impairment that substantially limits a major life activity;

(2) has a history or record of such impairment; and/or

(3) is perceived as having such an impairment.

The ADA does not link disability to a particular category or diagnosis. Rather, the definition is deliberately subjective and turns on whether the person's impairment substantially limits the performance of one or more major life activities. Major life activities are defined to include seeing, hearing, walking, learning, or working. Recently, the federal regulations were modified to include thinking, concentrating, and interacting with others as examples of major life activities that bring an individual within the definition

of a person with a disability. This modification clarifies that an individual with ADD is protected by the ADA if these major life activities are substantially limited.

An individual with a disability must also meet the criteria of being a "qualified individual with a disability." This means that the individual must meet the general requirements for participation in the program or activity offered by the private or public entity. For example, a student seeking admission to a college or university must meet certain objective criteria such as the completion of high school with a certain grade point average. These objective requirements are equally applicable to students with and without disabilities.

Title II of the ADA applies to all units of state and local government. The Title contains a broad mandate that prohibits discrimination against people with disabilities in all programs, services, or activities of such public entities. The general non-discrimination requirements of Title II include:

(1) Assuring equal opportunity to participate in the programs and services in the most integrated setting appropriate;

(2) Prohibiting the use of methods of administration or practices that are discriminatory; and

(3) Requiring reasonable modification of policies, practices, and procedures when necessary to avoid discrimination against people with disabilities.

These requirements must be met unless doing so would fundamentally alter the nature of the program or service offered or create an undue burden on the public entity. Also, public entities cannot use eligibility criteria that screen out or tend to screen out people with disabilities unless necessary for the provision of the service or activity. Finally, all state and local government entities must ensure program accessibility to all activities offered by the entity.

Education programs such as community college, adult education programs, and public universities are covered by the provisions of Title II. Requesting such modifications as provision of a quiet room for testing or permission to tape record a class to be replayed later for purposes of notetaking are the kinds of reasonable modifications contemplated under the ADA. Since many students with ADD have difficulty concentrating or paying attention in a noisy environment, reasonable modifications for these students may include a quiet place for testing, assignment of a carrel for studying in a quiet part of the library, or even a housing assignment to a dormitory designated as a "quiet dorm." Other reasonable accommodations may include use of an FM listening system to diminish external sounds and use of a lap-top computer to facilitate note-taking.

Some students may have ADD together with other recognized disabilities such as learning disabilities. These students may require other modifications, such as an extension of the time in which to take an exam or permission to create a work product on a computer to compensate for handwriting difficulties. These are also examples of reasonable modifications covered by the ADA.

Determinations as to the reasonableness of a requested modification are made on a case-by-case basis under the Act. Individuals with disabilities cannot be charged to offset any costs associated with providing program access. However, if provision of a modification would impose undue financial or administrative burdens on a school in light of all available resources, it may be permissible for the school to pay only a portion of the cost. Again, these determinations are based on the individual circumstances.

The provisions of Title II that apply to college students are enforced by the U. S. Department of Justice (DOJ). Individuals may file administrative charges directly with DOJ, which are typically routed to the Office of Civil Rights of the U. S. Department of Education, for investigation and possible compensation. Under some circumstances, an individual can also file directly in federal court for injunctive relief and, in certain cases, damages.

Title III of the ADA covers places of public accommodation, meaning privately owned entities that serve the public. Title III provides that no individual with a disability may be denied the full and equal enjoyment of the goods and services of a place of public accommodation. In delineating this mandate, the law states that private entities are required to make reasonable modifications in their policies, practices, or procedures to provide auxiliary aids and services where appropriate, and are prohibited from using eligibility criteria that screen or tend to screen on the basis of disability.

Most private universities are included within the reach of Title III of the ADA. However, religiously controlled entities are expressly exempt from this part of the federal law. For example, a Catholic university that is controlled by a board with a majority of representatives of the Catholic church would be considered a religiously controlled entity under the ADA. Thus, a private college or university that is controlled by a religious entity would not be covered by the ADA. However, if the private religious school receives federal financial assistance, it would be covered by the Rehabilitation Act of 1973 (Section 504).

As was true in the public university setting, the provisions of Title III can be used as the basis for reasonable modifications that assist the student with ADD in functioning effectively in the classroom. Examples of such modifications may include a quiet place for testing, extension of test time, and permission to use a tape recorder or computer for note-taking.

There are also particular requirements in Titles II and III of the ADA that relate to preparatory courses and administration of entrance exams for college, medical, law, or graduate school, and other professional or licensing exams. Title III of the ADA specifically requires that organizations that offer courses such as the preparation courses for the college SAT or ACT entrance exams and preparation courses for such exams as the LSAT or MCAT examinations provide materials in appropriate formats, insure accessible settings, and make other reasonable modifications for students with disabilities. In addition, under the requirements of Title II, the actual administration of such exams, if controlled by a public entity such as the Board of Bar Examiners for future attorneys, must be provided in an accessible location and an accessible manner. Thus, a college student who has been receiving the modification of testing in a quiet location has a basis to request such modification for the law school entrance exam, in law school, and in the eventual taking of the bar exam for licensing.

Title III can be enforced directly in the courts. Injunctive remedies, such as court orders providing for particular modifications, are available. Damages are not available to a private litigant under Title III. However, if an individual has filed an administrative complaint with the U. S. Department of Justice, DOJ can seek compensatory damages on behalf of an individual and also has the authority to assess penalties against entities that have violated the Act. There is no provision for punitive damages under Title III.

Students with disabilities are also protected from discrimination by the Rehabilitation Act of 1973, typically referred to as Section 504. The Rehabilitation Act prohibits discrimination on the basis of disability by any entity that receives federal financial assistance. Many colleges and universities, both public and private, are covered by the Rehabilitation Act because such schools typically receive federal funding in such areas as student financial aid or research grants. The language of the Rehabilitation Act is very broad and it does not contain the specific examples concerning higher education that are present in the ADA's legislative and regulatory history. However, there is an extensive body of administrative decisions and case law under Section 504 that makes clear the non-discrimination obligations of such institutions. Moreover, this wealth of administrative and judicial decisions is available to assist in the interpretation of the requirements of the ADA. Finally, Section 504 may provide a basis to reach a private religiously controlled school that is exempt under Title III, but receives federal financial assistance.

Many states also have broad civil rights laws that expressly include people with disabilities as a protected class. In order to determine whether such laws are applicable, one must look both at the definition of disability and the identification of activities or entities regulated by the state law. Some state's civil rights acts have specific provisions that relate to higher education. Also, particularly in major metropolitan areas, cities or counties may have enacted ordinances that prohibit discrimination on the basis of disability. Under some circumstances, the procedures for handling complaints under these laws may be more efficient or may provide alternative remedies to those that are available under federal law.

The legal rights that are available to students with disabilities can be used as effective leverage in advocating for change in student programs at the local level. Obviously, they also provide a judicial or administrative remedy where necessary. Most colleges and universities have student services departments that are familiar with the protections of the law. Students and their families are encouraged to educate themselves in order to advocate for their rights more effectively.

This article first appeared in the Fall 1996 issue of ATTENTION!

Lei Ann Marshall-Cohen, Esq. provides expertise on legal issues relating to the Americans with Disabilities Act (ADA) and disability rights law. Ms. Marshall-Cohen has served as a consultant to major corporations, hospitals, state, and local agencies and not-for-profit organizations on ADA compliance, as well as providing training on the ADA, disability awareness, and other disability rights issues. She successfully litigated two of the first ADA cases filed in Illinois, has written extensively on ADA, and was awarded the Council on Disability Rights' Gnawing Gargoyle Award for public policy in 1992.

Documenting ADD
for College Accommodations

by Peter S. Latham, J.D. and Patricia H. Latham, J.D.

INTRODUCTION

Many colleges offer outstanding services to students with ADD and learning disabilities, so much so that, occasionally, parents have observed that if they can just get their children through high school, things will be better in college,

Some colleges offer more services and accommodations than the law requires and will provide these services on the basis of minimal disability documentation. Perhaps because of budget considerations, greater numbers of students seeking disability services, or simply a greater awareness of the applicable laws, a number of colleges are beginning to question documentation of ADD and learning disabilities and develop policies as to the amount and type of documentation that is required for a student to qualify as an individual with a disability.

Before exploring the matter of documentation, we will provide an overview of the applicable federal laws.

LEGAL OVERVIEW

ADD that substantially limits a major life activity, such as learning, is considered a disability under the Rehabilitation Act of 1973, Section 504 (RA) and the Americans with Disabilities Act of 1990 (ADA). The RA applies to all colleges that receive federal funding. The ADA applies to private and public schools, regardless of whether they receive federal funds.

Individuals with ADD that is considered a disability are entitled to be free from discrimination and to receive reasonable accommodations in post-secondary educational programs, including courses and examinations and entrance and licensing testing. Such students are entitled to accommodations that recognize the individual communications needs of the student. The goal of this process is to communicate the entire educational experience on equal terms. (*United States v. Becker, C.P.A. Review*, CV 92-2879 [TFH] D.D.C. 1994.) A reasonable accommodation is one that does not alter the essential nature of a course or program and that does not cause an undue hardship. The question of whether providing the accommodation causes a financial hardship is measured by reference to the institution's budget and not to the amount of tuition paid to the institution by the student.

These laws are not self-executing. To obtain their protection, an individual must establish that he or she meets certain requirements.

THE STANDARD FOR ESTABLISHING ENTITLEMENT

To obtain the protections of the ADA and the RA, a student must show that he or she is a qualified individual with a disability. Two key elements must be established:

(1) THE STUDENT IS AN INDIVIDUAL WITH A DISABILITY.

An individual with a disability is one who has a physical or mental impairment that substantially limits a major life activity, such as caring for oneself, performing manual tasks, walking, seeing, hearing, speaking, breathing, learning, or working. The Equal Employment Opportunity Commission (EEOC), in 1995, provided guidance on employment issues and added to the list of major life activities mental and emotional processes such as thinking, concentrating, and interacting with others.

The impact of the impairment must be severe enough to result in an actual limitation of performance. The term "substantially limits" means that an individual either (1) is "[u]nable to perform a major life activity that the average person in the general population can perform", or (2) is "[s]ignificantly restricted as to the condition, manner, or duration" of the major life activity in question, when measured against the abilities of the "average person in the general population." [29 C.F.R. §§ 1630.2(j)(1)(i)-(ii)]

Does the comparison to average standard mean that a person with above average achievements can never be considered an individual with a disability? Consider a college student who achieves at an above average level overall. Specifically, suppose that, due to dyslexia and ADD, his reading speed is 50 percent of the average student's reading speed. Suppose further that he spends twice as much time as his classmates on reading assignments. Does his extraordinary effort, resulting in an overall above average performance, mean that he should not be permitted accommodations (eg. books on tape) for his reading difficulty? If we focus on the slow visual processing, which is part of the learning process, then we may be able to show that he is substantially limited in that learning process and therefore entitled to accommodations. Similarly, a student who breezes through all other academic courses but fails mathematics may be substantially limited in learning in the setting of the mathematics course and may be entitled to accommodations in mathematics.

Certainly, high achieving persons have been recognized as having learning disabilities and being entitled to accommodations. The case of *Pazer v. New York State Board of Law Examiners* (849 F. Supp. 284 [S.D.N.Y. 1994]) is instructive. There, the Court addressed the question of whether a law school graduate should be allowed accommodations on the bar exam. While the Court ruled against the law school graduate overall, in considering the case, the Court addressed the question of whether any person who graduated from law school could be considered to have a learning disability. The Court's answer was yes, and it said:

The Court therefore finds some merit to the argument that a disparity between inherent capacity and performance on a test may, in some circumstances, permit the inference that an individual has a learning disability, even though that individual's performance has met the standard of the ordinary person. (849 F. Supp. 284 at 287)

What about the possible impact of medication on the disability? The existence and seriousness of a disability must be judged without reference to corrective measures, including medications. Therefore, the question of whether a student with ADD has an impairment that substantially limits a major life activity should be judged without considering possible beneficial effects of medication.

(2) THE STUDENT WITH A DISABILITY IS OTHERWISE QUALIFIED.

Under both the ADA and RA, an "individual with a disability" must be one who is "otherwise qualified" for the educational program. An "otherwise qualified" individual is one who, though possessed of a disability, would be eligible for the education or program benefit, with or without a reasonable accommodation.

DOCUMENTING ENTITLEMENT TO ACCOMMODATIONS

Increasingly, students are being called upon to provide professional documentation of their disabilities and of their need for requested accommodations. Often, documentation that was prepared during high school, together with a record of accommodation, will be sufficient. Some students with ADD may not have received accommodations during high school and may not have medical or other reports to provide to a college as documentation of their disability. It would then be important to obtain documentation by a qualified professional. While particular documentation requirements vary from institution to institution, basic requirements are: (1) a diagnosis by a professional qualified to make it; (2) an evaluation of the impact of the diagnosed condition on the student's functioning; and (3) recommendations for specific reasonable accommodations. Let's consider each in turn.

(1) Diagnosis

A diagnosis is essentially a determination of the presence of a physical or mental impairment by one qualified to make that determination. In the case of ADD, there is no one test that with absolute accuracy can determine that ADD is present. Diagnoses should be based upon history, patient and family interviews, testing, medical or neurological examination, and/or clinical observations.

Reference should be made to published criteria, such as *DSM-IV* (the *Diagnostic & Statistical Manual of Mental Disorders* prepared by the American Psychiatric Association, now in its 4th edition). Ordinarily, this work should be cited in the documentation. In one case, a court found that the plaintiff had no learning disability because "the alleged learning disabilities claimed by Dr. Carter, the psychologist the plaintiff hired for this lawsuit, could not be found in *DSM-3R*, the nationally recognized directory of mental illnesses." (*Pandazides v. Virginia Board of Education*, 804 F. Supp. 794 [E.D. Va. 1992] at 803)

A diagnosis should be made by a qualified professional. Who is a qualified diagnostician? Diagnoses of adults are most often made by psychologists, neurologists, or psychiatrists. Diagnoses of children are made by pediatricians, psychologists, neurologists, and psychiatrists. In the case of learning disabilities, which frequently accompany ADD, diagnoses are most often made by psychologists and educational specialists following appropriate psycho-educational and/or neuro-psychological testing.

Can a postsecondary institution impose requirements as to professional qualifications acceptable to the institution? Certainly, reasonable requirements may be imposed. Clearly, an institution could legitimately refuse to accept the professional opinion of the family dentist that a student has ADD and needs accommodations in college. On the other hand, generally, it would be unreasonable to refuse to accept the professional opinion of a psychologist with substantial training and experience in diagnosing and treating ADD. It is likely that such a professional would be acceptable as an expert in a federal court proceeding.

What about requirements for current documentation? If a college student shows up with only a report from third grade to support a claim for services for ADD and learning disabilities, the college could reasonably request more current documentation. While neurological deficits do not go away, compensations over the years, in some cases, may result in little or no functional limitation in adulthood. Thus, the student may have been substantially limited in third grade but not in college. On the other hand, it may be unreasonable to require a whole new evaluation of a twenty-six-year-old who presents a thorough evaluation done at age twenty-two. In one case there was a suggestion that it may be discrimination to require burdensome current documentation requirements in connection with certain disabilities and not others. (Letter of Finding issued to University of Arizona, OCR Docket No. 09-91-2402; 2 NDLR Paragraph 285.) The ADA and the regulations that interpret it are clear in their expectation that documentation requirements will not be onerous. In this vein, they encourage giving weight to a record of accommodation in elementary and secondary education.

What about a recent diagnosis of ADD in a young adult? Can an institution reject the diagnosis on the ground that ADD should have been identified in childhood? The answer is no. At the same time, it would be important for the documentation to explore the history and to either indicate the presence of symptoms and functional impairment in childhood or explain why they were not evident earlier. For example, an individual with ADD and auditory processing difficulties may have performed at an acceptable level in third grade in a small, structured private school, but may exhibit significant functional impairment in a large state university with an emphasis on lectures.

(2) Evaluation of Impact

ADD presents differently in different people. An evaluation of impact is a description of the precise way in which a physical or mental impairment affects a particular individual. The evaluation ideally should answer the question of whether the impairment substantially limits one or more of this individual's major life activities. The major life tasks are considered to be caring for oneself, performing manual tasks, walking, seeing, hearing, speaking, breathing, learning, and working. As noted earlier, in 1995, the EEOC added thinking, concentrating, and interacting with others to the list of major life activities its investigators will recognize.

(3) Recommendations

The bottom line is set forth in the recommendations. These include proposed reasonable accommodations that will enable the individual to meet the essential requirements of the educational program without imposing an undue hardship on the institution. Recommendations must show that the accommodations address the particular individual's functional limitations and that, with accommodations, the individual is qualified to perform the academic work involved.

SPECIAL CONSIDERATIONS WHERE DOCUMENTATION IS FOR A LEGAL PURPOSE

The documentation discussed above differs from other medical and educational reports in that it is organized specifically around the demonstration that a particular person has a physical or mental impairment that substantially limits a major life activity, that specific course and/or test accommodations are necessary, and that, with proper accommodations, the individual is qualified. All information that is not relevant to these purposes need not appear in the documentation. For example, if an individual has several impairments, the documentation need cover only the ones that are relevant to the assertion of the particular legal rights. In contrast, many other medical and educational reports are more comprehensive in content.

HOW MUCH DOCUMENTATION IS ENOUGH?

The only legal requirement governing the amount of documentation is that "...[R]equests for documentation must be reasonable ...." (Preamble To Regulation on Nondiscrimination on the Basis of Disability by Public Accommodations and in Commercial Facilities; 28 C.F.R. Pt. 36; App. B [1991] at 617.) An individual may reach agreement with the college as to accommodations. If there is disagreement, the individual must be prepared to prove his or her case before a court, administrative agency, or in an alternative disputes resolution proceeding.

SUMMARY

Qualified students with ADD that substantially limits a major life activity, such as learning, are entitled, under the ADA and the RA, to reasonable accommodations in college courses and examinations. Colleges generally will require documentation of the disability.

Documentation of ADD for the purpose of obtaining accommodations in college should be prepared by a qualified professional and should include: diagnosis, evaluation of impact of the disorder on the student's functioning, and recommendations.

This article first appeared in the Fall 1996 issue of ATTENTION!

Peter S. Latham, J.D. and Patricia H. Latham, J.D. are partners in the Washington, D.C. law firm Latham & Latham, directors of JKL Communications, and founders and directors of the National Center for Law and Learning Disabilities (NCLLD). They have authored six books, contributed chapters to six additional books, and written numerous articles on ADD and learning disabilities.

Using Strategies and Services for Success in College

by Lois J. Burke

More and more college campuses across the nation are enrolling students with ADD. College is challenging for many students, but it can be particularly challenging for students with ADD, especially if strategies for successful management of the disorder are not employed. Students with ADD need to be aware of, and apply when necessary, some key strategies that can help foster success in the college environment.

ADVOCACY

On most college campuses, students with disabilities are responsible for informing necessary personnel about their need for assistance and/or accommodations. The key to advocacy is knowledge about what ADD is. Oftentimes, college students with ADD find that they are in a position of educating faculty members and other personnel about the disorder. It is very important that students with ADD know their legal rights so that they may obtain the most appropriate education possible. A disability services office can be very helpful in this area as office personnel can provide students with guidance on addressing faculty and staff regarding accommodations and services that are needed.

SELF-AWARENESS

It is also very important that individuals with ADD educate themselves and understand how the disorder impacts them. Some of the ways to become more aware include reading books and other resources, talking to professionals who are experienced in the field of adult ADD, and talking with other adults who have been diagnosed with ADD. These types of opportunities can be provided through participation in adult ADD support groups or through local and national organizations like CH.A.D.D.

Students with ADD also need to have a good understanding of how they respond to certain situations. Some important questions that can lead to this level of awareness are: "How do I react to failure?"; "How do I react to stress?"; "What do I do when I become overwhelmed?"; "How do I relate to others when I'm taking medication?"; "How do I relate to others when I'm not taking medication?".

Some other helpful keys students should use to develop a strong sense of self-awareness are: *Making time for transitions.* It is important that college students with ADD leave time between their classes and/or activities in order to take a break from the structured environment of the classroom, gather thoughts, get a snack, or do something to relax before another class begins. This procedure can aid in reducing the stress that commonly accompanies college.

Becoming aware of physical surroundings. Students should figure out what environments promote the best learning situations for them. For instance, do they concentrate better in an environment with no noise, some noise, or white noise? It is important that they consider both visual and auditory distractions as well as any temptations that are present in their study environments. A student may find it difficult to study in her apartment, for example, because of the many temptations that exist there, such as household chores or favorite television programs.

Students should try to choose environments that can provide them the most optimal learning environment and the fewest temptations and distractions.

Learning strengths, weaknesses, and learning style. Students with ADD often excel in areas like reading and written expression but have difficulties in subjects such as math. By recognizing their strengths and weaknesses, students can more appropriately plan for academic courses and balance course loads. Also, by understanding the type of learning style they have, students can better learn how to study and prepare for classes. For instance, some students require breaks between academic classes for optimal learning. Therefore, taking a few courses that provide recreational activities, such as aerobics or a sport, or classes that are not necessarily of an academic nature but are interesting and fun, may help students to relax and serve as a necessary break from academic stress.

Utilizing counseling. Students are encouraged to seek counseling if they are in need of help getting on task or keeping their focus – especially if the initial diagnosis of ADD was not made until adulthood. Counseling can help address any personal issues that have resulted from past experiences. If comorbid conditions such as depression are present, a personal counselor can provide additional support and help students develop strategies and techniques for effectively managing their ADD and related problems. Additionally, academic needs, such as time management and organizational skills can be addressed by disability services providers at many colleges and universities throughout the country.

ACCOMMODATIONS AND SERVICES

Typical services and accommodations in the college environment for students with ADD include a distraction-free space for testing and extended time on exams (usually time and one-half). For some students, the extra time provides an opportunity to take needed breaks. For other students, simply having a quiet space is a major benefit. Some students are easily distracted during the typical classroom setting, especially when other students finish exams before they do and are moving around and making noise.

Priority scheduling of classes is also beneficial for students with ADD as it allows them to schedule more appropriately for academic success. For example, some students are most alert in the morning; others are more alert in the afternoon. Priority scheduling allows students to schedule classes at times during the day when they are typically at their best.

Other services that are commonly available on college campuses include tutoring, access to personal counseling assistance, medication management, and stress reduction workshops. Students should investigate whether a peer support group exists if they feel that meeting other college students with ADD would be helpful. Some students may also benefit from assistance with note-taking or, on a rare occasion, a reader for exams.

TIME MANAGEMENT AND ORGANIZATIONAL STRATEGIES

The key word in developing skills in these areas is "effective." In many cases, developing or establishing structure can be a very effective tool in managing ADD. Some effective time management strategies can include using check lists and/or a daily planner, periodically writing notes about important information, and using a watch with a chime. Many students find it helpful to plan daily; others like making weekly plans. Whichever planning method is chosen, it is important that students with ADD set realistic dead-

lines and break large tasks into smaller, more manageable parts. If a student with ADD requires assistance in this area, a disabilities counselor who is familiar with organizational and time management strategies can be helpful. Some colleges have classes or workshops that provide assistance in effectively managing time and developing organizational strategies.

SETTING PRIORITIES

Students with ADD must try to set realistic goals for themselves. To do this, it may be helpful for the student to establish goals for each week, quarter, or semester. While students should plan for success when they establish their priorities and set their goals, it is also important that they not set themselves up for failure by attempting to accomplish too many tasks in too short a time period. They should also keep in mind that, even with the best attempts, some failures are inevitable. However, instead of seeing failures as stumbling blocks, students should try to learn from their failures and make appropriate adjustments to ensure more positive results in the future.

CAMPUS RESOURCES

In addition to using the disability services office, it is important that students learn what other resources are available on campus, such as quiet study rooms, tutoring facilities, libraries, and computer equipment. Getting to know personnel in the disability services office also can be useful, as they often have contacts in key departments and offices on campus, and knowing the right person to contact often saves time and frustration when it comes to addressing a number of issues and concerns.

These are but a few key strategies that may assist the college student with ADD in being successful in the college environment. Students typically develop strategies of their own during their college years, but the suggestions outlined above can serve as a preliminary guide. By avoiding negative, self-defeating behaviors and habits, such as not taking prescribed medication properly, and employing appropriate strategies like the ones highlighted in this article, students with ADD can achieve success in college.

This article first appeared in the Fall 1996 issue of ATTENTION!

Lois J. Burke is a Counselor at the Office for Disability Services at The Ohio State University. She works with students who have been diagnosed as having learning disabilities and ADD. Ms. Burke has been in the field of service provision for students with disabilities for over ten years and regularly makes presentations regarding accommodations and services for college students with learning disabilities. Her most recent presentations have focused on working with the college student with ADD.

Where There's A Will, There's A Way

by Nichole Payne Slabach

"Nichole Anjanette Payne, Bachelor of Arts degree in Interdepartmental Studies – Counseling and Psychology, with Honors Recognition," the Commencement speaker announced from the podium as I walked across the stage to receive my diploma from the University of Iowa. I don't think I had ever been so proud of hearing my name being announced. Despite all of the hard work that I had put forth over the years, it was hard to believe that my dream had actually become a reality, especially considering that three years prior to this graduation celebration, I had flirted with the idea of giving up my pursuit of a college degree.

During my third semester of college, I was almost ready to quit. I was failing Spanish despite long hours of studying and I didn't know what the problem was. But then, I never seemed to know what the problem was when it came to succeeding in THE academic setting. Since kindergarten, I could remember spending recesses inside because I didn't complete my work on time or was being punished for socializing with other students. My talent for making conversation was rarely appreciated by teachers. As a result of my behavior, SCHOOL was not my strong suit. I wanted to do well in school, but it was always such a struggle, and my failing grade in Spanish was a reminder that my academic pursuits would not be any easier at the college level.

Recognizing my constant struggles in school, a colleague suggested that I might have a learning disability, and she suggested that I get tested. I'm glad I took her advice. After hours of verbal and written testing, the psychologist testing me gave me a preliminary diagnosis of Attention Deficit Hyperactivity Disorder, but noted that she would need information about my childhood to confirm the diagnosis. I had never heard of ADD, but I did as the psychologist requested and asked my parents about my childhood behaviors. Once they had an open invitation to discuss my childhood, they began to enlighten me on the many adventures I had taken them on. I was overwhelmed by all of the stories they had to tell.

One of their favorite stories, which is still used as a threat to embarrass me, involves late night refrigerator raids. I hadn't been hungry when my parents had found me at two a.m. in the kitchen. Instead, my excessive energy and creativity had led me to produce unique artwork with large amounts of food. Unfortunately, because my parents were not art connoisseurs, they didn't exactly appreciate waking up consecutive nights to find me standing in the middle of my "masterpiece." To stifle my creative juices, my parents decided to secure the refrigerator doors with chains and a pad lock. Although my parents could now laugh at this and the many other childhood escapades I had led them on, my behavior as a child confirmed the psychologist's suspicions; my hyperactivity, inattentiveness, and distractibility were evidence that I had ADD.

I remember feeling numb as I read over the literature on ADD that I had received from the psychologist at my final session. I had always known that there was a reason for my struggles in school, but it was a bit unnerving to find out that an actual disorder had been the cause. I still wondered how receiving an "official" diagnosis would help me academically. I was relieved to find that there was an office on campus designated to assist college students with ADD. This made all the difference in the world. The staff were supportive and helped teach me how to study more effectively and perform better on tests; they were patient and willing to teach me how to accept and work with my ADD instead of beating myself up because school wasn't easy for me, as I had perceived it to be for all of my fellow classmates.

Despite their efforts, there were certain areas even they could not help me with. I had to endure many painful and difficult times throughout my college career. One time in particular comes to mind. During exams one semester, I found myself in an uncomfortable situation. My university had allocated a number of accommodations for students with ADD, including Alternative Testing Services, which provided extended testing time and testing rooms free of distractions. It is mandatory for educational institutions to provide accommodations for students in need of assistance, and professors are obligated to comply with these accommodations. A particular professor had agreed to bring a copy of the exam in a sealed envelope to the testing services center, but failed to show up. I knew I would have to go to him and I was not looking forward to it because of the embarrassing incident I had with him earlier in the semester.

In the beginning of the year, the professor had said that no food consumption was allowed in the auditorium while he lectured, even though the class met during the lunch hour. Unfortunately, I had totally forgotten about his warning one afternoon as I finished eating a rather crispy apple. I was quickly reminded, however, as I heard the professor bellowing at me from his podium. It is amazing how quiet a room full of 300-plus students can become when a professor is singling out one of his students. I was humiliated, not to mention angry with myself for not taking my morning medication, which would have helped me to think more clearly.

I was thinking of that incident as I approached the auditorium where my professor was administering the test he forgot to deliver to me. I had a horrible feeling that he would react negatively once again. Although I realized that I was making the ordeal worse than it was by focusing on the incident, I couldn't help but feel as though I was Daniel walking into the den of a merciless lion. I was thankful that a staff member from the student accommodation office had accompanied me to the "Lion's Den," especially since my fears would indeed be confirmed. The professor showed his disapproval with a raised voice and distinct posture as the staff member inquired as to the whereabouts of my exam. To say that I was embarrassed would be a gross understatement; I was extremely uncomfortable as I looked around the room to see many of my fellow classmates peering at me, wondering why I was not taking the test with them. Fortunately, once the professor realized that the error was on his part, he gave a copy of the exam to the staff member and we quickly exited the auditorium. It was pleasantly ironic to receive an A in that class, despite the many obstacles I had experienced with the professor.

Along with the knowledge I gained during college, I learned many valuable lessons. Most importantly, I learned that by accepting my differences and finding ways to accommodate for my disorder, I was able to find great freedom. Accepting myself enabled me to explore the gifts that I have. For example, I uncovered an intensity in myself that gives me a strong sense of creativity and the ability to complete tasks with passion and enthusiasm. My creativity has enabled me to successfully complete a senior honors research project, "Romancing the Inattentive," which explores the romantic relationships of couples in which one of the partners has ADD. In addition, as a result of my newly acquired study skills and my persistence, I was able to greatly improve my grade point average, so much so that I was able to graduate with honors and get accepted into graduate school, where I am currently working towards a Master's Degree in Clinical Psychology.

While I have endured many challenges throughout my academic career as a result of my ADD, I have been able to achieve success. I must admit, victory in the academic arena is truly sweet. My recollections of the obstacles I've encountered along the way are not meant to discourage individuals with ADD; rather, my hope is to paint a realistic picture of the challenges that may lie ahead. The key is to remember that challenges are merely potholes, not road blocks. Consider the challenges I have had to overcome. Who would have guessed that after my struggles in school, I would graduate with Honors from the University of Iowa? Who would have guessed that I would actually get accepted into graduate school? Who would have guessed that as my parents gazed at the chains that barricaded their daughter from creating havoc with the refrigerator over twenty years ago, that someday, it would all be worth it when they were able to sit proudly in the audience and watch their "holy terror" walk across the stage to receive her college degree? Take it from me; persistence does pay off – I'm living proof.

This article first appeared in the Spring 1996 issue of ATTENTION!

CHAPTER 6

RELATIONSHIPS

An Introduction by Arthur L. Robin, Ph.D.
Wayne State University, Detroit, Michigan
Professor, Psychiatry & Behavioral Neurosciences

In our fifteen-second sound bite, hedonistic, fast-paced, computer-driven culture, it is difficult enough for the average couple without any psychiatric problems to sustain a marriage or other long-term relationship. Good relationships are characterized by carefully measured combinations of love, friendship, and passion, and it takes hard work to maintain the proper balance of these ingredients, especially when children are part of the family. Don't let anyone tell you otherwise. Now add inattention, impulsivity, and hyperactivity to the picture, and such a relationship becomes exponentially more difficult to maintain. It is stressful enough if one spouse has ADD, but what if a child or both spouses have ADD? Then, life can really get interesting!

There are many ways that the core symptoms of ADD impair intimate relationships. We will give a few telling examples. Difficulties with attention can lead to communication problems, inconsistent task performance, negative attributions, and angry or depressed affect. The spouse with ADD may have a difficult time sustaining attention in conversations with the partner. As a result he or she makes mistakes carrying out household chores or parenting tasks, and after several such incidents, he or she comes across as "unreliable" or "inconsistent." Those who don't have ADD may infer that their spouses don't love them or aren't

committed to the marriage after the tenth time that their partner with ADD has missed an important communication, forgot to pick up the kids at the babysitter's, or brought home the wrong things from the supermarket.

How can the couple enjoy love making when the partner with ADD is thinking about work, the children, the clock ticking next to the bed, or any of other millions of distracting thoughts or stimuli which continuously stream through his or her head, or when he or she is hyper-sensitive to the partner's touch? What are the chances that the true causes of such "interference" with sexuality will be accurately communicated and discussed between the partners? Slim, indeed – more likely, one or both will feel unloved, will make negative attributions about the other and end up angry or depressed. In addition, many adults who have ADD get so hyper-focused on hobbies or work they are doing at home that by the time they get the bedroom, their frustrated spouse has given up any hopes of intimacy and gone to sleep.

Impulsivity often takes the form of poor frustration tolerance, easy loss of temper, sometimes lashing out aggressively, poor delay of gratification, and making non-thinking, spur-of-the-moment decisions about major purchases or other family events. At the end of the day when frustrated from work, it is very easy for the partner with ADD to "lose it" with the kids or spouse. When arguing with a spouse, it is easy for the impulsive adult to hit below the belt, seriously damaging the relationship. How many times have adults with ADD come home, to their spouse's horror, with an expensive new "toy" that they just had to have but did not need? Ideas for things like vacations may pop into the mind of the person with ADD, and before discussing it with the family, he or she has committed a large amount of money to airline tickets which cannot be refunded.

Hyperactivity, commonly experienced as mental restlessness and a need for constant stimulation and novelty, literally makes it difficult for some adults with ADD to remain committed to a longterm relationship; they get "bored" with their partner and often change relationships precipitously, leaving a trail of destruction in their wake. Some adults with ADD continue to have the high energy levels and physical restlessness which more often occurs in childhood. These restless souls often wear out their spouses, who can't keep up with their frenetic pace of living or non-stop talking.

Fifty percent of adults with ADD display comorbidity for other psychiatric conditions, most commonly mood disorders, substance abuse disorders, and anxiety disorders. Even those who don't have other psychiatric syndromes experience low self-esteem as a result of a lifetime of being criticized by family, friends, and others, creating fears of reaching out to others in intimate relationships. The emotional baggage these folks carry from their dysfunctional families of origin, which are also likely to have included mothers or fathers with ADD, further erode their ability to sustain intimacy and good communication. These additional problems only add insult to injury when it comes to intimate relationships. Thus, the legacies of ADD members of the previous generation indirectly impact the marriages of the current generation of adults with ADD.

When the honeymoon ends, the relationships of many adults who have ADD spiral downwards, slipping into bottomless pits of repetitive dysfunctional patterns of co-dependency. For example, one such pattern is the "messmaker" and the "cleaner upper." The partner with ADD constantly makes mistakes, forgets things, or doesn't follow through on commitments. The non-ADD partner constantly rescues his or her spouse and saves the day. Over time, the partner without ADD gets worn out and feels as if his or her spouse is another child.

Another such pattern is the daydreamer and the pest. The partner with ADD is disorganized, forgetful, and spaced out. The non-ADD partner is constantly nagging to get things done. The partner with ADD develops a great deal of resentment about being nagged, yet doesn't do things to avoid it. The non-ADD partner is chronically angry about failure of his or her spouse to keep commitments. Marriages characterized by such patterns become unbalanced, and the frequent anger and frustration of the partners make true intimacy difficult to sustain. Apathy, separation, and divorce may result.

The challenge for adults with ADD and their spouses or partners is to understand the many ways in which ADD and its associated problems can detract from their relationships, and to learn to avoid and/or compensate for these pitfalls in an effective manner. Specifically, partners need to learn to identify and self-monitor dysfunctional interactions fueled by the core symptoms of ADD, accurately attribute the negative outcomes to ADD-related factors rather than assuming the partner "doesn't love me" or "is out to get me," and to learn how to re-balance the instrumental and emotional tasks of their relationship to compensate for the difficulties which follow from ADD symptoms. Medication, personal education, and good psychotherapy can be very helpful to this process.

The challenge for professionals who work with couples is to understand the unique ways in which ADD contributes to relationship problems, and to tailor their interventions to couples with ADD, rather than mindlessly applying the same old interventions which they use with all other couples. Although there has been a great deal of excellent research on the treatment of marital problems, very little of this research to date has directly addressed ADD and marriage. Nonetheless, in the following chapter, the authors have fearlessly moved ahead to give their best clinical recommendations to adults with ADD and the professionals who wish to help them improve their relationships and cope with many of the pitfalls we have identified here.

The Impact of ADD Upon Couples

by John Capel, Ph.D. and Katherine Brown, M.H.S., M.A.

A couple sits facing each other across a room as their therapist tries to persuade them that, if they are to have a healthy relationship and keep their marriage intact, they must improve their communication skills and resolve some of the unfinished business from their childhood. There is a perplexed, sometimes despairing look on their faces as if they are thinking, "Doesn't anybody understand what I am going through? Does anybody get the reality of my situation?"

By making comments such as "Every couple experiences difficulties" or "Everybody forgets things," many therapists are ignorant to the daily problems confronted by couples with ADD. Those who have ADD or have a partner who has the disorder know that ADD can, and often does, have a serious impact on a relationship.

When we began conducting adult ADD support groups five years ago, our approach to couples therapy began to change as a result of the knowledge we gained. As we worked with couples with ADD, we began to recognize the limitations of our old therapeutic strategies. Now we see that ADD fits into a special category of couples' dynamics and that it is important not to sidestep the obvious symptoms created by the disorder when working with couples. ADD symptoms are so varied that it is impossible to present an all encompassing view. However, we have found some commonality and have developed special treatment methods to assist couples in working together to monitor medical treatment and respond to special issues that arise in the course of treatment.

WHY DOES SOMEONE CHOOSE A PARTNER WITH ADD?

Through our research, we have discovered what appears to be a pattern of mating in couples with ADD, which we refer to as "ships" and "anchors." Ships are adults with ADD who view life as an endless journey from one port to the next. Often, they are attracted to other adults with ADD with hopes of sailing off into a beautiful sunset together. The relationship is ideal until they enter rough waters, which usually happens when a child is born. Suddenly, the sailing days are over – at least for one parent, usually the mother. While one member of the couple may continue his journey, the other has become tied down. As the distance between the two increases, resentment eventually builds and the relationship suffers.

Adults with ADD may also be attracted to "anchors:" those individuals who do not have ADD and *appear* to be rock solid. Anchors may be unexciting realists who are methodical, analytical thinkers often exhibiting depressive qualities and obsessive-compulsive traits. In the beginning, the relationship works because the anchor keeps the relationship afloat. However, the partner with ADD inevitably drifts as far away from the anchor as the tether will allow. The anchor benefits from the relationship because his partner takes him away from the depths of solitary isolation. Eventually, however, many anchors complain that they are even more isolated than before, caring for the children alone while their spouse is rarely at home.

The most common experience of spouses who do not have ADD is the feeling that they are completely alone. They describe themselves as burned-out or depressed. They may recognize that they nag too much, but cannot stop. Many complain that they cannot have company over because they can't get ahead of the mess and fear that they will never get caught up on the unfinished projects their spouse has created around the house. These factors make conditions at home overwhelming for the partner without ADD, and tension results.

MEDICATION ADJUSTMENTS

The most effective treatment for ADD is built upon an accurate and complete diagnosis. Medical intervention will be an on-going issue in which both partners should take part. This does not merely require that the partner without ADD remind her spouse to take his medication; it requires that she provide specific feedback about the spouse's symptoms and allow him to decide if medication needs adjustment. Whether it is welcome or not, the spouse of someone with ADD has the best perspective on the effects of medication. It is important that information based on this perspective be communicated to the physician of the spouse with ADD.

Although medication can help some individuals with ADD, it does not completely resolve the symptoms of the disorder. Some report that they have been in "survival mode" for so long that when things have improved, they begin to feel their grief for "the lost years." Others, because of unspoken interdependencies, become depressed when their spouse's ADD symptoms improve. These individuals have become accustomed to a certain pattern of behavior from their spouse. When that changes, even if for the better, it requires an adjustment.

WHAT CAN YOU DO ABOUT AN EXPLOSIVE TEMPER OR MOOD SWINGS?

One area of particular concern for couples with ADD is the display of extreme mood swings or outbursts of anger by the partner who has the disorder. This can be a very frightening experience and carries a real potential for harm. It is difficult for the spouse who does not have ADD to understand that when her spouse is exploding, the real message often is "I hurt." When either spouse is too angry to keep from deliberately verbally or physically hurting one another, we recommend they take a "time-out." There is no way to reason with rage. Couples should pre-arrange a silent signal that a time-out has been initiated, predefine the minimum length of time required to cool off, and arrange designated "time-out zones."

THE EFFECTS OF ADD ON SEXUAL RELATIONS

There is a wide variety of sexual dysfunction that may be experienced by couples with ADD. For instance, some women with the disorder report hypersexual activity for certain periods of their lives. More frequently encountered, however, is the woman who reports that she is distracted from sexual feelings by such things as the answering machine, the kids stirring, or her own thoughts. One woman who was diagnosed with Hypoactive Sexual Desire received a sex re-education course, relaxation tapes, and sexually explicit videos in therapy, but with little success. However, when she was diagnosed with ADD and treated with a psychostimulant, she reported that for first time in her life, she was consistently able to sustain her interest in sex to fully experience and enjoy marital relations.

This is not to say that stimulants are aphrodisiacs; they are not. Merely being aware of one's own natural

processes can be therapeutic for many. In more cases than not, sexual functioning is disrupted by medication. For instance, some antidepressants may create side effects that impair sexual functioning, including loss of libido, vaginal dryness, problems sustaining an erection, or delayed ejaculation. However, that is not usually the case with psychostimulants.

PICK YOUR BATTLES; COUNT YOUR BLESSINGS

Couples with ADD should remember that there are many things worse than ADD. The divorce rate tells us that you do not have to have ADD to face a crisis in your relationship. In the light of eternity, stacks of papers are insignificant. It is important to find a degree of acceptance about having a spouse with ADD who is "organizationally challenged" and that this disability may never change. By learning to accept the adult with ADD "as is," the downward spiral of continuous bickering and resentment can be broken. It then becomes a question of learning ways to manage the clutter, rather than trying to make it disappear.

Since you are reading this article, you know that ADD is no picnic. Yet, it is important to know that ADD is treatable. It can be treated with a combination of medication, education, behavioral strategies, and counseling. With sufficient psychosocial support, individuals with ADD can overcome the obstacles that hinder their relationships.

To be in a relationship with someone who has ADD requires a great deal of courage, willingness to learn, and commitment. By working together, treatment strategies can be developed that ultimately benefit each person. Couples that come to understand ADD will not allow the pitfalls of the disorder to weaken or destroy their relationship. They begin each day seeking opportunities to learn and develop new ways to enhance and support their relationship.

Unlike many other neurobiological disorders, there are certain advantages to having ADD. When you look closely at the reason you were initially drawn to your spouse, you may find traits such as enthusiasm, spontaneity, creativity, high energy, extroversion, eagerness to learn, and a willingness to try new things. Instead of keeping a list of symptoms, remember to cherish these qualities and keep these gifts in focus.

This article first appeared in the Spring 1997 issue of ATTENTION!

John R. Capel, Ph.D., and Katherine G. Brown, M.H.S., M.A., are a couple who have personal and professional experience with ADD. They have designed special training programs for couples with ADD. They facilitate ADD adult support groups and lecture extensively on ADD and the treatment of children with behavior disorders.

PRACTICAL INTERVENTIONS

Cubby holes	Watches with alarms	Pill boxes
Key holders	White boards	Housekeepers
Phone message books	Armoires	Bookkeepers
Mail & message box	Electric organizers	Accountants
Glasses cases	Keeping lists	Secretaries
Penalty boxes	Calendars	Containers
Book cases	Daytimers	Organizers

COMMUNICATION

- Check-in when you come home. Turn off TV's, phones, computers, kids etc., until a plan is in place.

- Use red flags. Warn others to put up their guard.

- Make appointments to talk and listen. The goal is productive communication, with frequent feedback intended to assure that the message sent is the message received.

DISORGANIZATION

- Ritualize Daily and Weekly Cleanup Periods
  Make periods brief (5-10 minutes daily, 30-40 minutes weekly)
  Make the time period clear-cut with specific starting and ending times
  Make the area of cleanup confined, specific and quality controlled
  Plan to run "last person sweeps" over each other's areas
  Restrict phone calls, company and conversation during the time period
  Provide or restrict music or "white noise" according to the effect it has

- Use Obsessive-Compulsive Traits
  Prevention – Catch the "white lies" as they are told. Do it now!
    (e.g., "I'll remember to take care of this later.")
  Save perfectionist jobs for when they count
  Develop a "start and end on-time" ethic

MOOD SWINGS

- Understand the real message – "I hurt!"
- Is the medication properly adjusted? Answer the question first.
- Do not try to reason with rage. This is a time-out time.
- Be firm, without fueling the fire.
- Be supportive, not a door mat.

Living and Loving with ADD

by Edward M. Hallowell, M.D.

Knowing about ADD can save a marriage or relationship. If one member of the couple has ADD, daily arguments and bad feelings may be due to ADD rather than poisoned personalities or irreconcilable differences. Not knowing about ADD, a couple may feel lost or at war, while with the knowledge of ADD, they could be finding a new path for themselves.

In couples where one or both partners have ADD, life can list and yaw from day to day. As one member of a couple said to me, "I never know what to expect. I can't rely on him for anything. Why didn't he tell me he had ADD when we got married? I mean, it's really a circus." The distractibility, impulsivity, and excess energy often associated with ADD can disrupt intimate relationships in ways that leave each partner exhausted, angry, hurt, and misunderstood. In addition, ADD can affect one's sexuality adversely. However, if the situation is subtly regulated, both people can work together instead of being at odds and find satisfaction commensurate with the high energy they usually possess.

Since the diagnosis of ADD in adults is still relatively new, many couples living with ADD don't know much about the disorder. They find they are fighting over issues like attentiveness, responsibility, punctuality, or caring, and they think these matters are entirely under voluntary control. However, if ADD is present, these issues may not be entirely under the individual's voluntary control. The "fault" may lie not with either member of the couple, but with the neurobiological problem of ADD. Knowing this can save a marriage. The perspective of ADD can give a couple a whole new way of understanding each other, as well as provide a way for getting treatment.

The diagnosis is often overlooked because the couple's problems can look like ordinary couples' problems. A husband comes home and tunes out by reading the newspaper, has trouble paying attention when talking about feelings, drinks too much, and struggles with self-esteem, while not paying attention

to his wife's repeated attempts to get close to him. Or a wife daydreams chronically, feels depressed, complains of never having reached her potential, and feels trapped at home. These symptoms, in both instances, are entirely consistent with ADD, but few people would think of ADD because the symptoms also are consistent with ordinary, everyday couples' problems.

The impact of ADD upon sexuality is poorly understood. However, we have seen many people in our practice, both men and women, who complain of either an inability to pay attention during sex well enough to enjoy it, or the opposite: a hyperfocused, hypersexuality. How these traits relate to ADD is hard to say, but the symptoms occur often enough to deserve mention. Listen to one woman's account, contained in a note anonymously left for me after a lecture I had given:

Dear Dr. Hallowell:

I enjoyed your talk very much, and I wanted to ask you this question, or, more accurately, make this comment during the discussion period, but frankly I was too embarrassed. So I am leaving you this note in the hope that the concerns it raises can be of help to other people.

I am a forty-two-year-old woman. I'm quite attractive, if I do say so myself, and I love my husband. He is devoted to me. I am the woman of his dreams, he says. However, until I was diagnosed with ADD a year ago, my husband and I never had a satisfactory sex life. He had adored me from the start —I think that's why he stayed with me. But sex between us was boring at best.

For the longest while, I thought the problem was that I was just frigid. I was raised a Catholic, and If figured I just never got past the impact the nuns had on me. But it tore me up inside because I had sexual feelings. I had them all the time. I just couldn't focus on them when in bed with my husband. I read lots of erotic literature, had incredible urges toward other people, none of which I acted on, and I saw different therapists to work on what I thought was my mental block. How could I feel so sexy, look sexy, dress sexy, be married to an incredible man, and yet think of tomorrow's shopping list as he's making love to me? Once in a while, I guess that's normal, but all the time?

The worst part was I really started to hate myself for this and to feel tremendously inadequate. I hate to say this, but I even thought of just running away –you know, the slow boat to nowhere. But I never would have left. The kids, my husband – I couldn't leave them, although, as miserable as I was at times, I think they might have been happier without me.

Then I got lucky. A friend referred me to a new therapist, and this woman knew about ADD. She made the diagnosis in two sessions and started me on treatment. What a difference! I have never read anywhere about how ADD affects sexuality, but in my case, the change was incredible! Now I could focus and be there. After a while, I didn't even need medication. It was a matter of realizing that it was ADD and not some inadequacy or hidden guilt on my part. Then, it was a matter of taking steps to have sex at the right time, of providing soothing music to take over the day-dreaming part of my mind, and of talking to my husband openly about it. He was really great. It turns out he was blaming himself much as I had been blaming myself.

It is amazing how subtle, but how crucial, this discovery has been for me. I can't help but think there are a lot of women out there who are simply distractible but think they are sexually inadequate or just bored, instead.

Now... I approach sex with enthusiasm instead of dread.... I would never have done this if I had not found out about ADD. The treatment has helped me in all areas of my life, but is has helped me sexually more than anything.... And when I consider how relatively simple – yet powerful – the answer was, I just wanted to share it with you in the hope you will share it with others.

This note started me paying attention to an aspect of ADD most people have largely overlooked. So far, I have gathered a great deal of anecdotal evidence, though full of inconsistency; but many people do indeed report that ADD affects their sexuality, either in the direction of non-responsiveness or toward hypersexuality. Usually, the treatment helps both groups of people.

WHEN ONE PARTNER HAS ADD

Moving on to more general couples' issues: let's look at an example of a couple in which one member had ADD.

Sam and Mary were referred to me by Sam's therapist whom Sam had been seeing because Mary felt it was the only alternative to separation. Both in their early forties, they had been married eight years and had one child, David, age five.

They arrived fifteen minutes late for their first appointment. Sam blamed the traffic. "The traffic wouldn't have mattered if we had left on time," Mary quickly added.

"She's right," Sam said. "But that's the way I am. I'm late everywhere."

Sam had been an emergency room physician, but hadn't been practicing for a few years. He had tried his hand as a jazz musician and was currently trying to make it as a freelance writer. When I asked the couple why they scheduled their appointment with me, Mary replied, "Because, quite frankly, this man is making my life a living hell." She went on to explain why.

"He doesn't beat me or cheat on me or drink or gamble; he just behaves like an irresponsible little boy. I don't mind that he changes jobs because he finds being a doctor isn't interesting enough. I don't mind that he gets up in the middle of the night because he bored and wants to go flying. I don't mind that he makes plane reservations for Australia for all of us without even asking me about it and then calls me a "wet blanket" for not being overjoyed. What I do mind is that he doesn't know that I exist. He is so wrapped up in himself that I might as well be a robot. He doesn't know me. And what makes it hell is that he doesn't know that he doesn't know me. None of this bothers him. He's so oblivious."

Sam agreed, but insisted that he didn't do any of this on purpose.

As we reviewed Sam's history, the evidence mounted for a diagnosis of ADD. Mary wasn't easily convinced, asking, "How do you tell ADD from being selfish?" I explained that Sam seemed only to be aware of himself because he was constantly being distracted or being drawn to some form of high stimulation to avert boredom.

Even after my explanation, however, Mary's frustration was still apparent. "I'm tired of living this way. I want him to take some of the responsibility. I don't care whether you call it ADD or selfishness or just being a jerk. I'm tired of it! I want him to get to know me, and I don't want to feel like I have to squeeze everything I have to say into the five seconds of attention he gives me every day. I don't want to feel like I'm married to this immature person who's still trying to find himself. Can't he just grow up?"

Reactions like this one are typical of couples in which one partner has undiagnosed, untreated ADD. Once Sam's ADD was diagnosed, he began treatment, which included medication, and it worked very well. The medication allowed him to focus in a sustained way as he never had before. It took him out of the self-centered, fast-paced, constantly stimulated, always distracted cloud he'd come to live in and deposited him in the ordinary here and now. It allowed him to get to know his own feelings, to get to know his wife, and to be truly present wherever he was.

The struggle was not over with a mere diagnosis, however. Sam and Mary had to work very hard to make their marriage last. It took persistence and a daily, habitual tending to things. Sam had to unlearn a number of habits, and Mary had to get past a backlog of anger and resentment without killing Sam in the process. That they loved each other and wanted to be together provided the motivation, but it was by no means easy.

In addition to an adult receiving treatment for ADD, couples therapy is often helpful. ADD does not occur in a vacuum. The partner of an individual with ADD can benefit from a receptive forum as much as the person with ADD can. The stresses on the partner can mount as he or she tries to hold things together, keep the family from sinking, and generally try to bring some order out of the chaos.

CHAOS BROUGHT TO ORDER

Chaos surrounded Edgar when he first came to see me. He brought his wife with him, but he wanted to speak with me alone, first. Edgar came to see me because he had been thrown out of the system. His extended family decided they had had enough. Since they owned the car business Edgar worked for, they had the power to fire him. One day they called him in and told him that because he was so irresponsible, they could no longer employ him. They would see to it that he didn't starve, but he was no longer welcome in the business or in their homes.

"What can I tell you, Doc? I'm obnoxious," he said. "I'm extremely obnoxious. My family couldn't stand me anymore so they threw me out. It's probably just a matter of time before my wife does the same. But that's me. So I blow a few grand on a cruise to nowhere. Why shouldn't she be thrilled? So I ride down the highway with Dylan blasting, smoking a joint. That's how I do my best thinking. I like to go down to the showroom at three o'clock in the morning when I can't sleep and turn on the radios of all the cars on the floor and just let them blast. It's really a great feeling, standing in there with all the light on me and all the radios blaring when outside, everybody else is asleep. I can have the world to myself, the way I like it, on my own terms."

Although Edgar's behavior was peculiar, the description of an adult with ADD as immature or childish is not uncommon. People don't know how else to make sense of this kind of behavior, so they attack it as being beneath adult standards. They hope to shame the person into changing his ways. As is usually the case, Edgar's problem was not just ADD, but ADD was a big part of it. His impulsivity, high stimulus seeking, restlessness, tactlessness, and high energy all contributed to the fix he was in. Despite how obnoxious he said he was, he was also quite likable.

After a few weeks of getting to know Edgar and having him take some tests, I was confident that he had

ADD. His ADD had to be discriminated from mania, and it was on the basis of childhood history, his current situation – which showed periods of agitation but not mania – and psychological testing that the discrimination was made.

Rather than seeing Edgar individually, I decided to see him with his wife. It was important that she understand what was going on with him. His capacity for insight was minimal at first, and his ability to observe himself was not reliable. His wife became his coach, so to speak, reminding him of what he otherwise would forget. For most situations, this kind of couples therapy would not work because it identifies one member of the couple as the patient. But for ADD, it is a realistic way to proceed.

With his wife's help and with the help of medication, over time, Edgar was able to develop some capacity to reflect before acting, to find relaxation and focus by means other than fast cars, loud music, and marijuana, and to think before speaking. After six months, our sessions came to an end. By this time, his family had given him his job back on a conditional basis. The last I heard, Edgar and his wife were together, Edgar was working, and life was pretty good.

This article first appeared in the Spring/Summer 1993 issue of CH.A.D.D.er.

Edward Hallowell, M.D. is on the faculty of Harvard Medical School and is in private practice as a child and adult psychiatrist. He is the founder and director of The Hallowell Center for Cognitive and Emotional Health, an outpatient diagnosis and treatment center for children and adults located in Concord, Massachusetts, and is the author of several books.

25 TIPS ON THE MANAGEMENT OF ADD IN COUPLES

The following guidelines might be helpful settling the chaos that is so often present in couples living with ADD. These tips offer a starting point for discussion between members of couples. The best way to use them is to read them out loud, together. Pause over each suggestion and discuss whether it applies to you. As you do this, you can begin to set up your own way of dealing with ADD in your relationship. The key to it all is improving communication and resolving power struggles.

(1) Make sure you have an accurate diagnosis.

(2) Once you are sure of the diagnosis, learn as much as you can about ADD.

(3) Declare a truce.

(4) Set up a time for talking.

(5) Spill the beans. Tell each other what is on your minds. Try to say it all before you both start reacting.

(6) Write down your complaints and your recommendations. Otherwise, you'll forget them.

(7) Make a treatment plan. Brainstorm with each other as to how to reach your goals. You may want some professional help with this phase, but it is a good idea to try starting it on your own.

(8) Follow through on the plan.

(9) Make lists.

(10) Use bulletin boards.

(11) Put notepads in strategic places.

(12) Consider writing down what you want from the other person and give it to him or her in the form of a list every day.

(13) Take stock of your sex life in light of ADD.

(14) Avoid the pattern of mess-maker and cleaner-upper.

(15) Avoid the pattern of "pesterer"' and "tuner-outer."

(16) Avoid the pattern of the victim and the victimizer.

(17) Avoid the pattern of master and slave.

(18) Avoid the pattern of a sado-masochistic struggle as a routine way of interacting. Say, "I hate ADD," instead of "I hate you."

(19) In general, watch out for the dynamics of control, dominance, and submission that lurk in the background of most relationships where ADD is involved.

(20) Break the tapes of negativity.

(21) Use praise and encouragement frequently.

(22) Learn about mood management.

(23) Let the one who is the better organizer take on the job of organization.

(24) Make time for each other.

(25) Don't use ADD as an excuse. Each member of the couple has to take responsibility for his or her actions.

Interpersonal and Social Problems in Adults with ADD

by Kevin Murphy, Ph.D.

As is the case with many children with ADD, adults with ADD report problems with making and maintaining friendships and uneven interpersonal relations. In young children with ADD, over 50 percent are reported to have significant problems in peer relationships (Barkley, 1994). This percentage may be even higher in adults.

In fact, social functioning of adults with ADD is sometimes perceived by such individuals and their families as their single most crucial area of need. Adequate social skills are often viewed as a prerequisite for successful adaptive functioning in adulthood. School problems are finite; they have an endpoint and eventually go away. But social/interpersonal problems do not end with graduating or leaving school. They are usually chronic and pervasive and can continually interfere in one's vocational and family success, as well as one's overall mental health. For example, adults may report social difficulties in peer, family, marital, and job-related relations that can range from mildly disruptive to extremely debilitating. Social and interpersonal relationship problems can also contribute to deep-rooted feelings of loneliness, demoralization, and depression.

The purpose of this article is to describe some of the common social and interpersonal difficulties adults with ADD often encounter. Of course, not all children or adults with ADD experience problems with social relationships. For some, social skills may be a significant strength. For example, individuals with a high level of positive interpersonal qualities (such as being energetic, having a good sense of humor, and solid verbal abilities) may relate quite well with others. Their "proficiency" with people skills may lead others to cut them some slack or overlook other weaknesses they may have. Nonetheless, the majority of adults with ADD do experience some degree of social impairment.

It is crucial that readers appreciate the abysmal lack of controlled research on the social problems of adults with ADD. Much of what passes for wisdom in this area is based chiefly on clinical observations and opinions, which can be prejudiced by referral bias and selective memory of clinicians. It will be critical for future studies to compare adults with ADD to control groups of adults who do not have ADD and to those with other psychological disorders on valid measures of social skills to truly establish those social problems specific to ADD in adults. What follows, then, should be understood as the clinical option that it is and not as conclusions from research.

What are some of the factors that contribute to the social/interpersonal difficulties of adults with ADD? Like their younger counterparts, adults with ADD have been described as being more aggressive, disruptive, domineering, intrusive, noisy, and socially demanding than people without ADD (Barkley, 1994). Some may be perceived as overly demanding, impatient, self-centered, rude, obnoxious, uncooperative, irresponsible, unreliable, or immature. Due in part to their impulsivity, interrupting or intruding on others, forgetfulness, inattentiveness, hyperactivity, explosive temper, or mood swings, many adults with ADD have difficulty making and keeping friends. More than half show problems with stubbornness, defiance or refusal to obey, temper tantrums, and verbal hostility toward others (Barkley, 1994). These behavioral characteristics have been associated with peer rejection during the childhood and adolescent years and are likely to contribute to poor relations in the adult years as well.

Some adults with ADD complain of getting bored quickly and easily with boyfriends and girlfriends and have shorter dating relationships and more turnover in dating partners than others. They may impulsively say the wrong thing at the wrong time without regard for the feelings of others, contributing to their own alienation. Some of my patients have indicated that they often forget significant dates such as anniversaries, birthdays, trips or children's sporting events. They may over-commit themselves or inadvertently schedule multiple commitments at the same time, and have to back out of one at the last minute.

Poor emotional regulation and moodiness may

further contribute to the difficulties other people have in understanding and relating to those with ADD. For example, they may explode in anger at a spouse one minute and be fine the next. Exaggerated reactions and emotional displays may be confusing to others and further alienate the individual with ADD. Not surprisingly, communication between marital partners may be poor at times, resulting in poor resolution of hurt feelings and distorted beliefs about one another's intentions.

Communication and listening skills may also be deficient. Indeed, deficient communication and listening skills may represent a core deficit in the interpersonal repertoire of the adult with ADD. Adults with ADD are more likely to abruptly change topics during a conversation, interrupt others because they fear that they will forget what they want to say if they wait for an appropriate opening, have poor eye contact, and fail to listen consistently when others are talking. They may get distracted by an internal thought or something else in the external environment, drift off, and appear to be in a world of their own. Consequently, others may wonder if their message got through and may react with either anger, avoidance, or withdrawal. Spouses of adults with ADD may experience intense frustration with what they consider to be willful misconduct, insensitivity, and irresponsible behavior. They may also complain about inconsistency, lack of intimacy, not being listened to, or forgetfulness.

Adults with ADD may show a significant absence of social awareness and often fail to perceive or simply misperceive social cues that may communicate obvious messages to other people. For example, others may roll their eyes in frustration at the person with ADD who continues talking excessively when others are no longer listening. He or she may be totally unaware of this and the spouse may need to unobtrusively cue them before they will realize it. Other examples include not realizing when someone is joking or not getting the joke, or saying things that are inappropriate and out of context with the present conversation, causing others to wonder where that person was for the last several minutes. These types of social miscues can be embarrassing and humiliating. One of my patients summarized his social problems by saying, "For some reason, I just seem to turn people off."

Another area where social/interpersonal deficits may adversely impact the adult with ADD is in the workplace. As youth with ADD enter adulthood and assume jobs that require skilled labor, independence of supervision, acceptance of responsibility, and periodic training in new knowledge or skills, their deficits in attention, impulse control, regulation of activity level, and, sometimes, organizational and self-control skills

may begin to have a lasting impact (Barkley, 1994). Many adults with ADD from our clinic report problems with impulsive speech and temper, arguments with co-workers and supervisors, difficulty following or conforming to rules, forgetfulness, mood swings, failing to complete tasks in a timely manner, and generally inconsistent performance. They may get sidetracked from the task at hand and be perceived as needing frequent reminders and close supervision to get the job done. Some may feel overwhelmed and extremely stressed by their difficulty in juggling several balls at once and may react emotionally and impulsively by losing their temper or verbally assaulting another. These types of difficulties can be quite frustrating for supervisors and co-workers and can result in frequent criticism, hostility, and distancing from fellow workers.

It is important to keep in mind that much of this behavior is unintentional. Adults and children with ADD do not deliberately set out to sabotage their relationships. Most, if not all, want to perform better socially but just do not know the when's, where's, and how's of achieving change. Some have come to associate social interaction with either embarrassment, disappointment, criticism, or failure. When confronted with future opportunities for social interaction, some adults with ADD prefer to stay on the sidelines to avoid embarrassment and prevent another painful experience. This group tends to withdraw from people to protect themselves.

The following table summarizes the typical social difficulties many adults with ADD experience.

Intrusive Behaviors
disruptive behavior
domineering personality
loudness
impatience
excessive talking
forgetfulness

Poor Emotional Regulation
mood swings
impulsive temper
outbursts
exaggerated emotional reactions
easily angered
verbally aggressive
impatience

Poor Communication Skills
poor listening skills
poor eye contact
interrupting

difficulty staying focused on topic and
   abruptly shifting topics
inattentiveness/"spaciness"

Limited Self-awareness
   difficulty tuning into social cues
   misperceiving social cues

What kinds of interventions can assist adults with ADD and social skills problems and how successful are they? This is an under-researched area, but, generally speaking, treatment usually centers around medication; individual, couples, and group counseling; proper matching to jobs that "fit" well; and social skills education and training. Research with children shows that stimulant medication improves the social conduct and standing of children with ADD. Our clinical impression is much the same for adults, making medication part of a treatment program for many adults.

In summary, it is estimated that over 50 percent of adults with ADD have social skills deficits that may impair their family, peer, or workplace relationships.

These difficulties in some cases may adversely impact self-esteem and overall mental health. Despite the continuation of social skills difficulties into adulthood in many cases, with proper treatment and accommodations, most adults with ADD are able to lead successful and fulfilling lives.

This article first appeared in the October/November 1994 issue of CH.A.D.D.er Box.

Kevin Murphy, Ph.D. is Chief of the Adult AD/HD Clinic at the University of Massachusetts Medical Center and is an assistant professor in the department of psychiatry. He provides diagnostic and treatment services to adolescents and adults with AD/HD and conducts didactic training and clinical supervision for psychiatry residents.

REFERENCE

Barkley, R.A. (1994). *AD/HD in adults*. Program manual accompanying *AD/HD in Adults* videotape. New York Guilford Press.

Acclimated to AD/HD

by Kay E. Murray

As you look around your house, are there at least twenty-five projects left unfinished? Do the others in your family seem to talk to you non-stop at ninety miles an hour? Do you feel like you were cast as the tortoise in your family's version of the tortoise and the hare? Let me guess, you are the only adult without AD/HD in a household with a spouse and at least one child who have AD/HD.

Being the only person without AD/HD in a household can be a big challenge – one that sometimes you would just as soon not have. I have lived with my husband who has AD/HD for fourteen years and my son who has AD/HD for eight. Of course, I didn't have a name for it until about a year-and-a-half-ago (but I knew long before that).

Looking back over those years I see now that I have adapted myself to fit my role. I can honestly say that ninety-nine days out of 100, I don't notice or care about my unfinished kitchen (but, oh, look out for that 100th day). I have also tried to pick my battles and only worry about things that are truly important (most of the time). Now, before you think I've adapted perfectly to the AD/HD world (and could qualify for sainthood) let me confess. I do, sometimes, get tired of being the family organizer, the walking calendar that makes sure everyone gets to their appointments for the day, and the one who must remember where all the supplies are kept. I also must confess that I don't always listen when one or the other of them tells me about the ten thousand ideas they had today and what they did to act on each and every one of them. And, I know this is going to be hard to believe, sometimes I get grumpy and irritable and even blow my stack and tell them I'm moving to Alaska because I just know they are slowly driving me crazy.

But, there are some things about these two that I wouldn't trade for anything. I know, for example, that every night when I walk through that door I will hear from some far corner of the house, "Hi, Mom!" and that before I get my coat off, a smiling face will be right next to me telling me about some great revelation or another. I also look forward to the unexpected, the unconventional, and the impulsive – like the day they brought home a pig named George to live in the backyard (but that is a whole tale in itself). I just don't think I could truly go back to living a slow-paced, consistent, organized, and predictable lifestyle (but I can dream about it). So, for now, I will continue to plod along as the only tortoise in a two hare household.

After writing the above, I asked my husband what it was like to live with a spouse without AD/HD. Feeling quite smug at the time, I thought he would be telling me things like, I'm so grateful I live with someone who can keep me organized and remind me to finish all my projects around the house; but, instead he had quite different ideas. "You mean like what's it like to live with someone very predictable, with little imagination, and that can only manage to follow one train of thought at a time?" he said with a grin. Well, my father always told me never ask a question unless I really wanted to hear the answer!

After absorbing the reality of my husband's statement, I realized why we had gotten along so well all these years. We truly compliment each other's personalities (that, and we each have a very good sense of humor). After all, organization without creativity is pretty boring. Isn't it?

This essay first appeared in The Only Tortoise in a Two Hare Household *(3D Publishing, Federal Way, WA, 1997). Reprinted with permission of 3D Publishing.*

Kay Murray is married and the mother of two children. She works full-time as a Computer Aided Design Instructor for an aerospace company. Her unpaid job is to coordinate a local support group to help educate the community about ADD and to improve the lives of those touched by it.

The Search

by Karenne Bloomgarden

For practically all of my life I searched: I searched for the reasons why I felt so different from everyone; why I couldn't seem to fit in anywhere; what was wrong with me. Unfortunately, during my search I often chose the wrong places and relied upon the wrong people. I just wanted to find acceptance, understanding, and love, but the roads I chose to travel always seemed to lead me to dead ends. It wasn't until just five years ago, after a lifetime spent following the wrong path and making many poor choices, that I finally found the answer I had been desperately looking for, and my life has never been the same.

Even as a little girl I knew I was different from other children. I can remember sitting in class – fidgeting, squirming, my mind racing to a million places – while my classmates listened carefully as the teacher gave the class directions for assignments. By the time the teacher was through, I was either out of my seat or on a totally different subject. I just could not pay attention, and I certainly couldn't focus on my teacher's words long enough to follow directions. As a result, my grades were very poor. I did succeed, however, in being extremely loud and rambunctious. I was constantly clowning around and trying to make people laugh. Since I didn't have many friends, I suppose humor was just about the only thing that connected me to my peers. Unfortunately, my teachers and family members didn't usually find my antics so funny, as was evidenced in their insistent pleas for me to "Quiet down!", "Stop that!", "Pay attention!", and "Try harder!".

I'm sure my parents were looking for an answer of their own during this time – namely, a way to calm me down! They tried a variety of tactics, none of which worked. At one point, they thought ballet and piano lessons were the answer, believing that if I had something to take pride in, I might become better disciplined. Of course, that was merely wishful thinking on their part. I hated both and didn't take either seriously. In fact, all I did during class was joke around. The only thing I did enjoy doing was watching television, which I did as much as I possibly could. Because my grades were so poor, however, my parents thought limiting my TV time was appropriate. It was a pretty miserable time for me.

As I got older, the problems only worsened. During my teenage years, I felt even more alone and rejected. My grades were still bad and I was still acting out. Only now, my quest for acceptance and love led me to do everything in excess. One of the first areas my excessive behavior manifested itself in was my eating habits. I went through a period where I was constantly sneaking food into my room so that no one would know how much I was eating. Because I was eating so much, though, my problem eventually became impossible to hide, as I had gained noticeable weight.

During this stage of my life, I felt that the only attention I received from my parents was negative, so "negative" behavior became my primary focus. I started chasing boys, hanging out with the wrong crowd, experimenting with drugs, and acting out sexually. The people I was with were older than I was and thought drugs were "cool," so taking drugs made me feel accepted, and acceptance was something I had lacked until that time. Throughout my teen years I screamed for help and reached out in any way I knew how to find love and attention. On several occasions, my pursuit even led me to attempt suicide. I enjoyed staying in the hospital because of all the attention I received – it made me feel cared for, at least for a while – but it certainly never provided me with any answers for why I was feeling and behaving the way I was.

Despite my poor grades throughout school, I was able to make it into college. I suppose by this point I had learned how to manipulate the system. I had become such a crafty manipulator, in fact, that I was able to cheat in school on a regular basis without getting caught. While my grades remained poor overall, my peers and superiors constantly told me how intelligent I was. Because I was so determined to please people, I had somehow managed to give teachers and administrators the answers they wanted, but I was never able to retain the information I needed.

During college, my search continued to lead me down the wrong path – I was still hanging out with the wrong crowd and seeking attention from men the only way I knew how. I also continued to use drugs as a tool for acceptance. While I was not addicted, I had begun to use more powerful drugs by this time. Even though I had "friends" and "boyfriends," I couldn't have felt more alone, more dejected, more misunderstood. I was so busy trying to please others so they would like and accept me that I never took the time to figure out what it was that I needed. My behavior and attitude were not doing anything but fueling my insecurities and lack of self-esteem.

For years following college, I continued to blame myself for everything that went wrong in my life – and guilt becomes more and more difficult to carry around after decades of not confronting it – so my self-esteem continued to be low. On some level, I knew that I truly couldn't control my impulsive behavior as hard as I had tried, but a large part of me could not stop blaming myself for my problems. What stuck in my mind was all of the hurtful things people said about me, all the crazy stunts I had pulled to get attention, and all of the times I just wanted to die because it seemed I would never get better. The guilt continued to pile on.

Throughout all of the difficulties, there was one bright spot in my life: children. For some reason, I'd always been loved and accepted by children, and I felt safe enough with them to give them my unconditional love. One of the best choices I made in my life was to become a physical education teacher. I began working with children and spending my summers directing children's camps. My energy was finally getting channeled into something positive, and I was enjoying every minute of the time I spent with "my kids." I was finally a success at something in my life. At last, I had found what I had been searching for – or so I thought.

Although I had carved a niche for myself and found a career that was suitable for me and that I was good at, I had never identified the reasons for my destructive behavior. As a result, it continued. Through my involvement with the summer camp industry, I became executive director of the American Camping Association in New York. As an executive, I had a 9-5 office job – this was the first time I had no direct interaction with children. Extremely unhappy shuffling papers and working with many bosses, I once again started down that same, dark road that I had traveled so many times before. The road led me deeper into drug use, only this time, I became addicted. I was

no longer in control and it was becoming apparent to others. If it weren't for Morry Stein, a dear friend who convinced me that I needed help, I never would have survived. Thankfully, I did get help (I've been sober ever since), but I still hadn't uncovered the reason for my impulsive, often destructive, behavior.

Then, after nearly forty years of searching, I finally found that answer I had been looking for. As I impatiently awaited my turn to speak to a CH.A.D.D. meeting in New York on the subject, "how to prepare your child and select a summer camp," a man named Dr. A. Wachtel addressed the audience. I, of course, was listening to the traffic outside, thinking about what I had to do, and constantly looking at my watch, wondering when I would be able to speak. Then, Dr. Wachtel said something that grabbed my attention. My attention! He was telling a story about a teenage boy with AD/HD. He described the boy's symptoms and behavior. Then it all started to click. Maybe my excessive behavior hadn't been caused by me – as I had always assumed – after all. Maybe there really was a legitimate reason for my inability to control my inattention, hyperactivity, and impulsive behavior. It all began to make sense – I had all the symptoms Dr. Wachtel described.

I was, indeed, diagnosed with AD/HD and now take medication to control my impulsivity and hyperactivity. Thanks to Dr. Wachtel and CH.A.D.D., my search was finally complete, and the answers became known. Understanding what having AD/HD has meant in my life and learning how to effectively deal with the symptoms has made a dramatic difference in my life. Today, I am a special education and physical education teacher, a teacher trainer, and a successful entrepreneur. I teach children ages four to thirteen-years-old who have various neurological and/or physical disabilities. Having AD/HD, myself, allows me to communicate better with my students and be a much more effective teacher. In addition, I founded my own camp referral service, KB Camp Service, and am now in my twelfth successful year in business. I've actually become an expert of sorts on children's camps and have appeared on national television programs and in publications. I have to admit, I do still enjoy the attention, but at least now, it comes from a positive source.

Indeed my search was filled with many obstacles and many trials, and although my life is not perfect today, I am no longer following that destructive path that I once thought would provide me with acceptance. I know that there's only one person that I should seek acceptance from, and that's me. Understanding that AD/HD has had an impact on many of the decisions

I've made in my life and learning to manage my behavior, I've been able to accept myself for who I am. I used to say that I had to slow down so people could catch up – now I go at my own speed and try to surround myself with people who move at my pace. The energy I have as a result of my AD/HD has helped me to achieve success; recognition and effective management of my AD/HD has helped me to maintain it.

This article first appeared in the Spring 1996 issue of ATTENTION!

CHAPTER 7

TOPICS OF
SPECIAL INTEREST

In this chapter, we present a collection of articles offering insights into several unique issues that affect adults with ADD. From premenstrual syndrome, to substance abuse, to driving, to being the parent of a child with ADD when you, too, have the disorder, the authors on the following pages cover a broad range of subject matter. The common thread? – the interaction of ADD with the details and, sometimes, the struggles of everyday life.

There are, perhaps, two lessons to be learned from the articles in this chapter. First, ADD is a disorder that impacts all aspects of an individual's life. And second, there is still much to be learned about ADD.

Two of the nation's leading researchers, Russell Barkley, Ph.D. and Kevin Murphy, Ph.D., share the focus of – and some of the results from – their current research, including a look at the long term outcomes for individuals with ADD, and the health status and driving ability of young adults who have the disorder.

Some of the most troubling questions have always swirled around the interaction between ADD and substance abuse. Are young people with ADD more likely to become substance abusers? Are substance abusers more likely to have ADD? What are the treatment implications when ADD and substance abuse disorder are co-occurring? Timothy Wilens, M.D. presents a comprehensive look at what is known and not known about the issue in his article "ADD and Substance Abuse."

A burgeoning area of interest is how ADD presents itself in women and girls as compared to men and boys. Author Kathleen Nadeau, Ph.D., combines her extensive clinical experience with current research findings to help us understand why ADD may be a very different disorder for girls and women.

Finally, a very real life subject that has received little attention are the challenges facing adults who have ADD who are also the parents of children with ADD. In an article appearing for the first time anywhere, noted clinician and author Barbara Ingersoll, Ph.D., explores the trials and tribulations of this unique parent-child relationship.

We end this chapter with a brief article we call, "A Touch of Real Life." Four adults with ADD share their thoughts about living with this disorder, vignettes that originally appeared in the Spring 1997 issue of CH.A.D.D.'s magazine *ATTENTION!*

ADD and Substance Abuse: An Intoxicating Combination

by Timothy E. Wilens, M.D. and Colleen E. Lineham, B.A.

Within the past few years, there has been increasing interest in the overlap of ADD and the addictive disorder (Wilens et al., 1994). The concurrence of ADD and substance abuse (including alcohol abuse and dependence) has been frequently reported in clinical settings and is known to be associated with substantial impairment. While ADD onsets in early childhood and affects 6 to 9 percent of juveniles and approximately 2 to 3 percent of adults, substance use disorders onset in adolescence or early adulthood and may affect between 10 and 20 percent of adults. However, both disorders share several important characteristics: male predominance, family contributions, and genetic influences. Likewise, higher rates of other psychiatric disorders such as antisocial, conduct, anxiety, and mood disorders also occur with both disorders (Biederman et al., 1991).

SUBSTANCE ABUSE IN ADULTS WITH ADD

Recent studies have consistently shown elevated rates of substance abuse in adults with ADD as compared to the general population (Biederman et al., 1993). More specifically, in a group of adults with ADD, approximately one third have had alcohol abuse or dependence histories. In addition, a recent unpublished study at Massachusetts General Hospital indicates that most of the adults with ADD and substance abuse (generally alcohol and marijuana) also had mood, anxiety, or antisocial disorder.

ADD IN INDIVIDUALS WITH SUBSTANCE ABUSE

The majority of investigations on adolescents and adults with histories of substance abuse have demonstrated increased rates of ADD (Wilens et al., 1994). For instance, Dr. Tarter and associates (1977) reported elevated rates of ADD symptoms in alcohol dependent individuals, with those with more severe drinking habits having more severe ADD symptoms. Reports in cocaine and opioid abusers have also shown that between 17 and 45 percent of individuals in treatment had been diagnosed with ADD as children

(Wilens et al., 1994). A large group of those previously diagnosed with ADD as children also had conduct or antisocial disorder. In most of these studies, adolescents and adults with ADD were younger at presentation, had an earlier onset, had more severe substance abusing habits, and had higher rates of antisocial disorders than substance abusers who did not have ADD.

IS ADD A RISK FACTOR FOR DEVELOPMENT OF SUBSTANCE ABUSE?

Long-term studies of children with ADD have shown that 30 to 40 percent of these children do well as adults, 40 to 50 percent continue to have ADD symptoms, and 20 to 30 percent have problems with substance abuse (Weiss, 1992). In addition, these studies have shown that the group with ADD and elevated rates of substance abuse also had a continuation of their ADD symptoms as well as demoralization and evidence of conduct disorder. Research on children at risk for substance abuse also indicates that ADD plus conduct disorder may be an important antecedent to the onset of substance abuse.

FAMILY AND HIGH RISK STUDIES

Family studies have been used in psychiatric research to assess family and/or genetic influences, as well as to examine disorders that may be associated with ADD and substance abuse. Studies on the children of substance abusers and alcoholics show that these children are at elevated risk for developing emotional and behavioral problems including substance abuse, conduct disorder, and ADD (Wilens and Biederman, 1993). The link between ADD and substance abuse has been noted for many years to run in families, with studies showing elevated rates of substance abuse and antisocial problems in some relatives of children with ADD (Cantwell, 1972).

Hence, the current literature demonstrates several types of links between ADD and substance abuse. There is a large overlap between ADD and substance abuse in studies of individuals with either primary substance abuse or ADD. Children with ADD alone are at negligible risk for substance abuse; while children whose ADD persists as they get older may be at risk for substance abuse as adolescents and adults. ADD-like symptoms have been reported in children who develop substance abuse in later years. Elevated rates of substance abuse have also been found in the relatives of children with ADD, and elevated rates of ADD have been reported in the relatives of individuals with substance abuse. It appears that an important link between ADD and substance abuse is the presence of other disorders, particularly conduct and antisocial disorders (Wilens et al., 1994). However, the role of other disorders such as anxiety and depression may have an effect but have not yet been studied. In addition, abuse of substances in individuals with ADD may also be related to the "self-medication" of their ADD, accompanying demoralization, chronic failure, or other psychiatric problems.

Identifying the nature of the ADD influence on substance abuse and vice versa is an important issue, as substance abuse with psychiatric problems has been associated with treatment difficulties and poorer outcomes. Since ADD symptoms may exacerbate substance abuse and its treatment, the identification and treatment of ADD-related symptoms may reduce the associated impairment of both disorders.

Evaluation and treatment of co-occurring ADD and substance abuse should be part of a plan in which consideration is given to all aspects of the individual's life (see table). Any intervention in this group should follow a careful evaluation of the individual and his or her family including addiction, psychiatric, social, cognitive, and if applicable, educational evaluations. A thorough history of substance use – including past and current usage – should be obtained in all individuals with ADD. Careful attention should be paid to other problems, which may exist, including medical or neurological conditions, whose symptoms may be similar to those of ADD. Although no specific guidelines exist for evaluating the individual who is an active substance abuser, in our experience, at least one month of abstinence is helpful in assessing current ADD symptoms. Careful psychiatric assessments by a professional knowledgeable in both addiction and ADD is suggested.

The "core" ADD symptoms in substance abusing adults appear to be continuous with their childhood ADD symptoms. A history of ADD symptoms from childhood must be present in order to meet the criteria for ADD as an adult. In addition to inattention, distractibility, and frequent activity shifts, adults with ADD may also have marked stubbornness, low frustration tolerance, and chronic conflicts in social

relations. Because it reduces an individual's compliance with addiction treatment and recovery, ADD-related impulsivity appears to be particularly problematic in treating an individual's substance abuse problems.

When treating individuals with ADD and substance abuse, special attention should be given to other potential psychological and cognitive disorders. The presence of depression or anxiety not directly a result of the substance abuse needs to be further assessed. The overall evaluation should assist in the designing of a multi-modal treatment plan tailored to the needs of the individual.

The treatment of individuals with substance abuse and ADD needs to be addressed simultaneously with an initial emphasis on the substance abuse. It is noteworthy that ADD treatments should not be relied upon to correct the behavioral patterns of substance abuse. Additionally, these individuals often suffer from poor self-esteem, risk-taking behaviors, and difficulty sitting through 12-step programs and individual or group psychotherapy. Individuals with sufficient psychological distress from ADD and substance abuse should be referred to therapists familiar with both of these disorders. Effective psychotherapy for individuals with ADD and substance abuse generally combines structured and goal-directed sessions, active therapist involvement, and frequent reassessments. Substance abuse and ADD psychotherapies can be completed successfully in parallel with other addiction modalities (i.e. narcotics anonymous) and pharmacotherapy.

Pharmacotherapy serves an important role in reducing the core symptoms of ADD and other concurrent psychiatric disorders, and hence, may indirectly assist in substance abuse treatment. The pharmacological treatments for ADD (i.e., stimulants) do not appear to exacerbate substance use; however, studies of the scope of this problem are lacking, particularly in groups with substance abuse problems. Favorable reports of medication treatment for adults with ADD have included the use of psychostimulants (i.e. pemoline), antidepressants (i.e. tricyclics), and antihypertensives. When using drug therapy, frequent monitoring should include careful evaluation of treatment compliance, substance use status (random toxicology screens), and coordination of care with other caregivers.

In summary, there is a robust literature supporting a relationship between ADD and substance abuse. There appears to be family-genetic, environmental, and other psychiatric conditions relating ADD to substance abuse. Complex genetic, behavioral, and selfmedication influences contribute to the development and persistence of substance abuse in those with

ADD. Individuals with ADD and substance abuse require comprehensive multimodal intervention incorporating parallel addiction and mental health treatment.

This article first appeared in the Winter 1995 issue of ATTENTION!

Timothy E. Wilens, M.D. is Staff at the Pediatric Psychopharmacology unit at Massachusetts General Hospital, and Associate Professor of Psychiatry at Harvard Medical School.

REFERENCES

Biederman J, Farone SV, Spencer T, Wilens TE, Norman D, Lapey KA, Mick E, Lehman B, Doyle A (1993), Patterns of psychiatric comorbidity, cognitive, and psychosocial functioning in adults with attention deficit hyperactivity disorder. *American Journal of Psychiatry*, 150:1792-1798.

Biederman J, Newcom J, Sprich S (1991), Comorbidty of attention deficit hyperactivity disorder with conduct, depressive, anxiety, and other disorders. *American Journal of Psychiatry*, 148:546-57.

Cantwell D (1972), Psychiatric illness in the families of hyperactive children. *Archives of General Psychiatry*, 27: 414-417.

Tarter RE, McBride H, Buonpane N, Schneider DU (1977), Differentiation of alcoholics. *Archives of General Psychiatry*, 34: 761-768.

Weiss G (1992), *Attention Deficit Hyperactivity Disorder.* Philadelphia: W.B. Saunders Company.

Wilens T, Biederman J (1993), Psychopathology in pre-adolescent children at high risk for substance abuse: A review of the literature. *Harvard Review of Psychiatry*, 1: 207-218.

Wilens TE, Biederman J, Spencer TJ, Frances RJ (1994), Comorbidity of attention deficit hyperactivity disorder and the psychoactive substance use disorders. *Hospital and Community Psychiatry*, 45: 421-435.

EVALUATION AND TREATMENT OF INDIVIDUALS WITH ADD AND PSYCHOACTIVE SUBSTANCE USE DISORDER

Assessment	Guide
Psychiatric Evaluation	clinical interview; structured psychiatric interview; educational/cognitive screen
Addiction	History interview; questionnaires; urine toxicology screen
Sources of Information	individual; mate; parents; other caregivers
Psychosocial	Ask about current stressors and available supports.
Family Concerns	family history of emotional and behavioral problems, substance abuse, or underachievement
Differential Diagnosis	substance abuse symptoms (i.e., intoxication, withdrawal, sequela); medical and neurological concerns; psychiatric problems (i.e., depression, anxiety)
Treatment Strategies	review treatment expectations; develop multi-modal treatment plan
Specific Therapeutics	psychotherapies (individual and group) helpful for addictions; problematic behavioral patterns; intrapsychic and interpersonal distress; pharmacotherapy helpful for ADD and comorbid psychiatric disorders (i.e. depression)

ADD in Females:
From Childhood to Adulthood

by Kathleen G. Nadeau, Ph.D.

The majority of writing and research on ADD has traditionally focused on males, who were believed to make up 80 percent of all those with ADD. Today, more and more females are being identified, especially now that we are more aware of the non-hyperactive subtype of ADD. Girls and women with ADD face a variety of issues that are gender specific. This article will highlight some of those differences, and will explore some of the unique struggles faced by females with ADD.

CHILDHOOD ISSUES FOR GIRLS WITH ADD

Let's start with the recollections of childhood and adolescence by two women with ADD: Marie and Lauren. Marie is an introverted, "primarily inattentive" thirty-four-year-old woman with ADD who has struggled with anxiety and depression in addition to ADD, both in childhood and in adulthood:

"The thing I remember the most was always getting my feelings hurt. I was a lot happier when I played with just one friend. When someone teased me I never knew how to defend myself. I really tried in school, but I hated it when the teacher called on me. Half the time I didn't even know what the question was. Sometimes I would get stomach aches and beg my mother to let me stay home from school."

These recollections are very different from those of a typical elementary school-age boy with ADD. Marie was hypersensitive to criticism, had difficulty with the rapid give-and-take of group interactions, and felt socially "out of it," except in the company of her one best friend. She was a compliant girl whose greatest desire was to conform to teacher expectations and to avoid drawing attention to herself. Her distractibility created agony because of teacher disapproval and the resulting embarrassment in front of her peers.

On the other hand, Lauren's "hyperactive-impulsive" ADD patterns are more similar to those seen in many boys with ADD. Now twenty-seven, she recalls being stubborn, angry, defiant and rebellious, and physically hyperactive. She was also hyper-social:

"I can remember in grade school that everything felt frantic. I had a fight with my mom almost every morning. At school I was always jumping around, talking, and passing notes. Some of my teachers liked me, but some of them – the really strict ones – didn't like me. And I hated them. I argued a lot and lost my temper. I cried really easily too, and some of the mean kids in the class liked to tease me and make me cry."

Although we see the argumentativeness and defiance in Lauren, which we see more often in boys who have ADD, we also see that, like many girls with ADD, she was hyper-social and hyper-emotional. Life for Lauren, as for some other girls with ADD, was an emotional roller coaster. She was very disorganized and had very low tolerance for stress.

ADOLESCENT GIRLS WITH ADD

Let's take a look at Marie and Lauren's recollections of adolescence. Life for each of them seemed to become even more difficult. Adolescence is difficult enough as it is – when ADD is added to the mix, problems are amplified and stresses are intensified.

"High school just overwhelmed me. None of my teachers knew me because I never spoke up in class. Exams terrified me. I hated to study and write papers. They were really hard for me and I put them off until the last minute. I didn't date at all in high school. People didn't dislike me, but I bet if I went back to a class reunion, no one would remember who I was. I was pretty emotional, and it got ten times worse just before my period."

– Marie

"I was totally out of control in high school. I was smart, but a terrible student. I guess I worked on being a 'party animal' to make up for all the things I wasn't good at. At home I was angry and totally rebellious. I snuck out of the house after my parents went to sleep at night. I lied all the time. My parents tried to control me or punish me, but nothing worked. I couldn't sleep at night and was exhausted all day in school. Things were bad most of the time, but when I had PMS, I really lost it. School meant nothing to me."

– Lauren

Marie and Lauren presented very different pictures during their teenage years. Marie was shy, withdrawn, a daydreamer who was disorganized and felt overwhelmed. Lauren was hyperactive, hyper-emotional, and lived her life in a high stimulation, high risk mode. The differences in Marie's and Lauren's behaviors are obvious, but what do they have in common?

(1) Severe pre-menstrual syndrome.

During the teenage years, the neurochemical problems caused by ADD are greatly compounded by hormonal fluctuations. These combined dysregulated systems can result in tremendous mood swings, hyper-irritability, and emotional over-reaction.

(2) Tremendous concern with peer acceptance.

Girls with ADD seem to suffer more as a result of peer problems than do boys with ADD. Although Lauren had many friends, her emotionality repeatedly got in the way. Marie, by contrast, felt overwhelmed and withdrew, and felt most comfortable in the company of one close friend. Both, however, had a strong sense of "being different" from their peers.

(3) Among impulsive-hyperactive girls, a sense of shame.

Adolescent boys who are impulsive and hyperactive may be viewed as simply "sowing their oats." They may even gain peer approval as they rebel against authority, or as a result of their hard drinking, fast driving, and sexually-active lifestyle. Girls, however, tend to receive much more negative feedback from parents, teachers, and peers when they behave in such a manner. Later, as young women, they often join the chorus of accusation and outrage, blaming themselves and feeling a strong sense of shame for their earlier behavior.

RAISING GIRLS WITH ADD – SOME HELPFUL APPROACHES

Just like adolescent boys with ADD, girls with ADD need structure and guidelines at home. While males with ADD may behave in a very angry and rebellious fashion, for many girls, their life is an emotional roller coaster. They may withdraw and become depressed if they feel overwhelmed and socially rejected at school. Highly hyperactive impulsive girls may engage in constant, dramatic screaming battles at home, where it feels much safer to release their fears and frustrations. Helping them to re-establish emotional equilibrium, especially in relation to

hormonal fluctuations, is critical. For girls more so than for many boys, home needs to become a place to calm down and to refuel emotionally. All too often, however, parents are drawn into tumultuous battles rather than providing a much needed calming influence. How can you help as a parent?

(1) Teach your daughters to establish a "quiet zone" in their lives.

Whether shy and withdrawn or hyper and impulsive, girls with ADD often feel emotionally overwhelmed. They need to learn stress management techniques from an early age and to understand that they need emotional "time out" to regroup after an upset.

(2) Try to minimize corrections and criticism.

Too often, parents – with the best of intentions – shower girls who have ADD with corrections and criticisms. "Don't let them hurt your feelings like that." "You'd forget your head if it wasn't attached to your shoulders." "How do you expect to go to college with grades like that?" "If you just relaxed, dressed a little better..." These girls, whether loud and rebellious or shy and retiring, typically suffer from low self-esteem. Home is not only an important place to refuel, it is where confidence – so frequently eroded during the day at school – must be rebuilt.

(3) Help them look for ways to excel.

Girls with ADD typically feel that they are "not good at anything." Their distractibility, impulsivity, and disorganization often result in mediocre grades. Likewise, they often don't have the persistence, the "stick-to-it-iveness," to develop skills and talents like many of their friends. Helping girls with ADD find a skill or ability, and then praising and recognizing them for it are terrific boosts. Often, the life of an adolescent girl with ADD reaches a positive turning-point when she is lucky enough to find an activity that can raise her self-esteem.

(4) Seek medical treatment if PMS is severe.

PMS is something that many females with ADD may need to carefully manage throughout their lives. If PMS is severe in adolescence, it should be taken seriously and managed carefully. Sometimes severe PMS is managed through the use of anti-depressants with the dosage level being varied according to the menstrual cycle.

SPECIAL ISSUES FACED BY WOMEN WITH ADD

The same themes of social and physiological differences between males and females with ADD continue to play themselves out as adolescent girls become women with jobs, marriages, and families.

For a woman with ADD, her most painful challenge may be created by her own overwhelming sense of inadequacy at fulfilling the roles she feels that her family and society expect her to play. Both on the job and at home, women are often placed in the role of caretaker. While men with ADD are advised to build a support system around themselves, not only do few women have access to such a support system, but society has traditionally expected women to be the support system.

The emergence of "dual career couples" has intensified the struggles for women with ADD. Over the past two decades, more and more women have been required to fulfill not only the more traditional roles of wife and mother, but also to function efficiently and tirelessly as they juggle the demands of a full-time career. Divorce is also hitting women with ADD harder than their peers who do not have ADD. Divorce rates are close to 50 percent among all marriages in the United States; divorce becomes even more likely when ADD is added to the list of marital stressors. Following divorce, it continues to be predominantly mothers who act as primary parent for children. By adding ADD to the huge burden of singleparenting, the result is often chronic exhaustion and emotional depletion.

The hormonal fluctuations that commence at puberty continue to play a strong role in the lives of women with ADD. The problems they experience due to ADD are greatly exacerbated by their monthly hormonal fluctuations. Some women report that the stresses of parenting their children – who also may have ADD – while attempting to struggle with their own ADD, reaches crisis proportions on a monthly basis as they go through their premenstrual phase, often lasting as long as a week.

Although the number of older women yet identified with ADD is small, it seems quite reasonable to assume that the hormonal changes associated with menopause would be expected to, once again, exacerbate ADD symptoms of emotional reactivity.

IF YOU ARE A WOMAN WITH ADD, WHAT CAN YOU DO TO MANAGE YOUR LIFE BETTER?

Here's a list of twelve actions (and attitude changes) that could help make your life more manageable and, therefore, less stressful:

(1) Give yourself a break!

Often the biggest struggle is an internal one. Societal expectations have been deeply ingrained in many women. Even if a loving husband said, "Don't worry about it," women would place demands upon themselves. Breaking out of a mold that doesn't fit can take time and effort. Working with a therapist who really understands issues related to ADD may help shed the impossible expectations that you have of yourself.

(2) Educate your husband about ADD and how it affects you.

Your husband may feel anger and resentment about an ill-kept house or badly-behaved children, assuming that you "just don't care." He needs to appreciate the full brunt of ADD's impact upon you. Get him on your side; strategize how to make your life at home more "ADD-accommodating" and "ADD-friendly."

(3) It's only spilled milk!

Try to create an "ADD-friendly" environment in your home. If you can approach your ADD and your children's ADD with acceptance and good humor, explosions will decrease and you'll save more energy for the positive side of things.

(4) Simplify your life.

You are probably over-booked, and chances are, your children are too. Look for ways to reduce commitments so that you're not always pressed for time and hurried.

(5) Choose supportive friends.

So many women describe friends or neighbors who make them feel terrible by comparison – whose houses are immaculate, whose children are always clean, neat, and well-behaved. Don't put yourself in situations that will send you back to impossible expectations and negative comparisons.

(6) Build a support group for yourself.

One woman with ADD related that housework was such drudgery for her that she often couldn't bring herself to do it. One of her techniques, however, was to invite a friend, who shared similar tendencies, to keep her company while she completed some particularly odious task.

(7) Build in "time-outs" daily.

Time-outs are essential when you have ADD and are raising children. It's easy to not find time for time-outs, though, because they require planning. Make them routine so that you don't have to keep planning and juggling. For example, ask your husband to commit to two blocks of time each weekend when he will take the kids away from the house without you, or arrange for a regular baby-sitter several times a week.

(8) Don't place yourself in burn-out.

One mother with ADD, who is doing a great job of parenting her two children who also have ADD, is able to recognize her limitations. With two such challenging children, she arranges for a month-long, summer sleep-away camp each summer. She also arranges for each child to visit their grandparents one at a time. This allows her to spend time with each son without him having to compete with his brother.

(9) Eliminate and delegate.

Look at things that you require of yourself at home. Can some of these things be eliminated? Can you afford to hire someone to do some of them?

(10) Learn child behavior management techniques.

On the outside looking in, it may be easy for other parents to judge you if your children misbehave. What any parent of a child with ADD knows is that they don't respond to the usual admonishments and limits the way other children do. You have a super-challenging job. Get the best training you can find. There are excellent books on behavior management techniques for children with ADD.

(11) Get help for PMS or Menopausal Symptoms.

These symptoms are likely to be more severe in women with ADD than they may be in other women. Managing the destabilizing effect of your hormonal fluctuations is a critical part of managing your ADD.

(12) Focus more on the things you love.

There are many aspects of keeping a house and raising children that are rewarding and creative. Look for positive experiences to share with your children.

Women with ADD need to understand and accept themselves. They need to quit blaming themselves for not meeting the expected demands of two of life's most "ADD-unfriendly" jobs: that of housewife and mother. They also need the understanding and acceptance of their husbands, their families, and their friends. These are women who are struggling valiantly against demands that are difficult, if not impossible, to meet. Instead of measuring success in terms of clean dishes and folded laundry, women with ADD must learn to celebrate their gifts – their warmth, their creativity, their humor, their sensitivity, and their spirit – and to look for others who can appreciate the best in them as well.

This article, which appeared in the Spring 1996 issue of ATTENTION! *is adapted from* Adventures in Fast Forward, *by Kathleen G. Nadeau, a book on life, love and work for adults with ADD, which was published by Brunner/Mazel.*

Kathleen G. Nadeau, Ph.D. is Director of Chesapeake Psychological Services of Maryland, a private clinic that specializes in diagnosing and treating adolescents and adults with ADD. She is the editor of A Comprehensive Guide to Attention Deficit Disorder in Adults: Research, Diagnosis, and Treatment, *the first guide for professionals on adults with ADD and is the author of several books on ADD.*

ADD Research:
An Interview with
Russell A. Barkley, Ph.D.

(excerpted)

Russell A. Barkley, Ph.D. is a leading researcher in the field of ADD. In the following article, he discusses research he and his colleagues at the University of Massachusetts Medical Center are currently pursuing.

Here at the Medical Center, there are five avenues of research that we are pursuing at the moment – four of which are federally-funded initiatives and a fifth, which we are not receiving funding for.

The first and the longest running project is taking place in Milwaukee, Wisconsin, but is coordinated through the University of Massachusetts. This study has been going on for several years. Mary Ellen Fisher (the Medical College of Wisconsin) and I have been following a large group of hyperactive children and a comparison group of children. We have been tracking these individuals since I first saw them, when they were between five and nine-years-of-age. They are now in their mid-twenties. We recently finished bringing them back in for their young adult evaluation. We bring them back for evaluations roughly every five years.

Much of the information we have learned so far corroborates other follow-up studies, showing higher risks for educational problems, higher risks for conduct problems, and some delinquency. Difficulties with education, employment, and interpersonal functions are the three areas that seem to show widespread similarities with other findings. This study has also uncovered some additional risks that other studies really had not focused on.

One, for example, is in the area of medical risks, which I alluded to in my CH.A.D.D. presentation in 1995. This area explores the lifestyles that these individuals are leading their lack of concern for health-related behavior, such as diet, exercise and so forth; and the fact that they are smoking and drinking more than our control group. These factors lead us to believe that they are placing themselves at greater risk for cardiovascular disease as they get into later life. Also, their general risk-taking behavior puts them at greater risk for accidents. We have established higher incidence of motor vehicle accidents, speeding, and other areas as being linked to this group.

A second area of the medical risk category that we studied is the rather heedless sexual conduct of our subjects that leads them to have more partners than our control group has had. Though the rates of intercourse are actually the same for the AD/HD group and the control group, those in the AD/HD group have more partners and have significantly more unprotected sexual relations. As a result, over half of the AD/HD group have had themselves tested for HIV. Fortunately, none of them have tested positive. About 25 to 30 percent of them, however, have already had a sexually-transmitted disease for which they have sought treatment.

Also indicating this rather high-risk sexual lifestyle is the fact that, out of forty-two births that occurred in the two groups, forty-one were born to the AD/HD group. While the control group is behaving like the general U. S. population and are waiting to have their children until their later twenties or even early thirties, individuals in the AD/HD group are conceiving children while they are still quite young – in their late teens to early twenties which is about six years ahead of the control group. About 54 percent of the AD/HD group who have had children do not have custody of their children.

Another area we are studying is the driving ability of young adults with AD/HD. We are using a variety of tactics to measure driving ability – reviewing driving records, interviewing the individuals regarding their driving history, obtaining rating scales on their safety and driving behavior from parents and others who have driven with them, and conducting computer-generated driving simulations. So far, we are corroborating our earlier findings, which were that the individuals with AD/HD are in a high-risk category. They speed more and pay attention and obey the laws less; they are more erratic in their steering and braking; and they are not able to operate the motor vehicle as consistently as individuals who do not have AD/HD. Generally, those with AD/HD are not very good drivers. It has nothing to do with knowledge – they know how to drive a car and they know the rules – they simply do not know how to apply these rules when they get out on the road. By conducting studies like this one, we may be able to identify these high-risk drivers early, get them help, and forewarn their families....

What that gives us is a comparison of children who get the standard kindergarten, children who get the standard kindergarten plus parent training, and children who get our kindergarten program but no parent training. The program lasts for one year. Then we follow the children for two years after they leave the program to determine whether the program has reduced their educational and/or social risks. This process has not been completed, so the results are not yet available.

A fourth project we are involved with tests different family therapies for families with teenagers who have AD/HD in which there is a great deal of conflict. We are actually testing two different family programs: one is a program designed by Dr. Arthur Robin that focuses on problem-solving, communication skills, and changing belief systems; and the other combines Dr. Robin's program with behavior modification training for parents.

Finally, we are conducting some studies on my theory of AD/HD, particularly with regard to sense of time. To conduct these studies, we are using some very simple tests of time estimation and time production. What we are finding so far is that individuals with AD/HD over-estimate the time interval and under-produce it, which tells us that they are perceiving time as moving more slowly than it really does. There are at least two predictions that can be made as a result of these findings. The first is that individuals with AD/HD are always going to be late. For example, if a teacher gives a child twenty minutes to finish his assignment in class, he won't finish it on time because to him, twenty minutes is moving more slowly than it actually is – he thinks he has more time than he does. Therefore, not being punctual, not meeting deadlines, and that sort of thing all would be predicted for someone whose sense of time is not parallel to real time.

The second prediction is that individuals with AD/HD will get very impatient if they are asked to wait because they will sense that the waiting period lasts longer than it actually does. It can be expected, then, that adults with AD/HD may run red lights and drive on the shoulder of the road to get around a delay in traffic, and children with AD/HD may elbow their way to the front of the lunch line and yammer at their teacher, "I'm hungry let's get moving," in an effort to terminate the waiting interval.

I believe the field of ADD research is moving toward several areas. The first of those areas is neuro-imaging and other studies of brain function. As the technology has leap-frogged ahead here to allow us to look at the brain and brain function, I think that we are going to start seeing more studies like Dr. Judy Rapoport's brain imaging study and studies that not only show us the structure of the brain in very fine-grained detail, but also the function of the brain, much like Dr. Alan Zametkin's early studies have done. I believe we will see more sophisticated measures, such as this new functional MRI procedure, which is as good or better than PET scans and does not carry some of the risks that the PET does. I think these will help us to more clearly document the neuro-behavioral nature of AD/HD.

The second area is behavioral genetics. We have recently seen three separate reports of possible genes linked to AD/HD. I see this doing several things. The first is that it would certainly allow us to quickly develop a genetic test for the disorder. That would help for diagnostic purposes. We would no longer just be relying on behavior but would actually have a genetic marker that would help us. Secondly, it also may help us break down the disorder into more homogeneous subgroups; right now, we treat AD/HD as one large group. Third, I think, if we can identify the gene or the genes, we can learn what those genes do in the brain. If we could determine what gene is involved with AD/HD, we could actually develop medications that would very explicitly target that function in the nerve cells. Additionally, we will be able to learn much more about which combinations of treatments do and do not benefit individuals with AD/HD. It will be nice to know which of these treatments are really worthwhile, and which are not.

Finally, research has led to the development of several theories on AD/HD. It is encouraging to see this development as it marks a sign of scientific progress. A mature science is a theory-driven science.

This article first appeared in the Summer 1996 issue of ATTENTION!

Adults with AD/HD and the Driving Performance of Adolescents with AD/HD: An Interview with Kevin Murphy, Ph.D.

Kevin Murphy, Ph.D. is Chief of the Adult AD/HD Clinic at the University of Massachusetts Medical Center and one of the leading researchers in the field of ADD. Dr. Murphy and his associates are working on two exciting pieces of research In the following article, he discusses the focus of this research and what the results may be able to tell us.

At present, my colleagues and I are concentrating on two areas of research, one focusing on AD/HD in adults and the other on the motor vehicle driving habits of adolescents with AD/HD.

Through a three year grant from the National Institute of Mental Health (NIMH), our study on AD/HD in adults began with data collection during the summer of 1997, and we hope to have preliminary information available shortly after. This is very exciting because up until now, there has been little grant money allotted to studying this important aspect of the disorder. The purpose of the study is primarily to determine the nature of adult AD/HD symptoms. In particular, we have focused on determining if there is a more appropriate group of symptoms for adults with AD/HD than what is currently listed in *DSM-IV*, since criteria for these symptoms are based solely on field-tests of children and adolescents. Secondly, we will attempt to determine the value of "age of onset criteria." In other words, we hope to uncover any differences there may be between adult patients who reported symptoms in childhood with those who reported symptoms in adolescence or later in life. The answers will hopefully tell us how important the criteria of "age seven" is in diagnosing an adult with AD/HD. Third, we hope to bring to light the different types of outcomes and/or courses of the disorder in adults. Specifically, we are examining any adaptive impairments in the lives of adults with AD/HD, such as their educational attainment, marital satisfaction, work performance, and parenting stress/effectiveness.

Another area that is being explored in the course of this study is the utility of specific laboratory assessment measures in the diagnosis of AD/HD in adults. Certain tests that analyze the neuropsychological aspects, time concept, working memory, creativity, and sustained attention and distractibility are routinely given to children and adolescence who are tested for AD/HD. We hope to determine whether or not these same measures are helpful in the diagnostic process of adults. We are also focusing on gender differences, AD/HD and comorbidity, and skills such as organizational ability, time management, behavioral inhibition, and perception of time.

The second project we are working on is the study of motor vehicle driving habits of young adults with AD/HD. Data has been collected, and we are currently analyzing results. The main thrust of this study is to uncover differences in the driving knowledge and performance of young adults with AD/HD as compared with young adults who do not have the disorder. Data on this study has been collected from four primary sources: self report/rating of participants, rating by parents of participants, laboratory assessments, and official driving records. Driving performance in the context of this study is based on several factors, including the number of speeding tickets, accidents, and license suspensions and the severity of accidents. We are also looking at laboratory measures on reaction time and the ability to steer properly. Taking this research one step further, by obtaining driving records from the Motor Vehicle Administration, we will be able to correlate the accuracy between the self report and actual driving history of participants. We also hope to determine whether AD/HD is, itself, responsible for poor driving outcomes or whether a comorbid condition, such as substance abuse, may be a factor.

The implications of our findings in this study will be of particular interest to parents of adolescents with AD/HD as they are often concerned about insurance rates, safety issues, and discrimination. The real purpose here is to raise the level of consciousness about the risk factors associated with this population and offer possible interventions that can help in minimizing the risk and help prevent tragedy from occurring.

This article first appeared in the Summer 1997 issue of ATTENTION!

Parenting a Child with AD/HD: Hope and Help for the Harried and Hassled

by Barbara D. Ingersoll, Ph.D.

THE SCOPE OF THE PROBLEM

Since AD/HD has a strong genetic component, most children with AD/HD have at least one parent who also has AD/HD. In many cases, both parents have AD/HD because people tend to select mates who are like themselves – a phenomenon known technically as "assortative mating." Of course, this increases the likelihood that their children will have AD/HD since, as a friend of mine once observed, "When you breed Great Danes, you don't get Chihuahuas."

What does it mean to be the parent of a child with AD/HD when you, yourself, have AD/HD? Parenting is a complex and challenging job, even under the best of circumstances. It's safe to say that anything that adds an additional layer of complexity makes the job just that much more challenging. And, in your case, you've got at least a double layer of complexity – your child's AD/HD and your own. In the case of families in which both parents have AD/HD, the problems expand exponentially.

GETTING THE HELP YOU NEED

If you live in a multi-AD/HD family, what can you do? Like most thoughtful, intelligent parents today, you might begin by turning to mental health professionals who have some expertise in the area of AD/HD, and you might bone up on your reading on the subject.

What kind of advice are you likely to get? To answer this question, I turned to the manuscript of my most recent book (Ingersoll, 1997) and reviewed the recommendations I offered parents. What follows is a series of excerpted recommendations, along with my comments for parents who, themselves, have AD/HD.

Recommendation I: Help Your Child Organize Himself. Because children with AD/HD tend to be unorganized, they need all the help they can get to keep themselves and their belongings in order.

Comment for Parents: You already know that you're going to have difficulty in this arena, don't you?

Proposed Action: Clean out the clutter in your child's room. The more furniture, toys, and books in the room, the harder it is to clean. It's harder, too, to find the things your child needs when he needs them.

Comment for Parents: Oh, sure. You haven't seen the surface of your kitchen table for six years and your desk looks like who-did-it-and-ran but you're supposed to organize that snake's nest your child calls his room?

Don't aim for perfection or you'll never get off square one. There is an easier way, although it certainly wouldn't meet with Martha Stewart's approval. Take several large plastic garbage bags to the child's room. Allow the child to fill one bag with things to be kept in the room (clothes are not included). Place all other items into bags and immediately put the bags into whatever passes for a storage area in your house.

You might even use this as an opportunity to help your child sort items to give to less fortunate children. If you elect to do this, look up the telephone number of your favorite charity, write it down, and tape it to the appropriate bag. Carry the filled bag directly to the nearest telephone and make arrangements for pick up. Note: Do **not** leave the bag in your child's room or it will remain there until he or she leaves for college.

Proposed Action: Wardrobes should be simplified: many children have a favorite outfit or two that they virtually live in. Instead of scrambling frantically to wash the same shirt three times a week or dealing with wails of dismay when it's in the laundry, buy duplicates of favorite items of clothing.

Comment for Parents: This is a suggestion that

you *can* implement. Parents who are particularly disorganized can also avoid some of the morning chaos by insisting that the child shower and shampoo at night and allowing the child to sleep in his underwear – or even in his clothes for the next day. In this day of sweats and baggy jeans, who's going to notice?

Proposed Action: Spell out all expectations. Have your child make a chart and put it on the bathroom door to remind her that she needs to brush her teeth every morning and that taking a shower means using soap, as well as shampoo. You'll still have to check on her, but the charts will help a lot.

Recommendation II: Set Priorities and Keep Things in Perspective. Decide what's important and what doesn't really matter. Then act accordingly.

Comment for Parents: Hoo-ha! If there is one thing adults with AD/HD have difficulty doing, it is setting and adhering to priorities.

Proposed Action: If you and your child seem to lock horns over every little thing, stand back and consider what's really important in terms of the child's health, safety, and welfare. Hold your ground on those issues but be prepared to give ground on little things, like whether or not he folds his laundry before he puts it in the drawer: you might like a tidy drawer, with all underwear neatly folded, but your child probably couldn't care less. Remember, in all of recorded history, there is not a single known case of death due to wearing unfolded underwear.

Comment to Parents: Holidays can be difficult for children with AD/HD because they respond to the excitement around them and spiral out of control. Take a long, hard look at what is important to you about the holidays and then pare things down. If you wear yourself out with cooking, baking, decorating, and shopping, you won't have any patience left to deal with your child with AD/HD.

Proposed Action: Accept the fact that holidays at your house will be hectic, chaotic, and generally crazy. (They are at your neighbor's house, too, even though she has no children, a full-time housekeeper, and an apparently unlimited budget. You just aren't privy to the behind-the-scenes madness because she is slicker than you are at hiding the evidence.)

Begin by throwing out the holiday issues of all house-and-home type magazines: it's clear that the people who write these articles are all delusional. Then, pick **one thing** you really want to accomplish and pare it down to the bare bones so you can actually accomplish it. If you truly love to bake but can't stand the kids in the kitchen while you work, bribe somebody to take the kids to Funland for the day. If you genuinely want to share the baking with the children, THINK SMALL. Cookies? A big batch of chocolate chip

cookies is simple to prepare. But fourteen varieties of cookies, including several kinds of hand-decorated sugar cookies? Hello???

If you are a wrapping nut, wrap one present for each family member in the way you like to wrap packages, with neatly taped edges, fancy bows, and color-coordinated gift tags. The rest of the gifts should be wrapped in minimalist fashion – also known as "wham-bam-thank-you m'am" – or you might invest in a collection of pretty gift bags that are a godsend for the all-thumbs set. (You did keep the gift list down to just three or so per person, didn't you?)

Comment for Parents: Aren't you tired of those telephone calls from the teacher on days when you forget to give your child his medication in the morning?

Proposed Action: Because medication is often an important part of treatment for so many people with AD/HD, it's vital that you devise a system for ensuring that your child take his medication as prescribed. Mary Richard, past president of CH.A.D.D., points out that keeping medications straight is even more complicated when there are several family members who take medication. She suggests investing in unit dosage containers that hold up to four doses of medication per day and can be organized once a week for each person. You'll also know at a glance if any doses have been forgotten.

Recommendation III: Recognize and Respect Your Child's Limits. Because AD/HD is an invisible handicap, parents often forget that their child may have difficulty with tasks and responsibilities that others their age have mastered. If you find yourself constantly frustrated and disappointed with your child, it may be a red flag that you are overestimating his abilities and setting yourself up for disappointment.

Comment for Parents: It may also be a red flag indicating that your own AD/HD is not yet under good control. Poor frustration tolerance is a hallmark of AD/HD, as we all know.

Proposed Action: Think ahead in situations in which your child might have particular problems, and don't put him in a position of assured failure. If Aunt Ethel has dozens of knickknacks all over the house and won't put them out of reach when you visit, don't visit. If birthday parties and large family gatherings bring out the worst in your child, plan to arrive late and leave early. In between, watch for signs that the child is becoming overstimulated and be prepared to remove him before trouble starts.

Comment for Parents: You can do this. Even when you can't plan ahead, if the situation turns bad, get out before it turns into a disaster. Don't worry about social graces: when it's a problem situation, they'll probably be relieved to see you go.

Proposed Action: Make your expectations fit the child, not the other way around. Stick with the reality of what your child is able to do, and work from there. For example, even if other children your child's age can dress themselves in the morning, your child may not be able to do this without help. Either recognize this and adjust your morning schedule so you can provide this help, or be prepared for a nasty scene every morning – the choice is yours.

Comment for Parents: The most important thing is devising an arrangement that takes your needs and those of your child into consideration. Hate fixing lunches each morning? Fine – give the child lunch money or buy those snack-pack lunches in bulk. For kids who can't get organized in the morning without a valet, a maid, and a personal secretary, see tips about clothing (above) or keep a paper bag packed with a change of clothes and let the child dress in the car on the way to school in an emergency. The one thing you really should locate the night before, however, is the child's shoes: no matter how steely your resolve, it's pretty hard to make a kid leave the house barefoot in the winter!

Recommendation IV: Boost Your Child's Self Esteem. The term "self-esteem" seems on the way to becoming another buzz-word in the lexicon of American parents. It's too bad, because youngsters with AD/HD need all the help they can get in this department.

Comment for Parents: If you've had a lifetime of negative feedback about your own problems with AD/HD, you know what low self-esteem feels like.

Proposed Action: Remember to compliment your child as often as you can. This is especially important for children with AD/HD because they usually receive so many negative comments and so few compliments. Praise doesn't have to be lavish: a simple "Thanks" and a smile or a hug can be more powerful than you know.

Comment for Parents: You can do this one, too. Put ten pennies in one pocket and, for each time you compliment the child, transfer a penny to the other pocket. The catch is that you can't make a critical comment until after you've transferred all ten pennies to the other pocket. Think it's easy? Try it!

Proposed Action: Find and foster any activity in which your child excels, such as sports, music, or art. Because of their energy and intensity, many youngsters with AD/HD have a flair for the dramatic arts and find satisfaction and success in little theater groups and acting classes. Get the child involved in youth activities at

your church or synagogue where supportive people will express appreciation for the child's contributions.

Comment for Parents: Don't let yourself get carried away. Take a long, hard look at your schedule: if Jason's karate class is scheduled for 6:00 p.m., common sense dictates that you shouldn't also enroll Jessica in a gymnastics class that meets at 7:00 p.m. the same day.

TAKING IT ALL WITH A GRAIN OF SALT

As you can see, families with AD/HD must be judicious in the way they attempt to implement advice from "the pros." Twenty years later, I still cringe in embarrassment when I think of the hideously complex behavior management programs I enthusiastically foisted on parents of children with AD/HD, assuring them that the child's behavior would improve remarkably if they would just stick to the plan. Of course, it never occurred to me that these were busy parents with jobs and other family obligations who lacked my small army of medical students, interns, and residents to implement my carefully drafted plans. (To all those parents, wherever you are today, I apologize.)

Instead of trying to follow programs and recommendations that just won't work for you, think of these recommendations as a kind of smorgasbord or Chinese menu – much like the broad array of suggestions and tips that Sandra Rief lays out for teachers in her wonderful book *How to Reach and Teach ADD/AD/HD Children*. Those of you who have read this book know that Ms. Rief doesn't advocate a single solution to a problem: rather, she provides a potpourri of ideas from which teachers can select those best suited to their own style and temperament.

THE UP-SIDE

Is there an up-side to having a child with AD/HD? There certainly is, as many parents have already discovered.

These children, while often maddening in the extreme, are also an endless source of delight to parents who can appreciate a child whose imagination isn't limited to coloring within the lines. Parents who themselves have boundless energy and love to cram weekends and holidays with fun activities would be bored silly with a quiet little couch-potato.

Is there an up-side to being an adult with AD/HD who has a child with AD/HD? From what I've observed, the answer is also "Yes." In so many of the multi-AD/HD families with whom I've worked, I've observed that there's a special kind of bonding that often takes place between these parents and their children. Parents, knowing their own quirks, can be a little more tolerant when they see the same quirks in their children. And children, in turn, can look at a parent who has turned out pretty well overall and feel optimistic about their own future. Could we give our children a better gift?

Barbara D. Ingersoll, Ph.D. is a clinical psychologist who has worked with children and families for more than twenty-five years, Clinical Director of Montgomery Child and Family Health Services in Bethesda, MD, and the author of several books.

A Touch of Real Life

Attention Deficit Disorder is finally being recognized as more than a childhood disorder. For those of us dealing with this disorder, we can only say, "It is about time." After a lifetime of asking ourselves why being organized was almost impossible, forgetfulness was a natural part of each day, and education often required monumental effort, we finally have an explanation. You notice I didn't say excuse, but, rather, an explanation – an explanation that helps us to understand our behaviors and develop positive coping skills to deal with life's challenges.

While we do have more information than was available a few short years ago, there is also much we do not know about adults with ADD. In addition, we are being bombarded almost daily by advertisements for various treatments which claim to be the cure for ADD. Unfortunately, the list of benefit claims may also include a laundry list of other nagging physical ailments from headaches to foot pain. In this "buyer beware" world we live in, it is important for each of us to become knowledgeable about ourselves as individuals and the disorder that sometimes challenges us.

One of the most helpful things to me personally as an adult with ADD is the sharing of experiences with others like myself. While others around me consider time management, for instance, to be an inherent skill that everyone is born with (therefore either a non-issue or a matter of choice), other adults who have ADD understand what a significant challenge time management can present.

Hearing from others helps me to focus on my positive attributes, learn new strategies, feel comfortable with the fact that I am simply "differently-abled," and, most importantly, know that I am not alone.

Special thanks to those individuals who were willing to share their personal experiences in this book. We hope you will find them insightful as you travel on your own journey in search of knowledge and understanding.

Sheila Anderson
National President, CH.A.D.D.

MOVING BEYOND BAD CHOICES

My life was pretty much a mystery until I found out I had ADD. I've always been forgetful, done the wrong thing, and been at the wrong place at the wrong time. Unfortunately, I think that having ADD has also caused me to make some bad decisions. I've had two unsuccessful marriages, both with abusive husbands. I think I may have sought out this type of man because, self-consciously, I thought I deserved to be treated badly because of my inadequacies. My second husband actually thought that my being late and disorganized was passive-aggressive behavior I deliberately used to annoy him. I couldn't convince him that I simply couldn't help it. When I found out I had ADD,

it was really a blessing; I finally realized that I wasn't this horrible person I always thought I had been.

The biggest challenge I face on a daily basis is dealing with my unrealistic concept of time. I often compare myself to Alice in the fairy tale Alice in Wonderland. Alice is supposed to be following the White Rabbit who has the clock, but instead, she gets distracted and drifts off into the Mad Hatter's Tea Party, etc. and gets herself into trouble. That's the way my entire life has been; I am constantly getting distracted and drifting off. Even though I have timers all over the house to remind me of things I have to do and appointments to keep, my mind still takes off in another direction. Having an eight-year-old son and trying to keep track of his schedule and activities makes things even more difficult and takes a lot of energy.

My faith and having a sense of humor have helped me keep my life in perspective. I now refer to myself as "Better Late-Than-Never Murphy," realizing that it might take me longer than it takes others to complete a task, but I'll eventually get to it."

– Dorothy Murphy, Pittsburgh, PA

A SCHOOL PRINCIPAL STRUGGLES WITH SUCCESS

Growing up, I never had problems socially. I always had lots of friends and was involved in many activities, but I was easily distracted and would get off task easily. I found school very boring; it took all I had to sit there and not fall asleep, so I used to talk a lot, which frequently got me into trouble.

Nonetheless, I did quite well in school, graduating as valedictorian from high school and receiving a Master's Degree in Education. (I've completed everything for my doctorate except my dissertation. For all of the hours I've put in, I should have accomplished more than I have, but my distractibility and other symptoms of ADD have made it very difficult.) I think everyone just assumes that I have confidence in myself because of my successes, but I've actually always felt inadequate and unable to do all the things I think I'm capable of doing. This is the problem I struggle with the most, especially when it comes to my career. As a school principal, my reviews have always been good, but I've never felt on top of things and I don't feel I've reached my potential. I'm always running behind and I'm constantly nervous that I'll be unable to meet deadlines. I'm sure that it appears to others that I'm procrastinating or being lazy, but the truth is, I'm constantly working; I simply can't ever seem to do all that I have to. Most of the time, I feel as if I'm peddling a stationary bike, and I feel frustrated that I can't share my challenges with my supervisor."

I don't think many people know the real me because I rarely express my true opinions to others. I actually think much differently than most people, but I can't articulate my opinions in a way that they will understand, so I've learned to say what's appropriate and do what's expected of me.

– Carolyn O., Chicago, IL

DIVORCED AND UNEMPLOYED – ONE MAN'S HARD JOURNEY

I have had classic symptoms of ADD all of my life, but I was only diagnosed a few years ago.

Unfortunately, it was too late to save a twenty-three-year marriage, which fell apart primarily because of my addictive behavior. I truly believe that if I had been diagnosed ten years ago and received proper treatment, my marriage would still be intact today. I also believe my ADD symptoms have caused serious career challenges. I was an executive with a non-profit economic development group, but because of procrastination and disorganization, I was unable to maintain that position. For the past two years, I have been unemployed, so the price I've paid for having undiagnosed and untreated ADD has been very high.

ADD has presented many challenges in my life, but the most difficult for me has been structuring my time appropriately. I have a tendency to overattend to things I enjoy doing and completely avoid those things I don't like. For example, I spend much of my time and energy focusing on my current hobby, motorcycles I subscribe to just about every magazine about motorcycles there is and serve as the president of a local motorcycle group. On the other hand, when it comes to doing bills, I have no motivation whatsoever. It doesn't even matter how much money I have in the bank; I still hate to do the bills and I frequently receive past due notices because I just can't seem to get them together and pay them on time.

Simply because I know I have ADD doesn't make it easier, but at least I have become educated about the disorder and am finally learning how to deal with it effectively.

– Jeff Dunkle, Pittsburgh, PA

WHEN CHILDREN CAN'T FIND THEIR "ISLANDS OF COMPETENCE..."

I first thought I might have ADD when I saw my own behavior as a child in my two younger children, who were both diagnosed with the disorder in 1984. I assumed I had the disorder, but it wasn't for a number of years that the true impact of having ADD became clear. One day when I was on the Internet, I saw a list of typical adult ADD symptoms. Like a spiritual awakening, it hit me: there I was. As I started to look back over the years, I sat there and cried because I was beginning to realize how the disorder had affected my life.

The challenges I face run the gamut of all the complaints a person with ADD would have, but the one that is certainly most dominant is the issue of depression. It seems that depression co-exists with ADD – I don't know which came first, but it has affected me more than I ever really knew, and it gets worse the older I get. I believe it happened to me because I've experienced blocked goals and desires, and I've always been told "no you can't" or "you're not good enough" or "you can do better." I've also never seemed to fit in anywhere. I'm accepted by people I don't necessarily feel I have much in common with, but rejected by the people I have a high regard for and want to get to know, mainly because I miss important social cues. That's very frustrating for me.

Learning about the disorder has been the biggest help to me. I'm very thankful that my sons have information about their disorder at a young age so they'll have the opportunity to structure their lives accordingly. I know if I had had the same opportunity years ago, I probably would not have struggled as much as I have.

— *William Keller, Pittsburgh, PA*

CH.A.D.D.® Announces the
Second In Its "Strategies for Success" Series

ADD and Adults: Strategies for Success from CH.A.D.D.

You know how overwhelming ADD can be at times, how this "non-visible" disorder impacts every aspect of your life. From managing your time, to succeeding in the workplace, to navigating relationships, ADD presents unique challenges. Identify the strategies that work for you, and the energy and creativity that are hallmarks of ADD can help you achieve your potential. Fail to do so… well, you know how challenging life can be!

Now, for the first time from CH.A.D.D., the nation's preeminent organization working to improve the lives of individuals with ADD, comes the book you need. **ADD and Adults: Strategies for Success from CH.A.D.D.** *gives you practical advice on everything from finding the right clinician, to managing anger, to understanding your legal rights. – all from the nation's leading experts, including:*

• Russell Barkley, Ph.D. • Timothy Wilens, M.D. • Patricia Latham, J.D.

• Edward Hallowell, M.D. • MaryBeth Kravets, M.A., Counseling/College Consultant

• and more!

Order THIS book today. For yourself or somebody in your life
who is living with this disorder.

Regular Orders: $16.00 per Book + $2.75 Shipping and Handling
Bulk Pricing: $280.00 (Case of 20) + $15.00 Shipping and Handling

PLEASE SHIP THE FOLLOWING:

Regular Orders:
_____ Copies @ $18.75 each
(includes shipping) $_____.___

10% Member Discount:
_____ Copies @ $17.15 each $_____.___
($14.40/book + $2.75 shipping)

Bulk Orders:
_____ Cases @ $295.00 $_____.___
(includes shipping)
CASE PURCHASES REFLECT BULK DISCOUNT:
ADDITIONAL DISCOUNT NOT APPLICABLE

Florida residents add 6% sales tax $_____.___

International Orders add
shipping & handling; $10/book
$49/case $_____.___

TOTAL $ _____.___

Please provide complete shipping and payment information:

Name_____

Mailing Address:_____

City/State/Zip: _____

Telephone _____ Fax _____

Check all that apply:

☐ Parent of child with ADD   ☐ Educator   ☐ Health Care Professional   ☐ Other

PAYMENT (SPECIFY BELOW)
☐ Check Enclosed
☐ Credit Card (indicate card):   ☐ VISA   ☐ MasterCard   ☐ American Express

Name on card _____

Card Number _____ Expiration Date _____

Signature_____

All funds must be in U.S. dollars.
Please return this form wtih your remittance to:
CHILDREN AND ADULTS WITH ATTENTION DEFICIT DISORDERS
499 N.W. 70th AVENUE, SUITE 101
PLANTATION, FL 33317
Phone 954-587-3700 • Fax 954-587-4599

ADD and Adolescence:
Strategies for Success from CH.A.D.D.

Are you the parent of a teen or pre-teen who has ADD? A clinician or educator working with teenagers? If so, *ADD and Adolescence: Strategies for Success from CH.A.D.D.* is **THE** one book you and your teenager shouldn't be without.

This valuable resource is dedicated to helping teenagers with ADD and their parents address the many new challenges they are now facing, such as managing the increased workload of high school and building strong relationships with peers.

If you've been looking for sound advice and practical solutions, it's all here in one place! Don't delay. Order your copy of *ADD and Adolescence: Strategies for Success from CH.A.D.D.* right away.

Please provide complete shipping and payment information:

Name _____

Mailing Address _____

City _____ State _____ Zip _____

Telephone _____/_____ FAX number _____/_____

CHECK ALL THAT APPLY:

❑ Parent of child with ADD   ❑ Educator   ❑ Health Care Professional   ❑ Other

---

REGULAR ORDERS: $15.00 PER BOOK + $2.75 SHIPPING AND HANDLING
BULK PRICING: $260.00 (CASE OF 20) + $15.00 SHIPPING AND HANDLING

PLEASE SHIP THE FOLLOWING:

Regular Orders:

_____ Copies @ $17.75 each
(includes shipping) $_____.___

10% Member Discount:

_____ Copies @ $13.50 each $_____.___
($13.50/BOOK + $2.75 SHIPPING)

Bulk Orders:

_____ Cases @ $275.00
(includes shipping) $_____.___
CASE PURCHASES REFLECT
BULK DISCOUNT; ADDITIONAL
DISCOUNT NOT APPLICABLE

Florida residents
add 6% sales tax $_____.___

International Orders
add shipping & handling:
$10 per book; $49 per case $_____.___

TOTAL $ _____.___

PAYMENT (SPECIFY BELOW)

❑ Check Enclosed   ❑ VISA
❑ Credit Card   ❑ MasterCard
 (as indicated at right)   ❑ American Express

Name on card _____

Card # _____

Expiration Date _____

Signature _____

All funds must be in U.S. dollars.

Please return this form with your remittance to:

CHILDREN AND ADULTS WITH
ATTENTION DEFICIT DISORDERS
499 N.W. 70TH AVENUE, SUITE 101
PLANTATION, FL 33317

phone 954.587.3700 • *fax 954.587.4599*

CH.A.D.D. SUCCESS SIGN-UP

☐ **Yes** I want to succeed with CH.A.D.D.!

10th ANNIVERSARY
CH.A.D.D.®
1987 – 1997

Name _____

Occupation _____

Organization _____
(If organizational membership)

Address _____

City _____

State _____ Zip _____

Telephone:
Day _____

Evening _____

Fax number _____

☐ New Member   ☐ Renewal Membership

Regular Membership

☐ $35 family or educator membership

☐ $65 health care professional membership

☐ $100 individual international membership (outside of U.S. and Canada)

Organizational Membership

☐ $200 organizational membership

☐ $400 international organizational membership (outside of U.S. and Canada)

Payment

☐ Check   ☐ MasterCard   ☐ VISA   ☐ American Express

Name on Card _____   Card Number _____

Expiration Date _____   Signature _____

Chapter Affiliation _____

Detach and mail to:
Children and Adults with Attention Deficit Disorders
499 N.W. 70 Avenue • Suite 101 • Plantation, FL 33317

Questions or further information? Call CH.A.D.D. at 954-587-3700

(shipping and handling included in membership fee; all funds submitted must be in U.S. dollars)

the media of mass communication

..... **fifth edition**

John Vivian

WINONA STATE UNIVERSITY

Allyn and Bacon

BOSTON LONDON TORONTO SYDNEY TOKYO SINGAPORE

to Harold Vivian, my father,

who sparked my curiosity about the mass media at age
five by asking what was black and white and read all over.

and

to Elaine Vivian, my mother,

who nurtured this curiosity by keeping the house stocked
with books, magazines and reading material of every sort.

Vice President, Editor in Chief: Paul A. Smith
Series Editor: Karon Bowers
Developmental Editor: Carol Alper
Editorial Assistant: Leila Scott
Marketing Manager: Susan E. Ogar
Editorial-Production Administrator: Annette Joseph
Editorial-Production Service: Deborah Schneck
Copyeditor: Lehr Editorial Services
Composition and Prepress Buyer: Linda Cox
Photo Researcher: Sue C. Howard
Manufacturing Buyer: Megan Cochran
Cover Administrator: Linda Knowles
Text Designer: Deborah Schneck
Cover Designer: Susan Paradise

Copyright © 1999, 1997, 1995, 1993, 1991 by Allyn & Bacon
A Viacom Company
160 Gould Street
Needham Heights, MA 02494

Internet: www.abacon.com

Between the time Website information is gathered and then
published, it is not unusual for some sites to have closed.
Also, the transcription of URLs can result in unintended
typographical errors. The publisher would appreciate notifi-
cation where these occur so that they may be corrected in
subsequent editions. Thank you.

Library of Congress Cataloging-in-Publication Data
Vivian, John
    The media of mass communication / John Vivian. —
5th ed.
        p.   cm.
    Includes bibliographical references and index.
    ISBN 0-205-28739-5 (alk. paper)
    1. Mass media.   I. Title.
    P90.V53   1998   98-28087
    302.23—dc21   CIP

Printed in the United States of America

10 9 8 7 6 5 4   VHP 03 02 01 00

contents

Preface   xiii

1 the mass media   3

Learning Goals	3

Chapter-Opening Vignette: Chris Berman   3

Importance of Mass Media   5
Pervasiveness, 5 · Information Source, 5 ·
Entertainment Source, 6 · Persuasion
Forum, 7 · Binding Influence, 7

Primary Mass Media   7
Print Media, 8 · Electronic Media, 8 · Chemical
Media, 8

Mass Media Models   10
Hot-Cool Model, 10 · Entertainment-Information
Model, 11 · Elitist-Populist Model, 12 ·
Push-Pull Model, 13

Economics of Mass Media   14
Economic Foundation, 14 · Economic
Imperative, 17 · Upside and Downside, 17

Media Demassification   18
Technology and Demassification, 18 · Effects of
Demassification, 18

Media Conglomeration   19
Media Ownership Consolidation, 19 · Media
Ownership Collaboration, 19 · Dubious Effects
of Conglomeration, 24 · Positive Effects of
Conglomeration, 26

Media Globalization   28
Transnational Ownership, 28 · Effects of
Globalization, 29

Media Melding   31
Digitalization, 31 · Intracorporate Synergy, 31

Chapter Wrap-Up   32
Questions for Review   32
Questions for Critical Thinking   32
For Further Learning   33
For Keeping Up to Date   33

BOXES
● *Media Abroad: Mass Media and National Development*   6
● *Media Timeline: Media Technology*   9
● *Media Databank: Media Costs*   15
● *Media People: Sumner Redstone*   22
● *Media Abroad: U.S. Global Players*   29
● *Media Abroad: Overseas Heavyweights*   30

2 books   35

Learning Goals   35

Chapter-Opening Vignette:
Johannes Gutenberg   35

Importance of Books   37
Books in Human History, 37 · Books in
National Development, 37

Defining the Book Business   39
Trade Books, 40 · Textbooks, 40

Innovations in Books   40
Paperbacks, 41 · Electronic Books, 41

Book Marketing   42
Bookstores, 42 · Direct Marketing, 44

Commercial Success   46
    Best-Sellers, 46 · Best-Seller Lists, 47 ·
    Mass Marketing, 48 · Subsidiary Rights, 49

Mass-Marketing Debate   50
    Blockbuster Authors, 50 · Populist versus
    Elitist Views, 52

Book Publishers   52
    Major Houses, 52 · Small Presses, 54 ·
    Vanity Presses, 54

U.S. Government Printing Office   55

Chapter Wrap-Up   55
Questions for Review   55
Questions for Critical Thinking   56
For Further Learning   56
For Keeping Up to Date   57

BOXES
○ *Media Timeline: Development of Books*   *36*
● *Media People: Learning on the Porch*   *38*
● *Media People: Michael Hart*   *42*
● *Media Databank: Book Censorship*   *43*
● *Media People: Blockbuster Authors*   *51*
● *Media Databank: Corporate Connections*   *53*

3 magazines   59

Learning Goals   59

Chapter-Opening Vignette: Bonnie Fuller   59

Influence of Magazines   61
    Contributing to Nationhood, 61 · National
    Advertising Medium, 62 · Massive Magazine
    Audience, 62

Magazines as Media Innovators   63
    Investigative Reporting, 63 · Personality
    Profiles, 65 · Photojournalism, 65

Consumer Magazines   66
    Circulation Leaders, 66 · Newsmagazines, 67 ·
    Newspaper Supplements, 70 · Women's
    Magazines, 70 · Men's Magazines, 72

Non-Newsrack Magazines   72
    Sponsored Magazines, 72 · Trade
    Journals, 73 · Criticism of Trade Magazines, 73

Magazine Demassification   74
    Heyday of Mass Magazines, 74 · Assault from

    Television, 76 · A Narrower Focus, 76 · Critics
    of Demassification, 77 · New Competition, 79 ·
    Web Magazines, 79

Chapter Wrap-Up   79
Questions for Review   80
Questions for Critical Thinking   80
For Further Learning   80
For Keeping Up to Date   81

BOXES
○ *Media Timeline: Development of the Magazine*   *61*
● *Media People: Margaret Bourke White*   *64*
● *Media Databank: Magazine Circulation*   *67*
● *Media People: DeWitt and Lila Wallace*   *68*
○ *Media Abroad: Reader's Digest in China*   *69*
● *Media People: Sara Josepha Hale*   *71*
● *Media People: Jann Wenner*   *75*

4 newspapers   83

Learning Goals   83

Chapter-Opening Vignette: Joseph Patterson   83

Importance of Newspapers   85
    Newspaper Industry Dimensions, 85 · Content
    Diversity and Depth, 86

Newspaper Chain Ownership   86
    Trend Toward Chains, 86 · Assessing Chain
    Ownership, 87

National Dailies   89
    Wall Street Journal, 90 · *USA Today*, 93 ·
    Christian Science Monitor, 95 · National
    Editions, 97

Hometown Newspapers   97
    Metropolitan Dailies, 97 · Hometown
    Dailies, 100

Challenges for Daily Newspapers   101
    Circulation Patterns, 101 · Advertising
    Patterns, 102 · Prospects for the Daily
    Press, 103 · Newspaper Web Sites, 104

Weekly Newspapers   105
    Community Weeklies, 105 · Shoppers, 106

Alternative and Minority Newspapers   106
    Counterculture Newspapers, 106 · Gay
    Newspapers, 107 · Black Newspapers, 107 ·
    Foreign-Language Newspapers, 108

Chapter Wrap-Up   109
Questions for Review   109
Questions for Critical Thinking   110
For Further Learning   110
For Keeping Up to Date   111

BOXES
● *Media Databank: Newspaper Chains*   88
● *Media Databank: Newsroom Salaries*   90
● *Media People: Allen Neuharth*   94
● *Media People: Mary Baker Eddy*   96
● *Media Timeline: Notable Contemporary Newspapers*   99
● *Media Databank: Daily Newspaper Circulation*   102

5 records 113

Learning Goals   113
Chapter-Opening Vignette: Bob and Jakob Dylan   113

Recorded Music as a Social Force   115
    Rallying Power, 115 · Leading and Reflecting
    Change, 116

Sound Recording Technology   117
    Thomas Edison's Phonograph, 117 · Electrical
    Recording, 118 · Vinyl and Microgrooves, 118 ·
    Stereo Innovation, 118 · Digital Technology, 119

Evolution of Music   120
    American Folk Music, 121 · Early Rock 'n' Roll, 121

Artistic Autonomy   123
    Predictable Music, 124 · Cultural
    Homogenization, 125 · Restructured Record
    Industry, 125 · Music Demassification, 127

Marketing Records   127
    Measuring Commercial Success, 128 · Radio
    Airplay, 128 · Payola, 129 · Music Videos, 129

Conglomeration in Record-Making   130
    Big Six, 131 · Indies, 131

Censorship and Recorded Music   132
    Objectionable Music, 132 · Record
    Labeling, 132 · Lyrics and Young People, 133

Heisting Music   134
    Home-Dubbing, 134 · Piracy, 134

Chapter Wrap-Up   135
Questions for Review   136
Questions for Critical Thinking   136

For Further Learning   137
For Keeping Up to Date   137

BOXES
● *Media Timeline: Development of Record Industry*   117
● *Media Databank: Plethora of Formats*   120
● *Media People: Alan Freed*   122
● *Media Abroad: Canada: CanCon Requirement*   126
● *Media Databank: Conglomeration and Globalization*   130
● *Media Databank: Megadeals*   131

6 movies 139

Learning Goals   139
Chapter-Opening Vignette: Steven Spielberg   139

Importance of Movies   141
    Overwhelming Experience, 141 · Hollywood's
    Cultural Influence, 141

Technical Heritage of Movies   142
    Adaptation from Photography, 142 · Adding
    Sound to Pictures, 144

Three Crises That Reshaped Hollywood   144
    The Hollywood 10, 144 · Court Bans on
    Vertical Integration, 146 · Challenge from
    Television, 147

Hollywood's Response to Television   147
    Technical Innovation, 147 · Content
    Innovation, 148

Melding of Movies and Television   150
    Reconciliation of Competing Industries, 150 ·
    First Runs and After-Markets, 151

Movie Exhibitors   151
    Early Exhibition Facilities, 151 · Multiscreen
    Theaters, 151 · Box-Office Income, 152

Movie Finances   153
    The Lesson of Intolerance, 153 · Financing
    Sources, 153 · Artistic versus Budget Issues, 156

Movie Censorship   159
    Morality as an Issue, 159 · Movies and
    Changing Mores, 160 · Current Movie Code, 160

Chapter Wrap-Up   161
Questions for Review   162
Questions for Critical Thinking   162
For Further Learning   162
For Keeping Up to Date   163

BOXES

- *Media Timeline: Movie Technology* 142
- *Media People: Robert Flaherty* 143
- *Media Timeline: The Movie Industry* 146
- *Media Abroad: Movies of India* 148
- *Media Timeline: Movie Exhibition* 152
- *Media People: Spike Lee* 154
- *Media Databank: Top-Earning Movies* 155
- *Media People: Michael Eisner* 157
- *Media Timeline: Movie Censorship* 160

7 radio 165

Learning Goals 165

Chapter-Opening Vignette: Garrison Keillor 165

Significance of Radio 166
Radio as a Motivator, 166 · Ubiquity of
Radio, 167 · Scope of the Radio Industry, 167

Technical Development 168
Electromagnetic Spectrum, 168 · Transmitting
Voices, 168

Characteristics of American Radio 172
Radio in the Private Sector, 172 · Role of
Advertising, 172 · Noncommercial Radio, 172

Radio As Entertainment 173
Early Mass Programming, 173 · Formats for
Specific Audiences, 174

Radio News 175
Pioneer Radio News, 175 · McLendon
Influences, 176 · Decline of Radio News, 176 ·
Talk Radio, 177

Radio Networks 178
Four Traditional Networks, 178
Radio Networks Today, 180 · Affiliate-Network
Relations, 180

Broadcasting Regulation 181
Trusteeship Rationale, 181 · Regulating
Networks, 186 · Broadcast Deregulation, 187

Future of Radio 188
Risk-Free Bland Programming, 188 ·
Converting to Digital, 188 · Web Radio, 189

Chapter Wrap-Up 190
Questions for Review 190

Questions for Critical Thinking 190
For Further Learning 191
Keeping Up to Date 191

BOXES

- *Media Timeline: Radio Technology and Regulation* 168
- *Media Databank: Radio Formats* 174
- *Media Databank: Radio Chains* 181
- *Media People: John Brinkley* 183
- *Media People: Howard Stern* 184
- *Media Abroad: BBC: "This Is London"* 185
- *Media Abroad: Radio Martí* 186

8 television 193

Learning Goals 193

Opening Vignette: Jerry Seinfeld 193

Impact of Television 194
Cultural Impact, 194 · Mass Media
Shake-Up, 196

Technology of Television 197
Electronic Scanning, 197 · Integrated
Standardization, 197 · High-Definition
Television, 199 · Web-Television
Convergence, 199 · Interactive Television, 200

Structure of U.S. Television 201
Dual National System, 201 · Affiliate-Network
Relations, 201

Delivery Systems 203
Over-Air Stations, 203 · Cable Systems, 204 ·
Satellite Direct, 204

Over-Air Networks 205
Traditional Networks, 205 · NBC
Television, 205 · CBS Television, 205 · ABC
Television, 206 · Dumont Television, 206 ·
Fox Television, 207 · Late-Comers, 207

Cable Television 208
Roots of Cable, 208 · Gerald Levin and HBO,
208 · Turner Broadcasting System, 210 ·
Growth of Cable, 210 · Advertising, 212

Television Entertainment 212
Early Programming, 212 · Producing
Entertainment Programs, 213 · Changing
Program Standards, 214 · V-Chip, 214

Television News 215

Talking Heads and Newsreels, 215 · Shift in
Network News, 216 · 24-Hour Television
News, 216 · Local News, 218

Public Television   218
Corporation for Public Broadcasting, 218 ·
Debate Over Public Funding, 220

Chapter Wrap-Up   220
Questions for Review   221
Questions for Critical Thinking   221
For Further Learning   222
For Keeping Up to Date   223

BOXES
● *Media People: Philo Farnsworth*   198
● *Media Timeline: Television*   199
● *Media Abroad: Japanese Television*   202
● *Media Databank: Broadcast Numbers*   203
● *Media People: Ed Parsons*   209
● *Media People: Ted Turner*   211
● *Media People: Christine Craft*   217

9   the web   225

Learning Goals   225
Chapter-Opening Vignette: Tim Berners-Lee   225
World Wide Web   227
New Mass Medium, 227 · Web Terms, 228 ·
Web Limitations, 229 · New Video
Infrastructure, 230

Internet   231
The Information Highway, 231 · Online
Services, 233

Web Model   234
Users, 234 · Access Providers, 234 · Content
Providers, 234 · Advertisers, 235

Online Advertising   236
Growing Web Audience, 236 · Web's
Advertising Reach, 237

Web Technology   237
Transistors, 237 · Fiber Optics, 239

Nonlinear Communication   240
Hypertext and the Web, 240 · Hypermedia, 243

Hypertext in Practice   244
Pre-Hypertext Innovations, 244 · Hypertext
News, 245 · Hyperfiction, 246

Media Melding   246
Technological Convergence, 247 · Transition
Ahead, 249 · Government Deregulation, 249

Public Policy and the Web   250
Universal Access, 250 · Cyberpornography, 251

Chapter Wrap-Up   252
Questions for Review   252
Questions for Critical Thinking   253
For Further Learning   253
For Keeping Up to Date   253

BOXES
● *Media Timeline: Internet and Web*   228
● *Media People: Vint Cerf*   232
● *Media People: Bill Gates*   248
● *Media People: Neal Stephenson*   249

10   journalism   255

Learning Goals   255
Chapter-Opening Vignette: Christiane Amanpour   255
Journalism Traditions   257
Colonial Period, 257 · Partisan Period, 259 ·
Penny Period, 261 · Yellow Period, 263

Personal Values in News   265
Role of the Journalist, 265 · Journalists'
Personal Values, 266 · Journalistic Bias, 268

Variables Affecting News   270
News Hole, 270 · News Flow and Staffing, 270 ·
Perceptions About Audience, 271 ·
Availability of Material, 271 · Competition, 272

Nonnewsroom Influences on News   273
Executive Orders, 273 · Advertiser
Pressure, 274 · Pressure From Sources, 275

Gatekeeping in News   275
Gatekeepers' Responsibilities, 275 ·
Gatekeepers at Work, 276

Global Gatekeeping   277
Competition for Faraway News, 277 · News
Agencies, 277 · Supplemental Services, 279 ·
Video News Services, 279 · Effects of Video
Coverage, 280

Syndicates and News Products   281
Syndicates' Tradition, 281 · Syndicate
Services, 281

Journalism Trends   282
    Exploratory Reporting, 282 · Soft News, 285

Chapter Wrap-Up   285
Questions for Review   286
Questions for Critical Thinking   286
For Further Learning   287
For Keeping Up to Date   287

BOXES
○ *Media Timeline: Roots of Journalistic Practices*   *258*
● *Media People: Ida Wells-Barnett*   *260*
● *Media People: Ben Day*   *262*
● *Media People: The Composite Journalist*   *267*
● *Media People: Paul Julius Reuter*   *276*
● *Media People: Oriana Fallaci*   *283*

11 public relations   289

Learning Goals   289
Chapter-Opening Vignette: ValuJet   289
Importance of Public Relations   291
    Defining Public Relations, 291 · Public
    Relations in a Democracy, 292

Origins of Public Relations   292
    Moguls in Trouble, 292 · The Ideas of Ivy
    Lee, 293 · Public Relations on a New
    Scale, 295

Structure of Public Relations   298
    Policy Role of Public Relations, 298 · How
    Public Relations Is Organized, 298 · Public
    Relations Agencies, 299

Public Relations Services   300
    Activities Beyond Publicity, 300 · Public
    Relations and Advertising, 302 · Integrated
    Marketing, 302 · Joint Projects, 303

Media Relations   304
    Open Media Relations, 304 · Proactive Media
    Relations, 305 · Ambivalence in Media
    Relations, 306 · Adversarial Public
    Relations, 307

Professionalization   309
    A Tarnished Image, 309 · Standards and
    Certification, 309

Chapter Wrap-Up   311
Questions for Review   312
Questions for Critical Thinking   312
For Further Learning   312
For Keeping Up to Date   313

BOXES
○ *Media Timeline: Evolution of Public Relations*   *290*
● *Media People: Dorothea Lange*   *297*
● *Media Abroad: Russian Military Public Relations*   *299*
● *Media Databank: Major Public Relations Agencies*   *300*
● *Media People: Edward Bernays*   *310*

12 advertising   315

Learning Goals   315
Chapter-Opening Vignette: Volkswagen   315
Importance of Advertising   317
    Consumer Economies, 317 · Advertising and
    Prosperity, 317 · Advertising and
    Democracy, 318

Origins of Advertising   319
    Stepchild of Technology, 319 · Industrial
    Revolution, 319 · Pioneer Agencies, 320

Advertising Agencies   321
    Agency Structure, 321 · Agency
    Compensation, 322 · Advertiser Role in
    Advertising, 323

Placing Advertisements   323
    Media Plans, 323 · Media Choices, 324 ·
    Alternative Media, 325

Pitching Messages   326
    Importance of Brands, 326 · Lowest Common
    Denominator, 327 · Market Segments, 328 ·
    Redundancy Techniques, 328 · New
    Advertising Techniques, 329

Research and Psychology   330
    Motivational Research, 330 · Subliminal
    Advertising, 331

Conglomeration and Globalization   332
    Acquisition Binge, 333 · Agency Consolidation
    Problems, 333

Advertising Regulation   334
    Media Gatekeeping, 334 · Industry Self-
    Regulation, 335 · Government Regulation, 336

Problems and Issues   337
    Advertising Clutter, 337 · Creative
    Excesses, 338 · Advertising Effectiveness, 338

Chapter Wrap-Up   340
Questions for Review   340
Questions for Critical Thinking   340
For Further Learning   341
For Keeping Up to Date   341

BOXES
● *Media Databank: Advertising Spending*   *318*
● *Media Timeline: Development of Advertising*   *320*
● *Media Databank: Largest Advertising Agencies*   *322*
● *Media Abroad: Advertisement Cloning*   *338*
● *Media People: Calvin Klein*   *339*

13 media research   343

Learning Goals   343
Chapter-Opening Vignette: George Gallup   343
Public-Opinion Sampling   345
    The Surveying Industry, 345 · Probability
    Sampling, 345 · Quota Sampling, 347 ·
    Evaluating Surveys, 347 · Latter-Day Straw
    Polls, 348
Measuring Audience Size   348
    Newspaper and Magazine Audits, 349 ·
    Broadcast Ratings, 349 · Audience Measurement
    Techniques, 351 · Criticism of Ratings, 352
Measuring Audience Reaction   354
    Focus Groups, 355 · Galvanic Skin
    Checks, 355 · Prototype Research, 355
Audience Analysis   356
    Demographics, 356 · Geodemographics, 358 ·
    Psychographics, 358
Applied and Theoretical Research   360
    Media-Sponsored Research, 360 · Mass
    Communication Scholarship, 361
Chapter Wrap-Up   362
Questions for Review   362
Questions for Critical Thinking   362
For Further Learning   363
For Keeping Up-to-Date   363

BOXES
● *Media Timeline: Media Research*   *349*
● *Media Abroad: Global Television Ratings*   *353*

14 mass communication   365

Learning Goals   365
Chapter-Opening Vignette: Peter Arnett   365
Types of Communication   367
    Intrapersonal Communication, 367 ·
    Interpersonal Communication, 367 · Group
    Communication, 367 · Mass Communication, 368
Components of Mass Communication   369
    Mass Communicators, 369 · Mass
    Messages, 369 · Mass Media, 370 · Mass
    Communication, 370 · Mass Audiences, 370
Communication Models   370
    Role of Communication Models, 370 · Basic
    Model, 372 · Narrative Model, 373 · Concentric
    Circle Model, 373 · Mystery of Mass
    Communication, 373
Fundamentals in the Process   374
    Stimulation, 374 · Encoding, 374 ·
    Transmission, 374 · Decoding, 374 ·
    Internalization, 375
Players in the Process   375
    Gatekeepers, 375 · Regulators, 376 ·
    Gatekeeper-Regulator Hybrids, 376
Impediments to Communications   376
    Noise, 377 · Filters, 378
Results of Mass Communication   378
    Amplification, 378 · Feedback, 379 ·
    Effects, 380
Chapter Wrap-Up   380
Questions for Review   380
Questions for Critical Thinking   380
For Further Learning   381
For Keeping Up to Date   381

BOXES
● *Media People: David Sarnoff*   *368*

15 media effects   383

Learning Goals   383
Chapter-Opening Vignette: Orson Welles   383

Effects Studies   385
    Powerful Effects Theory, 385 · Minimal Effects
    Theory, 386 · Cumulative Effects Theory, 388

Uses and Gratifications Studies   388
    Challenges to Audience Passivity, 388 ·
    Surveillance Function, 389 · Socialization
    Function, 390 · Diversion Function, 390 ·
    Consistency Theory, 391

Individual Selectivity   391
    Selective Exposure, 391 · Selective
    Perception, 392 · Selection Retention and
    Recall, 392

Socialization   393
    Media's Initiating Role, 393 · Role
    Models, 395 · Stereotyping, 395 · Socialization
    Via Eavesdropping, 396

Media-Depicted Violence   397
    Learning About Violence, 397 · Media Violence
    as Positive, 397 · Prodding Socially Positive
    Action, 398 · Media Violence as Negative, 398 ·
    Catalytic Theory, 400 · Societally Debilitating
    Effects, 401 · Tolerance of Violence, 401

Media Agenda-Setting for Individuals   403
    Media Selection of Issues, 403 · Intramedia
    Agenda-Setting, 404

Media-Induced Anxiety   405
    Information Anxiety, 405 · Media-Induced
    Passivity, 406 · Well-Informed Futility, 406

Chapter Wrap-Up   407
Questions for Review   407
Questions for Critical Thinking   408
For Further Learning   408
For Keeping Up to Date   409

BOXES:
● *Media Timeline: Understanding Mass Media Effects*   386
● *Media People: Dorothy Day*   387
● *Media People: Peggy Charren*   394
● *Media People: George Gerbner*   402

16 mass media and society 411

Learning Goals   411
Chapter-Opening Vignette: Timothy Harris   411

Mass Media Role in Culture   413
    Elitism versus Populist Values, 413 · The Case
    Against Pop Art, 416 · Pop Art Revisionism, 417

Social Stability   418
    Media-Induced Ritual, 418 · The Media and
    the Status Quo, 419 · The Media and Cognitive
    Dissonance, 419 · Agenda-Setting and Status
    Conferral, 421 · Media and Morality, 421

Cultural Transmission   422
    Historical Transmission, 422 · Contemporary
    Transmission, 422

Mass Media and Fundamental Change   424
    Human Alienation, 424 · Television and the
    Global Village, 424

Cultural Intrusion   425
    Latter-Day Imperialism, 425 · Defending
    Western Hegemony, 426 · Emerging Global
    Media, 428 · Insidious Western Influence, 429 ·
    Transnational Cultural Enrichment, 429

Chapter Wrap-Up   429
Questions for Review   430
Questions for Critical Thinking   430
For Further Learning   430
For Keeping Up-to-Date   431

BOXES
● *Media Timeline: Mass Communication and Culture*   413
● *Media People: Linda and Robert Lichter*   414
● *Media Abroad: Americanizing the World*   427

17 mass media and governance 433

Learning Goals   433

Opening Vignette:
Mary Matalin and James Carville   433

Authoritarian Systems   435
    England Under Henry VIII, 435 · Methods of
    Authoritarian Control, 437 · Nature of Truth, 439

Libertarian Systems   440
    Optimism About the Human Mind, 440
    Marketplace of Ideas, 440 · First
    Amendment, 442

Freedom and Responsibility   443

Challenges to Libertarianism, 444 · Hutchins
Commission, 444

Media Role in Governance 445
Fourth Estate, 445 · Government-Media
Relations, 446

Media as an Information Source 447
Direct versus Indirect, 447 · Citizen
Preferences, 448 · Specialized Media, 448

Media Effects on Governance 450
Agenda-Setting, 451 · CNN Effect, 451 ·
Priming, 451 · Media Obsessions, 452

Government Manipulation of Media 455
Influencing Coverage, 455 · Trial Balloons and
Leaks, 456 · Stonewalling, 457 ·
Overwhelming information, 457

Media-Government Issues 458
Political Favors, 458 · Campaign
Spending, 458 · Free Air Time, 460 ·
Techno-Governance, 460

Chapter Wrap-Up 461
Questions for Review 462
Questions for Critical Thinking 462
For Further Learning 462
For Keeping Up to Date 463

BOXES
● *Media Timeline: Political-Media Theories* 435
● *Media People: John Twyn* 436
● *Media Abroad: Distinguishing Media Systems* 437
● *Media Abroad: Jailed Journalists* 438
● *Media People: Elijah Lovejoy* 443
● *Media People: Brian Lamb* 449
● *Media People: Roger Ailes* 453

18 mass media law 465

Learning Goals 465

Chapter-Opening Vignette: Oprah Winfrey 465

The U.S. Constitution 467
First Amendment, 467 · Scope of First
Amendment, 467

Prior Restraint 468
Public Nuisances, 468 · National Security, 470 ·
Military Operations, 471 · "Fire!" in a Crowded
Theater, 472

Slander and Mass Media 473
Concept of Libel Law, 474 · Sullivan
Case, 474 · Fair Comment and Criticism, 475

Privacy Law 476
Intruding on Solitude, 476 · Harassment, 477

Journalism Law 478
Court Coverage, 478 · Sunshine Laws, 479 ·
Confidential Sources, 480

Obscenity and Pornography 481
Import Restrictions, 481 · Postal
Restrictions, 481 · Pornography versus
Obscenity, 482

Censorship Today 482
Local Censorship, 483 · Library and School
Boards, 483 · Meese Pornography
Commission, 484

Copyright 484
How Copyright Works, 484 · Music
Licensing, 485

Chapter Wrap-Up 486
Questions for Review 486
Questions for Critical Thinking 486
For Further Learning 486
For Keeping Up to Date 487

BOXES
● *Media People: Jay Near* 469
● *Media Timeline: Landmarks in Media Law* 472
● *Media Abroad: Press Law in Britain* 473
● *Media Abroad: Norway and Reprography* 485

19 ethics and the mass media 489

Learning Goals 489

Chapter-Opening Vignette: Nike and CBS 489

The Difficulty of Ethics 491
Prescriptive Ethics Codes, 491 · Conflict in
Duties, 493

Moral Principles 494
Golden Mean, 494 · "Do Unto Others," 495 ·
Categorical Imperatives, 495 · Utilitarian
Ethics, 496 · Pragmatic Ethics, 496 · Egalitarian
Ethics, 496 · Social Responsibility Ethics, 496

Process versus Outcome   497
  Deontological Ethics, 497 · Teleological
  Ethics, 497 · Situational Ethics, 498

Potter's Box   498
  Four Quadrants, 499 · Limitations of Potter's
  Box, 500

Ethics and Other Issues   500
  Differentiating Ethics and Law, 500 · Accepted
  Practices, 501 · Prudence and Ethics, 501

Unsettled, Unsettling Questions   501
  Plagiarism, 502 · Misrepresentation, 504 ·
  Gifts, Junkets and Meals, 505

Chapter Wrap-Up   506
Questions for Review   507
Questions for Critical Thinking   507
For Further Learning   507

BOXES
● Media People: Arthur Ashe   492
◉ Media Timeline: Development of Media Ethics   495

About the Author   509
Index   511

preface

How did you keep up to date on the drama over Iraq's weapons of mass destruction? Or the Monica Lewinsky allegations? Why did you choose one brand of athletic shoes over another? Do you trust Al Gore? Newt Gingrich? Saddam Hussein? David Letterman? If you saw the movie *Titanic* but not *Scream 2,* why? How did you learn about the existence of the latest CD you purchased? Would you agree if your local library removed *Playboy* magazine from the shelves? Should *In the Night Kitchen* be banned? *Grapes of Wrath*? *Huckleberry Finn*? Who decides what music gets played on the radio? Who chooses news stories? Can you trust the New York *Times*? *Rolling Stone*? CNN? The *National Enquirer*? Should you worry about little children imitating Rambo? Barbie? Cartman and Stan? Is there too much sex on television?

Everybody faces these kinds of questions in this age of mass communication. The media are everywhere, and they affect almost every aspect of our lives, including the values we embrace. This fifth edition of *The Media of Mass Communication* is designed to help you become more informed and discerning as a consumer of mass media. It also is designed to provide a comprehensive foundation for further studies in mass communication.

This edition is thoroughly revised to keep you current on the mass media, but the most significant changes are in the chapter on the World Wide Web. In only a few years the web has emerged as a powerful new mass medium that will change how we think of the media and how we use them. You will learn, for example, that the next generation of college students probably won't be learning from a textbook like this one. What will replace it? Read on.

how this book is organized

- **Overview.** Chapter 1 orients you to the mass media. You will learn some of the themes that come up in later chapters.

- **The Media.** Separate chapters deal with each major mass medium in the sequence they developed: books, magazines, newspapers, sound recordings, movies, radio, television and the web.

- **Media Issues.** The remaining nine chapters focus on the process of mass communication, media research, theories, effects, law and ethics.

- **Questions for Review.** These questions are keyed to the major topics and themes in the chapter. Use them for a quick assessment of whether you caught the major points.

- **Questions for Critical Thinking.** These questions ask you both to recall specific information and to use your imagination and critical thinking abilities to restructure the material.

- **For Further Learning.** If you have a special interest in the material introduced in a chapter, you can use the end-of-chapter bibliographies to identify more detailed examinations in other sources. The notes can help orient you to the perspective of the authors of these sources, as well as to the level at which they are written. The sources range from easily digested articles in popular magazines to scholarly works that press the boundaries of human knowledge and understanding.

- **For Keeping Up to Date.** These sections list professional and trade journals, magazines, newspapers and other periodical references to help you keep current on media developments and issues. Most of these periodicals are available in college libraries.

- **Boxes.** Throughout the book, you will find four kinds of boxes that illustrate significant points. *Media People* boxes introduce personalities who have had a major impact on the media or whose story illustrates a major point of media history. *Media Abroad* boxes tell about practices in other countries to help you assess your own media's performance. The *Media Databank* boxes contain tables to help you see certain facts about the mass media at a glance. The *Media Timeline* boxes will help you see the sequence of media at a glance.

using this book

The Media of Mass Communication, fifth edition, contains many tools to help you master the material:

- **Introductory Vignettes.** Chapters open with colorful descriptions of major mass media traditions or issues. These are stories about people who contributed significantly to the mass media or who exemplify important aspects of media operations.

- **Learning Goals.** Chapters begin with learning goals to help you guide your thoughts as you read through the chapters.

- **Study Previews.** Chapters include frequent summaries of the material in subsequent paragraphs. These study previews can help prepare you for the material ahead.

- **Running Glossary.** You will find glossary definitions in the margins, on the same page as the name or concept is introduced in the text.

- **Media Online.** The margins also contain hundreds of World Wide Web addresses to guide your learning about the mass media beyond the textbook and the classroom.

- **Web Site.** You can go online for a great array of material designed especially to augment this edition. The MMC web site includes review questions, glossaries, information on key media personalities, media abroad vignettes and much more: www.abacon.com/vivian.

acknowledgments

This book represents many new approaches for introducing students to the media of mass communication. The imaginative and far-sighted team at Allyn and Bacon deserves much of the credit for these innovations. When Bill Barke was editorial director, he chose to make this the most colorful and visually oriented text available for mass communication survey courses. Communication editor Steve Hull, who has a passion for the mass media, especially movies, and who shared Bill's commitment to make this book as colorful and interesting as the media themselves, organized the people and resources to see the project to completion. Joe Opiela, humanities editor, shepherded innovations that kept *The Media of Mass Communication* at the head of its field, including the accompanying web site (www.abacon.com/vivian). This edition reflects the marketing background of Karon Bowers, now Allyn and Bacon's mass communication editor, who has worked with mass communication professors throughout the country to identify their ever-changing needs.

The greatest ongoing contributions have been those of Carol Alper, developmental editor for three editions. She not only has applied her lively imagination and good sense to the book's content but also has coordinated all the complexities of moving the manuscript to production.

With this level of support from the publisher, it's no wonder that almost 400 colleges and univerisities have adopted *The Media of Mass Communication.* Nor is it any wonder that the new Canadian edition, with my co-author Pete Maurin, has been well received.

In this edition, several researchers and writers have added sparkle with chapter-opening vignettes. Letha Dawson Scanzoni did the introductions for Chapter 3, on Bonnie Fuller; Chapter 10, on Christiane Amanpour; Chapter 12, on Volkswagen ads; Chapter 16, on Timothy Harris; Chapter 17, on Mary Matalin and James Carville; Chapter 18, on Oprah Winfrey; and Chapter 19, on Nike and CBS. Carolyn Smith did the opening vignettes for Chapter 1, on Chris Berman, and Chapter 8, on Jerry Seinfeld. Allen Workman did the vignette for Chapter 5, on Bob Dylan and Jakob Dylan.

Among students who have written thoughtful suggestions that have shaped this edition are Niele Anderson of Grambling State University; Lashaunda Carruth, Forest Park Community College; Mike Costache, Pepperdine University; Scott DeWitt, University of Montana; James Grades, Michigan State University; Dion Hillman, Grambling State University; Scott Wayne Joyner, Michigan State University; Nicholas Nabokov, University of Montana; June Siple, University of Montana; and Candace Webb, Oxnard College.

I also appreciate the thoughtful suggestions of colleagues who reviewed the manuscript in whole or in part, at various stages in the first or subsequent editions:

Edward Adams, Angelo State University;
Ralph D. Barney, Brigham Young University;
Thomas Beell, Iowa State University;
Robert Bellamy, Duquesne University;
ElDean Bennett, Arizona State University;
Lori Bergen, Wichita State University;
Bob Bode, Western Washington University;
Kevin Boneske, Stephen F. Austin State University;
E. W. Brody, University of Memphis;
Joe Camacho, California State University–Sacramento;
Patricia Cambridge, Ohio University;

Dom Caristi, Iowa State University;

Michael L. Carlebach, University of Miami;

Meta Carstarphen, University of North Texas;

Debbie Chasteen, Mercer University;

Danae Clark, University of Pittsburgh;

Jeremy Cohen, Stanford University;

Ross F. Collins, North Dakota State University;

David Donnelly, University of Houston;

Thomas R. Donohue, Virginia Commonwealth University;

Tom DuVal, University of North Dakota;

Kathleen A. Endres, University of Akron;

Donald Fishman, Boston College;

Kathy Flynn, Essex County College in Newark, New Jersey;

Ralph Frasca, University of Toledo;

Mary Lou Galician, Arizona State University;

Ronald Garay, Louisiana State University;

Bill Holden, University of North Dakota;

Peggy Holecek, Northern Illinois University;

Anita Howard, Austin Community College;

Wayne F. Kelly, California State University, Long Beach;

Bill Knowles, University of Montana;

Charles Lewis, Mankato State University;

Larry Lorenz, Loyola University;

Maclyn McClary, Humbolt State University;

Denis Mercier, Rowan College of New Jersey;

Gene Murray, Grambling State University;

Richard Alan Nelson, Kansas State University;

Thomas Notton, University of Wisconsin–Superior;

Terri Toles Patkin, Eastern Connecticut State University;

John V. Pavlik, Columbia University;

Deborah Petersen-Perlman, University of Minnesota–Duluth;

Tina Pieraccini, SUNY–Oswego;

Thom Prentice, Southwest Texas State University;

Hoyt Purvis, University of Arkansas;

Benjamin H. Resnick, Glassboro State College;

Ronald Roat, University of Southern Indiana;

Marshel Rossow, Mankato State University;

Quentin Schultz, Calvin College;

Scott Shaw, Operations Manager, WIZM-AM, La Crosse, Wisconsin;

Todd Simon, Michigan State University;

Howard L. Snider, Ball State University;

Penelope Summers, Northern Kentucky University;

Larry Timbs, Winthrop University;

John Tisdale, Baylor University;

Edgar D. Trotter, California State University–Fullerton;

Helen Varner, Hawaii Pacific University;

Michael Warden, Southern Methodist University;

Hazel G. Warlaumont, California State University–Fullerton;

Ron Weekes, Ricks College;

Bill Withers, Wartburg College;

Donald K. Wright, University of South Alabama;

Alan Zaremba, Northeastern University;

Eugenia Zerbinos, University of Maryland.

At Winona State University in Minnesota, several colleagues have been generous in sharing ideas from their teaching and reviewing portions of the manuscript. I especially want to thank Mike Cavanagh, whose web-saviness and wit yields continuing insights. I am deeply appreciative of academic secretary Paula Wiczek, who keeps abreast of pop culture better than anyone I know and who shares her currency, and who also helps in countless other ways. I also am appreciative of her successor as the mass communication department secretary, Trudie Gora. Both have found ways to weave my needs as an author into the flow of other activities in a very busy office.

The dazzling cover design reflects the talents of Linda Knowles, cover adminstrator, and Susan Paradise, cover designer, who built on the eye-catching yet functional interior design by Deborah Schneck. Thanks also go to Deborah for bringing the unprecedented number of components of the book together in production.

Appreciation goes also to Sue C. Howard, whose zest and energy as a photo researcher have contributed to this book's becoming a leader among mass communication textbooks in showing, not just telling, the story of mass media. I am also indebted to the copyeditor, Elisabeth Lehr, whose eagle eyes headed off a great many gremlins that inevitably creep into a manuscript.

While a tremendous amount of talent has gone into *The Media of Mass Communication*, fifth edition, a book like this is never finished. The media are rapidly changing, and the next edition will continue to reflect that. You as a student using this textbook can be the most significant contributor the next time. Please let me know how this book has helped you through your course and, also, how I can improve the next edition. My address is Route 1, Box 32, Lewiston, MN 55952-9706. You can also call or fax me at (507) 523-2294. On email, I'm at

jvivian@vax2.winona.msus.edu

May your experience with *The Media of Mass Communication*, fifth edition, be a good one.

John Vivian
Lewiston, Minnesota

the media of mass communication

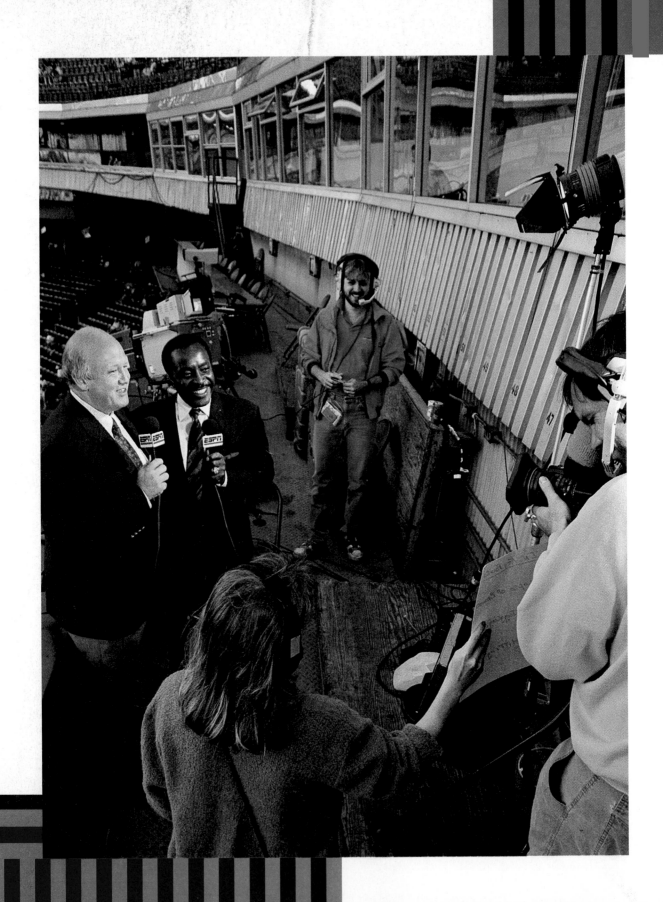

the mass media

in this chapter you will learn:

- The mass media are pervasive in our everyday lives.
- The primary mass media are built on print, electronic and photographic technologies.
- Scholars have devised models to explain the mass media.
- Most mass media organizations must be profitable to stay in business.
- Many mass media are focusing on narrower audiences.
- Mass media ownership is consolidating.
- Mass media ownership and message-crafting are undergoing global consolidation.
- Technology is melding traditional distinctions between mass media.

The NFL running back catches the football and breaks into the clear. "He—could—go—all—the—way!" booms ESPN's Chris "Boomer" Berman, in a vivid imitation of Howard Cosell, capturing the excitement of the moment for loyal NFL fans who aren't satisfied with just watching the game itself. They've already tuned in early for ESPN's pre-game programming and will tune in for more during ESPN's extensive highlight show. Plus they can tune in at any time of the day or night for game results and scores or to find out about any fast-breaking sports news stories.

ESPN's popularity with sports fans everywhere owes much to the personality of sports commentator Chris Berman. His combination of wit, enthusiasm and knowledge of sports has made him one of television's most respected commentators. For many loyal fans, it is as much Berman's ebullient style and his treasure-trove of sports knowledge that draws them to their television sets as the performances of the athletes themselves.

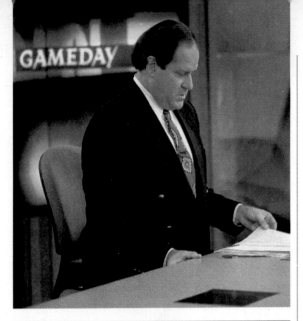

Sports Guy. Since ESPN's earliest days, Chris Berman has been with the cable sports channel. In many ways Berman is synonymous with the network, which—like many successful mass media companies—both reflects its audience's interests and also fuels them.

And Berman is as popular with the athletes as he is with the fans. Because he is as likely to make fun of himself for being "follically challenged" as he is to josh the players for "rumbling, tumbling and stumbling" their way through a game, they like and respect him. As part of the fun, Boomer makes up nicknames for players—like Roberto "Remember the Alomar," Bert "Be Home" Blyleven, or Von "Purple" Hayes. When players began to realize that the nicknames boosted their popularity, they began asking Boomer for the names. So far Berman has dubbed more than 800 happy players with one of his famous monikers and is constantly working on names for up-and-coming players.

Berman's career in sports broadcasting began while he was still in college. As a student at Brown University he served as sports director for the campus radio station and provided commentary for basketball, football and hockey games. After brief stints as disc jockey and talk-show host for a local radio station and weekend sports anchor for a local television station, Berman joined ESPN in 1979, just one month after its inception, and has been there ever since.

Back in the early days of ESPN, cable television was in its infancy. ESPN offered a specialized service for a narrow segment of the cable-viewing audience—the sports fan. Many people doubted that there would ever be much of a market for such specialized programming, but the founders of ESPN persevered. Then in 1987, when ESPN aired the America's Cup live from Australia, an overwhelming public response proved that lots of people were indeed willing to pay to see excellent sports coverage. A huge break came when ESPN landed its first NFL cable contract with programming beginning in the fall of 1987. Two years later ESPN reached an agreement with major league baseball. Telecasts began in 1990.

Today ESPN includes not only the flagship station but also ESPN2, which covers a wider range of sports programming both traditional and emerging, ESPNEWS, a 24-hour sports news network, and Classic Sports Network, featuring historic games and sports stories. Through its ESPN International entity, ESPN sports programming is available virtually around the world, broadcasting in 21 languages, in every country from Latin America to the Pacific Rim. Its international coverage is equally varied, including regionally popular sports such as Indian cricket, Argentine polo, Mexican baseball and the World Table Tennis Championship.

Like many modern mass media businesses, ESPN has been a part of the trend toward media conglomeration, beginning with ABC's acquisition of ESPN in 1984. Today ESPN is 80 percent owned by ABC, which is an indirect subsidiary of Disney. The Hearst Corporation holds the remaining 20 percent.

In addition to its television programming, ESPN satisfies sports fans' seemingly insatiable appetites for sports through a variety of other converging media. Over ESPN Radio you can hear commentaries and updates while driving to work, or listen to SportsBeat or GameNight on the way home. ESPN is also experimenting with several new ventures, including pay subscription programming, interactive software, home video and compact disks.

ESPN's most recent media foray is *ESPN* magazine, a flashy, large-format competitor for *Sports Illustrated*. Its premier issue featured stories on four up-and-coming young athletes, snowboarding, and the March Madness NCAA tournament.

Over the years Berman's popular style and dedication to entertaining and informing sports fans have netted him numerous honors and awards. On four occasions he's been named National Sportscaster of the Year, and three times he's been voted Best Cable Sportscaster. He has received five Emmy nominations as best sports host and was part of ESPN's Emmy-winning SportsCenter team in 1990.

Today Berman's responsibilities are as varied as ESPN itself. He hosts NFL GameDay, a Sunday morning pre-game show, a Sunday evening highlight show, NFL PrimeTime, and ESPN's Sunday night NFL telecasts. He also serves as a play-by-play commentator for major league baseball games, along with hosting Baseball Tonight, which combines baseball highlights, news and features. He is an occasional host of SportsCenter, ESPN's daily sports news program.

ESPN is also a major presence on the Internet. Its popular SportsZone is the equivalent of a 90,000-page newspaper that is constantly being updated with sports news, columns, chats, and video/audio clips. Athletic events are always in season. Sports fans, even in the dead of winter, can click on their RealAudio button, close their eyes, imagine a fielder with glove in the air, and hear Boomer's familiar words, "Back, back, back, back, back, back. Gone."

importance of mass media

(STUDY PREVIEW)   Mass media usually are thought of as sources of news and entertainment. They also carry messages of persuasion. Important, though often overlooked, is how mass messages bind people into communities, even into nations.

pervasiveness

Mass media are pervasive in modern life. Every morning millions of Americans wake up to clock radios. Political candidates spend most of their campaign dollars on television to woo voters. The U.S. consumer economy is dependent on advertising to create mass markets. American children see 30,000 to 40,000 commercial messages a year. With mass media so influential, we need to know as much as we can about how they work. Consider:

- Through the mass media, we learn almost everything we know about the world beyond our immediate environs. What would you know about the Whitewater deal or Princess Di or the Super Bowl if it were not for newspapers, television and other mass media?

- An informed and involved citizenry is possible in modern democracy only when the mass media work well.

- People need the mass media to express their ideas widely. Without mass media, your expression would be limited to people within earshot and to whom you write letters.

- Powerful forces use the mass media to influence us with their ideologies and for their commercial purposes. The mass media are the main tools of propagandists, advertisers and other persuaders.

information source

The most listened-for item in morning newscasts is the weather forecast. People want to know how to prepare for the day. The quality of their lives is at stake. Not

mass media and national development

The United Nations gathers data on the number of television and radio sets around the globe. The data for these Western democracies and developing countries indicate correlations between media use, education and prosperity.

	Radios per 1,000 people	TV sets per 1,000 people	Literacy rate
Western Democracies			
United States	2,123	815	98%
Australia	1,280	486	100%
United Kingdom	1,146	435	99%
Canada	1,026	641	99%
Japan	620	907	99%
Developing Countries			
Ethiopia	191	2.3	62%
India	79	32	48%
Bangladesh	42	4.6	35%
Haiti	40	4.6	39%
Burkina	26	5.3	18%

carrying an umbrella to work if rain is expected can mean getting wet on the way home, perhaps catching pneumonia, at worst dying. There used to be a joke that the most important thing the mass media did was to tell us whether a tornado was coming or whether the Russians were coming.

The heart of the media's informing function lies in messages called **news.** Journalists themselves are hard pressed to agree on a definition of news. One useful definition is that news is reports on things that people want or need to know. In the United States, reporters usually tell the news without taking sides.

Advertising also is part of the mass media's information function. The media, especially newspapers, are bulletin boards for trade and commerce. People look to grocery advertisements for specials. Classified advertisements provide useful information.

entertainment source

The mass media can be wonderful entertainers, bringing together huge audiences not otherwise possible. No matter how many people saw Charlie Chaplin on the vaudeville stage, more people saw him in movie houses. Even more have been entertained by his impersonator in the IBM personal computer advertisements on television and in magazines and newspapers.

Almost all mass media have an entertainment component. The thrust of the American movie industry is almost wholly entertainment, although there can be a strong informational and persuasive element. Even the most serious newspaper has an occasional humor column. Most mass media are a mix of information and entertainment—and also persuasion.

news
Nonfiction reports on what people want or need to know.

persuasion forum

People form opinions from the information and interpretations to which they are exposed, which means that even news coverage has an element of persuasion. The media's attempts to persuade, however, are usually in editorials and commentaries whose persuasive purpose is obvious. Most news media separate material designed to persuade from news. Newspapers package their opinion articles in an editorial section. Commentary on television is introduced as opinion.

The most obvious of the media messages designed to persuade is **advertising.** Ads exhort the audience to action—to go out and buy toothpaste, cornflakes and automobiles. **Public relations** is subtler, seeking to persuade but usually not to induce immediate action. Public relations tries to shape attitudes, usually by persuading mass media audiences to see an institution or activity in a particular light.

binding influence

The mass media bind communities together by giving messages that become a shared experience. In the United States, a rural newspaper editor scrambling to get out an issue may not be thinking how her work creates a common identity among readers, but it does. The town newspaper is something everyone in town has in common. In the same way, what subway riders in Philadelphia read on their way to work in the morning gives them something in common. A shared knowledge and a shared experience are created by mass media, and thus they create a base for community.

The same phenomenon occurs on a national level. Stories on the 1986 Challenger space shuttle disaster bound Americans in a nationwide grieving process. Coverage of the death of Princess Diana prompted a global dialogue on celebrity coverage. Stories on the Whitewater scandal help us figure out what we as a society regard as right and wrong. The importance of mass media in binding people into nationhood is clear in every revolution and coup d'état: The leaders try to take over the national media system right away.

Media in Revolution. Control of the mass media is a high priority for both the government and insurgents during a revolution. In 1989, in a revolution that ousted Romanian strongman Nicolae Ceauşescu, the fiercest fighting was at the government-controlled Bucharest television headquarters.

primary mass media

(STUDY PREVIEW) The mass media fall into three categories based on the technology by which they are produced—print, electronic and photographic. The primary **print media** are books, magazines and newspapers. The primary electronic media are television, major radio and sound recordings, and the web. The one primarily photographic medium is movies.

advertisements
Messages intended to persuade to buy.

public relations
Messages intended to win support.

print media
Books, magazines, newspapers.

print media

Books, magazines and newspapers generally can be distinguished in the following four categories: binding, regularity, content and timeliness:

	Books	Magazines	Newspapers
Binding	Stitched or glued	Stapled	Unbound
Regularity	Single issue	At least quarterly	At least weekly
Content	Single topic	Diverse topics	Diverse topics
Timeliness	Generally not timely	Timeliness not an issue	Timeliness important

Although these distinctions are helpful, they cannot be applied rigidly. For example, timeliness is critical to *Time* and *Newsweek*. Sunday newspaper supplements like *Parade* are magazines but are not bound. Over the past 20 years, book publishers have found ways to produce "instant books" on major news events within a couple of weeks so that their topics can be timely.

The definition problem was illustrated when comedian Carol Burnett sued the *National Enquirer* for reporting falsely that she had been tipsy at a restaurant. The case was tried in California, where state law was more tolerant of slanderous stories in newspapers than those in magazines. Defending itself, the *National Enquirer* tried to convince the judge that it was a newspaper. The judge did not buy the argument, and the *National Enquirer* was tried under the magazine rules and lost. But it was not an easy call. The *National Enquirer* has characteristics of both a newspaper and a magazine.

The technological basis of books, magazines and newspapers, as well as that of lesser print media such as brochures, pamphlets and billboards, is the printing press, which for practical purposes dates back to the 1440s. Print media messages are in tangible form. They can be picked up physically and laid down, stacked and filed and stored for later reference. Even though newspapers may be used to wrap up the leftovers from dinner for tomorrow's garbage, there also is a permanency about the print media.

electronic media

Television, radio and sound recordings flash their messages electronically. Pioneer work on **electronic media** began in the late 1800s, but they are mostly a 20th-century development. Unlike print messages, television and radio messages disappear as soon as they are transmitted. Messages can be stored on tape and other means, but usually they reach listeners and viewers in a nonconcrete form. Television is especially distinctive because it engages several senses at once with sound, sight and movement.

The newest mass medium, the World Wide Web, combines text, audio and visuals—both still and moving—in a global electronic network.

chemical media

The technology of movies is based on photographic chemistry. A lot of video production, including some prime-time television, is shot on videotape and stored electronically, but Hollywood still makes movies on strips of transparent celluloid that is "pulled through the soup"—a technology that dates back to 1888.

book
One-time, bound publication of enduring value on single topic.

magazine
Ongoing bound publication of continuing value with diverse topics.

newspaper
Unbound publication, generally weekly or daily, with diverse, timely content.

electronic media
Recordings, radio, television or web, whose messages are stored electronically for transmission and retrieval.

chemical media
Underlying technology for movies is photographic chemistry.

....media technology

1440s Primal Event
Johannes Gutenberg devised movable metal type, permitting mass production of printed materials.

1455 Books
Johannes Gutenberg printed first of his Bibles using movable type.

1690 Newspapers
Ben Harris printed *Publick Occurrences,* first newspaper in the Colonies.

1741 Magazines
Andrew Bradford printed *American Magazine* and Benjamin Franklin printed *General Magazine,* the first magazines in the Colonies.

1877 Recording
Thomas Edison introduced the Phonograph, which could record and play back sound.

1888 Movies
William Dickson devised the motion picture camera.

1895 Radio
Guglielmo Marconi transmitted the first message by radio wave.

1923 Television
Vladimir Zworykin invented the tube that picked up moving images for live transmission.

1969 Web
The U.S. Defense Department established the computer network that became the Internet.

In some respects, chemical technology is not only archaic but expensive. Studios make as many as 6,000 copies of major releases and ship them from movie house to movie house in cumbersome metal boxes. The freight bill alone is astronomical. How much easier—and cheaper—it would be to transmit movies via satellite to movie houses, which would cut film and distribution costs perhaps 85 percent. Engineers working on digital, electronic technology for movies are stymied, however, to match the image quality of film. A typical movie-house projector generates 80,000 lumens of light, equivalent to 46 100-watt incandescent bulbs, to penetrate the celluloid and cast an image on an 800 square foot screen. The most powerful digital projector, in contrast, will max out at only 6,000 lumens, and can't produce an acceptable image on a screen larger than 600 square feet. Most movie-house screens are at least 800 square feet. Many are larger. More powerful digital projectors would be, for the time being, prohibitively expensive.

Also in favor of chemistry technology is the efficiency of silver halide as a storage medium. A single frame of movie is coated with 40 million crystals of silver halide, each containing density and color that, when a projector beams light through the celluloid, creates the image on the screen. For a feature-length movie, that totals almost 5.5 trillion bits of data. A digital projector that could store and process such quantities of data is technically, but hardly economically, feasible. A celluloid projector runs about $20,000, while an advanced machine from Hughes-JVC is $250,000. But even the sophisticated Hughes-JVC machine can't project a clear image on a screen wider than 40 feet.

Eventually, as digital technology improves and costs come down, movies will shift from chemical to electronic technology. But don't hold your breath.

Digital Photography.
Today, images can be captured, stored, manipulated and reproduced digitally, without using chemicals. Kodak has a system that stores images on a CD-ROM, which allows them to be viewed on computer and television screen. And with a computer, the images can be easily enhanced in ways a photographer in a darkroom could never have done. This digital technology is rapidly replacing chemical-based technology that once was the sole basis of photography and movies.

mass media models

STUDY PREVIEW Scholars have devised numerous ways to dissect and categorize the mass media. These include the hot-cool, entertain-inform, elitist-populist and push-pull models. Each offers insights, but all of them have shortcomings in explaining the mass media.

hot-cool model

An innovative model that helps explain the mass media divides them hot and cold. This model is derived from the thinking of Canadian theorist **Marshall McLuhan,** who, although sometimes confusing and even contradictory, saw books, magazines and newspapers as **hot media.** Why hot? Because these media require a high degree of thinking to use. To read a book, for example, you must immerse yourself to derive anything from it. The relationship between medium and user is intimate. The same is true with magazines and newspapers. McLuhan also considered movies a hot medium because they involve viewers so completely. Huge screens command the viewers' full attention, and sealed, darkened viewing rooms shut out distractions.

In contrast, McLuhan classified electronic media, especially television, as cool because they can be used with less intellectual involvement and hardly any effort. Although television has many of the sensory appeals of movies, including sight, motion and sound, it does not overwhelm viewers to the point that all else is pushed out of their immediate consciousness. When radio is heard merely as background noise, it does not require any listener involvement at all, and McLuhan would call it a **cool medium.** Radio is warmer, however, when it engages listeners' imaginations, as with radio drama.

Marshall McLuhan
Devised hot-cool media model.

hot media
Print media, which require intimate audience involvement.

cool media
Can be used passively.

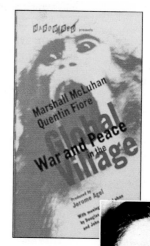

Digital Photography. Scholar Marshall McLuhan developed the idea of *hot* and *cool* media. The more that the audience is immersed in the message, the warmer McLuhan considered the medium. He saw movies as very warm because they can engage so many human senses simultaneously with a darkened environment and huge screen edging out competing stimuli.

McLuhan's point is underscored by research that has found people remember much more from reading a newspaper or magazine than from watching television or listening to the radio. The harder you work to receive a message from the media, the more you remember.

Marshall McLuhan

entertainment-information model

Many people find it helpful to define media by whether the thrust of their content is entertainment or information. By this definition, newspapers almost always are considered an information medium, and audio recording and movies are considered entertainment. As a medium, books both inform and entertain. So do television and radio, although some networks, stations and programs do more of one than the other. The same is true with magazines, with some titles geared more for informing, some for entertaining.

Although widely used, the entertainment-information dichotomy has limitations. Nothing inherent in newspapers, for example, precludes them from being entertaining. Consider the weirdest supermarket tabloids, which are newspapers but which hardly anybody takes seriously as an information source. The neatness of the entertainment-information dichotomy doesn't work well with mainstream newspapers either. Most daily newspapers have dozens of items intended to entertain. Open a paper and start counting with Calvin and Hobbs, Garfield and the astrology column.

The entertainment-information dichotomy has other weaknesses. It misses the potential of all mass media to do more than entertain and inform. The dichotomy misses the persuasion function, which you read about earlier in this chapter. People may consider most movies as entertainment, but there is no question that Steven Spielberg has broad social messages even in his most rollicking adventure sagas. In the same sense, just about every television sitcom is a morality tale wrapped up in an entertaining package. The persuasion may be soft-peddled, but it's everywhere.

Dividing mass media into entertainment and information categories is becoming increasingly difficult as newspapers, usually considered the leading information medium, back off from hard-hitting content to woo readers with softer, entertaining stuff. For better or worse, this same shift is taking place also at *Time* and *Newsweek.* This melding even has a name that's come into fashion: **infotainment.**

While the entertainment-information model will continue to be widely used, generally it is better to think in terms of four media functions—to entertain, to inform, to persuade, and to bind communities—and to recognize that all media do all of these things to a greater or lesser degree.

elitist-populist model

An ongoing tension in the mass media exists between advancing social and cultural interests and giving broad segments of the population what they want. This tension, between extremes on a continuum, takes many forms:

- Classical music versus pop music.
- Nudes in art books versus nudes in *Playboy* magazine.
- The New York *Times* versus the *National Enquirer.*
- A Salman Rushdie novel versus pulp romances.
- Ted Koppel's "Nightline" versus "Oprah Winfrey."
- A Public Broadcasting Service documentary on crime versus Fox Television's "Ten Most Wanted" re-creations.

At one end of the continuum is serious media content that appeals to people who can be called **elitists** because they feel the mass media have a responsibility to contribute to a better society and a refinement of the culture, regardless of whether the media attract large audiences. At the other end of the continuum are **populists,** who are entirely oriented to the marketplace. Populists feel the mass media are at their best when they give people what they want.

The mass media have been significant historically in shaping social and cultural values. Media committed to promoting these values generally forsake the largest possible audiences. In New York City, the serious-minded *Times,* which carries no comics, has generally lagged in street sales behind the *Daily News,* a screaming tabloid that emphasizes crime and disaster coverage, loves scandals and sex, and carries popular comics. The *Times* can be accused of elitism, gearing its coverage to a high level for an audience that appreciates thorough news coverage and serious commentary. The *Daily News,* on the other hand, can be charged with catering to a low level of audience and providing hardly any social or cultural leadership. The *Daily News* is in the populist tradition.

A lot of media criticism can be understood in the context of this elitist-populist continuum. People who see a responsibility for the mass media to provide cultural and intellectual leadership fall at one extreme. At the other extreme are people who trust the general population to determine media content through marketplace dynamics. Certainly there are economic incentives for the media to cater to mass tastes.

infotainment
Melding of media role as purveyor of information and entertainment.

elitists
Focus on media responsibility to society.

populists
Applaud media that attract large following.

Most mass media in the United States are somewhere in the middle of the elitist-populist continuum. Fox Television offers some serious fare, not only hyped crime re-creations, and the New York *Times* has a sense of humor that shows itself in the wit of its columnists and in other ways.

pull-push model

The communication revolution introduced by the World Wide Web in the mid-1990s required a new model to understand new ways that the media were working. The new model classifies some media as passive. These are **pull media,** which you steer. Examples are the traditional media, like radio and television, over which you have control to pull in a message. You can turn them on or off. You can pick up a book and put it down. You can go to a movie or not.

Push media, on the other hand, propel messages at you whether invited to or not. A simple, low-tech example is a recorded voice in a grocery store aisle that encourages you to buy a certain brand of corn flakes as you pass by the cereal display. Push media are taking sophisticated forms with the World Wide Web and new technologies that are making the media more pervasive than ever. They're always on.

Some push media you can program:

- A belt-loop beeper that updates the score on a football game you can't watch while you're doing something else.

- News and travel updates from Egypt you ask for after booking airline tickets for a vacation to the Pyramids.

Other push media intrude gently or in-your-face without you doing any programming:

- A heads-up automobile windshield display that flashes directions to nearby repair shops when sensors detect your engine is overheating.

- Banners across your computer screen that advertise products that your past online purchases indicate you're likely to want.

- Wall screens that push items at you based on assumptions about your interests—like music video samplers for a performing star who's popular on a radio station you listen to.

Because push media receivers are always on, like a beeper or wrist telephone, the messages find you. This is a radical departure from traditional pull media, in which mass messages are radiated everywhere to anyone who will tune in. Push media select to whom to send messages, which means the combination of messages you receive are personalized to you. An individual message may go to many, many people, but the combination of messages that you receive is unique to you—although this isn't done by a single transmitting source or a monolithic Big Brother. Many sources, possibly dozens, hundreds and thousands, target messages at you as someone with a presumed interest in what they have to say.

The editors of *Wired* magazine, describing push media, gave this example: "You are in your study, answering email from the office when you notice something happening on the walls. Ordinarily, the large expanse in front of you features a montage generated by Sci-Viz—a global news feed of scientific discoveries, plus classic movie scenes and 30-second comedy routines. You picked this service because it doesn't show you the usual disaster crap, yet the content is very lively, a sort of huge screen saver. Which you usually ignore. But just now you notice a scene from your hometown, something about an archeological find. You ask for the full video. This is always-on, mildly in-your-face networked media."

No model is perfect, which means push media and pull media are extremes that rarely exist in reality. Most media messages are push-pull hybrid. The "media wall" in the *Wired* magazine example intrudes without a specific invitation, but it also leaves it to you to choose what to pull in when you want more detail. Most emerging new media have such hybrid capabilities.

economics of mass media

(STUDY PREVIEW) With few exceptions, the U.S. mass media are privately owned and must turn profits to stay in business. Except for books, sound recordings and movies, most media income is from advertising, with lesser amounts directly from media consumers. These economic realities are potent shapers of media content.

economic foundation

The mass media are expensive to set up and operate. The equipment and facilities require major investment. Meeting the payroll requires a bankroll. Print media must buy paper by the ton. Broadcasters have gigantic electricity bills to pump their messages through the ether.

To meet their expenses, the mass media sell their product in two ways. Either they derive their income from selling a product directly to mass audiences, as do the movie, record and book industries, or they derive their income from advertisers who place advertisements for mass audiences that the media provide, as do newspapers, magazines, radio and television. In short, the mass media operate in a capitalistic environment, and, with few exceptions, they are in business to make money.

Advertising Revenue. Advertisers pay the mass media for access to potential customers. From print media, advertisers buy space. From broadcasters, they buy time.

Generally, the more potential customers a media company can deliver to advertisers, the more advertisers are charged for time or space. CBS had 40 million viewers for the 1996 Super Bowl, and it charged $1.3 million for a 30-second commercial. A spot on a daytime program, with a fraction of the Super Bowl audience, typically goes for $85,000. *Time* magazine, claiming a 4.6 million circulation, charges $138,200 for a full-page advertisement. If *Time*'s circulation were to plummet, so would its advertising rates. Although there are exceptions, newspapers, magazines, television and radio support themselves with advertising revenues.

Book publishers once relied solely on readers for revenue, but that has changed. Today, book publishers charge for film rights whenever Hollywood turns a book into a movie or a television program. The result is that publishing houses now profit indirectly from the advertising revenue that television networks pull in from broadcasting movies.

Movies too have come to benefit from advertising. Until the 1950s, movies relied entirely on box-office receipts for profits, but moviemakers now calculate what prof-

advertisements
Paid space or time in media for commercial message.

media databank

media costs

Here is a sampler of rates for time and space in major U.S. media for one-time placements. Major advertisers pay less because they are given discounts as repeat customers.

New York *Times*	Sunday full page	$ 53,000
Los Angeles *Times*	Sunday full page	52,900
Wall Street Journal	Full page	99,400
Time	Full page	138,200
Newsweek	Full page	111,100
Web Site (NBC)	6 months	350,000
NBC, "Seinfeld"	30-second spot	575,000
Fox, Super Bowl XXXI	30-second spot	1.3 million

its they can realize not only from "movie-house traffic" but also from recycling their movies through advertising-supported television and home videos. The home video aftermarket, in fact, now accounts for the lion's share of movie studio income. Today, moviemakers even pick up advertising directly by charging commercial companies to include their products in the scenes they shoot.

Circulation Revenue.   While some advertising-supported mass media, such as network television, do not charge their audiences, others do. *Wall Street Journal* readers pay 75 cents a copy at the newsrack. *Rolling Stone* costs $3.95. Little if any of the newsrack charge or even subscription revenue ends up with the *Wall Street Journal* or *Rolling Stone*. Distribution is costly, and distributors all along the way take their cut. For some publications, however, subscription income makes the difference between profit and loss.

Direct audience payments have emerged in recent years in broadcasting. Cable subscribers pay a monthly fee. Audience support is the basis of subscription television like commercial-free HBO. Noncommercial broadcasting, including the Public Broadcasting Service and National Public Radio, relies heavily on viewer and listener contributions. Record makers, moviemakers and book publishers depend on direct sales to the consumer.

Besides advertising and circulation revenue, some media units derive income from other sources, including donations.

Audience Donations.   Audience donations are important to some media operations. Public radio and television stations, which carry no advertising, solicit their audiences for contributions. On-air fund drives, usually running one week twice a year, raise as much as 30 percent of many stations' budgets. Why do listeners and viewers cough up $50 or more for public-station programming when there is so

> **circulation**
> Media revenue derived from sales to audience.

much free media available? On their fund drives, the stations emphasize their heavy emphasis on public affairs and high-brow cultural content, which is hard to find in advertising-supported media. The stations then state, quite frankly, the continuance of the programming is dependent on volunteer contributions. The pitches take many tacks, some of dubious logic, some guilt trips, and some carrying an implied threat. Even so, they raise significant funding:

- "You pay for your newspaper, so why not your news from NPR?"

- "Do your share. Don't leach on your neighbors' contributions."

- "If we don't receive your pledge, we may not be able to continue the quality of programming you've come to expect."

Private Support. The *Christian Science Monitor,* which maintains an expensive staff of foreign correspondents, has lost money for 30 years. Neither advertising nor subscription income is sufficient to meet expenses. In recent years, the *Monitor* has been in the red $12 million to $16 million a year. The losses were made up as always by the Christian Science Church, which sees part of its mission as providing quality news coverage of world affairs. Similarly, the Unification Church of the Reverend Sun Myung Moon underwrites the money-losing Washington *Times.*

Private support, largely from philanthropic organizations, helps keep the Public Broadcasting Service and National Public Radio on the air. The Federal Communications Commission does not allow PBS, NPR or their affiliate stations to accept advertising.

Many limited-circulation publications are supported by organizations that seek to influence limited audiences. Corporations like Exxon produce classy magazines geared for opinion leaders—state legislators, municipal officials and college professors. Special-interest groups such as the trucking industry, religious denominations and professional groups produce ad-free publications and video productions to promote their views.

Government Subsidies. The idea of government support for the mass media might seem contrary to the democratic ideal of a press that is fiercely independent of government, if not adversarial. The fact, however, is that Congress has provided as much as $286 million a year in tax-generated dollars for a quasi-government agency, the Corporation for Public Broadcasting, to funnel to the nation's noncommercial television and radio system. Buffers are built into the structure to prevent governmental interference in programming. The buffers seem generally to have worked. Some states, including Minnesota, New Mexico and Wisconsin, provide state tax dollars for noncommercial broadcasting.

Government dollars also constitute a small portion of mass media advertising revenue. State legislatures appropriate money to buy television and broadcast time, as well as newspaper and magazine space, to promote tourism and to attract new industry. The Defense Department buys space in publications for recruiting troops. The U.S. Postal Service promotes its services through advertising. Newspapers and magazines benefit from discount postal rates, a kind of government subsidy.

Some states require regulated industries, such as insurance companies, to buy space in the state's newspapers to publicize their financial reports. Although these reports, called *legal advertisements* or **legals,** are in tiny agate type, the same size as classified ads, the fees from them are important income for many publications. Some

legals
Government paid notices.

publications also have an indirect subsidy from school boards and other government units that are required by law to publish their minutes and sometimes budgets and other documents. These too are called legals.

Auxiliary Enterprises.   Many media companies have non-media enterprises that generate income that can relieve the profit pressure on their media operations. For years, the Chicago *Tribune* made handsome profits selling newsprint from its Canadian paper factories. Such auxiliary enterprises can tide the media properties through lean times. In 1997, the Public Broadcasting System decided to exploit its brand name by stepping up the marketing of PBS products and services. Many PBS and NPR affiliates issue catalogs with T-shirts, tapes, toys and trinkets that are spin-offs from programs.

economic imperative

Economics figures into which messages make it to print or the airwaves. To realize their profit potential, the media that seek large audiences choose to deal with subjects of wide appeal and to present them in ways that attract great numbers of people. A subject interesting only to small numbers of people does not make it into *Time* magazine. ABC, to take another example, drops programs that do not do well in the television ratings. This is a function of economics for those media that depend on advertising revenue to stay in business. The larger the audience, the more advertisers are willing to pay for time and space to pitch their goods and services.

Even media that seek narrow segments of the population need to reach as many people within their segments as possible to attract advertisers. A jazz radio station that attracts 90 percent of the jazz fans in a city will be more successful with advertisers than a competing jazz station that attracts only 10 percent.

Media that do not depend on advertising also are geared to finding large audiences. For example, a novel that flops does not go into a second printing. Only successful movies generate sequels.

upside and downside

The drive to attract advertising can affect media messages in sinister ways. For example, the television station that overplays the ribbon-cutting ceremony at a new store usually is motivated more by pleasing an advertiser than by telling news. The economic dependence of the mass media on advertising income gives considerable clout to advertisers who threaten to yank advertising out of a publication if a certain negative story appears. Such threats occur, although not frequently.

At a subtler level, lack of advertiser support can work against certain messages. During the 1950s, as racial injustice was emerging as an issue that would rip apart the nation a decade later, American television avoided documentaries on the subject. No advertisers were interested.

The quest for audience also affects how messages are put together. The effect is relatively benign, although real, when a television preacher like Oral Roberts avoids mentioning that he is a Methodist so as not to lose listeners of other faiths. Leaving things unsaid can be serious. For years, many high school science textbooks have danced gingerly around the subject of evolution rather than become embroiled with creationists and lose sales.

media demassification

(STUDY PREVIEW)   The idea that the mass audience is the largest number of people who can be assembled to hear mass messages is changing. Most media today seek narrow audience segments.

technology and demassification

Another contemporary economic phenomenon is **demassification.** The mass media are capable of reaching tremendous numbers of people, but most media today no longer try to reach the largest possible audience. They are demassifying, going after the narrower and narrower segments of the mass audience.

This demassification process, the result of technological breakthroughs and economic pressures, is changing the mass media dramatically. Radio demassified early, in the 1950s, replacing formats designed to reach the largest possible audiences with formats aimed at sectors of audience. Magazines followed in the 1960s and the 1970s, and today most of the 12,000 consumer magazines in the United States cater only to the special interests of carefully targeted groups of readers. Today, with dozens of television program services available via cable in most U.S. households, television also is going through demassification.

effects of demassification

The effects of demassification are only beginning to emerge. At first, advertisers welcomed demassification because they could target their pitches to groups of their likeliest customers. Although demassification dramatically changed the mass media—network radio went into a decline, for example—the economic base of the mass media remained advertising. Local radio stations found new profitability from advertisers anxious to support demassified formats. Today, however, technology has found ways for advertisers to bypass the mass media to reach mass audiences. The latest trend in demassification has advertisers producing their own media to carry their messages by mail to potential customers who, through computer sorting and other mechanisms, are more precisely targeted than magazines, newspapers, television and radio could ever do. The new **alternative media,** as they are called, include:

- Direct mail catalogs and flyers to selected addresses.

- Television commercials at the point of purchase, such as screens in grocery store shopping carts.

- Place-based media, such as magazines designed for distribution only in physicians' waiting rooms.

- Telemarketing, in which salespeople make their pitches by telephone to households determined by statistical profiles to be good potential customers.

If advertisers continue their shift to these and other alternative media, the revenue base of magazines, newspapers, radio and television will decline. Wholly new ways to structure the finances of these media will be necessary, probably with readers, listeners and viewers picking up the bill directly rather than indirectly by buying advertised products, which is the case today.

demassification
Media focus on narrower audience segments.
alternative media
Emerging, narrowly focused advertising vehicles.
conglomeration
Combining of companies into larger companies.

media conglomeration

(STUDY PREVIEW)   Giant corporations with diverse interests have consolidated the U.S. mass media into relatively few hands. One result is that new talent and messengers have a harder time winning media attention.

media ownership consolidation

The trend toward **conglomeration** involves a process of mergers, acquisitions and buyouts that consolidates the ownership of the media into fewer and fewer companies. The deep pockets of a wealthy corporate parent can see a financially troubled media unit, such as a radio station, through a rough period, but there is a price. In time, the corporate parent wants a financial return on its investment, and pressure builds on the station to generate more and more profit. This would not be so bad if the people running the radio station loved radio and had a sense of public service, but the process of conglomeration often doesn't work out that way. Parent corporations tend to replace media people with career-climbing, bottom-line managers whose motivation is looking good to their supervisors in faraway cities who are under serious pressure to increase profits. Management experts, not radio people, end up running the station, and the quality of media content suffers.

A myopic profit orientation is not surprising, considering that the executives of parent corporations are responsible to their shareholders to return the most profit possible from their diverse holdings. When a conglomerate's interests include enterprises as diverse as soccer teams, airlines, newspapers and timberland, as did the business empire of the late Robert Maxwell, it is easy to understand how the focus is more on the bottom line than on the product. The essence of this phenomenon was captured by *Esquire* magazine when it put this title on an article about the hotel magnate and financier who took over CBS in 1986 and, some say, hastened its decline: "Larry Tisch, Who Mistook His Network for a Spreadsheet."

media ownership collaboration

Besides a consolidation of media ownership, the remaining giant companies have joint deals, some very complex. Even Ted Turner, who created CNN, and Rupert Murdoch, who created Fox, and who snipe publicly at each other regularly, are intertwined in deals. One example: Time Warner, which owns CNN, carries Fox news on some of its cable systems. Murdoch's News Corporation, which owns Fox, carries Warner programming on its satellites. Ten percent of Time Warner is owned by Tele-Communications Inc., a giant cable system operator, which has a joint venture with Fox/Liberty Sports, which is owned by News Corporation. Got all that? It gets more complicated. News Corporation has deals with Disney,

On-Screen Directories. Program selection has gone digital with new interactive screen editions. You can scroll through television program listing services with a remote-control device, making your choices on-screen. Will the print edition of *TV Guide* disappear? Not for a while. To receive service you need a specially equipped television set that receives cable of satellite-direct programming.

GUIDE Plus+ and GUIDE Plus+ GOLD are trademarks of Gemstar Development Corporation. Reprinted by permission.

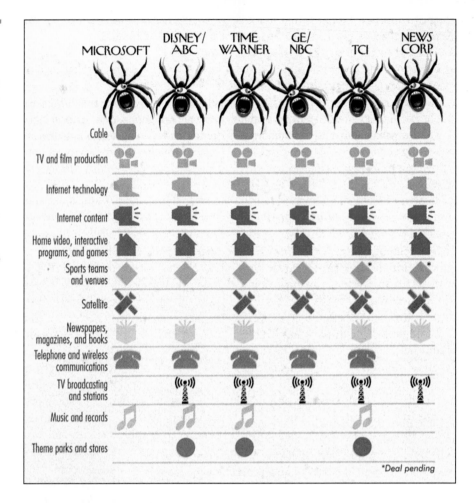

whose properties include ABC; General Electric, whose properties include NBC; Westinghouse, whose properties include CBS; and manifold others. All the big players are in television and film production, Internet content, home video, interactive programs, cable, electronic games, and sports teams. Most are also in books, music and records, television stations, newspapers, magazines, telephone and wireless communications. Disney, Time Warner and TCI own theme parks.

Sound like monopolies? The U.S. Justice Department thinks not. To use its trust-busting authority, the Justice Department needs to find collusion to fix prices. Media critic Ken Auletta, who studied the growing web of collaboration, concluded that fast-changing technology works against the restraints on competition that would make price-fixing likely. People have more ways than ever before to receive media messages.

More serious than sinister economic impact, says Auletta, is the potential for self-serving control of content, particularly journalism: "Is NBC likely to pursue a major investigative series on its partner Microsoft? Is Fox News going to go after its partner TCI? Is a junior ABC news producer going to think twice before chewing on the leg of a Disney partner?" Writing in the *New Yorker,* Auletta noted that Steven Brill complained that Time Warner had tried three times to wield its clout as part-owner of his law publications to influence coverage. In one case, Brill said, there was an attempt to

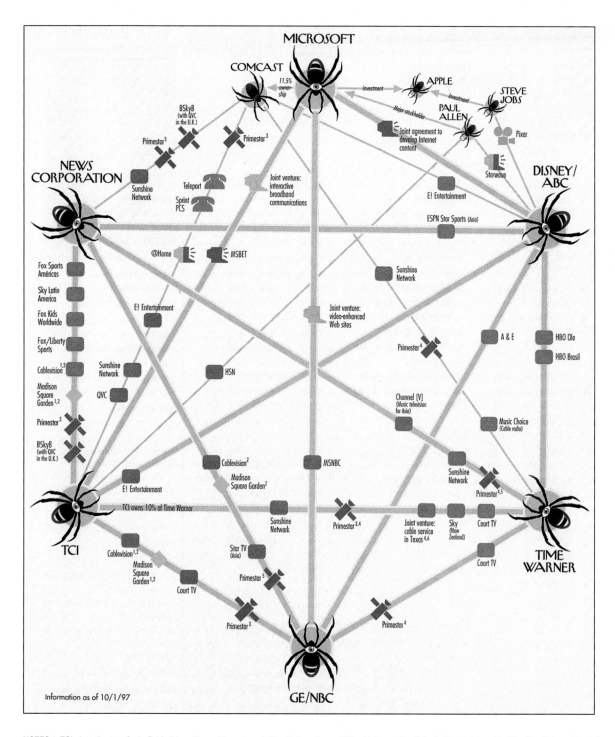

MICROSOFT

COMCAST

11.5% ownership

APPLE

investment

STEVE JOBS

PAUL ALLEN

Major stockholder

investment

Joint agreement to develop Internet content

Pixar

Starwave

BSkyB (with QVC in the U.K.)

Primestar[5]

Primestar[3]

NEWS CORPORATION

Sunshine Network

Teleport

Sprint PCS

Joint venture: interactive broadband communications

E! Entertainment

DISNEY/ ABC

ESPN Star Sports (Asia)

@Home

MSBET

Sunshine Network

Fox Sports Américas

Sky Latin America

Fox Kids Worldwide

Fox/Liberty Sports

Cablevision[1,2]

Madison Square Garden[1,2]

Primestar[3]

BSkyB (with QVC in the U.K.)

E! Entertainment

Sunshine Network

QVC

HSN

Joint venture: video-enhanced Web sites

Primestar[4]

A & E

HBO Ole

HBO Brasil

Channel [V] (Music television for Asia)

Music Choice (Cable radio)

Cablevision[2]

MSNBC

Madison Square Garden[2]

E! Entertainment

TCI owns 10% of Time Warner

Sunshine Network

Primestar[3,4]

Sunshine Network

Primestar[4,5]

Joint venture: cable service in Texas[4,6]

Sky (New Zealand)

Court TV

TCI

Cablevision[1,2]

Star TV (Asia)

Court TV

Madison Square Garden[1,2]

Court TV

Primestar[5]

TIME WARNER

Primestar[3]

Primestar[4]

GE/NBC

Information as of 10/1/97

NOTES 1: TCI plans the transfer to Cablevision of ten cable systems in New York and New Jersey in return for twelve million newly issued shares of Class A Cablevision stock. This will represent 33% of all outstanding shares. 2: Rainbow Media Holdings (25% owned by GE/NBC) and Fox/Liberty (News Corporation and TCI) have announced a deal to create a new twenty-four-hour national sports venture, to be called Fox Sports Net. The deal includes an ownership stake in Madison Square Garden. 3: TCI's interest in Primestar was spun off to the stockholders of the TCI Group as part of the new TCI Satellite Entertainment Company Company, chaired by

TCI's chief executive, John Malone. 4: Interest held by Time Warner Entertainment-Advance/Newhouse, a partnership. Advance Publications owns The New Yorker. 5: News Corporation's acquisition of an interest in Primestar is pending final government approval. 6: Joint venture is pending.

This chart has been assembled from reporting by Ken Auletta and Mike Uretsky, chairman of the Department of Information Systems, N.Y.U., and an inspection of proxies and S.E.C. filings.

⋯⋯sumner redstone's path to viacom

It's a wonder Sumner Redstone can keep track of everything in his Viacom media empire. In fact, there are many Viacom subsidiaries in which he has never set foot.

Redstone began building his empire in 1959 with drive-in theaters in the Northeast. It just kept growing, crowned by the 1994 acquisition of Paramount Communications. As with other media conglomerates, the enormity of the $26 billion company is hard to comprehend. The accompanying list of Viacom subsidiaries at the company's 1994 peak, gives a feel for it—and this list omits dozens of subsidiaries of subsidiaries.

When a company is so large, a strategic error ripples through hundreds, indeed thousands, of media projects. In 1994 Redstone made a mistake—a big one—in buying the Blockbuster video store chain. Within weeks, the profitability went out of video store business, and Blockbuster became a huge drain. The Blockbuster purchase, as well as the Paramount purchase, had been made with bor-rowed money, and Viacom found itself barely able to keep up with debt payments. Every Viacom subsidiary was pressed to pare costs, in some cases trimming personnel and dropping worthy but less-profitable media products.

In 1997, Redstone decided to sell off parts of the empire to raise cash. He targeted dozens of his Simon & Schuster book subsidiaries. He wanted to keep the imprints that put out consumer and juvenile titles—about a third of the company—because those kinds of books could be used to promote products from Viacom's entertainment companies, including the MTV and Nickelodeon cable channels. He put the textbook imprints on the auction block, thus dismantling Simon & Schuster, which had been the nation's largest book company and one of the most respected.

Economic necessity drove the proposed Simon & Schuster break-up, and time may prove Redstone's wisdom in refocusing the company as an enter-tainment entity with lots of potential for cross-promoting its myriad products.

There was a downside, however. When a media behemoth is in trouble, dislocations occur for thousands of media people and products in the subsidiaries that are sold off. One expected result: Many superb textbooks would be discontinued by whichever competing publishers buy part or all of Viacom's jetti-soned book subsidi-aries. The pattern in previous such deals was that the acquiring com-pany suddenly finds itself with too many directly competing titles and dis-continues some. The sell-off of Simon & Schuster's textbook operations sent jitters not only through S&S authors, but also through authors at com-peting companies that were considering buying the S&S imprints.

1020917 Ontario Inc.
Actrax International Corp.
Bardwire Inc.
Blockbuster Video
Broadcast Holding Ltd., L.P.
Broadcast Leasing Inc.
Broadview Television Co.
Cable TV Puget Sound Inc.

First the Drive-Ins.
Viacom chief Sumner Red-stone started his Viacom empire with a string of New England drive-in movie the-aters in 1959. Today Viacom ranks behind only Time Warner and Disney-ABC as a U.S.-based global media conglomerate.

Cable TV of Marin Inc.
Canada's Wonderland Inc.
Channel 3 Everett Inc.
Cineamerica Theaters, L.P.
Cinema International Corporation
Cinema International BV
Clear View Cable Systems Inc.
Com-Cable TV Inc.
Community Telecable of Seattle Inc.
Community Telecable of Bellevue Inc.
Computer Curriculum Corp.
Contra Costa Cable Co.
CPW Holdings Inc.
CPW Investments Ltd., L.P.
Crocket Cable Systems Inc.
Eighth Century Corp.
Everett Cablevision Inc.
Famous Players Inc.
Far-West Communications Inc.
Festival Inc.

Film Intex Corp
Games Productions Inc.
Games Animations Inc.
Glendale Property Corp.
Gulf & Western International NV
H-C-G Cablevision Inc.
International Raw Materials Ltd.
Jake & The Fat Man Productions Inc.
KBSG Inc.
KBSG-AM/FM
KDBK/KDBQ-FM
KHOW-AM/FM
KIKK-AM/FM
KIKK-FM Tower Corp.
Kings Island Co.
KMOV-TV
KNDD Inc.
KQLA-FM
KSLA-TV
KYSR Inc.
Low Key Production
Maarten Investings Partnership
Madison Square Garden Corp.
Marin Cable Television Inc.
Matlock Co.
MNYT-TV
Modern Curriculum Press Inc.
Monetas NV
MTV Songs Inc.
MTV Japan
MTV Brazil
MTV Europe
MTV Australia
MTV Asia
MTV Networks
MTV: Music Television
MTV Latino Inc.
MTV Australia Inc.
MTV Networks Co.
MTV Networks Europe Inc.
MTVN Shopping Inc.
Music by Nickelodeon Inc.
Music by Video Inc.
My Shadow Productions Inc.
National Amusements Inc.
Newtel Inc.
Nickelodeon/Nick At Nite

Nickelodeon Magazines Inc.
Nickelodeon Huggings U.L. Ltd.
Nieum Oranjestad Partnership
Nine W Inc.
Our Home Productions Inc.
Outatown Productions Inc.
Paramount Television Service Inc.
Paramount Stations Group of Philadelphia Inc.
Paramount Stations Holding Company Inc.
Paramount Stations Group Inc.
Paramount Pictures Corp.
Paramount Pictures (Canada) Ltd.
Paramount Parks Inc.
Paramount Home Video Inc.
Paramount Communications Realty Corp.
Paramount Communications Holding Co.
Paramount Communications (Canada) Ltd.
Paramount Communications BV
Paramount Communications Inc.
Paramount Communications Acquisition Corp.
PCI Canada Inc.
PCI's Holding Corp.
PMV Productions Inc.
Premier Advertiser Sales Inc.
Prentice-Hall Canada Inc.
Prentice-Hall International Inc.
Prentice-Hall, Inc.
Qwerty Inc.
Reality Check Productions Inc.
Remote Productions Inc.
Riverside Broadcasting Co. Inc.
Showtime Satellite Network Inc.
Showtime/The Movie Channel Inc.
Showtime Networks Satellite Programming Co.
Showtime Networks Inc.
Silver Burdett Ginn Inc.
Simon & Schuster Inc.
SNI Development Corp.

Tele-Vue Systems, Inc.
Television Signal Corp.
Theatre 59 Ltd.
They Productions Inc.
Toe-To-Toe Productions Inc.
Tunes by Nickelodeon Inc.
TV Scoop Inc.
United International Pictures BV
United Community Antenna Systems Inc.
United Cinemas International Multiplex BV
Uptown Productions Inc.
USA Networks
VE Television Inc.
VE Development Inc.
VE Productions Inc.
VE Drive Inc.
VH-1/Video Hits One
Viacom Networks Europe Inc.
Viacom VH-I Holding Co.
Viacom Pictures Development Co.
Viacom International Inc.
Viacom International Inc. Political Action Committee Corp.
Viacom MGS Services Inc.
Viacom Networks Inc.
Viacom Telecommunications (D.C.) Inc.
Viacom Sub Inc.
Viacom World Wide Ltd.
Viacom HA Holding Co.
Viacom First Run Ltd.
Viacom Pictures Songs Inc.
Viacom Pictures Inc.
Viacom Japan Inc. Viacom SA
Viacom Intl Pty Ltd.
Viacom Intl Ltd.
Viacom Enterprises Canada Ltd.
Viacom Canada Ltd.
Viacom Satellite Networks Inc.
Viacom Camden Lock Inc.
Viacom International Inc.
Viacom First Run Development Company Inc.
Viacom Cable

Viacom Networks Inc.
Viacom Productions Inc.
Viacom Enterprises
Viacom Entertainment
Viacom Broadcasting Inc.
Viacom International Ltd.
Viacom Broadcasting of Missouri Inc.
Viacom Broadcasting Co. Inc.
Viacom International Pty. Ltd.
Viacom Japan Inc.
Viacom Pacific Ltd.
Viacom Productions Inc.
Viacom Pictures Movie Music Inc.
Viacom International Inc.
Viacom Telecom Inc.
Viacom Shopping Inc.
Viacom K-Band Inc.
Viacom Cablevision of Northern California Inc.
Viacom Cablevision of Dayton Inc.
Viacom Bay Interconnect Inc.
Viacom Bay Area Sports Inc.
Viacom Cablevision Inc.
Viacom Pictures Overseas Inc.
Viacom Pictures
Viacom Video-Audio Comunicacoes Ltda.
Viacom Satellite News Inc.
Viacom Broadcasting West Inc.
Vista Television Cable Inc.
VJK Inc.
VNM Inc.
VP Programs Inc. Viacom SA
VSC Communications Inc.
VSC Productions Inc.
VSC Music Inc.
VSC Compositions Inc.
VSC Cable Inc.
WHEC-TV
WLIT-FM
WLTI-FM
WLTW-FM
WMZQ Inc.
WMZQ-AM/FM
WNYT Inc.
WVIT-TV

kill an article on Federal Trade Commission officials when the agency was reviewing the pending merger of Time Warner and Turner Broadcasting. Time Warner has denied Brill's allegation, but he has stood his ground. Whatever the truth of the Brill-Time Warner spat, corporate chain-of-command structures allow, if not encourage, meddling in media content.

dubious effects of conglomeration

Critics like Ben Bagdikian say conglomeration affects the diversity of messages offered by the mass media. Speaking at the Madison Institute, Bagdikian portrayed conglomeration in bleak terms: "They are trying to buy control or market domination not just in one medium but in all the media. The aim is to control the entire process from an original manuscript or new series to its use in as many forms as possible. A magazine article owned by *the company* becomes a book owned by *the company*. That becomes a television program owned by *the company*, which then becomes a movie owned by *the company*. It is shown in theaters owned by *the company*, and the movie sound track is issued on a record label owned by *the company*, featuring the vocalist on the cover of one of *the company* magazines. It does not take an angel from heaven to tell us that *the company* will be less enthusiastic about outside ideas and production that it does not own, and more and more we will be dealing with closed circuits to control access to most of the public."

As an example, **Viacom,** the conglomerate that owns MTV, lost no time in exploiting Beavis and Butt-head's notoriety when they reached icon status. Viacom's copyright became a book, a movie and a videogame, and hundreds of other applications were licensed. That began before 1994, when Viacom subsumed the already-gigantic Paramount Communications. Imagine the new vehicles available for exploiting the next Beavis and Butt-head phenomenon now that Viacom is a $26 billion empire that includes Blockbuster Video, Paramount Pictures, Paramount Television, Nickelodeon television and the huge book publisher, Simon & Schuster.

One of the negative effects of conglomeration occurs when a parent company looks to its subsidiaries only to enrich conglomerate coffers as quickly as possible and by any means possible, regardless of the quality of products that are produced. This is especially a problem when a conglomerate's subsidiaries include widget factories, cherry orchards, funeral homes and, by the way, also some book companies. The top management of such diverse conglomerates is inclined to take a cookie-cutter approach that deemphasizes or even ignores important traditions in book publishing, including a sense of social responsibility. Many of these conglomerates focus on profits alone. One result, according to many literary critics, has been a decline in quality.

Quality. Headquarters press subsidiaries to cut costs, hence increasing profits, which has devastated the quality of writing and editing. Fewer people do more work. At newspapers, for example, a reporter's story once went through several hands—editor, copy editor, headline writer, typesetter, proofreader. At every stage, the story could be improved. In today's streamlined newsrooms, proofreaders have been replaced by spell-check software, which not only introduces its own problems but which lacks the intelligence and judgment of a good proofer. The jobs of the reporter and typesetter have been consolidated. In many newsrooms, so have the jobs of copy editors and headline writers.

Los Angeles *Times* reporter Tom Rosentiel, writing in the *Columbia Journalism Review,* tells how reporters, pressured to increase productivity, take shortcuts to generate more copy: "Newspapers and newsmagazine interviews today are increasingly conducted over the phone, with reporters assembling stories as much as reporting them, combining elements from electronic transcripts, data bases and television. A growing number of major events, reporters acknowledge, are covered without going to the scene. The stories . . . lack the advantage of serendipity or the authenticity of having been there."

In the book industry, media critic Jacob Weisberg has documented how several major publishers, including Simon & Schuster and Random House, have routinely eliminated important stages in the editing process to rush new titles to print and turn quicker profits. In a revealing article in the *New Republic,* Weisberg lists these results of these accelerated schedules:

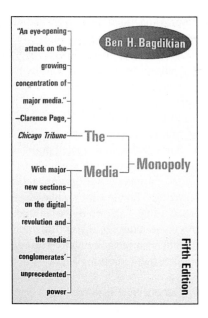

"An eye-opening attack on the growing concentration of major media."
—Clarence Page, *Chicago Tribune*

Ben H. Bagdikian

The Media Monopoly

With major new sections on the digital revolution and the media conglomerates' unprecedented power

Fifth Edition

Media Critic. Ben Bagdikian, called "one of the most considerate voices in journalism today," says huge media companies are ever more profit-obsessed. Their corporate strategies, he says, often sacrifice quality content and public service on the altar of increasing profits. Bagdikian has amassed distressing data on conglomeration in his book, *The Media Monopoly.*

- Factual errors, both major and minor, which in earlier times, he says, would have been caught by careful editing.

- Loose, flabby writing from deadline-pressured writers who once could rely on editors to tighten their work. Some books, Weisberg says, are running 100 pages longer than they should.

This issue of declining quality extends even to textbooks. In 1991 the Texas Board of Education found 250 errors, many of them glaring, in history books up for adoption. Among the errors:

- The United States used the atomic bomb to end the Korean conflict.

- Robert Kennedy and Martin Luther King Jr. were assassinated while Richard Nixon was president.

- George Bush defeated Michael Dukakis in 1989.

- Sputnik was the first intercontinental ballistic missile, and it carried a nuclear warhead.

- The Wisconsin senator who was the 1950s namesake for McCarthyism was General Douglas MacArthur.

Shocked at such errors, the Texas board delayed certifying the books and told publishers to get their act together.

Sameness. You can fly from the East to the West Coast on the same day and read the same Associated Press stories word for word. Newspaper publishers learned long ago that sharing stories via the AP could reduce costs. Although the audience is worse off for the lack of diverse coverage, nobody seems to mind much. This also has happened in network television. Whereas ABC, CBS and NBC once took pride in never using video their crews had not shot, the networks today have scaled back coverage to save costs and all subscribe to the same video coverage from outside sources: APTV, Reuters and Worldwide Television News.

Cultural sociologists fret at the sameness in recorded music. Major record companies encourage artists to imitate what is already popular. This result is that derivative music squeezes original artists and material out of the marketplace, or at least makes it more difficult for these artists to find an audience. Sociologists feel the movement of culture in new directions is slowed by this process.

Barry Diller, who created popular television programs at ABC and later at Fox, says the problem is the profit-driven trend to recycle existing material for a quick buck. In a speech to magazine executives, Diller pointed out the short-sightedness of recycling: "Taking a movie like *Jurassic Park* and turning it into a video game, that's repackaging. Taking a bestseller and putting it on tape, that's repackaging. Taking magazine articles and slapping them on-line, word for word, that's repackaging." He then likened repackaging to strip mining: "After you've extracted the riches from the surface, there's nothing left."

Corporate Instability. Conglomeration also has introduced instability. Profit-driven corporate parents are quick to sell subsidiaries that fall short of profit expectations even for a short term or just to raise cash. An alarming example of the cash problem unfolded in 1991 after media magnate **Robert Maxwell** died, apparently of suicide. Within days of his death it was discovered that Maxwell had been illegally shuffling vast amounts of money around his subsidiaries to cover loans he had taken out to expand his empire, which included Macmillan, the prestigious U.S. book-publishing company. Maxwell was not alone among conglomerate builders who found themselves in deep trouble after overextending themselves financially. The problem was not only in the instability wrought by their miscalculations and recklessness, but also in the products that their media subsidiaries produced. Michael Lennie, a San Diego textbook author attorney, put the problem this way: "The industry continues to grow more and more concentrated with large debt-ridden publishers too preoccupied with serving crippling debt to pay attention to the publishing of quality texts."

Anti-Intellectualism. Conglomeration worries book lovers because it means that conglomerate executives can use their chain-of-command authority to squash books they do not like and ramrod those they do into production. Generally these executives recognize that their professional expertise is in deal-making and management and leave judgments on literary quality and market potential to the editors at their book subsidiaries. Even so, the issue remains that the modern conglomerate structure of the American mass media, including the book industry, has created a whole new set of high-level gatekeepers who have unprecedented power to control media content.

positive effects of conglomeration

At the end of World War II, the mainline book-publishing business was dominated by family-run publishing houses, all relatively small by today's standards. Although there still are hundreds of small publishers in the United States today, consolidation has reduced the industry to six giants. Depending on whom you ask, the conglomeration has been a godsend or a disaster. Looking at the effects positively, the U.S. book industry is financially stronger:

Robert Maxwell
Global media mogul who overexpanded.

Another Merger. Ted Turner, who created the Turner cable broadcasting empire, and Gerald Levin, who headed Time Warner, were all triumphant in announcing their companies' merger in 1995. Time Warner was already the world's largest media company. The merger made it bigger. Just how big can media conglomerates become? A few weeks later, Disney bought Cap Cities/ABC to create a media company with $19 billion in annual revenues, moving into the same mega-media league as the new Time Warner enterprise.

- Parent corporations have infused cash into their new subsidiaries, financing expensive initiatives that were not financially possible before, including multimillion-dollar deals with authors.

- Because parent corporations often own newspapers, magazines and broadcast companies, book publishers have ready partners for repackaging books in additional media forms.

- Many of the new parent corporations own book companies abroad, which helps open up global markets.

Conglomeration, however, is not always good for book companies, or other companies either. Richard MacDonald, who specializes in media deals as equity research director at First Boston, says there are two kinds of people who operate conglomerates: builder entrepreneurs and monster entrepreneurs.

Builder Entrepreneurs. MacDonald, writing in the *Gannett Center Journal*, says the media and the public are well served by people who are "committed to the guts of the media business." He cites the late **William Paley** of CBS and **David Sarnoff** of RCA, who despite personal quirks were in the media business for the long haul and who recognized that attention to the quality of their product would pay dividends far into the future. MacDonald says contemporary media leaders of this sort include **Rupert Murdoch,** whose interests include News Corporation, HarperCollins and Fox, and **Ted Turner** of CNN. Among book publishers, these "builder entrepreneurs" would include **Alfred Knopf,** who emphasized outstanding European authors when he started a publishing house in 1915; **Bennett Cerf,** who cofounded Random House in 1927 to create "books of typographical excellence"; and **Barney Rosset,** founder of Grove Press, who waged numerous expensive battles against censorship of Henry Miller's *Tropic of Cancer.*

Monster Entrepreneurs. MacDonald uses the term "monster entrepreneurs" to describe people who are strictly in the media business for the money. They are motivated by greed, and, says MacDonald, they ask themselves: "How fast can I get the cash out?"

An example of a monster entrepreneur is London-based Robert Maxwell, who built a media empire without much concern about the content of his products. He

William Paley
Built CBS.

David Sarnoff
Built RCA.

Rupert Murdoch
Built News Corp.

Ted Turner
Built CNN.

Alfred Knopf
Built publishing house.

Bennett Cerf
Built Random House.

Barney Rosset
Anti-censorship crusader.

pressured the people he put in charge of his entities to make them profitable, and that, not content or quality, was his primary concern. As a result of this content neglect, Maxwell properties were not very good—and when he acquired respectable properties, they went into a decline.

Maxwell has become a favorite target of critics of conglomeration because of his obvious excesses —and in the end he failed. In 1991, to almost everyone's shock, including his bankers, Robert Maxwell died mysteriously, probably a suicide, when his finances began unraveling. It turned out that he built his empire with collateral from other properties that were already borrowed against to the hilt. His debt, including money taken illegally from employee pension funds, was $5 billion. Among properties he took down in the United States were the venerable Macmillan publishing house and the New York *Daily News*. Both had been recent acquisitions.

media globalization

(STUDY PREVIEW)   Foreign media conglomerates have acquired extensive media holdings in the United States. U.S. media companies, meanwhile, are extending their reach into other countries.

transnational ownership

One of the largest book publishers in the United States is a 150-year-old German company whose name most Americans do not even recognize: **Bertelsmann.** The Bertelsmann presence in the United States typifies the **globalization** of the mass media, a trend that is changing the structure of the mass media worldwide.

Bertelsmann owns 75 percent of Gruner & Jahn, a German-based magazine publisher which is a major player in France, Germany, Poland and Spain. With the 1994 acquisition of 14 women's magazines from the New York Times Company, Bertelsmann has been a major United States magazine producer. Worldwide, Bertelsmann owns 200 book companies, magazines and other operating units with 44,000 employees in 25 countries. These units generate almost $9 billion in sales a year, 30 percent of it from the United States. In the United States, Bertelsmann owns book companies with such familiar names as Random House, Bantam, Doubleday and Dell. It also owns RCA and Arista records. Worldwide, Bertelsmann dwarfs such better known media companies as CBS, Hearst and Murdoch.

Bertelsmann is one of many international media companies that, often quietly and behind the scenes, are changing the structure of media ownership. The French-Italian company Hachette Filipacchi has significant U.S. magazine holdings. PolyGram, of Britain, is aggressively positioning itself in the U.S. movie, television and pop music fields, including the 1993 acquisition of Motown Records and earlier Island, A&M and Mercury records. The Australia-based companies of Rupert Murdoch have major interests in U.S. magazines, television and newspapers. The biggest players in the magazine acquisition business in the United States in recent years have been Bertelsmann, Hachette and Murdoch, none of which is American owned.

In 1991 Time Warner, the result of the merger of Time-Life and Warner Communications, both old American media names, became 17.5 percent Japanese owned.

Bertelsmann
German media giant.
globalization
International media ownership.

u.s. global players

Four U.S. media rivals have established themselves as major players in other countries.

- **Time Warner Turner.** Time Warner, which operates in 70-plus countries, is among the world's largest media companies—a position strengthened with its 1995 acquisition of Turner Broadcasting, including CNN. Worldwide, Time Warner Turner revenues near $20 billion, roughly 40 percent from the United States.

   In Latin America, the company has adapted its HBO pay-television service and calls it HBO Olé. It's the most widely distributed cable network in Latin America. Elsewhere, the company has alliances with Itochu and Toshiba.

- **Disney-ABC.** Disney became one of the world's largest media company in 1995 when it acquired Cap Cities/ABC. The new company has annual revenues estimated at more than $19 billion. The consolidation included major assets in movies, television, newspapers and cable. Since 1995, the company has sold off some major properties, including several metro newspapers and also magazines to narrow its focus.

- **Viacom.** Viacom's MTV has been an entree into foreign markets. The music-video network reaches 240 million households in 63 countries, which is a model for Viacom to expand its VH-1 music and Nickelodeon satellite networks into other countries. There is a lot more that Viacom can market abroad. It holds 50,000 hours of television shows that it first sold to U.S. networks and now is recycling abroad.

- **News Corp.** Australian-born Rupert Murdoch owns News Corp., the interests of which go far beyond his 20th Century-Fox movie studio, the Fox television network and U.S. newspapers and magazines. In Asia, his satellite television service, Star TV, beams signals to China, India, Taiwan and Southeast Asia. Through Star TV, two-thirds of the world's population, 3 billion people, have access to programming that Murdoch's company creates or buys from other sources, including MTV, ESPN and Bart Simpson.

   Murdoch owns half of Sky Broadcasting, which sends signals from satellite to all of Europe. He also owns newspapers in Australia, Britain and the United States.

Japanese companies also have heavy stakes in the U.S. entertainment industry, including Columbia Pictures, CBS Records and MCA, whose full name, ironically, was once "Music Corporation of America."

Globalization is not only a matter of foreign ownership of U.S. media. American companies have extensive operations abroad, and in recent years the U.S. entertainment media industry has been a continuing bright spot in the nation's balance of trade. Far more is exported than imported.

effects of globalization

Experts disagree about the effect of globalization. Some critics, including respected media critic Ben Bagdikian, fret that "anonymous superpowers" like Bertelsmann are a potential threat to American cultural autonomy and the free flow of information and ideas. In his book *The Media Monopoly*, Bagdikian said: "The highest levels of world finance have become intertwined with the highest levels of mass

overseas heavyweights

Once U.S. media companies held the commanding lead for overseas markets, but home-grown companies are pumping out more content all the time. Some of these companies have become global players themselves.

- **Bertelsmann.** The German company Bertelsmann established itself globally as a book and magazine company. It has 200 subsidiaries in 25 countries, many of them operating under the name they had when Bertelsmann acquired them. In the United States, these include Random House, Bantam, Dell and Doubleday books. The company's U.S. interests include RCA records.

- **Hachette Filipacchi.** The French-Italian company Hachette Filipacchi publishes 74 magazines in 10 countries. This includes the 4.4 million circulation *Woman's Day,* which Hachette acquired when it bought the CBS magazine empire in 1988. Another Hachette magazine in the United States is the fashion magazine *Elle.*

- **Televisa.** Throughout Latin America, people watch soap operas, called *telenovelas.* Most of these originate from Televisa, a Mexican media giant.

Rockin' in New Delhi. The Star TV satellite-television service, owned by Australian-born U.S. citizen Rupert Murdoch, reaches all India and China. Among programs is the MTV channel in Hindi. Global media titans like Murdoch have been prompted by the success of emerging, indigenous media companies to customize programs to local markets.

- **TVB.** Hong Kong-based TVB has started an Asian television-satellite service. This company has plenty to put on the satellite. Its production runs about 6,000 hours a year in both Cantonese and Mandarin.

- **TV Globo.** A Brazilian media company, TV Globo, true to its name, has developed a global audience. Its telenovelas air in all the Spanish-speaking and Portuguese-speaking countries and beyond, including China.

media ownership, with the result of tighter control over the systems on which most of the public depends for its news and information." Other observers, such as Toni Heinzl and Robert Stevenson at the University of North Carolina, note that many global media companies, including Bertelsmann, have learned to let their local operating companies adapt to local cultures: "Following a global strategy, it is the company's policy to respect the national characteristics and cultural traditions in each of the more than two dozen countries in which it operates. It is impossible to detect even hints of German culture from the product lineup of Bertelsmann's companies abroad. Targeting specific preference of a national public or audience, the company has custom-tailored its products for each country: French culture in France, Spanish culture in Spain, American culture in the United States, and so on." The target is growth. In 1997, Bertelsmann launched a program to increase the percentage of its profits from the United States to 40 percent from 20 percent.

By and large, the agenda of media conglomerates is profits and nothing more. They do not promote ideology. American moviegoers did not see Japanese overtones in Columbia movies or CBS records after the Sony takeover, nor with MCA products after the Matsushita takeover. At the same time, it cannot be ignored that Bertelsmann tried to transplant its successful German geographic magazine *Geo* in the United States in 1979, only to give it up two years and $50 million later when it realized that *National Geographic*'s following was unshakable. Similarly, Hachette Filipacchi cloned its *Elle* fashion magazine for the United States, and Maxwell and Murdoch imported their British tabloid editors to reshape some of the American newspapers they bought. What can be said with certainty about media globalization is that it is occurring and that observers are divided about its consequences.

media melding

(STUDY PREVIEW)   The different mass media are moving into digital transmission, which is eroding the differences between them. This technological melding is being accelerated by the continuing consolidation of companies that own the mass media.

digitization

The eight primary mass media as we know them today are in a technological transition that is blurring the old distinctions that once clearly separated them. For example, newspapers are experimenting with electronic delivery via cable and telephone lines—"no paper" newspapers. Through personal computers, thousands of people have access to data banks to choose the news coverage they want. This is called **digitization,** a process that compresses, stores and transmits data, including text, sound and video, in extremely compact and efficient ways. An example of the potential of digitization was **configurable video,** developed at the Massachusetts Institute of Technology Media Lab in the 1980s. The MIT configurable video systems integrated printed articles and video segments that a person could read and view in any sequence desired. The MIT system was an integration of traditional print and electronic media with a new twist: An individual, sitting at a screen, could control the editing by passing unwanted portions and focusing on what was most valuable.

intracorporate synergy

Some media melding has come about because competitors have recognized how partnerships could be mutually beneficial. When television became a media force in the 1950s, Hollywood lost millions of moviegoers and declared war on its new rival. For several years, the movie industry even forbade television from playing movies, and Hollywood developed distinctive technical and content approaches that television could not duplicate. The rivalry eased in time, and today Hollywood and the television industry are major partners. Hollywood produces a significant amount of programming for the television networks, and there are all kinds of joint ventures.

> **melding**
> Conversion of all media to a common digital technology.
>
> **digitization**
> Efficient, compact storage and transmission of data.
>
> **configurable video**
> Integration of text, sound and video with audience controlling the sequence of presentation.

chapter wrap-up

The mass media are the vehicles that carry messages to large audiences. These media—books, magazines, newspapers, records, movies, radio, television and the Web—are so pervasive in modern life that many people do not even notice their influence. Because of that influence, however, we should take time to understand the mass media so that we can better assess whether they are affecting us for better or worse.

The mass media are essential for democracy. By keeping people on top of current issues, the media enable people to participate intelligently in public policy discussion and decision-making. The media also are the vehicles by which people debate the issues and try to persuade each other of different points of view. Even when they provide us with entertainment, the mass media are capable of portraying and shaping values that enrich our dialogue on social issues and public policy. Sometimes the media perform these functions well, sometimes not. Studying the media gives people the tools to know whether the media are living up to their potential as facilitators of democracy.

Technology is central to mass media. Magazines and newspapers are possible only because the printing process was invented. Television, likewise, is dependent on electronic equipment. Because media technology is complex, mass communication is possible only through organizations that bring together many people with a range of specialized skills. These organizations include television networks, book publishers and newspaper chains, almost all of which exist only because they generate profits for their owners. A related approach to studying the mass media, therefore, involves examining the competitive economic context within which they operate.

questions for review

1. How are the mass media pervasive in our everyday lives?

2. What are the three technologies on which the primary mass media are built?

3. Explain five models that scholars have devised to explain the mass media.

4. How do mass media organizations make money to stay in business?

5. Define demassification. Describe demassification that has occurred in radio, magazines and television.

6. Is conglomeration good for mass media consumers?

7. Why is globalization occurring in the mass media? Is it a good thing?

8. Where is technology taking the mass media?

questions for critical thinking

1. Some people were confused when Marshall McLuhan called electronic media cool and print media hot because, in their experience, radios and television sets heat up and newspapers are always at room temperature. What did McLuhan mean?

2. The effectiveness of messages communicated through the mass media is shaped by the technical limitations of each medium. A limitation of radio is that it cannot accommodate pictures. Is it a technical limitation that the *Wall Street Journal* does not carry photographs, or that the New York *Times* does not carry comics or that most radio news formats limit stories to 40 seconds? Can you provide examples of content limitations of certain media? What are the audience limitations inherent in all mass media?

3. For many years CBS television programs drew a generally older and more rural audience than the other networks. Did that make CBS a niche-seeking mass media unit? Did it make the CBS audience any less heterogeneous?

4. Which mass media perform the informing purpose best? The entertaining purpose? The persuading purpose? Which of these purposes does the advertising industry serve? Public relations?

5. Why do revolutionaries try to take over the mass media right away?

6. Which is more important to the American mass media—profits or doing social good? What about the goals of supermarket tabloids like the *National Enquirer*?

7. Which mass media rely directly on consumer purchases for their economic survival? Advertising provides almost all the revenue for commercial radio and television stations, but indirectly consumer purchases are an important factor. In what way?

8. Are any types of mass media not dependent on advertising or consumer purchases?

for further learning

Ken Auletta. "The Next Corporate Order: American Keiretsu." *New Yorker* (October 20–27, 1997). Pages 225–227. Auletta, a leading media critics, likens joint media ventures to the Japanese keiretsu, a multi-industry cartel. His focus is on Time Warner, Disney, News Corporation, Microsoft, General Electric and Tele-Communications Inc.

Ken Auletta. *Three Blind Mice: How the TV Networks Lost Their Way* (Random House, 1991). Auletta takes a dim view of media conglomeration in this examination of the corporate takeovers of ABC, CBS and NBC in the 1980s.

Ben H. Bagdikian. "Special Issue: The Lords of the Global Village." *The Nation* 248 (June 12, 1989): 23, Pages 805–20. Bagdikian, a media critic, argues that the concentration of media ownership into a few global conglomerates is diluting the vigor of news and other content.

Erik Barnouw and others. *Conglomerates and the Media* (The New Press, 1997). The reflections of broadcast historian Erik Barnouw and other media thinkers in a New York University lecture series are collected here. The theme is negative toward conglomerates, with oodles of examples of corporate owners who have used their power to influence media content for their financial benefit.

Barry Diller. "Don't Repackage—Redefine!" *Wired* (February 1995). Pages 82–85. This is a reprint of a 1994 speech in which media whiz Barry Diller implores magazine executives to focus more on original material and less on repackaging and recycling stories.

Kevin Kelly and Gary Wolf. "Kill Your Browser." *Wired* (March 1997). Cover, Pages 12-22. Kelly and Wolf project where mass media are going with this hep article on push and pull media.

Robert La Franco. "Where Analog Still Shines." *Forbes* (August 25, 1997), Page 82. La Franco explains why digital video technology remains inadequate for movie houses, which continue to use 19th-century technology to project images on big screens.

Richard J. MacDonald. "'Monster' Entrepreneurs and 'Builder' Entrepreneurs." *Gannett Center Journal 3* (Winter 1989): 1, Pages 11–17. In this issue, devoted to news-media barons, MacDonald shares his experience as an investment banker who deals with people who make media acquisitions.

Neil Postman. *Technopoly* (Vintage, 1993).

Tom Rosenstiel. "Yakety-Yak: The Lost Art of Interviewing." *Columbia Journalism Review* (January-February 1995). Pages 23–27. Rosenstiel, national correspondent for the Los Angeles *Times,* bemoans a shift from long-form interviews to quickie interviewing and story packaging.

Anthony Smith. *The Age of the Behemoths: The Globalization of Mass Media Firms* (Priority Press, 1991). In this brief volume, media scholar Smith details the recent growth of giant global media companies, including Bertelsmann, Sony and Time Warner, and discusses implications of this development.

for keeping up to date

Many mass media developments abroad are tracked in the monthly London-based *Censorship Index.*

Newsmagazines including *Time* and *Newsweek* cover major mass media issues more or less regularly, as do the New York *Times,* the *Wall Street Journal* and other major newspapers.

Periodicals that track the mass media as business include *Business Week, Forbes,* and *Fortune. Forbes* and *Fortune* magazines rank major U.S. companies annually by numerous criteria, including sales, assets and profits. *Fortune* ranks industrial companies in April and service companies in May. The *Forbes* rankings are in April.

Incipit prologus sancti theodori. presbiteri i parabolas salomonis iungat epistola quos iungit sacerdotium: immo carta non diuidat: quos xpi nedit amor. Cometarios in osee. amos. z zachariam malachiam. quoq; poscitis. Scripsisse: si licuisset pre valitudine. Mittitis solacia sumptuum. notarios nros et librarios sustentans: ut vobis potissimu nrm desudet ingeniu. Et ecce ex latere frequens turba diuisa poscetiu: quasi aut equu sit me vobis esurietibz alijs laborare: aut in ratione dati et accepti. cuisq; preter vos obnoxi9 sim. Itaq; longa egrotatione fractus: ne penitus hoc anno reticerem. z apud vos mutus essem. vidui opus nomini vro consecraui. interptatione videlicet triu salomonis voluminu: malloth qd hebrei pabolas vulgata editio puibia vocat: coeleth que grece ecclesiasten. latine ditionatorem possum9 dicere: sirasirim. qd i linguam nram vertit canticu canticoz. Fertur et panaretos. iusu filij sirach liber: z ali9 pseudographus. qui sapientia salomonis inscribit. Quoq; priore hebraicum reperi. non ecclesiasticu ut apud latinos: sed pabolas pnotatu. Cui iuncti erat ecclesiastes. et canticu canticoz: ut similitudinem salomonis. non solu numero librorum: sed etiam materiaz genere coequaret. Secundus apud hebreos nusqz est: quia et ipse stilus grecam eloquentiam redolet: et nonulli scriptoz veres hunc esse iudei filonis affirmant. Sicud ergo iudith z thobie z machabeoz libros legit quide eos ecclesia. sed inter canonicas scripturas non recipit: sic z hec duo volumina legat ad edificatione plebis: non ad auctoritatem ecclesiasticoz dogmatu confirmandam.

Si cui sane septuaginta interpretum magis editio place: habet eam a nobis olim emedata. Atq; eni noua sic cudim9: ut vetera destruam9. Et tame cu diligetissime legerit: sciat magis nra scripta intelligi: que non in terciu vas trasfusa coacuerit: sed statim de prelo purissime emedata teste: suu saprem seruauerit. Incipiut parabole salomois.

Arabole salomonis filij dauid regis isrl: ad sciendam sapientiam z disciplinam: ad intelligenda verba prudentie et suscipienda eruditione doctrine: iusticia et iudiciu z equitate: ut detur paruulis astutia: et adolescenti scientia et intellectus. Audies sapies sapientior erit: z intelliges gubernacla possidebit. Animaduertet parabolam et interpretationem: verba sapientiu z enigmata eoz. Timor dni principiu sapietie. Sapientiam atq; doctrinam stulti despiciut. Audi fili mi disciplina pris tui et ne dimittas legem mris tue: ut addatur gratia capiti tuo: z torques collo tuo. Fili mi si te lactauerint pctores: ne acquiescas eis. Si dixerit veni nobiscu insidiemur sanguini: abscodam9 rediculas ctra iusontem frustra. deglutiamus eu sicud infernus viuente z integrum quasi descedente in lacu: omne preiosa substantia reperiem9. implebim9 domus nras spolijs. Sortem mitte nobiscum. marsupiu sit vnum omniu nrm: fili mi ne ambules cu eis. Prohibe pedem tuu a semitis eoz. Pedes eni illoz ad malu currut: z festinat ut effundant sanguinem. Frustra auté iacitur rete ante oculos pinnatoz. Ipsi contra sanguine suu insidiant.

2

books

in this chapter you will learn:

- Mass production of the written word changed human history.

- Books today fall into two main categories: trade books and textbooks.

- Book innovations include paperbacks and now electronic books.

- Book retailing is dominated by chains with independent bookstores declining.

- A book's commercial success is measured in sales, but these are difficult to calculate.

- Elitists worry about the shift in book retailing to a marketing-driven model.

- The book industry worldwide is dominated by a few large and growing companies.

Johannes Gutenberg was eccentric—a secretive tinkerer with a passion for beauty, detail and craftsmanship. By trade, he was a metallurgist, but he never made much money at it. Like most of his fellow 15th-century Rhinelanders, he pressed his own grapes for wine. As a businessman, he was not very successful, and he died penniless. Despite his unpromising combination of traits, quirks and habits—perhaps because of them—Johannes Gutenberg

wrought the most significant change in history: the mass-produced written word. He invented movable metal type.

Despite the significance of his invention, there is much we do not know about Gutenberg. Even to friends, he seldom mentioned his experiments, and when he did he referred to them mysteriously as his "secret art." When he ran out of money, Gutenberg quietly sought investors, luring them partly by the mystique he attached to his work. What we know

First Mass-Produced Written Word. Johannes Gutenberg and his assistants could produce 50 to 60 imprints an hour with their modified wine press, but Gutenberg's real contribution was movable metal type. His movable type expedited the putting together of pages and opened the age of mass communication.

about Gutenberg's "secret art" was recorded only because Gutenberg's main backer didn't realize the quick financial return he expected on his investment and sued. The litigation left a record from which historians have pieced together the origins of modern printing.

The date that Johannes Gutenberg printed his first page with movable type is unknown, but historians usually settle on 1446. Gutenberg's printing process was widely copied—and quickly. By 1500, presses all over western Europe had published almost 40,000 books.

Today, Gutenberg is remembered for the Bibles he printed with movable type. Two hundred **Gutenberg Bibles,** each a printing masterpiece, were produced over several years. Gutenberg used the best paper. He concocted an especially black ink. The quality amazed everybody, and the Bibles sold quickly. Gutenberg could have printed hundreds more, perhaps thousands. With a couple of husky helpers, he and his modified wine press could have produced 50 to 60 imprints an hour. However, Johannes Gutenberg, who never had much business savvy, concentrated instead on quality. Forty-seven Gutenberg Bibles remain today, all collector's items. One sold in 1978 for $2.4 million.

Scribist Monk. Until the invention of movable metal type by Johannes Gutenberg in the 1440s, books were produced one at a time by scribes. It was tedious work, production was slow, and scribes were not always faithful to the original.

media timeline

····development of books

1440s Johannes Gutenberg printed Bible using movable type.

1638 Puritans established Cambridge Press.

1836 William Holmes McGuffey began influential reading textbooks.

1850s A distinct American literature emerged in novels.

1895 Congress established the Government Printing Office.

1971 Michael Hart began Project Gutenberg online archives.

importance of books

(STUDY PREVIEW) Mass-produced books, first intro-duced in the mid-1400s, changed human history by accel-erating the exchange of ideas and information among more people. Books have endured as a repository of culture. They are the primary vehicle by which new generations are educated to their society's values and by which they learn the lessons of the past.

books in human history

The introduction of mass-produced books in the 15th century marked a turning point in human history. Before then, books were handwritten, usually by scribist monks who copied existing books onto blank sheets of paper letter by letter, one page at a time. These **scribists** could turn out only a few hand-lettered books in a lifetime of tedium.

In the mid-1400s, **Johannes Gutenberg,** a tinkerer in what is now Germany, devised an innovation that made it possible to print pages using metal letters. Gutenberg's revolutionary contribution was in applying metallurgy to the printing process, which went back to ancient China. The idea for **movable metal type** occurred to Gutenberg in the mid-1430s. Instead of wood, which often cracked in the pressing process, he experimented with casting individual letters in a lead-based alloy. He built a frame the size of a book's page and then arranged the metal letters into words. Once a page was filled—with letters and words and sentences—he put the frame into a modified wine press, applied ink, laid paper and pressed. The process made it possible to produce dozens, even hundreds and thousands, of copies.

Gutenberg's impact cannot be overstated. The duplicative power of movable type put the written word into wide circulation and fueled quantum increases in literacy. One hundred years after Gutenberg, the state of communication in Europe had under-gone a revolution. Elaborate postal systems were in place. Standardized maps pro-duced by printing presses replaced hand-copied maps, with all their inaccuracies and idiosyncrasies. People began writing open letters to be distributed far and wide. News-papers followed. The exchange of scientific discoveries was hastened through special publications. Johannes Gutenberg stands at a dividing point in the history of human-kind. A scribist culture preceded him. The age of mass communication followed.

Gutenberg Masterpiece.
The craftsmanship that Johan-nes Gutenberg put into his Bibles made them sought after in the 1450s and still today. Of the 47 remaining, one sold at an auction for $2.4 million in 1978.

Gutenberg Bibles
Surviving Bibles all museum pieces.

scribists
Those who copied books manually.

Johannes Gutenberg
Transformed civilization with mass-produced written word.

movable metal type
Small blocks of type arranged into words, lines and pages.

Cambridge Press
First colonial publisher.

John Harvard
Owned a major personal library.

books in national development

Books were valued in the Colonial period. In Massachusetts in 1638, the Puritans set up **Cambridge Press,** the first book producer in what is now the United States. Just as today, personal libraries were a symbol of the intelligentsia. **John Harvard** of Cambridge, Massachusetts, was widely known for his personal collection of 300 books, a large library for the time. When Harvard died in 1638, he bequeathed his books to Newtowne College, which was so grateful that it renamed itself for him. Today it's Harvard University.

media | people

learning on the porch

William Holmes McGuffey

Just out of college, William Holmes McGuffey arrived at Miami University on horseback in 1826 with a few books on moral philosophy and languages. At the Ohio university he tested his theories on education with neighborhood kids who gathered on his porch next to the campus. McGuffey confirmed that children learn better when sentences are accompa-nied by a picture. He also noted that reading out loud helps and that spelling is not very impor-tant in learning to read. McGuffey took notes on his observations and tested his ideas on other age groups. He also col-lected a mass of stories from a great variety of places.

In 1833, the Truman & Smith publishing com-pany was scouting for someone to write a series of readers and found McGuffey. He culled his favorite stories for the new reader. Many were from the Bible, and most made a moral point. In 1836 the first of McGuffey's *Eclectic Readers* appeared. McGuffey still had lots of material that he had used with the children on his porch, and a second, a third and a fourth reader followed. Truman & Smith marketed the books vigor-ously, and they soon had a national following.

The company broke up and the publishing and marketing of McGuffey's books changed hands sev-eral times. As the years went on, many editors had a hand in revision, and McGuffey had less and less direction regarding their content. McGuffey's brother Alexander com-pleted the fifth and sixth readers in the series between 1843 and 1845 while McGuffey was busy with his teaching.

McGuffey's *Eclectic Readers* sold more than 122 million copies. A ver-sion was still being pro-duced for school use in 1920. Today some are in print for home schooling.

McGuffey Readers. For a century, McGuffey's readers taught American children to read, contributing to quantum increases in literacy. The McGuffey series first appeared in 1836.

William Holmes McGuffey
Wrote influential reading textbooks.

William Holmes McGuffey's reading textbook series brought the United States out of frontier illiteracy. More than 122 million of McGuffey's readers were sold beginning in 1836, coinciding with the boom in public-supported education as an American credo.

In the mid-1800s, American publishers brought out books that identified a distinctive new literary genre: the American novel. Still widely read are Nathaniel Hawthorne's *The Scarlet Letter* (1850), Herman Melville's *Moby Dick* (1851), Harriet

James Fenimore Cooper

Beecher Stowe's *Uncle Tom's Cabin* (1852), Mark Twain's *Huckleberry Finn* (1884) and Stephen Crane's *The Red Badge of Courage* (1895).

Today, most of the books that shape our culture are adapted to other media, which expands their influence. Magazine serialization put Ronald Reagan's memoirs in more hands than did the publisher of the book. More people have seen Carl Sagan on television than have read his books. Stephen King thrillers sell spectacularly, especially in paperback, but more people see the movie renditions. Books have a trickle-down effect through other media, their impact being felt even by those who cannot or do not read them. Although people are more in touch with other mass media day to day, books are the heart of creating American culture and passing it on to new generations.

defining the book business

(STUDY PREVIEW) When most people think about books, fiction and nonfiction aimed at general readers come to mind. These are called trade books, which are a major segment of the book industry. Also important are textbooks, which include not only schoolbooks but also reference books and even cookbooks.

trade books
General-interest titles.

textbooks
Educational, professional, reference titles.

paperbacks
Low-cost innovation.

Allen Lane
Built Penguin paperbacks in England.

Robert de Graff
Originated Pocket paperbacks in the United States.

electronic books
Stored and delivered digitally rather than printed.

bookstore downloads
Books created by local bookstores on site from text stored in distant computers.

peronal downloads
Books that individuals store in personal computers by drawing text from distant computers.

Project Gutenberg
Full-text online archive of major literature, reference works.

Michael Hart
Creator of Project Gutenberg.

trade books

The most visible part of the $15-billion-a-year American book-publishing industry produces **trade books,** which include general-interest titles. Trade books can be incredible best-sellers:

- J. R. R. Tolkien's *The Hobbit,* 35 million copies since 1937.
- Margaret Mitchell's *Gone With the Wind,* 28 million since 1936.
- William Peter Blatty's *The Exorcist,* 12 million since 1972.

While publishing trade books can be extremely profitable when a book takes off, trade books have always been a high-risk proposition. One estimate is that 60 percent of them lose money, 36 percent break even and 4 percent turn a good profit, and only a few in the latter category become best-sellers and make spectacular money.

textbooks

Although the typical successful trade book best-seller can be a spectacular money-maker for a few months, a successful **textbook** has a longer life with steady income. For example, Curtis MacDougall wrote a breakthrough textbook on journalism in 1932 that went through eight editions before he died in 1985. Then, the publisher brought out a ninth edition, with Robert Reid bringing it up to date. This has given MacDougall's *Interpretative Reporting* a life span of more than 60 years. Although textbook publishers don't routinely announce profits by title, *Interpretative Reporting* undoubtedly has generated more income than many trade book best-sellers.

Textbooks are the biggest segment of the book market. Textbooks, a book industry category that includes reference and professional books, generate a little more than half of the industry's profits. About one-third of those profits are from lawyers, physicians, journalists, scholars, accountants, engineers and other professionals who need personal libraries for reference.

Reference books, such as dictionaries, atlases and encyclopedias, represent about 10 percent of textbook revenue. Over the years, the Bible and Noah Webster's dictionary have led reference book sales, but others also have had exceptional, long-term success that rivals leading trade books. For example:

- Benjamin Spock's *Baby and Child Care,* 50 million copies since 1946.
- *Betty Crocker's Cookbook,* 21 million since 1950.
- *The Better Homes and Garden Cookbook,* 36 million since 1930.
- Dale Carnegie's *How to Win Friends and Influence People,* 15 million since 1940.

innovations in books

(STUDY PREVIEW) Paperback editions expanded the market for books during the Great Depression—an innovation that made books afforable to more people. New and forthcoming innovations involve digital storage and transmission of books in paper-less forms.

paperbacks

The modern **paperback** was the brainchild of **Allen Lane.** In 1935, in the middle of the Depression, Lane launched Penguin Books in London. He figured that low-cost books would find a following in poor times. It was a gamble. He printed only 20,000 copies of his first few books, popular novels and biographies. Then came a breakthrough. The Woolworth's dime store chain in the United States agreed to stock them.

Imitators followed. In New York **Robert de Graff** introduced Pocket Books in 1939. They were unabridged best-sellers that fit easily in pocket or purse. They cost only 25 cents. In their first two months on the market, sales reached 325,000 books. Almost everybody could spring a quarter for a book. "The paperback democratized reading in America," wrote Kenneth Davis in his book *Two-Bit Culture: The Paperbacking of America.* Today, paperback sales exceed 1 million copies a day. More than 120,000 titles are in print.

electronic books

Books as we know them, printed and bound, may be with us long into the future— but fundamental changes are under way. The bound ink-on-paper product that comes off mammoth presses for shipping by trucks to retail shelves will slip from dominance as a format for the written word. Futurologists agree that electronic books are coming. What form will they take? Two scenarios are emerging: bookstore downloads and personal downloads.

Bookstore Downloads. Instead of browsing through your favorite bookstore, you would go to a bookstore with no books. If you want a good mystery, you instead sit down at a computer screen, call up the latest mystery titles, and review electronic versions of book jacket blurbs. When you make your choice, you go to a clerk, who asks what form you would like the book in? Hard cover? Paperback? Leather bound? 8½ × 11? Folio size? Slick paper? Pulp? The clerk then hits a few keys and the manuscript is pulled off the publisher's computer, printed on the spot in the bookstore, and bound as you specified, all by automation. These store-bound books could be cheaper because shipping and shelf costs, major expenses in book retailing, are bypassed.

Crude versions of these downloads already exist in college course-packs. Campus stores can download material selected chapters from some textbooks and compile them in whatever sequence a professor specifies for the students.

Personal Downloads. Sometime, probably early in the 21st century, people will download books to their computers or even specialized portable devices. "You will be able to carry them with you to the beach," says Random House chief executive Alberto Vitale. Publishing houses are so confident about the electronic future of their products that they try to require authors to turn over electronic rights to their manuscripts, as well as the traditional rights to manufacture printed versions.

Project Gutenberg. The electronic future is already dawning with many books already online. **Project Gutenberg,** the brain-child of **Michael Hart** of Champaign-Urbana, Illinois, has been putting classic literature and reference works online since 1971. Hart's goal: 10,000 titles by the project's 30th anniversary in 2001.

media onvergence

Audio Books. Putting books on audio cassettes, with someone reading the text out loud, was first intended as a service for sight-impaired people. Then cassette players became standard issue in automobiles, and book publishers saw a whole new market: bored commuters. Today, the number of titles on tape has passed 30,000, including a lot of classics and self-improvement books besides the latest from Mary Higgins Clark.

michael hart

Sensing the potential of the Internet, Michael Hart typed the Declaration of Independence into the University of Illinois mainframe computer in 1971. Then he sent it to everybody on the old ARPA network that preceded the Internet. Thus began Project Gutenberg—a growing online collection of literature and reference works available free.

Hart's Declaration of Independence was a text-only, unglamorous presentation—and that's still how Gutenberg looks. The simple format makes material available to everybody. Says Hart: "I want people who still have old Atari 800s to be able to read these books." Hart likens himself to an electronic Johnny Appleseed, whose goal is straight-forward: Contribute to literacy by making literature universally available. In an interview with Dennis Hamilton for *Wired* magazine, Hart said: "Other than to redesign democracy, I can't think of anything more important than Gutenberg. It's the Archimedes leveler: Give me a place to stand, and I'll move the world."

The plain-vanilla Gutenberg format means blind people can run the text through a speech synthesizer. It also means libraries and other online sources can give their patrons access with no budget strain. And anybody with even the simplest computer and a modem can tap in free.

Hart, who has no regular, full-time job although he has been loosely associated with several universities off and on, keys in books himself. Over the years 750 people worldwide, sharing his enthusiasm, have volunteered to help with inputting and proofing. Two volunteer lawyers check that copyrights have indeed expired on everything that Gutenberg puts online.

About 10,000 Gutenberg files are downloaded from the University of Illinois computer on a typical day, but hundreds of libraries, online services and others recycle the books through their servers. Hart has never tried to keep records on usage: "I don't care where a book goes. I just want it to sprout legs and run."

More than 300 archives of public domain literature are in operation, some of them glitzy Web sites. The plain-vanilla Project Gutenberg, however, is the most widely known—partly because it was first and partly because of Hart's selfless, fervid commitment. Also, it's free.

book marketing

STUDY PREVIEW   Bookstore chains scored major gains in book retailing in the 1990s with the super bookstores and unprecedented inventories. This hurt independent bookstores and mall-based stores. An unexpected result was that publishers got stung by new dynamics introduced by the superstore phenomenon. Another phenomenon in book retailing, book clubs and online book shopping, reflects the move toward home-centered lifestyles.

bookstores

Book retailing is in rapid change. Traditionally shops were independently operated with owners who knew their patrons and were highly sensitive to their interests.

book censorship

How does censorship affect you? The American Library Association's Office for Intellectual Freedom receives reports on library materials that are most frequently challenged. Many acclaimed literary works have been attacked. The list in recent years has been led by:

- Robert Cormier's *The Chocolate War.*
- Salman Rushdie's *The Satanic Verses.*
- J. D. Salinger's *The Catcher in the Rye.*

- Maurice Sendak's *In the Night Kitchen.*
- John Steinbeck's *Of Mice and Men.*
- Mark Twain's *Huckleberry Finn.*
- *Playboy* magazine.
- All books on the occult.

In 1995, these became new targets of censors:

- Ernest Gaines' *The Autobiography of Miss Jane Pittman.*
- Toni Morrison's *Song of Solomon.*

- O. J. Simpson's *I Want to Tell You.*
- Jane Smiley's *A Thousand Acres.*
- Howard Stern's *Private Parts.*

Most complaints to the Office of Intellectual Freedom originate among conservatives, but in recent years a growing number have originated with liberals who want to be sensitive to people who might be offended. Such, for example, has been the heart of complaints

against Twain, who includes the word *nigger* in his late 19th-century dialogue. Critics say that's racist. Twain defenders note that the dialogue is typical of the period. More important, they say Twain was hardly a racist but sympathetic to the plight of blacks of the period.

In an offbeat request for sensitivity, a witch asked one library to take *Hansel and Gretel* off the shelves. The witch complained the book reflected poorly on witchery, a religion.

Then came the mall stores in the 1970s, reshaping how books were marketed. Today super bookstores are rewriting the rules again.

Independents. In Colonial Boston, the first seat of American intellectualism, book-selling was a local entrepreneurial business. The individuals who owned book shops catered to the reading interests of their particular customers. That customer-driven model of book retailing worked for almost 250 years. Even as the book business grew, sales representatives from the publishing houses still made individual calls on shop owners to chat about their wares, and the shop owners ordered what they intuitively knew their customers wanted. Shops maintained distinctive inventories.

Mall Stores. With the growth of mass merchandising and shopping malls in the 1970s, several bookstore chains emerged. Typified by B. Dalton and WaldenBooks, which together had 2,300 stores at their peak, these chains ordered books in huge lots from the publishers and stocked their stores coast to coast with rubber-stamp inventories. Often, these chains bought books even before they were printed, basing their decisions on publishers' promises for promotional blitzes and big discounts for bulk purchases. When huge stocks arrived, the mall stores had to move them—sometimes going to extraordinary steps with displays and discounts to fulfill their own projections, and sometimes without consideration for a book's literary qualities. Suddenly, book-selling became marketing-driven with flashy displays and other incentives prodding customers to buy—hardly a customer-driven way of doing business.

These formulaic stores focused on what could be moved rapidly without any attention to whether they had a balance represented on their shelves. Asked once where the books by the influential psychoanalyst Sigmund Freud could be found, a B. Dalton store manager answered: "Ahhh, I think we had one once." The new criteria was not literary or enlightenment but what products could be moved. The goal: fast inventory turnover.

Whatever their deficiencies, mall stores sold a lot of books—and it hurt the independents. In fact, by 1995, independent stores, which once dominated American book-selling, accounted for only 21.4 percent of sales.

Superstores. Marketing-driven book retailing entered a new dimension, literally, with stand-alone super bookstores in the 1990s. Barnes & Noble, Crown, Borders and Books-a-Million built 900 of the humungous stores, some bigger than grocery supermarkets and stocking 180,000 titles. The superstores do more than sell books. Part of their appeal has been to become a community center of sorts, with cafes, lectures, children's programs and poetry readings. The best news, though, is that with gigantic inventories, superstores have Freud in stock—an improvement over the mall stores.

There was, however, a dark side. By 1998, the superstore chains realized they had over-built. Trying to build customer traffic to maintain market share, these stores entered into a price war. Unable to compete, many mall stores closed. Even more severe was the impact on independents. Every year more went out of business.

While superstore customers liked the discounts, the price war profoundly damaged publishers. Unable to move all the new inventory, the superstores shipped truckloads of books back to publishers. Refunds had been common practice in publishing, almost a consignment relationship between stores and publishers. The volume of the new returns, however, caught publishers unaware. At HarperCollins, for example, operating profits fell 66 percent in 1996, forcing the publisher to take drastic steps. It canceled 106 books for which it had issued advances to authors. It also cut back its acquisition of new titles. In 1996, U.S. book output had reached 58,000 new titles. It was down to 56,000 in 1997 and still dropping. Book output, one measure of a culture's quality, suffered.

The super bookstores, as well as mall stores and independents, also faced growing competition from direct marketing.

direct marketing

Book clubs are becoming more important in creating best-sellers as people spend more time at home, not out shopping. Home-centered lifestyles also have contributed to the growth of online book shopping or a direct-to-consumer sales mechanism.

Book Clubs. A book's financial success can be boosted if a book club offers it to members, especially as a featured selection. Book club committees screen forthcoming books and then send them automatically to members, 12 to 15 times a year. With the **negative option** system, members receive a book unless they reject it after reading the club's promotion for it. The **Book-of-the-Month Club,** the oldest and largest, typically moves 200,000 copies of its featured selection.

Over its history, the Book-of-the-Month Club has shipped more than 500 million books. Started in 1926, BOMC originally saw its market as small-town and rural people without local book stores. The club offered packages of free books to entice people to join on condition they buy more books. Soon, using the same model, the **Literary Guild** was started. The Guild remains the second largest book club today. Dozens of smaller clubs, many of them offering books in specialized fields, have also come into existence. These smaller clubs usually sell about 10,000 copies of their featured selections.

Some kinds of books lend themselves to book clubs. More juvenile books are sold through clubs, led by Teen-Age Book Club, than through retail stores. The club promotes itself to teachers who encourage students to join. The club sells in 80 percent of U.S. elementary schools and 50 percent of the high schools.

Web Shopping. A startup Seattle company, Amazon.com, created an online bookstore with 1 million titles—far more than even the largest super-bookstore. In 1997, Barnes & Noble entered the online business, and soon both stores claimed more than 2.5 million titles. Those sites and other online bookstores are far more than ordering mechanisms. They carry book reviews, author biographies, chat rooms and other attractions. When competition was strongest, the online services offered steep discounts, sometimes 40 percent off retail, and made inroads into book sales through traditional bookstores and superstores.

Direct Mail. Several media companies, including Reader's Digest, Time, Meredith and American Heritage, sell books by mail. Promotional literature is sent to people on carefully selected mailing lists, and people order what they want. Professional and academic publishing houses, whose products wouldn't find space on bookstore shelves, market primarily through the mail. These publishers buy mailing lists from professional organizations, which, loaded with good prospects for particular titles, usually assures a profitable number of orders by return mail.

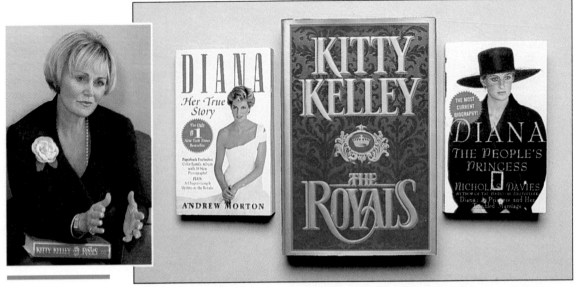

Kitty Kelley

Instant Books. When Lady Diana was killed in a Paris car wreck, many book publishers scrambled to capitalize on the public's obsession. Writers were hired to work day and night to compile breaking news into book form—and some titles were in stores within days. Old titles were re-issued. Warner Books speeded up production of Kitty Kelley's major unauthorized biography, *The Royals.* To critics who saw the instant books as ghoulish, publishers and book-sellers agreed to share some profits with Di's favorite charities. Ghoulish or not, the instant books sold.

commercial success

(STUDY PREVIEW) One measure of a book's success is sales, but because some books cost a lot more to bring to market than others, a great number of sales do not necessarily mean profits for the publisher. Strange as it may seem, sales are not a strong indicator of whether a book is read. People buy books for all kinds of reasons besides reading them.

best-sellers

What makes a **best-seller**? Traditional successful subjects have been Abraham Lincoln, physicians and dogs, which prompted one wag to suggest that a book about Lincoln's doctor's dog couldn't help but make a fortune. Books on the Kennedy family have done well over the past 30 years. Controversy also sells. Watergate books had a ready audience, and so did the memoirs and insider accounts of key figures in the Iran-Contra scandal of 1986 and 1987. Inspirational books sell well, and so does just about any book with a title that starts with "How to." Gossipy books, including autobiographies by celebrities, tend to do well. Biographies by celebrities' estranged children can be blockbusters.

> **best-seller**
> 75,000 copies hard cover, 100,000 paperback.

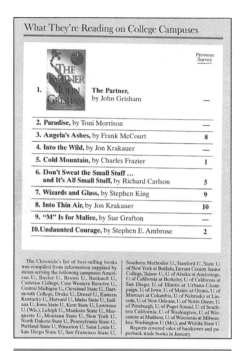

What They're Reading on College Campuses

		Previous Survey
1.	The Partner, by John Grisham	—
2.	Paradise, by Toni Morrison	—
3.	Angela's Ashes, by Frank McCourt	8
4.	Into the Wild, by Jon Krakauer	—
5.	Cold Mountain, by Charles Frazier	1
6.	Don't Sweat the Small Stuff ... and It's All Small Stuff, by Richard Carlson	5
7.	Wizards and Glass, by Stephen King	9
8.	Into Thin Air, by Jon Krakauer	10
9.	"M" Is for Malice, by Sue Grafton	—
10.	Undaunted Courage, by Stephen E. Ambrose	2

The Chronicle's list of best-selling books was compiled from information supplied by stores serving the following campuses: American U., Baylor U., Brown U., Bucknell U., Carleton College, Case Western Reserve U., Central Michigan U., Cleveland State U., Dartmouth College, Drake U., Drexel U., Eastern Kentucky U., Harvard U., Idaho State U., Indiana U., Iowa State U., Kent State U., Lawrence U. (Wis.), Lehigh U., Mankato State U., Marquette U., Montana State U., New York U., North Dakota State U., Pennsylvania State U., Portland State U., Princeton U., Saint Louis U., San Diego State U., San Francisco State U., Southern Methodist U., Stanford U., State U. of New York at Buffalo, Tarrant County Junior College, Tulane U., U. of Alaska at Anchorage, U. of California at Berkeley, U. of California at San Diego, U. of Illinois at Urbana-Champaign, U. of Iowa, U. of Maine at Orono, U. of Missouri at Columbia, U. of Nebraska at Lincoln, U. of New Orleans, U. of Notre Dame, U. of Pittsburgh, U. of Puget Sound, U. of Southern California, U. of Washington, U. of Wisconsin at Madison, U. of Wisconsin at Milwaukee, Washington U. (Mo.), and Wichita State U.

Reports covered sales of hardcover and paperback trade books in January.

Campus Best-Seller List. The *Chronicle of Higher Education,* a weekly newspaper read mostly by college administrators and faculty, checks campus bookstores at selected universities for a regular best-seller list among college people. The list bears some semblance to the New York *Times* weekly best-seller list, but there are differences that reflect issues and subjects with special attraction for people who frequent campus shops.

Best-Sellers. People in the book business track the list in the trade journal *Publishers Weekly.* The most quoted list, in the New York *Times,* ranks books by general categories. Critics say the *Times* gives too much weight to high-brow independent book stores, and its list undervalues a lot of paperback fiction. The *Wall Street Journal* list uses an index feature to show the relative sales of books on its lists. *USA Today* also has a weekly list, but it is a hodge-podge of formats and genres that, say critics, makes it a list of oranges and apples.

Usually publishers are pleased if a trade book sells more than 75,000 hardcover copies and 100,000 paperback copies—unless the book was part of a costly marketing program that required even more sales to break even.

best-seller lists

Best-seller lists compiled by numerous publications can spur sales. "If other people are buying the book, it must be good," people think. Then they buy it to read for themselves.

• The New York *Times* has the most-cited best-seller list. Despite the *Times'* claims that it samples "3,050 book stores plus wholesalers serving 38,000 other retailers," critics say the methodology is flawed. The critics say the *Times* favors independent book stores over the chains and drug store and airport outlets. That means popular mystery, romance, science fiction and western books and paperbacks in general are woefully under-reported. The *Times* disqualifies religious books from its list. Novelist Evan Maxwell faults the *Times* for a snobbish bias that under-counts books sold by independent distributors, rack jobbers, wholesalers and "beetle-browed teamsters who service smoke shops and newsstands."

The *Times* has been slow to respond to critics, even after an embarrassing revelation involving the highbrow *Closing of the American Mind* by Allan Bloom. It seems the *Times* was so impressed in reviewing an advance copy that it prematurely catapulted the book onto its best-seller list while most of the first printing was still on the shipping dock. To make it all the more embarrassing, the first printing was only 7,500 copies. Whatever the problems with the *Times* list, it is powerful. Bloom's book soon was Number 1 on just about every list in the country.

- The *Wall Street Journal* began its own list in 1994, based on national bookstore sales, which avoids the skewing effect of wholesale buys and statistical projections. The *Journal* gives an index of sales. In the first week, the current Danielle Steele novel led with an index of 100. Second was Michael Crichton's *Disclosure* with an index of 57. That meant Crichton was seeking 57 percent as many copies as Steele. Robert James Waller's *Bridges of Madison County* and *Slow Waltz in Cedar Creek* were third and fourth at an index of 38 and 32. The 15th fiction title, Tom Clancy's *Without Remorse*, was bottom on the fiction list, 15th with an index of 11. The indexing provides a comparison.

- *USA Today* samples over-the-counter sales at book stores and chains for its list, "Best-Selling Books: What People Across the USA Are Reading." It's a hodge-podge of 50 books, hard-back, trade-sized and paperback. Novelist Evan Maxwell, who tracks best-seller lists for Novelists Inc., an authors' association, doesn't much like the *USA Today* list. She says: "It lumps Rush Limbaugh with Howard Stern, Robert James Waller, Maya Angelou and cartoonist Bill Watterson. The undigested melange of titles, genres and formats gets thick and chunky real quick." Unlike the New York *Times, USA Today* lists the stores and chains that comprise its sample.

mass marketing

Book publishers once sent sample copies to influential magazines and newspapers and hoped for favorable reviews. They still do, but no longer is marketing so simple. Today, newspaper and magazine reviews are less important than television and radio interviews. ABC White House correspondent Sam Donaldson went on the publicity trail to promote his book, *Hold On, Mr. President*. In a two-week whirlwind, Donaldson hit 11 major cities, averaging six radio, television and newspaper interviews per city. There were appearances on the Larry King show and other network programs. He also fielded 75 telephone interviews during the book's first few weeks on bookstore shelves and made other appearances that nobody tallied. Almost immediately, the Donaldson book was on best-seller lists. The major publishing houses have whole departments assigned to promotion, whose job is to line up time on major broadcast programs for their authors to hawk their latest books.

Advertising campaigns have become important in book marketing. If a publisher has decided to push a book with advertising, bookstore chains take greater interest. So do book clubs, another important retail outlet.

Books lend themselves to what advertising people call point-of-purchase displays—especially paperbacks, which often are impulse purchases. Countertop and free-standing promotional racks are used more than ever. Lascivious covers and hyped subtitles improve paperback sales at the racks. The excesses once prompted humorist Art Buchwald to suggest that *Snow White and the Seven Dwarfs* be subtitled

Authors on Television. Media exposure for a new book, especially on television, enhances sales, as talk-show producers can attest. Every day the major shows are deluged with proposals to interview authors of new books. Here, Amy Tan, author of the novels *The Joy Luck Club* and *The Kitchen God's Wife,* appears on the "Charlie Rose" show. This late night PBS program is considered one of the more literate, author-friendly shows on television.

"The Story of a Ravishing Blonde Virgin Held Captive by Seven Deformed Men, All With Different Lusts." For *Alice in Wonderland,* he suggested "A Young Girl's Search for Happiness in a Weird, Depraved World of Animal Desires: Can She Ever Return to a Normal, Happy Life After Falling So Far?"

Controversy sells. After Stein & Day published Elia Kazan's *The Arrangement,* the Mount Pleasant, Iowa, Library Board sent it back as too racy for its shelves. Stein & Day's president mailed a letter to the Mount Pleasant *News,* offering a free copy to everyone in the community, urging them to read the book and decide for themselves and decrying the library board as censorious. Eight hundred people ordered their free copy, which created a bundle of publicity. Sales soared.

subsidiary rights

Book marketing increasingly involves recycling a title through variations, including paperback editions, **serialization,** and other **subsidiary rights.** There is income too in selling foreign rights. Selling these subsidiary rights, as they are called, also raises more income for authors.

Serialization of a book in magazines, usually in condensed form, dates to 1936 when **DeWitt Wallace,** the founder of *Reader's Digest,* approached Harper & Bros. with an idea. Wallace wanted to condense and reprint 50 pages from a new Harper book. He offered $1,000 for serialization rights. The proposition made no sense to Harper. The publishers supposed that condensation in a popular magazine would hurt book sales. Wallace argued the opposite, saying serialization would whet public interest, and he sweetened his offer to $5,000 if book sales did not increase after serialization began. Harper took him up on the deal, sales quadrupled, and the publishing house lost the $5,000. Today, publishing houses routinely figure income from magazine serialization into their budgets when planning a book. They know that serialization helps market the book.

Several theories exist on why serialization boosts book sales. One is that people who read a condensation then want to read the whole book. Another theory, which assumes human vanity, is that readers of a condensed version want the real book on their shelves to point to with pride as they talk about having read the book, even though they might never have opened the book itself.

serialization
Publishing book in segments in magazines, newspapers.

subsidiary rights
Rights to adapt book for additional markets.

DeWitt Wallace
Started first magazine serialization.

Publishers also sell paperback rights. Bantam paid $75,000 at an auction to put out *Jaws* as a mass-marketed paperback. By the mid-1980s, mass-marketed paperback rights had skyrocketed for blockbusters. Judith Krantz's *Princess Daisy* drew a reported $3.2 million for paperback rights.

Other income can come from movie rights. Movie producers will pay handsomely for rights to a book, and there can be a profitable second wave of interest in a book after it has been made into a movie.

A book's financial success can be further assured if a publisher interests a book club in offering it to members as a monthly selection. Book club committees screen forthcoming books and then send them automatically to members.

mass-marketing debate

(STUDY PREVIEW)   Some people praise the mass-marketing of books, noting that the book industry performs its best service when it provides great numbers of people what they want. Other people say that mass marketing detracts from the traditional literary and culture-enhancing role of books.

blockbuster authors

The competition for **blockbusters** approached frenzy in the late 1980s. Epic novelist James Clavell was given $5 million for his unwritten *Whirlwind* in 1985. It was an unprecedented risk that required sales of 1 million hardback and 3 million paperback copies for William Morrow and Avon Books, partners in the project, to break even. People who follow the book industry shuddered at the high stakes, but soon even the Clavell deal was eclipsed. Bursting with cash from corporate parents, other publishing houses upped the ante:

- Mary Higgins Clark, $32 million from Simon & Schuster for her next six thrillers in 1992.

- Jonathan Kellerman, $20 to $25 million for five new thrillers, from Random House, in 1997.

- Anne Rice, $17 million for three new vampire books in 1993.

- Novelist Stephen King, $10 million from Viking Penguin and New American Library for each of his next four horror stories.

- Pope John Paul II, $9 million for *Crossing the Threshold of Hope*, a 230-page collection of papal essays, from Knopf in 1994.

- Journalist Tom Wolfe, $7 million for a successor to his *Bonfire of the Vanities*. Out of loyalty to Farrar, Straus & Giroux, one of the few remaining independent houses, Wolfe turned down $15 million from a competing publisher.

- Southern author Alexandra Ripley, $4.9 million from Warner Books for a sequel to *Gone With the Wind*. Margaret Mitchell's advance for the 1936 original was $500.

blockbuster
Immensely successful title.

media people

blockbuster authors

Book sales are impossible to track precisely, but there is no doubt these authors produce regular blockbusters. The numbers here, for the typical hardcover sales by these authors, are culled from publishers' promotional materials, publishing insiders, interviews and other sources. Paperback sales compound these figures.

Tom Clancy	1.3 million
Stephen King	1.2 million
Danielle Steele	1.1 million
James Michener	850,000
Sidney Sheldon	840,000
Robert Ludlow	700,000
Judith Krantz	500,000
Jackie Collins	470,000
John Le Carré	460,000
Ken Follett	330,000
Jeffrey Archer	240,000

- Newt Gingrich, the speaker of the U.S. House of Representatives, $4.5 million for his *To Renew America* from HarperCollins in 1995. In a political hullabaloo over the advance, Gingrich ended up taking only a token $1 advance, although it was expected his royalties would top $4.5 million. Industry sources said he would be earning $9 a copy.

- Marcia Clark, the O.J. Simpson prosecutor, $4.2 million for *Without a Doubt,* from Viking in 1995.

- Mario Puzo, $4 million for an unwritten novel that Random House hoped would outdo *The Godfather.*

- George Stephanopolous, $2.8 million for his memoirs as a Clinton White House aide, from Little, Brown, in 1996.

- Dick Morris, $2.5 million for his memoirs, *Behind the Oval Office,* from Random House, in 1996.

Megabuck advances abated somewhat in the late 1990s when publishers, overwhelmed with unexpected returns from superstores, were forced to trim expenses. Stephen King, for example, found no takers for a proposed $17 million advance. Even so, multimillion advances continued for proven authors.

The publishers who invested so heavily in these authors continued to promote them as celebrities. The author star system, however, had a negative side. The blockbuster system concentrated the resources of publishing houses on a few major projects, which worked against the richness that the book industry could be contributing to the culture with a greater number of works. Brooks Thomas, president of HarperCollins' predecessor company, acknowledged that the system centers attention on commercial books instead of books that may be better literature or stronger contributors to the culture and society. Said Thomas: "God help poetry or criticism."

media online

Banned Books Online: A great collection of works (including classics) someone doesn't want you to see. www.cs.cmu.edu/Web/People/spok/banned-books.html

Internet Public Library: With teen, youth and cyber-savvy links www.ipl.org

populist versus elitist views

The mass-marketing debate can be boiled down to two contradictory traditions in American life. People in the **populist** tradition see the book industry and other mass media performing best when they satisfy the interests of the greatest number of people. The **elitist** tradition is not concerned with popularity or mass tastes but with quality. Elitists are not so unrealistic as to think that book publishers can survive by producing unpopular books. They emphasize, however, that the book industry has forsaken its traditional responsibility to produce books that are good for the society—not just those that sell well. Elitists tend to cast conglomeration in evil terms because parent corporations push their book subsidiaries to make ever greater profits, regardless of whether it is through publishing significant books or junk.

John Dessauer, a veteran publishing executive who is dismayed at what has happened, sounds a note of caution: "Publishers who consistently disrespect the demand for quality and worth in the manuscripts they publish will, despite temporary successes, find their enterprises dying of spiritual starvation in the end; just as publishers who consistently ignore the commercial needs of their establishments will find before long that cultural opportunities are negated by bankruptcy."

Critics of mass marketing may be overreacting. It has happened before when the book industry has gone in new directions. When Gutenberg introduced movable type, the Abbot of Sponheim exhorted his scribist monks to keep copying. He argued that it kept idle hands busy and encouraged diligence, devotion and knowledge of Scripture. When Robert de Graff introduced the 25-cent paperback, critics were concerned that the economics of the book industry would be so upset that the culture would be set back.

In a longer view, developments in the book industry all seem to have contributed to advances in the culture. Literacy, perhaps 10 percent in Gutenberg's time, is well past 90 percent in modern-day America. Not as many people are bookworms as might be, but more can read. Someday we may realize that the mass marketing of books has advanced literature and culture much as McGuffey's readers did in the 1800s, although in a different way. Some of the thunder in the elitists' criticism has been lost with the growth of superstores. While these stores cater to mass tastes, their huge inventories cover a broad range of subjects in some depth. Freud is there.

book publishers

(STUDY PREVIEW)   Conglomeration has reduced the book industry to fewer and fewer companies, all with global interests. Even so, small publishers continue, many profitably, in niches.

major houses

As with other mass media industries, book publishing has undergone consolidation with companies merging with each other, acquiring one another and buying lists from one another. Simon & Schuster, with more than 100 imprints, was the

---

populism
Value measured in sales.

elitism
Value measured in social good, quality.

Simon & Schuster
Largest commercial book publisher.

media databank

corporate connections

As late as World War II, most U.S. book publishing houses were family owned and independent. A lot has changed. The number of books issued annually, including revisions, has multiplied 12-fold to 60,000. Also, the major publishing houses are no longer family owned but part of media conglomerates with manifold interests.

Book Company	Corporate Parents and Siblings
Random House	Bertelsmann of Germany, whose interests in the United States include Bantam, Dell and Doubleday books, RCA and Arista records and numerous magazines.
Harcourt Brace	General Cinema, whose interests include HBJ insurance; Holt, Rinehart books; W. B. Saunders books; Neiman Marcus department stores; specialty retail outlets and movie theaters.
HarperCollins	News Corp., whose origins are in the Australian media empire of Rupert Murdoch and whose interests include Fox Television; Twentieth Century Fox movie studio; Ansett Airlines in Australia; the New York *Post;* newspapers in Australia, England, Hong Kong; a European satellite television network and Australian television stations.
William Morrow	Hearst, whose interests include Avon books; Hearst newspapers; *Esquire, Cosmopolitan, Redbook* and other magazines and television and radio stations.
G. P. Putnam's Sons	MCA, whose interests include Berkley Publishing; Universal movies; Decca, Kapp, Geffen and UNI records.
Simon & Schuster	Viacom, whose interests include Paramount movies; sports teams; Madison Square Garden; television stations; and movie houses.
Warner Books	Time Warner Turner, whose interests include CNN, HBO; Time-Life books; *Life, People* and *Time* magazines; Little, Brown books; local cable systems; Warner books; Warner Bros. movies; Warner Bros., Atlantic, Elektra, Reprise, Chappell records; Warner Home Video; Warner Amex and other cable television companies.
Addison-Wesley Longman	Pearson, of London, a fast-growing international company.

largest commercial book publisher in the world through most of the 1990s, with both extensive lists in trade books and also textbooks. Then in 1997, the parent company, Viacom, sold off everything but the trade book units. Through acquisitions, McGraw-Hill became the largest textbook publisher in the 1990s. Another major player was Bertelsmann of Germany.

Rankings vary by criteria and also are affected when companies sell portions of their lists to one another. An example was HarperCollins' 1995 decision to unload its extensive textbook operation to raise cash to pare down debt accumulated in earlier deals. The textbooks went to Pearson, a London media conglomerate, which folded the HarperCollins titles into its Addison-Wesley Longman textbook subsidiary in Boston. Got all that straight? The details are less important than the fact they illustrate an ongoing flux in the book industry. Amid all the flux, there is, however, a consistent thread: Fewer and fewer companies are dominating more and more of the world's book output.

It is true that thousands of small publishing houses exist, but outside their niches they are not major players.

small presses

Some universities, museums and research institutions publish scholarly titles that commercial publishing houses couldn't consider for economic reasons. Books from the **university presses,** as these publishing houses are known collectively, are purchased mostly by libraries and scholars. Some end up as textbooks.

By some counts, there are 12,000 book-publishing companies in the United States. The catalogs of most contain only a few titles. Among these small presses are some important regional publishers that publish only low-volume books with a long life. For example, Caxton Press in Caldwell, Idaho, produces Pacific Northwest books, many of them on historical topics with a selling life that can run decades. Other small presses specialize in poetry and special subjects for limited audiences that wouldn't otherwise be served. It's almost impossible, for example, to find more than a few token poetry books in a chain store.

vanity presses

It's easy for an author to get a book published—if the author is willing to pay all expenses up front. Family histories and club cookbooks are a staple in this part of the book industry. So are many who's-who books and directories, which list names and then are sold to those whose names are in the books.

Some book publishers, called **vanity presses,** go further by soliciting manuscripts and letting the author infer that the company can make it a best-seller. These companies direct their advertising at unpublished authors and promise a free manuscript review. A custom-addressed form letter then goes back to the author, saying, quite accurately no matter how good or how bad the manuscript, that the proposed book "is indicative of your talent." The letter also says the company would be pleased to publish the manuscript. Most vanity companies do little beyond printing, however. Their ability to promote and distribute a book is very limited, although an occasional best-seller emerges.

It can be argued that vanity publishers unscrupulously take advantage of unpublished authors who don't know how the book industry works. It can be argued too that a legitimate service is being provided. Ed Uhlan of Exposition Press, one of the largest vanity publishers, wrote an autobiographical book, *The Rogue of Publishers Row,* which details how slight the chance is that vanity press clients can make money. When he began including a free copy with the materials he sent inquiring authors, incredible as it seems, his business actually increased.

university presses
Academic and research publishers.

vanity presses
Author pays costs.

Government Printing Office
The U.S. government publisher.

u.s. government printing office

Many major book publishers are household names—Doubleday, Random House, **Simon & Schuster**—but not many people think of the federal government as a major player. The **Government Printing Office** produces more titles than even Simon & Schuster, the largest commercial book publisher in the world.

The GPO, established in 1895 for the systematic distribution of government publications, has 27,000 titles in print, including a few best-sellers. A 108-page paperback called *Infant Care,* published first in 1914, has sold 14 million copies. *Your Federal Income Tax* is a perennial big seller as April 15 approaches.

When significant government documents are published, such as the Warren Commission report on the assassination of President John Kennedy, the Nixon tapes, the Surgeon General's report on smoking or the Meese Commission report on pornography, the GPO can rival commercial publishing houses in the number of sales.

chapter wrap-up

Book publishing is a high-risk business, especially for works geared to general consumers. Most books do not make money, which means that publishing houses rely on best-sellers to offset the losses. Despite the risks, books can make enormous profits, which led many conglomerates to buy publishing houses in the 1980s. The new parent corporations pressed for more profitability. The result has been heightened competition for big-name authors and new attention to mass marketing. Multimillion-dollar advances to authors for popular, though not necessarily significant, works suggest that the book industry is backing away from its traditional role in furthering American culture and public enlightenment.

Conglomeration and increased pressure for profit are occurring in all mass media, and so is the question of cultural responsibility. The question is especially poignant for the book industry because it has been a central factor in American cultural values since the mid-19th century when a new literary genre, the American novel, emerged. These novels contributed to an American identity that was distinct from Europe's. With pride in their cultural contributions, major publishing houses integrated a profit consciousness with an explicit responsibility to publish worthy works for their own sake regardless of profit potential. There is evidence that the tradition is being lost with the new emphasis on mass marketing, which works almost exclusively with titles that sell quickly at mall bookstores.

questions for review

1. How did the mass production of the written word fundamentally change human history?

2. What are the main categories of books today?

3. What was the effect of paperback books? What about electronic books?

4. How has book retailing changed? What are the implications?

5. What makes a book a commercial success? How is this success measured?

6. Why do elitists worry about new forms of book retailing?

7. Do small specialized book publishers still have a place?

questions for critical thinking

1. Trace the development of the book industry through the innovations of these persons: Johannes Gutenberg, William Holmes McGuffey, Allen Lane and Robert de Graff.

2. What invention doomed the scribist culture that preceded the age of mass communication?

3. How do subsidiary rights multiply the profit potential of trade books?

4. Distinguish trade books and textbooks in terms of profit potential, duration on the market, distribution systems and the effect of mass-marketed paperbacks.

5. Subsidiary rights have become a major revenue source for book publishers. Discuss three kinds of subsidiary rights and their effect on the book industry.

6. For most people, book publishing brings McGraw-Hill, Simon & Schuster, HarperCollins and other major companies to mind. Describe how the following entities fit into the industry: Government Printing Office, Iowa State University Press, Caxton Press and Exposition Press.

7. Is there a threat to quality literature from subsidiary rights? From mass marketing? From conglomeration? From the quest for blockbusters? From projection models?

8. What are ways the book industry can assure its continued growth? How can the book industry protect itself from the need to retrench if growth stalls?

9. Where is the U.S. book industry heading with electronic publishing?

for further learning

Ken Auletta. "The Publishing World: The Impossible Business." *New Yorker* (October 6, 1997). Pages 50–63. Auletta, one of our time's best media reporters, identifies issues facing the U.S. book industry in this superb update.

Nicholson Baker. "The Author vs. the Library." *New Yorker* (October 14, 1996). Pages 50–62. Baker details the techno book-burning that has taken place at the San Francisco Public Library as part of computerization. Hundreds of thousands of books, many valuable and without duplicates in the collection, have been weeded. It's happening elsewhere too.

Book Industry Study Group. *Book Industry Trends.* New York: Book Industry Study Group. This voluminous compilation of data by book industry segments is updated annually.

John P. Dessauer. *Book Publishing: What It Is, What It Does,* 2nd edition. (R. R. Bowker, 1981). Dessauer, a veteran book publisher, is especially good on the organization of the book industry.

Wilson P. Dizard, Jr. *The Coming Information Age: An Overview of Technology, Economics and Politics* (Longman, 1982). Dizard, a futurist, explores the range of implications of postindustrialism, including the economics of media adaptation.

Elizabeth L. Eisenstein. *The Printing Press as an Agent of Change: Communications and Cultural Transformation in Early-Modern Europe,* 2 vols. (Cambridge University Press, 1980). Eisenstein offers a thorough examination of the advent of printing and how it changed even how we see ourselves.

Albert N. Greco. *The Book Publishing Industry.* Allyn & Bacon, 1996. Greco bases the thorough examination of the book business, including publishing and retailing, on data that he shares in numerous tables. The focus is on the 1980s and 1990s, with a good examination of major issues.

Nat Hentoff. *Free Speech for Me—But Not for Thee: How the American Left and Right Relentlessly Censor Each Other* (HarperCollins, 1992). Hentoff, an outspoken free-speech advocate, chronicles episodes in which people try to silence other voices and their rationales for doing so.

E. R. Hutchinson. *Tropic of Cancer on Trial* (Grove, 1968). Professor Hutchinson details the issues and the litigation trail of Grove Press's anticensorship battles in the 1960s on behalf of *Tropic of Cancer* by Henry Miller.

Bruce Porter. "B. Dalton: The Leader of the Chain Gang." *Saturday Review* (June 9, 1979). Porter worries about the effect of bookstore chains on the quality of books that Americans are reading.

James B. Stewart. "Moby Dick in Manhattan." *The New Yorker* (June 27/July 4, 1994). Pages 46–66. Stewart offers insight into how contemporary book publishing works in his detailing of the trials of acclaimed but poverty-stricken author James Wilcox.

André Schiffrin. "The Corporatization of Publishing." *Nation* (June 3, 1996). Pages 29–32. Schiffrin draws on 35 years experience as a book publishing executive to argue that conglomeration has damaged the amount of good literature that makes it to the book shelf.

John Tebbel. *A History of Book Publishing in the United States,* Vols. 1–3 (R. R. Bowker, 1972–1977).

Jacob Weisberg. "Rough Trade." *New Republic* (June 17, 1991). Weisberg stirred a hornet's nest in criticizing major profit-eager book publishers for deemphasizing the editing process to cut costs and rush books to market to score earlier revenue returns. See also the letters to editors in the subsequent July 15 *New Republic.*

John H. Westerhoff III. *McGuffey and His Reader: Piety, Morality and Education in 19th Century America* (Abington, 1978).

for keeping up to date

Publisher's Weekly is the trade journal of the book industry.

The C-SPAN cable television network runs a continuing program, "Booknotes," which focuses on authors and new titles as well as book industry issues.

Book Research Quarterly, published by Rutgers University, is a scholarly journal.

The Academic Author newsletter, published by the Text and Academic Authors Association, deals with textbook issues from the authors' perspective.

Many general interest magazines, including *Time* and *Newsweek,* cover book industry issues when they are topical, as do the New York *Times,* the *Wall Street Journal* and other major newspapers.

In recent years, the *New Republic* and the *Nation* have been especially enterprising in covering book industry practices as they change.

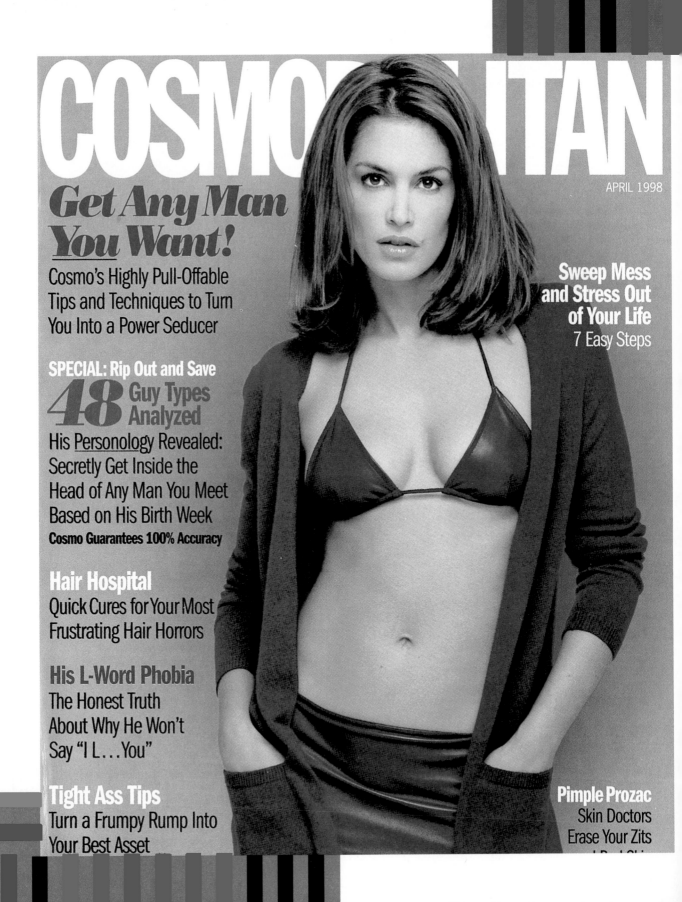

COSMOPOLITAN

APRIL 1998

Get Any Man You Want!

Cosmo's Highly Pull-Offable Tips and Techniques to Turn You Into a Power Seducer

SPECIAL: Rip Out and Save

48 Guy Types Analyzed

His <u>Personology</u> Revealed: Secretly Get Inside the Head of Any Man You Meet Based on His Birth Week

Cosmo Guarantees 100% Accuracy

Hair Hospital

Quick Cures for Your Most Frustrating Hair Horrors

His L-Word Phobia

The Honest Truth About Why He Won't Say "I L...You"

Tight Ass Tips

Turn a Frumpy Rump Into Your Best Asset

Sweep Mess and Stress Out of Your Life

7 Easy Steps

Pimple Prozac

Skin Doctors Erase Your Zits

3
magazines

in this chapter you will learn:

- Magazines have contributed importantly to American culture.

- Magazines have been journalistic, visual innovators.

- Most newsrack magazines aim at narrow audience segments.

- Sponsored magazines and trade journals outnumber newsrack magazines.

- Magazines continue to demassify.

- Magazines may be losing their influence in shaping the future.

A new editor comes into the job facing challenges—perhaps starting up an altogether new magazine, or relaunching an established magazine that has been languishing or heading up a well-established magazine that has already been enjoying enviable success.

Bonnie Fuller, the new editor of *Cosmopolitan* magazine, has met all these challenges in her editing career.

Canadian born, she began as an editor for *Women's Wear Daily.* Her interest in fashion found an outlet as a writer for the Toronto *Star,* and she later became editor of *Flare.* Under her six years of innovative leadership, *Flare* became the largest circulation fashion magazine in Canada. Fuller's talent for re-envisioning a magazine and carrying out a successful relaunch became further evident during her editorship of *YM,* a magazine for young women ages 15 to 24. Fuller turned what had formerly been known as *Young Miss* into *YM*—*"young and modern,"* more than doubling its circulation to over 2 million.

In 1994, Fuller joined Hearst Magazines where she launched an American edition of the French fashion, beauty and lifestyle magazine, *Marie Claire.* Hearst proclaimed it "the most successful launch in the history of Hearst titles." Under Fuller's editorship, the circulation increased from 250,000 to over 500,000.

She soon was faced with the challenge of taking a highly successful, well-established magazine and giving it new freshness and verve while retaining all the positive qualities that had made it such a success. The magazine was *Cosmopolitan,* whose editor, the legendary Helen Gurley Brown, now in her 70s, would be moving on to become the editor of the 33 international editions of *Cosmopolitan.*

Fuller knew a new editor cannot merely maintain the status quo and risk stagnation by doing nothing beyond emulating a former editor. On the other hand, a new editor cannot move too quickly and make too drastic changes that would drive loyal readers away. Nor can a new editor risk alienating the advertisers. In the case of *Cosmopolitan,* the advertisers had learned to count on the popularity of the magazine, with its vast and enthusiastic readership, which had made it the

world's largest-selling magazine for young women.

For years Helen Gurley Brown was virtually synonymous with the magazine. Brown had turned *Cosmopolitan* into one of the greatest success stories in magazine history. Her philosophy was that singleness could be a positive lifestyle in which a woman could enjoy beauty and comfort in her living arrangements, experience challenges in her career, and enjoy fashion, fitness, entertainment, romantic relationships, and yes, even sex. Singleness was not simply a holding pattern until marriage came along. It was a way of life.

Brown's *Cosmopolitan* exuded that philosophy, becoming a magazine for career-oriented women ages 18 to 35, whether single, married or divorced. The magazine soared from 800,00 subscribers to 2.5 million.

Under Brown, the magazine had been considered in the vanguard of the sexual revolution, but as that revolution waned in the age of AIDs, and as issues of sexual harassment came to the forefront in society, Brown's views were considered by some to be out of date. Brown, however, continued to emphasize the importance of sexuality to women and was convinced that woman-as-sex-object and woman-as-

feminist were not incompatible concepts.

As the new editor, Bonnie Fuller utilized reader focus groups to guide her in making changes and additions. She included articles on AIDs and sexual harassment in some of the first issues of the magazine under her editorship, persuaded that any issue of concern and relevance to women should be included in *Cosmopolitan.* At the same time, it was clear that the magazine would continue its saucy, sexy tone. Her fashion interests quickly showed up in the new *Cosmopolitan*'s greater emphasis on fashion and beauty, including updated cover photos, which Fuller said would continue to project "confidence and empowered sexuality." Fiction and recipes would disappear. But other basic emphases would remain, with articles on personal life and emotional issues, work, sex and love, health and fitness, men, entertainment and celebrities—all designed with the bright, independent, confident, energetic, and fun-loving "Cosmo girl" image in mind. To emphasize that image as a way of life, Fuller has given various departments and features such titles as "Cosmo Body," "Cosmo Health," "Cosmo Diet," "Cosmo Careers," "Cosmo Fashion," "Cosmo Hair," and

Bonnie Fuller

"Cosmo Mailbox." A cover line on the March 1998 issue announced "The Cosmo Orgasm."

Fuller has said she will discontinue the occasional centerfold, a practice Brown began with a pinup photo of film star Burt Reynolds in 1972. But Fuller has built upon the "Fun Fearless Female" theme that was begun for advertisements. The magazine now features profiles of outstanding women who embody the concept.

Under Fuller's first year as editor of *Cosmopolitan,* the magazine not only continued to flourish both in terms of readership and advertising, but her success attracted new advertisers as well. Her achievements earned her the 1997 *Advertising Age* editor of the year award.

influence of magazines

STUDY PREVIEW Today, as through their whole history, magazines are a mass medium through which the distinctive American culture is brought to a national audience. The periodicals pack great literature and ideas into formats that, unlike books, almost anybody can afford. Magazines are also a national unifier because they offer manufacturers a nation-wide audience for their goods.

contributing to nationhood

The first successful magazines in the United States, in the 1820s, were much less expensive than books. People of ordinary means could afford them. Unlike newspapers, which were oriented to their cities of publication, early magazines created national audiences. This contributed to a sense of nationhood at a time when an American culture, distinctive from its European heritage, had not yet emerged. The American people had their magazines in common. The *Saturday Evening Post,* founded in 1821, carried fiction by Edgar Allan Poe, Nathaniel Hawthorne and Harriet Beecher Stowe to readers who could not afford books. Their short stories and serialized novels flowed from the American experience and helped Americans establish a national identity.

With the **Postal Act of 1879,** Congress recognized the role of magazines in creating a national culture and promoting literacy—in effect, binding the nation. The law

> *Saturday Evening Post*
> Early contributor to identifiable American literature.
> **Postal Act of 1879**
> Discounted magazine mail rates.

media timeline

development of the magazine

1741 Andrew Bradford printed *American Magazine* and Benjamin Franklin printed *General Magazines,* first magazines in Colonies.

1821 *Saturday Evening Post* was launched, ushering in era of general-interest magazines.

1828 Sara Josepha Hale began editing the *Lady's Book,* first women's magazine.

1860s *Harper's Weekly* introduced visual news with Civil War illustration.

1879 Congress gave discount postal rates to magazines.

1899 Gilbert Grosvenor introduced photographs in *National Geographic.*

1902 Ida Tarbell wrote muckraking series on Standard Oil in *McClure's.*

1922 DeWitt and Lila Wallace founded *Reader's Digest.*

1923 Henry Luce and Briton Hadden founded *Time,* first newsmagazine.

1924 Harold Ross founded the *New Yorker* and introduced the modern personality profile.

1936 Henry Luce founded *Life* and coined the term photojournalism.

1960s Oversize general magazines, including *Life,* folded as advertisers moved to network television.

1962 Hugh Hefner introduced modern question-answer format in *Playboy.*

Fossil Ridge   Burgess Pass 7150 Ft.   Mt. Field 8645 Ft.   Cathedral Crags

Photojournalism Innovator. The *National Geographic,* a sponsored membership magazine, has been a leader in photographic coverage. A 1903 photo of a bare-breasted Filipino woman irked some people, but the *Geographic* defended itself as showing the peoples of the world as the

allowed a discount on mailing rates for magazines, a penny a pound. Magazines were being subsidized, which reduced distribution costs and sparked dramatic circulation growth. New magazines cropped up as a result.

national advertising medium

Advertisers used magazines through the 1800s to build national markets for their products, which was an important factor in transforming the United States from an agricultural and cottage industry economy into a modern economy. This too contributed to a sense of nationhood. The other mass media could not do that as effectively. Few books carried advertisements, and newspapers, with few exceptions, delivered only local readership to advertisers.

massive magazine audience

The American people have a tremendous appetite for magazines. According to magazine industry studies, almost 90 percent of U.S. adults read an average 10 issues a month. While magazines are affordable for most people, the household income of the typical reader is 5 percent more than the national average. In general, the more education and higher income a person has, the greater the person's magazine consumption.

In short, magazines are a pervasive mass medium. Magazines, however, are not only for the upper crust. Many magazines are edited for "downscale" audiences, which means the medium's role in society is spread across almost the whole range of people. Even illiterates can derive some pleasure and value from magazines, which by and large are visual and colorful.

The massiveness of the audience makes the magazine an exceptionally competitive medium. About 12,000 magazines vie for readers in the United States, ranging from general-interest publications such as *Reader's Digest* to such specialized publications as *Chili Pepper,* for people interested in hot foods, and *Spur,* for racehorse aficionados. In recent years, 500 to 600 new titles have been launched annually, magazine found them. In 1911 the *Geographic* demonstrated with a dramatic 17-page foldout of the Canadian Rockies that format need not limit photojournalism's portrayal of the world. The magazine also has led in underwater color and dramatic aviation and space photography.

although only one in five survives into the third year. Even among major magazines, a huge following at the moment is no guarantee of survival. Of the 23 U.S. magazines with a circulation of more than 1 million in 1946, 10 no longer exist. Magazine publishing is a risky business.

magazines as media innovators

(STUDY PREVIEW) Magazines have led other media with significant innovations in journalism, advertising and circulation. These include investigative reporting, in-depth personality profiles, and photojournalism.

investigative reporting

Muckraking, usually called "investigative reporting" today, was honed by magazines as a journalistic approach in the first years of the 20th century. Magazines ran lengthy explorations of abusive institutions in the society. It was **Theodore Roosevelt,** the reform president, who coined the term "muckraking." Roosevelt generally enjoyed investigative journalism, but one day in 1906, when the digging got too close to home, he likened it to the work of a character in a 17th-century novel who focused so much on raking muck that he missed the good news. The president meant the term derisively, but it came to be a badge of honor among journalists.

Muckraking established magazines as a powerful medium in shaping public policy. In 1902 **Ida Tarbell** wrote a 19-part series on the Standard Oil monopoly for *McClure's.* **Lincoln Steffens** detailed municipal corruption, and reforms followed. Other magazines picked up investigative thrusts. *Collier's* took on patent medicine frauds. *Cosmopolitan,* a leading muckraking journal of the period, tackled dishonesty

muckraking
Turn-of-century term for investigative reporting.

Theodore Roosevelt
Devised term "muckraking."

Ida Tarbell
Exposed Standard Oil.

McClure's
Turn-of-century muckraking magazine.

Lincoln Steffens
Exposed municipal corruption.

margaret bourke-white

The oversized *Life* magazine created by Henry Luce was the perfect forum for the work of Margaret Bourke-White. The giant pages, 13½ inches high and opening to 21-inch spreads, gave such impact to photos that they seemed to jump off the page at readers. Bourke-White was there at the beginning, shooting the immense Fort Peck Dam in Montana for *Life*'s first cover in 1936. Over her career, Bourke-White shot 284 assignments for *Life*, many of them enduring images from World War II. These included Holocaust victims in a Nazi concentration camp, great military movements, and the leaders of the time in both triumph and defeat. She was among the first great photojournalists.

Bourke-White's photojournalism went beyond the news and emotions of any given day to penetrate the core of great social problems. In collaboration with writer Erskine Caldwell, with whom she was later married, Bourke-White created a photo documentary on the tragic lives of sharecroppers in the American South. Later, in South Africa, she went

Margaret Bourke-White

Photojournalism Arrives. The oversize pages of *Life*, which opened to 13½ × 21 inches, did justice to great photography. Margaret Bourke-White's medieval tones captured the immensity of Fort Peck Dam under construction in Montana for the cover of the inaugural issue. Bourke-White became a star photographer for *Life*. She was among a handful of women journalists who covered World War II for American readers.

underground to photograph gold miners known only by numbers. Her haunting photos from the Midwest drought of the 1930s created indelible images in the minds of a generation. These were socially significant projects that moved people and changed public policy.

It was in college that Bourke-White learned photography, and she used it to pay tuition. First it was photographs of campus buildings, then full-fledged architectural photography. This turned into a fascination with modern technology, and eventually a job with the new *Fortune* magazine. She photographed industrial glass-making, the mining of bauxite, and the building of skyscrapers. It was her work at *Fortune* that caught Luce's eye when he created *Life,* and he brought her on board.

Margaret Bourke-White was fearless in her pursuit of photography. She took her camera, a weighty Speed Graphic, on the ledges of skyscrapers to get the feel she wanted in her images. She shot the ravages of the war in Europe from airplanes. She lived her work, and was quoted once as saying: "When I die I want to die living."

in the U.S. Senate. Muckraking expanded to books with **Upton Sinclair**'s *The Jungle.* Sinclair shocked the nation by detailing filth in meat-packing plants. Federal inspection laws resulted. Later newspapers joined muckraking, but it was magazines that had led the way.

personality profiles

The in-depth **personality profile** was a magazine invention. In the 1920s **Harold Ross** of the *New Yorker* began pushing writers to a thoroughness that was new in journalism. They used multiple interviews with a range of sources—talking not only with the subject of the profile but with just about everyone and anyone who could comment on the subject, including the subject's friends and enemies. Such depth required weeks, sometimes months of journalistic digging. It's not uncommon now in newspapers, broadcasting or magazines, but before Harold Ross, it didn't exist.

Under **Hugh Hefner,** *Playboy* took the interview in new directions in 1962 with in-depth profiles developed from a highly structured question-and-answer format. The *Playboy* Q-A format became widely imitated.

photojournalism

Magazines brought visuals to the mass media in a way books never had. *Harper's Weekly* sent artists to Civil War battles, leading the way to journalism that went beyond words.

The young editor of the *National Geographic,* Gilbert Grosvenor, drew a map proposing a route to the South Pole for an 1899 issue, putting the *Geographic* on the road to being a visually oriented magazine. For subsequent issues, Grosvenor borrowed government plates to reproduce photos, and he encouraged travelers to submit their photographs to the magazine. This was at a time when most magazines scorned photographs. However, Grosvenor was undeterred as an advocate for documentary photography, and membership in the National Geographic Society, a prerequisite for receiving the magazine, swelled. Eventually the magazine assembled its own staff of photographers and gradually became a model for other publications that discovered they needed to play catch-up.

Upton Sinclair
Exposed meat-packing industry.

personality profile
In-depth, balanced biographical article.

Harold Ross
Pioneered personality profile.

Hugh Hefner
Adapted personality profile to Q-A.

Harper's Weekly
Pioneered magazine visuals.

National Geographic
Introduced photography in magazines.

Aided by technological advances involving smaller, more portable cameras and faster film capable of recording images under extreme conditions, photographers working for the *Geographic* opened a whole new world of documentary coverage to their readers. Among *Geographic* accomplishments were:

- A photo of a bare-breasted Filipino woman field-worker shocked some *Geographic* readers in 1903, but Grosvenor persisted against Victorian sensitivities to show the peoples of the world as they lived.

- The first photographs from Tibet, by Russian explorers, appeared in 1905 in an 11-page spread—extraordinary visual coverage for the time that confirmed photography's role in journalism.

- A 17-page, eight-foot foldout panorama of the Canadian Rockies in 1911 showed that photojournalism need not be limited by format.

- The magazine's 100th anniversary cover in 1988 was the first hologram—a three-dimensional photograph—ever published in a mass-audience magazine. It was a significant production accomplishment.

Life magazine brought American photojournalism to new importance in the 1930s. The oversize pages of the magazine gave new intensity to photographs, and the magazine, a weekly, demonstrated that newsworthy events could be covered consistently by camera. *Life* captured the spirit of the times photographically and demonstrated that the whole range of human experience could be recorded visually. Both real life and *Life* could be shocking. A 1938 *Life* spread on human birth was so shocking for the time that censors succeeded in banning the issue in 33 cities.

consumer magazines

(STUDY PREVIEW)   The most visible category of magazines is general-interest magazines, which are available on newsracks and by subscription. Called **consumer magazines,** these include publications like ***Reader's Digest*** that try to offer something for everybody, but mostly they are magazines edited for narrower audiences.

circulation leaders

consumer magazines
Sold on newsracks.

Reader's Digest
Largest newsrack magazine.

Modern Maturity
Largest circulation, but limited to AARP members.

Henry Luce
Time founder, later *Life*.

Time
First newsmagazine.

Reader's Digest is usually considered to have the largest circulation of any U.S. magazine, selling 15.1 million copies a month, not counting foreign editions. However, *Reader's Digest's* lead in circulation is not technically correct because the circulation of the Sunday newspaper supplement *Parade* is twice that. Also, in recent years, with the graying of America, the magazine ***Modern Maturity,*** which is sent to members of the American Association of Retired Persons every two months, has reached a circulation of 21.1 million, considerably ahead of *Reader's Digest*.

The common notion that *Reader's Digest* is the largest magazine stems from its attempt to serve a true mass audience. Unlike *Modern Maturity,* the *Digest*'s easy-to-read articles cut across divisions of age, gender, occupation and geography. *Reader's*

magazine circulation

These are the circulation leaders among United States magazines. The figures do not include foreign editions, which add substantial circulation for some magazines. *Reader's Digest,* for example, publishes 40 editions in 18 languages for 12.2 million copies a month in addition to 15.1 million in the United States.

Reader's Digest	15.1 million
National Geographic	9.0 million
Better Homes and Gardens	7.6 million
Good Housekeeping	5.3 million
Ladies' Home Journal	5.0 million
Family Circle	5.0 million
Woman's Day	4.7 million
McCall's	4.5 million
Playboy	3.5 million
AAA World	3.4 million
Prevention	3.4 million
Redbook	3.2 million
American Legion Magazine	2.9 million

Sunday Supplements

Parade	37.2 million
USA Weekend	21.2 million

Weeklies

TV Guide	13.2 million
The Cable Guide	4.7 million
Time	4.0 million
People	3.3 million
Newsweek	3.2 million
Sports Illustrated	3.2 million
National Enquirer	2.6 million

Biweeklies

Rolling Stone	1.2 million

Bimonthlies

Modern Maturity	21.0 million

Non-Paid Circulation

Disney Channel	5.5 million
CompuServe Magazine	2.2 million
U–National College Magazine	1.5 million

Digest is a mass magazine in the truest sense of the word. It tries in every issue to have something for everybody. The Sunday newspaper supplements are also edited for a truly mass audience.

Led by *Reader's Digest,* about 1,200 magazines are published in the United States for newsrack and subscription sales. A few, including newsmagazines, deal with subjects of general interest. Most, however, have a narrower focus, such as *Motor Trend,* which is geared toward automobile enthusiasts; *Forbes,* which appeals to business people and investors; and *Family Circle,* which targets homemakers.

One thing that consumer magazines have in common is a heavy reliance on advertising. Exceptions include *Consumer Reports,* which wants to be above any suspicion that advertisers influence its reporting; the satire magazine *Mad,* whose editors like doing things their own way; the nondenominational religious magazine *Guideposts*; and the feminist *Ms.*

newsmagazines

Fresh out of Yale in 1923, classmates **Henry Luce** and Briton Hadden begged and borrowed $86,000 from friends and relatives and launched a new kind of magazine: *Time.* The magazine provided summaries of news by categories such as national affairs, sports and business. It took four years for *Time* to turn a profit, and some people doubted that the magazine would ever make money, noting that it merely rehashed

media online

***George* magazine:** Political commentary, interviews, and insight. www.georgemag.com

····dewitt and lila wallace

Lila and DeWitt Wallace

DeWitt and Lila Wallace had an idea, but hardly any money. The idea was a pocket-sized magazine that condensed informational, inspiring and entertaining nonfiction from other publications—a digest. With borrowed money, the Wallaces brought out their first issue of *Reader's Digest* in 1922.

The rest, as they say, is history. In 1947 the *Digest* became the first magazine to exceed a circulation of 9 million. Except for the Sunday newspaper supplement *Parade*, *Reader's*

Digest has been the nation's largest-circulation magazine most of the time since then. In 1996, *Reader's Digest's* circulation was 15.1 million— not counting an additional 12.2 million overseas in 18 languages.

The magazine has remained true to the Wallaces' successful formula. DeWitt and Lila Wallace, children of poor Presbyterian clergy, wanted "constructive articles," each with universal appeal. The thrust was upbeat but not Pollyanna. Digested as they were, the

articles could be quickly read. America loved it. More than 90 percent of *Reader's Digest* circulation is by subscription, representing long-term reader commitment.

For its first 33 years, *Reader's Digest* was wholly reader supported. It carried no advertising. Rising postal rates forced a change in 1955. There was scoffing about whether advertisers would go for "postage-stamp-sized ads" in *Reader's Digest* with its minipages, but the scoffers were wrong. The people who decide where to place

advertisements never doubted that *Reader's Digest* was well read. Today, advertisers—except for cigarette manufacturers—pay more than $100,000 a page for a color advertisement. Consistent with the Wallaces' standards, cigarette advertisements are not accepted and never have been.

media
online

Nation: Espouses levelheaded political reporting and writing. www.TheNation.com

People: Flashy magazine about ... well, people. www.pathfinder.com/people

U.S. News & World Report: News and features tailored to the net. www.usnews.com

what daily newspapers had already reported. Readers, however, came to like the handy compilation and the sprightly, often irreverent writing style that set *Time* apart.

The *Time* style, which came to be dubbed *Timespeak*, was carefully crafted by Luce and Hadden to give the magazine the tone of a single, knowledgeable, authoritative individual recapping the week's events and issues. *Timespeak*, which continues as part of *Time*'s personality, has two components:

- A snappy, informal, sometimes sassy writing style that includes calling people by unflattering nicknames, such as Scarface. To the consternation of English teachers everywhere, the style also took liberties with the English language, such as the reversed attributive "said Jones" instead of "Jones said." Testimony to *Time*'s impact on the culture is that reversed attributives are commonly accepted today in even the most formal writing.

- *Time* articles at first were written by a relatively small group of editors who strived for a consistent style and tone. Even after the magazine built a staff of reporters and stationed them around the globe, reporters seldom wrote stories. Instead, they wrote memos on what they considered important, and those memos, chock full of

readers digest in china

The Gansu People's Publishing House, in the remote western China city of Lanzhou, wasn't doing all that well in 1981. Hu Yaquan came to the rescue. He hired a few translators to digest foreign articles for a new monthly magazine. It was a low-cost venture modeled on the internationally successful *Reader's Digest* in the United States. In fact, Hu called it *Readers' Digest*. Within a year the circulation was 100,000.

Rigid government censors could find little fault with the magazine's upbeat mix of articles on personal and family issues, short morality tales, humor and soft current affairs treatments. And a growing class of Chinese aspiring to upward mobility bought the magazine. Circulation climbed. In 1993, however, the original *Reader's Digest,* in the United States, decided the rip-off was undermining its sales potential in China and forced some changes. The Lanzhou-based upstart changed its title to *Readers*—no apostrophe, no *Digest*. Content shifted too. Rather than boiling down foreign articles, *Readers* looked for Chinese prose and focused more on national issues like unemployment and corruption, but always with a solution-oriented angle that the government wouldn't find offensive.

With 4 million circulation today, *Readers* is the largest magazine in China. Its leadership, however, is not secure. Another magazine edited for a broad, national audience, *Family,* is a close second. Dozens of other magazines also compete for readers. Overall, the magazine business in China is expanding rapidly as the country moves into a market-based economy and people have more discretionary income. Nationwide, there are 8,300 magazines. In 1981

Leading China Magazine. The burgeoning China magazine industry is led by *Readers,* a monthly mix of short upbeat essays, gentle humor and mild treatments of public affairs. Circulation has topped 4 million. The magazine was founded in 1981 with the U.S.-based *Reader's Digest* as a model.

when Hu Yaquan founded *Readers,* there were 300.

---

information, quotations and comments, went to the magazine's editors in New York. The editors, after deciding what subjects to cover in the next issue, would put together stories from the reporter's field memos and other sources, such as newspaper and news service accounts. Still today, it is largely those editor-written stories, carefully controlled as to tone and style, that end up in the magazine.

A copycat, *Newsweek,* appeared in 1933. So did a third newsweekly, *U.S. News,* the forerunner to today's *U.S. News & World Report.* Despite the competition, *Time,* with 4 million copies weekly, has consistently led newsmagazine circulation.

While *Time, Newsweek* and *U.S. News & World Report* cover a broad range of subjects, specialized newsmagazines focus on narrower subjects. The largest category is those featuring celebrity news, including the gossipy sort. The supermarket tabloid **National Enquirer** focuses on the rich and famous, hyped-up medical research and sensational oddball news and is an incredible commercial success, with 2.6 million in circulation. Time-Life's *People* is at 3.3 million.

> **National Enquirer**
> Magazine or newspaper?

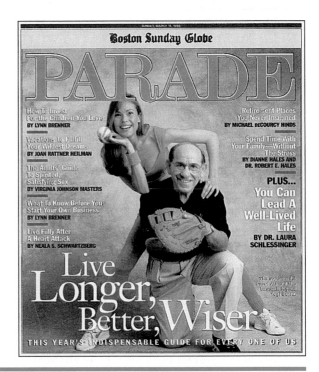

Massive Circulation. Some people quibble whether newspaper supplements are really magazines because they are neither stitched nor circulated as stand-alone products. Nobody can deny their reach, however. *USA Weekend,* owned by the Gannett chain, which also published the *USA Today* newspaper, has grown to 21.2 million copies weekly. That growth has eroded slightly the circulation of *Parade,* 37.2 million in 1998. (Left: Copyright 1998, *USA Weekend.* Reprinted with permission. Right: Gwendolen Cates/CP. ©1998, *Parade Magazine.* Reprinted with permission.)

newspaper supplements

Sometimes overlooked as magazines are **Parade** and **USA Weekend,** the independently produced supplements that newspapers buy and stuff inside their weekend editions. They are designed for general family reading.

The weekend supplements have built-in advantages over other magazines. Readers neither subscribe nor buy them directly. The supplements need only convince a newspaper to carry them, and they have instant circulation. *Parade*'s circulation exceeds 37 million, which, technically speaking, makes it easily the largest magazine in the nation. *USA Weekend* has a circulation in excess of 21 million.

women's magazines

The first U.S. magazine edited to interest only a portion of the mass audience, but otherwise to be of general interest, was *Lady's Magazine,* which later became *Godey's Lady's Book.* **Sara Josepha Hale** helped start the magazine in 1828 to uplift and glorify womanhood. Its advice on fashions, morals, taste, sewing and cooking developed a following, which peaked with a circulation of 150,000.

Sunday supplements
Free to buyers of Sunday newspapers.

Parade
Largest magazine circulation.

USA Weekend
Second largest weekend newspaper supplement

Sara Josepha Hale
Founded first women's magazine.

Seven Sisters
Leading women's magazines.

sara josepha hale

Sara Hale, widowed with five children, decided to write a novel to put the kids through college. *Northwood,* published in 1826, was one of the first books with America as its setting. The book attracted national attention, and all kinds of literary offers came Hale's way. She decided on the editorship of the new Boston-based *Ladies' Magazine.* While some magazines of the time had women's sections, no previous magazine had wholly devoted itself to women's interests. Hale's innovations and sensitivities made the magazine and its successor a familiar sight in households throughout the nation for half a century. During her tenure Hale defined women's issues and in indirect ways contributed importantly to women's liberation.

As editor of *Ladies' Magazine,* Hale departed from the frothy romance fiction and fashion coverage in the women's sections of other magazines. Her focus was on improving women's role in society. She campaigned vigorously for educational opportunities for women. When Matthew Vassar was setting up a women's college, she persuaded him to include women on the faculty—a novel idea for the time.

No fashion plate, Sara Hale encouraged women to dress comfortably yet attractively—no frills. For herself she preferred black for almost all occasions. When the owners of the magazine thought enthusiastic fashion coverage would boost circulation—and advertising—she went along, but in her own way. She pointed out how impractical and ridiculous the latest fashions were, and some she dismissed as trivial diversions.

Unlike other magazine editors of the time, she disdained reprinting articles from other publications. Hence, *Ladies' Magazine* created opportunities for new writers, particularly women, and enriched the nation's literary output. One issue, in 1843, was produced entirely by women. In her heyday, from the mid-1830s through the 1840s, Hale attracted the best writers to her pages: Ralph Waldo Emerson, Nathaniel Hawthorne, Oliver Wendell Holmes, Washington Irving, Henry Wadsworth Longfellow, Edgar Allan Poe, Harriet Beecher Stowe.

Hale edited *Ladies' Magazine* to 1837, when it was merged into the weaker *Godey's Lady's Book.* She moved to Philadelphia to become editor of the new magazine, which retained the *Godey* title. Circulation reached 150,000 in 1860.

Women's Magazine Pioneer. Sara Josepha Hale edited the first magazine designed for women, but just as important was the distinctive content. Unlike other magazines, which recycled articles from other magazines, mostly from England, Hale prided herself on original content. Her *Ladies' Journal* enriched the nation's literary output with original work by Ralph Waldo Emerson, Nathaniel Hawthorne, Oliver Wendell Holmes, Washington Irving, Henry Wadsworth Longfellow, Edgar Allan Poe, Harriet Beecher Stowe.

The *Godey's* tradition is maintained today in seven competing magazines known as the **Seven Sisters** because of their female following: *Better Homes & Gardens, Family Circle, Good Housekeeping, Ladies' Home Journal, McCall's, Redbook* and *Woman's Day.* While each sister can be distinguished from her siblings, there is a thematic connection: concern for home, family and quality living from a traditional woman's perspective.

An eighth sister is *Cosmopolitan,* although more aptly it is a distant cousin. Under Helen Gurley Brown, later Bonnie Fuller, *Cosmopolitan* has geared itself to a subcategory of women readers—young, unmarried and working. It's the most successful in a large group of women's magazines seeking narrow groups. Among them are *Elle,* focusing on fashion; *Playgirl,* with its soft pornography; *Essence,* for black women; *Seventeen,* for teenage girls; and *Self,* for women of the "me generation."

men's magazines

Founded in 1933, **Esquire** was the first classy men's magazine. It was as famous for its pin-ups as its literary content, which over the years has included articles from Ernest Hemingway, John Dos Passos and Gay Talese. Fashion has also been a cornerstone in the *Esquire* content mix.

Hugh Hefner learned about magazines as an *Esquire* staff member, and he applied those lessons when he created **Playboy** in 1953. With its lustier tone, *Playboy* quickly overtook *Esquire* in circulation. At its peak, *Playboy* sold 7 million copies a month. The magazine emphasized female nudity, but also carried journalistic and literary pieces whose merit attracted many readers. Readers embarrassed by their carnal curiosity could claim they bought the magazine for its articles. Critics sniped, however, that *Playboy* published the worst stuff of the best writers.

Playboy imitators added raunch—some a little, some a lot. The most successful, Bob Guccione's *Penthouse,* has never attracted as many readers or advertisers as *Playboy,* but it has been a commercial success. It is Hefner, however, whom sociologists credit with capitalizing on the post-World War II sexual revolution in the United States and fanning it.

Not all men's magazines dwell on sex. The outdoor life is exalted in *Field & Stream,* whose circulation tops 2 million. Fix-it magazines, led by *Popular Science* and *Popular Mechanics,* have a steady following.

non-newsrack magazines

(STUDY PREVIEW) Many organizations publish magazines for their members. While these sponsored magazines, including *National Geographic, Modern Maturity* and *Smithsonian,* resemble consumer magazines, they generally are not available at newsracks. In fact, consumer magazines are far outnumbered by sponsored magazines and by trade journals.

sponsored magazines

The founders of the National Geographic Society decided in 1888 to put out a magazine to promote the society and build membership. The idea was to entice people to join by bundling a subscription with membership and then to use the dues to finance the society's research and expeditions. Within a few years, the *National Geographic* had become a phenomenal success both in generating membership and as a profit center for the National Geographic Society. Today, more than 100 years old and with U.S. circulation at more than 9 million, the *Geographic* is the most widely recognized **sponsored magazine** in the nation. Other sponsored magazines include *Modern Maturity*, published by the American Association of Retired People for its members. Its circulation exceeds 21 million. Other major membership magazines include *Smithsonian*, by the Smithsonian Institute; *VFW*, by the Veterans of Foreign Wars; *American Legion*; and *Elks*, by the Elks lodge.

Many sponsored magazines carry advertising and are financially self-sufficient. In fact, the most successful sponsored magazines compete aggressively with consumer magazines for advertising. It is not unusual for an issue of *Smithsonian* to carry 100 pages of advertising.

While advertising has made some sponsored magazines into profit centers for their parent organizations, others come nowhere near breaking even. Typical is *Quill*, which the Society of Professional Journalists publishes as an organizational expense for the good of its membership. The society seeks advertising for *Quill*, but the magazine's relatively small readership has never attracted as much volume or the type of advertising as the *National Geographic*, the *Smithsonian* or *Modern Maturity*.

Many sponsored magazines do not seek advertising. These include many university magazines, which are considered something that a university should publish as an institutional expense to disseminate information about research and scholarly activities and, not incidentally, to promote itself. Other sponsored magazines that typically do not carry advertising include publications for union members, in-house publications for employees, and company publications for customers. These publications do not have the public recognition of consumer magazines, but many are as slick and professional as consumer magazines. All together, they employ far more editors, photographers and writers than consumer magazines.

trade journals

Everyone in a profession or trade has at least one magazine for keeping abreast of what is happening in the field. In entertainment, *Billboard* provides a solid journalistic coverage on a broad range of subjects in music: new recording releases, new acts, new technology and new merger deals. *Billboard*, a **trade journal,** is essential reading for people in the industry. About 4,000 trade journals cover a mind-boggling range of businesses and trades. Consider the diversity in these titles: *Rock and Dirt, Progressive Grocer, Plastics Technology, Hogs Today* and *Hardware Age*.

Like consumer magazines, the "trades" rely mostly on advertising for their income and profits. Some charge for subscriptions, but many are sent free to a carefully culled list of readers whom advertisers want to reach.

Many trade magazines are parts of companies that produce related publications, some with overlapping staffs. McGraw-Hill, the book publisher, produces more than 30 trade journals, including *Chemical Week* and *Modern Hospital*. Another trade magazine company is Crain Communications, whose titles include *Advertising Age, AutoWeek, Electronic Media* and two dozen other trades.

criticism of trade magazines

Many trade magazine companies, including McGraw-Hill and Crain, are recognized for honest, hard-hitting reporting of the industries they cover, but the trades have a mixed reputation. Some trade magazines are loaded with puffery exalting their advertisers and industries. For years, *Body Fashions,* formerly *Corset and Underwear Review,* unabashedly presented ads as news stories. As many trade journals do, it charged companies to run stories about them and covered only companies that were also advertisers. At some trades, the employees who solicit ads write news stories that echo the ads. These trades tend to be no more than boosters of the industries they pretend to cover. Kent MacDougall, writing in the *Wall Street Journal,* offered this especially egregious example: *America's Textile Reporter,* which promoted the textile industry from a management perspective, once dismissed the hazard of textile workers' contracting brown lung disease by inhaling cotton dust as "a thing brought up by venal doctors" at an international labor meeting in Africa, "where inferior races are bound to be afflicted by new diseases more superior people defeated years ago." At the time, in 1972, 100,000 U.S. textiles workers were afflicted with brown lung. Many trade magazines persist today in pandering to their trades, professions and industries, rather than approaching their subjects with journalistic truth-seeking and truth-telling.

Responsible trade journals are embarrassed by some of their brethren, many of which are upstarts put out by people with no journalistic experience or instincts. Because of this, and also because it takes relatively little capital to start a trade magazine, many bad trade magazines thrive. Several professional organizations, including the American Business Press and the Society of Business Press Editors, work to improve both their industry and its image. Even so, as former ABP President Charles Mill said, trades continue to be plagued "by fleabag outfits published in somebody's garage."

magazine demassification

(STUDY PREVIEW)   Giant mass-audience magazines, led by *Life,* were major influences in their heyday, but television killed them off by offering larger audiences to advertisers. Today, the magazine industry thrives through demassification, the process of seeking audiences with narrow interests. Critics feel demassification has changed the role of magazines in society for the worse.

heyday of mass magazines

Magazines once were epitomized by *Life.* Henry Luce used the fortune he amassed from *Time* to launch *Life* in 1936. The magazine exceeded Luce's expectations. He had planned on an initial circulation of 250,000, but almost right away it was 500,000. *Life* was perfect for its time. At 10 cents a copy, *Life* was within the reach of almost everyone, even during the Great Depression. It had quality—fiction from the best authors of the day. It had daring—flamboyant photography that seemed to jump off huge, oversize pages. The term "photo essay" was a *Life* creation.

Imitators followed. *Look,* introduced in 1937, was a knockoff in the same oversize dimension as *Life.* The historic *Saturday Evening Post* and *Collier's* were revamped as oversize magazines.

media

online

***Life* magazine:** Once too big for your lap, it now fits nicely on your screen.
www.lifemag.com

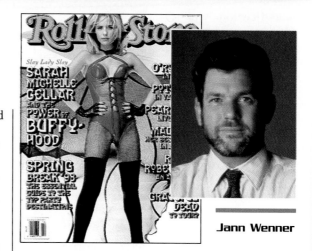

Jann Wenner

Jann Wenner was a student at the University of California's Berkeley campus as the hippie movement of the mid-1960s was flowering across the bay in San Francisco. Wenner dabbled in the loose, bohemian Haight-Ashbury life-style himself, including the drugs, but it was the music of the new generation that intrigued him the most—and he wanted to write about it.

In his second year at Berkeley, Wenner persuaded the editors of the campus newspaper, the *Daily Californian,* to give him a music column. In many ways, the column was a preview of Wenner's yet-to-come *Rolling Stone* magazine. Amid obscure egocentric references, Wenner reported music news seriously with a focus on his favorites: Bob Dylan, Mick Jagger, the Beatles. There were literary allusions, particularly to F. Scott Fitzgerald, and he found ways to tie the emerging psychedelic drug culture into politics. "One of these days," he wrote, "Lyndon Johnson is going to find out why the 'leaders of tomorrow' are hung up on LSD instead of LBJ."

Wenner gave up the column when he dropped out of college, but he tried to continue writing. The problem was that nobody would print his work. *Stereo Review* turned him down. So did the San Francisco dailies. Wenner went to London to propose covering the San Francisco music scene for *Melody Maker,* but that editor too said no.

Wenner decided to start his own magazine.

From friends, Wenner picked up venture capital totaling $6,500, and when his father gave him $1,000 in stock for his 21st birthday, he sold it to help fund the magazine. It was enough for Wenner, age 21, to launch *Rolling Stone.* That was in 1967. Within two years, *Rolling Stone* was widely regarded as the most authoritative rock 'n' roll magazine. It also became the voice for a new generation—not just the flower children of Haight-Ashbury but young people disenchanted with President Lyndon Johnson, the Vietnam war and the Establishment in general, and later with Richard Nixon and Watergate.

There were other magazines aimed at young people, but only Wenner realized that music was what bound the new generation together. Always at *Rolling Stone's* core, amid the fiction and political coverage, was rock 'n' roll.

The magazine became home for great writers of the new generation. Gonzo journalist Hunter Thompson was an early *Rolling Stone* regular, and later there were Truman Capote, Tom Wolfe and P. J. O'Rourke. Wenner encouraged writers to uninhibited truth-seeking and truth-telling. In his history of the magazine, Robert Draper wrote: "Wenner urged his writers to scrape away the bullshit. If the President lies, call him a liar; if Dylan is a poet, call him one."

By its sixth year, 1973, *Rolling Stone* turned profitable. No longer just "a little rock 'n' roll newspaper in San Francisco," as Wenner fondly referred to it in the early days, *Rolling Stone* has grown to maturity along with its original 1960s generation readership. The focus remains rock 'n' roll but without the beads and other symbols of the psychedelic era.

In middle age, *Rolling Stone* now is edited in New York. The instinctive seat-of-the-pants approach to editing that marked the early San Francisco days now is tempered by audience analysis from people who are comfortable in pin-stripe suits. The magazine's new mainstream respectability was cemented in 1985 when David Black won a National Magazine Award for a pioneering and explosive series on AIDs.

Today, circulation is 1.2 million. Wenner's company, Straight Arrow Publishers, is worth $250 million—more than 30,000 times the initial 1967 capitalization. Wenner himself is worth an estimated $100 million, not bad for a college dropout who started out with only $7,500 and a vision.

Calvin and Hobbes

by Bill Watterson

CPM
Cost per thousand.

assault from television

The oversize mass-audience magazines do not exist today, at least not as they did in the old days. *Collier's,* bankrupt, published its final issue in 1956. Hemorrhaging money despite a circulation of 4 million, *Saturday Evening Post* ceased in 1969. In 1971 *Look* died. *Life* was not even able to capitalize on the fact that it suddenly had less competition, and it went out of business the next year. It had lost $30 million over the previous three years. What had happened to the high-flying, oversize, mass-audience magazines? In a single word: television.

At its peak, *Life* had 8.5 million circulation, but in the 1950s the television networks had begun to deliver even bigger audiences. The villain for the giant magazines was not merely television's audience size, but **CPM,** advertising jargon for cost per 1,000 readers, listeners or viewers (the *M* standing for the Roman numeral for 1,000). In 1970 a full-page advertisement in *Life* ran $65,000. For less, an advertiser could have one minute of network television and reach far more potential customers. CPM-conscious advertising agencies could not conscientiously recommend *Life*'s $7.75 CPM when the networks' CPM was $3.60, and advertisers shifted to television.

a narrower focus

With the demise of *Life,* doomsayers predicted that magazines were a dying breed of media. The fact, however, was that advertisers withdrew only from magazines with broad readerships. What advertisers discovered was that although it was less expensive to use television to peddle universally used products like detergents, grooming aids and packaged foods, television, geared at the time for mass audiences, was too expensive for products appealing to narrow groups. Today, relatively few magazines seek a truly mass audience. These include *Reader's Digest,* the Sunday magazine supplements, and *Life,* which has been resurrected as a monthly and in a smaller, slimmer format that is a mere shadow of its flamboyant original self.

Special-interest magazines, whose content focused on limited subjects and whose advertising rates were lower, fit the bill better than either television or the giant mass-audience magazines for reaching customers with special interests. For manufacturers of $7,000 stereo systems, for example, it made sense to advertise in a narrowly focused audiophile magazine such as *Stereo Review.* In the same way, neither mass-audience magazines nor television was a medium of choice for top-of-the-line racing skis, but ski magazines were ideal. For fancy cookware, *Food & Wine* made sense.

Among new magazines that emerged with the demassification in the 1960s were regional and city magazines, offering a geographically defined audience to advertisers. Some of these magazines, which usually bore the name of their city or region, including *New York, Texas Monthly,* and *Washingtonian,* offered hard-hitting journalistic coverage of local issues. Many, though, focused on soft life-style subjects rather than antagonize powerful local interests and risk losing advertisers. Indeed, hypersensitivity to advertisers is a criticism of today's demassified magazines.

critics of demassification

Norman Cousins, once editor of the high-brow *Saturday Review of Literature,* criticized demassified magazines for betraying their traditional role of enriching the culture. Cousins said specialization had diluted the intellectual role of magazines in the society. Advertisers, he said, were shaping magazines' journalistic content for their commercial purposes—in contrast to magazine editors independently deciding content with loftier purposes in mind.

Scholar Dennis Holder put this "unholy alliance" of advertisers and readers this way: "The readers see themselves as members of small, and in some sense, elite groups—joggers, for example, or cat lovers—and they want to be told that they are terribly neat people for being in those groups. Advertisers, of course, want to reinforce the so-called positive self-image too, because joggers who feel good about themselves tend to buy those ridiculous suits and cat lovers who believe lavishing affection on their felines is a sign of warmth and sincerity are the ones who purchase cute little cat sweaters, or are they cat's pajamas." Magazine editors and writers, Holder said, are caught in the symbiotic advertiser-reader alliance and have no choice but to go along.

Norman Cousins and Dennis Holder were right that most consumer magazines today tend to a frothy mix of light, upbeat features, with little that is thoughtful or hard-hitting. However, most readers want to know about other people, particularly celebrities, and a great many trendy topics, and advertisers want to reach those readers, avoiding controversies that might hurt sales. So profitability for most magazines and their advertisers is locked into providing information their target audiences are interested in rather than serving an indefinable "public interest." The emphasis on profits and demassification saddens a number of people who believe that magazines have a higher calling than a cash register. These critics would agree with Cousins, who warned that emphasizing the superficial just because it sells magazines is a betrayal of the social trust that magazine publishers once held. "The purpose of a magazine," he said, "is not to tell you how to fix a leaky faucet, but to tell you what the world is about."

There is no question that demassification works against giving readers any kind of global view. In demassified magazines for auto enthusiasts, as an example, road test articles typically wax as enthusiastically as the advertisements about new cars. These demassified magazines, edited to target selected audiences and thereby attract advertisers, make no pretense of broadening their readers' understanding of substantive issues by exploring diverse perspectives. The narrowing of magazine editorial content appears destined to continue, not only because it is profitable but also because new

Netscape: Welcome to Slate

Back Forward Reload Home Search Guide Images Print Security Stop

Location: http://www.slate.com/toc/fp-Content.asp

Subscribe Now!

Slate™

SLATE USER NAME:

PASSWORD:

☐ From now on, sign me in automatically.

[Sign In]

Forgot your password?
Member Services
(Sign-in problems? Make sure you accept "cookies.")

DON'T GET CAUGHT OUT IN THE RAIN
Become a subscriber today, and get $10 off the regular price. Plus, get a Free Slate Umbrella... Subscribe Now!

FREE gift from Slate!
Your choice!
CLICK HERE!

Find Out More About Slate

MasterCard

Tuesday, March 31, 1998   - The Microsoft Network - ▼

WELCOME TO Slate --your smart take on the week's news, politics, and culture.
Slate is designed to inform and entertain--and to save you time with clever features that synthesize the news and media. We post new material every day. Subscribe and you'll also get Slate's e-mail-delivery services and our reader-discussion forum, "The Fray." Thanks.
To learn more about Slate, click here.
To subscribe (just $19.95 for a year), click here.
—Michael Kinsley, editor

FREE SAMPLES FROM TODAY'S SLATE

today's papers--What's in the New York Times, Washington Post, Wall Street Journal, Los Angeles Times, and USA Today.
the week/the spin--The news and how it's playing.
recycled--Tim Egan's virtual tour of Seattle cybermansions.
readme--"International Papers" by e-mail.
table of contents--A complete list of Slate's current offerings.
Slate search--Search our current issue and complete archive. (But only subscribers may access actual Slate contents.)

[   ] GO

boiler Slate --Advertisers, staff, the fine print.

Premier Zine. Microsoft, the dominant software manufacturer, moved into developing media content in the late 1990s with, among other things, the online magazine *Slate*. To edit the magazine, Microsoft hired Michael Kinsley, known for his commentaries on CNN and his editorship of the political and cultural journal *New Republic*, and Kinsley attracted a stable of prestigious, clever writers for the site. Like other zines, as online magazines are called, *Slate* didn't attract enough advertising to pay the bills, and Microsoft went to a subscription system in 1998.

technologies, like Time Warner's geodemographic TargetSelect program, make it possible for magazine publishers to identify narrower and narrower segments of the mass audience and then to gear their publications to those narrower and narrower interests.

new competition

An ominous sign for magazines is the cable television industry, which is eating into magazine advertising with an array of demassified channels, such as the ESPN sports channel, the Arts & Entertainment network and the CNBC financial news network. The demassified cable channels are picking up advertisers that once used magazines almost exclusively to reach narrow slices of the mass audience with a presumed interest in their products and services.

Another drain on magazine revenue is the growth of direct-mail advertising. Using sophisticated analysis of potential customer groups, advertisers can mail brochures, catalogs, fliers and other material, including video pitches, directly to potential customers at their homes or places of business. Every dollar that goes into direct-mail campaigns is a dollar that in an earlier period went into magazines and other traditional advertising media.

web magazines

Consumer and trade magazines adapted quickly to digital delivery in the late 1990s with World Wide Web editions. Time Warner created a massive web site, Pathfinder, for *Time, Sports Illustrated, People* and its other magazines. With substantial original content, Pathfinder wasn't merely an online version of Time Warner magazines but a distinctive product. There were hopes that advertisers would flock to online magazine sites and make them profitable, but ad revenue only trickled in. In 1998, Pathfinder went to subscriptions to supplement the meager advertising revenues. An access code was issued to *Entertainment Monthly* subscribers for an extra $30 a year. For the *Money* site, the fare was $30 to subscribers and $50 to everybody else. Even the giant Microsoft software company, with its deep pockets and a self-interest in promoting computer use, abandoned its esoteric, pop *Slate* as a free site.

media convergence

chapter wrap-up

Magazines have been an adaptable medium, adjusting with the times and with changing audience interests. *Cosmopolitan*, an especially good example of adaptability, was founded in 1886 as a home magazine, became a leading muckraking journal, switched into a general women's magazine and now is a specialized women's magazine. The adaptability of magazines is clear in the medium's long history of innovations, which, in time, other media have copied. These include in-depth personality profiles, photojournalism and muckraking.

The magazine industry once was defined by giant general-interest magazines, epitomized by *Life*, that offered something for everybody. Advertisers soured on these oversize giants when television offered more potential customers per advertising dollar. Magazines shifted to more specialized packages, and the focused approach worked. Magazines found advertisers who were seeking readers with narrow interests. Now, as other media—particularly television—are demassifying, magazines stand to lose advertisers, which poses new challenges.

A troubling question about contemporary magazines is whether they are still enriching American culture. Through most of their history, starting in the 1820s, magazines have made significant literature and ideas available at reasonable cost to the general public. Critics worry that many of today's specialized magazines have lost a sense of society's significant issues. Troubling too, say critics, is that these magazines have forsaken detached, neutral journalistic approaches in an enthusiasm for their specialized subjects, in effect selling out to the commercial interests of their advertisers rather than pursuing truth.

questions for review

1. How have magazines contributed to American culture?

2. How have magazines been innovative as a journalistic and as a visual medium?

3. Why are most magazines edited for the special interests of targeted audiences?

4. How do sponsored magazines and trade journals differ from the consumer magazines available at newsracks?

5. What is the status of demassification in the magazine industry?

6. Are magazines losing their influence as a shaper of the culture? Explain your answer.

questions for critical thinking

1. What characteristics does Bonnie Fuller have in common with these magazine founders: Sara Josepha Hale, Henry Luce, Jann Wenner, and DeWitt and Lila Wallace?

2. When American magazines came into their own in the 1820s, they represented a mass medium that was distinct from the existing book and newspaper media. How were magazines different?

3. How was the American identity that emerged in the 19th century fostered by magazines?

4. To some people, the word "muckraking" has a negative tone. Can you make the case that it should be regarded positively? Can you also argue the opposite?

5. Discuss the role of these innovators in contributing to magazines as a visual medium: Gilbert Grosvenor, Margaret Bourke-White and Henry Luce.

6. Can you name three consumer magazines in each of these categories: newsmagazines, Seven Sisters magazines, skin magazines, giant magazines and specialized magazines?

7. Considering that *Playboy* magazine relies less on newsrack sales than *Penthouse,* which would you as an advertiser prefer if all other things, including circulation, were equal?

8. The late Norman Cousins, a veteran social commentator and magazine editor, worried that trends in the magazine industry are undermining the historic role that magazines have had in enriching the culture. What is your response to Cousins's concerns?

for further learning

Walter M. Brasch. *Forerunners of Revolution: Muckrakers and the American Social Conscience* (University of America Press, 1990). Professor Brasch distinguishes muckraking from investigative reporting. Muckrakers, he says, seek to expose misdeeds that undermine the social fabric of society, while investigative reporters focus on abuses of the public trust and schemes that bilk people.

Robert Draper. *Rolling Stone Magazine: The Uncensored History* (Doubleday, 1990). In this lively and colorful account, Draper is enthusiastic about the early days of the music magazine *Rolling Stone* but less so about its founder, Jann Wenner, and what the magazine has become.

Amy Janello and Brennon Jones. *The American Magazine* (Harry N. Abrams, 1991). Janello and Jones focus on magazines as a creative medium, editorially and visually. The book includes essays by magazine people and more than 500 illustrations, including many magazine covers and spreads.

Alan and Barbara Nourie. *American Mass-Market Magazines* (Greenwood, 1990). The Nouries offer histories of 106 current and defunct consumer magazines.

Theodore Peterson. *Magazines in the Twentieth Century* (University of Illinois Press, 1964).

Sam G. Riley, ed. *Corporate Magazines in the United States* (Greenwood Press, 1992). This is a pioneering attempt at an overview of the publications that corporations produce for free circulation among employees, customers and other groups. The diversity of these publications makes a profile difficult. Sometimes called "public relations magazines," these publications employ many more people than the more visible consumer magazines.

Sam G. Riley and Gary W. Selnow, editors. *Regional Interest Magazines of the United States* (Greenwood Press, 1991). Riley and Selnow profile city and regional magazines, including *Arizona Highways, Southern Living, Texas Monthly, Chicago* and *Philadelphia.*

W. A. Swanberg. *Luce and His Empire* (Scribners, 1972). Swanberg, a biographer of major journalists, is at his best with Henry Luce of Time-Life.

William H. Taft. *American Magazines for the 1980s* (Hastings House, 1982). In this overview, Professor Taft describes the American magazine industry and trends at the start of the 1980s.

John Tebbel and Mary Ellen Zuckerman. *The Magazine in America, 1741–1990* (Oxford University Press, 1991). Tebbel and Zuckerman provide a great amount of information, much of it colorful, on the evolution of magazines in the United States. They make the case that magazines have been a major shaper of American life.

Eric Utne. "Tina's *New Yorker.*" *Columbia Journalism Review* 31 (March/April 1993). Pages 6, 31–37. Utne, a self-described magazine junkie, is far from convinced that the commercial-driven changes that former editor Tina Brown brought to the *New Yorker* are making a better magazine.

for keeping up to date

Folio is a trade journal on magazine management. Among major newspapers that track magazine issues in a fairly consistent way are the New York *Times,* the *Wall Street Journal* and *USA Today.*

4

newspapers

in this chapter you will learn:

- Newspapers are the major source of news for most Americans.

- Most U.S. newspapers are owned by chains, for better or worse.

- The United States is largely a nation of local and regional newspapers, with only three national dailies.

- Most of the leading U.S. newspapers are metropolitan dailies, which have dwindled in number with population and lifestyle shifts.

- Television and retailing changes have cut into newspaper display advertising, and newspapers may lose their dominance as an advertising medium.

- Community newspapers, especially suburban weeklies, are booming as people continue moving out of core cities.

- Thriving newspapers include counterculture, gay and Spanish-language papers aimed at narrow segments of readers.

Cousins **Joseph Patterson** and **Robert McCormick,** heirs to the McCormick reaper and Chicago *Tribune* fortunes, went off to fight in World War I. Little did they expect to see each other during the war, but one day during a lull in a battle they met. Full of war stories, Captain Patterson and Colonel McCormick stretched out on a dried-out manure pile behind a French farm house to catch up on each other's recent experiences.

The conversation turned to journalism, and Patterson described the flashy **tabloids** he had seen in London. There was nothing like them in the United States, and they seemed to be making lots of money. Then and there, the cousins decided to start a tabloid in New York after the war. Using Chicago *Tribune* money, they launched the **New York**

Triumphant Moment. Media mogul Robert Maxwell was all smiles when he bought the floundering New York *Daily News,* but mounting woes spelled doom for the empire and left the *Daily News'* future in continuing doubt.

Sold-out Edition. Perhaps the most famous news photograph of all time was Tom Howard's shot of the electric chair execution of murderer Ruth Snyder. Knowing the Sing Sing warden wouldn't agree to a photo, Howard strapped a tiny camera to his ankle and, at the right moment, lifted his trouser leg and snapped the shutter with a trip wire. The exclusive photo goosed street sales of the New York *Daily News,* which had followed the lurid trial of Snyder and her lover for killing her husband. Such stories and a focus on photo coverage, typical of the *Daily News* under founder Joseph Patterson, boosted the newspaper's circulation to more than 2 million, the largest in the nation, in the 1940s.

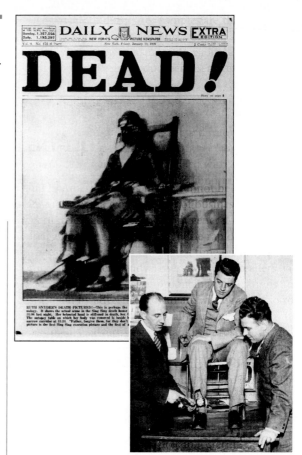

Daily News in 1919. Patterson ran the *Daily News,* while McCormick stayed in Chicago with the *Tribune.*

In 1919, when the *Daily News* was founded, there already were 18 dailies in New York. Within four years it was in the lead. Daily circulation broke through 2 million in 1944 and then climbed up to 2.4 million daily and more than 3 million Sunday— the largest in the nation.

From the beginning, Patterson's *Daily News* was an irreverent, borderline-tawdry tabloid. It had detractors who delighted in noting that it was a newspaper conceived on a dung heap—that dried-out manure pile back in France.

The *Daily News* was a paper for common people. Patterson followed the theory: "Tell it to **Sweeney**! The **Stuyvesants** will take care of themselves." In fact, the paper pointed out to advertisers that common people, taken all together, had tremendous buying power.

The newspaper screamed to be picked up with snappy heads on sensational stories: "Maid Back With Baby and Rape Tale" and "Trial Expected to Hear Lovelord Today." The *Daily News* called itself "New York's Picture Paper" and went after photos aggressively. When Ruth Snyder was electrocuted for murder at Sing Sing in 1928, prison officials barred cameras, but **Tom Howard** of the *Daily News* strapped a tiny camera to his leg and lifted his pant leg and snapped the shutter at the moment the current surged through the woman's body. The *Daily News* ran the picture as a full-page cover.

The *Daily News* had a sense of humor anyone could appreciate, whether a Sweeney or a Stuyvesant. When an Italian prosecutor accused actress Gina Lollobrigida of indecency in a film, the head read: "Charges Gina Was Obscena on La Screena." The gee-whiz, sometimes offbeat style endeared the *Daily News* to readers, at least until recent years. Today, there are doubts whether the *Daily News* can survive.

Despite its circulation, the New York *Daily News* never was a great newspaper, at least not in the sense of the serious, somber New York *Times,* and in the late 1960s circulation dropped precipitously. So did advertising and profits. As many *Daily News* readers moved upscale, with more education and more income, the *Daily News* no longer was their kind of newspaper. There were fewer Sweeneys in New York.

The Tribune Company in Chicago, which still owned the *Daily News,* put the paper up for sale in the 1980s, but there were no takers. Labor turmoil further weakened the paper, and many readers, sympathetic to the unions, boycotted the paper. At one low point, circulation reportedly slipped to 350,000. With losses mounting at $700,000 a day, the Tribune Company announced that it would shut down the paper.

Three days before the scheduled shutdown, British press tycoon **Robert Maxwell** agreed to buy the newspaper. But when he died a few weeks later, it was learned he was a world-class crook who had been raiding his employees' pension funds and committing other financial shenanigans. The *Daily News* went to Maxwell's creditors.

Although the future of the *Daily News* is unclear, the story of its rise and decline illustrates several fundamental realities of today's newspaper business. One is that many people love hyped news. In this sense, the *Daily News* could be considered a U.S. progenitor of today's supermarket tabloids. At the same time, people generally are more educated and sophisticated today than when the *Daily News* peaked. This has reduced markets for local gee-whiz scandal sheets. Also, television has cut into newspaper readership and led to a shakeout in the newspaper industry. Only the strongest newspapers survive.

The most fundamental lesson from the saga of the New York *Daily News* is that newspapers prosper when they attract a large audience that advertisers want to reach. When the audience diminishes or becomes an audience that advertisers aren't interested in, a newspaper is in trouble. If advertisers perceive that a newspaper doesn't reach the "right readers," they go elsewhere. So do the profits.

importance of newspapers

(STUDY PREVIEW) Newspapers are the primary mass medium from which people receive news. In most cities, no other news source comes close to the local newspaper's range and depth of coverage. This contributes to the popularity and influence of newspapers.

newspaper industry dimensions

The newspaper industry dwarfs other news media by almost every measure. Nearly one out of two people in the United States reads a newspaper every day, far more than tune in the network news on television in the evening. The data are staggering:

- About 1,570 daily newspapers put out 60 million copies a day, more on Sundays. Because each copy is passed along to an average of 2.2 people, daily newspapers reach 132 million people a day.
- Weekly newspapers put out 50 million copies. With their pass-along circulation of four people a copy, these newspapers reach somewhere around 200 million people a week.

Perhaps because television has stolen the glitz and romance that newspapers once had, the significance of newspapers is easy to miss. But the newspaper industry is large by every measure. In an article marveling at an issue of a newspaper as "the daily creation," the Washington *Post*'s Richard Harwood, writing about his own newspaper, said: "Roughly 11,000 people are involved in the production and distribution each day, enough bodies to fill all the billets of an Army light infantry division." Although Harwood stretched to include even the delivery boys and girls in his startling number, his point is valid: In Washington and everywhere else, newspapers far outdistance other news media in the number of people who gather, edit and disseminate news.

Newspapers are the medium of choice for more advertising than competing media. For local advertising, daily newspapers attracted $27.1 billion in 1992. Over-air television stations and cable systems were a distant second at $8.4 billion. Nationwide, including network television's tremendous advertising revenue, newspapers still lead with $30.7 billion in advertising revenue to television's $29.4 billion.

Joseph Patterson
Led New York *Daily News* to become largest-circulation U.S. daily.

Robert McCormick
Long-time publisher of Chicago *Tribune*.

tabloid
Half-size, easy-to-carry newspaper; not necessarily sensationalistic.

New York *Daily News*
Leader among metro tabloids.

Sweeneys
Common people.

Stuyvesants
Blue bloods.

Tom Howard
New York *Daily News* reporter who photographed Ruth Snyder in electric chair.

Robert Maxwell
Insatiable media mogul who "rescued" New York *Daily News*.

Except for brief downturns in the overall economy and an occasional exceptional situation, daily newspapers have been consistently profitable enterprises through the 20th century. Less than double-digit returns on investment are uncommon. As a mass medium, the newspaper is not to be underrated.

content diversity and depth

In most communities, newspapers cover more news at greater depth than competing media. A metropolitan daily like the Washington *Post* typically may carry 300 items, much more on Sundays—more than any Washington television or radio station and at greater length. City magazines in Washington, for example, offer more depth on selected stories, but the magazines are published relatively infrequently and run relatively few articles. Nationally, no broadcast organization comes close to the number of stories or the depth of the two major national newspapers, the *Wall Street Journal* and *USA Today*.

Newspapers have a rich mix of content—news, advice, comics, opinion, puzzles and data. It's all there to tap into at will. Some people go right for the stock market tables, others to sports or a favorite columnist. Unlike radio and television, you don't have to wait for what you want.

People like newspapers. Some talk affectionately of cuddling up in bed on a leisurely Sunday morning with their paper. The news and features give people something in common to talk about. Newspapers are important in people's lives, and as a medium they adapt to changing lifestyles. The number of Sunday newspapers, for example, grew from 600 in the 1970s to almost 900 today, reflecting an increase in people's weekend leisure time for reading and shopping. Ads in Sunday papers are their guide for shopping excursions.

All this does not mean that the newspaper industry is not facing problems from competing media, new technology and ongoing lifestyle shifts. But to date, newspapers have reacted to change with surprising effectiveness. To offset television's inroads, newspapers put new emphasis on being a visual medium and shed their drab graphics for color and aesthetics. To accommodate the work schedule transition of Americans over recent years from factory jobs starting at 7 a.m. to service jobs starting at 9 a.m., newspapers have emphasized morning editions and phased out afternoon editions. Knowing that the days of ink-on-paper technology are limited, the newspaper industry is examining **electronic delivery** methods for the 21st century.

Some problems are truly daunting, like the aversion of many young people to newspapers. Also, chain ownership has raised fundamental questions about how well newspapers can do their work and still meet the profit expectations of distant shareholders.

newspaper chain ownership

(STUDY PREVIEW) Through the 20th century, newspapers have been incredibly profitable, which, for better or worse, encouraged chain ownership. Today, chains own most U.S. newspapers.

electronic delivery
Sending news to readers' computer screens.

William Randolph Hearst
Chain owner who dictated content of all his newspapers.

trend toward chains

Reasoning that he could multiply profits by owning multiple newspapers, **William Randolph Hearst** put together a chain of big-city newspapers in the late 1880s.

Although Hearst's chain was not the first, his empire became the model in the public's mind for much that was both good and bad about **newspaper chains.** Like other chains, Hearst also expanded into magazines, radio and television. The trend toward chain ownership continues, and today 160 chains own four of every five dailies in the United States. Chain ownership is also coming to dominate weeklies, which had long been a bastion of independent ownership.

Newspaper profitability skyrocketed in the 1970s and 1980s, which prompted chains to buy up locally owned newspapers, sometimes in bidding frenzies. Single-newspaper cities were especially attractive because no competing media could match a local newspaper's large audience. It was possible for new owners to push ad rates up rapidly, and local retailers had to go along. The profit potential was enhanced because production costs were falling dramatically with less labor-intensive back-shop procedures, computerized typesetting and other automation. Profits were dramatic. Eight newspaper companies tracked by *Forbes* magazine from 1983 to 1988 earned the equivalent of 23.9 percent interest on a bank account. Only soft drink companies did better.

Federal tax law also accelerated the shift from family-owned to chain-owned newspapers in two ways. Inheritance taxes made it easier for families that owned independent newspapers to sell the papers than to leave them to their heirs. Also, chains were very eager to acquire more newspapers because they could avoid paying tax on income from their existing properties if they reinvested it in new holdings.

The **Gannett** media conglomerate's growth typifies how newspapers became chains and then grew into cross-media conglomerates. In 1906 the chain was six upstate New York newspapers. By 1982 Gannett had grown to almost 90 dailies, all profitable medium-size newspapers. Swimming in money, Gannett launched *USA Today.* Gannett not only absorbed *USA Today*'s tremendous start-up costs for several years but also had enough spare cash to outbid other companies for expensive metropolitan newspapers. In 1985 and 1986 Gannett paid $1.4 billion for the Detroit *News,* Des Moines *Register* and Louisville *Courier-Journal.* Along the way, Gannett acquired Combined Communications, which owned 20 broadcasting stations. Today Gannett owns 82 daily newspapers, 39 weeklies, 16 radio and 8 television stations, the largest billboard company in the nation and the Louis Harris polling organization. It renamed and beefed up a national Sunday newspaper magazine supplement. No longer just a newspaper chain, Gannett has become a mass media conglomerate.

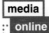

Knight-Ridder Newspapers: All in one place. www.nmc.infi.net/ kri/newsstand/pp

assessing chain ownership

Is chain ownership good for newspapers? The question raised in Hearst's time was whether diverse points of view were as likely to get into print if ownership were concentrated in fewer and fewer hands. That concern has dissipated as chains have become oriented more to profits than to participating in public dialogue. Executives at the headquarters of most chains focus on management and leave coverage and editorials to local editors. While **local autonomy** is consistent with American journalistic values, a corporate focus on profits raises a dark new question: Are chains so myopic about profits that they forget good journalism? The answer is that the emphasis varies among chains.

Journalistic Emphasis. Some chains, such as **Knight-Ridder,** whose properties include the Miami *Herald,* the Philadelphia *Inquirer* and the Detroit *Free Press,* are known for a strong corporate commitment to quality journalism. In 1988 Knight-Ridder newspapers won six of the 14 Pulitzer Prizes, including one by the Charlotte

newspaper chain
Company that owns several newspapers.

Gannett
A leading U.S. newspaper chain with 90 dailies.

local autonomy
Independence from chain headquarters.

Knight-Ridder
Newspaper chain widely respected for journalism.

····newspaper chains

Here are the largest U.S. newspaper chains, ranked by circulation, with a sample of their major properties:

	Daily Circulation	Number of Dailies
Gannett *USA Today*, Des Moines *Register*, Detroit *News*, Louisville *Courier-Journal*	5.5 million	82
Knight-Ridder Charlotte *Observer*, Detroit *Free Press*, Miami *Herald*, Philadelphia *Inquirer*, Seattle *Times*	3.6 million	27
Newhouse Cleveland *Plain Dealer*, Newark *Star Ledger*, New Orleans *Times-Picayune*, Portland *Oregonian*	2.9 million	26
Tribune Company Chicago *Tribune*	2.6 million	8
Times-Mirror Los Angeles *Times*, Hartford *Courant*, Denver *Post*, Long Island *Newsday*	2.5 million	22
Dow Jones *Wall Street Journal*, Ottaway Newspapers	2.4 million	8
New York Times New York *Times*, Florida dailies	1.7 million	26
Scripps Howard Albuquerque *Tribune*, Columbus *Citizen-Journal*, Cincinnati *Post*, Denver *Rocky Mountain News*, Memphis *Commercial Appeal*, Pittsburgh *Press*	1.6 million	21
News America Corp. Boston *Herald*, San Antonio *Express-News*	1.3 million	3

Observer for revealing the misuse of funds by the PTL ministry that opened up the televangelism scandals.

Balanced Emphasis. Most chains are known for undistinguished though profitable newspapers. This is an apt description for Gannett, the largest U.S. chain, measured by circulation.

Profit Emphasis. Several chains, including Thomson, Donrey and American Publishing, have a pattern of cutting costs aggressively, reducing staffs and trimming news coverage. It is not uncommon for a new chain owner to fire veteran reporters and editors, in some cases almost halving the staff. To save newsprint, some chains cut back the number of pages. They hire inexperienced reporters right out of college, pay them poorly and encourage them to move on after a few months so they can be replaced by other eager but inexperienced, and cheap, new reporters. The result is a reporting staff that lacks the kind of local expertise that is necessary for good journalism. Only the shareholders benefit.

In general, the following realities of chain ownership work against strong local journalistic enterprise:

Absentee Ownership. Chain executives are under pressure to run profitable enterprises, which works against good, aggressive journalism that can strain a newsroom budget. The top chain executives do not live in the communities that are short-changed by decisions to emphasize low-cost news.

Transient Management. The local managers of newspapers owned by chains tend to be career climbers who have no long-term stake in the community their newspaper serves. These people generally are not promoted from within a newspaper but are appointed by corporate headquarters, and generally they have short-term goals to look good to their corporate bosses so they can be promoted to better-paying jobs with more responsibility at bigger newspapers in the chain.

Weak Entry-Level Salaries. The focus of newspaper chains on enhancing profits to keep costs down has worked against strong salaries for journalists. The result is a "brain drain." Many talented reporters and editors leave newspapers for more lucrative jobs in public relations and other fields. In a report in *Quill* magazine, Wendy Govier and Neal Pattison offered this 1991 random collection of entry-level reporter salaries:

- St. Paul, Minnesota, *Pioneer Press*, owned by Knight-Ridder, circulation 200,000, $23,556 a year.

- Bremerton, Washington, *Sun*, owned by John P. Scripps Newspapers, circulation 41,500, $22,360 a year.

- Indianapolis *Star*, owned by Central Newspapers, circulation 244,000, $21,632 a year.

High Newsroom Turnover. Cost-conscious policies at many chain newspapers encourage newsroom employees to move on after a few pay raises, so they can be replaced by rookies at entry-level salaries. This turnover can denude a newsroom of people knowledgeable about the community the newspaper services, thus eroding coverage.

national dailies

(STUDY PREVIEW) Although the United States is a country of mostly local newspapers, three dailies have national circulation. The *Wall Street Journal* is the most solidly established with most of its readership anchored in business and finance. Prospects for the flashy *USA Today* and the dowdy but respected *Christian Science Monitor* are less certain.

absentee ownership
Company headquarters in far away city.
transient management
High turnover among executives.

media databank

....newsroom salaries

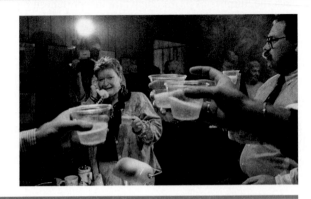

Reporters, photographers and copy editors at 134 U.S. and Canadian newspapers are represented in contract negotiations by the **Newspaper Guild.** Reporters at the New York *Times* had the most lucrative Guild contract in 1996, almost $1,300 a week, $67,000 a year, with two years' experience. Many earn more for merit, in bonuses, and for working odd hours.

The lowest Guild salary for experienced reporters was $346 a week at the Battle Creek, Michigan, *Enquirer.*

The Guild average was $711, almost $37,000 a year. The average for all newspapers, including

more than 1,400 non-union papers, is impossible to calculate because there's no reliable data-gathering mechanism.

Congratulations, and Here's $25. Betty Gray of the Washington, North Carolina, *Daily News* unearthed a major scandal that public officials knew about carcinogen-contaminated water and did nothing about it. Gray's work earned her a 1989 Pulitzer Prize—and a $25-a-week pay raise, which brought her annual salary to $15,000. The deplorable salary typifies the dubious success of many newspapers at boosting profits by keeping costs down.

	Salary per week
New York *Times*	$1,280 after 2 years
Boston *Globe*	1,090 after 5 years
Philadelphia *Inquirer* and *Daily News*	1,030 after 5 years
Chicago *Sun Times*	1,020 after 5 years
Reuters	990 after 6 years
St. Louis *Post-Dispatch*	980 after 5 years
Baltimore *Sun*	960 after 5 years
Agence France-Presse	950 after 7 years
Pittsburgh *Post-Gazette*	940 after 5 years
Cleveland *Plain Dealer*	930 after 4 years

wall street journal

The *Wall Street Journal,* the nation's largest newspaper, began humbly. **Charles Dow** and **Edward Jones** went into business in 1882, roaming the New York financial district for news and then scribbling notes by hand, which they sent by courier to their clients. As more information-hungry investors signed up, the service was expanded into a newsletter, and in 1889 the *Wall Street Journal* was founded. Advertisers eager to reach *Journal* readers bought space in the newspaper, which provided revenue to hire correspondents in Boston, Philadelphia and Washington. By 1900 circulation reached 10,000, and it grew to 30,000 by 1940.

The *Wall Street Journal* might have remained a relatively small albeit successful business paper had it not been for the legendary **Barney Kilgore,** who joined the newspaper's San Francisco bureau in 1929. Within two years, Kilgore was the *Journal*'s

Barney Kilgore

news editor and in a position to shift the newspaper's journalistic direction. Kilgore's formula was threefold:

- Simplify the *Journal*'s business coverage into plain English without sacrificing thoroughness.
- Provide detailed coverage of government but without the jargon that plagued Washington reporting most of the time.
- Expand the definition of the *Journal*'s field of coverage from "business" to "everything that somehow relates to earning a living."

The last part of the formula, expanded coverage, was a risk. Critics told Kilgore that the newspaper's existing readers might switch to other papers if they felt the *Journal* was slighting business. Kilgore's vision, however, was not to reduce business coverage but to seek business angles in other fields and cover them. It worked. Under Kilgore's leadership, *Journal* circulation reached 100,000 in 1947. When Kilgore died in 1967, a year after retiring as chairman of Dow Jones, publisher of the *Journal,* circulation had passed 1 million. Today, with circulation approaching 2 million, the *Journal* is the largest U.S. daily and, among the three national dailies, the most financially secure.

Although the *Journal* is edited for a general audience as well as for traditional business readers, it does not pander to a downscale audience. It carries no comics or horoscope columns, and its sports and entertainment coverage tends to focus on the front

Newspaper Guild
Collective bargaining agent at 134 U.S., Canadian newspapers.

Wall Street Journal
Financially successful U.S. national daily.

Charles Dow
Wall Street Journal co-founder.

Edward Jones
Wall Street Journal co-founder.

Barney Kilgore
Created modern *Wall Street Journal.*

office and the box office. A mark of the *Journal* is its grayness. The only art on Page 1 is an occasional one-column etching. Inside, advertisements are lavish with photography, but line art dominates the news sections. In 1991 the *Journal* began accepting limited color in advertisements, but even so, the visual impression, a correct one, is that the *Journal* is a newspaper for readers to take seriously. Advertisers take the *Journal* seriously too, knowing its readers' average household income is $147,000 a year. No other newspaper comes close to delivering such a prosperous audience.

The *Journal* puts significant resources into reporting. It is not unusual for a reporter to be given six weeks for research on a major story. This digging gives the *Journal* big breaks on significant stories. In 1988, as an example, the *Journal* reported in a lengthy biographical piece on evangelist Pat Robertson, who was seeking the Republican presidential nomination, that one of his children was conceived out of wedlock. It was a revelation that affected the course of the campaign, especially in view of Robertson's moral posture on family issues. While a serious newspaper, the *Journal* is neither stodgy nor prudish. Lengthy Page 1 pieces range from heavy-duty coverage of national politics to such diverse and unexpected stories as a black widow spider outbreak in Phoenix, archaeological research into human turds to understand lifestyles of lost civilizations, and how the admiral of landlocked Bolivia's navy keeps busy.

The *Wall Street Journal* has 500 editors and reporters, but not all are at the newspaper's Manhattan headquarters. The *Journal* has 11 foreign and 14 domestic bureaus, and its European and Asian editions have their own staffs.

The domestic U.S. editions are edited in New York, and page images are transmitted via orbiting satellite to 17 printing plants across the nation, so the paper is on the street and in the mail on the day of publication. Advertisers may pick and choose the editions in which they want their ads to appear.

The European and Asian editions are edited separately but lean heavily on the domestic U.S. edition for stories. The foreign editions are printed in Hong Kong, Japan, Malaysia, the Netherlands and Switzerland.

The challenge for the *Journal* has been finding a balance between its original forte, covering business, and its expanding coverage of broader issues. It is a precarious balance. Numerous business publications, including *Business Week* and the Los Angeles-based *Investor's Daily,* vie for the same readers and advertisers with compacter packages, and numerous other national publications, including the newsmagazines, offer general coverage. So far, the *Journal* has succeeded with a gradual broadening of general coverage without losing its business readers.

In brief, here are distinctive features of the *Wall Street Journal:*

Business Coverage.   The *Journal* is more consistently thorough in its coverage of business and finance than any other newspaper. The coverage, it is said accurately, "moves markets." The third section of the newspaper, typically 24 pages, is dominated by stock and financial tables.

Exploratory Reporting.   The *Journal* seeks out stories that might not be told unless a journalist went after them. This **exploratory reporting** includes what Kilgore called **leaders,** Page One in-depth stories on current events, trends and issues but not necessarily breaking news.

Commentary.   The editorial section is influential in political circles. Columnists represent a wide range of views. The *Journal*'s book, film, drama and other critics are widely followed and respected.

exploratory reporting
Enterprise coverage that goes beyond following events.

leaders
Leading stories in an edition.

USA Today
Gannett national daily founded in 1981.

McNewspaper
Derisive name for *USA Today.*

Allen Neuharth
Creator of *USA Today.*

Writing Style. Under Kilgore, the *Journal* encouraged writers to be simple, although not simplistic, in dealing with complex subjects. Part of the technique is a conversational tone, now widely used, that even includes contractions like "don't" and "we've."

usa today

A strict format, snappy visuals and crisp writing give **USA Today** an air of confidence and the trappings of success, and the newspaper has its strengths. In less than a decade, circulation reached 1.6 million, behind only the *Wall Street Journal,* and Gannett executives exude sureness about long-term prospects. The optimism is underscored by the confident if not brash Page One motto: "The Nation's Newspaper."

USA Today has had a significant impact since its founding. Like the *Wall Street Journal, USA Today* seeks well-heeled readers, although in different ways. *USA Today* has relatively few subscribers, going instead after single-copy sales, mostly to business people who are on the run and want a quick fix on the news. Many of *USA Today*'s sales are at airport newsracks, where many buyers are corporate executives and middle-management travelers who are away from home. Gannett offers deep discounts to upscale hotels to buy the papers in bulk and slip free under guests' doors as a morning courtesy. Stories strain to be lively and upbeat to make the experience of reading the paper a positive one. In contrast to the *Wall Street Journal,* almost all *USA Today* stories are short, which diverts little of a reader's time from pressing business. The brevity and crispness of *USA Today*, combined with the enticing graphics, has led some critics to liken the newspaper to fast food and dub it "**McNewspaper**"—not bad for you but not as nourishing as, say, the *Wall Street Journal.*

Despite its critics, *USA Today* has been true to founder **Allen Neuharth**'s original concept. Neuharth wanted to create a distinctive newspaper positioned below the *Wall Street Journal* and the New York *Times,* both of which are available nationally, and yet provide a kind of coverage not available in the metropolitan dailies. Because many corporate travelers change jobs fairly often and make career moves from state to state, Neuharth decided to provide two to three news and sports items every day from every state in the union. Not uncommon, for example, are items on Little League baseball championships in Idaho, if that happens to be the major sports event in Idaho on a particular day. Such tidbits from home are valuable to business travelers who have been on the road for days and cannot find such home-state items in local dailies or on television. Also for business people, the newspaper has a separate business section. This section lacks the depth of the *Wall Street Journal,* but readers can find several pages of stock data and stories, usually short, on breaking business news.

Graphics Innovator. Since its founding in 1981, *USA Today* has had a profound impact on many other newspapers. The most obvious influence has been to establish newspapers as a strong visual medium with color and graphics integrated with words. The newspaper's weather coverage and high story counts also have been widely imitated. *USA Today* is designed for travelers and as a "second buy" for people who already have read their hometown daily. Subscriptions are only a small part of *USA Today*'s circulation. Most sales are in distinctive TV-shaped newsracks and in airports, hotels and places where travelers pick it up for a fix on the news. Guaranteed in every issue are at least a few sentences of what's happening in news and sports from every state in the Union.

media
online

USA Today: The paper that was designed to look like TV now looks like the World Wide Web. www.usatoday.com

allen neuharth

Many people were sure that Al Neuharth had made a rare blunder. It was 1982, and Neuharth, chief of the enormously successful Gannett media conglomerate, was announcing that Gannett would launch a national daily newspaper—*USA Today*. Under Neuharth, Gannett had become a leading newspaper chain with more than 80 newspapers. Its profitability record was among the strongest of all American corporations, not just newspapers. But with Neuharth's *USA Today* announcements, Gannett stock tumbled on Wall Street. Within three days, the stock lost almost 1.8 percent of its value.

The doubters had cause. Historically the United States was a nation of **provincial newspapers,** reflecting the country's enormity, which made national distribution of a daily newspaper prohibitively expensive.

A second reason for the local thrust of U.S. newspapers is the nation's multi-layered, decentralized system of government. Many political decisions affecting people's lives are made at local levels, so naturally, news-papers track local issues. In contrast, most other nations, with strong central governments and not much local autonomy, have national newspapers.

Despite the provincial tradition and the conventional wisdom, Neuharth convinced Gannett directors that *USA Today* could be profitable. "Give me five years," he said. Four and one-half years later, Neuharth's daringly distinctive newspaper had its first profitable month. Even though the red ink returned the next month, Gannett executives were sure by then that the paper eventually could be a consistent money-maker, and they never wavered publicly on their commitment to keep it going. In 1993, in fact, some financial analysts figured that *USA Today* might break into black ink for the whole year for the first time—11 years after the newspaper was founded.

Neuharth, who was 58 when *USA Today* was born, had learned the newspaper business the hard way. After college and two years with the Associated Press in his native South Dakota, Neuharth and a friend started a weekly tabloid they

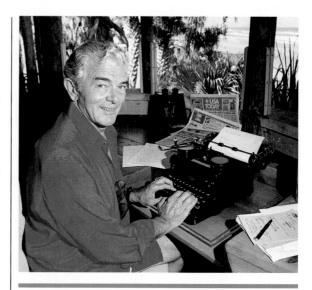

Old-Fashioned Way. After retiring from day-to-day operations at the Gannett chain, which owns *USA Today,* Al Neuharth, who created the national newspaper, took up reporting again. Neuharth trotted the globe in a Gannett corporate jet for a regular column that *USA Today* carried as "JetCapade." Ironic as it seems, the man who created the glitzy *USA Today* could not give up his Royal manual typewriter.

called *SoDak Sports.* Two years later and $50,000 in debt, they acknowledged that the paper was a failure and shut it down. However, lessons were learned. Years later, Neuharth told an interviewer, "Getting really bloodied as I did there at the age of 28, 29, was a tremendous stroke of good fortune for me. I thought I was a red-hot journalist then, a sportswriter who thought he ran great prose through the typewriter. And I thought if you did that, you would automatically succeed with a publication. Then I found out without advertising and other revenues, you couldn't pay the rent, no matter how much you and your friends enjoyed what you were writing and publishing."

Neuharth's goal of tapping into a corporate readership with the kind of discretionary income that attracts advertisers has succeeded in part. Gannett claims that one out of four readers has a $50,000-plus annual household income, unusually high for a newspaper but less than half the average of all *Wall Street Journal* readers.

USA Today has been a major innovator, especially in news and information packaging, and its techniques have caught on with many local newspapers. Innovations include:

High Story Counts.   Most stories run no more than 10 sentences, which creates room for many more stories per issue than in other newspapers. Even lengthier pieces, limited to only four per issue, are capped at 35 sentences. Among journalists, this is known as a "**high story count.**"

Splashy Design.   *USA Today* emphasizes color photographs and illustrations, moving away from words alone to tell the news and explain issues.

Graphs, Tables, Charts.   The newspaper offers data graphically, not just accompanying stories but standing alone in separate displays.

The introduction of *USA Today* came at a time when most newspapers were trying to distinguish themselves from television news with longer, exploratory and interpretive stories. While some major newspapers like the New York *Times* and the Los Angeles *Times* were unswayed by *USA Today*'s snappy, quick-to-read format, many other newspapers moved to shorter, easily digested stories, infographics and more data lists. Color became standard. *USA Today* has influenced today's newspaper style and format.

christian science monitor

Mary Baker Eddy, the influential founder of the Christian Science faith, was aghast at turn-of-the-century Boston newspapers. The Boston dailies, as in other major American cities, were sensationalistic, overplaying crime and gore in hyperbolic battles to steal readers from each other. Entering the fray, Eddy introduced a newspaper with a different mission. Her ***Christian Science Monitor,*** founded in 1908, sought to deal with issues and problems on a high plane and to help the world come up with solutions.

Nobody, least of all Mary Baker Eddy, expected such an intellectually oriented newspaper to make money, at least not right away, so the church underwrote expenses when subscriptions, newsstand sales and advertising revenue fell short. The *Monitor* sought subscriptions nationwide and abroad, and it developed a following. While edited in Boston, the *Monitor* was conceived as an international, not a local newspaper, and it became the first national daily newspaper in the United States.

The *Christian Science Monitor* tries to emphasize positive news, but it also deals with crime, disaster, war and other down-beat news, and it has won Pulitzer Prizes for covering them. The thrust, though, is interpretive, unlike the sensationalistic newspapers to which Mary Baker Eddy wanted an alternative. The *Monitor* does not cover events and issues to titillate its readers. Rather, as veteran Monitor editor Erwin Canham explained, the newspaper's mission is "to help give humankind the tools with which to work out its salvation." The *Monitor* is not preachy; in fact, only one plainly labeled religious article appears in each issue. The *Monitor* seeks to lead and influence by example.

provincial newspapers
Most U.S. newspapers focus coverage on their region; as opposed to a national press.

story count
Number of stories per edition.

Mary Baker Eddy
Founded *Christian Science Monitor* 1908.

Christian Science Monitor
Boston-based national U.S. newspaper.

·····mary baker eddy

Twenty-nine years after founding the Christian Science Church, Mary Baker Eddy, at age 88, started the *Christian Science Monitor.* That was in 1908 in Boston, and the newspaper clearly was an alternative to the sensationalistic press of the time. It quickly gained a reputation for international reporting and analysis. Although sponsored by the church, the *Monitor* never had an evangelical tone. The appeal was to intellectuals, and the emphasis was solution-oriented coverage of the great issues of the day.

Some biographers speculate that Eddy founded the *Monitor* to offset doubts and criticism about the Christian Science Church. She was a char-

ismatic leader, and there were questions whether the church, a distinctly American denomination she established in 1879, would survive her death. She was in great pain, probably from gallstones, and her physical condition was not strong. Mary Baker Eddy died in 1910, just short of the second anniversary of the *Monitor.*

Despite her years and frailties, Eddy was the force behind the *Monitor.* She insisted the newspaper have the church's name in the title. She came up with the motto that still graces the editorial page: "First the blade, then the ear, and then the full grain in the ear." She also wrote the *Monitor* statement of purpose: "To injure no man, but to bless all mankind."

Constructive Journalism. Since its 1908 founding, the *Christian Science Monitor* has emphasized solution-oriented journalism. The *Monitor,* based in Boston, began as an antidote to sensationalistic newspapers, emphasizing accurate and truthful coverage to help people address serious problems facing humankind.

Through its history, the *Monitor* has remained true to Eddy's original concept. Erwin Canham, who spent most of his career with the newspaper, finally serving as editor beginning in 1945, once explained the mission of *Monitor* as "to help give humankind the tools with which to work out its salvation."

A few seasoned foreign correspondents provide the backbone of the *Monitor*'s respected international coverage, and their stories are backed up with stories from reporters who work for other news organizations but who moonlight for the *Monitor.* A staff in Washington anchors domestic coverage. The cultural coverage and editorials are widely read.

Circulation peaked at 239,000 in 1971, the year when the *Monitor* joined several leading newspapers, including the New York *Times,* in printing secret Pentagon documents over the objections of the Nixon administration. By then, the *Monitor* was being printed at plants near Boston, Chicago, Los Angeles and New York for same-day mail delivery to much of the nation, as well as at a plant near London for foreign distribution. Since the 1971 peak, however, circulation has deteriorated to less than

140,000. Failing to find a sufficient following among national advertisers, the *Monitor* has shrunk from a full-size newspaper to a thinner and thinner tabloid. A handicap in finding advertising revenue is the church's doctrine-based refusal to accept ads for alcoholic beverages, tobacco products and drugs.

It is unclear how much longer the church, whose membership has dwindled to 150,000 and whose overall income is estimated at only $85 million a year, can afford to carry out Mary Baker Eddy's goal for a strong Christian Science presence in the news media.

national editions

The New York *Times* and the Los Angeles *Times* took to calling themselves national newspapers in the 1990s, but they really aren't. Both newspapers' national editions are mere add-on to a core product edited for provincial audiences in metropolitan New York and Los Angeles. For the national editions, editors replace local and regional coverage with Washington and foreign stories.

Even so, both the New York and Los Angeles *Times* have some characteristics of the three truly national dailies. For example, air delivery and satellite printing plants make the national editions available in many places the morning of publication. In some densely populated areas, home delivery is available.

These national editions are an attempt to capitalize on the strong reputations that the New York and Los Angeles *Times* have built over the years with their own Washington and foreign staffs. The newspapers hope to attract national advertisers—the same advertisers that have cottoned to the *Wall Street Journal, USA Today,* the newsmagazines and network television. Whether these national editions become profitable remains to be seen. The key to profitability is whether enough advertising can be found to cover distribution costs, which are high. The national editions themselves, as a repackaging of the existing core product, don't cost much to put out.

hometown newspapers

STUDY PREVIEW   The United States has 1,570 daily newspapers, most oriented to covering hometown news and carrying local advertising. Big-city dailies are the most visible hometown newspapers, but medium-size and small dailies have made significant strides in quality in recent decades and eroded the metros' outlying circulation.

metropolitan dailies

In every region of the United States, there is a newspaper whose name is a household word. These are metropolitan dailies with extensive regional circulation. In New England, for example, the Boston *Globe* covers Boston but also prides itself on extensive coverage of Massachusetts state government, as well as coverage of neighboring states. The *Globe* has a Washington bureau, and it sends reporters abroad on special assignments.

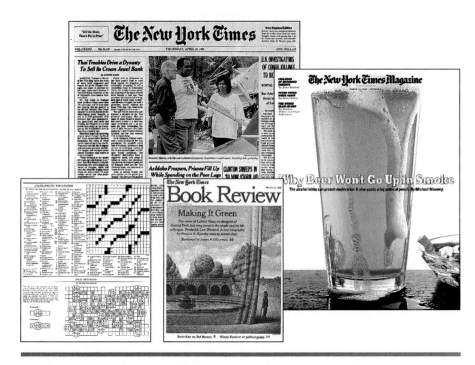

Old Gray Lady. True to the graphic spirit of the 19th century, when it rose in eminence, the New York *Times* is sometimes called the Old Gray Lady of American journalism. Even after color photos were added in 1997, the *Times* had a staid, somber visual personality. The coverage, writing and commentary, however, are anything but dull, and it is those things that have made the *Times'* reputation as the world's best newspaper. The paper is distinguished by international and Washington coverage, which is drawn mostly from its own staff reporters rather than the news services which most other newspapers rely on. Among Sunday features is the colorful, splashy *New York Times Magazine,* which runs lengthy examinations on serious issues. Also Sunday is a serious book review magazine. The New York *Times* crossword puzzle is one of the most followed in the world. The *Times* carries no comics or horoscopes, which contributes to the tone and mystique that set the newspaper apart.

When experts are asked to list the nation's best newspapers, the lists inevitably are led by the **New York *Times.*** Other newspapers with a continuing presence include the Baltimore *Sun,* Chicago *Tribune,* Dallas *Morning News,* Houston *Chronicle,* Los Angeles *Times,* Miami *Herald,* Minneapolis *Star Tribune,* Philadelphia *Inquirer,* St. Louis *Post Dispatch* and Washington *Post.*

Here are snapshots of three leading metro dailies:

New York *Times.* Not a librarian anywhere would want to be without a subscription to the New York *Times,* which is one reason that the *Times* boasts at least one subscriber in every county in the country. Since its founding in 1851, the *Times* has had a reputation for fair and thorough coverage of foreign news. A large, widely respected staff covers Washington. It is a newspaper of record, printing the president's annual state of the union address and other important documents in their entirety. The *Times* is an important research source, in part because the *Times* puts out a monthly and annual index that lists every story. The editorials are among the most quoted.

The *Times* news sections added color photographs in 1998, but the presentation remains somber and stolid, fitting the seriousness with which the *Times* takes its cov-

New York *Times*
Most respected U.S.
hometown daily.

1851 Henry Raymond founded New York *Times.*

1889 Newsletter editors Charles Dow and Edward Jones founded *Wall Street Journal.*

1908 Religious leader Mary Baker Eddy founded *Christian Science Monitor.*

1919 Joseph Patterson and Robert McCormick founded New York *Daily News.*

1955 Bohemian New York literati founded *Village Voice.*

1967 Jim Michaels founded Los Angeles-based *Advocate,* first gay newspaper.

1983 Gannett's Allen Neuharth founded *USA Today.*

erage. Inside, though, dazzling, colorful graphics have become standard in recent years. The Sunday edition includes the glitzy New York *Times Magazine,* a serious book review magazine, and one of the world's most followed crossword puzzles. Unusual for a United States newspaper, especially one with a large Sunday edition, the *Times* carries no comics.

Los Angeles *Times*. The **Los Angeles *Times*** edged out the declining New York *Daily News* in 1990 as the nation's largest metropolitan daily when circulation reached 1.3 million. By many measures, the *Times* is huge. A typical Sunday edition makes quite a thump on the doorstep at four pounds and 444 pages.

The *Times* has 1,300 editors and reporters, some in 27 foreign bureaus and 13 U.S. bureaus. Fifty-seven reporters cover the federal government in Washington alone. To cover the 1991 war against Iraq, the *Times* dispatched 20 reporters and photographers to the Gulf region, compared with 12 for the New York *Times* and 10 for the Washington *Post,* the traditional leading U.S. metro dailies for foreign coverage. Critics say the Los Angeles *Times* is sometimes disappointing in local coverage, but it is applauded for the coverage to which it channels resources.

Washington *Post*. The **Washington *Post*** cemented its reputation for investigative reporting by breaking revelation after revelation in the 1972 Watergate scandal, until finally Richard Nixon resigned the presidency in disgrace. The *Wall Street Journal,* New York *Times* and Los Angeles *Times,* all with large Washington staffs, compete aggressively with the *Post* for major federal stories, but the *Post* remains the most quoted newspaper for government coverage.

With the demise of the afternoon Washington *Daily News* and the *Star,* the *Post* was left the only local newspaper in the nation's capital, which upset critics who perceived a liberal bias in the *Post.* This prompted the Unification Church of the Reverend Sun Myung Moon to found the **Washington *Times*** as a rightist daily. The *Times* has only a fraction of the *Post*'s 840,000 circulation, but its scrappy coverage inserts local excitement into Washington journalism, as does its incessant sniping at the *Post* and *Post*-owned *Newsweek* magazine.

Los Angeles *Times*
Largest-circulation U.S. hometown daily.

Washington *Post*
Established reputation covering Watergate.

Washington *Times*
Conservative newspaper.

top newspapers

For years *Time* ranked U.S. newspapers once a year, but in 1984 the magazine dropped the much-watched list. So what are the best U.S. newspapers? In 1997 *Time*'s media watcher, Richard Zoglin declared categorically that the New York *Times* left everybody else a poor second. Here are excerpts from his comments on significant papers:

New York *Times*: Agreement is almost universal the the *Times* is the leading newspaper in the United States if not the world.

Anniston *Star*: This Alabama daily develops reporters who make reputations elsewhere.

Baltimore *Sun*: Reborn with enterprise reporting exemplified by two reporters who exposed slave trade in Sudan.

Cleveland *Plain Dealer*: One of the most improved U.S. newspapers.

Concord *Monitor*: Excellent statewide New Hampshire coverage.

Dallas *Morning News*: Innovative, feisty, hardly timid or formulaic.

Everett *Herald*: Creative, community-minded local reporting of this city north of Seattle.

Los Angeles *Times*: Still formidable despite major budget cutbacks. Coverage sometimes lumbering and hard to read.

New Orleans *Times-Picayune*: Shedding its fat, sleepy reputation with aggressive reporting.

Newsday: Good, gutty local coverage of Long Island. Eight Pulitzers in six years.

Orange County *Register*: Excellent local coverage that often skunks the Los Angeles *Times*. Glitzy design.

San Jose *Mercury News*: Covers Silicon Valley tech news and issues with verve.

St. Petersburg *Times*: Continues with outstanding enterprise reporting, crafted writing. Breeds great reporters.

Newark *Star-Ledger*: A rising star in the Newhouse chain.

Philadelphia *Inquirer*: Excellent at major investigations and splashy specials. Ragged everyday coverage.

Raleigh *News & Observer*: Tech-savvy newspaper whose Nando Web site sets the online standard.

Wall Street Journal: Excellent business, marketing and technology coverage. Slipping in enterprise reporting.

USA Today: Has added investigative reporting, thorough sports, smart business coverage, savvy trend spotting.

Washington *Post*: Improved local coverage. Has lost edge in political news.

hometown dailies

With their aggressive reporting on national and regional issues, the metro dailies receive more attention than smaller dailies, but most Americans read **hometown dailies.** By and large, these locally oriented newspapers, most of them chain-owned, have been incredibly profitable while making significant journalistic progress since World War II.

Fifty years ago, people in small towns generally bought both a metropolitan daily and a local newspaper. Hometown dailies were thin and coverage was hardly comprehensive. Editorial pages tended to offer only a single perspective. Readers had few alternative sources of information. Since then, these smaller dailies have hired better-prepared journalists, acquired new technology and strengthened their local advertising base.

Hometown dailies have grown larger and more comprehensive. The years between 1970 and 1980 were especially important for quantum increases in news coverage. The

hometown daily
Edited primarily for readers in a defined region.

news hole
Space in publication after ads are inserted.

space available for news, called the **news hole,** increased more than 25 percent. Many hometown dailies also gave much of their large news holes to bigger and more diverse opinion sections. Most editorial sections today are smorgasbords of perspectives.

challenges for daily newspapers

(STUDY PREVIEW)   Daily newspaper circulation in the United States is stagnant, and other media are eroding the dominance of the newspaper as an advertising medium. Even so, the newspaper industry is financially strong, and newspapers have inherent advantages over competing media.

circulation patterns

Confirming what was widely suspected, a 1990 study found that young people by and large don't read newspapers. According to the study, sponsored through the Los Angeles *Times,* only 30 percent of people under 35 read a newspaper the day before. Twenty-five years earlier, the Gallup polling people found the rate was 67 percent.

Newspaper executives have cause to worry. Unless they entice young readers, their medium will decline as older people, the bulk of their audience, die. But the problem may be even more serious. The Los Angeles *Times* study found that it isn't just newspapers that young people are avoiding but news itself. Of respondents between ages 18 and 29, 40 percent are less likely than their elders to be able to identify significant figures in the news, and 20 percent said they were less likely to follow even major events.

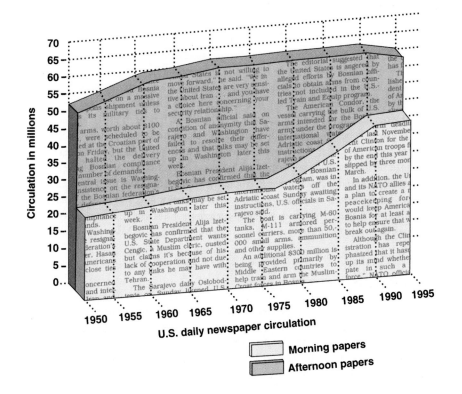

U.S. daily newspaper circulation

☐ Morning papers
▨ Afternoon papers

Death in the Afternoon. American newspaper circulation is almost stagnant at 60 million a day. Growth leveled off in the 1970s as evening television newscasts drew people away from afternoon newspapers. Some major afternoon newspapers folded; others switched to morning publication. Afternoon newspaper circulation, which peaked at 36.2 million in 1965, slipped to 17.7 million in 1972.

daily newspaper circulation

Daily Newspaper Circulation	Daily	Sunday
Wall Street Journal	1.8 million	
USA Today	1.6 million	
New York *Times*	1.1 million	1.8 million
Los Angeles *Times*	1.0 million	1.5 million
Washington *Post*	840,000	1.2 million
New York *Daily News*	726,000	974,000
Chicago *Tribune*	691,000	1.1 million
Long Island *Newsday*	670,000	745,000
Detroit *Free Press*	531,000	1.2 million
Dallas *Morning News*	515,000	822,000

The study overturned the notion that young people prefer television to newspapers for news. Only 4 of every 10 respondents under age 35 had watched television news the day before. Twenty-five years earlier it was 5 of 10. Except for sports and issues that affect them directly, like abortion, young people are less and less interested in news.

Overall, **circulation** growth has stalled after peaking at 62.8 million in 1988. More seriously, market penetration has declined sharply. The 1960 census found that the average American household subscribed to 1.12 newspapers. By 1990 the average was fewer than 0.7 subscription per household. Fewer people are reading newspapers.

The circulation decline has been heaviest among evening newspapers. Television is largely responsible. As television became the dominant evening activity in the nation, Americans spent less time with evening newspapers and eventually dropped their subscriptions. The decline in evening newspapers, called **PMs,** has been especially severe in blue-collar towns, where most families once built their lifestyle around 7 a.m. to 3 p.m. factory shifts. Today, as the United States shifts from an industrial to a service economy, more people work 9-to-5 jobs and have less discretionary time in the afternoon and evening to read a newspaper. Predictably, advertisers have followed readers from evenings to mornings, and one by one afternoon newspapers in two-newspaper cities folded. In many places, afternoon newspapers have followed their readers' lifestyle changes and converted to the morning cycle, publishing as **AMs.**

circulation
Number of copies of a periodical that are sold.

PMs
Afternoon newspapers.

AMs
Morning newspapers.

advertising patterns

Even morning papers are having advertising problems. The heady days when newspapers could count on more advertising every year seem over. Projections into the early 21st century indicate that newspaper advertising will be lucky to hold its own. Television's growth is a factor, but other media, including ads distributed by mail, are eating into the historic dominance of the newspaper as an advertising medium. In 1980 daily newspapers led all media with 27.6 percent of the total advertising pie. By 1992 the newspaper slice was down to 23.4 percent. The situation varied from city to city, but overall newspaper advertising was flattening out.

Besides television, daily newspaper advertising revenue has taken a hit from the **consolidation** of retailing into fewer albeit bigger companies. Grocery, discount and department store mergers cut down on advertising revenue. Fewer competing retail chains meant fewer ads.

This was a major loss because the grocery, discount and department stores were newspapers' largest source of income. The Los Angeles *Times* estimated it lost $12 million in ad revenue because of mergers in one year alone.

A growing advertising practice, bypassing the traditional mass media and sending circulars and catalogs directly to potential customers, also is cutting into newspaper advertising income. This **direct mail** trend took off in the 1970s and accelerated into the 1990s. Today, direct mail advertising accounts for 14 percent of the money spent nationwide by advertisers. To win back advertisers who switched to direct mail, newspapers are willing to tuck preprinted advertising circulars, mostly from large retailers, inside the regular paper. In one sense, **preprints,** as they are called, represent lost revenue because in the days before direct mail those ads would have been placed in the regular pages of the newspaper at full ad rates. Newspaper preprint rates are discounted deeply to compete with postal rates.

prospects for the daily press

While daily newspapers, both metros and smaller dailies, face problems, they hardly are on the verge of extinction. While competing media have taken away some newspaper retail advertising, the want ads, formally called **classified advertising,** continue to be highly profitable. At some newspapers, classifieds generate more than half of the revenue. The national average exceeds 40 percent. Television and radio have not found a way to offer a competing service, and not even free-distribution papers devoted to classified advertising have reversed the growth in daily newspaper classified revenue.

Also, the newspaper remains the dominant advertising medium for most major local advertisers: grocery stores, department stores, automobile dealerships and discount stores.

On the downside, daily newspapers have suffered major losses over the years in national advertising, mostly to magazines and network television. Despite the losses, newspapers have not given up on national advertising. Every newspaper has a broker, called a **national representative,** whose business is to line up national advertising for its client newspapers.

Daily newspapers have inherent advantages that competing media cannot match, at least not now.

Portability.   Newspapers are a portable medium. People can pick up a newspaper any time and take it with them, which is hardly possible with newspaper's biggest rival for advertisers, television. In the long term, as television sets are installed in more places and with the arrival of miniaturized, battery-operated television receivers, this newspaper advantage may erode.

Variety.   A newspaper has more room to cover a greater variety of events and provide a greater variety of features than competing media units. The entire script for a 30-minute television newscast can fit on a fraction of a single newspaper page. This

advertising consolidation
Retail mergers reduce number of major newspaper advertisers.

direct mail
Advertisements sent directly to consumers.

preprints
Separately printed ads inserted in a newspaper.

classified advertising
Want ads.

national representative
Newspaper's agency to solicit national advertisers.

portability
Newspapers are easy to tote, an advantage over some media.

advantage may dissipate as people have greater access to new specialized television services and zip and zap among them: the Weather Channel on cable, sports channels, consumer information channels, ticker-tape streamers on cable. Also, 900-number telephone services offer scores, game details and sports news on demand, although they are more expensive than buying a newspaper.

Indexed Content. Newspapers remain quick sources of information, ideas and entertainment. Readers can quickly find items that interest them by using headlines as an indexing device. With television, people have to wait for the items they want.

Depth Coverage. Newspapers have room for lengthy, in-depth treatments, which most contemporary broadcast formats preclude. Rare are radio newscasts with stories longer than 120 words, and most television focuses only on highlights.

These traditional advantages that accrue to the newspaper as a medium are being eroded, but the newspaper remains the only package that has them all. In general, newspaper companies are in a good position to survive because of an asset that competing media lack: the largest, most skilled newsroom staffs in their communities. Television stations have relatively minuscule news-gathering staffs, and they lack the tradition and experience to match the ongoing, thorough coverage of newspapers. The strength of newspaper companies is their news-gathering capability, not their means of delivery. Since the 1970s newspapers have experimented with facsimile, television text, and World Wide Web delivery, gaining familiarity with alternate technology for disseminating their main product, which is news, not newsprint.

newspaper web sites

Today almost every daily newspaper in the United States runs a web site. The people who run news organizations sense profits from the web at some future point, and they want to be on the ground floor. But how long will the wait be for these news sites to turn a profit? Hoag Levins, editor of mediainfo.com, published by the newspaper trade journal *Editor & Publisher,* expects advertisers will flock to the web when penetration reaches 50 percent of a city's households. In 1998, about 20 percent of U.S. homes had web access.

Levins: "A kind of critical mass can occur in metro areas when newspaper circulation drops to 50 percent of that area's households. Such declines can trigger a sudden, self-perpetuating downward spiral of cost-cutting, editorial quality decline, further readership loss and rapid erosion of advertiser confidence.

"Any good reporter can see that the same dynamics are at work on the World Wide Web, only in the other direction—up. The web is now being accessed by over 20 percent of American households, a demographic that is steadily increasing. As this digital equivalent of "circulation" increases to 50 percent of the households in any given community, it will achieve its own critical mass altering the communication and advertising realities of that community.

"Each year $66 billion is spent on advertising in local newspapers, magazines, shopper's guides, TV, cable, radio and other traditional outlets. And while the majority of local advertisers don't now consider the web a viable medium for effectively reaching their community, that will change. When household Internet access levels approach 50 percent, the web will suddenly provide those advertisers a 'door-to-door' electronic delivery system, for local neighborhoods comparable to that offered in printed newspapers."

Niche-Seeking. While many newspaper web sites offer the same wide range of coverage as the traditional print editions, many specialize with coverage for special audiences. Computer people worldwide, for example, tap into Mercury Center, a product of the daily San Jose *Mercury News* in California, for its concentration on nearby Silicon Valley. It's no surprise that the Milwaukee *Journal*'s news site offers concentrated coverage of the Green Bay Packers football team. The *Florida Today* site, out of Cocoa Beach, near Cape Canaveral and the Kennedy Space Center, has saturation coverage of the nation's space program.

That's not a pretty picture for the future of newspapers as an ink-on-paper product, but newspaper organizations with their own web sites are positioned for a transition in which their product—mostly news and information—is delivered by an alternate medium.

weekly newspapers

(STUDY PREVIEW) Many community weekly newspapers, especially in fast-growing suburbs, are thriving, while others, especially rural weeklies, have fallen on hard times. In all areas, free-distribution advertising sheets called shoppers have attracted strong followings.

community weeklies

Weekly newspapers are making strong circulation gains, especially in suburban communities, and some have moved into publishing twice a week. In all, almost 8,000 weekly newspapers are published in the United States, with circulation approaching 45 million. Weeklies are received in almost 60 percent of the nation's households, up almost one-third from 1970.

To the discomfort of metro dailies, many advertisers are following their customers to the suburban weeklies. Advertisers have found that they can buy space in weeklies for less and reach their likeliest customers. Ralph Ingersoll, whose weeklies give fits to the daily Long Island *Newsday* in New York, explained it this way in an interview with *Forbes:* "If you're an automobile dealer on Long Island, you can pay, say, $14,000 for a tabloid page in *Newsday,* most of which is wasted because the people that get it will never buy a car in your neck of the woods, or you can go into one of the weekender publications and pay a few hundred dollars and reach just the people likely to drive over to your shop."

Some weeklies, particularly those in upscale suburbs, offer sophisticated coverage of community issues. Others feature a homey mix of reports on social events such as who visited whom for Sunday dinner. The success of these weeklies sometimes is called "**telephone book journalism**" because of the emphasis on names, the somewhat over-drawn theory being that people buy papers to see their names in print. Weeklies have in common that they cover their communities with a detail that metro dailies have nei-ther staff nor space to match. There is no alternative to keeping up with local news.

Rural weeklies generally have fallen on rough times. Part of their problem is the diminishing significance of agriculture in the national economy and the continuing depopulation of rural America. In communities that remain retail centers, rural week-lies can maintain a strong advertising base. However, the Main Street of many small towns has declined as improved roads and the construction of major retail stores like Wal-Mart draw customers from 40 to 50 miles away. In earlier days, those customers patronized hometown retailers, who placed significant advertising in hometown week-lies. Today many of these Main Street retailers, unable to compete with giant discount stores, are out of business.

shoppers

Free-distribution papers that carry only advertisements have become increasingly important as vehicles for classified advertising. In recent years, **shoppers** have attracted display advertising that earlier would have gone to regular newspapers. Almost all shoppers undercut daily newspapers on advertising rates. The number of shoppers has grown to about 1,500 nationwide, and they no longer are merely an ignorable com-petitor for daily newspapers for advertising.

By definition, shoppers are strictly advertising sheets, but beginning in the 1970s some shoppers added editorial content, usually material that came free over the tran-som, such as publicity and occasional self-serving columns from legislators. Some shoppers have added staff members to compile calendars and provide a modicum of news coverage. Most of these papers, however, remain ad sheets with little that is journalistic. Their news-gathering efforts and expenses are minuscule compared with those of a daily newspaper.

alternative and minority newspapers

(STUDY PREVIEW)   Most newspapers attempt broad coverage for a broad audience, but more specialized newspapers are important in the lives of many people. These include counterculture, gay, black and Spanish-lan-guage newspapers, many of which are expanding and prospering today.

counterculture newspapers

A group of friends in the Greenwich Village neighborhood of New York, includ-ing novelist **Norman Mailer** and **Don Wolf,** decided to start a newspaper. Thus in 1955 was born the *Village Voice,* a free-wheeling weekly that became a prototype for a 1960s phenomenon called the **alternative press** and that has continued to thrive.

telephone book journalism
Listing readers' names.

shopper
An advertising paper without news.

counterculture newspapers
Challenge, defy mainstream values.

Norman Mailer
Among founders of *Village Voice.*

Don Wolf
Among founders of *Village Voice.*

Village Voice
Model for contemporary alternative press.

alternative press
Generally antiestablishment publication for young alienated audience.

In its early days, the *Village Voice* was a haven for bohemian writers of diverse competence who volunteered occasional pieces, some lengthy, many rambling. Many articles purported to be investigative examinations of hypocritical people and institutions, but, as *Voice* veteran Nat Hentoff has noted, nobody ever bothered to check "noisome facts," let alone the "self-righteous author." The *Voice* seemed to scorn traditional, detached, neutral reporting. Despite its flaws, the amateurism gave the *Voice* a charm, and it picked up readership.

The *Voice* today is more polished and journalistically serious. The characteristics that made it distinctive in its early history, and which were picked up by other counterculture newspapers, include:

- Antiestablishment political coverage with a strong antimilitary slant.

- Cultural coverage that emphasizes contrarian music and art and exalts sex and drugs.

- Interpretive coverage focusing more on issues of special concern to alienated young people.

- Extensive entertainment coverage and listings of events.

- Conversational, sometimes crude style that includes four-letter words and gratuitous expletives for their shock value.

- Extensive personals for dating and sex liaisons.

By delivering a loyal readership that was hard to reach through mainstream media, many counterculture newspapers became fat with advertising. Today, about 100 alternative newspapers are published in the United States, and many are prospering. With a circulation of 172,000, the *Village Voice* is widely available in big-city newsracks and by mail throughout the country.

gay newspapers

Jim Michaels began publishing the nation's first gay newspaper, the Los Angeles-based ***Advocate,*** out of his living room in 1967. Today, 125 gay newspapers have a total circulation of more than 1 million. Most are free papers distributed at gay bars, nightclubs and businesses, and many are financially marginal. However, mainstream advertisers are beginning to take notice of the loyalty of gay readers to their newspapers. In 1990 the "Columbia House Music Club" tested a membership ad offering eight discs for $1 in 12 gay newspapers. The response rate was so high that the club began placing the ad in 70 gay papers within a year.

The success of the Columbia ad confirmed a 1988 study that found unexpected affluence among readers of eight major gay newspapers. Individual incomes averaged $36,800, which was three times the national average, and household incomes averaged $55,430, which was $2\frac{1}{2}$ times the national average. The number of college graduates, 60 percent, and the number of people in professional and managerial jobs, 49 percent, were three times the national average. Other national advertisers followed Columbia into the gay press.

black newspapers

The ongoing integration of black and white people in American society has eroded the role of black newspapers since World War II, but 172 black newspapers remain in publication. In all, the black newspapers have a circulation of 3.6 million, a ratio of about 1:10 to the nation's black population. At their peak after World War II,

Jim Michaels
Founded the *Advocate.*

Advocate
First gay newspaper, 1967.

black newspapers included three nationally distributed dailies, from Baltimore, Chicago and Pittsburgh, whose combined circulation approached 600,000. The black dailies today, the Atlanta *Daily World,* **Chicago *Daily Defender*** and New York *Daily Challenge,* together have a circulation of 106,000, almost all local.

Black newspapers have been important in the U.S. civil rights movement, beginning in 1827 with John Russwurm and Samuel Cornish's ***Freedom's Journal,*** the first black newspaper. Frederick Douglass's ***North Star,*** founded in 1847, was a strident abolitionist sheet before the Civil War, and W. E. B. DuBois's ***Crisis,*** founded in 1910, was a militant voice for black advancement. Today, some black newspapers, like ***A.M. Journal,*** founded by American Muslim Malcolm X in 1961, crusade for causes in the tradition of their early predecessors. In the early 1990s, the Chicago *Defender* was alone among U.S. news media in covering the Haitian refugee situation until others picked up the issue and forced public attention on it. In general, though, black newspapers today focus on neighborhood social, church and sports events, and the tone is moderate.

Prospects for black newspapers generally do not appear strong. Only 15 percent of the advertising placed in black media, including television, radio and magazines, goes to newspapers. Media scholar James Tinney found that middle-income blacks look to establishment rather than black newspapers for information, even while relying on other black institutions, like the church and universities, for intellectual stimulation.

foreign-language newspapers

Through every wave of immigration, newspapers in foreign languages have sprouted to serve newcomers to the United States in their native tongue. In 1914, there were 140 foreign-language dailies published in the United States. About one-third were German, led by New York *Vorwarts* with a circulation of 175,000. The U.S. German-language press withered during World War I when its loyalty was challenged, but, like other foreign-language newspapers, it undoubtedly would have eventually disappeared anyway as the immigrants assimilated into the mainstream culture.

Today, the fast-growing Hispanic minority represents about 1 of every 15 Americans, and although most are bilingual, six daily newspapers and about 150 weeklies are published in Spanish. In general, these newspapers are thriving. The Knight-Ridder newspaper chain publishes *El Herald* as a daily Spanish-language companion to its Miami Herald and sells 67,000 copies a day. In New York, the Gannett chain operates the 63,000-circulation daily *El Diario-La Prensa*. Most Spanish-language newspapers are owned by Hispanics, but the presence of the gigantic, profitable Knight-Ridder and Gannett chains bespeaks the commercial viability of these papers.

The profitability of Spanish-language newspapers is fueled partly by the desire of many national advertisers to tap into the large Hispanic market. The newspapers' penetration, however, is not especially high. In heavily Hispanic Los Angeles, *La Opinion* has a circulation of only 55,000 a day. In Miami the competing *El Herald* and *Diario Las Americas* together sell only 130,000 copies a day. In New York *El Diario-La Prensa* and *Noticias del Mundo* together have a circulation of less than 130,000 in a metropolitan area with 2.5 million Hispanic people.

Whether Spanish-language newspapers will disappear as did earlier foreign-language newspapers is uncertain. While assimilation is occurring, many Hispanics are intent on maintaining their distinctive cultural identity and resist adopting English. Also, there is more sympathy for multiculturalism in the society than in the past. For the foreseeable future, Spanish-language newspapers will have a strong following among the continuing influx of people from Latin America and the Caribbean. With this immigration and a high fertility rate, the U.S. Hispanic population is growing about 4 percent a year.

Some analysts feel the Spanish-language media have peaked as Hispanics assimilate into the dominant U.S. culture. Frank Welzer, president of Sony's Latin music company, was quoted in a *Forbes* magazine analysis: "Hispanics watch as much English-language television as anyone else. It's only recent arrivals and the elderly who use Spanish media exclusively." Sigfredo Hernandez, a specialist in Hispanic marketing at Rider College in New Jersey, was quoted in the same article: "If you're trying to reach younger Hispanics, they've got to be addressed in English." Christopher Palmeri and Joshua Levine, who wrote the *Forbes* analysis, concluded: "Of course, there will always be a market for specialized advertising aimed at recent immigrants. Just recall the lively German, Italian and Yiddish language media of yore. But it is beginning to dawn on advertisers that the idea of a vast and unassimilated 'Hispanic market' is just a myth fostered by professional multiculturists and hucksters."

chapter wrap-up

Numerous, once powerful newspapers have disappeared since the middle of the century, among them the Chicago *Daily News,* Los Angeles *Herald Examiner,* New York *Herald Tribune,* Philadelphia *Bulletin* and Washington *Star.* U.S. dailies, which numbered 1,745 in 1980, are down to 1,570. Other media, particularly television and its evening newscasts, have siphoned readers away from evening newspapers. Also, while newspapers remain the largest U.S. advertising medium, television is making gains.

Can newspapers survive? Even if people were to stop buying newspapers tomorrow, newspaper organizations would survive because they have an asset that competing media lack: the largest, most skilled newsroom staffs in their communities. The presses and the ink-on-newsprint medium for carrying the message may not have a long future, but newspapers' news-gathering capability will endure. Already newspapers have experimented with facsimile, television text, and World Wide Web delivery, gaining familiarity with alternate technology for disseminating their main product, which is news, not newsprint.

Besides the daily national, metro and hometown newspapers, the United States has thousands of weekly community newspapers and special-interest papers. By focusing on audiences with special interests, many of these newspapers are attracting more advertisers and either solidifying their existing financial base or building strong new foundations for the future.

questions for review

1. Describe how newspapers are important in the lives of most Americans.

2. Explain the rise of newspaper chains. Have they been good for readers?

3. Why is the United States a nation mostly of provincial newspapers?

4. Many metropolitan daily newspapers have lost circulation and some have shut down. Why?

5. What challenges to their dominance as a news and advertising medium do newspapers face?

6. Community newspapers, especially suburban weeklies, are booming. Why?

7. What kinds of newspapers aimed at narrow audience segments are prospering?

questions for critical thinking

1. The United States is called a nation of provincial newspapers. Is the label correct? Do the *Wall Street Journal, USA Today* and *Christian Science Monitor* fit the provincial characterization?

2. How can you explain the declining number of U.S. newspapers and their losses in market penetration in view of the newspaper industry's profitability?

3. How have newspapers met challenges to their advertising revenue from radio, television, direct mail and shoppers?

4. Can you explain why a greater percentage of American newspapers are published for morning reading, not afternoon?

5. Identify advantages and disadvantages in the consolidation of U.S. newspapers, daily and weekly, into chains and cross-media conglomerates.

6. Can you identify how *USA Today* has changed American newspapers by comparing an issue of your hometown paper today with an issue from the 1970s?

7. How have improvements in U.S. newspapers led to fewer households taking more than a single newspaper?

8. Considering the business orientation that makes newspaper chains so profitable, does it seem unusual that someone like Al Neuharth, whose background was in journalism rather than business, led Gannett through its incredible and profitable growth?

for further learning

Norman Beasley. *Mary Baker Eddy: The Cross and the Crown.* (Duell, Sloan and Pearce, 1952).

Leo Bogart. *Preserving the Press: How Daily Newspapers Mobilized to Keep Their Readers* (Columbia University Press, 1991). Bogart, a newspaper industry analyst, describes the strengths and weaknesses of newspapers in times of changing technology, reader lifestyle changes and preferences, and new options for advertisers through other media.

Jonathan Curiel. "Gay Newspapers." *Editor & Publisher* 224 (August 3, 1991):32, 14–19. Curiel, a San Francisco Chronicle reporter, gives a history of gay newspapers and their growing attractiveness as an advertising medium.

Francis X. Dealy. *The Power and the Money: Inside the Wall Street Journal* (Birch Lane Press, 1993). Dealy, a former Dow Jones employee, claims the *Journal* has gone soft, citing a lack of investigative fervor on the 1980s' excesses in American business. Dealy argues that the newspaper missed scandals that would not have escaped its attention in an earlier era.

Edwin Diamond. *Behind the Times: Inside the New York Times* (Villard Books, 1994). Diamond, media columnist for *New York* magazine, updates Gay Talese's classic 1969 study of the most prestigious newspaper in the United States.

Katharine Graham. *Personal History* (Knopf, 1997). The longtime publisher of the Washington *Post* recounts the Pentagon Papers, Watergate, and other important episodes in the newspaper's history in this autobiography.

Lauren Kessler. *Against the Grain: The Dissident Press in America* (Sage, 1984). Kessler surveys the newspapers of minority and persecuted groups through U.S. history.

Richard McCord. *The Chain Gang: One Newspaper Versus the Gannett Empire* (University of Missouri Press, 1996). A case study on Gannett's Operation Demolition to run the weekly Salem, Oregon, *Community Press* out of business. McCord, himself a weekly publisher, includes a brief history of the Gannett chain.

Winthrop Neilson and Frances Neilson. *What's News: Dow Jones: Story of the Wall Street Journal* (Chilton Book Co., 1973).

Al Neuharth. *Confessions of an S.O.B.* (Doubleday, 1989). Neuharth, who created *USA Today,* explains his controversial newspaper management style in this sprightly autobiography.

Christopher Palmeri and Joshua Levine. "No Habla Espanol." *Forbes* (December 24, 1991), 140–142. These *Forbes* reporters conclude that the idea of a vast, unassimilated Spanish-language media market in the United States is "a myth fostered by professional multiculturists and hucksters."

Edward E. Scharff. *Worldly Power: The Making of the Wall Street Journal* (Beaufort, 1986). Traces the history of the *Journal* with emphasis on its editorial leadership since World War II.

William Shawcross. *Murdoch* (Simon & Schuster, 1992). Shawcross chronicles the rise of Rupert Murdoch as a global media baron and attempts to explain what motivates the man. Shawcross, a British journalist, relies extensively on interviews with people around Murdoch and Murdoch himself.

James D. Squires. *Read All About It! The Corporate Takeover of America's Newspapers* (Times Books, 1993). Squires, a former Chicago *Tribune* executive, makes a case that newspaper managers are preoccupied with advertising and profits. As a result, the traditional separation of advertising and news staffs has been eroded, which in turn has led to news coverage that is compromised by newspapers' financial interests.

Jim Strader. "Black on Black." *Washington Journalism Review* 14 (March 1992):2, 33–36. Strader, a Pittsburgh reporter, discusses the decline of national black newspapers and their hopes to beef up local coverage to restore their influence.

Times Mirror Center for the People and the Press. *The Age of Indifference* (Times Mirror Company, 1990). This major study found that young people have significantly less interest in news than the generations before them. They read fewer newspapers and watch less news on television.

Richard Zoglin "The Last Great Newspaper." *Time* (September 29, 1997). Zoglin, *Time*'s media watcher, offers an enthusiastic status report on the New York *Times,* which he attributes to gradual improvements in management and the editing and reporting staff.

for keeping up to date

Editor & Publisher is a weekly trade journal for the newspaper industry.

mediainfo.com. The trade journal *Editor & Publisher* launched this new print magazine in 1997 to cover the emerging online news industry. http://www.mediainfo.com

Newspaper Research Journal is a quarterly dealing mostly with applied research.

Presstime is published monthly by the American Newspaper Publishers Association.

5
records

in this chapter you will learn:

- Records compound the effect of music on human emotions.

- Sound reproduction has shifted from acoustic to analog to digital forms.

- Popular American music today is rooted in black slave and hillbilly white genres.

- Artistic dynamics and corporate forces both shape popular music.

- The recording industry depends on radio and music videos to promote new music.

- Six companies dominate the U.S. recording business.

- Moralists long have objected to some lyrics and pressured record-makers to change.

- Home-dubbing and piracy are major drains on record industry profits.

With their gold record "Bringing Down the Horse," the young folk rock group "The Wallflowers" with Jakob Dylan showed enough fresh talent to get Grammy nominations for two years running for songs from the same CD. In their second try, the Wallflowers and Jakob's song "One Headlight" finally gained performance and songwriting Grammys for two out of three nominations in 1998—the year that not so coincidentally saw three awards go to Jakob's father, the classic folk-rock icon Bob Dylan. With this father-and-son combination, the Grammy ceremony managed to recognize new and old musical talent in one explosive flourish, while fueling journalism's endless hunger for nostalgia and for speculation about Jakob's struggle to "live with the legacy of a famous dad."

Dodging such media hype, both Dylans avoided appearing together, and Jakob had continually deflected interviews that pushed the father-son connection. "I think it's more of an issue with the media than it is with me," he told

Bob Dylan and the Pope. Popular music from the United States has an international following, even in high places. Bob Dylan's audiences have included the Pope in a Vatican performance.

a New York *Times* interviewer, "I don't need to figure out whether the Dylan legacy is really important or not." Having seen little of his father after his parents' bitter 1977 divorce, Jakob avoided showbiz early to study painting in New York. But by 1990 he was back in Los Angeles with the new band, Wallflowers, doing Tuesday night jam gigs in bars around town. Asked by a Salt Lake *Tribune* interviewer about this turn toward music, Jakob said, "I just started.... Everybody lives under shadows. I obviously have one but I don't pretend it's any worse than anyone else's." Nevertheless, with his incredibly bright blue eyes, rangy frame, tousled hair, and slightly nasal singing voice, Jakob bears more than a passing resemblance to the world-famed image of his father Bob Dylan.

With Jakob's songs, later called "long on soul, smarts and feeling," and with distinctive keyboard sounds created by band regular Rami Jaffee, the Wallflowers were picked up fairly quickly by a small *indie* label, Virgin records, for a first CD titled with their name. The album got top reviews but sold poorly, and Jakob, haunted by his famous family name, later told an interviewer, "I was never interested in that record selling.... Selling 30,000 records when you're only 21 years old isn't bad. But

people assume that when someone like me is in the group, it's a failure if it doesn't sell a million copies.... People at the label expected [the CD] to fly out of the bag," Jakob said. "Once they realized that it wasn't, then they tried to get me to do a lot of crap I wasn't interested in doing. I didn't want to do junk TV shows and junk magazines. I made their jobs a little harder." To another interviewer Jakob went on to describe this first-record experience: "It's a business, and, when you're on a record label, certain groups need exposure. We didn't feel like anyone [left at that company] was behind the group," he recalled. "They all say 'We're in it for the long haul. We're behind you.' We learned the hard way it wasn't true."

Free agents again, Jakob with Rami Jaffee and others played two shows a week at Los Angeles clubs for more than a year while shopping a demo of new songs including "6th Avenue Heartache" to other labels. Finally, with enough new material, a distinctive style, and with Jakob's voice often compared to a young Bruce Springsteen, the Wallflowers were picked up for a second record by another small company, Interscope Records. The result in mid-1996 was "Bringing Down the Horse," which reviewer Karen Schoermer called

Creating His Own Footsteps. When Bob Dylan and son Jakob Dylan both won 1998 Grammys, people jumped to father-like-son comparisons. But Jakob Dylan, flanked here by fellow Wallflowers Greg Richlin and Michael Ward, has drawn little from his father's work in creating a distinctive kind of music for a new generation of young people.

"rootless root music: vaguely retro country-folk-rock, with plenty of '60's antecedents in the mellow Hammond organ, tart slide guitar and rustic pedal steel, but with a keen sense for modern production and sturdy hooks. In other words, they're widely derivative, but songs like 'One Headlight' and 'Three Marlenas' feel so comfortably, soulfully right that you won't care." Touring with several other famous rock groups, the Wallflowers sold more than one million copies and finally hit the big time with two Grammy awards in the year that Jakob's dad received three. "I don't think there should be any boundaries in songwriting," Jakob said, reflecting on his music to *US* magazine's Jancee Dunn. "You don't have to

have lived through the experiences to have a good song, as long as you sing truthfully."

Even Jakob Dylan's youngest fans were aware that his father Bob Dylan had been an idol of the previous generation's young baby boomers. It was Bob Dylan who launched the folk-rock era in the early 1960s with "Mr. Tambourine Man," yet left the folk scene to pursue his own highly personal form of rock. As critic Dave Marsh later summarized, "His surreal lyrical stance and mercurial persona quickly made him 'the voice of his generation.' He drove himself hard until breaking his neck in a motorcycle crash in 1966, then he reined himself in and grew up. But Bob Dylan's successes were only occasional after "Blood on the Tracks," his famous "divorce album" of 1975.

Then in 1997, after a slow recovery in concerts that showed some of his earlier energy, Bob Dylan's first CD of original material since 1990, "Time Out Of Mind," earned him a strong comeback. Many critics declared that he had revisited the lost ground of "Blood on the Tracks." The new CD's atmospheric and contemplative lyrics, critically described as "dark-toned emotional struggle balanced by an ironic sense of humor and lively one-liners," were set to raw, bluesy shuffles and jaunty rock numbers. Backed by a band using sound distortion and heavy-handed organ, the album reminded some of the effects popularized by more contemporary groups, including his son Jakob's Wallflowers. "Time Out Of Mind" went on to take the 1998 Grammy awards for Contemporary Folk Album as well as Album of the Year. His "Cold Irons Bound" won Best Male Rock Performance. With these three awards—one for excellence, one for folk, and another for a rock performance—Bob Dylan's recording was acclaimed as a distillation and rebirth of the folk-rock tradition which he himself had largely invented. Perhaps, in the spirit of the CD's lead classic song "Not Dark Yet," the awards may even have shown some recognition that this continually reborn star's ability to recreate himself might not be infinite.

Bob Dylan himself seemed to reflect this feeling in an introspective Associated Press interview about his album and his anguished lyrics. "It's certainly not an album of felicity," Bob acknowledged. "I try to live within that line between despondency and hope. I'm suited to walk that line, right between the fire.... I see [this album] right straight down the middle of the line, really." Asked whether the new CD's success had helped him find satisfaction in the revival of his career, he said "I think that it's hard to find happiness as a whole in anything. The days of tender youth are gone."

The hoopla from the Grammy ceremony, and the sudden convergence of father-son Grammy awards raises interesting issues for the recording industry: Can the mass media reflect genuine demand from audiences for new styles of music that emerge with new generations? Or do the media mostly support music that connects popular audiences to older styles from previous generations? And does the media audience look for new waves in music or echoes of older styles? An answer to this question requires us to look at the flow of popular music over time as well as the role of record companies.

Other questions: Can the recording industry encourage new artists and new kinds of music, or does it does it regularly look for derivative work, or new but predictable ways to sell old, reliable music formulas? Does Jakob Dylan's early rise through the "indie" record labels show appreciation for his originality, or was it more an exploitation of his father's name? And finally, how much truth is in the criticism that the annual self-admiration ceremony, the Grammy Awards, is an empty promotional event designed to sell trendy, reliable styles of popular recordings at the expense of talented and innovative artists? In fact, why didn't the Wallflowers' "Bringing Down the Horse" win an award the first year it was nominated?

recorded music as a social force

(STUDY PREVIEW) Music is a potent form of human expression that can mobilize hearts and minds. Think about the effects of hymns and anthems, martial music and love songs. For better or worse, these powerful effects are magnified by the technology of sound recording.

rallying power

Released in 1984, "We Are the World" right away was the fastest-climbing record of the decade. Four million copies were sold within six weeks. Profits from the record, produced by big-name entertainers who volunteered, went to the USA for Africa pro-

media
online

1-800 Music Now: Try (free) before you buy. www.1800musicnow.com

Axiom Music: This site invites you to destroy all rational thought. With illuminating histories. www.hyperreal.com/music/labels/axiom/index.html

Classical Music Online: Can classical music be this hep? Find out. www.crl.com./~virtualv/cmo

Consumable: Alternative music with international reviewers. www.westnet.com/consumable/Consumable.html

Country Connection: A comprehensive treatment of the country music world. digiserve.com/country

ject. The marketplace success paled, however, next to the social impact. The record's message of the oneness of humankind inspired one of the most massive outpourings of donations in history. Americans pumped $20 million into USA for Africa in the first six weeks the record was out. Within six months, $50 million in medical and financial support was en route to drought-stricken parts of Africa. "We Are the World," a single song, had directly saved lives.

The power of recorded music is not a recent phenomenon. In World War I, "Over There" and other records reflected an enthusiasm for American involvement in the war. Composers who felt strongly about the Vietnam war wrote songs that put their views on vinyl. "The Ballad of the Green Berets" cast American soldiers in a heroic vein, "An Okie From Muskogee" glorified blind patriotism, and there were antiwar songs, dozens of them.

Political speech writers know the political value of tapping into popular music. It was no accident in the 1992 primaries when George Bush paraphrased a Nitty Gritty Dirt Band song to a New Hampshire crowd: "If you want to see a rainbow, you've got to stand a little rain." In his state-of-the-union message, the president borrowed from Paul Simon's "Boy in the Bubble" to make a point on the economy: "If this age of miracles and wonders has taught us anything, it's that if we can change the world, we can change America."

In short, music has tremendous effects on human beings, and the technology of sound recording amplifies these effects. The bugle boy was essential to Company B in earlier times, but today reveille is on tape to wake the troops. Mothers still sing Brahms's lullaby, but more babies probably are lulled to sleep by Brahms on tape. For romance, lovers today lean more on recorded music than their own vocal cords. The technology of sound recording gives composers, lyricists and performers far larger audiences than would ever be possible through live performances.

leading and reflecting change

Besides explicit advocacy and its immediate, obvious effects, recorded music can have subtle impact on the course of human events. **Elvis Presley,** "the white boy who sang colored," hardly realized in the mid-1950s that his music was helping pave the way for American racial integration. It was the black roots of much of Presley's music, as well as his suggestive gyrations, that made him such a controversial performer. Whatever the fuss, white teenagers liked the music, and it blazed a trail for many black singers who became popular beyond the black community. A major black influence entered mainstream American culture. There also was a hillbilly element in early rock, bringing the concerns and issues of poor, rural whites—another oppressed, neglected minority—into the mainstream consciousness. Nashville ceased to be an American cultural ghetto.

While recorded music has the power to move people to war and peace, to love and to sleep, it also reflects changing human values. In 1991, as U.S. troops were massing at the Persian Gulf to reclaim Kuwait, American record-makers issued music that reflected public enthusiasm for the war. Arista records put Whitney Houston's Super Bowl version of "The Star Spangled Banner" on a single, which sold 750,000 audio copies in only eight days. It was the fastest-selling single in Arista's history. Boston Dawn's remake of the Shirelle's oldie "Soldier Boy," expressing a woman's love for her soldier overseas, included some rap lines from the soldier. It was very much a song of the times, and the record company, American Sound, had 25,000 back orders for the record almost as soon as it was released.

Elvis Presley
Artist who melded black and white genres into rockabilly in 1950s.

1877 Thomas Edison introduced recording-playback device, the Phonograph.

1887 Emile Berliner introduced technology to record discs simultaneously.

1920s Joseph Maxwell introduced electrical microphones and recording system.

1948 Peter Goldmark introduced long-play

microgroove vinyl 33⅓-rpm records.

1950s Rock 'n' roll, a new musical genre, shook up record industry.

1960 Stereo recordings and playback equipment introduced.

1983 Digital recording on CDs introduced.

sound recording technology

(STUDY PREVIEW) The recording industry, as with all mass media, has been built on technological advances and breakthroughs, beginning with Thomas Edison's mechanical phonograph. Today, the technology is all electrical and digital.

thomas edison's phonograph

For years scientific journals had speculated on ways to reproduce sound, but not until 1877 did anyone build a machine that could do it. That was when American inventor **Thomas Edison** applied for a patent for a talking machine. He used the trade name **Phonograph,** which was taken from Greek words meaning "to write sound."

The heart of Edison's invention was a cylinder wrapped in tin foil. The cylinder was rotated as a singer shouted into a large metal funnel. The funnel channeled the voice against a diaphragm, which fluttered to the vibrations. A stylus, which most people called a "needle," was connected to the diaphragm and cut a groove in the foil, the depth of the groove reflecting the vibrations. To listen to a recording, you put the cylinder on a player and set a needle in the groove that had been created in the recording process. Then you placed your ear to a megaphone-like horn and rotated the cylinder. The needle tracked the groove, and the vibrations created by the varying depths of the groove were fed through the horn. This process was called **acoustic recording.**

Edison's system contained a major impediment to commercial success: A recording could not be duplicated. In 1887 **Emile Berliner** introduced a breakthrough. Rather than recording on a cylinder covered with flimsy foil, as Edison did, Berliner used a sturdy metal disc. From the metal disc, Berliner made a mold and then poured a thermoplastic material into the mold. When the material hardened, Berliner had a near-perfect copy of the original disc—and he could make hundreds of them. Berliner's system, called the gramophone, led to mass production.

> **Thomas Edison**
> Built first audio recorder-playback machine.
>
> **Phonograph**
> First recorder-playback machine.
>
> **acoustic recording**
> Vibration-sensitive recording technology.
>
> **Emile Berliner**
> His machine played discs that could be mass-produced.

Thomas Edison. Prolific U.S. inventor Thomas Edison devised a machine that took sound waves and etched them into grooves on a foil drum. When the drum was put on a replacing mechanism and rotated, you could hear the recorded sound. Edison's Phonograph, as he called it, was never a commercial success because his recordings could not be duplicated. It was a later inventor, Emile Berliner, who found a way to mass produce recorded music.

electrical recording

In the 1920s, the Columbia and Victor record companies introduced records based on an electrical system perfected by **Joseph Maxwell** of Bell Laboratories. Metal funnels were replaced by microphones, which had superior sensitivity. For listening, it was no longer a matter of putting an ear to a mechanical amplifying horn that had only a narrow frequency response. Instead, loudspeakers amplified the sound electromagnetically.

Magnetic tape was developed in Germany and used to broadcast propaganda in World War II. In 1945 American troops brought the German technology home with them. Ampex began building recording and playback machines. The 3M Company perfected tape. Recording companies shifted from discs to magnetic tape to record master discs. An advantage of tape was that bobbles could be edited out. Creative editing became possible.

While magnetic tape suggested the possibility of long-playing records, the industry continued to use brittle shellac discs that revolved 78 times a minute. One problem with the 10-inch **78-rpm** disc was that it could accommodate only three to four minutes of sound on a side.

vinyl and microgrooves

One day **Peter Goldmark,** chief engineer at Columbia Records, was listening to a 78-rpm recording of Brahms's Second Piano Concerto, Arturo Toscanini conducting. The concerto was divided onto six discs, 12 sides. Fed up with flipping discs, Goldmark got out his pencil and calculated whether a slower spin and narrower grooves could get the whole concerto on one disc. It was possible, although it would take both sides. At least the break could come between movements.

In 1948 Goldmark's long-playing record was introduced. Each side had 240 **microgrooves** per inch and contained up to 25 minutes of music. Offering several advantages, **LP**s soon replaced the 78-rpm record. Not only did each record have more music, but also the sound was better. The records were of vinyl plastic, which

---

Joseph Maxwell
Introduced electrical recording in 1920s.

magnetic tape
German invention that allowed sound editing.

78-rpm
Shellac records; rotated 78 times per minute; up to four minutes per side.

Peter Goldmark
Devised successful long-play records.

microgrooves
240 grooves per inch; 25 minutes per side at 33⅓-rpm.

LP
Long-play record, 33⅓-rpm, plastic, larger disc than 78s.

meant less hissing and scratching than shellac records. Also, vinyl discs were harder to break than the brittle 78s.

stereo innovation

Technical progress until the late 1970s produced nothing as revolutionary as the microgroove, but the improvements, taken all together, made for dramatically better sound. Anyone who has grown up with the B-52s would hardly believe that record-buyers accepted the sound quality of Bill Haley records only 30 years earlier. Better fidelity, called high fidelity, or **hi-fi,** was introduced in the early 1950s. The full audio range of the human ear could be delivered to listeners exactly as it was recorded. **Stereo** came in 1961. Multiple microphones recorded on separate tracks. Records played the sound back through two speakers, simulating the way people hear— through their left and their right ears. Consumers went for the new quality. FM stereo radio was introduced about the same time.

Except for tapes, Edison's 1877 technology, refined by Maxwell half a century later, was at the heart of sound recording for 101 years. The technology was called **analog recording** because it converted the waves that were physically engraved in the grooves of the record into electrical pulses that coincided analogously with the waves in the grooves.

digital technology

Record-makers developed a technological revolution in 1978: the **digital recording.** No longer were continuous sound waves inscribed physically on a disc. Instead, sound waves were sampled at millisecond intervals, and each sample was logged in computer language as an isolated on-off binary number. When discs were played back, the digits were translated back to the sound at the same millisecond intervals they were recorded. The intervals would be replayed so fast that the sound would seem continuous, just as the individual frames in a motion picture become a moving blur that is perceived by the eye as continuous motion.

hi-fi
High fidelity.

stereo
Left and right tracks.

analog recording
Sound waves physically engraved in record.

digital recording
Recording and playback system using on-off binary code for sound.

....plethora of formats

When record-makers introduce new formats, they are gambling that the public will accept them and begin replacing their music collections in the new format. This worked with CDs, which have become the dominant format since the 1980s. The risk is that alternative formats may scare off music buyers, who put off buying records so they don't get stuck with an orphaned format. Lots of consumers felt burned when Betamax home-video format flopped. In the late 1940s, when CBS and RCA were in a duel-till-death competition over 33⅓ versus 45 rpm, sales slumped for months. Here are today's alternatives:

Compact discs. Silvery 4.7-inch disks with embedded binary data that are read by a laser light.

Digital audio tape. Japanese manufacturers introduced DAT, which has CD clarity with the additional feature of dubbing capability.

Digital compact cassettes. Philips introduced DCC, which lacks DAT's audio range but can play both digital and ordinary tapes.

Mini Discs. Sony is pushing 2½-inch MDs, which can carry as much as 70 minutes of music, albeit with less quality than a regular CD. Sony hopes MDs will find a market among people who like portable Walkman-like players.

Tape cassettes. This is an analog magnetic for-mat that was dominant before CDs.

Which will end up on the scrap heap, where already rest 33⅓-rpm LPs, 45-rpm LPs, eight-track tapes and Edison's discs, all of which had their day in the sun? Probably all, considering disappointing consumer acceptance of DAT, DCC and MD and the inevitability of technology finding improvements on the CD.

By 1983 digital recordings were available to consumers in the form of **compact discs,** silvery 4.7-inch platters. The binary numbers were pits on the disc that were read by a laser light in the latest version of the phonograph: the **CD** player. The player itself converted the numbers to sound.

Each disc could carry 70 minutes of uninterrupted sound, more than Peter Goldmark dared dream. Consumers raved about the purity. Some critics argued, however, that there was a sterility in digital recording. The sound was too perfect, they said. Instead of reproducing performances, said the critics, compact discs produced a quality more perfect than a performance. Traditional audiophiles had sought to reproduce live music perfectly, not to create a perfection that could never be heard in a live performance.

evolution of music

compact disc
Digital record format; now dominant.

CD
Short for compact disc.

(STUDY PREVIEW) Evolving African-American folk music and hillbilly white music came together in the 1950s to create rock 'n' roll. This hybrid musical genre fueled the record industry and popular culture explosively. In the process of becoming big business, the authenticity of early rock was compromised.

american folk music

Most music historians trace contemporary popular music to roots in two distinctive types of American folk music, both of which emerged in the South.

Black Music. Black slaves who were brought to the Colonies used music to soothe their difficult lives. Much of the music reflected their oppression and hopeless poverty. Known as **black music,** it was distinctive in that it carried strains of slaves' African roots and at the same time reflected the black American experience. This music also included strong religious themes, expressing the slaves' indefatigable faith in a glorious afterlife. Flowing from the heart and the soul, this was folk music of the most authentic sort.

After the Civil War, black musicians found a white audience on riverboats and saloons and pleasure palaces of various sorts. That introduced a commercial component into black music and fueled numerous variations, including jazz. Even with the growing white following, the creation of these latter-day forms of black music remained almost entirely with African-American musicians. White musicians who picked up on the growing popularity of black music drew heavily on black songwriters. Much of Benny Goodman's swing music, for example, came from black arranger Fletcher Henderson.

In the 1930s and 1940s, a distinctive new form of black music, rhythm and blues, emerged. The people who enjoyed this music were all over the country, and these fans included both blacks and whites. Mainstream American music had come to include a firm African-American presence.

Hillbilly Music. Another authentic American folk music form, **hillbilly music,** flowed from the lives of Appalachian and Southern whites. Early hillbilly music had a strong colonial heritage in English ballads and ditties, but over time hillbilly music evolved into a genre in its own right. Like black music, hillbilly fiddles and twangy lyrics reflected the poverty and hopelessness of rural folk, "hillbillies" as they called themselves. Also like black music, hillbilly music reflected the joys, frustrations and sorrows of love and family. Hillbilly music, however, failed to develop more than a regional following—that is, until the 1950s when a great confluence of the black and hillbilly traditions occurred. This distinctive new form of American music, called **rockabilly** early on, became rock 'n' roll.

early rock 'n' roll

Music aficionados quibble about who invented the term rock 'n' roll. There is no doubt, though, that Memphis disc jockey **Sam Phillips** was a key figure. From his job at WREC, Phillips found an extra $75 a month to rent a 20-foot by 35-foot storefront, the paint peeling from the ceiling, to go into business recording, as he put it, "anything, anywhere, anytime." His first jobs, in 1949, were weddings and bar mitzvahs, but in 1951 Phillips put out his first record, "Gotta Let You Go" by a one-man blues singer Joe Hill Louis, who played his own guitar, harmonica and drums for accompaniment. In 1951 he recorded B. B. King and then **Jackie Brenston**'s "Rocket 88," which many musicologists call the first rock 'n' roll record. Phillips sold his early recordings, all by black musicians, mostly in the blues tradition, to other labels.

In 1952, Phillips began his own Sun Records label and a quest to broaden the appeal of the black music he loved to a wide audience. "If I could find a white man who had the Negro sound and the Negro feel, I could make a billion dollars," he said.

black music
Folk genre from American black slave experience.

hillbilly music
Folk genre from rural Appalachian, Southern white experience.

rockabilly
Black-hillbilly hybrid that emerged in 1950s.

Sam Phillips
Pioneered rockabilly, rock 'n' roll; discovered Elvis Presley.

Jackie Brenston
"Rocket 88" first rock 'n' roll record; 1951.

alan freed

Alan Freed had always liked music. At Ohio State University, Freed played trombone in a jazz band called the Sultans of Swing. After an army stint during World War II, he landed an announcing job at a classical radio station in Pennsylvania. Later Freed went to Cleveland and became host for a late-night radio show. He played records by Frank Sinatra, Jo Stafford, Frankie Laine and other popular performers of the day.

That was before rock 'n' roll. In 1951 Cleveland record store owner Leo Mintz, who sponsored Freed's "Record Rendezvous" on WJW, decided one day to show Freed his shop. Neither the radio nor the record industry was ever the same again. Freed saw Mintz's shop full of white teenagers. They weren't listening to Perry Como or Rosemary Clooney. They were dancing in the aisles to rhythm 'n' blues—"Negro music," as it was called then. And they were buying it.

Freed went back to WJW and talked management into a new show, "Moon Dog House." With the new show and a variety of promotions, Freed built a white audience for black music in Cleveland. Word spread. Soon Freed was syndicated on faraway stations with music that soon everyone was calling "rock 'n' roll." Within three years he was the top disc jockey in New York City. Rock 'n' roll was here to stay, and the U.S. record industry would be shaken to its roots.

Alan Freed embodied the best and the worst of the intertwined businesses of music, records and radio. He was an innovator at a pivotal point in

Alan Freed. On his "Moon Dog House" radio show in Cleveland, Alan Freed laid the groundwork for rock 'n' roll in the early 1950s. By the time he reached New York, Freed was a major influence in the success of young, new performers.

music history. The rock 'n' roll he played transformed musical tastes almost overnight. Critics charged that his rock 'n' roll was corrupting a generation of teenagers, the same kind of controversy that still plagues the record business today. For Freed, as with many people in the music industry, life was in the fast lane. He became involved in shady deals with record-makers eager for him to play their music on the air, and he was prosecuted—some say persecuted—in the first of many **payola** scandals. Like many in the faddish record and music industry, Freed rose fast and died young, in 1965 at age 43.

Alan Freed
Disc jockey who integrated black music, rock into playlists.

payola
Bribes to radio people to promote records.

In a group he recorded in 1954, the Starlight Wranglers, Sam Phillips found Elvis Presley.

Elvis's first Sun recording, "That's All Right," with Scotty Moore and Bill Black, found only moderate success on country radio stations, but Sam Phillips knew he was onto something. It wasn't quite country or quite blues, but it was a sound that could move both white country fans and black blues fans. Elvis moved on to RCA, a major label, and by 1956 had two of the nation's best-selling records, the flip-side hits "Don't Be Cruel" and "Hound Dog," plus three others among the year's top 16. Meanwhile, Sam Phillips was recording Carl Perkins, Roy Orbison, Johnny Cash and

Early Rock 'n' Roll. Memphis music promoter Sam Phillips was the visionary who saw a mass audience for a hybrid of hillbilly music and black soul music. Looking for "a white boy who can sing colored," Phillips found Elvis Presley in a threesome that put out four singles beginning with "That's All Right" in 1954, on Phillips' Sun label. Most musicologists trace the first rock 'n' roll recording to 1951 when Jackie Brenston recorded "Rocket 88" at Sam Phillips' Memphis studio.

Elvis Presley

Sam Phillips

Jerry Lee Lewis, adding to the distinctively American country-blues hybrid: wild, thrashing, sometimes reckless rock 'n' roll.

The new music found a following on radio stations that picked up on the music mix that Cleveland disc jockey **Alan Freed** had pioneered as early as 1951—occasional rhythm 'n' blues amid the mainstream Frank Sinatra and Peggy Lee. By 1955, Freed was in New York and clearly on a roll. Freed helped propel Bill Haley and the Comets' "Rock Around the Clock" to Number One. Rock's future was cemented when "Rock Around the Clock" was the musical bed under the credits for the 1955 movie *Blackboard Jungle*. Young people flocked to the movie not only for its theme on teen disenchantment and rebellion but also for the music.

artistic autonomy

(STUDY PREVIEW) Cultural sociologists worry that commercialism is undercutting the vibrancy of music's evolution. "It's all alike," they say. On the other hand, many new artists are using low-cost recording equipment to do original and innovative work. And major record-makers have had to give these artists room to do things their way.

media

online

Beatles: For links to countless Beatles web sites, check this one out. www.primenet.com/ ~dhaber/beatles.http

Blue Highway: An excellent history and chronology of the blues. Get your mojo workin' here! vivanet.com/~blues

Elvis: A fan maintains this elaborate Elvis site, with links to dozens of Elvis pages. These include a tour of Graceland, Elvis' home in Memphis; poetry about Elvis, and lyrics to Elvis songs. sunsite.unc.edu/elvis/ elvishom.html

Music Central Online: Sure Microsoft is everywhere, but the content is good. www.mus-iccentral.msn.com/Home.htm

Vibe: Funky and hip happenings in music. metaverse.com/vibe

Covering. When Little Richard's 1955 recording "Tutti Frutti" picked up a following, there were white parents who didn't want the kids listening to "black music." That racist phobia contributed to the practice of covering, in which major labels issued the same music, sometimes toned down, with white artists. Pat Boone, for example, covered "Tutti Frutti." The kids, though, both black and white, wanted the real thing, and that's how rock 'n' roll furthered the cultural integration of American society. Looking back, Little Richard is amused: "Pat Boone was on the dresser, but I was in the drawer. At least I was in the same house."

Pat Boone

Little Richard

predictable music

After World War II the big record companies saw a profitable future with adaptations of music that was already popular. They signed huge contracts with proven performers like Frank Sinatra and Rosemary Clooney. The companies were so confident in themselves that they gave performers little room for originality. In his book *Solid Gold*, Serge Denisoff quotes a former Capitol executive about how the system worked: "The company would pick out 12 songs for Peggy Lee and tell her to be at the studio Wednesday at 8, and she'd show up and sing what you told her. And she'd leave three hours later and Capitol'd take her songs and do anything it wanted with them. Her art was totally out of her—the artist's—hands. That was a time when the artist was supposed to show up and put up with anything the almighty recording company wanted." What the company wanted was predictable music.

When rock 'n' roll came along, the major record-makers first ignored it as a momentary flash. How wrong they were. Almost overnight, small niche companies that specialized in the new music, like Sun Records in Memphis, were swamped with orders. From 1955 to 1957 the number of records on the trade journal *Billboard*'s Top 10 list from independent companies quintupled from 8 to 40.

Even though losing market share, the major companies were slow to respond. One cautious reaction was to issue toned-down remakes of rock 'n' roll songs that were catching on, a practice called **covering.** An example was "Roll With Me, Henry" by Etta James, an answer song to "Work With Me, Annie" by the Midnighters, a black group. In the covered version by major pop-label singer Georgia Gibbs, the suggestive title was toned down to "Dance With Me, Henry," and the lyrics were tamed too.

covering
Redoing authentic songs in bid for success with mass audience.

World Tour. British pop group Spice Girls open their 1998 world tour in Dublin before a 6,000-capacity crowd. The odds were against the Spice Girls sustaining their popularity in the generally short-lived pop music field. Fans shift their enthusiasm quickly, with a lot of one-hit wonders never regaining a following.

It became a hit. This process of modifying a song to appeal to vanilla mass-market tastes, and to avoid the risks inherent in doing new things, was repeated hundreds of times. Each time, say cultural historians, artistic authenticity was compromised.

cultural homogenization

The sameness of sound that major record companies were seeking, called **cultural homogenization,** worried many social historians terribly. In their book *Rock 'n' Roll Is Here to Pay,* Steven Chapple and Reebee Garofalo argue that historically many of the great creative contributions in music have come from lean and hungry independent companies, or indies. Rockabilly innovators like Elvis Presley and Carl Perkins, for example, were at their best when recording with scrappy little risk-taking indies. The result was a new richness and diversity in the culture. At that time, the majors were discouraging risk and innovation.

Chapple and Garofalo contrast the rockabilly innovations with "the Philadelphia schlock" of slick packager **Dick Clark,** whose television dance program, "American Bandstand," which began in the 1950s, sought a teenage audience featuring watered-down adaptations of the original, innovative works. The result was commercially safe pop that would sell to a mass audience.

This cultural homogenization was an elitist-populist issue. As elitists saw it, the sameness, even if popular, was undesirable because art should always be exploring new ground. Otherwise, the culture stagnates. Populists, on the other hand, trusted the marketplace to shape the direction of the culture.

restructured record industry

In the late 1950s, the relationship between indies and majors changed substantially. In effect, the indies became the talent research and development arm of the majors. When an indie's talent showed promise, the artist or group moved to a major label, or the indie entered a joint venture or distribution deal with a major.

Even so, the elitist-populist tension continued. Today, reviewers still pan the record industry's **Grammy Awards** for favoring derivative artists, who may be as popular as Georgia Gibbs in her day but whose artistic merits are second rate. In

> **cultural homogenization**
> A sameness in popular music that works against artistic innovation.
>
> **Dick Clark**
> Promoted watered-down rock 'n' roll for mass audience.
>
> **Grammy Awards**
> Annual record industry recognitions for artists, technicians.

canada: cancon requirement

Since 1970 the Canadian Radio-Television Commission has required that Canadian radio stations play 30 percent Canadian content between 6 a.m. and midnight. The CanCon regulations were designed:

• To promote Canadian culture as distinctive, particularly to stave off heavy U.S. influence

• To strengthen the Canadian music industry. Given the rise of Canadian artists and songs, the music industry clearly is stronger. As for promoting Canadian culture, CanCon has done little.

The inherent CanCon problem is defining what's Canadian. Just because a song has a Canadian composer, lyricist or performer doesn't make it truly Canadian, as CanCon's designers have learned. Of 19 chart-topping "Canadian" songs in CanCon's first 13 years, four were recorded by Americans. These included "It Doesn't Matter Anymore," written by Canadian Paul Anka but recorded by yankee Buddy Holly. These songs, in essence, were written for the U.S. market.

Two top songs that had Canadian origins under CanCon's definitions gained popularity by being on soundtracks for American movies—"Born to Be Wild" by Steppenwolf for the movie *Easy Rider,* and "One Tin Soldier" by Original Cast for *Billy Jack.* These songs promoted the American myths of the biker and the cowboy. There wasn't much Canadian about them.

Several songs written by Canadians reflected American or British values instead of mirroring Canadian culture. Example: "Diana" by Paul Anka.

Two songs were Canadian but in offbeat ways. One was "Clear the Track, Here Comes Shack," a tribute to hockey player Eddie Shack. The other was "Take Off" by comics Bob and Doug Mackenzie, whose popularity rested at its novelty. Guess Who's "American Woman" was Canadian-conceived, but in making clear distinctions between Canadian and American culture the song was thematically more binational than Canadian.

Other Number One songs were nondescript American-style music, like "Put Your Hand in the Hand" by Ocean, "Sweet City Woman" by the Stampeders, "Heart of Gold," by Neil Young, "Seasons in the Sun" by Terry Jacks, "New World Man" by Rush, and three songs by Bachman Turner Overdrive—"Taking Care of Business," "You Ain't Seen Nothing Yet" and "Hey You."

1991, **Sinéad O'Connor,** an especially talented and innovative artist, boycotted the Grammy ceremony. The awards, she said, were merely the record industry's hype to promote sales and had little to do with authentic artistry. Her point was underscored by reviewers who, in covering O'Connor's defection, noted that previous Grammy winners included such dubious talents as Debby Boone and the group Toto.

Profit can be made by imitating what's gone before and been successful. It's safer to be derivative than innovative. Critics note that conglomerate parent companies persistently pressure their record subsidiaries to increase profits, which, in effect, discourages artistic innovation and risk. This is not to say that there is no innovation, but there are financial lures and rewards for homogenization that supersede a sense of responsibility to foster artistic contributions. Music commentator David Hadelman, writing in *Rolling Stone,* made the point this way: "It's no revelation that teenybopper acts like Abdul, the New Kids, Milli Vanilli, Rick Astley and Kylie Minogue are primarily poster-ready hunks and babes and barely singers at all." About the Grammys, *Time*

Sinéad O'Connor
Outspoken against commercialism in recording industry.

music critic Jay Cocks said: "The Grammys have the most unfortunate reputation for often making saccharine choices that toady shamelessly to the marketplace."

Joe Smith, president of Capitol records, was unwittingly revealing about the profit-over-art orientation of the major record companies when he defended the televised Grammy awards by saying: "They get good ratings. This is not the International Red Cross."

music demassification

While company-dictated commercialism and homogenization are a factor in popular music, they are less a problem than in Peggy Lee's time. Many performers today come from a different tradition. They won't put up with corporate A&R people choosing everything from their music to their wardrobe. The South Carolina quartet Hootie and the Blowfish, as an example, started by making the rounds at college bars and frat houses in the late 1980s and along the way found the cash to produce the album "Kootchypop." It was a distinctive work, hardly something manufactured by corporate marketing people, and Hootie gradually built a following. In fact, the group self-marketed an astounding 50,000 copies of "Kootchypop," which headed them to the big time. Their 1994 album "Cracked Rear View," on the major Atlantic label, sold 3 million the first year out, 2 million the next.

Technology has put sophisticated low-cost recording and mixing equipment within the means of a lot of **garage bands.** As little as $15,000 can buy 16-track recorders and 24-channel mixing boards, plus remodeling, to do what only a major studio could a few years ago. Back then, only big-name artists could afford their own studios. Now almost everyone can. Home recording studios in the United States now number more than 100,000. Since 1980 commercial studios have dwindled from 10,000 to 1,000. Dan Daley, an editor at the trade journal *Mix*, calls this the "democratization" of the recording industry, which has returned an independent attitude among artists that record companies have been forced to recognize. Nobody gets treated like Peggy Lee any more.

The widespread availability of **mini-studios** is contributing to a demassification in recorded music that, in some respects, should please elitists. Music that flows from the soul and heart of the musicians, reflecting the life experiences of the artists without strong commercial imperatives, is being recorded. And some of this music moves the culture in new directions. Early rap and hip-hop, for example, had authenticity. So did the early Seattle grunge. Elitists note, though, that breakthroughs are always subsumed by derivative artists who try to pick up on a new sound that's become popular. The result, at worst, is a cultural setback, and at best, the cultural stagnation that comes from homogenization.

marketing records

(STUDY PREVIEW) The success of the record industry is highly dependent on free airplay over radio and also music video outlets like MTV. This dependence is no better illustrated than in the payola scandals that first surfaced in the 1950s.

---

demassification
Low-cost equipment allowing more artists to record more music.

garage bands
Low budget, aspiring groups.

mini-studios
Use consumer-, not professional-quality equipment.

measuring commercial success

The measure of success in the record-making business is the **gold record.** Once a single sells 1 million or an album sells 500,000 copies, the **Recording Industry Association of America** confers a gold-record award. A **platinum record** is awarded for 2 million singles sold or 1 million albums. RCA's Tchaikovsky treatment by the pianist Van Cliburn is one of only two classical recordings ever to receive a gold record.

About half the records sold in the United States today are pop, a broad category that ranges from Barry Manilow's mellow sentimentalism to Mötley Crüe's hard-edged rock. The rest are country, classical, jazz and the other musical genres, as well as children's records and the minor although growing category of recorded literature and self-help cassettes.

Discount stores account for 50 percent of U.S. record sales; 25 percent are through department stores; and 15 to 20 percent are through record stores, including chains like Musicland. Mail-order outlets, including record clubs, account for the rest.

radio airplay

Record companies ship new releases free to radio stations in hope of **airplay.** Few make it. Stations are inundated with more records than they can possibly audition. Also, most stations stick to a playlist of already popular music rather than risk losing listeners by playing untried records. To minimize the risk and yet offer some fresh sounds, most radio station music directors rely heavily on charts of what music is selling and being played elsewhere. The most-followed charts appear in the trade journal *Billboard.* There also are **tip sheets,** which leading disc jockeys and music directors put out as a sideline and sell by subscription.

Airplay is valuable because it is the way in which most people are first exposed to new releases that they might go out and buy. Also, airplay is efficient for record-makers because it is free except for the cost of shipping the sample records. Because an estimated 13 percent of record purchases are on impulse, promotional point-of-purchase displays also are important.

The relationship between the radio and record industries is a two-way street. Not only do radio stations need records, but record-makers need radio to air their products. Records that win airplay are almost assured success. This interdependence expanded to television in the 1980s when cable television services, such as MTV and VH-1, built their programming on video versions of popular music.

Erykah Badu. With a sultry style as distinctive as her Afro-goddess headdresses, Erykah Badu fuses blues, jazz, soul and hip-hop. While drawing on numerous traditions, Badu's renditions are hardly derivative, yet she has garnered both pop and critical acclaim. In 1998 she won two Grammys—best rhythm and blues album for "Baduism" and best female R&B vocal performance for "On and On."

Celine Dion. Doubts were aplenty whether Celine Dion's strong voice was right for "The Heart Will Go On," the title song for the movie *Titanic.* She restrained her usual style, giving the song a hesitancy that overcame movie director James Cameron's doubts. It was perfect, and the song became a continuing bestseller and won the Canadian singer a Grammy.

payola

The relationship between the radio and record industries has had problems, notably **payola.** In 1958 the grapevine was full of stories about record companies' bribes to disc jockeys to play certain records. One audit found that $263,000 in "consulting fees" had been paid to radio announcers in 23 cities. The **Federal Trade Commission** filed unfair competition complaints against record companies. Radio station managers, ever conscious that their licenses from the Federal Communications Commission could be yanked for improprieties, began demanding signed statements from disc jockeys that they had not accepted payola. Dozens of disc jockeys in major markets quietly left town.

Payola scandals did not end with the 1950s. Competition for airplay has continued to tempt record promoters to "buy" airtime under the table. There were indictments again in the 1970s. And in 1988 two independent promoters were charged with paying $270,000 to program directors at nine widely imitated radio stations to place records on their playlists. One station executive was charged with receiving $100,000 over two years. Some payola bribery involved drugs.

Payola scandals illustrate the relationship that has taken shape between the record and radio industries. It is an interdependent relationship, but radio holds the upper hand. It is the record industry's need for airplay that precipitates the scandals.

music videos

Since 1981, when the Warner media conglomerate made **MTV** available to local cable television systems, music videos have been important in marketing records in the United States. The actual introduction of music videos, however, predates MTV. In Europe in the 1970s, when state-regulated radio avoided pop music, record-makers needed to be especially innovative in promoting new music. Seeking new ways to interest young people in their products, European record companies created videos that featured recording artists acting out their music. Dance clubs played the videos, and record sales picked up. American record-makers, desperate to reverse slumping sales, borrowed the idea and made videos available to cable television channels to play between movies. The videos developed a following.

gold record
Award for sales of 500,000 albums, 1 million singles.

Recording Industry Association of America
Record industry trade organization.

platinum record
Award for sales of 1 million albums, 2 million singles.

airplay
When a record receives free time on radio or video channel.

Billboard
Weekly music trade journal.

tip sheets
Music newsletters.

payola
Bribes to radio people to promote new records.

Federal Trade Commission
U.S. government agency that assures fairness in commerce.

MTV
First U.S. cable television service built on music videos.

conglomeration and globalization

The major record companies are all part of larger corporations with diverse interests. Japan-based Sony, which acquired CBS Records in 1988 and Columbia Pictures in 1989, represents the extent to which media conglomeration and globalization are occurring. Here is a thumbnail list of Sony's U.S. units, excluding its subsidiaries elsewhere, and a sampler of their products:

CBS Records	Michael Jackson
Digital Audio Disc Corp.	Compact discs
Sony Magnetic Products Group	Video- and audiotape
Sony Engineering and Manufacturing	Television, video, audio hardware
Columbia Pictures	First-run movies
Tri-Star Pictures	First-run movies
Columbia Pictures Television	"Wheel of Fortune"
Columbia Tri-Star Home Video	Recycled movies for home video
Loews Theaters	Movie houses
Sony Electronic Publishing	Electronic games
SVS	Video distribution
Material Research Corp.	Semiconductors
Sony Trans Com Corp.	In-flight entertainment

Big Six
Dominant U.S. record companies.

indies
Short for independent record companies.

In 1981 the Warner media conglomerate, whose divisions included Warner records, gambled that a full-time music video cable channel would attract enough viewers to interest advertisers and make money, while simultaneously promoting records. At first there were doubters, but by 1984 the Music Television Channel, MTV for short, claimed 24 million viewers, more than any other cable channel. Warner was right, too, about a correlation between music videos on television and record sales. The MTV audience was mostly teenagers and young adults, the same people who buy most records. It was no surprise when surveys found that almost three out of four record-buyers reported that MTV influenced their choices at the record shop.

The record industry gave itself another shot in the arm in the 1980s by switching to compact disc digital playback equipment and software. The quality of CD sound attracted attention, and many people began replacing their tape and record collections with CDs. By the mid-1980s, the record industry was clearly out of its slump.

conglomeration in record-making

(STUDY PREVIEW) The U.S. record industry is concentrated in six major companies. This consolidation worries cultural sociologists, who say that the industry's size and bent for profits discourage musical innovation.

Big-star megadeals have returned to fashion after almost ruining the U.S. record industry in 1979. The question, again, is whether the industry may be over-extending itself financially. Recent deals surpass any of those of the 1970s. Many are multi-year packages, sometimes including more than records. Both Madonna and Michael Jackson's deals, for example, include movies. Here, according to industry insiders, are among the best deals of recent years:

Prince	Warner	$108 million
Madonna	Warner	$75 million
Michael Jackson	Sony	$65 million
ZZ Top	BMG	$50 million
Aerosmith	Sony	$50 million
Janet Jackson	Virgin	$40 million

big six

Records, like the other mass media, are big business. Six companies, the **Big Six**, dominate the U.S. recording industry with 90 percent of the market. Each of these majors is, in turn, part of a larger media conglomerate:

- Sony Music is owned by Sony, the Japanese electronic hardware company, which purchased it in 1988 from CBS Inc. Labels include Columbia, Epic and WTG.
- Capitol is owned by Electrical and Musical Instruments of England and Paramount Communications of the United States. Labels include Chrysalis.
- MCA, formerly Music Corporation of America, is owned by Seagram of Canada, which purchased it in 1994 from Matsushita Electrical Industrial Corp. of Japan. It has numerous media interests, including Universal Pictures. Labels include MCA, Decca, Kapp, Geffen and UNI.
- PolyGram is part of a Dutch-owned, London-based company owned by Philips of the Netherlands. Labels include A&M, Deutsche Grammophon, Island, Mercury and Motown.
- RCA Records is a subsidiary of the German media giant Bertelsmann, which purchased it in 1988 from General Electric. RCA labels include Arista.
- Warner Music is owned by Time Warner, the conglomerate that resulted from the 1989 merger of Warner Communications, whose interests included Warner movies and Time-Life, the magazine giant. Labels include Atco, Atlantic, East West, Elektra, Giant, Interscope, Nonesuch, Reprise, Sire and Warner Brothers.

indies

About 10 percent of the U.S. record market is held by independent companies. Although many **indies** are financially marginal, they are not to be written off. Some indies prosper in market niches. Windham Hill succeeded with high-tech jazz recordings in the 1980s, as did 415 Records with its own brand of rock. A single hit can propel an independent label from a relatively obscure market niche into a major independent. For Rounder Records, it was releases by George Thorogood and the Destroyers in the late 1970s. For Windham Hill, it was a hit by pianist George Winston. IRS scored with the group R.E.M.

censorship and recorded music

(STUDY PREVIEW) A perennial problem for record-makers is pressure to sanitize lyrics to protect young listeners. Some would-be censors are at the reactionary and radical fringes of society, but others have received serious attention from congressional committees. By and large, the record industry has headed off government sanctions with voluntary labels on records.

objectionable music

Campaigns to ban records are nothing new. In the Roaring '20s, some people saw jazz as morally loose. White racists of the 1950s called Bill Haley's rock "nigger music." War protest songs of the Vietnam period angered many Americans.

Government attempts to censor records have been rare, yet the **Federal Communications Commission** indirectly keeps some records off the market. The FCC can take a dim view of stations that air objectionable music, which guides broadcasters toward caution. Stations do not want to risk their licenses. Because the record industry is so dependent on airplay, hardly any music that might offend makes it to market.

The FCC has been explicit about obnoxious lyrics. In 1971 the commission said stations have a responsibility to know "the content of the lyrics." Not to do so, said the commission, would raise "serious questions as to whether continued operation of the station is in the public interest." The issue at the time was music that glorified drugs.

record labeling

In the 1980s complaints about lyrics narrowed to drugs, sexual promiscuity and violence. A group led by Tipper Gore and wives of several other influential members of Congress, **Parents Music Resource Center,** claimed links between explicit rock music and teen suicide, teen pregnancy, abusive parents, broken homes and other social ills. The group objected to lyrics like Prince's "Sister," which extols incest; Mötley Crüe's "Live Wire," with its psychopathic enthusiasm for strangulation; Guns n' Roses' white racism; and Ice-T and other rap artists' hate music.

The Parents Music Resource Center argued that consumer protection laws should be invoked to require that records with offensive lyrics be labeled as dangerous, like cigarette warning labels or the movie industry's rating system. After the group went to the FCC and the **National Association of Broadcasters,** record companies began labeling potentially offensive records: "Explicit Lyrics—Parental Advisory." In some cases, the companies printed lyrics on album covers as a warning.

Federal Communications Commission
U.S. government agency that licenses broadcast stations.

Parents Music Resource Center
Crusaded for labels on "objectionable" music.

National Association of Broadcasters
Radio, television trade organization.

Sam Brownback. Senator Sam Brownback, a new Congressman in 1997, picked up on the sometimes effective jawboning tactic to get the music industry to clean up its act. Brownback, from Kansas, ordered a hearing to explore the negative effect of "virtual violence" on kids who buy music, games and videos that depict violence. Such political pressure, which implies the possibility of government regulation, earlier prompted Time Warner to unload record subsidiaries that specialized in themes that alarmed a lot of parents.

In the preliminaries to the 1996 presidential campaign, former Senate majority leader **Bob Dole,** a presidential hopeful, attacked record-makers in a bid to rally support. In his early posturing, Dole said: "We must hold Hollywood and the entire entertainment industry responsible for putting profit ahead of common decency." Another White House aspirant, **William Bennett,** focused on Time Warner, urging the media giant's bosses to remove objectionable lyrics. When Time Warner execs tried counter-arguments, Bennett said: "Are you folks morally disabled?" House Speaker **Newt Gingrich** proposed boycotting radio stations that play "explicitly vicious" music.

The campaign found a new champion in Bob Dole's successor in the U.S. Senate in 1997. Newly elected Senator **Sam Brownback,** a Kansas Republican, announced a hearing called "An Examination of Violent Music on Youth Behavior and Well Being," and invited the news corps in. To the assembled reporters, as their tapes rolled, Brownback disgustingly recited lyrics from Marilyn Manson's "Irresponsible Hate Anthem." He then took testimony from music industry critics, including C. Delores Tucker. Robert Love, the managing editor of the music magazine *Rolling Stone,* lambasted Brownstone for grandstanding, but also found ironic humor in the senator's promise to keep the heat on music-makers: "That's good news for Marilyn Manson, since the only sure outcome of such government attention will be to send kids to the record store."

lyrics and young people

Despite countless studies, it is unclear whether mores are affected by lyrics. Two scholars from California State University at Fullerton found that most high school students are hazy on the meaning of their favorite songs. Asked to explain Bruce Springsteen's "Born in the U.S.A.," about the hopelessness of being born in a blue-collar environment, many teenagers were simplistically literal. "It's about the town Bruce Springsteen lives in," said one. Led Zeppelin's "Stairway to Heaven" has been criticized for glorifying drug or sexual rushes, but many teenagers in the study were incredibly literal, saying the song was about climbing steps into the sky. What does this mean? Professor Lorraine Prinsky of the Fullerton study concluded that teenagers use rock music as background noise. At most 3 percent, she said, are fully attentive to the lyrics.

Critics, however, see an insidious subliminal effect. Some songs repeat their simple and explicitly sexual messages over and over, as many as 15 to 30 times in one song. Said a spokesperson from the Parents Music Resource Center: "I can't believe it's not getting through. It's getting into the subconscious, even if they can't recite the lyrics."

Bob Dole
Sought 1996 political support by criticizing music, movies.

William Bennett
Attacked Time Warner as "morally disabled" for certain of its music, movies.

Newt Gingrich
Congressional leader who proposed radio station boycott.

Sam Brownback
Kansas senator who held hearings to explore negative effect of violence in media on kids.

heisting music

(STUDY PREVIEW) Record companies claim home-dubbing has eroded 20 percent of their sales—$1.5 billion a year worldwide. About the same is lost to pirates who are in the business of dubbing recorded music for the black market.

home-dubbing

The lopsidedness of the relationship between the radio and record industries became obvious in another way in the 1970s. Instead of buying records and tapes at $9 each, people began sharing records and dubbing them onto relatively inexpensive blank tapes. Phonograph manufacturers offered machines that not only could dub tapes from records but also could record from the air at the flick of a toggle. Many FM stereo radio stations catered to home dubbers by announcing when they would play uninterrupted albums.

The economic effect of **home-dubbing** on the record industry is hard to measure precisely, but the Recording Industry Association of America estimates that the industry loses $1.5 billion a year, one-fifth of its sales.

Record companies tried to dissuade stations from playing albums uninterrupted, but it did not work. Stations were not about to give up the audience they had cultivated for their made-for-dubbing programs. The record companies had no recourse. Cutting off pre-releases to radio stations would mean throwing away free airplay, and airplay was too important. Again, the record industry's dependence on radio was clear. Record-makers were powerless to close a major drain on their revenues.

The dependence of the record industry on radio again was demonstrated in the 1980s when many radio stations shifted to oldies. Traditionally, the record industry derived most of its profits from new music, whose marketing was boosted by radio airplay. In the 1980s, however, stations played more old songs to reach the huge audience of baby boomers who grew up in the 1950s and 1960s and who, like generations before them, preferred the music that was popular when they were young. The change in radio programming worked against the record industry, which, although it was in an economic partnership with radio, was not in control of the relationship.

While record-makers were unable to strike a deal with the radio industry to plug the home-dubbing revenue drain, progress was made on another front in 1991. The record-makers and their longtime foe on the home-dubbing issue, the manufacturers of home electronic equipment, agreed on a "taping tax." Anyone purchasing a blank tape would pay a 1 percent fee to be passed on to songwriters, music publishers and others who lose royalty income from home-dubbing. Congress approved the taping tax in 1992.

piracy

Criminal **piracy** involves dubbing records and videos and selling the dubs. An estimated 18 percent of the records and tapes sold are from shadowy pirate sources, mostly in Asia but also in other countries, including Saudi Arabia. These pirate operations have no A&R, royalty or promotion expenses. They dub tapes produced by

home-dubbing
Recording music from a purchased record onto a blank tape for personal use.

piracy
Manufacturing recorded music for sale without permission from record company, artists

legitimate companies and sell them through black-market channels. Their costs are low, and their profits are high.

These pirate operations are well financed and organized. It is not uncommon for a Bangkok pirate operation to have 100 "slave" tape-copying machines going simultaneously 24 hours a day and even to ship illegal copies before the official release by the U.S. distributor. Both the Recording Industry Association of

Recording Piracy. Pirating operations in Bangkok are so well organized that illegal copies of music and videotapes find their way into local shops ahead of their release through legal channels. A tape of the movie *Pretty Woman* went for $5 in a blank cassette box weeks before the U.S. distributor put it on the market.

America and the Motion Picture Association of America spend millions of dollars a year on formal trade complaints and private investigations in Bangkok and other piracy centers, but with limited success. Local authorities have other priorities and antipiracy laws are weak. In an interview with *Fortune* magazine, Frank Knight, a Bangkok investigator who specializes in these cases, said: "Anybody who's been involved in past mischief, such as drug exports, finds this to be a highly lucrative crime that's easier and less punishable." Knight has tracked exports of illegal tapes to South Africa, to the Indian subcontinent, throughout the Asian Rim and to the United States. The RIAA estimates that $1.5 billion in music revenue is lost to pirates every year, and the MPAA estimates the loss to filmmakers at $1.2 billion a year.

chapter wrap-up

For most of the 20th century, recorded music has been a banner that successive generations have used to identify themselves and their values: jazz, rock 'n' roll, be-bop, disco, hip-hop, grunge. The record industry's continuing success depends on how well it can help each new generation set itself apart from mom and dad. The generational differences, however, are a two-edged issue for record-makers. Through most of the 20th century, record-makers have had to deal with critics, always older people and authorities, who feel pop music is undermining traditional social values.

From one perspective, concern about music's potential as an insidious social force is understandable. From personal experience, everybody knows the emotive power of music. Armies march to war to martial music. Babies ease into sleep with lullabies. Lovers find inspiration in the strains and lyrics of romantic music. Recordings, of course, exponentially increase the audience for music, which gives the critics cause for alarm. There is little evidence, however, that music moves young people to antisocial acts, as some critics suggest in blaming music for a growing number of teen suicides and other social problems.

The mainstream of today's popular music has grown out of rock 'n' roll in the 1950s. Early rock was itself a result of a confluence of two distinct streams of American music—one that can be traced to black slave music from the Deep South and one that can be traced to the hillbilly music of Appalachian and Southern whites. While early rock was a wonderful entertainer, historians and sociologists say its importance far transcended its entertainment value. It helped bridge gaps between black and white Americans, drawing on the distinctive musical genres from both races. Some musicologists see a pivotal moment in American social history in 1954, when an upstart Memphis record-maker, Sam Phillips, went looking for a white who "had the Negro sound and the Negro feel." He found Elvis Presley.

While the recording industry is enormously profitable today, not all is well. Critics say the industry is concentrated in too few companies, which, they say, results in a sameness in music that discourages innovation and retards the evolution of the culture. Populists, on the other hand, trust the marketplace. As populists see it, record-makers are producing the right stuff if it's popular and sells.

The future holds challenges for the record industry. Home-dubbing equipment has given young people an alternative to buying records. This is a major leak on industry profits. So far it has proven unstoppable. Another leak is piracy. Hundreds of outfits, mostly abroad, churn out unauthorized copies of popular records for the black market. Attempts to stem this piracy have been mixed.

The record industry also risks overextending itself financially with megadeals to artists. Another risk is confusing consumers with too many formats besides the currently dominant compact disc.

The greatest challenge, however, is staying in tune with young people. This can be difficult because young people can be fickle. When record sales plummeted in 1924, young people were turning on the radio. In 1979 they played video games and sent the record industry into a depression. For the most part, though, young people have been a loyal, growing market, and they will continue to be as long as recordings are an affordable vehicle to identify their generation, to celebrate their values, to demonstrate youthful rebellion and to dance to.

questions for review

1. Why is recorded music important?

2. What were the innovations of Thomas Edison, Emile Berliner, Joseph Maxwell and Peter Goldmark? How is digital reproduction different?

3. What are the roots of American popular music? How has it evolved?

4. Has conglomeration affected innovation in popular music?

5. What is the relationship between the record and radio industries?

6. What role do independent record companies play?

7. How do would-be censors affect the record business?

8. What effects do home-dubbing, piracy, new formats and megadeals with performers have?

questions for critical thinking

1. Discuss the effect of moralists and others who would like to change the content of some recorded music. How do these people go about trying to accomplish their goals? What common threads have there been to their criticism through the 20th century?

2. What has been the role of small independent record-makers like Sam Phillips in the music industry? How has that role changed?

3. How has the relationship between artists and recording companies changed since World War II? Why has the change occurred?

4. Three principal methods for storing sound for replaying have been developed. Distinguish each type, explain the advantages of each and place them in a

historical perspective. The methods are mechanical media, like the phonograph disc; magnetic media, like cassette tapes; and digital media, like compact discs.

5. Two types of piracy are plaguing the United States recording industry. Describe illegal copying of both records and tapes for resale and home-dubbing, and discuss what can be done.

6. Of the major technological developments in sound recording, which was the most significant? Support your case. Consider, but do not limit yourself to these developments: the Phonograph of Thomas Edison in 1877, electromagnetic applications by Joseph Maxwell in 1924, the 33⅓ LP by Peter Goldmark and the compact disc.

7. What are the common and the distinguishing characteristics of the six major U.S. recording companies? They are Capitol, Sony, MCA, PolyGram, RCA and Warner.

8. Discuss the relationship of the independent recording companies and the majors, with particular attention to Windham Hill, Rounder and Motown. Consider that Motown was acquired by a major label in 1988.

for further learning

Steve Chapple and Reebee Garofalo. *Rock 'n' Roll Is Here to Pay: The History and Politics of the Music Industry* (Nelson-Hall, 1977). This interpretive look at the music industry is built on the premise that authentic cultural contributions are co-opted by profit motives.

R. Serge Denisoff with William Schurk. *Tarnished Gold: The Record Industry Revisited* (Transaction Books, 1986). Denisoff, a sociologist, examines the recording industry by accepting popular music as a cultural phenomenon within a commercial framework. This is an update of his 1975 book, *Solid Gold.*

Colin Escott with Martin Hawkins. *Good Rockin' Tonight: Sun Records and the Birth of Rock 'n' Roll* (St. Martin's, 1991).

Discographers Escott and Hawkins update their earlier work on Sam Phillips and his Memphis recording studio.

Peter Fornatale and Joshua E. Mills. *Radio in the Television Age* (Overlook Press, 1980). This interestingly written account of radio from the 1950s through the 1970s suggests that the payola scandals were overplayed in the media because of other events of the time.

Roland Gelatt. *The Fabulous Phonograph: From Tin Foil to High Fidelity* (J.B. Lippincott, 1955). This is a comprehensive history through the battle of the speeds and the demise of the 78-rpm record.

Fred Goodman. "Between Rock and a Hard Place." *Worth* (March 1995), 102–106. A former *Rolling Stone* editor tracks the financial vagaries of the Minneapolis rock band Jayhawks. He says the economics of rock 'n' roll are weird, "a $5 billion industry in which everyone makes a decent living except most musicians."

Robert Palmer. *Rock & Roll: An Unruly History* (Harmony Books, 1995). Palmer, former New York *Times* rock critic, tracks the evolution and influence of rock, from blues and gospel to reggae, punk and rock.

Barry L. Sherman and Joseph R. Dominick. "Violence and Sex in Music Videos: TV and Rock 'n' Roll." *Journal of Communication* 36 (Winter 1986):1, 79–93. Scholars Sherman and Dominick tackle the influence of music videos from numerous perspectives. Their report is part of a 68-page special music video section in this issue of the *Journal of Communication.*

for keeping up to date

The weekly *Billboard* is the recording industry's leading trade journal.

Consumer magazines that track popular music and report on the record industry include *Rolling Stone* and *Spin.*

Entertainment Weekly has a regular section on music.

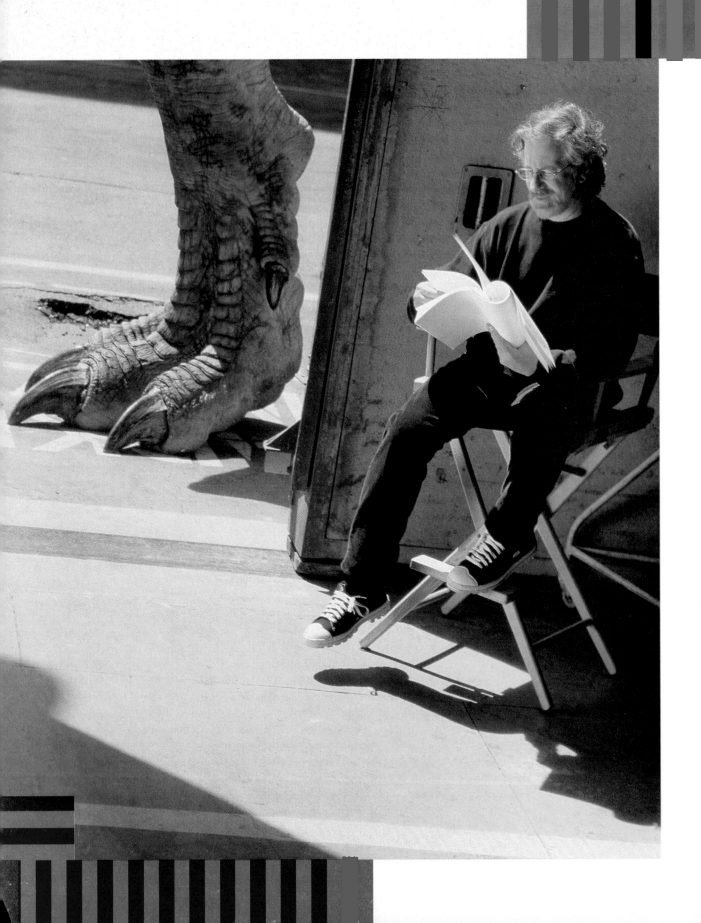

6

movies

Steven Spielberg was infected young with a love for movies—not just seeing them but making them. When he was 12, he put two Lionel toy trains on a collision course, turned up the juice to both engines and made a home movie of the crash. By that time, he already had shot dozens of short movies. For one of them, he coaxed his mother into donning a pith helmet and Army surplus uniform, and then he rolled the film as she bounced the family Jeep through backhill potholes near Phoenix.

That was his family war movie.

Imagine Steven Spielberg's excitement, at age 17, when a family visit to Los Angeles included a tour of the Universal studios. Imagine his disappointment when the tour bus bypassed the sound stages. At the next break, he gave the tour group the slip and headed straight back to the sound stages, somehow managed to get in, and ended up chatting for an hour with editorial head Chuck Silvers. The next day, with a pass signed by Silvers, Spielberg was back

in this chapter you will learn:

- Movies have powerful impact.

- The technological basis of movies is photography chemistry.

- Movies had their heyday as a mass medium in the 1940s.

- Anti-Communism, the courts and television threatened Hollywood, beginning in the late 1940s.

- Hollywood responded to external threats in the 1950s with technical and content innovations.

- Hollywood today is a major producer of television programming.

- The movie exhibition business faces challenges from home video.

- Moviemakers are in an expensive, high-risk business.

- Hollywood always opts for self-policing to quell censorship threats.

to show him four of his 8-millimeter home movies. Silvers liked what he saw but told the young Spielberg that he could not issue another pass for the next day. Undaunted, Spielberg put on a suit and tie the next day and, carrying his father's briefcase, walked through the Universal gates, faking a familiar wave to the guard. It worked. Spielberg spent the whole summer in and out of Universal, hanging around as movies were being made.

Today, Spielberg is one of the world's best-known movie-makers. The gross return from his 1993 movie, *Jurassic Park,* topped $900 million in less than a year and was heading toward $1 billion with home video and other after-market releases. That surpassed 1982's *E.T.: The Extra-Terrestrial,* another Spielberg film, which had been the top Hollywood moneymaker. Spielberg's *Indiana Jones and the Last Crusade* is fifth and *Jaws* eighth. His *Raiders of the Lost Ark, Indiana Jones and the Temple of Doom* and *Close Encounters of the Third Kind* all are in the top 20. In all, his 15 movies have grossed more than $4 billion.

Steven Spielberg's work embodies a whole range of qualities that tell us a lot about Hollywood and the role of movies in our culture. He is a wonderful, audience-oriented storyteller: "I want people to love my movies, and I'll be a whore to get them into theaters," he once said.

Spielberg's films also represent the glitz and glamour of Hollywood. Most are spectacularly filmed with dazzling special effects. And their box-office success has helped fuel the extravagances that are part of the image Hollywood cultivates for itself.

But Spielberg is deeper than that. He entwines observations from his personal life into film commentary on fundamental human issues. The fantasy *E.T.* centers on a boy growing up alienated in a broken home, who identifies with the alien E.T. Movie analysts see the boy as a metaphorical stand-in for Spielberg, who was taunted as a Jew when he transferred into a new high school and found himself alienated for something over which he had no control.

Moviegoers entranced by Spielberg's adventure stories sometimes forget his serious works. His 1985 *The Color Purple,* adapted from Alice Walker's Pulitzer Prize-winning book, was a painful, insightful account of a southern African-American family during the first half of the century. *Schindler's List,* his acclaimed 1993 account of the Holocaust, flows from his own heritage. These movies, some say Spiel-

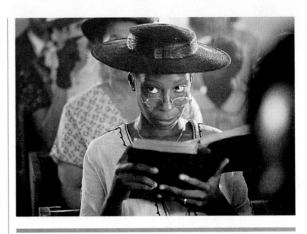

Box Office and Critical Success. Perhaps no other moviemaker can project stories so compellingly across such a diverse range as Steven Spielberg. His 1993 *Jurassic Park,* which raised questions about DNA preservation of extinct life forms, became the most profitable movie in history, until being eclipsed by James Cameron's *Titanic* later in the decade. Spielberg's 1985 *Color Purple* was an insightful, painful inquiry into the southern black families during the first half of the century. Among his other accomplishments: *Amistad,* on an early American slave revolt; *Schindler's List,* on the Nazi Holocaust; *E.T.: The Extra-Terrestrial*; and *Jaws.*

berg's best, represent the potential of the medium to help us individually and collectively sort through the dilemmas of the human condition.

Schindler's List swept the Oscars in 1993, casting Spielberg in a whole new light as a director. Until then, Spielberg's critical success seemed to count against him at Oscar time, and even critics who liked his work for its seamless craft and visceral punch dismissed him as a serious director. Though he had tackled serious themes before, he always seemed uncomfortable with the material, as if he were trying too hard to make a

point. All that changed with *Schindler's List.* The film, from the novel by Thomas Keneally, has been universally praised as one of the great films of the decade, and with it Spielberg has assured himself a place in film history not only as the highest-grossing director of all time, but as one of the great U.S. directors of the postwar period.

In this chapter, you will learn how the movie industry is structured, including the historical influences that have reshaped the industry. You also will learn about issues that will shape Hollywood in the years ahead.

importance of movies

(STUDY PREVIEW) The experience of watching a movie, uninterrupted in a darkened auditorium, has entranced people since the medium's earliest days. It is an all-encompassing experience, which has given movies a special power in shaping cultural values.

overwhelming experience

Movies have a hold on people, at least while they are watching one, that is more intense than any other medium. It is not unusual for a movie reviewer to recommend taking a handkerchief, but never will you hear such advice from a record reviewer and seldom from a book reviewer. Why do movies have such powerful effects? It is not movies themselves. With rare exception, these evocative efforts occur only when movies are shown in a theater. The viewer sits in a darkened auditorium in front of a giant screen, with nothing to interrupt the experience. The rest of the world is excluded. Movies, of course, can be shown outdoors at drive-in theaters and on television, but the experience is strongest in the darkened cocoon of a movie house.

People have been fascinated with movies almost from the invention of the technology that made it possible, even when the pictures were nothing more than wobbly, fuzzy images on a whitewashed wall. The medium seemed to possess magical powers. With the introduction of sound in the late 1920s, and then color and a host of later technical enhancements, movies have kept people in awe. Going to the movies remains a thrill—an experience unmatched by other media.

hollywood's cultural influence

When Clark Gable took off his shirt in the 1934 movie *It Happened One Night* and revealed that he was not wearing anything underneath, American men, in great numbers, decided that they too would go without undershirts. Nationwide, undershirt sales plummeted. Whether men prefer wearing underwear is trivial compared with some concerns about how Hollywood portrays American life and its influence:

- Sociologist Norman Denzin says the treatment of drinking in American movies has contributed to a misleading bittersweet romanticism about alcoholism in the public consciousness.

- Scholars using content analysis have found exponential increases in movie violence that far outpace violence in real life and contribute to perceptions that violence is a growing social problem in modern life.

- Utility company executives were none too pleased with the widespread public concern about nuclear power created by James Bridges' 1979 movie, *The China Syndrome.*

- Political leaders express concern from time to time that movies corrupt the morals of young people and glamorize deviant behavior.

- Congressman Parnell Thomas once raised questions that Hollywood was advocating the violent overthrow of the government.

Steven Spielberg
Leading director whose work includes *Jurassic Park, Schindler's List, E.T.*

Movies are part of our everyday lives in more ways than we realize. Even the way we talk is loaded with movie metaphors. The *New Yorker* magazine noted this introducing an issue on Hollywood: "Our personal scenarios unspool in a sequence of flashbacks, voice-overs and cameos. We zoom in, cut to the chase, fade to black."

Because of the perceived influence of movies, some real, some not, it is important to know about the industry that creates them. This is especially true now that television entertainment programming has been largely subsumed by Hollywood and that the book, magazine and sound recording industries are closely tied into it.

technical heritage of movies

(STUDY PREVIEW) Motion picture technology is based on the same chemical process as photography. The medium developed in the 1880s and 1890s. By the 1930s movie houses everywhere were showing "talkies."

adaptation from photography

The technical heritage of motion pictures is photography. The 1727 discovery that light causes silver nitrate to darken was basic to the development of motion picture technology. So was a human phenomenon called **persistence of vision.** The human eye retains an image for a fraction of a second. If a series of photographs capture something in motion and if those photographs are flipped quickly, the human eye will perceive continuous motion.

The persistence of vision phenomenon was demonstrated photographically in 1877 by **Eadweard Muybridge** in California. Former Governor Leland Stanford found himself in a wager on whether horses ever had all their legs off the ground when galloping. It was something the human eye could not perceive. All anyone could make

persistence of vision
Fast-changing still photos create illusion of motion.

Eadweard Muybridge
Demonstrated persistence of vision with galloping horses.

Robert Flaherty
First documentary-maker.

Nanook of the North
First documentary.

media timeline

movie technology

1877 Eadweard Muybridge used sequential photographs to create illusion of motion.

1888 William Dickson devised motion picture camera.

1891 George Eastman devised flexible celluloid for motion pictures.

1922 Fox used sound in newsreels.

1927 Warner Brothers distributed first talkie, ***The Jazz Singer***.

1932 Disney issued first full-color movie, *Flowers and Trees.*

1937 Disney issued first animated feature, *Snow White.*

Explorer **Robert Flaherty** took a camera to the Arctic in 1921 to record the life of an Eskimo family. The result was a new kind of movie: the documentary. While other movies of the time were theatrical productions with scripts, sets and actors, Flaherty tried something different—recording reality.

His 57-minute ***Nanook of the North*** was compelling on its own merits when it started on the movie house circuit in 1922, but the film received an unexpected macabre boost a few days later when Nanook, the father of the Eskimo family, died of hunger on the ice. News stories of Nanook's death stirred public interest—and also attendance at the movie, which helped establish the documentary as an important new film genre.

Flaherty's innovative approach took a new twist in the 1930s, when propagandists saw reality-based movies as a tool to pro-mote their causes. In Germany the Nazi government produced propaganda films, and other countries followed. Frank Capra directed the vigorous five-film series *Why We Fight* for the U.S. War Office in 1942.

After World War II, there was a revival of documentaries in Flaherty's style—a neutral recording of natural history. Walt Disney produced a variety of such documentaries, including the popular *Living Desert* in the 1950s.

Today, documentaries are unusual in American movie houses, with occasional exceptions like *Mother Teresa* in 1986 and movies built on rock concerts.

The CBS television network gained a reputation in the 1950s and 1960s for picking up on the documentary tradition with *Harvest of Shame*, on migrant workers, and *Hunger in America*. In the same period, the National Geographic Society established a documentary unit, and French explorer Jacques Cousteau went into the television documentary business.

Such full-length documentaries mostly are relegated to the Public Broadcasting Service and cable networks today. The major networks, meanwhile, shifted most documentaries away from full-length treatments. Typical was CBS's "60 Minutes," a weekly one-hour program of three minidocumentaries. These new network projects, which included ABC's "20/20," combined reality programming and entertainment in slick packages that attracted larger audiences than traditional documentaries.

Nanook of the North.
The documentary became a film genre with explorer Robert Flaherty's *Nanook of the North* in 1922. This film was an attempt to record reality—no actors, no props. The film was especially potent not only because it was a new approach and on a fascinating subject but also because, coincidentally, Nanook died of starvation on the ice about the time that it was released.

Robert Flaherty

Edison's Kinetoscope.
Among the earliest mechanisms for watching movies was inventor Thomas Edison's kinetoscope. A person would look through a peephole as a strip of film was wound over a lightbulb. The effect was shaky. Later, Edison borrowed a technique from the Lumière brothers of Paris for the Vitascope system of projecting images on a wall.

William Dickson
Developed first movie camera.

George Eastman
Devised celluloid film.

Lumière brothers
Opened first movie exhibition hall.

Warner brothers
Introduced sound.

The Jazz Singer
First feature sound movie.

out of the legs of a galloping horse was a blur. Stanford asked Muybridge if photography could settle the question. Muybridge stationed 24 cameras along a track with trip strings to open the shutters. The galloping horse hit the strings, and Muybridge had 24 sequential photographs that showed that galloping horses take all four legs off the ground at the same time. Stanford won his $25,000 bet.

More significant to us was that the illusion of a horse in motion was possible by flipping Muybridge's photographs quickly. The sequential photographic images, when run rapidly by the human eye, made it appear that the horse was moving. All that was needed was the right kind of camera and film to capture about 16 images per second. Those appeared in 1888. **William Dickson** of Thomas Edison's laboratory developed a workable motion picture camera. Dickson and Edison used celluloid film perfected by **George Eastman,** who had just introduced his Kodak camera. By 1891 Edison began producing movies.

Edison movies were viewed by looking into a box. In France, brothers **Auguste** and **Louis Lumière** brought projection to motion pictures. By running the film in front of a specially aimed powerful lightbulb, the Lumières projected movie images on a wall. In 1895 they opened an exhibition hall in Paris—the first movie house. Edison recognized the commercial advantage of projection, and himself patented the Vitascope projector, which he put on the market in 1896.

adding sound to pictures

Dickson, at Edison's lab, came up with a sound system for movies in 1889. In the first successful commercial application, Fox used sound in its 1922 Movietone newsreels. But it was four upstart moviemakers, the brothers **Albert, Harry, Jack** and **Sam Warner,** who revolutionized movies with sound. In 1927 the Warners released *The Jazz Singer* starring Al Jolson. There was sound for only two segments, but it caught the public's fancy. By 1930, 9,000 movie houses around the country were equipped for sound.

three crises that reshaped hollywood

(STUDY PREVIEW)   In quick succession, Hollywood took three body blows in the late 1940s. Right-wing political leaders sent some directors and screenwriters to jail in 1947 and intimidated moviemakers into creative cowardice. In 1948 the U.S. Supreme Court broke up the economic structure of the movie industry. Then television stole people from the box office.

the hollywood 10

Hollywood had a creative crisis in 1947 when Congressman Parnell Thomas, chair of the House Un-American Activities Subcommittee, began hearings on Communists in Hollywood. Thomas summoned 47 screenwriters, directors and actors and demanded answers to accusations about leftist influences in Hollywood and the Screen Writers Guild. Ten witnesses who refused to answer insulting accusations went to jail

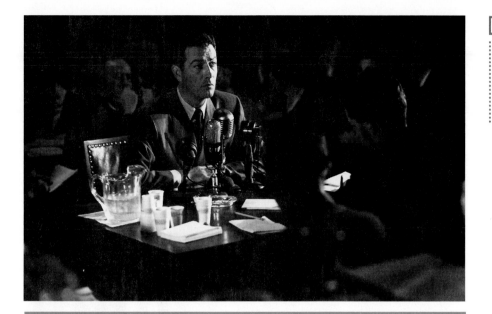

media
online

National Film Board of Canada:
Charged with defining what
makes Canada the country it is.
www.nfb.ca

Divided Hollywood. When some members of Congress set out in 1947 to unearth
Communist infiltration in Hollywood, they heard what they wanted to hear from actor Robert
Taylor. He testified that he had seen plenty of things "on the pink side" in Hollywood. Other
Hollywood people saw through the congressional probe as a witch hunt, and refused even to
testify. Ten of them went to jail.

for contempt of Congress. It was one of the most highly visible manifestations of
McCarthyism, a post-World War II overreaction to Soviet Communism as a national
threat.

The Thomas hearings had longer deleterious effects. Movie producers, afraid the
smear would extend to them, declined to hire the **Hollywood 10.** Other careers were
also ruined. One expert identified 11 directors, 36 actors, 106 writers and 61 others
who suddenly were unwelcome in their old circles and could not find work.

Among the Hollywood 10 was screenwriter **Dalton Trumbo.** His powerful pacifist
novel *Johnny Got His Gun* made Trumbo an obvious target for the jingoist Thomas
committee. After Trumbo refused to answer committee questions, he was jailed. On
his release, Trumbo could not find anybody who would accept his screenplays, so he
resorted to writing under the pseudonym Robert Rich. The best he could earn was
$15,000 per script, one-fifth his former rate. When his screenplay for *The Brave One*
won an Academy Award in 1957, Robert Rich did not dare show up to accept it.

In a courageous act, **Kirk Douglas** hired Trumbo in 1959 to write *Spartacus.* Then
Otto Preminger did the same with *Exodus.* Besides Trumbo, only screenwriter **Ring
Lardner, Jr.** rose from the 1947 ashes. In 1970, after two decades on the blacklist,
Lardner won an Academy Award for *M*A*S*H.*

The personal tragedies resulting from the Thomas excesses were bad enough, but
the broader ramification was a paucity of substantial treatments of major social and
political issues. Eventually, movie-makers rallied with sophisticated treatments of controversial subjects that, it can be argued, were more intense than they might otherwise
have been. It was an anti-McCarthy backlash, which did not occur until the mid-1950s,
when Hollywood began to reestablish movies as a serious medium.

Hollywood 10
Film industry people who
were jailed for refusing to
testify at congressional
anti-Red hearings.

Dalton Trumbo
Blackballed screenwriter.

Kirk Douglas
Courage to hire Dalton
Trumbo despite anti-Red
critics.

Ring Lardner, Jr.
Blacklisted screenwriter
who reemerged with
*M*A*S*H.*

media timeline

....the movie industry

1912 Carle Laemmle founded Universal, first major Hollywood studio.

1916 Investors took role in the art and creativity after financial disaster of D. W. Griffith's *Intolerance*.

1919 Charlie Chaplin, Douglas Fairbanks, D. W.

Griffith and Mary Pickford founded United Artists studio.

1923 Warner brothers founded studio bearing their name.

1923 Walt Disney formed studio.

1924 Metro-Goldwyn-Mayer founded.

1924 Columbia Pictures founded.

1929 RKO founded.

1948 Congressional hearings label leading

Hollywood people as Communist sympathizers.

1952 U.S. Supreme Court rules First Amendment protects movies.

1950s Television eroded movie attendance.

court bans on vertical integration

The government has acted twice to break up the movie industry when it became so consolidated that there was no alternative to preventing abuses. **Adolph Zukor**'s Paramount became a major success as a producer and distributor of feature films in the 1920s, but Zukor wanted more. He began buying movie houses, and eventually owned 1,400 of them. It was a classic case of **vertical integration**, a business practice in which a company controls its product all the way from inception to consumption. Paramount not only was producing and distributing movies, but also, through its own movie houses, was exhibiting them. It was profitable, and soon other major Hollywood studios also expanded vertically.

Still not satisfied with his power and profits, Zukor introduced the practice of **blockbooking**, which required non-Paramount movie houses to book Paramount films in batches. Good movies could be rented only along with the clunkers. The practice was good for Zukor because it guaranteed him a market for the failures. Exhibitors, however, felt coerced, which fueled resentment against the big studios.

The U.S. Justice Department began litigation against vertical integration in 1938, using **Paramount** as a test case. Ten years later, in 1948, the U.S. Supreme Court told Paramount and four other major studios to divest. They had a choice of selling off either their production or distribution or exhibition interests. Most sold their theater chains.

The effect shook the whole economic structure on which Hollywood was based. No longer could the major studios guarantee an audience for their movies by booking them into their own theaters, and what had come to be known as the **studio system** began to collapse. There was now risk in producing movies because movie houses decided what to show, and there was also a hitherto missing competition among studios.

Movie scholars say the court-ordered divestiture, coming when it did, had a more damaging effect than the Justice Department and the courts foresaw. It was about this time that Parnell Thomas and his congressional committee were bashing producers,

Adolph Zukor
Movie mogul whose Paramount epitomized vertical integration.

vertical integration
Controlling whole creation-production-exhibition sequence.

blockbooking
Studio requirement that movie houses rent clunkers to get good movies.

Paramount decision
Required studios to loosen control on whole creation-distribution-exhibition sequence.

studio system
The centralized studio-controlled movie industry disassembled by the Paramount decision.

which undermined Hollywood's creative output. Now the whole way in which the industry operated was required to change overnight. Hollywood was coming apart.

challenge from television

Movie attendance in the United States peaked in 1946 at 90 million tickets a week. Every neighborhood had a movie house, and people went as families to see the latest shows, even those that were not very good. Movies, rivaled only by radio, had become the nation's dominant entertainment medium.

Then came television. The early television sets were expensive, and it was a major decision in many families whether to buy one. In many households there were family conferences to decide whether to divert the weekly movie budget to buying a television. By 1950 movie attendance plummeted to 60 million a week and then 46 million by 1955. Today, fewer than 20 million people go to the movies in a typical week.

Not only had the movie industry been pummeled by Congress into creative timidity, and then been broken up by the courts, but also it had lost the bulk of its audience. Doomsayers predicted an end to Hollywood.

hollywood's response to television

•••• (STUDY PREVIEW) Ironic as it seems, television has been the greatest force shaping the modern movie industry. When television began eroding movie attendance in the 1950s, moviemakers responded with technical innovations such as wrap-around screens. There also were major shifts in movie content, including treatments of social issues that early television would not touch.

technical innovation

When television began squeezing movies in the late 1940s, movie-makers scrambled for special effects to hold their audience. Color movies had been introduced in the 1930s. In the 1950s they came to be the standard—something that early television could not offer. Other technical responses included wrap-around **Cinerama** screens, which put images not only in front of audiences but also in their peripheral vision. Television's small screen could not match it. Cinerama also permitted movie-makers to outdo television with sweeping panoramas that were lost on small television screens. Offsetting its advantages, Cinerama was a costly attempt to increase audience involvement. It required multicamera production, and theaters had to be equipped with special projectors and remodeled for the curved screens. **CinemaScope** gave much the same effect as Cinerama but less expensively, with an image 2½ times wider than it was high, on a flat screen. CinemaScope did not fill peripheral vision, but it seemed more realistic than the earlier squarish screen images. Gimmicky innovations included three-dimensional pictures, which gave viewers not only width and height but also depth. Smell-o-vision was a dubious, short-lived technique. Odors wafted through movie houses to enhance the audience's sensual involvement.

Cinerama
Wraparound screens
CinemaScope
Horizontal screens.

media abroad

movies of india

Indian Fan Mags. Prolific moviemakers in India crank out movies, most of them not very good, in 16 languages to meet a seemingly insatiable public demand. Fans track the off-screen antics of their favorite stars in celebrity magazines like these in English, Gujerato and Hindi.

At 85 cents a seat, people jam Indian movie houses in such numbers that some exhibitors schedule five showings a day starting at 9 a.m. Better seats sell out days in advance in some cities. There is no question that movies are the country's strongest mass medium. Even though per capita income is only $1,360 a year, Indians find enough rupees to support an industry that cranks out 900 movies a year, three times more than American moviemakers. Most are B-grade formula melodramas and action stories. Screen credits often include a director of fights. Despite their flaws, Indian movies are so popular that it is not unusual for a movie house in a Hindi-speaking area to be packed for a film in another Indian language that nobody understands. Movies are produced in 16 Indian languages.

The movie mania centers on stars. Incredible as it may seem, M. G. Ramachandran, who played folk warriors, and M. R. Radha, who played villains, got into a real-life gun duel one day. Both survived their wounds, but Ramachandran exploited the incident to bid for public office. He campaigned with posters that showed him bound in head bandages and was elected chief minister of his state. While in office, Ramachandran continued to make B-grade movies, always as the hero.

Billboards, fan clubs and scurrilous magazines fuel the obsession with stars. Scholars Erik Barnouw and Subrahmanyam Krishna, in their book *Indian Film,* characterize the portrayals of stars as "mythological demigods who live on a highly physical and erotic plane, indulging in amours." With some magazines, compromising photos are a specialty.

A few Indian moviemakers have been recognized abroad for innovation and excellence, but they generally have an uphill battle against B-movies in attracting Indian audiences. Many internationally recognized Indian films, such as those by Satyajit Ray, flop commercially at home.

In the late 1990s, Indian movies developed a cult following in the United States. The major Indian movie export market, however, was in Hindi-speaking parts of the world. In Sri Lanka, for example, whose language Sinhala is closely related to Hindi, the domestic movie industry is overshadowed by imported Indian movies.

content innovation

Besides technical innovations, moviemakers attempted to regain their audiences with high-budget movies, with innovative themes and, finally, by abandoning their traditional mass audiences and appealing to subgroups within the mass audiences.

High-budget movies called **spectaculars** became popular in the 1950s. How could anybody, no matter how entranced by television, ignore the epic *Quo Vadis,* with one scene using 5,500 extras? There were limits, however, to luring Americans from their

spectaculars
Big-budget epic movies.

James Cameron

television sets with publicity-generating big-budget epics. The lavish *Cleopatra* of 1963 cost $44 million, much of which 20th Century-Fox lost. It just cost too much to make. Even so, moviemakers continued to risk occasional big-budget spectaculars. No television network in the 1960s would have put up $20 million to produce the profitable *Sound of Music.* Later, the *Star Wars* movies by George Lucas were huge successes of the sort television could not contemplate.

Television's capture of the broad mass audience was a mixed blessing. Television was in a content trap that had confined movies earlier. To avoid offending big sections of the mass audience, television stuck with safe subjects. Movie-makers, seeking to distinguish their products from television, began producing films on serious, disturbing social issues. In 1955 *Blackboard Jungle* tackled disruptive classroom behavior, hardly a sufficiently nonthreatening subject for television. Also in 1955 there was *Rebel Without a Cause,* with James Dean as a teenager seeking identity. Marital intimacy and implied homosexuality were elements in the movie adaptation of Tennessee Williams's *Cat on a Hot Tin Roof,* starring Paul Newman and Elizabeth Taylor.

Television continued to be squeamish about many social issues into the 1960s, but movies continued testing new waters, notably with violence and sex. The slow-motion machine-gun deaths of bank robbers Bonnie and Clyde in Arthur Penn's 1967 classic left audiences awed in sickened silence. Nevertheless, people kept coming back to movies with graphic violence. Sex was taboo on television but not at the movies. It was the theme in *Bob and Carol and Ted and Alice, Carnal Knowledge,* and *I Am Curious, Yellow.* Sex went about as far as it could with the hard-core *Deep Throat* of 1973, which was produced for porno houses but achieved crossover commercial success in regular movie houses.

Movies came to be made for a younger crowd. By 1985, regular moviegoers fell into a relatively narrow age group—from teenagers through college age. Fifty-nine

The Oscars. Screenwriters and actors Ben Affleck and Matt Damon taking home the 1998 Oscars for their *Good Will Hunting.* The Oscar is recognized as a mark of accomplishment because it is the film industry itself, the Academy of Motion Picture Arts and Sciences, that selects the winners.

percent of the tickets were purchased by people between the ages of 12 and 24. Even so, the industry did not produce exclusively for a young audience. Moviemakers recognized that the highest profits came from movies with a crossover audience. These were movies that attracted not only the regular box-office crowd but also infrequent movie-goers. Essential, however, was the youth audience. Without it, a movie could not achieve extraordinary success. The immensely profitable *E.T.* was an example. It appealed to the youth audience, to parents who took their small children and to film aficionados who were fascinated with the special effects.

melding of movies and television

(STUDY PREVIEW) Hollywood's initial response to television was to fight the new medium, an effort that had mixed results. Next, Hollywood adopted the idea that if you can't beat them, join them. Today, most of the entertainment fare on television comes from Hollywood.

reconciliation of competing industries

Despite Hollywood's best attempts to stem the erosion in attendance caused by television, box-office sales continued to dwindle. Today, an average of only 19 million tickets are sold a week, about one-fifth of attendance at the 1946 box-office peak. Considering that the U.S. population has grown steadily during the period, the decline has been an even more severe indication of television's impact on movie attendance.

Despite a near 50-year slide in box-office traffic, Hollywood has hardly lost its war with television. The movie industry today, a $4-billion-a-year component of the U.S. economy, is so intertwined with television that it is hard to distinguish them. Three-quarters of the movie industry's production today is for television.

media

online

Alfred Hitchcock: The master of suspense unmasked. http://nextdch.mty.itesm.mx/~plopezg/Kaplan/Hitchcock.html

Lion's Den: MGM/UA was one of the first major studios to go online. www.mgmua.com

Lucasfilm: The force behind a generation's most influential pictures. www.lucasarts.com

Star Trek: First Contact: Engage yourself in a technical, elaborate site. http://firstcontact.msn.com/index.html

Worldcam: The planet's moving picture show. http://ovd.com

There remains, however, an uneasy tension between the exhibitors who own movie houses and television. Theater traffic has not recovered, and while moviemakers and distributors are profiting from new distribution channels, especially home videos, these new outlets are hurting theater traffic.

first runs and after-markets

When movie-makers plan films today, they build budgets around anticipated revenues that go beyond first runs in movie houses. Unlike the old days, when movies either made it or didn't at the box office, today moviemakers earn more than 17 percent of their revenue from pay television services like HBO after the movie has played itself out in movie houses. Another 8 percent comes from selling videotapes.

For most movies, foreign release is important. Movies are usually released in the United States and abroad simultaneously. Foreign distribution revenues can be significant. The box-office revenue from U.S. movies abroad, in fact, is significant in balance-of-trade figures with other nations. After-market revenue comes from pay-per-view television channels and the home video market.

movie exhibitors

(STUDY PREVIEW) Most movie-goers today go to multiscreen theaters that show a wide range of movies. These multiplexes are a far cry from the first commercially successful exhibition vehicles, peep show machines that only one viewer at a time could watch. Intermediate exhibition vehicles ranged from humble neighborhood movie houses to downtown palaces.

early exhibition facilities

In the early days, movie patrons peered into a box as they cranked a 50-foot loop over sprockets. These were called peep shows. When Thomas Edison's powerful incandescent lamp was introduced, peep show parlors added a room for projecting movies on a wall. Business thrived. Typical admission was a nickel. By 1908 just about every town had a nickelodeon, as these early exhibition places were called.

Exhibition parlors multiplied and became grander. In 1913 the elegant Strand Theater, the first of the movie palaces, opened in New York. By the early 1940s there were more than 20,000 movie houses in the United States. Every neighborhood had one.

As television gained prominence in the 1950s, many movie houses fell into disrepair. One by one they were boarded up. Drive-in movies eased the loss. At their peak, there were 4,000 drive-ins, but that did not offset the 7,000 movie houses that had closed. Furthermore, **drive-ins** were hardly 365-day operations, especially in northern climates.

multiscreen theaters

Since a nadir in 1971, when annual attendance dropped to 875 million, the exhibition business has evolved into new patterns. Exhibitors have copied the European practice of **multiscreen theaters**—and they built them mostly in suburbs. The new

drive-ins
Outdoor screens viewable from automobiles.
multiscreen theaters
Several screens with central infrastructure.

media | timeline

movie exhibition

1895 Auguste and Louis Lumière opened movie house in Paris.

1896 Koster and Bial's Music Hall is site of first public motion picture showing in United States.

1946 U.S. box office peaked at 90 million a week.

1970s Multiscreen movie houses became the norm.

multiscreen theaters allow movie-goers to choose among several first-run movies, all nearby in a multiplex theater with as many as 12 screens. A family can split up in the lobby—mom and dad to one screen, teenagers to another, and the little kids to a G-rated flick.

Showing rooms are smaller today, averaging 340 seats compared with 750 in 1950. Most multiplexes have large and small showing rooms. An advantage for exhibitors is that they can shift popular films to their bigger rooms to accommodate large crowds and move other films to smaller rooms.

Multiplex theaters have lower overhead. There might be 12 projectors, but only one projectionist, one ticket taker and one concession stand. The system has been profitable. Today there are more than 23,000 screens in the United States—more than double the number in 1970 and more than the total number of theaters when movies were the only game in town. In the 1990s, ticket sales have fluctuated from year to year, but the trend in attendance has been downward.

box-office income

Movie houses usually split box-office receipts with a movie's distributor. The movie-house percentage is called the **nut.** Deals vary, but a 50-50 split is common the first week. **Exhibitors,** as the movie houses are called, take a higher percentage the longer the run. A frequent formula is 60 percent the second week and 70 percent the third, and sometimes more after that. Besides the nut, the concession stand is an important revenue source for exhibitors. Concessions are so profitable that exhibitors sometimes agree to give up their nut entirely for a blockbuster and rely on popcorn and Milk Duds to make money. Movie-house markups on confections are typically 60 percent, even more on popcorn.

The **distributors** that market and promote movies claim a share of movie revenue, taking part of the nut from exhibitors and charging booking fees plus expenses to the movie-makers. Distribution expenses can be significant. Advertising and marketing average $6 million per movie. Making multiple prints, 1,200 copies at $1,200 apiece, and shipping them around the country is expensive too. Distributors also take care of after-markets, including foreign exhibition, videocassette distributors and television—for a fee plus expenses.

nut
Movie-house share of box-office revenue.

exhibitors
Movie-house business.

distributors
Arrange circulation of movies on behalf of studios to exhibitors.

D. W. Griffith
Early producer known for innovations in *The Birth of a Nation,* loose-spending in *Intolerance.*

major studios
Include Warner Brothers, Paramount, Disney, MGM.

independent producer
Makes movies outside major studios but sometimes with major studio's cooperation.

With some movies not enough box-office income is generated for the producers to recoup their production expenses. These expenses can be staggering, about $43 million on average. However, when production budgets are kept low and the movie succeeds at the box office, the return to the producers can be phenomenal.

movie finances

(STUDY PREVIEW) The financing of movies is based more on hardball assessments of their prospects for commercial success than on artistic merit. The money to produce movies comes from major movie studios, banks and investment groups. Studios sometimes draw on the resources of their corporate parents.

the lesson of intolerance

The great cinematic innovator **D. W. Griffith** was riding high after the success of his 1915 Civil War epic, *The Birth of a Nation.* Griffith poured the profits into a new venture, *Intolerance.* It was a complex movie that examined social injustice in ancient Babylon, Renaissance France, early 20th-century America and the Holy Land at the time of Christ. It was a critical success, a masterpiece, but film audiences had not developed the sophistication to follow a theme through disparate historical periods. At the box office it failed.

Intolerance cost $2 million to make, unbelievable by 1916 standards. Griffith had used huge sets and hundreds of extras. He ended up broke. To make more movies, Griffith had to seek outside financing. The result, say movie historians, was a dilution in creativity. Financiers were unwilling to bankroll projects with dubious prospects at the box office. Whether creativity is sacrificed by the realities of capitalism remains a debated issue, but there is no doubt that moviemaking is big business.

financing sources

Just as in D. W. Griffith's time, movies are expensive to make—about $43 million on average. Then there are the big-budget movies. Depending on how the expenses are tallied, the 1997 movie *Titanic* cost somewhere between $200 million to $240 million to make. Where does the money come from?

Major Studios. **Major studios** finance many movies with profits from their earlier movies. Most movies, however, do not originate with major studios but with **independent producers.** While these producers are autonomous in many respects, most of them rely on major studios for financing. The studios hedge their risks by requiring that they distribute the movies, a profitable enterprise involving rentals to movie houses and television, home video sales and merchandise licensing.

The studios, as well as other financial backers, do more than write checks. To protect their investments, some involve themselves directly in film projects. They

spike lee

Spike Lee, a bright, clever young film director, was in deep trouble in 1992. He had persuaded Warner Brothers, the big Hollywood studio, to put up $20 million for a film biography of controversial black leader Malcolm X, one of his heroes. Lee insisted on expensive foreign shooting in Cairo and Soweto, and now, not only was the $20 million from Warner gone but so was $8 million from other investors. To finish the movie, Lee put up his own $3 million up-front salary to pay, he hoped, all the production bills.

The crisis was not the first for Lee, whose experience as a moviemaker illustrates several realities about the American movie industry, not all of them flattering:

- Hollywood is the heart of the American movie industry, and it is difficult, if not impossible, for feature filmmakers to succeed outside of the Hollywood establishment.

- Hollywood, with rare exception, favors movies that follow themes that already have proven successful rather than taking risks on innovative, controversial themes.

- Fortunes come and go in Hollywood, even studio fortunes. Although Warner is a major studio and often flush with money, it was on an austerity binge when Spike Lee came back for more money in 1992.

- The American movie industry has been taken over by conglomerates, which, as in the case of Warner Brothers, a subsidiary of Time Warner, was being pressured in 1992 to maximize profits to see the parent company through a difficult economic period.

To hear Spike Lee tell it, his problem also was symptomatic of racism in the movie industry. Addressing the Los Angeles Advertising Club during the *Malcolm X* crisis, Lee, who is black, was blunt: "I think there's a ceiling on how much money Hollywood's going to spend on black films or films with a black theme."

Although studio executives would deny Lee's charge, his perceptions were born of experience in making five movies, all critically acclaimed and all profitable but all filmed on shoestring budgets and with little or no studio promotion.

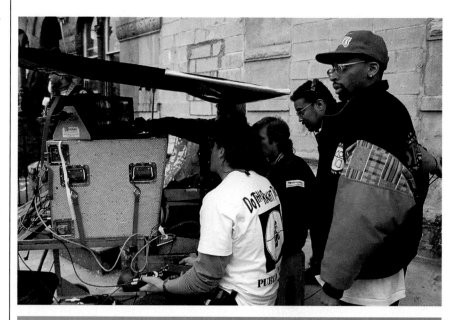

Public Enemy. Between movie projects, Spike Lee produces television commercials and videos, including the popular *Public Enemy.* There have been many slow periods between movies for Lee, who finds Hollywood money hard to come by for his work, even though he is acclaimed as one of his generation's great moviemakers. Lee blames racism among those who control Hollywood purse strings.

media | databank

....top-earning movies

These are the top-earning movies of all time, listed by domestic gross revenue. By some measures, *Jurassic Park* leads the list with global grosses exceeding $900 million.

Movie	Director	Domestic Gross	Year
Titanic	James Cameron	$471 million	1997
E.T.: The Extra-Terrestrial	Steven Spielberg	$407 million	1982
Jurassic Park	Steven Spielberg	$357 million	1993
Forrest Gump	Robert Zemeckis	$327 million	1994
Star Wars	George Lucas	$323 million	1977
The Lion King	Roger Allers and Rob Minkoff	$313 million	1994
Home Alone	Chris Columbus	$285 million	1990
Return of the Jedi	George Lucas	$264 million	1983
Jaws	Steven Spielberg	$260 million	1975
Batman	Leslie Martinson	$251 million	1989
Indiana Jones: Raiders of the Lost Ark	Steven Spielberg	$242 million	1981

examine budgets and production schedules in considering a loan request. It's common for them to send representatives to shooting sites to guard against budget overruns.

Major studios that are part of conglomerates can draw on the resources of their corporate parents. In 1952 giant MCA acquired the ailing Universal studio and plowed its recording business profits into the studio. Universal turned profitable and MCA became even stronger by having another profitable subsidiary. The Gulf and Western conglomerate later did the same with Paramount. Coca-Cola acquired Columbia in 1982 with a promise to help Columbia through the rough times that had beset the movie company.

In the 1980s several studios acquired new corporate parents, which made it easier to finance movies. The Japanese electronics giant Sony bought Columbia in 1989. At $3.4 billion, it was the biggest Japanese takeover of an American corporation in history. The size of the deal was a sign of the new resources Columbia could tap to make movies. By the early 1990s three of the largest U.S. studios were owned by giant foreign companies with the ability to generate cash from other enterprises to strengthen their new U.S. movie subsidiaries.

Investor Groups. Special investment groups sometimes are put together to fund movies for major studios. Among them is Silver Screen Partners, which provided millions of dollars in financing for Disney projects at a critical point in Disney's revival in the 1980s.

Disney Animation   Animator Walt Disney catapulted his success with Mickey Mouse (nee Steamboat Willie) movie cartoons, introduced in 1928, into full-length features with *Snow White and the Seven Dwarfs* nine years later. *Snow White* was a high-risk endeavor, costing $1.5 million to put together, a lot at the time, with nobody knowing how much market there would be. The public loved it, leading to new animinated Disney features, including such enduring favorites as *Pinocchio* and *Bambi*. Although Walt Disney died in 1966, the company's tradition in animation has lived on. The Christmas 1995 animated feature, *Toy Story,* was one of the season's blockbusters. That followed the unprecedented success of *Pocahontas,* which five months after its release was still showing in more than 200 screens. The company also has also expanded into a broad range of entertainment, including movies with mature themes from its Miramax subsidiary. In 1995, Disney turned a long relationship with ABC television into a full-fledged $19 billion merger that combined Cap Cities/ABC and Disney.

Less proven producers, or those whose track records are marred by budget overruns and loose production schedules, often seek financing from **risk investors,** who include venture capitalists, tax-shelter organizers and foreign distributors. Risk investors often take a bigger share of revenue in exchange for their bigger risk. It sometimes is a surprise who puts up the money. For *Willie Wonka and the Chocolate Factory,* it was Quaker Oats.

Banks.   To meet front-end production expenses, studios go to banks for loans against their assets, which include their production facilities and warehouses of vintage films awaiting rerelease. By bankrolling movies early in Hollywood's history, California-based **Bank of America** grew into one of the nation's biggest banks.

artistic versus budget issues

Movie-makers are expanding their supplemental incomes by charging other companies to use movie characters, themes and music for other purposes. This has raised questions about whether commercial imperatives have more priority than artistic considerations.

Merchandise Tie-Ins.   Fortunes can be made by licensing other companies to use characters and signature items from a movie. In one of the most successful **merchandise tie-ins,** 20th Century-Fox and George Lucas licensed Ewok dolls, R2D2 posters and even *Star Wars* bed sheets and pillowcases. By 1985, seven years after the movie's release, tie-ins had racked up sales of $2 billion. The licensing fee typically is 10 percent of the retail price of the merchandise. *Batman* tie-ins rang up $500 mil-

risk investors
Put money into projects at interest rates commensurate with risk.

Bank of America
Became giant institution by loaning money for movies.

merchandise tie-ins
Studio deals to profit from merchandise carrying movie names and logos.

When he was a kid, Michael Eisner wanted to be a doctor. It didn't work out. Today, as chief executive of the Walt Disney Company, Eisner is credited with the vision that put together a 1995 merger of Disney and CapCities/ABC into one of the world's largest media companies. It is a corporate marriage that financial observers agree makes sense. Disney's strength, producing media content, is being merged with ABC's strength, its delivery system.

An early upshot of the merger was Disney taking over Saturday morning programming on the ABC television network. Even that was more than it seemed. The newly merged company began using "Disney" as a brand to sell advertisers integrated marketing packages. Advertisers not only bought time on children's programming on Saturday mornings but also could get first dibs on Disney product promotions and licensing.

Where is Disney/ABC going? Speculation includes staging ABC-televised sports events at new arenas at Disney theme parks. Additional possibilities lie in the fact that the ESPN sports cable channel is part of the combined company.

Meanwhile, a string of successful Disney movies fuels the corporate coffers for new initiatives. *Pocahontas* and *Toy Story* were 1995 blockbusters. Even cutting-edge and niche 1995 movies from Disney subsidiaries, including *Dangerous Minds, Powder* and *While You Were Sleeping,* pulled in more than expected. The *Dangerous Minds* soundtrack, targeted at black Americans, swelled corporate coffers.

On another front, the financially uneven Disney theme parks have seen recent turnarounds.

The key to Disney's success under Eisner has been building the Disney brand name; cross-promoting Disney initiatives, like inscribing Disney's name on ABC television programming; extending product lines in additional directions; recycling Disney products, like reissuing classic animated Disney movies, such as *Cinderella,* on a schedule; repackaging existing products for new markets; and licensing the use of Disney logos to other companies for promotions, like the hamburger chains.

Michael Eisner. Media observers call Michael Eisner the most powerful person in Hollywood. Eisner, chief executive of Walt Disney Company, has presided over a string of successful but diverse movies, ranging in recent years from *The Lion King* to *Crimson Tide* and *Dead Presidents.* Even more significant, he engineered the 1995 Disney merger with Cap Cities/ABC, which gives Disney a new outlet for its creative output.

lion in sales in 1989, within six months of the movie's release, and Warner Brothers was earning 20 percent of the retail revenue on some products.

Toys. For the 1995 film *Batman Forever,* Warner Brothers let the Hasbro toy company dress the Riddler. Hasbro wanted tight pants, not the baggy ones in the script, so the Riddler action toy would look better. The result? The Riddler wore tight pants on screen. A recurrent report from *Pocahontas* animators is that their bosses ordered them to have the raccoon Meeko braid the Indian maiden's hair so Mattel could market Braided Beauty Pocahontas dolls.

Some movie-makers deny that the cart is ahead of the horse. Disney officials, for example, say Mattel had no hand in the script for *Pocahontas:* The script comes first, the toys second. Even so, movie-makers have huge financial incentives to do whatever it takes to assure success. Toy makers pay licensing fees, typically 10 percent of a toy's retail price. Disney earned $16 million, the record, for the 1994 movie *The Lion King.* In 1995 *Batman Forever* paraphernalia generated $13 million, *Pocahontas* $10 million. Power Ranger gear, tied into both the movie and the television series, has totaled $300 million, of which an estimated $30 million went back to Fox—a significant revenue source requiring hardly any studio expense.

Is this kind of commercialism undermining the artistic autonomy that normally is associated with creative enterprises like movie-making? This is the same elitist-populist issue that's at the heart of the ongoing debate about media content. At one extreme is the pristine elitist preference for creative forces to drive content oblivious to commercial considerations. At the other extreme is the laissez-faire populist belief that nothing's wrong with marketplace forces. Populists say that if a movie's box office suffers because toy-makers have had too much sway on script decisions, moviemakers will make future adjustments—and an appropriate balance will result eventually. Some elitists accept that argument but worry nonetheless about the commercial contamination that occurs in the meantime.

Music. Tie-ins are not new. Music, for example, was a revenue source for moviemakers even before talkies. Just about every early movie house had a piano player who kept one eye on the screen and hammered out supportive mood music, and sheet-music publishers bought the rights to print and sell the music to musicians who wanted to perform it on their own. This was no small enterprise. D. W. Griffith's *The Birth of a Nation* of 1915 had an accompanying score for a 70-piece symphony.

Today, music has assumed importance besides supporting the screen drama. It has become a movie-making profit center. *Saturday Night Fever* was the vehicle for a host of hit songs. *Urban Cowboy* was as much a film endeavor as a recording industry enterprise.

Product Placement. Moviemakers also have begun building commercial products into story lines in a subtle form of advertising. It was no coincidence that Tom Cruise downed Pepsi in *Top Gun.* Some movie producers work brand names into their movies for a fee. When the alien E.T. was coaxed out of hiding with a handful of candy, it was with Reese's Pieces. The Hershey company, which makes Reese's, paid to have its candy used. Sales soared in the next few months. Producers first offered the Mars company a chance for the candy to be M&Ms, but Mars executives were squeamish about their candy being associated with anything as ugly as E.T. They did not realize that movie-goers would fall in love with the little alien.

After *E.T.,* the product placement business boomed. Miller beer paid to have 21 references in *Bull Durham.* The same movie also included seven references for Budweiser, four for Pepsi, three for Jim Beam, and two for Oscar Meyer. A simple shot of a product in the foreground typically goes for $25,000 to $50,000. Some advertisers have paid $350,000 for multiple on-screen plugs.

Critics claim that **product placements** are sneaky. Some want them banned. Others say the word "advertisement" should be flashed on the screen when the products appear. Movie people, on the other hand, argue that using real products adds credibility. In the old days, directors assiduously avoided implicit endorsements. In a bar scene, the players would drink from cans marked "beer"—no brand name. Today, says Marvin Cohen, whose agency matches advertisers and movies, "A can that says 'Beer' isn't going to make it anymore." The unanswered question is how much product-placement deals affect artistic decisions.

movie censorship

STUDY PREVIEW The movie industry has devised a five-step rating system that alerts people to movies they might find objectionable. Despite problems inherent in any rating scheme, the NC-17, R, PG-13, P and G system has been more successful than earlier self-regulation attempts to quiet critics.

morality as an issue

It was no wonder in Victorian 1896 that a movie called *Dolorita in the Passion Dance* caused an uproar. There were demands that it be banned—the first but hardly last such call against a movie. In 1907 Chicago passed a law restricting objectionable motion pictures. State legislators across the land were insisting that something be done. Worried moviemakers created the **Motion Picture Producers and Distributors of America** in 1922 to clean up movies. **Will Hays,** a prominent Republican who was an elder in his Presbyterian church, was put in charge. Despite his efforts, movies with titillating titles continued to be produced. A lot of people shuddered at titles such as *Sinners in Silk* and *Red Hot Romance,* and Hollywood scandals were no help. Actor William Reid died from drugs. Fatty Arbuckle was tried for the drunken slaying of a young actress. When the Depression struck, many people linked the nation's economic failure with "moral bankruptcy." Movies were a target.

Under pressure, the movie industry adopted the **Motion Picture Production Code** in 1930, which codified the kind of thing that Will Hays had been doing. There was to be no naughty language, nothing sexually suggestive, and no bad guys going unpunished.

Church people led intensified efforts to clean up movies. The 1930 code was largely the product of Father **Daniel Lord,** a Roman Catholic priest, and **Martin Quigley,** a Catholic layperson. In 1934, after an apostolic delegate from the Vatican berated movies in an address to a New York church convention, United States bishops organized the **Legion of Decency,** which worked closely with the movie industry's code administrators.

The legion, which was endorsed by religious leaders of many faiths, moved on several fronts. Chapters sprouted in major cities. Some chapters boycotted theaters for six weeks if they showed condemned films. Members slapped stickers marked "We Demand Clean Movies" on car bumpers. Many theater owners responded,

product placement
When manufacturer pays for products to be used as props.

Motion Picture Producers and Distributors of America (MPPDA)
1922 Hollywood attempt to establish moral code for movies.

Will Hays
Led MPPDA.

Motion Picture Production Code
1930 Hollywood attempt to quiet critical moralists.

Daniel Lord
Priest who led morality crusade against Hollywood.

Martin Quigley
Partner of Father Daniel Lord.

Legion of Decency
Church listing of acceptable movies.

1896 Moralists outraged at *Dolorita in the Passion Dance.*

1907 Chicago ordinance banned objectionable movies.

1915 U.S. Supreme Court dismissed movies as

"circuses" unworthy of First Amendment protection.

1922 Motion Picture Producers and Distributors of America tried to eliminate objectionable content to quiet critics.

1934 Hollywood established mandatory production code to quiet critics.

1934 Roman Catholic leaders created Legion of Decency to deter people from certain movies.

1952 U.S. Supreme Court ruled First Amendment protects movies in *The Miracle* case.

1960 Hollywood created rating system to quiet critics.

vowing to show only approved movies. Meanwhile, the industry itself added teeth to its own code. Any members of the Motion Picture Producers and Distributors of America who released movies without approval were fined $25,000.

movies and changing mores

In the late 1940s the influence of the policing agencies began to wane. The 1948 Paramount court decision was one factor. It took major studios out of the exhibition business. As a result, many movie houses could rent films from independent producers, many of whom never subscribed to the code. A second factor was the movie **The Miracle,** which became a First Amendment issue in 1952. The movie was about a simple woman who was sure St. Joseph had seduced her. Her baby, she felt, was Christ. Critics wanted the movie banned as sacrilege, but the Supreme Court sided with exhibitors on grounds of free expression. Film-makers became a bit more venturesome.

At the same time, with mores changing in the wake of World War II, the influence of the Legion of Decency was slipping. In 1953 the legion condemned *The Moon Is Blue,* which had failed to receive code approval for being a bit racy. Despite the legion's condemnation, the movie was a box-office smash. The legion contributed to its own undoing with a series of incomprehensible recommendations. It condemned significant movies such as Ingmar Bergman's *The Silence* and Michelangelo Antonioni's *Blow Up* in the early 1960s while endorsing the likes of *Godzilla vs. the Thing.*

current movie code

Movie-makers sensed the change in public attitudes in the 1950s but realized that audiences still wanted guidance they could trust on movies. Also, there remained some moralist critics. In 1968 several industry organizations established a new rating system. No movies were banned. Fines were out. Instead, a board representing movie producers, distributors, importers and exhibitors, the **Classification and Rating Administration Board,** placed movies in categories to help parents determine what movies their children should see. The categories, as modified through the years, are:

- **G:** Suitable for general audiences and all ages.

- **PG:** Parental guidance suggested because some content may be considered unsuitable for preteens.

- **PG-13:** Parental guidance especially suggested for children younger than 13 because of partial nudity, swearing or violence.

- **R:** Restricted for anyone younger than 17 unless accompanied by an adult.

- **NC-17:** No children under age 17 should be admitted.

Whether the rating system is widely used by parents is questionable. One survey found two out of three parents couldn't name a movie their teenagers had seen in recent weeks.

chapter wrap-up

Movies passed their 100th birthday in the 1980s as an entertainment medium with an especially strong following among young adults and teenagers. From the beginning, movies were a glamorous medium, but beneath the glitz were dramatic struggles between competing businesspeople whose success depended on catching the public's fancy.

The most dramatic period for the movie industry came at midcentury. Fanatic anti-Communists in Congress intimidated movie-makers into backing away from cutting-edge explorations of social and political issues, and then a government antitrust action forced the major studios to break up their operations. Meanwhile, television was siphoning people away from the box office. Movie attendance fell from 90 million to 16 million per week.

It took a few years, but the movie industry regrouped. More than ever, political activism and social inquiry have become themes in American movies. Movie-makers met the threat from television by becoming a primary supplier of TV programming. In response to the antitrust orders, the big studios sold their movie houses and concentrated on financing independent productions and then distributing them. In short, the movie industry has proved itself remarkably resilient and adaptive.

The movie industry has three primary components: production, marketing and exhibition. Most movie fans follow production, which involves stars, screenplays and big money. Major studios control most production, either by producing movies themselves or by putting up the money for independent producers to create movies, which the studios then market. Marketing, called "distribution" in the trade, involves promotion and profitable after-markets like television and home video sales. Since the 1948 antitrust action, exhibition has been largely independent of Hollywood, although the corporations that own the major studios have again begun moving into the movie-house business.

> **_Miracle_ case**
> U.S. Supreme Court ruled First Amendment protected movies from censorship.
>
> **Classification and Rating Administration Board**
> Rates movies on G, PG, PG-13, R, NC-17 scale.

Throughout their history, movies have been scrutinized by moralists who fear their influence. Today, the critics seem fairly satisfied with the NC-17, R, PG-13, PG and G rating system that alerts parents to movies that they might find unsuitable for their children.

questions for review

1. Why do movies as a mass medium have such a strong impact on people?

2. How does the technological basis of movies differ from the other primary mass media?

3. Why did movies begin fading in popularity in the late 1940s?

4. What was Hollywood's initial response to television?

5. What is the relationship between Hollywood and the television industry today?

6. How has the movie exhibition business changed over the years?

7. How do movie-makers raise cash for their expensive, high-risk projects?

8. How has Hollywood responded to criticism of movie content?

questions for critical thinking

1. How would you describe the success of these innovations—Cinerama, CinemaScope, 3-D and Smell-o-vision—in the movie industry's competition against television?

2. Epic spectaculars marked one period of moviemaking, social causes another, sex and violence another. Have these genres had lasting effect?

3. Can you explain why films geared to baby boomers, sometimes called teen films, dominated Hollywood in the 1970s and well into the 1980s? Why are they less important now?

4. How did Eadweard Muybridge demonstrate persistence of vision, and how did that lead to early movie-making? Cite the contributions of William Dickson, George Eastman and the Lumière brothers.

5. Explain how these three developments forced a major change in Hollywood in the 1950s: the 1947 Thomas hearings, the 1948 Paramount court decision, and the advent of television.

6. Once the number of movie exhibitors in the nation was measured in terms of movie houses. Today it is measured by the number of screens. Why?

7. Explain how moviemakers finance their movies. What are the advantages and disadvantages of each method?

8. What has been the role of these institutions in shaping movie content: Motion Picture Producers and Distributors of America, Legion of Decency, and Classification and Rating Administration Board?

9. Describe government censorship of movies in the United States.

for further learning

Thomas W. Bohn and Richard L. Stromgren. *Light and Shadows: A History of Motion Pictures* (Alfred Publishing, 1975). This is a lively, comprehensive examination.

Larry Ceplair and Steven Englund. *The Inquisition in Hollywood: Politics in the Film Community, 1930–1960* (Doubleday, 1980). Ceplair and Englund examine the 1947 congressional smear that depopulated Hollywood of some of its most talented screenwriters and directors.

Norman K. Denzin. *Hollywood Shot by Shot: Alcoholism in American Cinema* (de Gruyter, 1991). Denzin, a sociologist, tracks Hollywood portrayals of alcoholism from 1932 to 1989 for trends to interpret how they came to be and their effects.

Joan Didion. "In Hollywood." *The White Album* (Pocket, 1979). Didion discredits the notion that the major studios are dying with the emergence of independent producers. The studios both bankroll and distribute independent films and, she says, make lots of money in the process.

Douglas Gomery. *The Hollywood Studio System* (St. Martin's, 1986). Gomery examines the movie industry of the 1930s and 1940s, a period when Hollywood moved into mass production, global marketing and a centralized distribution system.

Thomas Guback. "The Evolution of the Motion Picture Theater Business in the 1980s." *Journal of Communication* (Spring 1987), pages 70–77. Why are so many new movie screens being built in the United States even though a smaller percentage of the population goes to movies? Guback lays out an array of economic factors from popcorn prices to new vertical integration schemes.

Garth Jowett and James M. Linton. *Movies as Mass Communication* (Sage, 1980). Jowett and Linton examine the social impact of movies and the economic determinants of the movie industry in this brief, scholarly book.

Lary May. *Screening Out the Past: The Birth of Mass Culture and the Motion Picture Industry* (Oxford University Press, 1980). A thoroughly documented early history.

Victor Navasky. *Naming Names* (Viking, 1980). This is another treatment of the congressional investigation into the film industry.

Murray Schumach. *The Face on the Cutting Room Floor: The Story of Movie and Television Censorship* (Da Capo, 1974).

for keeping up to date

People serious about movies as art will find *American Film* and *Film Comment* valuable sources of information.

Trade journals include *Variety* and *Hollywood Reporter.*

Among consumer magazines with significant movie coverage are *Premiere, Entertainment Weekly* and *Rolling Stone.*

The *Wall Street Journal, Business Week, Forbes* and *Fortune* track the movie industry.

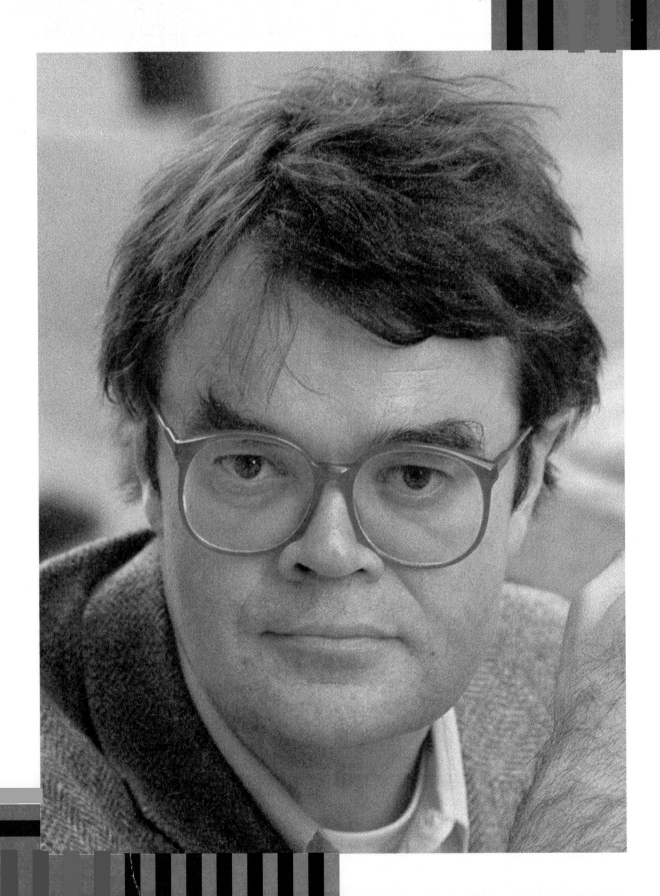

radio

**in this chapter
you will learn:**

- Radio reaches people everywhere with opinion, news, entertainment and advertising.

- Radio signals move through the air by piggy-backing on already existing electromagnetic waves.

- Most American radio operates in the private sector of the economy and relies on advertising.

- Radio in the United States has an entertainment rather than an educational thrust.

- News is becoming less important in the programming mix of U.S. radio.

- National networks have been influential since the 1920s in shaping American radio.

- Radio is regulated by the federal government. So is television.

- New technology may trigger programming innovations.

With his butterscotch voice, **Garrison Keillor** purred Hank Snow's "Hello Love" into a radio microphone one Saturday night in 1974. Twenty years after live drama, comedy and theater had departed the airwaves, replaced by disc jockeys and records, Keillor was inaugurating a radio show that brought back the good old days for many Americans and intrigued a whole younger generation with gentle stories about Norwegian bachelor farmers, poems and homey music.

The show, **"A Prairie Home Companion,"** soon went national, attracting 4 million listeners a week, becoming a cult hit among sophisticated noncommercial radio listeners, and landing Keillor on the cover of *Time* magazine. Except for a two-year sabbatical, Keillor has been on the air ever since with stories from his fictional **Lake Wobegon,** somewhere in Minnesota, "where all the men are strong, all the women are good looking and all the children are above average." Today, the two-hour broadcasts remain a staple at 350 noncommercial radio stations around the country on Saturday nights—an unlikely time, it would seem, to amass great numbers of people around their radios.

A lot of "APHC," as it's called in the trade, is unlikely. There are the tongue-in-cheek commercials from Wobegon merchants and the 20-minute monologues about Lake Wobegon's Lutherans and Catholics, old Plymouths, and picnics at the lake.

The success of Garrison Keillor's show may rest on its nostalgic feel. As in radio's early days, the show is aired live before an audience. It has spontaneity. It's down-home, not slick— just like local radio used to be. It has a powerful intimacy and immediacy, putting listeners' imaginations to work as they conjure up impressions from the drowsy voices of

Live Radio. Garrison Keillor and his radio company perform "A Prairie Home Companion" on stage live at the old Globe Theater in downtown St. Paul, Minnesota, before a studio audience. The show, reminiscent of old-time radio, began in 1974. Quickly a cult hit, the show always sold out the 900-seat theater, and 4 million people tuned in weekly. Now slightly updated and revised, the show remains a romanticized link to America's small-town, agrarian past.

Keillor and his companions and their old-fashioned sound effects.

Lake Wobegon, "the little town that time forgot and the decades cannot improve," is everybody's hometown. It is rustic, cozy, warm—a refuge in Americana. It is also radio at its traditional old-time best.

In this chapter, you will learn that radio's heyday was dominated by live bands, drama and comedy, like Garrison Keillor's show today. You will also learn why radio dropped all that in the 1950s, almost instantly switching to canned music and formulaic disc jockey patter. And you will learn where radio is likely headed, which probably is not back to Lake Wobegon.

significance of radio

(STUDY PREVIEW)   Radio is an important medium for opinion, news, entertainment and advertising. The portability of radio means it is everywhere in our daily lives.

radio as a motivator

Radio can motivate people to action. When members of Congress were mulling a 51 percent pay hike for themselves in 1988, radio talk show host **Jerry Williams** decided it was time for another Boston tea party. He stirred his Boston listeners to send thousands of tea bags to Congress as a not-so-subtle reminder of the 1773 colonial frustration over taxes that led to the Revolutionary War. Talk show hosts elsewhere joined the campaign, and Congress, swamped with tea bags, scuttled the pay raise proposal.

Recording companies know the power of radio. Without radio stations playing new music, a new record release is almost certainly doomed. Airplay spurs people to go out and buy a record.

Advertisers value radio to reach buyers. Only newspapers, television and direct mail have a larger share of the advertising dollars spent nationwide, and radio's share is growing. From $7 billion in 1986, radio ad revenue soared almost 30 percent to beyond $11 billion in 1998.

ubiquity of radio

Radio is everywhere. The signals piggyback on naturally occurring waves in the electromagnetic spectrum and reach every nook and cranny. Hardly a place in the world is beyond the reach of radio.

There are 6.6 radio receivers on average in U.S. households. Nineteen of 20 automobiles come with radios. People wake up with clock radios, jog with headset radios, party with boom boxes and commute with car radios. People listen to sports events on the radio, even if they're in the stadium. Thousands of people build their day around commentators like Paul Harvey. Millions rely on hourly newscasts to be up to date. People develop personal attachments to their favorite announcers and disc jockeys.

Statistics abound about radio's importance:

- **Arbitron,** a company that surveys radio listenership, says teenagers and adults average 22 hours a week listening to radio.

- People in the United States own 520 million radio sets. Looked at another way, radios outnumber people 2:1.

- More people receive their morning news from radio than from any other medium.

scope of the radio industry

More than 11,000 radio stations are on the air in the United States. Communities as small as a few hundred people have stations.

Although significant as a $11 billion a year industry, the financial health of radio is uneven. The big radio chains, four with more than 100 stations, do spectacularly. In 1997, Jacor, for example, had second-quarter net revenue of $186.8 million—its best quarter ever, triple a year earlier. But many stations struggle, especially AM. In 1991, a particularly bad year, 153 stations signed off for the final time.

The potential for profit drives the price of some stations to astronomical levels. A sampler of 1997 sales:

- Alabama: Little Rock: WAGG-AM, WENN-FM, WBHK-FM, WBHJ—$32 million.
- California: Salinas and Monterey: KDON-AM, KDON-FM, KTOM-AM and FM, KRQC-FM and KOCN-FM—$23.7 million.
- Ohio: Dayton and Springfield: WGTZ-FM, WING-AM and FM—$18.4 million.
- Pennsylvania: Allentown: WFMZ-FM—$26 million.

Arbitron
Radio listener survey company.

radio technology and regulation

1895 Guglielmo Marconi transmitted message by radio.

1906 Lee De Forest created audion tube that allowed voice transmission.

1912 David Sarnoff used radio to learn news of

Titanic disaster, putting radio in public eye.

1920 Westinghouse puts KDKA, Pittsburgh, on air as first licensed commercial station.

1927 Congress created Federal Radio Communi-

cations Commission to regulate radio.

1934 Congress created Federal Communications Commission to regulate radio, telephone, television.

1939 Edwin Armstrong put FM station on air.

1967 Congress established Corporation for Public Broadcasting to create a national noncommercial system.

technical development

(STUDY PREVIEW) Human mastery of the electromagnetic spectrum, through which radio is possible, is only a century old. In 1895 an Italian physicist and inventor, Guglielmo Marconi, was the first to transmit a message through the air. Later came voice transmissions and better sound.

electromagnetic spectrum

Radio waves are part of the physical universe. They have existed forever, moving through the air and the ether. Like light waves, they are silent—a part of a continuing spectrum of energies—the **electromagnetic spectrum.** As early as 1873, physicists speculated that the electromagnetic spectrum existed, but it was an Italian nobleman, **Guglielmo Marconi,** who made practical application of the physicists' theories.

Young Marconi became obsessed with the possibilities of the electromagnetic spectrum and built equipment that could ring a bell by remote control—no strings, no wires. The Marconi device shaped a radio wave in such a way that another device could intercept it and decipher a message from the wave's shape. In 1895, when he was 21, Marconi used his wireless method to transmit codes for more than a mile on his father's Bologna estate. Marconi patented his invention in England, and his mother, a well-connected Irish woman, arranged British financing to set up the Marconi Wireless Telegraph Company. Soon ocean-going ships were equipped with Marconi radiotelegraphy equipment to communicate at sea, even when they were beyond the horizon, something never possible before. Marconi made a fortune.

transmitting voices

Breakthroughs came quickly. In 1906 a message was sent across the Atlantic. In 1906 **Lee De Forest,** a promoter who fancied himself an inventor, created what he

David Sarnoff
His monitoring of the sinking of the *Titanic* familiarized people with radio; later NBC president.

electromagnetic spectrum
Energy waves on which radio messages are piggybacked.

Guglielmo Marconi
Produced the first wireless transmission.

Lee De Forest
Inventor whose projects included the audion tube.

audion tube
Made voice transmission possible.

Reginald Fessenden
First radio program, 1906.

Who Invented Radio? Numerous theorists conceived of wireless transmission ahead of the Irish-Italian inventor Guglielmo Marconi. A dentist, Mahlon Loomis, detected signals between two mountains in Virginia in 1866 and won a patent for wireless telegraphy in 1872. Scottish mathematician James Maxwell and German physicist Heinrich Hertz did important theorizing. Who, then, invented radio? Marconi became interested in radio in 1894 and succeeded in a wireless transmission in 1895, and he aggressively exploited the potential of his experiments into a commercial success that tightly linked his name with the invention of radio in the public's mind. But admirers of a reclusive but brilliant Croatia-born American scientist, Nikola Tesla, have mounted a campaign for him to be recognized as the inventor of radio. Among their evidence is a 1943 U.S. Supreme Court decision recognizing that Tesla had transmitted on the electromagnetic spectrum before Marconi. The debate remains open, however, whether Tesla really conceived of the electromagnetic spectrum as a vehicle for transmitting messages. Tesla's focus at the time was wireless transmission of electricity.

Nikola Tesla

called the **audion tube** to make voice transmission possible. Some say he stole the underlying technology from Canadian inventor **Reginald Fessenden.** Whatever the truth of the matter, it was Fessenden who broadcasted the first radio program, also in 1906. From Brant Rock, Massachusetts, where he had a laboratory, Fessenden played some recorded Christmas carols, shocking wireless operators on ships at sea.

Bounce-Back Effect. When AM electromagnetic waves are transmitted, many of them follow the contour of the earth, which extends their range beyond the line-of-sight from the transmitter. Some AM waves go upward, and many of these are bounced back to earth by reflective layers in the ionosphere, which further extends a station's range. The bounce-back effect is weaker during the day when the sun warms the ionosphere and reduces its reflective properties. FM transmissions have a shorter range than AM because the signals move in straight lines and tend not to adhere to the earth's contours. Also, upward-moving FM waves pass through the ionosphere rather than being reflected back.

technical development   **169**

Guglielmo Marconi

Unmodulated Wave. If you could see electromagnetic waves, they would look like the cross-section of a ripple moving across a pond, except they would be steady and unending. Guglielmo Marconi figured out how to hitch a ride on these waves to send messages in 1895.

Lee De Forest

Amplitude-Modulated Wave. Lee De Forest discovered how to adjust the height of electromagnetic waves to coincide with the human voice and other sounds. De Forest's audion tube made voice transmission possible, including an Enrico Caruso concert in 1910.

Edwin Armstrong

Frequency-Modulated Wave. FM radio transmissions squeeze and expand electromagnetic waves without changing their height. Edwin Armstrong introduced this form of broadcasting, which had superior clarity and fidelity, in the 1930s. Not even lightning interferes with transmission.

"Radio" Becomes a Household Word. When the *Titanic* sank in 1912, newspapers relied on young radio operator David Sarnoff for information on what was happening in the mid-Atlantic. For 72 hours Sarnoff sat at his primitive receiver, which happened to be on exhibit in a department store, to pick up details from rescue ships. The newspaper coverage of the disaster made "radio" a household word, which paved the way for consumer acceptance over the next few years.

Instead of the dots and dashes of Morse code, suddenly there was music. De Forest, however, took the limelight with show-off broadcasts from the Eiffel Tower and other stunts. In 1910, De Forest clearly demonstrated radio's potential as an entertainment medium with a magnificent performance by the tenor Enrico Caruso from the New York Metropolitan Opera House.

Technical development stalled during World War I. Military and civilian research concentrated on other things, and work on the newfangled wireless was put off. After the war, Americans were wary as never before about the dangers of dependence on foreign goods. They worried about being cut off if another war disrupted transoceanic commerce. The worry extended to patents, even those in friendly countries, like Marconi's British wireless patent. At the urging of the federal government, three American companies—General Electric, Westinghouse and American Telephone & Telegraph—pooled their resources in 1919 and bought Marconi's American subsidiary and patents. Although the consortium broke up within a few years, it helped to refine the technology further. In this same period, physics department experiments at many U.S. colleges added to the technology, which gave further impetus to radio's development.

Static-free transmission was developed by **Edwin Armstrong,** a Columbia University researcher. In 1939 Armstrong built an experimental station in New Jersey using a new system called **frequency modulation,** FM for short. FM's system, piggybacking sound on airwaves, was different from the older **amplitude modulation,** or AM method. In time, Armstrong developed FM stereo with two soundtracks, one for each ear, duplicating the sensation of hearing a performance live.

Edwin Armstrong
Invented FM as alternative transmission method.
frequency modulation
FM
amplitude modulation
AM

characteristics of american radio

(STUDY PREVIEW) The radio industry established itself early in the private, free enterprise sector of the economy. It chose entertainment, rather than news, information and education, as its main programming thrust.

radio in the private sector

A Westinghouse engineer in Pittsburgh, **Frank Conrad,** fiddled with radiotelegraphy in his home garage, playing music as he experimented. People with homemade receivers liked what they heard from Conrad's transmitter, and soon he had a following. When Conrad's Westinghouse bosses learned that he had become a local celebrity, they saw profit in building receivers that consumers could buy at $10 a set and take home to listen to. To encourage sales of the receivers, Westinghouse built a station to provide regular programming of news, sports and music—mostly music. That station, **KDKA,** became the nation's first licensed commercial station in 1920.

The licensing of KDKA by the government was important because it demonstrated the United States' commitment to placing radio in the private sector. In Europe, broadcasting was a government monopoly. KDKA's entertainment programming also sent American broadcasting in a certain direction. In many other countries, radio was used mostly for education and high culture, not mass entertainment.

role of advertising

Westinghouse never expected KDKA itself to make money, only to spur sales of $10 Westinghouse home receivers. The economic base of KDKA and the rest of American broadcasting changed in 1922 when **WEAF** in New York accepted $50 from a real estate developer and allowed him 10 minutes to pitch his new Long Island apartments. Then the Gimbel's department store tried radio advertising. Within months, companies were clamoring for air time. The Lucky Strike Orchestra produced programs, as did the Taystee Loafers from the Taystee bread company, and the A&P Gypsies, the Goodrich Silvertown Orchestra, and the Interwoven Pair from the sock company.

In those first few years of the 1920s, American radio took on these distinctive traits:

* Private rather than state ownership of the broadcast system.

* An entertainment thrust to programming that emphasized popular culture.

* An economic foundation based on selling time to advertisers who needed to reach a mass audience of consumers.

noncommercial radio

American radio was already solidly established as a commercially supported medium when Congress established a regulatory agency in 1927, the **Federal Radio Commission.** To assure that radio's potential as an educational medium was not lost, the FRC reserved some licenses for noncommercial stations. These went mostly to

---

Frank Conrad
Pioneer whose work led to KDKA.

KDKA
First licensed commercial station.

WEAF
New York station that carried first commercial.

noncommercial radio
Stations licensed on condition that they not carry commercials.

Federal Radio Commission
Original government regulatory agency for radio.

stations operated by colleges and other institutions that would finance their operation without advertising. Today, about 10 percent of the nation's radio stations hold noncommercial licenses. Many of these are low-power stations that colleges operate as training facilities.

In 1967 Congress passed the **Public Broadcasting Act** to create a national noncommercial radio system. Every major city and most college towns have a public radio station, most of which carry specialized programs that do not have large enough audiences to attract advertisers. Classical music, news and documentaries are programming mainstays at most public stations.

Many noncommercial stations are affiliates of **National Public Radio,** a network that went on the air in 1970. NPR was created with support from the **Corporation for Public Broadcasting,** a quasi-governmental agency that channels federal funds into the national public radio system. Two NPR news programs, "Morning Edition" and "All Things Considered," have earned a loyal following. NPR offers about 50 hours of programming a week to affiliate stations. Beginning in 1981 American Public Radio of St. Paul, Minnesota, also offered programs to noncommercial stations. Today, APR has been subsumed by **Public Radio International,** which is a major alternative and also a complementary programming source to NPR.

Neither noncommercial stations nor their networks carry advertising, but supporting foundations and corporations are acknowledged on the air as underwriters. In recent years some of these acknowledgements have come to resemble advertising but without exhortations, which the FCC prohibits.

radio as entertainment

(STUDY PREVIEW) Radio stations today are known by a wide range of formats, each geared to attracting narrow segments of the population. In earlier times, radio stations sought broader mass audiences with programs that had wide appeal. The programming was a culturally unifying influence on the nation. Today's more segmented programming came about when radio began losing the mass audience to television in the 1950s.

early mass programming

In the early days, most stations were on the air at night with hotel tea-time music. It was pleasant programming, offensive to no one. Sandwiched among the **potted-palm music,** as it was called, were occasional soloists, poets and public speakers. As broadcasting expanded into the daytime, stations used more recordings, which introduced a bit more variety. In the late 1920s, evening programming became more varied. Potted-palm music gave way to symphonies and big bands. Guy Lombardo, the Dorsey Brothers and Benny Goodman all found that radio helped promote their record sales. In Nashville, WSM built a country music program on the Saturday night Southern tradition of picking, singing and gossiping with your neighbors on the courthouse yard. In 1927 the program was named the "Grand Ole Opry."

With more varied programs, radio attracted a true mass audience in the 1930s. Fred Waring and His Pennsylvanians demonstrated that variety shows could attract large audiences. Jack Benny, Milton Berle and Bob Hope did the same with comedy. Drama series were introduced—murders, soap operas, Westerns, thrillers. Quiz

Public Broadcasting Act
Channels federal dollars to develop national noncommercial radio, television system.

National Public Radio
Network linking noncommercial stations.

Corporation for Public Broadcasting
Quasi-public agency to administer federal funds for noncommercial radio, television.

Public Radio International
Alternative noncommercial radio programming source.

potted-palm music
Popular, inoffensive early programming.

media databank

····radio formats

Commercial radio stations, dependent on advertising revenue, change formats to find the large, profitable niches of listeners. Classification of formats is tricky because so many overlap. By the mid-1990s, however, it was clear that a mix of adult and light rock, usually called "adult contemporary," had displaced country, the 1980s leader. The leading formats:

Format	Stations	Percentage
Adult contemporary	2,014	18.3
Top 40	1,310	11.9
News and talk	1,607	14.6
Country	1,211	11.0
Album-oriented rock	1,001	9.1
Urban contemporary	968	8.8
Oldies	693	6.3
Spanish	451	4.1
Adult standard	385	3.5
Classic rock	363	3.3
Easy listening	275	2.5
Adult alternative	231	2.1
Religious	220	2.0
Classical	188	1.7

media

online

R&R: The radio and records trade journal offers playlists and station ratings online, as well as links to many station homepages. www.rronline.com

KHMX-FM, Houston: You start with a map of Mix 96.5's facilities and click your way to the studios and offices. Includes a mini-bite of the morning show in Real Audio. www.khmx.com

WKDF-FM, Nashville, Tennessee: From one KDF link you can request your favorite music over the air. By clicking a skull, you can see what's requested to death. www.edge.net/kdf/

WFLN-FM, Philadelphia: One of the nation's premiere commercial classical stations includes its history and mission statement on its web site. www.beethoven.com/wfln/

shows became part of the mix. In 1940 Texaco began sponsoring Saturday matinees of the Metropolitan Opera from New York, which remains the longest continuously sponsored program on radio.

The early radio programming, geared to attract large audiences, was a culturally unifying factor for the nation. Almost everyone had a common experience in the radio programs of the time.

formats for specific audiences

Comedies, dramas and quiz shows moved to television beginning in the late 1940s, and so did the huge audience that radio had cultivated. The radio networks, losing advertisers to television, scaled back what they offered stations. As the number of listeners dropped, local stations switched more to recorded music, which was far cheaper than producing programs.

Although most stations in the pre-television period offered diversity, a few stations emphasized certain kinds of programming. Country music stations dotted the South. Some stations carried only religious programs. In the 1950s, Cleveland announcer Alan Freed introduced rock 'n' roll, which became the fare at hundreds of stations and began wide-scale fragmentation in radio programming. Today, hardly any station tries to offer something for everyone, but everyone can find something on the radio to like. There is a format for everyone.

After Freed came the **Top 40** format, in which the day's top songs were repeated in rotation. The wizard of radio formatting, **Gordon McLendon,** perfected the format at **KLIF** in Dallas, Texas, by mixing fast-paced newscasts, disc jockey chatter, lively commercials and promotional jingles and hype with the music. It was catchy, almost hypnotizing—and widely imitated.

McLendon also designed beautiful music as a format at **KABL,** San Francisco, in 1959; all-news at **XTRA,** Tijuana, Mexico, aimed at southern California, in 1961; all-classified ads at **KADS,** Los Angeles, 1967. In all of his innovations, McLendon was firm about a strict structure. In Top 40, for example, there were no deviations from music in rotation, news every 20 minutes, naming the station by call letters twice between songs, upbeat jingles and no dead-pan commercials. McLendon's classified-ad format bombed, but the others have survived.

Radio's fragmented programming has reduced its role as a culturally unifying factor. Almost everyone listens to radio, but listening to a hard-rock station gives a person hardly anything in common with people who listen to public affairs-oriented stations or soul stations or beautiful-music stations. Today, the shared experience of radio does not extend beyond narrow segments of the population.

Gordon McLendon. The views of radio programming guru Gordon McLendon were widely sought in the 1950s. It was McLendon who created the Top 40 and all-news formats that enabled radio to survive massive audience losses to television.

radio news

(STUDY PREVIEW)   Radio became a significant news source for many Americans during World War II. Today, a few large cities have at least one excellent all-news station, but in general radio has declined as a news medium. Listener call-in programs have become a popular format that has potential as a forum on public issues.

pioneer radio news

Radio news preceded radio stations. In November 1916, Lee De Forest arranged with a New York newspaper, the *American,* to broadcast election returns. Hundreds of people tuned in with home-built receivers to an experimental transmission to hear De Forest proclaim: "Charles Evans Hughes will be the next President of the United States." In November 1920, when KDKA in Pittsburgh became the nation's first licensed commercial station, it began by reporting returns in the Harding-Cox presidential race as they were being counted at the Pittsburgh *Post.* This time radio had the winner right.

The Detroit *News* began regular newscasts with its **WWJ** a few months later. While the *News* and some other newspapers built radio stations to promote interest in news and strengthen circulation, the newspaper industry was not enthusiastic. Worried that radio might steal away readers, newspapers tried to deny stations access to faraway news from the Associated Press. In 1933 the AP, which was controlled by newspapers, finally offered its news to stations only if they agreed to limit newscasts to five minutes twice a day. Furthermore, the morning newscast could be aired only after 9:30 a.m. and the evening newscast only after 9 p.m. to protect morning and evening newspaper sales. No single story could exceed 30 words. Bulletins on breaking stories were banned, as were commercial sponsors for newscasts. The restrictions fell apart within two years as the NBC and CBS networks set up their own news-gathering organizations. CBS World News Roundup began in 1938, with correspondents reporting from five European cities.

Top 40
Format that replays pop records.
Gordon McLendon
Program innovator; devised Top 40, all-news, beautiful music formats.
KLIF
Top 40 innovator, Dallas.
KABL
Beautiful music innovator, San Francisco.
XTRA
All-news innovator, Tijuana, Mexico.
KADS
All-ad innovator, Los Angeles.
WWJ
First regular newscasts, Detroit.

Spanning Generations.
Newscaster and commentator Paul Harvey, reportedly the highest-paid person in radio, survived the change from radio's heyday to today's specialized programming with his touch for the ironic. His clipped delivery and signature items, such as his drawn-out "good day," have made his ABC programs a fixture in the lives of millions of people.

Radio news came into its own in World War II, when the networks sent more correspondents abroad. Americans, eager for news from Europe, developed the habit of listening to the likes of **Edward R. Murrow** for first-person accounts of what was happening. Murrow's reporting compared with the best that newspapers were offering. Consider the potency of this 1940 Murrow report from London: "Today I went to buy a hat. My favorite shop had gone, blown to bits. The windows of my shoe store were blown out. I decided to have a haircut. The windows of the barbershop were gone, but the Italian barber was still doing business. 'Some day', he said, 'we smile again, but the food it doesn't taste so good since being bombed.'"

mclendon influence

Local radio news improved after the war when reporters began using tape recorders to interview and to capture the sounds of the news. It was the innovation of tape that gave Gordon McLendon's KLIF newscasts the you-are-there quality that helped propel the station to the top of the ratings in the 1950s. After XTRA in Tijuana turned profitable in the early 1960s, McLendon took over a Chicago station, renamed it WNUS and converted it to all-news. He used the same low-budget approach that worked at XTRA—a skeletal announcing staff reading wire copy.

Taking notice, the Group W broadcasting chain began converting to all-news in 1965, but with strong local coverage by station reporters. CBS followed in 1967 with some of the stations it owned. Unlike McLendon, Group W and CBS went beyond spot news and invested in well-known commentators and included features. It worked. An estimated 35 percent of all New York listeners tuned in to either Group W's WINS or CBS's WCBS at least once a week. So successful were Group W and CBS that McLendon surrendered the all-news market in Chicago to CBS's WBBM and in Los Angeles to Group W's KFWB in 1968.

All-news stations have prospered in a few major cities. New York, Los Angeles, Chicago and some other cities have sustained all-news stations with large reporting staffs that provide on-scene competitive coverage. Such news operations maintain the tradition of radio news at its best—instantaneous, informed and intelligent coverage of a sort that other media cannot match.

In many markets, however, some stations that call themselves all-news are all-news in name only and provide scant local coverage amid piped-in network newscasts, like the 24-hour CNN audio network. So-called all-news stations in many markets actually run mostly listener call-in and lengthy interviews, and they originate less local coverage than some competitors who, although not all-news, have kept a stronger commitment to news.

decline of radio news

When the United States launched the air war against Iraq on January 16, 1991, ABC radio did not even try to cover what was happening. That whole evening, the network plugged its radio affiliates into the audio of the ABC television coverage being anchored by Peter Jennings. It was a telling moment, and a sad one, in the history of American radio as a news medium. Instead of leading the way in originating coverage, ABC and other traditional radio networks gave a poor showing of themselves throughout the Persian Gulf war, mostly picking up audio from official briefings and sandwiching it inside brief scripts rewritten from the AP and other news services.

> **Edward R. Murrow**
> Eyewitness World War II accounts from London.

By the 1990s, radio had become primarily an entertainment medium with low-cost programming based on playing records. Even the historic KDKA in Pittsburgh, which aired the first news reports as early as 1920, had by 1991 suspended local newscasts after 8 p.m. Many metropolitan stations had cut news to minimal local staffs, sometimes using just one or two people who anchored brief newscasts during commuting hours, and relied for global and national coverage on brief network summaries. Some stations don't even commit a person full-time to local news.

Nor do the commercial networks put much energy into gathering news for radio. Former congressional correspondent Edward Connors, writing in *Washington Journalism Review* in 1991, reported that radio network reporters in the nation's capital seldom go out after a story any more. Instead they spend most of their time in studios, picking up audio feeds and watching coverage of scheduled events on the C-SPAN public affairs television network. ABC was down to four full-time radio reporters in Washington. CBS had only two. Every radio network except CBS subscribes to an audio-feed service which, for fees starting at $31,000 a year, provides raw coverage from which newscasters extract a few sentences to combine with boiled-down copy from the AP.

This remote coverage lacks the advantages of having a reporter at the scene. For example, when confirmation hearings for Supreme Court Justice David Souter were under way in 1990, newscasters in remote studios had no idea from their audio feeds that a demonstration had broken out in the back of the hearing room. They heard only the official exchange from microphones fixed to pick up senators' questions and Souter's responses. Incredible as it seems, only one radio reporter was at the hearing: Louise Schiavone of the AP. Schiavone scrambled with her recorder to the back of the room and had the only sound on a significant aspect of a major story.

Another disadvantage to remote coverage is that if reporters aren't present, they cannot ask questions to follow up on the official dialogue or to seek added perspective. David Oziel, UPI Radio news director, put it this way: "You are there to see expressions on people's faces and other human elements that can only be described by a reporter on the scene."

Despite the decline of radio news, there are bright spots. One is National Public Radio, which has the largest radio network reporting staff in the nation's capital, with 12 people. NPR has many of the sources of the commercial networks—news services like AP and audio services—but it is different in the emphasis it places on staffing events. The reporters also approach stories differently. Instead of keeping stories to 25 seconds, a recommended maximum at commercial networks, NPR allows reporters the airtime to tell their stories thoroughly and in depth.

Alone among the radio networks, NPR offers extended newscasts in the tradition of commercial networks in radio's heyday—"Morning Edition" and "All Things Considered." NPR's staff beyond Washington is limited, however, and the network leans heavily on the BBC for international coverage and its noncommercial affiliates for coverage beyond the Potomac. Occasionally NPR sends reporters abroad and into the hinterlands of the United States, but with no advertising base, NPR has perennial budget problems that limit its full inheritance of the tradition of Edward R. Murrow and other radio news pioneers.

talk radio

Talk formats that feature live listener telephone calls emerged as a major genre in American radio in the 1980s. Many AM stations, which couldn't compete with FM's

Talking on the Right.
Political observers say talk radio shows, which are overwhelmingly conservative, were a key in the 1994 Republican takeover of Congress. In San Francisco, KSFO is an all-conservative format headlined by J. Paul Emerson. He holds back nothing. Pounding his fist on the broadcast studio console, he bellows that he "hates Japs." In Denver, Ken Hamblin, who calls himself the Black Avenger, holds forth with outspoken right-wing talk. Hamblin is syndicated on 63 stations around the nation. The effect of "talkers," as they're known in the trade, cannot be overstated. A Los Angeles Times-funded poll found 44 percent of Americans pick up most of their political information from these shows.

sound quality for music, realized they were better suited to talk, which doesn't require high fidelity.

Call-in formats were greeted enthusiastically at first because of their potential as forums for discussion of the great public issues. Some stations, including WCCO in Minneapolis and WHO in Des Moines, were models whose long-running talkers raised expectations. So did Ray Suarez' "Talk of the Nation" on National Public Radio. Many talkers, however, went other directions, focusing less on issues than on wacky, often vitriolic personalities. Much of the format degenerated into advice programs on hemorrhoids, psoriasis, face-lifts and psychoses. Sports trivia went over big; so did pet care. Talk shows gave an illusion of news but in reality were low-brow entertainment.

Whatever the downside of **talkers,** as they're known in the trade, they have huge followings. **Rush Limbaugh** was syndicated to 660 stations at his peak, reaching an estimated 20 million people a week. A survey by the Times Mirror Center for the People and the Press found 44 percent of Americans received most of their political information from talk radio. On AM radio, talk became the most common format in the 1990s.

Talk Listenership. The influence of talkers can be overrated. A 1996 Media Studies Center survey of people who listen to political talk shows found they're hardly representative of mainstream Americans.

The political talk show audience is largely white, male, Republican and financially well off. It is much more politically engaged than the general population, but on the right-wing. Also, these people have distrust in the mainstream media, which they perceive as biased to the left.

Effect on News. Many stations with music-based formats used the advent of news and talk stations to reduce their news programming. In effect, many music stations were saying, "Let those guys do news and talk, and we'll do music." The rationale really was a profit-motivated guise to get out of news and public affairs, which is expensive. Playing records is cheap. The result was fewer stations offering serious news and public affairs programming.

radio networks

(STUDY PREVIEW)   Although the major networks, ABC, CBS, NBC and Mutual, have different roots, they all contributed to the shaping of the American broadcasting industry. They were at the heart of radio in its heyday. Today, the networks are leaders in demographic programming.

four traditional networks

NBC. The Radio Corporation of America station in Newark, New Jersey, **WJZ,** and a station in Schenectady, New York, linked themselves by telegraph line and simultaneously carried the same broadcast of the 1923 World Series. It was the first network. More linkups with more stations followed. RCA recognized the commercial

Imus in the Morning. Sometimes it's difficult to tell whether irreverent radio talk-show host Don Imus is running a spoof or interviewing real people. Despite his lack of orthodoxy, Imus lines up high-level guests who sometimes shed restraint and display another side of their personas. The Imus program is simulcast on the MSNBC cable television network and segments sometimes are live on NBC's "Today" show.

potential of networks and formed the **National Broadcasting Company** in 1926 as a service to local stations that eventually would link stations coast to coast.

Meanwhile, **American Telephone & Telegraph** developed a 27-station network that stretched as far west as Kansas City. However, in 1926, just as NBC was being formed, AT&T decided to get out of radio. AT&T was aware that the government was looking at restraint-of-trade issues and could break up the company. Also, the company wanted to concentrate on activities that promised more profit than it foresaw in radio. AT&T sold the network to NBC, which operated it as a separate enterprise.

ABC. Although NBC operated the two networks independently, the Federal Communications Commission became increasingly doubtful about "chain broadcasting," as it was called. Under government pressure, NBC sold the old AT&T network in 1943 to **Edward Nobel,** who had made a fortune with Lifesavers candy. Nobel named his new corporation the **American Broadcasting Company,** and the ABC network was born with 168 stations.

CBS. The new ABC network was in competition not only with the scaled-down NBC but also with the **Columbia Broadcasting System.** CBS had its roots in a 1927 experiment by **William Paley,** who was advertising manager for his father's Philadelphia cigar company. To see if radio advertising could boost sales, young Paley placed advertisements on **United Independent Broadcasters,** a 16-station upstart network. Within six months sales skyrocketed from 400,000 to 1 million cigars a day. Impressed, Paley bought the network, called it CBS, and remained at the helm almost 50 years.

Mutual. When NBC and CBS signed up local affiliates, they guaranteed that no competing station would be given the network's programs, which put independent stations without popular network programs at a disadvantage. To compete, independents exchanged programs and sometimes linked up for one-shot coverage of events. In 1934, independent stations led by **WGN** in Chicago and **WOR** in New York created a new kind of network, the **Mutual Broadcasting System.** Any station could pick up Mutual programs no matter who else was airing them. Furthermore, in a

talkers
Talk shows.

Rush Limbaugh
Most listened-to talk show host in 1990s.

WJZ
First station linkup, New York.

National Broadcasting Company
First network; established by Radio Corporation of America.

American Telephone & Telegraph
Created network in 1926; later sold to NBC.

Edward Nobel
Financed creation of ABC.

American Broadcasting Company
Created from one of NBC's two networks.

Columbia Broadcasting System
Primary early competitor to NBC.

William Paley
Founded CBS.

United Independent Broadcasters
Predecessor to CBS.

WGN
Partner with WOR in establishing Mutual, Chicago.

WOR
Partner with WGN in establishing Mutual, New York.

Mutual Broadcasting System
Provides programming on non-exclusive basis.

departure from policy at NBC and CBS, Mutual stations were not required to carry programs they did not want. Many independent stations tapped into Mutual, and the network eventually claimed more affiliates than the other networks, although few stations carried all that Mutual made available.

radio networks today

Today, inexpensive satellite relays have spawned a bevy of national and regional programming services, but these pale compared to the original Big Four networks in their heyday. In news, only four major players remain—and NBC exists in name only. NBC sold off its radio network in the 1980s to a Los Angeles company, Westwood One, which also bought the old Mutual operation. These are the major news networks:

ABC. The original ABC is now split into demographic networks. Today they are called the Excel, Galaxy, Genesis, Platinum and Prime networks.

Westwood. Westwood has six networks, some with familiar names from the past: CNN-Plus, Country, Mutual, NBC, The Source and Young Adult.

CBS. CBS still operates a network called CBS, plus a youth-oriented network called Spectrum. Beginning in 1997, Westwood operated the advertising part of the operation.

American Urban. This company uses its namesake for its network: American Urban Radio.

affiliate–network relations

The early networks were attractive vehicles to advertisers seeking a national audience, which is how the networks made their money and how they still do. Networks base their fees for running commercials on the size of their huge multistation audiences. In general, the more **affiliate** stations and the larger the audience, the higher a network's revenue.

ABC, CBS and NBC each owns stations called **o-and-o's,** short for network owned and operated, but most of a network's strength is in its affiliates. That is why networks look to popular local stations to carry their programs and advertisements. Affiliate-network relationships are mutually advantageous. Local stations profit from network affiliations in two ways. Networks pay affiliates for running their national advertisements. These network payments average about 5 percent of the station's income. Also, strong network programs are audience builders. The larger a station's audience, generally, the more it can charge local advertisers to carry their messages.

A network and an affiliate define their relationship in a contract that is subject to periodic renegotiation and renewal. In radio's heyday, which ran into the early 1950s, network affiliations were so attractive and profitable to local stations that the networks could dictate terms. As television displaced radio as the preferred national entertainment medium, however, the networks relaxed exclusivity and other requirements. Today, local stations are in a stronger position in negotiating affiliation contracts and terms. There are also more possible affiliations because, with the economies possible through satellite hook-up, so many networks have come into existence. About 40 percent of American stations have a network affiliation.

affiliate
Station that subscribes to network for programming.
o-and-o
Station owned and operated by network; not to be confused with affiliate.

broadcast regulation

(STUDY PREVIEW) Complex regulations govern American broadcasting today. These regulations govern station engineering and ownership. The Federal Communications Commission also regulates content in a limited way.

media **online**

Federal Communications Commission: A comprehensive web site with an overview of the agency and links to agency documents, including the 1996 Telecommunication Act
www.fcc.gov/telecom.html

trusteeship rationale

Radio in the United States is regulated by the federal government, as is television—although not the print media. To understand why, you need to go back to the days after World War I when radio stations with powerful signals boomed their way onto the airwaves. There were not enough frequencies, and the airwaves became a deafening cacophony. A station finding itself drowned out might boost power to keep listeners, thereby drowning out weaker signals in a kind of king-of-the-mountain competition. An alternative was jumping to a less cluttered frequency and asking listeners to follow. It was chaos.

Failing to solve the problem among themselves, radio station owners finally called on the federal government for a solution. In 1927 Congress borrowed language from 19th-century railroad regulatory legislation and established the **Federal Radio Commission.** The commission was given broad licensing authority. The authorizing legislation, the Federal Radio Act, said licenses would be for limited terms. The FRC could specify frequency, power and hours of operation.

Federal Radio Commission
Assigned frequencies starting in 1927.

---

media databank

radio chains

For years, the government restricted a radio company to owning no more than seven AM and seven FM stations, but the restrictions gradually relaxed. Then the 1996 Telecommunications Act eliminated any cap, except that a single company could own no more than eight stations in a large market and scaled-down maximums for smaller markets. Right away, radio chains began gobbling up stations and also other chains. These are the biggest:

Radio Chain	Stations
CapStar, Dallas	413 stations
Westinghouse/CBS, New York	174 stations
Clear Channel, San Antonio	171 stations
Jacor, Cincinnati	156 stations
Sinclair, Baltimore	59 stations
Cox Communications, Atlanta	49 stations
Heftel	37 stations
Disney/ABC, New York	26 stations
Beasley, Naples, Florida	26 stations

The new commission's immediate problem was that 732 stations were on the air, but the technology of the time allowed room for only 568. In the end, the commission allowed 649 to remain on the air with strict limits on transmission to prevent signal overlaps. Even so, some stations were silenced, solid evidence that government was in the business of broadcast regulation.

As might be expected in a nation of libertarian traditions, there was uneasiness about licensing a medium that not only purveyed information and ideas but that also was a forum for artistic creativity. What about the First Amendment? As a practical matter, the broadcast spectrum had a real and absolute capacity. Someone had to be the arbiter of the airwaves, or a scarce resource would be rendered unusable. The **trusteeship concept** developed. It held that the airwaves are public property and should be subject to regulation for the public good, just as are public roads. The test of who should be granted licenses, and who denied, would be service to the "**public interest, convenience and necessity,**" a phrase from the 1927 Federal Radio Act that remains a cornerstone of American broadcasting.

With the Federal Communications Act of 1934, Congress replaced the FRC with the **Federal Communications Commission.** Television, under development at the time, was incorporated into the FCC's charge. Otherwise, the FCC largely continued the FRC's regulatory responsibility.

Engineering Regulations.   Over the years, the FCC has used its regulatory authority to find room in the radio spectrum for more and more stations. Almost 5,000 AM stations are broadcasting today, compared with 649 when the FRC was set up, and there are more than 5,000 FM stations.

By limiting the power of station signals, the FCC squeezes many stations onto a single frequency. For example, WBAL in Baltimore, Maryland, and KAAY in Little Rock, Arkansas, both broadcast at 1090 on the dial, but restrictions on their signal strengths prevent overlapping. Dozens of stations, scattered around the nation, are sandwiched at some frequencies. At night, when the atmosphere extends the range of AM transmissions, many stations are required to reduce their power; go off the air; or transmit directionally, like north-south, to avoid overlap. The FCC, with its licensing authority, insists that stations comply strictly with engineering restrictions to avoid the pre-1927 chaos.

Ownership Regulations.   The FCC regulates station ownership. To encourage diverse programming, the FCC limits how many stations a single individual or company may own. Whether diverse ownership creates diverse programming is debatable, but the FCC has prevented local broadcast monopolies.

The FCC insists that licensees be of good character, follow sound business practices and operate within the letter and spirit of the law and FCC regulations. No nonsense is tolerated. Consider the case of WLBT-TV in Jackson, Mississippi, which made no attempt to bring blacks onto its staff even though Jackson was largely a black community. The station carried virtually no black-oriented programming and lost its license license in a 1969 court order.

Content Regulations.   The 1934 Federal Communications Act specifically forbids censorship, and the government has never had agents sitting at any radio stations to keep things off the air. Yet the FCC has a powerful influence over what is aired because broadcasters are accountable for what they have aired when license renewal time comes up. Licenses are granted for eight years.

The government has provided clues aplenty to broadcasters on what it, as trustee for the public, does not want on the air. Although FCC policy today has shifted some-

trusteeship concept
Government regulates broadcasting in public interest.

"public interest, convenience and necessity"
Criteria for awarding broadcast licenses.

Federal Communications Commission
Replaced FRC; added mandate that included television, telephone.

John Brinkley
Quack doctor who lost appeal that broadcast regulation was an infringement on free expression.

john brinkley

John Brinkley and his bride arrived in Milford, Kansas, population 200, in 1917 and rented the old drug store for $8 a month. Mrs. Brinkley sold patent medicines out front, while Brinkley talked to patients in a back room. One day an elderly gentleman called on "Dr. Brinkley" to do something about his failing manhood. As the story goes, the conversation turned to Brinkley's experience with goats in the medical office of the Swift meat-packing company, a job he had held for barely three weeks. Said Brinkley, "You wouldn't have any trouble if you had a pair of those buck glands in you." The operation was performed in the back room, and word spread. Soon the goat gland surgeon was charging $750 for the service, then $1,000, then $1,500. In 1918 Brinkley, whose only credentials were two mail-order medical degrees, opened the Brinkley Hospital. Five years later he set up a radio station, KFKB, to spread the word about his cures.

Six nights a week, Brinkley extolled the virtues of his hospital over the air. "Don't let your

doctor two-dollar you to death," he said. "Come to Dr. Brinkley." If a trip to Milford was not possible, listeners were encouraged to send for Brinkley compounds. Soon the mail-order demand was so great that Brinkley reported he was buying goats from Arkansas by the boxcar. "Dr. Brinkley" became a household word. *Radio Digest* awarded Brinkley's KFKB (for Kansas First, Kansas Best) its Golden Microphone Award as the most popular radio station in the country. The station had received 356,827 votes in the magazine's write-in poll. Brinkley was a 1930 write-in candidate for governor. Harry Woodring won with 217,171 votes to Brinkley's 183,278, but Brinkley would have won it had it not been for misspellings that disqualified thousands of write-in ballots.

Also in 1930 the KFKB broadcast license came up for renewal by the Federal Radio Commission, which had been set up to regulate broadcasting. The American Medical Association wanted the license to be revoked. The medical profession had been outraged by Brinkley but had not found a way to derail his

thriving quackery. In fact, Brinkley played to the hearts of thousands of Middle America's listeners when he attacked the AMA as "the meat-cutter's union." At the license hearing, Brinkley argued that the First Amendment guaranteed him freedom to speak his views on medicine, goat glands and anything else he wanted. He noted that Congress had specifically forbidden the FRC to censor. It would be a censorious affront to the First Amendment, he said, to take away KFKB's license for what the station put on the air. Despite Brinkley's arguments, the FRC denied renewal.

Brinkley challenged the denial in federal court, and the case became a landmark on the relationship between the First Amendment and American broadcasting. The appeals court sided with the FRC, declaring that broadcast licenses should be awarded for serving "the public interest, convenience and necessity." It was appropriate, said the court, for the commission to review a station's programming to decide on renewal. Brinkley appealed to the U.S. Supreme Court, which

Goat Gland Surgeon. Eager for publicity, John Brinkley obliges a photographer by placing a healing hand on a supposedly insane patient he is about to cure. Broadcasting such claims from his Kansas radio station, Brinkley developed a wide market for his potions. Because of his quackery, he lost the station in a significant First Amendment case.

declined to hear the case. The goat gland surgeon was off the air, but not for long. In 1932 Dr. Brinkley, proving himself unsinkable, bought a powerful station in Villa Acuna, Mexico, just across the Rio Grande from Del Rio, Texas, to continue peddling his potions. By telephone linkup from his home in Milford, Brinkley continued to reach much of the United States until 1942, when the Mexican government nationalized foreign-owned property.

howard stern

No wonder they call **Howard Stern** a "**shock jock.**" The New York disc jockey is outrageous, cynical and vulgar. But people listen to his bathroom-wall jokes and his topless female studio guests. Not surprisingly, the Federal Communications Commission, which regulates U.S. broadcast stations, doesn't cotton well to Stern's brand of humor. That hasn't bothered Stern much. In fact, he told listeners he was praying that the prostate cancer of FCC Chairman Alfred Sikes would spread.

No matter how obnoxious, Stern has a following. In fact, he is the crown jewel air personality of Infinity Broadcasting, which became part of the giant CBS radio system in 1996, and is syndicated.

Stern was expensive for Infinity Broadcasting, not just because he commanded top dollar in salary but because the FCC fined stations carrying Stern $1.7 million for his "references to sexual and excretory activities and functions." Infinity could afford to pay the fine, but challenged it on First Amendment grounds. Infinity's president, Mel Karmazin, calls it a harass-ing attempt at censorship of something that thousands of people want to hear. Those who don't like it can listen elsewhere, Karmazin says: "That's why they make on-off buttons."

Howard Stern has known controversy a long time. At Boston University, he worked at the campus radio station—until they fired him for a show on Godzilla going to Harlem. Later at WNBC in New York, a bit called "Bestiality Dial-a-Porn" got him fired again.

At WXRK in New York, Stern proved he could draw listeners. The station shot from Number 21 to Number 1 in morning ratings after he signed on in 1985. At his current Infinity home, the blue humor, as well as his racism, sexism, homophobia, misogyny and bad taste, continue to attract a large, profitable audience.

Depending on who you talk to, Howard Stern represents the best in American radio, meeting the interests and needs of a mass audience, or the worst, pandering to the lowest instincts in society and getting rich in the process.

His autobiographical 1993 book, *Private Parts,* was further evidence of his commercial success. Publisher Simon & Schuster was into a sixth printing within weeks of the release. In 1995 came a second book, *Miss America.* HarperCollins's first printing, the largest in its history, was 1.4 million.

Shock Jock. Blunt and uninhibited on the air, radio personality Howard Stern is the epitome of the "shock jock." He has expanded into television on the E! channel, and in 1993 he wrote a best-selling autobiographical book, *Private Parts,* and followed up in 1995 with another, *Miss America.* Although his New York–based program has strong listenership, Stern's crude humor is not universally popular. Fox television boss Rupert Murdoch got cold feet about creating a program for Stern in 1994, and the FCC has fined stations that carry his radio program $1.7 million.

what, many broadcasters, not wanting to risk their licenses, still regard the lessons from these cases as indelible:

- **Unanswered personal attacks.** In 1962 a station in Pennsylvania aired an attack by a right-wing evangelist on author Fred Cook. Cook was called a liar, and it was implied that he championed Communist causes. Cook asked for time to respond, but the station refused. The FCC sided with Cook, and eventually so did the U.S. Supreme Court in a decision called Red Lion after the name of the company that owned the station.

- **Realistic, alarming spoofs.** The FCC fined a St. Louis station, KSHE, $25,000 in 1991 after disc jockey John Ulett broadcast a mock nuclear attack on the United States. The FCC was not amused.

- **Exclusive forum for licensee.** A Methodist preacher used his church-owned station, KGEF in Los Angeles, as an extension of the pulpit to attack Catholics, Jews, lawyers, judges, labor unions and other groups. The FRC denied renewal in 1930. On appeal, the courts said a licensee has no unlimited right to spread hatred.

- **Dirty words.** WBAI-FM in New York, a noncommercial station, included a George Carlin comedy cut in a 1975 program examining social attitudes toward language. The Carlin monologue included "dirty words," which the FCC ruled indecent at times of day when children might be listening. The U.S. Supreme Court agreed.

Howard Stern
Controversial New York talk show host.

shock jock
Announcer whose style includes vulgarities, taboos.

British Broadcasting Corporation
Provides international service.

radio martí

Six years after Fidel Castro took over Cuba and allied himself with the former Soviet Union, the U.S. government set up a radio station, **Radio Martí,** to blanket the Caribbean island, 90 miles off Key West, with news, commentary and entertainment. Outraged, Castro countered with a super-powered station of his own that drowned out some U.S. commercial stations, including one as far away as WHO in Des Moines, Iowa.

Radio Martí, founded in 1985 and funded at $20 million a year, broadcasts 24 hours a day. It has 165 employees, all Spanish-speaking. The signal goes out on shortwave from the government-operated U.S. Information Agency's **Voice of America** headquarters in Washington. Two Miami AM stations also carry Martí programming an hour a day.

In 1990, USIA added TV Martí, a $13 million a year, 80-staff operation that beams 2½ hours of programming a day at Cuba from a balloon antenna tethered above the Florida Straits.

Martí has been controversial not only with Castro. As with earlier U.S. government-sponsored transnational broadcast services, Radio Free Europe and Radio Liberty, there are continuing charges of political bias. The U.S. Information Service defends Martí news and commentary as dispassionate, albeit from a U.S. perspective.

Part of the suspicion about Martí stems from U.S. government lies about **Radio Free Europe** and **Radio Liberty,** which were set up after World War II to reach into the former Soviet Union and its Central Europe satellite countries. Both services were ostensibly operated by private interests, but it was later discovered that the CIA funded them.

At their peak, various Radio Free Europe and Radio Liberty transmitters were beaming 1,000 hours a week of programming behind the Iron Curtain. Reporting every bungle and misstep of the communist governments, the U.S.-funded stations clearly were fomenting dissent. The Soviet Union countered by building 1,000 transmitters that broadcast shrieks and howls to drown out the incoming signals. When the United States objected, the Soviet Union pointed to a 1936 treaty that condemned broadcasts calculated "to incite the population of any territory to acts incompatible with internal order."

The Soviet Union had its own international propaganda service, **Radio Moscow,** which pumped out almost 2,000 hours of shortwave programming a week in 64 languages.

While stations are subject to discipline, the FCC provides only general guidance on what it does want aired. It encourages local origination over network programming, and it also encourages public affairs and community-oriented programming, but the FCC assiduously avoids dictating what goes on the air, even when under pressure to do so. Pressure shows up inevitably when a classical music station switches to another format. To classical music lovers who ask the FCC to intervene, the commission has said again and again that it considers formats a function of the marketplace. If a station cannot find enough listeners with one format to attract advertisers, then it should be free to try another.

regulating networks

The networks deliver programming to local stations, and local stations pass network programming on to listeners. Because networks do not themselves broadcast on the public airwaves, they have never been subject to FCC licensing as stations are. Even so, the government can put a lot of pressure on the networks. Consider:

- **Affiliate Pressure.** As licensed entities, affiliate stations are answerable to the FCC, which means that network programming must conform to FCC standards. The networks have entire departments to review programs to ensure that they comply with acceptable guidelines.

- **Antitrust.** The size of the major networks leaves them vulnerable to **antitrust** action. It was after the FCC's rumblings that NBC was too powerful that the network sold one branch to candy manufacturer Edward Nobel in 1943 rather than risk an FCC recommendation to the Justice Department to dismantle the company.

- **Network Licensees.** The networks themselves own radio and television stations, which are subject to licensing. The stations, all in major cities, are significant profit sources for the networks, which do not want to risk losing the FCC licenses to operate them.

broadcast deregulation

Ronald Reagan proclaimed his presidency would "get government off the backs of business." In 1996, seven years after Reagan left office, it seemed that his deregulation dream had come true—at least in broadcasting. The government relaxed its age-old limits on how many radio stations a single company could own. Right away, radio companies began gobbling up one another in mergers that had some pundits predicting all of radio being in only a few corporate hands before long.

In one deal, the Westinghouse-CBS broadcast conglomerate and the Infinity radio chain merged. Together they had 89 stations and dominated 10 top markets. In Philadelphia alone, the newly merged company had 44 percent of the radio revenues; in Boston, 39 percent; in New York, 39 percent; and in Los Angeles, 26 percent.

Within six months of when the traditional ownership limits were lifted, the U.S. Justice Department learned that the Jacor radio chain was planning to buy two Citicaster stations in Cincinnati. The deal would have given Jacor 53 percent of the radio dollars in Cincinnati. Justice threatened an antitrust action, and Jacor agreed to sell one station to fall below a 50 percent cap that Justice said it would tolerate.

The current federal limits:

- In markets of 45-plus stations, a single company can own no more than eight stations, with a maximum of five FM or five AM.

- In markets of 30 to 44 stations, no more than seven stations, with a maximum of four being either FM or AM.

- In markets of 15 to 29 stations, no more than six stations, with a maximum of four being either FM or AM.

- In markets of less than 15 stations, no more than five stations, with a maximum of three being either FM or AM.

- No company can regularly have more than 50 percent of a market's audience share.

- No company may earn more than 50 percent of the radio advertising revenues in a market.

- No foreign ownership is allowed.

Radio Martí
U.S. government radio targeted at Cuba.

Voice of America
U.S. government radio targeted at the former Soviet Union.

Radio Free Europe
U.S. government radio targeted at the former Soviet Union.

Radio Liberty
U.S. government radio targeted at the former Soviet Union.

Radio Moscow
Russian government radio targeted at foreign listeners.

antitrust
Government action against monopolies.

future of radio

(STUDY PREVIEW) Innovations are unusual in radio programming, and the dynamics that contribute to a sameness can be expected to continue. Technology, however, is introducing changes, including digital transmission and satellite-direct delivery, which could upend the U.S. radio industry and possibly trigger fundamental rethinking on content.

risk-free bland programming

Like most mass media, radio in the United States is imitative. When major programming innovations occur, which is rare, the cloning begins. In the 1980s, when audiences glommed onto talk radio, for example, hundreds of stations copied the format. The coast-to-coast sameness of radio formats, and even the on-air voices and personalities, has been reinforced by the growth of chain ownership. Chain managers prefer tried-and-true routes to profits. They avoid the risks attendant to striking out in fresh directions.

National program services, which pipe programs to stations to relay to listeners, also contribute to the uniformity. In seeking large overall audiences in diverse parts of the country, these syndicates stick to safe, middle ground even within their format niches. The future bodes much of the same, unless something occurs that upends the whole industry.

What innovations occur in the immediate future probably will be incremental technical upgrades. One such recent development has been equipment that permits stations to embed supplementary data in their signals. These data show up mostly today in new receivers that display a word or two identifying the station's call letters and the format. Eventually this technology can lead to bigger display screens with headlines, weather and advertisements.

converting to digital

The quality of radio transmissions made a quantum leap when Edwin Armstrong's FM finally took hold in the 1960s. When the economics make it possible—and don't hold your breath—we face another sound break-through: digital radio.

Digital Radio. In the late 1980s, when radio stations tore out their turntables and began playing CDs, many proclaimed a giant step forward in broadcasting. It was hollow hype. While CDs have superior sound to old analog records, stations still transmitted in the same old analog way—and still do.

Technically it is possible for stations to upgrade to digital transmission, picking up the long chain of binary 0s and 1s from CDs, with the transmission corresponding precisely to the binary encoding on the CD. The hitch is that the receivers most people own today—in their cars, at home, at work, wherever—cannot pick up digital signals. Digital receivers, really mini-computers, run $200 to $300, and few people are so dissatisfied with the current quality of radio sound that they will invest in expensive, duplicate equipment. Digital radio will come, but not tomorrow nor even the day after.

National Radio. Radio station owners are losing sleep over a new Federal Communication Commission rule approved in 1997. The rule allows for radio superstations to be built to send signals from satellites directly to people's receivers. The result: national radio stations. The local station, necessary in the past for relaying network signals to listeners, would be out of the loop.

The FCC allowed room for 20 radio channels in the direct-satellite rules. These channels, transmitting digitally, could be attractive to national advertisers, but several things need to happen first. Today the number of people with digital receivers hardly constitutes the critical mass that advertisers need. Also, technology needs to be found so digital signals can penetrate urban areas where buildings and other structures impede signals.

Local stations have an ace to play against satellite-direct competitors: reviving their local orientation. Rather than inundating listeners with the cultural output of Nashville, Hollywood and New York, local stations could work harder at identifying and playing back distinctive local cultures. Stations that slight local news today might rediscover that community journalism can set them apart from interlopers beaming slick programming down from satellites.

In one respect, national radio is already here. The major satellite-direct television services, including Dish network, offer commercial-free music on 20 to 30 audio channels, each carrying a different genre. Part of a subscription service, this is, in effect, pay radio.

web radio

Many radio stations, and also other companies, have established music sites on the World Wide Web. Theoretically the quality of sound, being digital, should be excellent, but for the time being, the web's bandwidth limitations can't handle enough digital data for smooth delivery. Until bandwidth is expanded to accommodate real-time listening, there is software available that picks up web music and stores it for playback. Also, technology is finding ways to compress digital signals so more and more data, including the binary 0 and 1 codes that underlie digital music, can be squeezed through the bottlenecks on the Internet pipelines.

Once technology catches up with the web's potential, probably when the Internet is upgraded entirely to fiber-optic cable, people might look to the web for radio-type services. On-demand programming is a possibility. Instead of waiting for your favorite song or the latest sports, you could call up what you want and it would be played instantly for you—just for you when you want it. It is the telephone and cable television companies, which now are rewiring the nation and the world, that will offer this on-demand service.

Radio would still have a role for people on the go, commuting or at the beach, where they can't plug in. But the rest of today's radio audience would leave for on-demand music and news services offered on the web and cable.

In the distant future, digital compression may be able to squeeze so many messages onto the electromagnetic spectrum that on-demand services can be delivered over the air. It may still be radio stations that deliver these services, but the programming would be listener-determined, not station-determined. Radio would be like a giant jukebox.

This raises fundamental questions about the structure of tomorrow's radio industry: How will advertising fit in? Will advertising fit in at all? Who would want to listen to happy-idiot disc jockey patter if they could get the music they want whenever they want? Or the latest sports or news? In short, the kind of services offered by radio today will likely be subsumed in the broader media services that are being created by companies installing interactive cable links.

chapter wrap-up

The proliferation in radio programming can be expected to continue with stations narrowcasting into more and more specialized niches. Broadcast industry commentator Erik Zorn predicts hundreds of formats, some as narrow as all-blues music stations, business news stations, Czech-language stations and full-time stations for the blind. In this new world of demand programming, any listener will be able to choose among literally hundreds of programs at any time—a far cry from pre-television days when mainstream radio was truly a mass medium and sought the whole audience with every program.

Technology has created problems. The advent of FM stereo drew listeners away from AM in the 1980s. With its superior quality of sound, FM held more than 70 percent of the U.S. radio audience by the 1990s. Many AM stations shifted to news and talk formats, which did not require stereo transmissions to attract an audience, but these audiences were smaller and AM ended up with fewer listeners. The resale value of AM stations sank, even for old-line big-name stations. Some AM stations entered bankruptcy.

There is no question that radio will continue as a strong medium of mass communication, but the shape of the radio industry is less certain. As in the past, government regulation, technological innovation and competition from other mass media will be major players in determining radio's future.

questions for review

1. Why is radio called a ubiquitous and influential medium?

2. How does radio move invisibly through on electromagnetic waves?

3. What are characteristics of the radio industry in the United States?

4. Why has U.S. radio historically had an entertainment rather than educational thrust?

5. What is the status of news in U.S. radio today?

6. Why did the government begin broadcast regulation in 1927? What has happened since?

7. What forces contribute to a sameness in U.S. radio programming? Will technology affect programming in the future?

8. How have the national networks shaped American radio?

questions for critical thinking

1. The telegraph was invented by Samuel Morse in 1844. Roughly 50 years later Guglielmo Marconi introduced radio wireless telegraphy. What was the difference?

2. Lee De Forest was a technical and programming innovator. Explain the significance of his audion tube and his 1916 broadcast of election returns.

3. A new way of transmitting radio was developed by Edwin Armstrong in the 1930s, and by the 1980s it had left the nation's original AM broadcast system in economic peril. Discuss Armstrong's invention and how it has reshaped American radio.

4. American radio was shaped by the networks in the 1920s and 1930s and reshaped by the advent of television in the 1950s. Explain these influences, and be sure to cite radio's transition from literal *broadcasting* toward *narrowcasting*. What about the influence of Gordon McLendon? What of the future?

5. Explain the significance of KDKA of Pittsburgh, WEAF of New York, WOR of New York and WGN of Chicago.

6. How does demographic programming today differ from the potted-palm music of early radio? From newscasts of the 1930s when the networks set up their own reporting staffs? From newscasts of the late 1950s when AM stations improved local coverage?

for further learning

Erik Barnouw. *A Tower in Babel, A History of Broadcasting in the United States to 1933* (Oxford, 1966); *The Golden Web, A History of Broadcasting in the United States, 1933–1953* (Oxford, 1968); *The Image Empire, A History of Broadcasting in the United States, 1953–On* (Oxford, 1970). Barnouw's trilogy is thorough and readable.

John R. Bittner. *Law and Regulation of the Electronic Media,* 2nd ed. (Prentice Hall, 1993).

Gerald Carson. *The Roguish World of Dr. Brinkley* (Holt, Rinehart & Winston, 1960). Carson's lightly written account tells how the Goat Gland Surgeon took the issue of broadcast regulation to court and lost.

Stanley Cloud and Lynne Olson. *The Murrow Boys: Pioneers on the Front Lines of Broadcast Journalism* (Houghton Mifflin, 1997). Cloud and Olson, both journalists, offer a fascinating chronicle of the rise of CBS radio news during World War II, and then the post-war struggles, including corporate obstacles that contributed to decline.

Richard Corliss. "Look Who's Talking: The Explosion of Radio Call-In Shows Has Created a New Form of Electronic Populism and Demagoguery," *Time* (January 23, 1995), pp. 22–25.

Jack Ladd. *Radio Waves: Life and Revolution on the FM Dial.* (St. Martin's Press, 1992). Ladd, a pioneer in the free-form FM format in the 1960s, tracks the evolution of the format. He revels in tales of profit-obsessed and FCC-paranoid station managers whose caution worked against innovation.

Lynne Schafer Gross. *Telecommunications: An Introduction to Radio, Television and Other Electronic Media,* 5th ed. (Wm. C. Brown, 1995). Professor Gross's survey of broadcasting includes an excellent explanation of how the electromagnetic spectrum works.

for keeping up to date

The weekly trade journals *Broadcasting* and *Electronic Media* keep abreast of news and issues.

Other news coverage can be found in the *Wall Street Journal,* the New York *Times,* the Los Angeles *Times* and other major daily newspapers.

Scholarly articles can be found in the *Journal of Broadcasting, Electronic Media, Journal of Communication* and *Journalism Quarterly.*

On regulation, see the *Federal Communications Law Journal.*

Talkers magazine will keep you posted on talk shows.

R&R, a weekly trade journal published by Radio & Records, carries charts and playlists that not only reflect what's getting airtime but also shape what will be getting airtime.

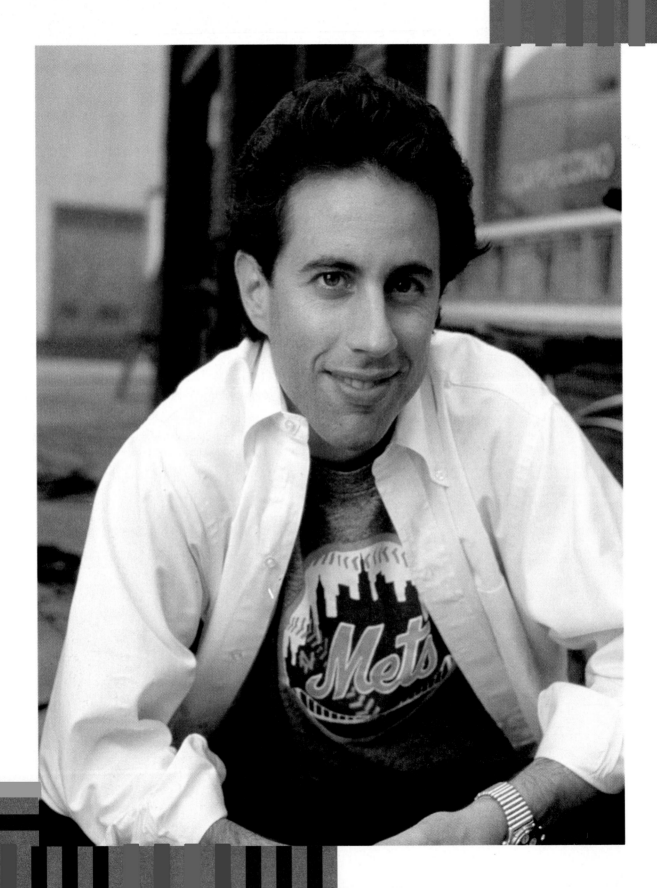

8

television

in this chapter you will learn:

● Television influences people, culture and other media.

● Television technology is electronic.

● U.S. television has a tiered national-local structure.

● Television has expanded beyond over-air delivery.

● Networks dominate programming to local over-air television stations.

● Federal money helps fund noncommercial television.

● Cable today rivals over-air networks and affiliates.

● Radio was the model for early television programs.

● Television is an efficient purveyor of news.

Jerry Seinfeld always knew he was funny. Almost from birth he made his friends laugh. At age 8 he became fascinated with comedians like Abbott and Costello on television. Then and there he decided that his destiny was to become a comedian. At Queens College he worked part time as a telephone lightbulb salesman and a street jewelry vendor, but he never lost sight of his dream. The dream came true in 1987 when his first television special, "Jerry Seinfeld's Stand-up Confidential," appeared on

HBO. Since then he has won critical acclaim as a stand-up comic, TV actor, best-selling author, and advertising pitchman. His book, *SeinLanguage,* stayed on the New York *Times* best-seller list for 33 weeks.

But it is as creator, producer and star of his own comedy series that Jerry Seinfeld made cultural history—as well as millions of dollars in advertising revenue for NBC. Over nine seasons the show became the highest-rated comedy series on television, with every episode watched by an average of more than 30 million viewers. It has won 10 Emmy Awards.

What was "Seinfeld" about? The show's four main characters—Seinfeld as himself, his former girlfriend Elaine, his friend George, and his nutty neighbor Kramer—are self-absorbed New Yorkers coping with the ups and downs of day-to-day life, from working for an eccentric boss to losing a car in a parking garage. Even though the action occurs in New York City, the series has universal appeal. Many scenes take place in a corner diner that could be anywhere, complete with the standard plastic ketchup and mustard containers, tuna salad and rye toast.

"Seinfeld" has been described as "a cultural signpost for the '90s" and "the defining sitcom of our age." Like most of us, its characters stumble through life trying to deal with such mysteries as how to find a good job, how to behave on a date and how to cope with the unexpected. Nothing is too trivial. Even soup had its day on "Seinfeld" when the Soup Nazi terrorized his customers into eating whatever soup he chose. Then there's Seinfeld's nemesis, the mailman named Newman who will assassinate pets for pay.

"Seinfeld" tickles the intellect as well as the funny bone. Each episode is carefully crafted so the story unfolds in a logical fashion and is intertwined with all the other episodes. In one episode, for example, Elaine's life falls dramatically from a high to a low in which she loses both her job and her boyfriend, while George's soars in the opposite direction as he lands a job with the New York Yankees and gains a beautiful girlfriend. By the end of each episode the stories of all the characters have gone full circle. There are no loose ends.

With the series doing so well, many were shocked by the announcement that the 1997–98 season would be the last. The decision was made by Seinfeld himself. It was, he said, "all about timing. As a comedian, my sense of timing is everything." It was important to him that the show go out on a high note. "I wanted to end the show on the same kind of peak we've been doing it on for years," he said. "I wanted the end to be from a point of strength. I wanted the end to be graceful."

Seinfeld fans across the nation were stunned. NBC was stunned too. "Seinfeld" was the second-highest rated show on the air, generating about $200 million a year in profit for the network. The series was so valuable to NBC that in its last season Seinfeld was being paid $1 million per episode and the supporting stars were each receiving $600,000. Seinfeld reportedly turned down an offer of $5 million per episode for a 10th season.

Seinfeld's popularity with viewers throughout the nation demonstrates the cultural impact of television. Even the language of the show—"yada, yada, yada," "Not that there's anything wrong with that," and "Master of your domain"—has become part of daily conversations from New York to Seattle. The series also illustrates the importance of popular programs to the major networks. Advertising revenues are directly tied to ratings, and "Seinfeld" rated an impressive 20.5 average. Little wonder that NBC would have done almost anything to keep the cameras rolling on Jerry Seinfeld and his quirky friends.

impact of television

(STUDY PREVIEW) Television has strong influences on people, on the culture, and on other media. In a remarkably short time, television has become the most popular U.S. medium for entertainment. Television has eroded newspapers' dominance for news.

cultural impact

Ninety-eight percent of American households have at least one television set. On average, a set is on about seven hours a day in these households. There is no question that television has changed American life-styles, drawing people away from other diversions that once occupied their time. Churches, lodges and neighborhood taverns once were central in the lives of many people, and today they are less so. For 26 million people "60 Minutes" is a Sunday night ritual that was not available three generations ago.

Television can move people. Revlon was an obscure cosmetics brand before it took on sponsorship of the "$64,000 Question" quiz show in the 1950s. Overnight, Revlon became a household word and an exceptionally successful product. In 1995, Procter & Gamble and General Motors spent $1.5 billion advertising their wares on television; Philip Morris, $1.4 billion (for its non-cigarette products); and Chrysler, $950 million.

The role of television in riveting the nation on serious matters was demonstrated in 1962, when President John Kennedy spoke into the camera and told the American people that the nation was in a nuclear showdown with the Soviet Union. People rallied to the president's decision to blockade Cuba until the Soviet Union removed the ballistic missiles it was secretly installing. Today, it is rare for a candidate for public office not to use television to solicit support. In fact, as presidential campaigns geared up for the year 2000, campaign managers looked less for volunteers to make door-to-door and other in-person contacts with voters than to help raise funds for television advertising. In state and many local races too, television had emerged as the most cost-efficient and also effective way to reach voters.

Fictional television characters can capture the imagination of the public. Perry Mason did wonders for the reputation of the law profession. Mary Tyler Moore's role as a television news executive showed that women could succeed in male-dominated industries. Roles played by Alan Alda were the counter-macho models for the bright, gentle man of the 1970s. In this same vein, however, Bart Simpson's bratty irreverence toward authority figures sent quivers through parents and teachers in the 1990s. Then came the alarm that Beavis and Butt-Head's fun with matches might lead kids all over the country to set everything in sight on fire.

While television can be effective in creating short-term impressions, there also are long-term effects. A whole generation of children grew up with Teenage Mutant Ninja Turtles as part of their generational identity. Then came Power Rangers. These long-term effects exist at both a superficial level, as with Teenage Mutant Ninja Turtles, and at a serious level. Social critic **Michael Novak** puts the effect of television in broad terms: "Television is a molder of the soul's geography. It builds up incrementally a psychic structure of expectations. It does so in much the same way that school lessons slowly, over the years, tutor the unformed mind and teach it how to think."

What are the "lessons" to which Novak refers? Scholars **Linda and Robert Lichter** and **Stanley Rothman,** who have surveyed the television creative community, make a case that the creators of television programs are social reformers who build their political ideas into their scripts. The Lichters and Rothman identify the television creative community as largely secular and politically liberal. Among program creators whom they quote is Garry Marshall, the creative force behind "Happy Days" and later "Mork and Mindy": "The tag on 'Mork' is almost like the sermon of the week. But it doesn't look like that. It is very cleverly disguised to look like something else, but that's what it is." In many ways, Norman Lear, the creator of Archie Bunker, is the archetype program creator for the Lichter-Rothman profile. And Lear's liberal political and social agenda lived on in series like "Ellen," with the controversial lesbian coming-out show in 1997.

Sick But Popular. How sick can television humor get? For critics, the answer came in "South Park" in 1997. The animated cast, led by Kenny, Cartman, Kyle and Stan, gives adults some perverse memories of growing up, which creators say is the goal. But kids watch the Comedy Central show too, which gives critics fits. Every episode ends with Kenny getting killed. Cute, right?

Michael Novak
Believes TV is broad shaper of issues.
Linda and Robert Lichter, Stanley Rothman
Scholars who claim TV is reformist.

Scholars have different views on the potency of television's effect on the society, but they all agree that there is some degree of influence. Media scholar George Comstock, in his book *Television in America,* wrote: "Television has become an unavoidable and unremitting factor in shaping what we are and what we will become."

mass media shake-up

In a brash moment in 1981, television tycoon Ted Turner predicted the end of newspapers within 10 years. The year 1991 came and went, and, as Turner had predicted, television was even more entrenched as a mass medium—but newspapers too were still in business. Turner had overstated the impact of television, but he was right that television would continue taking readers and advertisers from newspapers, just as it had from the other mass media.

Since its introduction in the early 1950s, the presence of television has reshaped the other media. Consider the following areas of impact:

Books. The discretionary time people spend on television today is time that once went to other activities, including reading, for diversion and information. To stem the decline in reading, book publishers have responded with more extravagant promotions to draw attention to their products. A major consideration with fiction manuscripts at publishing houses is their potential as screenplays, many of which end up on television. Also, in deciding which manuscripts to accept, some publishers even consider how well an author will come across in television interviews when the book is published.

Newspapers. Evening television newscasts have been a major factor in the steady decline of afternoon newspapers, many of which have ceased publication or switched to mornings. Also, hometown newspapers have lost almost all of their national advertisers, primarily to television. Most newspaper redesigns today, including Gannett's *USA Today,* attempt to be visual in ways that newspapers never were before television.

Magazine. Television took advertisers from the big mass circulation magazines like *Life,* forcing magazine companies to shift to magazines that catered to smaller segments of the mass audience that television could not serve.

Recordings. The success of recorded music today hinges in many cases on the airplay that music videos receive on television.

Movies. Just as magazines demassified after television took away many of their advertisers, Hollywood demassified after television stole the bulk of its audience. Today, savvy movie-makers plan their projects for both the big screen and for reissuing, to be shown on television via the networks and for home video rental. These aftermarkets, in fact, have come to account for far more revenue to major Hollywood studios than their movie-making.

Radio. Radio demassified with the arrival of television. The television networks first took radio's most successful programs and moved them to the screen. Having lost its traditional programming strengths, radio then lost both the mass audience and advertisers it had built up since the 1920s. For survival, individual radio stations shifted almost entirely to recorded music and geared the music to narrower and narrower audience segments.

technology of television

(STUDY PREVIEW) Television is based on electronic technology. Light-sensitive cameras scan a scene with incredibly fast sweeps across several hundred horizontally stacked lines. The resulting electronic blips are transmitted to receivers, which recreate the original image by sending electrons across horizontally stacked lines on a screen.

electronic scanning

In the 1920s an Idaho farm boy, **Philo Farnsworth,** came up with the idea for using a vacuum tube to pick up moving images and then display them electronically on a screen. Farnsworth found financial backers to build a lab, and in 1927 the first live moving image was transmitted. At age 21, Philo Farnsworth had invented television. Farnsworth's tube, which he called the **image dissector,** was an incredible feat considering that some of the world's great corporate research labs, including RCA's, were trying to accomplish the same thing.

Not wanting to be upstaged, RCA claimed its **Vladimir Zworykin** had invented a tube, the **iconoscope,** and deserved the credit for television. That would have meant, of course, that RCA would reap a fortune from patent rights. In a patent trial, however, it was learned that both Zworykin and his boss, RCA chief David Sarnoff, had visited Farnsworth's lab and had the opportunity to pirate his invention. Zworykin claimed he had the idea for the iconoscope as early as 1923, but his evidence was not forthcoming. RCA ended up paying Farnsworth a license fee to use his technology.

In retrospect, the technology seems simple. A camera picks up light reflected off a moving subject and converts the light to electrons. The electrons are zapped one at a time across stacked horizontal lines on a screen. The electrons follow each other back and forth so fast that they seem to show the movement picked up by the camera. As with the motion picture, the system freezes movement at fraction-of-second intervals and then replays it to create an illusion of movement—the **persistence of vision** phenomenon. There is a difference, however. Motion pictures use chemical-based photographic processes. Television uses electronics, not chemicals, and images recorded by the camera are transmitted instantly to a receiving tube.

integrated standardization

Westinghouse, RCA and General Electric pooled their television research in 1930, and Zworykin was put in charge to develop a national television system. By the time the United States entered World War II in 1941, there were 10 commercial stations licensed, and several companies were manufacturing home receivers. With war, however, all these energies were diverted to the war effort.

Even after the war, there were delays. The Federal Communications Commission, wanting to head off topsy-turvy expansion that might create problems later, halted further station licensing in 1948. Not until 1952 did the FCC settle on a comprehensive licensing and frequency allocation system and lift the freeze. The freeze gave the FCC time to settle on a uniform system for the next step in television's evolution: color. RCA wanted a system that could transmit to both existing black-and-white

Philo Farnsworth
Invented technology that uses electrons to transmit moving images live.

image dissector
Farnsworth's television vacuum tube.

Vladimir Zworykin
RCA engineer who claimed to invent television.

iconoscope
Zworykin's television vacuum tube.

persistence of vision
Retina's capability to retain an image briefly, allowing brain to fill in gaps between successive images.

philo farnsworth

Farm Boy Invention. Harvesting an Idaho potato field in 1921, the 13-year Philo Farnsworth came up with the idea to transmit moving pictures live on a magnetically deflected electron beam. Crafting his own materials, including hand-blown tubes, Farnsworth completed his first image dissector while barely in his 20s. Later, RCA used the technology for its flamboyant public introduction of television.

Philo Farnsworth was 11 when his family loaded three covered wagons to move to a farm near Rigby in eastern Idaho. Cresting a ridge, young Farnsworth, at the reins of one wagon, surveyed the homestead below and saw wires linking the buildings. "This place has electricity!" he exclaimed. Philo obsessed on the electricity, and soon he was an expert at fixing anything electrical that went wrong.

That day when the Farnsworths settled near Rigby, in 1919, was a pivotal moment in young Farnsworth's life that led to technology on which television is based.

The next pivotal moment came two years later when Philo Farnsworth was 13. He found an article that scientists were working on ways to add pictures to radio but they couldn't figure out how. He then went out to hitch the horses to a harvesting machine to bring in the potatoes. As he guided the horses back and forth across the field, up one row, down the next, he visualized how moving pictures could be captured live and transmitted to a faraway place. If the light that enables people to see could be converted to electrons and then transmitted one at a time but very fast as a beam, back and forth on a surface, then, perhaps, television could work.

The ideas simmered a few months and then, when he was 14, Farnsworth chalked a complicated diagram for "electronic television" on his chemistry teacher's blackboard. The teacher, Justin Tolman, was impressed. In fact, 15 years later Tolman would reconstruct those blackboard schematics so convincingly that Farnsworth would win a patent war with RCA and cloud RCA's claim that its Vladimir Zworykin invented television.

Farnsworth's native intelligence, earnestness and charm helped win over the people around him. When he was 19, working in Salt Lake City, Farnsworth found a man with connections to San Francisco investors. With their backing, the third pivotal moment in Farnsworth's work, he set up a lab in Los Angeles, and later in San Francisco, and put his drawings and theories to work. In 1927, with hand-blown tubes and hand-soldered connections, Farnsworth had a gizmo he called the image dissector. It picked up the image of a glass slide and transmitted it. The Idaho farm boy had invented television.

When David Sarnoff, the patent-mongering vice president at RCA, hired Vladimir Zworykin in 1930 to develop television, he told Zworykin first thing to pay a visit on Farnsworth in California. Not knowing Zworykin was with RCA, Farnsworth gave him the run of the lab for three days. Not long thereafter Sarnoff himself came by and saw television for the first time. He offered $100,000 for everything. The answer was no.

Three years later, RCA began touting a camera system based on something called an Iconoscope developed by its own Vladimir Zworykin. Indignant and feeling conned, Farnsworth challenged RCA's patent. It turned out that Zworykin's claim to being first, way back in 1923, was mushy. Farnsworth won the patent case. The RCA publicity machine, however, placed Zworykin in the public's mind as the father of the technology that begat television. To many people, rightly or wrongly, Farnsworth gets only honorable mention. The fact is that, in the end, RCA paid Farnsworth royalties to use his technology.

1927 Philo Farnsworth devised tube that picked up moving images for transmission.

1939 RCA demonstrated television at New York World's Fair.

1947 CBS began newscast with Douglas Edwards, and NBC with John Cameron Swayze.

1951 Edward R. Murrow and Fred Friendly began CBS documentaries.

1951 "I Love Lucy" became filmed and edited program, starting Hollywood in television production.

1952 FCC adopted national standard for compatible black-and-

white and color transmission.

1967 Congress authorized funds to create Public Broadcasting System.

1975 Gerald Levin put HBO on satellite for cable systems.

1976 Ted Turner put WTBS, Atlanta, on satellite for cable systems.

1986 Rupert Murdoch created Fox network.

1995 Time Warner created WB network.

1995 Viacom created UPN network.

and new color sets. CBS favored a system that had superior clarity, but people would have to buy new sets to pick it up, and even then they would not be able to receive black-and-white programs. Finally, in 1953, the FCC settled on the RCA system.

high-definition television

Just as the FCC was slow to approve a color television system, it also moved slowly on technology to improve on-screen picture quality. European television, with images created on 825 horizontal lines across the screen, was always sharper than the 525-line U.S. system. In the 1980s the Japanese introduced HDTV, short for high-definition television, with 1,124 lines. After exhaustive evaluations, the FCC acted in 1997, not only to catch up but to leapfrog European and Japanese technology. The commission ordered a reshuffling of bandwidth, and gave stations an additional channel to accommodate digital transmissions that can make super-sharp screen images possible. By the year 2006, all U.S. broadcasters are obligated to be transmitting in the new digital formats.

web-television convergence

Theoretically the transition to digital television will facilitate the convergence of television with other media. Images could be so crisp that it would be possible to read text on-screen—not just today's billboard-type huge-letter messages, but fine type. Newspaper and magazine articles would be able to deliver the kind of word-driven products they now put on paper. The images could even rival movies for image quality. Importantly, people would be able to shift seamlessly from what they today watch on television to what they do on the World Wide Web.

Online Peacock. A 1995 joint venture of NBC television and the Microsoft computer giant stepped up the competition to be on the ground floor of the emerging cybermedia. In a high-tech news conference, NBC President Bob Wright in New York and Microsoft Chairman Bill Gates in Hong Kong announced that NBC's America's Talking cable network would become MSNBC. Microsoft put up $250 million for the stake in television; NBC, meanwhile, is creating news content for the new Microsoft online service.

Whether the full potential of this convergence will be realized is up in the air. In 1997 the computer industry suffered a serious setback in trying to convince the FCC to base the new HDTV standards on computer rather than television onscreen technology. The technologies aren't compatible, and the computer people were hopeful that the commission would go for their approach, which yields superior visuals. The commission rejected the PCTV plan (PCTV is short for "personal computer television") as too complex.

Disappointed but undeterred, computer companies charged ahead with products like WebTV that manipulate on-screen television images to display text-driven messages like e-mail. While the quality is far short of PCTV, the market potential seemed strong enough to prompt Bill Gates, chief of the giant Microsoft computer company, to pay $425 million to buy WebTV's parent company to exploit the potential.

interactive television

WebTV and PCTV both are examples of interactive television, using a receiver screen to display incoming and outgoing communications. In time, such two-way communication may actually be piggy-backed on over-air television signals, but now it is merely a jazzed-up telephone connection in most cases. The internet messages—e-mail as well as the web—actually are coming and going through telephone jacks when viewers switch from the television mode to the web mode.

The next stage in upgrading interactive television will be when telephone and cable companies complete their fiber-optic networks all the way to individual consumers. Fiber-optic cables will have the capacity to accommodate so much data that single-route two-way communication will be possible.

Also, some over-air stations that now have extra channel space, which was assigned by the FCC to deliver HDTV signals eventually, are expected to instead use the expended bandwidth to offer two-way communication services.

structure of u.s. television

(STUDY PREVIEW)   The U.S. television system was built on both a local and a national foundation. As it did with radio, the FCC licensed local stations with the goal of a diversified system. At the same time, networks gave the system a national character.

dual national system

Congress and the Federal Communications Commission were generally satisfied with the American radio system that had taken form by the 1930s, and they set up a similar structure for television. The FCC invited people who wanted to build stations in local communities to apply for a federal license. As a condition of their FCC license, station owners raised the money to build the technical facilities, to develop an economic base and to provide programming. These stations, which broadcast over the airwaves, the same as radio, became the core of a locally based national television system. It was the same regulated yet free-enterprise approach that had developed for radio. By contrast, governments in most other countries financed and built centralized national television systems.

Even though the FCC regulated a locally based television system, the U.S. system soon had a national flavor. NBC and CBS modeled television networks on their radio networks and provided programs to the new local television stations. Today, American television still has a backbone in the networks. Of 1,160 full-power local over-air commercial stations, two-thirds are affiliates of one of the three major networks, ABC, CBS or NBC. In almost every city, it is the network-affiliated stations that have the most viewers.

affiliate–network relations

A network affiliation is an asset to local stations. Programs offered by the networks are of a quality that an individual station cannot afford to produce. With quality network programs, stations attract larger audiences than they could on their own. Larger audiences mean that stations can charge higher rates for local advertisements in the six to eight minutes per hour the networks leave open for affiliates to fill. Stations also profit directly from affiliations. The networks share their advertising revenue with affiliates, paying each affiliate 30 percent of the local advertising rate for time that network-sold advertisements take. Typically almost 10 percent of a station's income is from the network.

Affiliate-network relations are not entirely money-making bliss. The networks, whose advertising rates are based on the number of viewers they have, would prefer that all affiliates carry all their programs. Affiliates, however, sometimes have sufficient financial incentives to preempt network programming. Broadcasting a state basketball tournament can generate lots of local advertising. The networks also would prefer that affiliates confine their quest for advertising to their home areas, leaving national ads to the networks. Local stations, however, accept national advertising on their own, which they schedule inside and between programs, just as they do local advertising.

....japanese television

Anyone who owns a television set in Japan can expect a knock on the door every couple of months. It is the collector from NHK, the Japan Broadcast Corporation, to pick up the $16 reception fee. This ritual occurs six times a year in 31 million doorways. The reception fee, required by law since 1950, produces $2.6 billion annually to support the NHK network.

NHK is a Japanese tradition. It went on the air in 1926, a single radio station, the first broadcast of which was the enthronement of Emperor Hirohito. Today, NHK operates three radio and two domestic television networks. It also runs Radio Japan, the national overseas shortwave service, which transmits 40 hours of programs a day in 21 languages.

The primary NHK television network, Channel One, offers mostly highbrow programming, which gives NHK its reputation as the good gray network. Medieval samurai epics have been a long-term staple. NHK also is known for programs like the 1980 "Silk Road," 30 hours total, which traced early Europe-Japan trade across Asia. NHK airs about 600 hours a year of British and American documentaries and dramas from the BBC and PBS. The network prides itself on its news.

Some NHK programs, such as the 15-minute Sunday morning "Serial Novel," have huge followings. Ratings regularly are 50 percent. Most Japanese viewers, however, spend most of their television time with stations served by four networks, all with headquarters in Tokyo: Fuji, NHK, NTV and Tokyo Broadcasting System. A few independent stations complete Japan's television system.

The commercial stations all offer similar fare: comedies, pop concerts and videos, quiz shows, sports and talk shows. In recent years, news has gained importance in attracting viewers and advertisers, encroaching on one of NHK's traditional strengths.

The networks have learned to pay more heed to affiliate relations in recent years. Unhappy affiliates have been known to leave one network for another. Television chains like Group W or Gannett have a major bargaining chip with networks because, with a single stroke of a pen, they can change the affiliations of several stations. This happened in 1994 when Fox lured 12 stations away from the Big-Three networks, eight of them from CBS alone.

Also, affiliates are organized to deal en masse with their networks. In 1982 the affiliates forced CBS and NBC to abandon plans to expand the evening network newscasts to 60 minutes. An hour-long newscast would have lost lucrative station slots for local advertising. One estimate is that the stations would have lost $260 million a year in advertising revenue, far more than network payments would have brought in.

Networks once required affiliates to carry most network programs, which guaranteed network advertisers a large audience. Most stations were not bothered by the requirement, which dated to network radio's early days, because they received a slice of the network advertising revenue. Even so, the requirement eventually was declared coercive by the FCC, which put an end to it. There remains pressure on affiliates, however, to carry a high percentage of network programs. If a station does not, the network might transfer the affiliation to a competing station. At the same time, the FCC decision increased the opportunities for affiliates to seek programming from nonnetwork sources, which increased pressure on networks to provide popular programs.

delivery systems

(STUDY PREVIEW) Engineers, broadcast leaders and the Federal Communications Commission structured television delivery much like radio. The original over-air system is now supplemented with cable and satellite-direct delivery.

over-air stations

The engineers and corporate leaders who conceived television really thought in terms of **radio with pictures.** That's not surprising. These people, from Vladimir Zworykin to David Sarnoff, were radio people. The television systems they built used towers, just like radio, to send signals via the electromagnetic spectrum to homes, just like radio. And just like radio, the Federal Communications Commission issued licenses to local station operators to encourage localism and diversity in programming.

The networks, primarily CBS and NBC, thwarted localism and diversity to a great extent by creating popular national programs for local stations. Just like radio, this created a two-tier national television system. Stations were local and offered local programs, but the most popular shows came from the national networks. The networks really came into their own, with strong advertising revenue, when **coaxial cable** linked the East and West coasts in 1951. Pioneer broadcast newsman Edward R. Murrow opened his "See It Now" with live pictures from cameras on the Atlantic and Pacific oceans. People marveled.

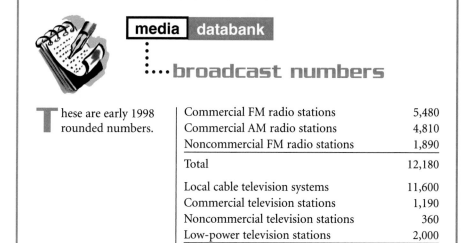

media   databank

broadcast numbers

These are early 1998 rounded numbers.

Commercial FM radio stations	5,480
Commercial AM radio stations	4,810
Noncommercial FM radio stations	1,890
Total	12,180
Local cable television systems	11,600
Commercial television stations	1,190
Noncommercial television stations	360
Low-power television stations	2,000
Total	15,150

radio with pictures
Simplistic definition of TV.
coaxial cable
Heavy-duty landline for video signals.

Satellite Delivery. With the notable exception of sparsely populated Siberia, CNN reaches most of the earth's land mass with overlapping signals from 15 satellites. You almost have to work at being beyond the reach of the "birds" on which the net work buys signal-relay capacity. The satellites, in geosynchronous orbit, pick up signals that CNN aims upward, then the on-board equipment amplifies and relays the signals back to earth, feeding local cable systems, over-air stations, and hotels and other in-house distribution systems.

cable systems

Two-thirds of U.S. households today receive television via wire. Beginning in the early 1950s, entrepreneurs in outlying towns with poor reception built towers to capture signals and then send them by wire to local viewers. In the 1980s, major cities were wired. These cable systems carry programs from over-air stations in their area plus, since the late 1970s, a lot of exclusive programming picked up from satellites.

Cable companies tacked their wires on utility poles, but their coaxial cable was, in fact, much better than telephone wire because it had to carry much more sophisticated signals. Today, cable companies and phone companies are in a race to replace their wires with **optical fiber cable** to deliver more data and sharper pictures. Fiber optics can carry signals that can make on-screen delivery as sharp as a computer screen's visuals. In fact, cable and phone companies see their future in offering a vast array of telecomputer services.

satellite direct

Stanley Hubbard owned a profitable over-air station in Minnesota, but he came to see that his KSTP was a dinosaur in an age of satellite communication. Why should people need to tune into his station, which picked up network signals from satellite, when they could tune in directly to the satellite? For more than a decade, Hubbard poured millions of dollars into his vision for **direct-broadcast satellite** delivery, DBS for short. In 1994, Hubbard and a General Motors subsidiary, DirecTV, launched **Digital Satellite Service.** Since then, other satellite direct services have begun operation, not only to serve viewers in the United States but all over the world.

optical fiber cable
High-capacity glass filament for video signals.

Stanley Hubbard
Pioneer of direct broadcast transmission.

DBS
Direct-broadcast satellite with transmission from orbit to receiver; no TV station or cable system intermediary.

Digital Satellite Service
Pioneer DBS company.

over-air networks

(STUDY PREVIEW) Three national networks, first NBC and CBS, then ABC, have dominated programming to local over-air stations since World War II. Today, newcomers Fox, Time Warner and Viacom are trying for a slice of the audience.

traditional networks

For 40 years, television in the United States was dominated by three national networks—**ABC, CBS** and **NBC.** Their only early competitor, the Dumont network, couldn't make it and began a slow withering in 1955 and died three years later. The **Big Three** networks built up local affiliates, about 200 each, to carry their programs in every major market and a lot of smaller ones.

nbc television

The federal government licensed the first television stations in 1941, on the eve of U.S. entry into World War II. But when factories converted to war production, there were no more television sets manufactured until after peace arrived in 1945. By 1948, the coaxial cables that were necessary to carry television signals had been laid to the Midwest, and NBC began feeding programs to affiliates. The coaxial linkup, with some stretches connected by **microwave relays,** connected the East and West coasts in 1951.

NBC innovations included two brainstorms by **Pat Weaver,** an ad executive recruited to the network as a vice president. In 1951 Weaver created a late-night comedy-variety talk show, precursor to the venerable "Tonight Show." Weaver also created an early morning entry, the still-viable "Today." With those shows, NBC owned the early morning and insomniac audiences for years. Weaver also authorized special one-shot programs, spectaculars he called them, which preempted regular programs and drew regular viewers from other networks without losing NBC's regulars.

In 1985, **General Electric** bought NBC. During a three-year period, 1982 to 1985, all of the Big Three networks moved out of the hands of the broadcast executives, like NBC's **David Sarnoff,** who grew up in the business and nurtured these giant influential entities. As it turned out, the Big Three heyday was over with new competitive pressures from cable and other quarters. The new owners, with their focus on the bottom line and their cost-cutting instincts, fundamentally changed network television for a new era.

cbs television

CBS was outmaneuvered by NBC in lining up affiliates after World War II but caught up. By 1953, CBS edged out NBC in audience size by acquiring affiliates and creating popular programs.

The old CBS radio soap operas, transported to television in 1951, were a factor. So was a science fiction anthology, which paved the way for "The Twilight Zone." Also by 1953, the "I Love Lucy" sitcom series, which eventually included 140 episodes, was a major draw.

ABC Television
American Broadcasting Company. Built from ABC radio network. One of Big Three over-air networks.

CBS Television
Columbia Broadcasting System. Built from CBS radio network under William Paley. One of Big Three over-air networks.

NBC Television
National Broadcast Company. Built from NBC radio network under David Sarnoff. One of Big Three over-air networks.

Big Three
ABC, CBS, NBC.

microwave relays
Towers re-angle over-air signals to match earth's curvature.

Pat Weaver
Created NBC's "Tonight Show," "Today."

General Electric
Current NBC owner.

David Sarnoff
Longtime NBC boss.

Edward R. Murrow
Reporter who criticized Joseph McCarthy.

William Paley
Longtime CBS boss.

United Paramount Theaters
Strengthened ABC in 1953 merger.

Roone Arledge
Created ABC's "Wide World of Sports."

CapCities
Owner of ABC before purchase by Disney.

Allen Dumont
Operated early fourth network.

Dumont network
1950–1958.

CBS established its legacy in television public affairs programming when **Edward R. Murrow,** famous for his live radio reporting from Europe, started "See It Now." Three years later, when Senator Joseph McCarthy was using his office to smear people, it was Murrow on "See It Now" who exposed the senator's dubious tactics. Many scholars credit Murrow with undoing McCarthy and easing the Red Scare that McCarthy was promoting.

The CBS television network was shepherded in its early years by **Bill Paley,** who had earlier created the CBS radio network. Paley retired in 1982, and Laurence Tisch, a hotel mogul, came into control of CBS. Today, Westinghouse owns the network.

abc television

ABC established its television network in 1948 but ran a poor third. Things began changing in 1953 when ABC merged with **United Paramount Theaters,** whose properties included several television stations. The new company went into fast production schedules of programs that were aimed at Hollywood-like mass audiences. Live programming, the hallmark of early network television, was not part of ABC's recipe. By 1969 more than 90 percent of the network's programs were on film, tightly edited and with no live gaffes. It worked. ABC's 1964 fall lineup made national network television a three-way race for the first time.

ABC's growth was pegged largely to two Disney programs, "Disneyland" in 1954 and "The Mickey Mouse Club" in 1955. Another audience-builder was ABC's decision not to carry gavel-to-gavel coverage of the national political conventions. That brought criticism that ABC was abdicating its public responsibility, but by leaving the conventions mostly to CBS and NBC, ABC cleaned up in the ratings with an entertainment alternative. ABC picked up more steam in 1961 with its "Wide World of Sports," a weekend anthology with appeal that extended beyond sports fans. **Roone Arledge,** the network sports chief, created "Monday Night Football" in 1969. Network television not only was a three-way race again, but in 1975 ABC was leading by a hair.

CapCities Communications, a profitable Kansas City-based television station chain, bought ABC in 1985. The network's parent company operated as ABC/CapCities until Disney bought the operation in 1996.

dumont television

Allen Dumont sometimes ends up merely a footnote in television history, which is unfortunate. He was telecasting in New York as early as CBS, in 1939, and his station and NBC both aired the 1940 presidential election returns. After World War II, Dumont was the right person in the right place. He had a company that manufactured the first television receivers, coinciding with the new public demand for them. Dumont, in fact, beat RCA to the market by several weeks. With his manufacturing profits, Dumont built stations in the District of Columbia and Pittsburgh. In 1950 he created the **Dumont network.**

At its peak, the Dumont network transmitted 21 hours of prime-time shows to 160 affiliates, but it never rivaled ABC, CBS and NBC. The Big Three had a foundation of radio experience on which to build their television networks. Dumont didn't. Revenues, at best, were only a third that of the bigger networks. Dumont affiliates were mostly the poorest stations in their markets, with the smallest audiences. In 1955, when the investors were queuing up to buy television stations, Dumont sold his Pittsburgh station for $9.8 million—almost 10 times the value of its physical assets—and began deemphasizing the network, which went dark in 1958.

For many years nobody attempted a fourth network. The national television field was the exclusive domain of ABC, CBS and NBC from 1955 until 1986 when Fox came along.

fox television

In the 1980s media baron **Rupert Murdoch** bought seven non-network stations in major cities and also the 20th Century-Fox movie studio. The stations gave Murdoch the nucleus for a fourth over-air television network, and 20th Century-Fox gave him production facilities and a huge movie library. Murdoch recruited **Barry Diller,** whose track record included impressive programming successes at ABC, to head his proposed **Fox** network. In 1986 Fox went on the air, the signal going to Murdoch's stations and to affiliates among other independent stations nationwide. First there was a late-night talk show, then Sunday night shows and then Saturday night shows. Today Fox has at least two hours of prime-time programming every night. With 190 affiliates, Fox is close to the 200 of the other networks although the Fox affiliates generally have smaller local followings.

Fox became profitable quickly. The plan was to build an audience one night at a time with relatively inexpensive programming. This included the crude, dysfunctional Bundys in "Married . . . With Children" and the Bart Simpson cartoon series. Those programs attracted mostly young people in their free-spending years, as did Fox's "Beverly Hills 90210" and "Melrose Place." That audience made the network hot with advertisers. Controlling expenses was essential in the Murdoch-Diller plan. To keep costs down, for example, Fox had no news division in its start-up years. Programs like "Cops" and "America's Most Wanted," built around live police footage and recreated crimes, were inexpensive to produce.

late-comers

Over-air television network competition intensified in the latter 1990s with three upstart networks. The Warner Brothers and United Paramount networks signed on in 1995, both admittedly trying to ape Fox's approach for a young audience. In 1997, the Pax Net signed on.

Warner Brothers. Back in 1955 some people found the Warner Brothers cartoon "One Froggy Evening" funny. You judge for yourself. There was this frog that would break into song, usually "I'm Just Wild About Harry." His owner sensed a fast buck in this performing frog, but at every audition the frog would emit only a faint ribit. Funny? Regardless, Time Warner chose Michigan J. Frog as the mascot for the new over-air television network it launched in 1995.

The **WB Television Network** took $300 million to start up, but Time Warner thought it would work. Using much the same formula as Fox a few years earlier, WB started with a limited schedule, two hours prime-time on Wednesdays, with the goal of building it up. In charge were two former Fox executives, Garth Ancier and Jamie Kellner. And, no surprise, they aimed for a young adult audience, as had Fox.

Warner started with 43 affiliates, far short of roughly the 200 traditional networks, but Chicago super station WGN, which is picked up by many cable systems, also carried WB programs. The company claimed Michigan G. Frog was reaching 72 percent of the population.

Talk Shows. When CBS put David Letterman opposite the venerable "Tonight" show, the network had a lot at stake. The success of the show depended on how many of the network's affiliates would air it rather than the profitable sitcom reruns and old movies. Letterman survived the test, with offbeat humor and guests performing wild antics, like actress Drew Barrymore dancing on his desk.

Rupert Murdoch
Created Fox network.
Barry Diller
Created early successful Fox programming.
Fox
Launched 1986.
WBTV
New network for over-air affiliates; started in 1995.

United Paramount. A week after WB Television went on the air in 1995, **United Paramount Network** began beaming four hours of programming, on Mondays and Tuesdays, to stations that reached 79 percent of the country via 96 affiliates. Paramount predicted it would match Fox's audience right away, primarily on the strength of yet another Star Trek series, "Voyager." Like Fox and WB, United Paramount played for a young audience. In fact, early programs were Fox look-alikes, including "Unhappily Ever After," remarkably similar to Fox's "Married . . . With Children." Other programs included former Fox stars Robert Townsend and brothers Shawn and Marlon Wayans.

Like Fox and WB, United Paramount was well financed. Paramount Communications was a subsidiary of the deep-pocketed Viacom media giant.

Pax Net. Over the years Bud Paxson cobbled together a group of television stations in disparate markets. By 1998 he calculated that he had a critical mass to launch a seventh over-air national network. He signed on some additional stations as affiliates, and Pax Net was a reality. Paxson differentiated his network by aiming programs at women, with old episodes of "Touched by an Angel," "Sisters" and "Dr. Quinn." When Pax Net signed on, 65 stations in the network could reach roughly 60 percent of the nation's television sets.

cable television

(STUDY PREVIEW) The cable television industry has grown from independent small-town community antenna systems into a well-heeled, consolidated industry. Today cable is a major threat to the traditional networks and their over-air affiliates.

roots of cable

Cable companies, which deliver pictures by wire, often on utility poles strung through alleys, have siphoned millions of viewers from television stations that deliver programming over the air. Cable and over-air broadcasters are now rivals, but it was not always so.

In the early 1950s, the Big Three networks and their local affiliates reached only major cities. Television signals, like FM radio, do not follow the curvature of the earth, so communities 40 to 50 miles away were pretty much out of range. Rough terrain kept even nearer towns from receiving television. One by one, small-town entrepreneurs hoisted antennas on nearby hilltops to catch television signals from the nearest cities with over-air stations. These local cable television systems, called **CATV,** for community antenna television, ran a cable down into town and stretched wire on telephone poles to deliver pictures to houses from the hilltop antenna. Everybody was happy. Small-town America got big-city television, local entrepreneurs made money, and the networks and their stations gained viewers they couldn't otherwise reach. With this larger, cable-enhanced audience, the networks and stations were able to hike advertising rates.

gerald levin and hbo

Television entered a new era in 1975 when **Gerald Levin** took over **HBO,** a Time-Life subsidiary. HBO had been offering movies and special events, such as champi-

UPN
New network for over-air affiliates; started in 1995.

CATV
Short for Community Antenna Television. An early name for cable systems.

Gerald Levin
Offered exclusive HBO programming to cable systems.

HBO
Short for Home Box Office. First cable programming via satellite.

ed parsons

In Astoria, Oregon, downriver from Portland at the mouth of the Columbia, Ed Parsons built the first cable television system. Parsons had tinkered with radio since he was a kid, and nobody in Astoria had been surprised when he built the local station, KAST. In 1946, with hundreds of fellow station operators from around the country, Ed and his wife Grace attended a national broadcast convention in Chicago. There they saw a demonstration of television—and Grace was hooked. Two years later, when they heard that a Seattle station was beginning experimental telecasting. Grace told Ed that if anybody could figure out how to get the television signal from Seattle, 125 miles north, it was him.

There were problems. One was that television signals travel straight rather than follow the earth's curvature. As a result, reception is chancy beyond 50 miles. Another

problem was the 4,000-foot coastal range, which not only blocked reception from Seattle but also diverted signals helter-skelter across the landscape.

Parsons, a pilot, took a modified FM receiver and flew around Clatsop County to find the Seattle station's audio signal. He also roamed backroads with another receiver to find a place to raise an antenna, but none was practicable. Then he discovered a suitable signal came in at the roof of the eight-story John Jacob Astor Hotel downtown—a bit more than a stone's throw from his and Grace's apartment.

Parsons jury-rigged an antenna, mounted it on the hotel roof, and strung a line from the hotel penthouse to his living room. On Thanksgiving Day 1948, Grace turned on the set in their living room while Ed, listening to her reports on a walkie-talkie, adjusted the antenna on the Astor Hotel roof until, eventually, the Seattle station came in.

That, however, was hardly a cable system. But what happened next, and Ed Parsons' response to it, led to Astoria's community cable system. As Ed Parsons recalled years later: "We literally lost our house. People would drive for hundreds of miles to see television. When people drove down from Portland or came from The Dalles or from Klamath Falls to see television, you couldn't tell them no." In her book, *CATV: The History of Community Antenna Television,* Mary Alice Mayer Philips said the situation got so bad on Christmas Eve that Parsons chased everyone out and locked the door.

Parsons' first solution was a proposal to the manager of the Astor Hotel. Parsons said he would drop a cable down the elevator shaft if the hotel would make a television set available in the lobby. The manager thought it would be good for business, little realizing

that the television would draw so many people to the hotel lobby that guests wouldn't be able to squeeze their way to the registration desk.

Next Parsons persuaded a music store down the street to put a set in a display window. It, too, seemed like a good idea—until traffic jams prompted the police chief to urge Parsons to try something else. At that point, however, in March 1949, Parsons had made history, using cable to connect a television reception antenna with a customer: Cliff Poole's music store.

To alleviate congestion at the store windows, Parsons' next step was to extend the cable through underground utility tunnels to more stores, to taverns and homes. Later he strung cable on utility poles. Within a year Parsons had 25 places hooked up. Six months later there were 75. He charged $125 for installation, then $3 a month.

---

onship boxing, to local cable systems, which sold the programs to subscribers willing to pay an extra fee. It was a **pay-per-view** service. Levin wanted to expand HBO to a pay-per-month service with 24-hour programming, mostly movies. If it worked, this would give local cable systems a premium channel from which to derive extra revenue.

For an expanded HBO to succeed, Levin needed to cut the tremendous expense of relaying HBO transmission across the country from microwave tower to microwave

> **pay-per-view**
> With PPV, cable companies charge subscribers for each program they watch.

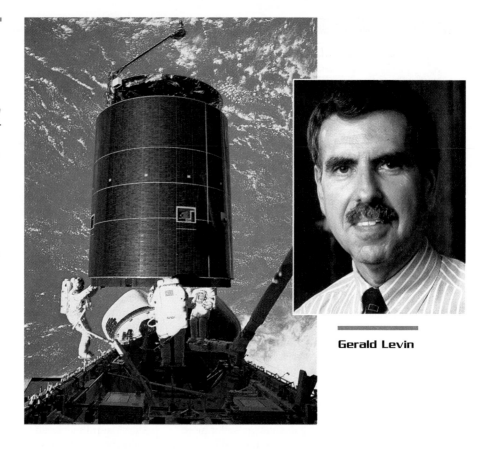

Satellite Delivery. Gerald Levin, president of media titan Time Warner since 1992, made a name for himself by putting HBO on satellite to be transmitted to local cable systems in the 1970s. This revolutionized television by offering distinctive programming, besides that of over-air stations, for customers of local cable systems nationwide. The television industry has never been the same since. Although the cost of orbiting and maintaining complex communication satellites is steep, it is far cheaper than the old landline and microwave relay systems.

Gerald Levin

tower. Then it occurred to Levin: Why not bypass microwaving and instead send the HBO signal to an orbiting satellite, which could then send it back to earth in one relay to every local cable system in the country? Levin put up $7.5 million to use the Satcom 1 satellite. That allowed him to cut microwave costs while expanding programming and making HBO available to more of the country.

turner broadcasting system

The potential of HBO's satellite delivery was not lost on **Ted Turner,** who owned a near down-and-out, non-network UHF station in Atlanta. Turner took a flier, dubbing his WTBS a **superstation** and putting it on satellite. Cable systems stumbled over themselves to sign up. Turner was giving them an additional channel to entice people to hook up—even if they were already getting over-air stations without cable.

In 1980 Turner put together **CNN,** a 24-hour news service which enticed more people to subscribe to local cable services. Turner charged cable companies modestly for his services, a few pennies per month per local subscriber. He also worked at developing a stream of revenue from national advertisers.

growth of cable

HBO barely dented the over-air stations' viewership, reaching only 265,000 homes at the outset, but everyone recognized that HBO was leading the way toward a restructuring of the U.S. television industry. On Wall Street, cable became hot. Invest-

Ted Turner
Cable pioneer with WTBS superstation, CNN, and other program services to cable systems.

superstation
Over-air station available by satellite to local cable systems.

CNN
Short for Cable News Network. First 24-hour TV news network.

media people

····ted turner

Ted Turner

When his father died, Ted Turner inherited a floundering Atlanta television station that hardly anybody watched. Back then, in 1963, many television sets could not pick up channels higher than 13, which meant that Turners' WTGC, like other UHF stations, was nonexistent in many households. Advertising revenue was thin, and it was not easy to make the rent for the decrepit building that housed the studios. Only 60 people were on the payroll. Fumigators sprayed for fleas weekly.

Young Turner threw himself energetically into making something of the inheritance. He did everything himself, even stocking the soda machine. More important, he recognized that WTGC was condemned to a shoe-string future unless he could offer viewers more than old B movies and sitcom reruns. Desperate to diversify programming, Turner borrowed enough money to buy the cellar-dwelling Atlanta Braves and Atlanta Hawks teams in the mid-1970s. The purchases spread Turner's finances even thinner, but they gave WTGC something distinctive to offer.

Turner then turned to his other major problem—WTGC's obscure UHF channel. Learning that HBO was planning to beam programs to an orbiting satellite for retransmission to local cable systems nationwide, he decided to do the same. Turner redubbed his station WTBS in 1976, bought satellite time and persuaded cable systems to add his "superstation" to their package of services. Overnight, Turner multiplied the audience for his old movies, sitcom reruns, and Atlanta pro sports. WTBS began attracting national advertising, something WTGC never could.

Ted Turner stopped refilling the soda machine himself, but he still worked hard. He kept an old bathrobe at his office and slept on the couch when he worked late. His mind never stopped. He considered a second cable network—a 24-hour television news service. In 1980, again stretching his finances to the limit, Turner bought an old mansion, outfitted it with the latest electronic news-gathering and editing equipment, hired a couple dozen anchors and launched Cable News Network. A few months later, with CNN still deep in red ink, Turner learned that ABC and Westinghouse were setting up the Satellite News Channel, which would compete with CNN. To discourage cable systems from picking up the competitor, Turner decided over a weekend to establish a second news network himself, and "Headline News" was born. The gamble worked, and ABC and Westinghouse sold their news network to Turner, who promptly shut it down.

Almost overnight in 1991, a key part of Turner's vision came to fruition. CNN leaped to industry dominance with its 24-hour coverage of the Persian Gulf war. Government and industry leaders worldwide watched it for quicker and better information than they could obtain through their own sources. Not infrequently, other news organizations ended up quoting CNN because they couldn't match the network's no-holds-barred commitment to thoroughness and timeliness. Turner's audience swelled, as each day CNN earned greater and wider respect. Back when it went on the air, CNN had been laughed at as "Chicken Noodle News." No more.

Turner sold CNN and the whole bevy of his other networks to Time Warner in 1995, but he remains in charge of them all as a Time Warner, vice president.

ors poured in dollars. This financed more cable network startups, construction of new cable systems and buy-outs of existing cable systems.

Networkstart-Ups. Ted Turner's operation became a money machine that financed a second news channel, CNN Headline News, and the TNT entertainment network. Soon there were other players: the ESPN sports network, a weather network, music video networks, home-shopping networks. While people once had a choice of ABC, CBS, NBC, PBS and perhaps an independent station or two, they now could choose among dozens of channels. The audience that was once the exclusive province of over-air networks and stations was fragmenting rapidly.

Urban Cable Construction.   The original cable industry was comprised of small-town operations to bring in distant signals. With the new satellite programs, however, companies with deep pockets smelled huge profits if they could wire major cities, which they did. Today, more than 90 percent of the U.S. population has access to cable, and about 65 percent subscribes.

Cable System Buyouts.   The prospects of huge profits led to a consolidation of the cable industry. TeleCommunications Inc. of Denver, usually called TCI, bought up small cable companies around the country and emerged a major player in U.S. mass media. Other companies, including Time Warner and Cox, built urban systems and bought up existing cable companies.

advertising

Like the original CATV systems, the new cable companies made their money by charging subscribers a monthly fee to be hooked up. Soon, though, cable companies went after a second stream of revenue: advertisers. There was a model in the early satellite program services, like Turner's WTBS and CNN, which had aggressively pursued advertisers from ABC, CBS and NBC. Local cable systems did it locally, however, going after advertisers that over-air stations had regarded as exclusively theirs for 40 years.

The original cozy relationship between over-air broadcasters and those little CATV companies in small-town America was all over. The cable industry had become a giant.

television entertainment

(**STUDY PREVIEW**)   Early national television networks patterned their programs on their successful radio experience, even adapting specific radio programs to the screen. Until "I Love Lucy" in 1951, programs were aired live. Today, most entertainment programming is taped and then polished by editing.

early programming

In the early days of television, the networks provided their affiliate stations with video versions of popular radio programs, mostly comedy and variety shows. Like radio, the programs originated in New York. With videotape still to be invented, almost everything was broadcast live. Early television drama had a live theatrical on-stage quality that is lost with today's multiple taping of scenes and slick editing. Comedy shows like Milton Berle's and variety shows like Ed Sullivan's, also live, had a spontaneity that typified early television.

The Innovative "Lucy." The long-running television series "I Love Lucy," starting in 1951, was taped and then edited for polish. This practice was a departure from other television programs, which, being broadcast live, lacked "Lucy's" slickness. The program also was significant because Desi Arnaz and Lucille Ball, who created the series, refused to live in New York where most television programs were being produced. The show thus became a Hollywood production and marked the beginning of the shift of television entertainment program production to California.

Desi Arnaz and **Lucille Ball**'s "I Love Lucy" situation comedy, introduced in 1951, was significant not just because it was such a hit but because it was not transmitted live. Rather, multiple cameras filmed several takes. Film editors then chose the best shots, the best lines and the best facial expressions for the final production. Just as in movie production, sequences could be rearranged in the cutting room. Even comedic pacing and timing could be improved. Final responsibility for what went on the air shifted from actors to editors. Taping also made possible the libraries of programs that are reissued by syndicates for rerunning.

"I Love Lucy" also marked the start of television's shift to Hollywood. Because Arnaz and Ball, who were married at the time, wanted to continue to live in California, they refused to commute to New York to produce the show. Thus, "Lucy" became television's first Los Angeles show. Gradually, most of television's entertainment production went west.

Entertainment programming has grown through phases. Cowboy programs became popular in the 1950s, later supplemented by quiz shows. The cowboy genre was replaced by cop shows in the late 1960s. Through the changes, sitcoms have remained popular, although they have changed with the times, from "Father Knows Best" in the 1950s through "All in the Family" in the 1970s to "Friends" and "Seinfeld" in the 1990s.

producing entertainment programs

Until 1995, the networks produced some entertainment programs but relied on independent companies for the majority of their shows. The independent companies create prototype episodes called **pilots** to entice the networks to buy the whole series, usually a season in advance. When a network buys a series, the show's producers work closely with network programming people on details.

> **Desi Arnaz and Lucille Ball**
> Introduced taping; led the television industry's move to Hollywood.
>
> **pilot**
> Prototype show for a series.

In addition to buying programs from independent producers, networks buy motion pictures from Hollywood, some that have already been on the movie-house circuit and on pay television and others made expressly for the networks. Hollywood studios are among the largest producers of network entertainment programs.

Like the networks, stations buy independently produced entertainment programs. To do this, stations go to distributors, called **syndicators,** who package programs specifically for sale to individual stations, usually for one-time use. Syndicators also sell programs that previously appeared on the networks. These off-network programs, as they are called, sometimes include old episodes of programs still playing on the networks. "Murder, She Wrote," a successful CBS program, went off-net in 1987 to the USA cable network even while new episodes were still being produced for CBS. Local stations, like the networks, also buy old movies from motion picture companies for one-time showing.

changing program standards

Because the networks are responsible for the programs they feed their affiliates, the networks have **standards and practices** units that review every program for content acceptability and sometimes order changes. Although it is gate-keeping, not true censorship, standards and practices people sometimes are called "censors."

At all three major networks, the censorship units once were cautious not to offend viewers, advertisers or the FCC. At one time, censors regularly sent suggestive commercials back to agencies for revision, insisted that Rob and Laura Petrie of "The Dick Van Dyke Show" sleep in separate beds, and even banned the Smothers Brothers' anti-war jabs at President Lyndon Johnson.

The standards and practices units have been downsized in recent years—in part because of greater audience and government acceptance of risqué language and forthright dramatizations. Today, sitcom couples no longer sleep in separate beds and hardly ever in pajamas.

This does not mean there are no limits. In 1993, ABC pushed the limit of some people's tolerance with "NYPD Blue." Many advertisers were at first cautious about signing up for the program. The criticism, mostly from the religious right, led by the Reverend **David Wildmon,** was offset by the critical acclaim the program received. The program also drew large audiences. Many advertisers, despite the criticism, couldn't pass up "NYPD Blue" as an effective vehicle to get out their messages. Undeterred, Wildmon and his followers launched a $3 million campaign against the program, the network and the sponsors in 1994, but decision-makers, including regulators, weren't listening.

syndicators
Independent program producers and distributors.

standards and practices
Network offices to review programs for suitability.

David Wildmon
Anti-smut crusader.

Douglas Edwards
Pioneer anchor.

John Cameron Swayze
Pioneer anchor.

v-chip

While public concern over violence and rough language on television is difficult to measure, Congress decided in 1996 to do something about it. The Telecommunications Act of 1996 required a new kind of electronic chip in every television set—except tiny sets with mini-screens. The V-chip, as it was called, was designed to permit parents to intercept objectionable programs their kids might watch when unattended. The law, part of the 1996 Telecommunications Act, required broadcasters and cable companies to code objectionable programs beginning in February 1997 so the V-chips could do their job. There were delays, however, in making the chip workable, and implementation was postponed.

When it finally is introduced, will the V-Chip work? Moralists and parent groups that lobbied for the V-Chip hailed the new law as a triumph, but rating programs is not an easy matter. Is it an act of violence when a boulder falls on Bugs Bunny's head, driving him halfway to China? Should a single act of violence render an entire episode unacceptable? How much skin is too much? These are imponderables that will remain in debate until after solutions are found to technical hitches with the V-chip and people try it out.

television news

(STUDY PREVIEW)   The television networks began newscasts in 1947 with anchors reading stories into cameras, embellished only with occasional newsreel clips. Networks expanded their staffs and programming over the years. Documentaries, introduced in the 1950s, demonstrated that television could cover serious issues in depth.

talking heads and newsreels

The networks began news programs in 1947, CBS with "**Douglas Edwards** and the News" and NBC with **John Cameron Swayze**'s "Camel News Caravan." The 15-minute evening programs rehashed AP and UP dispatches and ran film clips from movie newsreel companies. The networks eventually built up their own reporting staffs and abandoned the photogenic but predictable newsreel coverage of events like beauty contests and ship launchings. With on-scene reporters, network news focused more on public issues. In 1963 the evening newscasts expanded to 30 minutes with NBC's **Chet**

Walter Crokite on a 1952 Set. More than anyone else, Walter Cronkite is associated with the rise of television as a news medium. He began his career with a series of newspaper, radio station and news-service jobs, and then he became well known for his United Press stories from Europe during World War II. He joined CBS in 1950 and began anchoring the network's evening television news in 1962. Surveys found him to be the most trusted person in the nation in the 1960s and 1970s, primarily for his centrist approach to news. He retired from full-time anchoring in 1981.

Huntley-David Brinkley team and CBS's **Walter Cronkite** in nightly competition for serious yet interesting accounts of what was happening. When Cronkite retired in 1981, surveys found him the most trusted man in the country—testimony to how important television news had become. Although news originally was an unprofitable network activity, sometimes referred to as a "glorious burden," it had become a profit center by the 1980s as news programs attracted larger audiences, which in turn attracted more advertisers.

Television's potential as a serious news medium was demonstrated in 1951 when producer **Fred W. Friendly** and reporter **Edward R. Murrow** created "See It Now," a weekly investigative program. Television gained new respect when Friendly and Murrow exposed the false, hysterical charges of Senator Joseph McCarthy about Communist infiltration of federal agencies.

shift in network news

Some say television news was at its best during the Murrow period. It is a fact that the Big Three networks have scaled down their global news-gathering systems since the mid-1980s. New, bottom line-oriented owners and budget problems forced the changes. Newscasts have suffered most, losing a lot of original coverage from abroad.

Prime-time **magazine** programs, like "60 Minutes" and "20/20," once were a sideline of network news divisions. Today, those programs have become so popular with viewers that ABC, CBS and NBC news divisions have shifted resources to produce more of them. NBC's "Dateline," for example, airs four nights a week. The proliferation of magazine programs has further reduced the talent and budget for the newscasts that once were the main identity of the network's news. Critics point out that some network magazine projects are of the tabloid mold—flashy but not much substance. Edward R. Murrow set a higher standard.

24-Hour Television News

When Ted Turner launched Cable News Network as an around-the-clock news services in 1980, critics belittled the shoe-string operation as Chicken Noodle News. Gradually CNN built up its resources and an audience and advertiser base. CNN proved its mettle in the 1991 Persian Gulf War, routinely outdoing the Big Three networks in coverage from the Gulf and being wholly competitive from Washington and other world centers. Some ABC, CBS and NBC affiliates pre-empted their networks' war coverage to feed viewers CNN's reports. Newspapers around the world quoted the network. CNN viewership shot to 10 million U.S. households—almost one in 10. After the war, the CNN audience slipped to 700,000 on many slow news days, sometimes lower, but there were dramatic spikes when major news broke. People had

media people

christine craft

Christine Craft

Kansas City television anchor **Christine Craft** was stunned. Her boss, the news director, had sat her down in his office and announced he was taking her off the anchor desk. He flashed a consultant's report at her. "We've just gotten our research back," he said. "You are too old, too unattractive, and not sufficiently deferential to men." He went on, "When the people of Kansas City see your face, they turn the dial."

Christine Craft was incredulous. During her few months at KMBC, in 1981, the station had climbed to Number One for the first time in three years. She was an experienced television journalist who had anchored in her hometown, at KEYT in Santa Barbara; reported in San Francisco, at KPIX; and anchored a sports show on the CBS network. At 36, she was hardly over the hill. What did her news director mean that she was "not sufficiently deferential to men"? He explained that she had not played second fiddle to male co-anchors. "You don't hide your intelligence to make the guys look smarter. People don't like that you know the difference between the American and the National League."

Angry, Chris Craft sued. She charged that KMBC was demoting her on sexist grounds, claiming that male anchors were not held to the same standards in age, appearance or deference. Further, she said, the station had paid her unfairly, $38,500 compared with $75,000 for her male co-anchor. It was an important moment in American television, triggering an overdue sensitivity to equal opportunity and treatment for women and men. Craft won her jury trial and even an appeal trial before a second jury. In further appeals, the Metromedia conglomerate, which owned KMBC,

prevailed, but Craft had made her point on behalf of women broadcasters throughout the land.

Within two years, Craft was back as an anchor and happy at KRBK in Sacramento. Then she was named news director and managing editor, the first woman to hold the positions at a Sacramento television station.

learned to count on CNN for breaking news. One CNN strength was international news built around staff coverage from 19 bureaus—more than any other network. In 1997, veteran CBS anchor Dan Rather seriously considered jumping to CNN. Although he stayed at CBS, he acknowledged CNN as a worthy competitor.

By the late 1990s, other players joined the 24-her news competition.

Fox News. Fox hired a corps of respected Washington reporters, including Brit Hume from ABC, and launched the Fox News cable network. The Fox overage was supplemented with feeds from local stations affiliated with the Fox over-air network, as well as with video reports from three global news agencies—AP Television, Reuters and World Television News—that also served ABC, CBS, NBC and CNN. Trendy sets and irreverent anchor banter, along with a Murdochian taste for the sensational, set Fox News apart. Slick presentation and an underdog's drive gave coverage an edge.

MSNBC. A Microsoft-NBC alliance evolved into the all-news MSNBC cable network. The network drew on NBC's resources, including widely recognized anchors like Tim Brokaw and Jane Pauley and also NBC's film archives going back to the 1950s. MSNBC had the depth to inspire viewer confidence.

> **Christine Craft**
> Fought for greater equity in on-air assignments

The all-news networks overrode scheduled newscasts and news programs for live coverage of major events, always with expert analysis—a new dimension in television news.

Meanwhile, other all-news networks came on the air. A CNN spin-off, Headline News, offered quick summaries of news in 20-minute cycles. The Hubbard satellite-direct service operated a low-budget summary service out of St. Paul, Minnesota, emphasizing hometown news from local stations around the country. All-news services emerged elsewhere too. The Canadian Broadcasting Corporation established the Newsworld International cable service. The British Broadcast Corporation also went into the all-news business. CNN established foreign centers to serve regions abroad with distinctive news packages. Continental pride prompted a European consortium to create Euronews to counter CNN's inroads. In the United States, meanwhile, local cable companies in major markets, first New York, then second-tier markets like Tampa, went into the 24-hour news business.

One upshot on the proliferating news channels was further deterioration in Big Three news audiences. By 1998, the ABC, CBS and NBC evening newscasts commanded less than half of the television sets in the nation, contrasted to 95 percent 20 years earlier. Of course, other media choices also were fragmenting the old Big Three audiences. The all-news networks also lessened the pressure on other networks to provide breaking coverage of news, and the cleavage widened between entertainment networks and news networks rather than the hybrid Big Three model.

local news

Local television news imitated network formats in the early days, but by the 1970s many innovations were occurring at the local level. Local reporting staffs grew, and some stations went beyond a headline service to enterprising and investigative reports. Many stations were quick to latch onto possibilities of satellite technology in the 1980s to do their own locally oriented coverage of faraway events. This reduced the dependence of stations on networks for national stories. Today, large stations send their own reporters and crews with **uplink** vans to transmit live reports back home via satellite. At the 1996 Democratic and Republican national conventions, for example, viewers could see local delegates being interviewed by local reporters who knew local issues, which was something the networks, always looking for broad, general stories, could not do.

public television

(STUDY PREVIEW)   The quasi-government Corporation for Public Broadcasting funnels federal dollars into noncommercial television, including the PBS network. Despite attempts to buffer CPB from political meddling, President Nixon tried tampering with it in the 1970s, as did the new Republican-controlled House of Representatives in 1995.

corporation for public broadcasting

Many school districts and universities set up noncommercial television stations in the 1960s in attempts to broaden their reach. The experiments had mixed results.

Puppets on Chopping Block. When Republicans in the 1995 Congress talked about cutting off funding for PBS, New York Democrat Nita Lowey brought out Bert and Ernie. "Sesame Street" should not be on the chopping block, said Lowey. Republicans said the nation could no longer afford public funding for PBS and suggested privatization. That, said PBS backers, would mean commercialization and change the nature of public television fundamentally from its original mission.

Most programs were dull lectures, and the following was small. In some cities, meanwhile, citizen groups obtained licenses for noncommercial stations. By the late 1960s there were more than 300 of these stations. It was a grossly undeveloped national resource.

In 1967, a blue-ribbon group, the **Carnegie Commission on Educational Television,** examined the situation and recommended the educational television concept be changed to **public television** to "serve the full needs of the American public." This put to rest the dowdy **ETV** image of the early noncommercial stations.

Within months, Congress responded by creating the **Corporation for Public Broadcasting** to develop a national noncommercial broadcasting system for both television and radio. The goal was to offer quality programming distinct from that of the commercial networks, which, by their nature, pandered to mass markets.

In its early days CPB helped build the **Public Broadcasting Service,** a network for noncommercial television stations, and also **National Public Radio.** Later CPB channeled more dollars to individual stations to buy programs from either PBS or other sources and thus made for more diversity.

Unlike commercial networks, PBS does not pay affiliates to carry its programs. Affiliates pay the network. Besides revenue from affiliates, PBS has income from corporations, foundations and viewers themselves—in addition to federal money from CPB.

PBS does not produce programs. Rather, it acquires many programs from a handful of stations. These are mostly the production powerhouses KQED in San Francisco; WGBH, Boston; WNET, New York: WQED, Philadelphia, and WTTW, Chicago. For diversity, PBS also buys programs from independent producers.

PBS made its mark in 1970 with "Sesame Street," produced by the **Children's Television Workshop,** an independent producer. A drama aired the same year, "The Andersonville Trial," won an Emmy. Other early fare included Julia Child on cooking, "Mr. Rogers' Neighborhood," "Black Report" and the "MacNeil/ Lehrer NewsHour." PBS also carried a lot of high-brow BBC programs, which led one wag to say PBS stood for "Primarily British Shows." This was all distinctive programming that was not economically feasible for the commercial networks because, in general, the audiences were smaller than advertisers wanted.

As the years went on, cable began to encroach on what had been PBS's domain. The Discovery cable channel, for example, featured old documentaries and nature shows. PBS lost a distinctive edge. Also many noncommercial stations blurred their own images when they began offering old movies and other programs that, said crit-

Carnegie Commission
Recommended upgrading noncommercial broadcast system.

public TV
Post-Carnegie term for noncommercial TV.

ETV
Educational TV. Early term for noncommerical TV.

CPB
Short for Corporation for Public Broadasting. Funnels federal money to public broadcast system.

PBS
Short for Public Broadcasting System. National TV network for noncommercial television stations.

NPR
National Public Radio. A national network for noncommercial radio stations.

Children's Television Workshop
Created "Sesame Street."

ics, were redundant to the commercial networks. Concerned that they would lose viewers to PBS, commercial broadcasters cried foul that a government-subsidized operation was intruding into their free-enterprise turf. PBS affiliates conceded they were trying to expand their audience, but they also said their movies were classics and shown as cultural fare. That debate continues.

The greatest threat to PBS, however, has been from conservative ideologues who charge that the network is politically biased and liberal.

debate over public funding

A knotty problem when CPB was created was the possibility of government interference in programming. This was addressed in the 1967 Public Broadcasting Act, which specified that congressional funding go—no strings attached—to CPB in advance of programming decisions. While the president appoints CPB's directors with the Senate's approval, the law is specific that CPB is not a government agency. That provision was intended to prevent the corporation from becoming a political lackey.

Even so, there have been problems. In the early 1970s President **Richard Nixon** was upset over unflattering PBS documentaries. His telecommunications director, **Clay Whitehead,** went to broadcasters and proposed that public television emphasize local programs. The stated rationale was that the commercial networks offered enough national programming. Unstated was that locally originated programming was less likely to focus on national issues, reducing the administration's exposure to critical coverage.

In 1972, Nixon vetoed a two-year $154 million congressional funding package for CPB, saying the corporation was too powerful over local stations. Outraged, key CPB officials resigned. That gave the president an opportunity to appoint people more to his liking. The new CPB appointees wanted more cultural and local-origination programs and fewer documentaries. Coincidentally, just as a divisive battle was shaping up, the Watergate scandal erupted. The attention of the White House shifted to its own survival, not ideological games over public television.

Ideological opposition to PBS, and also to NPR, erupted again in the mid-1990s, cast more distinctly as liberalism versus conservatism. The new 1995 Republican-controlled House, with its distinct conservative bent, threatened to take a hatchet to CPB's proposed $286 million budget. In the background was campaign rhetoric over PBS being a haven of leftist ideology, but hearings focused on whether the debt-plagued federal government could afford to keep subsidizing noncommercial television and radio.

The House GOP minority picked up "privatization" as a buzz word and seemed to favor phasing out federal support over five or seven years. PBS president Ervin Duggan said privatization would mean commercialization. That, he said, would fundamentally alter PBS by putting the network in a race for audience size and advertising dollars.

Richard Nixon
U.S. president who vetoed CPB funding.

Clay Whitehead
Proposed bypassing CPB to localize noncommercial broadcasting during the Nixon administration.

chapter wrap-up

American television patterned itself after radio. From the beginning, television was a dual national system of locally owned commercial stations and national networks. Companies that were heavily involved in radio were also the television heavyweights. Even television's programming mimicked radio's. The Big Three networks, NBC, CBS and ABC, were the most powerful shapers of television, leading in entertainment programming and news. They also pioneered many of the technological advances. Today, program packaging and further technical innovations are challenging the Big Three dominance, and the television industry is undergoing a major restructuring.

Gerald Levin and then Ted Turner led the restructuring when they realized that they could deliver programs to local cable companies via orbiting satellite. Levin's HBO and Turner's WTBS, both movie services, became unique features of cable companies in the 1970s. The threat to local over-air stations and the Big Three networks was minor at first, but cable companies began wiring more neighborhoods, and additional cable networks came to be, among them Turner's 24-hour CNN news service. With cable into more than 60 percent of the nation's homes today, the cable networks are siphoning major advertising from the Big Three, and many local cable companies are going after local advertisers. In some cities, non-network, independent local stations have become major players for advertising, which further contributes to the restructuring.

Satellite technology is contributing to major changes in a second way. Network affiliates discovered in the 1980s that they could use their new downlink equipment, which received network transmissions from satellites, to pick up programming from other sources. Suddenly, these stations could pick and choose programs, even news video, as never before. Many stations expanded their newscasts and assembled their own faraway coverage with video from a variety of network and non-network sources. Larger stations acquired mobile uplink equipment and sent crews great distances to cover news. It was not unusual for some stations to send crews abroad several times a year. No longer were local over-air stations so dependent on their networks to succeed.

questions for review

1. How is television influential on people and society in the short term and the long term?

2. How is television technology different than movie technology?

3. How was radio the role model for early television programming?

4. How has television expanded beyond over-air delivery?

5. What is the relationship between the television networks and their local over-air affiliates?

6. What is the connection between Congress and public television?

7. What is the relationship between the cable and over-air television industries today?

8. Why did early television programs resemble their radio predecessors?

9. Why do critics say television news is in decline?

questions for critical thinking

1. How did Philo Farnsworth's image dissector employ electronics to pick up moving images and relay them to faraway screens? Explain the difference between television and film technology.

2. What was the relationship of radio and early television programming? You might want to review Chapter 7 to explain the effect of television on radio.

3. Trace the development of television news from the newsreel days. Include the heyday of documentaries and explain what happened to them. What was the contribution of Fred Friendly and Edward R. Murrow? Explain expanded network newscasts and the importance of Walter Cronkite. What contribution has PBS made? Include magazine and talk show programs in your answer.

4. Outline the development of television networks. Besides the three major networks, include Allen

Dumont's, Ted Turner's and Rupert Murdoch's networks. Explain challenges faced today by the major networks, including how independent stations have become stronger, the innovation pioneered by Gerald Levin, the effect of FCC deregulation, expanded program production by syndicators and new technologies. How do you regard the observation of some critics that the Big Three networks will not exist in their present form a few years into the 21st century?

5. Historically, why have television stations sought affiliations with ABC, CBS and NBC? Discuss changes in network-affiliate relations. Is a network affiliation as attractive today as it was 20 years ago? Why or why not?

6. What happened to network Standards and Practices Departments in the late 1980s? Why?

7. How is the television industry funded? Remember that the financial base is different for the commercial networks, network-affiliated stations, independent stations, noncommercial networks and stations, superstations, cable networks, cable systems and subscriber services.

8. How does the career of Ted Turner epitomize the emergence of new program and delivery systems as a challenge to the traditional structure of television in the United States?

for further learning

Erik Barnouw. *Tube of Plenty: The Evolution of American Television* (Oxford, 1975). Barnouw, the preeminent biographer of broadcasting, deals with evolutions in network programming and the powerful personalities that shaped the television industry.

James Day. *The Vanishing Vision: The Inside Story of Public Television.* (University of California Press, 1995). Professor Day, a veteran on public television, draws on his experience, documentary sources and interviews to trace the evolution of the noncommercial station patchwork into a coherent national broadcast system. In the end, though, Day is pessimistic over the floundering sense of mission that marks public television today.

Stephen Frantzich and John Sullivan. *The C-SPAN Revolution* (University of Oklahoma Press, 1997). Professors Frantzich and Sullivan built this engaging, detailed history of C-SPAN from more than 100 interviews, from documents and the network's own coverage. They argue that the network has enhanced if not revolutionized political debate in the United States.

Lynn Boyd Hinds. *Broadcasting the Local News, The Early Years of Pittsburgh's KDKA-TV* (Pennsylvania State University Press, 1995). This is an excellent case study on the evolution of local television news at a pioneer station.

Laurence Jarvik. *PBS: Behind the Screen* (Capitol Research Center, 1997). Jarvik, a conservative scholar, argues that the Public Broadcasting Service is over-funded and mired in inept bureaucratic management.

Leland L. Johnson. *Toward Competition in Cable Television* (MIT Press, 1994). Johnson analyzes the growing competition that cable is facing from telephone, direct broadcast satellites, wireless cable, as well as the continuing competition with over-air stations.

Jeff Kisseloff. *An Oral History of Television, 1920–1961* (Viking, 1995).

George Mannes. "The Birth of Cable TV." *Invention & Technology* (Fall 1996). Pages 42–50. Mannes drew on oral histories at the National Cable Television Center and Museum for this colorful account of cable's pioneers, including Ed Parsons of Astoria, Oregon, and the people behind various small-town Pennsylvania systems.

Cary O'Dell. *Women Pioneers in Television: Biographies of Fifteen Industry Leaders* (McFarland, 1996). O'Dell, curator of the Museum of Broadcast Communication at the Chicago Cultural Center, covers Milfred Freed Alberg, Lucille Ball, Gertrude Berg, Peggy Charren, Joan Ganz Cooney, Faye Emerson, Pauline Frederick, Dorothy Fuldheim, Betty Furness, Freida Hennock, Lucy Jarvis, Ida Lupino, Irna Phillips, Judith Walker and Betty White.

Patrick R. Parsons. "Two Tales of a City: John Walson Sr., Mahonoy City, and the 'Founding' of Cable TV." *Journal of Broadcasting & Electronic Media* (Summer 1996). Pages 354–365. Professor Parsons debunks the often-told story that Walson, of Mahonoy City, Pennsylvania, built the first cable television system. This is historical scholarship of the first order.

Charles Platt. "The Great HDTV Swindle." *Wired* (February 1997), Pages 57–60, 186–192. Platt blames the delay in introducing high-quality television pictures on the television industry, which he criticizes as self-serving and greedy.

Paul Schlatzkin. *The Farnsworth Chronicles.* National Online Music Alliance, 1996. This web site is as enthusiastic about Philo Farnsworth's invention of television as it is harsh on Vladimir Zworykin and David Sarnoff. Good reading. Great pictures. (songs.com/noma/philo/index.htm)

Christopher H. Sterling and John M. Kittross. *Stay Tuned: A Concise History of American Broadcasting* (Wadsworth, 1990). The authors track the history of radio and television with special attention to the impact of technology, programming innovation, and social effects.

for keeping up to date

Broadcasting & Cable is broadcasting's major trade journal. Coverage of federal regulation, programming and ownership is consistently solid. Every issue inlcudes a comprehensive table on prime-time Nielsens for the six over-air networks.

Journal of Broadcasting and *Electronic Media* is a quarterly scholarly journal published by the Broadcast Education Association.

Television/Radio Age is a trade journal.

Videography is a trade journal focusing on production issues in corporate video and production.

Consumer magazines that deal extensively with television programming include *Entertainment* and *TV Guide*.

Newsmagazines that report television issues more or less regularly include *Newsweek* and *Time*.

Business Week, Forbes and *Fortune* track television as a business.

Major newspapers with strong television coverage include the Los Angeles *Times*, the New York *Times* and the *Wall Street Journal*.

9

the web

**in this chapter
you will learn:**

- The World Wide Web is emerging as a major mass medium.

- The web operates on a global Internet that links many far-flung computer networks.

- The web can be understood by dissecting it into functional components.

- Advertising will be the primary revenue source for web services.

- Transistors and fiber-optic cable have increased the capacity for exchanging data.

- The web is based on a nonlinear communication form called hypertext.

- Hypertext is revolutionizing news-telling, but its effect on other story-telling forms is uncertain.

- Digitization is propelling the transition of some traditional media to the web.

- Should government assure universal web access? Can cyberpornography be curbed?

After the trade magazine *InfoWorld* announced its 1994 annual award for computer-tech accomplishments, a couple of especially knowledgeable readers complained: "Aren't you overlooking **Tim Berners-Lee**?" The callers were not so much protesting who had won but asking why TBL, as he refers to himself, wasn't considered. To the first of the queries, *InfoWorld* columnist Bob Metcalfe asked, "Tim who?"

Metcalfe learned from one caller that TBL had recently arrived at the Massachusetts Institute of Technology, so Metcalfe went to Cambridge looking for him. There, at a computer screen, was Tim Berners-Lee wholly engrossed in unscrambling an ill-conceived encryption mess that the U.S. National Security Agency had devised. Metcalfe, it turned out, had found the person who, more than any other, is revolutionizing human communication.

What is it that Tim Berners-Lee has done? No less than invent the World Wide Web, the global information infrastructure that has emerged as the mass medium that may, given time, eclipse many of our current media. Some liken Berners-Lee to Johannes Gutenberg, who 400 years earlier launched the Age of Mass Communication with the movable type that made mass production of the written word possible.

While Berners-Lee is widely respected in academic circles, he remains obscure to most people. He was interviewed once in 1993 on Carl Malamud's "Geek of the Week" radio program, and his résumé is heavy with scholarly presentations at lofty academic conferences. To most of the human race, though, even people who rely on the World Wide Web every day, TBL's name is not yet a household word.

Tim Berners-Lee was graduated from Oxford in 1976 and went to work as a software engineer in England. Over the next few years he put in a couple of stints at **CERN,** the high-power European particle physics lab in Geneva, and dabbled with software programs for storing data so it could be reassembled with random associations. In 1989 he joined CERN on a permanent basis. In October that year he proposed a new project dubbed the **World Wide Web.** His goal was to create a system that would allow physicists, on just about any computer anywhere, to tap into any of several computer networks, called internets, and to move freely around among interconnected documents. Working with four software engineers and a programmer, Berners-Lee had a demonstration up and running by Christmas.

As Berners-Lee traveled the globe to introduce the web at scientific conferences, the potential of what he had devised became clear. The web was a system that could put information in interface with all other information.

In 1992, leading research organizations in the Netherlands, Germany and the United States committed to the web. As enthusiasm grew in the scientific research community, word spread to other quarters. In one eight-month period in 1993, web use multiplied 414 times. While technophiles had been connecting

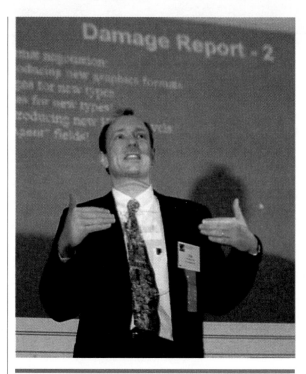

Original Webmaster. Tim Berners-Lee and his associates at a Swiss research facility created new internet coding in 1989, dubbing it the World Wide Web. Today the coding is the heart of global computer communication.

to the web in growing numbers, several products came on the market in 1994, led by Internet in a Box, that allowed a greater number of people to connect at home. This was a major factor ushering in widespread access.

In this chapter you will learn how the web has sprung upon us not only as the eighth major mass medium, joining books, magazines, newspapers, records, movies, radio and television. It also is a medium that eventually may absorb some of the others. Welcome to the 21st century.

world wide web

(STUDY PREVIEW)   The World Wide Web has emerged as the eighth major mass medium. Many newspaper and magazine companies are delivering colorful, often expanded editions electronically to people at computer screens. The web is more flexible than other media. Users can navigate paths among millions of on-screen messages.

new mass medium

From a dizzying array of new technologies, the World Wide Web emerged in the mid-1990s as a powerful new mass medium. What is the web? It is where ordinary people can go on their computer screens and, with a few clicks of a mouse button, can find a vast array of information and entertainment that originates all over the world. Make no mistake, though: The web is not just singular on-screen pages. The genius of the web is that on-screen pages are linked to others. It is the people browsing the web, not editors and programmers, who choose which on-screen pages to go to, and which to pass by, and in what sequence. People don't need to go linearly from Newscast Story 1 to Newscast Story 2. By using all kinds of on-screen indexing and cross-referencing, they can switch instantly to what interests them. It's an almost seamless journey from a Viacom promotion message for a new movie, to a biography on the movie's leading lady in the *USA Today* archives, to things as disparate as L. L. Bean's mail-order catalog and somebody's personal collection of family snapshots. In short, the web is an interface for computers that allows people anywhere to connect to any information anywhere else on the system.

Every major mass media company has put products on the web. Thousands of start-up companies are establishing themselves on the ground floor. The technology

---

media
online

CERN: Tim Berners-Lee quietly created the World Wide Web while working at this European particle physics lab. www.cern.ch

Home Gopher: Granddaddy of the World Wide Web. gopher://gopher.micro.umn.edu:70/1

24 hours in Cyberspace: A day in the life of the web, it chronicles the event. www.cyber24.com

---

Tim Berners-Lee
Devised protocols, codes for web.

CERN
Physics lab in Geneva where web was invented.

World Wide Web
System that allows global linking of information modules in user-determined sequences.

News Online. The first major newspaper to go online with hypertext news was *USA Today.* By clicking the cursor on any of many hot spots, you can move to more detail or special sections. Hot spots on this web page include the headlines, the photograph, and the sections Life, Money, Sports and Weather. On each of those web pages are more options that link to hundreds of other web pages. Some links go to earlier editions. You can, for example, link to dozens of movie reviews that *USA Today* has carried over recent months. (Copyright 1998, *USA Weekend.* Reprinted with permission.)

1945 Vannevar Bush proposed "a memex machine" for associative links among all human knowledge.

1947 AT&T developed transistor.

1962 Ted Nelson introduced term *hypertext.*

1969 U.S. Defense Department created ARPAnet network

linking military contractors and researchers.

1973 Mead Data Central went online via telephone line with Lexis, first online full-text database.

1978 Mead Data Central went online with Nexis, first online database with national news publications.

1979 CompuServe began service to consumers.

1980s Telephone and cable companies began upgrade to fiber-optic lines.

1983 National Science Foundation linked researchers to supercomputers with Internet.

1984 William Gibson coined term *cyberspace* in sci-fi novel *Neuromancers.*

1989 Tim Berners-Lee devised coding that made World Wide Web possible.

1992 Albuquerque, New Mexico, *Tribune* went online.

---

is so straightforward and access so inexpensive that thousands of individuals have set up their own web sites.

How significant is the web as a mass medium? A 1995 study found 17.6 million adults in North America using the web—more than one of every 20. The percentage of web-knowledgeable people promises to mushroom as personal computers become standard household equipment and as virtually every schoolchild becomes "computer literate."

The significance of the web is measurable in other ways too. There are people who have given up reading the print edition of the *Wall Street Journal* and instead browse through one of the *Journal*'s constantly updated web editions. Hundreds of publications went **online** in the mid-1990s, from the venerable but tech-savvy New York *Times* to local papers in the hinterlands like the Casper *Star Tribune* in Wyoming. Hundreds of magazines have online versions too.

web terms

Ask a techie to define the web. You will be told it's interconnected computer servers that use universal codes to allow people who are not tech-savvy to choose from among thousands of interconnected web sites on every computer server in the system. At each web site, the user can choose subsets of screen images that also are interconnected. Here are terms that will make this clearer:

- **Web site.** An institution's or individual's presence on the web is called a site. A site can be a magazine, for example. If you tap into *Business Week* magazine's site on your screen, you will find a gateway to hundreds of "pages" that the editors have compiled for you to browse through.

online
Being connected to the web or an internet.
web site
Where an institution establishes its web presence.

- **Web page.** Once you are at a web site, you can move your computer cursor to icons, boxes and shaded images and click to move to related web pages that interest you. A web page can include words, pictures and graphics. It works this way:

You call up *USA Today*'s web site. Your screen fills with a web page that lists a few headlines on breaking news stories. If you click on the headline that most interests you, you will find a summary of the story, perhaps five sentences. That summary is on a web page. Also on the page are options to go to more information on the story. But unlike the print edition, which was edited to be read from the top of the story all the way through to the end, you can choose to switch to what interests you most. In the case of a plane crash, you could choose to go to a file photo and technical data on the aircraft, or to a list of victims, or to a history of the airline whose plane went down, or an eyewitness account of the crash or any of dozens of other related web pages. At each new page you visit, you have options to other pages—or to return to a page you have already read.

You also can choose at any point to move your cursor to other categories of the web site's content: a summary of other breaking news, sports, weather, stock tables, celebrity gossip.

- **Browsing.** The process of moving through web sites and pages is called browsing or sometimes **surfing.**

- **Server.** The computers that connect web sites are called servers. An individual server can carry many web sites.

- **Internet.** An internet, with a small *i*, is a system that connects other, usually local networks of computers. In recent years, various internets linked up with each other into a single internet. The whole system has come to be called the **Internet,** with a capital *I*. Among users, it's known as the Net, a term used with affection and also awe.

The World Wide Web is the system of protocols and codes that has opened up the Internet to wider use and created opportunities for advertising. This advertising revenue will drive the web's further development. Futurists quibble on whether people will end up calling this new medium the Net or the Web. Ten years from now, millions of users worldwide probably will have settled on one or the other.

- **Cyber-.** The prefix cyber- is affixed almost casually to anything involving communication via computer. *Cyberspace* is the intangible place where the communication occurs. *Cyberporn* is sexual naughtiness delivered on-screen. A *cyberpunk* is a kid obsessed with computer protocols and coding.

Science-fiction novelist **William Gibson** introduced the term *cyberspace* in his book *Neuromancer.* At that point, in 1984, he saw a kind of integration of computers and human beings. Paraphrasing a bit, here is Gibson's definition of *cyberspace:* "A consensual hallucination experienced daily by billions of people in every nation. A graphic representation of data abstracted from the banks of every computer in the human system. Unthinkable complexity. Lines of light ranged in the nonspace of the mind. Clusters and constellations of data."

web limitations

To date, newspapers and magazines have made the greater strides in delivering web products, and book publishers are not far behind. Text and simple graphics take

web page
A single computer screen containing words, pictures, graphics.

browsing
Moving through web sites and pages.

surfing
Synonymous with browsing.

server
Computers that connect web sites.

internet
Any network that connects computer networks.

Internet
With capital *I*, the backbone network for web communication.

cyber-
Prefix for human connection via computers.

William Gibson
Sci-fi writer who coined term *cyberspace*.

	Today's Modem 56 kilobits per second	Future Modem, Upgraded Bandwidth 4 megabits per second
Simple image 2 megabits	35.7 seconds	0.5 seconds
Short animation 72 megabits	21.5 minutes	18 seconds
Long animation 4.3 gigabits	21.4 hours	18 minutes

bandwidth
Room available in a medium, such as cable or the electromagnetic waves, to carry messages.

interstate highways
Frequent analogy for Internet.

information highway
Loose term for Internet.

ARPAnet
Military network that preceded Internet.

National Science Foundation
Developed current Internet to give scholars access to supercomputers.

relatively little **bandwidth,** or space, to transmit on cable, or the airwaves for that matter. Fancy graphics take more bandwidth, which means they require more time to transmit. Super-detailed photographs take several minutes.

To understand the bandwidth issue, compare the Internet with a pipeline system. The section of pipe with the narrowest diameter governs the capacity of the system. The Internet has a lot of narrow pipes, or, put another way, there are bottlenecks with very limited bandwidth. In time, as the Internet undergoes continuing improvements, capacity will grow, and fancier content—like complex graphics—will take less time to arrive on users' screens.

Music and video require lots of bandwidth, which raises the question: Will there ever be enough Internet space for real-time radio and television and full-length movies? Barring an unanticipated technological breakthrough, probably not for a long time. The broadcast networks and many stations have established stakes on the web, but the content is mostly text and graphics. Audio is limited to snippets, generally with poor sound quality. Moving visuals are brief. As delivery capacity increases with more super-fast, high-capacity lines, the web will deliver more audio and moving-image products that require high-capacity transmission systems. Authorities urge caution, however, on whether whole television and radio programs or movies will be transmitted via the Internet any time soon.

new video infrastructure

While the Internet infrastructure is growing and improving, local cable television systems and telephone companies are in frantic competition to upgrade their existing community wiring. These projects are creating a second infrastructure, separate from the Internet, whose capabilities to deliver video and audio surpass the web. These systems also will exceed the capabilities of current cable television and telephone systems. For example, people will be able to call up television programs and also music and movies whenever they want—no waiting until the top of the hour for your favorite show or until your favorite song comes up on a disc jockey's rotation list. Images and sound will be sharper than is now possible. These services will be delivered via satellite to the local cable system and telephone infrastructures, then distributed locally via the upgraded cable systems that are being installed. This new infrastructure is a massive project estimated to cost between $300 billion and $1 trillion in the United States alone.

Some breathless, enthusiastic futurists see the web eventually subsuming all seven traditional mass media—books, magazines, newspapers, recordings, movies, radio and television. That, however, could be a long time coming. The web does not, for example, handle audio and video very well. Also, in the foreseeable future, there will still be people without computers who will look to traditional media for entertainment, information and ideas. Even among people with computer access, many will prefer media forms they are accustomed to.

internet

(STUDY PREVIEW) The Internet is the wired infrastructure on which web messages move. It began as a military communication system, which expanded into a government-funded civilian research network. Today, the Internet is a user-financed system tying institutions of many sorts together into an "information highway."

the information highway

Some historians say the most important contribution of Dwight Eisenhower's presidency in the 1950s was the U.S. **interstate highway** system. It was a massive project, easily surpassing the scale of such previous human endeavors as the Pyramids, the Great Wall of China and the Panama Canal. Eisenhower's interstates bound the nation together in new ways and facilitated major economic growth by making commerce less expensive. Today, what is called the **information highway** is being built—an electronic network that connects libraries, corporations, government agencies and individuals. This electronic highway is called the Internet, and it is the backbone of the World Wide Web.

The Internet had its origins in a 1969 U.S. Defense Department computer network called **ARPAnet,** for Advanced Research Project Agency. The Pentagon built the network for military contractors and universities doing military research to exchange information. In 1983, the **National Science Foundation,** whose mandate is to promote science, took over part of the network to give researchers access to four costly supercomputers at Cornell, Illinois, Pittsburgh and San Diego. The new civilian network was an expensive undertaking, but the ARPAnet infrastructure was already in place. Also, the expense of the new component was far less than installing dozens of additional $10 million supercomputers that would have duplicated those at the original four core computer sites.

This new National Science Foundation network attracted more and more institutional users, many of which had their own internal networks. For example, most universities that joined the NSF network had intracampus computer networks. The NSF network, then, became a connector for thousands of other networks. As a backbone system that interconnects networks, *internet* was a name that fit.

vint cerf

Even as a kid, Vinton Cerf liked tech stuff. When he was 10, back in 1953, he built a volcano out of plaster of paris and potassium permanganate. Then he decorated the mountain with gelatin-coated glycerine capsules and waited for the gelatin to melt. The result: A thermite grenade that impressed and also scared his folks.

Today Cerf is called the Father of the Internet. Although he's uncomfortable with the title, the fact is that he was there. Cerf, "Vint" to his friends, and co-researcher Bob Kahn created the coding that allowed various computers to talk to each other over phone lines. In 1974 Cerf and Kahn, both at the University of California at Los Angeles, published an article explaining their inter-computer language protocols.

Kahn's interests shifted to other things, but Cerf kept working on details for linking the military's Advanced Research Projects Agency network to other networks in a way that would seem seamless to users.

Why does Cerf object to being called the Father of the Internet? "It's not right to think of the Internet as having only one father," he says. "It has at least two, and in reality thousands, because of the number of people who contributed to what it is today." Even so, it was Kahn who took the project to Stanford when he switched universities and shepherded it into maturity through 1982.

Later, in 1992, Cerf created the nonprofit Internet Society that coordinates Internet policy so the system remains universally useful.

The expense of operating the Internet is borne by the institutions and organizations that tie their computers into it. The institutions pay an average of $43,000 a year to hook in.

The Internet is undergoing significant upgrading. The 1992 **High-Performance Computing Act** authorized $3 billion to develop and install computers at leading research centers so they can exchange information. These Internet enhancements, called the **National Research and Education Network,** permit the exchange of more and lengthier material, even full-motion video. Data will move at least 100 times faster than it does today. With the high-capacity cable that's being installed, the volume of data will swell exponentially.

As the improvements come on-stream, the Internet is becoming not just an information highway but also an information superhighway. These kinds of new activities are becoming possible:

- Physicians send x-rays and CAT scans instantly to faraway experts for analysis.

- Students zip through the entire Library of Congress index and have entire books transmitted back to them.

- Farmers receive climatology forecasts and detailed weather maps from satellite photos to make decisions on planting and harvesting.

High-Performance Computing Act
1992 law to upgrade, expand Internet.

National Research and Education Network
An in-process upgrade of the Internet.

The Eyeball as a Screen. A Seattle company, Micro Vision, is hoping to market a device that projects images directly onto the human eyeball. This VRD, short for "virtual retina display," is not much more cumbersome to wear than a pair of glasses, and it gives a sharper image than a 70-millimeter IMAX screen. With VRD, people would not need television or computer screens. Micro Vision says this device can be made for less than $100.

online services

The World Wide Web became operational in the 1990s, but commercial online services go back another 20 years. **Mead Data Central,** an Ohio company, offered **Lexis,** the first online full-text database, in 1973. Lexis carried state and federal statutes, court decisions and other legal documents. A lawyer could tap into Lexis for research and cut back on maintaining and updating the traditional expensive office law library. Because Lexis was delivered via telephone lines whose capacity precluded data-intensive graphics, there was nothing fancy about how Lexis looked—simple text on the computer screen. But it was just what lawyers and legal scholars needed, and they paid handsomely for the service.

Building on its Lexis success, Mead launched **Nexis** in 1978. Nexis was the first online database with national news organizations, including the New York *Times,* the Washington *Post,* the Associated Press and *U.S. News & World Report.* Nexis proved invaluable to researchers, who could tap into not only recent editions of participating newspapers and magazines but also back issues. Today, Nexis includes thousands of publications from around the world.

Lexis and Nexis remain full-text services, with massive amounts of unadorned, gray content. While they are still important to many people, especially as a research source, they have been eclipsed by flashy graphic-oriented services designed for mass audiences. Nexis comes nowhere near the glitz of America Online.

> **Mead Data Central**
> Created Lexis, Nexis.
> **Lexis**
> First online full-text database; carries legal documents.
> **Nexis**
> First online database with national news.

users
Subscribers to commercial online services.

access providers
Offer web access on subscription basis.

content providers
Creators and packagers of online information.

commercial online services
Content providers that derive income from subscriptions or advertising or both.

America Online
Largest commercial online service.

CompuServe
First successful general-interest online service.

Prodigy
First online service with 1 million subscribers.

web model

(STUDY PREVIEW) One way to understand the web is to look at how the major components function. Mass communicators, called *content providers,* create the messages that move on the Internet to *access providers,* which make them available to the people who tap into the web. These web consumers are called users. The costs are borne by site sponsors and advertising, although at this infant point the web hasn't realized its potential as an advertising medium.

users

Not surprisingly, people who use the web are called **users.** Anyone with a computer, a modem that hooks the computer into a telephone line, and software like Netscape or Internet Explorer can be a user. How many web users are there? Nobody knows for sure, but one benchmark was a 1995 study that extrapolated 17.6 million adults in North America. Some experts believe that number doubled within a year.

access providers

Users connect to the web through computers called servers. The companies that operate servers, called **access providers,** charge users a modest fee, typically $20 monthly. Some access providers are free, but part of the deal is that they can send advertising to your screen without a specific invitation.

Generally, anyone connected with an institution with an in-house server gives web access to employees at no charge. For example, students, faculty and employees assigned a computer account at their college have full web access.

content providers

Anyone who creates a web site is a **content provider**—even college students who post a résumé on a personal site. The content providers that are most visited are **commercial online services** like America Online. Online services offer massive arrays of entertainment and information. Besides online service, content providers include commercial sites operated by companies that are selling wares and promoting themselves over the web. Other content providers include professional associations and other institutions. Many media organizations have become content providers, both adapting content from their other products to the web and also creating web-unique material.

Online services. Although a latecomer to the commercial online business, **America Online** grew rapidly. By 1998, it was the largest, at 11.6 million subscribers after acquiring its main competitor, **CompuServe.** The Microsoft Network, with 2.6 million subscribers, is a distant second. **Prodigy** has fewer than 1 million subscribers. Online services have a variety of subscription structures, but generally they charge $20 a month.

Besides providing their wide range of content, including games, online services offer gateways to the rest of the web. This makes them both content providers and access providers. Their services include email.

Commercial Sites. Every major U.S. company has a web site, some just to let you know they exist and what they are about. Some companies use the web to sell products. An example is the upstart Seattle company **amazon.com,** which is revolutionizing the book industry. You can order books online from an inventory of every book in print. Although amazon.com didn't realize any early profits, it forced traditional book-sellers, including Barnes & Noble, to scramble to establish their own web sales outlets.

Many art galleries display their collections online and are ready to make sales over the Internet. Payment is by credit card. Not surprisingly, computer retailers sell a lot of hardware and software from their sites. Airlines sell tickets from web sites. Some airline sites permit people to check their frequent-flier accounts any time and even cash in accumulated points in online transactions. Online pornography sites, which by some estimates constitute about 1 percent of all web visits, frequently charge by the minute.

Institutional Sites. Many professional associations maintain sites as a service to members. Among media associations with sites: International Association of Business Communicators, Society of Professional Journalists, and the Text and Academic Authors Association. The sites typically include online newsletters, member lists, and membership application forms.

A simple site can be built and maintained relatively inexpensively. The expense can be as little as buying time on a server and producing messages—a few hundred dollars a month. This is not to say that all web sites are cheaply done. Some companies spend more than $500,000 a year to maintain complex sites.

Media Sites. Prominent content providers include media companies that have built sites based mostly on recycled content from their existing products but more and more with distinctive, fresh material too. Time Warner has one of the most elaborate sites, **Pathfinder,** with material from its numerous magazines, including *Time, Life, Fortune, Sports Illustrated,* and *People,* and CNN. In addition, Pathfinder offers coverage that is exclusively online. The television networks have sites. So do local stations. Many media sites are free, including *USA Today.* Some charge for access, like the *Wall Street Journal.*

advertisers

Commercial online services have established a second revenue stream, in addition to subscriber fees, from advertising. America Online was the first service to take advertising, charging American Express $300,000 for a year of messages. Just as in the traditional advertising-supported media, advertisers pay to have their commercial messages interspersed among the various offerings on the commercial online services.

Media companies moved aggressively to create a web presence in the mid-1990s for two reasons. They wanted to be on the ground floor of an emerging medium that it seemed might eventually make their traditional delivery systems obsolete. Also,

amazon.com
Pioneer online bookstore.

Pathfinder
Time Warner web site that includes all the company's magazines and more.

they saw the web's potential advertising revenue. Media sites were slow to take off as a profitable advertising medium. Not until 1997 was any profit reported from a web site intended to be advertising supported. The first was Channel 4000 site, operated by Minneapolis television station WCCO, which said it was in the black for several months running.

Promising new web advertising vehicles are **webcasting** companies that package content that downloads automatically into users' computers. **PointCast,** as an example, delivers news, sports, weather and stock prices—whatever the individual user specifies in advance—to users' computer screens. Another webcaster offers 80 radio stations, streaming programs into users' computers for playing as soon as it's all downloaded. One webcaster does the same with sports 70 hours a week. These and other webcasters are two-way, interactive media products, delivering exactly the type of information that the users want. By tracking their users' information preferences, webcasters amass data that advertisers can use to identify likely customers. These ads are then downloaded with the content that individual users specified. Advertising can be tailored specifically to narrow audiences. "There's no other medium where you know your customer as well as you do on the web," media security analyst Betty Lyter told *Business Week.*

Webcasting is a departure from the original relationship between web users and content providers. Instead of users being proactive in searching out sites, "surfing the web," as it's called, webcasters surf to the user. Advertisers call it **push media,** because ads are pushed at users rather than users pulling them in.

online advertising

(STUDY PREVIEW)   The Internet's reach grew to 13 percent of the North American population in 1995, fueling interest in cyberspace as an effective place for advertisers to reach consumers. A problem, however, is that nobody has solid data on how many people are tapping into web sites that carry ads.

growing web audience

Until 1995 nobody knew how many people were using the Internet, and some promoters with vested interests were using suspiciously high guesstimates. Hard data began emerging in 1995, however. Nielsen Media Research conducted an exhaustive study that found that 37 million people over age 16 in the United States and Canada had access to the Internet, almost 13 percent of the population, and 24 million were using it—11 percent. The number exceeded most of the guesstimates. The study also found 17.6 million people using the World Wide Web, which was rapidly evolving into an electronic news, information and advertising medium with fancy typefaces, color and graphics.

The Nielsen study demonstrated the web's potential as an advertising medium. The study also found most web users had loads of discretionary income. The average annual household income exceeded $80,000.

web's advertising reach

Despite upbeat Nielsen data about people who use the web, there remains a hitch in developing the web as a major advertising medium. Nobody has devised tools to measure traffic at a web site in meaningful ways. Such data are needed to establish advertising rates that will give advertisers confidence that they're spending their money wisely on web advertising. For traditional media, advertisers look to standard measures like **cost per thousand (CPM)** to calculate the cost effectiveness of ads in competing media. Across-the-board comparisons aren't possible with the web, however—at least not yet. In some ways, buying space for cyber-ads is a crap shoot.

The most-cited measure of web audiences is the **hit.** Every time someone browsing the web clicks an on-screen icon or on-screen highlighted section, the computer server that offers the web page records a hit. Some companies that operate web sites tout hits as a measure of audience, but savvy advertisers know hits are a misleading indicator of audience size. The online edition of *Wired* magazine, HotWired, for example, records an average 100 hits from everybody who taps in. HotWired's 600,000 hits on a heavy day come from a mere 6,000 people.

Another measure of web usage is the **visit,** a count of the people who visit a site. But visits too are misleading. At *Playboy* magazine's web site, 200,000 visits are scored on a typical day, but that doesn't mean *Playboy* cyber-ads receive exposure to 200,000 different people. The fact is many of the same people visit again and again on a given day.

Some electronic publications charge advertisers by the day, others by the month, others by the hit. But because of the vagaries of audience measurements, there is no standard pricing. Knowing that the web cannot mature as an advertising medium until advertisers can be given better audience data, electronic publications have asked several companies, including Nielsen, to devise tracking mechanisms. But no one expects data as accurate as press runs and broadcast ratings any time soon. In the meantime, advertisers are making seat-of-the-pants assessments on which web sites are hot.

web technology

(STUDY PREVIEW)   The 1947 invention of the transistor led to data digitization and compression. Without transistors, the web would never have come into being. Nor would the other mass media be anything like we know them today. Another invention, Corning Glass' fiber-optic cable, makes it possible to transmit huge amounts of digitized data.

transistors

Three researchers at AT&T's **Bell Labs** developed the **semiconductor** switch in 1947. **Walter Brattain, John Bardeen** and **William Shockley,** who would receive the 1956 Nobel Prize, took pieces of glasslike silicon (just sand, really) and devised a way to make them respond to a negative or positive electrical charge. These tiny units, first called **transistors,** now more commonly called semiconductors or chips, functioned very rapidly as on-off switches. The on-off technology, in which data are converted to on-off codes, is called **digitization** because data are reduced to a series of digits, 1 for on, 0 for off.

---

cost per thousand (CPM)
Advertising term to measure an ad's reach.

hit
Tallied every time someone goes to a web page.

visit
Tallied for every person who visits a web site.

Bell Labs
AT&T facility where transistor invented.

semiconductor
Tiny sand-based transistor that responds to weak on-off charges.

Walter Brattain
Co-developer of transistor.

John Bardeen
Co-developer of transistor.

William Shockley
Co-developer of transistor.

transistor
Semiconductor.

digitization
Converting on-off coding for storage and for transmission.

Digitization. As might be expected, Bell researchers tried applying **digitization** to telephone communication. Soon they found ways to convert the human voice to a series of coded pulses for transmission on telephone lines to a receiver that would change them into a simulation of the voice. These pulses were digital on-off signals that were recorded so fast at one end of the line and reconstructed so fast at the other that they sounded like the real thing. The rapid on-off signals worked like the persistence of vision phenomenon that creates the illusion of movement in motion pictures.

A milestone event occurred in 1962 when AT&T sent a message to Chicago from suburban Skokie using transistor technology—the first digital telephone call. Until that moment, telephone communication was based on sound waves being converted to varying electrical currents for transmission. At the receiving end, the currents were changed back to sound waves. With digital transmission, voices were instead converted to an incredibly fast-moving stream of discrete on-off digital pulses.

Compression. Bell Labs also devised techniques to squeeze different calls onto the same line simultaneously, which increased the capacity of the nation's telephone network. With traditional telephone technology, dating to Alexander Graham Bell's 1876 invention of the telephone, only one message could be carried at a time on a telephone line. With digitization, however, a new process called **multiplexing** became possible. Tiny bits of one message could be interspersed with tiny bits of other messages for transmission and then sorted out at the other end.

AT&T introduced multiplex telephone services in 1965. People marveled that 51 calls could be carried at the same time on a copper wire with on-off digital switching technology. The capacity of the nation's telephone communication system was dramatically increased without laying even a single new mile of wire.

compression
Squeezing data to increase storage and transmission capacity.

multiplexing
Compressing messages for simultaneous transmission on same line or radio wave.

Few people foresaw that digitization and compression would revolutionize human existence, let alone do it so quickly. The web wasn't even a glimmer in anyone's eye. Nonetheless, the building blocks for the web were being created.

Miniaturization. Radio and television were the first mass media beneficiaries of the transistor. In the 1940s, broadcast equipment was built around electrical tubes, which looked somewhat like light bulbs. These tubes heated up and eventually burned out. In addition, they consumed massive amounts of electricity. Transistors, on the other hand, could perform the same functions with hardly any electricity and no heat. Important too, transistors were much, much smaller than tubes and much more reliable.

Consumers began benefitting directly from transistors in the mid-1950s. Until then, even the smallest radios, called "table models," were hunky pieces of furniture. Then came a new product: hand-held, battery-powered transistor radios that people could carry anywhere. Those tiny radios, however, were merely glimpses at the mass communication revolution that transistors were ushering in.

Not only did the use of transistors dramatically reduce the size and weight of broadcast equipment, the size of computers shrank as well. In the 1940s, early computers, based on tube technology, were so big it took entire buildings to house them and large staffs of technicians to operate them. Today, the Marquardt Corporation estimates that all the information recorded in the past 10,000 years can be stored in a cube six feet by six feet by six feet. All 12 million books in the Library of Congress would take fewer than two of those cubic inches.

There seems no end to miniaturization. IBM has developed a computer drive that, using **giant magneto-resistance** technology, crams an incredible 100 million digital characters on a thumbtack-size disk. IBM now expects to be producing GMR disks that can accommodate 2 billion characters on a thumbtack. That's equivalent to 2,000 novels.

Efficiencies. Transistor-based equipment costs less to manufacture and operates with incredible efficiency. The National Academy of Science estimates it cost $130,000 to make 125 multiplications when the forerunners of today's computers were introduced in the 1940s. By 1970 the cost was a mere $4. Today, it can be done for pennies.

fiber optics

While AT&T was building on its off-on digital technology to improve telephone service in the 1960s, **Corning Glass** developed a cable that was capable of carrying light at incredible speeds—theoretically 186,000 miles per second. It was apparent immediately that this new **fiber-optic cable,** made out of silicon, could carry far more digitized multiplex messages than could copper. The messages were encoded as light pulses rather than as the traditional electrical pulses for transmission.

By the 1980s, new equipment to convert data to light pulses for transmission was in place, and long-distance telephone companies were replacing their copper lines with fiber optics, as were local cable television systems. Today, with semiconductor switching combined with optical fiber cable, a single line can carry 60,000 telephone calls simultaneously. In addition to voice, the lines can carry all kinds of other messages that have been broken into digitized pulses. With fiber-optic cable, the entire *Oxford English Dictionary* can be sent in just seconds. Such speed is what has made the web a mass medium that can deliver unprecedented quantities of information so quickly.

miniaturization
Reducing size of devices for data recording, storage, retrieval.

giant magneto-resistance (GMR)
Allows super-miniaturization.

Corning Glass
Company that developed fiber-optic cable.

fiber-optic cable
Glass strands capable of carrying data as light.

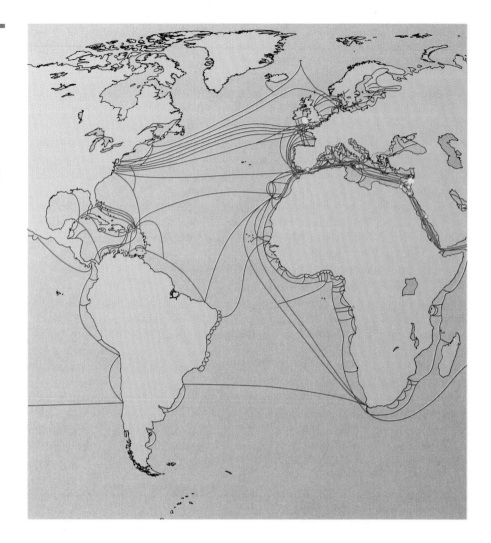

Global Fiber-Optics. The Fiberoptic Link Around the Globe, "FLAG" for short, is the longest engineering project in human history—a 17,400-mile communication link of England and Japan. The blue lines are other undersea fiber-optic routes that are planned or in place. The world is being wired for faster World Wide Web communication.

nonlinear communication

(STUDY PREVIEW) Hypertext, a relatively recent concept for creating messages, is the heart of the web as a mass medium. With hypertext, the people who receive messages can influence the sequence of the messages they receive. Once, it was only the communicators who had such power.

hypertext and the web

Until recently, we were all accustomed to mass messages flowing from start to finish in the sequence that mass communicators figured would be most effective for most people. Many mass messages still flow linearly. Newscasts, as an example, start with the most important item first. A novel builds climatically to the final chapter. A

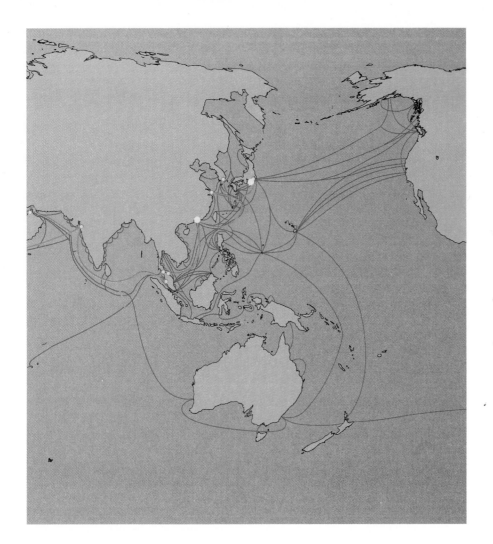

television commercial catches your attention at the start and names the advertiser in the sign-off. This is **linear communication.**

Vannevar Bush, a leading thinker of his time, noted to *Atlantic* magazine readers in 1945 that knowledge had expanded exponentially in the 20th century, but the means for "threading through" the maze was "the same as used in the days of square-rigged ships." Bush proposed a machine he called **memex** to mimic human thinking in organizing material. With his memex, people could retrieve information through automated association with related information.

Alas, Bush's memex was never built, but a generation later, technologist **Ted Nelson,** who may have heard his grandfather read Bush's article aloud, picked up on the idea. In his 1962 book *Literary Machines,* Nelson coined the term **hypertext** for an alternate way for people to send and receive information. Nelson also used the term *nonsequential writing,* but it was *hypertext* that stuck.

To see how hypertext works, pretend you're a few years into the future and you're studying a new edition of this book. You're at your computer screen because the book is in on-screen nonlinear hypertext. Your professor has assigned you to study

linear communication
Messages in a specified start-to-end sequence.

Vannevar Bush
Proposed machine for relational information retrieval.

memex
Machine proposed by Vannevar Bush for nonlinear information access.

Ted Nelson
Coined term *hypertext* for nonlinear communication.

hypertext
Method of interrelating messages so users control their sequence.

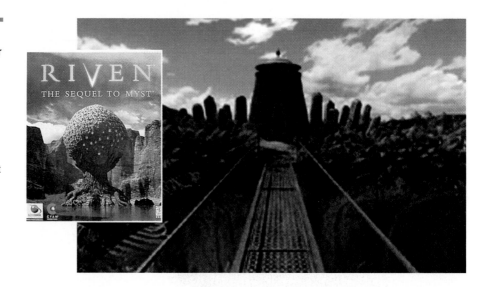

Nonlinear Communication. Computer games like Riven are a sophisticated form of hypertext with the players choosing options that shape the course of the game. The term *hypertext* was introduced by technologist Ted Nelson in his 1962 book *Literary Machines.* The concept was outlined in a 1945 *Atlantic* magazine article, "As We May Think," by intellectual Vannevar Bush. Hypertext is a nonlinear way for people to receive information.

Chapter 10, which you open up on-screen. You can read the chapter linearly from start to finish, or you also can move your on-screen cursor to highlighted words, called hot spots, hot keys or links, and click on them to switch elsewhere in the book or to other documents for detail that interests you.

Years later, reflecting on the instant success of his New York *Sun,* Benjamin Day shook his head in wonderment. He hadn't realized at the time that the *Sun* was such a milestone. Whether he was being falsely modest is something historians can quibble over. The fact is that the *Sun,* which Day founded in 1833, discovered mass audiences on a scale never before envisioned and ushered in the era of modern mass media.

At Chapter 10's Media People box on Ben Day, you can click on New York *Sun* and go to a screen with a thumbnail history of the newspaper with its own hot spots. You decide to click the penny newspapers hot spot. Up comes a list of 14 leading one-cent newspapers. You could click on any of the 14 to go to screens with information about them. Instead, you choose a hot spot on a list of options at the bottom of the screen: Scholarship 1960–69. There you find a list of nine books and 61 articles in academic journals on the Penny Press Period from the 1960s, and you can go to summaries, tables of contents or full texts of any of them. The hyperlinks are limitless, and at any time you can reverse your course to a previous screen to choose a hot term to go on yet another pathway.

In primitive ways, people have done a kind of hypertext learning for centuries. In the library, a researcher may have two dozen books open and piled on a desk, with dozens more reference books handy on a shelf. Moving back and forth among the books, checking indexes and footnotes, and fetching additional volumes from the library stacks, the researcher is creating new meanings by combining information in new sequences. The computer has accelerated that process and opened up thousands of resources, all on-screen, for today's scholars.

One way to understand the World Wide Web is to plot dots for various web sites randomly on a sheet of paper and then connect every dot with every other dot. It will look like a spider web, hence the name World Wide Web. You also can jump

media

online

Vannevar Bush: Bush's 1945 *Atlantic* magazine article, proposing a new relationship between human beings and knowledge, is available online: www.isg.sfu.ca/"duchier/misc/vbush

from page to page *within* a web site. This fundamentally sets the web apart from other mass media.

hypermedia

Hyperlinks can take you not only to more than just other text but also to sounds, images and movies. These nontext links are called **hypermedia.** Kevin Hughes of Honolulu Community College, in a primer on the World Wide Web, offered these possibilities for hypermedia:

- You are reading a text on the Hawaiian language. You select a Hawaiian phrase, then hear the phrase spoken in the native tongue.

- You are a law student studying the Hawaii Revised Statutes. By selecting a passage, you find precedents from a 1920 Supreme Court ruling stored at Cornell University. Cross-referenced hyperlinks allow you to view any one of 520 related cases with audio annotations.

- Looking at a company's floor plan, you are able to select an office by touching a room on screen. The employee's name and picture appears with a list of current projects.

- You are a scientist doing work on the cooling of steel springs. Selecting text in a research paper, you are able to view a computer movie of a cooling spring. Selecting a button you are able to receive a program that will perform thermodynamic calculations.

- You are a student reading a digital version of an art magazine and select a work to print or display in full. If the piece is a sculpture, you can request to see a movie of the sculpture rotating. By interactively controlling the movie, you can zoom in to see more detail.

> **hypermedia**
> Hypertext with sound, image and movie links.

How Hypertext Works.
At a glance, on-screen hypertext looks like any other text, but there is a difference. Hypertext contains links within the text to other documents. By clicking your cursor on shaded, under-lined or colored text, or graphics, you can go instantly to your choice of other documents. This illustration, adapted from one by Kevin Hughes, a student systems programmer at Honolulu Community College, shows how you can move from the term *hypertext* in one document to a history of hypertext, or to a dictionary definition of *hypertext*. These new documents themselves have links to other documents. As Hughes puts it: "Continually selecting text would take you on a free-associative tour of information. In this way, hypertext links, called hyperlinks, can create a complex virtual web of connections." Those connections can include hypermedia—sounds, images and movies.

Hypertext is basically the same as regular text – it can be stored, read, searched, or edited – with an important exception: hypertext contains connections within the text to other documents.

Selecting a piece of hypertext...

...can take you to more hypertext, books, movies, sounds, and images.

hypertext in practice

STUDY PREVIEW   Major news media are creating hypertext products that are revolutionizing how news is told. Whether hypertext will revolutionize other forms of story-telling, like the novel, is unclear.

pre-hypertext innovations

Although hypertext itself is not new, the shift from linear presentation in traditional media has been gradual. A preliminary stage was merely casting text in digital form for storage and transmission. This is what other early online services like Nexis did, providing linear full-text of news stories from cooperating newspapers. While a major step forward at the time, full-text is derisively called **shovelware** by hypertext enthusiasts because it is simply moved from a traditional medium to another without much adaptation to the unique characteristics of the new medium. Shovelware falls short of the potential of the web.

The **Media Lab** at the Massachusetts Institute of Technology came up with the next refinement: the *Daily Me,* an experimental digital newspaper that provided sub-scribers information only on subjects they specified in advance. Take, for example, a car buff who follows baseball and who earns a living running a grocery store in Spokane, Washington. For this person, a customized *Daily Me* would include news on the automobile industry, the American and National Leagues and the Spokane Indians farm club, livestock and produce market reports, news summaries from the

shovelware
Computer-delivered products without modification from linear original.
Media Lab
Massachusetts Institute of Technology research facility.
Daily Me
Experimental computer newspaper with reader-determined content.

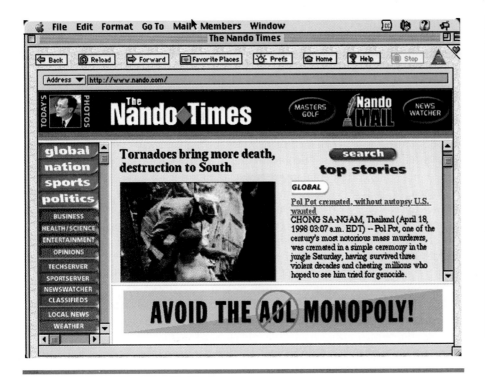

Online News. The Raleigh, North Carolina, *News & Observer* went online with Nando in 1994, pioneering the news site concept. About 650 households were hooked up then. Within 14 months, however, Nando had grown into an incredible success with seven million hits in a typical week. To meet consumer demand, the company was using 844 phone lines.

Spokane area and neighboring British Columbia and Idaho and a brief summary of major national and world news.

MIT's *Daily Me* innovation took commercial form at the *Wall Street Journal,* which in 1995 launched the first customizable electronic newspaper. It was called **Personal Journal,** with the subtitle: "Published for a Circulation of One." *Personal Journal,* which cost $18 a month plus 50 cents per update, offered whatever combination a subscriber wanted of business and general coverage by category, market tables and selected quotes, sports and weather.

hypertext news

The potential of digital news was realized with the web. When **USA Today** established a web site, it offered a hypertext product—not shovelware. *USA Today* webmasters broke the newspaper's content into web page-size components, updated them 24 hours a day as events warranted, and linked every page with others. Every day, readers can choose among thousands of connections, in effect creating their own news package by moving around among the entire content of the newspaper. Hot spots include links to archived material from previous coverage that *USA Today*'s webmasters figured some readers would want to draw on for background.

> **Personal Journal**
> *Wall Street Journal* computer newspaper with reader-determined content.
>
> **USA Today**
> Newspaper with one of first nonlinear computer editions.

All the major news products coming online today are state-of-the-art hypertext ventures. Some web sites offer users an opportunity to communicate immediately back to the creators of the products.

hyperfiction

While digital technology is revolutionizing many aspects of human communication, it is unclear whether all literary forms will be fundamentally affected. Scholar John Pavlik has indicated that fiction, for example, has undergone a revolution in production in recent centuries but, unlike news, not in form:

"When the Brothers Grimm wrote their fairy tales in the Middle Ages, the quill pen was the writing tool of choice and the words were intended to be read in a linear fashion, from start to finish. Every story had a single plot, a beginning, middle and end, and every reader, even 20th century ones, read the same story.

"Although the technology of writing changed significantly from the days of the Brothers Grimm into the middle of the 20th century, the notion of story-telling evolved very little until relatively recently. By and large, stories still had a beginning, middle and end, and readers still digested a single plot or set of facts. Even the 'new' electronic media of radio and television did little to change the editorial process, although the written word became the spoken word, and images only imagined, drawn or in still form became animated and life-like. Nevertheless, facts or narration still unfolded in linear fashion, from start to finish."

Today there are experiments with hypertext fiction. The computer games Myst and Riven put players in dream-like landscapes where they wander through adventures in which they choose the course of events. Options, of course, are limited to those the authors put into the game, but the player has a feeling of creating the story rather than following an author's plot. Myst and Riven represent a new dimension in exploration as an experiential literary form.

Some futurists see interactivity overtaking traditional forms of human story-telling, and the term *hyperfiction* has been applied to a few dozen pioneer hypertext novels. One hyperfiction enthusiast, Trip Hawkins, who creates video games, laid out both sides in a New York *Times* interview: "Given the choice, do viewers really want to interact with their entertainment? Watching, say, *Jurassic Park,* wouldn't they prefer to have Steven Spielberg spin the tale of dinosaurs munching on their keepers in an island theme park?" For himself, however, Hawkins says: "I want to be on the island. I want to show that I could have done better than those idiots did. I could have gotten out of that situation."

media convergence

hyperfiction
Nonlinear novels, games, other fiction.

media melding

(STUDY PREVIEW) Many mass media as we know them are converging into digitized formats. Complementing and hastening this technological melding is ownership conglomeration and joint ventures. Government deregulation is contributing to a freer business environment that encourages new ventures.

Latter-Day Pathfinder. Pathfinder is the Time Warner web site that links to hundreds of online services originating with the conglomerate's media subsidiaries. These are as diverse as *People* and *Sports Illustrated* magazines, the *Progressive Farmer* trade journal, the HBO cable television programming service, and Elektra Records. Where did the whimsical Time Warner folks who created Pathfinder come up with the name? Their online explanation: "It's meant to suggest an adventure into unknown territory, your compass or guide into a new realm. Pathfinder also is a tribute to a great character in a dreadful novel: Natty Bumppo, the uncorrupted natural man who followed the wilderness westward in James Fenimore Cooper's novel that threatened to turn us off to reading when we were in high school. As he meanders his way through Cooper's works, he picks up a bunch of other names, but most of us agreed that Pathfinder was a better name for an Internet service than Leatherstocking or Deerslayer."

technological convergence

Johannes Gutenberg brought mass production to books, and the other primary print media, magazines and newspapers followed. People never had a problem recognizing differences among books, magazines and newspapers. When sound recording and movies came along, they too were distinctive, and later so were radio and television. Today, the traditional primary media are in various stages of transition to digital form.

Whether a convergence of the cable television systems and the Internet occurs is too far distant to consider. There is, however, a convergence in digital technology. This convergence is fueled by accelerated miniaturization of equipment and the ability to compress data into tiny digital bits for storage and transmission. And all the media companies, whether their products traditionally relied on print, electronic or photographic technology, are involved in the convergence.

As the magazine *The Economist* noted, once-discrete media industries "are being whirled into an extraordinary whole." Writing in *Quill* magazine, *USA Today*'s Kevin

technological convergence
Melding of print, electronic and photographic media into digitized form.

....bill gates

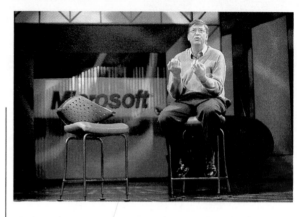

Bill Gates was well into his courses at Harvard when his high school buddy Paul Allen drove across the country from Seattle to convince him to drop out. Gates did. The pair went to Albuquerque and set up shop to do computer stuff. Their company, Microsoft, today is the world's largest software producer, and it is moving rapidly into creating a dominant web presence. It also is becoming a major creator of media content. With the company's success, Gates became the world's richest person. In 1997, at age 41, he was worth $23.9 billion. His assets were growing at $30 million a day.

In Albuquerque in 1976, Gates wrote the code for the Microsoft Disk Operating System, usually abbreviated as MS-DOS and pronounced m-s DOSS. Allen and Gates persuaded computer hardware manufacturers to bundle MS-DOS with their units, which pre-empted competitors. The bundling also gave Micro-

soft a growing and gigantic market for software application programs that operated only on MS-DOS. The company's word-processing program, Microsoft Word, for example, dominates globally. So do various Microsoft Windows operating systems that have updated MS-DOS.

With their initial success, Gates and Allen moved the company to their hometown, Seattle, where it remains. Allen bowed out after a debilitating disease was diagnosed (falsely, it turned out). Allen's departure left Gates in charge. Today the company operates out of a 35-building campus in suburban Redmond.

Critics say Microsoft products are neither the best nor the most innovative. These critics attribute the company's success to cut-throat competitive practices and marketing muscle, rather than product excellence. Detractors have built web sites that revile Gates as an unconscionable monopolist.

Several times the federal government has considered antitrust action to force Microsoft to scale back. Gates, who subscribes to Darwin's "survival of the fittest" theory, explains away the criticism as envy.

In the mid-1990s Gates became concerned that Microsoft's software dominance would be eroded by Internet-based systems, like Sun Microsystem's Java, that allow people to tap remote computers for the applications they need—rather than storing dozens or hundreds of applications inside their own personal computers. Responding to the changing landscape, Gates set Microsoft on a new course. The company introduced a browser, Internet Explorer, to go against the innova-

tive, fast-growing Netscape Navigator browser. He bundled Explorer inside major Microsoft software packages so customers would have it on hand as the company developed advertiser-supported content products with easy access through Explorer.

To jump-start Microsoft's move into real-time delivery of content, Gates created an alliance with the NBC television network. One component of the alliance is the MS Network, an online computer service which includes NBC-generated news, information and entertainment content, plus a growing array of content from Microsoft. Another component is the MSNBC cable television network that draws on both companies' resources.

Manay put it this way: "All the devices people use for communicating and all the kinds of communication have started crashing together into one massive megamedia industry. The result is that telephone lines will soon carry TV shows. Cable TV will carry telephone calls. Desktop computers will be used to watch and edit

Neal Stephenson emerged as an important new-tech novelist with his 1992 *Snow Crash,* which became the rage of Silicon Valley. The novel, a thriller, originally intended as a Macintosh game, is set in a near-future when the United States has lost its leadership in everything but movies, software and high-speed pizza delivery.

It's a bustling, not unfriendly "megaverse." Characteristic of Stephenson's work, *Snow Crash* has disparate story lines that culminate quickly in the last few pages.

Critics applaud Stephenson's sense of language and culture, especially the interactions between groups of individuals and changing technology. He

also has demonstrated a good sense of what's technologically just ahead. His *Zodiac,* in 1988, was intended to be "day after tomorrow" fiction—a future that was very close. One of his characters writes computer games for 32-bit home computers, which soon became the norm in the marketplace.

Stephenson, born in

1959, has been hailed as a possible successor to William Gibson, author of *Neuromancer,* in the techno-thriller genre. Stephenson's works include *The Big U,* 1984; *Zodiac: The Eco-Thriller,* 1988; *Interface,* 1994; and *Diamond Age,* 1995, which was co-authored with his uncle under the pseudonym Stephen Bury.

movies. Cellular phone-computers the size of a notepad will dial into interactive magazines that combine text, sound and video to tell stories."

transition ahead

Nobody expects the printed newspaper to disappear overnight, or for movie houses, video rental shops and over-air broadcasters to go out of business all at once. But the fact is that all the big media companies have established stakes on the web, and in time, digitized messages delivered over the web may dominate.

Outside of the web itself, major media companies also are trying to establish a future for themselves in reaching audiences in new digital ways. Companies that identify voids in their ability to capitalize on new technology have created joint ventures to assure they won't be left out. The NBC television network, for example, has agreed to provide news on Microsoft's MSN online service. All of the regional Bell telephone companies have picked up partners to develop video delivery systems. Cable companies are gearing for telephone-like two-way interactive communication systems that will, for example, permit customers not only to receive messages but also to send them.

government deregulation

Until recent years, a stumbling block to the melding of digital media was the U.S. government. Major components of today's melded media—the telephone, television and computer industries—grew up separately, and government policy kept many of

media
online

FedWorld: The information buck starts here. www.fedworld.gov

White House: First user-friendly site to bring you closer to the government you deserve. www.whitehouse.gov/WH/Welcome.html

Thomas: Jefferson, that is. Legislative information on the Web. http://thomas.loc.gov/home/thomas.html

Blue Ribbon Campaign for Free Speech Online: The First Amendment battle over the web started here. www.eff.org/blueribbon.html

them from venturing into the others' staked-out territory of services. Telephone companies, for example, were limited to being common carriers. They couldn't create their own media messages, just deliver other people's. Cable companies were barred from building two-way communication into their systems.

In the 1970s, government agencies began to ease restrictions on business. In 1984, President **Ronald Reagan** stepped up this **deregulation,** and more barriers came down. The pro-business Reagan administration also took no major actions against the stampede of media company mergers that created fewer and bigger media companies. George Bush, elected in 1988, and Bill Clinton, elected in 1992, continued Reagan's deregulation initiatives and also his soft stance on mergers. The Clinton position, however, is less ideological and more pragmatic. Clinton's thinking was based on the view that regulation and antitrust actions would hamstring U.S. media companies, and other enterprises too, in global competition.

In 1996, Congress approved a new telecommunications law that wiped out many of the barriers that heeded full-bore exploitation of the potential of new media. The law repealed a federal ban against telephone companies providing video programming. Just as significant, cable television systems were given a green light to offer two-way local telephone. The law, the **Telecommunications Act of 1996,** accelerated the competition that had been emerging between telephone and cable television companies to rewire communities for higher quality, faster delivery of new audio and video services.

public policy and the web

STUDY PREVIEW The web is a content-neutral medium whose content is more directly user-driven than the traditional media. This makes the web hard to regulate, which has created problems for moralists concerned about indecent material, and for authoritarian governments that find traditional media easier to censor. The difficulty is compounded by the volume of messages scooting around in cyberspace.

universal access

Ronald Reagan
President who pushed deregulation.

deregulation
Government policy to reduce regulation of business.

Telecommunications Act of 1996
Repealed many limits on services that telephone and cable companies could offer.

universal access
Giving everyone the means to use the Web.

Although web use is growing dramatically, the fact is that not everybody has access or, probably, ever will. Those who can afford computers and access charges will benefit tremendously. What about everybody else? This is a profound public policy question, especially in a democracy that prides itself on assuring equality for every citizen on basic matters like access to information.

One line of reasoning is that the government should not guarantee **universal access.** This rationale draws on the interstate highway system as an analogy. The government builds the roads, but individuals provide the vehicles to drive around on the system.

The counterargument is that access to information will become so essential to everyone's well-being that we could end up with a stratified society of info-rich and info-poor people. Such a knowledge gap hardly is the democratic ideal.

The National Telecommunications and Information Administration, recognizing the problem, issued $62 million in grants in 1995 to schools, libraries and communities to devise innovative ways to get people online. Larry Irving, the assistant U.S. Secretary of Commerce responsible for administering the program, sees the key as hooking children on the Internet. As they grow up, the kids then will demand public policies that assure access as a right of citizenship. That was part of the Clinton administration's reason for grants like one to a school in Hall, Montana, population 95. Kids learned about the Internet during the day, and the community had access in the evening.

cyberpornography

Robert Thomas was tired of moving furniture for a living, so in 1991 he decided to try making money from his computer hobby. He set up an Internet bulletin board from which anyone on the Net could download sex photos. Thomas started with 12 photos. He charged for access, and business boomed. Within three years he had a stock of 25,000 photos and was pulling in $800,000 a year. In 1994, a government agent in Memphis downloaded some of Thomas' offerings, and soon Thomas, who lived in California, was serving a three-year jail term for transmitting obscene material.

Thomas is not the only provider of **cyberpornography** to the Internet. Authorities are trying to eradicate indecency from cyberspace, especially if children have access. How serious is the problem? No one is certain how much cyberporn is out there. Vanderbilt University business professors Donna Hoffman and Thomas Novak estimate that only one-half of 1 percent of the files available on the Internet could be described as pornographic. And how often kids visit those sites is impossible to measure. Some people would argue that even a single child's exposure to pornography is too much and justifies sanctions. In Congress, Senator **James Exon** of Nebraska led a crusade for two-year prison terms and $100,000 in fines for anyone making indecent material available to minors online. The crusade resulted in the **Communications Decency Act of 1996,** but the law was attacked by free-expression advocates and the U.S. Supreme Court struck it down because it also limited the material that adults could put on and read off the web. Public policy in the United States generally is tolerant of sexual material, except when children are involved. The question is whether laws protecting children can work without violating the constitutionally guaranteed freedom of adults to create, transmit and receive such material.

Policing the Internet, including web sites, presents unique challenges. The nature of the web is that it is unstructured and unregulated, and the available material is in ongoing flux. The anarchy of the web is its inherent virtue. The immensity of cyberspace is another problem for would-be regulators. The web system that Tim Berners-Lee and his associates devised has infinite capacity.

Among alternatives to protect children are desktop programs that have come on the market to identify objectionable Internet bulletin boards and web sites. **SurfWatch,** for example, blocks access to such sites as soon as they are discovered. Bill Duvall of Los Altos, California, who created SurfWatch, hires college students to monitor cyberspace for sexual explicitness, and updates SurfWatch regularly. He identifies five to 10 new smut sites a day.

Commercial online services keep close tabs on what goes on in their bulletin boards and chat rooms, and occasionally excise bawdy material. In addition, the industry is working on a rating system, somewhat like Hollywood's movie ratings, to

---

cyberpornography
Indecency delivered by computer.

James Exon
U.S. senator who backed penalties for delivery of indecency to children.

Communications Decency Act
Federal law intended to keep indecency aimed at children off the web; Supreme Court found act unconstitutional.

SurfWatch
Software that intercepts indecent material.

help parents screen things they deem inappropriate for the kids. Since 1993, however, the commercial online services have been able to give their subscribers access to the unregulated Internet. Once out of an online service's gate, subscribers are beyond the protection of the service's in-house standards of acceptability.

chapter wrap-up

The web utilizes the global Internet, so computers anywhere can exchange digitized data—including text, visuals and audio. Many media companies are investing heavily in cyberspace, and the expansion of high-capacity fiber-optic cable networks will increase capacity tremendously so that audio and moving visuals are on tap live on any computer screen connected to the Internet. Two-way communication via the web already is standard fare. With every passing day, more mass communication is occurring on the web.

The web is rooted in digital technology, which has led to compression of data into smaller and smaller forms for transmission. This has been followed by fiber-optic cables having mega-capacities to transmit data. A single fiber-optic strand can carry 50 copies of a medium-size novel in a second—hundreds of times faster than can copper cable television lines and thousands of times faster than can copper telephone lines.

Public policy will need rethinking as the media converge. The old regulatory distinctions between print and broadcast media, which involve fundamental First Amendment issues, will need to be reassessed. There also are global implications because of the virtual impossibility of stopping media signals at national borders. Because of the web, authoritarian governments will find that their traditional controls of media content no longer work.

Whatever changes are ahead, however, the heart of mass communication remains with trained and talented people preparing messages for mass audiences. The work of mass communicators is in gathering, digesting and packaging information, whether it be news, entertainment or persuasion. Newspapers as we know them may disappear, along with television and books and the other traditional media. But the demand for creating media messages of all kinds will grow as technology enables mass communicators to cater to more specific audience segments. For mass communicators, the future is in the content, not the hardware.

questions for review

1. How can the World Wide Web be defined as a new and distinctive mass medium?

2. How is the World Wide Web related to the Internet?

3. What is the future for commercial online services?

4. What is the difficulty with the web as an advertising medium?

5. What is the effect of digitization and fiber-optic cable on mass communication?

6. What is the connection between the web and hypertext?

7. Will hypertext change the way that human beings create stories and receive them?

8. Why was digitizing a necessary prelude to the web?

9. Should public policy guarantee everyone, including children, total access to the web?

questions for critical thinking

1. Will it ever be possible to condense all human knowledge into an area smaller than the 36-square-foot cube described by the Marquardt Corporation?

2. What makes books, magazines, newspapers, sound recordings, movies, radio and television different from one another? What will become of these distinctions in coming years?

3. Trace the development of the technology that has made the web possible.

4. What were the innovations that Tim Berners-Lee introduced that are revolutionizing mass communication?

5. Compare and contrast commercial online services and the web. What are the long-term prospects for each? Why?

6. How does hypertext depart from traditional human communication? And does hypertext have a future as a literary form?

7. What obstacles would you have in designing public policy to assure access for every citizen to the web?

8. Some people say there is no point in trying to regulate cybersmut. Do you agree? Disagree? Why?

9. Some mass media may be subsumed by the web. Pretend you are a futurist and create a timeline for this to happen.

for further learning

Vannevar Bush. "As We May Think." *Atlantic Monthly* (July 1945). In this seminal article, Bush, president of the Carnegie Institution, proposed a machine for associative retrieval of information—a precursor for the web.

Martha FitzSimons, editor. *Media, Democracy and the Information Highway* (Freedom Forum Media Studies Center, 1993). This conference report on national information policy is an excellent starting point on the major issues involving rapidly changing technology.

Robert Lucky. *Silicon Dreams* (St. Martin's, 1989). Lucky argues that words are more important in mass communication than images. This is fortunate, he notes, because more words can be stored digitally than can photographs.

Kevin Maney. "Will the Techno Tsunami Wash Us Out?" *Quill* (March 1994), pp. 16–18. Maney, a newspaper reporter, discusses implications of media convergence on the careers of media people. This issue of *Quill* has additional articles on the subject.

John V. Pavlik. *New Media Technology: Cultural and Commercial Perspectives* (Allyn & Bacon, 1995). Pavlik, a scholar, provides a sweeping view of the technology landscape, including major corporate players and both the flamboyant and obscure leaders of the media revolution.

Mark Slouka. *War of the Worlds* (Basic Books, 1996). Slouka, of the University of California, San Diego, addresses how the continuing transition away from face-to-face communication is affecting what it means to be human.

for keeping up to date

The magazine *Wired* offers hep coverage of cyberdevelopments, issues and people.

Trade journals *Editor & Publisher, Advertising Age* and *Broadcast/Cable* have excellent ongoing coverage of their fields.

InfoWorld covers the gamut of cybernews.

Widely available news media that explore cyberissues include *Time, Newsweek*, the *Wall Street Journal* and the New York *Times*.

Don't overlook surfing the web for sites that track web developments.

10
journalism

in this chapter you will learn:

- Many mass media practices originated during major periods in American history.

- Journalists bring many personal, social and political values to their work.

- Many variables beyond journalists' control affect what ends up being reported.

- Factors outside the newsroom influence how news is reported.

- Gatekeeping is both essential and hazardous in the news process.

- Exploratory reporting and soft news are journalistic trends going in opposite directions.

- News organizations rely heavily on common sources like news services and syndicates.

They all wanted her—ABC, CBS, NBC. The Cable News Network already had her, but her contract was expiring. **Christiane Amanpour,** having achieved worldwide acclaim as a war correspondent, was now the object of a bidding war. In the end, there were three winners: Amanpour herself, reportedly offered close to $2 million, making her the highest paid foreign correspondent in the world; CNN, which would retain her as senior international correspondent; and CBS, which would fea-ture her special reports on "60 Minutes."

Thirteen years had passed since the day in 1983 when Amanpour entered CNN's building in Atlanta to begin her entry-level job as an assistant to the international assignment desk. Ted Turner's news network was only three years old. Amanpour would grow with the company, becoming a reporter working out of CNN's bureaus in New York, Frankfort and Paris.

But it was her work as a correspondent in the hot spots around the globe that caused the world to take notice. Wherever civil unrest and conflict broke out, wherever there arose political crises, turmoil, military actions, and all the human tragedies associated with such events, TV viewers could expect Amanpour to be there, showing and telling them what was happening. CNN's global audience expanded rapidly; government leaders and ordinary citizens alike were tuning in to see on-the-spot coverage of breaking news. The vast changes in Central Europe, the break-up of the Soviet Union, the events in Sarajevo, Algeria, Haiti, Rwanda, Somalia, the Persian Gulf—all were covered in Amanpour's unique reporting style.

Colleagues in broadcast journalism praised her for her fearlessness. Martin Bell, a veteran correspondent for the BBC, who worked alongside Amanpour for a time and who suffered wounds during the Bosnian conflict, said Amanpour "was very lucky not to have become a casualty" during her four years there because she defied danger and went everywhere the camera crew went. A sound technician who worked with her in another conflict area admired her instinctual ability to know exactly when to enter and exit perilous situations—"like a cat." A *TV Guide* writer remembers some American soldiers who asked her to pose for a picture with them. One of them quipped that being seen in a picture with Christiane Amanpour would prove they deserved their danger pay.

Amanpour's fearlessness also showed up in another way, bringing both praise and criticism and sparking heated debates over "bias," "balance" and "neutrality" in the media. The most talked about example of her boldness occurred in May 1994 when, during a live satellite broadcast of CNN's "Global Forum," she accused President Clinton of "flip-flopping" over Bosnia. Looking into the camera, she asked why the United States was delaying so long in forming a policy on the issue. And why was the President permitting the U.S. and the West "to be held hostage to those who do have a clear policy, the Bosnian Serbs"? The President was visibly angry and denied the charge of wavering. In that moment, Amanpour had gone from reporting news to making news—as was evident by the media's attention to the exchange.

Many critics charged she had overstepped the boundaries between objective reporting and advocating a position. They reminded her that reporters are expected to remain detached from what they report. They are to provide facts and information, simply tell what happens, and not give their opinions. Correspondents should not take sides.

For Amanpour, it was impossible not to take sides. To her, the Bosnian conflict was a war waged by military forces against civilians who wanted only to go about their daily lives. She had witnessed the carnage. She had stood with weeping wives, mothers and children as they grieved over the thousands of men and boys who were massacred and shoved into mass graves.

For a New York *Times* forum, she reflected on a visit to the Holocaust Museum in Washington, D.C. "In war," she said, "it is the reporter's duty to confront the lies, not simply to repeat them as slaves to some misplaced notion of objectivity." She expressed disagreement with the idea that objectivity means "treating all sides equally" if to do so conveys the notion that all sides are morally equivalent. "If you draw a moral equivalence between victim and aggressor, then you are just a step away from being neutral, and when you are neutral, you are just a step away from being an accomplice." In the case of Bosnia, Amanpour said, that would mean being "an accomplice to genocide." When interviewed for Brown University's alumni magazine, she put it more succinctly: "Should we have said Hitler had a point?"

Amanpour credits her awareness of her job's "moral dimension" to the experience of reporting the horrors of ethnic cleansing. Her reporting on any topic has earned her a reputation of being authoritative, uncompromising, extremely well versed in foreign affairs, skillful in explaining complexities, and always compelling in the human drama she presents. "It really makes a difference when you can find the people affected the most by war and conflict, the innocent victims, to tell the story of the effects such events have on their lives," she told a group of TV news staff members in South Africa, inspiring them to want to apply the same approach in reporting the events in their country.

In a commencement speech at Emory University, Amanpour spoke of being "offended, angered, horrified and frankly dispirited" over the political apathy so many Americans display with regard to international turmoil. "You cannot pretend that what happens in this world won't affect this country and won't affect each and every one of you and your families and friends," she told the 1997 graduates.

Her own vast knowledge of the international scene, combined with her extensive travels, her background as the daughter of an Iranian father and British mother, her ability to speak French and Farsi as well as English, have all contributed to another asset Amanpour possesses—her enviable access to many world leaders. In early 1998, she was granted a rare televised interview with Iran's new moderate president, Mohammad Khatami, who told her that, although Iran was not yet ready to talk with U.S. government leaders, it was ready for dialogue through "the exchange of professors, writers, scholars, artists, journalists and tourists." Again, the call was for journalistic involvement in world affairs, raising once more the question of whether true objectivity is possible or desirable in today's world.

journalism traditions

(STUDY PREVIEW) · United States journalism has evolved through four distinctive eras—the colonial, partisan, penny and yellow press periods. Each of these periods made distinctive contributions to contemporary news media practices.

colonial period

Benjamin Harris published the first colonial newspaper, **Publick Occurrences,** in Boston in 1690. He was in hot water right away. Harris scandalized Puritan sensitivities, alleging that the king of France had dallied with his son's wife. In the colonies just as in England, a newspaper needed royal consent. The governor had not consented, and Harris was put out of business after one issue.

Even so, Harris' daring was a precursor for emerging press defiance against authority. In 1733 **John Peter Zenger** started a paper in New York in competition with the existing Crown-supported newspaper. Zenger's New York *Journal* was backed by mer-

Christiane Amanpour
Foreign correspondent known for CNN work from world hot spots.

colonial period
To the Revolution.

Benjamin Harris
Published *Publick Occurrences.*

Publick Occurrences
First Colonial newspaper, Boston, 1690.

John Peter Zenger
Defied authorities in New York *Journal.*

When Words Failed, 1798-Style. The partisanship during the crude partisan period peaked in 1798 when Roger Griswold impugned the war record of fellow congressman Matthew Lyon. Lyon spat in Griswold's eye. The next day, on the floor of the U.S. House of Representatives, Griswold went after Lyon with his cane, and Lyon beat him back with a handy set of fire tongs. This political cartoon, one of the first, captured the hand-to-hand combat. Later, after Lyon mildly insulted President Adams in print, the Federalists put him in jail.

Andrew Hamilton
Urged truth as defense for libel.
Arthur Schlesinger
Viewed newspapers as instigating Revolution.

chants and lawyers who disliked the royal governor. From the beginning the newspaper antagonized the governor with items challenging his competence, and finally the governor arrested Zenger. The trial made history. Zenger's attorney, **Andrew Hamilton,** argued that there should be no punishment for printing articles that are true. The argument was a dramatic departure from the legal practice of the day, which allowed royal governors to prosecute for articles that might undermine their authority, regardless of whether the articles were true. Hamilton's argument prevailed, and Zenger, who had become a hero for standing up to the Crown, was freed. To the governor's chagrin, there was great public celebration in the streets of New York that night.

Zenger's success against the Crown foreshadowed the explosive colonial reaction after Parliament passed a stamp tax in 1765. The colonies did not have elected representatives in Parliament, so the cry was a defiant "No taxation without representation." The campaign, however, was less ideological than economic. Colonial printers, who stood to lose from the new tax, which was levied on printed materials, led the campaign. Historian **Arthur Schlesinger** has called it the newspaper war on Britain. The newspapers won: the tax was withdrawn. Having seen their potential to force the government's hand, newspapers then led the way in stirring other ill feelings against England and precipitating the American Revolution.

These traditions from the colonial period remain today:

- The news media, both print and broadcast, relish their independence from government censorship and control.

- The news media, especially newspapers and magazines, actively try to mold government policy and mobilize public sentiment. Today this is done primarily on the editorial page.

- Journalists are committed to seeking truth, which was articulated as a social value in Zenger's "truth defense."

- The public comes down in favor of independent news media when government becomes too heavy-handed, as demonstrated by Zenger's popularity.

- In a capitalistic system, the news media are economic entities that sometimes react in their own self-interest when their profit-making ability is threatened.

partisan period

After the Revolution, newspapers divided along partisan lines. What is called the Federalist period in American history is also referred to as the **partisan period** among newspaper historians. Intense partisanship characterized newspapers of the period, which spanned roughly 50 years to the 1830s.

Initially the issue was over a constitution. Should the nation have a strong central government or remain a loose coalition of states? James Madison, Alexander Hamilton, Thomas Jefferson, John Jay and other leading thinkers exchanged ideas with articles and essays in newspapers. The *Federalist Papers,* a series of essays printed and reprinted in newspapers throughout the nation, were part of the debate. Typical of the extreme partisanship of the era were journalists who reveled in nasty barbs and rhetorical excesses. It was not unusual for an ideological opponent to be called "a spaniel" or "a traitor."

After the Constitution was drafted, partisanship intensified, finally culminating lopsidedly when the Federalist party both controlled the Congress and had their leader, **John Adams,** in the presidency. In firm control and bent on silencing their detractors, the Federalists ramrodded a series of laws through Congress in 1798. One of the things these laws, the **Alien and Sedition acts,** prohibited was "false, scandalous, malicious" statements about government. Using these laws, the Federalists made 25 indictments, which culminated in 10 convictions. Among those indicted was **David Bowen,** a Revolutionary War veteran who felt strongly about free expression. He put up a sign in Dedham, Massachusetts, that said: "No stamp tax. No sedition. No alien bills. No land tax. Downfall to tyrants of America. Peace and retirement to the president [the Federalist John Adams]. Long live the vice president [the Anti-Federalist **Thomas Jefferson**] and the minority [the Anti-Federalists]. May moral virtues be the basis of civil government." If only critics of recent presidents were so mild! But the Federalists were not of a tolerant mind. Bowen was fined $400 and sentenced to 18 months in prison.

Federalist excesses were at their most extreme when **Matthew Lyon,** a member of Congress, was jailed for a letter to a newspaper editor that accused President Adams of "ridiculous pomp, foolish adulation, selfish avarice." Lyon, an anti-Federalist, was sentenced to four months in jail and fined $1,000. Although he was tried in Rutland, Vermont, he was sent to a filthy jail 40 miles away. When editor Anthony Haswell printed an advertisement to raise money for Lyon's fine, he was jailed for abetting a criminal. The public was outraged at Federalist heavy-handedness. The $1,000 was quickly raised, and Lyon, while still in prison, was re-elected by a two-to-one margin. After his release from prison, Lyon's supporters followed his carriage for 12 miles as he began his way back to Philadelphia, the national capital. Public outrage showed itself in the election of 1800. Jefferson was elected president, and the Federalists were thumped out of office, never to rise again. The people had spoken.

Here are traditions from the partisan period that continue today:

- Government should keep its hands off the press. The First Amendment to the Constitution, which set a tone for this period, declared that "Congress shall make no law . . . abridging freedom . . . of the press."

- The news media are a forum for discussion and debate, as newspapers were in the *Federalist Papers* dialogue on what form the Constitution should take.

ida wells-barnett

Ida Wells bought a first-class ticket for a car at the front of the train, but when the conductor saw she was black he told her to go to the rear. First-class, he said, was "set apart for white ladies and gentlemen." Wells, a small, sturdy woman, refused, and the conductor, who was white, threw her off the train. Wells sued, citing various constitutional guarantees, and won before a Memphis jury. The Tennessee Supreme Court, however, said she was harassing the railroad and overturned the jury verdict.

The case, in 1885, was among the first involving racial equality in public transportation, and the attention it received made it clear to Wells, a 21-year-old school teacher, that the press could be a powerful vehicle to bring about change. She bought into a small weekly newspaper, the *Free Speech,* and began crusading for better schools for black children. The school board, embarrassed, fired her. So she went into journalism full time as editor of her newspaper.

In 1892 three black grocers, whose store had been successful against white competitors, were lynched. Wells pulled all stops in coverage, reporting the details that led to the lynchings and denouncing the community for condoning what happened. It was thorough, courageous reporting, and it received wide attention. Soon she was writing for the New York *Age,* with her articles a fixture in almost all of the nation's 400 black newspapers. She continued her work on lynchings as mob vigilanteeism, amassing data that they were becoming more common. In 1892 she counted 2,565, triple the number 10 years earlier. She urged black readers to arm themselves for self-protection: "A Win-chester rifle should have a place of honor in every home." Her office was attacked.

To continue her crusade, Wells went to England, beyond the mobs' reach, to rail against U.S. racial injustice, including lynchings of black men, on every forum she could find. Her book, *A Red Record,* contained alarming statistics on U.S. lynchings. By now an internationally recognized figure, Wells felt relatively safe to return to the United States on the lecture circuit with the press sure to follow her every word. States began prosecutions for lynchings, and the number declined. Memphis had none for 25 years.

Wells eventually settled in Chicago, married, and reared four children, all the while continuing her journalistic crusade for racial justice and also other reforms, including women's

Dynamite in a Small Package. When she was 21 she sued a railroad for throwing her out of a whites-only car. Ida Wells learned the power of journalism. She went on to a distinguished career as a crusader for racial justice and, in particular, against the growing 1890s practice of lynching.

rights. In fearless pursuit of facts, she went alone to lynchings and riots. Her factual reports, published widely, provided indisputable evidence of injustice and persecution and built general sympathy for both law enforcement and for legislation to correct social wrongs.

- The news media should comment vigorously on public issues.
- Government transgressions against the news media will ultimately be met by public rejection of those committing the excesses, which has happened periodically throughout American history.

penny period

In 1833, when he was 22, the enterprising **Benjamin Day** started a newspaper that changed American journalism: the **New York *Sun.*** At a penny a copy, the *Sun* was within reach of just about everybody. Other papers were expensive, an annual subscription costing as much as a full week's wages. Unlike other papers, distributed mostly by mail, the *Sun* was hawked every day on the streets. The *Sun*'s content was different too. It avoided the political and economic thrust of the traditional papers, concentrating instead on items of interest to common folk. The writing was simple, straightforward and easy to follow. For a motto for the *Sun,* Day came up with "It Shines for All," his pun fully intended.

Day's *Sun* was an immediate success. Naturally, it was quickly imitated, and the penny press period began. Partisan papers that characterized the partisan period continued, but the mainstream of American newspapers came to be in the mold of the *Sun.*

Merchants saw the unprecedented circulation of the penny papers as a way to reach great numbers of potential customers. Advertising revenue meant bigger papers, which attracted more readers, which attracted more advertisers. A snowballing momentum began that continues today with more and more advertising being carried by the mass media. A significant result was a shift in newspaper revenues from subscriptions to advertisers. Day, as a matter of fact, did not meet expenses by selling the *Sun* for a penny a copy. He counted on advertisers to pick up a good part of his production cost. In effect, advertisers subsidized readers, just as they do today.

Several social and economic factors, all resulting from the Industrial Revolution, made the penny press possible:

- **Industrialization.** With new steam-powered presses, hundreds of copies an hour could be printed. Earlier presses were hand operated.

- **Urbanization.** Workers flocked to the cities to work in new factories, creating a great pool of potential newspaper readers within delivery range. Until the urbanization of the 1820s and 1830s, the U.S. population had been almost wholly agricultural and scattered across the countryside. Even the most populous cities had been relatively small.

- **Immigration.** Waves of immigrants arrived from impoverished parts of Europe. Most were eager to learn English and found that penny papers, with their simple style, were good tutors.

- **Literacy.** As immigrants learned English, they hungered for reading material within their economic means. Also, literacy in general was increasing, which contributed to the rise of mass-circulation newspapers and magazines.

A leading penny press editor was **James Gordon Bennett,** who, in the 1830s, organized the first newsroom and reporting staff. Earlier newspapers had been either sidelines of printers, who put whatever was handy into their papers, or projects of ideologues, whose writing was in an essay vein. Bennett hired reporters and sent them out on rounds to gather information for readers of his New York *Herald.*

Horace Greeley developed editorials as a distinctive journalistic form in his New York *Tribune,* which he founded in 1841. More than his competitors, Greeley used his newspaper to fight social ills that accompanied industrialization. Greeley's

penny period
One-cent newspapers geared to mass audience and mass advertising.

Benjamin Day
Published New York *Sun.*

New York *Sun*
First penny newspaper, 1833.

James Gordon Bennett
Organized first methodical news coverage.

Horace Greeley
Pioneered editorials.

media people

...ben day

Years later, reflecting on the instant success of his **New York** *Sun,* **Benjamin Day** shook his head in wonderment. He hadn't realized at the time that the *Sun* was such a milestone. Whether he was being falsely modest is something historians can debate. The fact is the *Sun,* which Day founded in 1833, discovered mass audiences on a scale never before envisioned and ushered in the era of modern mass media.

Ben Day, a printer, set up a shop in 1833, but business was slow. With time on his hands, he began a little people-oriented handbill with brief news items and, most important, an advertisement for his printing business. He printed 1,000 copies, which he sold for a penny apiece. The tiny paper, four pages of three

columns of type, sold well, so Day decided to keep it going. In six months the *Sun,* the first of a new era of **penny papers,** had the highest circulation in New York. By 1836, circulation had zoomed to 20,000.

Fifty years later Day told an interviewer that the *Sun's* success was "more by accident than by design." Even so, the *Sun* was the first newspaper that, at a penny a copy, was within the economic means of almost everyone. He filled the paper with the local police court news, which is the stuff about which there is universal interest. True to its masthead motto, "It Shines for All," the *Sun* was a paper for the masses.

At a penny a copy, Day knew he couldn't pay his bills, so he built the paper's economic foundation on advertising. This

remains the financial basis of most mass media today—newspapers, magazines, television and radio. Just as today, advertisers subsidized the product to make it affordable to great multitudes of people.

Today it is technology that makes the media possible. The *Sun* was a pioneer in using the technology of its time, engine-driven presses. The *Sun's* messages—the articles—were crafted to interest large, diverse audiences, as are mass messages today. Also like today, advertising drove the enterprise financially. The story of Day's *Sun* also demonstrates a reality, as true then as now, that the mass media must be businesses first and purveyors of information and entertainment second.

Day's financial experience with the *Sun* has

been duplicated time and again in the history of the modern mass media. He got rich. Within five years of launching the *Sun,* on his way to a fortune, he sold out. That, he recalled later, noting the *Sun's* continuing success under subsequent owners, was "the silliest thing I ever did." But the profit from the sale enabled him to continue with other papers and magazines, many of them also successful because they were priced low so everyone could buy them. When he died in 1889, Day was a wealthy man.

New York *Sun*
Harbinger of modern mass media.

Benjamin Day
Introduced first penny-paper newspaper.

penny papers
Affordable by almost everyone.

Tribune was a voice against poverty and slums, an advocate of labor unions and an opponent of slavery. It was a lively forum for discussions of ideas. Karl Marx, the communist philosopher, was a *Tribune* columnist for a while. So was Albert Brisbane, who advocated collective living. Firm in Greeley's concept of a newspaper was that it should be used for social good. He saw the *Tribune* as a voice for those who did not have a voice; a defender for those unable to articulate a defense; and a champion for the underdog, the deprived and the underprivileged.

In 1844, late in the penny press period, **Samuel Morse** invented the telegraph. Within months, the nation was being wired. When the Civil War came in 1861, correspondents used the telegraph to get battle news to eager readers. It was called **lightning**

news, delivered electrically and instantly. The Civil War also gave rise to a new convention in writing news, the **inverted pyramid.** Editors instructed their war correspondents to tell the most important information first in case telegraph lines failed—or were snipped by the enemy—as a story was being transmitted. That way, when a story was interrupted, editors would have at least a few usable sentences. The inverted pyramid, it turned out, was popular with readers because it allowed them to learn what was most important at a glance. They did not have to wade through a whole story if they were in a hurry. Also, the inverted pyramid helped editors fit stories into the limited confines of a page—a story could be cut off at any paragraph and the most important parts remained intact. The inverted pyramid remains a standard expository form for telling event-based stories in newspapers, radio and television.

Several New York newspaper publishers, concerned about the escalating expense of sending reporters to gather faraway news, got together in 1848 to share stories. By together sending one reporter, the newspapers cut costs dramatically. They called their cooperative venture the **Associated Press,** a predecessor of today's giant global news service. The AP introduced a new tone in news reporting. So that AP stories could be used by member newspapers of different political persuasions, reporters were told to write from a nonpartisan point of view. The result was a fact-oriented kind of news writing often called **objective reporting.** It was widely imitated and still is the dominant reporting style for event-based news stories in all the news media.

There are traditions of today's news media, both print and electronic, that can be traced to the penny press period:

- Inverted pyramid story structures.

- Coverage and writing that appeals to a general audience, sometimes by trying to be entertaining or even sensationalistic. It's worth noting that the egalitarian thinking of Andrew Jackson's 1829–1837 presidency, which placed special value on the "common man," coincided with the start of the penny press and its appeal to a large audience of "everyday people."

- A strong orientation to covering events, including the aggressive ferreting out of news.

- A commitment to social improvement, which included a willingness to crusade against corruption.

- Being on top of unfolding events and providing information to readers quickly, something made possible by the telegraph but that also came to be valued in local reporting.

- A detached, neutral perspective in reporting events, a tradition fostered by the Associated Press.

yellow period

The quest to sell more copies led to excesses that are illustrated by the Pulitzer-Hearst circulation war in New York in the 1890s.

Joseph Pulitzer, a poor immigrant, made the St. Louis *Post-Dispatch* into a financial success. In 1883, Pulitzer decided to try a bigger city. He bought the New York *World* and applied his St. Louis formula. He emphasized human interest, crusaded for worthy causes, and ran lots of promotional hoopla. Pulitzer's *World* also featured solid journalism. His star reporter, **Nellie Bly,** epitomized the two faces of the Pulitzer for-

Stunt Journalism. When newspaper owner Joseph Pulitzer sent reporter Nellie Bly on an around-the-world trip in 1890 to try to outdo the fictional Phileas Fogg's 80-day trip, stunt journalism was approaching its peak. Her feat took 72 days.

Samuel Morse
Invented telegraph.

lightning news
Delivered by telegraph.

inverted pyramid
Most important information first.

Associated Press
Co-op to gather, distribute news.

objective reporting
Telling news without bias.

yellow period
Late 1800s; marked by sensationalism.

Joseph Pulitzer
Emphasized human interest in newspapers; later sensationalized.

Nellie Bly
Stunt reporter.

Joseph Pulitzer

William Randolph Hearst

Journalistic Sensationalism. Rival New York newspaper publishers Joseph Pulitzer and William Randolph Hearst tried to outdo each other daily with anti-Spanish atrocity stories from Cuba, many of them trumped up. Some historians say the public hysteria fueled by Pulitzer and Hearst helped precipitate the Spanish-American War, especially after the U.S. battleship *Maine* exploded in Havana harbor. Both Pulitzer and Hearst claimed it was a Spanish attack on an American vessel, although a case can be made that the explosion was accidental.

William Randolph Hearst
Built circulation with sensationalism.

Frederic Remington
Illustrator sent by Hearst to find atrocities in Cuba.

mula for journalistic success. For one story, Bly feigned mental illness, entered an insane asylum and emerged with scandalous tales about how patients were treated. It was enterprising journalism of great significance. Reforms resulted. Later, showing the less serious, show biz side of Pulitzer's formula, Nellie Bly was sent out to circle the globe in 80 days, like the fictitious Phileas Fogg. Her journalism stunt took 72 days.

In San Francisco, Pulitzer had a young admirer, **William Randolph Hearst.** With his father's Nevada mining fortune and mimicking Pulitzer's New York formula, Hearst made the San Francisco *Examiner* a great success. In 1895 Hearst decided to go to New York and take on the master. He bought the New York *Journal* and vowed to "out-Pulitzer" Pulitzer. The inevitable resulted. To outdo each other, Pulitzer and Hearst launched crazier and crazier stunts. Not even the comic pages escaped the competitive frenzy. Pulitzer ran the *Yellow Kid,* and then Hearst hired the cartoonist away. Pulitzer hired a new one, and both papers ran the yellow character and plastered the city with yellow promotional posters. The circulation war was nicknamed yellow journalism, and the term came to be a derisive reference to sensational excesses in news coverage.

The yellow excesses reached a feverish peak as Hearst and Pulitzer covered the growing tensions between Spain and the United States. Fueled by hyped atrocity stories, the tension eventually exploded in war. One story, perhaps apocryphal, epitomizes the no-holds-barred competition between Pulitzer and Hearst. Although Spain had consented to all demands by the United States, Hearst sent the artist **Frederic Remington** to Cuba to cover the situation. Remington cabled back: "Everything is quiet. There is no trouble here. There will be no war. Wish to return." Hearst replied: "Please remain. You furnish the pictures. I'll furnish the war."

Yellow journalism had its imitators in New York and elsewhere. It is important to note, however, that not all American journalism went the yellow route. **Adolph Ochs** bought the New York *Times* in 1896 and built it into a newspaper that avoided sideshows to report and comment seriously on important issues and events. The *Times,* still true to that approach, outlived the Pulitzer and Hearst newspapers in New York and today is considered the best newspaper in the world.

The yellow tradition, however, still lives. The New York *Daily News,* founded in 1919 and almost an immediate hit, ushered in a period that some historians characterize as **jazz journalism.** It was just Hearst and Pulitzer updated in tabloid form with an emphasis on photography. Today, newspapers like the commercially successful *National Enquirer* are in the yellow tradition. So are a handful of metropolitan dailies, including Rupert Murdoch's San Antonio, Texas, *Express-News.* It is obvious too in tabloid television programs like "Hard Copy" and "A Current Affair" and interview programs like "Jerry Springer," which pander to the offbeat and the sensational.

While not as important in forming distinctive journalistic traditions as the earlier penny papers, yellow newspapers were significant in contributing to the growing feeling of nationhood in the United States, especially among the diverse immigrants arriving in massive numbers. Journalism historian Larry Lorenz put it this way: "The publishers reached out to the widest possible audience by trying to find a common denominator, and that turned out to be the human interest story. Similarities among groups were emphasized rather than differences. Readers, in their quest to be real Americans, seized on those common elements to pattern themselves after, and soon their distinctive characteristics and awareness of themselves as special groups began to fade."

Yellow Journalism's Namesake. The Yellow Kid, a popular cartoon character in New York newspapers, became the namesake for the sensationalist "yellow journalism" of the 1880s and 1890s. Many newspapers of the period, especially in New York, hyperbolized and fabricated the news to attract readers. The tradition remains in isolated areas of modern journalism, such as the supermarket tabloids and trash documentary programs on television.

personal values in news

(STUDY PREVIEW) Journalists make important decisions on which events, phenomena and issues are reported and which are not. The personal values journalists bring to their work and that therefore determine which stories are told, and also how they are told, generally coincide with mainstream American values.

role of the journalist

After years of wrestling to come up with a definition for *news,* NBC newscaster Chet Huntley threw up his hands and declared: "News is what I decide is news." Huntley was not being arrogant. Rather, he was pointing out that events that go unreported aren't news. Regardless of an event's intrinsic qualities, such as the prominence of the people involved and the event's consequence and drama, it becomes news only when it's reported. Huntley's point was that the journalist's judgment is indispensable in deciding what's news.

Huntley's conclusion underscores the high degree of autonomy that individual journalists have in shaping what is reported. Even a reporter hired fresh out of college

Adolph Ochs
Developed New York *Times* as serious newspaper.

jazz journalism
Latter-day yellow journalism.

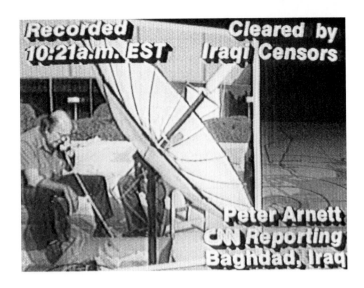

Peter Arnett in Baghdad. CNN's Peter Arnett provided exclusive coverage from Baghdad during the 1991 Persian Gulf war. The coverage troubled many Americans and some journalists who, in their ethnocentrism, saw Arnett as being used by the enemy. While the Iraqis controlled much of Arnett's access to information, he wrote his own dispatches. He consistently reminded viewers of the conditions under which he was gathering information, including that Iraqi officials were his primary source.

by a small daily newspaper and assigned to city hall has a great deal of independence in deciding what to report and how to report it. Such trust is unheard of in most other fields, which dole out responsibility to newcomers in small bits over a lengthy period. Of course, rookie journalists are monitored by their newsroom supervisors, and editors give them assignments and review their stories, but it is the city hall reporter, no matter how green, who is the news organization's expert on city government.

The First Amendment guarantee of a free press also contributes to the independence and autonomy that characterize news work. Journalists know they have a high level of constitutional protection in deciding what to report as news. While most reporters will agree on the newsworthiness of some events and issues, such as a catastrophic storm or a tax proposal, their judgments will result in stories that take different slants and angles. On events and issues whose newsworthiness is less obvious, reporters will differ even on whether to do a story.

journalists' personal values

The journalistic ideal, an unbiased seeking of truth and an unvarnished telling of it, dictates that the work be done without partisanship. Yet as human beings, journalists have personal values that influence all that they do, including their work. Because the news judgment decisions that journalists make are so important to an informed citizenry, we need to know what makes these people tick. Are they left-wingers? Are they ideological zealots? Are they quirky and unpredictable? Are they conscientious?

A sociologist who studied stories in the American news media for 20 years, **Herbert Gans,** concluded that journalists have a typical American values system. Gans identified primary values, all in the American mainstream, that journalists use in making their news judgments:

Ethnocentrism. American journalists see things through American eyes, which colors news coverage. In the 1960s and 1970s, Gans notes, North Vietnam was consistently characterized as "the enemy." American reporters took the view of the American government and military, which was hardly detached or neutral. This ethnocentricity was clear at the end of the war, which American media headlined as "the *fall* of South Vietnam." By other values, Gans said, the communist takeover of Saigon could be considered a *liberation*. In neutral terms, it was a *change in government*.

Herbert Gans
Concluded journalists have mainstream values.

ethnocentrism
Seeing things on basis of personal experience, values.

....the composite journalist

Here is a look at American journalists, drawn from numerous studies in recent years:

- **Age.** Journalism is more a young person's line of work than most career areas, probably because of stresses from deadlines, uncooperative news sources and difficult reporting assignments. Forty-five percent are 25 to 34 years old, compared with 28 percent for the civilian U.S. workforce.

- **Gender.** Women comprise 53 percent of the new reporters hired by the media. Many women leave the field, however. Among long-term reporters, 65 percent are men. The number of women in management is increasing but remains small. Of managing editors, 26 percent are women; of editors, 16 percent; of general managers, 8 percent; of publishers, 6 percent.

- **Education.** Most young journalists hold college degrees in journalism or mass communication, and gradually such degrees are increasing. Among television journalists, the percentage of journalism and mass communication degrees is 63 percent; daily newspapers, 56 percent; news services, 53 percent; radio, 53 percent; weekly newspapers, 50 percent; and newsmagazines, 26 percent.

This ethnocentrism creates problems as the news media become global. During the Persian Gulf war in 1991, CNN discovered that the commonly used word "foreign," which to American audiences meant anything non-American, was confusing to CNN audiences in other countries. Eager to build a global audience, CNN boss Ted Turner banned the word "foreign" and told anchors and scriptwriters that they would be fired for uttering the word. "International" became the substitute word, as awkward as it sometimes sounded to American ears. The semantic change was cosmetic, however, for the CNN war coverage continued, inevitably, to be largely from the American perspective, just as Gans found in his earlier studies. It is hard for all people, including journalists, to transcend their own skins.

Commitment to Democracy and Capitalism. Gans found that American journalists favor democracy of the American style. Coverage of other governmental forms dwells on corruption, conflict, protest and bureaucratic malfunction. The unstated idea of most U.S. journalists, said Gans, is that other societies do best when they follow the American ideal of serving the public interest.

Gans also found that American journalists are committed to the capitalist economic system. When they report corruption and misbehavior in American business, journalists treat them as aberrations. The underlying posture of the news coverage of the U.S. economy, Gans said, is "an optimistic faith" that businesspeople refrain from unreasonable profits and gross exploitation of workers or customers while competing to create increased prosperity for all. In covering controlled foreign economies, American journalists emphasize the downside.

It may seem only natural to most Americans that democracy and capitalism should be core values of any reasonable human being. This sense itself is an ethnocentric value, which many people do not even think about but which nonetheless shapes how they conduct their lives. Knowing that American journalists by and large share this value explains a lot about the news coverage they create.

media

online

Accuracy In Media: View of the news from the right. www.aim.org

Columbia Journalism Review: Respected and topical discussion of the issues of the day. www.cjr.org

Small-Town Pastoralism. Like most of their fellow citizens, American journalists romanticize about rural life. Given similar stories from metropolitan Portland and tiny Sweet Home, Oregon, editors usually opt for the small town.

Cities are covered as places with problems; rural life is celebrated. Suburbs are largely ignored. This small-town pastoralism, said Gans, helps explain the success of Charles Kuralt's long-running "On the Road" series on CBS television.

Individualism Tempered by Moderation. Gans found that American journalists love stories about rugged individuals who overcome adversity and defeat powerful forces. This is a value that contributes to a negative coverage of technology as something to be feared because it can stifle individuality. Gans again cited "On the Road," noting how Charles Kuralt found a following for his pastoral features on rugged individuals.

Journalists like to turn ordinary individuals into heroes, but there are limits. Rebels and deviates are panned as extremists who go beyond another value—moderation. To illustrate this propensity toward moderation, Gans noted that "the news treats atheists as extremists and uses the same approach, if more gingerly, with religious fanatics. People who consume conspicuously are criticized, but so are people such as hippies who turn their backs on consumer goods. The news is scornful both of the overly academic scholar and the oversimplifying popularizer; it is kind neither to high-brows nor to low-brows, to users of jargon or users of slang. College students who play when they should study receive disapproval, but so do 'grinds.' Lack of moderation is wrong, whether it involves excesses or abstention."

In politics, Gans says, both ideologues and politicians who lack ideology are treated with suspicion: "Political candidates who talk openly about issues may be described as dull; those who avoid issues entirely evoke doubts about their fitness for office."

Social Order. Journalists cover disorder—earthquakes, industrial catastrophes, protest marches, the disintegrating nuclear family, and transgressions of laws and mores. This coverage, noted Gans, is concerned not with glamorizing disorder but with finding ways to restore order. To critics who claim that the news media concentrate on disruption and the negative, Gans noted a study of television coverage of the 1967 race riots: Only 3 percent of the sequences covered the riots, and only 2 percent dealt with injuries and deaths. A full 34 percent of the coverage focused on restoring order. *Newsweek*'s coverage, according to the same study, devoted four times as many words to police and Army attempts to restore order as to describing the disturbances.

The journalistic commitment to social order also is evident in how heavily reporters rely on persons in leadership roles as primary sources of information. These leaders, largely representing the Establishment and the status quo, are the people in the best position to maintain social order and to restore it if there's a disruption. This means government representatives often shape news media reports and thus their audiences' understanding of what is important, "true" or meaningful. No one receives more media attention than the president of the United States, who is seen, said Gans, "as the ultimate protector of order."

journalistic bias

Critics of the news media come in many colors. Conservatives are the most vocal, charging that the media slant news to favor liberal causes. Liberal critics see it in the opposite light. The most recurrent charge, however, is that the media are leftist, favoring Democrats over Republicans, liberals over conservatives, and change over the status quo.

The fact is that journalists generally fall near the political center. A landmark 1971 survey by **John Johnstone** found 84.6 percent of journalists considered themselves middle-of-the-road or a little to the left or right. In 1983 **David Weaver** and **Cleveland Wilhoit** found 91.1 percent in those categories. At the same time, Gallup surveys put 90 percent of Americans at the center or a little left or right. The breakdown is as follows:

Political Leanings	Journalists 1971	Journalists 1983*	U.S. Adults 1982
Pretty far left	7.5	3.8	0.0
A little left	30.5	18.3	21.0
Middle of road	38.5	57.6	37.0
A little right	15.6	16.3	32.0
Pretty far right	3.4	1.6	0.0
No answer	4.5	2.5	10.0

*Percentages add up to 100.1 due to rounding.

The number of journalists who claimed to be a little leftist dropped considerably during the 12 years. Journalists had moved even more to the middle politically.

On party affiliation, Weaver and Wilhoit found that journalists identify themselves as independents more than the general population:

Political Leanings	Journalists 1971	Journalists 1983*	U.S. Adults 1982
Democrat	33.5	38.5	45.0
Independent	32.5	39.1	30.0
Republican	25.7	18.8	25.0
Other	5.8	1.6	0.0
No answer	0.5	2.1	0.0

*Percentages add up to 100.1 due to rounding.

Despite such evidence, charges persist that journalists are biased. The charges are all the stranger considering that most American news organizations pride themselves on a neutral presentation and go to extraordinary lengths to prove it. To avoid confusion between straight reporting and commentary, opinion pieces are set apart in clearly labeled editorial sections. Most journalists, even those with left or right leanings, have a zealous regard for detached, neutral reporting. Although they see their truth-seeking as unfettered by partisanship, they recognize that their news judgments often are made in confusing situations against deadline pressure, and they are the first, in self-flagellating postmortems, to criticize themselves when they fall short of the journalistic goals of accuracy, balance and fairness.

Considering the media's obsession with avoiding partisanship, how do the charges of bias retain any currency? First, critics who paint the media as leftist usually are forgetting that news, by its nature, is concerned with change. Everybody, journalists and media consumers alike, is more interested in a volcano that is blowing its top than in one that remains dormant. This interest in what is happening, as opposed to what is not happening, does not mean that anyone favors volcanic eruptions. However, the fact is that change almost always is more interesting than the status quo, although it is often more threatening and less comfortable. When journalists spend time on a presidential candidate's ideas to eliminate farm subsidies, it is not that the journalists favor the change, just that the topic is more interesting than stories about government programs that are unchallenged. Because conservatives favor the status quo, it is natural that they

John Johnstone
Found most journalists see selves as politically centrist.
David Weaver
Found journalists' political positions shift with population.
Cleveland Wilhoit
Collaborator with David Weaver.

would feel threatened by news coverage of change and proposals for change, no matter how disinterested and dispassionate the coverage, but this is hardly liberal bias.

The news media also are criticized because of an American journalistic tradition that is implicit in the U.S. Constitution: a belief that democracy requires the press to serve a watchdog function. Since the founding of the Republic, journalists have been expected to keep government honest and responsive to the electorate by reporting on its activities, especially on shortcomings. Unless the people have full reports on the government, they cannot intelligently discuss public issues, let alone vote intelligently on whether or not to keep their representatives. Sometimes to the dismay of those in power, the news media are part of the American system to facilitate change when it is needed.

In short, journalists' concern with change is not born of political bias. It is inherent in the nature of their work.

variables affecting news

(STUDY PREVIEW) The variables that determine what is reported include things beyond a journalist's control, such as how much space or time is available to tell stories. Also, a story that might receive top billing on a slow news day might not even appear on a day when an overwhelming number of major stories are breaking.

news hole

A variable affecting what ends up being reported as news is called the **news hole.** In newspapers the news hole is the space left after the advertising department has placed all the ads it has sold in the paper. The volume of advertising determines the number of total pages, and generally, the bigger the issue, the more room for news. Newspaper editors can squeeze fewer stories into a thin Monday issue than a fat Wednesday issue.

In broadcasting, the news hole tends to be more consistent. A 30-minute television newscast may have room for only 23 minutes of news, but the format doesn't vary. When the advertising department doesn't sell all the seven minutes available for advertising, it usually is public service announcements, promotional messages and program notes—not news—that pick up the slack. Even so, the news hole can vary in broadcasting. A 10-minute newscast can accommodate more stories than a 5-minute newscast, and, as with newspapers, it is the judgment of journalists that determines which events make it.

news flow and staffing

Besides the news hole, the **flow** of news varies from day to day. A story that might be played prominently on a slow news day can be passed over entirely in the competition for space on a heavy news day.

On one of the heaviest news days of all time, in 1989, death claimed Iran's Ayatollah Khomeini, a central figure in U.S. foreign policy; Chinese young people and the government were locked in a showdown in Tiananmen Square; the Polish people were voting to reject their one-party Communist political system; and a revolt was

news hole
Space for news in a newspaper after ads inserted; time in newscast for news after ads.
news flow
Significance of events worth covering varies day to day.

under way in the Soviet republic of Uzbekistan. That was a heavy news day, and the flow of major nation-rattling events preempted stories that otherwise would have been news.

Staffing affects news coverage, like whether reporters are in the right place at the right time. A newsworthy event in Nigeria will receive short shrift on U.S. television if the network correspondents for Africa are occupied with a natural disaster in next-door Cameroon. A radio station's city government coverage will slip when the city hall reporter is on vacation or if the station can't afford a regular reporter at city hall. When Iraq invaded Kuwait by surprise in August 1990, it so happened that almost all the U.S. and European reporters assigned to the Persian Gulf were on vacation or elsewhere on assignment. An exception was Caryle Murphy of the Washington *Post*. Like everyone else, Murphy hadn't expected the invasion, but she had decided to make a routine trip from her Cairo bureau for a first-hand look at Kuwaiti affairs. Only by happenstance did Murphy have what she called "a front-row seat for witnessing a small nation being crushed." Competing news organizations were devoid of eyewitness staff coverage until they scrambled to fly people into the region.

perceptions about audience

How a news organization perceives its audience affects news coverage. The *National Enquirer* lavishes attention on unproven cancer cures that the New York *Times* treats briefly if at all. The *Wall Street Journal* sees its purpose as news for readers who have special interests in finance, the economy and business. Ted Turner's CNNfx was established to serve an audience more interested in quick market updates, brief analysis and trendy consumer news than the kind of depth offered by the *Journal*.

The perception that a news organization has of its audience is evident in a comparison of stories on different networks' newscasts. CNN may lead newscasts with a coup d'état in another country, while CNNfx leads with a new government economic forecast, MTV with the announcement of a rock group's tour and "A Current Affair" with a six-month-old gory homicide that none of the others covered at all.

availability of material

The availability of photographs and video also is a factor in what ends up being news. Television is often faulted for overplaying visually titillating stories, such as fires, and underplaying or ignoring more significant stories that are not photogenic. Newspapers and magazines also are partial to stories with strong accompanying visuals, as shown in an especially poignant way when a Boston woman and child sought refuge on their apartment's balcony when the building caught fire. Then the balcony collapsed. The woman died on impact; the child somehow survived. The tragedy was all the more dramatic because it occurred just as firefighters were about to rescue the woman and child. Most journalists would report such an event, but in this case the coverage was far more extensive than would normally be the case because Stanley Forman of the Boston *Herald-American* photographed the woman and child plunging to the ground. On its own merits, the event probably would not have been reported beyond Boston, but with Forman's series of dramatic photographs, clicked in quick succession, the story was reported in visual media—newspapers, magazines and television—around the world.

Radio news people revel in stories when sound is available, which influences what is reported and how. A barnyard interview with a farm leader, with cows snorting in the

news staffing
Available staff resources to cover news varies.

Everybody's Chasing the President.
Competition among journalists has an unfortunate
side. Nobody wants to be scooped, so producers,
editors and reporters all look at what each other is
doing to be sure not to miss it. The result is herd
journalism with a lot of coverage being the same
and redundant. Scholar Leon Sigal devised the term
"consensible nature of news" to explain these similarities. The downside is fewer resources go into
digging fresh and distinctive coverage.

background, is likelier to make the air than the same farm leader saying virtually the
same thing in the sterile confines of a legislative committee chamber.

competition

One trigger of adrenaline for journalists is landing a scoop and, conversely, being
scooped. Journalism is a competitive business, and the drive to outdo other news
organizations keeps news publications and newscasts fresh with new material.

Competition has an unglamorous side. Journalists constantly monitor each other
to identify events that they missed and need to catch up on to be competitive. This
catch-up aspect of the news business contributes to similarities in coverage, which
scholar Leon Sigal calls the **consensible nature of news.** It also is called "pack" and
"herd" journalism.

In the final analysis, news is the result of journalists scanning their environment
and making decisions, first on whether to cover certain events and then on how to

**consensible nature of
news**
News organization second-
guesses competition in
deciding coverage.

The Watchdog Press. The news media's role
in a democracy as the people's watchdog for government wrong-doings sometimes shows itself in
unpleasant news. Matt Drudge, editor of the scandal-mongering *Drudge Report* newsletter, broke the
1998 coverage that President Clinton was being
investigated for a charge he had encouraged White
House intern Monica Lewinsky to lie about a sexual
liaison. Although a tawdry subject, it was the kind of
media attention that not only exposes lapses in governance but discourages others in leadership roles
from repeating old mistakes.

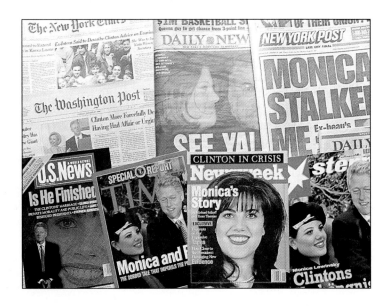

cover them. The decisions are made against a backdrop of countless variables, many of them changing during the reporting, writing and editing processes.

nonnewsroom influences on news

(STUDY PREVIEW) While journalists are key in deciding what to report and how, nonnewsroom forces in news organizations sometimes play a role too. These forces include advertiser-sensitive executives, who do not always share the truth-seeking and truth-telling agendas of journalists.

executive orders

While reporters have significant roles in deciding what makes news, news organizations are corporate structures. The people in charge have the final word on matters big and small. It is publishers and general managers and their immediate lieutenants who are in charge. Some of these executives make self-serving decisions on coverage that gall the journalists who work for them, but such is how chains of command work.

An egregious example of front-office meddling in news judgments was alleged in a 1990 complaint to the Federal Communications Commission by radio station KCDA in Coeur d'Alene, Idaho. The station charged that the local newspaper, the Coeur d'Alene *Press,* lavished news coverage on the radio station owned by the newspaper's owner but ignored KCDA despite KCDA's extensive participation in community activities that were as newsworthy as the activities that garnered coverage for the newspaper-owned station. In one *Press* story in which mentioning KCDA was unavoidable, it was referred to only as "an obscure local radio station."

Also appalling is excessive pandering to advertiser interests. It is impossible to catalog the extent to which journalistic autonomy is sacrificed to curry favor from advertisers, but it can occur even at generally respected news organizations. The Denver *Post,* a metro daily, once offered a shopping mall 1,820 column inches of free publicity, equivalent roughly to 72,000 words, a small book, as a bonus if the mall bought 30 pages of advertising. The puffery cut into space that might have been used for substantive news.

Some news organizations obsequiously lean over backwards not to alienate advertisers, which also can undermine journalistic autonomy. NBC once invited Coca-Cola, a major advertiser, to preview a television documentary that reported the company benefited from exploited migrant agricultural workers. NBC then acceded to Coca-Cola's requests to drop certain scenes.

Such policy decisions are more common among smaller, less financially solid news organizations, whose existence can be in jeopardy if they lose advertisers. To avoid rankling advertisers, the Las Cruces, New Mexico, *Sun-News,* as an example, once had a policy against naming local businesses that were in the news in an unsavory way. When police raided a local hotel room, the *Sun-News* offered not even a hint of which hotel was the site of the raid.

Rarely do media owners acknowledge that they manipulate news coverage to their own economic interests, which is why it is difficult to document the frequency of these abuses. Sociologists who have studied newsrooms note that publishers hire managers whose thinking coincides with their own, and these managers hire editors

Trailing Ted. News reporters sometimes operate in packs, all seeking to stay on top of the same story. This is because most reporters use the same values in deciding what their audiences want to know. They are surrogates who ask questions for their readers, viewers and listeners. This happened after federal agents arrested Theodore Kaczynski near Lincoln, Montana, for the Unabomber mail bombings. Reporters were seeking information and asking questions that the public wanted to know.

media
online

Australian Football League: www.cadability.com.au/AFL/news/

ESPNet SportsZone: www.espnet.sportzone.com

National Football League: www.nflhome.com

National Basketball Association: www.nba.com

National Hockey League: www.nhl.com

Perth Heat: microbase.com.au/theheat/ph.home.htm

and reporters of the same sort. The result is that decisions made by reporters do not differ much from those the publisher would make in the same situation. With the sociology of the newsroom shaped by largely like-minded people, seldom does anyone need to order manipulation explicitly. This means most instances of slanting coverage to the wishes of advertisers or other special interests are neither recorded nor reported.

In fairness, it must be said that media owners generally are sensitive to their truth-seeking and truth-telling journalistic responsibilities and assiduously avoid calling the shots on news coverage. Those who answer to a call other than journalistic soundness are within their court-recognized First Amendment rights, which allow media people to exercise their freedom responsibly as well as irresponsibly. Journalists who are bothered by wrong-headed news decisions have three choices: persuade wayward owners of the wrongness of their ways, comply with directives, or quit and go work for a respectable journalistic organization.

advertiser pressure

Special interests try to exert influence on coverage, such as squelching a story or insisting on self-serving angles. Advertiser pressure can be overt. The managing editor of the Laramie, Wyoming, *Boomerang* complied with a request from the newspaper's own advertising manager not to carry a state agency's news release warning people that Bon Vivant vichyssoise, possibly tainted with lethal botulism bacteria, had been found on the shelves at a local grocery. The ad manager was fearful of losing the store's advertising. In fact, the store did yank its advertising from a Laramie radio station when it aired the story, and the station's news director reported that he was warned to back off from the story and later fired.

Generally, advertiser clout is applied quietly, as when Ralph's grocery chain cancelled a $250,000 advertising contract with the Los Angeles *Herald Examiner* after a story on supermarket overcharging and shortweighting. From a journalistic perspective, the sinister result of cancelling advertising is the possible chilling effect on future coverage.

Advertiser pressure can be even more subtle. Many airlines insist that their ads be deleted from newscasts with stories about airline crashes. This is reasonable from an airline's perspective, but it also is a policy that has the effect of encouraging stations, especially financially marginal stations, to omit crash stories, even though these stories would contribute to listeners' having a clearer sense about air safety.

To their credit, most news organizations place allegiance to their audiences ahead of pleasing advertisers, as Terry Berger, president of an advertising agency representing the Brazilian airline Varig, found out from *Condé Nast's Traveler,* a travel magazine. After an article on air pollution in Rio de Janeiro, Berger wrote the magazine: "Is your editorial policy then to see how quickly you can alienate present and potential advertisers and at the same time convince your readers to stick closer to home? I really think that if you continue with this kind of editorial information, you are doing both your readers and your advertisers a disservice. For this kind of information, people read the New York *Times*. I therefore find it necessary to remove *Condé Nast's Traveler* from Varig's media schedule." Unintimidated, the magazine's editor, Harold Evans, did not recant. Not only did Evans print the letter but he followed with this comment: "Mrs. Berger is, of course, entitled to use her judgment about where she advertises Brazil's national airline. I write not about that narrow commercial issue, but about her assertion that it is a disservice to readers and advertisers for us to print true but unattractive facts when they are relevant. This goes to the heart of the editorial policy of this magazine. . . . We rejoice in the enrichments of travel, but our aim is to give readers the fullest information, frankly and fairly, so they can make their own judgments."

pressure from sources

Journalists sometimes feel external pressure directly. At the court house, valuable sources turn cold after a story appears that they don't like. A tearful husband begs an editor not to use the name of his wife in a story that points to her as a bank embezzler. A bottle of Chivas Regal arrives at Christmas from a sports publicist who says she appreciates excellent coverage over the past year. Most journalists will tell you that their commitment to truth overrides external assaults on their autonomy. Even so, external pressures exist.

The relationship between journalists and publicists can be troublesome. In general, the relationship works well. Publicists want news coverage for their clients and provide information and help reporters line up interviews. Some publicists, however, are more committed to advancing their clients than to advancing truth, and they work to manipulate journalists into providing coverage that unduly glorifies their clients.

Staging events is a publicity tactic to gain news coverage that a cause would not otherwise attract. Some staged events are obvious hucksterism, such as Evel Knievel's ballyhooed motorcycle leaps across vast canyons in the 1970s and local flagpole-sitting stunts by celebrity disc jockeys. Covering such events usually is part of the softer side of news and, in the spirit of fun and games and diversion, is relatively harmless.

Of more serious concern are staged events about which publicists create a mirage of significance to suck journalists and the public into giving more attention than they deserve. For example, consider:

- The false impression created when hundreds of federal workers are released from work for an hour to see an incumbent's campaign speech outside a government office building.
- The contrived "photo opportunity" at which people, props and lighting are carefully, even meticulously arranged to create an image on television.
- Stunts that bring attention to a new product and give it an undeserved boost in the marketplace.

Staged events distort a balanced journalistic portrayal of the world. Worse, they divert attention from truly significant events.

gatekeeping in news

(STUDY PREVIEW) The individual reporter has a lot of independence in determining what to report, but news work is a team effort. No individual acts entirely alone, and there are factors, such as gatekeeping, that affect what ends up on the printed page or over the air.

gatekeepers' responsibilities

News dispatches and photographs are subject to changes at many points in the communication chain. At these points, called gates, **gatekeepers** delete, trim, embellish and otherwise try to improve messages.

gatekeeper
Throttles and shapes flow of news from origin to media outlet.

Just as a reporter exercises judgment in deciding what to report and how to report it, judgment also is at the heart of the gatekeeping process. Hardly any message, except live reporting, reaches its audience in its original form. Along the path from its originator to the eventual audience, a message is subject to all kinds of deletions, additions and changes of emphasis. With large news organizations, this process may involve dozens of editors and other persons.

The gatekeeping process affects all news. A public relations practitioner who doesn't tell the whole story is a gatekeeper. A reporter who emphasizes one aspect of an event and neglects others is a gatekeeper. Even live, on-scene television coverage involves gatekeeping because it's a gatekeeper who decides where to point the camera, and that's a decision that affects the type of information that reaches viewers. The C-SPAN network's live, unedited coverage of Congress, for example, never shows members of Congress sleeping or reading a newspaper during debate, even though such happens.

Gatekeeping can be a creative force. Trimming a news story can add potency. A news producer can enhance a reporter's field report with file footage. An editor can call a public relations person for additional detail to illuminate a point in a reporter's story. A newsmagazine's editor can consolidate related stories and add context that makes an important interpretive point.

gatekeepers at work

Most gatekeepers are invisible to the news audience, working behind the scenes and making crucial decisions in near-anonymity on how the world will be portrayed in the evening newscast and the next morning's newspaper. Here, slightly updated, is how mass communication scholar Wilbur Schramm explained gatekeeping in 1960: "Suppose we follow a news item, let us say, from India to Indiana. The first gatekeeper is the person who sees an event happen. This person sees the event selectively, noticing some things, not others. The second gatekeeper is the reporter who talks to this 'news source.' Now, of course, we could complicate this picture by giving the reporter

media people

Paul Julius Reuter

Much of Europe had been linked by telegraph by the late 1840s, but a 100-mile gap remained between the financial centers of Brussels in Belgium and Aachen in Prussia. Young Paul Julius Reuter established a carrier pigeon service, with birds carrying dispatches strapped to their feet. News by pigeon wasn't new. In fact, Reuter had picked up the idea from Charles Havas who had established London-to-Paris and Brussels-to-Paris pigeon routes in 1835.

The significance of Reuter's work was that he parlayed it into a global news agency that bears his name. With profits from his first Brussels customers, Reuter moved to London to pick up American news from the new trans-Atlantic cable for his pigeon delivery. In 1858 he offered his service to newspapers via telegraph.

In time, the ownership of Reuters fell to newspaper owners in Australia, Britain and New Zealand. In 1984, the company became publicly traded, which attracted investors whose money funded further expansion.

a number of news sources to talk to about the same event, but in any case the reporter has to decide which facts to pass along the chain, what to write, what shape and color and importance to give to the event. The reporter gives his message to an editor, who must decide how to edit the story, whether to cut or add or change. Then the message goes to a news service where someone must decide which of many hundreds of items will be picked up and telegraphed to other towns, and how important the story is, and therefore how much space it deserves.

"At a further link in the chain, this story will come to a United States news service and here again an editor must decide what is worth passing on to the American news-papers and broadcasting stations. The chain leads us on to a regional and perhaps a state news service bureau, where the same decisions must be made; always there is more news than can be sent on—which items, and how much of the items, shall be retained and retransmitted? And finally when the item comes to a local newspaper, an editor must go through the same process, deciding which items to print in the paper.

"Out of news stories gathered by tens of thousands of reporters around the world, only a few hundred will pass the gatekeepers along the chains and reach a local news-paper editor, who will be able to pass only a few dozen of those on to the newspaper reader."

global gatekeeping

(STUDY PREVIEW)   Because gathering news is expensive, especially when it comes from far away, news organizations set up agencies, usually called wire services, news services or networks, to reduce the cost and then share the resulting stories. Today, global news services, led by the Associated Press, have more influence than most people realize on what is reported and how it is told.

competition for faraway news

Sam Gilbert took great pride in his coffee house. At seven stories, it was the tallest building in the United States. It dominated the Boston waterfront. Gilbert's was a popular place, partly because of an extensive collection of the latest European news-papers that he maintained in a reading room. In 1811, with a second war imminent with Britain, Gilbert announced that his patrons no longer would have to wait for ships to dock to have the latest news. Forthwith, he said, an employee would row out to ships waiting to enter the harbor and rush back with packets of the latest news. Newspapers up and down the seaboard picked up Gilbert's idea, and publishers scrambled to outdo each other by buying the fastest sloops.

In time, complex courier systems caught ships arriving at Halifax, Nova Scotia, and rushed news by pony and sloop to Boston and New York. Competition escalated, especially after Samuel Morse invented the telegraph in 1844 and coastal cities began to be linked by wire.

news agencies

The competition was spirited, especially in New York, where 10 newspapers raced to beat each other with foreign dispatches. The competition escalated costs, and in

Sam Gilbert
Emphasized providing news quickly.

1846, one of New York's scrappiest news merchants, **David Hale** of the *Journal of Commerce,* brought five of his competitors together to discuss combining their efforts in order to reduce expenses. The concept was simple. Competing newspapers would rely on a common organization, Harbor News Association, and share both the material and the expenses. The name evolved into the *Associated Press.*

Associated Press. Today the AP provides state, national and international news, photos, graphics, radio and television services to more than 15,000 outlets worldwide. The AP, the world's largest news-gathering organization, estimates its news reaches more than 1 billion people a day. It operates bureaus in 71 countries. In the United States, the AP has 142 bureaus in state capitals and major cities. Like its predecessor organization, it remains a nonprofit cooperative. Member newspapers each own a share based on circulation and numerous other factors. Each newspaper is obligated to furnish its local stories to the AP for distribution to other member newspapers. The AP also has its own staff, 1,100 journalists in the United States and 480 abroad, to generate stories for all members. Periodically the expense of operating the AP is tallied, and members are billed for their share. The budget is about $300 million. Policies are set by member newspapers, which meet regularly.

The AP sells its news to magazines and even government agencies, and it operates profit-making news script, audio and video services for radio and television newsrooms. Only newspapers, however, are full members with a controlling voice in the organization's policies.

These numbers give a sense of the AP's size:

* 3,000 employees nationwide, including journalists, management and support personnel.
* 1,700 United States newspapers, including 1,460 daily newspaper members.
* 6,000 television, cable and station outlets.
* 1,000 radio subscribers to AP Network News, which is the largest single radio network in the United States.
* 8,500 foreign subscribers in 112 countries.

United Press International. As the AP evolved, it limited membership to one newspaper per city. The policy upset newspaper-chain owner E. W. Scripps, who was denied AP membership for the new papers he was founding in the 1880s because older papers already had exclusive AP franchises. In 1907 Scripps founded the United Press for newspapers that the AP shut out. The heart of Scripps' new service was his own newspapers, but the service also was a profit-seeking enterprise available to any and all newspapers willing to subscribe.

William Randolph Hearst followed in 1909 with the International News Service. Both UP and INS tried to match the comprehensive Washington and foreign service of the Associated Press, but the AP proved impossible to derail. Even when the AP suffered a major setback, losing a 1945 U.S. Supreme Court decision that forced it to abandon exclusivity, the result spurred AP growth. Non-AP newspapers joined the co-op by the dozen, which hurt United Press and Hearst's INS.

In 1958 UP and INS merged to form the United Press International, but the new company, in reality a subsidiary of the Scripps-Howard newspaper chain, failed to meet profit expectations and eventually went on the selling block. Nobody wanted it. The British news service Reuters, anxious for a toehold in the United States, surveyed UPI's assets and decided against buying. In the 1980s UPI went through a series of owners. There were attempts at corporate reorganization, technological economies and sales blitzes, but several owners later the service was anything but secure.

David Hale
Organized predecessor to Associated Press.
Associated Press
U.S.-based global news service; largest news-gathering organization in the world.
United Press International
Faded major news agency.

Reuters. Much of Europe had been linked by telegraph by the late 1840s, but a 100-mile gap remained between the financial centers of Brussels in Belgium and Aachen in Prussia. Young Paul Julius Reuter established a carrier pigeon service, with the birds carrying dispatches tied to their legs, and he immediately attracted banking customers. Reuter then moved to London to pick up the latest American news from the new trans-Atlantic cable for his pigeon delivery. In 1858 he offered his service to newspapers via telegraph.

In 1984, after years of being owned by newspapers in Britain, Australia and New Zealand, Reuters became a publicly traded company. Newly aggressive, the company beefed up its financial market reporting and expanded its domestic U.S. service. Today, Reuters serves 6,500 media organizations worldwide, including 290 in the United States. Including clients in the business and financial community, Reuters has 27,000 subscribers worldwide. The service is offered in 11 languages.

Agence France-Presse. Paris-based Agence France-Presse, the world's third-largest news agency today, was founded by Charles Havas in 1835. Using carrier pigeons, Havas provided Paris newspapers by noon with morning news from London and Brussels. Today AFP has 1,100 journalists in 150 bureaus worldwide. AFP is strongest in French-speaking parts of the world, but it also transmits text, photo, audio and video reports in Arabic, English, German, Spanish and Portuguese to 500 newspaper, 350 radio and 200 television clients and to 100 national news agencies that pass AFP stories on to more media outlets. AFP has more than 50 U.S. media clients.

The agency's leadership is intent on global expansion, but a close association with the French government hurts its credibility. Almost half of AFP's subscription income comes from government agencies, and the government wields that financial stick from time to time. In 1996, Prime Minister Alain Juppé complained to AFP's chairman, Lionel Fleury, about coverage of huge labor strikes prompted by Juppé's policy to cut state pensions. Neither did Juppé like stories that he had cut the rent on a city-owned luxury apartment for his son. Not long after Juppé complained, AFP board of directors, which includes five government members, replaced Fleury with someone more to Juppé's liking.

supplemental services

One UPI problem was the emergence of supplemental news services in the 1960s. The New York *Times* began packaging its stories, opinion pieces and columnists for other newspapers. The Washington *Post* and Los Angeles *Times* followed. By the mid-1970s, many newspapers that had used both AP and UPI were being tempted to drop one of them and buy one of the supplementals for distinctive, in-depth reporting, top-flight opinion pieces and colorful columnists—things that were strengths of neither AP nor UPI. It was UPI that usually got the ax. The reasoning was that AP and UPI were largely duplicative. Both had large worldwide news-gathering systems, but AP had more correspondents in more bureaus. Both provided state and regional coverage, but again, in most states, AP had more staff. Neither missed major events, which meant that one was expendable.

video news services

The major news networks, ABC, CBS, CNN and NBC, prefer to cover foreign stories with their own crews, but they also subscribe to global video services for stories and pictures they miss. Europe-based **Visnews** was an early supplier of video. Today, the London-based Reuters, capitalizing on the prestige of its name, has rechristened

media
online

Reuters NewMedia: This text site might be criticized as shovelware, but it downloads quickly and is unusually thorough. The content comes from the British-based news service Reuters. www.yahoo.com/headlines/current/news

Reuters
British-based global news agency.

Agence France-Presse
Paris-based global news agency.

supplemental services
Agencies that provide back-up, depth coverage.

Visnews
Video news service now known as Reuters.

Visnews simply as *Reuters*. ABC is primary owner of a second video service, **World-wide Television News.** In 1994, the Associated Press launched **APTV** as a third major player in global video news coverage. The video news business grew rapidly in the 1990s for several reasons:

Network Cutbacks. Beginning in the early 1980s corporate bosses at ABC, CBS and NBC slashed their news divisions' budgets. The cuts forced news executives to make painful decisions. At each network, foreign staffing took the hardest hits. At CBS, the cuts were wrenching. Since 1938 when it launched "World News Roundup" radio newscasts with staff reporters in Europe, CBS had prided itself on distinctive foreign coverage.

Critics lamented the decline of the networks' foreign coverage, but others said the size of foreign staffs was bloated and reductions were overdue. Also, relatively few foreign stories made it on the air. Newscast producers recognized that Americans are not international minded and, all other things being equal, favor domestic over foreign stories.

Today, ABC, CBS and NBC operate only a handful of foreign bureaus. From those bureaus, reporters fly to hot spots. Always short-staffed, these bureaus miss stories, so producers in New York pick up material from APTV, Reuters and WTN. Unlike the other U.S. networks, CNN has expanded its foreign bureaus, but even CNN's foreign staff cannot feed producers enough stories to satisfy the 24-hour news network's voracious appetite. So CNN too leans heavily on the video news services.

Government Regulation. Several European nations have deregulated broadcasting, and entrepreneurs have launched networks and stations. Stephen Claypole, an old Reuters hand who joined the new APTV in 1994, estimates the market for international news will grow 50 percent by the turn of this century.

Independent Stations. Years ago, network-affiliated stations learned that news is a good lead-in to build audiences for other programming. Today, many independent stations have established newscasts that draw on the video news stories for faraway coverage. Affiliates of the Fox network, which didn't offer network news its first few years of existence, were among subscribers to the video news services to provide at least some distant coverage.

New Technologies. The video that APTV, Reuters and WTN shoot is digital, which means it can be adapted easily to other media. Reuters, for example, can provide its subscribing newspapers and magazines with stills from its television service. The market will expand as newspapers and magazines shift to digital delivery that includes moving images.

effects of video coverage

The entry of the Associated Press into the video news business in 1994 was heralded for its potential to expand global news coverage. Lou Prato, writing in *American Journalism Review,* quoted WTN Vice President Terry O'Reilly: "History teaches us that diversity in journalism leads us to better journalism. If the AP produces the quality of services it promises, then the public will benefit."

Others, less enthusiastic, don't buy O'Reilly's diversity argument. They see numerous smaller video services being squeezed out by three giants: APTV, Reuters and WTN. The result could be more **herd journalism** as the three major services concentrate on major stories, essentially duplicating each other. The small, scrappy outfits that now produce offbeat but insightful pieces would go under.

WTN
ABC's video news service.
APTV
Associated Press video news service.
herd journalism
Copy-cat coverage.

There also was concern that AP and Reuters are diverting resources from their core print services. Staff members who once carried a pad and pencil now lug High-8 cameras and need to think also in terms of video packaging. To their credit, both AP and Reuters have expanded their foreign bureaus for the greater workload, but the fact remains that reporters have additional obligations. In his *AJR* article on the growth of video services, Lou Prato quoted Reuters executive Paul Eedle: "Our aim will be to make everyone more flexible. We want to train our text journalists in how to use a camera and transmit a picture, and some camera crews in writing stories so that we have the flexibility we need."

syndicates and news products

(STUDY PREVIEW)   News organizations buy ready-to-run features, including political columns, from organizations called syndicates. Because syndicates sell the same features to many organizations, their influence is substantial.

syndicates' tradition

After Union recruiters swept through Baraboo, Wisconsin, and signed up the local boys for the Civil War, **Ansell Kellogg** lacked the staff to get out his four-page Baraboo *Republic,* so he took to borrowing the inside pages of another newspaper. The practice not only saw Kellogg through a staffing crisis but also sparked an idea to save costs by supplying inside pages at a fee to other short-handed publishers. By 1865 Kellogg was in Chicago providing ready-to-print material for newspapers nationwide. In journalism history, Kellogg is remembered as the father of the newspaper syndicate.

In the 1880s **S. S. McClure** had a thriving syndicate, putting out 50,000 words a week in timeless features on fashion, homemaking, manners and literature. McClure and other syndicators charged subscribing newspapers a fraction of what each would have to pay to generate such material with its own staff. Features, poetry, opinion and serialized stories by the period's great literary figures, including Jack London, Rudyard Kipling, George Bernard Shaw, Robert Louis Stevenson and Mark Twain, became standard fare in many newspapers through syndication.

syndicate services

Today, syndicates offer a wide range of material, usually on an exclusive basis. In major cities with competing newspapers, some features go to the highest bidder. Generally, rates are based on circulation. A small daily might spend $150 a week for 30 to 50 syndicated features. A metropolitan newspaper might spend $500 a week for a single comic strip.

Here are the major features distributed by syndicates, some of which are important as news and commentary, others of which are pure diversion:

- **Political Columns.** Commentator **David Lawrence** introduced the syndicated political column in 1916, providing modest-budget local newspapers with a low-cost tie to Washington. **Walter Lippmann,** the most influential columnist in U.S. history, appeared in hundreds of newspapers as a syndicated feature from 1929 into the 1960s.

syndicates
Provide low-cost, high-quality content to many news outlets.

Ansell Kellogg
Founded first syndicate.

S. S. McClure
Expanded syndicate concept.

David Lawrence
First syndicated political columnist.

Walter Lippmann
Influential political columnist.

- **Political Cartoons. Bill Mauldin's** powerful World War II cartoons received a nationwide audience by syndication. Look at political cartoons on your local newspaper's editorial page, and you will see a note that identifies the cartoonist's home newspaper and, unless the cartoonist is local, the name of the syndicate that distributed it.

- **Comics.** Early syndicates offered stand-alone cartoons. In 1907 "Mutt and Jeff" became the first daily strip. Comics were packed on a single page in the 1920s and became a major circulation builder. In 1984 Charles Schulz's "Peanuts" established a landmark as the first strip to appear in 2,000 newspapers.

- **Lovelorn Columns.** Writing as **Dorothy Dix,** Elizabeth Meriwether Gilmer became "Mother Confessor" to millions in 1916 with the first column to the lovelorn. It was predecessor to today's columns by sisters **Abigail Van Buren** and **Ann Landers.** In the 1920s Gilmer earned an unheard-of $90,000 a year from syndication, more than any single newspaper could have paid a columnist.

- **How-to Columns.** Among available columns are "Shelby Lyman on Chess" and June Roth's "Nutrition Hotline."

- **Reviews.** Book, movie, television and video reviews are provided by syndicates. They range from high-brow criticism to the low-brow "Joe Bob Goes to the Drive-In."

- **Games.** Syndicates offer dozens of crosswords, games and puzzles. Horoscopes and astrology columns are other staples.

- **Literature.** Some syndicates buy serialization rights to memoirs and books, giving newspapers that sign up for them a truncated prepublication series. Leading magazines also supply stories to newspapers through syndicates.

Syndicates also offer picture, graphics and art services. Many syndicates offer all the editorial copy that's needed for topical advertising supplements, such as spring car-care tabloids and September back-to-school issues.

journalism trends

(STUDY PREVIEW)   News has taken two divergent paths in content in recent years. Some news organizations have moved into sophisticated, interpretative and investigative reporting. Others have emphasized superficial, tantalizing news.

exploratory reporting

Norman Cousins acquired his reputation as a thinker when he edited the magazine *Saturday Review.* A premier journal under Cousins, the magazine tackled issues in depth and with intelligence. A few years later, Cousins said he couldn't find much of that kind of journalism in magazines any more: "The best magazine articles in the U.S. today are appearing not in magazines but in newspapers." Cousins was taking note of a profound late 20th-century change in the concept of news. Newspapers and

Bill Mauldin
Political cartoonist.

Dorothy Dix
First lovelorn columnist.

Abigail Van Buren
Personal advice columnist.

Ann Landers
Personal advice columnist.

exploratory reporting
Proactive news-gathering.

media people

oriana fallaci

Of necessity, **Oriana Fallaci** grew up fast. A teenager in Mussolini's Italy, she figured out early whose side she was on. She delivered grenades inside cabbage heads for the antifascist resistance. She had a keen sense of who were the good guys and who the bad—and later, as a journalist, she devised interview techniques to smoke them out. She is one of the foremost journalists of her time.

Both bright and hardworking, she learns a whole language to conduct interviews in her sources' native tongue. Sometimes she puts six months into preparing for one of her marathon interviews. She flouts danger. In fact, she was shot twice covering stories in Mexico. She adapts to whatever the situation to get a story. Although not Muslim, she agreed to wear a Muslim veil, a chador, to interview Iranian leader Ayatollah Khomeini. As an interviewer, she keeps her sights on finding revealing truths about important people through cleverness, disquieting and unexpected questions, and persistence.

Those qualities show in Fallaci's famous interview with Ayatollah Khomeini in his Teheran quarters. In deference, she wore the chador veil, which gave her an opportunity for a question that would so unsettle the ayatollah that she learned things no earlier interviewer had about his temper and his temperament. From her own account: "I was wearing the thing, all seven meters of it, pins everywhere, perspiring, and I began to ask him about the chador as a symbol of women's role in Iran." The question penetrated to the core of Khomeini's value system. Off guard, he instantly turned nasty. In a revealing outburst he shouted: "If you don't like the chador, don't wear it, because the chador is for young, proper women!" Insulted, she ripped the veil off: "This is what I do with your stupid medieval rag!" Shocked, the ayatollah shot up and left, with Fallaci calling after him: "Where do you go? Do you go to make pee-pee?" Quick-witted Fallaci's pee-pee afterthought was calculated to elicit further personal revelations, but Khomeini didn't turn around.

Fallaci's detractors see her **caustic interview style** as grand theater. Whatever the criticism, her unconventional approach gives her readers fresh insights into her sources' characters.

Once an interview is under way, Fallaci won't take no for an answer.

When Khomeini stomped out, she sat waiting for him to return. Again and again, aides asked her to leave. Finally, Khomeini's son came pleading for her to leave. On his fifth time back, he said Khomeini would see her the next day if she left. By that point, she recalled later, she too needed to pee-pee.

At the appointed hour the next day, Khomeini, faithful to his promise, arrived to continue the interview. And Fallaci, true to her goal, looked him in the eye: "Now Imam, let's start where we left off yesterday. We were talking about my being an indecent woman."

---

to a lesser extent television were tackling difficult issues that earlier were almost the exclusive provinces of magazines. Cousins especially admired the Los Angeles *Times,* which runs thoroughly researched, thoughtful pieces. It is not unusual for the Los Angeles *Times* to commit weeks, even months, of reporters' time to develop major stories, nor is that unusual at other major newspapers and some smaller ones.

Although American newspapers have never been devoid of in-depth coverage, the thrust through most of their history has been to chronicle events: meetings, speeches, deaths, catastrophes. The emphasis began changing noticeably in the 1960s as it dawned on journalists that chronicling easily identifiable events was insufficient to capture larger, more significant issues and trends.

> **Oriana Fallaci**
> Leading journalistic interviewer.
>
> **caustic interview**
> Adversarial approach to subjects.

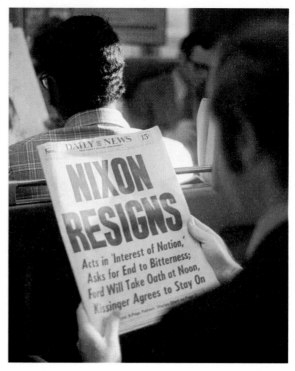

Investigative Journalism. Dogged pursuit of meticulous factual detail became a new wrinkle in 20th-century journalism after Washington *Post* reporters Carl Bernstein and Bob Woodward unearthed the Watergate scandal. For months they pursued tips that a break-in at the Democratic Party national headquarters in the Watergate hotel, office and apartment complex in Washington, D.C., had been authorized high in the Republican White House and that the White House then had tried to cover it up. In the end, for the first time in American history, a president, Richard Nixon, resigned.

The failure of event-based reporting became clear when Northern cities were burning in race riots in the late 1960s. Journalists had missed one of the 20th century's most significant changes: the northward migration of Southern blacks. Had journalists covered the migration and provided information on the festering social divisions that resulted, there might have been a chance to develop public policies before frustration over racial injustices blew up, with heavy losses of life and property and great disruption.

The superficiality of mere chronicling was underscored in early coverage of the Vietnam War. By focusing on events, journalists missed asking significant questions about the flawed policies until it was too late.

Newspapers expanded significantly beyond a myopic focus on events in the 1970s for three reasons:

- Recognition that old ways of reporting news were not enough.

- Larger reporting staffs that permitted time-consuming enterprise reporting.

- Better-educated reporters and editors, many with graduate degrees.

Newspapers, profitable as never before, were able to hire larger staffs that permitted them to try more labor-intensive, exploratory kinds of journalism. Instead of merely responding to events, newspapers, particularly big ones, began digging for stories. Much of this **investigative journalism** was modeled on the Washington *Post*'s doggedness in covering Watergate, the White House-authorized break-in at the Democratic national headquarters during the 1972 presidential campaign. Twenty years earlier, the **Watergate** break-in scandal probably would not have gone beyond three paragraphs from the police beat. In 1972, however, the persistence of *Post* reporters **Carl Bernstein** and **Bob Woodward** posed so many questions about morality in the White House that eventually President Nixon resigned and 25 aides went to jail.

investigative journalism
Seeking stories that would not surface on their own and which subjects would prefer not be told.

Watergate
Reporting of Nixon administration scandal.

Carl Bernstein
Washington *Post* reporter who dug up Watergate.

Bob Woodward
Bernstein colleague on Watergate.

As late as 1960, many daily newspapers were still hiring reporters without college degrees. By 1970 that had changed, and many newspaper reporters were acquiring advanced degrees and developing specialties. Major newspapers hired reporters with law degrees for special work and encouraged promising reporters to go back to college for graduate work in science, business, medicine and the environment. The result was a new emphasis on proactive reporting in which journalists did not wait for events to happen but went out looking, even digging, for things worth telling.

soft news

The success of the *National Enquirer,* whose circulation began to skyrocket in the 1960s, was not unnoticed, and when Time-Life, Inc. launched *People* magazine and the New York *Times* launched *Us* magazine, gossipy celebrity news gained a kind of respectability. In this period, the newspaper industry began sophisticated research to identify what readers wanted, then fine-tuned the content mix that would improve market penetration. As a result, many dailies added "People" columns. The news services began receiving requests for more off-beat, gee-whiz items of the sensational sort. Newspapers had always run such material, but more is being printed today to appeal to a broader audience. Many newspapers today also carry more consumer-oriented stories, lifestyle tips, and entertainment news. This is called **soft news.**

Traditionalists decry the space that soft news takes in many newspapers today, but soft news generally has not displaced hard news. Rather, newspapers fit additional hard news, as well as soft news, into larger newspapers. The news hole, the space left after advertisements are put in a newspaper, increased from 19 pages on average in 1970 to 24 pages today.

chapter wrap-up

Journalism is an art, not a science. Judgments, rather than formulas, determine which events and issues are reported and how—and no two journalists approach any story exactly the same way. This leaves the whole process of gathering and telling news subject to second-guessing and criticism. Journalists ask themselves all the time if there are ways to do a better job. All journalists can do is try to find truth and to relate it accurately. Even then, the complexity of modern news-gathering—which involves many people, each with an opportunity to change or even kill a story—includes dozens of points at which inaccuracy and imprecision can creep into a story that started out well.

The hazards of the news-gathering process are most obvious with foreign coverage. Even if the reporter is able to gather information and put it into a meaningful context, the story passes through many gatekeepers, all of whom can modify it, before it reaches newsroom in the United States. Then copyeditors, headline writers, photo editors, caption writers and others can take even more cracks at a story.

It is no wonder that the coverage that ends up in print and on the air does not please everyone. At the same time, the news media receive some unfair criticism. The most frequent is the charge that the media slant coverage. The fact, according to respected surveys, is that the political orientation of U.S. journalists largely coincides with that of the majority of the American people. Other studies have found that the

soft news
Geared to satisfying audience's information wants, not needs.

values that journalists bring to their work are mainstream cultural values, including ethnocentrism and faith in democracy and capitalism.

The consolidation of news-gathering, through services like the Associated Press, has created great economies in covering faraway events and issues. These services permit local newspapers and broadcast stations to offer more thorough coverage than they could with their own resources. The flip side is that faraway coverage is less expensive than hiring local reporters, which raises serious questions about the appropriate balance between hometown and faraway coverage. The same questions can be raised about syndicates, which provide high-quality political commentary, cartoons, comics and other materials inexpensively to local newspapers and stations.

questions for review

1. What contemporary news practices are rooted in the colonial, partisan, penny and yellow periods of U.S. history?

2. What personal values do journalists bring to their work? Does this affect what is reported and how?

3. What variables beyond journalists' control affect news?

4. What external pressures, from outside the media, affect news reporting?

5. What responsibilities do journalists have as gatekeepers?

6. What is the relationship between global news services and the newspapers you read and the newscasts you hear?

7. What is the relationship between syndicates and the newspapers you read?

8. Is there a contradiction between the two contemporary journalistic trends of exploratory reporting and soft news?

questions for critical thinking

1. The 19-year-old son of the premier of a troubled Central American country in which the CIA has deep involvement died, perhaps of a drug overdose, aboard a Northwest Airlines plane en route from Tokyo to Singapore. On the plane was a young female country-western singer, his frequent companion in recent weeks. The plane was a Boeing 747 manufactured in Washington state. Northwest's corporate headquarters is in Minnesota. The death occurred at 4 a.m. Eastern time. Consider the six elements of news—proximity, prominence, timeliness, consequence, currency and drama—and discuss how this event might be reported on morning

television newscasts in Miami, Minneapolis, Nashville, Seattle and the District of Columbia. How about in Managua? Singapore? Tokyo? Rome? Istanbul? Johannesburg? What if the victim were an ordinary college student? What if the death occurred a week ago?

2. Explain news judgment.

3. How do news hole and news flow affect what is reported in the news media?

4. *Time* and *Newsweek* carry cover stories on the same subject one week. Does this indicate that executives of the magazine have conspired, or is it more likely to be caused by what Leon Sigal calls the *consensible nature of news*?

5. How does the nature of news provide ammunition to conservatives to criticize the news media as leftist promoters of change?

6. Discuss whether the American news media reflect mainstream American values. Do you see evidence in your news media of an underlying belief that democracy, capitalism, rural small-town life, individualism and moderation are virtues?

7. Do you feel that the mass media revel in disorder? Consider Herbert Gans' view that the media cover disorder from the perspective of identifying ways to restore order.

8. If a college president calls a news conference and makes a major announcement, who are the gatekeepers who determine how the announcement is covered in the campus newspaper?

9. Three major global news services are the Associated Press, Reuters and United Press International. Discuss their similarities and differences.

10. Consider the advantages and disadvantages of your local daily newspaper running both the Ann Landers and the Dear Abby advice columns.

for further learning

Peter Arnett. *Live From the Battlefield: From Vietnam to Baghdad, 35 Years in the World's War Zones* (Simon & Schuster Touchstone, 1994).

Ben Bradlee. *A Good Life: Newspapering and Other Stories* (Simon & Schuster, 1996). In this memoir veteran Washington *Post* editor Ben Bradlee, the most visible editor of his generation, takes you on an inside expedition through the Kennedy years, the Pentagon Papers, Watergate and the Janet Cooke scandal.

Daniel J. Czitrom. *Media and the American Mind: From Morse to McLuhan* (University of North Carolina Press, 1982). Czitrom explores the effect of technological innovations, particularly the telegraph, movies and radio, and popular and scholarly responses to them.

Hazel Dicken-Garcia. *Journalistic Standards in the Nineteenth Century* (University of Wisconsin Press, 1989). Dicken-Garcia traces the idea that the press should be a purveyor of information, not only a forum for partisanship, back to the time before the penny press period.

Edwin and Michael Emery with Nancy L. Roberts. *The Press and America*, 8th ed. (Prentice Hall, 1995). The Emerys offer an encyclopedic chronology of American mass media back to its roots in authoritarian England.

James Fallows. *How the Media Undermine American Democracy* (Pantheon, 1996). Fallows, an *Atlantic* magazine editor, has assembled a rich collection of stories that don't reflect well on the news media to explain what he sees as public disaffection.

Mark Fishman. *Manufacturing the News* (University of Texas Press, 1980). Fishman argues that the conventions of gathering news shape what ends up being reported as much as events themselves.

Thomas L. Friedman. *From Beirut to Jerusalem* (Farrar, Straus & Giroux, 1989). Friedman, of the New York *Times,* reveals a lot about being a foreign correspondent in this insightful look at anarchy in Beirut, Arab-Israeli tensions and Arab politics.

Herbert J. Gans. *Deciding What's News: A Study of CBS Evening News, NBC Nightly News, Newsweek and Time* (Pantheon, 1979). A sociologist examines how the values journalists bring to their work affect the news that is reported.

Jane T. Harrigan. *Read All About It! A Day in the Life of a Metropolitan Newspaper* (Globe Pequot Press, 1987). Harrigan, a journalist, tracks hundreds of newspaper people from 6 a.m. through midnight as they produce an issue of the Boston *Globe.* Along the way, she explains how journalists decide which events to report.

Norman E. Isaacs. *Untended Gates: The Mismanaged Press* (Columbia University Press, 1986). Isaacs, who has edited several major American dailies, argues that the lapses of media ethics can be blamed on top-level managers who are reluctant to involve themselves in newsroom decisions.

Brooke Kroeger. *Nellie Bly: Daredevil, Reporter, Feminist* (Random House, 1994). Kroeger, a former news reporter, unearthed court documents and lost letters for this meticulous, detailed account of an innovative reporting pioneer.

Molly Moore. *A Woman at War: Storming Kuwait With the U.S. Marines* (Scribner's, 1993). Moore, a Washington *Post* reporter, explains the difficulties of getting breaking stories back to the newsroom when military personnel control your movement and access. Moore is especially good at recounting the psychological impact of pending combat on soldiers.

Michael Parenti. *Inventing Reality: The Politics of the Mass Media,* 2nd edition (St. Martin's, 1993).

Lou Prato. "The Business of Broadcasting: Expect More TV News From Abroad." *American Journalism Review* (December 1994). Page 52.

Michael Schudson. *Discovering the News: A Social History of American Newspapers* (Basic Books, 1978). Schudson chronicles the development of journalism as a profession in the United States, focusing on changing concepts of news values and objectivity along the way.

David H. Weaver and G. Cleveland Wilhoit. *The American Journalist: A Portrait of U.S. News People and Their Work,* 2nd edition (Indiana University Press, 1991). This comprehensive profile updates the authors' 1986 work and an earlier 1971 study, which also bears reading: John W. C. Johnstone, Edward J. Slawski and William W. Bowman. *The News People: A Sociological Portrait of American Journalists and Their Work* (University of Illinois Press, 1976).

for keeping up to date

Among publications that keep current on journalistic issues are *Columbia Journalism Review, Quill, American Journalism Review, Editor & Publisher* and *Forbes Media Critic.*

Bridging the gap between scholarly and professional work is *Newspaper Research Journal.*

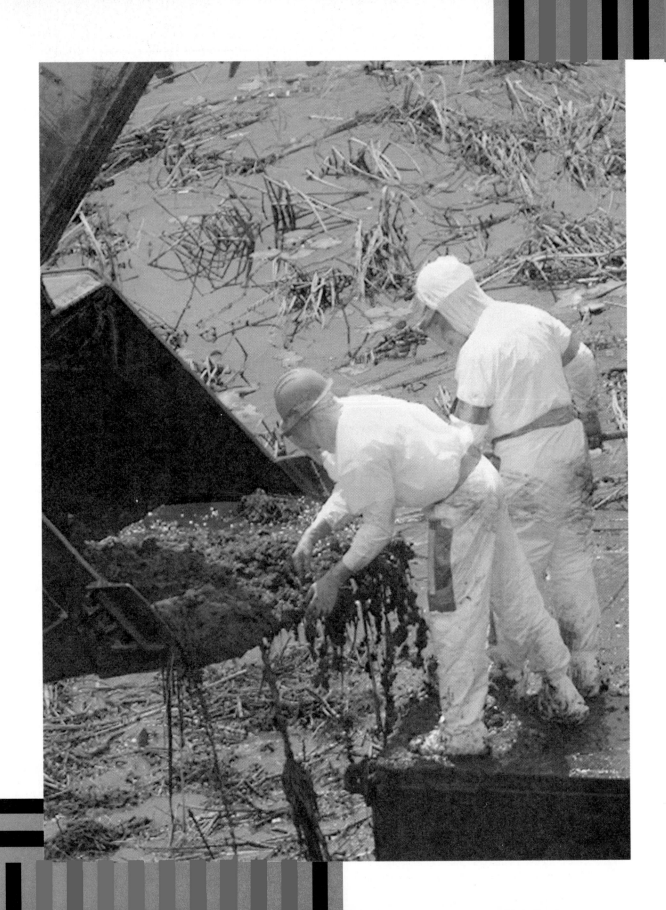

public relations

in this chapter you will learn:

- Public relations is a persuasive communication tool that uses mass media.
- Public relations grew out of public disfavor with big business.
- Public relations is an important management tool.
- Public relations includes promotion, publicity, lobbying, fundraising, crisis management.
- Public relations usually involves a candid, proactive relationship with mass media.
- Public relations organizations are working to improve the image of their craft.

Marcia Scott's pager buzzed at 2:30 p.m., May 11, 1996—a moment she will never forget. As public relations director for the discount airline ValuJet, Scott was coordinating photo coverage of a good-deed event— the construction of a Habitat for Humanity house by 27 ValuJet employees, including the company president. That's when the pager sounded.

The message: A ValuJet plane had disappeared from radar out of Miami.

Recognizing the inevitability of a crash at some point, every airline has a contingency plan to guide it through the crisis. A team from ValuJet's Atlanta headquarters was dispatched to Miami, and the company flew in employees from throughout its system and assigned one to the family of each of the 110 people

Swamp Recovery. When a ValuJet plane went down in the Florida Everglades, the airline activated a contingency plan that they put together for the inevitability of such a crisis. ValuJet did everything right in the hours following the crash, but that was not enough to offset the tarnish that resulted from the intense scrutiny of its safety practices and the operational problems that followed the crash. The airline retired the ValuJet name and logo a year later.

aboard. The company arranged lodging in Miami and set up a system to keep them up-to-date as the wreckage recovery in the Florida Everglades progressed. The ValuJet people were there to help the families through their grieving. They organized a trip to the recovery site, where the fuselage and fragments were being drudged from a mucky crater in the swamp.

Scott's role in implementing the contingency plan was mostly in the background. Consistent with usual public relations practice, it was the company's chief executive, president Lewis Jordan, who was ValuJet's public face. At a news conference, Jordan expressed regret and promised ValuJet's full

cooperation with investigators. He then was available on an ongoing basis to reporters through news conferences, while Scott and her public relations people handled interim queries. Carrying out other aspects of the contingency plan, Jordan called on the chief executives of other airlines to honor the tickets of ValuJet customers whose flights were canceled. In the meantime, ValuJet advertising, with its "good times, great fares" theme, was furloughed lest it be tastelessly juxtapositioned with news about the grisly crash. There was also a plan to keep shareholders informed on the impact on their investment.

Even the best-laid contingency plans don't always work. ValuJet was

Lewis Jordan

burdened by its three-year advertising that emphasized low fares, which, combined with questions posed about its safety practices, eroded public confidence. The rush to judgment—combined with a shambled schedule resulting from inspections

of the entire ValuJet fleet—were something from which the airline couldn't recover. In 1997, ValuJet was folded into another carrier and the company's catchy but tarnished name, as well as its Critter logo, was retired.

media timeline

evolution of public relations

1859 Charles Darwin advanced survival-of-fittest theory, which led to social Darwinism.

1880s Public dissatisfied with unconscionable business practices justified with social Darwinism.

1906 Ivy Lee began first public relations agency.

1917 George Creel headed federal agency that generated support for World War I.

1927 Arthur Page became first corporate public relations vice president.

1930s Paul Garrett created term *enlightened self-interest* at General Motors.

1942 Elmer Davis headed federal agency that generated support for World War II.

1965 Public Relations Society of America created accreditation system.

1970s Herb Schmertz pioneered adversarial public relations at Mobil Oil.

1987 PRSA adopted ethics code.

importance of public relations

(STUDY PREVIEW) Public relations is a persuasive communication tool that people can use to motivate other people and institutions to help them achieve their goals.

defining public relations

Edward Bernays, the public relations pioneer, lamented how loosely the term **public relations** is used. To illustrate his concern, Bernays told about a young woman who approached him for career advice. He asked her what she did for a living. "I'm in public relations," she said. He pressed her for details, and she explained that she handed out circulars in Harvard Square. Bernays was dismayed at how casually people regard the work of public relations. There are receptionists and secretaries who list public relations on their résumés. To some people, public relations is glad-handing and back-slapping and smiling prettily to make people feel good. The fact, however, is that public relations goes far beyond good interpersonal skills. A useful definition is that public relations is a management tool for leaders in business, government and other institutions to establish beneficial *relationships* with other institutions and groups. Four steps are necessary for public relations to accomplish its goals:

Identifying Existing Relationships. In modern society, institutions have many relationships. A college, for example, has relationships with its students, its faculty, its staff, its alumni, its benefactors, the neighborhood, the community, the legislature, other colleges, accreditors of its programs, perhaps unions. The list could go on and on. Each of these constituencies is called a public—hence the term *public relations.*

Evaluate the Relationships. Through research, the public relations practitioner studies these relationships to determine how well they are working. This evaluation is an ongoing process. A college may have excellent relations with the legislature one year and win major appropriations, but after a scandal related to the president's budget the next year, legislators may be downright unfriendly.

Design Policies to Improve the Relationships. The job of public relations people is to recommend policies to top management to make these relationships work better, not only for the organization but also for the partners in each relationship. **Paul Garrett,** a pioneer in corporate relations, found that General Motors was not seen in friendly terms during the Great Depression, which put the giant auto-maker at risk with many publics, including its own employees. GM, he advised, needed new policies to seem neighborly—rather than as a far-removed, impersonal, monolithic industrial giant.

Implement the Policies. Garrett used the term **enlightened self-interest** for his series of policies intended to downsize GM in the eyes of many of the company's publics. Garrett set up municipal programs in towns with GM plants, and grants for schools and scholarships for employees' children. General Motors benefited from a revised image and, in the spirit of enlightened self-interest, so did GM employees, their children and their communities.

media
online

Autonomy Publishing Corp.: Big list of PR firms on the web. www.autonomy.com/pubrel.htm

Medialink: PR with a decidedly broadcast slant. www.medialinkworldwide.com

National Investor Relations: Institute on the Big Money side of the equation. www.niri.org

PRNewswire: News about companies searchable by industry. www.prnewswire.com

public relations
A management tool to establish beneficial relationships.

Paul Garrett
Devised notion of enlightened self-interest.

enlightened self-interest
Mutually beneficial public relations.

Public relations is not a mass medium itself, but PR often uses the media as tools to accomplish its goals. To announce GM's initiatives to change its image in the 1930s, Paul Garrett issued news releases that he hoped newspapers, magazines and radio stations would pick up. The number of people in most of the publics with which public relations practitioners need to communicate is so large that it can be reached only through the mass media. The influence of public relations on the news media is extensive. Half of the news in many newspapers originates with formal statements or news releases from organizations that want something in the paper. It is the same with radio and television.

public relations in a democracy

Misconceptions about public relations include the idea that it is a one-way street for institutions and individuals to communicate to the public. Actually, the good practice of public relations seeks two-way communication between and among all the people and institutions concerned with an issue.

A task force established by the **Public Relations Society of America** to explore the stature and role of the profession concluded that public relations has the potential to improve the functioning of democracy by encouraging the exchange of information and ideas on public issues. The task force made these points:

- Public relations is a means for the public to have its desires and interests felt by the institutions in our society. It interprets and speaks for the public to organizations that otherwise might be unresponsive, and it speaks for those organizations to the public.

- Public relations is a means to achieve mutual adjustments between institutions and groups, establishing smoother relationships that benefit the public.

- Public relations is a safety valve for freedom. By providing means of working out accommodations, it makes arbitrary action or coercion less likely.

- Public relations is an essential element in the communication system that enables individuals to be informed on many aspects of subjects that affect their lives.

- Public relations people can help activate the social conscience of the organizations for which they work.

origins of public relations

(STUDY PREVIEW) Many big companies found themselves in disfavor in the late 1800s for ignoring the public good to make profits. Feeling misunderstood, some moguls of industry turned to Ivy Lee, the founder of modern public relations, for counsel on gaining public support.

moguls in trouble

Nobody would be tempted to think of **William Henry Vanderbilt** as very good at public relations. In 1882, it was Vanderbilt, president of the New York Central Railroad,

Public Relations Society of America
Professional public relations association.

William Henry Vanderbilt
Embodies bad corporate images of 1880s, 1890s with "let public be damned."

who said, "The public be damned," when asked about the effect of changing train schedules. Vanderbilt's utterance so infuriated people that it became a banner in the populist crusade against robber barons and tycoons in the late 1800s. Under populist pressure, state governments set up agencies to regulate railroads. Then the national government established the **Interstate Commerce Commission** to control freight and passenger rates. Government began insisting on safety standards. Labor unions formed in the industries with the worst working conditions, safety records and pay. Journalists added pressure with muckraking exposés on excesses in the railroad, coal and oil trusts; on meat-packing industry frauds; and on patent medicines.

The leaders of industry were slow to recognize the effect of populist objections on their practices. They were comfortable with **social Darwinism,** an adaptation of **Charles Darwin**'s survival-of-the-fittest theory. In fact, they thought themselves forward-thinking in applying Darwin's theory to business and social issues. It had been only a few years earlier, in 1859, that Darwin laid out his biological theory in *On the Origin of Species by Means of Natural Selection.* To cushion the harshness of social Darwinism, many tycoons espoused paternalism toward those whose "fitness" had not brought them fortune and power. No matter how carefully put, paternalism seemed arrogant to the "less fit."

George Baer, a railroad president, epitomized both social Darwinism and paternalism in commenting on a labor strike: "The rights and interests of the laboring man will be protected and cared for not by labor agitators but by the Christian men to whom God in His infinite wisdom has given the control of the property interests of the country." Baer was quoted widely, further fueling sentiment against big business. Baer may have been sincere, but his position was read as a cover for excessive business practices by barons who assumed superiority to everyone else.

Meanwhile, social Darwinism came under attack as circuitous reasoning: economic success accomplished by abusive practices could be used to justify further abusive practices, which would lead to further success. Social Darwinism was a dog-eat-dog outlook that hardly jibed with democratic ideals, especially not as described in the preamble to the U.S. Constitution, which sought to "promote the general welfare, and secure the blessings of liberty" for everyone—not for only the chosen "fittest." Into these tensions at the turn of the century came public relations pioneer Ivy Lee.

the ideas of ivy lee

Coal mine operators, like the railroad magnates, were held in the public's contempt at the turn of the century. Obsessed with profits, caring little about public sentiment or even the well-being of their employees, the mine operators were vulnerable in the new populist wave. Mine workers organized, and 150,000 in Pennsylvania went out on strike in 1902, shutting down the anthracite industry and disrupting coal-dependent industries, including the railroads. The mine operators snubbed reporters, which probably contributed to a pro-union slant in many news stories and worsened the operators' public image. Not until six months into the strike, when President Theodore Roosevelt threatened to take over the mines with Army troops, did the operators settle.

Shaken finally by Roosevelt's threat and recognizing Roosevelt's responsiveness to public opinion, the mine operators began reconsidering how they went about their business. In 1906, with another strike looming, one operator heard about **Ivy Lee,** a young publicist in New York who had new ideas about winning public support. He was hired. In a turnabout in press relations, Lee issued a news release that announced, "The anthracite coal operators, realizing the general public interest in conditions in

Interstate Commerce Commission
First federal agency to rein in excessive business practices, 1890.

social Darwinism
Application of Darwin's survival-of-fittest theory to society.

Charles Darwin
Devised survival-of-fittest theory.

George Baer
Epitomized offensive corporate paternalism 1890s.

Ivy Lee
Laid out fundamentals of public relations.

Ivy Lee

Ludlow Massacre. Colorado militiamen opened fire during a 1914 mine labor dispute and killed women and children. Overnight, John D. Rockefeller became the object of public hatred. It was a Rockefeller company that owned the mine, and even in New York, where Rockefeller lived, there were rallies asking for his head. Public relations pioneer Ivy Lee advised Rockefeller to tour the Ludlow area as soon as tempers cooled to show his sincere concern and to begin work on a labor contract to meet the concerns of miners. Rockefeller ended up a popular character in the Colorado mining camps.

the mining regions, have arranged to supply the press with all possible information." Then followed a series of releases with information attributed to the mine operators by name—the same people who earlier had preferred anonymity and refused all interview requests. There were no more secret strike strategy meetings. When operators planned a meeting, reporters covering the impending strike were informed. Although reporters were not admitted to the meetings, summaries of the proceedings were given to them immediately afterward. This relative openness eased long-standing hostility toward the operators, and a strike was averted.

Lee's success with the mine operators began a career that rewrote the rules on how corporations deal with their various publics. Among his accomplishments were:

Converting Industry Toward Openness. Railroads had notoriously secretive policies not only about their business practices but even about accidents. When the **Pennsylvania Railroad** sought Ivy Lee's counsel, he advised against suppressing news—especially on things that inevitably would leak out anyway. When a train jumped the rails near Gap, Pennsylvania, Lee arranged for a special car to take reporters to the scene and even take pictures. The Pennsylvania line was applauded in the press for the openness, and coverage of the railroad, which had been negative for years, began changing. A "bad press" continued plaguing other railroads that persisted in their secretive tradition.

Turning Negative News into Positive News. When the U.S. Senate proposed investigating International Harvester for monopolistic practices, Lee advised the giant farm implement manufacturer against reflexive obstructionism and silence. A statement went out announcing that the company, confident in its business practices, not only welcomed but also would facilitate an investigation. Then began a campaign that pointed out International Harvester's beneficence toward its employees. The campaign also emphasized other upbeat information about the company.

Pennsylvania Railroad
Ivy Lee favorably changed railroad's approach to public relations.

Putting Corporate Executives on Display. When workers at a Colorado mine went on strike, company guards fired machine guns and killed several men. More battling followed, during which two women and 11 children were killed. It was called the **Ludlow Massacre,** and **John D. Rockefeller Jr.,** the chief mine owner, was pilloried for what had happened. Rockefeller was an easy target. Like his father, widely despised for the earlier Standard Oil monopolistic practices, John Jr. tried to keep himself out of the spotlight, but suddenly mobs were protesting at his mansion in New York and calling out: "Shoot him down like a dog." Rockefeller asked Ivy Lee what he should do. Lee began whipping up articles about Rockefeller's human side, his family and his generosity. Then, on Lee's advice, Rockefeller announced he would visit Colorado to see conditions himself. He spent two weeks talking with miners at work and in their homes and meeting their families. It was a news story that reporters could not resist, and it unveiled Rockefeller as a human being, not a far-removed, callous captain of industry. A myth-shattering episode occurred one evening when Rockefeller, after a brief address to miners and their wives, suggested that the floor be cleared for a dance. Before it was all over, John D. Rockefeller Jr. had danced with almost every miner's wife, and the news stories about the evening did a great deal to mitigate antagonism and distrust toward Rockefeller. Back in New York, with Lee's help, Rockefeller put together a proposal for a grievance procedure, which he asked the Colorado miners to approve. It was ratified overwhelmingly.

Avoiding Puffery and Fluff. Ivy Lee came on the scene at a time when many organizations were making extravagant claims about themselves and their products. Circus promoter **P. T. Barnum** made this kind of hyping a fine art in the late 1800s, and he had many imitators. It was an age of puffed-up advertising claims and fluffy rhetoric. Lee noted, however, that people soon saw through hyperbolic claims and lost faith in those who made them. In launching his public relations agency in 1906, he vowed to be accurate in everything he said and to provide whatever verification anyone requested. This became part of the creed of good practice in public relations, and it remains so today.

public relations on a new scale

The potential of public relations to rally support for a cause was demonstrated on a gigantic scale in World War I and again in World War II.

World War I. In 1917 President Woodrow Wilson, concerned about widespread antiwar sentiment, asked **George Creel** to head a new government agency whose job was to make the war popular. The Creel Committee cranked out news releases, magazine pieces, posters, even movies. A list of 75,000 local speakers was put together to talk nationwide at school programs, church groups and civic organizations about making the world safe for democracy. More than 15,000 committee articles were printed. Never before had public relations been attempted on such a scale—and it worked. World War I became a popular cause even to the point of inspiring people to buy Liberty Bonds, putting up their own money to finance the war outside the usual taxation apparatus.

World War II. When World War II began, an agency akin to the Creel Committee was formed. Veteran journalist **Elmer Davis** was put in charge. The new Office of War Information was public relations on a bigger scale than ever before.

Ludlow Massacre
Colorado tragedy that Ivy Lee converted into public relations victory.

John D. Rockefeller Jr.
Ivy client who had been target of public hatred.

puffery
Inflated claims.

P. T. Barnum
Known for exaggerated promotion.

George Creel
Demonstrated public relations works on mammoth scale; World War I.

Elmer Davis
Led Office of War Information; World War II.

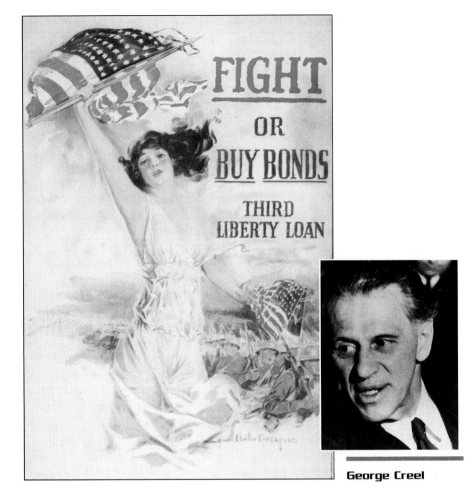

George Creel

The Creel and Davis committees employed hundreds of people. Davis had 250 employees handling news releases alone. These staff members, mostly young, carried new lessons about public relations into the private sector after the war. These were the people who shaped corporate public relations as we know it today.

Corporate Giving. One manifestation of the growing presence of public relations people in business was corporate giving. Paul Garrett had pioneered the "give back" concept at General Motors in the 1930s, and the idea spread after World War II. In 1946, the Minnesota-based Dayton H. Hudson department store company began donating 5 percent of its pre-tax income to community projects. Today many corporations employ full-time managers to address community and social needs and to work at assuring that their companies are good citizens.

Taking the Dayton Hudson example, the Greater Minneapolis Chamber of Commerce created the 5% Club in 1976 to encourage more corporations to make community investments. Within a few years, such corporate giants as 3M, Burlington Northern, FirstBank, General Mills, Honeywell, Northwestern Bell and Pillsbury were channeling significant money into a broad range of projects. The 5% Club was the first such program in the country. Today, corporate leaders from around the world visit Minnesota to learn how to develop corporate giving programs at home.

dorothea lange

Dorothea Lange.

The power of mass media messages to change public policy was never better illustrated than in the emotional, telling photographs of Dorothea Lange. Her images from the Depression, showing impoverished, broken people, many homeless and hungry, generated government assistance to help the poor. After she and economist Paul Taylor documented conditions among California migrant workers, the government built migrant camps. Finally, the federal government hired Lange to photograph the American West. Her most famous photograph, "Migrant Mother," came on government assignment. For many people, that image, a woman in rags with three grimy children, her face and body showing anxiety and care, epitomized the Depression of the 1930s and helped neutralize opposition to unprecedented, large-scale federal relief programs.

Lange studied photography at Columbia University, then set up a portrait business in San Francisco. Soon, though, she moved into photo documentaries. Her 1932 photo, "White Angel Bread Line," brought her work to wide attention. It showed a grizzled, unshaven, broken man, his back to a bread line. The stark contrasts, typical of Lange's work, made it, along with "Migrant Mother" one of the great images of the era.

Her work was widely disseminated by the government and appears still today to illustrate the Depression. When Archibald MacLeish published his poem *Land of the Free*, her photographs accompanied it. With Paul Taylor, she produced *An American Exodus*, a book on the Dust Bowl migrations, which moved audiences and shaped government policy.

Like the first corporate ventures into public relations back in Ivy Lee's days, corporations had numerous motives for developing corporate giving programs. Bill King, an early administrator of the Minnesota 5% Club, is frank that the club originated amid declining public warmth toward business: "Although business had gone through a recession, there were perceptions of excess corporate profits, accompanied by disregard for the environment, allegations of profiteering during the Vietnam war, and other social phenomena such as the civil rights movement, the women's movement, and the consumer rights movement. Business was a primary target of the voting public's dissatisfaction. Obviously it was time for business to respond or risk changes in the free enterprise system."

This is hardly to say that some corporate leaders aren't interested in improving their communities just because it's a good and right thing to do. As King wrote about the Minnesota experience: "A social responsibility stakeholder management philosophy began to emerge." There were other incentives too. Since 1935, Congress has allowed a 5 percent deduction to corporations for charitable contributions. Also, while giving 5 percent of pre-tax profits means a lot for community projects, Dayton Hudson says it's not a lot for a corporation. The company says that to cut its giving from 5 percent to 1 percent would mean a mere 5.4 cents less in earnings per share—a small price to pay for a better quality of community life, an improved public image, and a conducive atmosphere for corporate growth.

media
online

Propaganda: Aaron Delwiche, of the University of Washington, takes a critical look at the Creel Commission's work in World War I. This site has been recognized widely as one the best student projects.
http://weber.u.washington.edu/~scmuweb/propag/home.htm

structure of public relations

(STUDY PREVIEW)   In developing sound policies, corporations and other institutions depend on public relations experts who are sensitive to the implications of policy on the public consciousness. This makes public relations a vital management function. Besides a role in policymaking, public relations people play key roles in carrying out institutional policy.

policy role of public relations

When giant AT&T needed somebody to take over public relations in 1927, the president of the company went to magazine editor **Arthur Page** and offered him a vice presidency. Before accepting, Page laid out several conditions. One was that he have a voice in AT&T policy. Page was hardly on an ego trip. He had seen too many corporations that regarded their public relations arm merely as an executor of policy. Page considered PR itself as a management function. To be effective as vice president for public relations, Page knew that he must contribute to the making of high-level corporate decisions as well as executing them.

Today, experts on public relations agree with Arthur Page's concept: When institutions are making policy, they need to consider the effects on their many publics. That can be done best when the person in charge of public relations, ideally at the vice presidential level, is intimately involved in decision-making. The public relations executive advises the rest of the institution's leaders on public perceptions and the effects that policy options might have on perceptions. Also, the public relations vice president is in a better position to implement the institution's policy for having been a part of developing it.

how public relations is organized

No two institutions are organized in precisely the same way. At General Motors, 200 people work in public relations. In smaller organizations, PR may be one of several hats worn by a single person. Except in the smallest operations, the public relations department usually has three functional areas of responsibility:

External Relations.   This involves communication with groups and people outside the organization, including customers, dealers, suppliers and community leaders. The external-relations unit usually is responsible for encouraging employees to participate in civic activities. Other responsibilities include arranging promotional activities like exhibits, trade shows, conferences and tours.

Public relations people also lobby government agencies and legislators on behalf of their organization, keep the organization abreast of government regulations and legislation and coordinate relations with political candidates. This may include fundraising for candidates and coordinating political action committees.

In hospitals and nonprofit organizations, a public relations function may include recruiting and scheduling volunteer workers.

Internal Relations.   This involves developing optimal relations with employees, managers, unions, shareholders and other internal groups. In-house newsletters,

russian military public relations

The architects of Russian democratization in the 1990s recognized that the old Soviet Union's heavy-handed propaganda wouldn't do. Information minister Valery Manilov, concerned especially about the military's relations with the mass media, turned to the Pentagon to see how the U.S. military told its story to the media. A series of exchanges between Russian and U.S. military people resulted in revised Russian military doctrines that resemble the U.S. model. The fundamental doctrine: "Maximum disclosure, minimum delay."

Colonel Rick Kiernan, a U.S. Army public affairs officer who spent time in Russia explaining Pentagon policies, said the Russians were quick to pick up on the idea that people want information but only if they can trust it. People are much more interested in information than political party themes and propaganda, he said.

In restructuring its public relations, the Russian military chose the widely used three-function U.S. military model. This involves separate units:

- **Command information.** For internal military audiences, including the troops.

- **Community affairs.** Outreach programs mostly for communities that neighbor military bases.

- **Media relations.** For conveying messages to large groups of people through the media.

The Russian military has a fourth unit, issues management, which focus on broad issues like the environment and health care.

---

magazines and brochures are important media for communicating with organizations' internal audiences.

Media Relations. Communication with large groups of people outside an organization is practicable only through the mass media. An organization's coordinator of media relations responds to news media queries, arranges news conferences and issues news releases. These coordinators coach executives for news interviews and sometimes serve as their organization's spokesperson.

public relations agencies

Even though many organizations have their own public relations staff, they may go to public relations agencies for help on specific projects or problems. In the United States today, hundreds of companies specialize in public relations counsel and related services. It is a big business. Income at global PR agencies like Burson-Marsteller runs about $200 million a year.

The biggest agencies offer a full range of services on a global scale. Hill & Knowlton has offices in Cleveland, its original home; Dallas; Frankfurt; Geneva; London; Los Angeles; New York, now its headquarters; Paris; Rome; Seattle; and Washington, D.C. The agency will take on projects anywhere in the world, either on its own or by working with local agencies.

Besides full-service agencies, there are specialized public relations companies, which focus on a narrow range of services. For example, clipping services cut out and provide newspaper and magazine articles and radio and television items of interest to clients.

Arthur Page
Established public relations role as top management tool.

external public relations
Gearing messages to outside organization, constituencies, individuals.

internal public relations
Gearing messages to inside groups, constituencies, individuals.

media relations
Using mass media to convey messages.

public relations agencies
Companies that provide public relations services.

media | databank

major public relations agencies

These are the largest U.S.-based public relations agencies. Because some agencies are part of larger companies that don't break out data on their subordinate units, some data here are estimates.

Company	Income Worldwide	Employees Worldwide
Burson-Marsteller	$204 million	2,100
Shandick	160 million	1,800
Hill & Knowlton	149 million	1,200
Edelman	80 million	800
Omnicon	66 million	1,000
Fleishman-Hillard	59 million	600
Ketchum	45 million	500
Rowland	44 million	500
Ogilvy Adams & Rinehart	36 million	300
Manning, Selvage & Lee	31 million	300

Among specialized agencies are those that focus exclusively on political campaigns. Others coach corporate executives for news interviews. Others coordinate trade shows.

Some agencies bill clients only for services rendered. Others charge clients just to be on call. Hill & Knowlton, for example, has a minimum $5,000-a-month retainer fee. Agency expenses for specific projects are billed in addition. Staff time usually is at an hourly rate that covers the agency's overhead and allows a profit margin. Other expenses are usually billed with a 15 to 17 percent markup.

public relations services

(STUDY PREVIEW) Public relations deals with publicity and promotion, but it also involves less visible activities. These include lobbying, fund-raising and crisis management. Public relations is distinct from advertising.

activities beyond publicity

publicity
Brings public attention to something.
promotion
Promoting a cause, idea.

Full-service public relations agencies provide a wide range of services built on two of the cornerstones of the business: **publicity** and **promotion.** These agencies are ready to conduct media campaigns to rally support for a cause, create an image or turn a problem into an asset. Publicity and promotion, however, are only the most visible services offered by public relations agencies. Others include:

Lobbying. Every state capital has hundreds of public relations practitioners whose specialty is representing their clients to legislative bodies and government agencies. In North Dakota, hardly a populous state, more than 300 persons are registered as lobbyists in the capital city of Bismarck.

Lobbying has been called a "growth industry." The number of registered lobbyists in Washington, D.C., has grown from 3,400 in 1976 to almost 10,000 today. In addition, there are an estimated 20,000 other people in the nation's capital who have slipped through registration requirements but who nonetheless ply the halls of government to plead their clients' interests.

In one sense, lobbyists are expediters. They know local traditions and customs, and they know who is in a position to affect policy. Lobbyists advise their clients, which include trade associations, corporations, public interest groups and regulated utilities and industries, on how to achieve their goals by working with legislators and government regulators. Many lobbyists call themselves "government relations specialists."

Political Communication. Every capital has political consultants whose work mostly is advising candidates for public office. Services include campaign management, survey research, publicity, media relations and image consulting. Political consultants also work on elections, referendums, recalls and other public policy issues.

Image Consulting. Image consulting has been a growing specialized branch of public relations since the first energy crisis in the 1970s. Oil companies, realizing that their side of the story was not getting across, turned to image consultants to groom corporate spokespersons, often chief executives, to meet reporters one on one and go on talk shows. The groomers did a brisk business, and it paid off in countering the stories and rumors that were blaming the oil companies for skyrocketing fuel prices.

Financial Public Relations. Financial public relations dates to the 1920s and 1930s, when the U.S. Securities and Exchange Commission cracked down on abuses in the financial industry. Regulations on promoting sales of securities are complex. It is the job of people in financial PR to know not only the principles of public relations but also the complex regulations governing the promotion of securities in corporate mergers, acquisitions, new issues and stock splits.

Fund-Raising. Some public relations people specialize in fund-raising and membership drives. Many colleges, for example, have their own staffs to perform these functions. Others look to fund-raising firms to manage capital drives. Such an agency employs a variety of techniques, from mass mailings to phonathon soliciting, and charges a percentage of the amount raised.

Perrier Is Back. In 1990, when traces of cancer-causing benzene were found in Perrier, the bottled French mineral water, Perrier's reputation was in jeopardy. So were sales of $100 million a year in the United States alone. The company acted promptly to meet this challenge. First, release all available information about the contamination. Second, explain there was no significant health risk from the minute amounts of benzene. Third, point out that the company voluntarily recalled 160 million bottles from distribution channels worldwide because it did not meet its standards. Fourth, relaunch the product. Fifth, put Perrier President Ronald V. Davis in touch with the public, vouching for Perrier's purity and quality controls. Photographs of Davis quaffing Perrier were soon in the news media everywhere. This was all followed, three weeks after the recall, by an advertising campaign, "Perrier Is Back." Sales rebounded.

lobbying
Influencing public policy, usually legislation regulations.

political communication
Advising candidates, groups on public policy issues, usually in elections.

image consulting
Coaching individuals for media contacts.

Contingency Planning. Many organizations rely on public relations people to design programs to address problems that can be expected to occur. Airlines, for example, need detailed plans for handling inevitable plane crashes—situations requiring quick, appropriate responses under tremendous pressure. When a crisis occurs, an organization can turn to public relations people for advice on dealing with it. Some agencies specialize in **crisis management,** which involves picking up the pieces either when a contingency plan fails or when there was no plan to deal with a crisis.

Polling. Public-opinion sampling is essential in many public relations projects. Full-service agencies can either conduct surveys themselves or contract with companies that specialize in surveying.

Events Coordination. Many public relations people are involved in coordinating a broad range of events, including product announcements, news conferences and convention planning. Some in-house public relations departments and agencies have their own artistic and audio-visual production talent to produce brochures, tapes and other promotional materials. Other agencies contract for these services.

public relations and advertising

Both public relations and advertising involve persuasion through the mass media, but most of the similarities end there.

Management Function. Public relations people help shape an organization's policy. This is a management activity, ideally with the organization's chief public relations person offering counsel to other key policy-makers at the vice-presidential level. **Advertising,** in contrast, is not a management function. The work of advertising is much narrower. It focuses on developing persuasive messages, mostly to sell products or services, after all the management decisions have been made.

Measuring Success. Public relations "sells" points of view and images. These are intangibles and therefore hard to measure. In advertising, success is measurable with tangibles, like sales, that can be calculated from the bottom line.

Control of Messages. When an organization decides it needs a persuasive campaign, there is a choice between public relations and advertising. One advantage of advertising is that the organization controls the message. By buying space or time in the mass media, an organization has the final say on the content of its advertising messages. In public relations, in contrast, an organization tries to influence the media to tell its story a certain way, but the message that goes out actually is up to the media. A news reporter, for example, may lean heavily on a public relations person for information about an organization, but the reporter also may gather information from other sources. In the end, it is the reporter who writes the story. The upside of this is that the message, coming from a journalist, has a credibility with the mass audience that advertisements don't. Advertisements are patently self-serving. The downside of leaving it to the media to create the messages that reach the audience is surrendering control over the messages that go to the public.

integrated marketing

For many persuasive campaigns, organizations use both public relations and advertising. Increasingly, public relations and advertising people find themselves working together. This is especially true in corporations that have adopted **integrated marketing communication,** which attempts to coordinate advertising as a marketing tool with promotion and publicity of the sort that public relations experts can provide. Several major advertising agencies, aware of their clients' shift to integrated marketing, have acquired or established public relations subsidiaries to provide a wider range of services under their roof.

It's this overlap that has prompted some advertising agencies to move more into public relations. The WWP Group of London, a global advertising agency, has acquired both Hill & Knowlton, the third-largest public relations company in the United States, and the Ogilvy PR Group, the ninth largest. The Young & Rubicam advertising agency has three public relations subsidiaries: Burson-Marsteller, the largest; Cohn & Wolf, the 13th; and Creswell, Munsell, Fultz & Zirbel, the 50th. These are giant enterprises, which reflect the conglomeration and globalization of both advertising and public relations.

Public relations and advertising also overlap in **institutional advertising,** which involves producing ads not to sell goods or services but to promote an institution's image or position on a public issue.

joint projects

For many persuasive campaigns, organizations use both public relations and advertising. Increasingly, public relations and advertising people find themselves working together—an overlap resulting from the decisions of many major ad agencies to acquire public relations agencies. The acquisition of Hill & Knowlton, one of the largest U.S. public relations agencies, by the WWP Group of London, a global ad agency, was repeated many times in the 1990s.

Institutional Advertising. Public relations and advertising cross-overs are hardly new. One area of traditional overlap is **institutional advertising,** which involves producing ads to promote an image rather than a product. The fuzzy, feel-good ads of agricultural conglomerate Archer Daniels Midland, which pepper Sunday morning network television, are typical.

Integrated Marketing. The new **integrated marketing communication** hybrid, with elements of public relations, advertising and marketing, emerged in the 1990s. The idea is to use any and all means to make a product part of a targeted consumer's mindset. It is not enough to advertise in the traditional media to mass audience or even subgroups. Rather, the goal is to immerse a product in the mindset of individual consumers by focusing a diverse array of messages in their experience.

To describe integrated marketing communication, called IMC, media critic James Ledbetter suggests thinking of the old Charlie the Tuna ads, in which a cartoon fish made you chuckle and identify with the product—and established a brand name. That's not good enough for IMC. "By contrast," Ledbetter says, "IMC encourages tuna buyers to think about all aspects of the product. If polls find that consumers are worried about dolphins caught in tuna nets, then you might stick a big "Dolphin Safe" label on the tins and set up a web site featuring interviews with tuna fishermen. The new wave of IMC, according to one of its primary texts, is "respectful, not patronizing; dialogue-seeking, not monologuic; responsive, not formula-driven. It speaks to the highest point of common interest—not the lowest common denominator."

As advertising has shifted toward IMC, ad agencies have acquired or created public relations divisions or subsidiaries to provide a wide range of the services under one roof.

> **integrated marketing communication**
> Comprehensive program that links public relations, advertising.
>
> **institutional advertising**
> Paid space and time to promote institution's image, position.

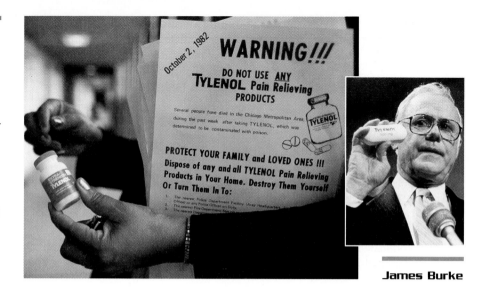

James Burke

Product-Tampering Crisis. When cyanide-laced Tylenol capsules killed seven people in Chicago, the manufacturer, Johnson & Johnson, responded quickly. Company President James Burke immediately pulled the product off retailers' shelves and ordered company publicists to set up a press center to answer news media inquiries as fully as possible. Burke's action and candor helped restore the public's shaken confidence in Tylenol, and the product resumed its significant market share after the crisis ended. It turned out that it had been a crazy person outside Johnson & Johnson's production and distribution system who had contaminated the capsules rather than a manufacturing lapse.

media relations

(STUDY PREVIEW) Public relations people generally favor candor in working with the news media. Even so, some organizations opt to stonewall journalistic inquiries. An emerging school of thought in public relations is to challenge negative news coverage aggressively and publicly.

open media relations

The common wisdom among public relations people today is to be open and candid with the mass media. It is a principle that dates to Ivy Lee, and case studies abound to confirm its effectiveness. A classic case study on this point is the Tylenol crisis.

Johnson & Johnson had spent many years and millions of dollars to inspire public confidence in its product Tylenol, and by 1982 the product was the leader in a crowded field of headache remedies with 36 percent of the market. Then disaster struck. Seven people in Chicago died after taking Tylenol capsules laced with cyanide. James Burke, president of Johnson & Johnson, and Lawrence Foster, vice president for public relations, moved quickly. Within hours, Johnson & Johnson:

- Halted the manufacture and distribution of Tylenol.

- Removed Tylenol products from retailers' shelves.

- Launched a massive advertising campaign requesting people to exchange Tylenol capsules for a safe replacement.

- Summoned 50 public relations employees from Johnson & Johnson and its subsidiary companies to staff a press center to answer media and consumer questions forthrightly.

- Ordered an internal company investigation of the Tylenol manufacturing and distribution process.

- Promised full cooperation with government investigators.

- Ordered the development of tamper-proof packaging for the reintroduction of Tylenol products after the contamination problem was resolved.

Investigators determined within days that an urban terrorist had poisoned the capsules. Although the news media exonerated Johnson & Johnson of negligence, the company nonetheless had a tremendous problem: how to restore public confidence in Tylenol. Many former Tylenol users were reluctant to take a chance, and the Tylenol share of the analgesic market dropped to 6 percent.

To address the problem, Johnson & Johnson called in the Burson-Marsteller public relations agency. Burson-Marsteller recommended a media campaign to capitalize on the high marks the news media had given the company for openness during the crisis. Mailgrams went out inviting journalists to a 30-city video teleconference to hear James Burke announce the reintroduction of the product. Six-hundred reporters turned out, and Johnson & Johnson officials took their questions live.

To stir even wider attention, 7,500 **media kits** had been sent to newsrooms the day before the teleconference. The kits included a news release and a bevy of supporting materials: photographs, charts and background information.

The resulting news coverage was extensive. On average, newspapers carried 32 column inches of copy on the announcement. Network television and radio as well as local stations also afforded heavy coverage. Meanwhile, Johnson & Johnson executives, who had attended a workshop on how to make favorable television appearances, made themselves available as guests on the network morning shows and talk shows such as "Donahue" and "Nightline." At the same time, Johnson & Johnson distributed 80 million free coupons to encourage people to use Tylenol again.

The massive media-based public relations campaign worked. Within a year, Tylenol had regained 80 percent of its former market share, and today, in an increasingly crowded analgesic field, Tylenol is again the market leader with annual sales of $670 million, compared with $520 million before the cyanide crisis.

proactive media relations

Although public relations campaigns cannot control what the media say, public relations people can help shape how news media report issues by taking the initiative. In the Tylenol crisis, for example, Johnson & Johnson reacted quickly and decisively and took control of disseminating information, which, coupled with full disclosure, headed off false rumors that could have caused further damage.

Proactive Crisis Responses. A principle in crisis management is to seize leadership on the story. This involves anticipating what journalists will want to know and providing it to them before they even have time to formulate their questions. Ivy Lee did this time and again, and Johnson & Johnson did it in 1982.

For successful crisis management, public relations people need strong ongoing relationships with an organization's top officials. Otherwise, when a crisis strikes, they likely will have difficulty rounding up the kind of breaking information they need to deal effectively with the news media. During the 1991 Persian Gulf war, Pentagon spokesperson Pete Williams received high marks as a public relations person for shaping news coverage of the conflict. Williams did this by tapping his close working relationships with Defense Secretary Dick Cheney and the Joint Chiefs of Staff for information favorable to the war effort. At regular news briefings, sometimes

> **media kit**
> A packet provided news reporters to tell the story in an advantageous way.

several a day, Williams provided so much grist for the journalistic mill that reporters were overwhelmed putting it together for stories, which reduced the time available for them to go after stories on their own. The war was reported largely as the Pentagon wanted.

Ongoing Media Relationships. Good media relations cannot be forged in the fire of a crisis. Organizations that survive a crisis generally have a history of solid media relations. Their public relations staff people know reporters, editors and news directors on a first-name basis. They avoid hyping news releases on routine matters, and they work hard at earning the trust of journalists.

Many public relations people, in fact, are seasoned journalists themselves, and they understand how journalists go about their work. It is their journalistic background that made them attractive candidates for their PR jobs. Pete Williams, for example, was a television news reporter in Wyoming before making a midcareer shift to join Dick Cheney's staff in Washington when Cheney was first elected to Congress from Wyoming.

Sound Operating Principles. An underlying strength that helped see Johnson & Johnson through the Tylenol crisis was the company's credo. The credo was a written vow that Johnson & Johnson's first responsibility was to "those who use our products and services." The credo, which had been promoted in-house for years, said: "Every time a business hires, builds, sells or buys, it is acting *for the people* as well as *for itself,* and it must be prepared to accept full responsibility."

With such a sound operating principle, Johnson & Johnson's crisis response was, in some respects, almost reflexive. Going silent, for example, would have run counter to the principles that Johnson & Johnson people had accepted as part of their corporate culture for years.

ambivalence in media relations

Despite the advantages of open media relations, there are companies that choose not to embrace that approach. The business magazine *Fortune* has listed these major corporations as notorious for not even returning phone calls from journalists:

- Amerada Hess, the huge crude oil and natural gas company.

- Winn-Dixie, the Southern supermarket chain.

- Texas Instruments, the semiconductor company.

Some corporations take a middle ground, currying media coverage selectively. Giant IBM, which receives 30,000 media queries a year, frets that news coverage would underscore its sheer size and invite federal antitrust scrutiny. IBM turns away questions on many issues, including the company's long-term planning. The corporation's PR chief, Seth McCormick, spurns Ivy Lee's maxim that corporate executives should be "on display." In an interview, McCormick told *Fortune:* "We control what is said about the company through the sparsity of heads for the outside world to talk to. We like it that way."

Procter & Gamble is another major U.S. company that generally is tight-lipped about how it conducts its business, with the notable exception of product promotions. Another notable exception was Procter & Gamble's full-scale public relations campaign in the 1980s to squelch persistent rumors that its corporate symbol—the moon and stars—had roots in Satanism.

> **proactive media relations**
> Taking initiative to release information.
> **ambivalent media relations**
> Mix of proactive, reactive and inactive media contacts.

Herb Schmertz

adversarial public relations

Public relations took on aggressive, even feisty tactics when Mobil Oil decided in the 1970s not to take media criticism lightly any more. **Herb Schmertz,** vice president for Mobil's public affairs, charted a new course by:

- Filing formal complaints with news organizations when coverage was unfair in the company's view.

- Taking Mobil's case directly to the general public with paid advertising, *advertorials* as they are called, a splicing of the words "advertising" and "editorial," that explained the company's views.

- Sending corporate representatives on media tours to spread Mobil's side to as many constituencies as possible.

Schmertz's energetic counterattacks were a departure from conventional wisdom in public relations, which was to let criticism go unanswered or, at most, to complain privately to executives of news organizations about negative coverage as unwarranted. The conventional wisdom was that a public response would only bring more attention to the negative coverage.

In abandoning passivity, Mobil was adapting what sports fans call the Red Auerbach technique. Auerbach, the legendary coach of the Boston Celtics, was known for criticizing referees. He realized he would never get a ref to change a call, but he believed that refs would be less inclined to make questionable calls against the Celtics in the future if they knew that Auerbach would jump all over them. Mobil President Rawleigh Warner Jr. explained the new Mobil policy this way: "People know that if they take a swipe at us, we will fight back."

> **adversarial public relations**
> Attacking critics openly.
> **Herb Schmertz**
> Pioneered advertorials.
> **advertorials**
> Paid advertisements that state an editorial position.

Schmertz employed the full range of PR tools in 1974 when ABC aired a television documentary that raised critical questions about the U.S. oil industry. Mobil objected first to ABC and then fired off a formal complaint to the National News Council, a volunteer media watchdog group. Mobil claimed 32 inaccuracies and instances of unfairness and requested that the council investigate. Mobil also issued an unusually lengthy news release, quoting from the documentary and offering point-by-point rebuttals.

Six Mobil executives were given a crash course on giving good interviews and sent out to meet the news media. In two years, the executives and other Mobil representatives appeared on 365 television and 211 radio shows and talked with 80 newspaper reporters. Schmertz encouraged them to take the offensive. To counter the ABC impression that the oil industry still engaged in the bad practices of its past, Schmertz told executives to stress that such information was outdated. "Put the shoe on the other foot," he said, advising the Mobil executives to say the impression left by the ABC documentary was "comparable to Mobil's producing a documentary about today's television industry and pointing to a 1941 FCC decree requiring RCA to rid itself of one of its networks as evidence of a current conspiracy."

Advertorials were part of Mobil's initiatives. Under Schmertz, as much as $6 million a year went into newspaper and magazine ads, explaining the company's position. Mobil also began producing its own television programs on energy issues and providing them free to stations. The programs had a journalistic tone, and many stations ran them as if they were actual documentaries rather than part of Mobil's media campaign.

The jury is still out on whether Schmertz's aggressive sparring is good policy. Most organizations continue to follow the traditional thinking that taking on the media only generates more attention on the original bad news. On the other hand, Schmertz's approach has been tried by some major corporations. Bechtel, Illinois Power and Kaiser Aluminum all have called for independent investigations of stories that reflected badly on them.

Another adversarial approach, although not recommended by most public relations people, is for an offended organization to sever relations with the source of unfavorable news—an **information boycott**. In 1954, in a spectacular pout, General Motors cut off contact with *Wall Street Journal* reporters and withdrew advertising from the newspaper. This approach carries great risks:

- By going silent, an organization loses avenues for conveying its message to mass audiences.

- An organization that yanks advertising to punish detractors is perceived negatively for coercively wielding its economic might.

- An organization that quits advertising in an effective advertising medium will lose sales.

A boycott differs from Schmertz's adversarial approach in an important respect. Schmertz responds to negative news by contributing to the exchange of information and ideas, which is positive in a democratic society. An information boycott, on the other hand, restricts the flow of information. Today, GM's policy has returned to the conventional wisdom of not arguing with anyone who buys paper by the ton and ink by the barrel with the exception of its suit against NBC for faking the explosion of a GMC truck.

information boycott
Severing ties with news media.

professionalization

(STUDY PREVIEW) Public relations has a tarnished image that stems from shortsighted promotion and whitewashing techniques of the late 1800s. While some dubious practices continue, PR leaders are working to improve standards.

a tarnished image

Unsavory elements in the heritage of public relations remain a heavy burden. P. T. Barnum, whose name became synonymous with hype, attracted crowds to his stunts and shows in the late 1800s with extravagant promises. Sad to say, some promoters still use Barnum's tactics. The claims for snake oils and elixirs from Barnum's era live on in commercials for pain relievers and cold remedies. The early response of tycoons to muckraking attacks, before Ivy Lee came along, was **whitewashing**—covering up the abuses but not correcting them. It is no wonder that the term "PR" sometimes is used derisively. To say something is "all PR" means it lacks substance. Of people whose apparent positive qualities are a mere façade, it may be said that they have "good PR."

Although journalists rely heavily on public relations people for information, many journalists look at PR practitioners with suspicion. Not uncommon among seasoned journalists are utterances like: "I've never met a PR person I couldn't distrust." Such cynicism flows partly from the journalists' self-image as unfettered truth-seekers whose only obligation is serving their audiences' needs. PR people, on the other hand, are seen as obligated to their employers, whose interests do not always dovetail with the public good. Behind their backs, PR people are called "flaks," a takeoff on the World War II slang for antiaircraft bursts intended to stop enemy bombers. PR **flakkers,** as journalists use the term, interfere with journalistic truth-seeking by putting forth slanted, self-serving information, which is not necessarily the whole story.

The journalism-PR tension is exacerbated by a common newsroom view that PR people try to get free news hole space for their messages rather than buy airtime and column inches. This view may seem strange considering that 50 to 90 percent of all news stories either originate with or contain information supplied by PR people. It is also strange considering that many PR people are former news reporters and editors. No matter how uncomfortable PR people and journalists are as bedfellows, they are bedfellows nonetheless.

Some public relations people have tried to leapfrog the negative baggage attached to the term "PR" by abandoning it. The U.S. military shucked "PR" and tried **public information,** but it found itself still dogged by the same distrust that surrounded "public relations." The military then tried *public affairs,* but that was no solution either. Many organizations have tried *communication* as a way around the problem. Common labels today include the military's current *public affairs* offices and businesses' *corporate communication* departments.

standards and certification

The Public Relations Society of America, which has grown to 12,000 members, has a different approach: improving the quality of public relations work, whatever

media online

Hill & Knowlton: At this Web site, Hill & Knowlton details its international services. These include crisis and issue management, business-to-business communication, media relations, research, design, event management, and sponsorship. www.100.nmius.com/index.html

whitewash
Cover-up.

flakkers
Derisive word for public relations people.

public information
Among alternate words for public relations; others are public affairs, corporate communication.

professionalization **309**

edward bernays

After graduation from college in 1912, Edward Bernays tried press agentry. He was good at it, landing free publicity for whoever would hire him. Soon his bosses included famous tenor Enrico Caruso and actor Otis Skinner. Bernays felt, however, that his success was tainted by the disdain in which press agents were held in general. He also saw far greater potential for affecting public opinion than his fellow press agents. From Bernays' discomfort and vision was born the concept of modern public relations. His 1923 book, *Crystallizing Public Opinion,* outlined a new craft he called public relations.

Bernays saw good public relations as counsel to clients. He called the public relations practitioner a "special pleader." The concept was modeled partly on the long-established lawyer-client relationship in which the lawyer, or counselor, suggests courses of actions. Because of his seminal role in defining what public relations is, Bernays sometimes is called the "Father of PR," although some people say the honor should be shared with Ivy Lee.

No matter, there is no question of Bernays' ongoing contributions. He taught the first course in public relations in 1923 at New York University. Bernays encouraged firm methodology in public relations, a notion captured in the title of a book he edited in 1955: *The Engineering of Consent.* He long advocated the professionalization of the field,

which laid the groundwork for the accreditation of the sort the Public Relations Society of America has developed.

Throughout his career, Bernays stressed that public relations people need a strong sense of responsibility. In one reflective essay, he wrote:

"Public relations practiced as a profession is an art applied to a science in which the public interest and not pecuniary motivation is the primary consideration. The engineering of consent in this sense assumes a constructive social role. Regrettably, public relations, like other professions, can be abused and used for anti-social purposes. I have tried to make the profession socially responsible as well as economically viable."

Edward Bernays. Integrity was important to public relations pioneer Edward Bernays. When he was asked by agents of fascist dictators Francisco Franco and Adolf Hitler to improve their images in the United States, he said no. "I wouldn't do for money what I wouldn't do without money," Bernays said.

Bernays became the Grand Old Man of public relations, still attending PRSA and other professional meetings past his 100th birthday. He died in 1993 at age 102.

APR
Indicates PRSA accreditation.
IABC
Professional public relations organization.
PRSSA
Student public relations organization.

the label. In 1951, the association adopted a code of professional standards. In a further professionalization step in 1965, PRSA established a certification process. Those who meet the criteria and pass exams are allowed to place **APR,** which stands for accredited public relations professional, after their names. The criteria are:

- Being recommended by an already accredited PRSA member.

- Five years of professional experience.

- Passing an eight-hour written examination on public relations principles, techniques, history and ethics.

- Passing an oral exam conducted by three professionals.

The process is rigorous. Typically, a third of those who attempt the examination fail it the first time. Once earned, certification needs to be renewed through continuing education, and the right to use "APR" can be taken away if a member violates the PRSA code. About 3,800 PRSA members hold APR certification.

The PRSA set of professional standards, intended to encourage a high level of practice, says a member shall:

- Deal fairly with clients or employees, past, present or potential; with fellow practitioners; and with the general public.

- Conduct his or her professional life in accord with the public interest.

- Adhere to truth and accuracy and to generally accepted standards of good taste.

- Not engage in any practice that tends to corrupt the integrity of channels of communication or the process of government.

- Not intentionally communicate false or misleading information.

PRSA is not alone in encouraging the practice of public relations at a high level. The **International Association of Business Communicators,** with 125 chapters, also keeps dialogue going on professional issues with seminars and conferences. Some professional groups are highly specialized, like the Library Public Relations Council, the Bank Marketing Association and the Religious PR Council. The International Public Relations Association, with members in 60 countries, sponsors the World Congress of Public Relations every third year. The student arm of PRSA, the **Public Relations Student Society of America,** works through 145 campus chapters at improving standards.

chapter wrap-up

When Ivy Lee hung up a shingle in New York for a new publicity agency in 1906, he wanted to distance himself from the huckstering that marked most publicity at the time. To do that, Lee issued a declaration of principles for the new agency and sent it out to editors. Today, Lee's declaration remains a classic statement on the practice of public relations. It promised that the agency would deal only in legitimate news about its clients, and no fluff. It invited journalists to pursue more information about the agency's clients. It also vowed to be honest and accurate.

Here's Lee's declaration: "This is not a secret press bureau. All our work is done in the open. We aim to supply news. This is not an advertising agency; if you think any of our matter ought properly to go to your business office, do not use it. Our matter is accurate. Further details on any subject treated will be supplied promptly, and any editor will be assisted most cheerfully in verifying directly any statement of fact. Upon inquiry, full information will be given to any editor concerning those on whose behalf an article is sent out. In brief, our plan is, frankly and openly, on behalf of the business concerns and public institutions, to supply to the press and the public of the United States prompt and accurate information concerning subjects which are of value and interest to the public to know about."

The declaration hangs in many public relations shops today.

questions for review

1. What is public relations? How is public relations connected to the mass media?

2. Why did big business become interested in the techniques and principles of public relations beginning in the late 1800s?

3. How is public relations a management tool?

4. What is the range of activities in which public relations people are involved?

5. What kind of relationship do most people strive to have with the mass media?

6. Why does public relations have a bad image? What are public relations professionals doing about it?

questions for critical thinking

1. When Ivy Lee accepted the Pennsylvania Railroad as a client in 1906, he saw the job as "interpreting the Pennsylvania Railroad to the public and interpreting the public to the Pennsylvania Railroad." Compare Lee's point with Arthur Page's view of public relations as a management function.

2. How are public relations practitioners trying to overcome the complaints from journalists that they are flakkers interfering with an unfettered pursuit of truth?

3. What was the contribution of the Committee on Public Information, usually called the Creel Committee, to public relations after World War I?

4. How do public relations agencies turn profits?

5. When does an institution with its own in-house public relations operation need to hire a PR agency?

6. Explain the concept of enlightened self-interest.

7. How did the confluence of the following three phenomena at the turn of the century contribute to the emergence of modern public relations?

   • The related concepts of social Darwinism, a social theory; laissez-faire, a government philosophy; and paternalism, a practice of business.

   • Muckraking, which attacked prevalent abuses of the public interest.

   • Advertising, which had grown since the 1830s as a way to reach great numbers of people.

8. Showman P. T. Barnum epitomized 19th-century press agentry with extravagant claims, like promoting the midget Tom Thumb as a Civil War general. To attract crowds to a tour by an unknown European soprano, Jenny Lind, Barnum labeled her "the Swedish Nightingale." Would such promotional methods work today? Keep in mind that Barnum, explaining his methods, once said, "There's a sucker born every minute."

for further learning

Scott M. Cutlip. *The Unseen Power: Public Relations—A History* (Erlbaum, 1994). Cutlip, a pioneer in public relations education, integrates the history of public relations in the larger scheme of U.S. life in this definitive, 800-page work.

Scott M. Cutlip, Allen H. Center and Glen M. Broom. *Effective Public Relations,* 7th edition (Prentice Hall, 1994). This widely used introductory textbook touches all bases.

James E. Grunig, editor. *Excellence in Public Relations and Communications Management* (Erlbaum, 1992). This 660-page volume, based on a comprehensive study of the profession, offers insights for anyone considering a public relations career.

Ray Eldon Hiebert. *Courtier to the Crowd: The Story of Ivy Lee and the Development of Public Relations* (Iowa State University Press, 1966). Professor Hiebert's flattering biography focuses on the enduring public relations principles articulated, if not always practiced, by Ivy Lee.

George S. McGovern and Leonard F. Guttridge. *The Great Coalfield War* (Houghton Mifflin, 1972). This account of the Ludlow Massacre includes the success of the Ivy Lee–inspired campaign to rescue the Rockefeller reputation but is less than enthusiastic about Lee's corporate-oriented perspective and sometimes shoddy fact gathering.

Lael M. Moynihan. "Horrendous PR Crises: What They Did When the Unthinkable Happened." *Media History Digest* (Spring-Summer 1988). Pages 19–25. Moynihan, a consumer relations specialist, details eight major cases of crisis management through proven public relations principles.

Herbert Schmertz and William Novak. *Good-bye to the Low Profile: The Art of Creative Confrontation* (Little, Brown, 1986). Combative Herb Schmertz passes on the lessons he learned as Mobil Oil's innovative public relations chief, including how-tos for advertorials and preparation of executives for interviews with journalists.

for keeping up to date

The trade journal *O'Dwyer's PR Services* tracks the industry on a monthly basis.

Other sources of ongoing information are *Public Relations Journal, Public Relations Quarterly* and *Public Relations Review.*

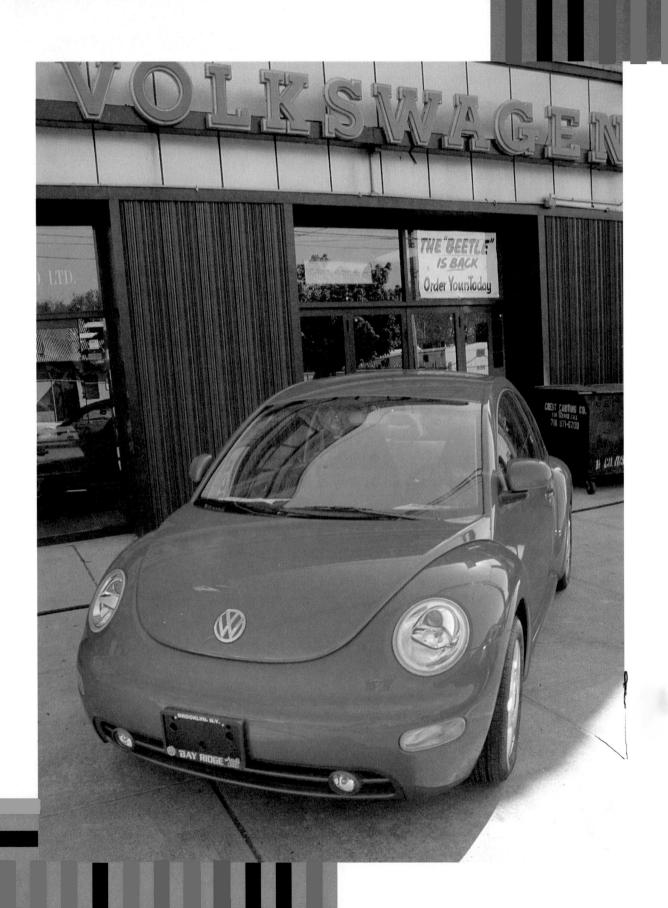

12
advertising

in this chapter you will learn:

- Advertising is a keystone in a consumer economy, a democracy and the mass media.

- Most advertising messages are carried through the mass media.

- Advertising agencies create and place ads for advertisers.

- Advertisements are placed with care in media to reach appropriate audiences for advertised products and services.

- Advertising tactics include brand names, lowest common denominators, positioning and redundancy.

- Advertising uses psychology to tap audience interests.

- Globalization of the advertising industry has created opportunities and problems.

- Advertising messages have shifted from a "buyer beware" to a "seller beware" sensitivity.

- Advertising people need to solve problems created by ad clutter and creative excesses.

When Volkswagen introduced the new Beetle in March 1998, one of its ads asked, "Is it possible to go backwards and forwards at the same time?" The question could apply to the advertising campaign behind the ad as well as to the car it promoted. Could a modern campaign live up to the classic VW ads of an earlier period?

Arnold Communications, the Boston-based agency that won the coveted Volkswagen of America advertising account in 1995, is out to demonstrate a "yes" answer to that question. The agency had wowed the Volkswagen executives with an integrated theme to be used throughout VW's entire line of cars. The ad campaign would target active, independent, energetic, younger, technology-minded people—people who kept abreast of new developments and liked innovation and fun.

The campaign's unifying motif was the brainchild of Ron Lawner, Arnold Communication's chief creative officer and one of the agency's managing partners. Lawner divided people into two categories: drivers and passengers. It was an overly simplistic dichotomy, but it worked. Drivers were people who found it exciting to be at the wheel, who enjoyed the sense of control and power as a car spun around a curve or zipped along an expressway. Passengers were people who went along for the ride. Volkswagen cars were built for drivers. The theme of the ad campaign would be "Drivers wanted."

The idea was to create understated presentations without a lot of verbiage. More show, less tell. As one example, rather than talking about a car's horsepower, one TV commercial featured a horse farm. When a champion breeder whistles, he is followed by VW Golfs and Jettas. They nudge him gently as he holds up a gas can for feeding time; one of them is soaped down to keep its coat "clean and glossy." The cars race around as the breeder talks about their need for exercise and comments on their happiness, which shows up in "the gleam in their daytime running lights." The VW logo comes on with the words, "Drivers wanted." The announcer mentions the two classes of people on the road of life: passengers and drivers. The commercial ends with the horse breeder

asking viewers if they wouldn't "just like to take one home?"

This clever, offbeat, story-telling approach is in the tradition of the advertising campaign that Bill Bernbach and his agency developed for Volkswagen three decades earlier. According to a Boston *Globe* article, Ron Lawner considers the Doyle Dane Bernbach Volkswagen campaign of the 1960s and 1970s to be "one of the best two or three advertising campaigns ever done in the world." That opinion is shared by many others, who consider Bernbach's honest, creative, soft-sell and humorous approach to have given a new look to advertising.

Advertising Age named a Doyle Dane Bernbach Volkswagen commercial as one of the 50 best commercials of the past half-century. Aired during the early 1970s, it showed a funeral procession entering a cemetery. The voice-over is that of a deceased wealthy tycoon reading his will, which leaves virtually nothing to his wife, sons and partner, who are riding in limousines and accustomed to opulence. After rebuking them for their lavish lifestyles, he announces that his "entire fortune of $100 billion dollars" will go to his nephew, who is seen driving a VW Beetle. Such commercials are remem-

bered many years later. And, like sales, recall is an important gauge of an advertisement's effectiveness. Recalling an advertisement indicates its message has gotten through and is likely to be talked about and perhaps acted upon.

One of the 1997 commercials produced by the Arnold Communications team also seems to be earning itself a spot in viewer's memories. Immediately after it ran, people began talking about it. The Volkswagen toll-free number and its web site were inundated with comments from people saying how much they liked the commercial. The demand was so great for the music (a song called "You Don't Love Me; Da, Da, Da," recorded in 1982 by the German group Trio) that Mercury Records re-released it and included a scene from the Volkswagen commercial on the CD case.

The commercial was a simple one, two guys in their early 20s just driving around on a Sunday afternoon in a VW Golf. There is no dialogue, only the music from the car's radio. They pick up an old discarded armchair, open the hatchback and load it into the car (subtly illustrating the Golf's roominess and the hatchback feature). But after driving a short distance, they notice the chair has an odd odor. They stop, open the

car's hatchback again and unload the smelly armchair on another corner. The announcer says, "The German-engineered Volkswagen Golf. It fits your life, or your complete lack thereof."

The commercial was not only chosen to receive top honors in the 17th Annual Best of Broadcasting awards ceremony, it also drew attention for another reason. Its first airing was during the episode of ABC's "Ellen" in which she revealed her lesbian orientation. A number of advertisers had chosen not to run commercials during this episode. To those who raised questions about Volkswagen's willingness to be associated with a program considered controversial by many, a spokesperson for Arnold Communications pointed out that Volkswagen was a "cool, progressive company" that was not into prejudice and that, furthermore, people living in alternative lifestyles also earn income and buy cars. The commercial was saying nothing one way or the other about the young men's relationship.

The special challenge of moving backward (to the earlier Bernbach touch) in order to go forward with the new campaign was especially evident as the creative Arnold team worked on the print ads and commercials for the

1998 redesigned Beetle after 19 Beetleless years.

The original Beetle was first introduced into the United States in 1949 and sales got off to an extremely slow start, largely because of an awareness that it had been designed in the 1930s under Hitler's orders for an affordable family car. Bernbach was Jewish, yet it was his unique creativity and vision that helped the Beetle achieve the status of a cultural icon somehow dissociated from its Nazi past. One of the basic tenets of Bernbach's advertising philosophy was to know the product and let the product tell its own story in a simple, honest, persuasive way. His funny ads, such as "Think Small," or one with a picture of a Beetle labeled "Lemon" (because of a blemished chrome strip on the glove compartment), are remembered to this day.

Building upon that memory, the Arnold team has one ad showing a green new Beetle with the headline, "Lime." Other Arnold ads also blend a celebration of the new with a nostalgic look at the old, hoping to appeal to the generation that fell in love with the Beetle during the 1960s and 1970s. Unlike the original model, the new Beetle has its engine in the front "but its heart is in the same place," says one ad. A television commercial shows the peppy new Beetle demonstrating "less flower, more power." Some ads emphasize the new Beetle's cuteness qualities, which caused some owners to think of their Beetles almost as pets rather than as vehicles. Thus the question: "Hug it? Drive it?" But in spite of some "nods to the past," said Ron Lawner in a New York *Times* interview, this is "a very contemporary campaign for a very modern car." A number of ads therefore also target a technologically sophisticated younger generation. But the main point stressed by Lawner is very much in keeping with the philosophy of Bernbach decades earlier. "The car is the star," Lawner insists and "speaks for itself."

What does it say? No doubt Lawner would answer, "Drivers Wanted."

importance of advertising

(STUDY PREVIEW)   Advertising is key in a consumer economy. Without it, people would have a hard time even knowing what products and services are available. Advertising, in fact, is essential to a prosperous society. Advertising also is the financial basis of important contemporary mass media.

consumer economies

Advertising is a major component of modern economies. In the United States, the best estimates are that advertisers spend about 2 percent of the gross domestic product to promote their wares. When the nation's production of goods and services is up, so is advertising spending. When production falters, as it did in the early 1990s, many manufacturers, distributors and retailers pull back their advertising expenditures.

The essential role of advertising in a modern consumer economy is obvious if you think about how people decide what to buy. If a shoe manufacturer were unable to tout the virtues of its footwear by advertising in the mass media, people would have a hard time learning about the product, let alone knowing whether it is what they want.

advertising and prosperity

Advertising's phenomenal continuing growth has been a product of a plentiful society. In a poor society with a shortage of goods, people line up for necessities like food and clothing. Advertising has no role and serves no purpose when survival is the question. With prosperity, however, people have not only discretionary income

Here are the biggest-spending advertisers in the United States. One way to put these figures in everyday terms is to think about the percentage of the price of products that is spent on advertising. Procter & Gamble, for example, spends about $1 on advertising for every $6.70 in sales. Looked at another way, 25 cents of the $1.69 you spend for a tube of Procter & Gamble toothpaste goes into advertising.

Procter & Gamble	$2.6 billion
General Motors	2.4 billion
Philip Morris	2.3 billion
Chrysler	1.4 billion
Time Warner	1.4 billion
Sears, Roebuck	1.3 billion
Walt Disney	1.3 billion
PepsiCo	1.3 billion
Grand Metropolitan	1.3 billion
Ford	1.2 billion

but also a choice of ways to spend it. Advertising is the vehicle that provides information and rationales to help them decide how to enjoy their prosperity.

Besides being a product of economic prosperity, advertising contributes to prosperity. By dangling desirable commodities and services before mass audiences, advertising can inspire people to greater individual productivity, so that they can have more income to buy the things that are advertised.

Advertising also can introduce efficiency into the economy by allowing comparison shopping without in-person inspections of all the alternatives. Efficiencies also can result when advertising alerts consumers to superior and less costly products and services, which displace outdated, outmoded and inefficient offerings.

Said Howard Morgens when he was president of Procter & Gamble: "Advertising is the most effective and efficient way to sell to the consumer. If we should ever find better methods of selling our type of products to the consumer, we'll leave advertising and turn to these other methods." Veteran advertising executive David Ogilvy made the point this way: "Advertising is still the cheapest form of selling. It would cost you $25,000 to have salesmen call on a thousand homes. A television commercial can do it for $4.69." McGraw-Hill, which publishes trade magazines, has offered research that a salesperson's typical call costs $178, a letter $6.63, and a phone call $6.35. For 17 cents, says McGraw-Hill, an advertiser can reach a prospect through advertising. Although advertising does not close a sale for all products, it introduces products and makes the salesperson's job easier and quicker.

advertising and democracy

Advertising first took off as a modern phenomenon in the United States, which has given rise to a theory that advertising and democracy are connected. This theory notes that Americans, early in their history as a democracy, were required by their political system to hold individual opinions. They looked for information so that they could evaluate their leaders and vote on public policy. This emphasis on individuality and reason paved the way for advertising: Just as Americans looked to the mass media for information on political matters, they also came to look to the media for information on buying decisions.

In authoritarian countries, on the other hand, people tend to look to strong personal leaders, not reason, for ideas to embrace. This, according to the theory, diminishes the demand for information in these nondemocracies, including the kind of information provided by advertising.

Advertising has another important role in democratic societies in generating most of the operating revenue for newspapers, magazines, television and radio. Without advertising, many of the media on which people rely for information, for entertainment and for the exchange of ideas on public issues would not exist as we know them.

origins of advertising

(STUDY PREVIEW) Advertising is the product of great forces that have shaped modern society, beginning with Gutenberg's movable type, which made mass-produced messages possible. Without the mass media, there would be no vehicle to carry advertisements to mass audiences. Advertising also is a product of the democratic experience; of the Industrial Revolution and its spin-offs, including vast transportation networks and mass markets; and of continuing economic growth.

stepchild of technology

Advertising is not a mass medium, but it relies on media to carry its messages. **Johannes Gutenberg**'s movable type, which permitted mass production of the printed word, made mass-produced advertising possible. First came flyers, then advertisements as newspapers and magazines were introduced. In the 1800s, when technology created high-speed presses that could produce enough copies for larger audiences, advertising used them to expand markets. With the introduction of radio, advertisers learned how to use electronic communication. Then came television.

Flyers were the first form of printed advertising. The British printer **William Caxton** issued the first printed advertisement in 1468 to promote one of his books. In America, publisher **John Campbell** of the Boston *News-Letter* ran the first advertisement in 1704, a notice from somebody wanting to sell an estate on Long Island. Colonial newspapers listed cargo arriving from Europe and invited readers to come, look and buy.

industrial revolution

The genius of **Benjamin Day**'s New York *Sun,* in 1833 the first penny newspaper, was that it recognized and exploited so many changes spawned by the Industrial Revolution. Steam-powered presses made large press runs possible. Factories drew great numbers of people to jobs within geographically small areas to which newspapers could be distributed quickly. The jobs also drew immigrants who were eager to learn—

Johannes Gutenberg
Progenitor of advertising media.

William Caxton
Printed first advertisement.

John Campbell
First ad in British colonies.

Benjamin Day
Penny newspaper brought advertising to new level.

1468 William Caxton promoted book with first printed advertisement.

1704 Joseph Campbell included advertisements in Boston *News-Letter*.

1833 Benjamin Day created New York *Sun* as combination news and advertising vehicle.

1869 Wayland Ayer opened first advertising agency, Philadelphia.

1890s Brand names emerged as advertising technique.

1903 New York Legislature barred unauthorized commercial exploitation.

1910 Edward Bok of *Ladies' Home Journal* established magazine advertising code.

1914 Congress created Federal Trade Commission

to combat unfair advertising.

1929 NBC established code of acceptable advertising.

1942 Media industries created predecessor to Ad Council.

1950s Ernest Dichter pioneered motivational research.

1950s David Ogilvy devised brand imaging technique.

1950s Jack Trout devised positioning technique.

1957 James Vicary claimed success for subliminal advertising.

1960s Rosser Reeves devised unique selling proposition technique.

from newspapers as well as other sources—about their adopted country. Industrialization, coupled with the labor union movement, created unprecedented wealth, giving even laborers a share of the new prosperity. A consumer economy was emerging, although it was primitive by today's standards.

A key to the success of Day's *Sun* was that, at a penny a copy, it was affordable for almost everyone. Of course, Day's production expenses exceeded a penny a copy. Just as the commercial media do today, Day looked to advertisers to pick up the slack. As Day wrote in his first issue: "The object of this paper is to lay before the public, at a price within the means of everyone, all the news of the day, and at the same time afford an advantageous medium for advertising." Day and imitator penny press publishers sought larger and larger circulations, knowing that merchants would see the value in buying space to reach so much buying power.

National advertising took root in the 1840s as railroads, another creation of the Industrial Revolution, spawned new networks for mass distribution of manufactured goods. National brands developed, and their producers looked to magazines, also delivered by rail, to promote sales. By 1869 the rail network linked the Atlantic and Pacific coasts.

pioneer agencies

By 1869 most merchants recognized the value of advertising, but they grumbled about the time it took away from their other work. In that grumbling, a young Philadelphia man sensed opportunity. **Wayland Ayer,** age 20, speculated that merchants, and even national manufacturers, would welcome a service company to help them create advertisements and place them in publications. Ayer feared, however, that his idea might not be taken seriously by potential clients because of his youth and

Wayland Ayer
Founded first ad agency.

creative director
Key person in ad campaigns.

account executives
Agency reps to clients.

media buyers
Decide where to place ads.

inexperience. So when Wayland Ayer opened a shop, he borrowed his father's name for the shingle. The father was never part of the business, but the agency's name, N. W. Ayer & Son, gave young Ayer access to potential clients, and the first advertising agency was born. The Ayer agency not only created ads but also offered the array of services that agencies still offer clients today:

- Counsel on selling products and services.
- Design services, that is, actually creating advertisements and campaigns.
- Expertise on placing advertisements in advantageous media.

advertising agencies

⬤●●●●● (STUDY PREVIEW) Central in modern advertising are the agencies that create and place ads on behalf of their clients. These agencies are generally funded by the media in which they place ads. In effect, this makes agency services free to advertisers.

agency structure

Full-service advertising agencies conduct market research for their clients, design and produce advertisements and choose the media in which the advertisement will run. The 500 leading U.S. agencies employ 120,000 people worldwide. In the United States, they employ about 73,000. The responsibilities of people who work at advertising agencies fall into these broad categories:

Creativity. This category includes copywriters, graphics experts and layout people. These creative people generally report to **creative directors,** art directors and copy supervisors.

Liaison. Most of these people are **account executives,** who work with clients. Account executives are responsible for understanding clients' needs, communicating those needs to the creative staff and going back to clients with the creative staff's ideas.

Buying. Agency employees called **media buyers** determine the most effective media in which to place ads and then place them.

Research. Agency research staffs generate information on target consumer groups, data that can guide the creative and media staffs.

MILK
Where's your mustache?

Mustache Success. Something happened to reverse declining U.S. milk consumption in 1995, and the milk industry thinks it was the Bozell agency's mustache campaign. The industry's promotion board doubled spending on the campaign, to $110 million the next year, and Bozell signed up more celebrities, like Spike Lee. Bozell's Joel Kushins was named *Advertising Age* magazine's Media Maven of the Year for putting humor in a campaign for a mundane commodity product.

largest advertising agencies

Here are the largest global advertising agencies ranked by their annual income.

Agency	Headquarters	Annual Income
WWP Group	London	$2.8 billion
Interpublic	New York	2.0 billion
Omnicom	New York	1.8 billion
Saatchi & Saatchi	London	1.7 billion
Dentsu	Tokyo	1.4 billion
Young & Rubicam	New York	1.0 billion
Euro RSCG	Paris	1.0 billion
Grey	New York	700 million
Foote, Cone & Belding	Chicago	700 million
Hakuhodo	Tokyo	700 million

commission system
Agencies bill clients 15 percent more than media charge for time and space.

Many agencies also employ technicians and producers who turn ideas into camera-ready proofs, color plates, videotape and film and audio cartridges, although a lot of production work is contracted to specialty companies. Besides full-service agencies, there are creative boutiques, which specialize in preparing messages; media buying houses, which recommend strategy on placing ads; and other narrowly focused agencies.

agency compensation

Advertising agencies generally earn 15 percent of what their clients spend to buy space and time. An agency that can land a mega-account, like Procter & Gamble, which spends almost $3 billion a year, can realize $450 million in revenue. That isn't all gravy, however. Agencies have significant overhead, and the cost of producing a spectacular television ad can be astronomical. Also, it's worth noting, big advertisers like P&G spread their advertising among many agencies.

Commissions. The 15 percent **commission system** is rooted in an old magazine and newspaper practice. Knowing agencies were influential in deciding where advertisements were placed, publications offered them 15 percent discounts. A newspaper that listed $100 per column inch as its standard rate would charge agencies only $85. The agency, however, billed clients the full $100 and kept the 15 percent difference. To clients, it seemed like agency services were free. There was nothing secret about the arrangement, and it remains standard practice for most national and some local advertising.

Fees. Although in place more than 100 years, the commission system has problems. For agencies, income fluctuates with changes in ad frequency. Also, advertisers suspect agencies are self-serving when they recommend bigger campaigns. To address these problems, some agencies have gone to a **fee system.** Arrangements vary, but agencies usually bill clients for expenses as they are incurred, plus an agreed-upon percentage as profit.

Performance.   Procter & Gamble, which spends more on advertising than any other U.S. company most years, has discussed a **performance system** to compensate agencies. The company would cover only an agency's costs plus a modest profit. If a campaign strikes bonanza, then the agency shares in the treasure.

advertiser role in advertising

Most companies, although they hire agencies for advertising services, have their own advertising expertise among the in-house people who develop marketing strategies. These companies look to ad agencies to develop the advertising campaigns that will help them meet their marketing goals. For some companies, the **advertising director** is the liaison between the company's marketing strategists and the ad agency's tacticians. Large companies with many products have in-house **brand managers** for this liaison. Although it is not the usual pattern, some companies have in-house advertising departments and rely hardly at all on agencies.

placing advertisements

(STUDY PREVIEW)   The placement of advertisements is a sophisticated business. Not only do different media have inherent advantages and disadvantages in reaching potential customers, but so do individual publications and broadcast outlets.

media plans

Agencies create **media plans** to ensure that advertisements reach the right target audience. Developing a media plan is no small task. Consider the number of media outlets available: 1,400 daily newspapers in the United States alone, 8,000 weeklies, 1,200 general-interest magazines, 10,000 radio stations and 1,000 television stations. Other possibilities include direct mail, billboards, blimps, skywriting and even printing the company's name on pencils.

Media buyers use formulas, some very complex, to decide which media are best for reaching potential customers. Most of these formulas begin with a factor called **CPM,** short for cost per thousand. If airtime for a radio advertisement costs 7.2 cents per thousand listeners, it's probably a better deal than a magazine with a 7.3-cent CPM, assuming both reach the same audience. CPM by itself is just a starting point in choosing media. Other variables that media buyers consider include whether a message lends itself to a particular medium. For example, radio wouldn't work for a product that lends itself to a visual pitch and sight gags.

Media buyers have numerous sources of data to help them decide where advertisements can be placed for the best results. The **Audit Bureau of Circulations,** created by the newspaper industry in 1914, provides reliable information based on

fee system
Agencies bill clients for expenses plus add-on percentage as profit.

performance system
Agency bills for expenses and modest profit, but is rewarded extra for successful campaigns.

advertising director
Coordinates marketing and advertising.

brand manager
Coordinates marketing and advertising for specific brand.

media plan
Lays out where ads are placed.

CPM
Cost per thousand; a tool to determine cost effectiveness of different media.

Audit Bureau of Circulations
Verifies circulation claims.

shelf life
How long a periodical remains in use.
pass-along circulation
All the people who see a periodical.

independent audits of the circulation of most newspapers. Survey organizations like Nielsen and Arbitron conduct surveys on television and radio audiences. Standard Rate and Data Service publishes volumes of information on media audiences, circulations and advertising rates.

media choices

Here are the pluses and minuses of major media as advertising vehicles:

Newspapers. The hot relationship that media theorist Marshall McLuhan described between newspapers and their readers attracts advertisers. Newspaper readers are predisposed to consider information in advertisements seriously. Studies show that people, when ready to buy, look more to newspapers than to other media. Because newspapers are tangible, readers can refer back to advertisements just by picking up the paper a second time, which is not possible with ephemeral media like television and radio. Coupons are possible in newspapers. Newspaper readers tend to be older, better educated and higher earning than television and radio audiences. Space for newspaper ads usually can be reserved as late as 48 hours ahead, and 11th-hour changes are possible.

However, newspapers are becoming less valuable for reaching young adults. To the consternation of newspaper publishers, there has been an alarming drop in readership among these people in recent years, and it appears that, unlike their parents, young adults are not picking up the newspaper habit as they mature.

Another drawback to newspapers is printing on newsprint, a relatively cheap paper that absorbs ink like a slow blotter. The result is that ads do not look as good as in slick magazines. Slick, stand-alone inserts offset the newsprint drawback somewhat, but many readers pull them out and discard them first thing when they open the paper. Also, most people use their newspaper to wrap the garbage or line the bird cage within a day or so, which means that, unlike magazines, there is not much opportunity for readers to happen across an ad a second or third time.

Magazines. As another print medium, magazines have many of the advantages of newspapers, plus longer **shelf life,** an advertising term for the amount of time that an advertisement remains available to readers. Magazines remain in the home for weeks, sometimes months, which offers greater exposure to advertisements. People share magazines, which gives them high **pass-along circulation.** Magazines are more prestigious, with slick paper and splashier graphics. With precise color separations and enameled papers, magazine advertisements can be beautiful in ways that newspaper advertisements cannot. Magazines, specializing as they do, offer more narrowly defined audiences than do newspapers.

On the downside, magazines require reservations for advertising space up to three months in advance. Opportunities for last-minute changes are limited, often impossible.

Radio. Radio stations with narrow formats offer easily identified target audiences. Time can be bought on short notice, with changes possible almost until airtime. Comparatively inexpensive, radio lends itself to repeated play of advertisements to drive home a message introduced in more expensive media like television. Radio lends itself to jingles that can contribute to a lasting image.

However, radio offers no opportunity for a visual display, although the images listeners create in their minds from audio suggestions can be more potent than those set out visually on television. Radio is a mobile medium that people carry with them. The extensive availability of radio is offset, however, by the fact that people tune in and out. Another negative is that many listeners are inattentive. Also, there is no shelf life.

Television. As a moving and visual medium, television can offer unmatched impact, and the rapid growth of both network and local television advertising, far outpacing other media, indicates its effectiveness in reaching a diverse mass audience.

Drawbacks include the fact that production costs can be high. So are rates. The expense of television time has forced advertisers to go to shorter and shorter advertisements. A result is **ad clutter,** a phenomenon in which advertisements compete against each other and reduce the impact of all of them. Placing advertisements on television is a problem because demand outstrips the supply of slots, especially during prime hours. Slots for some hours are locked up months, even whole seasons, in advance. Because of the audience's diversity and size, targeting potential customers with any precision is difficult with television—with the exception of emerging narrowly focused cable services.

Online Services. Like many other newspapers in the mid-1990s, the San Jose, California *Mercury News* established a news web site on the Internet. Editors put news from the newspaper on the web site, so people with computers could pick up news online. Every time an electronic reader tapped into Mercury Center, as the Mercury's web site was dubbed, it was recorded as a **hit.** In 1995, Mercury Center was receiving 325,000 hits a day, compared with the 270,000 circulation of the newsprint product. The potential of web sites as advertising vehicles has not been lost on newspapers or other organizations, including AT&T and Microsoft, which also have established news sites online.

One advantage of online advertising is that readers can click deeper and deeper levels of information about advertised products. A lot more information can be packed into a layered online message than within the space and time confines of a print or broadcast ad. High-resolution color is standard, and the technology is available for moving pictures and audio.

Advertisers are not abandoning traditional media, but they are experimenting with online possibilities. For mail-order products, orders can be placed over the Internet right from the ad. For some groups of potential customers, online advertising has major advantages. To reach college students, almost all of whom have computer access, online advertising makes sense.

Another online advantage is cost. Because production costs are low, ad rates also can be low. One weekly college newspaper, *The Independent* at Winona State University in Minnesota, cut production costs from $2,400 to $75 a month by going online as the *CyberIndee.* Advertisers who had paid $300 a month for quarter-page ads in the newsprint edition found themselves paying only $50 for online ads.

The downside of web-site advertising is that the Internet is accessible only to people with computers, modems and online subscriptions. Of course, the percentage of the computer-knowledgeable population is mushrooming and will continue to do so.

alternative media

The leading 100 U.S. advertisers put $52.1 billion into ads in 1996—a 10.4 percent increase from the year before. There had been similar increases in previous years. Yet the national advertising dollars to the traditional media, magazines, newspapers,

ad clutter
So many competing ads that all lose impact.
online services
Provide messages to computers.
hit
A recorded viewing of an online site.

radio and television hasn't been keeping pace. Where is the leakage? To follow fragmenting audiences, advertisers have moved into alternative media for reaching potential customers.

Every city has a business magazine, none of which by itself puts much of a dint into national magazine or local newspaper advertising, but they lure some dollars. The continuing growth in gay newspaper advertising, up almost 20 percent in 1996, was hardly missed by the giant media, but it contributed to a further division of the advertising pie. The Spanish-language television networks Univison and Telemundo, as well as local stations and Spanish radio, newspapers and magazines, brought in $1.2 billion in 1996. Direct-mail advertising sidesteps traditional media entirely, with advertisers making direct contact with potentiual customers. In the first quarter of 1997, advertisers paid $133 million for World Wide Web advertising—six times a year earlier.

All tolled, alternative media have taken a chunk away from traditional major media.

pitching messages

(STUDY PREVIEW) When the age of mass production and mass markets arrived, common wisdom in advertising favored aiming at the largest possible audience of potential customers. These are called lowest common denominator approaches, and such advertisements tend to be heavy-handed, so that no one can possibly miss the point. Narrower pitches, going for segments of the mass audience, permit more deftness, subtlety and imagination.

importance of brands

A challenge for advertising people is the modern-day reality that mass-produced products aimed at large markets are essentially alike: Toothpaste is toothpaste is toothpaste. When a product is virtually identical to the competition, how can one toothpaste-maker move more tubes?

Brand Names.   By trial and error, tactics were devised in the late 1800s to set similar products apart. One tactic, promoting a product as a **brand name,** aims to make a product a household word. When it is successful, a brand name becomes almost the generic identifier, like Coke for cola and Kleenex for facial tissue.

Techniques of successful brand name advertising came together in the 1890s for an English product, Pears' soap. A key element in the campaign was multi-media saturation. Advertisements for Pears' were everywhere, in newspapers and magazines and on posters, vacant walls, fences, buses and street posts. Redundancy hammered home the brand name. "Good morning. Have you used Pears' today?" became a good-natured greeting among Britons that was still being repeated 50 years later. Each repetition reinforced the brand name.

Brand Image.   **David Ogilvy,** who headed the Ogilvy & Mather agency, developed the **brand image** in the 1950s. Ogilvy's advice: "Give your product a first-class ticket through life."

brand name
Product widely recognized by its given, not generic name.
David Ogilvy
Championed brand imaging.
brand image
Spin put on a brand name.

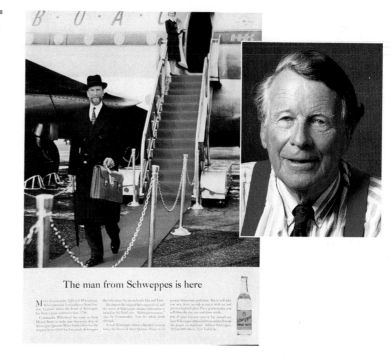

First-Class Ticket. In one of his most noted campaigns, advertising genius David Ogilvy featured the distinguished chair of the company that bottled Schweppes mixers in classy locations. Said Ogilvy: "It pays to give products an image of quality—a first-class ticket." Ogilvy realized how advertising creates impressions. "Nobody wants to be seen using shoddy products," he said.

The man from Schweppes is here

Ogilvy created shirt advertisements with the distinguished Baron Wrangell, who really was a European nobleman, wearing a black eye patch—and a Hathaway shirt. The classy image was reinforced with the accoutrements around Wrangell: exquisite models of sailing ships, antique weapons, silver dinnerware. To some, seeing Wrangell's setting, the patch suggested all kinds of exotica. Perhaps he had lost an eye in a romantic duel or a sporting accident.

Explaining the importance of image, Ogilvy once said: "Take whisky. Why do some people choose Jack Daniels, while others choose Grand Dad or Taylor? Have they tried all three and compared the taste? Don't make me laugh. The reality is that these three brands have different images which appeal to different kinds of people. It isn't the whisky they choose, it's the image. The brand image is 90 percent of what the distiller has to sell. Give people a taste of Old Crow, and tell them it's Old Crow. Then give them another taste of Old Crow, but tell them it's Jack Daniels. Ask them which they prefer. They'll think the two drinks are quite different. They are tasting images."

lowest common denominator

Early brand-name campaigns were geared to the largest possible audience, sometimes called an LCD, or **lowest common denominator,** approach. The term "LCD" is adapted from mathematics. To reach an audience that includes members with IQs of 100, the pitch cannot exceed their level of understanding, even if some people in the audience have IQs of 150. The opportunity for deft touches and even cleverness is limited by the fact they might be lost on some potential customers.

Lowest common denominator advertising is best epitomized in contemporary advertising by USP, short for **unique selling proposition,** a term coined by **Rosser Reeves** of the giant Ted Bates agency in the 1960s. Reeves's prescription was simple: Create a benefit of the product, even if from thin air, and then tout the benefit authoritatively and repeatedly as if the competition doesn't have it. One early USP campaign flaunted that Schlitz beer bottles were "washed with live steam." The claim sounded good—who would want to drink from dirty bottles? However, the fact was that every brewery used steam to clean reusable bottles before filling them again. Furthermore, what is "live steam"? Although the implication of a competitive edge was hollow, it was done dramatically and pounded home with emphasis, and it sold

> **lowest common denominator**
> Messages for broadest audience possible.
>
> **unique selling proposition**
> Emphasizing a single feature.
>
> **Rosser Reeves**
> Devised unique selling proposition.

beer. Just as hollow as a competitive advantage was the USP claim for Colgate toothpaste: "Cleans Your Breath While It Cleans Your Teeth."

Perhaps to compensate for a lack of substance, many USP ads are heavy-handed. Hardly an American has not heard about fast-fast-fast relief from headache remedies or that heartburn relief is spelled R-O-L-A-I-D-S. USP can be unappealing, as acknowledged even by the chairman of Warner-Lambert, which makes Rolaids, who once laughed that his company owed the American people an apology for insulting their intelligence over and over with Bates's USP slogans. Warner-Lambert was also laughing all the way to the bank over the USP-spurred success of Rolaids, Efferdent, Listermint and Bubblicious.

A unique selling proposition, however, need be neither hollow nor insulting. Leo Burnett, founder of the agency bearing his name, refined the USP concept by insisting that the unique point be real. For Maytag, Burnett took the company's slight advantage in reliability and dramatized it with the lonely Maytag repairman.

market segments

Rather than pitching to the lowest common denominator, advertising executive **Jack Trout** developed the idea of **positioning.** Trout worked to establish product identities that appealed not to the whole audience but to a specific audience. The cowboy image for Marlboro cigarettes, for example, established a macho attraction beginning in 1958. Later, something similar was done with Virginia Slims, aimed at women.

Positioning helps distinguish products from all the LCD clamor and noise. Advocates of positioning note that there are more and more advertisements and that they are becoming noisier and noisier. Ad clutter, as it is called, drowns out individual advertisements. With positioning, the appeal is focused and caters to audience segments, and it need not be done in such broad strokes.

Campaigns based on positioning have included:

- Johnson & Johnson's baby oil and baby shampoo, which were positioned as an adult product by advertisements featuring athletes.

- Alka-Seltzer, once a hangover and headache remedy, which was positioned as an upmarket product for stress relief among health-conscious, success-driven people.

redundancy techniques

Advertising people learned the importance of redundancy early on. To be effective, an advertising message must be repeated, perhaps thousands of times. Redundancy, however, is expensive. To increase effectiveness at less cost, advertisers use several techniques:

- **Barrages.** Scheduling advertisements in intensive bursts called **flights** or **waves.**

- **Bunching.** Promoting a product in a limited period, like running advertisements for school supplies in late August and September.

- **Trailing.** Running condensed versions of advertisements after the original has been introduced, as automakers do when they introduce new models with multipage magazine spreads, following with single-page placements.

- **Multimedia Trailing.** Using less expensive media to reinforce expensive advertisements. Relatively cheap drive-time radio in major markets is a favorite follow-

Jack Trout
Devised positioning.

positioning
Targeting ads for specific consumer groups.

barrages
Intensive repetition of ads.

flights
Intensive repetition of ads.

waves
Intensive repetition of ads.

bunching
Short-term ad campaign.

trailing
Shorter, smaller ads after campaign is introduced.

through to expensive television advertisements created for major events like the Super Bowl.

Saturation.   An emerging twist on advertisement placement is saturation advertising. With this approach, an advertiser selects a media vehicle that seems right for its product or service, and then buys all the space that is available. Besides saturating a targeted audience, saturation advertising blocks out the competition.

Chris Whittle, an advocate of saturation advertising, once suggested that General Motors become the sole sponsor of the Olympic games. Whittle also suggested GM buy all the newspaper and magazine ad space, and also all the television and radio time, for one week a year to tout its products, as well as every commercial slot on CNN for the whole year.

In practice, saturation advertising is more modest—like Chrysler buying all the space in a special thematic *Newsweek* issue or Hallmark buying all the time on a seasonal network program.

new advertising techniques

Inundated with advertisements, 6,000 a week on network television, double since 1983, many people tune out. Some do it literally with their remotes. Ad people are concerned that traditional modes are losing effectiveness. People are overwhelmed. Consider, for example, that a major grocery store carries 30,000 items, each with packaging that screams "buy me." There are more commercial messages put there than a human being can handle. The problem is ad clutter. Advertisers are trying to address the clutter in numerous ways, including stealth ads, new-site ads and alternative media. Although not hidden or subliminal, stealth ads are subtle—even covert. You don't know you're being pitched unless you're attentive, really attentive.

Stealth Ads.   Stealth ads fit so neatly into the landscape that the commercial pitch seems part of the story line. In 1996, the writers for four CBS television programs, including *Nanny* and *High Society,* wrote Elizabeth Taylor into their scripts. And there she was, over two hours of programming one winter night, wandering in and out sets looking for a missing string of black pearls. Hardly coincidentally, her new line of perfume, Black Pearls, was being introduced at the time.

The gradual convergence of information and entertainment, called infotainment, has a new element—advertising. *Seinfeld* characters on NBC munched Junior Mints. The M&M/Mars candy company bought a role for Snickers in the Nintendo game *Biker Mice From Mars.* In 1997 Unilever's British brand Van den Bergh Foods introduced a video game in 1997 that stars its Peperami snack sausage. In movies, promotional plugs have become a big budget item. The idea is to seamlessly work the presence of commercial products into a script without a cue—nothing like the hopelessly dated "And now a word from our sponsors."

Less subtle is the **infomercial,** a program-length television commercial dolled up to look like a newscast, a live-audience participation show or a chatty talk show. With the proliferation of 24-hour television service and of cable channels, air time is so cheap at certain hours that advertisers of even off-beat products can afford it. Hardly anybody is fooled that infomercials are anything but advertisements, but some full-length media advertisements, like Liz Taylor wandering through CBS sitcoms, are cleverly disguised.

A print media variation is the **'zine**—a magazine published by a manufacturer to plug a single line of products with varying degrees of subtlety. 'Zine publishers, includ-

stealth ads
Advertisements, often subtle, in nontraditional, unexpected places.

infomercial
Program-length broadcast commercial

'zine
Magazine-like publication that pitches the publisher's product in both articles and ads. The term also is used for online magazines, many of them self-published by individuals.

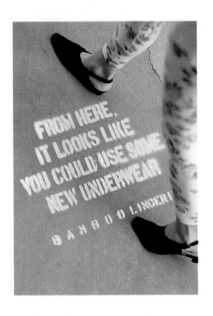

ing such stalwarts as IBM and Sony, have even been so brazen as to sell these wall-to-wall advertising vehicles at news stands. In 1996, if you bought a splashy new magazine called *Colors,* you paid $4.50 for it. Once inside, you probably would realize it was a thinly veiled ad for Benetton casual clothes. *Guess Journal* may look like a magazine, but guess who puts it out as a 'zine: The makers of the Guess fashion brand.

Stealth advertisements try "to morph into the very entertainment it sponsors," wrote Mary Kuntz, Joseph Weber and Heidi Dawley in *Business Week*. The goal, they said, is "to create messages so entertaining, so compelling—and maybe so disguised—that rapt audiences will swallow them whole, oblivious to the sales component."

New-Site Ads. Solving the problem of ad clutter by going underground with stealth ads, ironically, contributes to the clutter. Sooner or later, it would seem, people would also tire of advertising omnipresence. Snapple stickers adorn kiwis and mangoes at the grocery. Sports stadiums named for department stores, like the Target Center in Minneapolis, try to weave product names into everyday conversation and the news. Sports events galore bear the names of high-bidding sponsors. How omnipresent can advertising become? Consider the Bamboo lingerie company that stenciled messages on Manhattan sidewalks in 1994: "From here, it looks like you could use some new underwear."

research and psychology

(STUDY PREVIEW) Freudian ideas about the human subconscious influenced advertising in the 1950s, and research tried to tap hidden motivations that could be exploited to sell products and services. The extreme in appealing to the subconscious, called subliminal advertising, worried many people, but it was an approach whose effectiveness was never demonstrated.

motivational research

Whatever naïveté Americans had about opinion-shaping was dispelled by the mid-20th century. Sinister possibilities were evident in the work of **Joseph Goebbels,** the Nazi minister of propaganda and public enlightenment. In the Pacific, the Japanese beamed the infamous Tokyo Rose radio broadcasts to GIs to lower their morale. Then, during the Korean War, a macabre fascination developed with the so-called brainwashing techniques used on American prisoners of war. In this same period, the work of Austrian psychiatrist **Sigmund Freud,** which emphasized hidden motivations and repressed sexual impulses, was being popularized in countless books and articles.

No wonder, considering this intellectual context, advertising people in the 1950s looked to the social sciences to find new ways to woo customers. Among the advertising pioneers of this period was **Ernest Dichter,** who accepted Freud's claim that people act on motivations that they are not even aware of. Depth interviewing, Dichter felt, could reveal these motivations, which could then be exploited in advertising messages.

Dichter used his interviewing, called **motivational research,** for automotive clients. Rightly or wrongly, Dichter determined that the American male was loyal to his wife but fantasized about a mistress. Men, he noted, usually were the decision makers in purchasing a car. Then, in what seemed a quantum leap, Dichter equated sedans, which were what most people drove, with wives. Sedans were familiar, reliable. Convertibles, impractical for many people and also beyond their reach financially, were equated with mistresses—romantic, daring, glamorous. With these conclusions in hand, Dichter devised advertisements for a new kind of sedan without a center door pillar. The hardtop, as it was called, gave a convertible effect when the windows were down. The advertisements, dripping with sexual innuendo, clearly reflected Dichter's thinking: "You'll find something new to love every time you drive it." Although they were not as solid as sedans and tended to leak air and water, hardtops were popular among automobile buyers for the next 25 years.

Dichter's motivational research led to numerous campaigns that exploited sexual images. For Ronson lighters, the flame, in phallic form, was reproduced in extraordinary proportions. A campaign for Ajax cleanser, hardly a glamour product, had a white knight charging through the street, ignoring law and regulation with a great phallic lance. Whether consumers were motivated by sexual imagery is hard to establish. Even so, many campaigns based on motivational research worked.

subliminal advertising

The idea that advertising can be persuasive at subconscious levels was taken a step further by market researcher **Jim Vicary,** who coined the term **subliminal advertising.** Vicary claimed in 1957 that he had studied the effect of inserting messages like "Drink Coca-Cola" and "Eat popcorn" into movies. The messages, although flashed too fast to be recognized by the human eye, still registered in the brain and, said Vicary, prompted moviegoers to rush to the snack bar. In experiments at a New Jersey movie house, he said, Coke sales increased 18 percent and popcorn almost 60 percent. Vicary's report stirred great interest, and also alarm, but researchers who tried to replicate his study found no evidence to support his claim.

Despite doubts about Vicary's claims, psychologists have identified a phenomenon they call **subception,** in which certain behavior sometimes seems to be triggered by messages perceived subliminally. Whether the effect works outside laboratory experiments and whether the effect is strong enough to prod a consumer to go out and buy is uncertain. Nevertheless, there remains a widespread belief among the general population that subliminal advertising works, and fortunes are being made by people who peddle various devices and systems with extravagant claims that they can control human behavior. Among these are the "hidden" messages in stores' sound systems that say shoplifting is not nice.

This idea that advertising is loaded with hidden messages has been taken to extremes by **Wilson Bryan Key,** who spins out books alleging that plugs are hidden in all kinds of places for devil worship, homosexuality and a variety of libertine activities. He has accused the Nabisco people of baking the word "sex" into Ritz crackers. At Howard Johnson restaurants, he has charged, placemat pictures of plates

Ernest Dichter
Pioneered motivational research.

motivational research
Seeks subconscious appeals that can be used in advertising.

Jim Vicary
Dubious subliminal advertising claims.

subliminal advertising
Ads that cannot be consciously perceived.

subception
Receiving subconscious messages that trigger behavior.

Wilson Bryan Key
Sees subliminal advertising widely used.

Sex in the Clams? Author Wilson Bryan Key is convinced that Madison Avenue hides sex in advertisements to attract attention and sell products. To demonstrate his point, he outlined the human figures that he saw in an orgy in a photograph of clam strips on a Howard Johnson restaurant menu. Most advertising people dismiss Key's claims.

heaped with clams portray orgies and bestiality. Though widely read, Key offers no evidence beyond his own observations and interpretations. In advertising circles, his views are dismissed as amusing but wacky. The view of Nabisco and Howard Johnson is less charitable.

In 1990 Wilson Bryan Key's views suffered a serious setback. He was a primary witness in a highly publicized Nevada trial on whether the Judas Priest heavy-metal album "Stained Class" had triggered the suicide of an 18-year-old youth and the attempted suicide of his 20-year-old friend. The families said that the pair had obsessed on a Judas Priest album that dealt with suicide and that one song was subliminally embedded with the words "Do it" over and over. The families' attorneys hired Key as an expert witness to help make their point. From Key's perspective, the case did not go well. Millions of television viewers who followed the trial strained to make out the supposed words "Do it," but even when isolated from the rest of the music, they were almost impossible to make out. It turned out the sounds were neither lyrics nor even vocal but rather instrumental effects. Members of Judas Priest testified that they had not equated the sound to any words at all and had inserted it for artistic effect, hardly to encourage suicide. The jury sided with Judas Priest, and Key left town with his wobbly ideas on subliminal messages having taken a serious blow under a jury's scrutiny.

David Ogilvy, founder of the Ogilvy & Mather agency, once made fun of claims like Key's, pointing out the absurdity of "millions of suggestible consumers getting up from their armchairs and rushing like zombies through the traffic on their way to buy the product at the nearest store." The danger of "Vote Bolshevik" being flashed during the "NBC Nightly News" is remote, and whether it would have any effect is dubious.

conglomeration and globalization

STUDY PREVIEW A tremendous consolidation in the advertising business occurred in the 1980s. Agencies bought agencies, and some of the resulting super agencies continued their acquisitions abroad. Today, these global agencies are beset with problems that came with the early 1990s worldwide recession.

acquisition binge

In the late 1970s, under President Carter, the federal government backed off on antitrust actions and other regulatory controls, fueling a great number of mergers and consolidations in American business. Advertising was no exception, and many agencies swallowed up others. The Reagan, Bush and Clinton administrations continued the hands-off-business approach into the 1990s, and dominant big businesses, including major advertising agencies, became even more so.

The demassification of the mass media was also a factor. Several big agencies, whose favored choice for most clients had been network television for 40 years, realized that the network audience was fragmenting, and they had to find a new way to do business. These agencies lacked in-house expertise at direct-mail advertising and other emerging advertising media, so they began buying smaller, specialized ad shops, successful regional agencies and public relations companies to fill in the gaps.

While U.S. agencies were consolidating, there was also an international consolidation occurring that wiped out the traditional dominance of U.S. advertising agencies abroad. Not only did some foreign agencies like Dentsu of Japan become giant multinational organizations, but an upstart London agency, Saatchi & Saatchi, went on an acquisition binge that absorbed several U.S. agencies. The result is fewer but bigger agencies.

This globalization of the advertising business had detractors who were concerned that the new super agencies, all based in leading Western societies, would further diminish indigenous values in less developed countries under the steamroller they called "cultural imperialism." Many ad people saw the situation differently, arguing that people buy only what they want and that it would be the choice of Third World people whether to respond to advertising that originates with multinational advertising agencies. Also, noted advertising guru David Ogilvy, successful advertising always is adapted to local conditions: "The advertising campaigns for these brands will emanate from the headquarters of multinational agencies but will be adapted to respect differences in local culture." If local appeals and themes are necessary to sell a product, those are the ones that will be employed.

agency consolidation problems

The agency consolidation of the 1980s was driven mostly by two factors. First, agencies that were turning huge profits had money to spend on acquisitions, and other profitable agencies were attractive acquisition targets. Second, banks and other lending institutions were willing to finance highly leveraged acquisitions. The pace of acquisitions came to a halt during the worldwide recession that developed in 1990, and some of the new super agencies began to unravel.

With the recession, many manufacturers, retailers and other advertisers cut back on spending. Agency revenue plummeted. As a result, the source of money for super agencies to repay loans disappeared. Some agencies shut down subsidiary agencies or consolidated them. There were massive layoffs, and businesses were scaled back.

Advertising Globalization Manufacturers on every continent are seeking markets elsewhere, which is generating accounts and revenues for advertising agencies with international operations. Gap's new high-fashion outlet in Tokyo's ritzy Ginza district is among thousands of examples. Some of the greatest advertising agency expansion is in China, where by one count 50 foreign agencies are trying to carve a share out of a virtually untapped market of 1.2 billion people. The effect is tremendous. Steven Strasser, writing in *Newsweek,* said: "China cares about its athlete's foot problem. Johnson & Johnson's subsidiary made sure of that. When its recent J&J commercial revealed that a fungus caused the itch, sales of Daktarin fungicidal cream soared from Shanghai to Xian."

Some agencies bought time to get their finances back in order under the auspices of bankruptcy courts. Even still, the prospects for some of these troubled agencies remain unsure.

media
online

Ad Council: The Ad Council's web site includes a brief history and a list of memorable campaigns: Loose Lips Sink Ships, Friends Don't Let Friends Drive Drunk, and Take a Big Bite Out of Crime. www.adcouncil.org

***Advertising Age* Online:** The industry's magazine's web site with top stories of the day. www.adage.com

American Association of Advertising Agencies: Exclusive country club of advertising professionals. www.commercepark.com/AAAA

Blacklist of Internet Advertisers: Whatcha' gonna do when they come for you? http://math-www.unipaderborn.de/~axel/BL/blacklist.html#list

International Advertising Association: A global partnership of advertisers, agencies and media. ww1.usa1.com/~ibnet/iaahp.html

Internet Advertising Resource Guide: Complete resource list for ad professionals and students. www.voyager.net/adv/internet-advertising-guide.html

advertising regulation

(STUDY PREVIEW)   The "buyer beware" underpinning of much of 19th-century advertising has given way to "seller beware." Today, advertising is regulated on many fronts, by the media that carry advertisements, by the advertising industry itself and by governmental agencies.

media gatekeeping

A dramatic reversal in thinking about advertising has occurred in the 20th century. The earlier *caveat emptor* mindset, "buyer beware," tolerated extravagant claims. Anybody who believed that the same elixir could cure dandruff, halitosis and cancer deserved to be conned, or so went the thinking. Over the years, due partly to the growing consumer movement, the thinking changed to *caveat venditor,* "seller beware," placing the onus on the advertiser to avoid misleading claims and to demonstrate the truth of claims.

In advertising's early days, newspapers and magazines skirted the ethics question posed by false advertisements by saying their pages were open to all advertisers. Under growing pressure, publications sometimes criticized dubious advertisements editorially, but most did not ban them. **Edward Bok,** who made *Ladies' Home Journal* a runaway success in the 1890s, crusaded against dishonest advertising. In one exposé on Lydia E. Pinkham's remedies for "female maladies," Bok reported that Lydia, to whom women readers were invited in advertisements to write for advice, had been dead for 22 years. Yet the advertisements continued.

In 1929, NBC adopted a code of ethics to preclude false or exaggerated claims. Other networks followed. At the peak of the networks' concern about broadcast standards, it was estimated that half the commercials for products were turned away for violating network codes. Codes for broadcast advertising have come and gone over the years, all voluntary with stations that choose to subscribe.

The print media also have seen a variety of industry-wide codes, all voluntary. Most publications spurn misleading advertisements. Typical is the Minot *Daily News* in North Dakota, which refuses advertisements for "clairvoyance, fortune telling, magnetic healing, doubtful medicines and fake sales." Many college newspapers refuse advertisements from term-paper services. Some metropolitan papers turn away advertisements for pornographic movies.

A case can be made that the media do not go far enough in exercising their prerogative to ban dubious advertisements. Critics argue that on nettling questions, such as the morality of printing ads for carcinogenic tobacco products, with major revenue at stake, many newspapers and magazines sidestep a moral judgment, run the advertisements, and reap the revenue. The critics note, for example, that most commercial broadcasters ran cigarette advertisements until the federal government intervened. The media, so goes the argument, are too devoted to profits to do all the regulating they should.

caveat emptor
Buyer beware.

caveat venditor
Seller beware.

Edward Bok
Set media standards for ads.

industry self-regulation

The advertising industry itself has numerous organizations that try, through ethics codes and moral suasion, to eradicate falsity and deception. Besides the explicit purposes of these self-policing mechanisms, their existence can be cited by advertising people to argue that their industry is able to deal with misdeeds itself with a minimum of government regulation.

National Advertising Review Council. The **National Advertising Review Council** investigates complaints from anybody. When it finds a problem, the council asks the offending advertiser to correct the situation. If that does not work, the council turns its file over to whichever government agency it thinks is appropriate.

Although it is a creation of advertising trade associations, the National Advertising Review Council has earned a reputation as a dispassionate attempt at self-regulation. Its 50 members include 10 people appointed from the public—with no connection to the advertising business. Of the complaints the council investigates, two-thirds typically are found to be deceptive advertising. About half of those advertisements are discontinued or modified under council pressure. The council has no legal authority, but its willingness to go to federal agencies or to state attorneys general, in effect recommending prosecution, is a powerful tool for honesty in advertising.

Codes. Typical of codes of advertising trade groups is that of the **American Association of Advertising Agencies,** which says member agencies are expected never to produce ads with:

- False, misleading statements or exaggerations, visual or verbal, including misleading price claims.

- Testimonials from unknowledgeable people.

- Unfair disparagement of competitive products.

- Distorted or insufficiently supported claims.

- Anything offending public decency.

Acceptance of the code is a kind of loose condition of membership—more a statement of the association's values than an enforcement tool.

Public Interest Advertising. The advertising industry has set up an organization, the Ad Council, which creates advertisements free for worthy causes. For almost 60 years the council's existence has helped offset criticism that the advertising business is an unscrupulous manipulator.

The **Ad Council** has roots in World War II when the ad industry, major media organizations and advertisers created the War Advertising Council to create ads for the war effort. Advertisers funded the council, agencies created the advertisements gratis and media ran donated time and space for them. The first campaign, to recruit military nurses, stressed, "Nursing is a proud profession." Within weeks, 500,000 women applied for the Cadet Nurses Corps—almost eight times more than needed. After the war the Ad Council was formed to continue *pro bono* work on behalf of socially significant national issues.

Because the ads are well done, the media are pleased to run them as a contribution to the public good. Magazines, newspapers and broadcasters donate about $800 million a year in time and space to the Ad Council's ads.

Joe Namath's Newsworthiness. The 1969 Super Bowl led to a new fine-line distinction in expropriation law. *Sports Illustrated* used a news photo from the game to solicit subscriptions, and player Joe Namath objected that the magazine was exploiting his likeness without permission. Generally, the courts have found against unauthorized use of someone's likeness for commercial purposes, but this time the court said that "incidental use" of once-newsworthy photos was all right. Namath lost.

National Advertising Review Council
Reviews complaints about ads.

American Association of Advertising Agencies
Trade association.

Ad Council
Ad industry group that creates free campaigns for worthy causes.

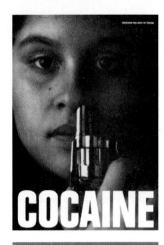

Public Service. The DDB Needham Worldwide agency created this advertisement free for the Partnership for a Drug-Free America, which distributed it to publications that ran it at no cost. Every year, major agencies and the media donate their services to the Partnership on behalf of the anti-drug organization.

Federal Trade Commission
Regulates advertising.

puffery
Legally permissible excesses in advertising.

In a typical year, 300 noncommercial organizations ask the Ad Council to take them on. The council chooses a dozen, which are turned over to agencies that rotate their services. The United Way has received continuing support from the council. Other campaigns have included restoring the Statue of Liberty, combating illiteracy and improving American productivity. Campaigns that have left an imprint on the public mind have included:

- Forest fire prevention with the character Smoky Bear.

- Environmental protection with the memorable "Don't be fuelish" slogan.

- Fund-raising for the United Negro College Fund, with the line, "A mind is a terrible thing to waste."

government regulation

The federal government began regulating advertisements in 1914 when Congress created the **Federal Trade Commission.** The commission was charged with protecting honest companies that were being disadvantaged by competitors that made false claims. Today, nine federal agencies besides the FTC are involved heavily in regulating advertising. These include the Food and Drug Administration, the Postal Service, the Federal Communications Commission and the Securities and Exchange Commission. In addition, most states have laws against advertising fraud.

In its early days, the Federal Trade Commission went about its work meekly, but fueled by the consumer movement in the 1960s, it became aggressive. Although the agency never had the authority to review advertisements ahead of their publication or airing, the FTC let it be known that it would crack down on violations of truth-in-packaging and truth-in-lending requirements. The FTC also began insisting on clarity so that even someone with low intelligence would not be confused. The FTC took particular aim at the overused word "free." To be advertised as "free," an offer had to be without conditions. The FTC moved further to protect the gullible. It was unacceptable, said the FTC, to leave the impression that actors in white coats speaking authoritatively about over-the-counter drugs and toothpastes were physicians or dentists. When Ocean Spray claimed that its cranberry juice offered "food energy," the FTC insisted that the language be changed to "calories." The FTC clamped down on a claim that Profile bread helped people lose weight, noting that the only difference from regular bread was thinner slices. The FTC pressed the Kroger grocery chain on its claim that it carried 150 everyday items cheaper than the competition, found that the claim was misleading and told Kroger to drop it.

Even with its crackdown, the FTC never ventured into regulating taste. Advertisements in poor taste were allowed, as long as they were not deceptive or unfair. **Puffery** was allowed, as long as there was no misstatement of fact. In borderline cases about what constituted puffery, an advertiser could always appeal to the courts.

The FTC has been less aggressive in regulating advertising since the Reagan administration, which deemphasized government regulation. Consumer activists, however, continue to complain to the FTC and other federal and state agencies and to bring pressure on the media not to run certain advertisements. Most of the concerns today are to protect impressionable children.

Today, some advertisers—especially the tobacco and liquor industries—face regulation of a different sort. To settle and head off civil law suits, tobacco companies have withdrawn advertising aimed at kids. There are fewer pictures of healthy, young people holding a cigarette or taking a puff. The liquor industry faces a different kind of government pressure. Historically the industry has refrained from advertising hard liquor on television and radio, and many networks and stations had policies against it too. In the late 1990s, under increasing competitive pressure, the Canadian conglomerate Seagrams and some broadcasters broke ranks and began dabbling with television advertising. That prompted Federal Communications Commission rumbling on possibly banning such ads. Some congressional leaders also began talking tough. An FCC crackdown seemed unlikely, however, considering the general deregulation mood in government that left it to the marketplace to determine what's acceptable and what's not.

problems and issues

(STUDY PREVIEW)   People are exposed to such a blur of ads that advertisers worry that their messages are being lost in the clutter. Some advertising people see more creativity as the answer so people will want to see and read ads, but there is evidence that creativity can work against an ad's effectiveness.

advertising clutter

Leo Bogart of the Newspaper Advertising Bureau noted that the number of advertising messages doubled through the 1960s and 1970s, and except for the recession at the start of the 1990s, the trend continues. This proliferation of advertising creates a problem—too many ads. CBS squeezed so many ads into its coverage of the 1992 winter Olympics that some viewers felt the network regarded the games as a sideshow. Even in regular programming, the frequency of ads has led advertisers to fret that their individual ads are being lost in the clutter. The problem has been exacerbated by the shortening of ads from 60 seconds in the early days of television to today's widely used 15-second format.

At one time, the National Association of Broadcasters had a code limiting the quantity of commercials. The Federal Communications Commission let station owners know that it supported the NAB code, but in 1981, as part of the Reagan administration's deregulation, the FCC backed away from any limitation. In 1983 a federal court threw out the NAB limitation as a monopolistic practice.

Ad clutter is less an issue in the print media. Many people buy magazines and newspapers to look at ads as part of the comparative shopping process. Even so, some advertisers, concerned that their ads are overlooked in massive editions, such as a seven-pound metro Sunday newspaper or a 700-page bridal magazine, are looking to alternative means to reach potential customers in a less cluttered environment.

The clutter that marks much of commercial television and radio today may be alleviated as the media fragment further. Not only will demassification create more specialized outlets, such as narrowly focused cable television services, but there will be new media. Videodiscs, for example, can be delivered by mail, and videotext can be called up on home computer screens. The result will be advertising aimed at narrower audiences.

media
online

Federal Trade Commission: Contains copies of daily press releases, speeches and documents. Also information about the FTC's mission and structure of the agency. www.ftc.gov/

Ad Parody: Take aim and fire at will at the ads you love to hate. www.dnai.com/~sharrow/parody.html

Adjacency: Multimedia brand designer. adjacency.com

University of Texas-Austin Department of Advertising: Home of the Advertising Research Resource Center—the last word in links. www.utexas.edu/coc/adv

L.L. Bean: Clothing, gear, and national parks. www.llbean.com

Benetton: Offers previews of upcoming Benetton campaigns: www.benetton.com

Chase Online Marketing Strategies: For out-of-print advertising. http://advert.com/who.html

Club Med: The Club Med resort chain offers a brochure and a $50 discount offer. Users may not realize it, but registering gives Club Med a data base of potential customers. www.hotwired.com/Coin/Spnsrs/ClubMed

MCI: Products, tools and customer service. www.mci.com

advertisement cloning

Procter & Gamble, the Cincinnati-based global household product conglomerate, has taken aim at marketing costs to boost profits. The goal: Reduce marketing outflow to less than 20 percent of sales—a major cut from 1996's 24 percent.

How to do it?

One tactic is to reduce creative costs in advertising by cloning campaigns that succeed in one country and use them elsewhere.

Eventually this could also mean lower costs for producing advertisements.

In a 1996 trial of ad-cloning, the "Demanding Experts" campaign for Tide detergent in the United States was exported to Mexico and Puerto Rico for P&G's Ariel brand.

Similarly, the company recycled its "Show and Smell" campaign for Gain detergent in the United States for its Daz brand in Britain.

creative excesses

Advertisers are reviewing whether creativity is as effective an approach as hard sell. **Harry McMahan** studied **Clio** Awards for creativity in advertising and discovered that 36 agencies that produced 81 winners of the prestigious awards for advertisements had either lost the winning account or gone out of business.

Predicts advertising commentator E. B. Weiss: "Extravagant license for creative people will be curtailed." The future may hold more heavy-handed pitches, perhaps with over-the-counter regimens not only promising fast-fast-fast relief but also spelling it out in all caps and boldface with exclamation marks: **F-A-S-T! F-A-S-T! F-A-S-T!!!**

advertising effectiveness

Long-held assumptions about the effectiveness of advertising itself are being questioned. **Gerald Tellis,** a University of Iowa researcher, put together a sophisticated statistical model that found that people are relatively unmoved by television advertisements in making brand choices, especially on mundane everyday products like toilet paper and laundry detergents. Tellis's conclusions began with consumer purchasing studies in Eau Claire, Wisconsin. Not surprisingly, considering its self-interest, the advertising industry has challenged the Tellis's studies.

Meanwhile, other researchers have continued work on what makes effective advertising and which media work best. A 1995 study by **Yankelovich Partners** found magazine ads entice only 13 percent of Americans to try new products; newspaper ads, 15 percent; and television ads, 25 percent. The study, with a statistically impressive sample of 1,000 consumers, shook the conventional wisdom that celebrity endorsements work. Only 3 percent of the respondents said they would try a product based on a celebrity's testimonial. A Yankelovich official, Hal Quinley, explained the dismal report card on advertising's effectiveness on weak credibility. "Advertising has little confidence among consumers," he told the *Wall Street Journal*. "It rates below the fed-

calvin klein

The name Calvin Klein may be associated mostly with designer jeans, fancy-priced underwear and high-end perfumes, but the people around the *man* Calvin Klein say his real forté is advertising. Indeed, it has been titillating advertisements and the attention they brought, much of it critical, that has propelled Klein's brand into a $1.9 billion company. Those campaigns came from Klein's in-house ad agency. His creative staff comes up with ideas, but Klein chooses what to go with. His competitors say he has had an uncanny knack for eroticizing young models in ways that both entice and disturb the people who see his ads.

The fuss over Klein's ads, which feature models in various states of undress as much as they do his products, only draws them more attention. Noted *Advertising Age* columnist Bob Garfield: "If you make a small amount of the right kind of noise, the media will deliver you tens or hundreds of millions of dollars in free publicity."

Klein hit advertising pay dirt in 1980. The slogan for his form-fitting jeans was "What comes between me and my Calvins? Nothing." Not only was the slogan racy, so were the shots of actress Brooke Shields, then 15. It was enough to provoke feminist leader Gloria Steinem into a public protest. During the resulting Klein-Steinem media spat, his jean sales nearly doubled.

Hunky actor Marky Mark, grinning anatomically correct in his Calvin Klein undershorts, raised a furor in 1992, and Klein continued laughing all the way to the bank. Nudity and intertwined bodies marked ads for Klein perfumes, again stirring critics. To *Newsweek* reporter Michele Ingassia, Klein once defended the sexuality of his ads, including frontal nudity: "These products are about the body."

In 1995, Klein perhaps went too far with skimpily clad models, some looking barely pubescent, in back-alley and tawdry bare-room settings. Critics saw a leering quality in the ads. In one television commercial, an older gravely male voice coached the model: "You think you could rip that shirt off of you? That's a real nice body. You work out? I can tell." The campaign was nothing slapdash. Klein, impressed with a high-concept fashion pictorial in *L'Uomo Vogue*, an Italian magazine, went to the photographer, Steven Meisel. Klein and Meisel had worked together before, and as Klein told it, the intention was "not to create controversy."

This time the "small amount of the right kind of noise," as *Ad Age*'s Garfield put it, got out of hand. The giant Dayton Hudson retail chain asked Klein to yank its name from the ads. The U.S. Justice Department, flexing its muscle with a new anti-child pornography law, asked whether the models were as young as they looked and threatened criminal action if they were. Some politicians and moralists called for store boycotts.

Under pressure, Klein pulled the ads and said there was no intent to offend. "Yeah, right," said the critics. Meisel, the photographer, said the models all were adults. In fact, he said, one was 29. The feds backed off. The criticism ebbed. What the critics sensed as victory, however, ended up a mixed bag. The controversial campaign was scheduled to run only one more week and the print ads only six more. Already, the product had received more attention in the media, which dutifully reproduced the ads in news accounts, than it would have on its own without the firefight.

Did the controversy dampen sales? Fashion writer Alan Millstein said the fuss ended a slump for Calvin Klein jeans and they were "flying out of stores."

eral government." A lot of people trust their friends, however. Six out of 10 would try a new product recommended by a friend or relative.

For advertisers, the lesson from the Tellis and Yankelovich studies is not that advertising doesn't work but that throwing money into campaigns without careful study can be wasteful. For some products, some media are better than others. For new products, according to Yankelovich's findings, free samples are the best way to pique consumer interest. So are cents-off coupons. In short, though, advertising may be overrated. With countless variables affecting consumer decisions, advertisers cannot place total faith in advertising to move their products and services.

chapter wrap-up

The role of advertising in American mass media cannot be overstated. Without advertising, most media would go out of business. In fact, in the 1960s, when advertisers switched to television from the giant general-interest magazines like *Life* and *Look,* those magazines went under. Today, the rapid expansion of cable networks is possible only because advertisers are buying time on the new networks to reach potential customers. In one sense, advertisers subsidize readers, viewers and listeners who pay only a fraction of the cost of producing publications and broadcasts. The bulk of the cost is paid by advertisers, who are willing to do so to make their pitches to potential customers who, coincidentally, are media consumers.

Besides underwriting the mass media, advertising is vital for a prosperous, growing consumer economy. It triggers demand for goods and services, and it enables people to make wise choices by providing information on competing products. The result is efficiency in the marketplace, which frees more capital for expansion. This all speaks to an intimate interrelationship involving advertising in a democratic and capitalistic society.

Today, as democracy and capitalism are reintroduced in Central and Eastern Europe, advertising can be expected to have an essential role in fostering new consumer economies. American, European and Japanese advertising agencies will be called on for their expertise to develop campaigns for goods and services that will make for better lives and stronger economies. This process will provide a greater revenue base for the mass media in these countries, which will result in better journalistic and entertainment content.

questions for review

1. Why is advertising essential in a capitalistic society?

2. Trace the development of advertising since the time of Johannes Gutenberg.

3. What is the role of advertising agencies?

4. Why do some advertisements appear in some media and not other media?

5. What are the major tactics used in advertising? Who devised each one?

6. How do advertising people use psychology and research to shape their messages?

7. What are the advantages and the problems of the globalization of the advertising industry?

8. Does advertising still follow the "buyer beware" dictum?

9. What are some problems and unanswered issues in advertising?

questions for critical thinking

1. How does the development of modern advertising relate to Johannes Gutenberg's technological innovation? To the Industrial Revolution? To long-distance mass transportation? To mass marketing?

2. Why does advertising flourish more in democratic than in autocratic societies? In a capitalistic more than in a controlled economy? In a prosperous society?

3. What were the contributions to advertising of Wayland Ayer, Rosser Reeves, Jack Trout, Ernest Dichter, Wilson Bryan Key and David Ogilvy?

4. What are the responsibilities of advertising account executives, copywriters, media buyers, researchers, brand managers, ad reps, brokers?

5. What are the advantages of the commission system for advertising agency revenue? Of the fee system? The disadvantages of both?

6. Describe these advertising tactics: brand name promotion, unique selling proposition, lowest common denominator approach, positioning and redundancy.

7. Ad clutter is an emerging problem. How is it a problem? What can be done about it?

8. How has the Ad Council improved the image of companies that advertise, agencies that create advertisements and media that carry advertisements? Give examples.

for further learning

Mary Billard. "Heavy Metal Goes on Trial." *Rolling Stone* (July 12–26, 1990, double issue). Pages 83–88, 132. Billard examines the events leading to a shotgun suicide of a Nevada youth whose family claimed that subliminal messages in a Judas Priest song led him to do it.

Stephen Fox. *The Mirror Makers: A History of American Advertising and Its Creators* (Morrow, 1984).

Wilson Bryan Key. *Subliminal Seduction: Ad Media's Manipulation of a Not So Innocent America* (New American Library, 1972). Sex appeal has a special dimension for Key, who argues that an advertisement for Gilbey's gin has the letters s-e-x carefully carved in ice cubes in an expensive *Time* magazine advertisement. Key offers no corroborating evidence in this and later books, *Media Sexploitation* (New American Library, 1976), *The Clam-Plate Orgy: And Other Subliminal Techniques for Manipulating Your Behavior* (New America, 1980) and *The Age of Manipulation* (Holt, 1989).

Mary Kuntz, Joseph Weber and Heidi Dawley. "The New Hucksterism." *Business Week* (July 1, 1996). These magazine reporters tell how advertisers have become part of the info-tainment mix. They document commercial messages, sometimes disguised, sometimes not, the advertisers have built into television sitcom plots and other places never before considered ad forums.

Bob Levenson. *Bill Bernbach's Book: A History of the Advertising That Changed the History of Advertising* (Random House, 1987). Levenson focuses on the "creative revolution" typified in the Bernbach agency's "Think Small" Volkswagen advertisements of the 1950s and early 1960s.

Nancy Millman. *Emperors of Adland: Inside the Advertising Revolution* (Warner Books, 1988). This fast-paced book by a Chicago newspaper columnist traces the mergers of advertising agencies in the 1980s and questions whether mega-agencies are good for advertising.

David Ogilvy. *Confessions of an Advertising Man* (Atheneum, 1963). The man who created a leading agency explains his philosophy in this autobiography. In *Ogilvy on Advertising* (Vintage, 1985), Ogilvy offers lively advice about effective advertising.

Anthony Pratkanis and Elliot Aronson. *Age of Propaganda: The Everyday Use and Abuse of Persuasion* (W. H. Freeman, 1992). Pratkanis and Aronson, both scholars, provide a particularly good, lively status report on "subliminal sorcery."

Michael Schudson. *Advertising: The Uneasy Persuasion: Its Dubious Impact on American Society* (Basic Books, 1984). Schudson, a media theorist, challenges the effectiveness of advertising while exploring the ideological impact of advertisements.

for keeping up to date

Weekly trade journals are *Advertising Age* and *AdWeek*. Scholarly publications include *Journal of Marketing Research* and *Journal of Advertising*. The New York *Times* regularly reports on the industry.

13
media research

in this chapter you will learn:

- Surveys tell the mass media about their audiences.

- The size of mass media audiences is measured by monitoring press runs and sales and by surveying.

- Mass media organizations measure the reaction of people to make informed decisions on content.

- Audience analysis techniques include demographic, geodemographic and psychographic breakdowns.

- Mass media organizations are more interested in applied than theoretical research.

George Gallup was excited. His mother-in-law, Ola Babcock Miller, had decided to run for secretary of state. If elected, she would become not only Iowa's first Democrat but also the first woman to hold the state-wide office. Gallup's excitement, however, went beyond the novelty of his mother-in-law's candidacy. The campaign gave him an opportunity to pull together his three primary intellectual interests: survey research, public opinion and politics. In that 1932 campaign, George

Gallup conducted the first serious poll in history for a political candidate. Gallup's surveying provided important barometers of public sentiment that helped Miller gear her campaign to the issues most on voters' minds. She won and was reelected twice by large margins.

Four years after that first 1932 election campaign, Gallup tried his polling techniques in the presidential race and correctly predicted that Franklin Roosevelt would beat Alf Landon. Calling another Roosevelt victory accurately, his Gallup Poll organization had clients knocking at his door.

Gallup devoted himself to accuracy. Even though he predicted Roosevelt's 1936 victory, Gallup was bothered that his reliability was not better. His method, quota sampling, could not call a two-way race within 4 percentage points. With **quota sampling,** a representative percentage of women and men was surveyed, as was a representative percentage of Democrats and Republicans, Westerners and Easterners, Christians and Jews and other constituencies.

In 1948 Gallup was correct that Thomas Dewey was not a shoo-in for president. Nonetheless, his pre-election poll was 5.3 percentage points off. So he decided to switch to a tighter method, **probability sampling,** which theoretically gave everyone in the population being sampled an equal chance to be surveyed. With probability sampling, there was no

Public Pulse Beat. The Gallup organization conducts ongoing polls on political issues. Check them out: www.gallup.com

need for quotas because, as Gallup explained in his folksy Midwestern way, it was like a cook making soup: "When a housewife wants to test the quality of the soup she is making, she tastes only a teaspoonful or two. She knows that if the soup is thoroughly stirred, one teaspoonful is enough to tell her whether she has the right mixture of ingredients." With the new **sta-**

tistical extrapolation method, Gallup narrowed his error rate to less than 2 percentage points.

Even with improvements pioneered by Gallup, public opinion surveying has detractors. Some critics say polls influence undecided voters toward the front-runner—a bandwagon effect. Other critics say polls make elected officials too

responsive to the momentary whims of the electorate, discouraging courageous leadership. George Gallup, who died in 1984, tirelessly defended polling, arguing that good surveys give voice to the "inarticulate minority" that legislators otherwise might not hear. Gallup was convinced that public-opinion surveys help make democracy work.

public-opinion sampling

media
online

Find/SVP:
www.etrg.findsvp.com

NetGravity: www.netgravity.com

A.C. Nielsen:
www.nielsenmedia.com

O'Reilly & Associates:
www.website.ora.com

(STUDY PREVIEW)   Public-opinion polling is an important ancillary activity for the mass media. One polling technique, probability sampling, relies on statistical guidelines that can be incredibly accurate. Sad to say, less reliable survey techniques also are used, which sullies the reputation of serious sampling.

the surveying industry

Public-opinion surveying is approaching a $1 billion-a-year business whose clients include major corporations, political candidates and the mass media. Today, just as in 1935, the **Institute of American Public Opinion,** founded by George Gallup, cranks out regular columns for newspaper clients. Major news organizations hire survey companies to tap public sentiment regularly on specific issues.

About 300 companies are in the survey business in the United States, most performing advertising and product-related opinion research for private clients. During election campaigns, political candidates become major clients. There are dozens of other survey companies that do confidential research for and about the media. Their findings are important because they determine what kind of advertising will run and where, what programs will be developed and broadcast and which ones will be canceled. Some television stations even use such research to choose anchors for major newscasts.

probability sampling

Although polling has become a high-profile business, many people do not understand how questions to a few hundred individuals can tell the mood of 250 million Americans. In the probability sampling method pioneered by George Gallup in the 1940s, four factors figure into accurate surveying:

Sample Size.   To learn how Layne College students feel about abortion on demand, you start by asking one student. Because you can hardly generalize from one student to the whole student body of 2,000, you ask a second student. If both agree, you start developing a tentative sense of how Layne students feel, but because you cannot have much confidence in such a tiny sample, you ask a third student, and a fourth and a fifth. At some point between interviewing just one and all 2,000 Layne students, you can draw a reasonable conclusion.

Statisticians have found that **384** is a magic number for many surveys. Put simply, no matter how large the **population** being sampled, if every member has an equal opportunity to be polled, you need ask only 384 people to be 95 percent confident that you are within 5 percentage points of a precise reading. For a lot of surveys, that is close enough. Here is a breakdown, from Philip Meyer's *Precision Journalism,* a book for journalists on surveying, on necessary sample sizes for 95 percent confidence and being within 5 percentage points:

George Gallup
Introduced probability sampling.

quota sampling
Demographics coincide with whole population.

probability sampling
Everyone in population being surveyed has an equal chance to be sampled.

statistical extrapolation
Drawing conclusions from segment of whole.

Institute of American Public Opinion
Gallup polling organization.

sample size
Number of people surveyed.

384
Number of people in properly selected sample for results to provide 95 percent confidence that results have less than 5 percent margin error.

population size
Number of people in group being studied.

Population Size	Sample Size
Infinity	384
500,000	384
100,000	383
50,000	381
10,000	370
5,000	357
3,000	341
2,000	322
1,000	278

At Layne, with a total enrollment of 2,000, the sample size would need to be 322 students.

Sample Selection. Essential in probability sampling is giving every member of the population being sampled an equal chance to be interviewed. If, for example, you want to know how Kansans intend to vote, you cannot merely go to a Wichita street corner and survey the first 384 people who pass by. You would need to check a list of the state's 675,000 registered voters and then divide by the magic number, 384:

$$\frac{675,000}{384} = 1,758$$

You would need to talk with every 1,758th person on the list. At Layne College, 2,000 divided by 322 would mean an interval of 6.2. Every sixth person in the student body would need to be polled.

Besides the right sample size and proper interval selection, two other significant variables affect survey accuracy: margin of error and confidence level.

Margin of Error. For absolute precision, every person in the population must be interviewed, but such precision is hardly ever needed, and the process would be prohibitively expensive and impracticable. Pollsters, therefore, must decide what is an acceptable margin of error for every survey they conduct. This is a complex matter, but, in simple terms, you can have a fairly high level of confidence that a properly designed survey with 384 respondents can yield results within 5 percentage points, either way, of being correct. If the survey finds that two candidates for statewide office are running 51 to 49 percent, for example, the race is too close to call with a sample of 384. If, however, the survey says that the candidates are running 56 to 44 percent, you can be reasonably confident who is ahead in the race because, even if the survey is 5 points off on the high side for the leader, the candidate at the very least has 51 percent support (56 percent minus a maximum 5 percentage points for possible error). At best, the trailing candidate has 49 percent (44 percent plus a maximum 5 percentage points for possible error).

Increasing the sample size will reduce the margin of error. Meyer gives this breakdown:

Population Size	Sample Size	Margin of Error
Infinity	384	5 percentage points
Infinity	600	4 percentage points
Infinity	1,067	3 percentage points
Infinity	2,401	2 percentage points
Infinity	9,605	1 percentage point

Professional polling organizations that sample American voters typically use sample sizes between 1,500 and 3,000 to increase accuracy. Also, measuring subgroups within the population being sampled requires that each subgroup, such as men and women, Catholics and non-Catholics, or Northerners and Southerners, be represented by 384 properly selected people.

Confidence Level. With a sample of 384, pollsters can claim a relatively high 95 percent confidence level, that is, that they are within 5 percentage points of being on the mark. For many surveys, this is sufficient statistical validity. If the confidence level needs to be higher, or if the margin of error needs to be decreased, the number of people surveyed will need to be increased. In short, the level of confidence and margin of error are inversely related. A larger sample can improve confidence, just as it also can reduce the margin of error.

quota sampling

Besides probability sampling, pollsters survey cross-sections of the whole population. This quota sampling technique gave Gallup his historic 1936 conclusions about the Roosevelt-Landon presidential race. With quota sampling, a pollster checking an election campaign interviews a sample of people that includes a quota of men and women that corresponds to the number of male and female registered voters. The sample might also include an appropriate quota of Democrats, Republicans and independents; of poor, middle-income and wealthy people; of Catholics, Jews and Protestants; of Southerners, Midwesterners and New Englanders; of the employed and unemployed; and other breakdowns significant to the pollster.

Both quota and probability sampling are valid if done correctly, but Gallup abandoned quota sampling because he could not pinpoint public opinion closer than 4 percentage points on average. With probability sampling, he regularly came within 2 percentage points.

evaluating surveys

Sidewalk interviews cannot be expected to reflect the views of the population. The people who respond to such polls are self-selected by virtue of being at a given place at a given time. Just as unreliable are call-in polls with 800 or 900 telephone numbers. These polls test the views only of people who are aware of the poll and who have sufficiently strong opinions to want to be heard.

Journalists run the risk of being duped when special-interest groups suggest that news stories be written based on their privately conducted surveys. Some organizations selectively release self-serving conclusions.

To guard against being duped, the Associated Press insists on knowing methodology details before running poll stories. The AP tells reporters to ask:

- **How many persons were interviewed and how were they selected?** Any survey of fewer than 384 persons selected randomly from the population group has a greater margin for error than usually is tolerated.

- **When was the poll taken?** Opinions shift over time. During election campaigns, shifts can be quick, even overnight.

- **Who paid for the poll?** With privately commissioned polls, reporters should be skeptical, asking whether the results being released constitute everything learned

> **confidence level**
> Degree of certainty that a survey is accurate.

in the survey. The timing of the release of political polls to be politically advantageous is not uncommon.

- **What was the sampling error?** Margins of error exist in all surveys unless everyone in the population is surveyed.

- **How was the poll conducted?** Whether a survey was conducted over the telephone or face to face in homes is important. Polls conducted on street corners or in shopping malls are not worth much statistically. Mail surveys are flawed unless surveyors follow up on people who do not answer the original questionnaires.

- **How were questions worded and in what order were they asked?** Drafting questions is an art. Sloppily worded questions yield sloppy conclusions. Leading questions and loaded questions can skew results. So can question sequencing.

It is at great risk that a polling company's client misrepresents survey results. Most polling companies, concerned about protecting their reputations, include a clause in their contracts with clients that gives the pollster the right to approve the release of findings. The clause usually reads: "When misinterpretation appears, we shall publicly disclose what is required to correct it, notwithstanding our obligation for client confidentiality in all other respects."

latter-day straw polls

The ABC and CNN television networks dabble, some say irresponsibly, with phone-in polling on public issues. The vehicle was the **900 telephone number,** which listeners could dial at 50 cents a call to register yea or nay on a question. These **straw polls** can be fun, but statistically they are meaningless.

Just as dubious are the candid camera features, popular in weekly newspapers, in which a question is put to citizens on the street. The photos of half a dozen individuals and their comments are then published, often on the editorial page. These features are circulation builders for small publications whose financial success depends on how many local names and mug shots can be crammed into an issue, but it is only coincidental when the views expressed are representative of the population as a whole.

These **roving-photographer** features are at their worst when people are not given time to formulate an intelligent response. The result too often is contributions to the public babble, not public understanding. The result is irresponsible pseudojournalism.

900 numbers
Used for call-in surveys; respondents select selves to participate.

straw poll
Respondents select selves to be polled; unreliable indicator of public opinion.

roving photographer
Statistically unsound way to tap public opinion.

measuring audience size

(STUDY PREVIEW) To attract advertisers, the mass media need to know the number and kinds of people they reach. This is done for the print media by audits and for the broadcast media by surveys. Although surveying is widely accepted for obtaining such data, some approaches are more reliable than others.

newspaper and magazine audits

The number of copies a newspaper or magazine puts out, called **circulation,** is fairly easy to calculate. It is simple arithmetic involving data like press runs, subscription sales and unsold copies returned from newsracks. Many publishers follow strict procedures, which are checked by independent audit organizations, such as the **Audit Bureau of Circulations,** to assure advertisers that the system is honest and circulation claims comparable.

The Audit Bureau of Circulations was formed in 1914 to remove the temptation for publishers to inflate their claims to attract advertisers and hike ad rates. Inflated claims, contagious in some cities, were working to the disadvantage of honest publishers. Today, most newspapers and magazines belong to ABC, which means that they follow the bureau's standards for reporting circulation and are subject to the bureau's audits.

broadcast ratings

Radio and television audiences are harder to measure, but advertisers have no less need for counts to help them decide where to place ads and to know what is a fair price. To keep track of broadcast audiences, a whole industry, now with about 200 companies, has developed. The **A.C. Nielsen Co.** tracks network television viewership. The American Research Bureau, usually called **Arbitron,** is the leader in measuring radio audiences.

Radio ratings began in 1929 when advertisers asked pollster **Archibald Crossley** to determine how many people were listening to network programs. Crossley checked a small sample of households and then extrapolated the data into national ratings, the same process that radio and television audience tracking companies still use, although there have been refinements.

In the 1940s, Nielsen began telling advertisers which radio programs were especially popular among men, women and children. Nielsen also divided listenership into age brackets: 18–34, 35–49, and 50 plus. These were called **demographic breakdowns.** When Nielsen moved into television monitoring in 1950, it expanded audience data

circulation
Number of readers of a publication.

Audit Bureau of Circulations
Checks newspaper, magazine circulation claims.

ratings
Measurements of broadcast audience size.

A. C. Nielsen Co.
Surveys television viewership.

Arbitron
Surveys radio listenership.

Archibald Crossley
First broadcast audience surveys.

demographics
Characteristics of groups within a population being sampled, including age, gender, affiliations.

Broadcasting &Cable PEOPLE'S CHOICE
Ratings according to Nielsen
March 16-22

KEY: RANKING/SHOW [PROGRAM RATING/SHARE] • TOP TEN SHOWS OF THE WEEK ARE NUMBERED IN RED • TELEVISION UNIVERSE ESTIMATED AT 98.0 MILLION HOUSEHOLDS; ONE RATINGS POINT=980,000 TV HOMES
YELLOW TINT IS WINNER OF TIME SLOT • (NR)=NOT RANKED; RATING/SHARE ESTIMATED FOR PERIOD SHOWN • *PREMIERE • SOURCES: NIELSEN MEDIA RESEARCH, CBS RESEARCH • GRAPHIC BY KENNETH RAY

Week 26

	abc	CBS	NBC	FOX	UPN	WB
	8.7/14	**7.0/11**	**8.4/13**	**9.1/14**	**2.2/3**	**2.9/4**
MONDAY 8:00	55. America's Funniest Home Videos 7.7/12	47. Cosby 8.2/13	66. Suddenly Susan 7.2/11	63. Melrose Place 7.3/11	114. In the House 2.0/3	95. 7th Heaven 3.8/6
8:30		45. Ev Loves Raymd 8.3/13	75. House Rules 6.4/10		109. Mal & Eddie 2.2/3	
9:00	19. 20/20 9.9/15	68. The Closer 7.1/11	73. Caroline in/City 6.6/10	16. Ally McBeal 10.8/16	107. Good News 2.3/3	114. Three 2.0/3
9:30		72. George & Leo 6.7/10	82. Suddenly Susan 5.8/9		109. Sparks 2.2/3	
10:00 10:30	34. The Practice 8.6/15	82. Brooklyn South 5.8/10	10. Dateline NBC 12.1/21			
	8.9/15	**7.7/13**	**10.3/17**	**4.8/8**	**1.9/5**	**4.1/6**
TUESDAY 8:00	33. Home Imprvmt 8.7/14	25. JAG 9.3/15	17. Mad About You 10.5/17	90. 12th Annual American Comedy Awards 4.8/8	111. Moesha 2.1/4	101. Buffy/Vampire Slayer 3.4/5
8:30	49. Smthg So Right 8.0/13		25. For Your Love* 9.3/15		111. Clueless 2.1/3	
9:00	14. Home Imprvmt 11.6/18	63. Public Eye with Bryant Gumbel 7.3/12	12. Frasier 12.0/19		117. Mal & Eddie 1.7/3	90. Dawson's Creek 4.8/8
9:30	49. That's Life 8.0/13		18. Lateline 10.2/16		116. In the House 1.9/3	
10:00 10:30	41. NYPD Blue 8.4/15	77. 48 Hours Special 6.3/11	19. Dateline NBC 9.9/18			
	9.6/16	**7.4/12**	**9.3/15**	**6.4/10**	**2.7/4**	**3.7/6**
WEDNESDAY 8:00	31. Spin City 9.0/15	56. The Nanny 7.6/13	81. NewsRadio 5.9/10	41. Beverly Hills, 90210 8.4/14	102. Star Trek: Voyager 3.1/5	99. Sister, Sistr 3.6/6
8:30	22. Dharma & Greg 9.7/16	79. Cybill 6.2/10	56. Seinfeld 7.6/12			97. Smart Guy 3.7/6
9:00	13. Drew Carey 11.8/19	70. Michael Hayes 7.0/11	37. 3rd Rock fr/Sun 8.5/14	93. Significant Others 4.3/7	107. The Sentinel 2.3/4	97. Wayans Bros 3.7/6
9:30	24. Two Guys/Girl* 9.4/15		23. Working 9.5/15			95. Steve Harvey 3.8/5
10:00 10:30	31. PrimeTime Live 9.0/16	41. Chicago Hope 8.4/15	10. Dateline NBC 12.1/21			
	6.6/11	**7.8/13**	**16.4/26**	**6.1/9**		
THURSDAY 8:00	94. Prey 4.0/6	54. NCAA Basketball Championship 7.8/13	3. Friends 15.9/26	61. Busted on the Job 7.4/12		
8:30			4. Just Shoot Me 15.7/25			
9:00	52. ABC Thursday Night Movie—Waterworld, Part 2 7.9/13		1. Seinfeld 20.8/31	92. New York Undercover 4.7/7		
9:30			4. Caroline in/City 15.7/24			
10:00		75. NCAA Basketball Championship 6.4/13	2. Seinfeld 16.3/27			
10:30			6. Frasier 14.2/25			
	9.3/17	**7.6/14**	**7.4/13**	**5.5/10**		
FRIDAY 8:00	37. Sabrina/Witch 8.5/16	66. NCAA Basketball Championship 7.2/14	87. Players 5.7/11	88. Beyond Belief: Fact or Fiction 5.2/10		
8:30	45. Boy Meets Wrld 8.3/15					
9:00	47. Sabrina/Witch 8.2/14		27. Dateline NBC 9.1/16	82. Millennium 5.8/10		
9:30	60. Boy Meets Wrld 7.5/13					
10:00 10:30	12. 20/20 11.6/21	52. NCAA Basketball Championship 7.9/16	56. Homicide: Life on the Street 7.6/14			
	5.5/10	**8.1/15**	**6.5/12**	**7.0/13**		
SATURDAY 8:00	82. Saturday Night at the Movies—Beverly Hills Cop 3 5.8/10	49. Dr. Quinn, Medicine Woman 8.0/15	80. TV Censored Bloopers 6.1/11	77. Cops 6.3/12		
8:30				68. Cops 7.1/13		
9:00		56. The Magnificent Seven 7.6/14	74. The Pretender 6.5/12	63. AMW: America Fights Back 7.3/13		
9:30						
10:00 10:30	89. ABC News Saturday Night 4.9/9	27. Walker, Texas Ranger 9.1/18	71. Profiler 6.9/13			
	8.2/13	**13.9/22**	**8.8/14**	**7.7/12**		**2.7/4**
SUNDAY 7:00	27. ABC Family Movie—The Little Rascals 9.1/15	(nr) NCAA Bsktb Ch 11.5/24	34. Dateline NBC 8.6/15	82. World's Funniest! 5.8/10		111. Nick Freno 2.1/4
7:30		6. 60 Minutes 14.2/23				104. Parent 'Hood 2.4/4
8:00			19. Dateline NBC 9.9/15	27. The Simpsons 9.1/14		104. Sister, Sister 2.8/4
8:30		9. Touched by an Angel 12.9/20		34. Damon* 8.6/13		102. Jamie Foxx 3.1/5
9:00	61. ABC Sunday Night Movie—Blood on Her Hands 7.4/12		41. NBC Sunday Night Movie—I've Been Waiting for You 8.4/14	37. The X-Files 8.5/13		100. Unhap Ev Af 3.5/5
9:30		8. CBS Sunday Movie—It Could Happen to You 14.0/23				105. Alright Alrdy 2.4/4
10:00 10:30						
WEEK AVG	**8.1/14**	**8.8/15**	**9.6/16**	**6.7/11**	**2.3/4**	**3.3/5**
STD AVG	**8.5/14**	**9.9/16**	**10.4/17**	**7.2/12**	**2.9/5**	**3.1/5**

42

March 30 1998 **Broadcasting & Cable**

Ratings and Shares. The trade journal *Broadcasting & Cable* reports the network Nielsens weekly. The number before each show indicates its place. NBC's "Seinfeld," at 9 p.m. Thursday, led this week. One measure of audience is the "rating," the percentage of television-equipped households viewing a program. "Seinfeld's" rating was 20.8 percent. Because 97 million U.S. households have television sets, each percentage point is valued at 970,000 households, which means 20,176,000 households were watching. A second audience measure is called "share," which is the percentage of all households with a television on. "Seinfeld" had a 31 share, far outdistancing CBS' basketball championships, 13; ABC's movie, 13; and Fox's "New York Undercover," 7. The other 26 percent of households that were watching television had something else on.

into more breakdowns. Today breakdowns include income, education, religion, occupation, neighborhood and even which products the viewers of certain programs use frequently.

While Archibald Crossley's early ratings were sponsored by advertisers, today networks and individual stations also commission ratings to be done. The television networks pass ratings data on to advertisers immediately. Local stations usually recast the raw data for brochures that display the data in ways that put the station in the most favorable light. These brochures are distributed by station sales representatives to advertisers. While advertisers receive ratings data from the stations and networks, major advertising agencies have contracts with Nielsen, Arbitron and other market research companies to gather audience data to meet their specifications.

audience measurement techniques

The primary techniques, sometimes used in combination, for measuring broadcast audiences are:

Interviews. In his pioneer 1929 listenership polling, Archibald Crossley placed telephone calls to randomly selected households. Today, many polling companies use telephone interviews exclusively. Some companies conduct face-to-face interviews, which can elicit fuller information, although it is more expensive and time-consuming.

Diaries. Many ratings companies give forms to selected households to record what stations were on at particular times. Some companies distribute diaries to every member of a household. Arbitron's diaries go to everybody over age 12 in selected households, which provide data on age and gender preferences for certain stations and programs. Participants mail these diaries back to Arbitron, which tabulates the results.

Meters. For television ratings, Nielsen installs meters to record when television sets are on and to which channels they are tuned. Early devices like Nielsen's **audimeter** recorded data on film cartridges, which were mailed back every two weeks to Nielsen. Today, new devices transmit data daily by telephone to Nielsen's central computer. With the new meters, Nielsen is able to generate next-day reports, called **overnights,** for the networks.

Ratings companies make ongoing adjustments to their sample sizes and methods. Nielsen once said that the 1,170 homes that had audimeters provided a sound sample. Later, Nielsen added diaries to 2,000 more homes to widen the statistical base. With a larger base, audiences could be subdivided into categories to determine viewing prefer-

interviews
Face-to-face, mail, telephone survey technique.

diaries
Sampling technique in which respondents keep their own records.

audimeter
Mechanical monitor that tracks viewing habits.

overnights
Next-morning reports on network viewership.

Measuring Broadcast Audiences. Many audience measurement companies ask selected households to keep diaries on their listening and viewing habits. Through statistical extrapolations, these companies claim they can discover the size of the total audience for particular programs and stations. This Nielsen diary asks participants to list who is watching, which allows broadcast executives and advertisers to learn demographic details about this audience. Under pressure for more accurate television ratings, Nielsen, Arbitron and other audience measurement companies are shifting from written diaries to electronic meters. With a meter, members of participating households punch in when they start watching. With more advanced meters, punching in is not even required. The meters sense who is watching by body mass, which is programmed into the meter for every member of the household when it is installed.

ences by age groups, regions and other breakdowns. Today, Nielsen has 4,000 selected households wired with meters.

Though an improvement over interviews and diaries in several respects, the early meters recorded only whether a television set was turned on and to which channel it was tuned—not whether anybody was watching. In many households, it came to be realized, people left the television on as background noise, which distorted the final data. To address this problem, Nielsen and Arbitron installed new push-button devices called **peoplemeters** and asked people in the surveyed households to punch in personal codes to identify who was watching certain programs—mom, dad, oldsters, teenagers, little kids, or nobody at all.

Like diaries, the first peoplemeters required participants to log their viewing dutifully. It was recognized that not everyone in every wired household could be expected to be equally conscientious about recording their "entries" and "exits." To address this problem, new **passive meters** can recognize household members automatically by body mass, which eliminates the hazard of some viewers' failing to record their watching.

criticism of ratings

However sophisticated the ratings services have become, they have critics. Many fans question the accuracy of ratings when their favorite television program is cancelled because the network finds the ratings inadequate. Something is wrong, they say, when the viewing preferences of a few thousand households determine network programming for the entire nation. Though it seems incredible to someone unknowledgeable about statistical probability, the sample base of major ratings services

peoplemeter
Monitor that tracks individual viewing habits.

passive meters
Recognize individuals by body mass to track viewing habits.

global television ratings

Colgate-Palmolive, the global toiletries company, has a problem figuring out how much its ad dollars are buying in different countries because audience rating agencies in different countries have developed separate terminology. In Austria, the word "housewife" means anyone, male or female, 18 or older, who maintains a house. The French, however, define "housewife" as a female shopper. Colgate isn't alone. All multinational advertisers end up comparing apples and oranges when they try to get a clear idea on how much to invest in different countries to reach comparable audiences of likely customers.

Several major advertising and television trade groups now are working up definitions to standardize television audience measurement terminologies. It's no small task. Should ratings include only live viewing or also VCR viewing? Should a 4-year-old count equally with an adult? How do you count viewers where one set serves a whole village that gathers and watches together? Should an impoverished minority-group member count as much as an affluent elite whose discretionary income glimmers in advertisers' eyes? And, yes, for the sake of Colgate-Palmolive, who is and who isn't a housewife?

Hashing out these questions, and also whether national and regional traditions and preferences will surrender to universal standards, are:

- Advertising Research Foundation, a United States organization.
- European Broadcasting Union.
- European Association of Advertising Agencies.
- Group of European Audience Researchers.
- World Federation of Advertisers.

The goal is to generate data that can be exchanged meaningfully across borders.

---

like Nielsen generally is considered sufficient to extrapolate reliably on viewership in the 97 million U.S. households.

It was not always so. Doubts peaked in the 1940s and 1950s when it was learned that some ratings services lied about sample size and were less than scientific in choosing samples. A congressional investigation in 1963 prompted the networks to create the **Broadcast Ratings Council** to accredit ratings companies and audit their reports.

Ratings have problems, some inherent in differing methodologies and some attributable to human error and fudging:

Discrepancies. When different ratings services come up with widely divergent findings in the same market, advertisers become suspicious. Minor discrepancies can be explained by different sampling methods, but significant discrepancies point to flawed methodology or execution. It was discrepancies of this sort that led to the creation of the Broadcast Ratings Council.

Slanted Results. Sales reps of some local stations, eager to demonstrate to advertisers that their stations have large audiences, extract only the favorable data from survey results. It takes a sophisticated local advertiser to reconcile slanted and fudged claims.

Sample Selection. Some ratings services select their samples meticulously, giving every household in a market a statistically equal opportunity to be sampled.

> **Broadcast Ratings Council**
> Accredits ratings companies.

Fickle Audience. Television executives look to survey research to find ways to reach more viewers. In 1994, CNN's ratings were down 25 percent from a year earlier. That prompted the network to scrap some soft-news programs, including "Living in the '90s," and to create new call-in sports and news programs, one with a live audience. CNN's problem is that it cannot sustain the huge audience it draws when everybody is intently interested in major news, like the O. J. Simpson case or Operation Desert Storm. The network typically draws only about 400,000 viewers. Although CNN's audience is educated, affluent and attractive to advertisers, more viewers would mean more revenue. CNN accounted for 70 percent of Turner Broadcasting's operating earnings before Turner was subsumed into Time Warner.

Some sample selections are seriously flawed: How reliable, for example, are the listenership claims of a rock 'n' roll station that puts a disc jockey's face on billboards all over town and then sends the disc jockey to a teenage dance palace to ask about listening preferences?

Hyping. Ratings-hungry stations have learned how to build audiences during **sweeps** weeks in February, May and November when major local television ratings are done. Consider:

- Radio give-aways often coincide with ratings periods.

- Many news departments promote sensationalistic series for the sweeps and then retreat to routine coverage when the ratings period is over. Just ahead of one 1988 Minneapolis sweeps, one station mailed out thousands of questionnaires, asking people to watch its programs and mail back the form. Accused of trickery to look good in the ratings, the station responded with a straight face that it merely was trying a new technique to strengthen viewership. The timing, it argued, was mere coincidence.

- Besides sweep weeks, there are **black weeks** when no ratings are conducted. In these periods, some stations run all kinds of odd and dull serve-the-public programs that they would never consider during a sweeps period.

Respondent Accuracy. Respondents don't always answer truthfully. People have an opportunity to tell interviewers or diaries that they watched "Masterpiece Theater" on PBS instead of less classy fare. Shock radio and trash television may have more audience than the ratings show.

Zipping, Zapping and Flushing. Ratings services measure audiences for programs and for different times of day, but they do not measure whether commercials are watched. Advertisers are interested, of course, in whether the programs in which their ads are sandwiched are popular, but more important to them is whether people are watching the ads.

This vacuum in audience measurements was documented in the 1960s when somebody with a sense of humor correlated a major drop in Chicago water pressure with the Super Bowl halftime. Football fans were getting off the couch by the thousands at halftime to go to the bathroom. Advertisers were missing many people because viewers were watching the program but not the ads.

This problem has been exacerbated with the advent of handheld television remote controls. Viewers can zip from station to station to avoid commercials, and when they record programs for later viewing they can zap out the commercials.

measuring audience reaction

(STUDY PREVIEW)   The television ratings business has moved beyond measuring audience size to measuring audience reaction. Researchers measure audience reaction with numerous methods including focus groups, galvanic skin checks and prototypes.

focus groups

Television consulting companies measure audience reaction with **focus groups.** Typically an interview crew goes to a shopping center, chooses a dozen individuals by gender and age, and offers them cookies, soft drinks and $25 each to sit down and watch a taped local newscast. A moderator then asks their reactions, sometimes with loaded and leading questions to open them up. It is a tricky research method that depends highly on the skill of the moderator. In one court case, an anchor who lost her job as a result of responses to a focus group complained that the moderator contaminated the process with prejudicial assertions and questions:

- "This is your chance to get rid of the things you don't like to see on the news."

- "Come on, unload on those sons of bitches who make $100,000 a year."

- "This is your chance to do more than just yell at the TV. You can speak up and say I really hate that guy or I really like that broad."

- "Let's spend 30 seconds destroying this anchor. Is she a mutt? Be honest about this."

Even when conducted skillfully, focus groups have the disadvantage of reflecting the opinion of the loudest respondent.

galvanic skin checks

Consulting companies hired by television stations run a great variety of studies to determine audience reaction. Local stations, which originate news programs and not much else, look to these consultants for advice on news sets, story selection, and even which anchors and reporters are most popular. Besides surveys, these consultants sometimes use **galvanic skin checks.** Wires are attached to individuals in a sample group of viewers to measure pulse and skin reactions, such as perspiration. Advocates of these tests claim that they reveal how much interest a newscast evokes and whether it is positive or negative.

These tests were first used to check audience reaction to advertisements, but today some stations look to them in deciding whether to remodel a studio. A dubious use, from a journalistic perspective, is using galvanic skin checks to determine what kinds of stories to cover and whether to find new anchors and reporters. The skin checks reward short, photogenic stories like fires and accidents rather than significant stories, which tend to be longer and don't lend themselves to flashy video. The checks also favor good-looking, smooth anchors and reporters regardless of their journalistic competence. One wag was literally correct when he called this "a heartthrob approach to journalism."

prototype research

Before making major investments, media executives need as much information as they can obtain to determine how to enhance a project's chances for success or whether it has a chance at all. The **American Research Institute** of Los Angeles specializes in showing previews of television programs and even promotional ads to sample audiences. It is a method originated by movie studios, which invite people to advance showings and watch their reaction to decide how to advertise a new film most effectively, how to time the film's release and even whether to re-edit the film.

hyping
Intensive promotion to attract audience during ratings periods.

sweeps
When broadcast ratings are conducted.

black weeks
Periods when ratings not conducted.

zipping
Viewers change television channels to avoid commercials.

zapping
Viewers record programs and eliminate commercial breaks.

flush factor
Viewers leave during commercials to go to refrigerator, bathroom, etc.

focus groups
Small groups interviewed in loosely structured ways for opinion, reactions.

galvanic skin checks
Monitor pulse, skin responses to stimuli.

prototype research
Checks response to product still in development.

American Research Institute
Movie prototype research.

When Gannett decided to establish a new newspaper, *USA Today,* it created proto-types, each designed differently, to test readers' reactions. Many new magazines are preceded with at least one trial issue to sample marketplace reaction and to show to potential advertisers.

In network television, a prototype may even make it on the air in the form of a pilot. One or a few episodes are tested, usually in prime time with a lot of promotion, to see if the audience goes for the program concept. Some made-for-television movies actually are test runs to determine whether a series might be spun off from the movies.

audience analysis

(STUDY PREVIEW) Traditional demographic polling methods divided people by gender, age and other easily identifiable population characteristics. Today, media people use sophisticated lifestyle breakdowns such as geodemographics and psychographics to match the content of their publications, broadcast programs and advertising to the audiences they seek.

demographics

Early in the development of public-opinion surveying, pollsters learned that broad breakdowns had limited usefulness. Archibald Crossley's pioneering radio sur-veys, for example, told the number of people who were listening to network pro-grams, which was valuable to the networks and their advertisers, but Crossley's figures did not tell how many listeners were men or women, urban or rural, old or young. Such breakdowns of overall survey data, called demographics, were developed in the 1930s as Crossley, Gallup and other early pollsters refined their work.

Today, if demographic data indicate a political candidate is weak in the Midwest, campaign strategists can gear the candidate's message to Midwestern concerns. Through demographics, advertisers keen on reaching young women can identify mag-azines that will carry their ads to that audience. If advertisers seek an elderly audience, they can use demographic data to determine where to place their television ads.

While demographics remains valuable today, newer methods can break the popu-lation into categories that have even greater usefulness. These newer methods, which include geodemography, provide lifestyle breakdowns.

Marketing people have developed **cohort analysis,** a specialized form of demo-graphics, to identify generations and then design and produce products with genera-tional appeal. Advertising people then gear media messages with the images, music, humor and other generational variables that appeal to the target cohort. The major cohorts are dubbed

- **Generation X,** who came of age in the 1980s.

- **Baby-Boomers,** who came of age in the late 1960s and 1970s.

- **Post-War Generation,** who came of age in the 1950s.

- **World War II Veterans,** who came of age in the 1940s.

- **Depression Survivors,** who came of age during the economic depression of the 1930s.

demographics
Age, race, gender, ethnicity, affiliations and other char-acteristics of a subgroup of people.

cohort analysis
demographic tool to identify marketing targets by common characteristics.

Generation X
today's 20-something generation.

Baby boomers
today's 30-something and 40-something generation.

Post-war generation
today's 50-something generation.

World War II Veterans
today's 60-something generation.

Depression survivors
today's 70-something generation.

Cohort analysis has jarred traditional thinking that people, as they get older, simply adopt their parents' values. The new 50-plus generation, for example, grew up on Coke and Pepsi drinks and, to the dismay of coffee growers, prefers to start the day with cola—not the coffee their parents drank.

The Chrysler automobile company was early to recognize that Baby-Boomers aren't interested in buying Cadillac-type luxury cars even when they have amassed the money to afford them. In 1996, Chrysler scrapped plans for a new luxury car to compete with Cadillac and instead introduced the $35,000 open-top 1997 Plymouth Prowler that gave Baby-Boomers a nostalgic feel for the hot rods of their youth. Chrysler also determined that graying Baby-Boomers preferred upscale Jeeps to the luxo-barge cars that appealed to the Post-War generation.

Advertising people who use cohort analysis know that Baby-Boomers, although now in their 50s, are still turned on to pizzas and the Rolling Stones. In short, the habits of their youth stick with a generation as it gets older. What appealed to the 30-something a decade ago won't necessarily sail with today's 30-something set. David Bostwick, Chrysler's marketing research director, puts it this way: "Nobody wants to become their parents."

Cohort Analysis. When Oldsmobile realized in the 1980s that young buyers weren't maturing into clones of their parents, the company flaunted its cars with the advertising slogan "It's not your father's Oldsmobile." Unfortunately for Olds, the cars were not much different and sales continued to skid. Today, marketing and advertising people are using cohort analysis to develop products, not just slogans, to appeal to different generations. Chrysler did this in the late 1990s, dropping plans for the LHX luxury car which might have appealed to people in their 50s a generation ago but not to today's aging baby-boomers. For the new 50-something generation, Chrysler created the Plymouth Prowler hotrod, which stirred wonderful memories of affluent car-buyers who grew up in the 1960s and 1970s.

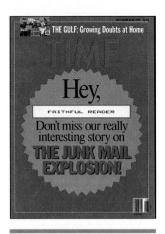

Geodemographics. Many magazines can customize their advertising and editorial content to match the interests of readers through sophisticated geodemographic audience analysis. *Time* demonstrated the potential of its TargetSelect geodemographic program by printing the name of each subscriber as part of the cover art for the November 26, 1990, issue. The cover underscored the point of the lead article about the sort of TargetSelect sophistication also used by "junk mail" companies to match fliers sent through the mail with the likeliest customers for their products.

Jonathan Robbin
Devised PRIZM geodemography system.

PRIZM
Identifies population characteristics by zip code.

geodemography
Demographic characteristics by geographic area.

psychographics
Breaking down a population by lifestyle characteristics.

VALS
Psychographic analysis by values, lifestyle, life stage.

geodemographics

While demographics, including cohort analysis, remain valuable today, new methods can break the population into categories that have even greater usefulness. These newer methods, which include geodemography, provide lifestyle breakdowns.

Computer whiz **Jonathan Robbin** provided the basis for more sophisticated breakdowns in 1974 when he began developing his **PRIZM** system for **geodemography.** From census data, Robbin grouped every zip code by ethnicity, family life cycle, housing style, mobility and social rank. Then he identified 34 factors that statistically distinguished neighborhoods from each other. All this information was cranked through a computer programmed by Robbin to plug every zip code into 1 of 40 clusters. Here are the most frequent clusters created through PRIZM, which stands for Potential Rating Index for Zip Markets, with the labels Robbin put on them:

- **Blue-Chip Blues.** These are the wealthiest blue-collar suburbs with a median household income of $32,000 and house value of $72,600. These Blue-Chip Blues, as Robbin calls them, comprise about 6 percent of U.S. households. About 13 percent of these people are college graduates.

- **Young Suburbia.** Child-rearing outlying suburbs, 5.3 percent of U.S. population; median income, $38,600; median house value, $93,300; college grads, 24 percent.

- **Golden Ponds.** Rustic mountain, seashore or lakeside cottage communities, 5.2 percent; income, $20,100; house, $51,500; college grads, 13 percent.

The potential of Robbin's PRIZM system was clear at *Time, Newsweek* and *McCall's,* which re-sorted subscriber lists and created new zoned editions to allow advertisers to mix and match their messages with a great variety of subaudiences of potential customers. Cadillac could choose editions aimed at these PRIZM neighborhoods:

- **Blue-Blood Estates.** Wealthiest neighborhoods; income, $70,300; house, $200,000 plus; college grads, 51 percent.

- **Money and Brains.** Posh big-city enclaves of townhouses, condos and apartments; income, $45,800; house, $159,800; college grads, 46 percent.

For household products, Colgate-Palmolive might focus on:

- **Blue-Collar Nursery.** Middle-class, child-rearing towns; income, $30,000; house, $67,300; college grads, 10 percent.

Geodemographic breakdowns are used not only for magazine advertising but also for editorial content. At Time Warner magazines, geodemographic analysis permits issues to be edited for special audiences. *Time,* for example, has a 600,000 circulation edition for company owners, directors, board chairs, presidents, other titled officers and department heads. Among others are editions for physicians and college students.

psychographics

A refined lifestyle breakdown introduced in the late 1970s, **psychographics,** divides the population into lifestyle segments. One leading psychographics approach, the Values and Life-Styles program, known as **VALS** for short, uses an 85-page survey that was used to identify broad categories of people:

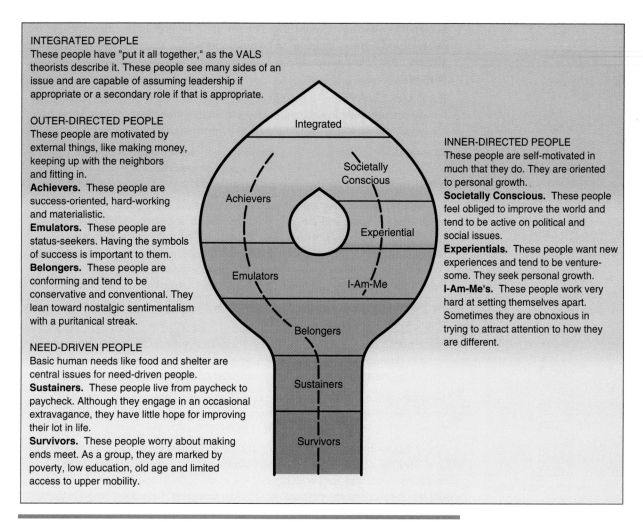

INTEGRATED PEOPLE
These people have "put it all together," as the VALS theorists describe it. These people see many sides of an issue and are capable of assuming leadership if appropriate or a secondary role if that is appropriate.

OUTER-DIRECTED PEOPLE
These people are motivated by external things, like making money, keeping up with the neighbors and fitting in.
Achievers. These people are success-oriented, hard-working and materialistic.
Emulators. These people are status-seekers. Having the symbols of success is important to them.
Belongers. These people are conforming and tend to be conservative and conventional. They lean toward nostalgic sentimentalism with a puritanical streak.

NEED-DRIVEN PEOPLE
Basic human needs like food and shelter are central issues for need-driven people.
Sustainers. These people live from paycheck to paycheck. Although they engage in an occasional extravagance, they have little hope for improving their lot in life.
Survivors. These people worry about making ends meet. As a group, they are marked by poverty, low education, old age and limited access to upper mobility.

INNER-DIRECTED PEOPLE
These people are self-motivated in much that they do. They are oriented to personal growth.
Societally Conscious. These people feel obliged to improve the world and tend to be active on political and social issues.
Experientials. These people want new experiences and tend to be venturesome. They seek personal growth.
I-Am-Me's. These people work very hard at setting themselves apart. Sometimes they are obnoxious in trying to attract attention to how they are different.

VALS Hierarchy. Developmental psychologists have long told us that people change their values as they mature. Today, many advertisers rely on the Values and Life-Styles model, VALS for short, which was derived from developmental psychology, to identify potential consumers and to design effective messages. Relatively few advertising messages are aimed at survivors and sustainers, who have little discretionary income. However, belongers and people on the divergent outer-directed or inner-directed paths are lucrative advertising targets for many products and services.

- **Belongers.** Comprising about 38 percent of the U.S. population, these people are conformists who are satisfied with mainstream values and are reluctant to change brands once they're satisfied. Belongers are not very venturesome and fit the stereotype of Middle America. They tend to be churchgoers and television watchers.

- **Achievers.** Comprising about 20 percent of the population, these are prosperous people who fit into a broader category of inner-directed consumers. Achievers pride themselves on making their own decisions. They're an upscale audience to which a lot of advertising is directed. As a group, achievers aren't heavy television watchers.

media
online

VALS: Now that you've read all about VALS in the textbook, see where you fit on the value and lifestyle hierarchy. You might be surprised after responding to this site's questionnaire. You will also learn that SRI has updated the hierarchy with VALS2.
http:future.sricom/vals/vals-home.html

- **Societally Conscious.** Comprising 11 percent of the population, these people are aware of social issues and tend to be politically active. The societally conscious also are upscale and inner-directed, and they tend to prefer reading to watching television.

- **Emulators.** Comprising 10 percent of the population, these people aspire to a better life but, not quite understanding how to do it, go for the trappings of prosperity. Emulators are status seekers, prone to suggestions on what makes the good life.

- **Experientials.** Comprising 5 percent of the population, these people are venturesome, willing to try new things in an attempt to experience life fully. They are a promising upscale audience for many advertisers.

- **I-Am-Me's.** Comprising 3 percent of the population, these people work hard to set themselves apart and are susceptible to advertising pitches that offer ways to differentiate themselves, which gives them a kind of subculture conformity. SRI International, which developed the VALS technique, characterized I-Am-Me's as "a guitar-playing punk rocker who goes around in shades and sports an earring." Rebellious youth, angry and maladjusted, fit this category.

- **Survivors.** This is a small downscale category that includes pensioners who worry about making ends meet.

- **Sustainers.** These people live from paycheck to paycheck. Although they indulge in an occasional extravagance, they have slight hope for improving their lot in life. Sustainers are a downscale category and aren't frequent advertising targets.

- **Integrateds.** Comprising only 2 percent of the population, integrateds are both creative and prosperous—willing to try different products and ways of doing things, and they have the wherewithal to do it.

Applying psychographics is not without hazard. The categories are in flux as society and lifestyles change. SRI researchers charted growth in the percentage of I-Am-Me's, experientials and the societally conscious in the 1980s and projected that they would be one-third of the population within a few years. Belongers were declining.

Another complication is that no person fits absolutely the mold of any one category. Even for individuals who fit one category better than another, there is no single mass medium to reach them. VALS research may show that achievers constitute the biggest market for antihistamines, but belongers also head to the medicine cabinet when they're congested.

applied and theoretical research

(STUDY PREVIEW) Media-sponsored research looks for ways to build audiences, to enhance profits and to program responsibly. In contrast, mass communication scholarship asks theoretical questions that can yield new understandings, regardless of whether there is a practical application.

media-sponsored research

applied research
Usefulness, usually economic, is apparent.

Studies sponsored by mass media companies seek knowledge that can be put to use. This is called **applied research.** When broadcasters underwrite research on media violence, they want answers to help make programming decisions. Audience measures and analysis are applied research, which can be put to work to enhance profits.

Mass media research ranges from developing new technology to seeking historical lessons from previous practices. Here are some fields of applied media research:

Technological Research.   Mass media companies and their suppliers finance research into technology to take economic advantage of new opportunities. Early television in the United States, for example, was spearheaded in the 1930s by RCA, which saw new opportunities for its NBC radio subsidiary.

Policy Analysis.   The media have intense interests in how changes in public policy will affect their business. The importance of good policy analysis was illustrated by the 1979 decision of the Federal Communications Commission to allow people to install backyard satellite dishes to pick up television signals. Analysts anticipated correctly that the television networks would go to satellites to send programs to their affiliates.

Opinion Surveys.   When anchor Dan Rather began wearing a sweater on the CBS Evening News, ratings improved. The network learned about the "sweater factor" from audience surveys. Survey research helps media executives make content decisions—whether to expand sports coverage, to hire a disc jockey away from the competition or to ax a dubious sitcom. Advertisers and public relations practitioners also look to public-opinion surveys.

mass communication scholarship

In contrast to applied research, theoretical research looks for truths regardless of practical application. Scholars consider most theoretical research on a higher level than applied research, partly because the force that drives it is the seeking of truths for their own sake rather than for any economic goal.

Profit motivated as they are, media organizations are not especially enthusiastic about funding theoretical research. There usually is no apparent or short-term economic return from theoretical scholarship. For this reason, most theoretical research occurs at major universities, whose institutional commitments include pushing back the frontiers of human knowledge, even if no economic reward is likely. Here are some of the kinds of studies and analyses that are the subject of **theoretical research:**

Effects Studies.   The greatest ferment in mass communication scholarship has involved questions about effects. In the 1920s, as mass communication theory took form, scholars began exploring the effects of mass communication and of the mass media themselves on society and individuals. Conversely, scholars are also interested in how ongoing changes and adjustments in society influence the mass media and their content.

Process Studies.   A continuing interest among scholars is the mystery of how the process of mass communication works. Just as human beings have developed theories to explain other great mysteries, such as thunder being caused by unhappy gods thrashing about in the heavens, mass communication scholars have developed a great many explanations to help us understand mass communication.

Gratifications Studies.   Beginning in the 1940s, studies about how and why individuals use the mass media attracted scholarly interest. These today are called **uses and gratifications studies.**

technological research
To improve, find new technology.

policy analysis
Seeks implications of public policy, future effects.

opinion surveys
Seek audience reaction, views.

theoretical research
Goal to advance knowledge.

effects studies
Impact of media on society, of society on media.

process studies
To understand the mass communication process.

uses and gratifications studies
To explain why people choose their media outlets.

Content Analysis. George Gerbner, a scholar of media violence, studied the 8 p.m. hour of network television for 19 years and found an average of 168 violent acts a week. Gerbner arrived at his disturbing statistic through **content analysis,** a research method involving the systematic counting of media content. Gerbner's tallying became a basic reference point for important further studies that correlated media-depicted violence with changes in incidents of violence in society at large.

It is also content analysis when a researcher tallies the column inches of sports in a newspaper to determine what percentage of available space goes to sports. While interesting for its own sake, such information can become a significant indicator of the changing role of sports in American life.

chapter wrap-up

The mass media are a rich field for study, partly because there are so many mysteries about how the process of mass communication works. Scholars have devised fascinating theories to explain the process, but their theories are widely divergent, and they squabble among themselves even about basic premises. Students aspiring to media careers have the special problem of trying to sort out these theories, which stem from scholarship and research on the same campuses where the work of journalism, advertising, broadcasting and public relations is taught.

Besides scholarship, often of an abstract sort, media research includes work that is distinctly practical. Publishers and broadcast executives need data on their circulations and reach in order to attract advertisers, and they are eager for research that can help them to reduce costs and tailor their product to larger or more profitable audiences. Both the media themselves and special research companies perform this kind of research.

Both theoretical research, which mostly is campus-based, and applied research, which the media eagerly fund, use many of the same tools. A unifying tool of these disparate research approaches is public-opinion sampling. It is used to track public opinion, which is essential in public relations work; to learn which television programs are the most watched, which is essential in programming and advertising decisions; and to determine the effects of media and how people use the media, which are scholarly endeavors.

content analysis
Measuring media content to establish database for analysis.

questions for review

1. What do surveys tell the mass media about their audiences?

2. How is the size of mass media audiences measured?

3. How is the reaction of people to the mass media measured?

4. What are techniques of audience analysis?

5. Why are mass media organizations more interested in applied than theoretical research?

questions for critical thinking

1. Street-corner polls are called straw polls because they are based on such weak methodology. Explain how quota sampling and probability sampling are improvements.

2. What is the basis for arguments that public-opinion surveys subvert democracy? What is the counterargument?

3. The Audit Bureau of Circulations and television rating services like A. C. Nielsen and Arbitron are essential media services to advertisers. How are these services similar? How different?

4. How can local television and radio stations manipulate their ratings? Why can't the Broadcast Ratings Council do anything about it?

5. Explain how applied research and theoretical research differ.

for further learning

Charles O. Bennett. *Facts Without Opinion: First Fifty Years of the Audit Bureau of Circulations* (Audit Bureau of Circulations, 1965).

George Gallup. *The Sophisticated Poll Watcher's Guide* (Princeton Opinion Press, 1972). Gallup, a pioneer pollster, answers critics who charge that polls pervert the democratic process. Gallup argues that polling oils the wheels of democracy by helping elected leaders determine the majority will.

Shearson A. Lowery and Melvin L. DeFleur. *Milestones in Mass Communication Research: Media Effects,* 3rd edition. (Longman, 1995). Beginners will find Lowery and DeFleur's chronicle an easily followed primer on developments in mass communication research.

Philip Meyer. *New Precision Journalism* (Indiana University Press, 1991). Meyer, a reporter who became a professor, explains how scholarly research methods, including survey research, can be applied in journalistic truth seeking.

William S. Rubens. "A Personal History of TV Ratings, 1929 to 1989 and Beyond." *Feedback* 30 (Fall 1989):4. Pages 3–15. Rubens, a former NBC vice president for research, draws on his experience for this thumbnail history of measuring broadcast audience.

Michael J. Weiss. *The Clustering of America* (Harper & Row, 1988). Weiss, a clever writer, describes Jonathan Robbin's geodemographic research and then takes the reader on a tour to view America through PRIZM eyes.

Roger D. Wimmer and Joseph R. Dominick. *Mass Media Research: An Introduction,* fifth edition. (Wadsworth, 1997.) The authors include the history of audience measures and research, including the techniques used in television ratings. Wimmer and Dominick also examine fundamentals of polling tecniques.

for keeping up to date

Public Opinion Quarterly is a scholarly publication. *American Demographics* and *Public Opinion* have a lot of general-interest content for media observers.

14

mass communication

in this chapter you will learn:

- The potentially most influential form of human communication is through mass media.

- Mass communicators reach mass audiences via mass media through a mysterious process called mass communication.

- Models are imperfect but useful vehicles for seeing how mass communication works.

- Mass communication and other human communication forms have the same fundamentals.

- Media gatekeepers and non-media regulators influence media messages.

- Impediments to the success of mass communication include noise and filters.

- The mass media amplify messages to reach large audiences.

The hour and minute, 2:32 a.m., will remain forever in **Peter Arnett**'s memory. That's when the 1991 war against Iraq escalated with allied bombing runs on Baghdad. Every dog in the neighborhood began barking like they were deranged. It was "dog radar," Arnett later surmised. In the next instant, the southern sky lit up in a huge flash. Bernard Shaw, who happened to be in Baghdad to interview the deputy foreign minister, grabbed for the microphone connected to a special four-wire circuit CNN had arranged to communicate out of the country. "Something is happening!" Shaw shouted into the mike as he stabbed at a control button to raise the network's headquarters in Atlanta. "Something is happening!" He was patched through to the anchor, and CNN's three reporters in Baghdad, Peter Arnett, John Holliman and Bernie Shaw, were live describing the first allied attack on the Iraqi capital. The whole world was listening.

The next morning CNN pulled most of its crew out of Baghdad, but Arnett, along with a producer and a technician, opted to stay. For the next few days, CNN was exclusive from Baghdad, a climactic point in the career of Peter Arnett. A New Zealander, he knocked around southeast Asia as a young reporter and landed finally with the Associated Press. He won a Pulitzer prize for his AP work in Vietnam. Later he covered war and crises in Cyprus, Lebanon, Iran and Central America for the AP, then CNN. Wars are what Peter Arnett does. His reports from Baghdad made his name a household word all over the world.

Arnett's courageous reporting from Baghdad illustrates many things about the mysterious process of mass communication, which is the subject of this chapter. Reflexively, Arnett converted his observations into messages and sent them out. Those are fundamentals in the communication process.

To understand Arnett's reports, viewers needed to put them into the framework of their own individual experience and values. This is true of all communication. Some viewers, including President George Bush, were angered at some Arnett stories, including one on a U.S. attack that, his source claimed, destroyed Iraq's only powdered milk factory. White House spokesperson Marlin Fitzwater called him "a conduit for Iraqi disinformation." Arnett stood by his story. Members of Congress denounced his reporting as somehow traitorous because it was from behind enemy lines. Some derisively called him "Baghdad Pete." Keep this in mind when you read about "filters" in the pages ahead.

Arnett was not free in his reporting from Baghdad. The Iraqi government assigned escorts who were selective where they took him. These "minders," as the escorts were called, also monitored his reports and could pull the plug. In his memoirs, *Live From the Battlefield,* Arnett describes how he told as much as he could without becoming an Iraqi propagandist, while always being accurate. These minders were what we call "regulators" in the mass communication process.

When Arnett wasn't live, his reports were edited by CNN people in Atlanta. These were "gatekeepers," another hurdle in a message's route from the source to the audience. Another impediment in Arnett's message getting through was equipment. He used a variety of means to get his stories out, including a satellite telephone with three backup signals. There also were transmissions to an intermediary CNN base in Jordan. The success of Arnett getting through to his audience was dependent on millions of electronic and mechanical components all working, including the controls on each individual viewer's television set.

Through all of this, Arnett received "feedback," another mass communication term. He was buoyed when Atlanta anchors congratulated him. When he learned the White House was vilifying him, he took note. When he saw military vehicles on a trip in the country and an Iraqi minder touched his fingers to his lips in a silent warning, Arnett knew he could not report that. Feedback is another element in the complex mass communication process.

Mass communication, in fact, has so many variables that we probably will never understand it well enough to predict reliably what the effect of a given message will be. Despite the complexity, however, we have no choice but to try to improve our understanding. Mass communication is too important for us not to.

Baghdad Pete. Iraqi government press aides took CNN reporter Peter Arnett to a bombed-out plant in Baghdad during the U.S. bombing raids. It was, his Iraqi source claimed, the country's only baby milk plant, and Arnett showed viewers powdered milk containers he found in the debris. The Pentagon was furious, claiming the plant was a biological weapons testing center. Arnett stood by his report despite criticism from people who could not understand how a reporter behind enemy lines could be trusted. They coined the derisive nickname "Baghdad Pete."

types of communication

(STUDY PREVIEW)   The communication in which the mass media engage is only one form of **communication.** One way to begin understanding the process of mass communication is to differentiate it from other forms of communication.

intrapersonal communication

We engage in **intrapersonal communication** when we talk to ourselves to develop our thoughts and ideas. This intrapersonal communication precedes our speaking or acting.

interpersonal communication

When people talk to each other, they are engaging in **interpersonal communication.** In its simplest form, interpersonal communication is between two persons physically located in the same place. It can occur, however, if they are physically separated but emotionally connected, like lovers over the telephone.

The difference between the prefixes *intra-* and *inter-* is the key difference between intrapersonal and interpersonal communication. Just as intrasquad athletic games are within a team, intrapersonal communication is within one's self. Just as intercollegiate games are between schools, interpersonal communication is between individuals.

group communication

There comes a point when the number of people involved reduces the intimacy of the communication process. That's when the situation becomes **group communication.** A club meeting is an example. So is a speech to an audience in an auditorium.

Group and Mass Communication. When Boyz II Men go on stage, they are engaging in group communication. A spontaneous relationship with their audience is part of their performance—their communication. In the recording studio, Boyz II Men has to intuitively adjust their performance to an audience they cannot see. This lack of immediate feedback is a characteristic of mass communication that separates it from interpersonal and group communication.

Peter Arnett
AP, later CNN war reporter.

communication
Exchange of ideas, information.

intrapersonal communication
Talking to oneself.

interpersonal communication
Usually two people face to face.

group communication
More than two people; in person.

media | people

david sarnoff

David Sarnoff had no childhood. In 1901, when he was 10, Sarnoff and his mother and two brothers arrived penniless in New York from Russia. Two days later he had a job as a delivery boy, then he added a newspaper route, then a newsstand. In spare moments, he went to the library to read technical books. At 16, he landed a job with American Marconi, which sent him to an island station to exchange messages with ships at sea with the new technology of radio telegraphy. He earned $70 a month, of which $25 went to room and board at a nearby farm. He sent $40 back to his mother.

In 1912 Sarnoff was working at a Marconi demonstration in a New York department store when he picked up the first signals that the steamship *Titanic* had sunk. President Taft ordered every other radio telegraphy station off the air to reduce interference. For the whole world, young David Sarnoff was the only link to the rescue drama unfolding out in the North Atlantic. He stayed at his post 72 hours straight, then went to another site for better reception until the lists of living and dead were complete.

When he collapsed in bed sometime during the fourth day, Sarnoff, then 21, was a national hero and *radio* had become a household word. Through Sarnoff, the whole world suddenly recognized the importance of radio for point-to-point communication, which was the business American Marconi was into. Sarnoff's most significant work, however, was yet to come.

In 1916 Sarnoff drafted a memo to his boss that demonstrated he grasped a potential for radio that everyone else at Marconi had missed. He proposed building "radio music boxes," to be sold as household appliances so people at home could listen to music, news, weather and sports. Sarnoff saw profit in manufacturing these home receivers and selling them for $75. His boss scoffed, but Sarnoff kept refining his proposal. By 1920 he won the ear of the people running RCA, which had succeeded American Marconi.

Sarnoff's proposal for radio music boxes demonstrated his genius. He grasped that radio could be more than a vehicle for telegraph-like point-to-point communication. He saw radio as a mass medium, which could send signals from a central source to dozens, hundreds, thousands, indeed millions of people simultaneously. Sarnoff was not alone in conceptualizing radio as a mass medium. Lee De Forest, for example, had been broadcasting music, but as historian Erik Barnouw noted, "Sarnoff translated the idea into a business plan that began with the consumer." That business plan included a financial base for radio in advertising.

Under RCA auspices, Sarnoff went on to build NBC, the first radio network, and then NBC television. He also pioneered the business of mass producing music for mass audiences with RCA records. From humble origins, through hard work, insight and genius, Sarnoff came to preside for the rest of his life over one of the world's largest and most significant media empires—RCA. He died in 1971.

---

mass communication
Many recipients; not face to face; a process.

mass communication

Capable of reaching thousands, even millions, of people is **mass communication,** which is accomplished through a mass medium like television or newspapers. Mass communication can be defined as the process of using a mass medium to send messages to large audiences for the purpose of informing, entertaining or persuading.

In many respects the process of mass communication and other communication forms is the same: Someone conceives a message, essentially an intrapersonal act. The message then is encoded into a common code, such as language. Then it's transmitted. Another person receives the message, decodes it and internalizes it. Internalizing a message is also an intrapersonal act.

In other respects, mass communication is distinctive. Crafting an effective message for thousands of people of diverse backgrounds and interests requires different skills than chatting with a friend across the table. Encoding the message is more complex because a device is always used—for example, a printing press, a camera or a recorder.

One aspect of mass communication that should not be a mystery is spelling the often-misused word "communication." The word takes no "s" if you are using it to refer to a *process*. If you are referring to a communication as *a thing,* such as a letter, a movie, a telegram or a television program, rather than a process, the word is "communication" in singular form and "communications" in plural. The term "mass communication" refers to a process, so it is spelled without the "s."

components of
mass communication

(STUDY PREVIEW)   Mass communication is the process that mass communicators use to send their mass messages to mass audiences. They do this through the mass media. Think of these as the Five Ms: mass communicators, mass messages, mass media, mass communication and mass audience.

mass communicators

The heart of mass communication is the people who produce the messages that are carried in the mass media. These people include journalists, scriptwriters, lyricists, television anchors, radio disk jockeys, public relations practitioners and advertising copywriters. The list could go on and on.

Mass communicators are unlike other communicators because they cannot see their audience. David Letterman knows hundreds of thousands of people are watching as he unveils his latest Top 10 list, but can't see them or hear them chuckle and laugh. He receives no immediate feedback from his mass audience. This communicating with an unseen audience distinguishes mass communication from other forms of communication. Storytellers of yore told their stories face to face, and they could adjust their pacing and gestures and even their vocabulary to how they sensed they were being received. Mass communicators don't have that advantage.

mass messages

A news item is a **mass message,** as are a movie, a novel, a recorded song and a billboard advertisement. The *message* is the most apparent part of our relationship to the

mass communicators
Message crafters.

mass messages
What is communicated.

mass media. It is for the messages that we pay attention to the media. We don't listen to the radio, for example, to marvel at the technology but to hear the music.

mass media

The **mass media** are the vehicles that carry messages. The primary mass media are books, magazines, newspapers, television, radio, sound recordings, movies and the web. Most theorists view media as neutral carriers of messages. The people who are experts at media include technicians who keep the presses running and who keep the television transmitters on the air. Media experts also are tinkerers and inventors who come up with technical improvements, such as compact discs, AM stereo radio and newspaper presses that can produce high-quality color.

mass communication

The process through which messages reach the audience via the mass media is called "mass communication." This is a mysterious process about which we know far less than we should. Researchers and scholars have unraveled some of the mystery, but most of how it works remains a matter of wonderment. For example: Why do people pay more attention to some messages than to others? How does one advertisement generate more sales than another? Is behavior, including violent behavior, triggered through the mass communication process? There is reason to believe that mass communication affects voting behavior, but how does this work? Which is most correct—to say that people can be controlled, manipulated or influenced by mass communication? Nobody has the answer.

mass audiences

The size and diversity of **mass audiences** add complexity to mass communication. Only indirectly do mass communicators learn whether their messages have been received. Mass communicators are never sure exactly of the size of audiences, let alone of the effect of their messages. Mass audiences are fickle. What attracts great attention one day may not the next. The challenge of trying to communicate to a mass audience is even more complex because people are tuning in and tuning out all the time, and when they are tuned in, it is with varying degrees of attentiveness.

communication models

mass media
Vehicles that carry messages.

mass audiences
Recipients of mass messages.

basic model
Shows sender, encoding, transmission, decoding, receiver.

(STUDY PREVIEW)   Scholars have devised models of the communication process in an attempt to understand how the process works. Like all models, these are simplifications and are imperfect. Even so, these models bring some illumination to the mysterious communication process.

role of communication models

Hobbyists build models of ships, planes, automobiles and all kinds of things. These models help them see whatever they are modeling in different ways. Industrial

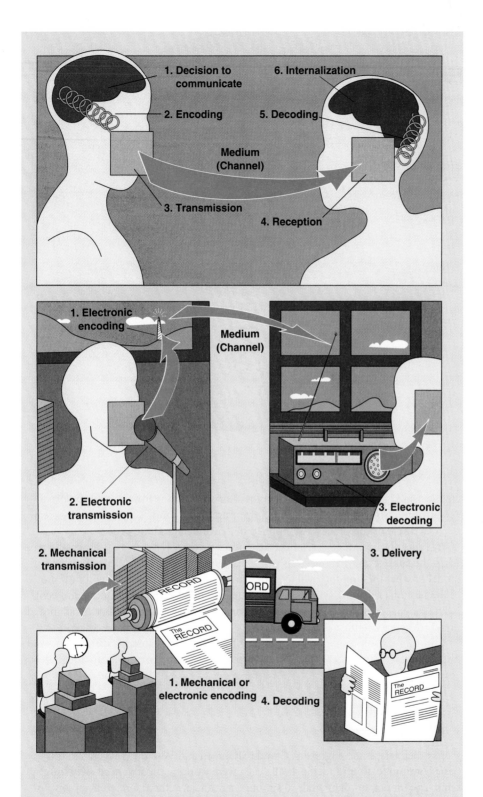

1. Decision to communicate
2. Encoding
6. Internalization
5. Decoding
Medium (Channel)
3. Transmission
4. Reception

1. Electronic encoding
2. Electronic transmission
Medium (Channel)
3. Electronic decoding

2. Mechanical transmission
3. Delivery
1. Mechanical or electronic encoding
4. Decoding

RECORD
The RECORD
ORD
The RECORD

Fundamentals of the Process. Claude Shannon and Warren Weaver reduced communication to fundamental elements in their classic model. Communication, they said, begins in the human mind. Messages then are encoded into language or gesture and transmitted. A recipient sees or hears the message, decodes from the language or other form in which it was transmitted and internalizes it. Those fundamental elements are also present in mass communication except there is a double encoding and double decoding. In mass communication, not only does the communicator encode the message into language or another form to be communicated but also the message then is encoded technologically for transmission through a mass medium. In radio, for example, the words are encoded into electronic impulses. At the decoding site, a piece of machinery, a radio receiver, for example, decodes the impulses into words, which then are decoded again by the human recipient in order to internalize them. With print media, the two steps in decoding are not as obvious because the steps are so integrated. One is reading the words. The other is converting those representations into concepts.

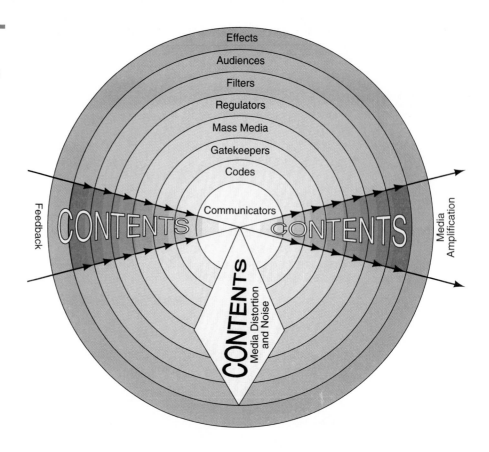

engineers and scientists do the same thing, learning lessons from models before they actually build something to full scale. Communication models are similar. By creating a facsimile of the process, we hope to better understand the process.

A reality about models is that they are never perfect. This reality is especially true when the subject being modeled is complex. An architect, for example, may have a model of what the building will look like to passersby, but there also will be a model of the building's heating system, traffic patterns, and electrical, plumbing and ventilation systems. None of these models are complete or accurate in every detail, but all nonetheless are useful.

Communication models are like that. Different models illustrate different aspects of the process. The process itself is so complex that no single model can adequately cover it.

basic model

Two Bell telephone engineers, **Claude Shannon** and **Warren Weaver,** laid out a basic communication model in 1948. They were working on advanced switching systems. The model, fundamentally a simple diagram, gave them a reference point for their work. That model has become a standard baseline for describing the communication process. The Shannon-Weaver model identifies five fundamental steps in the communication process:

- The human stimulation that results in a thought.
- The encoding of the thought into a message.
- The transmission of the message.
- The decoding of the message by the recipient into a thought.
- The internalization of the message by the recipient.

narrative model

Yale professor **Harold Lasswell,** an early mass communication theorist, developed a useful yet simple model that was all words—no diagram. Lasswell's **narrative model** poses four questions: Who says what? In which channel? To whom? With what effect?

You can easily apply the model. Pick any bylined story from the front page of a newspaper.

- *Who says what?* The newspaper reporter tells a story, often quoting someone who is especially knowledgeable on the subject.
- *In which channel?* In this case, the story is told through the newspaper, a mass medium.
- *To whom?* The story is told to a newspaper reader.
- *With what effect?* The reader decides to vote for Candidate A or B, or perhaps readers just add the information to their reservoir of knowledge.

concentric circle model

The Shannon-Weaver model can be applied to all communication, but it misses some things unique to mass communication. In 1974 scholars Ray Hiebert, Donald Ungurait and **Thomas Bohn** presented an important new model—a series of concentric circles with the encoding source at the center. One of the outer rings was the receiving audience. In between were several elements that are important in the mass communication process but less so in other communication processes.

The concentric circle is one of the most complete models for identifying elements in the mass communication process, but it misses many complexities. It takes only one message from its point of origin, but in reality thousands of messages are being issued simultaneously. Audiences receive many of these messages, but not all of them, and the messages are received imperfectly. Feedback resonates back to communicators unevenly, often muted, often ill-based. Gatekeeping too is uneven. In short, there are so many variables that it is impossible to track what happens in any kind of comprehensive way.

mystery of mass communication

The mass communication process is full of mystery. Major corporations commit millions of dollars to advertising a new product and then anxiously hope the promo-

Harold Lasswell
Devised narrative model.

narrative model
Describes process in words, not schematic.

Thomas Bohn
Devised concentric circle model, with Ray Hiebert, Donald Ungurait.

tional campaign works. Sometimes it does. Sometimes it doesn't. Even experts at mass communication, such as the people at advertising agencies, haven't unlocked the mysteries of the process, nor have scholars who try to understand the influence of mass communication on society and individuals. One of the enduring questions of our time is whether the media trigger violent behavior.

Despite the mystery and the uncertainties, there is no alternative to mass communication in modern society. Therefore, it is important for people who create mass media messages to learn all that can be known about the process. It is no less important that people who receive the messages have a sense of the process that is being used to inform, entertain and persuade them.

fundamentals in the process

(STUDY PREVIEW)   Most models for mass communication as well as other communication forms share some fundamental elements. The elements are sequential, beginning with whatever stimulates a person to want to communicate and continuing through encoding and transmission. To complete the communication process, the recipient of the message must decode and internalize it.

stimulation

Both the Shannon-Weaver and the concentric circle models begin with a source who is stimulated to want to communicate a message. The **stimulation** can result from many things. Emotions can be stimuli, as can something that is sensed. The stimulation can be as diverse as seeing a beautiful panorama, feeling a draft, or hearing a child cry.

encoding

The second step is **encoding.** The source puts thoughts into symbols that can be understood by whomever is destined to receive the message. The symbols take many forms—for example, the written word, smoke signals or pictographs.

transmission

stimulation
Stirs someone to communicate.
encoding
Putting something into symbols.
transmission
Sending a message.

The message is the representation of the thought. In interpersonal communication, the message is almost always delivered face to face. In mass communication, however, the message is encoded so that it is suitable for the equipment being used for **transmission.** Shannon and Weaver, being telephone engineers, offered the example of the sound pressure of a voice being changed into proportional electrical current for transmission over telephone lines. In technical terms, telephone lines were channels for Shannon and Weaver's messages. On a more conceptual basis, the telephone lines were the *media,* in the same way that the printed page or a broadcast signal is.

decoding

The receiver picks up signals sent by the transmitter. In interpersonal communication, the receiver is a person who hears the message or sees it, or both. An angry message encoded as a fist banging a table is heard and perhaps felt. An insulting message encoded as a puff of cigar smoke in the face is smelled. In mass communication, the first receiver of the message is not a person but the equipment that picks up and then reconstructs the message from the signal. This mechanical **decoding** is necessary so that the human receiver of the message can understand it. As Shannon and Weaver put it: "The receiver ordinarily performs the inverse operation that was done by the transmitter."

internalization

In mass communication, a second kind of decoding occurs with the person who receives the message from the receiving equipment. This is an intrapersonal act, **internalizing** the message. For this second kind of decoding to work, the receiver must understand the communication form chosen by the source in encoding. Someone who reads only English will not be able to decode a message in Greek. Someone whose sensitivities are limited to punk rock will not understand Handel's water music. In other words, the source and the receiver must have enough in common for communication to occur. This common experience, which can be as simple as speaking the same tongue, is called **homophyly.** In mass communication, the encoder must know the audience well enough to shape messages that can be decoded accurately and with the intended effect.

Internalization. A consumer who has seen and heard ads for a product retrieves those messages from memory to weigh whether to make a purchase. Those retrieved messages are considered with packaging messages, which also are a form of mass communication.

players in the process

(STUDY PREVIEW)   Two great influences on the mass communication process are gatekeepers and regulators. Gatekeepers are media people who influence messages. Regulators are non-media people who do the same.

gatekeepers

The most visible people in the mass communication process are the communicators. These are the Tom Brokaws, Danielle Steeles and Rush Limbaughs. But mass communication is not a solo endeavor. Dozens, sometimes hundreds, of individuals are involved. A Stephen King thriller passes through several editors before being published. When it's adapted as a screenplay, substantial modifications are made by many other individuals, all expert in the medium of the movie. Later, when it is adapted for television, experts in television as a mass medium make further changes, and so might the network program standards office. Any media person who can stop or alter a mes-

decoding
Translating a symbolic message.

internalization
Making sense of a decoded message.

homophyly
A coding oneness that makes communication possible.

sage en route to the audience is a **gatekeeper.** Newscast producers are gatekeepers because they decide what is aired and what is not. They make decisions about what to emphasize and what to deemphasize. Magazine and newspaper editors do the same, sorting through hundreds of stories to choose the relatively few that will fit in their publications.

Gatekeepers have tremendous responsibility because they shape the messages that reach us. They even decide which messages don't reach us. When gatekeepers make a mistake the communication process and also the message suffer.

regulators

Non-media people and institutions who try to influence mass-communicated messages before they reach the audience are **regulators.** The Federal Communications Commission is a government agency that serves as a regulator with its authority to fine a radio station for on-air indecency. The specter of FCC fines keeps most stations in line. Advertisers know the Federal Trade Commission and two dozen other federal regulatory agencies are looking over their shoulders. Local cable commissions throughout the country have a strong voice in what cable systems offer their subscribers.

Regulators in the mass communication process also include **pressure groups.** For several years the Parents Music Resource Center campaigned for controls on recorded music and videos, including album covers, that it found objectionable. The PMRC's plan for a rating system fell apart, but it was influential in persuading record-makers to place warning labels for parents on certain records. The Communications Office of the United Church of Christ prevailed in yanking the license of a racist television station, WLBT, in Jackson, Alabama. Community groups that threaten media boycotts also are regulators.

gatekeeper-regulator hybrids

Media trade and professional organizations influence media content. For many years the National Association of Broadcasters television programming standards influenced what many stations aired. An NAB maximum, the number of radio commercials per hour, became an industry standard. Ethics codes from the Society of Professional Journalists and many other groups of media people have had wide influence.

Are organizations like the NAB and SPJ gatekeepers or regulators? Comprised of media people, they would seem to be gatekeepers, but because they do not operate on the front line of making content decisions directly, they have many characteristics of regulators. They are, in fact, a hybrid which institutionalizes peer pressure among media people to influence media content.

gatekeepers
Media people who influence messages en route.

regulators
Non-media people who influence messages.

pressure groups
Try to influence media messages, policies; include citizen groups, government agencies.

gatekeeper-regulator hybrids
Media trade, professional groups.

impediments to communication

STUDY PREVIEW Some models emphasize things that interfere with a message being communicated. Feedback can influence a communicator to change a message. Noise is transmission interference. Filters are recipient factors that interfere with an easy or correct reception of the message.

noise

If speakers slur their words, the effectiveness of their messages is jeopardized. Slurring and other impediments in the communication process before the message reaches the audience are called **noise.** In mass communication, which is based on complex mechanical and electronic equipment, the opportunities for noise interference are countless because so many things can go wrong. Noise occurs in three forms: channel noise, environmental noise and semantic noise.

Semantic Noise. Mass communicators themselves can interfere with the success of their own messages by sloppiness. This is called **semantic noise.** Sloppy wording is an example. Slurring is also a semantic impediment to communication.

Channel Noise. When you're listening to an AM radio station and static interrupts the transmission, you are experiencing **channel noise.** Other forms of channel noise also include smudged ink on a magazine page and a faulty microphone on a television anchor's desk set.

Environmental Noise. An intrusion that occurs at the reception site is **environmental noise.** This would include a doorbell interrupting someone's reading of an article. So would shouting kids who distract a viewer from the 6 o'clock news, which interferes with the decoding process.

Mass communicators go to special lengths to guard against noise interfering with their messages. For example, in encoding, broadcast scriptwriters avoid "s" sounds as much as possible because they can hiss gratingly if listeners are not tuned precisely on the frequency. Because words can be unintentionally dropped in typesetting, many newspaper reporters write that a verdict was "innocent" rather than "not guilty." It would be a serious matter if noise resulted in the deletion of "not."

To keep noise at a minimum, technicians strive to keep their equipment in top-notch condition. Even so, things can go wrong. Also, mass communicators cannot control noise that affects individual members of their audience—such as the siren of a passing fire truck, a migraine headache or the distraction of a pot boiling over on the stove. Clear enunciation, whether sharp writing in a magazine or clear pronunci-

The Lower case

Family meals became lonesome without dad when reports came that

U.S. soldiers attacked Pearl Harbor
Wednesday Republican-American (Conn.) · 12-6-97

Police jail nurse shot to death while driving home on freeway
Antelope Valley Press (Ca.) · 10/21/97

In 1995, Shelby received the Ida B. Wells Award for "exemplary achievement in the hiring and firing of minorities in the news media."
LA Weekly · 10/31/97

Man inured when car plunges down an embankment
Montgomery Journal (Md.) · 12/6/97

Meet the new head of UConn's board of trustees
PAGE A3
The Hartford Courant (Conn.) · 6/11/97

5 Skinheads Arrested in Denver Hate Beating
San Francisco Chronicle · 11/26/97

A chart in Business Day ranking the Big Six public accounting firms on several measures included some incorrect figures supplied by Bowman's Accounting Report for Ernst & Young and thus ranked the firms incorrectly in several categories. A corrected chart appears today on page X96.
The New York Times · 8/2/97

After a 12 year courtship, Greenspan and NBC News correspondent Andrea Mitchell were married by Supreme Court justice Ruth Bader Ginsburg in April. They live in her house near the Chain Bridge in Washington.
Vanity Fair · December '97

Man kills himself hours before appearing in court
Richmond Hill-Bryan County News (Ga.) · 8-6-97

Department requests swell town budget
Greenwich Time (Conn.) · 12/11/97

Home Depot purchases wallpaper, blinds retailers
The Atlanta Journal-Constitution · 11/25/97

James Bond spat in court
The Martinez Gazette · 11-19-97

School bond worries dog trustees
The Davis Enterprise (Calif.) · 12/3/97

CJR offers $25 for items published in The Lower case. Please send only original, unmutilated clippings suitable for reproduction, together with name and date of publication, and include your social security number for payment.

Semantic Noise. In every issue, the *Columbia Journalism Review* delights in reproducing bad headlines and other newspaper gaffes as a reminder to journalists to be more careful. These gaffes are examples of semantic noise, in which ambiguous wording and other poor word choices interfere with clear communication.

---

noise
Impedes communication before message reaches receiver.

semantic noise
Sloppy message-crafting.

channel noise
Interference during transmission.

environmental noise
Interference at reception site.

ation on the radio, can minimize such interference, but most noise is beyond the communicator's control.

Repetition is the mass communicator's best antidote against noise. If the message does not get through the first time, it is repeated. Rare is an advertisement that plays only once. Radio newscasters repeat the same major news stories every hour, although they rehash the scripts so they will not bore people who heard the stories earlier.

filters

Unwittingly, people who tune in to mass messages may themselves interfere with the success of the mass communication process.

Informational Filters. If someone doesn't understand the language or symbols a communicator uses, the communication process becomes flawed. It is a matter of an individual lacking information to decipher a message. This deficiency is called an **informational filter.** This filter can be partly the responsibility of the communicator, whose vocabulary may not be in tune with the audience's. More clearly, though, it is an audience deficiency.

Physical Filters. When a receiver's mind is dimmed by fatigue, a **physical filter** is interfering with the mass communication process. A drunk whose focus fades in and out also suffers from a physical filter. Mass communicators have little control over physical filters.

Psychological Filters. If a receiver is a zealous animal rights activist, **psychological filters** likely will affect the reception of news on medical research involving animals. Being on a different wavelength can be a factor. Imagine two women friends going to the movie *Fatal Attraction* together. One woman is married and monogamous, the other is involved with a married man. Having different ideas on and experiences with marital fidelity, which is at the heart of the movie, the women hear the same words and see the same images, but they see two "different" movies.

results of mass communication

(STUDY PREVIEW) Because mass communication reaches such large audiences, the process amplifies messages like a giant megaphone. Things that are mass communicated stand a better chance of becoming important than things that are not. Mass communication has its greatest influence when it moves people to action.

amplification

The technology of the mass media gives mass communicators a megaphone. This is something other communicators don't have. A letter writer, for example, generally aims a message at one other person. A magazine writer, in contrast, has the printing press to reach thousands, if not millions, of readers. The printing press is a mega-

filters
Receiver factor that impedes communication.

informational filter
Receiver's knowledge limits impede deciphering symbols.

physical filter
Receiver's alertness impedes deciphering.

psychological filter
Receiver's state of mind impedes deciphering.

amplification
Spreading message.

phone. Broadcasters have their transmission equipment. The equipment of the mass media allows mass communicators to amplify messages in ways that are not possible with interpersonal or even group communication.

Things that mass communicators choose to communicate have a status conferred on them. This is gatekeeping at work. Stories and views that don't survive the gatekeeping process have little chance of gaining widespread attention. Those that make it through the process have some inherent credibility just because they made it through so many hurdles.

Status conferral can work positively and negatively. For example, some scholars claim that the U.S. government overreacted in 1980 to the 444-day Iran hostage situation because media coverage kept fueling public reaction. In the same vein, Oliver North's name would not have become a household word had it not been for saturation media coverage of the Iran-Contra issue.

Status conferral is not limited to the news media. Ballads and music, amplified through the mass media, can capture the public's imagination and keep an issue alive and even enlarge it. In World War I, catchy songs such as "Over There" helped rally support for the cause. Fifty years later, "An Okie From Muskogee" lent legitimacy to the hawkish position on Vietnam. Bob Dylan's 1975 song "Hurricane" reopened the investigation into the murder conviction of Reuben "Hurricane" Carter. Movies also have the power to move people and sustain issues. Sidney Poitier movies of the 1960s, including *Guess Who's Coming to Dinner,* helped keep racial integration on the American agenda.

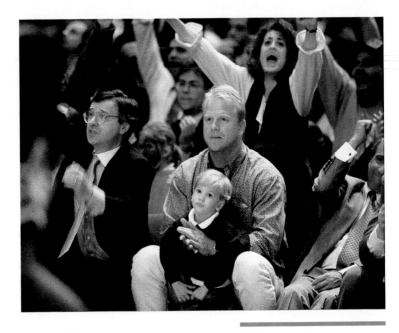

Media Amplification.
After Super Bowl quarterback Boomer Esiason of the Cincinnati Bengals found out that his infant son Gunnar had cystic fibrosis, he vowed to make his fight to cure Gunnar a crusade, however quixotic it might turn out. The media picked up on Esiason's campaign, which not only has raised research funds but has shown that professional athletes, who seem so carefree and indestructible, have real problems just like the rest of us.

feedback

Because mass communication is not the one-way street that the Shannon-Weaver model indicated, later theorists embellished the model by looping the process back on itself. The recipient of a message, after decoding, responds. The original recipient then becomes the sender, encoding a response and sending it via a medium back to the original sender, who becomes the new destination and decodes the response. This reverse process is called **feedback.**

In interpersonal communication, you know if your listener does not understand. If you hear "Uhh?" or see a puzzled look, you restate your point. In mass communication, feedback is delayed. It might be a week after an article is published before a reader's letter arrives in the newsroom. Because feedback is delayed and because there usually is not very much of it, precise expression in mass communication is especially important. There is little chance to restate the point immediately if the television viewer does not understand. A mass communicator cannot hear the "Uhh?"

status conferral
Credence that a topic or issue receives because of media attention.
feedback
Recipient response to sender.

effects

The whole point of communicating a message is to have an **effect.** A jokester wants to evoke at least a chuckle. A eulogist wants to inspire memories. A cheerleader wants to stir school spirit. The vast size of the mass communicator's audience compounds the potential for powerful effects. Because the potential effect is so great, we need to understand as much as possible about the process that leads to effects.

chapter wrap-up

Mass communication is a mysterious process. Many scholars have developed theories and models to help us understand some aspects of mass communication, but the process is so complex that we will never master it to the point of being able to predict reliably the outcome of the process. There are just too many variables. This does not mean, however, that the quest for understanding is pointless. The more we know about how mass communication works, the better mass communicators can use the process for good effects and the better media consumers can intelligently assess media messages before using them as a basis for action.

An understanding of the mass communication process begins with understanding the fundamentals of all human communication. These fundamentals are the conceptualizing, encoding and transmitting of messages, and also decoding and internalizing messages. Mass communication has additional complexities, though. These include gatekeeping changes within the media as messages move between the originating communicator and the audience. Non-media forces also influence mass messages. The technology itself presents hazards for mass communication to work. A television tower is vulnerable to lightning strikes. A newspaper delivery truck can go off a cliff.

The greatest advantage of mass communication over other communication forms is that it amplifies messages. In interpersonal communication, you can reach another person with what you have to say. At a rally, you can reach a few dozen. Even at a super-rally, like an evangelist at a football stadium, the maximum audience is the seating of the stadium. With mass communication, however, a message can be amplified so millions of people pick it up. This potential for mass communicators to reach such vast audiences, and perhaps motivate them to action, is what makes the study of the mass communication process important.

effect
Result of mass communication.

questions for review

1. Can you create a sentence that uses the Five Ms: mass communicators, mass messages, mass media, mass communication, and mass audiences?

2. What good are mass communication and other models? And what do models fail to do?

3. How does mass communication differ from other human communication?

4. How do gatekeepers and regulators influence media messages? How are they different from each other?

5. How do noise and filters impede mass communication?

6. Status conferral is one effect of mass media amplification. How does this work?

questions for critical thinking

1. How is each of these types of communication—intrapersonal, interpersonal, group and mass—difficult to master?

2. All communication involves conceiving, encoding, transmitting, receiving and decoding, but some of these steps are more complicated for mass communication. In what way?

3. Different mass communication models offer different insights into the mass communication process. Describe the different perspectives of these models: Shannon-Weaver, concentric circle and narrative.

4. From your own experience, describe a message that went awry as it moved through the mass communication process. Did the problem involve gatekeepers? Regulators? Noise? Filters?

5. People in the physical sciences can predict with great accuracy how certain phenomena will work. Why will social scientists never be able to do this with the mass communication process?

6. From your own experience, describe how a lack of homophyly has damaged a mass communication attempt.

for further learning

Peter Arnett. *Live From the Battlefield: From Vietnam to Baghdad, 35 Years in the World's War Zones* (Simon & Schuster Touchstone, 1994).

Stephen W. Littlejohn. *Theories of Human Communication,* 5th edition (Wadsworth, 1996). Professor Littlejohn traces developments in communication theory and synthesizes current research. One chapter focuses on mass communication.

Denis McQuail and Sven Windahl. *Communication Models for the Study of Mass Communication,* 2nd edition (Longman, 1993). McQuail and Windahl show dozens of models from the first 30 years of mass communication research with explanatory comments. Included is discussion on the narrative, Shannon-Weaver and helix models.

Alexis S. Tan. *Mass Communication Theories and Research* (Macmillan, 1986). Drawing on the growing body of behavioral communication research, Professor Tan explains mass communication functions, processes and effects. Although it is written for serious students, the book requires no background in communication theory, methodology or statistics.

for keeping up to date

Scholarly discussion on the communication process can be found in *Communication Yearbook,* published since 1977, and *Mass Communication Review Yearbook,* published since 1986.

The *Journal of Communication* is a quarterly scholarly publication from Oxford University Press.

15
media effects

in this chapter you will learn:

- Most media scholars today believe the effects of the mass media generally are cumulative over time.

- Individuals choose some mass media over others for the satisfactions they anticipate.

- Individuals have substantial control over mass media effects on them.

- Mass media have a significant role helping children learn society's expectations of them.

- Scholars differ on whether media-depicted violence triggers aggressive behavior.

- The mass media set the agenda for what people are interested in and talk about.

- The mass media can work against citizen involvement in political processes.

The boy genius **Orson Welles** was on a roll. By 1938, at age 23, Welles's dramatic flair had landed him a network radio show, "Mercury Theater on the Air," at prime time on CBS on Sunday nights. The program featured adaptations of well-known literature. For their October 30 program, Welles and his colleagues decided on a scary 1898 British novel. Their enthusiasm faded five days before airtime when writer Howard Koch concluded that the novel did not lend itself to radio. Koch said that he, in effect, was required to create a one-hour original play and five days was not enough time, but neither was there time to switch to another play. The Thursday rehearsal was flat. Koch, frantic, scrambled to rewrite the script, but the Saturday rehearsal was disappointing too. Little did Welles expect that Koch's loose adaptation of H. G. Wells' **"War of the Worlds"** would become one of broadcasting's most memorable programs.

Orson Welles opened with the voice of a wizened chronicler from some future time, intoning eerily:

"We know now that in the early years of the 20th century this world was being watched closely by intelligences greater than man's...." Welles's unsettling monologue was followed by an innocuous weather forecast, then hotel dance music. To casual listeners, the monologue seemed a mistake dropped inadvertently into typical radio music. Then the music was interrupted by a news bulletin. An astronomer reported several explosions on Mars, propelling something at enormous velocity toward Earth. The bulletin over, listeners were transported back to the hotel orchestra. After applause, the orchestra started up again, only to be interrupted: Seismologists had picked up an earthquake-like shock in New Jersey. Then it was one bulletin after another. A huge cylinder had crashed into a New Jersey farm. On the scene, a reporter asked what happened.

Farmer: A hissing sound. Like this: sssssssss ... kinda like a fourt' of July rocket.

Reporter: Then what?

Farmer: Turned my head out the window and would have swore I was to sleep and dreamin'.

Reporter: Yes?

Farmer: I seen a kinda greenish streak and then zingo! Somethin' smacked the ground. Knocked me clear out of my chair!

The story line accelerated. Giant Martians moved across the countryside spewing fatal gas. One at a time, reporters at remote sites vanished off the air. The Secretary of the Interior came on: "Citizens of the nation: I shall not try to conceal the gravity of the situation.... Placing our faith in God we must continue the performance of our duties, each and every one of us, so that we may confront this destructive adversary with a nation united, courageous, and consecrated to the preservation of human supremacy on this earth."

Meanwhile, the Martians decimated the Army and were wading across the Hudson River. Amid sirens and other sounds of emergency, a reporter on a Manhattan rooftop described the monsters advancing through the streets. He passed on bulletins that Martian cylinders were coming down in St. Louis, Chicago, near Buffalo, all over the country. From his vantage, he described the Martians felling people by the thousands and moving in on him, the gas crossing Sixth Avenue, then Fifth Avenue, then 100 yards away, then 50 feet. Then silence. A lonely ham radio voice somehow became patched into the network: 2X2L calling CQ ... 2X2L calling CQ ... 2X2L calling CQ, New York ... Isn't there anyone on the air? ...

Orson Welles. Young Orson Welles scared the living daylights out of several million radio listeners with the 1939 radio drama "War of the Worlds." Most of the fright was short-lived, though. All but the most naive listeners quickly realized that Martians, as they marched toward the Hudson River to destroy Manhattan, really had not devastated the New Jersey militia.

Isn't there anyone? ... Anyone? ..." Silence.

To the surprise of Orson Welles and his crew, the drama triggered widespread mayhem. Neighbors gathered in streets all over the country, wet towels to their faces to slow the gas. In Newark, New Jersey, people, many undressed, fled their apartments. Said a New York woman: "I never hugged my radio so closely.... I held a crucifix in my hand and prayed while looking out my open window to get a faint whiff of gas so that I would know when to close my window and hermetically seal my room with waterproof cement or anything else I could get a hold of. My plan was to stay in the room and hope that I would not suffocate before the gas blew away." A Midwest man told of his grandparents, uncles, aunts and children, on their knees, "God knows but we prayed.... My mother went out and looked for Mars. Dad was hard to convince or skeptical or sumpin', but he even got to believing it. Brother Joe, as usual, got more excited than he could show. Brother George wasn't home. Aunt Gracie, a good Catholic, began to pray with Uncle Henry. Lily got sick to her stomach. I prayed harder and more earnestly than ever before. Just as soon as we were convinced that this thing was real, how petty all things on earth seemed; how soon we put our trust in God."

In one Pacific Northwest village, a power outage reinforced the panic. Switchboards throughout the country were swamped by people trying to call relatives, fueling the hysteria. The telephone volume in northern New Jersey was up 39 percent. Most CBS stations reported a six-fold increase in calls. Many people jumped into their cars to drive to safety but did not know where to go and so just drove around, which put hysterical strangers in touch with each other.

Researchers estimate that one out of six people who heard the program, more than one million in all, suspended disbelief and braced for the worst.

The effects were especially amazing considering that:

- An announcer identified the program as fiction at four points.

- Almost 10 times as many people were tuned to a popular comedy show on another network.

- The program ran only one hour, an impossibly short time for the sequence that began with the blastoffs on Mars, included a major military battle in New Jersey, and ended with New York's destruction.

Unwittingly, Orson Welles and his Mercury Theater crew had created an evening of infamy and raised questions about media effects to new intensity. In this chapter, you will learn what scholars have found out about the effects of the mass media on individuals.

effects studies

(STUDY PREVIEW) Early mass communication scholars assumed that the mass media were so powerful that ideas and even ballot-box instructions could be inserted as if by hypodermic needle into the body politic. Doubts arose in the 1940s about whether the media were really that powerful, and scholars began shaping their research questions on assumptions that media effects were more modest. Recent studies are asking about long-term, cumulative media effects.

powerful effects theory

The first generation of mass communication scholars thought the mass media had a profound, direct effect on people. Their idea, called effects theory, drew heavily on social commentator **Walter Lippmann**'s influential 1922 book, *Public Opinion*. Lippmann argued that we see the world not as it really is but as "pictures in our heads." The "pictures" of things we have not experienced personally, he said, are shaped by the mass media. The powerful impact that Lippmann ascribed to the media was a precursor of the effects theory that evolved among scholars over the next few years.

Yale psychologist **Harold Lasswell,** who studied World War II propaganda, embodied the effects theory in his famous model of mass communication: *Who, Says what, In which channel, To whom, With what effect.* At their extreme, effects theory devotees assumed that the media could inject information, ideas and even propaganda hypodermically into the public. The theory was explained in terms of a hypodermic needle model or bullet model. Early effects scholars would agree that newspaper coverage and endorsements of political candidates decided elections.

The early scholars did not see that the hypodermic metaphor was hopelessly simplistic. They assumed wrongly that individuals are passive and absorb uncritically and unconditionally whatever the media spew forth. The fact is that individuals read, hear

Orson Welles
His radio drama cast doubt on powerful effects theory.

"War of the Worlds"
Radio drama that became test bed on ability of media to instill panic.

powerful effects
Theory that media have immediate, direct influence.

Walter Lippmann
His *Public Opinion* assumed powerful media effects in 1920s.

Harold Lasswell
His mass communication model assumed powerful effects.

⋯⋯understanding mass media effects

1922 Walter Lippmann attributed powerful effects to mass media.

1938 Hadley Cantril concluded "War of the Worlds" panic drastically overstated.

1940s Mass communication scholars shifted from studying effects to uses and gratification.

1948 Paul Lazarsfeld challenged powerful effects theory in voter studies.

1967 George Gerbner launched his television violence index.

1970s Mass communication scholars shifted to cumulative effects theory.

1972 Maxwell McCombs and Don Shaw concluded media create public agendas, not opinion.

and see the same things differently. Even if they did not, people are exposed to many, many media—hardly a single, monolithic voice. Also, there is a skepticism among media consumers that is manifested at its extreme in the saying: "You can't believe a thing you read in the paper." People are not mindless, uncritical blotters.

minimalist effects theory

Scholarly enthusiasm for the hypodermic needle model dwindled after two massive studies of voter behavior, one in Erie County, Ohio, in 1940 and the other in Elmira, New York, in 1948. The studies, led by sociologist **Paul Lazarsfeld** of Columbia University, were the first rigorous tests of media effects on an election. Lazarsfeld's researchers went back to 600 people several times to discover how they developed their campaign opinions. Rather than citing particular newspapers, magazines or radio stations, as had been expected, these people generally mentioned friends and acquaintances. The media had hardly any direct effect. Clearly, the hypodermic needle model was off base, and the effects theory needed rethinking. From that rethinking emerged the **minimalist effects** theory, which included:

Paul Lazarsfeld
Found voters more influenced by other people than mass media.

minimalist effects
Theory that media effects mostly indirect.

two-step flow
Media effects on individuals are through opinion leaders.

opinion leaders
Influential on friends, acquaintances.

multistep flow
Media effects on individuals come through complex interpersonal connections.

status conferral
Media attention enhances attention to people, subjects, issues.

Two-Step Flow Model. Minimalist scholars devised the **two-step flow** model to show that voters are motivated less by the mass media than by people they know personally and respect. These people, called **opinion leaders,** include many clergy, teachers and neighborhood merchants, although it is impossible to list categorically all those who comprise opinion leaders. Not all clergy, for example, are influential, and opinion leaders are not necessarily in an authority role. The minimalist scholars' point is that personal contact is more important than media contact. The two-step flow model, which replaced the hypodermic needle model, showed that whatever effect the media have with the majority of the population is through opinion leaders. Later, as mass communication research became more sophisticated, the two-step model was expanded into a **multistep flow** model to capture the complex web of social relationships that affects individuals.

Status Conferral. Minimalist scholars acknowledge that the media create prominence for issues and people by giving them coverage. Conversely, neglect rele-

media people

···dorothy day

Dorothy Day believed in social reform—racial justice, women's rights, fair wages, disarmament, and prison reform. A pacifist, she opposed war. Eight times Dorothy Day went to jail for her beliefs. Her activism took journalistic form in the *Catholic Worker,* which she founded with her husband Peter Maurin in 1933. The newspaper, a tabloid visually distinctive for its woodcut art, became a mainstay in social reform movements, its circulation reaching 100,000 in less than a year. *The Catholic Worker* and Dorothy Day exemplified the mass media's potential to bring about change and leave the world a better place.

Born in 1897, Dorothy Day was the daughter of

Reform Journalist. Dorothy Day combined her political Socialism, her Roman Catholic beliefs and a cerebral commitment to social reform in both the Catholic Worker movement and the *Catholic Worker* newspaper. Beginning in 1933, Day campaigned for labor reform, social justice and women's rights in the *Worker,* whose circulation reached 150,000.

an itinerant sports writer. The family moved a lot, so she developed an early picture of what the whole country was like. At the University of Illinois she read Upton Sinclair's *Kropotkin,* which she credited with crystallizing her commitment to social justice. She moved to New York and wrote for the *Socialist Call* and then the *Masses,* alongside such radical thinkers as Max Eastman and John Reed. Her feeling for society's down-trodden became ever-keener.

Meanwhile, an interest in Catholicism matured into her conversion.

In 1932, in the middle of the Depression, Day and Peter Maurin developed a program of social action to bring scholars, workers and the needy together in houses of hospitality, farming communes and roundtable discussions—and they created a newspaper to spread the word. Thus was born the *Catholic Worker.* The Day-Maurin movement took tangible form in Houses of Hospitality in

many major cities. The poor could come for meals, lodging and moral support. These initiatives came to be called the Catholic Worker movement, and while Day was traversing the country to establish more Houses of Hospitality she also remained as publisher and editor of the *Catholic Worker,* stridently calling for reforms in labor law and other public policy to help poor people. At one point the paper's circulation reached 150,000.

gates issues and personalities to obscurity. Related to this **status conferral** phenomenon is **agenda-setting.** Professors **Maxwell McCombs** and **Don Shaw,** describing the agenda-setting phenomenon in 1972, said the media do not tell people *what to think* but tell them *what to think about.* This is a profound distinction. In covering a political campaign, explain McCombs and Shaw, the media choose which issues or topics to emphasize, thereby helping set the campaign's agenda. "This ability to affect cognitive change among individuals," say McCombs and Shaw, "is one of the most important aspects of the power of mass communication."

Narcoticizing Dysfunction. Some minimalists claim that the media rarely energize people into action, such as getting them to go out to vote for a candidate. Rather, they say, the media lull people into passivity. This effect, called **narcoticizing dysfunction,** is supported by studies that find that many people are so overwhelmed by the volume of news and information available to them that they tend to withdraw

agenda-setting
Media tell people what to think about, not what to think.

Maxwell McCombs and Don Shaw
Articulated agenda-setting theory.

narcoticizing dysfunction
People deceive selves into believing they're involved when actually they're only informed.

from involvement in public issues. Narcoticizing dysfunction occurs also when people pick up a great deal of information from the media on a particular subject—poverty, for example—and believe that they are doing something about a problem when they are really only smugly well informed. Intellectual involvement becomes a substitute for active involvement.

cumulative effects theory

In recent years some mass communication scholars have parted from the minimalists and resurrected the powerful effects theory, although with a twist that avoids the simplistic hypodermic needle model. German scholar **Elisabeth Noelle-Neumann,** a leader of this school, conceded that the media do not have powerful immediate effects but argues that effects over time are profound. Her **cumulative effects** theory notes that nobody can escape either the media, which are ubiquitous, or the media's messages, which are driven home with redundancy. To support her point, Noelle-Neumann cites multimedia advertising campaigns that hammer away with the same message over and over. There's no missing the point. Even in news reports there is a redundancy, with the media all focusing on the same events.

Noelle-Neumann's cumulative effects theory has troubling implications. She says that the media, despite surface appearances, work against diverse, robust public consideration of issues. Noelle-Neumann bases her observation on human psychology, which she says encourages people who feel they hold majority viewpoints to speak out confidently. Those views gain credibility in their claim to be dominant when they are carried by the media, whether they are really dominant or not. Meanwhile, says Noelle-Neumann, people who perceive that they are in a minority are inclined to speak out less, perhaps not at all. The result is that dominant views can snowball through the media and become consensus views without being sufficiently challenged.

To demonstrate her intriguing theory, Noelle-Neumann has devised the ominously labeled **spiral of silence** model, in which minority views are intimidated into silence and obscurity. Noelle-Neumann's model raises doubts about the libertarian concept that the media provide a marketplace in which conflicting ideas fight it out fairly, each receiving a full hearing.

uses and gratifications studies

(STUDY PREVIEW)   Beginning in the 1940s, many mass communication scholars shifted from studying the media to studying media audiences. These scholars assumed that individuals use the media to gratify needs. Their work, known as uses and gratifications studies, focused on how individuals use mass media—and why.

challenges to audience passivity

As disillusionment with the powerful effects theory set in after the Lazarsfeld studies of the 1940s, scholars reevaluated many of their assumptions, including the idea that people are merely passive consumers of the mass media. From the reevaluation came

Elisabeth Noelle-Neumann
Leading cumulative effects theorist.

cumulative effects
Theory that media influence gradual over time.

spiral of silence
Vocal majority intimidates others into silence.

research questions about why individuals tap into the mass media. This research, called **uses and gratifications** studies, explored how individuals choose certain media outlets. One vein of research said people seek certain media to gratify certain needs.

These scholars worked with social science theories about people being motivated to do certain things by human needs and wants, such as seeking water, food and shelter as necessities and wanting to be socially accepted and loved. These scholars identified dozens of reasons why people use the media, among them surveillance, socialization and diversion.

surveillance function

With their acute sense of smell and sound, deer scan their environment constantly for approaching danger. In modern human society, surveillance is provided for individuals by the mass media, which scan local and global environments for information that helps individuals make decisions to live better, even survive.

News coverage is the most evident form through which the mass media serve this **surveillance function.** From a weather report, people decide whether to wear a raincoat; from the Wall Street averages, whether to invest; from the news, whether the president will have their support. Although most people don't obsess about being on top of all that's happening in the world, there is a touch of the news junkie in everybody. All people need reliable information on their immediate environment. Are tornadoes expected? Is the bridge fixed? Are vegetable prices coming down? Most of us are curious about developments in politics, economics, science and other fields. The news media provide a surveillance function for their audiences, surveying the world for information that people want and need to know.

It is not only news that provides surveillance. From drama and literature, people learn about great human issues that give them a better feel for the human condition.

uses and gratifications
Theory that people choose media that meet needs, interests.
surveillance function
Media provide information on what's going on.

Popular music and entertainment, conveyed by the mass media, give people a feel for the emotional reactions of other human beings, many very far away, and for things going on in their world.

socialization function

Except for recluses, people are always seeking information that helps them fit in with other people. This **socialization function,** a lifelong process, is greatly assisted by the mass media. Without paying attention to the media, for example, it is hard to participate in conversations about how the Yankees did last night, or Tom Cruise's latest movie or the current Pentagon scandal. Jay Leno's monologues give late-night television watchers a common experience with their friends and associates the next day, as do the latest movie and the evening news.

Using the media can be a social activity, bringing people together. Gathering around the radio on Sunday night for the Mercury Theater in the 1930s was a family activity. Going to the movies with friends is a group activity.

The media also contribute to togetherness by creating commonality. Friends who subscribe to *Newsweek* have a shared experience in reading the weekly cover story, even though they do it separately. The magazine helps individuals maintain social relationships by giving them something in common. In this sense, the media are important in creating community, even nationhood and perhaps, with global communication, a fellowship of humankind.

Less positive as a social function of the mass media is **parasocial interaction.** When a television anchor looks directly into the camera, as if talking with individual viewers, it is not a true social relationship that is being created. The communication is one-way without audience feedback. However, because many people enjoy the sense of interaction, no matter how false it is, many local stations encourage on-camera members of the news team to chat among themselves, which furthers the impression of an ongoing conversation with an extended peer group that includes the individual viewer.

This same false sense of reciprocal dialogue exists also among individuals and their favorite political columnists, lovelorn and other advice writers and humorists. Some people have the illusion that the friends David Letterman interviews on his program are their friends, and so are Jay Leno's and Larry King's. It is also illusory parasocial interaction when someone has the television set on for companionship.

diversion function

Through the mass media, people can escape everyday drudgery, immersing themselves in a soap opera, a murder mystery or pop music. The result can be stimulation, relaxation or emotional release.

Stimulation. Everybody is bored occasionally. When our senses—sight, hearing, smell, taste and touch—are without sufficient external stimuli, a sensory vacuum results. Following the physicist's law that a vacuum must be filled, we seek new stimuli to correct our sensory deprivation. In modern society the mass media are almost always handy as boredom-offsetting stimulants. It's not only in boring situations that the mass media can be a stimulant. To accelerate the pace of an already lively party, for example, someone can put on quicker music and turn up the volume.

Relaxation. When someone's sensory abilities are overloaded, the media can be relaxing. Slower, softer music sometimes can help. Relaxation, in fact, can come

socialization function
Media help people fit into society.

parasocial interaction
A fake sense of participating in dialogue.

diversion function
Media entertain.

through any change of pace. In some situations, a high-tension movie or book can be as effective as a lullaby.

Release. People can use the mass media to blow off steam. Somehow a Friday night horror movie dissipates the frustration pent up all week. So can a good cry over a tear-jerking book.

Using the mass media as a stimulant, relaxant or release is quick, healthy escapism. Escapism, however, can go further, as when soap-opera fans so enmesh themselves in the programs that they perceive themselves as characters in the story line. Carried too far, escapism becomes withdrawal. When people build on media portrayals to the point that their existence revolves on living out the lives of, say, Elvis Presley or Marilyn Monroe, the withdrawal from reality has become a serious psychological disorder.

consistency theory

Gratifications scholars learned that people generally are conservative in choosing media, looking for media that reinforce their personal views. Faced with messages consistent with their own views and ones that are radically different, people pay attention to the one they're comfortable with and have slight recall of contrary views. These phenomena—selective exposure, selective perception, selective retention and selective recall—came to be called **consistency theory.**

Consistency theory does a lot to explain media habits. People read, watch and listen to media with messages that don't jar them. The theory raised serious questions about how well the media can meet the democratic ideal that the media be a forum for the robust exchange of divergent ideas. The media can't fulfill their role as a forum if people hear only what they want to hear.

individual selectivity

(STUDY PREVIEW) Individuals choose to expose themselves to media whose perspective and approach reinforce their personal interests and values. These choices, called selective exposure, are consciously made. Similar selectivity phenomena are at work subconsciously in how individuals perceive and retain media content.

selective exposure

People make deliberate decisions in choosing media. For example, outdoors enthusiasts choose *Field & Stream* at the newsrack. Academics subscribe to the *Chronicle of Higher Education.* Young rock fans watch MTV. People expose themselves to media whose content relates to their interests. In this sense, individuals exercise control over the media's effects on them. Nobody forces these selections on anybody.

This process of choosing media, called **selective exposure,** continues once an individual is involved in a publication or a broadcast. A hunter who seldom fishes will gravitate to the hunting articles in *Field & Stream,* perhaps even skipping the fishing pieces entirely. On MTV, a hard-rock aficionado will be attentive to wild music but

> **consistency theory**
> People choose media, messages consistent with their individual views, values.
>
> **selective exposure**
> People choose some media messages over others.

will take a break when the video jock announces that a mellow piece will follow the commercial.

selective perception

The selectivity that occurs in actually reading, watching and listening is less conscious than in selective exposure. No matter how clear a message is, people see and hear egocentrically. This phenomenon, known as **selective** or **autistic perception,** was demonstrated in the 1950s by researcher Roy Carter, who found that physicians concerned about socialized medicine at the time would hear "social aspects of medicine" as "socialized medicine." Rural folks in North Carolina, anxious for news about farming, thought they heard the words "farm news" on the radio when the announcer said "foreign news."

Scholars Eugene Webb and Jerry Salancik explain it this way: "Exposure to information is hedonistic." People pick up what they want to pick up. Webb and Salancik state that nonsmokers who read an article about smoking focus subconsciously on passages that link smoking with cancer, being secure and content, even joyful, in the information that reinforces the wisdom of their decision not to smoke. In contrast, smokers are more attentive to passages that hedge the smoking-cancer link. In using the mass media for information, people tend to perceive what they want. As social commentator Walter Lippmann put it, "For the most part we do not first see and then define, we define first and then see." Sometimes the human mind distorts facts to square with predispositions and preconceptions.

selective retention and recall

Experts say that the brain records forever everything to which it is exposed. The problem is recall. While people remember many things that were extremely pleasurable or that coincided with their beliefs, they have a harder time calling up the memory's file on other things.

"Selective forgetting" happens to mothers when they tend to deemphasize or even forget the illnesses or disturbances of pregnancy and the pain of birth. This phenomenon works the opposite way when individuals encounter things that reinforce their beliefs.

Nostalgia also can affect recall. For example, many mothers grossly predate when undesirable behavior like thumb sucking was abandoned. Mothers tend also to suggest precocity about the age at which Suzy or José first walked or cut the first tooth. In the same way, people often use rose-colored lenses, not 20/20 vision, in recalling information and ideas from the media.

In summary, individuals have a large degree of control over how the mass media affect them. Not only do individuals make conscious choices in exposing themselves to particular media, but also their beliefs and values subconsciously shape how their minds pick up and store information and ideas. The phenomena of selective exposure, selective perception and selective retention and recall are overlooked by people who portray the mass media as omnipotent and individuals as helpless and manipulated pawns.

The 1938 "War of the Worlds" scare demonstrates this point. The immediate response was to heap blame on the media, particularly Orson Welles and CBS, but panic-stricken listeners bore responsibility too. A Princeton University team led by psychologist **Hadley Cantril,** which studied the panic, noted that radio listeners brought

---

selective perception
People tend to hear what they want or expect to hear.

autistic perception
Synonym for selective perception.

selective retention
Subconsciously, people retain some media messages, not others.

selective recall
People recollect some media messages for long term but not others.

Hadley Cantril
Concluded less media effect than had been thought.

to their radio sets predispositions and preconceptions that contributed to what happened. Among their subconscious baggage:

- A preconception, almost a reverence, about radio, especially CBS, as a reliable medium for major, breaking news.

- A predisposition to expect bad news, created by a decade of disastrous global economic developments and another war imminent in Europe.

- Selective perception, which caused them to miss announcements that the program was a dramatization. While many listeners tuned in late and missed the initial announcement, others listened straight through the announcements without registering them.

- An awe about scientific discoveries, technological progress and new weapons, which contributed to gullibility.

- Memories from World War I about the horror of gas warfare.

- An inability to test the radio story with their own common sense. How, for example, could the Army mobilize for a battle against the Martians within 20 minutes of the invasion?

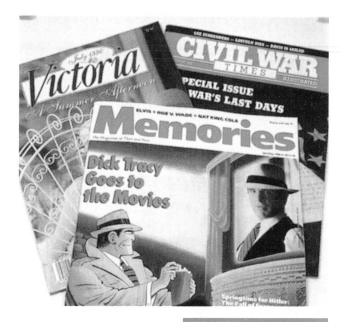

Selective Retention. The influence of the mass media is a function of both media and audience. The success of nostalgia magazines like *Memories*, which was introduced in 1989 and whose circulation soared to 650,000, is a result of the rose-colored lenses through which most people view the past. This is an example of selective retention at work.

socialization

(STUDY PREVIEW) The mass media have a large role in initiating children into the society. This socialization process is essential to perpetuating cultural values, but some people worry that it can be negative if the media report and portray undesirable behavior and attitudes, such as violence and racism.

media's initiating role

Nobody is born knowing how to fit into society. This is learned through a process that begins at home. Children imitate their parents and brothers and sisters. From listening and observing, children learn values. Some behavior is applauded, some is scolded. Gradually this culturization and **socialization** process expands to include friends, neighbors, school and at some point the mass media.

In earlier times, the role of the mass media came late because books, magazines and newspapers required reading skills that were learned in school. The media were only a modest part of early childhood socialization. Today, however, television is omnipresent from the cradle. A young person turning 18 will have spent more time watching television than in any other activity except sleep. Television, which requires no special skills

> **socialization**
> Learning to fit into society.

····peggy charren

Children's Television. Peggy Charren, a homemaker and concerned mother, led a campaign in Washington for better kids' television, persuading the Federal Communications Commission, the Federal Trade Commission and Congress that reform was needed. After the Children's Television Act was passed in 1990, Charren disbanded her lobbying group, Action for Children's Television.

After watching television with her two young daughters, Peggy Charren decided something needed doing. "Children television time was filled with cartoon adventures, often violent and rarely creative, in story or animation form," she said. "Youngsters were being told to want unhealthy food and expensive toys." Charren invited neighborhood moms to her livinggroom to discuss the "wall-to-wall monster cartoons." Thus, in 1968, was born Action for Children's Television. which, with Charren in charge, became the most influential nongovernment entity shaping American television for the next two decades.

The first target was "Romper Room," a Boston-produced show that was little more than a program-length commercial aimed at kids. The host shamelessly hawked "Romper Room's" own line of toys from sign-on to sign-off. ACT sponsored a university study of "Romper Room" and was ready to take the findings to the Federal Communications Commission when station WHDH, which produced the show, stopped the "host-selling" to get Charren off its back—ACT's first victory.

Action for Children's Television then requested meetings with the three big networks, but ABC and NBC said no. Insulted, Charren and her growing organization decided to take their cause to the government. In 1970, ACT became the first public interest group to request a meeting with the FCC. The commission responded by creating a permanent group to oversee children's television issues. With the new government pressure, the National Association of Broadcasters, the major industry trade group, established new standards for children's television. The new guidelines barred "host-selling" and put a 12-minute per hour cap on commercials during children's television. The lesson for ACT was that government pressure works. "We found that when the regulators make noise the industry takes action to keep the rules away," Charren said.

There were other battles, but the major victory for Charren and Action for Children's Television was the Children's Television Act of 1990. The law established government expectations for children's programming across a wide range of issues, including advertising, content and quantity. In 1992, to the surprise of many people, Charren announced she was disbanding ACT. After 24 years, she said, ACT has met the objectives that she had set out to accomplish. With the Children's Television Act in effect, the need for ACT had passed. At that point, ACT had 10,000 members.

Through all her crusading for better children's programming, Charren never called for censorship. Her battle cry was choice. "Censorship meant fewer choices. We needed more choice, not less." She did, however, admit to pushing "to eliminate commercial abuses targeted to children."

Even with violent programs, about which she had grave reservations, Charren never called for censorship. Her view:

"Violent television teaches children that violence is the solution to problems, that violent behavior can be fun and funny, that criminals and police make up a larger percentage of the population than they really do, and that violent behavior is practiced by heroes as well as by villains. But you can't say that there shouldn't be any violence on television. It is the *context* that is really important. Too often, children are the excuse for banning speech: words and pictures in comic books, movies, classic stories, textbooks and television. But government censorship is not the way to protect children from inappropriate content."

to use, has displaced much of the socializing influence that once came from parents. "Sesame Street" imparts more information on the value of nutrition than Mom's admonition to eat spinach.

By definition, socialization is **prosocial.** Children learn that motherhood, baseball and apple pie are valued, that buddies frown on tattling, that honesty is virtuous and that hard work is rewarded. The stability of a society is assured through the transmission of such values to the next generation.

role models

The extent of media influence on individuals may never be sorted out with any precision, in part because every individual is a distinct person and because media exposure varies from person to person. Even so, some media influence is undeniable. Consider the effect of entertainment idols as they come across through the media. Many individuals, especially young people casting about for an identity all their own, groom themselves in conformity with the latest heartthrob. Consider the Mickey Mantle butch haircuts in the 1950s and then Elvis Presley ducktails, Beatle mopheads in the 1960s and punk spiking in the 1980s. Remember all the Madonna look-alikes in high schools a few years ago? This imitation, called **role modeling,** even includes speech mannerisms from whoever is hip at the moment—"Know what I mean?" "Grody to the max." "Isn't that special." "Not!"

No matter how quirky, fashion fads are not terribly consequential, but serious questions can be raised about whether role modeling extends to behavior. Many people who produce media messages recognize a responsibility for role modeling. Whenever Batman and Robin leaped into their Batmobile in the campy 1960s television series, the camera always managed to show them fastening their seat belts. Many newspapers have a policy to mention in accident stories whether seat belts were in use. In the 1980s, as concern about AIDS mounted, movie-makers went out of their way to show condoms as a precaution in social situations. For example, in the movie *Broadcast News,* the producer character slips a condom into her purse before leaving the house on the night of the awards dinner.

If role modeling can work for good purposes, such as promoting safety consciousness and disease prevention, it would seem that it could also have a negative effect. Such was the argument against the 1988 movie *Colors,* which was built around Los Angeles gang violence. Said Curtis Sliwa, leader of the Guardian Angels, which opposed the movie, "It doesn't take much creative analysis to know that this could foment a problem.... It's almost like a how-to movie. It starts with a drive-by shooting." When the movie opened, two teenagers at one movie house were shot, one fatally, and police made 13 arrests at another theater. Experts were divided, as might be expected, on whether the violence was inspired by depictions on the screen.

stereotyping

Close your eyes. Think "professor." What image forms in your mind? Before 1973 most people would have envisioned a harmless, absent-minded eccentric. Today, the image is more likely to be the brilliant, sometimes brutal Professor Kingsfield portrayed by John Houseman in the 1973 movie and subsequent television series "The Paper Chase." Both the absent-minded pre-1973 professor and the steel-trap post-1973 Kingsfield are images known as stereotypes. Both flow from the mass media. While neither is an accurate generalization about professors, both have long-term impact.

Stereotyping is a kind of shorthand that can facilitate communication. Putting a cowboy in a black hat allows a movie director to sidestep complex character explanation and move quickly into a story line, because movie-goers hold a generalization about cowboys in black hats. They are the bad guys—a stereotype. Newspaper editors pack lots of information into headlines by drawing on stereotypes held by the readers. Consider the extra meanings implicit in headlines that refer to the "Castro regime," or a "Southern belle," or a "college jock." Stereotypes paint broad strokes that help create impact in media messages, but they are also a problem. A generalization, no matter how useful, is inaccurate. Not all Scots are cheap, nor are all Wall Street brokers crooked, nor are all college jocks dumb—not even a majority.

By using stereotypes, the mass media perpetuate them. With benign stereotypes, there is no problem, but the media can perpetuate social injustice with stereotypes. In the late 1970s, the U.S. Civil Rights Commission found that blacks on network television were portrayed disproportionately in immature, demeaning or comic roles. By using a stereotype, television was not only perpetuating false generalizations but also being racist. Worse, network thoughtlessness was robbing black people of strong role models.

Feminists have leveled objections that women are both underrepresented and misrepresented in the media. One study by sociologist Eve Simson found that most female television parts were decorative, played by pretty California women in their 20s. Worse were the occupations represented by women, said Simson. Most frequent were prostitutes, at 16 percent. Traditional female occupations—secretaries, nurses, flight attendants and receptionists—represented 17 percent. Career women tended to be man-haters or domestic failures. Said Simson: "With nearly every family, regardless of socioeconomic class, having at least one TV set and the average set being turned on 6.3 hours per day, TV has emerged as an important source for promulgating attitudes, values and customs. For some viewers, it is the only major contact with outside 'reality,' including how to relate to women. Thus, not only is TV's sexism insulting, but it is also detrimental to the status of women."

Media critics like Simson call for the media to become activists to revise demeaning stereotypes. While often right-minded, such calls can interfere with accurate portrayals. In the 1970s, Italian-American activists, for example, lobbied successfully against Mafia characters being identified as Italian.

socialization via eavesdropping

The mass media, especially television, have eroded the boundaries that people once respected between the generations, genders and other social institutions. Once adults whispered when they wanted to discuss certain subjects, like sex, when children were around. Today, children eavesdrop on all kinds of adult topics by seeing them depicted on television. Though meant as a joke, these lines ring true today to many squirming parents:

Father to a Friend: My son and I had that father-and-son talk about the birds and the bees yesterday.
Friend: Did you learn anything?

Joshua Meyrowitz, a communication scholar at the University of New Hampshire, brought the new socialization effects of intergenerational eavesdropping to wide attention with his 1985 book, *No Sense of Place.* In effect, the old socially recognized institution of childhood, which long had been protected from "big-people issues" like

---

stereotyping
Using broad strokes to facilitate story-telling.

Joshua Meyrowitz
Noted media have reduced generational, gender barriers.

money, divorce and sex, was disappearing. From television sitcoms, kids today learn that adults fight and goof up and sometimes are just plain silly. These are things kids may always have been aware of in a vague sense, but now they have front row seats.

Television also cracked other protected societal institutions, such as the "man's world." Through television, many women entered the man's world of the locker room, the fishing trip and the workplace beyond the home. Older mass media, including books, had dealt with a diversity of topics and allowed people in on the "secrets" of other groups, but the ubiquity of television and the ease of access to it accelerated the breakdown of traditional institutional barriers.

media-depicted violence

(STUDY PREVIEW) Some individuals mimic aggressive behavior they see in the media, but such incidents are exceptions. Some experts argue, in fact, that media-depicted violence actually reduces real-life aggressive behavior.

learning about violence

The mass media help bring young people into society's mainstream by demonstrating dominant behaviors and norms. This prosocial process, called **observational learning,** turns dark, however, when children learn deviant behaviors from the media. In Manteca, California, two teenagers, one only 13, lay in wait for a friend's father in his own house and attacked him. They beat him with a fireplace poker, kicked him and stabbed him, and choked him to death with a dog chain. Then they poured salt in his wounds. Why the final act of violence, the salt in the wounds? The 13-year-old explained that he had seen it on television. While there is no question that people can learn about violent behavior from the media, a major issue of our time is whether the mass media are the cause of aberrant behavior.

Individuals on trial for criminal acts occasionally plead that "the media made me do it." That was the defense in a 1974 California case in which two young girls playing on a beach were raped with a beer bottle by four teenagers. The rapists told police they had picked up the idea from a television movie they had seen four days earlier. In the movie, a young woman was raped with a broom handle, and in court, the youths' attorneys blamed the movie. The judge, as is typical in such cases, threw out media-projected violence as an unacceptable scapegoating defense and held the young perpetrators responsible.

Although the courts have never accepted transfer of responsibility as a legal defense, it is clear that violent behavior can be imitated from the media. Some experts, however, say that the negative effect of media-depicted violence is too often overstated and that media violence actually has a positive side.

media violence as positive

People who downplay the effect of media portrayals of blood, guts and violence often refer to a **cathartic effect.** This theory, which dates to ancient Greece and the

media online

Mediascope Study: You can read the conclusions of the 1996 National Television Violence Study, commissioned by the cable television industry, at this site. www.mediascope.org/mediascope/ntvs.html

Mediascope Interviews: At this site you will find the transcript of a MacNeil-Lehrer Newshour segment on the release of the 1996 Mediascope television violence study. www1.pbs.org/newshour/bb/entertainment/tviolence_2-7.html

Television Violence Act: Julia Schlegal, an Indiana University law student, wrote this constitutional anlysis of Senator Paul Simon's proposal for reducing television violence. www.house.gov/white/internetcaucus/netcauc.html

UCLA Television Monitoring Project: This site carries the text of the exhaustive UCLA Center for Telecommunication Policy 1995 report on television violence. www.ucla.edu/current/hotline/violence/i.htm

observational learning
Theory that people learn behavior seeing it in real life, in depictions.

cathartic effect
People release violent inclinations by seeing them portrayed.

philosopher **Aristotle,** suggests that watching violence allows individuals vicariously to release pent-up everyday frustration that might otherwise explode dangerously. By seeing violence, so goes the theory, people let off steam. Most advocates of the cathartic effect claim that individuals who see violent activity are stimulated to fantasy violence, which drains off latent tendencies toward real-life violence.

In more recent times, scholar **Seymour Feshbach** has conducted studies that lend support to the cathartic effect theory. In one study, Feshbach lined up 625 junior high school boys at seven California boarding schools and showed half of them a steady diet of violent television programs for six weeks. The other half were shown nonviolent fare. Every day during the study, teachers and supervisors reported on each boy's behavior in and out of class. Feshbach found no difference in aggressive behavior between the two groups. Further, there was a decline in aggression among boys watching violence who were determined by personality tests to be more inclined toward aggressive behavior.

Opponents of the cathartic effect theory, who include both respected researchers as well as reflexive media bashers, were quick to point out flaws in Feshbach's research methods. Nonetheless, his conclusions carried a lot of influence because of the study's unprecedented massiveness—625 individuals. Also, the study was conducted in a real-life environment rather than in a laboratory, and there was a consistency in the findings.

prodding socially positive action

Besides the cathartic effects theory, an argument for portraying violence is that it prompts people to socially positive action. This happened after NBC aired "The Burning Bed," a television movie about an abused woman who could not take any more and set fire to her sleeping husband. The night the movie was shown, battered-spouse centers nationwide were overwhelmed with calls from women who had been putting off doing anything to extricate themselves from relationships with abusive mates.

On the negative side, one man set his estranged wife afire and explained that he was inspired by "The Burning Bed." Another man who beat his wife senseless gave the same explanation.

media violence as negative

The preponderance of evidence is that media-depicted violence has the potential to cue real-life violence, and most catharsis theorists concede this possibility. The **aggressive stimulation** theory, however, is often overstated to the point that it comes across smacking of the now generally discredited bullet, or hypodermic needle, theory of mass communication. The fact is that few people act out media violence in their own lives.

An exaggerated reading of the aggressive stimulation theory became impressed in the public mind, indelibly it seems, after a 1963 *Look* magazine article by Stanford researcher **Albert Bandura.** In his research, Bandura had found that there was an increase in aggressive responses by children shown films of people aggressively punching and beating on large inflated clowns called Bobos. After the film, the children's toys were taken away except for a Bobo doll, which, Bandura reported, was given a beating—just like in the film. The inference was that the children modeled their behavior

Aristotle
Defended portrayals of violence.

Seymour Feshbach
Found evidence for media violence as a release.

aggressive stimulation
Theory that people are inspired to violence from media depictions.

Albert Bandura
Found media violence stimulated aggression in children.

on the film violence. Bandura also conducted other experiments that all pointed in the same direction.

The **Bobo doll studies** gained wide attention, but, as with most research on the contentious media-triggered violence issue, other scholars eventually became critical of Bandura's research methodologies. One criticism is that he mistook child playfulness with the Bobo dolls for aggressiveness. Even so, everyone who has been stirred to excitement by a violent movie knows from personal experience that there is an effect, and the early publicity on the Bobo studies seemed to verify that growing societal violence was caused by the media.

Such cause-and-effect connections frequently are inferred from individual incidents that are widely played in the news media. Here is a sampler:

- Fifteen-year-old Ronald Zamora of Miami, a fan of the television police shows "Kojak" and "Police Woman," murdered an 83-year-old neighbor woman, and then said he was the victim of "involuntary subliminal television intoxication."

- Before going to the electric chair, serial killer Ted Bundy reported that media depictions inspired him to stalk women and kill them.

- Twenty-nine people shot themselves playing Russian roulette in separate incidents across the nation after watching the movie *The Deer Hunter*, which keeps cutting to a high-tension Russian roulette Saigon gambling scene.

Inferences from such anecdotal cases have contributed to the common notion that media-depicted violence leads directly to aggressive and violent behavior. This widely

Wow, Pow, Zap. The notion that media-depicted violence triggers real-life violence gained currency in the 1960s after researcher Albert Bandura wrote a *Look* magazine article about his Bobo doll research. Kids in a laboratory began really whacking Bobos after seeing people doing the same thing in a film. There is a continuing debate, however, whether people were accurate in inferring that media violence directly causes real violence. Bandura himself has been dismayed at some of the simplistic conclusions that have been drawn from the *Look* article.

Bobo doll studies
Kids seemed more violent after seeing violence in movies.

held notion was also supported by casual readings of numerous serious studies, among them:

- In upstate New York, researcher Monroe Lefkowitz identified third graders who watched a lot of violent television, and then, 10 years later, found that these individuals were rated by their peers as "aggressive."

- Psychologist Leonard Berkowitz of Wisconsin showed violent film scenes to children and college students and then moved them to a lab where they were given push buttons and told that they could administer electric shocks to an individual who, depending on the experiment, either had insulted them or resembled a violent character in the film, or who, they were told, had made a mistake on an exam and needed a reminder. Those who had seen the violence on film pushed their shock buttons more and longer than other subjects who had not seen the film.

- The National Institute of Mental Health reported that serious fights in high schools were more common among students who watched violent television programs.

These studies, however, do not prove that media-depicted violence leads to real-life violence. There are other plausible explanations for a correlation between media-depicted and actual violence. One is that people whose feelings and general view of the world tend toward aggressiveness and violence gravitate to violent movies and television shows because of their predisposition. This leads us to the catalytic theory, which sees media-depicted violence as a bystander, not a trigger, to violent behavior.

catalytic theory

Simplistic readings of both cathartic and aggressive stimulation effects research can yield extreme conclusions. A careful reading, however, points more to the media having a role in real-life violence but not necessarily triggering it and doing so only infrequently—and only if several non-media factors are also present. For example, evidence suggests that television and movie violence, even in cartoons, is arousing and can excite some children to violence, especially hyperactive and easily excitable children. These children, like unstable adults, become wrapped up psychologically with the portrayals and are stirred to the point of acting out. However, this happens only when a combination of other influences are also present. Among these other influences are:

- *Whether violence portrayed on the media is rewarded.* In 1984 David Phillips of the University of California at San Diego found that the murder rate increases after publicized prizefights, in which the victor is rewarded, and decreases after publicized murder trials and executions, in which, of course, violence is punished.

- *Whether media exposure is heavy.* A lesson from Monroe Lefkowitz's upstate New York research and dozens of other studies is that aggressive behavioral tendencies are strongest among people who see a lot of media-depicted violence. This suggests a cumulative media effect rather than a single hypodermic injection leading to violence.

- *Whether a violent person fits other profiles.* Studies have found correlations between aggressive behavior and many variables besides violence viewing. These include income, education, intelligence and parental child-rearing practices. This

catalytic theory
Media violence is among factors that sometimes contribute to real-life violence.

is not to say that any of these third variables cause violent behavior. The suggestion, rather, is that violence is far too complex to be explained by a single factor.

Most researchers note too that screen-triggered violence is increased if the aggression:

- Is realistic and exciting, like a chase or suspense sequence that sends adrenalin levels surging.

- Succeeds in righting a wrong, like helping an abused or ridiculed character get even.

- Includes situations or characters similar to those in the viewer's own experience.

All these things would prompt a scientist to call media violence a catalyst. Just as the presence of a certain element will allow other elements to react explosively but itself not be part of the explosion, the presence of media violence can be a factor in real-life violence but not a cause by itself. This catalytic theory was articulated by scholars **Wilbur Schramm,** Jack Lyle and Edwin Parker, who investigated the effects of television on children and came up with this statement in their 1961 book, *Television in the Lives of Our Children,* which has become a classic on the effects of media-depicted violence on individuals: "For *some* children under *some* conditions, *some* television is harmful. For *other* children under the same conditions, or for the same children under *other* conditions, it may be beneficial. For *most* children, under *most* conditions, *most* television is probably neither particularly harmful nor particularly beneficial."

societally debilitating effects

Media-depicted violence scares far more people than it inspires to violence, and this, according to **George Gerbner,** a leading researcher on screen violence, leads some people to believe the world is more dangerous than it really is. Gerbner calculates that 1 in 10 television characters is involved in violence in any given week. In real life, the chances are only about 1 in 100 per *year*. People who watch a lot of television, Gerbner found, see their own chances of being involved in violence nearer the distorted television level than their local crime statistics or even their own experience would suggest. It seems that television violence leads people to think they are in far greater real-life jeopardy than they really are.

The implications of Gerbner's findings go to the heart of a free and democratic society. With exaggerated fears about their safety, Gerbner says, people will demand greater police protection. They are also likelier, he says, to submit to established authority and even to accept police violence as a tradeoff for their own security.

tolerance of violence

An especially serious concern about media-depicted violence is that it has a numbing, callousing effect on people. This **desensitizing theory,** which is widely held, says not only that individuals are becoming hardened by media violence but also that society's tolerance for such antisocial behavior is increasing.

Media critics say the media are responsible for this desensitization, but many media people, particularly movie and television directors, respond that it is the

Scapegoating. On the eve of his execution, serial killer Ted Bundy claimed his violence was sparked by girlie magazines. Whatever the truth of Bundy's claim, scholars are divided about whether media depictions precipitate violent behavior. At one extreme is the view that media violence is a safety valve for people inclined to violence. At the other extreme is the aggressive stimulation theory that media violence causes real-life violence. Most thinking, to paraphrase a pioneer 1961 study on television and children, is that certain depictions under certain conditions may prompt violence in certain persons.

Wilbur Schramm
Concluded minimal effects of television on children.

George Gerbner
Speculated that democracy endangered by media violence.

desensitizing theory
Tolerance of real-life violence grows because of media-depicted violence.

george gerbner

George Gerbner worries a lot about media violence. And he's been doing this longer than just about anybody else. In 1967, Gerbner and colleagues at the University of Pennsylvania created a television violence index and began counting acts of violence. Today, almost three decades later, the numbers are startling. Gerbner calculates the typical American 18-year-old has seen 32,000 murders and 40,000 attempted murders at home on television.

In a dubious sense, there may be good news for those who fear the effects of media violence. Gerbner's index has found no significant change in the volume of violence since the mid-1970s. It may be maxed out.

Gerbner theorizes that the media violence has

negative effects on society. It's what he calls "the mean-world syndrome." As he sees it, people exposed to so much violence come to perceive the world as a far more dangerous place than it really is. One of his concerns is that people become overly concerned for their own safety and, in time, may become willing to accept a police state to assure their personal security. That, he says, has dire consequences for the free and open society that has been a valued hallmark of the American life-style.

Are there answers? Gerbner notes that the global conglomeration of mass media companies works against any kind of media self-policing. These companies are seeking worldwide outlets for their products, whether

movies, television programs or music, and violence doesn't require any kind of costly translations. "Violence travels well," he says. Also, violence has low production costs.

Gerbner notes that violence is an easy fill for weak spots in a television story line. Also, in television, violence is an effective cliff-hanger before a commercial break.

While Gerbner's stats are unsettling, he has critics who say his numbers make the situation seem worse than it really is. The Gerbner index scores acts of violence without considering their context. That means when Bugs Bunny is bopped on the head, it counts the same as Rambo doing the same thing to a vile villain in a skull-crushing, blood-spurting scene. A poke in the eye on "The

It's a Mean World. Scholar George Gerbner, who has been tracking television violence since 1967, says a typical American child sees 32,000 on-screen murders before age 18. The result, he says, is many people see the world as much meaner than it really is.

Three Stooges" also scores as a violent act.

Despite his critics, Gerbner has provided a baseline for measuring changes in the quantity of television violence. Virtually every scholar cites him in the ongoing struggle to figure out whether media violence is something that should worry us all.

desensitization that has forced them to make the violence in their shows even more graphic. They explain that they have run out of alternatives to get the point across when the story line requires that the audience be repulsed. Some movie critics, of course, find this explanation a little too convenient for gore-inclined movie-makers and television directors, but even directors not inclined to gratuitous violence feel their options for stirring the audience have become scarcer. The critics respond that this is a chicken-or-egg question and that the media are in no position to use the desensitization theory to excuse increasing violence in their products if they themselves contributed to the desensitization. And so the argument goes on about who is to blame.

Desensitization is apparent in news also. The absolute ban on showing the bodies of crime and accident victims in newspapers and on television newscasts, almost universal a few years ago, is becoming a thing of the past. No longer do newsroom practices forbid showing body bags or even bodies. During the 1991 Persian Gulf war, U.S. television had no reluctance about airing videos of allied troops picking up the bodies of hundreds of strafed Iraqi soldiers and hurling them, like sacks of flour, onto flatbed trucks for hauling to deep trenches, where the cameras recorded the heaped bodies being unceremoniously bulldozed over with sand.

In summary, we know far less about media violence than we need to. Various theories explain some phenomena, but the theories themselves do not dovetail. The desensitizing theory, for example, explains audience acceptance of more violence, but it hardly explains research findings that people who watch a lot of television actually have heightened anxiety about their personal safety. People fretting about their own safety hardly are desensitized.

Desensitization. Critics of media violence say slasher movies like the *Scream* series desensitize people, especially teenagers, to the horrors of violence. That concern extends to video games. In one, Carmaggedon, kids are encouraged on the packaging blurb: "Don't slow down to avoid hitting that pedestrian crossing the street—aim, rev up and rack up those points." In one sequence in the Mortal Kombat video game, a crowd shouts encouragement for Kano to rip the heart out of Scorpion, his downed protagonist. Kano waves the dismembered heart to the crowd, which roars approvingly. Although scholars disagree about whether media violence begets real-life violence, most do agree that media violence leaves people more accepting of violence around them in their everyday lives.

media agenda-setting for individuals

(STUDY PREVIEW) Media coverage helps define the things people think about and worry about. This is called agenda-setting. It occurs as the media create awareness of issues through their coverage, which lends importance to those issues. The media don't set agendas unilaterally, but they look to their audiences in deciding their priorities for coverage.

media selection of issues

When the New York police wanted more subway patrols, their union public relations person, Morty Martz, asked officers to call him with every subway crime. Martz passed the accounts, all of them, on to newspapers and television and radio stations. Martz could not have been more pleased with his media blitz. News coverage of subway crime, he later boasted, increased several thousand percent, although there had been no appreciable change in the crime rate itself. Suddenly, for no reason other than dramatically stepped-up coverage, people were alarmed. Their personal agendas of what to think about—and worry about—had changed. The sudden new concern, which made it easier for the union to argue for more subway patrols, was an example of media agenda-setting at work. Martz lured news media decision-makers into putting subway crime higher on their lists of issues to be covered, and individuals moved it up on their lists of personal concerns.

The agenda-setting phenomenon has been recognized for a long time. Sociologist **Robert Park,** writing in the 1920s, articulated the theory in rejecting the once-popular notion that the media tell people what to think. As Park saw it, the media create awareness of issues more than they create knowledge or attitudes. Today, agenda-setting theorists put it this way: The media do not tell people what to think but what to think about. Agenda-setting occurs at several levels:

Creating Awareness. Only if individuals are aware of an issue can they be concerned about it. Concern about parents who kill their children becomes a major issue with media coverage of spectacular cases. In 1994 Susan Smith, a South Carolina woman, attracted wide attention with her horrific report that her sons, ages 3 and 1, had been kidnapped. The story darkened later when the woman confessed to driving the family car into the lake and drowning the boys herself. Over several days of intense media attention, the nation learned not only the morbid details of what happened but also became better informed about a wide range of parental, family and legal issues that the coverage brought to the fore.

Establishing Priorities. People trust the news media to sort through the events of the day and make order of them. Lead-off stories on a newscast or on Page One are expected to be the most significant. Not only does how a story is played affect people's agendas, but so do the time and space afforded it. Lavish graphics can propel an item higher.

Perpetuating Issues. Continuing coverage lends importance to an issue. A single story on a bribed senator might soon be forgotten, but day-after-day follow-ups can fuel ethics reforms. Conversely, if gatekeepers are diverted to other stories, a hot issue can cool overnight—out of sight, out of mind.

intramedia agenda-setting

Agenda-setting also is a phenomenon that affects media people, who constantly monitor one another. Reporters and editors many times are concerned more with how their peers are handling a story than with what their audience wants. Sometimes the media harp on one topic, making it seem more important than it really is, until it becomes tedious.

Robert Park
Argued media create awareness.

The media's agenda-setting role extends beyond news. Over time, life-styles and values portrayed in the media can influence not just what people think about but what they do. Hugh Hefner's *Playboy* magazine of the 1950s helped to usher in the sexual revolution. Advertising has created a redefinition of American values by whetting an appetite for possessions and glamorizing immediate gratification.

Even so, individuals exercise a high degree of control in their personal agendas. For decades, William Randolph Hearst campaigned with front-page editorials in all his newspapers against using animals in research, but animal rights did not become a pressing public issue. Even with the extensive media coverage of the Vietnam war, polls late in the 1960s found that many Americans still were unmoved. For the most part, these were people who chose to tune out the war coverage. The fact is that journalists and other creators of media messages cannot automatically impose their agendas on individuals. If people are not interested, an issue won't become part of their agendas. The individual values at work in the processes of selective exposure, perception and retention can thwart media leadership in agenda-setting.

Also, media agendas are not decided in a vacuum. Dependent as they are on having mass audiences, the media take cues for their coverage from their audiences. Penny press editors in the 1830s looked over the shoulders of newspaper readers on the street to see what stories attracted them and then shaped their coverage accordingly. Today, news organizations tap the public pulse through scientific sampling to deliver what people want. The mass media both exert leadership in agenda-setting and mirror the agendas of their audiences.

media-induced anxiety and apathy

(STUDY PREVIEW)   The pervasiveness of the mass media is not necessarily a good thing, according to some theorists who say a plethora of information and access to ideas and entertainment can induce information anxiety. Another theory is that the news media even encourage passivity by leaving an impression that their reporting is so complete that there's nothing left to know or do.

information anxiety

The New York *Times* had a landmark day on November 13, 1987. It published its largest edition ever—12 pounds, 1,612 pages and 12 million words. How could anyone, even on a quiet Sunday, manage all that information? One of the problems in contemporary life is the sheer quantity of information technology allows us as a society to gather and disseminate. Even a relatively slender weekday edition of the New York *Times* contains more information than the average person in the 17th century was likely to come across in a lifetime, according to Richard Saul Wurman in his book *Information Anxiety*.

While educated people traditionally have thirsted for information, the quantity has become such that many people feel overwhelmed by what is called **information pollution.** We are awash in it and drowning, and the mass media are a factor in this. Consider college students at a major metropolitan campus:

- They pass newspaper vending machines and racks with a dozen different papers—dailies, weeklies, freebies—en route to class.

- On the radio, they have access to 40 stations.

- In their mailbox, they find a solicitation for discount subscriptions to 240 magazines.

- They turn on their television during a study break and need to choose among 50 channels.

- At lunch, they notice advertisements everywhere—on the placemat, on the milk carton, on table standups, on the butter pat, on the walls, on the radio coming over the public-address system, on the pen used to write a check.

- At the library, they have almost instant online access through computer systems to more information than any human being could possibly deal with.

Compounding the quantity of information available is the accelerating rate at which it is available. Trend analyst John Naisbitt has made the point with this example: When President Lincoln was shot in 1865, people in London learned about it five days later. When President Reagan was shot in 1981, journalist Henry Fairlie, in his office one block away, heard about the assassination attempt from his London editor who had seen it on television and phoned Fairlie to get him to go to the scene. Databases to which almost every college student today has access are updated day by day, hour by hour, even second by second.

It is no wonder that conscientious people who want good and current data to form their judgments and opinions, even to go about their jobs, feel overwhelmed. Wurman, who has written exclusively on this frustration, describes information anxiety as the result of "the ever-widening gap between what we understand and what we think we should understand."

The solution is knowing how to locate relevant information and tune out the rest, but even this is increasingly difficult. Naisbitt reported in *Megatrends* that scientists planning an experiment are spending more time figuring out whether someone somewhere already has done the experiment than conducting the experiment itself.

On some matters, many people do not even try to sort through all the information that they have available. Their solution to information anxiety is to give up. Other people have a false sense of being on top of things, especially public issues, because so much information is available.

media-induced passivity

One effect of the mass media is embodied in the stereotypical couch potato, whose greatest physical and mental exercise is heading to the refrigerator during commercials. Studies indicate that the typical American spends four to six hours a day with the mass media, mostly with television. The experience is primarily passive, and it has

information pollution
Media deluge people with information and no sense of order, priority.

media-induced passivity
Media entice people away from social involvement.

been blamed, along with greater mobility and access to more leisure activities, for major changes in how people live their lives.

- **Worship Services.** In 1955 Gallup found that 49 percent of Americans attended worship services weekly. Today, it is less than 40 percent.

- **Churches and Lodges.** The role of church auxiliaries and lodges, like the Masons, Odd Fellows and Knights of Pythias, once central in community social life with weekly activities, has diminished.

- **Neighborhood Taverns.** Taverns at busy neighborhood corners and rural crossroads once were the center of political discussion in many areas, but this is less true today.

- **Participatory Sports.** Despite the fitness and wellness craze, more people than ever are overweight and out of shape, which can be partly attributed to physical passivity induced by television and media-based homebound activities.

While these phenomena may be explained in part by people's increased use of the mass media and the attendant passivity, it would be a mistake not to recognize that social forces besides the media have contributed to them.

well-informed futility

The news media take pride in purveying information to help people be active and involved in public matters, but, ironically, the media contribute insidiously to passivity by lulling people into accepting news reports as the last word on a subject. To attract and impress audiences, reporters use techniques to enhance their credibility, coming across as more authoritative than they really are and making their stories seem comprehensive and complete. Consider the well-groomed, clear-spoken television reporter on the Capitol steps whose 40-second report seems to address all inherent questions. The slickness in presentation works against the journalistic ideal of promoting intelligent citizen involvement in the political and social process by seeming to be so complete that nothing more can be said. The result is called the syndrome of **well-informed futility.** Readers, listeners and viewers feel satisfied that they're fully informed, which becomes an end in itself rather than actual involvement. This phenomenon works against democracy, which is predicated on citizen involvement, not apathy.

As agenda-setters, the mass media may also be working against the democratic ideal. The greater the role of the media in choosing the society's issues and fashions and even setting the values, the less the role of the people at a grassroots level.

chapter wrap-up

The mass media influence us, but scholars are divided about how much. There is agreement that the media help initiate children into society by portraying social and cultural values. This is a serious responsibility because portrayals of aberrant behavior, like violence, have effects, although we are not sure about their extent. This is not to say that individuals are unwitting pawns of the mass

well-informed futility
Media make people feel involved when actually only informed.

media. People choose what they read and what they tune in to, and they generally filter the information and images to conform with their preconceived notions and personal values.

In other respects too, the mass media are a stabilizing influence. The media try to fit into the lives of their audiences. An example is children's television programs on weekend mornings when kids are home from school but still on an early-rising schedule. The media not only react to audience life-styles but also contribute to the patterns by which people live their lives, like going to bed after the late news. In short, the media have effects on individuals and on society, but it is a two-way street. Society is a shaper of media content, but individuals make the ultimate decisions about subscribing, listening and watching. The influence issue is a complex one that merits further research and thought.

questions for review

1. Why have most media scholars abandoned the powerful and minimalist effect theories for the cumulative theory?

2. What is the uses and gratifications approach to mass media studies?

3. Do individuals have any control over mass media effects on them?

4. What role do the mass media have in socializing children?

5. How do scholars differ on whether media-depicted violence triggers aggressive behavior?

6. What is meant when someone says: "The mass media don't tell people what to think as much as tell them what to think about"?

7. Does being informed by mass media necessarily improve citizen involvement in political processes?

questions for critical thinking

1. Although generally discredited by scholars now, the powerful effects theory once had many adherents. How do you explain the lingering popularity of this thinking among many people?

2. Name at least three opinion leaders who influence you on issues that you do not follow closely in the media. On what issues are you yourself an opinion leader?

3. Give specific examples of each of the eight primary mass media contributing to the lifelong socialization process. For starters, consider a current nonfiction best-selling book.

4. Explain how selective exposure, selective perception and selective retention would work in the imaginary case of a devout Muslim who was studying English literature at Harvard University at the time Salman Rushdie's book, *The Satanic Verses,* was published. You may want to check newsmagazines in February and March 1989 for background.

5. Discuss the human needs that the mass media help satisfy in terms of the news and entertainment media.

6. Among the functions that the mass media serve for individuals are diversion and escape. Is this healthy?

7. Explain the prosocial potential of the mass media in culturization and socialization. What about the media as an antisocial force in observational learning?

8. Cite at least three contemporary role models who you can argue are positive. Explain how they might also be viewed as negative. Cite three role models who you can argue are negative.

9. What stereotype comes to your mind with the term "Uncle Remus"? Is your image of Uncle Remus one that would be held universally? Why or why not?

10. How can serious scholars of mass communication hold such diverse ideas as the cathartic, aggressive stimulation and catalytic theories? Which camp is right?

for further learning

Cham Eyal, Jim Winter and Maxwell McCombs. "The Agenda-Setting Role in Mass Communication." In Michael Emery and Ted Curtis Smythe, *Reading in Mass Communication: Concepts and Issues in the Mass Media,* 6th ed. (Wm. C. Brown, 1986). Pages 169–174. The authors, all scholars, trace the development of agenda-setting theory and identify the status of research.

Leo W. Jeffres. *Mass Media: Processes and Effects,* 2nd ed. (Waveland, 1994). Professor Jeffres discusses the variety of perspectives that attempt to understand the mysterious process of mass communication and then focuses on effects of the media on individuals and on society.

Robert M. Liebert, Joyce N. Spafkin and Emily S. Davidson. *The Early Window: Effects of Television on Children and Youth,* 3rd edition (Pergamon, 1988). This compendium covers the broad range of studies on television and children with special emphasis on research into media-depicted violence.

Joshua Meyrowitz. *No Sense of Place: The Impact of Electronic Media on Social Behavior* (Oxford, 1985). Professor Meyrowitz says television allows everybody, adult and child alike, to eavesdrop into other generations, which has eroded if not undone intergenerational distinctions that once were essential components of the social structure.

John Naisbitt. *Megatrends: Ten New Directions Transforming Our Lives* (Warner, 1982). Naisbitt identifies trends in society, particularly the shift from the industrial age to the information age. Naisbitt's later thoughts are in *Megatrends 2000* (Avon, 1990).

Williard D. Rowland, Jr. *The Politics of TV Violence: Policy Uses of Communication Research* (Sage, 1983). Rowland argues that the mass media have used a heavy hand behind the scenes to dilute research findings that screen violence begets real-life violence. Rowland, a scholar, goes back to the Payne studies in the late 1920s.

Richard Saul Wurman. *Information Anxiety* (Doubleday, 1989). Wurman discusses information overload as a modern problem for individuals and suggests ways to deal with it.

for keeping up to date

Among numerous scholarly journals that publish research on media effects are the *Journal of Communication, Journalism Quarterly, Journal of Broadcasting & Electronic Media* and *Mass Communication Review.*

Also valuable is *Mass Communication Review Yearbook* published annually by Sage of Beverly Hills, California.

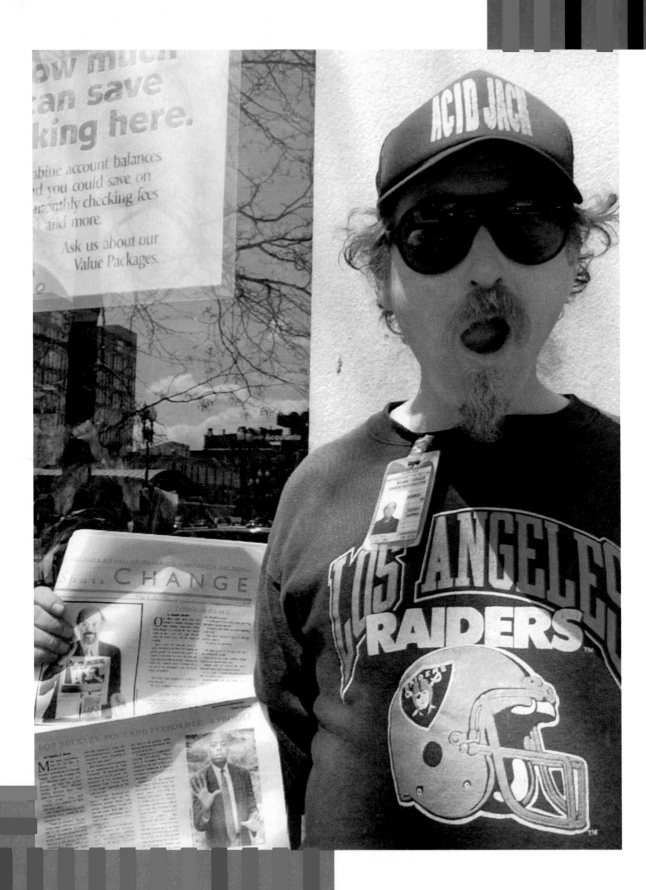

16

mass media and society

- The mass media seek to reach large audiences rather than to extend cultural sensitivity.

- The mass media contribute to stability in the society by providing common rituals.

- People communicate with generations into the future and with faraway people through the mass media.

- Scholar Marshall McLuhan foresaw television easing the alienation of human beings from their true nature.

- Societies that dominate economically and politically export their values elsewhere for better or worse.

As the two women walked along a Chicago street, one woman grabbed her friend's arm to hurry past the man who had courteously asked if they wanted to buy a newspaper. Surveying his clothing with disdain, she mumbled to her friend, "Another homeless person asking for a handout." The friend said, "No, he isn't begging for money. He wants to give us something in exchange." As she handed him a dollar and heard his polite "Thank you," she noticed he was wearing a badge designating him as an official vendor for the newspaper. She opened the paper and found herself marveling at the writing quality—especially the poetry. She had just purchased *StreetWise*, one of the approximately 125 "homeless newspapers" now being published in cities around the world.

"The modern street newspaper movement is generally considered to have begun in the late 1980s with a paper called

Street News, which was sold by poor people in New York," says Timothy Harris, chair of the North American Street Newspaper Association. Although the original Street News ran into severe internal difficulties, the concept sparked the imagination of a number of advocates for the poor. This could be a way to inform the public about poverty issues, while at the same time providing flexible employment for people with neither jobs nor homes.

A spontaneous movement was soon underway. In 1991 and 1992, four papers in widely separate geographical areas sprang up without any contact among their founders. A grant from The Body Shop provided funds to launch The Big Issue in London, its staff dedicated to producing a quality publication that would support poor people both ideologically and economically. In the United States, Chicago's StreetWise, San Francisco's Street Sheet, and Boston's Spare Change got underway.

Timothy Harris, the founder of Spare Change, admits that his idealism caused him to make mistakes in the beginning. He was so committed to getting out the voice of the homeless that he attempted a completely democratic model, with homeless people totally in charge—a task for which many were unprepared. In hindsight, he views that model as "fairly extreme," and it gave rise to many problems. The paper has since changed its mode of operation and "has become more stable."

That experience helped shape Harris's vision for the next paper he started, Seattle's monthly Real Change, which he now directs. This time, he said, he wanted to "moderate the model" so that it "worked better and had greater stability." Equipped only with his firm belief in the power of street newspapers to be both a voice and an organizing tool for poor and homeless people, he moved to Seattle in March 1994. Although he had no start-up funds, he was able to sell $3,000 worth of endorsement ads and obtain enough other support to publish the first issue within six months. Since that first issue, Real Change has paid for itself through circulation, donations, ad sales, and reliance on its dedicated volunteers for staffing needs.

Harris has since written a manual on how to start a street newspaper. "A lot of the folks who are doing street newspapers are organizers more than they are editors and publishers," he points out, "so there's a learning curve there."

One reason 45 street newspapers in the United States and Canada have joined together to form the North American Street Newspaper Association "is so that people who are doing street newspapers don't have to reinvent the wheel." Harris points out that "there are a whole lot of things that different papers have figured out and are able to share with other papers." The organization gives members a sense of involvement in a dynamic movement, creates solidarity, and encourages the start-ups of new papers. The goal is to produce street newspapers that will be effective, that will empower the poor and homeless, and that will survive and grow as businesses that are also able to support other kinds of organizing. Similar purposes lie behind the International Network of Street Newspapers, composed mainly of European-based street papers as well as papers in South Africa and Australia.

Harris brings to his work not only his academic training in social thought, political economy and journalism at the University of Massachusetts, but also his practical experience as a political activist. He started an alternative newspaper during his college days, then worked in a magazine that focused on poverty issues, and later became director of an organization called Jobs with Peace, which he says "did poor people's grass-roots organizing and made broader connections to the overall military economy and how that creates poverty." He also brings to his work his personal experience of having been a teenage runaway who was himself homeless for a time.

Real Change is in partnership with poor and homeless people in many different ways. They can contribute material for publication, for example, or they can sell the paper. Those who wish to be vendors are given 10 newspapers free to sell on the streets for the $1 cover price, and they can purchase additional copies for 30 cents each and earn 70 cents for each paper sold. Street newspapers hold vendors to a strict code of conduct, including the requirement that they refrain from drugs and alcohol and wear an identifying badge when selling the papers.

Real Change is one of several street newspapers that has a site on the World Wide Web (www.speakeasy.org/realchange/sitemap.html). A unique feature is Hobson's Choice, an electronic game. Harris explains, " We wanted to create a situation where it's easier for people to understand who homeless people are and why they're homeless and what life is like for them. I think it's very easy for people, when they don't know very many poor people, to believe the stereotypes and accept rationalizations about why people are poor—rationalizations that support the status quo."

Harris hopes that street newspapers will make the public "more aware of the issues, and a lot more aware of who poor and homeless people are, and a lot more able to empathize with their situation" and then that readers "will move from that position of empathy to one of action-to try to change things."

To Timothy Harris, each paper going out is like a stone cast into a pond and creating ripples. "You don't know where those ripples are going," he says. "But you know every once in awhile one will come back, and you'll see something that has happened or someone who has been changed because of contact with the paper. I think street newspapers are one of the most profound organizing tools for poor and homeless people that have come along in the last several decades."

mass media role in culture

STUDY PREVIEW The mass media are inextricably linked with culture because it is through the media that creative people have their strongest sway. While the media have the potential to disseminate the best creative work of the human mind and soul, some critics say the media are obsessive about trendy, often silly subjects. These critics find serious fault with the media's concern for pop culture, claiming it squeezes out things of significance.

elitist versus populist values

The mass media can enrich society by disseminating the best of human creativity, including great literature, music and art. The media also carry a lot of lesser things that reflect the culture and, for better or worse, contribute to it. Over time, a continuum has been devised that covers this vast range of artistic production. At one extreme is artistic material that requires sophisticated and cultivated tastes to appreciate. This is called **high art.** At the other extreme is **low art,** which requires little sophistication to enjoy.

high art
Requires sophisticated taste to be appreciated.
low art
Can be appreciated by almost everybody.

media **timeline**

mass communication and culture

1960s Marshall McLuhan theorized that television could end human alienation caused by print media.

1960s Dwight Macdonald equated pop art and kitsch.

1965 Susan Sontag saw pop art as emotive high art.

1969 Herbert Schiller articulated cultural imperialism concerns.

1976 Herbert Gans related cultural sensitivity to social and economic status.

linda and robert lichter

It was love over the statistics. **Linda and Robert Lichter** met while working on a massive study of major media decision-makers and married. Later they formed the **Center for Media and Public Affairs** in Washington, which today is a leading research organization on the mass media and social change. One of the most troubling findings of the Lichters and co-researcher **Stanley Rothman** is that the major U.S. media are out of touch with the American people. This conclusion comes out of massive studies of the people who run the entertainment media.

The Lichter-Rothman studies say that television executives and key creative people are overwhelmingly liberal on the great social issues of our time. More significantly, the studies have found that the programming these people produce reflects their political and social agenda. For example:

• Television scripts favor feminist positions in 71 percent of the shows, far more than public-opinion surveys find among the general population.

• Three percent of television murders are committed by blacks, compared with half in real life.

• Two out of three people are portrayed in positive occupations on television, but only one out of three businesspeople is depicted in a positive role.

These examples, according to the Lichters and Rothman, indicate a bias toward feminism and minority people and against businesspeople. The Lichter-Rothman work documents a dramatic turnaround in television entertainment fare. Two generations ago, leading programs, ranging from sitcoms like "Leave It to Beaver" and dramatic programs like "Wagon Train" extolled traditional values. In the 1970s came programs like "Mork and Mindy" and "All in the Family" that questioned some values. Today, network schedules make plenty of room for programs like "L.A. Law" and "Murphy Brown" that examine nontraditional views and exhibit a dramatically different social orientation than, say, "Leave It to Beaver."

It is hazardous, of course, to paint too broad a picture of contemporary television, where a sitcom

Stanley Rothman

like "The Cosby Show" is much in the 1950s mode, but the Lichters and Rothman, by analyzing 620 shows over a 30-year period, argue persuasively that there has been a dramatic shift. They characterize the shift this way: "Television's America may once have looked like Los Angeles' Orange County writ large—Waspish, businesslike, religious, patriotic and middle class. Today it better resembles San Francisco's Marin County—trendy, self-expressive, culturally diverse and cosmopolitan."

The Lichter-Rothman studies indicate that this liberal, urban and secular "media elite," which creates television entertainment programming, is moving further and further away from traditional values. This might be just an interesting phenomenon,

Linda and Robert Lichter

except that, to critics, this media elite is subverting American culture by glamorizing alternative lifestyles and values. The Lichters and Rothman add fuel to this concern by noting that television's creative people not only deal with vexsome issues but, both subtly and overtly, slant the issues to their point of view.

This raises all kinds of serious questions about the mass media's effects on society. Can the media change bedrock social values? If values can be changed, are they really bedrock? While there is no doubt that the media affect society, how much? And how do these effects work?

One strain of traditional media criticism has been that the media underplay great works and concentrate on low art. This **elitist** view argues that the mass media do society a disservice by pandering to low tastes. To describe low art, elitists sometimes use the German word *kitsch,* which translates roughly as garish or trashy. The word captures their disdain. In contrast, the **populist** view is that there is nothing unbecoming in the mass media's catering to mass tastes in a democratic, capitalistic society.

In a widely cited 1960 essay, "Masscult and Midcult," social commentator **Dwight Macdonald** made a virulent case that all popular art is kitsch. The mass media, which depend on finding large audiences for their economic base, can hardly ever come out at the higher reaches of Macdonald's spectrum.

This kind of elitist analysis was given a larger framework in 1976 when sociologist **Herbert Gans** categorized cultural work along socioeconomic and intellectual lines. Gans said that classical music, as an example, appealed by and large to people of academic and professional accomplishments and higher incomes. These were **high-culture** audiences, which enjoyed complexities and subtleties in their art and entertainment. Next came **middle-culture** audiences, which were less abstract in their interests and liked Norman Rockwell and prime-time television. **Low-culture** audiences were factory and service workers whose interests were more basic; whose educational accomplishments, incomes and social status were lower; and whose media tastes leaned toward kung fu movies, comic books and supermarket tabloids.

Gans was applying his contemporary observations to flesh out the distinctions that had been taking form in art criticism for centuries—the distinctions between high art and low art.

High-Brow. The high art favored by elitists generally can be identified by its technical and thematic complexity and originality. High art often is highly individualistic because the creator, whether a novelist or a television producer, has explored issues in fresh ways and often with new and different methods. Even when a collaborative effort, a piece of high art is distinctive. High art requires a sophisticated audience to appreciate it fully. Often it has enduring value, surviving time's test as to its significance and worth.

The sophistication that permits an opera aficionado to appreciate the intricacies of a composer's score, the poetry of the lyricist and the excellence of the performance sometimes is called **high-brow.** The label has grim origins in the idea that a person must have great intelligence to have refined tastes, and a high "brow" is necessary to accommodate such a big brain. Generally the term is used by people who disdain those who have not developed the sophistication to enjoy, for example, the abstractions of a Fellini film, a Matisse sculpture or a Picasso painting. High-brows generally are people who, as Gans noted, are interested in issues by which society is defining itself and look in literature and drama for stories on conflicts inherent in the human condition and between the individual and society.

Middle-Brow. Middle-brow tastes recognize some artistic merit but without a high level of sophistication. There is more interest in action than abstractions, in Captain Kirk aboard the starship Enterprise, for example, than in the childhood struggles of Ingmar Bergman that shaped his films. In socioeconomic terms, middle-brow appeals to people who take comfort in media portrayals that support their status quo orientation and values.

Low-Brow. Someone once made this often-repeated distinction: High-brows talk about ideas, middle-brows talk about things, and **low-brows** talk about people.

Linda and Robert Lichter
Research indicates liberal agenda in entertainment programming; colleague of Stanley Rothman.

Center for Media and Public Affairs
Media research organization.

Stanley Rothman
Research indicates liberal agenda in entertainment programming; colleague of Lichters.

elitism
Mass media should gear to sophisticated audiences.

kitsch
Pejorative word for trendy, trashy, low art.

populism
Mass media should seek largest possible audiences.

Dwight Macdonald
All pop art is kitsch.

Herbert Gans
Social, economic and intellectual levels of audience coincide.

high-, middle- and low-culture audience
Continuum identified by Herbert Gans.

high-, middle- and low-brow
Levels of media content sophistication that coincide with audience tastes.

Judging from the circulation success of the *National Enquirer* and other supermarket tabloids, there must be a lot of low-brows in contemporary America. Hardly any sophistication is needed to recognize the machismo of Rambo, the villainy of Simon Legree, the heroism of Superman or the sexiness of Madonna.

the case against pop art

Pop art is of the moment, including things like mood rings, hula-hoops and grunge garb—and trendy media fare. Even elitists may have fun with pop, but they traditionally have drawn the line at anyone who mistakes it as having serious artistic merit. Pop art is low art that has immense although generally short-lived popularity.

Elitists see pop art as contrived and artificial. In their view, the people who create **popular art** are masters at identifying what will succeed in the marketplace and then providing it. Pop art, according to this view, succeeds by conning people into liking it. When Nehru jackets were the fashion rage in the late 1960s, it was not because they were superior in comfort or utility or aesthetics, but because promoters sensed profits could be made in touting them via the mass media as new and cashing in on easily manipulated mass tastes. It was the same with Cabbage Patch dolls, pet rocks, showy petticoats and countless other faddy products.

The mass media, according to the critics, are obsessed with pop art. Partly this is because the media are the carriers of the promotional campaigns that create popular followings but also because competition within the media creates pressure to be first, to be ahead, to be on top of things. The result, say elitists, is that junk takes precedence over quality.

Much is to be said for this criticism of pop art. The promotion by CBS of the screwball 1960s sitcom "Beverly Hillbillies," as an example, created an eager audience that otherwise might have been reading Steinbeck's critically respected *Grapes of Wrath*. An elitist might chortle, even laugh at the unbelievable antics and travails of the Beverly Hillbillies, who had their own charm and attractiveness, but an elitist

popular art
Art that tries to succeed in marketplace.

would be concerned all the while that low art was displacing high art in the marketplace and that the society was the poorer for it.

pop art revisionism

Pop art has always had a few champions among intellectuals, although their voices were usually drowned out in the din of elitist pooh-poohing. In 1965, however, essayist **Susan Sontag** wrote an influential piece, "One Culture and the New Sensibility," which prompted many elitists to take a fresh look at pop art.

Pop Art as Evocative. Sontag made the case that pop art could raise serious issues, just as could high art. She wrote: "The feeling given off by a Rauschenberg painting might be like that of a song by the Supremes." Sontag soon was being called the high priestess of pop intellectualism. More significantly, the Supremes were being taken more seriously, as were a great number of Sontag's avant-garde and obscure pop artist friends.

Popularization of High Art. Sontag's argument noted that the mass appeal of pop artists meant that they could convey high art to the masses. A pop pianist like Liberace might omit the trills and other intricacies in performing a sonata, but he nonetheless gave a mass audience an access to Mozart that otherwise would never occur. Sontag saw a valuable service being performed by artists who both understood high art and could "translate" it for unsophisticated audiences, a process known as **popularization.**

As Sontag saw it, the mass media were at the fulcrum in a process that brings diverse kinds of cultural products and audiences together in exciting, enriching ways. The result of popularization, Sontag said, was an elevation of the cultural sensitivity of the whole society.

Pop Art as a Societal Unifier. In effect, Sontag encouraged people not to look at art on the traditional divisive, class-conscious, elitist-populist continuum. Artistic value, she said, could be found almost anywhere. The word "camp" gained circulation among 1960s elitists who were influenced by Sontag. These high-brows began finding a perversely sophisticated appeal in pop art as diverse as Andy Warhol's banal soup cans and ABC's outrageous "Batman." The mass media, through which most people experienced Warhol and all people experienced "Batman," became recognized more broadly than ever as a societal unifier.

The Sontag-inspired revisionist look at pop art coincides with the view of many mass media historians that the media have helped bind the society rather than divide it. In the 1840s, these historians note, books and magazines with national distribution provided Americans of diverse backgrounds and regions with common reference points. Radio did the same even more effectively in the 1940s. Later, so did network television. In short, the mass media are purveyors of cultural production that contributes to social cohesion, whether it be high art or low art.

High Art as Popular. While kitsch may be prominent in media programming, it hardly elbows out all substantive content. In 1991, for example, Ken Burns's public television documentary, "The Civil War," outdrew low art primetime programs on ABC, CBS and NBC five nights in a row. It was a glaring example that high art can appeal to people across almost the whole range of socioeconomic levels and

pop art revisionism
Pop art has inherent value.

Susan Sontag
Saw cultural, social value in pop art.

popularization
Adjust media content to appeal to broader audience.

is not necessarily driven out by low art. Burns's documentary was hardly a lone example. Another, also from 1991, was Franco Zeffirelli's movie *Hamlet*, starring pop movie star Mel Gibson, which was marketed to a mass audience and yet could hardly be dismissed by elitists as kitsch. In radio, public broadcasting stations, marked by high-brow programming, in some cities have become major players for ratings.

social stability

(STUDY PREVIEW) The mass media create rituals around which people structure their lives. This is one of many ways that the media contribute to social stability. The media foster socialization through adulthood, contributing to social cohesion by affirming beliefs and values and helping reconcile inconsistent values and discrepancies between private behavior and public morality.

media-induced ritual

Northwest Airlines pilots, flying their Stratocruisers over the Dakotas in the 1950s, could tell when the late-night news ended on WCCO, the powerful Minneapolis radio station. They could see lights at ranches and towns all across the Dakotas going off as people, having heard the news, went to bed. The 10 o'clock WCCO news had become embedded as a ritual. Today, for people on the East and West coasts, where most television stations run their late news at 11 p.m., the commonest time to go to bed is 11:30, after the news. In the Midwest, where late newscasts are at 10 o'clock, people tend to go to bed an hour earlier and also to rise an hour earlier. Like other rituals that mark a society, media-induced rituals contribute order and structure to the lives of individuals.

The effect of media-induced rituals extends even further. Collectively, the lifestyles of individuals have broad social effect. Consider just these two effects of evening newspapers, an 1878 media innovation:

Evening News. E. W. Scripps changed people's habits with his evening newspapers, first in Cleveland in 1878, then elsewhere. Soon, PM papers outnumbered AM papers. The new habit, however, was not so much for evening newspapers as for evening news, as newspaper publishers discovered a hundred years later when television siphoned readers away with evening newscasts. The evening ritual persists, even though the medium is changing as PMs go out of business or retreat to mornings.

Competitive Shopping. In the era before refrigeration and packaged food, household shopping was a daily necessity. When evening newspapers appeared, housewives, who were the primary shoppers of the period, adjusted their routines to read the paper the evening before their morning trips to the market. The new ritual allowed time for more methodical bargain hunting, which sharpened retail competition.

Besides shaping routines, ritual contributes to the mass media's influence as a shaper of culture. At 8:15 a.m. every Sunday, half the television sets in Japan are tuned to "Serial Novel," a tear-jerking series that began in the 1950s. Because so many people watch, it is a common experience that is one element in the identification of contemporary Japanese society. In American society, a ritual that marked the society for years was "Dallas," Friday, 9 p.m. Eastern time, 8 p.m. Central time. Other rituals are going to Saturday movie matinees, reading a book at bedtime and watching Monday night football.

the media and the status quo

In their quest for profits through large audiences, the mass media need to tap into their audience's common knowledge and widely felt feelings. Writers for network sitcoms avoid obscure, arcane language. Heroes and villains reflect current morals. Catering this way to a mass audience, the media reinforce existing cultural beliefs and values. People take comfort in learning through the media that they fit into their community and society, which furthers social cohesion. This is socialization continued beyond the formative years. It also is socialization in reverse, with the media taking cues from the society and playing them back.

The media's role in social cohesion has a negative side. Critics say that the media pander to the lowest common denominator by dealing only with things that fit the status quo easily. The result, the critics note, is a thwarting of artistic exploration beyond the mainstream. Critics are especially disparaging of predictable, wooden characters in movies and television and of predictability in the subjects chosen for the news.

A related negative aspect of the media's role as a contributor to social cohesion is that dominant values too often go unchallenged, which means that some wrong values and practices persist. Dudley Clendinen, a newspaper editor who grew up in the South, faults journalists for, in effect, defending racism by not covering it: "The news columns of Southern papers weren't very curious or deep or original in the late 1940s and 1950s. They followed sports and politics actively enough, but the whole rational thrust of Southern culture from the time of John C. Calhoun on had been self-defensive and maintaining. It had to be, to justify the unjustifiable in a society dedicated first to slavery and then to segregation and subservience. Tradition was everything, and the news pages were simply not in the habit of examining the traditions of the South."

the media and cognitive dissonance

The media are not always complacent. Beginning in the late 1950s, after the period to which Clendinen was referring, media attention turned to racial segregation. News coverage, literary comment and dramatic and comedy portrayals began to point up flaws in the status quo. Consider the effect, through the mass media, of these individuals on American racism:

- **John Howard Griffin.** In 1959 Griffin, a white journalist, dyed his skin black for a six-week odyssey through the South. His book, *Black Like Me,* was an inside look at being black in America. It had special credibility for the white majority because Griffin was white.

If you forget to bring along a designated driver, remember, you can always rent one.

MADD
Mothers Against Drunk Driving

Public Service. Major agencies produce public service advertisements on a rotating basis for the Ad Council. These magazines and newspaper ads, as well as television and radio public-service announcements, are distributed free. The media run them at no cost. The Council chooses about a dozen organizations a year to benefit from the in-house creative genius at the agencies that produce the ads *pro bono.*

Cognitive Dissonance. Many white Americans from racist backgrounds found themselves challenging their own values when the federal government adopted proactive civil rights policies in the 1950s and 1960s. This dissonance escalated as these people followed news coverage of the long-overdue demands of blacks for fair treatment, as in this 1963 march. Some white racists resolved the discrepancy by abandoning racism. Many others simply retreated from discussion on the issue.

Agenda-Setting. Media attention to certain events puts a spotlight on issues that might otherwise not receive wide public attention. The Christmas 1996 slaying of JonBenet Ramsey, a regular on the child beauty-pageant circuit, raised the issue of "stage moms" who energetically push their kids into activities beyond the norm for their age.

---

cognitive dissonance
Occurs when people realize their values are inconsistent.

- **George Wallace.** The mass audience saw the issue of segregation personified in news coverage of Governor George Wallace physically blocking black students from attending the University of Alabama. The indelible impression was that segregation could be defended only by a clenched fist and not by reason.

- **Martin Luther King Jr.** News photographers captured the courage and conviction of Martin Luther King Jr. and other civil rights activists, black and white, taking great risks through civil disobedience to object to racist public policies.

- **Archie Bunker.** Archie Bunker, a television sitcom character, made a laughing stock of bigots.

To some people, the media coverage and portrayals seemed to exacerbate racial tensions. In the longer run, however, media attention contributed to a new consensus through a phenomenon that psychologists call **cognitive dissonance.** Imagine white racists as they saw George Wallace giving way to federal troops under orders from the White House. The situation pitted against each other two values held by individual racists—segregation as a value and an ordered society as symbolized by the presidency. Suddenly aware that their personal values were in terrible disharmony, or dissonance, many of these racists avoided the issue. Instead of continuing to express racism among family and friends, many tended to be silent. They may have been as racist as ever, but they were quiet, or watched their words carefully. Gradually their untenable view is fading into social unacceptability. This is not to say that racism does not persist. It does, and continues to manifest itself in American life although, in many ways, in forms much muted since the media focused on the experiment of John Howard Griffin, the clenched fist of George Wallace and the crusade of Martin Luther King Jr.

When the media go beyond pap and the predictable, they are examining the cutting-edge issues by which the society defines its values. Newsmagazines, newspapers and television, utilizing new printing, photography and video technology in the late 1960s, put war graphically into American living rooms, pointing up all kinds of discrepancies between Pentagon claims and the Vietnam reality. Even the glamorized, heroic view of war, which had persisted through history, was countered by media depictions of the blood and death. Unable to resolve the discrepancies, some people withdrew into silence. Others reassessed their views and then, with changed positions or more confident in their original positions, they engaged in a dialogue from which a consensus emerged. And the United States, the mightiest power in history, began a militarily humiliating withdrawal. It was democracy at work, slowly and painfully, but at work.

agenda-setting and status conferral

Media attention lends a legitimacy to events, individuals and issues that does not extend to things that go uncovered. This conferring of status occurs through the media's role as agenda-setters. It puts everybody on the same wavelength, or at least a similar one, which contributes to social cohesion by focusing our collective attention on issues we can address together. Otherwise, each of us could be going in separate directions, which would make collective action difficult if not impossible.

media and morality

A small-town wag once noted that people read the local newspaper not to find out what is going on, which everybody already knows, but to find out who got caught. The observation was profound. The mass media, by reporting deviant behavior, help enforce society's moral order. When someone is arrested for burglary and sentenced, it reaffirms for everybody that human beings have property rights.

Beyond police blotter news, the mass media are agents for reconciling discrepancies between **private actions** and **public morality.** Individually, people tolerate minor infractions of public morality, like taking pencils home from work. Some people even let life-threatening behavior go unreported, like child abuse. When the deviant behavior is publicly exposed, however, toleration ceases and social processes come into action that reconcile the deviance with public morality. The reconciling process maintains public norms and values. Consider Douglas Ginsburg. In the 1970s, Ginsburg, a young law professor, smoked marijuana at a few parties. It was a misdemeanor, but Ginsburg's friends tolerated it, and not a word was said publicly. In 1988, however, when President Reagan nominated Ginsburg to the U.S. Supreme Court, reporter Nina Totenberg of National Public Radio reported Ginsburg's transgressions. Exposed, he withdrew his name. There was no choice. His private action, publicly exposed, could not be tolerated, and his withdrawal maintained public norms and values, without which a society cannot exist.

This same phenomenon occurred in the 1980s when homelessness became a national issue. For years, homeless people in every major city had slept in doorways and alleys and, during winter, at steam vents. The homeless were seen but invisible. When social policies and economic factors in the 1980s sent the numbers skyrocketing, homelessness became a media issue that could not be ignored, and the society had to do something. Under the glare of media attention, people brought their private behavior, which had been to overlook the problem, into conformity with the tenet of public morality that says we are all our brothers' keepers. Across the nation, reform policies to relieve homelessness began moving through legislative channels.

Sherry Turkle. Some people create new personalities for themselves when they're online in Internet chat rooms. This has given rise to computer sociolgy as a specialized academic field. Sherry Turkle, a professor at the Massachusetts Institute of Technology, is in the vangard exploring the Internet's influence on behavior. Some people, Turkle has discovered, like the anonymity of the Net to play with personas they wouldn't dare experiment with in face-to-face, real-life situations. Some individuals like their new Net personality so much they integrate it into other aspects of their lives.

---

private actions versus public morality
Dichotomy that exposes discrepancies between behavior and values.

Values Transmission.
If not for mass media attention on the flamboyant, some would say weird, attire and manners of basketball player Dennis Rodman, not so many kids would be doing strange things to their hair. In trivial ways, as with Rodman, and in significant ways, as with fundamental social change, the mass media are a factor in diffusing "innovations" that lead eventually to change.

cultural transmission

(STUDY PREVIEW)   The mass media transmit cultural values through history. Past generations talk to us through mass media, mostly books, just as we, often not realizing it, talk to future generations. The media also diffuse values and ideas contemporaneously.

historical transmission

Human beings have a compulsion to leave the wisdom they have accumulated for future generations. There is a compulsion, too, to learn from the past. In olden times, people gathered around campfires and in temples to hear storytellers. It was a ritual through which people learned the values that governed their community.

Five-thousand years ago, the oral tradition was augmented when Middle Eastern traders devised an alphabet to keep track of inventories, transactions and rates of exchange. When paper was invented, clay tablets gave way to scrolls and eventually books, which became the primary vehicle for storytelling. Religious values were passed on in holy books. Military chronicles laid out the lessons of war. Literature provided lessons by exploring the nooks and crannies of the human condition.

Books remain the primary repository of our culture. For several centuries, it has been between hard covers, in black ink on paper, that the experiences, lessons and wisdom of our forebears have been recorded for posterity. Other mass media today share in the preservation and transmission of our culture over time. Consider these archives:

- Museum of Broadcasting in New York, with 1,200 hours of television documentaries; great performances, productions, debuts and series; and a sample of top-rated shows.

- Library for Communication and Graphic Arts at Ohio State University, whose collection includes editorial cartoons.

- Vanderbilt Television News Archive in Nashville, Tennessee, with 7,000 hours of network nightly news programs and special coverage such as political conventions and space shots.

contemporary transmission

The mass media also transmit values among contemporary communities and societies, sometimes causing changes that otherwise would not occur. Anthropologists have documented that mass communication can change society. When Edmund Carpenter introduced movies in an isolated New Guinea village, the men adjusted their clothing toward the Western style and even remodeled their houses. This phenomenon, which scholars call **diffusion of innovations,** occurs when ideas move through the mass media. Consider the following:

- **American Revolution.** Colonists up and down the Atlantic seaboard took cues on what to think and how to act, from newspaper reports on radical activities, mostly

historical transmission
Communication of cultural values to later generations.

contemporary transmission
Communication of cultural values to different cultures.

diffusion of innovations
Process through which news, ideas, values, information spread.

Demanding a Better Life. Muscovites rioted against their government in 1993 when it became clear that the first-wave, post-Communist reformers could not deliver the Western-style prosperity that the Russian people had learned about through the mass media. They were acting out a process called diffusion of innovation. Through media coverage of Western consumer economies, the people knew there was a better way, and they wanted their leaders to adopt the innovations that would make them prosperous also.

in Boston, in the decade before the Declaration of Independence. These included inflammatory articles against the 1765 Stamp Act and accounts of the Boston Tea Party in 1773.

- **Music, Fashion and Pop Culture.** In modern-day pop culture, the cues come through the media, mostly from New York, Hollywood and Nashville.

- **Third World Innovation.** The United Nations creates instructional films and radio programs to promote agricultural reform in less developed parts of the world. Overpopulated areas have been targets of birth control campaigns.

- **Democracy in China.** As China opened itself to Western tourists, commerce and mass media in the 1980s, the people glimpsed Western democracy and prosperity, which precipitated pressure on the Communist government to westernize and resulted in the 1989 Tiananmen Square confrontation. A similar phenomenon was a factor in the glasnost relaxations in the Soviet Union in the late 1980s.

- **Demise of Main Street.** Small-town businesses are boarding up throughout the United States as rural people see advertisements from regional shopping malls, which are farther away but offer greater variety and lower prices than Main Street.

Scholars note that the mass media can be given too much credit for the diffusion of innovations. Diffusion almost always needs reinforcement through interpersonal communication. Also, the diffusion hardly ever is a one-shot hypodermic injection but a process that requires redundancy in messages over an extended period. The 1989 outburst for democracy in China did not happen because one Chinese person read Thomas Paine one afternoon, nor do rural people suddenly abandon their local Main Street for a Wal-Mart 40 miles away. The diffusion of innovations typically involves three initial steps in which the mass media can be pivotal:

- **Awareness.** Individuals and groups learn about alternatives, new options and possibilities.

- **Interest.** Once aware, people need to have their interest further whetted.
- **Evaluation.** By considering the experience of other people, as relayed by the mass media, individuals evaluate whether they wish to adopt an innovation.

The adoption process has two additional steps in which the media play a small role: the trial stage, in which an innovation is given a try, and the final stage, in which the innovation is either adopted or rejected.

mass media and fundamental change

(STUDY PREVIEW) The detribalization theory says the written word changed tribal communities by de-emphasizing interpersonal communication. Written communication engaged the mind, not the senses, and, according to the theory, a lonely, cerebral-based culture resulted. Now, as sense-intensive television displaces written communication, retribalization is creating a global village.

human alienation

An intriguing, contrarian assessment of the media's effects on human society was laid out by Canadian theorist **Marshall McLuhan** in the 1960s. McLuhan argued that the print media had alienated human beings from their natural state. In pre-mass media times, McLuhan said, people acquired their awareness about their world through their own observation and experience and through their fellow human beings, whom they saw face to face and with whom they communicated orally. As McLuhan saw it, this was a pristine communal existence—rich in that it involved all the senses—sight, sound, smell, taste and touch. This communal, tribal state was eroded by the written word, which involved the insular, meditative act of reading. The printing press, he said, compounded this alienation from humankind's tribal roots. The written word, by engaging the mind, not the senses, begat **detribalization,** and the printing press accelerated it.

According to McLuhan, the printed word even changed human thought processes. In their tribal state, he said, human beings responded spontaneously to everything that was happening around them. The written word, in contrast, required people to concentrate on an author's relatively narrow, contrived set of data that led from Point A to Point B to Point C. Following the linear serial order of the written word was a lonely, cerebral activity, unlike participatory tribal communication, which had an undirected, helter-skelter spontaneity.

television and the global village

McLuhan saw television bringing back tribalization. While books, magazines and newspapers engaged the mind, television engaged the senses. In fact, the television screen could be so loaded with data that it could approximate the high level of sen-

---

human alienation
Dissatisfaction with individual and cultural deviations from basic nature.

Marshall McLuhan
Blamed human alienation on mass-produced written word.

detribalization
The removal of humankind from natural, tribal state.

sual stimuli that people found in their environments back in the tribal period of human history. **Retribalization,** he said, was at hand because of the new, intensely sensual communication that television could facilitate. Because television could far exceed the reach of any previous interpersonal communication, McLuhan called the new tribal village a **global village.**

With retribalization, McLuhan said, people will abandon the print media's linear intrusions on human nature. Was McLuhan right? His disciples claim that certain earmarks of written communication—complex story lines, logical progression and causality—are less important to today's young people, who grew up with sense intensive television. They point to the music videos of the 1980s, which excited the senses but made no linear sense. Many teachers say children are having a harder time finding significance in the totality of a lesson. Instead, children fasten on to details.

As fascinating as McLuhan was, he left himself vulnerable to critics who point out that, in a true nonlinear spirit, he was selective with evidence and never put his ideas to rigorous scholarly examination. McLuhan died in 1980. Today the jury remains divided, agreeing only that he was a provocative thinker.

cultural intrusion

STUDY PREVIEW Some experts claim that the export of American and Western popular culture is latter-day imperialism motivated by profit and without concern for its effect on other societies. This theory of cultural dominance claims too that Third World countries are pawns of the Western-based global entertainment media and news services. Other experts disagree, saying the charges of cultural imperialism are overblown and hysterical.

latter-day imperialism

Some scholars claim that international communication has a dark side, which they call **cultural imperialism.** Their view is that the media are like the 19th-century European colonial powers, exporting Western values, often uninvited, to other cultures. At stake, these critics say, is the cultural sovereignty of non-Western nations. These critics note that the international communication media have their headquarters in the United States and also in the former European colonial powers. The communication flow, they claim, is one way, from the powerful nations to the weak ones. The result, as they see it, is that Western values are imposed in an impossible-to-resist way. A Third World television station, for example, can buy a recycled American television program for far less than it costs to produce an indigenous program.

Scholar **Herbert Schiller,** who wrote *Mass Communications and American Empire,* argued that the one-way communication flow is especially insidious because the Western productions, especially movies and television, are so slick that they easily outdraw locally produced programs. As a result, says Schiller, the Western-controlled international mass media preempt native culture, a situation he sees as robbery, just like the earlier colonial tapping of natural resources to enrich the home countries.

India is a fascinating recent example of cultural intrusion, if not cultural imperialism. Until 1991 this nation had only one television network, which ran programs that

---

retribalization
Restoring humankind to natural, tribal state.

global village
Instantaneous connection of every human being.

cultural imperialism
One culture's dominance of another.

Herbert Schiller
Saw Western cultures subsuming others.

Television Everywhere. The influence of Western society has permeated cultures around the world, which critics say results in a superimposition of Western values and styles that erode worthy but fragile cultural values elsewhere. Here, cultural intrusion shows itself with latter-day Bedouins outside Ragga, Syria, with Detroit pickup trucks and television.

originated in India almost exclusively. Then came Star TV, global media mogul Rupert Murdoch's satellite service from Hong Kong, that carried lots of U.S.-originated programming. Writing in *Media Studies Journal,* India media critic Shailaja Bajpai offered these observations:

• Many Indians now dress like the Americans they see on "Baywatch."

• While Indian boys once wanted to grow up to be great cricket players, they now want to shoot baskets like Michael Jordan.

Other anecdotal evidence of American culture rubbing off elsewhere is in South Africa. According to Sebiletso Mokone-Matabane, an executive with the Independent Broadcasting authority there, robbers now shout "freeze," a word that has no roots in Afrikaans or the indigenous languages, when they storm into a bank. The robbers have been watching too much American television.

defending western hegemony

Being leaders of pop culture abroad, says advertising executive David Ogilvy, does not necessarily mean that American values are being imposed abroad. Most Ogilvy & Mather employees abroad, he notes, are not American. When agencies use American campaigns, they modify them to fit the local culture. In addition, local subsidiaries of multinational agencies create many of their campaigns. Some of the outcry against American agencies abroad, according to Ogilvy, has little to do with any cultural invasion but is a cry for profits. Locally owned agencies, he says, "have a habit of wrapping themselves in their national flag and appealing to their governments for protection against foreign invaders. They accuse us of imposing an alien culture, particularly in countries that have little culture of their own."

Some people could accuse Ogilvy of insensitivity, but he also defines another way of viewing transcultural mass communication. The goal of advertising, Ogilvy reminds

media abroad
....americanizing the world

British traders introduced opium in China in the 1600s. The habit spread, and soon the British had a profitable trade importing opium to Chinese ports and exporting silver to pay for it. Resentful at British profits from the death and misery they had introduced, the Chinese government acted in 1839 against any further opium importation. In response, the British bombarded Canton, and the Opium War ensued.

Today, a similar struggle, dubbed the Second Opium War, is under way. Yielding to American trade pressure, Japan, South Korea and Taiwan lifted

Samurai Cowboy. For better or worse, American culture has permeated cultures almost everywhere on the globe. In Tokyo, a number of country and western bars have found legions of customers eager to don a Stetson, light a Marlboro, twang a guitar and sing Willie Nelson music. American beer is big too. Critics fret that American cultural icons and values are squeezing out indigenous cultural production and values. "Cultural imperialism," they call it.

bans on foreign tobacco in 1987, and the Marlboro man instantly became a familiar poster figure. Propelled by huge advertising budgets and American-style promotion, United States tobacco sales increased 24-fold almost overnight in Taiwan, to 5.1 billion cigarettes a year.

Is this cultural imperialism at its worst? Massa-chusetts Congressman Chet Atkins called it "the ultimate ugly Americanism." Noting that the U.S. government had mounted an extensive domestic campaign against smoking, Atkins said, "We are sending a message through our trade negotiators that Asian lungs are more expendable than American lungs." In Taiwan, a lead-ing antismoking activist, David Yen, said, "We want American friendship, machinery and food—but not your drugs."

Meanwhile, the Marlboro man, taller in the saddle than ever, rides on. Smoking in Japan, South Korea and Taiwan continues to grow to record levels.

critics, is to sell goods—regardless of where advertisements originate. Just because a campaign was invented elsewhere does not necessarily make it an insult to anyone's self-respect.

In some ways, cultural imperialism is in the eyes of the beholder. Some Latin American countries, for example, scream "cultural imperialism" at the United States but don't object when Mexico exports soap operas to the rest of Latin America, as do Brazil and Argentina. Although they are exercising a form of cultural imperialism, nobody puts the label on them. Media observer Larry Lorenz, who has studied this phenomenon, explains it this way: "What is occurring is simply internationalism brought on by the ever more sophisticated media of mass communication."

The cultural imperialism theory has other doubters among scholars. The doubters note that the theory is a simplistic application of the now-discredited hypodermic needle model of mass communication. Media messages do not have immediate direct effects.

Also overstated are charges that news from Europe and the United States dominates coverage in other parts of the world. One study found that 60 to 75 percent of

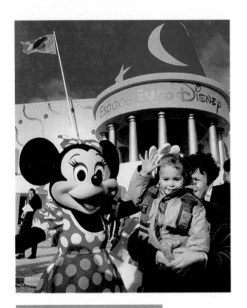

the foreign news in the Third World is about other Third World countries, mostly those nearby. While the giant Western news services, AP, Agence France-Presse and Reuters, are the main purveyors of foreign news, the coverage that reaches Third World audiences is extremely parochial.

emerging global media

Concern about Western cultural imperialism is slowly changing as two related things occur. First, the number of international media players, many neither in Europe nor the United States, is increasing. Second, rather than merely recycling domestic products abroad, United States-based media companies are creating new, local-oriented content in the countries where they do business.

Prime-time U.S. television soap operas "Dallas" and "Dynasty" once were on prime-time fare throughout the world, either with subtitles or dubbed awkwardly into local languages. Today, local media people who have mastered Western production techniques are producing local media content. Their programs go over big, attracting viewers and advertisers better than imported programs. Allan Ng, a Far East investment analyst, has seen the change at the giant Hong Kong satellite television service TVB. To *Business Week* reporter Joyce Barnathan, Ng said: "TVB dares not show 'Dynasty' until 11 at night."

Cultural Intrusion. When French children grow up loving American pop culture characters like Minnie and Mickey Mouse, is native French culture being lost? EuroDisney, outside Paris, and the presence of other U.S.-spawned cultural icons and output, including music and movies, has led some scholars to question whether American culture and values are displacing others around the globe. Some scholars call this phenomenon cultural imperialism.

Indigenous local programming not only is taking hold in other countries, especially those with a developing middle class, but also many of these emerging media are exporting their material. Throughout Latin America, for example, people watch soap operas produced by TV Globo in Brazil and Televisa in Mexico. The Belgian broadcast company RTL, which once spent most of its programming dollars on imports like "Dallas" and "Dynasty," now produces most of its own shows. The French TF-1 and Italian Rai Uno television services have cut back substantially on U.S. programs. The turnaround in Europe has been fueled not only by audience preferences for local material but also by a European Union policy that half of each nation's broadcast programming must originate within the union.

There is also new competition, much of it well financed. In Europe, the television service Canal One has teamed up with Bertelsmann of Germany to create a formidable competitor for the whole European audience. TVB in Hong Kong has its eye on dominating media fare to China, Southeast Asia and the Subcontinent. What once were easy pickings for U.S. media companies are now tough markets.

To compete, U.S. media companies are investing in other countries to develop local programming. MTV and ESPN both are building advanced production studios in Singapore. In 1995 Viacom relaunched its MTV service to Asia with local hosts. In Europe, U.S. companies are forming local partnerships. NBC, for example, which bought the European Super Channel cable network in 1983, has added business news from the *Financial Times,* a London newspaper. NBC has teamed up with TV Azteca in Mexico to tap into local programming and marketing savvy. Time Warner's HBO is in partnership with Omnivision, a Venezuelan cable company, for the HBO Olé pay-television service in Latin America.

While many countries are developing significant, local media powerhouses, some countries are decades away from having their own media production facilities, financing and know-how. Their complaint today is not solely about cultural imperialism from the United States but from Bonn, Caracas, Hong Kong, London, Mexico City, Paris and Sao Paulo.

insidious western influence

While more media content is being originated in home countries, some critics say don't be fooled. Shailaja Bajpai, editor of an Indian television magazine, says Indian TV producers clone U.S. television: "The American talk show has inspired Indian imitations. Never have so many Indians revealed so much about their private lives to such a wide audience. Every day a new show is planned. If nothing else, American television has loosened tongues (to say nothing of our morals). Subjects long taboo are receiving a good airing." Those Indian programs may be produced in India, but the concept is hardly Indian.

transnational cultural enrichment

Some scholars see transnational cultural flow in more benign terms than Herbert Schiller and his fellow cultural imperialism theorists. George Steiner has noted that European and American culture have been enriched, not corrupted, by the continuing presence of Greek mythology over 2,000 years. In a homey way, sociologist Michael Tracey makes a similar point:

"I was born in a working-class neighborhood called Oldham in the north of England. Before the First World War, Oldham produced most of the world's spun cotton. It is a place of mills and chimneys, and I was born and raised in one of the areas of housing—called St. Mary's—built to serve those mills. I recently heard a record by a local group of folk singers called the Oldham Tinkers, and one track was about Charlie Chaplin. This song was apparently very popular with local children in the years immediately after the First World War. Was that evidence of the cultural influences of Hollywood, a primeval moment of the imperialism of one culture, the subjugation of another? It seems almost boorish to think of it that way. Was the little man not a deep well of pleasure through laughter, a pleasure that was simply universal in appeal? Was it not Chaplin's real genius to strike some common chord, uniting the whole of humanity? Is that not, in fact, the real genius of American popular culture, to bind together, better than anything, common humanity?"

Despite the controversy alleging cultural imperialism and the arguments to debunk it, the issue is not settled. Many Third World countries, speaking through the United Nations, have demanded subsidies from Western nations to finance local cultural enterprises. They also have demanded a policy voice in the major Western-operated global news services.

chapter wrap-up

The mass media have caused fundamental changes in human communication. When Gutenberg introduced movable type in the 15th century, people began shifting from largely intuitive interpersonal communication to reading, which, says communication theorist Marshall McLuhan, required a different kind of concentration. The result, according to McLuhan, was less spontaneous communication, an alienation among individuals and a fragmented society. With electronic, visual media like television, which engage numerous senses and require less cerebral participation than reading, McLuhan saw a return to communication more consistent with human nature. He called it retribalization. Not everyone accepts McLuhan's vision, but there is agreement that the mass media profoundly affect society.

The mass media do not operate in a vacuum. The people who decide media content are products of the society, and the necessity to turn a profit requires that the media be in touch with the society's values or lose audience. In one sense, this reality of capitalism works against the media venturing too far from mainstream values. Critics say the media pander too much to popular tastes and ignore culturally significant works that could enrich society. An alternate view, more charitable to the media, is that great works trickle down to mass audiences through media popularization.

The media contribute both to social stability and to change. A lot of media content gives comfort to audiences by reinforcing existing social values. At the same time, media attention to nonmainstream ideas, in both news and fiction forms, requires people to reassess their values and, over time, contributes to social change.

questions for review

1. Why are mass media more interested in reaching large audiences rather than contributing to cultural sensitivity?

2. How do the mass media contribute to stability in the society?

3. What are historical and cultural transmission?

4. How did scholar Marshall McLuhan foresee that television would ease the human alienation that he said was created by the mass-produced written word?

5. Are there disadvantages when dominant societies export their values elsewhere?

questions for critical thinking

1. Why do the mass media find little room for great works that could elevate the cultural sensitivity of the society?

2. Explain essayist Susan Sontag's point that the mass media bring culturally significant works to mass audiences through the popularization process.

3. Give examples of how people shape their everyday lives around rituals created by the mass media. Also, give examples of how the mass media respond to social rituals in deciding what to present and how and when to do it.

4. Why would a radical social reformer object to most mass media content?

5. How has cognitive dissonance created through the mass media worked against racial separatism in American society since the 1950s?

6. How do the mass media help determine the issues that society sees as important?

7. How do the media contribute to social order and cohesion by reporting private acts that deviate from public morality? You might want to consider the case of Dick Morris in the 1996 presidential campaign of Bill Clinton.

8. Give examples of the mass media allowing cultural values to be communicated through history to future societies. Also, give examples of contemporary cultural transmission.

9. Explain scholar Marshall McLuhan's theory that the mass-produced written word has contributed to an alienation of human beings from their true nature. How did McLuhan think television could reverse this alienation?

10. Is *imperialism,* a word with strong negative implications, the best term to describe the transmission of cultural ideas and values from developed to less developed societies?

for further learning

"Global Views on U.S. Media," *Media Studies Journal* (Fall 1995). This special issue carries 21 articles on perceptions of U.S. media abroad, including ones by Shailaja Bajpai of India and Sebiletso Mokone-Matabane of South Africa, both of which are cited in this chapter.

S. Robert Lichter, Linda S. Lichter and Stanley Rothman. *Watching America: What Television Tells Us about Our Lives* (Prentice Hall, 1991).

Marshall McLuhan. *The Gutenberg Galaxy: The Making of Typographic Man* (University of Toronto Press, 1967). Most of the array of McLuhan's speculations about media effects can be found in this book and in his earlier *Understanding Media: The Extensions of Man* (McGraw Hill, 1964).

Herbert Schiller. *Mass Communications and American Empire* (Kelley, 1969). Schiller sees "an imperial network" of American forces, including the media, building a cultural dominance in less developed parts of the world.

Susan Sontag. "One Culture and New Sensibility." *Against Interpretation* (Farrar Straus & Giroux, 1966). Sontag sees pop art as a vehicle for bringing cultural sensitivity to mass audiences.

for keeping up to date

Recommended are *Journal of Popular Culture, Journal of American Culture* and *Journal of International Popular Culture*, all scholarly publications.

17

mass media and governance

in this chapter you will learn:

- Authoritarian media systems are subject to censorship, licensing, bribes and repression.

- Libertarian media systems are optimistic about human intellectual capabilities.

- The U.S. media system has shifted from libertarianism to social responsibility.

- The U.S. news media are a watchdog on government in the people's behalf.

- The news media influence people mostly through opinion leaders.

- The mass media are major shapers of the public's agenda of issues.

- Government has many tools for manipulating media coverage.

- Credibility is at the heart of many unsettled government-media issues.

He sent her fresh flowers and his special food creations. He charmed her office staff and made everybody laugh. And, although he was in his 40s, everybody referred to him as her "boyfriend." The two had so much in common—especially their immersion in politics and their work as political consultants.

But they differed in one important respect. He was a Democrat, and she was a Republican. Not a unique situation. Couples have had such differences before.

Mary Matalin was not just any Republican, however. At the time, she was chief of staff of the Republican National Committee, working out of their Washington, D.C., headquarters. She was hoping to be chosen for an important position in President George Bush's re-election campaign.

And James Carville, the man she was dating, was not just any Democrat. On that evening in November 1991 when they joined some friends for dinner,

Carville had just returned from Pennsylvania where he and his business partner, Paul Begala, helped a Democratic candidate win a U.S. Senate seat. Matalin considered that victory to be one of Carville's "really annoying string of successes, putting Democrats in places that without him would probably have gone to Republicans." Now Democratic presidential hopefuls were vying for the services of the Carville-Begala strategy team for the primary races. But neither of the two men was interested in "doing a presidential."

So as the couple sat in the restaurant that November evening, Mary Matalin was totally unprepared when one of their dinner companions, a reporter, asked Carville when he would be officially starting the Clinton campaign. Matalin felt as though she had been kicked. She felt hurt, betrayed and physically ill. She rushed to the restroom and stayed long enough to regain composure. Carville had not only neglected to inform her personally of his decision, he had earlier assured her he didn't want to work on a presidential race. Matalin feared that her close association with Clinton's designated campaign manager would ruin any chance she had of being chosen to be the political director of the Bush campaign.

After they left the restaurant, an angry exchange broke out. Matalin was sure Clinton would win the primaries and then, if she got the position she was hoping for, it would be a campaign with her candidate trying to beat Carville's candidate. "Before me flashed the whole next year," she later wrote in a book she and Carville co-authored, "something that had never happened in the annals of presidential politics: a boyfriend and girlfriend working against each other."

To make sure Matalin's job aspirations weren't hurt, Carville asked the reporter to hold off on publishing his acceptance of the Clinton campaign job. Although the reporter acted out of friendship in delaying publication of the story, the incident provided a preview of what lay ahead—the carefully planned use of the media to carry out the Carville strategy.

A week later, Mary Matalin was appointed political director of the campaign to re-elect President George Bush. The battle was on.

Like her Democratic counterpart, Matalin used the media to her candidate's advantage. "When in doubt, spin," she explained at one point in their book. The 1992 presidential campaign was taking place at a time when terms like "candidate packaging," "image building," "stonewalling," "spin doctors," "handlers," "leaks," "crisis resolution" and "damage control strategy" were becoming part of the common parlance.

Perhaps no concept sums up modern political strategizing so much as the notion of *spin*—an intentional slant to the way information is presented so that the public will interpret and respond to events in ways favorable to the candidate or political party. The term comes from a baseball pitcher's ability to spin a ball so that its trajectory is not what the opposing team expects.

Carville and Matalin were unabashedly masters of spin. Each of them tried to keep one step ahead of what the media would say about the candidates they served. That meant helping their candidates present an image and message that would appeal to voters. It was Carville who insisted the Clinton campaign stay on the dollar issues that concerned the American people and who coined the phrase, "It's the economy, stupid."

This was not, however, a competition between two political strategists, each out to better the other. Both Matalin and Carville were ideologically committed to their respective parties. Although Matalin had come from a family of Democrats and for a time had even embraced the "hippie" culture, she had undergone a complete turnabout after writing a paper on political conservatism for a college course. Carville had grown up in a segregated Southern culture and found his thinking changing when, as a schoolboy, he had read *To Kill a Mockingbird.* He had also observed that it was the intervention of federal agents who made sure school integration was carried out, which helped convince him of the federal government's power to do good.

In the end, Bill Clinton won the election, the romance between Carville and Matalin survived the campaign, and they later married and became parents. Carville continued his work as a political consultant and presidential advisor. Matalin found avenues for sharing her political views as a television commentator and radio talk show host.

Together, Carville and Matalin wrote their campaign memoirs in *All's Fair: Love, War, and Running for President,* providing a captivating, behind-the-scenes account of a presidential campaign and showing the crucial role the media plays in the election of government leaders.

authoritarian systems

(STUDY PREVIEW)   Authoritarian governments, including modern-day dictatorships, regard the mass media as subservient: The government is beyond challenge.

england under henry VIII

When Johannes Gutenberg invented movable type in the 1400s, making mass production of the written word possible, authorities were enthusiastic. Early printers produced Bibles and religious tracts, which were consistent with the values of the intertwined institutions of state and church. It did not occur to anybody that the new invention might be used for heretical or traitorous purposes. Later, occasional tracts appeared that challenged the authorities, but their threat was easily dismissed because, even in the early 1500s, printing still was mostly in Latin, which could be read only by the ruling elite. Most common people were unable to read even their native language, let alone Latin. The printed word seemed an unlikely vehicle for the foment of popular revolution.

Within two generations, however, the comfortable relationship between the authorities and the fast-growing printing industry changed, and the authorities clamped down. What happened in England was typical. In 1529, after Dutch tracts that challenged royal authority began showing up, King Henry VIII outlawed imported publications. He also decreed that every English printer must be licensed. Printers caught producing anything objectionable to the Crown lost their licenses, in effect being put out of business. Remaining in the government's good graces brought favors. A license was a guaranteed local monopoly and a lock on government and church printing jobs.

Divine Right. King James I, who fancied himself a scholar, wrote a treatise in 1598 that claimed monarchies were legitimate because of a pipeline to God. His theory, called the divine right of kings, is a classic defense for authoritarian political and media systems.

---

media timeline

political-media theories

1529 Henry VIII barred imported publications.

1529 Henry VIII established Stationers Company to license printers.

1591 James I articulated divine right of kings theory.

1644 John Milton laid out libertarian theory in *Areopagitica.*

1791 United States reconstituted, again, as libertarian state.

1947 Hutchins Commission urged media to be socially responsible.

1961 Columbia University founded *Columbia Journalism Review.*

1962 Louisville *Courier-Journal* named Norman Isaacs as ombudsman.

1970 New York *Times* expanded commentary with daily op-ed page.

john twyn

John Twyn died a particularly gruesome death. In 1663 Twyn, a printer, published a book that held that the monarch should be accountable to the people. While hardly a radical concept today, the idea was heretical in 17th-century England, where kings considered themselves divinely appointed. Twyn, who had not even written the book but merely printed it, was arrested and convicted of seditious libel. His sentence: "You shall be hanged by the neck, and being alive, shall be cut down and your privy members shall be cut off, your entrails shall be taken from your body, and you living, the same to be burnt before your eyes."

The political climate in England and the other modern Western democracies has changed dramatically since John Twyn's time. But mass communicators are still profoundly affected by the political systems within which they operate. The Committee to Protect Journalists, which tracks repression against the press, reports that dozens of reporters are jailed every year. In 1995 there were 182 journalists in 22 countries in prison or held hostage. Fifty-one died, 45 by assassination.

Even in the United States, a democracy with a constitution guaranteeing free expression and a free press, journalists are sentenced to jail from time to time, usually for refusing to identify their confidential sources when asked to do so by a judge. There are even stories of reporters' lives being threatened. Washington *Post* reporters Carl Bernstein and Bob Woodward said they learned their lives were in danger as they dug into 1972 Nixon re-election campaign scandals. In that same period, columnist Jack Anderson reported that a government plot had been hatched in the Justice Department to assassinate him for his Watergate reporting.

Frederick Siebert, a scholar on the authoritarian English press, describes the main function of the mass media in an authoritarian system this way: "to support and advance the policies of government as determined by the political machinery then in operation." Siebert's phrase "then in operation" points out how fickle an authoritarian system can be. In 1530, when England under Henry VIII was still a Catholic state, a man was executed for selling a book by a Protestant author. Only 50 years later, after the government had rejected Catholicism, a printer was executed for printing a Catholic pamphlet. In an authoritarian system, the media are subservient to government and adjust their content to coincide with changes in government policy.

Authoritarian Execution. Authoritarian governments prevent mass media criticism of their policies with numerous methods, including execution. In authoritarian England, the Crown made public spectacles of executions, as in the case of John of Barneveld in 1619, shown here, which had a chilling effect on other people who might have challenged the Crown.

media abroad

····distinguishing media systems

Scholars Fred Siebert, Theodore Peterson and Wilbur Schramm created models for looking at national media systems in a pioneering work, *Four Theories of the Press*. Their book, published in 1956, helped many later scholars make sense of the roles that mass media play in vastly different political systems.

Siebert, Peterson and Schramm identified authoritarian, communist and libertarian models, and also a latter-day adaptation of libertarianism that they called social responsibility. There is quibbling about whether social responsibility should be a separate model, but the point really is how these models offer a systematic picture of the mass media in different nations.

Review the characteristics of media in different systems in the following table, and then see where a national media system that you or your classmates know about fits in. A good starting point would be England in the latter years of Henry VIII's reign. How about the United States? Classmates who have lived abroad or studied foreign political systems can help with other countries.

Remember, a model is never perfect, and no national media system fits into a Siebert, Peterson and Schramm pigeonhole exactly. Some developed, relatively stable countries, like the United States, are better fits than countries in the developing world that are still working out their political systems. A special challenge is where to plug in Mexico: The country has privately owned media, but criticism of government, while allowed, can bring indirect sanctions from the government.

	Authoritarian	Communist	Libertarian	Social Responsibility
Who Owns the Mass Media?	Privately owned	State owned	Privately owned	Privately owned
Is Criticism of Government Allowed?	No	Yes, but ideology is off-limits	Yes, even encouraged	Yes, as long as it is responsible
Who Decides What the Media Will Say?	The media	The state	The media	Experts
Who Decides What the Media Will Not Say?	The state	The state	The media	Experts
Who Enforces Decisions on Media Content?	The state	The state	Nobody	Ideally the media, perhaps the state

methods of authoritarian control

Censorship usually comes to mind as an authoritarian method to control the mass media, but censorship is labor intensive and inefficient. Other methods include licensing, bribery and repression.

Censorship. Authoritarian regimes have found numerous ways, both blatant and subtle, to control the mass media. **Censorship** is one. The most thorough censoring requires that manuscripts be read by governmental agents before being printed or aired. To work, prepublication censorship requires a governmental agent in every

> **censorship**
> Government restrictions on expression either before or after dissemination.

media abroad

⋯⋯jailed journalists

Freedom House, a New York agency that tracks attacks on the news media worldwide, reported 26 journalists were murdered in 14 countries in 1997 because of their reporting. In addition:

- 30 journalists were kidnapped or disappeared.

- 231 were beaten, assaulted or tortured.

Reporter on Trial. Reuters correspondent Aliza Marcus awaits her verdict in an Istanbul court on charges of inciting racial hatred by reporting on the Turkish-Kurdish conflict. She was acquitted.

- 284 were arrested.

- 147 suffered various forms of harassment.

   The figures were all improved substantially

from the year before, but Freedom House cautioned that forces for repression remain a concern. In 43 countries, 33 different kinds of laws were drafted

in 1997 to threaten or regulate the activities of journalists.

media
online ⋯⋯⋯⋯⋯⋯

Freedom House: Freedom House was established in 1941 by Eleanor Roosevelt and Wendell Willkie to promote democracy around the world. Its programs include surveys on freedom, including economic and press freedom. www.freedomhouse.org

licensing
Authoritarian technique that allows only authorized mass media to operate.

Stationers Company
Printers' trade association through which Henry VIII maintained control of press.

Joseph Goebbels
Nazi propaganda chief.

Francisco Franco
Spanish dictator.

newsroom and everywhere else that mass media messages are produced. This is hardly practicable, although governments sometimes establish elaborate censorship bureaucracies during wartime to protect sensitive military information and to ban information that runs counter to their propaganda. Even democracies like the United States and Israel have required reporters to run battlefield stories past censors.

Licensing. Authoritarian governments generally favor less obtrusive methods of control than censorship. Henry VIII introduced a **licensing** system that limited the printing trade to people who held royal patents. The mechanism for bestowing these licenses rested with the **Stationers Company,** a printers' trade association. Royal patents were available only to association members, and membership was tightly controlled. To stay in the Crown's favor, the Stationers Company expelled members who produced forbidden materials, in effect putting them out of business.

   Four hundred years later, Nazi Germany used a more complex system. Under the guise of improving the quality of news, entertainment and culture, **Joseph Goebbels,** the minister of propaganda and public enlightenment, established guilds to which "cultural workers" had to belong. There were "chambers," as these guilds were called, for advertising, film, literature, music, the press, radio and theater. The chambers could deny membership to cultural workers whose work did not qualify. As Nazi anti-Semitism became frenzied, however, the chambers shifted their membership criteria to exclude Jews. Membership in the press chamber, for example, was limited to third-generation Aryans.

   The Spanish dictator **Francisco Franco,** who came to power in 1936, employed rigid licensing. News organizations could hire only people listed on an official register of journalists. To be on the list required graduation from one of Franco's three-year journalism schools, which wove political indoctrination into the curriculum. The success of the schools, from Franco's perspective, was further assured because admission was limited to students who were sympathetic to the generalissimo.

Bribery. Germany's "Iron Chancellor," **Otto von Bismarck,** maintained an immense fund for bribing editors, which kept much of the German press of the 1860s on his side. The practice is institutionalized in much of the impoverished Third World today, where journalists, earning barely subsistence salaries, accept gratuities on the side for putting certain stories in the paper and on the air.

Bribery also can occur when a government controls supplies that are necessary for the media to function. Franco cut newsprint deliveries to a Spanish newspaper in the early 1960s after several pro-monarchist articles appeared. In Mexico, a country with no newsprint manufacturing plants, **PIPSA,** a quasi-government agency, allocates imported newsprint. The goal, purportedly, is to assure an even stream of paper to newspapers and magazines. In practice, however, a correlation exists between articles unfavorable to the regime and either interruptions in paper delivery or the delivery of inferior paper. The publisher of a slick magazine gets the message quickly when PIPSA will supply only rough pulp. This is subtle bribery: Publications that play ball with the regime receive a payoff in supplies essential for doing business.

Repression. Authoritarian rulers are at their most obvious when they arrest journalists who challenge their authority. Execution is the ultimate sanction. While such extreme action usually comes only after, not before, an article critical of the regime appears, it still has a chilling effect on other journalists. To learn that a fellow journalist was dragged away in the middle of the night for writing a critical article is mighty intimidating to other journalists considering similar pieces.

Camcorders in the Amazon. Video technology gives oppressed people a low-cost weapon to document promises by governments they don't trust. In the Amazon, the Kayapo tribe videotaped negotiations with Brazilian officials about a proposed dam.

nature of truth

Authoritarian media systems make sense to anyone who accepts the premise that the government, whether embodied in a king or a dictator, is right in all that it says and does. Such a premise is anathema to most Americans, but a mere 400 years ago it was mainstream Western thought. King James VI of Scotland, who later became King **James I** of England, made an eloquent argument for the **divine right of kings** in 1598. He claimed that legitimate kings were anointed by the Almighty and thereby were better able to express righteousness and truth than anyone else. By definition, therefore, anybody who differed with the king was embracing falsity and probably heresy.

The authoritarian line of reasoning justifies suppression on numerous grounds:

- Truth is a monopoly of the regime. Commoners can come to know it only through the ruler, who, in King James's thinking, has an exclusive pipeline to the Almighty. Advocates of authoritarianism have little confidence in individuals.

- Challenges to the government are based on falsity. It could not be otherwise, considering the premise that government is infallible.

- Without strong government, the stability necessary for society to function may be disrupted. Because challenges to government tend to undermine stability and because the challenges are presumed to be false to begin with, they must be suppressed.

bribery
Incentives, usually financial, for mass media to conform to government line.

Otto von Bismarck
German chancellor who bribed editors.

PIPSA
Quasi-government Mexican agency that controls distribution of newsprint.

James I
English monarch who articulated divine right of kings theory.

divine right of kings
Monarchs have monopoly on righteousness and truth because they are selected by God.

To the authoritarian mind, journalists who support the government are purveying truth and should be rewarded. The unfaithful, who criticize, are spreading falsity and should be banished. It all makes sense if King James was right with his divine right theory. It was no wonder that sedition was a high crime.

An inherent contradiction in authoritarianism is the premise that the ruler is uniquely equipped to know truth. Experience over the centuries makes it clear that monarchs and dictators come in many stripes. Regimes have been known to change in midstream, as in Henry VIII's change of heart on Roman Catholicism. A fair question to put to authoritarian advocates is whether Henry was right when he was a Catholic, or later when he was an Anglican.

libertarian systems

STUDY PREVIEW   Libertarian thinkers have faith in the ability of human beings to come to know great truths by applying reason. Libertarians feel that a robust, open exchange of ideas will eliminate flawed notions and reinforce good ones. This process, however, may take time because people individually and collectively make short-term mistakes.

optimism about the human mind

Physicists love telling young science pupils the story of an English lad, **Isaac Newton,** who, sitting in an orchard one late-summer day, was struck on the head by a falling apple. Voilà! At that moment the law of gravity was instantly clear to Isaac Newton. It is a good story, though not a true one. Deriving the law of gravitation was a much more sophisticated matter for Newton, the leading 17th-century physicist, but the orchard story lives on. It is a story also told to pupils in their first world history class to illustrate a period in intellectual history called the Enlightenment. In this version, young Newton not only discovered gravity at the very instant that he was bumped on the head, but he also realized that he could come to know great truths like the law of gravity by using his own mind. He did not need to rely on a priest or a monarch or anyone else claiming a special relationship with God. He could do it on his own. This revelation, say the history teachers, was a profound challenge to authoritarian premises and ushered in the era of rationalist thinking that marks the modern age. Individually and together, people were capable of learning the great truths, called the **natural law,** unassisted by governing authorities. The insight of the Enlightenment was that human beings are rational beings. It marked the beginning of quantum progress in the sciences. The insight also contributed to the development of libertarianism, which held the intellectual roots of modern democracy.

marketplace of ideas

An English writer, **John Milton,** was the pioneer libertarian. In his 1644 pamphlet *Areopagitica,* Milton made a case for free expression based on the idea that individual

FREE   PARTLY FREE   PRESS NOT FREE

The Map of Press Freedom reflects the flow of news and information within and between 186 countries. Those with *free* print and broadcast media are shown in ☐ . Countries with *partly free* news media appear in ☐. Nations whose news media are *not free* are colored ☐ . Universal criteria determine the judgements, starting with Article 19 of the United Nations' Universal Declaration of Human Rights.

Criteria include the degree of independence of the news media from governmental ownership and influence; economicpressures on news content, and diverse violations of press freedom from the murder of journalists to other physical abuses and harassments.

Everyone has the right to freedom of opinion and expression; this right include freedom to hold opinions without interference and to seek, receive and impart information and ideas through any media and regardless of frontiers. Article 19, Universal Declaration of Human Rights - UN General Assembly, 1948

Congress shall make no law...abridging the freedom of speech, or of the press... The First Amendment to the Constitution of the United States.

*(We) note the expansion in the dissemination of information...and express the hope for the continuation of this process, so as to meet the interest of mutual understanding among peoples...*Final Act of the 35 nations. East and West, in the Commission on Security and Cooperation in Europe, (CSCE, 1975)

This is the fourth edition of the Map of Press Freedom. Since 1979, Freedom House has regularly assessed press freedom worldwide. For a full report on freedom of the press, please contact Freedom House.
Freedom House
120 Wall Street
New York, NY 10005
Phone: (212) 514-8040
Fax: (212) 514-8055
www.freedomhouse.org

Press Freedom. Freedom House, which tracks press freedom worldwide, reports relatively few countries with news and information flowing freely within and across their borders. Massive sections of Africa and Asia, plus Cuba and scattered small European countries, do not have free flows and exchanges. In making its determinations, Freedom House considered media independence from government ownership and economic pressure.

human beings were capable of discovering truth if given the opportunity. Milton called for a **marketplace of ideas** in which people could choose from the range of human ideas and values, just as shoppers pinch a lot of fruits and vegetables at the produce market until they find the best. Milton's marketplace of ideas was not a place but a concept. It existed whenever people exchanged ideas, whether in conversation or letters or the printed word.

> **marketplace of ideas**
> People can come to know truth only if they have access to all information, opinions.

Marketplace of Ideas.
John Milton gave the world the marketplace of ideas concept in his 1644 pamphlet *Areopagitica,* which paved the way for libertarianism. Milton said that everyone should be free to express ideas, no matter how traitorous, blasphemous, deleterious or just plain silly, for the consideration of other people. It was a strong argument against restrictions on free expression.

self-righting process
People make occasional errors in their truth-seeking but eventually discover them.

First Amendment
The free expression section of the U.S. Constitution.

Thomas Paine
Pamphleteer who helped inspire the American Revolution.

natural rights
Fundamental human rights, including self-determination.

Milton was eloquent in his call for free expression. He saw no reason to fear any ideas, no matter how subversive, because human beings inevitably would choose the best ideas and values. "Let [Truth] and Falsehood grapple: whoever knew Truth put to the worse in a free and open encounter?" he wrote. Milton reasoned that people would gain confidence in their own ideas and values if they tested them continually against alternative views. It was an argument against censorship. People need to have the fullest possible selection in the marketplace if they are going to go home with the best product, whether vegetables or ideas. Also, bad ideas should be present in the marketplace because, no matter how obnoxious, they might contain a grain of truth worth considering.

Milton acknowledged that people sometimes err in sorting out alternatives, but these mistakes are corrected as people continually reassess their values against competing values in the marketplace. Milton saw this truth-seeking as a never-ending, life-long human pursuit, which meant that people would shed flawed ideas and values for better ones over time. This came to be called a **self-righting process.**

first amendment

Libertarian ideas took strong root in England's North American colonies in the 1700s. Pamphleteer **Thomas Paine** stirred people against British authoritarianism and incited them to revolution. The rhetoric of the Enlightenment was clear in the Declaration of Independence, which was drafted by the libertarian philosopher Thomas Jefferson. His document declared that people possessed **natural rights** and were capable of deciding their own destiny. No king was needed. There was an emphasis on liberty and individual rights. Libertarianism spread rapidly as colonists rallied against Britain in the Revolutionary War. Not everyone who favored independence was a firm libertarian, however, and when it came time to write a constitution for the new republic, there was a struggle between libertarian and authoritarian principles. The libertarians had the greater influence, but sitting there prominently were Alexander Hamilton and a coterie of individuals who would have severely restricted the liberties of the common people. The Constitution that resulted was a compromise. Throughout the Constitution an implicit trust of the people vies with an implicit distrust. Even so, the government that emerged was the first so influenced by libertarian principles, and "the great experiment in democracy," as it has been called, began.

In 1791 the Constitution was expanded to include the First Amendment, which barred governmental interference in the exchange of ideas. The First Amendment declares that "Congress shall make no law . . . abridging the freedom of speech, or of the press. . . ." In practice, there have been limits on both free speech and free expression since the beginning of the republic. Legal scholars debate where to draw the line when the First Amendment comes into conflict with other rights, such as the right not to be slandered and the right to privacy. Even so, for 200 years the First Amendment has embodied the ideals of the Enlightenment. The United States clearly is in the libertarian tradition, as are the other Western-style democracies that followed.

elijah lovejoy

Elijah Lovejoy

Presbyterian social reformers founded the St. Louis *Observer* as a reform newspaper in 1833. They asked **Elijah Lovejoy** to be the editor. It made sense. Lovejoy was a minister sympathetic to reform, including abolition of slavery, and he was an experienced journalist. He accepted. Over the next three years, Lovejoy became increasingly opposed to slavery—a controversial position in Missouri before the Civil War. The fervor of his editorials grew.

Although Lovejoy's followers were abolitionists, most St. Louis people either favored slavery or hated seeing the issue split their city. Hostile public meetings were called to protest Lovejoy's abolitionist crusade. At one meeting it was decided that the free press provision of the U.S. Constitution should be ignored if the peace of the community was threatened. The resolution was aimed at Lovejoy.

At first Lovejoy refused to yield. However, after his printshop was vandalized and he heard that a mob was intent on beating him up or killing him, he decided to move the *Observer* a few miles up the Mississippi River to Alton, Illinois. While the steamboat carrying his press sat on the Alton dock, a new mob showed up with sledgehammers and crowbars, uncrated the press and dumped it in the river.

Undeterred, Lovejoy appealed to abolitionists nationally for money for a new press. Three weeks later, with a new press, he published the first Alton *Observer*. Still undeterred in his crusade, Lovejoy called on readers to help create a state abolitionist society. Within a few days, the mob responded by destroying Lovejoy's new press. Again, with financial support from the national abolitionist movement, Lovejoy ordered another press. On arrival, it was locked up in a warehouse, but the mob broke in and dumped it in the river. At a public meeting, Lovejoy declared he would not give in to any mob, and he ordered yet another press. The mob destroyed this fourth press too, and this time they shot and killed Elijah Lovejoy.

Elijah Lovejoy stands today as testimony to the importance of the mass media as a way for people of strong opinions to persuade others to their point of view. While Lovejoy did not prevail against the mob, his murder made him a martyr. Other abolitionist editors invoked his memory as a battle cry, and eventually their view became public policy. Black slavery was over.

freedom and responsibility

(STUDY PREVIEW) An uneasiness developed in the 20th century over the validity of the libertarian assumptions necessary for the marketplace of ideas to work. In 1947 a private panel, the Hutchins Commission, gave voice to this uneasiness in identifying abuses of press freedom and recommending a change in emphasis from a free to a responsible press. This new emphasis came to be called the social responsibility concept.

challenges to libertarianism

The novelist and muckraker **Upton Sinclair** raised questions about the integrity of newspapers in his novel *The Brass Check,* published in 1919. Sinclair offered a look inside an imaginary newsroom in which powerful interests could bribe their way into print. He outlined how newspapers could abuse their freedom. The doubts that Sinclair planted about the news media grew. Many people were bothered about one-sidedness in newspapers, especially as consolidations reduced the number of competing newspapers. Orson Welles's 1941 movie ***Citizen Kane,*** based on newspaper publisher William Randolph Hearst, undermined public confidence in the people who ran newspapers. So did the quirkiness of other prominent publishers, such as **Robert McCormick,** who turned the Chicago *Tribune* into a campaign vehicle for simplified spellings like "thru" for "through," "frate" for "freight" and "buro" for "bureau." McCormick was always quick to defend his eccentricities, as well as the *Tribune*'s blatantly right-wing news coverage, in the name of a free press. Americans, imbued with libertarian idealism, were hesitant to challenge McCormick and other media barons, but there were growing doubts by the late 1940s about whether modern society provided a proper environment for Milton's marketplace of ideas. These doubts concerned basic libertarian assumptions:

- **People Are Capable of Distinguishing Truth.** In their enthusiasm about human nature, libertarians assumed that people are involved in a life-long quest for knowledge, truth and wisdom. There was evidence aplenty, however, that many people could not care less about the great questions of human existence. People might be capable of sorting truth from falsity in the marketplace of ideas, but many do not work at it.

- **Media Are Diverse.** Libertarians imagined a world of so many diverse publications that there would be room for every outlook. In the 20th century, however, some people saw a reduction in media diversity. Cities with several newspapers lost papers one by one to the point that in the 1940s few cities had more than two newspapers. Only three broadcast networks dominated radio coverage of national and international affairs.

- **Media Independence.** Libertarianism assumed that truth-seeking individuals exchange ideas in an unstructured, free-wheeling marketplace. As governments picked up public relations skills, however, the media have experienced varying degrees of manipulation, which has detracted from their role as the vehicles of the marketplace. Also, the reliance of American media on advertising means that media whose coverage is not attractive to advertisers are squeezed out of existence.

- **Easy Access to Media.** The libertarian notion of all citizens engaging in great dialogues through the media seemed naïve to some people. Few newspapers published more than a half a dozen reader letters a day, and the reduction in the number of cities with multiple newspapers had further devalued newspapers as a vehicle for citizen exchange.

hutchins commission

Doubts about some libertarian assumptions took firm shape in 1947 when magazine tycoon **Henry Luce** gave a grant of $200,000 to an old college friend, **Robert Hutchins,** to study the American press. Hutchins, chancellor of the University of

---

Upton Sinclair
Novelist who exposed journalistic abuses in *The Brass Check* (1919).

Citizen Kane
Movie loosely based on newspaper publisher William Randolph Hearst (1941); exposed journalistic abuses.

Robert McCormick
Strong-willed, eccentric publisher of Chicago *Tribune* who championed libertarianism.

Henry Luce
Magazine publisher who financed 1947 Hutchins Commission evaluation of press freedom.

Robert Hutchins
Intellectual who led commission that identified flaws in libertarian premises.

Chicago, assembled a group of scholars. The Hutchins Commission, as it was called, issued a bombshell report that expressed concern that the news media were becoming too powerful. The commission cited the growth of newspaper chains. To Luce's dismay, the commission also seemed concerned about the power of magazine groups like his own *Time, Life* and *Fortune.* The commission said the news media needed to be more responsible and specifically called on the press to provide:

- A truthful, comprehensive and intelligent account of the day's events in a context that makes them meaningful.

- A forum for exchange of comment and criticism, including contrary ideas.

- A representative picture of society's constituent groups, including blacks and other minorities.

- Coverage that challenges society's goals and values and helps clarify them.

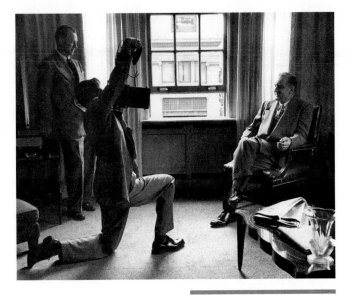

Luce was livid. He had established the commission hoping to blunt criticism that his own magazines were one-sided and too powerful. It backfired. The commission raised serious questions about news media practices that Luce and other media barons had defended in the name of freedom of the press. Robert McCormick, publisher of the Chicago *Tribune,* mounted a tirade and commissioned a book to rip the commission's report apart. Newspaper trade associations went on record that the republic was best served when nobody was looking over journalists' shoulders. Freedom of the press, they argued, was at stake when government or anybody else, including a private group of eggheads under Robert Hutchins' direction, tried to prescribe what the press should do.

Despite the negative initial reception, the Hutchins Commission's recommendations have shaped how the most respected news organizations go about their work today.

Impetus to Social Responsibility. The blue-ribbon Hutchins Commission called in 1947 for the media to be more socially responsible, but not until the 1950s did news people begin a serious self-assessment of their practices. One trigger of the self-assessment was the damage that resulted from news coverage of false charges by Wisconsin Senator Joseph McCarthy that Communists had infiltrated federal agencies. The reporting that McCarthy made the allegations was literally accurate, but it failed to raise essential questions about McCarthy's credibility. When the news media realized they had been duped by McCarthy, and that the American people had been duped through them, there developed an emphasis on reporting to put events "in a context that makes them meaningful," as the Hutchins Commission had recommended in 1947.

media role in governance

(STUDY PREVIEW) The news media sometimes are called the fourth estate or the fourth branch of government. These terms identify the independent role of the media in reporting on the government. The media are a kind of watchdog on behalf of the citizens.

fourth estate

Medieval English and French society were highly structured into classes of people called estates. The first estate was the clergy. The second was the nobility. The third was the common people. After Gutenberg, the mass-produced written word began

Freedom Forum: The Gannett media chain created the Freedom Forum to study and explore media issues, including issues of press freedom, press-government relations, and media coverage. www.freedomforum.org/whoweare/media.asp

Fairness and Accuracy in Reporting: Includes reports from the FAIR media watchdog group. You can also find FAIR's analysis of talk show host Rush Limbaugh for accuracy, and Limbaugh's lame, often evasive, responses. www.igc.apc.org/fair/

fourth estate
The press as a player in medieval power structures, in addition to the clerical, temporal and common estates.

Edmund Burke
British member of parliament who sometimes is credited with coining the term *fourth estate.*

fourth branch
The press as an informally structured check on the legislative, executive and judicial branches of government.

watchdog role
Concept of the press as a skeptical and critical monitor of government.

equal time rule
Government requirement for stations to offer competing political candidates the same time and the same rate for advertising.

fairness doctrine
Former government requirement that stations air all sides of public issues.

emerging as a player in the power structure, but it couldn't be pigeon-holed as part of one or another of the three estates. In time, the press came to be called the **fourth estate.** Where the term came from isn't clear, but **Edmund Burke,** a member of the British Parliament, used it in the mid-1700s. Pointing to the reporters' gallery, Burke said: "There sat a Fourth Estate more important by far than them all." The term remains for all journalistic activity today. The news media report on the other estates, ideally with roots in none and a commitment only to truth.

The fourth-estate concept underwent an adaptation when the United States was created. The Constitution of the new republic, drafted in 1787, set up a balanced form of government with three branches—the legislative, the executive and the judicial. The republic's founders implied a role for the press in the new governance structure when they declared in the Constitution's First Amendment that the government should not interfere with the press. The press, however, was not part of the structure. This led to the press being called the **fourth branch** of government. Its job was to monitor the other branches as an external check on behalf of the people. This is the **watchdog role** of the press. As one wag put it, the founders saw the role of the press as keeping tabs on the rascals in power to keep them honest.

government-media relations

Although the First Amendment says the government shouldn't place restrictions of the press, the reality is that exceptions have evolved.

Broadcast Regulation. In the early days of commercial radio, stations drowned out one another. Unable to work out mutually agreeable transmission rules to help the new medium realize its potential, station owners went to the government for help. Congress obliged by creating the Federal Radio Commission in 1927. The commission's job was to limit the number of stations and their transmitting power to avoid signal overlaps. This the commission did by requiring stations to have a government-issued license that specified technical limitations. Because more stations were broadcasting than could be licensed, the commission issued and denied licenses on the basis of each applicant's potential to operate in the public interest. Over time, this criterion led to numerous requirements for broadcasters, in radio and later television, in their coverage of public issues.

Because of the limited number of available channels, Congress tried to assure an even-handedness in political content through the **equal time rule.** If a station allows one candidate to advertise, it must allow competing candidates to do so under the same conditions, including time of day and rates. The equal time requirement is in the law that established the Federal Radio Commission and also the 1934 law that established its successor, the Federal Communications Commission. The rule has since been expanded to require stations to carry a response from the opposition party immediately after broadcasts that can be construed as political, like the President's state of the union address.

From 1949 to 1987 the Federal Communications Commission also required stations to air all sides of public issues. The requirement, called the **fairness doctrine,** was abandoned in the belief that a growing number of stations, possible by improved technology, meant the public could find plenty of diverse views. Also, the FCC figured the public's disdain for unfairness would undermine the ability of lopsided stations to keep an audience. The commission, in effect, acknowledged the marketplace could be an effective force for fairness—without further need for a government requirement.

Abandonment of the fairness doctrine was part of the general movement to ease government regulation on business. This shift has eased the First Amendment difficulties inherent in the federal regulation of broadcasting. Even so, the FCC remains firm against imbalanced political broadcasting. In 1975, for example, the commission refused to renew the licenses of stations owned by **Don Burden** after learning that he was using them on behalf of political friends. At KISN in Vancouver, Washington, Burden had instructed the news staff to run only favorable stories on one U.S. Senate candidate and negative stories on the other. At WIFE in Indianapolis, he ordered "frequent, favorable mention" of one U.S. senator. The FCC declared it would not put up with "attempts to use broadcast facilities to subvert the political process." Although the Burden case is almost a quarter-century old, the FCC has sent no signals that it has modified its position on blatant slanting.

Print Regulation. The U.S. Supreme Court gave legitimacy to government regulation of broadcasting, despite the First Amendment issue, in its 1975 **Tornillo** opinion. Pat Tornillo, a candidate for the Florida Legislature, sued the Miami *Herald* for refusing to print his response to an editorial urging voters to the other candidate. The issue was whether the FCC's fairness doctrine could apply to the print media— and the Supreme Court said no. As the Court sees it, the First Amendment applies more directly to print than broadcast media.

This does not mean, however, that the First Amendment always protects print media from government interference. The Union Army shut down dissident newspapers in Chicago and Ohio during the Civil War. While those incidents were never challenged in the courts, the U.S. Supreme Court has consistently said it could envision circumstances in which government censorship would be justified. Even so, the court has laid so many prerequisites for government interference that censorship seems an extremely remote possibility.

Internet Regulation. The Internet and all its permutations, including chat rooms and web sites, are almost entirely unregulated in terms of political content. The massive quantities of material and its constant flux makes government regulation virtually impossible. Even Congress' attempt to ban Internet indecency in 1996 fell apart under judicial review. The only inhibition on Internet political content is not through government restriction but civil suits between individuals on issues like libel and invasion of privacy.

media as an information source

(STUDY PREVIEW) Most news media influence is through opinion leaders. Newspapers and magazines are especially important to these opinion leaders. For the public, television is the preferred source of political news. For politically engaged people, talk radio and online media are also significant sources.

direct versus indirect

Early libertarians, with their emphasis on the reasoning ability of individual human beings, saw a direct link between press reports and individual decision-

Don Burden
Radio station owner who lost licenses for favoring some political candidates over others.

Tornillo case
The U.S. Supreme Court upheld First Amendment protection for the print media even if they are imbalanced and unfair.

making. Today we know the linkage between the media and individuals generally is less direct. **Paul Lazarsfeld**'s pioneering studies on voter behavior in 1940 and 1948 found most people rely on personal acquaintances for information about politics and governance. Lazarsfeld called this a **two-step flow** process, with **opinion leaders** relying heavily on the news media for information and ideas, and other people relying on the opinion leaders. In reality, this is hardly a clinically neat process. The influence of opinion leaders varies significantly from issue to issue and even day to day, and people who normally don't use the media much may do so at some points and then rely less on opinion. As Lazarsfeld came to recognize the complexity of the process, he renamed it **multi-step flow.**

In short, news coverage and media commentary have influence on the public, but usually it is through the intermediaries who Lazarsfeld called opinion leaders. Lazarsfeld's observation is underscored every time network television reporters talk on-camera with political leaders and refer to the public in the third person as "they," as if *they* aren't even watching. Implicit in the third person is the reporters and political leaders' understanding that their audience is comprised more of opinion leaders than the body politic.

citizen preferences

Which media do people use most for political news? Opinion leaders lean heavily on newspapers and magazines, which generally are more comprehensive and thorough than broadcast sources. Not surprisingly, scholar Doris Graber found better-educated people favor newspapers. Even so, there is no denying that television has supplanted newspapers as the primary source for most people. Political scientist William Mayer found people relied more on television than newspapers by a 3:1 margin in the 1992 presidential campaign. For national coverage, the television networks present news attractively and concisely.

For local and state political news, however, television isn't as respected. Newspapers, Mayer found, are the primary source for most people on local political campaigns. In many communities, local television coverage is superficial and radio coverage almost nonexistent. In state-level gubernatorial and senatorial races, television is favored 5:3 as a primary information source, according to Mayer's studies—only half as much as at the national level.

Media preference studies generally ask people to rank their preference, which can lead to a false conclusion that the second-ranked preference isn't relied on at all. While people may use television most, this hardly means they don't read newspapers at all. The daily press turns out more than 60 million copies a day nationwide. Also, newspapers and magazines too, especially those with veteran political reporters and commentaries, are looked to by broadcast assignment editors for ideas on stories to pursue. Daniel Patrick Moynihan, the New York senator, once noted that the New York *Times* is the standard by which other media decide what's worth covering.

specialized media

Sometimes overlooked in considering the influence of media political coverage are the specialized sources.

Paul Lazarsfeld
Sociologist who concluded that media influence on voters generally is indirect.

two-step flow
Media effect on individuals is through opinion leaders.

opinion leaders
Media-savvy individuals who influence friends and acquaintances.

multi-step flow
Political information moves from the media to individuals though complex, ever-changing interpersonal connections.

Brian Lamb
Created C-SPAN.

talking heads
Negative term for dialogue-based television shows.

C-SPAN
Cable network for public and cultural affairs; covers Congress live.

America's town hall
Fanciful term for C-SPAN.

wired nation
The United States, now that it is linked by cable.

media people
brian lamb

Conducting the Town Hall. Brian Lamb, who might be called the ultimate news junkie, had a brainstorm to aim cameras on whatever was happening— like sessions of the U.S. House, coffee klatches in Iowa during the presidential primaries, the governor's state of the state address in Alabama, a radio talk show host on the air—and broadcast it live. He talked cable industry leaders into the idea, and C-SPAN went on satellite to local cable systems in 1978. No fancy, expensive editing—just the cameras showing whatever they see. C-SPAN calls itself "America's town hall."

Brian Lamb, a quiet, contemplative man, had knocked around news in Washington for 22 years. He had seen government as a UPI radio reporter. He had plied public relations on the Hill and at the White House. In the 1970s, as satellite-relayed television came into being and as cable was growing, Brian Lamb saw something no one else did— possibilities for television that dealt exclusively with public affairs.

In Lamb's mind, this would be a television network using relatively cheap satellite time to cover sessions of Congress live and beam them down to cable systems. The network wouldn't try expensive production. It would just have somebody with a camera at places where news was occurring and turn it on. Why would anybody want to carry such **talking head** programs? Lamb told cable industry leaders it would give them prestige with public-minded viewers. The cable people saw it as a low-cost way to blunt elitists' criticism that they weren't offering anything much worth watching. They agreed to offer the

new network free to every subscriber and give Lamb a few pennies a month for each of those subscribers.

In 1978, **C-SPAN,** short for Cable-Satellite Public Affairs Network, began a 24-hour service that showed the U.S. House of Representatives live when it was in session and filled the rest of the time with interviews and discussions on public affairs. With its headquarters only a couple of blocks from the Capitol, C-SPAN has become a regular stopping point for major players on the issues of the day. Viewers call in and exchange their thoughts with the nation's movers and shakers. C-SPAN calls itself "**America's town hall.**"

C-SPAN's budget, only $29 million in 1996, would keep NBC or CBS on the air only a few days, but it has brought incredible content to cable viewers.

When budget allows, C-SPAN sends crews out into the country with lightweight video equipment. They use no complicated production techniques. They just turn the camera on and record America's pulse beat. These forays beyond the Beltway, according to media com-

mentator Jeff Greenfield, are C-SPAN at its best: "The real pearls come when C-SPAN picks up its camera and winds up at a coffee klatch in Iowa, or a lobster dinner in New Hampshire, when a presidential hopeful is speaking. Or when it covers a conversation between a political strategist and a group of reporters and editors over coffee and doughnuts. Or when it shows up at the hundreds of seminars in Washington on media coverage of politics."

The C-SPAN audience is not huge. Perhaps 10 million people tune in at least once a month. But the audience is an important one—educated, bright, concerned.

C-SPAN exemplifies many of the revolutionary changes taking place in television. The network could never have come into existence were it not for the high-tech equipment that has improved reliability and reduced production and distribution costs. C-SPAN is a product of our **wired nation,** in which just about everybody, except people in rural areas, has access to cable television. Also, with its relatively small audi-

ence, C-SPAN typifies the audience fragmentation that is occurring in television. The days are gone when a few behemoth networks dominated programming.

Political Journals. Intellectual magazines, like the *Nation* and the *New Republic,* have small circulations, but their audiences have a higher proportion of opinion leaders than many larger publications. This gives them great potency when you consider Lazarsfeld's trickle-down multi-step flow.

The specialization that the mass media have undergone through demassification, with individual media units seeking narrow audience segments, has spawned new forums devoted to political news and exchanges.

Demassified Television. The C-SPAN television network never claimed a large audience, but its emphasis on Washington has made it a place that many opinion leaders tap into. The proliferation of all-news networks, including CNN, MSNBC and Fox News Channel, all with around-the-clock coverage from Washington, add to the diversity of sources for national political and government news. So has the growth of specialized programs on over-air networks, like the nightly News Hour with Jim Lehrer on PBS and the Sunday discussion programs on the other networks.

Talk Radio. Demassification reached massive audiences with the advent of **talk radio** in the 1980s. **Rush Limbaugh,** the most popular talker host, went on the air in 1988 and built an audience of 20 million a week over a network of 600-plus stations. The topic: politics. With seven of the nine leading talk shows, the slant is conservative. Some studies found these shows appeal mostly to "angry white males," and those were, in fact, the voters who turned out the Democratic Congress in 1994.

The influence of talkers may have peaked. By the 1996 election, when Bill Clinton won a second term by a large margin, the talkers, led by the Clinton-bashing Limbaugh, were unable to deliver a critical mass of voters. Whatever the political potency of talkers, they nonetheless are a source of information and ideas for a politically engaged audience.

Web. The World Wide Web is a significant source of political information. Every candidate for dog catcher, it seems, has a web site come election time. Online magazines, like the '**zine** *Slate,* are digital versions of the traditional political journals. In fact, Michael Kinsley left the editorship of the *New Republic* in Washington to edit *Slate* out of Seattle. The finances of 'zines are uncertain—not even Microsoft-backed *Slate* has been profitable, but neither have most of the traditional intellectual magazines.

An immeasurable quantity of political dialogue occurs on the Internet. **Chat rooms** devoted to candidates, issues, causes and politics in general come and go regularly, some with only a handful of followers, others with thousands.

talk radio
Stations or programs based on discussion, some with listener participation.

talkers
Informal term for talk radio.

Rush Limbaugh
Conservative radio personality with the largest talk-show following.

'zine
Informal term for an online magazine.

chat room
An Internet site, usually for an assigned topic, at which people may sign in and read other people's messages and contribute their own.

media effects on governance

(STUDY PREVIEW) Media coverage shapes what we think about as well as how to think about it. This means the media are a powerful linkage between the government and how people view their government. A negative aspect is the trend of the media to pander to transitory public interest in less substantive subjects, like scandals, gaffes and negative events.

agenda-setting

A lot of people think the news media are powerful, affecting the course of events in god-like ways. It's true the media are powerful, but scholars, going back to sociologist Paul Lazarsfeld in the 1940s and even Robert Park in the 1920s, have concluded it's not in a direct tell-them-how-to-vote-and-they-will kind of way. Political scientist Bernard Cohen cast media effects succinctly when he said: The media don't tell people *what to think* but rather *what to think about*. This has come to be called **agenda-setting.**

Civil Rights.   The civil rights of American blacks were horribly ignored for the century following the Civil War, then came news coverage of a growing reform movement in the 1960s. That coverage, of marches and demonstrations by Martin Luther King Jr. and others, got the public thinking about racial injustice. In 1964, Congress passed the Civil Rights Act that explicitly forbids discrimination in hotels and eateries, government aid and employment practices. Without media coverage, the public agenda would not have included civil rights at a high enough level to have precipitated change as early as 1964.

Watergate.   Had the Washington *Post* not doggedly followed up on a break-in at the Democratic Party's national headquarters in 1972, the public would never have learned that people around the Republican president, Richard Nixon, were behind it. The *Post* set the national agenda.

Lewinsky.   Nobody would have spent much time pondering whether President Bill Clinton engaged in sexual indiscretions if David Brock, writing in the *American Spectator* in 1993, had not reported allegations by Paula Jones. Nor would the issue have reached a feverish level of public attention without Matt Drudge's 1997 report in his online *Drudge Report* about Monica Lewinsky.

By and large, news coverage does not call for people to take positions, but based on what they learn from coverage, people do take positions. It's a catalytic effect. The coverage doesn't cause change directly, but serves rather as a catalyst.

cnn effect

Television is especially potent as an agenda-setter. For years nobody outside Ethiopia cared much about a devastating famine. Not even after four articles in the New York *Times* was there much response. The Washington *Post* ran three articles, and the Associated Press distributed 228 stories—still hardly any response. The next year, however, disturbing videos aired by the BBC captured public attention and triggered a massive relief effort. In recent years, many scholars looking at the agenda-setting effect of television vis-à-vis other media have focused on CNN, whose extensive coverage lends itself to study. As a result, the power of television to put faraway issues in the minds of domestic audiences has been labeled the **CNN effect.**

priming

Media coverage not only creates public awareness but it also can trigger dramatic shifts in opinion. An example was the fate of George Bush. In 1991 his approval ratings were at record highs. In 1992 the people thumped him out of office. What happened? During the Persian Gulf war in 1991, the media put almost everything

agenda-setting
The process through which issues bubble up into public attention through mass media selection on what to cover.

CNN effect
The ability of television, through emotion-raising video, to elevate distant issues on the domestic public agenda.

else on the back burner to cover the war. The president's role in the coverage was as commander-in-chief. Primed by the coverage, the public gave Bush exceptionally favorable ratings. When the war ended, media coverage shifted to the economy, which was ailing, and the president was hardly portrayed heroically. His ratings plummeted, and in 1992 he lost a re-election bid.

In 1991 the media coverage created an environment that primed the public to see the president positively, and in 1992 the environment changed. It was a classic example of **priming,** the process in which the media affect the standard that people use to evaluate political figures and issues. This is hardly to say that the media manipulate the environments in which people see political figures and issues. No one, for example, would argue that the Persian Gulf war should not have been covered. The fact, however, is that it was through the media that people were aware of the war and concluded the president was doing a great job.

media obsessions

Although critics argue the media are politically biased, studies don't support this. Reporters perceive themselves as middle-of-the road politically, and by and large they work to suppress personal biases. Even so, reporters gravitate toward certain kinds of stories to the neglect of others—and this flavors coverage.

Presidential Coverage. News reporters and editors have long recognized that people like stories about people, so any time an issue can be personified, the better. In Washington coverage, this has meant focusing on the president to treat issues. A 1980 study of the CBS Evening News found 60 percent of the opening stories featured the president. Even in non-election years, the media have a near-myopic fix on the White House. This displaces coverage of other important governmental institutions, like Congress and the courts, and also state and local government.

Conflict. Journalists learn two things about conflict early in their careers. First, their audiences like conflict. Second, conflict often illustrates the great issues by which society is defining and redefining its values. Take, for example, capital punishment or abortion or the draft. People get excited about these issues because of the fundamental values involved.

Part of journalists' predilection toward conflict is that conflict involves change—whether to do something differently. All news involves change, and conflict almost always is a signal to the kind of change that's most worth reporting. Conflict generally is a useful indicator of newsworthiness.

Sometimes, though, journalists latch on to conflict and slight other stories worth reporting. Political columnist David Broder made the point well: "A piece of videotape showing Democratic Rep. Pete Stark of California denouncing the Republicans for 'cutting' Medicare will play over and over. Tape of a Democrat praising a Republican for the successful 'culmination of a long, bipartisan effort to re-examine and refocus the federal role in education and training of America's workers' will never make it out of the editing room."

Scandals. Journalists know too that their audiences like scandal stories—a fact that trivializes political coverage. Talking about coverage of Bill Clinton early in his presidency, political scientists Morris Fiorina and Paul Peterson said: "The public was bombarded with stories about Whitewater, Vince Foster's suicide, $200 haircuts, parties

priming
Process in which the media affect the standard that people use to evaluate political figures and issues.
Roger Ailes
Influential former Republican political consultant.

···· roger ailes

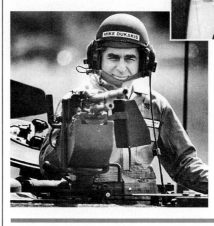

Roger Ailes

Roger Ailes learned what works on television when he was producing "The Mike Douglas Show," a celebrity interview television program, in the 1960s. Ahead of the show, Ailes commanded guests to be interesting, brief, funny and quotable. Years later, Ailes gave himself that same advice when, as our era's most sought-after political consultant, he had the power to say yea or nay on campaign commercials, to groom candidates for interviews and even to order changes in presidential speeches.

Ailes was good at what he did. Even those who loathed the Willie Horton commercial in the 1988 Bush presidential campaign admitted it worked. In that commercial, the Democratic candidate, Michael Dukakis, was lambasted for paroling murder-rapist Willie Horton, who was black. Many say the ad aimed unfairly at inciting latent white racism against Dukakis. A lot of Bush people had a hand in the ad, including Floyd Brown, who produced it, but it was Ailes who was in charge. To *Time* magazine Ailes said: "The only question is whether we depict Willie Horton with a knife in his hand or without it." Ailes has an uncanny feel for what's quotable.

Not only did Ailes okay the Bush ad that criticized Dukakis' environmental record by using Boston Harbor as a setting, he also had a hand in Bush's memorable line: "About as clear as Boston Harbor." And then there was the line about Dukakis being "a card-carrying member of the ACLU." Remember Bush invoking Clint Eastwood's line, "Read my lips," to underscore his commitment to no new taxes.

In the Bush campaign, Ailes was responsible for what became known as the "Tank Spot." Dukakis had gone to an Army post to ride around in a tank, giving photographers a chance to show him in a military setting. What Ailes saw in the news footage, however, was Dukakis' Army-issue communication headset looking like Mickey Mouse ears. The footage became the Tank Spot, which some observers say was the most devastating political ad of all time. Voters who were unsure about the Massachusetts governor on foreign issues be-

Negative Ads. Swipes at opposition candidates have become a mainstay in U.S. elections. The 1988 Bush presidential campaign used this news footage to cast doubts on opponent Michael Dukakis as a commander in chief. Political consultant Roger Ailes knew viewers would see the headset as Mickey Mouse ears. Bush won.

came really cautious when they saw the spot. Said Ailes: "They're afraid of this guy in the Mickey Mouse hat becoming commander in chief."

While Ailes knows how to needle the opposition with sophisticated twists, he also likes the plain and simple. His most effective Bush ad, he says, had Bush looking straight into the camera and saying: "You hear anybody say I want to raise your taxes, you tell them you know George Bush and that isn't so."

Ailes learned elections in the successful 1968 Nixon campaign. Then he did Reagan in 1983, then Bush. More recently he has produced the Rush Limbaugh television show, where many Limbaugh lines have an Ailes ring to them. Limbaugh's critics have called Ailes the brains behind the show.

Today, Ailes runs the Fox all-news network.

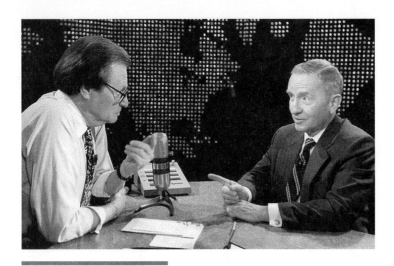

Electronic Town Hall.
Ross Perot took his second bid for the presidency directly to the people with live, televised speeches and appearances on talk shows. This bypassed the usual processes that the news media use in boiling down, summarizing and packaging the news. By bypassing media gatekeepers, Perot maintained more control over his messages. Other candidates also are using new technology to communicate directly with voters.

with Sharon Stone, the White House travel office, Hilary Clinton's investments, and numerous other matters that readers will not remember. The reason you do not remember is that, however important these matters were to the individuals involved, they were not important for the overall operation of government. Hence, they have been forgotten."

No matter how transitory their news value, scandal and gaffe stories build audiences, which explains their increase. Robert Lichter and Daniel Amundson, analysts who monitor Washington news coverage, found policy stories outnumbered scandal stories 13:1 in 1972 but only 3:1 in 1992. During that same period, news media have been become savvy at catering to audience interests and less interested in covering issues of significance. This also has led to more negative news. Lichter and Amundson found negative stories from Congress outnumbered positive stories 3:1 in 1972 but 9:1 in 1992.

Horse Races. In reporting political campaigns, the news media obsess on reporting the polls. Critics say this treating of campaigns as **horse races** results in substantive issues being underplayed. Even when issues are the focus, as when a candidate announces a major policy position, reporters connect the issue to its potential impact in the polls.

Brevity. People who design media packages, like a newspaper or newscast, have devised presentation formats that favor shorter stories. This trend has been driven in part by broadcasting's severe time constraints. Network anchors, most notably Dan Rather, have complained for years that they have to condense the world's news into 23 minutes on their evening newscasts. The result: Short, often superficial treatments. The short-story format shifted to many newspapers and magazines, beginning with the launch of *USA Today* in 1981. *USA Today* obtained extremely high story counts, covering a great many events, by running short stories—many only a half-dozen sentences. The effect on political coverage has been profound:

The **sound bites** in campaign stories, the actual voice of a candidate in a broadcast news story, dropped from 47 seconds in 1968 to 10 seconds in 1988. Issues that require lengthy explorations, say critics, get passed up. Candidates, eager for air time, have learned to offer quippy, catchy, clever capsules that are likely to be picked up rather than articulating thoughtful persuasive statements. The same dynamic is available in *USA Today*-style brevity.

Some people defend brevity, saying it's the only way to reach people whose increasingly busy lives don't leave them much time to track politics and government. In one generalization, brevity's defenders note, the short attention span of the MTV generation can't handle much more than 10-second sound bites. Sanford Ungar, the communication dean at American University, applauds the news media for devising writing and reporting styles that boil down complex issues so they can be readily understood by great masses of people. Ungar: "If *USA Today* encourages people not to think deeply, or not to go into more detail about what's happening, then it will be a

---

horse races
An election campaign treated by reporters like a game—who's ahead, who's falling back, who's coming up the rail.

sound bite
The actual words of someone in the news, sandwiched in a correspondent's report.

disservice. But if *USA Today* teaches people how to be concise and get the main points across sometimes, they're doing nothing worse than what television is doing, and doing it at least as well."

While many news organizations have moved to briefer and trendier government and political coverage, it's unfair to paint too broad a stroke. The New York *Times,* the Washington *Post* and the Los Angeles *Times* don't scrimp on coverage, and even *USA Today* runs four lengthy articles every issue, occasionally on government and politics. The television networks, which have been rapped the most for sound-bite coverage, also offer in-depth treatments outside of newscast—like the Sunday morning programs.

Campaigning with a Sax. Political candidates have learned to take their campaigns live directly to the people via radio and television. Bill Clinton did it with entertainment program appearances during the 1992 elections, including the "Arsenio Hall Show" where he played the saxophone. This form of campaigning through electronic media bypasses journalists who once were an intermediary between candidates and voters.

Candidates have also discovered alternatives to being condensed and packaged. In 1992, presidential hopeful Ross Perot made the hour-long Larry King interview program on CNN a frequent forum for his views. Bill Clinton bypassed reporters and went directly to the people by playing the sax and discussing his platform on the Arsenio Hall late-night show. With dozens of cable networks, all with more talk and interview shows than ever, news junkies have no problem getting their fixes. To critics who note that the Big 3 networks all have abandoned gavel-to-gavel coverage of the national political conventions, it should be pointed out that CNN filled the void.

government manipulation of media

(STUDY PREVIEW) Many political leaders preoccupy themselves with media coverage because they know the power it can have. Over the years they have developed mechanisms to influence coverage to their advantage.

influencing coverage

Many political leaders stay up nights figuring out ways to influence media coverage. James Fallows, in his book *Breaking the News,* quoted a Clinton White House official: "When I was there, absolutely nothing was more important than figuring out what the news was going to be. . . . There is no such thing as a substantive discussion that is not shaped or dominated by how it is going to play in the press."

The game of trying to outsmart the news media is nothing new. Theodore Roosevelt, at the turn of the century, chose Sundays to issue many announcements. Roosevelt recognized that editors producing Monday newspapers usually had a dearth of news because weekends, with government and business shut down, didn't generate much worth telling. Roosevelt's Sunday announcements, therefore, received more prominent play in Monday editions. With typical bullishness, Teddy claimed he had

Presidents and the Media. Franklin Roosevelt was not popular with most newspaper and magazine publishers. Editorials opposed his election in 1932, and whatever sparse support there was for his ideas to end the Great Depression was fading. Two months after taking office, Roosevelt decided to try radio to communicate directly to the people, bypassing the traditional reporting and editing process that didn't always work to his favor. In his first national radio address, Roosevelt explained the steps he had taken to meet the nation's financial emergency. It worked. The president came across well on radio, and people were fascinated hearing their leader live and direct. Roosevelt's "fireside chats" became a fixture of his administration, which despite editorial negativism would continue 13 years—longer than any in U.S. history. John Kennedy used television as Roosevelt had used radio, and every political leader since, for better or worse, has recognized the value of the mass media as a vehicle for governance.

"discovered Mondays." Compared to how sophisticated government leaders have become at manipulating press coverage today, Roosevelt was a piker.

trial balloons and leaks

To check weather conditions, meteorologists send up balloons. To get an advance peek at public reaction, political leaders also float **trial balloons.** When Richard Nixon was considering shutting down radio and television stations at night to conserve electricity during the 1973 energy crisis, the idea was floated to the press by a subordinate. The reaction was so swift and so negative that the idea was shelved. Had there not been a negative reaction or if reaction was positive, then the president himself would have unveiled the plan as his own.

Trial balloons are not the only way that the media can be used. Partisans and dissidents use **leaks** to bring attention to their opponents and people they don't much like. When leaking, someone passes information to reporters on condition they not be identified as the source. While reporters are leery of many leakers, some information is so significant and from such reliable sources that it's hard to pass up.

The quantity of off-the-record leaks became so great in the 1960s—and it hasn't abated since—that Alfred Friendly, managing editor of the Washington *Post*, put labels on how reporters should handle information from sources:

trial balloon
A deliberate leak of a potential policy, usually from a diversionary source, to test public response.

leak
A deliberate disclosure of confidential or classified information by someone who wants to advance the public interest, embarrass a bureaucratic rival or supervisor, or disclose incompetence or skullduggery.

On the Record. Anything said may be used and attributed by name to the source. This is what journalist prefer. News conferences, of course, are on-the-record, and so are most interviews. Example: "Flanders Domingo, a deputy assistant secretary of the Navy, said. . . ."

Off the Record. This information is not to be passed on, not even in conversation. Information is offered off the record for many reasons. Sometimes a source wants to help a reporter better understand a confusing or potentially harmful situation. Or it may be intended to head off a damaging error that a source thinks a reporter might make if not informed.

On Background. What's said may be used in print or on the air, but the source cannot be identified. For example: "A source close to the Secretary of Defense said. . . ."

On Deep Background. The source's information may be used but with no attribution whatsoever—not even a hint as to the source. As a result, the information must stand on the reporter's reputation alone. "The 7th Fleet is standing by to sail into the South China Sea." Period.

It's essential that reporters understand how their sources intend information to be used. It's also important for sources to have some control over what they tell reporters. Even so, reporter-source relationships lend themselves to abuse by manipulative government officials. Worse, the structures of these relationships allow officials to throttle what's told to the people. As political scientists Karen O'Connor and Larry Sabato said: "Every public official knows that journalists are pledged to protect the confidentiality of sources, and therefore the rules can be used to an official's own benefit—but, say, giving reporters derogatory information to print about a source without having to be identified with the source." This manipulation is a regrettable though unavoidable part of the news-gathering process.

stonewalling

When Richard Nixon was under fire for ordering a cover-up of the Watergate break-in, he went months without a news conference. His aides plotted his movements to avoid even informal, shouted questions from reporters. He hunkered down in the White House in a classic example of **stonewalling.** Experts in the branch of public relations called political communications generally advise against stonewalling because people infer guilt or something to hide. Nonetheless, it is one way to deal with difficult media questions.

A variation on stonewalling is the **news blackout.** When U.S. troops invaded Grenada, the Pentagon barred the press. Reporters who hired runabout boats to get to the island were intercepted by a naval blockade. While heavy-handed, such limitations on media coverage do, for a limited time, give the government the opportunity to report what's happening from its self-serving perspective.

overwhelming information

During the Persian Gulf buildup in 1990 and the war itself, the Pentagon tried a new approach in media relations. Pete Williams, the Pentagon's chief spokesperson, provided so much information, including video, sound bites and data, that reporters

stonewall
To refuse to answer questions, sometimes refusing even to meet with reporters.

news blackout
When a person or institution decides to issue no statements despite public interest, and also declines news media questions.

were overwhelmed. The result was that reporters spent so much time sorting through material, all of it worthy, that they didn't have time to compose difficult questions or pursue fresh story angles. The result: War coverage was almost entirely favorable to the Bush administration.

media-government issues

STUDY PREVIEW Serious questions of trust are at stake as media owners become more business oriented. Other issues: Can news be trusted if reporters pick up outside income from special interests? Does political advertising pander to emotional and superficial instincts? Should television be required to give candidates free airtime? Should we look to the Internet to make government instantly responsive to public will?

political favors

Public confidence in media coverage suffers whenever doubts arise about whether the media are truly the public's watchdogs on government. Such doubts have grown as media control has been concentrated in fewer hands through conglomeration, and with the concomitant growth in media leaders being business people first and media people second. Rupert Murdoch, whose media empire includes the Fox television network, lost tremendous credibility when it was discovered he had offered House Speaker Newt Gingrich $4.5 million for a yet-unwritten manuscript to be published by Murdoch's HarperCollins book subsidiary. At the time, Murdoch was facing a federal challenge to his ownership of Fox. Book industry experts said there was no way Gingrich's book could earn $4.5 million—and, in fact, it flopped. When the deal was exposed, Murdoch and Gingrich both backpedaled and proclaimed Murdoch's problems on the Hill and the book deal were unfortunate coincidences.

Whatever the truth of the Murdoch-Gingrich deal, the interplay of media and government raises questions about whether the media are more responsive to their financial interest or to the public interest. Murdoch once yanked BBC off his Star-TV satellite service to China after Chinese government leaders objected to BBC coverage. At the time, Murdoch had numerous business initiatives needing Chinese governmental approval. In a similar incident, in 1998, Murdoch canceled a forthcoming book from HarperCollins because of passages critical of China's human rights record. Murdoch's action became known only because the author, the respected former British governor of Hong Kong, went public with his objections.

It's impossible to know how many media decisions are driven by business rather than public interests because the participants don't advertise them as such. They become public only through roundabout ways, and while they embarrass the participants, it doesn't seem they derive any lessons and change their ways—at least not in the case of Rupert Murdoch.

campaign spending

The mass media have become essential tools not only for national political leaders. Even candidates for state and many local offices have media advisers. Critics note that

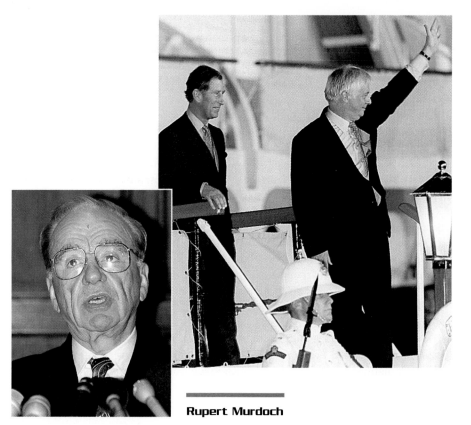

Rupert Murdoch

this techno-politics has serious downsides. In the age of television, photogenic candidates have an unfair built-in advantage. According to the critics, good looks rather than good ideas sway the electorate. Perhaps more serious, in some critics' view, is that slick presentation is more important than substance when it comes to 15-second TV spots.

Can candidates buy their way to office with advertising? While a candidate who vastly outspends another would seem to have an advantage, well-heeled campaigns can fail. In the most expensive U.S. Senate campaign in history, in California in 1994, Michael Huffington spent $18 million—78 cents per registered voter. Still, he lost to Diane Feinstein, who spent only $9 million. Also in 1994, Oliver North of Iran-Contra fame rounded up $15 million, mostly from political rightists, to run for Virginia's Senate seat. Although North far outspent Charles Robb, he lost.

In presidential campaigns too, no correlation has been established between winning and media spending. **Herbert Alexander,** a University of Southern California political scientist who tracks campaign spending, noted that George Bush outspent Bill Clinton $43 million to $32 million in 1991 and lost. Ross Perot also outspent Clinton, buying almost $40 million in media time and space. In 1988, however, Bush outspent Michael Dukakis $32 million to $24 million and won. The data point to campaign advertising being only one of many variables in elections.

The fact remains, however, that a political campaign has a cost of admission. Candidates need media exposure, and a campaign without advertising would almost certainly be doomed.

It would be a mistake to conclude that political advertising has no effect. A major 1976 study by **Thomas Patterson** and **Robert McClure** concluded that 7 percent of

---

Herbert Alexander
His studies conclude media advertising is only one of many variables in political campaigns.

Thomas Patterson and Robert McClure
Effect of political advertising on voters critical only in close campaigns.

the people in a 2,700-person sample were influenced by ads on whether to vote for Richard Nixon or George McGovern for president. While that was a small percentage, many campaigns are decided by even slimmer margins. The lesson from the Patterson-McClure study is that political advertising can make a critical difference.

free air time

Television advertising comprises most of candidates' campaign budgets, which has put growing pressure on candidates to raise funds to buy the time. This pressure has resulted in campaign finance irregularities that end up haunting candidates later. Many political observers, for example, questioned whether Al Gore's Year 2000 presidential hopes could survive the Buddhist Temple fund-raising scandal back during the 1996 Clinton-Bush campaign. Not surprisingly, Gore became an advocate of requiring television stations to give free airtime to candidates.

One proposal, from the Center for Governmental Studies in Los Angeles, would require stations to give two hours to candidates in the 60 days before an election. To allay station objections to losing revenue, the center proposed tax credits to offset station costs. Broadcasters still objected on numerous grounds. Shelby Scott, of the American Federation of Television and Radio Artists, said: "I don't want any more 30-second spots. I don't think they inform the electorate." Other television people noted that political ads, which are sold at cheap rates, would displace more lucrative commercial ads. Broadcasters also noted a coerciveness in being required to give free airtime to political candidates, noting that stations are beholden to the federal government for their licenses to remain in business.

techno-governance

The populist **Ross Perot,** an underdog 1992 presidential hopeful, excited many people with a proposal to televise expert discussions on public issues and ask viewers to tap their telephone keypads or computer keyboards to direct the nation's leaders on what to do. It would be an instant plebiscite on issues of war and peace, taxes and everything else. It was hardly a surprise that Perot was championing techno-governance. He had made a fortune in cutting-edge electronics, and he knew the technology was available for 1-800 toll-free plebiscites. It all seemed so efficient, and at first blush it seemed to many people to be a major step toward true democracy with grass-roots participation. The idea appealed particularly to people who felt disenfranchised and cynical about how political parties, primaries and elected representatives were performing.

The Perot proposal faltered, however, as analysts voiced doubts that had developed earlier when less-visible technicians and engineers had proposed electronic plebiscites. Among doubts was whether an electronic town hall could be representative.

Unrepresentative. Not everyone has access to a telephone or computer to participate in **electronic town halls,** which means a whole lower-economic stratum of the population is excluded. Further, millions of people aren't interested in keeping on top of public policy issues day in and day out. The town hall would be overrepresented with news hounds, political junkies, and people with a special interest in the issues at hand on a given day.

Simplistic. Many issues are too complex to be understood in a brief exchange of views on television. The options possible on a keypad are too limited—yes and

Ross Perot
Presidential candidate who advocates electronic town hall.

electronic town hall
Electronic mechanism for immediate public feedback to elected leaders.

no, at the least. Even detailed options, like a multiple-choice exam, cannot include enough options to represent informed citizen participation. With the current system, the people assign their elected representatives to do homework that's needed to sort through complex issues and make the best decision.

Vulnerable to Manipulation.   No matter how well intentioned the producers of Perot's proposed television discussions might be, a neutral presentation is impossible. Nuances in scripts can make a difference, especially with a nationwide audience of people who bring widely different backgrounds and sensitivities, even vocabularies, to their viewing. Even the sequence of speakers can slant the response.

Demagogic.   Good public policy is not always popular. People predictably favor lower taxes, for example, but lower taxes can mean less government service. Good public policy can also be painful. People might flinch at short-term hardships of a free-trade policy, even though it is better in the long term. Decisions on such matters, political scientists argue, should come from serious deliberation and the give-and-take of the political process. Also, say the political scientists, tough public policy decisions require leadership and courage—which the electronic town hall would short-circuit.

chapter wrap-up

A nation's political and media systems mirror each other. Democracies have libertarian media systems in which government functions under the watchful eye of the independent news media. The media, in fact, are called "watchdogs" because they are expected to identify misdeeds by government and bring them to public attention.

The United States was the pioneer democracy with a libertarian media system, and others followed. Today, most developed Western nations are in the libertarian tradition. The development of these governing and media systems was a reaction to authoritarian systems in which the government operated dictatorially and controlled the media through a variety of means, including censorship, licensing, bribery and repression.

Authoritarian and libertarian systems spring from philosophically distinct premises. Authoritarianism, which operates today in much of the world, is doubtful about the ability of people to govern themselves. Trust is placed in a dictator, monarch or other ruler, sometimes assumed to be divinely appointed. In authoritarian systems, the media follow the leadership of the infallible governing authority. Libertarianism, on the other hand, has confidence in the ability of human beings, individually and collectively, to conduct their own affairs.

American libertarianism has mellowed into a new framework that emphasizes responsibility more than the unbounded freedom of early libertarians. This shift has been prompted in part by lapses in the media living up to libertarians' expectations. As a watchdog, for example, the media generally perform well but not always. Lapses are serious, such as Rupert Murdoch unplugging BBC from his satellite television service to China because Chinese leaders, whose approval he needed for numerous business ventures, were piqued at BBC coverage of their policies. Other questions about media credibility flow from the growing sophistication with which government leaders manipulate coverage to their political advantage. Critics of libertarianism argue that it's time to reconsider the premises of the school of thought.

No one denies that the news media are influential, but the influence generally is indirect through media-savvy opinion leaders. Although the media have limited immediate direct influence on voters, the media are powerful players in public life because they shape the public's agenda by reporting some issues and ignoring or downplaying others. The media also frame issues and prime how people see the issues.

questions for review

1. How do authoritarian governments control the mass media?

2. Why are libertarian and authoritarian media systems different?

3. Explain the shift among U.S. media systems from libertarianism to social responsibility.

4. What does the term *Fourth Estate* mean?

5. How do the news media influence people on political issues?

6. How does media agenda-setting and priming work?

7. How do government leaders manipulate media coverage?

questions for critical thinking

1. Does the U.S. news media live up to its watchdog role?

2. Who are opinion leaders in your life? How do they influence your views?

3. What personal values would influence you as a news reporter who sets public agendas and frames issues and primes how people see them?

4. What perils face a reporter who accepts information off-the-record from one source and later receives the same information on deep background from another source?

5. Considering the dynamics in government-media relations, what are the prospects for plans to require television to give free airtime to political candidates?

for further learning

"1-800-Trouble." New York *Times* (June 13, 1992). Page 14. This editorial makes a strong, compact case against electronic plebiscites of the sort proposed by presidential candidate Ross Perot in the 1992 election.

Ken Auletta. "Fee Speech" *New Yorker* (September 12, 1994), Pages 20–42, and "New Speech Rules Anger TV Vets" *American Journalism Review* (September 1994). Pages 40–47.

Bernard Cohen. *The Press and Foreign Policy* (Princeton University Press, 1963). This is the classic treatment of the subject.

Commission on Freedom of the Press. *A Free and Responsible Press* (University of Chicago, 1947). This is the Hutchins Commission report from which have sprung the social responsibility modifications of libertarian thinking about the press.

Stephen Craig, editor. *Broken Contract* (Westview, 1996). Political scientist Diane Owen discusses talk shows and their audiences in a chapter, "Who's Talking, Who's Listening? The New Politics of Radio Talk Shows," Pages 127–146.

Ronald Elving. "On Radio, All Politics Is a Lot Less Vocal," *Congressional Quarterly Weekly Report* (May 10, 1997). Page 1102.

Morris T. Fiorina and Paul E. Peterson. *The New American Democracy* (Allyn & Bacon, 1998).

Doris Graber. *Mass Media and American Politics* (CQ Press, 1993). Graber, a media scholar, discusses the media as a source of information about politics and government for the public.

S. Robert Lichter and Daniel Amundson. "Less News Is Worse News: Television News Coverage of Congress, 1972–1992," in Thomas Mann and Norman Ornstein, editors. *Congress, the Press, and the Public* (American Enterprise Institute, 1994). Pages 131–140.

William Mayer. "Trends in Media Usage," *Public Opinion Quarterly* 57 (1993). Pages 593–611.

Larry McCarthy. "The Selling of the President: An Interview With Roger Ailes." *Gannett Center Journal* (Fall 1988), 65–72. McCarthy, a political advertising consultant, offers a succinct biography on Ailes. This issue of the journal focuses on the media and elections.

Karen O'Connor and Larry J. Sabato. *American Government: Continuity and Change* (Allyn & Bacon, 1997).

Thomas E. Patterson and Robert C. McClure. *The Unseeing Eye: The Myth of Television Power in National Elections.* Putnam, 1976. This classic study found most people are reinforced in their pre-existing values and views by television campaign news and political advertising.

Ronald E. Pynn. *American Politics: Changing Expectations,* fifth edition (Simon & Schuster, 1997). Chapter 7 of Professor Pynn's survey textbook deals with mass media in American political life.

Alicia Sheppard. "Talk Is Expensive" *American Journalism Review* (May 1994), Pages 20–42, and "New Speech Rules Anger TV Vets" *American Journalism Review* (September 1994). Page 19.

Fred Siebert, Theodore Peterson and Wilbur Schramm. *Four Theories of the Press* (University of Illinois Press, 1956). Siebert, Peterson and Schramm root national political and media systems in philosophical premises about the nature of knowledge, humankind and society. *Four Theories* remains the seminal work for later treatments of the subject.

James P. Winter and Chaim H. Eyal. "Agenda-Setting for the Civil Rights Issue." *Public Opinion Quarterly* 7 (October 1979).

for keeping up to date

Index on Censorship, published in London, provides monthly country-by-country status reports.

Scholarly journals that carry articles on foreign media systems, international communication and media responsibility include the *Journal of Broadcasting & Electronic Media,* the *Journal of Communication* and *Journalism Quarterly.*

Professional journals that carry articles on foreign media systems and on media responsibility include *Columbia Journalism Review, Quill* and *American Journalism Review.*

Ongoing discussion on media responsibility also appears in the *Journal of Mass Media Ethics.*

18
mass media law

in this chapter you will learn:

- The heart of U.S. mass media law is the First Amendment's guarantee of free expression.

- The government may only rarely prohibit expression.

- Anyone who is falsely slandered by the mass media may sue for libel.

- The mass media generally may not intrude on someone's solitude.

- The news media may cover the courts and government however they see fit.

- Obscenity is not protected by the First Amendment, but pornography is.

- Most censorship battles today are fought at the local level.

- Copyright law protects intellectual property from being stolen from its owners.

The crowd outside the federal courthouse in Amarillo, Texas waited expectantly for the jury's verdict. When the doors opened, a confident and beaming Oprah Winfrey walked out, thrusting her fist upward and outward to signal a triumphant "Yes!" The country's Number One talk show host had just won an important legal victory.

"Free speech not only lives, it rocks!" Winfrey told the cheering well-wishers that February morning in 1998. She vowed never again to take free speech for granted. And she would not stop speaking out. "I come from a people who struggled and died to use their voice in this country, and I refuse to be muzzled," she said.

For nearly six weeks, she had sat as a defendant in a lawsuit over the April 16, 1996, broadcast of "The Oprah Winfrey Show," which had featured a segment on mad cow disease. When cattle prices plummeted shortly after the program aired, a group of cattlemen blamed Winfrey for their financial losses and sued.

Winfrey told the court her programs are designed to "inform, enlighten, uplift and entertain" through a discussion format. For a feature on food safety, it seemed appropriate to discuss mad cow disease.

First discovered among cattle in the United Kingdom during the mid-1980s, mad cow disease is an always fatal disease of the central nervous system occurring after a long incubation period. Epidemiological evidence suggested that the disease may have entered the food chain through diseased carcasses taken to rendering plants and made into protein additives for cattle feed. Such animal-based feed supplements were banned by the British government in 1988.

At first, it was thought that humans could not contract the disease. But when a new variant form of a related disease showed up among 10 people in the United Kingdom, the British government notified the World Health Organization, which quickly called together an international panel of experts to study the situation and make further recommendations. This was just two weeks before Winfrey's 1996 program.

Thus, the timely topic had already been reported and discussed through various media outlets before Winfrey's show was aired. Why then was Winfrey's program singled out for the lawsuit?

The program's content was one factor. A former cattle rancher turned vegetarian activist, also named as a defendant in the suit, was one of Winfrey's guests. He had expressed his opinion that an outbreak of mad cow disease in the United States could "make AIDS look like a common cold." As he talked about animal carcasses being processed for cattle feed (a practice the U.S. Food and Drug Administration prohibited a year after the broadcast), Winfrey had interjected, "It has just stopped me cold from eating another burger." The audience applauded at what Winfrey later called her "gut reaction" to hearing about "cows eating cows," which struck her as an unnatural practice.

Second, the plaintiffs took issue with the program's presentation and editing. Winfrey was accused of interrupting her two other guests, a lobbyist for the National Cattlemen's Beef Association and a representative of the U.S. Department of Agriculture. Her production company was accused of cutting many of their taped comments during the final editing. From the witness stand, Winfrey explained that only rambling repetitions were edited. She had provided a forum for debate, she said; and it was up to her guests, not her, to refute the points they disagreed with. She emphasized that her show was not a news program or documentary. It was a talk show, and the talk show format requires guests with opposing viewpoints to jump in quickly at the "pivotal moment." She said balance doesn't mean "every game is going to end in a tie." The Beef Association representative had been invited to appear on a follow-up program the next week, where he talked further about measures the U.S. has taken to ensure beef safety and safeguard public health. But an attorney for the plaintiffs called this second program an example of "shutting the barn door after the horse is out."

Winfrey's influence was a third factor in the suit brought against her. Because she had announced she wouldn't eat another hamburger, the plaintiffs' attorneys suggested that other people would stop eating beef. Winfrey's influence was well-known. Book publishers coveted the "Oprah effect"—the best seller status conferred on any book chosen for her book club. And her weight loss success had inspired many people to change their eating and exercise habits. But Winfrey said it was "absurd" to think her off-the-cuff statement would alter the beef eating practices of her viewers, who "are intelligent enough to make decisions on their own." (In an after-trial interview with ABC's Diane Sawyer, Winfrey said she had received the "cutest note" which said, "Did you ever think you'd see the day when a black woman would be on trial for having too much influence?")

No doubt the major factor in the suit against Oprah Winfrey was the existence of a Texas law that holds a person liable for falsely disparaging a "food product of agriculture or aquaculture that is sold or distributed in a form that will perish or decay beyond marketability within a limited period of time."

Such "perishable food defamation statutes," often called "veggie libel laws," were passed by 13 states after Washington state's apple growers had unsuccessfully tried to sue CBS in 1989. The growers had wanted compensation for losses incurred after a broadcast of "60 Minutes" linked the widely used apple ripening chemical, Alar, to health hazards in humans. But the case was dismissed, and its dismissal was upheld by the U.S. Supreme Court. Apples could not be libeled. Agricultural organizations then began lobbying for legislation to protect generic perishable food products from libel and slander, just as individuals and brand name products are protected.

While proponents of such laws say they are necessary to protect livelihood, opponents say they stifle free speech by intimidating, squelching debates and impeding investigations that help ensure food safety. Winfrey's attorney said that whereas he once considered veggie libel laws silly, he now considers them scary.

The Winfrey trial was expected to test the constitutionality of such laws. It did not. The judge ruled the suit did not fit the perishable agricultural products disparagement law (cattle, as live cattle, are not perishable products). Instead, the suit had to proceed under conventional business defamation law in which plaintiffs must prove malice and the deliberate spreading of falsehoods about a plaintiff's business. The jury could not be convinced that this had occurred.

During the trial, Winfrey had voiced her firm belief in the First Amendment. At one point she remarked that just as the cattle ranchers didn't like some of her comments, she hasn't liked many of the things people have said about her. "But this is America," she said. "People are allowed to say things about you that you don't like." This conviction sustained her through what she calls "the most painful experience" of her entire life, and prompted her to celebrate "free speech that rocks."

the u.s. constitution

(STUDY PREVIEW) The First Amendment to the Constitution bars the government from limiting freedom of expression, including expression in the mass media, or so it seems. However, for the first 134 years of the amendment's existence, it appeared that the states could ignore the federal constitution and put their own restrictions on free expression because it did not apply to them.

first amendment

The legal foundation for free expression in the United States is the **First Amendment** to the Constitution. The amendment, penned by **James Madison,** boiled down the eloquence of Benjamin Franklin, Thomas Jefferson and earlier libertarian thinkers during the American colonial experience to a mere 45 words: "Congress shall make no law respecting an establishment of religion, or prohibiting the free exercise thereof; or abridging the freedom of speech, or of the press; or of the right of the people peaceably to assemble, and to petition the Government for a redress of grievances."

The amendment, which became part of the Constitution in 1791, seemed a definitive statement that set the United States apart from all other nations at the time in guaranteeing that the government wouldn't interfere with free expression. It turned out, however, that the First Amendment did not settle all the questions that could be raised about free expression. This chapter looks at many of these unsettled issues and attempts to clarify them.

scope of first amendment

The First Amendment explicitly prohibited only Congress from limiting free expression, but there was never a serious legal question that it applied also to the executive branch of the national government. There was a question, however, about whether the First Amendment prohibited the states from squelching free expression.

> **First Amendment**
> Bars government from limiting free expression.
> **James Madison**
> Author of First Amendment.

From the early days of the republic, many states had laws that limited free expression, and nobody seemed to mind much. In fact, all the way through the 1800s the First Amendment seemed largely ignored. Not until 1925, when the U.S. Supreme Court considered the case of **Benjamin Gitlow,** was the First Amendment applied to the states. In this case, Gitlow, a small-time New York agitator, rankled authorities by publishing his "Left Wing Manifesto" and distributing a Socialist paper. He was arrested and convicted of violating a state law that forbade advocating "criminal anarchy." Gitlow appealed that the First Amendment to the U.S. Constitution should override any state law that contravenes it, and the U.S. Supreme Court agreed. Gitlow, by the way, lost his appeal on other grounds. Even so, his case was a significant clarification of the scope of the First Amendment.

prior restraint

(STUDY PREVIEW)   When the government heads off an utterance before it is made, it is engaging in prior restraint. Since the 1930s, the U.S. Supreme Court has consistently found that prior restraint violates the First Amendment. At the same time, the Court says there may be circumstances, although rare, in which the public good would justify such censorship.

public nuisances

The U.S. Supreme Court was still finding its voice on First Amendment issues when a Minnesota case came to its attention. The Minnesota Legislature had created a "public nuisance" law that allowed authorities to shut down "obnoxious" newspapers. The Legislature's rationale was that government has the right to remove things that work against the common good: Just as a community can remove obnoxious weeds, so can it remove obnoxious "rags." In 1927 in Minneapolis, authorities used the law to padlock the *Saturday Press,* a feisty scandal sheet owned by **Jay Near** and **Howard Guilford.**

Most right-minded people would agree that the *Saturday Press* was obnoxious, especially its racist hate-mongering. Other people, however, including publisher **Robert McCormick** of the Chicago *Tribune* and the fledgling **American Civil Liberties Union,** saw another issue. To their thinking, the First Amendment protected all expression from government interference, no matter how obnoxious. They also were bothered that government, in this case the county prosecutor, was the determiner of what was obnoxious.

Three and one-half years after the *Saturday Press* was silenced, the U.S. Supreme Court, in a 5–4 decision, threw out the Minnesota law. The Court ruled that **prior restraint,** prohibiting expression before it is made, was disallowed under the U.S. Constitution. Said Chief Justice **Charles Evans Hughes:** "The fact that the liberty of the press may be abused by miscreant purveyors of scandal does not make any less the immunity of the press from previous restraint in dealing with official misconduct."

The decision was a landmark limitation on governmental censorship, although the Court noted, as it always does in such cases, that protection for the press "is not absolutely unlimited." The Court has always noted that it can conceive of circumstances, such as a national emergency, when prior restraint might be justified.

Benjamin Gitlow
His appeal resulted in ban on state laws that restrict free expression.

Jay Near
His appeal resulted in strong ruling against government prior restraint on expression.

Howard Guilford
Colleague of Jay Near in producing *Saturday Press.*

Robert McCormick
Chicago *Tribune* publisher who supported *Near v. Minnesota.*

American Civil Liberties Union
Backed *Near v. Minnesota.*

prior restraint
Prohibiting expression in advance.

Charles Evans Hughes
Chief justice who wrote *Near v. Minnesota.*

....jay near

Jay Near and Howard Guilford, who started a scandal sheet in Minneapolis in 1927, did not have far to look for stories on corruption. Prohibition was in effect, and Minneapolis, because of geography, was a key American distribution point for bootleg Canadian whiskey going south to Chicago, St. Louis and other cities. A former county prosecutor was knee-deep in the illicit whiskey trade. Mose Barnett, the leading local gangster, never needed an appointment with the police chief. He could walk into the chief's office any time. The mayor was on the take. A standard joke was that city hall had been moved to McCormick's Cafe, notorious for its payoff activity. Gambling, prostitution and booze palaces flourished in blatant violation of the law. Mobsters extorted protection payments from local merchants. Contract murder went for $500, on slow days $200.

Hearing about the kind of newspaper that Near and Guilford had in mind, the crooked police chief, aware of his own vulnerability, told his men to yank every copy off the newsstands as soon as they appeared. The *Saturday Press* thus became the first American newspaper banned even before a single issue had been published.

The confrontation between the corrupt Minneapolis establishment and the Near-Guilford scandal-mongering team worsened. One afternoon a few days after the first issue, gunmen pulled up beside Guilford's car at an intersection and fired four bullets at him, one into his abdomen. Not even that silenced *The Saturday Press*. While Guilford lay critically wounded in the hospital, Near stepped up their crusade, pointing out that mob kingpin Mose Barnett had threatened Guilford before the attack. Near also went after Barnett for ordering thugs to terrorize an immigrant launderer who had bought his own dry cleaning equipment rather than send his customers' laundry to a mob-controlled plant. Near's other targets included the mayor, the police chief, the head of the law enforcement league, the grand jury and the county prosecutor.

Two months after the first issue of *The Saturday Press,* Floyd Olson, the prosecutor, was fed up, and he went to court and obtained an order to ban Near and Guilford from producing any more issues. Olson based his case on a 1925 Minnesota gag law that declared that "a malicious, scandalous and defamatory newspaper"

The Saturday Press

Vol 1, No. 1   Minneapolis, Minn., Sept. 21, 1927   Price 5 Cents

Jay Near

CONTENTS

Following a Custom
Page 2

A Friendly Tip
Page 4

Home Town Gambling
Page 11

Tom and Jake
Page 8

Gil's Chatterbox
Page 9

CHAFF!
Page 13

Just Kidding
Page 3

Two Toms Beat One Tom's Tom-Tom
Page 6

1927 Scandal Sheet. Page One of Jay Near and Howard Guilford's inaugural issue looked bland enough, but inside were stories that infuriated officials. The officials eventually declared *The Saturday Press* a public nuisance and shut it down to head off further incriminating coverage of local corruption. In the landmark court case that resulted, *Near v. Minnesota,* the U.S. Supreme Court ruled that such "prior restraint" was unconstitutional.

could be banned as a public nuisance.

Despite their crusading for good causes, Near and Guilford's brand of journalism was hard to like. Both were bigots, who peppered their writing with references to "niggers," "yids," "bohunks" and "spades." Could they get away with saying such things in print?

The U.S. Supreme Court said "no" in a landmark decision known as *Near v. Minnesota.* The court said that no government at any level has the right to suppress a publication because of what it might say in its next issue. Except in highly exceptional circumstances, such as life-and-death issues in war time, legal action

against a publication can come only after something has been published.

After the ruling, Near resumed *The Saturday Press* and Guilford rejoined the enterprise. The paper floundered commercially, however, and Guilford quit. In 1934 Guilford announced for mayor and promised to campaign against the underworld. Before campaigning got started, gangsters crowded Guilford's car to the curb and fired a shotgun into his head.

Two years later, Near, age 62, died of natural causes. The local obituary didn't even mention *Near v. Minnesota* despite its being one of the most important court decisions in American media history.

Vietnam Archive: Pentagon Study Traces 3 Decades of Growing U. S. Involvement

By NEIL SHEEHAN

A massive study of how the United States went to war in Indochina, conducted by the Pentagon three years ago, demonstrates that four administrations progressively developed a sense of commitmen... a readi... tect the... tion wit... extent... knowle...

The 4,000 ... append... tary of... and co... in Sout... mid-196...

Three pages of documentary material from the Pentagon study begin on Page 35.

Though far from a complete history, ... e study ... rnment ... er three ... 40 au... broad ... ngs, in... ion's de... ance in ... munist... ed" the ... set" the

¶That the Kennedy Administration, though ultimately spared from major escalation decisions by the death of its leader, transformed a policy of "limited-risk gamble," which it inherited, into a "broad commitment" that left ... tween ... ation, ... t and ... s, in... gainst ... ng in ... war, ... realed ... id its ... ; clan... 1964

Daniel Ellsberg   **Neil Sheehan**

national security

The U.S. Supreme Court, which is the ultimate interpreter on constitutional questions, has been consistent that government has a censorship right when national security is at stake. This position was underscored in the **Pentagon Papers** case. A government contract researcher, **Daniel Ellsberg,** spent several years with a team preparing an internal Pentagon study on U.S. policy in Vietnam. In 1971, at the height of the war, Ellsberg decided that the public should have an inside look at Pentagon decision-making. He secretly photocopied the whole 47-volume study, even though it was stamped "top secret," and handed it over to New York *Times* reporter Neil Sheehan. After several weeks, the *Times* began a front-page series drawn from the Pentagon Papers. Saying that the study could hurt national security, but also knowing that it could embarrass the government, the Nixon administration ordered the *Times* to stop the series.

The *Times* objected that the government was attempting prior restraint but agreed to suspend the series while it appealed the government order. Meanwhile, the Washington *Post* somehow obtained a second copy of the Pentagon Papers and began its own series, to which the government also objected. Before the U.S. Supreme Court, the government argument that national security was at stake proved weak, and the *Times* and the *Post* resumed their series. So did dozens of other newspapers, and the Pentagon Papers eventually were published in their entirety and sold at bookstores throughout the land.

Despite the journalistic victory in the Pentagon Papers case, the Court said that it could conceive of circumstances in which the national security could override the First Amendment guarantees against prior restraint. In earlier cases, justices had said that the government would be on solid ground to restrain reports on troop movements and other military activities in wartime if the reports constituted "a clear and present danger."

military operations

At times the United States has employed battlefield censorship, requiring correspondents to submit their copy for review before transmission. This practice was discarded by the time of the Vietnam War, but it appeared in a variant form in 1983 when the Reagan administration ordered troops to the Caribbean island of Grenada. The Pentagon, which controlled all transportation to the battle area, refused to take reporters along. A few print reporters rented yachts and airplanes and made it through a naval barricade, but photographers and television crews, their equipment giving away their identity as journalists, were turned back.

Journalists objected strenuously to the Grenada news blackout. As a result, the Pentagon agreed to include a few **pool reporters** in future military actions. These reporters' stories then would be made available to other news organizations. The pool system was used in the 1989 invasion of Panama, but the military manipulated the arrangement. Reporters were confined to a windowless briefing room at a U.S. Army post and given history lessons on U.S.-Panama relations, not current information on what was happening. Overall, the pool arrangement was to the liking of the military, not the media.

Most journalists were skeptical of the military's argument that it needed to control reporters to keep information on its activities from the enemy. Journalists said the true motive was to prevent honest and truthful reporting that might undermine public support at home for the military intervention. This skepticism proved well founded in 1991 when the Pentagon went to extraordinary lengths to shape field reporting from the Persian Gulf war. These were the main Pentagon tactics, none involving explicit censorship but being nonetheless effective in shaping news coverage:

- The military arranged reporter pools for some coverage, which facilitated showing reporters what the military wanted seen.

- The military placed vast areas off limits to reporters with a variety of explanations, including sensitivity to the policies of "host nations" such as Saudi Arabia.

War Coverage. Whatever the political system, the rules of government-media relations can be lost in combat. Reporters covering the Persian Gulf war found strict rules imposed on their movements by the military. In the Croatian war in 1991, reporters had other problems. In one situation, reporters fled into a cornfield when they found their car being fired on, and then a Croatian soldier moved in and used the car for cover. This was all despite the large and universally recognized "TV" taped on the windshield.

pool reporters
News media-selected reporters who share stories, photos with others.

media timeline

····landmarks in media law

1791 States ratified First Amendment, free expression section of U.S. Constitution.

1901 Iowa Supreme Court ruled performers must accept criticism of performances.

1919 Justice Oliver Wendell Holmes coined "fire in crowded theater" example for prior restraint.

1927 Congress created agency to regulate radio.

1930 Court overrules import ban on *Ulysses.*

1931 U.S. Supreme Court banned prior restraint in *Near v. Minnesota.*

1952 U.S. Supreme Court accorded First Amendment protection to movies.

1964 U.S. Supreme Court ruled public figures can

sue for libel only if media reckless.

1966 U.S. Supreme Court ruled that courts, not media, responsible for assuring fair trials.

1966 Congress passed Freedom of Information Act.

1968 U.S. Supreme Court ruled local community standards determine obscenity.

1971 U.S. Supreme Court banned prior restraint in *New York Times v. United States* national security case.

1972 U.S. Supreme Court ruled journalists can be compelled to name confidential sources.

1980s Reagan deregulation of business, including mass media, began.

■■■■■■■■

- Pentagon public relations people overwhelmed reporters with carefully structured news briefings and news conferences with top brass, and provided so much data, including spectacular video, that reporters had scant time left for pursuing alternate perspectives.

"fire!" in a crowded theater

Prior restraint has been justified in situations other than national security. Supreme Court Justice **Oliver Wendell Holmes** wrote in a 1919 case: "The most stringent protection of free speech would not protect a man in falsely shouting 'fire' in a theater and causing panic." In other words, the government would be justified in stopping the man. The problem, however, is for government agents to draw the line between speech that must be banned and letting go all the rest. To help, Holmes developed what he called the **clear and present and danger test.** Using this test, the courts place a heavy burden on the government to demonstrate that the expression would have caused so serious an effect that prior restraint was justified. Yes or no, was there a clear and present danger?

It is a judgment call whether an anticipated negative effect warrants suppression, but the Court has rendered decisions that give some sense of when prior restraint is justified. In one case, the Supreme Court upheld the conviction of Philadelphia Socialist **Charles Schenck,** who published 15,000 leaflets during World War I that described that war as a Wall Street scheme and encouraged young men to defy their draft orders. Although Schenck's case did not involve prior restraint, the Court's line of reasoning included a guideline on when restraint may be permissible. The Court

Oliver Wendell Holmes
Justice who wrote "Fire!" in crowded theater justification for prior restraint.

clear and present danger test
A long-lived justification for government prior restraint.

Charles Schenck
His appeal resulted in first articulation of clear and present danger.

declined to say that Schenck's leaflets constituted a clear and present danger, but it ruled that they were unacceptable in a time of war. This was called the **bad tendency test,** which could be applied in times of domestic unrest and riot.

The bad tendency and the clear and present danger tests are closely related, but there is a distinction. It is harder for the government to make a convincing case that an article or utterance represents a clear and present danger than it is to argue that there is merely a bad tendency. Over the years since the Schenck case, the courts generally have insisted that the government be held to the stiffer clear and present danger test, and the bad tendency rationale is hardly ever considered in prior-restraint cases anymore. Today, the right to free expression has very few exceptions.

slander and mass media

STUDY PREVIEW   When the mass media carry disparaging descriptions and comments, they risk being sued for libel. The media have a strong defense if the libel was accurate. If not, there can be big trouble. Libel is a serious matter. Not only are reputations at stake when defamation occurs, but also losing a suit can be so costly that it can put a publication or broadcast organization out of business.

bad tendency test
An early justification for government prior restraint.

concept of libel law

If someone punches you in the face for no good reason, knocking out several teeth, breaking your nose and causing permanent disfigurement, most courts would rule that your attacker should pay your medical bills. If your disfigurement or psychological upset causes you to lose your job, to be ridiculed or shunned by friends and family or perhaps to retreat from social interaction, the court probably would order your attacker to pay additional amounts. Like fists, words can cause damage. If someone says or writes false, damaging things about you, you can sue for **libel.** Freedom of speech and the press is not a license to say absolutely anything about anybody.

If a libeling statement is false, the utterer may be liable for millions of dollars in damages. This is serious for the mass media. When the *Saturday Evening Post* reported that Alabama football coach Bear Bryant and Georgia athletic director Wally Butts fixed a game, Butts sued. The magazine lost the case, and it was ordered to pay $6 million in damages. Although the amount was eventually reduced, the judgment contributed to the demise of the magazine. When a former Miss Wyoming felt embarrassed by a fictitious article in *Penthouse* magazine, she was awarded $26.5 million even though she was not even named in the article. The verdict was set aside on appeal, but there was concern for a time about the magazine's well-being. A $9.2 million judgment against the Alton, Illinois, *Telegraph* forced the newspaper to file for bankruptcy protection.

The largest jury award to date, in 1997 against the *Wall Street Journal,* was almost twice the earnings that year of the *Journal*'s parent company, Dow Jones Inc. The award was reduced substantially on appeal, but the fact remains that awards have grown dramatically in recent years and can hurt a media company seriously.

sullivan case

Elected officials have a hard time winning libel suits today. Noting that democracy is best served by robust, unbridled discussion of public issues and that public officials are inseparable from public policy, the U.S. Supreme Court has ruled that public figures can win libel suits only in extreme circumstances. The Court also has said that people who foist themselves into the limelight forfeit some of the protection available to other citizens.

The key court decision in developing current U.S. libel standards originated in an advertisement carried by the New York *Times* in 1960. A civil rights coalition, the Committee to Defend Martin Luther King and the Struggle for Freedom in the South, escalated its antisegregationist cause by placing a full-page advertisement in the *Times.* The advertisement accused public officials in the South of violence and illegal tactics against the civil rights struggle. While the advertisement was by and large truthful, it was marred by minor factual errors. Police Commissioner L. B. Sullivan of Montgomery, Alabama, filed a libel action saying that the errors damaged him, and he won $500,000 in an Alabama trial. On appeal to the U.S. Supreme Court, the case, **New York *Times* v. Sullivan,** became a landmark in libel law. The Supreme Court said that the importance of "free debate" in a democratic society generally was more important than factual errors that might upset and damage public officials. To win a libel suit, the Court said, public officials needed to prove that damaging statements were uttered or printed with the knowledge that they were false. The question in the Sullivan case became whether the *Times* was guilty of "**reckless disregard** of the truth." The Supreme Court said it was not, and the newspaper won.

libel
A defamation; synonymous with slander.

New York Times v. Sullivan
Libel case that largely barred public figures from the right to sue for libel.

reckless disregard
Supreme Court language for situation in which public figures may sue for libel.

Questions lingered after the Sullivan decision about exactly who was and who was not a *public official*. The courts struggled for definition, and the Supreme Court eventually changed the term to *public figure*. In later years, as the Court refined its view on issues raised in the Sullivan case through several decisions, it remained consistent in giving the mass media a lot of room for error, even damaging error, in discussing government officials, political candidates and publicity hounds.

- **Government Officials.** All elected government officials and appointed officials with high-level policy responsibilities are "public figures" as far as their performance in office is concerned. A member of a state governor's cabinet fits this category. A cafeteria worker in the state capitol does not.

- **Political Candidates.** Anyone seeking public office is subject to intense public review, during which the courts are willing to excuse false statements as part of robust, wide-open discussion.

- **Publicity Hounds.** Court decisions have gone both ways, but generally people who seek publicity or intentionally draw attention to themselves must prove "reckless disregard of the truth" if they sue for libel.

How far can the media go in making disparaging comments? It was all right, said a Vermont court, when the Barre *Times Argus* ran an editorial that said a political candidate was "a horse's ass, a jerk, an idiot and a paranoid." The court said open discussion on public issues excused even such insulting, abusive and unpleasant verbiage. Courts have generally been more tolerant of excessive language in opinion pieces, such as the Barre editorial, than in fact-based articles.

fair comment and criticism

People flocked to see the **Cherry Sisters'** act. Effie, Addie, Jessie, Lizzie and Ella toured the country with a song and dance act that drew big crowds. They were just awful. They could neither sing nor dance, but people turned out because the sisters were so funny. Sad to say, the Cherry Sisters took themselves seriously. In 1901, desperate for respect, they decided to sue the next newspaper reviewer who gave them a bad notice. The reviewer, it turned out, was Billy Hamilton, who included a lot of equine metaphors in his piece for the Des Moines *Leader*: "Effie is an old jade of 50 summers, Jessie a frisky filly of 40, and Addie, the flower of the family, a capering monstrosity of 35. Their long skinny arms, equipped with talons at the extremities, swung mechanically, and anon waved frantically at the suffering audience. The mouths of their rancid features opened like caverns, and sounds like the wailings of damned souls issued therefrom. They pranced around the stage with a motion that suggested a cross between the *danse du ventre* and the fox trot—strange creatures with painted faces and hideous mien. Effie is spavined, Addie is stringhalt, and Jessie, the only one who showed her stockings, has legs with calves as classic in their outlines as the curves of a broom handle."

The outcome of the suit was another setback for the Cherrys. They lost in a case that established that actors or others who perform for the public must be willing to accept both positive and negative comments about their performance. This right of **fair comment and criticism,** however, does not make it open season on performers in aspects of their lives that do not relate to public performance. The *National Enquirer* could not defend itself when entertainer Carol Burnett sued for a story that described her as obnoxiously drunk at a restaurant. Not only was the description false (Carol

Cherry Sisters
Complainants in case that barred performers from suing critics.

fair comment and criticism
Doctrine that permits criticism of performers, performances.

Fair Comment and Criticism.
Upset with what an Iowa reviewer said about their show, the Cherry Sisters sued. The important 1901 court decision that resulted said that journalists, critics and anybody else can say whatever they want about a public performance. The rationale was that someone who puts on a performance for public acceptance has to take a risk also of public rejection.

Burnett abstains from alcohol), but Burnett was in no public or performing role at the restaurant. This distinction between an individual's public and private life also has been recognized in cases involving public officials and candidates.

privacy law

(STUDY PREVIEW) The idea that people have a right to limit intrusions on their privacy has been taking form in American law through much of this century. In general, permission is not required in news coverage, although the courts have been consistent in saying that there are limits on how far news reporters can go with their cameras and in writing about personal information.

intruding on solitude

The courts have recognized a person's right to solitude and punished overzealous news reporters who tap telephone lines, plant hidden microphones, use telephoto lenses, and break into homes and offices for stories. In general, reporters are free to pursue stories in public places and, when invited, in private places. Sometimes the courts have had to draw the line between public and private places. Here are some examples:

- **A hospital room. Dorothy Barber** entered a Kansas City hospital with a metabolic disorder. No matter how much she ate, she lost weight. One day, two newspaper

privacy law
Recognizes a right to be left alone.
Dorothy Barber
Successfully sued when photos of her in hospital published.
Ron Galella
Celebrity photographer.
Jacqueline Kennedy Onassis
Successfully barred photographer from hounding children, herself.

reporters, one with a camera, paid Barber a visit for a story and took a picture without permission. United Press International distributed the photograph, showing Dorothy Barber in her hospital bed, and *Time* magazine ran the picture. The caption read: "The starving glutton." Barber sued *Time* and won. The court said that reporters have a right to pursue people in public places, but the right of privacy protects a person in bed for treatment and recuperation.

- **Inside a private business.** A Seattle television photographer wanted to tape a pharmacist charged with Medicaid fraud, but the man would not cooperate. The photographer then set himself on the sidewalk outside the pharmacy and filmed the pharmacist through a front window. The pharmacist sued, charging the television station with photographic eavesdropping, but the court dismissed the suit, ruling that the photographer recorded only what any passerby was free to see. The outcome would have been different had the photographer gone into the shop, a private place, and taped the same scene without permission.

- **Expectation of privacy.** Some intrusion cases have hinged on whether the person being reported upon had "a reasonable expectation of privacy." Someone lounging nude at a fenced-in backyard pool would have a strong case against a photographer who climbed a steep, seldom-scaled cliff with a telephoto lens for a picture. A similar case can be made against hidden cameras and microphones.

Paparazzi at Fault? A lingering question in the Paris accident that killed three people, including Princess Di, was whether celebrity-chasing photographers were somehow at fault. In Europe, the pursuit of photos had become a daring, some say daredevil, acitivity, with paparazzi on motorcycles chasing movie stars and other celebrities, sometimes at high speeds on crowded motorways.

harassment

By being in a public place, a person surrenders most privacy protections, but this does not mean that journalists have a right to hound people mercilessly. **Ron Galella,** a free-lance celebrity photographer, learned this lesson, or should have, in two lawsuits filed by **Jacqueline Kennedy Onassis.** Galella stalked the former First Lady, darting and jumping and grunting at her to catch off-guard facial expressions that would make interesting photographs that he could sell to magazines and photo archives. Mrs. Onassis became Galella's specialty, but he also was building a photo file on the Kennedy children. Galella broke Mrs. Onassis's patience in 1973 when he frightened a horse ridden by young John Kennedy, and the horse bolted. John Kennedy escaped serious injury, but Mrs. Onassis asked her Secret Service protection detail to intervene to prevent Galella from endangering her children. Not long thereafter, the guards and Galella got into a tussle. Galella filed a $1.3 million suit, claiming he had

Aggressive Journalism. Photographer Ron Galella made a living by shadowing former First Lady Jacqueline Kennedy Onassis and selling the pictures. Although not pleased, Mrs. Onassis tolerated the paparazzi photographer until he began scaring her and the Kennedy children in an effort to get fresh shots. She asked a judge for an order to keep Galella away, and it was granted.

been roughed up and that the guards were interfering with his right to earn a livelihood. He also claimed that his First Amendment rights were being violated. Mrs. Onassis responded with a $1.5 million suit, asking for an injunction to halt Galella.

A federal judge acknowledged that Galella could photograph whomever he wanted in public places and write stories about them, but that the First Amendment could not justify incessant pursuits that "went far beyond the reasonable bounds of news gathering." The judge said that harassment was impermissible, and he ordered Galella to stay 300 feet from the Onassis and Kennedy homes and the schools of the Kennedy children, 225 feet from the children in public places, and 150 feet from Mrs. Onassis.

Nine years later, Mrs. Onassis returned to court to object to Galella's over-zealous journalistic techniques. He was found in contempt of court for violating the 1973 order on 12 separate occasions. The Onassis-Galella issue was a further recognition that a **right to be left alone** exists among other constitutional rights, including the right of a free press.

journalism law

(STUDY PREVIEW) The Constitution gives journalists great liberty in covering trials, seeking access to information held by the government and even in withholding confidential information from the government.

court coverage

News media have great liberty under the First Amendment to cover events as they see fit. Such was the case with **Sam Sheppard,** a Cleveland osteopath who was convicted of murder in a media circus. Even when he was acquitted after 12 years in prison, it was too late for him. He was unable to reestablish his medical practice. He died, a ruined man, a few years later.

A free press does not come without cost, and some people, like Sheppard, end up paying dearly. It is from such cases, however, that we learn the implications of the First Amendment and how to sidestep some of the problems it creates. When the U.S. Supreme Court ordered a new trial for Sheppard in 1966, it declared that it is the responsibility of the courts to assure citizens a fair trial regardless of media irresponsibility. The justices were specific about what the judge presiding at Sheppard's trial could have done. Among options:

- Seat only jurors who had not formed prejudicial conclusions.

- Move the trial to another city not so contaminated by news coverage.

- Delay trial until publicity subsided.

- Put jurors under 24-hour supervision so they would not have access to newspapers and newscasts during the trial.

- Insist that reporters respect appropriate courtroom decorum.

- Order attorneys, litigants and witnesses not to talk with reporters.

- Issue gag orders against the media but only in "extraordinary circumstances."

right to be left alone
Principle underlying most privacy cases and law.

Sam Sheppard Case
Judges told they, not news media, responsible for fair trial.

In other cases, the U.S. Supreme Court has allowed actions against the media to preclude unfavorable, prejudicial coverage of hearings, but those involve unusual circumstances. In the main, the news media have First Amendment-guaranteed access to the courts and the freedom to cover court stories regardless of whether the courts are pleased with the coverage. The same applies to news coverage of government in general.

sunshine laws

Implicit in any democracy is that public policy is developed in open sessions where the people can follow their elected and appointed leaders as they discuss issues. Every state has an open meeting law that specifically declares that legislative units, including state boards and commissions, city councils, school boards and county governing bodies, be open to the public, including journalists. The idea is for public policy to be created and executed in the bright sunshine, not in the secrecy of back rooms.

Open meeting laws vary. Some insist that almost every session be open, while others are not nearly as strict with the state legislatures that created them as they are with city, county and school units and with state executive agencies. Some of these laws proclaim the virtues of openness but lack teeth to enforce openness. In contrast, some states specify heavy fines and jail terms for public officials who shut the doors. Here are provisions of strong open meeting laws:

- Legislative units are required to meet at regular times and places and to announce their agendas ahead of time.

- Citizens can insist on quick judicial review if a meeting is closed.

- Closed sessions are allowed for only a few reasons, which are specifically identified, such as discussion on sensitive personnel matters, collective bargaining strategy and deciding security arrangements.

- Any vote in a closed session must be announced immediately afterward.

- Decisions made at a closed meeting are nullified if the meeting is later declared to have been closed illegally.

- Penalties are specified for any official who illegally authorizes a closed meeting.

Besides open meeting laws, the federal and state governments have open record laws to assure public access to government documents. These laws are important to journalists in tracking policy decisions and actions that they could not cover personally. Journalists especially value documents because, unlike human sources, they do not change their stories.

The federal **Freedom of Information Act** was passed in 1966, specifying how people could request documents. Since 1974 federal agencies have been required to list all their documents to help people identify what documents they are seeking and help the agencies locate them quickly. Despite penalties for noncompliance, some agencies sometimes drag their feet and stretch the FOI Act's provisions in order to keep sensitive documents off-limits. Even so, the law was a landmark of legislative commitment to governmental openness that allowed only a few exceptions. Among those exceptions are:

- Documents classified to protect national security.

sunshine laws
Require government meetings, documents be open.
Freedom of Information Act
Requires many federal documents to be available to public.

- Trade secrets and internal corporate information obtained on a confidential basis by the government.

- Preliminary drafts of agency documents and working papers.

- Medical and personnel files for which confidentiality is necessary to protect individual privacy.

- Police files that, if disclosed, might jeopardize an investigation by tipping off guilty people or, worse, falsely incriminating innocent people.

confidential sources

One unresolved conflict between government and the news media involves confidential sources. There are important stories, although not many, that would never be written if reporters were required to divulge their sources. In 1969, at a time of racial unrest in the United States, **Earl Caldwell** of the New York *Times* spent 14 months cultivating sources within the Black Panthers organization and produced a series of insightful stories on black activism. A federal grand jury in San Francisco, where Caldwell was assigned, was investigating bombings and other violence blamed on the Black Panthers, and Caldwell's stories caught the jury's attention, especially quotations attributed to unnamed Black Panther leaders, such as "We advocate the direct overthrow of the government by ways of force and violence." The grand jury asked to see Caldwell's notebooks, tapes and anything else that could help its investigation. Caldwell defied the subpoena, saying his appearance before the grand jury would interfere with his relationship with his sources. Furthermore, he had promised these sources that he would not identify them. Journalists watching the showdown were mindful of the historical responsibility of the press as an independent watchdog on government. If Caldwell testified, he in effect would become part of the investigative arm of the government. Tension mounted when a federal judge supported the grand jury, noting that all citizens are required to cooperate with criminal investigations and that journalists are no different.

A federal appeals judge ruled, however, that "the public's First Amendment right to be informed would be jeopardized by requiring a journalist to submit to secret grand jury interrogation." The government, said the judge, could command a journalist to testify only if it demonstrated "a compelling need." Meanwhile, journalists were running the risk of going to jail for contempt of court for refusing to respond to government subpoenas for their testimony, notes and films. In 1972 the U.S. Supreme Court considered the issue and ruled that journalists "are not exempt from the normal duty of all citizens."

After that Supreme Court decision, several states adopted **shield laws,** which reorganized reporter-source confidentiality. A problem with shield laws is that they require government to define who is a journalist. This raises the specter of the government's deciding who is and who is

Defying a Subpoena.
New York *Times* reporter Earl Caldwell faced jail for defying court orders to reveal the sources of his 1970 articles about urban terrorism. Caldwell argued that he had obtained his information on a confidential basis and that he would not break the covenant he had made with his sources. Others argued that journalists, like all citizens, have an obligation to tell all they know to officials who are investigating criminal activity.

not a journalist, which smacks of authoritarian press control. As an example, the Ohio shield law protects "bona fide journalists," who are defined as people employed by or connected to newspapers, radio stations, television stations and news services. Not only is it disturbing when government defines who is a journalist in a free society, but such attempts are destined to fail. The Ohio definition, for example, fails to protect free-lance journalists and writers who do their work on their own in the hope that they might eventually sell it.

obscenity and pornography

(STUDY PREVIEW) Despite the First Amendment's guarantee of free expression, the U.S. government has tried numerous ways during this century to regulate obscenity and pornography.

import restrictions

A 1930 tariff law was used as an import restriction to intercept James Joyce's *Ulysses* at the docks because of four-letter words and explicit sexual references. The importer, **Random House,** went to court, and the judge ruled that the government was out of line. The judge, **John Woolsey,** acknowledged "unusual frankness" in *Ulysses*, but said he could not "detect anywhere the leer of the sensualist." The judge, who was not without humor, made a strong case for freedom in literary expression: "The words which are criticized as dirty are old Saxon words known to almost all men, and, I venture, to many women, and are such words as would be naturally and habitually used, I believe, by the types of folks whose life, physical and mental, Joyce is seeking to describe. In respect to the recurrent emergence of the theme of sex in the minds of the characters, it must always be remembered that his locale was Celtic and his season Spring."

Woolsey was upheld on appeal, and Ulysses, still critically acclaimed as a pioneer in stream-of-consciousness writing, remains in print today.

postal restrictions

Postal restrictions were used against a 1928 English novel, *Lady Chatterly's Lover,* by D. H. Lawrence. The book was sold in the United States in expurgated editions for years, but in 1959, **Grove Press** issued the complete version. Postal officials denied mailing privileges. Grove sued and won.

In some respects, the Grove case was *Ulysses* all over again. Grove argued that Lawrence, a major author, had produced a work of literary merit. Grove said the explicit, rugged love scenes between Lady Chatterly and Mellors the gamekeeper were essential in establishing their violent yet loving relationship, the heart of the story. The distinction between the *Ulysses* and *Lady Chatterly* cases was that one ruling was against the customs service and the other against the postmaster general.

Communications Decency Act. The federal government's latest foray into systematically regulating media content was the ill-conceived 1996 Communications Decency Act. Without hearings or formal debate, Congress created the act to keep smut away from children using the Internet. While hardly anyone defends giving kids indecent material, the law had two flaws—the difficulty of defining indecency, and

Earl Caldwell
Refused to reveal confidential news sources.

shield laws
Allow journalists to protect identification of confidential sources.

Random House
Fought against censorship of James Joyce's *Ulysses*.

John Woolsey
Judge who barred import law censorship of *Ulysses*.

Grove Press
Fought against censorship of D. H. Lawrence's *Lady Chatterly's Lover*.

the impossibility of denying questionable material to children without restricting freedom of speech for adults.

Definition. Through history, the courts have found it impossible to define indecency clearly. Before a Philadelphia federal appeals court that reviewed the Communications Decency Act, witnesses from the Justice Department testified that the law required them to prosecute certain AIDS information, museum exhibits, prize-winning plays and even the *Vanity Fair* magazine cover of actress Demi Moore nude and pregnant.

Access. When it reviewed the law in 1997, the U.S. Supreme Court noted that the Internet is the most democratic of the media, enabling almost anyone to become a town crier or pamphleteer. Enforcing the law would necessarily inhibit a free expression of the sort that has roots in the Revolution that resulted in the creation of the Republic and the First Amendment, the court said. The decision, 7-2, purged the law from the books.

How, then, are government bans of indecency on radio and television justified, but not on the Internet? Justice John Stevens, who wrote the majority Supreme Court opinion, said the Internet is hardly as "invasive." The odds of people encountering pornography on the Internet are slim unless they're seeking it, he said. Underpinning the Court's rejection of the Communications Decency Act was the fact that the Internet lends itself to free-for-all discussions and exchanges with everybody participating who wants to, whereas other media are dominated by carefully crafted messages aimed at people whose opportunity to participate in dialogue with the message producers is so indirect as to be virtually nil.

pornography versus obscenity

Since the *Ulysses* and *Lady Chatterly* cases, much more has happened to discourage federal censorship. The U.S. Supreme Court has ruled that pornography, material aimed at sexual arousal, cannot be stopped. Import and postal restrictions, however, still can be employed against obscene materials, which the Court has defined as going beyond pornography. Obscenity restrictions apply, said the Court, if the answer is yes to *all* of the following questions:

- Would a typical person applying local standards see the material as appealing mainly for its sexually arousing effect?

- Is the material devoid of serious literary, artistic, political or scientific value?

- Is sexual activity depicted offensively, in a way that violates state law that explicitly defines offensiveness?

censorship today

(STUDY PREVIEW) Local governments have tried numerous ways to restrict distribution of sexually explicit material. Local libraries and schools also sometimes act to ban materials, but these attempts at censorship are not restricted to obscenity and pornography. Anything to which a majority of a local board objects can be fair game.

local censorship

Municipalities and counties have tried heavy-handed restrictions against sexually explicit publications and video material, generally without lasting success. Outright bans fail if they are challenged in the courts, unless the material is legally obscene. The U.S. Supreme Court spoke on this issue after Mount Ephraim, New Jersey, revised zoning laws to ban all live entertainment from commercial areas. The Court said the rezoning was a blatant attempt to ban lawful activities, and the decision was widely interpreted to apply to porn shops and other businesses that are often targets of local censorship campaigns. A federal court applied the same reasoning when it threw out a Keego Harbor, Michigan, zoning ordinance that forbade an adult theater within 500 feet of a school, church or bar. In Keego Harbor, there was no site not within 500 feet of a school, church or bar.

Some local governments have been innovative in acting against sexually explicit materials. One successful approach has been through zoning laws to rid neighborhoods of porn shops by forcing them into so-called **war zones.** Owners of adult-oriented businesses generally have been pleased to go along. By complying, they face less heat from police and other official harassment. The courts have found that war zone ordinances are legitimate applications of the principle underlying zoning laws in general, which is to preserve and protect the character of neighborhoods. So just as local governments can create single-residence, apartment, retail and other zones, they also can create zones for adult bookstores and theaters.

An opposite zoning approach, to disperse these kinds of businesses instead of concentrating them, has also been upheld in court. In Detroit, an ordinance insists that a 1,000-foot space separate "problem businesses," which include porn shops, adults-only theaters, pool halls and cabarets. This is all right, say the courts, as long as it does not exclude such businesses entirely.

Unlike the publishers in the landmark *Ulysses* and *Lady Chatterly* cases, in recent years book publishers have not taken the initiative against local restrictions aimed at pornography distributors and porn shops. Litigation is expensive, and major publishing houses do not produce porn-shop merchandise. Magazine publishers, notably *Playboy* and *Penthouse*, have fought some battles, but the issue has become fragmented since the Supreme Court's insistence that local standards be a measure of acceptability. Because what is obscene to people in one town may not be to people in another, it is impossible for the producers of nationally distributed books and magazines to go after all the restrictive local actions.

library and school boards

Local libraries sometimes decide to keep certain books off the shelves, usually because of content that offends the sensitivities of a majority of the library board. This kind of censorship survives challenges only when legal obscenity is the issue, which is seldom. Also, the wide availability of banned books renders library bans merely symbolic.

Some school boards still attempt censorship, although there is little support in the courts unless the issue is legal obscenity, which is rare. Whatever latitude school boards once had was strictly limited in 1982 when the U.S. Supreme Court decided against the Island Trees, New York, school board after several members had gone

war zones
Neighborhoods where pornography permitted.

Smut Battler. Edwin Meese, former U.S. attorney general for President Reagan, was the namesake of a commission that examined pornography. The commission came up with the politically acceptable conclusion that pornography was a serious threat to society and that government should take a tough stance against it. The problem, however, was that the commission ignored scientific evidence on the issue, which is far from conclusive.

into the high school library and removed 60 books. Among them were *The Fixer* by Bernard Malamud and *Laughing Boy* by Oliver Lafarge, both of which had won Pulitzer Prizes. School board members argued that the 60 books were anti-American, anti-Semitic, anti-Christian, and "just plain filthy." The Court did not accept that. School boards, said the Court, "may not remove books from library shelves simply because they dislike the ideas in those books and seek their removal to prescribe what shall be orthodox in politics, nationalism, religion or other matters of opinion."

meese pornography commission

A presidential commission concluded in 1970 that pornography had hardly any ill effects and recommended the repeal of most obscenity laws. The commission's report did not sit well with President Richard Nixon, who denounced it. When Ronald Reagan became president, he told Attorney General **Edwin Meese** to appoint a new commission to reassess the effects of pornography, except this time the commission was set up to develop the kinds of conclusions that the White House could endorse.

The new commission was packed with prominent members of the antipornography movement. Notably absent were civil libertarians. The Meese commission staff ignored scientific research on pornographic effects. For testimony, the staff lined up antiporn witnesses with personal stories and anecdotes but no hard evidence that pornography causes crime and other antisocial behavior.

copyright

(STUDY PREVIEW) Mass media people are vulnerable to thievery. Because it is so easy for someone to copy someone else's creative work, copyright laws prohibit the unauthorized re-creation of intellectual property, including books, music, movies and other creative production.

how copyright works

Congress has had a copyright law on the books since 1790. The law protects authors and other creators of intellectual property from having someone profit by reproducing their works without permission. Permission is usually granted for a fee.

Almost all books have copyright protection the moment they are created in a tangible form. So do most movies, television programs, newspaper and magazine articles, songs and records, and advertisements. It used to be that a creative work needed to be registered with the Library of Congress for a $10 fee. Formal registration is no longer required, but many people still do it for the fullest legal protection against someone pirating their work.

The current copyright law protects a creative work for the lifetime of the author plus 50 years. After the 50 years, a work enters what is called the **public domain,** and anyone may reproduce it without permission.

The creator of an original work may sell the copyright, and many do. Authors, for example, typically give their copyright to a publisher in exchange for a percentage of income from the book's profits.

media
online

Copyright Law: The Norwegian reprography agency Kopinor offers a wide array of essays on international reprography issues. www.kopinor.no

music licensing

Song-writers have a complex system to make money from their copyrighted works through music licensing organizations every time their music is played. These organizations collect fees from broadcast stations and other places that play recorded music, even restaurants and bowling alleys. The licensing organizations pass the fees on to their members. The largest licensing organizations are known in the trade by their abbreviations, the **American Society of Composers, Authors and Performers,** known as ASCAP, and **Broadcast Music Inc.,** known in the field as BMI:

ASCAP. For a commercial radio station to play ASCAP-licensed music, there is a charge of 2 percent of the station's gross receipts. ASCAP tapes six-hour segments from selected radio stations to determine whose music is being played. From the analysis, a complex formula is derived to divvy the license income among song-writers, music publishers and other members of ASCAP who own the music.

BMI. The organization known as BMI, which licenses most country-western and soul music, checks radio station playlists every 12 to 14 months to create a formula for distributing license income.

American Society of Composers, Authors and Performers
Music licensing organization.
Broadcast Music Inc.
Music licensing organization.

chapter wrap-up

The American mass media enjoy great freedom under the First Amendment, which forbids the government from impinging on expression. Even so, the freedom has limits. When the First Amendment guarantee of a free press runs against the constitutional guarantee of a free trial, there is a conflict of values that must be resolved. This is also true when the mass media violate someone's right to be left alone, which, although not an explicit constitutional guarantee, has come to be recognized as a basic human right. An understanding of mass media law and regulation involves studying how the American judicial system, headed by the U.S. Supreme Court, has reconciled conflicting interests. In short, the First Amendment is not inviolate.

Major restrictions on the mass media involve prior restraint, censorship, commercial exploitation, invasion of privacy, libel, fair trials and obscenity. The courts have struggled to square these restrictions with the absolutist language of the First Amendment, finding a balance between the guarantee of free expression with other interests, such as national security, and other rights, such as personal privacy.

questions for review

1. Why is the First Amendment important to mass media in the United States?

2. In what situations may the government exercise prior restraint to silence someone?

3. Who can sue the mass media for libel?

4. Do the mass media face limits on intruding on an individual's privacy?

5. Do the mass media face limits in covering government meetings or the courts? Or digging into government documents?

6. How is obscenity different from pornography?

7. How did a U.S. Supreme Court decision pretty much end federal concern about pornography?

8. How does copyright law protect intellectual property from being stolen from its owners?

questions for critical thinking

1. How can any restriction on free expression by the mass media or by individuals be consistent with the absolutist language of the First Amendment?

2. Define censorship. In a strict sense, who is a censor?

3. What lessons about prior restraint are contained in *Near v. Minnesota* (1931) and *New York Times Co. v. United States* (1971)?

4. How could Judge Blythin, who presided at the 1954 murder trial of Cleveland osteopath Sam Sheppard, have headed off the news media orgy that led to an appeal to the U.S. Supreme Court and an acquittal?

5. How do authors and creators of other intellectual property copyright their works, and why do they do it?

6. What kinds of meetings by public agencies can be closed to the public and the news media under the terms of open meeting laws? Are the public and the press barred from seeking any government documents under the U.S. Freedom of Information Act and sunshine laws?

7. Discuss the role of book publishers in the struggle for free expression through the *Ulysses* and Grove Press cases. Why have book publishers moved out of the forefront of the free expression struggle on today's most pressing issue—municipal pornography bans?

8. What is the trend with local censorship by library boards and school boards?

for further learning

Ellen Alderman and Caroline Kennedy. *The Right to Privacy* (Knopf, 1995). This best-seller will bring you up to date on privacy law. Includes chapter on privacy and the press.

Fred W. Friendly. *Minnesota Rag: The Dramatic Story of the Landmark Supreme Court Case That Gave New Meaning to Freedom of the Press* (Random House, 1981). Friendly, a pioneer television journalist, colorfully traces the *Near v. Minnesota* prior-restraint case.

Michael Gartner. "Fair Comment," *American Heritage* (October–November 1982). Pages 28–31. Gartner, a newspaper and television executive, delights in digging up the details of the colorful Cherry Sisters case that decided that almost anything could be said by reviewers of public performances.

Clark R. Mollenhoff. "25 Years of *Times v. Sullivan*," *Quill* (March 1989). Pages 27–31. A veteran investigative reporter argues that journalists have abused the landmark *Sullivan* decision and have been irresponsibly hard on public figures.

Philip Nobile and Eric Nadler. *United States of America vs. Sex: How the Meese Commission Lied About Pornography* (Minotaur, 1986). Nobile and Nadler, editors of the *Penthouse* magazine spinoff *Forum*, discredit the 1986 attorney general's report on pornography, which called for stricter laws against adult material. They argue that the commission ignored and distorted scientific evidence on the effects of pornography.

Sanford J. Ungar. *The Papers & the Papers: An Account of the Legal and Political Battle Over the Pentagon Papers* (Dutton, 1975). Ungar, a news reporter, provides a comprehensive chronology of our era's major prior-restraint case.

Robert J. Wagman. *The First Amendment Book* (Pharos, 1991). This lively history of the First Amendment is endorsed by leading journalists as a primer on the subject.

for keeping up to date

Censorship News is published by the National Coalition Against Censorship.

Media Law Bulletin tracks developments in media law.

News Media and the Law is published by the Reporters' Committee for Freedom of the Press.

Media Law Reporter is an annual collection of major court cases.

Student Press Law Reports, from the Student Press Law Center, follows events in the high school and college press and broadcast media.

The *Wall Street Journal* has a daily law section that includes media cases.

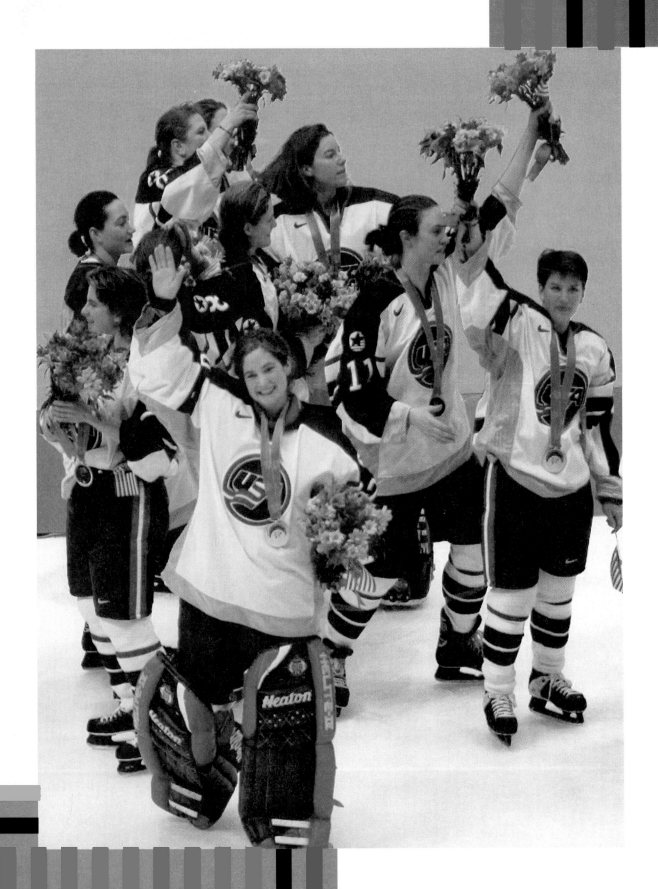

19

ethics and the mass media

in this chapter you will learn:

- Mass media ethics codes cannot anticipate all moral questions.

- Mass media people draw on numerous moral principles, some inconsistent with each other.

- Some mass media people prefer process-based ethics systems, while some prefer outcome-based systems.

- Potter's Box is a useful tool to sort through ethics issues.

- Some mass media people confuse ethics, law, prudence and accepted practices.

- Dubious mass media practices confound efforts to establish universal standards.

In Greek mythology, Nike, the winged goddess of victory, presided over athletic contests and military battles. During the 1998 Olympic Winter Games in Nagano, Japan, Nike was involved in another kind of skirmish— a heated controversy over media ethics. The dispute wasn't centered around Nike-the-goddess, but around Nike-the-athletic shoe company that was named after her.

It began with a deal. CBS had purchased the exclusive rights to televise the Winter Olympics for $375 million, and Nike signed on as one of the network's sponsors. As part of the contract, Nike provided CBS correspondents with free apparel displaying the company's trademark "swoosh." Nike's stated purpose was to "help build awareness" of its products, not only through the commercials to be aired, but through the on- and off-air presence of the CBS reporters at the Winter Games.

The reporters (like many of Nike's advertisements) wouldn't have to say a word; the familiar swoosh would say it all. Designed by a college student in 1971 and representing a wing of the goddess, the logo is as recognizable to sports fans as are the five Olympic rings. One commentator has dubbed it "the Esperanto of the day" in the athletic world and beyond.

Criticisms of the CBS-Nike agreement surfaced quickly. "Can you possibly imagine Edward R. Murrow or Walter Cronkite wearing the Nike swoosh while delivering the news?" wrote Bob Herbert of the New York *Times*. Arguing that a decision based on money had "turned its announcers into billboards," Josh Dubow, an Associated Press sports writer asked, "If the time comes at these games for CBS to do hard-news reporting on Nike, will the credibility of its announcers be tarnished?"

One of CBS's own reporters, Roberta Baskin, saw in the swooshes on the jackets an even more ominous sign—the implication that CBS would simply refuse to air any such hard-news story. She fired off a strong memo to CBS news executives saying that she now understood why her 1996 "48 Hours" report on labor conditions in Nike's Asian factories had not been re-broadcast and why she hadn't been permitted to do follow-up reports. CBS News president Andrew Heyward and other executives forcefully denied any such Nike influence over news content and were disturbed by Baskin's suggestion that such an eventuality might occur.

Nevertheless, the backlash over the on-air wearing of the logos was effective in getting the practice stopped. Some of the correspondents themselves had been uneasy about wearing the swooshes and had either not worn the jackets or had tried to make sure the swooshes weren't seen. Although the sports division of CBS was said to have approved or even required the wearing of the logos, the news division was unaware of the practice and, under the barrage of criticism, directed that there be no more swooshes during live broadcasts. The reporters' previously taped spots were permitted to be shown.

Part of the onslaught of criticism came from the U.S. Olympic Committee, which considers the wearing of corporate logos by broadcasters "a bad idea." The Committee has stated that it does not want NBC's correspondents to wear corporate symbols during the Summer Olympics in the year 2000 when that network broadcasts the Sydney games.

CBS's problem was compounded by the fact that although Nike was a sponsor of the television broadcasts, it was neither an official Worldwide Partner nor a Gold Sponsor of the Olympics themselves and had none of the rights such official sponsorships convey—such as permission to use the Olympic symbols in advertising and promotional activities. The rules are strictly followed, as an incident at a news conference illustrates. Because Nike was not an official sponsor of the Nagano Games, officials asked Prince Albert of Monaco to remove his swoosh-decorated jacket and sweatshirt before he could be interviewed on camera about his participation in a bobsled team. He was also asked to roll down his turtleneck so that the Nike logo wouldn't show.

During the 1996 Summer Olympics in Atlanta, Nike's promotional tactics had also drawn sharp criticism. Australian journalist Michael Stutchbury wrote, "The world's leading sports shoemaker, Nike, has found a simple way to market its link to the world's biggest sporting event without coughing up the . . . Olympic sponsorship fees forked out [by other global corporations]." Stutchbury said that "instead of sponsorship rights, Nike buys the world's top athletes to wear its shoes and sing its praises." In Atlanta, as in Nagano, the swoosh logo had been ubiquitous. Various critics called the company's high visibility "ambush marketing" and "parasitic."

Thus, the voices raised against the display of the logo by CBS on-air correspondents echoed earlier negative responses to Nike's aggressive promotional efforts, and CBS was caught up in the criticism. But perhaps more than anything else, the discussion centered around ethics. Steve Geimann, chair of the ethics committee of the Society for Professional Journalists expressed disagreement with the idea that sports coverage differs from other news. He and a number of other journalists wrote an open letter to CBS accusing the network of crossing "the line between professional journalism and commercial endorsements."

The ethical codes of various professional associations have warned of the danger of blurring the lines between advertisements and the news. In its pre-television days, the organization now called the Radio-Television News Directors Association urged its members to have commercials read by a voice other than that of the newscaster to clearly mark the boundaries between advertisements and news content. Its present code also instructs its members to "strive to conduct themselves in a manner that protects them from conflicts of interest, real or perceived." They are to "decline gifts or favors which could influence or appear to influence their judgments." A similar and even more comprehensive statement is found in the Society of Professional Journalists' Code of Ethics.

The media are constantly faced with ethical questions and decisions of many kinds. How its representatives struggle with the complexities of such decision-making is the focus of this chapter.

the difficulty of ethics

....• (STUDY PREVIEW) Mass media organizations have put together codes of ethics that prescribe how practitioners should go about their work. While useful in many ways, these codes neither sort through the bedeviling problems that result from conflicting prescriptions nor help much when the only open options are negative.

prescriptive ethics codes

The mass media abound with **codes of ethics.** The earliest was adopted in 1923, the **Canons of Journalism of the American Society of Newspaper Editors.** Advertising, broadcast and public relations practitioners also have codes. Many newcomers to the mass media make an erroneous assumption that the answers to all the moral choices in their work exist in the **prescriptions** of these codes. While the codes can be helpful, ethics is not so easy.

The difficulty of ethics becomes clear when a mass communicator is confronted with a conflict between moral responsibilities to different concepts. Consider:

Respect for Privacy. The code of the Society of Professional Journalists prescribes that reporters will show respect for the dignity, **privacy,** rights and well-being of people "at all times." The SPJ prescription sounds excellent, but moral priorities such as dignity and privacy sometimes seem less important than other priorities. The public interest, for example, also overrode privacy in 1988 when the Miami *Herald* staked out presidential candidate Gary Hart overnight when he had a woman friend in his Washington townhouse.

Commitment to Timeliness. The code of the Radio-Television News Directors Association prescribes that reporters be "**timely** and accurate." In practice, however, the virtue of accuracy is jeopardized when reporters rush to the air with stories. It takes time to confirm details and be accurate—and that delays stories.

Being Fair. The code of the Public Relations Society of America prescribes dealing fairly with both clients and the general public. However, a persuasive message prepared on behalf of a client is not always the same message that would be prepared on behalf of the general public. Persuasive communication is not necessarily dishonest, but how information is marshaled to create the message depends on whom the PR person is serving.

codes of ethics
Statement that defines acceptable, unacceptable behavior.

ASNE Ethics Code
First media code, 1923.

prescriptive ethics
Follow the rules and your decision will be the correct one.

privacy
Respect for privacy common in ethics codes.

timeliness
A virtue in most news ethics codes.

fairness
A virtue in most media ethics codes.

media people

arthur ashe

Private Issue? Tennis hero Arthur Ashe objected that news media inquiries about his AIDS violated his privacy.

Tennis champion Arthur Ashe was glad but then leery to hear his old high school chum Doug Smith on the phone. Smith, tennis reporter for *USA Today,* wanted to see him for an interview. It was not unusual for reporters to call on Ashe. He was the first world-class American black male tennis player, and after his athletic prime he had campaigned vigorously against apartheid. But by 1992, he worried with every interview that the question of whether he had AIDS would surface.

Ashe, in fact, had AIDS. He had contracted the virus apparently in 1983 during surgery. Five years later when doctors found the infection, Ashe began therapy for the debilitating and inevitably fatal disease. He decided against going public that he had the disease, and his family and friends went along with what Ashe called "a silent and generous conspiracy to assist me in maintaining my privacy."

When Doug Smith showed up for the interview, he asked the dreaded question: "Do you have AIDS?" Although Ashe re-

alized that some reporter some day would ask the question, it nonetheless caught him off guard. "Could be," he quipped. Then he recognized how much more revealing his words were than he intended. The secret was out.

The next afternoon, before Smith's article could appear, Ashe called a news conference to announce that he suffered from AIDS. Although he was gentle on *USA Today,* Ashe criticized the mass media for intruding into the private lives of people. In the news conference, carried live by CNN, Ashe said: "I am sorry that I have been forced to make this revelation at this time. After all, I am not running for some office of public trust, nor do I have stockholders to account to. It is only that I fall in the dubious umbrella of, quote, public figure, end of quote."

Ironically, *USA Today* had decided against going with the story, but Ashe's news conference nonetheless epitomized one of the great media ethics questions of our time: Who prevails when the mass media are at the intersection of the public's interest

in knowing certain information and an individual's interest in preserving personal privacy? Like all vexsome ethics questions, people on both sides feel strongly and mount powerful arguments for their positions. Journalists themselves are hardly of one mind.

Among those supporting *USA Today*'s initiative was Gerry Callahan of the Boston *Herald.* Callahan said the violation of Ashe's privacy was committed by whoever in his circle of friends tipped the newspaper anonymously. The newspaper, he said, merely was performing its function to check out tips.

Not everyone saw it that way. *USA Today* received almost 1,100 calls, with 60 people canceling their subscriptions. Among journalists, there were negative reactions too: Mona Charen, a syndicated columnist, wrote that the fact that Ashe was a great athlete who established a milestone for blacks was "no reason to treat his personal struggle as a peep show."

Much of the criticism of *USA Today*'s initiative centered on "cheap

scoops." Jeff Cohen, who heads the FAIR media watchdog group, said: "In recent years, mass media have been sliding down the slippery slope in pursuit of private lives of celebrities. These stories sell newspapers and pump up TV ratings, but they do little for public discourse."

Paul McMasters, executive director of the Freedom Forum, cast the incident as a no-win situation all around, as is the case with many ethics issues. Said McMasters: "The fact that Arthur Ashe is stricken with AIDS is a tragedy. The fact that he lost a measure of his privacy is a tragedy."

conflict in duties

Media ethics codes are well-intended, usually helpful guides, but they are simplistic when it comes to knotty moral questions. When media ethicians Clifford Christians, Mark Fackler and Kim Rotzoll compiled a list of five duties of mass media practitioners, some of these inherent problems became obvious.

Duty to Self. Self-preservation is a basic human instinct, but is a photojournalist shirking a duty to subscribers by avoiding a dangerous combat zone?

Self-aggrandizement can be an issue too. Many college newspaper editors are invited, all expenses paid, to Hollywood movie premieres. The duty-to-self principle favors going: The trip would be fun. In addition, it is a good story opportunity, and, as a free favor, it would not cost the newspaper anything. However, what of an editor's responsibility to readers? Readers have a right to expect writers to provide honest accounts that are not colored by favoritism. Can a reporter write straight after being wined and dined and flown across the continent by movie producers who want a gung-ho story? Even if reporters rise above being affected and are true to conscience, there are the duty-to-employer and the duty-to-profession principles to consider. The newspaper and the profession itself can be tarnished by suspicions, no matter whether they are unfounded, that a reporter has been bought off.

Duty to Audience. Television programs that reenact violence are popular with audiences, but are they a disservice because they frighten many viewers into also inferring that the streets are more dangerous than they really are?

Tom Wicker of the New York *Times* tells a story about his early days as a reporter in Aberdeen, North Carolina. He was covering a divorce case involving one spouse chasing the other with an ax. Nobody was hurt physically, and everyone who heard the story in the courtroom, except the divorcing couple, had a good laugh. "It was human comedy at its most ribald, and the courtroom rocked with laughter," Wicker recalled years later. In writing his story, Wicker captured the darkly comedic details so skillfully that his editor put the story on Page One. Wicker was proud of the piece until the next day when the woman in the case called on him. Worn out, haggard, hurt and angry, she asked, "Mr. Wicker, why did you think you had a right to make fun of me in your paper?"

The lesson stayed with Wicker for the rest of his career. He had unthinkingly hurt a fellow human being for no better reason than evoking a chuckle, or perhaps a belly laugh, from his readers. To Wicker, the duty-to-audience principle never again would transcend his moral duty to the dignity of the subjects of his stories. Similar ethics questions involve whether to cite AIDS as a contributor to death in an obituary, to identify victims in rape stories, and to name juveniles charged with crimes.

Duty to Employer. Does loyalty to an employer transcend the ideal of pursuing and telling the truth when a news reporter discovers dubious business deals involving the parent corporation? This is a growing issue as the mass media become consolidated into fewer gigantic companies owned by conglomerates. In 1989, for example, investigative reporter Peter Karl of Chicago television station WMAQ broke a story that General Electric had manufactured jet engines with untested and sometimes defective bolts. Although WMAQ is owned by NBC which in turn is owned by General Electric, Karl's exclusive, documented and accurate story aired. However,

Public People, Private Moments. Photographers who waited in the bushes to snap pictures of Bill and Hilary Clinton on the beach were putting their duty to their audience ahead of other duties. Such is the heart of ethics: Finding your way when duties are in conflict. The President contended the photos, during a Caribbean vacation, were an invasion of privacy.

media
online

Journalism Ethics: How can journalists practice ethics at a high level. This site, drawn from the book *Doing Ethics in Journalism,* has checklists to help. chestnut.enmu.edu/ ~lozanom/check.htm

Paparazzi. An ethics dilemma stems from the conflict that photojournalists face between their duty to serve their audience's interests and their duty to respect the rights of people they photograph. Before she died in a car wreck while being pursued by photographers, Diana, princess of Wales, complained that media people go too far when pursuing a story becomes hounding a person.

when the story was passed on to the network itself, Marty Ryan, executive producer of the "Today" show, ordered that the references to General Electric be edited out.

Duty to the Profession. At what point does an ethically motivated advertising-agency person blow the whistle on misleading claims by other advertising people?

Duty to Society. Does duty to society ever transcend duty to self? To audience? To employer? To colleagues? Does ideology affect a media worker's sense of duty to society? Consider how Joseph Stalin, Adolf Hitler and Franklin Roosevelt would be covered by highly motivated communist, fascist and libertarian journalists.

Are there occasions when the duty-to-society and the duty-to-audience principles are incompatible? Nobody enjoys seeing the horrors of war, for example, but journalists may feel that their duty to society demands that they go after the most grisly photographs of combat to show how horrible war is and, thereby, in a small way, contribute to public pressure toward a cessation of hostilities and eventual peace.

moral principles

STUDY PREVIEW Concern about doing the right thing is part of human nature, and leading thinkers have developed a great number of enduring moral principles over the centuries. The mass media, like other institutions and also like individuals, draw on these principles, but this does not always make moral decisions easy. The principles are not entirely consistent, especially in sorting through dilemmas.

the golden mean

The Greek philosopher **Aristotle,** writing almost 2,400 years ago, devised the **golden mean** as a basis for moral decision making. The golden mean sounds simple and straightforward: Avoid extremes and seek moderation. Modern journalistic balance and fairness are founded on this principle.

The golden mean's dictate, however, is not as simple as it sounds. As with all moral principles, application of the golden mean can present difficulties. Consider the federal law that requires over-the-air broadcasters to give "equal opportunity" to candidates for public office. If one candidate buys 30 seconds at 7 p.m. for $120, a station is obligated to allow other candidates for the same office to buy 30 seconds at the same time for the same rate. On the surface, this application of the golden mean, embodied in federal law, might seem to be reasonable, fair and morally right, but the issue is far more complex. The equality requirement, for example, gives an advantage to candidates who hold simplistic positions that can be expressed compactly. Good and able candidates whose positions require more time to explain are disadvantaged, and the society is damaged when inferior candidates win public office.

While minute-for-minute equality in broadcasting can be a flawed application of the golden mean, Aristotle's principle is valuable to media people when making moral decisions, as long as they do not abdicate their power of reason to embrace formulaic tit-for-tat measurable equality. It takes the human mind, not a formula, to determine

Golden Mean. The Greek thinker Aristotle told his students almost 2,400 years ago that right courses of action avoid extremes. His recommendation: moderation.

| media | timeline |

....development of media ethics

400 B.C. Aristotle laid out golden mean.

20s Jesus Christ articulated "Do unto others as you would have them do unto you."

1785 Immanuel Kant advanced categorical imperative.

1865 John Stuart Mill proposed utilitarianism.

1903 John Dewey advanced pragmatism.

1919 Upton Sinclair exposed newsroom abuses in novel *The Brass Check*.

1923 American Society of Newspaper Editors adopted media ethics code.

1947 Hutchins Commission urged media to be socially responsible.

1971 John Rawls advanced veil of ignorance.

fairness. And therein lies the complexity of the golden mean. No two human beings think exactly alike, which means that applying the golden mean involves individuals making judgment calls that are not necessarily the same. This element of judgment in moral decisions can make ethics intellectually exciting. It takes a sharp mind to sort through issues of balance and fairness.

do unto others

The Judeo-Christian principle of "**Do unto others** as you would have them do unto you" appeals to most Americans. Not even the do-unto-others prescription, however, is without problems. Consider the photojournalist who sees virtue in serving a mass audience with a truthful account of the human condition. This might manifest itself in portrayals of great emotions, like grief. But would the photojournalist appreciate being photographed herself in a grieving moment after learning that her own infant son had died in an accident? If not, her pursuit of truth through photography for a mass audience would be contrary to the "do-unto-others" dictum.

categorical imperatives

About 200 years ago, German philosopher **Immanuel Kant** wrote that moral decisions should flow from thoroughly considered principles. As he put it, "Act on the maxim that you would want to become universal law." He called his maxim the categorical imperative. A **categorical imperative,** well thought out, is a principle that the individual who devised it would be willing to apply in all moral questions of a similar sort.

Kant's categorical imperative does not dictate specifically what actions are morally right or wrong. Moral choices, says Kant, go deeper than the context of the immediate issue. He encourages a philosophical approach to moral questions, with people using their intellect to identify principles that they, as individuals, would find acceptable if applied universally.

Aristotle
Advocate of golden mean.

golden mean
Moderation is best course.

"Do unto others"
Judeo-Christian principle for ethical behavior.

Immanuel Kant
Advocated categorical imperative.

categorical imperative
Follow principles as if they had universal application.

Universal Law. Immanuel Kant, an 18th-century German philosopher, urged people to find principles that they would be comfortable having applied in all situations. He called these principles categorical imperatives.

Kant does not encourage the kind of standardized approach to ethics represented by professional codes. His emphasis, rather, is on hard thinking. Says philosopher Patricia Smith, of the University of Kentucky, writing in the *Journal of Mass Media Ethics*: "A philosophical approach to ethics embodies a commitment to consistency, clarity, the principled evaluation of arguments and unrelenting persistence to get to the bottom of things."

utilitarian ethics

In the mid-1800s, British thinker **John Stuart Mill** declared that morally right decisions are those that result in "happiness for the greatest number." Mill called his idea the principle of utility. It sounds good to many of us because it parallels the democratic principle of majority rule, with its emphasis on the greatest good for the greatest number of people.

By and large, journalists embrace Mill's utilitarianism today, as evinced in notions like the *people's right to know,* a concept originally meant to support journalistic pursuit of information about government, putting the public's interests ahead of government's interests, but which has come to be almost reflexively invoked to defend pursuing very personal information about individuals, no matter what the human toll.

pragmatic ethics

John Dewey, an American thinker who wrote in the late 1800s and early 1900s, argued that the virtue of moral decisions had to be judged by their results. Dewey's **pragmatic ethics,** like other ethics systems, has problems. One is that people do not have perfect crystal balls to tell them for sure whether their moral actions will have good consequences.

egalitarian ethics

In this century, philosopher **John Rawls** introduced the **veil of ignorance** as an element in ethics decisions. Choosing a right course of action, said Rawls, requires blindness to social position or other discriminating factors. An ethical decision requires that all people be given an equal hearing and the same fair consideration.

To Rawls, a brutal slaying in an upscale suburb deserves the same journalistic attention as a slaying in a poor urban neighborhood. All other things being equal, a $20,000 bank burglary is no more newsworthy than a $20,000 embezzlement.

Utilitarianism. American journalists tend to like 19th-century British thinker John Stuart Mill's utilitarianism, which favors actions that result in the greatest good for the greatest number of people. This approach to ethics dovetails well with majority rule and modern democracy.

social responsibility ethics

The **Hutchins Commission,** a learned group that studied the American mass media in the 1940s, recommended that journalists and other media people make decisions that serve the society responsibly. For all its virtues, the **social responsibility** system, like all ethics systems, has difficulties. For one thing, decision makers can only imperfectly foresee the effects of their decisions. It is not possible to predict with 100 percent confidence whether every decision will turn out to be socially responsible. Also, well-meaning people may differ honestly about how society is most responsibly served.

process versus outcome

(STUDY PREVIEW) The various approaches to ethics fall into two broad categories: deontological ethics and teleological ethics. Deontologists say people need to follow good rules. Teleologists judge morality not by the rules but by the consequences of decisions.

deontological ethics

The Greek word *deon,* which means "duty," is the heart of **deontological** ethics, which holds that people act morally when they follow good rules. Deontologists feel that people are duty bound to identify these rules.

Deontologists include people who believe that Scripture holds all the answers for right living. Their equivalent among media practitioners are those who rely entirely on codes of ethics drafted by organizations they trust. Following rules is a prescriptive form of ethics. At first consideration, ethics might seem as easy as following the rules, but not all questions are clear-cut. In complicated situations, the rules sometimes contradict each other. Some cases are dilemmas with no right option—only a choice among less-than-desirable options.

Deontological ethics becomes complicated, and also more intellectually interesting, when individuals, unsatisfied with other people's rules, try to work out their own universally applicable moral principles.

Here are some major deontological approaches:

- **Theory of divine command.** This theory holds that proper moral decisions come from obeying the commands of God, with blind trust that the consequences will be good.

- **Theory of divine right of kings.** This theory sees virtue in allegiance to a divinely anointed monarch.

- **Theory of secular command.** This theory is a nonreligious variation that stresses allegiance to a dictator or other political leader from whom the people take cues when making moral decisions.

- **Libertarian theory.** This theory stresses a laissez-faire approach to ethics: Give free rein to the human ability to think through problems, and people almost always will make morally right decisions.

- **Categorical imperative theory.** This theory holds that virtue results when people identify and apply universal principles.

teleological ethics

Unlike deontological ethics, which is concerned with the right actions, teleological ethics is concerned with the consequences of actions. The word **teleological** comes from the Greek word *teleos,* which means "result" or "consequence."

Teleologists see flaws in the formal, legalistic duty to rules of deontologists, noting that great harm sometimes flows from blind allegiance to rules.

Here are some major teleological approaches:

utilitarianism
Best course bestows the most good for the most people; also known as the principle of utility.

John Stuart Mill
Advocated utilitarianism.

John Dewey
Advocate of pragmatism.

pragmatism
Judge acts by their results.

egalitarianism
Treat everyone the same.

John Rawls
Advocated egalitarianism.

veil of ignorance
Making decisions with blind eye to extraneous factors that could affect decision.

Hutchins Commission
Advocated social responsibility as goal and result of media activities.

social responsibility
Making decisions that serve society responsibly.

deontology
Good actions flow from good processes.

divine command theory
Proper decisions follow God's will.

divine right of kings theory
Proper decisions follow monarch's will.

secular command theory
Good decisions follow ruler's will.

libertarian theory
Given good information and time, people ultimately make right decisions.

teleology
Good decisions are those with good consequences.

- **Pragmatic theory.** This theory encourages people to look at human experience to determine the probable consequences of an action and then decide its desirability.

- **Utilitarian theory.** This theory favors ethics actions that benefit more people than they damage—the greatest good for the greatest number.

- **Social-responsibility theory.** This theory judges actions by the good effect they have on society.

situational ethics

Firm deontologists see two primary flaws in teleological ethics:

- Imperfect foresight.
- Lack of guiding principles.

Despite these flaws, many media practitioners apply teleological approaches, sometimes labeled **situational ethics,** to arrive at moral decisions. They gather as much information as they can about a situation and then decide, not on the basis of principle but on the facts of the situation. Critics of situational ethics worry about decisions governed by situations. Much better, they argue, would be decisions flowing from principles of enduring value. With situational ethics, the same person might do one thing one day and on another day go another direction in a similar situation.

Consider a case at the *Rocky Mountain News* in Denver. Editors learned that the president of a major suburban newspaper chain had killed his parents and sister in another state when he was 18. After seven years in a mental hospital, the man completed college, moved to Colorado, lived a model life and became a successful newspaper executive. The *Rocky Mountain News* decided not to make a story of it. Said a *News* official: "The only reason for dredging up [his] past would be to titillate morbid curiosity or to shoot down, maliciously, a successful citizen."

However, when another newspaper revealed the man's past, the *Rocky Mountain News* reversed itself and published a lengthy piece of its own. Why? The newspaper that broke the story had suggested that *News* editors knew about the man's past and decided to protect him as a fellow member of the journalistic fraternity. *News* editors denied that their motivation was to protect the man. To prove it, they reversed their decision and published a story on him. The *News* explained its change of mind by saying that the situation had changed. *News* editors, concerned that their newspaper's credibility had been challenged, felt that printing a story would set that straight. Of less concern, suddenly, was that the story would titillate morbid curiosity or contribute to the destruction of a successful citizen. It was a classic case of situational ethics.

Flip-flops on moral issues, such as happened at the *Rocky Mountain News,* bother critics of situational ethics. The critics say decisions should be based on deeply rooted moral principles—not immediate, transient facts or changing peripheral contexts.

potter's box

situational ethics
Make ethics decisions on basis of situation at hand.

(STUDY PREVIEW)   Moral problems in the mass media can be so complex that it may seem there is no solution. While ideal answers without any negative results may be impossible, a process exists for identifying a course of action that integrates an individual's personal values with moral principles, and then tests conclusions against loyalties.

four quadrants

A Harvard Divinity School professor, **Ralph Potter,** has devised a four-quadrant model for sorting through ethics problems. The quadrants of the square-like model called **Potter's Box,** each pose a category of questions. Working through these categories helps clarify the issues and lead to a morally justifiable position. These are the quadrants of Potter's Box:

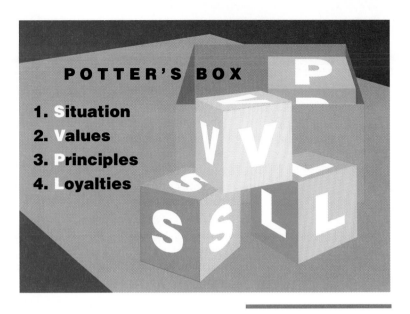

POTTER'S BOX

1. **S**ituation
2. **V**alues
3. **P**rinciples
4. **L**oyalties

Definition. In Quadrant 1, the facts of the issue are decided. Consider a newsroom in which a series of articles on rape is being developed, and the question arises whether to identify rape victims by name. Here is how the situation could be defined: The newspaper has access to a young mother who had been abducted and raped, and who is willing to describe the assault in graphic detail and to discuss her experience as a witness at the assailant's trial. Also, the woman is willing to be identified in the story.

Values. Moving to Quadrant 2 of Potter's Box, editors and reporters identify the values that underlie all the available choices. This process involves listing the positive and negative values that flow from conscience. One editor might argue: Full, frank discussion on social issues is necessary to deal with them. Another might say: Identifying the rape victim by name might discourage others from even reporting the crime. Other positions: Publishing the name is in poor taste. The newspaper has an obligation to protect the victim from her own bad decision to allow her name to be used. The purpose of the rape series can be accomplished without using the name. Readers have a right to all the relevant information that the newspaper can gather. An editor who is torn between such antiethical thoughts is making progress toward a decision by at least identifying all the values that can be posited.

Principles. In Potter's Quadrant 3, decision-makers search for moral principles that uphold the values they identified in Quadrant 2. John Stuart Mill's principle of utility, which favors the majority over individuals, would support using the victim's name because it could add poignancy to the story, enhancing the chances of improved public sensitivity and perhaps even lead to improved public policy, all of which, Mill would say, outweighs the harm that might come to an individual. On the other hand, people who have used Immanuel Kant's ideas to develop inviolable operating principles—categorical imperatives—look to their rule book: We never publish information that might offend readers. One value of Potter's Quadrant 3 is that it gives people confidence in the values that emerged in their debates over Quadrant 2.

Loyalties. In Quadrant 4, the decision-maker folds in an additional layer of complexity that must be sorted through: loyalties. The challenge is to establish a hierarchy of loyalties. Is the first loyalty to a code of ethics, and if so, to which code? To readers, and if so, to which ones? To society? To employer? To self? Out of duty to

Clarifying Process. Potter's Box offers four categories of questions to help develop morally justifiable positions. Ralph Potter, the divinity professor who devised the categories, said to start by establishing the facts of the situation. Then identify the values that underpin the options, recognizing that some values may be incompatible with others. Then consider the moral principles that support each of the values. Finally, sort through loyalties to all the affected interests. Potter's Box is not panacea, but it gives people the assurance that they have worked through ethics issues in a thorough way.

Ralph Potter
Ethicist who devised Potter's Box.
Potter's Box
Tool for sorting through pros and cons of ethics question.

self, some reporters and editors might want to make the rape series as potent as possible, with as much detail as possible, to win awards and bring honor to themselves and perhaps a raise or promotion or bigger job with another newspaper. Others might be motivated by their duty to their employer: The more detail in the story, the more newspapers it will sell. For others, their duty to society may be paramount: The newspaper has a social obligation to present issues in as powerful a way as possible to spur reforms in general attitudes and perhaps public policy.

limitations of potter's box

Potter's Box does not provide answers. Rather, it offers a process through which the key elements in ethics questions can be sorted out.

Also, Potter's Box focuses on moral aspects of a problem, leaving it to the decision-maker to examine practical considerations separately, such as whether prudence supports making the morally best decision. Moral decisions should not be made in a vacuum. For example, would it be wise to go ahead with the rape victim's name if 90 percent of the newspaper's subscribers would become so offended that they would quit buying the paper and, as a result, the paper would go out of business?

Other practical questions can involve the law. If the morally best decision is to publish the name but the law forbids it, should the newspaper proceed anyway? Does journalistic virtue transcend the law? Is it worth it to publish the name to create a First Amendment issue? Are there legal implications, like going to jail or piling up legal defense costs?

Is it worth it to go against accepted practices and publish the victim's name? Deciding on a course of action that runs contrary to tradition, perhaps even contrary to some ethics codes, could mean being ostracized by other media people, whose decisions might have gone another way. Doing right can be lonely.

ethics and other issues

STUDY PREVIEW   Right and wrong are issues in both ethics and law, but they are different issues. Obedience to law, or even to professional codes of ethics, will not always lead to moral action. There are also times when practical issues can enter moral decisions.

differentiating ethics and law

Ethics is an individual matter that relates closely to conscience. Because conscience is unique to each individual, no two people have exactly the same moral framework. There are, however, issues about which there is consensus. No right-minded person condones murder, for example. When there is a universal feeling, ethics becomes codified in law, but laws do not address all moral questions. It is the issues of right and wrong that do not have a consensus that make ethics difficult. Was it morally right for *USA Today* to initiate coverage of Arthur Ashe's AIDS?

Ethics and law are related but separate. The law will allow a mass media practitioner to do many things that the practitioner would refuse to do. Since the 1964 *New*

York Times v. Sullivan case, the U.S. Supreme Court has allowed the news media to cause tremendous damage to public officials, even with false information. However, rare is the journalist who would intentionally push the *Sullivan* latitudes to their limits to pillory a public official.

The ethics decisions of an individual mass media practitioner usually are more limiting than the law. There are times, though, when a journalist may choose to break the law on the grounds of ethics. Applying John Stuart Mill's principle of "the greatest good," a radio reporter might choose to break the speed limit to reach a chemical plant where an accident is threatening to send a deadly cloud toward where her listeners live. Breaking a speed limit may seem petty, but it demonstrates that obeying the law and obeying one's conscience do not always coincide.

accepted practices

Just as there is not a reliable correlation between law and ethics, neither is there one between accepted media practices and ethics. What is acceptable at one advertising agency to make a product look good in photographs might be unacceptable at another. Even universally **accepted practices** should not go unexamined, for unless accepted practices are examined and reconsidered on a continuing basis, media practitioners can come to rely more on habit than on principles in their work.

prudence and ethics

Prudence is the application of wisdom in a practical situation. It can be a leveling factor in moral questions. Consider the case of Irvin Leiberman, who had built his *Main Line Chronicle* and several other weeklies in the Philadelphia suburbs into aggressive, journalistically excellent newspapers. After being hit with nine libel suits, all costly to defend, Leiberman abandoned the editorial thrust of his newspapers. "I decided not to do any investigative work," he said. "It was a matter of either feeding my family or spending my whole life in court." Out of prudence, Leiberman decided to abandon his commitment to hard-hitting, effective journalism.

Courageous pursuit of morally lofty ends can, as a practical matter, be foolish. Whether Irvin Leiberman was exhibiting a moral weakness by bending to the chilling factor of libel suits, which are costly to fight, or being prudent is an issue that could be debated forever. The point, however, is that prudence cannot be ignored as a factor in moral decisions.

unsettled, unsettling issues

•••• (STUDY PREVIEW) When mass media people discuss ethics, they talk about right and wrong behavior, but creating policies on ethics issues is not easy. Many standard media practices press the line between right and wrong, which muddies clear-cut standards that are universally applicable and recognized. There is further muddiness because many ethics codes confuse unethical behavior and behavior that may appear unethical but that is not necessarily so.

accepted practices
What media do as a matter of routine, sometimes without considering ethics implications.

prudence
Applying wisdom, not principles, to an ethics situation.

plagiarism

Perhaps the most fiercely loyal media fans are those who read romance novels and swear by a favorite author. In an Internet chat room in 1997, romance writer Janet Dailey found herself boxed into an admission that she had plagiarized from rival writer Nora Roberts. There is no scorn like that of creative people for those who steal their work, and Roberts was "very, very upset." HarperCollins recalled *Notorious*, Dailey's book that contained the plagiarism, and Roberts' fans, many of them long-time Dailey detractors, began a hunt for other purloined passages.

What is plagiarism? Generally it's considered passing off someone else's creative work as your own, without permission. It's still plagiarism if it's changed a bit, as was Dailey's loose paraphrasing.

The fact that Dailey's 93 books over 20 years had sold an average of more than 2 million each made the scandal all the juicier. In the end, Roberts proposed a financial settlement, and the proceeds went to promote literacy.

Everyone agrees plagiarism, a form of thievery, is unethical, but the issue is not simple. The fact is that in many media people draw heavily on other people's ideas and work. Think about sitcom story lines that mimic each other, or the bandwagon of movies that follow an unexpected hit with an oddball theme that suddenly becomes mainstream. Journalists, most of whom consider themselves especially pristine compared to their media brethren, have standard practices that encourage a lot of "borrowing."

Among factors that make journalists uncomfortable when pressed hard on plagiary questions are:

- Institutionalized exchanging of stories.
- The role of public relations in generating news stories.
- Monitoring the competition.
- Subliminal memory and innocent recall.

Swapping Stories. Some creative work, like scholarship, requires that information and ideas be attributed to their sources. Journalists are not so strict, as shown

---

Romance Plagiarism.
Cynics think all romance novels are the same, but aficionados know the difference. It shook Janet Dailey fans in 1997 to learn that she had loosely paraphrased a passage from rival Nora Roberts. The publisher withdrew Dailey's book with the plagiarized passages, and the question was whether Dailey, whose 93 titles had sold more than 200 million copies, would ever recover from the tarnish. You decide how serious the transgression:

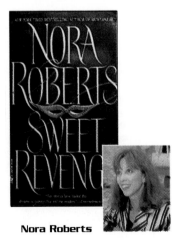

Nora Roberts

"Talk to me."
"It was just a dream as you said."
"You're hurting." He touched her cheek. This time she didn't jerk away, only closed her eyes. "You talk, I'll listen."
"I don't need anyone."
"I'm not going away until you talk to me."

—From *Sweet Revenge* (1989) by Nora Roberts

"Talk to me, Eden."
"It was only a dream, just as you said."
His fingers brushed her cheek. . . . She closed her eyes at the contact. "You need to talk about it. I'll listen."
"I don't need anyone," she insisted stiffly.
"I'm not leaving until you tell me about it."

—From *Notorious* (1996) by Janet Dailey

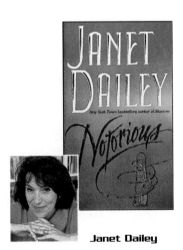

Janet Dailey

by story swapping through the Associated Press. The AP picks up stories from its members and distributes them to other members, generally without any reference to the source. Some AP publications and broadcasters do not even acknowledge AP as the intermediary.

Conditioned by 150 years of the AP's being a journalistic model and under pressure to gather information quickly, many journalists have a high tolerance for "borrowing." When the Chicago *Tribune* was apologizing for a story cribbed from the Jerusalem *Post,* for example, one of the writer's colleagues defended the story: "Everybody rewrites the Jerusalem *Post.* That's how foreign correspondents work."

Incredible as it seems, journalistic tolerance for plagiarism even allows radio stations to pirate the local newspaper for newscasts. Sometimes you can hear the announcer turning the pages. A sad joke that acknowledges this practice is that some stations buy their news at 50 cents a copy, which is cheaper than hiring reporters to cover the community. So pervasive is the journalistic tolerance for "borrowing" that few newspapers even mildly protest when their stories are pirated.

News Releases. In many newsrooms, the plagiarism question is clouded further by the practice of using news releases from public relations people word for word without citing the source. Even in newsrooms that rewrite releases to avoid the embarrassment of running a story that is exactly the same as the competition's, it is standard practice not to cite the source. Public relations people, who are paid for writing favorable stories on their clients, have no objections to being plagiarized, and news organizations find it an easy, inexpensive way to fill space. Despite the mutual convenience, the arrangement raises serious questions of ethics to which many in the media have not responded. The practice leaves the false impression that stories originating with news releases actually originated with the news organization. More serious is that the uncredited stories are a disservice to democracy. Marie Dunn White, in the *Journal of Mass Media Ethics,* wrote: "In order for the reader to evaluate the information he or she is receiving correctly and completely, he or she must know which information came from a press release and, therefore, may be biased."

Monitoring Competition. Competitive pressure also contributes to fuzziness on the plagiarism issue. To avoid being skunked on stories, reporters monitor each other closely to pick up tips and ideas. Generally, reporters are not particular about where they pick up information as long as they are confident that it is accurate. For background, reporters tap newsroom libraries, databases, journals, books and other sources, and, in the interest of not cluttering their stories, they do not use footnotes.

Subliminal Memory. Covering breaking events has its own pressure that puts journalists at special risk. Almost every journalist who writes under the pressure of a deadline has had the experience of writing a story and later discovering that phrases that came easily at the keyboard were actually somebody else's. In their voracious pursuit of information, reporters store phrases and perhaps whole passages subliminally in their memories. This happened to a drama critic at the St. Paul, Minnesota, *Pioneer Press,* who was horrified when a reader pointed out the similarity between his review of a play and an earlier review of the same play in the New York *Times.* Once aware of what he had done unwittingly, the critic offered his resignation. His editors instead moved him to the copy desk.

The muddiness on the issue of journalistic plagiarism is encapsulated in the fact that the Society of Professional Journalists' ethics code makes a flat statement that plagiarism is "dishonest and unacceptable," but then sidesteps the knotty part of the issue by declining to define *plagiarism.*

> **plagiarism**
> Using someone else's work without permission or credit.

misrepresentation

Janet Cooke's meteoric rise at the Washington *Post* unraveled quickly the day after she received a Pulitzer Prize. Her editors had been so impressed with her story, "Jimmy's World," about a child who was addicted to heroin, that they nominated it for a Pulitzer Prize. The gripping tale began: "Jimmy is 8 years old and a third-generation heroin addict, a precocious little boy with sandy hair, velvety brown eyes and needle marks freckling the baby-smooth skin of his thin brown arms." Janet Cooke claimed that she had won the confidence of Jimmy's mother and her live-in man friend, a drug dealer, to do the story. Cooke said she had promised not to reveal their identities as a condition for her access to Jimmy.

The story, played on the front page, so shocked Washington that people demanded that Jimmy be taken away from his mother and placed in a foster home. The *Post* declined to help authorities, citing Cooke's promise of confidentiality to her sources. The mayor ordered the police to find Jimmy with or without the newspaper's help, and millions of dollars in police resources went into a door-to-door search. After 17 days, the police gave up knocking on doors for tips on Jimmy. Some doubts emerged at the *Post* about the story, but the newspaper stood behind its reporter.

Janet Cooke, 25 when she was hired by the *Post*, had extraordinary credentials. Her résumé showed a baccalaureate degree, magna cum laude, from Vassar; study at the Sorbonne in Paris; a master's degree from the University of Toledo; abilities in several languages; and two years of journalistic experience with the Toledo *Blade*. Said Ben Bradlee, editor of the *Post*, "She had it all. She was bright. She was well-spoken. She was pretty. She wrote well." She was black, which made her especially attractive to the *Post*, which was working to bring the percentage of black staff reporters nearer to the percentage of blacks in its circulation area.

"Jimmy's World" was published in September 1980. Six months later, the Pulitzer committee announced its decision and issued a biographical sheet on Janet Cooke. The Associated Press, trying to flesh out the biographical information, spotted discrepancies right away. Janet Cooke, it turned out, had attended Vassar one year but had not been graduated with the honors she claimed. The University of Toledo had no record of awarding her a master's. Suddenly, doubts that had surfaced in the days immediately after "Jimmy's World" was published took on a new intensity. The editors sat Cooke down and grilled her on the claims on which she was hired. No, she admitted, she was not multilingual. The Sorbonne claim was fuzzy. More importantly, they grilled her on whether there was really a Jimmy. The interrogation continued into the night, and finally Janet Cooke confessed all: There were no confidential sources, and there was no Jimmy. She had fabricated the story. She resigned, and the *Post*, terribly embarrassed, returned the Pulitzer.

In cases of outright fabrication, as in "Jimmy's World," it is easy to identify the lapses in ethics. When Janet Cooke emerged briefly from seclusion to explain herself, she said that she was responding to pressures in the *Post* newsroom to produce flashy, sensational copy. Most people found the explanation unsatisfying, considering the pattern of deception that went back to her falsified résumé.

There are misrepresentations, however, that are not as clearly unacceptable. Much debated are:

Staging News. To attract favorable attention to their clients, public relations people organize media events. These are designed to be irresistible to journalists. Rallies and demonstrations on topical issues, for example, find their way onto front pages, magazine covers and evening newscasts because their photogenic qualities give

misrepresentation
Deception in gathering or telling information.

Janet Cooke
Classic case of representing fiction as true.

staging news
Creating an event to attract news media attention and coverage.

them an edge over less visual although sometimes more significant events. The ethics question is less important for publicists, who generally are up-front about what they are doing. The ethics question is more serious for journalists, who claim that their job is to present an accurate, balanced account of a day's events but who regularly over-play staged events that are designed by publicists to be photogenic and easy to cover.

Re-Creations. A wave of **reality programs** on television that began in the late 1980s featured reenactments that were not always labeled as such. Philip Weiss, writing in *Columbia Journalism Review,* offered this litany: shadows on the wall of a woman taking a hammer to her husband, a faceless actor grabbing a tin of kerosene to blow up his son, a corpse in a wheelbarrow with a hand dangling, a detective opening the trunk of a car and reeling from the smell of a decomposing body. While mixing re-creations with strictly news footage rankles many critics, others argue that it helps people under-stand the situation. The same question arises with docudramas, which mix actual events and dramatic re-creations.

Selective Editing. The editing process, by its nature, requires journalists to make decisions on what is most worth emphasizing and what is least worth even including. In this sense, all editing is selective, but the term **selective editing** refers to making decisions with the goal of distorting. Selective editing can occur in drama too, when writers, editors and other media people take literary license too far and intentionally misrepresent.

Fictional Methods. In the late 1960s, many experiments in media portrayals of people and issues came to be called the **new journalism.** The term was hard to define because it included so many approaches. Among the most controversial were applica-tions of fiction-writing methods on topical issues, an approach widely accepted in book publishing but suddenly controversial when it appeared in the news media. Character development became more important than before, including presumed insights into the thinking of people being covered. The view of the writer became an essential element in much of this reporting. The defense for these approaches was that traditional, facts-only reporting could not approach complex truths that merited journalistic explorations. The profound ethics questions that these approaches posed were usually mitigated by clear statements about what the writer was attempting. Nonetheless, it was a controver-sial approach to the issues of the day. There was no defense when the fictional approach was complete fabrication passing itself off as reality, as in "Jimmy's World."

gifts, junkets and meals

In his 1919 book *The Brass Check,* a pioneer examination of newsroom ethics, **Upton Sinclair** told how news people took bribes to put stories in the paper. Today, media ethics codes universally condemn gifts and certainly bribes, but there still are many people who curry favor with the mass media through gifts, such as a college sports information director who gives a fifth of whisky at Christmas to a sports writer as a gesture of goodwill. Favors can take many forms: media-appreciation luncheons, free trips abroad for the experience necessary to do a travel article, season passes to cover the opera, discounts at certain stores.

Despite the consistent exhortation of the ethics codes against gifts, favors, free travel and special treatment and privileges, there is nothing inherently wrong in tak-ing them if they do not influence coverage and if the journalist's benefactor under-stands that. The problem with favors is more a practical one than one of ethics. Taking a favor may or may not be bad, but it *looks* bad. Many ethics codes do not

re-creations
Re-creating real events.

reality programs
Broadcast shows with a non-fiction basis.

selective editing
Misrepresentation through omission and juxtaposition.

new journalism
Mixing fiction based in non-fiction.

junket
Trip with expenses paid by someone who may expect favors in return.

The Brass Check
1919 book that exposed newsroom corruption.

Upton Sinclair
Author of *The Brass Check*.

make this important distinction. One that does is the code of the Associated Press Managing Editors, which states: "Journalists must avoid impropriety and *the appearance of impropriety* as well as any conflict of interest or *the appearance of conflict.* They should neither accept anything nor pursue any activity that might compromise or *seem to compromise* their integrity." The APME admonitions at least recognize the distinction between the inherent wrongness of impropriety, which is an ethics question, and the perception that something may be wrong, which is an unwise perception to encourage but which is not necessarily unethical.

While ethics codes are uniform against **freebies,** as gifts and favors are called, many news organizations accept free movie, drama, concert and other tickets, as well as recordings, books and other materials for review. The justification usually is that their budgets allow them to review only materials that arrive free and that their audiences would be denied reviews if the materials had to be purchased. A counterargument is that a news organization that cannot afford to do business right should not be in business. Many news organizations, however, insist on buying tickets for their reporters to beauty pageants, sports events and other things to which there is an admission fee. A frequent exception occurs when a press box or special media facility is available. With recordings, books and free samples, some media organizations return them or pass them on to charity to avoid any appearance that they have been bought off.

When junkets are proposed, some organizations send reporters only if they can pay the fare and other expenses. The Louisville *Courier-Journal* is firm: "Even on chartered trips, such as accompanying a sports team, or hitchhiking on a State Police plane, we insist on being billed for our pro-rata share of the expense." An exception is made by some news organizations for trips that they could not possibly arrange on their own, such as covering a two-week naval exercise aboard a ship.

Some media organizations address the issue of impropriety by acknowledging favors. Many quiz shows say that "promotional consideration" has been provided to companies that give them travel, lodging and prizes. Just as forthright are publications that state that reviews are made possible through season passes or free samples. Acknowledging favors does not remove the questions but at least it is up-front.

chapter wrap-up

Mass media people need to be concerned about ethics because they can have powerful effects. But answers do not come easily. Personal information can embarrass a person inexcusably. However, it can be argued that privacy is less important, for example, with candidates for high office.

Philosophers have devised numerous systems to help individuals address moral issues. Influential is John Stuart Mill's utilitarianism, which favors choices that lead to the greatest good for the most people. Mill's reasoning was implicit when some media people defended their coverage of Gary Hart by saying that choosing a president of high moral character overrode the discomfort that intense coverage caused an individual. Other moral principles favor more respect for individual privacy.

Moral decision-making is rooted in conscience, which makes it highly individual. Attempts to bring order to moral issues in journalism and the mass media have included codes of ethics. These codes identify behaviors that are recognized as ethically troublesome, but because they are generalized statements, the codes cannot anticipate all situations. There is no substitute for human reason and common sense.

freebie
Gift for which the giver may expect favor in return

questions for review

1. Why cannot ethics codes anticipate all moral questions? And does this limit the value of codes for mass media people?

2. List and explain moral principles that mass media people can use to sort through ethics questions.

3. How can mass media people come to different conclusions depending on whether they use process-based or outcome-based ethics?

4. How is Potter's Box a useful tool to sort through ethics issues?

5. Is ethics the same as law? As prudence? As accepted practice?

6. Discuss dubious mass media practices that are inconsistent with many moral principles.

questions for critical thinking

1. The Manchester, New Hampshire, *Union Leader* has been criticized for giving more space to some candidates than to others in presidential primaries. Is this disparity necessarily a sign of unfair coverage? You may want to check the index for the *Union Leader* which is discussed in Chapter 17.

2. How are traditional libertarians deontological in their approach to ethics? How is the social responsibility approach teleological?

3. As someone who reads newspapers and watches newscasts, would you favor deontological or teleological ethics? Which is easier? Which system do you think most journalists prefer?

4. Can you identify the ethics principle or system most associated with Aristotle? Immanuel Kant? John Stuart Mill? John Dewey? John Rawls? Robert Maynard Hutchins?

5. How can codes of ethics help mass media people make the right decisions? Do codes always work? Why or why not?

6. A candidate for mayor tells a news reporter that the incumbent mayor is in cahoots with organized crime. What should the reporter do before going on the air with this bombshell accusation? Why?

7. Can media people ever defend breaking the law as ethical?

8. Is there a difference between ethics and accepted practices?

for further learning

Jay Black, Bob Steele and Ralph Barney. *Doing Ethics in Journalism: A Handbook with Case Studies,* revised edition (Allyn & Bacon, 1994).

Clifford G. Christians, Kim B. Rotzoll and Mark Fackler. *Media Ethics,* 4th ed. (Longman, 1995). These scholars are especially good at describing Kant's categorical imperative and other philosophical systems on which media ethics can be based.

Roy Peter Clark. "The Original Sin: How Plagiarism Poisons the Press," *Washington Journalism Review* (March 1983), 43–47.

Carl Hausman. *The Decision-Making Process in Journalism* (Nelson-Hall, 1990). Hausman, a journalism professor, provides a checklist to help sort the way through ethics problems.

Walter B. Jaehnig. "Harrison Cochran—The Publisher with a Past," *Journal of Mass Media Ethics* 2 (Fall/Winter 1986–87):1, 80–88. This is a case study examination of the Rocky Mountain News situational ethics case. Every issue of this journal contains a media ethics problem with commentary from professional and scholarly observers.

Janet Malcolm. *The Journalist and the Murderer* (Knopf, 1990). Malcolm argues that journalists exploit their sources of information, using the relationship of author Joe McGinniss and a convicted murderer for the book *Fatal Vision.*

John C. Merrill. *The Dialectic in Journalism: Toward a Responsible Use of Press Freedom* (Louisiana State University Press, 1990). Professor Merrill, who has written several books on journalism ethics, favors philosophical frameworks for solving ethics questions rather than codes of ethics.

Greg Retsinas. "Reporter's Ception Denounced," *Editor & Publisher* 128 (May 6, 1995):18, 16, 39.

Phillip Weiss. "Bad Rap for TV Tabs," *Columbia Journalism Review* 28 (May/June 1989):1, 39–42. Weiss deals with ethics questions raised by tabloid television programs, including dramatized re-creations.

Marie Dunn White. "Plagiarism and the News Media," *Journal of Mass Media Ethics* 4 (1989):2, 265–280. White examines the hazards when journalists read their competitors for story ideas and information.

for keeping up to date

Ethicists sort through moral dilemmas involving mass communication in the scholarly *Journal of Mass Media Ethics.*

Many trade and professional journals also deal with media ethics, including *Quill, Columbia Journalism Review* and *American Journalism Review.*

about the author

John Vivian is a professor of journalism at Winona State University in Minnesota, where he has taught mass media survey courses for 15 years. Earlier he taught at Marquette University, the University of North Dakota, New Mexico State University and the University of Wisconsin centers in Waukesha and West Bend. He holds an honorary faculty appointment at the U.S. Defense Information School.

He is a past president of the Text and Academic Authors Association, and has been active in the Society of Professional Journalists and College Media Advisers.

His professional media experience began with his hometown newspaper in Kellogg, Idaho, and continued through college at Gonzaga University with United Press International and the Associated Press. After a master's degree from Northwestern University's Medill School of Journalism, he returned to the AP in Seattle, Denver and Cheyenne. Besides Gonzaga and Northwestern, he has done advanced studies at Marquette University, the University of Minnesota and the University of North Dakota.

His work as an Army command information officer earned numerous Minaret, Fourth Estate and other awards. In college he was editor of the Gonzaga *Bulletin*. He was faculty adviser to the Marquette *Tribune*, and later founded the multi-college *Winona Campus Life* lab newspaper. He has edited numerous publications, including *The Academic Author*, and two online news sites: *Text and Academic Authors* (www.winonanet.com/taa) and the *CyberIndee* (www.winonanet.com/cyberindee).

Vivian introduced his widely used college textbook, *The Media of Mass Communication*, in 1991. Vivian and co-author Alfred Lawrence Lorenz, of Loyola University in New Orleans, wrote *News: Reporting and Writing*, a college journalism textbook, in 1995. Vivian's scholarly, professional and trade articles have appeared in numerous publications, including *American Journalism*, *American Speech*, *Journalism Educator*, *Journalism History*, *Journalism Quarterly*, *Masthead* and *Newspaper Research Journal*.

award for excellence

The Media of Mass Communication by John Vivian has been awarded the Text and Academic Authors award for excellence. Affectionately called "the Texty," the award has been characterized as the Oscar for textbooks. The award was in a broad range of academic disciplines that included college textbooks in communication, education and the performing and visual arts. The judges, all veteran textbook authors, evaluated books on four criteria: Is the book interesting and informative? Is the book well organized and presented? Is the book up to date and appealing? Does the book possess "teachability"? The judges gave *The Media of Mass Communication* perfect scores on all criteria. Said one judge: "By all measures, superior." John Vivian said he was especially pleased with the award because fellow textbook authors were the judges. "There is no more meaningful recognition than that which comes from peers," he said.

The Text and Academic Authors Association sponsors the Texty awards to promote excellence by identifying outstanding textbooks and other learning materials. TAA is the nation's leading organization for textbook authors. Its headquarters are at the University of South Florida–St. Petersburg.

The Media of Mass Communication was introduced in 1991 and quickly became the most-adopted textbook for introductory mass media and mass communication courses. The book's popularity has grown among college professors and their students with every new edition.

index

Page numbers followed by letter "b" refer to entries appearing in boxes.
Page numbers followed by letter "f" refer to entries appearing in photo captions.

AAAA (American Association of Advertising Agencies), 335
AAP (Association of American Publishers), 39b
ABC (American Broadcasting Company), 4, 17, 20b, 21b, 179-180, 206
ABC (Audit Bureau of Circulations), 323, 349
A.C. Nielson Co., 349
accepted practices, 501
account executives, 320
achievers, 359
acoustic recording, 117
acquisition binge, 333
ad clutter, 325
Ad Council, 336
Advanced Research Project Agency network (see ARPAnet)
advertisements, 7b, 14
advertiser pressure, 274
advertiser role, 323
advertising
  account executives, 320
  agencies, 320-321, 322b
  agency consolidation, 334
  agency structure, 321
  brand manager, 323
  brands, 326
  bunching, 328
  cloning, 339b
  clutter, 337
  commissions, 322
  conglomeration and regulation, 334
  consumer economies and, 317
  control of messages, 302
  creative director, 320-321
  creativity, 321
  democracy and, 318
  development of, 320
  effectiveness, 340
  flights, 328

  government regulation, 336
  importance of, 317, 326
  importance of brands, 326
  infomercials, 329
  institutional, 303
  integrated marketing, 303
  largest agencies, 322b
  liaison, 321
  magazines and, 62
  media buyers, 321
  motivational research, 331
  origins of, 319
  pass-along circulation, 324
  pitching messages, 326
  problems and issues, 337
  prosperity, 317
  radio, 172
  redundancy techniques, 328
  research, 321
  research and psychology, 330
  revenue, 14
  shelf life, 324
  spending, 318
  stepchild of technology, 319
  subception, 331
  subliminal, 331
  television, 212
  trailing, 328
  'zine, 329
advertorials, 307
The Advocate, 107
affiliate-network relations, 180, 201
after-markets, movie, 151
Agence France-Presse, 279, 334
agencies
  advertising, 320-321, 322b, 322, 323, 334
  public relations, and, 299-300
agenda-setting, 387, 402, 451
aggressive stimulation, 398
Ailes, Roger, 452, 453b
airplay, 127

Alderman, Ellen, 486
Alexander, Herbert, 459
Alien and Sedition acts, 259
alienation, 423
alternative media, 18, 325
Amanpour, Christiane, 255
A.M. Journal, 108
AM radio (see amplitude modulation)
America Online, 234
American Association of Advertising Agencies (see AAAA)
American Broadcasting Company (see ABC)
American Civil Liberties Union, 468
American Research Institute, 355
American Society of Composers, Authors and Performers (see ASCAP)
American Society of Newspaper Editors (see ASNE)
American Telephone & Telegraph (see AT&T)
American Urban network, 180
"America's town hall," 448
amplitude modulation (AM), 170-171
Amundson, Daniel, 462
analog recording, 119
Anniston Star, 100
anti-intellectualism, 26
AP (Associated Press), 263, 268
applied research, 360
APR, 310
APTV (Associated Press Television), 280
Arbitron, 167, 349
Areopagiticia, 440
Aristotle, 398, 495
Arledge, Roone, 206

Armstrong, Edwin, 170-171
Arnaz, Desi, 213
Arnett, Peter, 287, 365-367, 380
Aronson, Elliot, 342
ARPAnet, 230
artistic autonomy, 123
ASCAP (American Society of Composers, Authors and Performers), 485
Ashe, Arthur, 492
ASNE Ethics Code, 491
Associated Press (see AP)
Associated Press video news service (see APTV)
Association of American Publishers (see AAP)
AT&T, 179
audience
  analysis, 356
  demassification, 62
  donations, 14
  measurement, 346, 348, 351, 354
  passivity, 388
audimeter, 351
audion tube, 168-169
audits, circulation, 349
Audit Bureau of Circulations (see ABC)
Auletta, Ken, 21, 33, 56, 462
authoritarian systems, 435-436
authors, blockbuster, 50, 51b
autistic perception, 392
auxiliary enterprises, 17
Avon books, 40b
Ayer, Wayland, 320

baby-boomers, 356
background, deep, 457
bad tendency test, 473
Baer, George, 293
Bagdikian, Ben H., 24b, 33
Baker, Nicholas, 56

Ball, Lucille, 213
Baltimore *Sun*, 100
Bandura, Albert, 398
bandwidth, 230
Bank of America, 156
banks and movies, 156
Barber, Dorothy, 476
Bardeen, John, 237
Barney, Ralph, 597
Barnouw, Erik, 33, 191, 222
Barnum, P.T., 295
barrages, 328
basic model, 370, 372
BBC (British Broadcasting
    Corporation), 185, 185b
BDD Online, 40
Beasley, Norman, 110
Bell labs, 237
belongers, 359
Bennett, Charles O., 363
Bennett, James Gordon, 261
Bennett, William, 133
Berlin, Isaiah, 462
Berliner, Emile, 117
Berman, Chris, 4
Bernays, Edward, 310
Berners-Lee, Tim, 225-228
Bernstein, Carl, 284-285
Bertelsmann, 28b, 30
Big Three (television), 205
Big Six (records), 130
Billard, Mary, 341
Billboard, 128
binding influence, 7
Bismark, Otto von, 439
Bittner, John, 191
Black, Jay, 507
black weeks, 355
block-booking, 146
Bly, Nellie, 263
BMI (Broadcast Music Inc.),
    485
Bok, Edward, 334
Bogart, Leo, 110
Bohn, Thomas W.,1 62, 373
book clubs, 44
Book-of-the-Month Club, 44
books
    campus best-sellers, 47
    censorship, 43
    definition of, 8, 39
    development of, 36
    importance of, 37
    innovations in, 40
    audio, 41f

instant, 46
publishers, 52
best-seller lists, 47
best-sellers, 46, 47
electronic, 40-41
paperbacks, 40b, 41
television and, 196
text, 40
trade, 40
bookstore downloads, 40b, 41
bounce-back effect, 169
Bourke-White, Margaret, 64
Bowen, David, 259
box-office income, 152
Bradford, Andrew, 61b
Bradlee, Ben, 287
brand image, 326
brand name, 326
brand manager, 323
Brasch, Walter M., 80
The Brass Check, 505
Brattain, Walter, 237
Brenston, Jackie, 121
brevity, in news, 454
bribery, 439
Brinkley, David, 216
Brinkley, John, 182-183b
British Broadcasting Corpo-
    ration (see BBC)
broadcast (see also radio;
    television)
    deregulation, 187
    regulation, 446
Broadcast Music Inc. (see
    BMI)
Broadcast Ratings Council,
    353
Brown, Helen Gurley, 60
Brownback, Sam, 133
browsing, 229
bunching, 328
Bunker, Archie, 420
Burden, Don, 447
Burke, Edmund, 446
Bush, Vannevar, 241, 253

C-SPAN (Cable-Satellite Pub-
    lic Affairs Network), 448
cable television, 4, 204, 208,
    210, 212
Cable News Network (see
    CNN)
Cable-Satellite Public Affairs
    Network (see C-SPAN)
Cablevision, 20f

Caldwell, Earl, 480
Campbell, John, 319
Cambridge Press, 37
campaign spending, 458
campus best-sellers, 47
Cantril, Hadley, 392
CanCon requirement, 126
CapCities, 206
Carnegie Commission, 219
Carson, Gerald, 191
categorical imperative, 495
CATV (community-antenna
    television), 208
caustic interview, 284
caveat emptor, 334
caveat venditor, 334
Caxton, William, 319
CBS (Columbia Broadcasting
    System), 19, 179-180,
    205-206
CDs (compact disks), 120
censorship
    definition of, 437, 482
    movies, 159-160
Center for Media and Public
    Affairs, 414-415
Ceplair, Larry, 162
Cerf, Bennett, 27
Cerf, Vint, 232
CERN, 226-228
chains
    radio, 181
channel noise, 376
Chapple, Steve, 137
chatroom, 450
chemical media, 8
Cherry sisters, 475
Chicago *Daily Defender*, 108
Chicago *Tribune*, 17
Children's Television Work-
    shop, 219
Christian Science Church, 16
Christian Science Monitor, 95
Christians, Clifford G., 507
*Chronicle of Higher Educa-
    tion*, 47
CinemaScope, 147
Cinerama, 147
circulation, 15, 349
Citizen Kane, 444
civil rights, 451
Clark, Dick, 125
Clark, Roy Peter, 507
Classic Sports Network, 4
Cleveland, Ohio, *Plain Dealer*,

100
Clio awards, 339
cloning, advertisement, 339b
Cloud, Stanley, 191
clutter, ad, 337
CMP (cost per thousand), 76
CNN (Cable News Network),
    19, 210
CNN effect, 451
coaxial cable, 203
codes
    movie, 160
    records, 132
codes of ethics, 491
cognitive dissonance, 419
Cohen, Bernard, 462
cohort analysis, 356
collaboration, web of, 21b
Columbia Broadcasting Sys-
    tem (see CBS)
commercial success, 46
commission system, 322
communication
    group, 367
    interpersonal, 367
    intrapersonal, 367
    mass (see mass communica-
        tion)
Communication Decency
    Act, 251, 481
communication models, 370
community-antenna televi-
    sion (see CATV)
compact disks (see CDs)
competition, journalistic, 272
compression, 238
CompuServe, 234
concentric circle model, 372-
    373
Concord, New Hampshire,
    Monitor, 100
confidence level, in surveying,
    347
confidential sources, 480
conflict, in news, 452
conglomeration, 18b, 19
    advertising and, 334
    defintion of, 18b
    dubious effects, 24
    media, 19
    positive effects, 26
    record industry, 130
Conrad, Frank, 172
consensible nature of news, 272
consistency theory, 391

Constitution, U.S., 467
consumer economies, 5
content analysis, 361
contingency planning, 302
Cooke, Janet, 504
cool medium, 10b, 317
Cooper, James Fenimore, 39
copyright, 484
Corliss, Richard, 191
Corning Glass, 239
corporate connections, 53b
corporate giving, 296
corporate instability, 26
Corporation for Public
    Broadcasting (see CPB)
Cosmopolitan, 59-60, 72
cost per thousand (see CPM)
court coverage, 478
covering, 124
CPB (Corporation for Public
    Broadcasting), 16, 173,
    219
CPM (cost per thousand),
    237
Craft, Christine, 217b
Craig, Stephen, 462
creative director, 320-321
creative excesses, advertising,
    336
Creel, George, 295
Crisis, 108
Cronkite, Walter, 215-216
Crossley, Archibald, 349
cultural homogenization, 125
cultural imperialism, 425
cultural intrusion, 424
cultural values, 12
cumulative effects theory, 388
Curiel, Jonathan, 110
Cutlip, Scott M., 312
cyber-, 229
cyberpornography, 251
Czitrom, Daniell J., 287

Daily Me, 244
Dallas *Morning News,* 100
Darwin, Charles, 293
Davidson, Emily S., 408
Davis, Elmer, 295
Day, Benjamin, 261-262, 319
Day, Dorothy, 387
Day, James, 222
Dawley, Heidi, 341
DBS (see direct broadcast
    satellite)

De Forest, Lee, 168
de Graff, Robert, 40b, 41
Dealy, Francis X., 110
DeFleur, Melvin L., 363
decoding, 374-375
deep background, 457
demassification
    effects of, 18, 18b
    magazine, 76, 77
demographics, 349, 356, 358
Denisoff, R. Serge, 137
Denzin, Norman K., 162
deontology, 497
Depression survivors, 356
deregulation, broadcast, 187
Dessauer, John P., 56
detribalization, 424
Dewey, John, 497
Diamond, Edwin, 110
diaries, 351
Dichter, Ernest, 331
Dicken-Garcia, Hazel, 287
Dickson, William, 144
Didion, Joan, 162
differentiating ethics and law,
    500
diffusion of innovations, 421
digital satellite service, 204
digital photography, 10b, 11
digital radio, 188
digital recording, 119-120
digitzation, 31, 237-238
Diller, Barry, 26, 33, 207
direct broadcast satellite
    (DBS), 204
direct mail, 45
direct marketing, 44
dirty words, 185
DiSanto, Ronald L., 56
discrepancies, 353
Disney, 20b, 21b
distributors, movie, 152
diversion function, 390
divine command theory, 497
divine rights of kings theory,
    439
Dix, Dorothy, 282
Dizard, Wilson P., 56
Dole, Bob, 133
Dominick, Joseph R., 137
Douglas, Kirk, 145
Dow, Charles, 90, 91b
downscale audience, 62
Draper, Robert, 80
Dumont, Allen, 206

Dumont network, 206
drive-ins, movie, 151

Eastman, George, 144
economic imperative, 17
economic foundation, 14
economics of mass media, 14
Eddy, Mary Baker, 95-96
Edison, Thomas, 117
educational television, 219
Edwards, Douglas, 214-215
effects, of video coverage, 280
effects studies, 361, 385
egalitarianism, 496
Einstein, Elizabeth L., 56
Eisner, Michael, 157
electronic media, 8
electronic recording, 118
electronic town hall, 460
electromagnetic spectrum,
    168, 169
elitist-populist model, 12-13
elitism, 12, 12b, 52, 415
Ellsberg, Daniel, 470
Elving, Ronald, 462
Emery, Edwin and Michael,
    287
encoding, 374
Englund, Steven, 162
enlightened self-interest, 291
enterpreneurs
    monster, 27
    builder, 27
entertainment-information
    model, 11
entertainment source, 6
environmental noise, 376
equal time law, 446
Escott, Colin, 137
ESPN magazine, 4
ESPN radio, 4
ESPN, 4-5
ESPNEWS, 4
Esquire magazine, 19, 72
ethics
    categorical imperatives,
        495-496
    conflict, 492
    deontological, 497
    development of, 495b
    difficulty of, 491
    egalitarian, 496
    and law, 500-501
    moral principles, 494
    pragmatic, 496

prescriptive, 491
situational, 498
social responsibility, 496
teleological, 497-498
utilitarianism, 496-497
ethnocentrism, 266
Everett, Washington, *Herald,*
    100
events coordination, 302
exhibitors, movie, 151
Exon, James, 251
external public relations, 298-
    299
Eyal, Cham, 308, 463

Fackler, Mark, 507
fair comment and criticism,
    475
fairness doctrine, 446, 491
Fallaci, Oriana, 284
Fallows, James, 287
Farnsworth, Philo, 197-198
FCC (Federal Communica-
    tions Commission), 132-
    133, 173, 181-187, 184b,
    199, 201-203, 214, 337,
    361, 367
fee system, 323
Federalist Papers, 257
Fessenden, Reginald, 168
fiber-optic cable, 239
filters, 376
finances, movie, 153
financial public relations, 301
Fiorina, Morris T., 462
First Amendment, 442, 467
first runs, 151
Fishman, Mark, 287
FitzSimons, Martha, 253
Flaherty, Robert, 142-142
flakkers, 309
flights, 328
flush factor, 355
FM (see frequency modula-
    tion)
focus groups, 355
formats, radio, 174
Fornatale, Peter, 137
four quadrants, 499
fourth branch, 446
Fourth Estate, 446
Fox, Stephen, 342
Fox news, 19
Fox television, 207, 217
Franco, Francisco, 438

Frantzich, Stephen, 222
FRC (Federal Radio Commission), 168b, 172-173, 181-182
free air-time, 460
freebie, 506
Freed, Alan, 122
Freedom's Journal, 108
Freedom of Information Act, 479
frequency modulation, 170-171
Freud, Sigmund, 330
Friedman, Thomas L., 287
Friendly, Fred, 216, 487
frontier literature, 39
FTC (Federal Trade Commission), 320b, 336-337, 376
Fuller, Bonnie, 59-60
functions, mass media
    diversion, 398
    socialization, 390, 393
    surveillance, 389
fund-raising, 301

Galella, Ron, 476
Gallup, George, 343, 345, 363
galvanic skin checks, 355
Gannett, 24, 87
Gans, Herbert, 266-267, 287, 415
Garofalo, Reebee, 137
Garrett, Paul, 291
Gartner, Michael, 487
gatekeepers, 375-376
gatekeeping, 275-276, 334
Gates, Bill, 248b
GE (General Electric), 20b, 21b, 205
Gelatt, Roland, 137
General Electric (see GE)
Generation X, 356
George, 67
giant magneto-resistance (see GMR)
Gilbert, Sam, 277
Gilson, William, 229
Gingrich, Newt, 133
Gitlow, Benjamin, 467
global gatekeeping, 277
global media, 426
global village, 424
globalization
    advertising and, 332
    conglomeration, and, 332

effects, 29
    record industry, 130
GMR (giant magneto-resistance), 239
Goebbels, Joseph, 330, 438
golden mean, 494-495
Goldmark, Peter, 118
gold records, 128
Gomery, Douglas, 162
Goodman, Fred, 137
governance
    direct versus indirect, 447
Government Printing Office, 54b, 55
government deregulation, 249
government regulation, 336
government subsidies, 16
Grabner, Doris, 462
Graham, Katharine, 110
Grammy Awards, 125
gratifications studies, 361
Greco, Albert N., 56
Greeley, Horace, 261
Griffith, D.W., 152-153
Gross, Lynne Schafer, 191
Grosvenor, Gilbert, 61b, 65-66
group communication, 367
Grove Press, 481
Gruning, James E., 321
Guback, Thomas, 162
Guilford, Howard, 468
Gutenberg Bible, 36, 37b
Gutenberg, Johannes, 35-36, 319
Guttridge, Leonard F., 312

Hachette Filipacchi, 30b
Hale, David, 278
Hale, Sara Josepha, 61b, 71b
Hamilton, Andrew, 258
harassment, 477
HarperCollins, 40
HarperCollins Interactive, 40
Harper's Weekly, 61, 65
Harrington, Jane T., 287
Harris, Benjamin, 257
Hart, Michael, 40b, 41, 42
Harvard, John, 37
Hausman, Carl, 507
Hawkins, Martin, 137
Hays, Will, 159
HBO (Home Box Office), 15, 208

HDTV (high-definition television), 199
Hearst, William Randolph, 86, 264
heisting music, 134
Hefner, Hugh, 61b, 65
Hentoff, Nat, 56
El Herald, 108
herd journalism, 280
Hertz, Heinrich, 169f
Hiebert, Ray Eldon, 312
high-definition television (see HDTV)
hi-fi, 119
High-Performance Computing Act, 232
Hinds, Lynn Boyd, 222
hit, web, 237
Holmes, Oliver Wendell, 472
Home Box Office (see HBO)
home-dubbing, 134
home video, 15
horse-race news coverage, 454
hot media, 10b
hot-cool model, 10
Howard, Tom, 84, 85
Hubbard, Stanley, 204
Hughes, Charles Evans, 468
human alienation, 423
Huntley, Chet, 216
Hutchins Commission, 444, 497
Hutchins, Robert 444
Hutchinson, E.R., 56
hyperfiction, 246
hypermedia, 243
hypertext news, 245
hyping, 354-355

IABC (International Association of Business Communicators), 311
ICC (Interstate Commerce Commission), 293
iconoscope, 197
image consulting, 301
image dissector, 197
immigration, 261
import restriction, 481
importance of (see influence of)
indecency, 185
independents (indies), 131-132
    book-sellers, 43

recording, 130-131
    producers, 152-153
indies (see independents)
individual selectivity, 391
Industrial Revolution, 319
industrialization, 261
influence, of
    advertising, 317
    magazines, 61
    mass media, 5
    movies, 141
    public relations, 291
    radio, 166
    television, 194
influences on news, 273
infomercials, 329
informational filter, 376
infotainment, 12-12b
initiating role, 393
Institute of American Public Opinion, 345
integrated standardization, 197
interactive television, 200
internal public relations, 298-299
International Association of Business Communicators (see IABC)
internalization, 375
Internet, 229, 231
intrapersonal communication, 367
Interstate Commerce Commission (see ICC)
interviews, survey, 351
intracorporate synergy, 31
inverted pyramid, 263
investigative reporting, 63, 283
investor groups, 155
Isaacs, Norman E., 287

Jaehnig, Walter B., 507
James I, 439
Janello, Amy, 80
Japan television, 202b
Jarvik, Laurence, 222=20
jazz journalism, 265
Jazz Singer, The 144
Jefferson, Thomas, 259
Jeffres, Leo W., 408
Johnson, Leland L., 222
Johnstone, John, 269
Jones, Brennon, 80

Jones, Edward, 90, 91b
journalism
    colonial period, 257
    exploratory reporting, 282
    herd, 280
    investigative, 283
    jazz, 265
    law, 478
    penny period, 261-262
    roots of, 258b
    soft news, 285
    traditions, 257
    trends, 282
    yellow period, 263
journalistic bias, 268
journalists
    composite of, 267b
    ethnocentricism, 266
    personal values, 265-266
    role of, 265
junket, 505

KABL radio, 175
KADS radio, 175
Kant, Immanuel, 495
KDKA radio, 172
Keillor, Garrison, 165
Kellogg, Ansell, 281
Kelly, Keving, 33
Kennedy, Caroline, 486
Kessler, Lauren, 110
Key, Wilson Bryan, 331, 341
Kilgore, Barney, 90, 91b
King, Martin Luther Jr., 420
Kisseloff, Jeff, 222
kitsch, 415
Kittross, John M., 222
Klein, Calvin, 338b
KLIF radio, 175
Knight-Ridder Newspapers, 87
Knopf, Alfred, 27
Kroeger, Brooke, 287
Kuntz, Mary, 341

La Franco, Robert, 33
labeling, record, 132
Ladd, Jack, 191
Lake Wobegon, 165
Lamb, Brian, 448, 449b
Landers, Ann, 282
Lane, Allen, 40b, 41
Lange, Dorothea, 297
Lasswell, Harold, 373, 385

Lardner, Ring Jr., 145
law (see media law)
Lawrence, David, 281
Lazarsfeld, Paul, 386, 448
leak, 456
Lee, Spike, 154
legals, 16-17
Legion of Decency, 159
Leibert, Robert M., 408
Levenson, Bob, 341
Levin, Gerald, 208-210
Levine, Joshua, 110
Lewinsky, Monica, 451
Lexis, 233
libel law, 474
libertarianism, 440, 444, 497
licensing, 438
Lichter, Linda and Robert, 195, 414b, 415, 430, 462
Life magazine, 61b, 74
lightning news, 263
Limbaugh, Rush, 179, 450
linear communication, 241
Lippmann, Walter, 281
literacy, 261
Literary Guild, 44b, 45
Littlejohn, Stephen W., 380
live radio, 166
lobbying, 301
long-play records (see LPs)
Loomis, Mahlon, 169f
Lord, Daniel, 159
Los Angeles Times, 97, 99-100
Lovejoy, Elijah, 443b
Lowrery, Shearson A., 363
lowest common denominator, 327
LPs, 118
Luce, Henry, 61b, 66-67, 444
Lucky, Robert, 253
Ludlow Massacre, 295
Lumière brothers, 144
Lyon, Matthew, 259

Macdonald, Dwight, 415
MacDonald, Richard J., 33
Madison, James, 467
magazine, television, 216
magazines
    audience, 62
    audits, 349
    circulation, 67, 349
    consumer, 66
    Cosmopolitan, 59-60, 72
    definition of, 8

development of, 61
Esquire, 72
George, 67
Harper's Weekly, 61, 65
influence of, 61, 324
Life, 61b, 64, 74
McClure's, 63
Modern Healthcare, 72
Modern Maturity, 66
National Enquirer, 69
National Geographic, 62-63, 65, 69, 72-73
Newsweek, 68-69
Playboy, 72
Reader's Digest, 62, 66-67
Saturday Evening Post, 61
sponsored, 72
television and, 76, 196
Time, 66-69
magnetic tape, 118
major movie studios, 152-153
Mailer, Norman, 106
Malcomb, Janet, 507
mall stores, 43
Maney, Kevin, 253
Mannes, George, 222
Marconi, Guglielmo, 168, 169
margin of error, 346
market segments, 328
marketplace of ideas, 440, 442
mass audiences, 370
mass communication (see also mass media)
    agenda-setting, 387
    amplification, 378
    audience passivity, 388
    audience preferences, 448
    austistic perception, 392
    communicators, 369
    components of, 369
    consistency theory, 391
    culture and, 413
    cumulative effects theory, 388
    demassification, 18
    diversion function, 390
    effects, 379
    effects on governance, 450
    effects studies, 385
    feedback, 379
    fundamentals, 371b, 374
    globalization, 28
    governance and, 445
    government issues, 458
    government manipulation

of, 455
high-brow, 415
individual selectivity, 391
initiating role, 393
low-brow, 415
melding, 31, 246
messages, 369
minimalist effects theory, 386
models of, 372-373
multi-step flow, 386
mystery of, 373
narcoticizing dysfunction, 387
obsessions, 452
powerful effects theory, 385
regulation of, 447
revolution, and, 7f
role models, 395
timeline, 9b
opinion leaders, 386
ownership, 19
parasocial interaction, 390
prosocial, 395
relaxation, 390
release, 391
results of, 378
scholarship, 361
selective exposure, 391
selective perception, 392
selective recall, 392
selective retention, 392
socialization function, 390, 393
specialized, 448
spiral of silence, 388
status conferral, 386
sterotyping, 395-396
stimulation, 390
surveillance function, 389
systems, 437b
theories of, 435
two-step flow, 386
understanding effects, 386
uses and gratification studies, 388
mass marketing, 48
mass-marketing debate, 50
mass media
    advertising revenue, 16
    agenda-setting, 420
    conglomeration, 19
    contemporary transmission, 422
    convergence, 13
    costs, 15b

cultural transmission, 421
definition of, 370
diffusion of innovations, 421
elitist versus populist values, 413
fundamental change and, 423
historical transmission, 421
licensing of, 438
models, 10-14
morality, 420
national development and, 6b
role in culture, 413
technology, 9b
transnational cultural enrichment, 428
western influence, 428
Mauldin, Bill, 282
Maxwell, James, 169f
Maxwell, Joseph, 118
Maxwell, Robert, 19, 26b, 84, 85
Mayer, William, 462
MBS (Mutual Broadcasting System), 179
McCarthy, Joseph, 445f
McCarthy, Larry M., 462
McClure, Robert C., 459, 462-463
McClure, S.S., 281
McClure's magazine, 63
McCombs, Maxwell, 408
McCord, Richard, 110
McCormick, Robert, 83, 85, 444, 468
McGovern, Geroge S., 321
McGuffey readers, 38
McGuffey, William Holmes, 38
McLendon, Gordon, 174, 176
McLuhan, Marshall, 10b, 11f, 423, 430
McMahon, Harry, 339
McNewspaper, 92-93
McQuail, Denis, 380
Mead Data Central, 233
MDs (mini-disks), 120
media buyers, 320, 321
media kit, 305
Media Lab, 244
media law
    Britain press, 473
    censorship, 482-484

confidential sources, 480-481
copyright, 484-485
court coverage, 478
intellectual property, 484-485
journalism, 478
landmarks in, 472
libel, 473-476
obscenity, 481-482
pornography, 481-482
privacy, 476-478
sunshine, 479-480
media plans, 323
media relations, 299, 304-307
media-sponsored research, 360-361
Meese, Edwin, 484
megadeals, record industry, 131
memex, 241
merchandise tie-ins, 156-157
Merrill, John C., 507
Meyer, Philip, 363
Meyrowitz, Joshua, 396, 408
Michaels, Jim, 106
microgrooves, 118
Microsoft, 20b, 21b
microwave relays, 205
military, law and, 471
military public relations, 299
Mill, John Stuart, 497
Millman, Nancy, 342
Mills, Joshua E., 137
Milton, John, 440
mini-disks (see MDs)
mini-studios, 127
miniaturization, 239
Minnich, Harvey C., 56
Miracle case, 161
misrepresentation, 504
models, mass communication
    basic, 372
    concentric circle, 372-373
    narrative, 373
Modern Healthcare magazine, 73
Modern Maturity magazine, 66
Mollenhoff, Clark R., 487
Moon, Reverend Sun Myung, 16
Moore, Molly, 287
Morse, Samuel, 262-263
Motion Picture Producers

and Distributors of America, 159
Motion Picture Production Code, 159
motivational research, 331
movable metal type, 37
movies
    adaptation from photography, 142
    after-markets, 151
    block-booking, 146
    box-office income, 152
    censorship, 159-160
    changing mores, 160
    Classification and Rating Administration Board, 161
    code, 160
    content innovation, 148
    cultural influence, 141
    definition of, 9b
    distributors, 152
    drive-ins, 151
    exhibitors, 151
    finances, 153
    first runs, 151
    home video market, 15
    Hollywood, 10, 144, 145
    importance of, 141
    independent producers, 152-153
    investor groups, 155
    major studios, 152-153
    merchandise tie-ins, 156-157
    morality, 159
    multiscreen theaters, 151
    music and, 158
    nut, 152
    ratings, 160
    risk investors, 156
    sound, 144
    studio system, 146
    technical heritage, 142
    technical innovation, 147
    television and, 150, 156, 196
    top earning, 155b
    vertical integration, 146
Moynihan, Lael M., 312
MSNBC, 217
MTV, 129
muckraking, 63
multiplexing, 238
multi-screen theaters, 151
multi-step flow, 386, 448

Murdoch, Rupert, 19, 27, 207
Murrow, Edward R., 176, 206, 216b
music
    culture, 422
    demassification of, 127
    garage bands, 127
    licensing, 485
    movies and, 158, 159
    objectionable, 126
    styles, 121
Music Television (see MTV)
music videos, 129
Mutual Broadcasting System (see MBS)
Muybridge, Eadweard, 142

NAB (National Association of Broadcasters), 132
Nadler, Eric, 487
Naisbitt, John, 408
Nanook of the North, 142
narcoticizing dysfunction, 387
narrative model, 373
National Advertising Review Council, 335
National Association of Broadcasters (see NAB)
National Broadcasting Company (see NBC)
National Geographic, 62-63, 65, 72-73
National Public Radio (see NPR)
national radio, 189
National Research and Education Network (see NERN)
National Science Foundation, 230
national security, 470
natural law, 440
natural rights, 442
NBC (National Broadcasting Company), 20b, 21b, 178, 205-206
Near, Jay, 468, 469b
negative news, 294
negative option, 44
Neilson, Frances and Winthrop, 110
Nelson, Ted, 241
NERN (National Research and Education Net-

work), 232
networks, broadcast
  affiliate pressure, 187
  American Broadcasting
    Company (see ABC)
  antitrust, 187
  Big Three, 205
  cable, 208
  Cable News Network (see
    CNN)
  Columbia Broadcasting Sys-
    tem (see CBS)
  cutbacks, 280
  Dumont network, 206
  Fox, 207, 217
  government regulation, 186,
    280
  Home Box Office (see
    HBO)
  licensees, 187
  magazine, 216
  MSNBC, 217
  National Broadcasting
    Company (see NBC)
  news, 216
  over-air, 205
  Pax Net, 208
  radio, 178, 180
  regulation (see government
    regulation)
  shift in news, 216
  start-ups, 211
  technologies, 280
  traditional, 205
  United Paramount (see
    UPN)
  Turner Broadcasting Sys-
    tem, 210
  Warner brothers, 207
Neuharth, Al, 92b, 93, 94, 110
new journalism, 505
New Orleans, Louisiana,
  Times-Picayune, 100
New York *Daily News*, 12, 83,
  85
New York *Times*, 12, 97, 98,
  100
New York *Times v. Sullivan*,
  474
New York *Sun*, 261-262
Newark, New Jersey, *Star-
  Ledger*, 100
news
  agencies, 277
  conditions for, 457

definition of, 6
negative, 294
soft, 285
television, 216
news hole, 270
news flow, 279
news staffing, 271
News Corporation, 19, 20b
Newsday, 100
Newspaper Guild, 91
newspapers
  absentee ownership, 89
  advertising, 102, 103
  The Advocate, 107
  alternative, 106
  A.M. Journal, 108
  AMs, 102
  Anniston, Alabama, *Star*,
    100
  audits, 349
  balanced emphasis, 88
  Baltimore *Sun*, 100
  black, 107
  blackout, 457
  business coverage, 92
  chain ownership, 86-89
  challenges, 101
  Chicago *Daily Defender*, 108
  Chicago *Tribune*, 17
  circulation, 101, 102, 349
  classified advertising, 103
  Cleveland *Plain Dealer*, 100
  commentary, 92
  community weeklies, 105
  Concord, New Hampshire,
    Monitor, 100
  counterculture, 106
  Crisis, 108
  Dallas *Morning News*, 100
  definition of, 8
  depth coverage, 104
  direct mail, 103
  diversity and depth, 86
  electronic delivery, 86
  El Herald, 108
  Everett, Washington, *Her-
    ald*, 100
  exploratory reporting, 92
  Freedom's Journal, 108
  gay, 107
  high story counts, 95
  hometown dailies, 100
  importance of, 85
  indexed content, 104
  industry dimensions, 85

leaders, 92
leading, 100
local autonomy, 95
Los Angeles *Times*, 97, 99-
  100
metropolitan dailies, 97
minority, 106
national dailies, 89
national editions, 97
national representatives,
  103
Newark, New Jersey, *Star-
  Ledger*, 100
New Orleans, Louisiana,
  Times-Picayune, 100
New York *Daily News*, 12,
  83, 85
New York *Times*, 12, 97, 98,
  100, 261-262
Newsday, 100
news hole, 100
Newspaper Guild, 91
North Star, 108
Orange County, California,
  Register, 100
Philadelphia *Inquirer*, 100
PMs, 102
portability, 103
preprints, 103
profit emphasis, 88
provincial newspapers, 95
Raleigh, North Carolina,
  News & Observer, 100
salaries, 89, 90b,
San Jose, California, *Mercury News*, 100
St. Petersburg, Florida,
  Times, 100
shoppers, 106
splashy design, 95
story count, 95
television and, 196
top, 100
transient management, 90
turnover, 90
USA Today, 92-93, 100
variety, 103
Village Voice, 106
Wall Street Journal, 90, 91,
  100
Washington *Post*, 97, 99, 100
web sites, 104
weeklies, 105
writing style, 93
newspaper supplements

Parade, 70
USA Weekend, 70
Newsweek magazine, 68-89
Newton, Isaac, 440
Nexis, 233
NFL cable contract, 4
Nielsen, A.C. Co. (see A.C.
  Nielsen Co.)
900 numbers, for surveying,
  348
Nixon, Richard, 220
Nobel, Edward, 179
Nobile, Philip, 487
noise, 376
noncommercial radio, 172
nonlinear communication,
  230
North Star, 108
Nourie, Alan and Barbara, 80
Novak, Michael, 195
Novak, William, 313
NPR (National Public Radio),
  15-17, 173, 219
nut, 152

o-and-o (see owned and operated)
objectionable music, 132
objective reporting, 263
obscenity, 481
O'Connor, Karen, 462
O'Connor, Sinead, 126
Ochs, Adolph, 265
O'Dell, Cary, 222
off the record, 457
Ogilvy, David, 326, 342
Olson, Lynne, 191
Onassis, Jacqueline Kennedy,
  476
on the record, 457
online
  access providers, 234
  advertising, 235-236=09
  commercial sites, 235
  content providers, 234
  definition of, 228
  growing audience, 236
  institutional sites, 235
  media sites, 235
  services, 324
  users, 234
  webcasting, 236
on-screen directories, 19b
opinion leaders, 386, 448
optical fiber cable, 204

Orange County, California, *Register,* 100
over-air television, 205
overnights, 351
owned and operated stations, (o-and-o's), 180
ownership, broadcast station, 182

Page, Arthur, 299
Paine, Thomas, 442
Paley, William, 27, 179, 206
Palmer, Robert, 137
Palmeri, Christopher, 110
Paramount, 146
parasocial interaction, 390
Parenti, Michael, 287
Parents Music Resource Center, 132
Parsons, Ed, 209
Parsons, Patrick P., 222
partisan period, 259
pass-along circulation, 324
passive meters, 352
Patterson, Joseph, 83
Patterson, Joyce, 85
Patterson, Thomas, E., 459, 463
Pavlik, John V., 253
Pax Net, 208
Paxon, Bud, 208
payola, 129
pay-per-view television, 208
Penguin USA, 40
penny period, 261-262
Pennsylvania Railroad, 294
Pentagon papers, 470
peoplemeter, 352
performance system, 323
Perot, Ross, 460
persistence of vision, 142, 197
personal downloads, 40b, 41
Personal Journal, 245
personal values in journalism, 265-266
personality profiles, 65
persuasion forum, 7
Peterson, Paul E., 462
Peterson, Theodore, 80, 463
pervasiveness, 5
Philadelphia *Inquirer,* 100
Phillips, Sam, 121
Phonograph, 117
photojournalism, 65
physical filter, 376

pilot programs, 213
PIPSA, 439
piracy, music, 134
pitching messages, 326
plagiarism, 502
platinum records, 128
Platt, Charles, 222
Playboy magazine, 72
Pointcast, 236
political communication, 301
political favors, 458
political journals, 450
polling, 302
pool reporters, 471
popular art, 416-417
popularization, 417
population size, 345
populism, 12, 52, 415
populist tradition, 12
populist versus elitist views, 52
pornography, 481
Porter, Bruce, 56
postal restrictions, 481
positioning, 328
Postman, Neil, 33
post-war generation, 356
Postal Act of 1879, 61
potted-palm music, 173
Potter, Ralph, 499
Potter's Box, 498-500
powerful effects theory, 385
"A Prairie Home Companion," 165
pragmatism, 497
Pratkanis, Anthony, 342
Prato, Lou, 287
Presley, Elvis, 116
presses (book)
   university, 54
   vanity, 54
pressure from sources, 275
pressure groups, 376
PRI (Public Radio International), 173
primal event, 9b
primary mass media, 7
priming, 451-452
print media, 7b, 8
prior restraint, 468
privacy law, 476, 491
private actions, in morals, 421
private support, in morals, 16
PRIZM, 358
proactive crisis responses, 305

probability sampling, 344-345
process studies, 361
process versus outcome, 497
Prodigy, 234
product placement, 158-159
program standards, television, 214
Project Gutenberg, 40b, 41, 43
promotion, 300
propaganda, 297
prosocial effects, 395
prototype research, 355
PRSA (Public Relations Society of America), 309-310
PRSSA (Public Relations Student Society of America), 311
prudence, 501
psychographics, 358
psychological filters, 387
Public Broadcasting Act, 173
Public Broadcasting System, 16-17
public domain, 484
public information, 309
public interest, 336
"public interest, convenience and necessity," 182
public morality, 421
public nuisances, 468
public opinion sampling, 345
Public Radio International (see PRI)
public relations, 7b
   activities beyond, 300
   adversarial, 307
   agencies, 299-300
   contingency planning, 302
   corporate giving, 296
   crisis management, 302
   democracy and, 292
   enlightened self-interest, 291
   events coordination, 302
   evolution of, 290
   external relations, 298-299
   financial, 301
   fund-raising, 301
   how organized, 298
   image, 309
   image consulting, 301
   importance of, 291
   internal relations, 298-299
   lobbying, 301
   management function, 302

measuring success, 302
   military, 299
   moguls, 292
   negative news, 294
   openness, 294
   origin of, 292
   political communication, 301
   services, 300
   standards, 309
   structure of, 298
   polling, 302
   policy role, 298
   professionalization, 309
   Russian military, 299
Public Relations Society of America (see PRSA)
Public Relations Student Society of America (see PRSSA)
public television, 218-219, 220
publication
   circulation, 349
   ratings, 349
publicity, 300
Publick Occurrences, 257
puffery, 295, 337
Pulitzer, Joseph, 263
pull-push model, 13
push media, 13
Pynn, Ronald E., 463

Quigley, Martin, 159
quota sampling, 344, 347

radio
   advertising, 172, 324
   affiliate network relations, 180
   amplitude-modulated wave, 170-171
   bland programming, 188
   bounce-back effect, 169
   chains, 181b
   characteristics of, 172
   content regulations, 182
   decline of news, 176
   definition of, 9b
   digital, 188
   dirty words, 185
   early mass programming, 173
   effect on news, 178
   electromagnetic spectrum,

168
engineering regulations, 182
as entertainment, 173
exclusive forum for licensee, 185
formats, 174
frequency-modulated wave, 170-171
future of, 188
live, 166
McLendon influence, 176
as motivator, 166
national, 189
networks, 178, 180
news, 175
noncommercial, 172
owned and operated stations, (o and o's), 180
ownership regulations, 182
private sector and, 172
"public interest, convenience and necessity," 182
regulation, 180
scope of industry, 167
significance of, 166
talk, 177
talkers, 179
technical development, 168
technology and regulation, 168b
television and, 196
transmitting voices, 168
trusteeship rationale, 180, 182
ubiquity of, 167
unmodulated wave, 170
web and, 189
Radio Free Europe, 186b, 187b
Radio Liberty, 186b, 187b
Radio Martí, 186b
Radio Moscow, 186b, 187b
Raleigh, North Carolina, News & Observer, 100
Random House, 481
ratings
  broadcast, 349
  criticism of, 352
  global, 353b
  movie, 160
Rawls, John, 497
Reader's Digest, 62, 66-67
Reagan, Ronald, 250
re-creations, 505

reality programs, 505
reckless disregard, 474
record, off the, 457
record, on the, 457
record industry
  conglomeration, 130
  development of, 117
  globalization, 130
  indies, 130-131
  megadeals, 131
  reflecting change, 116
  restructed, 125
  technology, 117
recording
  acoustic, 117
  analog recording, 119
  compact disks (see CDs)
  censorship, 132
  CDs, 120
  digital technology, 119-120
  electronic, 118
  hi-fi, 119
  mini-disks (see MDs)
  MDs, 120
  labeling, 132
  objectional music, 132
  piracy, 134
  stereo innovation, 119
  tape cassettes, 120
  television and, 196
Recording Industry Association of America (see RIAA)
records
  airplay, 127
  gold, 128
  marketing, 127
  platinum, 128
  tip sheets, 128
Redstone, Sumner, 22
redundancy techniques, 328
Reeves, Rosser, 327
regulation
  advertising, 334
  broadcast, 180
regulators, 376
relaxation, through media, 390
release, through media, 391
Remington, Frederic, 264
reporting, exploratory, 282
repression, 439
reprography, 485
research
  advertising and, 321

applied, 360
audience, 356
cohort analysis, 356
effects studies, 361
gratifications studies, 361
media-sponsored, 360-361
psychology and, 330
respondent accuracy, 354
retribalization, 424
Reuters, 279
RIAA (Recording Industry Association of America), 128
right to be left alone, 478
Riley, Sam G., 80, 81
risk investors, 156
Robbin, Jonathan, 358
Rockefeller, John D. Jr., 295
role models, 395
Rolling Stone magazine, 15
Roosevelt, Theodore, 63
Rosenstiel, Tom, 33
Ross, Harold, 61b, 65
Rosset, Barney, 27
Rothman, Stanley, 195, 414b, 415, 430
Rotzoll, Kim B., 507
roving photographer, 348
Rowland, Williard D., 408
Rubens, William S., 363
Russia military public relations, 299

Sabato, Larry J., 462
sample selection, 346, 353
sample size, 345
San Jose Mercury News, 100
Sarnoff, David, 27, 168, 205, 368b
satellite delivery, 204
saturation advertising, 329
Saturday Evening Post, 61
scandals, 452
Scharff, Edward E., 110
Schenck, Charles, 472
Schiffrin, André, 57
Schiller, Herbert, 425, 430
Schlatzkin, Paul, 222
Schlesinger, Arthur, 258
Schmertz, Herb, 307, 313
Schramm, Wilbur, 463
Schudson, Michael, 287, 342
Schurk, William, 137
scribists, 37
secular command theory, 497

selective editing, 505
selective exposure, 391
selective perception, 392
selective recall, 392
selective retention and recall, 392
self-regulation, 335
self-righting process, 442
Selnow, Gary W., 81
semantic noise, 376
semiconductor, 237
serialization, 49
server, 229
Seven Sisters, 70-72
78-rpm, 118
Shannon, Claude, 372
Shawcross, William, 110
Sheehan, Neil, 470f
shelf life, 324
Shepard, Alicia, 463
Sheppard, Sam, 478
Sherman, Barry L., 137
Siebert, Fred, 462
shield laws, 480
Shockley, William, 237
shovelware, 244
Simon & Schuster, 52b
Sinclair, Upton, 65, 444, 505
situational ethics, 498
slander and mass media, 473
slanted surveys, 353
Slouka, Mark, 253
small presses, 54
small-town pastoralism, 268
Smith, Anthony, 33
social Darwinism, 293
social order, 268
social responsibility, 497
social stability, 418
social values, 12
socialization function, 390, 393
soft news, 285
Sontag, Susan, 417, 430
sound bite, 454
Spafkin, Joyce N., 408
spectaculars, movie, 148
Spielberg, Steven, 139
spiral of silence, 388
Squires, James D., 110
staging news, 504
Stationers Company, 438
statistical extrapolation, 344
status conferral, 386
status quo, 419

stealth ads, 329
Steele, Bob, 507
Steele, Thomas J., 56
Steffens, Lincoln, 63
Stephenson, Neal, 249b
stereo recording, 119
Sterling, Christopher H., 222
Stern, Howard, 184b
Stewart, James B., 57
stimulation, 374, 390
stonewall, 457
St. Petersburg, Florida, *Times*, 100
Strader, Jim, 111
straw polls, 348
Stromgren, Richard L., 162
studio system, 146
Stuyvesants, 84, 85
subception, 331
subliminal memory, 331, 503
subsidiary rights, 49
Sullivan, John, 222
sunshine laws, 479-480
supermarket tabloids, 11
superstations, 210
superstores, 44
supplemental services, 279
SurfWatch, 251
surveillance function, 389
surveys
   evaluating, 347
   margin of error, 346
   quota, 344, 347
   respondent accuracy, 354
   sample selection, 346
   sample size, 345
   slanted, 353
   straw polls, 348
Swanberg, W.A., 81
Swayze, John Cameron, 214-215
Sweeneys, 84, 85
sweeps, 355
syndicates, 281
syndicators, television, 214

tabloids, 11, 83, 85
Taft, William H., 81
talk radio, 177, 450
talkers, 179, 450
talking heads, 448
Tan, Alexis S., 380
tape cassettes (audio), 120
Tarbell, Ida, 61b, 63

TCI, 20b, 21b
Tebbel, John, 57, 81
techno-governance, 460
technological convergence, 247
technology
   demassification and, 18
   mass media, 7-9
   movies, 142-144
   printing, 35
   radio, 168-170
   records, 117-119
   television, 197-200
   web, 237-239
Telecommunication Act of 1996, 250
teleology, 497
telemarketing, 18
telephone book journalism, 106
Televisa, 30b
television
   advertising, 212
   affiliate-network relations, 201
   black weeks, 355
   books and, 196
   broadcast numbers, 302b
   cable systems, 204, 212
   Corporation for Public Broadcasting (see CPB)
   cultural impact, 194
   delivery systems, 203
   dual national system, 201
   early programming, 212
   educational, 219
   electronic scanning, 197
   entertainment, 212-213
   flush factor, 355
   focus groups, 355
   global ratings, 353b
   global village and, 424
   growth of cable, 210, 325
   hyping, 354-355
   high-definition, 199
   iconoscope, 197
   impact of, 194
   image dissector, 197
   integrated standardization, 197
   interactive, 200
   Japan, 202b
   magazines and, 196
   microwave relays, 205
   movies and, 196

newspapers and, 196
   pay-per-view, 208
   pilot, 213
   program standards, 214
   public, 218-219
   public funding, 220
   persistence of vision, 197
   radio and, 196
   recording, 196
   satellite delivery, 204
   standards and practices, 214
   structure, 201
   sweeps, 355
   syndicators, 214
   technology of, 197
   timeline, 199
   urban cable construction, 212
   V-chip, 214-215
   web convergence, 199
   zapping and zipping, 355
Tellis, Gerald, 340
Tesla, Nikola, 169
textbooks, 40
theories
   aggressive stimulation, 398
   catalytic, 400
   cathartic, 397
   consistency, 391
   cumulative effects, 388
   four theories of press, 437, 462
   minimalist effects, 386
   multi-step flow, 386
   powerful effects, 385-386
   spiral of silence, 389
   two-step flow, 386
   uses and gratification, 388
   violence, of, 397-402
Thomson, 24
timeliness, 491
Time magazine, 14, 17, 66-69
Timespeak, 68
Time Warner, 19, 20b, 21b
tip sheets, 128
Top 40, 174
Tornillo case, 447
trade journal, 72, 73
trailing, 328
trial balloon, 456
transistors, 237
transmission, 374
transnational ownership, 28
Trout, Jack, 328
Trumbo, Dalton, 145

trusteeship rationale, 180, 182
Turkle, Sherry, 421f
Turner Broadcasting System, 210
Turner, Ted, 19, 27, 210-211
TV Globo, 30b
TVB, 30b
two-step flow, 386, 448
Twyn, John, 436b

Unification Church, 16
unique selling proposition (see USP)
United Independent Broadcasters, 179
United Paramount Network (see UPN)
United Paramount Theaters, 206
United Press International (see UPI)
Ungar, Sanford J., 487
unmodulated wave, 170
universal access to web, 250
university presses, 54
UPI (United Press International), 278
UPN, 207, 208
urbanization, 261
USA Today, 92-93, 100, 245
uses and gratification studies, 388
U.S. Constitution, 467
USP (unique selling proposition), 327
utilitarianism, 496-497
Utne, Eric, 81

VALS, 358
values, social and cultural, 12
Van Buren, Abigail, 282
Vanderbilt, William Henry, 92
vanity presses, 54
V-chip, 214-215
veil of ignorance, 497
vertical integration, 146
Viacom, 22-23
Vicary, Jim, 331
video news services, 279
Village Voice, 106
Visnews, 279
Voice of America, 186b, 187b

Wagman, Robert J., 487
Wall Street Journal, 15, 90, 100

Wallace, DeWitt, 49, 61b, 68b
Wallace, Lila, 61b, 68b
war zones, 483
Warner brothers, 144
Warner Brothers Television
    (see WBTV)
Watergate, 284-285
Washington *Post*, 97, 99, 100
Washington *Times*, 16
watchdog role, 446
Watergate, 451
waves, 328
WBTV, 207
WEAF radio, 172
Weaver, David H., 269, 287
Weaver, Pat, 205
Weaver, Warren, 372
web (World Wide Web)
    advertising reach, 237
    communication revo-
        lution, 13
    convergence, 199

definition of, 227-228
hypertext, 240-241, 244
limitations, 229
magazines, 79
model, 234
political information and,
    450
public policy, 250
radio and, 189
shopping, 45
technology, 237
terms, 228-234
transition ahead, 249
Weber, Joseph, 341
Wells-Barnett, Ida, 260b
Weiss, Michael J., 363
Weiss, Phillip, 507
Wenner, Jann, 75b
Westerhoff III, John H., 57
Westwood, 180
WGN radio, 179
White, Marie Dunn, 507

Whitehead, Clay, 220
whitewash, 309
Whittle, Chris, 329
Wildmon, David, 214
Wilhoit, G. Cleveland, 269,
    287
Williams, Jerry, 166-167
Wimmer, Roger D., 363
Windahl, Sven, 380
Winfrey, Oprah, 45
Winter, Jim, 408, 463
Wired magazine, 13
wired nation, 448
WJZ radio, 179
Wolf, Don, 106
Wolf, Gary, 33
women's magazines, 70
Woodward, Bob, 284-285
Woolsey, John, 481
WOR radio, 179
World War II veterans, 356
World Wide Web (see web)

Worldwide Television News
    (WTN), 26
Wurman, Richard Saul, 408
WWJ radio, 175

XTRA radio, 175

Yankelovich Partners, 340
yellow period, 263

zapping, zipping, flushing,
    355
Zenger, John Peter, 257
'zine, 329, 450
Zoglin, Richard, 111
Zuckerman, Mary Ellen, 81
Zukor, Adolph, 146
Zworykin, Vladimir, 197

photo credits

Chapter 1

p. 3, © James Schnepf/ Gamma Liaison; p. 4, AP/ Wide World Photos; p. 7, AP/ Wide World Photos; p. 10, © J. Barr/ Gamma Liaison; p. 11, (right) AP/ Wide World Photos (left) © David M. Grossman; p. 22, © Evan Agostini/ Gamma Liaison; p. 25, © David M. Grossman; p. 27, AP/ Wide World Photos; p. 30, © Dilio Mehta/ Contact Press Images

Chapter 2

p. 34, North Wind Picture Archives; p. 36, (left) North Wind Picture Archives; p. 36, (right) North Wind Picture Archives; p. 37, North Wind Picture Archives; p. 38, (left) Culver Pictures; p. 38, (right) The Granger Collection, New York; p. 39, (left) Stock Montage; p. 39, (right) Culver Pictures; p. 41, © David M. Grossman; p. 45, AP/ Wide World Photos; p. 46, (right) © David M. Grossman; p. 46, (left) AP/ Wide World Photos; p. 47, (left) The Chronicle of Higher Education; p. 47, (middle) Copyright © 1998 by Publishers Weekly; p. 47, (right) Copyright © 1997 by THE NEW YORK TIMES Company. Reprinted by permission; p. 49, © Charlie Rose/ PBS

Chapter 3

p. 60, Courtesy of Cosmopolitan; p. 62, © Charles Walcott/ National Geographic Society; p. 64, (left) Margaret Bourke-White/ LIFE Magazine © TIME, Inc.; p. 64, (middle) Margaret Bourke-White/ LIFE Magazine © 1936 TIME, Inc.; p. 64, (right) © George Strock, LIFE Magazine © 1944 Time, Inc.; p. 68, Reader's Digest; p. 69, Courtesy of Gansu People's Publishing House, Lanzhou, China; p. 70, (left) Copyright © 1998, USA Weekend (right) © 1998 Parade Magazine; p. 71, The Granger Collection, New York; p. 75, (left) Photograph by Mark Seliger from *Rolling Stone*. April 1998. By Straight Arrow Publishers Company. L. P. 1998. All rights reserved. Reprinted by permission; p. 75, (right) Straight Arrow Publishers; p. 76, Copyright © 1998 Watterson. Reprinted with permission of Universal Press Syndicate. All rights reserved; p. 78, first published in Slate. www.slate.com

Chapter 4

p. 82, © Vogel/ Gamma Liaison; p. 84, (back) New York Daily News Photo; p. 84, (front)

New York Daily News Photo; p. 90, © Ric Carter; p. 91, (right) Reprinted with permissin of THE WALL STREET JOURNAL © 1998, Dow Jones & Company, Inc. All rights reserved; p. 91, (inset) THE WALL STREET JOURNAL; p. 93, Copyright 1998, USA TODAY. Reprinted with permission; p. 94, © Scott Maclay/ The Freedom Forum; p. 96, (right) Reprinted by permission of The Christian Science Monitor, photos by Reuters and AP/ Wide World Photos; p. 96, (left) The Granger Collection, New York; p. 98, all photos Copyright © 1998 by THE NEW YORK TIMES Company. Reprinted by permission; p. 105, Reprinted with permission of the San Jose *Mercury News* and Mercury Center (www.mercurycenter.com), all rights reserved © 1998.

Chapter 5

p. 112, © Livio Anticoli/ Gamma Liaison; p. 114, AP/ Wide World Photos; p. 118, UPI/ Corbis-Bettmann; p. 119, Corbis-Bettmann; p. 122, Corbis-Bettmann; p. 123, (right) © Alain Benainous/ Gamma Liaison; p. 123, (left) UPI/ Corbis-Bettmann; p. 124, (left) UPI/ Corbis-Bettmann; p. 124, (right) Corbis-Bettmann; p. 125, AP/ Wide World Photos; p. 128, © Evan Agostini/ Gamma Liaison; p. 129, AP/ Wide World Photos; p. 133, © Brad Markel/ Gamma Liaison; p. 135, © Peter Charlesworth/ JB Pictures

Chapter 6

p. 138, © Gregory Heisler/ Putline; p. 140, Warner Bros. (Courtesy Kobal); p. 143, (right) Culver Pictures; p. 143, (left) AP/ Wide World Photos; p. 144, Corbis-Bettmann; p. 145, AP/ Wide World Photos; p. 148, © Van Bucher; p. 149, (right) Gamma Liaison; p. 149, (left) AP/ Wide World Photos; p. 150, AP/ Wide World Photos; p. 154, © Steve Allen/ Gamma Liaison; p. 156, AP/ Wide World Photos; p. 157, AP/ Wide World Photos

Chapter 7

p. 164, AP/ Wide World Photos; p. 166, Minnesota Public Radio; p. 169, The Granger Collection, New York; p. 170, (top) AP/ Wide World Photos; p. 170, (middle) AP/ Wide World Photos; p. 170, (bottom) AP/ Wide World Photos; p. 171, (left) Corbis-Bettmann; p. 171, (right) Corbis-Bettmann;

p. 175, AP/ Wide World Photos; p. 176, UPI/ Corbis-Bettmann; p. 178, (top) © Mark Richards; p. 178, (bottom) © Barry Stover, TIME Magazine; p. 179, © Jacques Chenet/ Gamma Liaison; p. 183, UPI/ Corbis-Bettmann; p. 184, © Jeff Slocomb/ Outline

Chapter 8

p. 192, © Summa/ Gamma Liaison; p. 195, AP/ Wide World Photos; p. 198, UPI/ Corbis-Bettmann; p. 200, (left) AP/ Wide World Photos; p. 200, (right) AP/ Wide World Photos; p. 207, AP/ Wide World Photos; p. 210, (left) NASA; p. 210, (right) AP/ Wide World Photos; p. 211, © Bill Swersey/ Gamma Liaison; p. 213, UPI/ Corbis-Bettmann; p. 215, AP/ Wide World Photos; p. 216, AP/ Wide World Photos; p. 217, © Mike Maple/ Woodfin Camp & Associates; p. 219, AP/ Wide World Photos

Chapter 9

p. 224, AP/ Wide World Photos; p. 226, AP/ Wide World Photos; p. 232, AP/ Wide World Photos; p. 233, © Kevin R. Morris; p. 238, UPI/ Corbis-Bettmann; pp. 240, 241, © 1998 Spaceshots/Living Earth, Inc. Reprinted by permission; p. 242, © David M. Grossman; p. 242, © 1993 Cyan, Inc. All rights reserved. Myst ® Cyan, Inc. All Riven, indicia, sounds, images and text © 1996, 1997 Cyan, Inc. All rights reserved. Riven ® Cyan, Inc.; p. 243, Corbis-Bettmann; p. 245, courtesy of www.nando.net; p. 248, © Jeff Scheid/ Gamma Liaison

Chapter 10

p. 254, © Noel Quidu/ Gamma Liaison; p. 257, Corbis-Bettmann, hand coloring by North Wind Picture Archives; p. 260, The Granger Collection, New York; p. 262, Corbis-Bettmann; p. 263, UPI/ Corbis-Bettmann; p. 264, (right) Corbis-Bettmann; p. 264, (top left) Culver Pictures; p. 264, (bottom left) Culver Pictures; p. 265, Culver Pictures; p. 266, © John Chiasson/ Gamma Liaison; p. 272, (top) © Ira Wyman/ Sygma; p. 272, (bottom) © Allen Tannenbaum/ Sygma; p. 273, AP/Wide World Photos; p. 283, (left) Superstock; p. 283, (right) UPI/ Corbis-Bettmann; p. 284, AP/ Wide World Photos

Chapter 11
p. 288, AP/ Wide World Photos; p. 290, © Erik Lesser/ Gamma Liaison; p. 294, (left) Colorado History Society; p. 294, (right) AP/ Wide World Photos; p. 296, (left) The Granger Collection, New York; p. 296, (right) AP/ Wide World Photos; p. 297, The Granger Collection; p. 301, © Anthony Barboza; p. 304, (left) © Kevin Horan; p. 304, (right) Sygma; p. 307, (right) © Van Bucher; p. 307, (left) Courtesy of Herb Schmertz; p. 310, UPI/ Corbis-Bettmann

Chapter 12
p. 314, © David Grossman; p. 327, (left) Ogilvy & Mather; p. 327, (right) Ogilvy & Mather; p. 330, Reprinted by permission of Bamboo; p. 332, (left) Wilson Bryan Key; p. 332, (right) Wilson Bryan Key; p. 333, © Tom Wagner/ SABA; p. 335, AP/ Wide World Photos; p. 336, Partnership for a Drug-Free America

Chapter 13
p. 342, AP/ Wide World Photos; p. 350, Courtesy Broadcasting & Cable, March 30, 1998; p. 352, (left) Nielsen Media Research; p. 352, (right) Nielsen Media Research; p. 354, © Roger Hutchings/ Woodfin Camp & Associates; p. 357, (top) © Douglas Burrows/ Gamma Liaison; p. 357, (bottom left) Reuters/ John C. Hillery/ Archive Photos; p. 357, (bottom right) Reuters/ John C. Hillery/ Archive Photos

Chapter 14
p. 364, © John Chiasson/ Gamma Liaison; p. 366, © John Chiasson/ Gamma Liaison; p. 367, (right) © Sam Jones; p. 367, (left) AP/ Wide World Photos; p. 368, UPI/ Corbis-Bettmann; p. 375, © Jacques Chenet/ Woodfin Camp & Associates; p. 377, Reprinted from The Columbia Journalism

Review. March/April © 1998; p. 379, © John Barnett/ Globe Photos

Chapter 15
p. 382, Culver Pictures; p. 384, Culver Pictures; p. 387, Archive Photos; p. 389, © 1998 Los Angeles Daily News/ Tina Gerson/ Sygma; p. 393, © David Dempster; p. 394, AP/ Wide World Photos; p. 399, Dr. Albert Bandura; p. 401, UPI/ Corbis-Bettmann; p. 402, Heikki Saukkoma; p. 403, (left) © 1998 SCi (Sales Curve Interactive) limited. All rights reserved. (right) Archive Photos

Chapter 16
p. 410, AP/ Wide World Photos; p. 414, (right) Center for Media and Public Affairs; p. 414, (left) © Fredrich Cantor; p. 416, (center) Copyright © 1998 by THE NEW YORK TIMES Company. Reprinted by permission; p. 416, (right) New York Post; p. 416, (left) New York Daily News; p. 419, AP/ Wide World Photos; p. 420, © Dave Sartin/ Gamma Liaison; p. 421, Steven Klein; p. 422, © Henry McGee/ Globe Photos; p. 423, © Robert Nickelsberg/ Gamma Liaison; p. 425, © Stephen Ferry/ The Image Works; p. 426, Reuters/ Corbis-Bettmann; p. 427, Catherine Karnow/ Woodfin Camp & Associates

Chapter 17
p. 432, © Bruce Cotler/ Globe Photos; p. 435, Stock Montage; p. 436, North Wind Picutre Archives; p. 438, AP/ Wide World Photos; p. 439, Stephen Ferry/ The Image Works; p. 442, Culver Pictures; p. 443, Illinois State Historical Society; p. 445, © Carl Mydans/ LIFE Magazine; p. 449, AP/ Wide World Photos; p. 453, (left) UPI/ Corbis-Bettmann; p. 453, (right) AP/ Wide World Photos; p. 454, Reuters/ Corbis-Bettmann; p. 455, AP/ Wide World Photos; p. 456, (left) UPI/ Corbis-Bettmann; p. 456, (right) Archive Photos;

p. 459, (right) Reuters/ Jeff Topping/ Archive Photos; p. 459, (left) Reuters/ Ira Schwartz/ Archive Photos

Chapter 18
p. 464, AP/ Wide World Photos; p. 469, (right) From The Collection of the Minnesota Historical Society; p. 469, (left) From The Collection of the Minnesota Historical Society; p. 470, (background) © Copyright The New York Times Company; p. 470, (left) AP/ Wide World Photos; p. 470, (right) AP/ Wide World Photos; p. 471, (right) © Chris Morris/ Black Star; p. 471, (left) AP/ Wide World Photos; p. 476, George Mills; p. 477, (top) Reuters/ Jean-Christophe Kahn/ Archive Photos; p. 477, (bottom) Joy Smith/ Ron Galella Ltd.; p. 480, AP/ Wide World Photos; p. 484, AP/ Wide World Photos

Chapter 19
p. 488, AP/ Wide World Photos; p. 492, AP/ Wide World Photos; p. 493, Sygma; p. 494, (top) Big Picture/ Archive Photos; p. 494, (bottom) Corbis-Bettmann; p. 494, (top) North Wind Picture Archives; p. 496, (bottom) North Wind Picture Archives; p. 502, (left) © David M. Grossman; p. 502, (right) AP/ Wide World Photos; p. 503, (right) © David M. Grossman; p. 503, (left) © Ed Lallo/ Gamma Liaison